MACRO ECONOMICS

CANADA IN THE GLOBAL ECONOMY

SEVENTH CANADIAN EDITION

MACRO ECONOMICS

CANADA IN THE GLOBAL ECONOMY

SEVENTH CANADIAN EDITION

CAMPBELL R. McCONNELL
University of Nebraska, Lincoln

STANLEY L. BRUE
Pacific Lutheran University

THOMAS P. BARBIERO
Ryerson Polytechnic University

McGraw-Hill Ryerson Limited

Toronto New York Auckland Bogotá Caracas
Lisbon London Madrid Mexico Milan New Delhi
San Juan Singapore Sydney Tokyo

ISBN: 0-07-552614-X

2 3 4 5 6 7 8 9 10 BBM 5 4 3 2 1 0 9 8 7

Printed and bound in Canada

SENIOR EDITOR: Jennifer Mix
SUPERVISING EDITOR: Margaret Henderson
DEVELOPMENT EDITOR: Daphne Scriabin
PRODUCTION EDITOR: Wendy Thomas
COVER & TEXT DESIGN: Lisa Kinloch, David Murphy/ArtPlus Limited
PRINTING & BINDING: Best Book Manufacturers

Canadian Cataloguing in Publication Data

McConnell, Campbell R.
        Macroeconomics

7th Canadian ed.
Includes index.
ISBN 0-07-552614-X

1. Macroeconomics. I. Brue, Stanley, L., 1945–   .
II. Barbiero, Thomas Paul, 1952–   .
III. Title.

HB172.5.M24 1996   339   C95-932133-0

This edition is dedicated to my dear wife, Elsa.

ABOUT THE AUTHORS

Campbell R. McConnell earned his Ph.D. from the University of Iowa after receiving degrees from Cornell College and the University of Illinois. He taught at the University of Nebraska — Lincoln from 1953 until his retirement in 1990. He is also coauthor of **Contemporary Labor Economics,** 4th ed. (McGraw-Hill) and has edited readers for the principles and labour economics courses. He is a recipient of both the University of Nebraska Distinguished Teaching Award and the James A. Lake Academic Freedom Award, and is past-president of the Midwest Economics Association. Professor McConnell was awarded an honorary Doctor of Laws degree from Cornell College in 1973 and received its Distinguished Achievement Award in 1994. His primary areas of interest are labour economics and economic education. He has an extensive collection of jazz recordings and enjoys reading jazz history.

Stanley L. Brue did his undergraduate work at Augustana College (S.D.) and received his Ph.D. from the University of Nebraska — Lincoln. He teaches at Pacific Lutheran University, where he has been honoured as a recipient of the Burlington Northern Faculty Achievement Award. He has also received the national Leavey Award for excellence in economic education. Professor Brue is national President and member of the International Executive Board of Omicron Delta Epsilon International Economics Honorary. He is coauthor of **Economic Scenes,** 5th ed. (Prentice-Hall) and **Contemporary Labor Economics,** 4th ed. (McGraw-Hill) and author of **The Evolution of Economic Thought,** 5th ed. (HB/Dryden). For relaxation, he enjoys boating on Puget Sound and skiing trips with his family.

Thomas P. Barbiero received his Ph.D. from the University of Toronto after completing undergraduate studies at the same university. He has published papers on the role of the agricultural sector in the industrial development of northern Italy in the period 1861–1914. His research interests in the last few years have turned to economic methodology and the application of economic theory to explain social phenomena. Professor Barbiero is presently associate professor of economics at Ryerson Polytechnic University. He spends his summer in Italy with his wife and three children. While there, apart from following his interest in the country's economic history, he assiduously pursues good food and wine.

CONTENTS IN BRIEF

CONTENTS

PREFACE

We are pleased to present the seventh Canadian edition of *Macroeconomics* and *Microeconomics*. *Macroeconomics* and *Microeconomics* continue to be leading economics texts in both Canada and the United States. Moreover, the Russian language versions of *Macroeconomics* and *Microeconomics* are the leading economics texts in Russia. More than 1 million Russians have used this book since the fall of communism.

Capitalism in Russia, interest rate hikes, GATT and NAFTA, pollution rights, governments' pursuit of balanced budgets — what a remarkable time for teaching and learning economics! The message of our day is clear: People who comprehend economic principles will have an advantage functioning in, and making sense of, the emerging world. We thank each of you using *Macroeconomics* and *Microeconomics* for granting us a modest role in your efforts to teach or learn this vital subject.

WHAT'S NEW?

This edition has been thoroughly revised, polished, and updated. Many of the changes have been motivated by the comments of nine reviewers. We sincerely thank each of them and acknowledge them by name at the end of this preface.

Here, we strive only for an overview of the changes in the seventh Canadian edition; chapter-by-chapter details are provided in the *Instructor's Resource Manual*.

NEW CHAPTERS

We have added three new chapters for this edition of *Macroeconomics*.

• **THE PUBLIC SECTOR.** Responding to reviewers' suggestions, we have added a chapter on the government sector in the introductory part of the text (Chapter 5). Reviewers rightly pointed out the important role of government in the Canadian economy and that the public sector should be introduced early in the text. The economic functions of government, externalities, and public goods are introduced, and the size of government as measured by expenditures and revenues is discussed. The public sector is then put into the circular flow model introduced in Chapter 2.

• **CANADA IN THE GLOBAL ECONOMY.** The material of Part I has been condensed and rearranged to allow an early and comprehensive chapter (Chapter 6) on the global economy. This chapter contains not only descriptive material (volume and pattern of world trade), but also essential theory (comparative advantage, exchange rates) and institutional features (trade barriers, GATT, EU, NAFTA). By providing the basics of international trade and finance, the chapter is a springboard for the instructor who wishes to fully integrate micro and macro materials into a global framework.

- **ALTERNATIVE ECONOMIC SYSTEMS IN TRANSITION.** The last decade of the twentieth century has seen previously centrally planned economies attempting to transform themselves closer to existing models of market-dominated economies. The most prominent case has been the former Soviet Union, which divided into a number of states after it broke up in 1989. In the new chapter, found in *Macroeconomics* (Chapter 24), we focus particularly on Russia, the largest economy still in existence of what was the Soviet Union. We investigate the prevailing ideology of the Soviet Union, its economic problems, and the economic factors that led to its demise. We then review the success of Russia in its attempted transition to a market economy, and look at its future prospects, along with those of other previously centrally planned economies trying to make that transition.

NEW FEATURES

The seventh edition contains three new "features" — one adding another global dimension to *Macroeconomics*, the other two making the book more interactive.

- **THE BIG PICTURE.** Responding to reviewers' comments, we have added a box at the beginning of each chapter that connects the material already learned with the new materials still to be covered, to give the reader "The Big Picture." Sometimes students lose the forest for the trees, and this new feature helps them to avoid it.

- **IN THE MEDIA.** In the sixth edition we introduced "In the Media" boxes — newspaper articles about current economic events. These have been updated and economic analysis has been added. A question at the end of the analysis allows students to test their understanding of the economic theory behind the story.

- **GLOBAL PERSPECTIVES.** We have added Global Perspective sections — most containing charts — throughout the book to compare the Canadian economy with other nations. To merely state, for example, Canada's rates of inflation, unemployment, or taxes or the size of Canadian farm subsidies without international comparisons denies students the context needed for meaningful comparisons.

- **KEY QUESTIONS (WITH ANSWERS).** We have designated two to five end-of-chapter questions as "Key Questions," answering them in the back of the text. Many of these questions are quantitative and are designed to help the student work through and understand basic concepts. The reader is alerted within the chapters as to when a particular Key Question is relevant. Students wanting to immediately test their understanding can turn to the specially marked Key Question, checking their answer against the end-of-book answer. Others may want to wait until they have read the full chapter before answering the Key Questions. Either way, the Key Questions make *Macroeconomics* more interactive.

RECONSTITUTED MACROECONOMICS

The macro analysis has been carefully rethought and restructured for logical development of the ideas and to provide greater flexibility for instructors. Because these changes are extensive, we wish to provide detail.

- *Chapters 7, 8, and 9* on national income accounting, macroeconomic instability, and the simple Aggregate Expenditure (AE) model have undergone only minor revision.
- *Chapter 10* examines changes in equilibrium GDP and the multiplier in the private closed economy. It then brings in the net export and government components of the aggregate expenditures model, the latter from the previous edition's chapter on fiscal policy. Then, recessionary and inflationary gaps are considered, along with historical applications of these concepts.
- *Chapter 11* develops the aggregate demand-aggregate supply (AD-AS) model, with two optional sections that (1) derive the AD curve from the AE model, and (2) show how shifts in the AD curve and AE curve are related. We anticipate that most instructors will assign the AE chapters, but instructors wishing to use only AD-AS can delete the AE chapters along with these optional sections in Chapter 11. With in-class supplementation, Chapter 11's section on the multiplier with inflation could serve as a springboard for instructors to develop the concepts of the MPC, MPS, and multiplier.
- *Chapter 12* on fiscal policy is cast entirely in terms of AD-AS.

We believe the new organization of the macro accomplishes three goals.

- Most importantly, by eliminating the previous "jumping" between models, the AE and AD-AS models are better integrated for the majority of professors who teach both. The new progression is: National income accounting, macroeconomic instability, the AE model, derivation of AD from the AE model, addition of AS, and application of the AD-AS model to fiscal policy (and later to monetary policy).
- Second, the new organization provides an exclusive AD-AS option (Chapters 11 and 12 and beyond) for those desiring it.
- Finally, the two AE chapters are now unencumbered with AD-AS sections for instructors wishing to emphasize the AE model throughout the course.

THE ECONOMIC PERSPECTIVE

We have placed greater emphasis on the economic way of thinking. In Chapter 1 we have greatly expanded the section on the economic perspective, discussing scarcity and choice, rational behaviour, and marginal analysis. In Chapter 2 we use the ideas of marginal benefits and marginal costs (Figure 2-2) to determine the optimal position on the production possibilities curve. We then take opportunities to reinforce the economic perspective in the remainder of the book.

CULLING AND TIGHTENING

Our considerable culling and tightening in the sixth edition has been well-received by reviewers and the marketplace. Buoyed by that response, we have again looked for places to delete the archaic, remove redundancy, tighten sentences, and reduce formality. In further economizing on words, we were careful *not* to reduce the thoroughness of our explanations. Where needed, the "extra sentence of explanation" remains a distinguishing characteristic of our textbook.

OTHER NEW TOPICS AND REVISED DISCUSSIONS

Along with the changes just discussed, there are many other revisions worth noting.

- **Part 1.** *Chapter 1*: Reorganization of the "policy" section; new discussion of the correlation-causation fallacy. *Chapter 2*: Clarification of productive vs. allocative efficiency; new applica-

tion on lumber vs. owls. *Chapter 3*: Expanded discussion of property rights. *Chapter 4*: New examples: Increased demand for broccoli, carrots, guns; reduced supply of haddock.

- **Part 2.** *Chapter 8*: New Figure 8-8 on nominal vs. real interest rate. *Chapter 10*:; Major new aggregate expenditure applications: Great Depression; inflation of the late 1960s and early 1970s. *Chapter 12*: new presentation of fiscal policy in the AD-AS framework (Figures 12-1 and 12-2); revised discussion of the full-employment budget (new Figure 12-4).
- **Part 3.** *Chapter 15*: New AD-AS presentation of monetary policy (Figure 15-3); new discussions of recent successes of monetary policy, the "loss of control" issue; and the effect of interest rate changes on interest income. New Figure 15-4 provides an AD-AS "overview" of macro theory and policy.
- **Part 4.** *Chapter 16*: New discussion of employment and training policy. *Chapter 18*: New topics: Ownership of the public debt (Figure 18-1); and debt as a curb on fiscal policy. *Chapter 19*: Clarification of demand and efficiency factors in growth (Figure 19-1); discussions of the new doomsday models (Figure 19-6).
- **Part 5.** *Chapter 20*: New topics: supply and demand analysis of exports and imports (Figures 20-3, 20-4, and 20-5); and government export promotion policies. *Chapter 21*: Revised discussion of the manage float. *Chapter 23*: New table on the distribution of world income (Table 23-1); new perspectives on the population problem; new discussion of the difficulties associated with foreign aid; reworked discussion of the debt crisis; new section on the "New Global Compact." *Chapter 24*: Progress report on the Russian transition to capitalism.

APPLYING THE THEORY

These selections serve several purposes: some provide current or historical real-world applications of economic concepts; others reveal "human interest" aspects of economic problems; some present contrasting or "non-mainstream" points of view; and still others present economic concepts or issues in a global context. In the sixth edition these selections were placed in boxes without any heading. Besides unifying these "minireadings" through giving them a heading, we have placed a question about the story at the end of the chapter. Ten of the Applying the Theory boxes are new and others have been revised and updated.

The new topics are: Cuba's declining production possibilities (Chapter 2); alternative views on why Europe's unemployment rate is so high (Chapter 11); the use of the dollar around the world (Chapter 13); pros and cons of economic growth (Chapter 19); speculation in currency markets (Chapter 21); and China as an emerging economic power (Chapter 24).

We trust that the outcome of these revision efforts is a text and set of ancillaries superior to their predecessors.

FUNDAMENTAL GOALS

Although the seventh edition bears only a modest resemblance to the first, the basic purpose remains the same — to introduce the beginning economics student to principles essential to an understanding of the economizing problem and the policy alternatives available for dealing with it. We hope that an ability to reason accurately and objectively about economic matters and a lasting interest in economics will be two byproducts of this basic objective. Our intention remains to present the principles and problems of economics in a straightforward, logical fashion. Therefore, we continue to put great stress on clarity of presentation and organization.

ACKNOWLEDGEMENTS

The publication of this seventh edition will extend the life of *Macroeconomics* well into its second decade. The acceptance of the parent text, *Economics*, which was generous from the outset, has expanded with each edition. This gracious reception has no doubt been fostered by the many teachers and students who have been kind enough to provide their suggestions and criticisms.

Our colleagues at the University of Nebraska-Lincoln, Pacific Lutheran University, and Ryerson Polytechnic University have generously shared knowledge of their specialties with us and have provided encouragement. We are especially indebted to Ryerson professors John Hughes, David Cape, Dagmar Rajagopal, Gus Zaks, George Carter, Ingrid Bryan, Tom Tushingham, and Mark Lovewell, who

have been most helpful in offsetting our comparative ignorance in their areas of specialty.

As indicated, the seventh edition has benefitted from a number of perceptive reviews. In both quality and quantity, they provided the richest possible source of suggestions for this revision. We wish to thank the following instructors who participated in the formal review process:

T. Andersen	Red Deer College
B. Abbott	Northern Alberta Institute of Technology
B. Cook	University of New Brunswick
M. Dore	Brock University
H. Grant	University of Winnipeg
I. Hayani	Seneca College
J. Hughes	Ryerson Polytechnic University
L. Ifill	Algonquin College
S. Law	University of New Brunswick

We also owe a debt of gratitude to all those instructors who contributed in an informal manner their comments and suggestions to authors, editors, and McGraw-Hill Ryerson representatives over the life of the sixth edition. In this connection, I. Hayani of Centennial College, Sage Traviza of the International Centre for Tax Studies, Faculty of Management Studies, University of Toronto, and Torben Andersen of Red Deer College were particularly helpful, and we are grateful to them.

We also wish to thank the following instructors who participated in the formal review process of the sixth edition:

M. Benarroch	University of Winnipeg
E. Black	Brandon University
D. Box	University College of the Fraser Valley
C. Burke	Lethbridge Community College
N. Clegg	Kwantlen College
K. Dawson	Conestoga College
C. Dickhoff	British Columbia Institute of Technology
S. Dodaro	St. Francis Xavier University
S. Fefferman	Northern Alberta Institute of Technology
P. Fortura	Algonquin College
B. Gayle-Anyiwe	Seneca College
P. Jacobs	Champlain Regional College
E. Jacobson	Northern Alberta Institute of Technology

M. Moy	University College of Cape Breton
V. Nallainayagam	Mount Royal College
A. Nimarko	Vanier College
D. Pepper	British Columbia Institute of Technology
R. Schwindt	Simon Fraser University
L. Smith	University of Waterloo
T. Tushingham	Ryerson Polytechnic University

We are greatly indebted to the many professionals at McGraw-Hill Ryerson — and in particular to Daphne Scriabin, Margaret Henderson, and Gary Bennett — for their expertise in the production and distribution of the book. Wendy Thomas's editing has been invaluable. Without her constant vigilance, such a major revision of *Macroeconomics* would undoubtedly have had many more errors. Whatever errors or omissions remain are clearly due to our own oversight.

With such quality assistance, we see no compelling reason that the authors should assume full responsibility for errors of omission or commission. But we bow to tradition.

Our greatest debt is to Jennifer Mix for her conscientious and imaginative supervision of this revision. Her patience and many positive contributions are gratefully acknowledged.

Campbell R. McConnell
Stanley L. Brue
Thomas P. Barbiero

TO THE STUDENT

Economics is concerned with efficiency — accomplishing goals using the best methods. Therefore, we offer some brief introductory comments on how to improve your efficiency — and your understanding and grade — in studying economics. Several features of this book will aid your learning.

- **APPENDIX ON GRAPHS** Being comfortable with graphical analysis and a few related quantitative concepts will be a big advantage to you in understanding principles of economics. The appendix to Chapter 1 reviews graphing, line slopes, and linear equations. Be sure not to skip it!

- **THE BIG PICTURE** The new Big Picture in each chapter is designed to stimulate interest, state the main objectives, and present an organizational overview of the chapter and its connection with previously covered chapters.

- **TERMINOLOGY** A significant portion of any introductory course is terminology. To designate key terms, we have put them in boldface type, listed them at the end of each chapter, and provided a glossary of definitions at the end of the book.

- **REVIEWS** Important things should be said more than once. You will find a chapter summary at the conclusion of every chapter as well as two or three "Quick Reviews" within each chapter. These review statements will help you focus on the essential ideas of each chapter and also to study for exams. If any of these statements is unclear, you should reread the appropriate section of the text.

- **KEY GRAPHS** We have labelled graphs having special relevance as "Key Graphs." Your instructor may or may not emphasize each of these figures, but pay special attention to those your instructor discusses in class. You can bet there will be exam questions on them!

- **FIGURE LEGENDS** Economics is known for its many graphs. The legends accompanying the diagrams in this book are self-contained analyses of the concepts shown. Study these legends carefully — they are quick synopses of important ideas.

- **GLOBALIZATION** Each nation functions increasingly in a global economy. To gain appreciation of this wider economic environment, be sure to take a look at the "Global Perspectives," which compare Canada to other selected nations.

- **APPLYING THE THEORY** While it is tempting to ignore these boxes, doing so is a mistake. Some "Applying the Theory" boxes are revealing applications of economic concepts; some are short case studies; still others present views that contrast with mainstream thinking. All will deepen and broaden your grasp of economics.

• IN THE MEDIA   Interesting stories have been selected from the printed media that show the real-world application of the economic theory just learned. Each of these stories ends with a question to test your understanding of the chapter's materials.

• QUESTIONS   A comprehensive list of questions is located at the end of each chapter. The old cliché that you "learn by doing" is very relevant to economics. Use of these questions will enhance your understanding. We designate several of them as "Key Questions" and answer them at the end of the book. You can immediately turn to these particular questions when they are cited in each chapter, or later after you have read the full chapter.

• SOFTWARE   Many of the end-of-chapter questions deal with subject matter reinforced by the computerized tutorial, *Concept Master III*, which complements this text. A floppy disk symbol appears in connection with questions whose underlying content correlates to a lesson in the tutorial program.

• STUDY GUIDE   We enthusiastically recommend the *Study Guide* accompanying this text. This "portable tutor" contains not only a broad sampling of various kinds of questions, but a host of useful learning aids.

You will find in Chapter 1 that economics involves a special way of thinking — a unique approach to analyzing problems. The overriding goal of this book is to help you acquire that skill. If our co-operative efforts — yours, ours, and your instructor's — are successful, you will be able to comprehend a whole range of economic, social, and political problems that otherwise would have remained murky and elusive.

So much for the pep talk. Let's get on with the show.

Drabble reprinted by permission of United Feature Syndicate, Inc.

AN INTRODUCTION TO ECONOMICS

CHAPTER 1

THE NATURE AND METHOD OF ECONOMICS

Human beings, unfortunate creatures, are plagued with many material wants. The fact is, however, that the total of all our material wants is beyond the productive capacity of all available resources. Thus, scarcity is pervasive in all aspects of our lives. This unyielding fact is the basis of our definition of economics: ***Economics is concerned with the efficient use (or management) of limited productive resources to attain the maximum satisfaction of human material wants.*** Though it may not be self-evident, all the headline-grabbing issues of the day — inflation, unemployment, the federal budget deficit, poverty and inequality, pollution, government regulation of business — have their roots in the issue of using scarce resources efficiently.

In this chapter, however, we will not plunge into the problem and issues of the moment. Our immediate concern is with some basic preliminary questions:

1. Of what importance or consequence is the study of economics?

2. How should we study economics — what are the proper procedures? What is the methodology of this subject?

3. What specific problems, limitations, and pitfalls might we encounter in studying economics?

4. How do economists think about problems? What is the economic perspective?

BOX 1-1   THE BIG PICTURE

You are about to embark on the study of economics, a discipline that can help you understand a vast array of human issues and problems. Economics is about *scarcity, wants,* and *choices.* Try to think of any goods or services of which there is such an abundance that *everyone* in the world has as much as he or she wants. You will not have much success! Even time must be carefully budgeted because there is less of it than we would like. As George Stigler, a Nobel Prize winner in economics, points out, "Anything that is an object of conscious desire must be scarce: One does not consciously desire the air breathed, or to hear bad jokes. Scarce things are costly. If they weren't, everyone would get so much of each that they would not be scarce anymore. So anything scarce, and worth having, has been costly for someone to obtain."*

The only reason you do not consciously think about breathing is that you have as much oxygen as you could possibly want. If you didn't, you would have to carefully budget even the air you breathe! It is

* G.J. Stigler, *Memoirs of an Unregulated Economist* (New York: Basic Books, 1988).

because economics deals with an issue — scarcity — that pervades our daily lives that its study is relevant to a large spectrum of interests and pursuits.

If we wanted or needed very little in relation to available resources, the scarcity problem would be less pronounced. But because there are so many goods and services we need and want, we must make choices about which goods and services we most desire. Despite often being referred to as the "dismal science," economics is really about getting enjoyment out of life: getting as much enjoyment as possible out of the limited resources available to us; the study of economics may thus be your ticket to "happiness"! More realistically, you may come to better understand and appreciate the ubiquitous problem of scarcity in our daily lives.

You need to understand the scarcity problem if you are to succeed in the study of economics, particularly microeconomics. "The Big Picture" boxes have been written to continuously remind you of the raison d'être of economics, and to put the information in each chapter within the larger context of scarcity, wants, and choices.

THE RELEVANCE OF ECONOMICS

Why should you study economics? Is studying economics worth your time and effort? Half a century ago John Maynard Keynes (1883–1946) — one of the most influential economists of this century — offered a telling response:

> The ideas of economists and political philosophers, both when they are right and when they are wrong, are more powerful than is commonly understood. Indeed the world is ruled by little else. Practical men, who believe themselves to be quite exempt from any intellectual influences, are usually the slaves of some defunct economist.

The ideologies of the modern world have been shaped in substantial measure by the great economists of the past — for example, Adam Smith, David Ricardo, John Stuart Mill, Karl Marx, and

John Maynard Keynes. And it is currently common for world leaders to ask for and receive the advice and policy prescriptions of economists.

The Government of Canada has more than a thousand economists in its various ministries and agencies — and the advice of this army of economists is considered essential to the functioning of modern government. The areas economists advise on include unemployment and inflation, economic growth and productivity, taxation and public expenditures, poverty and income maintenance, the balance of payments and the international monetary system, labour-management relations, health care, pollution, immigration, competition, and industrial regulation, among others.

ECONOMICS FOR CITIZENSHIP

A basic understanding of economics is essential if we are to be well-informed citizens. Many of today's problems have important economic aspects, and as informed voters we can influence the decisions of our political leaders in these matters. What are the causes and consequences of the federal budget deficit that is often a main item in the news? What of the depressing stories of homeless people? Are mergers of corporations good or bad? Why is inflation undesirable? What can be done to reduce unemployment? Are existing welfare programs effective and justifiable? Should we continue to subsidize farmers? Do we need further reform of our tax system? Will free trade with the United States and Mexico help or hurt our industries, employment, and incomes?

Since the answers to such questions are determined largely by our elected officials, intelligence in the voting booth depends on a basic working knowledge of economics. Needless to say, a sound grasp of economics is more than helpful to politicians themselves!

PERSONAL APPLICATIONS

Economics is also important in business. An understanding of the overall operation of the economic system puts the business executive in a better position to decide on policies. The executive who understands the causes and consequences of inflation is better equipped, during inflationary periods, to make more intelligent business decisions. Indeed, that is why economists are on the payrolls of most large corporations. Their job is to gather and interpret economic information on which rational business decisions can be made.

Economics also gives the individual as consumer and worker some insights as to how to make wiser buying and employment decisions. How can you "hedge" against the reduction in the purchasing power of the dollar that accompanies inflation? Which occupations pay well; which are most immune to unemployment? Should you buy or lease a car? Should you use a credit card or pay cash? Similarly, an individual who understands, for example, the relationship between budget deficits and security (stock and bond) values will be able to make more enlightened personal financial investment decisions.

METHODOLOGY

Mastering the discipline of economics will be much easier if you understand the methodology used by economists. You will be studying theories of economic relationships that economists have assembled in the last several hundred years. How have they constructed these theories and how can we be sure that these theories adequately describe the workings of a market economy?

The methodology used by economists to arrive at an understanding of economic phenomena is no different than that used in other social sciences and the natural sciences. It is generally referred to as the scientific method. Economists try to formulate economic *theories* (also known as principles, models, or laws) that shed light on economic phenomena, economic *policies* that aim to solve economic *problems*.

The procedures employed by economists to arrive at theories are summarized in Figure 1-1.

1. Sometimes economists begin by gathering facts relevant to a specific economic problem. This task is referred to as *descriptive* or *empirical economics*.

2. From the facts a general principle or **theory** may be derived. A theory seeks to explain the relationship among facts. When theories are distilled from facts we refer to such a derivation as **induction**. The inductive method begins with an accumulation of facts, which are then arranged systematically and analyzed so as to permit a generalization or principle. Induction moves from facts to theory, from the particular to the general. The induction method is represented by the left upward arrow from box 1 to box 2 in Figure 1-1.

Economists also arrive at new theories by drawing on insight, logic, or intuition. We refer to such a process as **deduction**. When a new theory is formed through the deductive method, it is in the first instance tentative until verified by facts. Until the theory is verified by facts, we refer to it as a hypothesis. For example, we may conjecture that it is rational for consumers to buy more of a product when price is low than when it is high.

To test the validity of the hypothesis they have deduced, economists must subject it to the systematic and repeated examination of relevant facts. Do data in fact reveal a negative or inverse relationship between price and the amount purchased? This testing process is represented by the right downward arrow from box 2 to box 1 in Figure 1-1.

Deduction and induction are complementary, rather than opposing, techniques of investigation. Hypotheses formulated by deduction provide guidelines

FIGURE 1-1   The relationship between facts, principles, and policies in economics

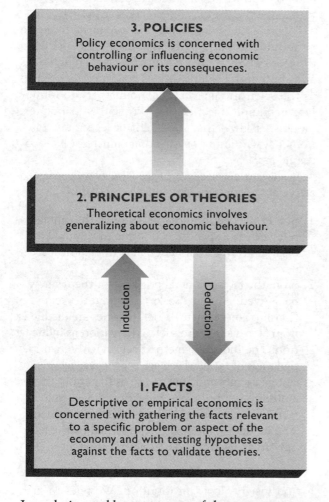

3. POLICIES
Policy economics is concerned with controlling or influencing economic behaviour or its consequences.

2. PRINCIPLES OR THEORIES
Theoretical economics involves generalizing about economic behaviour.

Induction

Deduction

1. FACTS
Descriptive or empirical economics is concerned with gathering the facts relevant to a specific problem or aspect of the economy and with testing hypotheses against the facts to validate theories.

In analyzing problems or aspects of the economy, economists may use the inductive method, whereby they gather, systematically arrange, and generalize on facts. Alternatively, the deductive method develops hypotheses that are then tested against facts. Generalizations derived from either method of inquiry are useful not only in explaining economic behaviour, but also as a basis for formulating economic policies.

for economists as they gather and systematize empirical data. Conversely, some understanding of factual evidence — of the "real world" — is a prerequisite to the formulation of meaningful hypotheses.

The general knowledge of economic behaviour that economic principles provide can then be used in formulating policies for correcting or avoiding the problem under scrutiny. This aspect of the field is sometimes called "applied economics" or **policy economics** (box 3).

Continuing to use Figure 1-1 as a point of reference, let us now examine the economist's methodology in more detail.

DESCRIPTIVE ECONOMICS

All sciences are empirical. That means all sciences are based on observable and verifiable behaviour of certain data or subject matter. In the physical sciences, the factual data are inorganic. As a social science, economics is concerned with the behaviour of individuals and institutions engaged in the production, exchange, and consumption of goods and services.

The gathering of economic data can be a complex task. Because the world of reality is cluttered with a multitude of interrelated facts, economists must use discretion in gathering them. They must distinguish economic from noneconomic facts and then determine which economic facts are relevant and which are irrelevant for the particular problem under consideration. But even when this sorting process has been completed, the relevant economic facts may appear diverse and unrelated.

ECONOMIC THEORY

Economic theory systematically arranges, interprets, and generalizes on economic data or facts. Principles and theories bring order and meaning to facts by tying them together, determining the relationship to one another, and generalizing on them. But facts in turn serve as a check on the validity of principles already established. Since how individuals and institutions actually behave in producing, exchanging, and consuming goods and services may change with time, it is essential that economists continuously check theories against the changing economic environment.

TERMINOLOGY   Economists talk about "laws," "principles," "theories," and "models." These terms all mean essentially the same thing: generalizations, or statements of regularity, concerning the economic behaviour of individuals and institutions. The term "economic law" is a bit misleading because it implies a high degree of precision, universal application, and even moral rightness. Some people incorrectly assume "theory" has nothing to do with the facts and realities of the world. In truth, theory helps us to understand the facts and realities of the world. The term "model" has much to commend it. A model is a simplified picture of reality, an abstract generalization of how relevant data actually behave.

In this book the four terms (laws, principles, theories, and models) will be used synonymously. The choice of terms in labelling any particular generalization will be governed by custom or convenience. Thus, the relationship between the price of a product and the quantity consumers purchase will be called the "law" of demand, rather than the theory or principle of demand, simply because this is the customary designation.

Several other points regarding the character and derivation of economic principles are in order.

GENERALIZATIONS Economic principles are generalizations. They are frequently stated as averages or statistical probabilities. For example, when economists say that the average Canadian family earned an income of $52,000 in 1994, they are generalizing. It is recognized that some families earned much more and many families earned less. Yet this generalization, properly handled and interpreted, can be very meaningful and useful.

Similarly, economic generalizations are often stated in terms of probabilities. For example, a researcher may tell us that there is a 95% probability that every $1 reduction in personal income taxes will result in a $0.90 increase in consumer spending.

"OTHER THINGS EQUAL" ASSUMPTION Like other scientists, economists make use of the **ceteris paribus,** or **other things being equal assumption** to construct their generalizations. We assume that all other variables, except those under immediate consideration, are held constant. This simplifies the reasoning process by isolating the relationship under consideration. To illustrate: In considering the relationship between the price of Pepsi and the amount purchased, it is helpful to assume that of all factors that might influence the amount of Pepsi purchased (for example, the prices of other goods, such as Coke, and consumer incomes and preferences), only the price of Pepsi varies. The economist is then able to focus on the "price of Pepsi–purchases of Pepsi" relationship without reasoning being blurred or confused by the intrusion of other variables.

In the natural sciences, controlled experiments usually can be performed where "all other things" are in fact held constant, or virtually so. Thus the scientist can test the assumed relationship between two variables with great precision. But economics is not a laboratory science. The economist's process of empirical verification is based on "real world" data generated by the actual operation of the economy. In this rather bewildering environment, "other things" *do* change. Despite the development of rather complex statistical techniques designed to hold other things equal, such controls are less than perfect. As a result, economic theories are sometimes less certain and less precise in application than those of the laboratory sciences.

ABSTRACTIONS Economic principles, or theories, are necessarily abstractions. The very process of sorting out noneconomic and irrelevant facts in the fact-gathering process involves abstracting from "reality." Unfortunately, the abstractness of economic theory prompts the uninformed to identify theory as something that is impractical and unrealistic. This is nonsense!

Economic theories are practical, in fact, *because* they are abstractions. Economists theorize in order to give meaning to a maze of facts that would otherwise be confusing and useless, and to put facts into a more usable, practical form. Thus, to generalize is to abstract or purposely simplify; generalization for this purpose is practical, and therefore so is abstraction. An economic theory is a model — a simplified picture or map — for some segment of the economy. This model enables us to better understand reality *because* it avoids confusing details. Theories — *good* theories — are grounded on facts and therefore are realistic. Theories that do not fit the facts are simply not good theories.

MACRO AND MICRO There are two levels of analysis at which the economist can derive laws concerning economic behaviour. Macroeconomics deals with the economy as a whole or with the basic subdivisions or aggregates — such as the household, business, government, and foreign trade sectors — making up the economy. An aggregate is a collection of specific economic units treated *as though* they were one unit. Thus we might find it convenient to lump together the many businesses in our economy and treat them as though they were one huge unit.

Macroeconomics is concerned with obtaining an overview, or general outline, of the structure of the economy and the relationships between the major aggregates that make up the economy. It deals with such magnitudes as *total* output, the *total* level of employment, *total* income, *aggregate* expenditures, and the *general* level of prices, in analyzing various economic problems. Macroeconomics examines the forest, not the trees. It gives us a bird's-eye view of the economy.

Microeconomics deals with *specific* economic units and a *detailed* consideration of the behaviour of these individual units. Here we analyze an individual industry, firm, or household and concentrate on such magnitudes as the output or price of a *specific* product, the number of workers employed by a single firm, the revenue or income of a particular firm or household, and the expenditures of a given firm or family. In microeconomics we examine the trees, not the forest.

Many topics and subdivisions of economics are rooted in both "micro" and "macro." There has been a convergence of macro and micro in important areas in recent years. While the problem of unemployment was once treated as a macroeconomic topic ("unemployment depends on *aggregate* spending"), economists now recognize that decisions made by *individual* workers in searching for jobs and the way specific product and labour markets function are also critical in determining the unemployment rate. (**Key Question 5**)

GRAPHIC EXPRESSION Many of the economic models or principles in this book will be expressed graphically. The most important of these are labelled "**Key Graphs.**" You should read the appendix to this chapter to review graphing and other relevant quantitative relationships.

QUICK REVIEW 1-1

1. Economics is concerned with the efficient management of scarce resources.

2. Induction is the observation of regularities in factual data and drawing generalizations from them; deduction uses logic to create hypotheses that are then tested with factual data.

3. Economic theories ("laws," "principles," or "models") are generalizations, based on facts, concerning the economic behaviour of individuals and institutions.

4. Macroeconomics deals with the economy as a whole; microeconomics focuses on specific units that make up the economy.

DESIGNING ECONOMIC POLICY

Economic theories should provide the basis for *economic policy*. Our understanding of economic principles can be applied in resolving or alleviating specific problems and in furthering the realization of society's overall goals (box 3 of Figure 1-1). Economic principles are valuable as predictive devices. And prediction, even if not completely accurate, is required if we want to alter some event or outcome. If some undesirable event such as unemployment or inflation can be predicted or understood through economic theory, we may then be able to influence or control that event.

FORMULATING ECONOMIC POLICY The creation of policies designed to achieve specific goals is no simple matter. Here's a brief examination of the basic steps in policy formulation.

1. **STATING GOALS** The first step is to make a clear statement of a goal. If we say that we want "full employment," do we mean that everyone between, say, 16 and 65 years of age should have a job? Or do we mean that everyone who wants to work should have a job? Should we allow for some "normal" unemployment caused by inevitable changes in the structure of industry and workers' voluntarily changing jobs?

2. **POLICY OPTIONS** Next, we must state and recognize the possible effects of alternative policies designed to achieve the goal. This requires a clear understanding of the economic impact benefits, costs, and political feasibility of alternative programs. For example, economists debate the relative merits and demerits of fiscal policy (which involves changing government spending and taxes) and monetary policy (which entails altering the supply of money) as alternative means of achieving and maintaining full employment.

3. **EVALUATION** We are obligated to ourselves and future generations to review our experiences with chosen policies and evaluate their effectiveness; it is only through this evaluation that we can hope to improve policy applications. Did a specific change in taxes or the supply of money alter the level of employment to the extent originally predicted? Did deregulation of a particular industry (for example, the

airlines) yield the predicted beneficial results? If not why not? (**Key Question 1**)

ECONOMIC GOALS   Economic policies are designed to achieve certain economic goals that are widely accepted in our own and many other societies. They include:

1. ECONOMIC GROWTH   The production of more and better goods and services, for the purpose of attaining a higher standard of living, is desired.

2. FULL EMPLOYMENT   Suitable jobs should be available for all who are willing and able to work.

3. PRICE LEVEL STABILITY   Sizable upswings or downswings in the general price level, that is, inflation and deflation, should be avoided.

4. AN EQUITABLE DISTRIBUTION OF INCOME   No group of citizens should face stark poverty while other citizens enjoy extreme luxury.

5. BALANCE OF TRADE   We seek a reasonable balance in our international trade and financial transactions.

This list of goals provides the basis for several significant points.

1. INTERPRETATION   This and any other statement of basic economic goals inevitably results in problems of interpretation. What, for example, is an "equitable" distribution of income? On the other hand, most of us might accept the above goals, but might disagree as to the types of policies needed to attain these goals.

2. COMPLEMENTARY   Certain of these goals are complementary in that when one goal is achieved, some other goal or goals will also tend to be realized. For example, growth (goal 1) will help achieve full employment (goal 2).

3. CONFLICTING   Some goals *may* be conflicting or mutually exclusive. Thus, there are **trade-offs**, meaning that to achieve one goal we must sacrifice some other goal. Some economists argue that those forces that further the attainment of economic growth and full employment may be the very same forces that cause inflation. In fact, the possible conflict between

goals 2 and 3 has been at the forefront of economic research and debate in recent years. Goals 1 and 4 may also be in conflict. Some economists point out that efforts to achieve greater equality in the distribution of income may weaken incentives to work, invest, innovate, and take business risks, all of which promote rapid economic growth.

4. PRIORITIES   When goals do conflict, society must develop a system of priorities for the objectives it seeks. If full employment and price stability are to some extent mutually exclusive, that is, if full employment is accompanied by some inflation *and* price stability entails some unemployment, society must decide on the relative importance of these two goals. There is clearly ample room for disagreement here. But society must assess the trade-offs and make decisions.

POSITIVE AND NORMATIVE   As we move from the fact and principles levels (boxes 1 and 2) of Figure 1-1 to the policy level (box 3) we are making a leap from positive to normative economics.

Positive economics attempts to set forth statements about economic behaviour that are devoid of value judgements. Positive statements are verifiable by appealing to facts. In contrast, **normative economics** embodies someone's value judgements. Normative statements cannot be tested against facts to determine whether they are true. Positive economics is concerned with *what* is, while normative economics embodies subjective feelings about *what ought* to be.

Positive economics is concerned with what the economy is actually like; normative economics has to do with whether certain conditions or aspects of the economy are desirable.

Consider the following examples. Positive statement: "Unemployment is 7% of the labour force." Normative statement: "Unemployment ought to be reduced." Positive statement: "Other things being the same, if tuition is increased, enrolment at Informed University (IU) will fall." Normative statement: "Tuition should be lowered at IU so that more students can obtain an education." Indeed, whenever such words as "ought" or "should" appear in a sentence, there is a strong chance that you are dealing with a normative statement. However, it is worth noting that the choice of what positive statement to make may, in itself, be a normative statement. (**Key Question 6**)

QUICK REVIEW 1-2

1. Designing economic policy requires the clear statement of goals, the assessing of policy options, and the evaluation of policy results.

2. Some of society's economic goals are complementary while others are conflicting.

3. Positive economics deals with factual statements ("what is"), while normative economics concerns value judgements ("what ought to be").

PITFALLS TO OBJECTIVE THINKING

You should be aware that there are pitfalls to thinking objectively about economic problems. Avoiding these pitfalls will greatly facilitate your grasp of economic reasoning. The following are pitfalls to objective thinking that you should guard against.

BIAS

In contrast to neophyte physicists or chemists, budding economists often launch into their field of study with a bundle of biases and preconceptions. For example, you might be suspicious of business profits or feel that deficit spending is evil. Biases may cloud your thinking and interfere with objective analysis. Students beginning their studies in economics must be willing to shed biases and preconceptions not warranted by facts.

LOADED TERMINOLOGY

The economic terminology in newspapers and popular magazines is sometimes emotionally loaded. The writer — or the particular interest group represented — may have a cause to further or an axe to grind, and the terms will be slanted to solicit the support of the reader. A governmental flood-control project in the Prairies may be called "creeping socialism" by its opponents and "protecting the national interest" by its proponents. We must be prepared to discount such terminology to objectively understand economic issues.

DEFINITIONS

No scientist is obligated to use immediately understandable definitions of terms. The economists may find it convenient and essential to define terms in such a way that they are at odds with the definitions held by most people in everyday speech. No problem, so long as the economist is explicit and consistent in these definitions. For example, the term "investment" to John Q. Citizen is associated with the buying of bonds and stocks in the securities market. How often have we heard someone talk of investing in Bell Canada stock or government bonds? But to the economist, "investment" means the purchase of real capital assets such as machinery and equipment, or the construction of a new factory building.

FALLACY OF COMPOSITION

Another pitfall in economic thinking is assuming "what is true for the individual or part of a group is *necessarily* true for the group or whole." This is a logical **fallacy of composition;** it is *not* correct. For example, a wage increase for Smith is desirable because, with constant product prices, it increases Smith's purchasing power and standard of living. But if everyone gets a wage increase, product prices will likely rise; that is, inflation will occur. Thus Smith's standard of living may be unchanged as higher prices offset this larger salary.

Second illustration: An *individual* farmer who is fortunate enough to realize a bumper (particularly large) crop is likely to realize a sharp increase in income. But this generalization does not apply to farmers as a *group*. An individual farmer's bumper crop will not influence crop prices because it is such a negligible fraction of the total farm output, but for farmers as a group prices vary inversely with total output. Thus if *all* farmers realize bumper crops, the total output of farm products rises, thereby depressing crop prices. If price declines are relatively greater than the increased output, farm incomes will *fall*.

CAUSATION FALLACIES

Economists often try to discern if economic phenomenon A actually affects economic phenomenon B. Causation, however, is sometimes difficult to discern in economics. Beware of these two fallacies:

POST HOC FALLACY   You must be very careful before concluding that because event A precedes event B, A is the cause of B. This kind of faulty reasoning is known as the **post hoc, ergo propter hoc,** or **after this, therefore because of this, fallacy.**

Example: Suppose early each spring the medicine man of a tribe performs his ritual by cavorting around the village in a green costume. A week or so later the trees and grass turn green. Can we conclude that event A, the medicine man's gyrations, has caused event B, the landscape's turning green? Obviously not. The rooster crows before dawn, but this doesn't mean the rooster is responsible for the sunrise!

Informed University hires a new hockey coach and the team's record improves. Is the new coach the cause? Maybe. But perhaps the presence of more experienced players or an easier schedule is the true cause.

CORRELATION VERSUS CAUSATION We must not confuse **correlation** with **causation.** *Correlation* is a technical term indicating that two sets of data are associated in some systematic and dependable way. For example, we may find that when X increases, Y also increases. But this does not necessarily mean that X is the cause of Y. The relationship could be purely coincidental or determined by some other factor, Z, not included in the analysis.

Example: Economists have found a positive correlation between education and income. In general, people with more education earn higher incomes than people with less education. Common sense suggests education is the cause and higher incomes are the effect; more education suggests a more productive worker and such workers receive larger monetary rewards.

But might not causation run the other way? Do people with higher incomes buy more education, just as they buy more automobiles and steaks? Or is the relationship explainable in terms of still other factors? Are education and income positively correlated because the bundle of characteristics — ability, motivation, personal habits — required to succeed in education are the same characteristics required to be a productive and highly paid worker? **(Key Question 9)**

THE ECONOMIC PERSPECTIVE

The methodology used by economists to help them come up with good theories is common to all the natural and social sciences. And all scholars try to avoid the reasoning errors just discussed. Thus, economists do *not* think in a special way. But they *do* think about things from a special perspective.

The **economic perspective** has several critical and closely interrelated features, including scarcity, rational behaviour, and benefit-cost comparisons.

SCARCITY AND CHOICE

Recall that economists view the world from the vantage point of scarcity. Human and property resources are scarce. It follows that outputs of goods and services must be scarce as well. Scarcity limits our options and necessitates choices. If we cannot have it all, what should we choose to have?

At the core of economics is the ever-present reality of scarcity in relation to our material wants, and thus the idea that "there is no free lunch" (no wonder economics is referred to as the "dismal science"!). Someone may treat you to lunch, making it "free" to you. But there is a cost to someone. The lunch requires scarce inputs of farm products and the labour of cooks and waiters. These resources could have been used in alternative productive activities and those activities — those other goods and services — are sacrificed in providing your lunch.

RATIONAL BEHAVIOUR

Economics assumes "rational self-interest." This means that individuals make decisions that yield them the greatest satisfaction or maximum fulfilment of some goal. As consumers, workers, and businesspersons, people have goals and make rational decisions to achieve those objectives. Thus, consumers seek to spend their incomes to get the greatest satisfaction from the goods and services their limited incomes allow them to buy. It is in this sense that consumers are rational.

Rational behaviour does not mean everyone will make similar choices because their circumstances (constraints), preferences, and available information may differ. You may decide that it is in your self-interest to attend college or university before entering the labour force. But a high school classmate decides to forgo additional schooling and take a job. Why the different choices? Your academic abilities, along with your family's income and wealth, may be significantly greater than those of your classmate; or perhaps your job preferences are different from your classmate's. You may also be better informed, realizing for example that college- and university-educated workers earn much higher incomes and are less likely to be unemployed than are workers with just a high school education. Thus, you opt for college or university while your high school classmate with either very different job preferences, or with fewer human and financial resources and less information, chooses a job. Both are rational choices, but based on differing constraints, information, or preferences.

Our example implies that rational decisions may change as circumstances change. Suppose the federal government decides it is in the national interest to increase the supply of college- and university-educated workers. As a result, government policy changes to provide greater financial assistance to post-secondary students. Under these new conditions, your high school classmate may opt for college or university rather than a job after graduating from high school.

Rational self-interest is *not* the same as selfishness. People make personal sacrifices to help family members or friends and contribute to charities because they derive pleasure from doing so. Parents contribute financially to their children's education because they derive satisfaction from that choice.

MARGINAL ANALYSIS: BENEFITS AND COSTS

The economic perspective focuses largely on *marginal analysis* — decisions that compare marginal benefits and marginal costs. Marginal means "extra" or "additional." Most economic choices result in changes to the status quo. When you graduated from high school, you faced the question of whether you should get *additional* education. Similarly, businesses are continuously deciding whether to employ more or fewer workers or to produce more or less output.

In making such choices rationally, we must compare marginal benefits and marginal costs. Because of scarcity, any choice will result in *both* extra benefits and additional costs. Example: Your time is scarce. What to do with, say, two "free" hours on a Saturday afternoon? Option: Watch the Vancouver Canucks play the Montreal Canadiens on television. Marginal benefit: The pleasure of seeing the game. Marginal cost: Any of the other things you sacrifice by spending an extra two hours in front of the tube, including studying (economics, we hope), jogging, or taking a nap. If the marginal benefit exceeds the marginal cost, then it is rational to watch the game. But if you perceive the marginal cost of watching the game to exceed its marginal benefits, then one of the other options will be chosen.

BOX 1-2   APPLYING THE THEORY

The key to understanding economic behaviour is to *constantly* apply the marginal cost-benefit perspective. An illuminating example of its application can be had by economists' response to the automobile safety legislation that ensued in Canada and the United States after Ralph Nader published *Unsafe at Any Speed*, which pointed out the danger to passengers of available car models. Economists predicted that once padded dashboards, seat belts, collapsible steering columns, and other safety enhancement features were introduced, the number of automobile accidents would increase! It is the type of response that would not likely come from a non-economist. Economists reasoned that if drivers felt the threat to being killed in an automobile accident diminished with the new safety features, they would, on average, be less careful.

In 1975 Sam Peltzman of the University of Chicago investigated the impact of the new safety features on automobile accidents. He found that there *were* more accidents, but the number of deaths remained the same as previously, presumably on account of the enhanced safety features on the later-model automobiles.

If you are still in doubt about the applicability of the marginal cost-benefit perspective, consider the comments of Armen Alchian of the University of California at Los Angeles. He was certain the accident rate for automobiles would fall if automobile manufacturers were required to install a spear on the steering wheel aimed directly at the driver's heart! Who could argue with Alchian that drivers would be much more careful with a spear aimed at their heart? The marginal cost could be very high!

Adapted from Steven E. Landsburg, *The Armchair Economist.* (New York: The Free Press, 1993), Chapter 1.

BOX 1-3   APPLYING THE THEORY

FAST-FOOD LINES: AN ECONOMIC PERSPECTIVE

How might the economic perspective help us understand the behaviour of fast-food consumers?

When you enter a fast-food restaurant, which line do you select? What do you do when you are in a long line in the restaurant and a new station opens? Have you ever gone to a fast-food restaurant, only to see long lines, and then leave? Have you ever had someone in front of you in a fast-food line place an order that takes a long time to fill?

The economic perspective is useful in analyzing the behaviour of fast-food customers. These customers are at the restaurant because they expect the marginal benefit or satisfaction from the food they buy to match or exceed its cost. When customers enter the restaurant, they scurry to the shortest line — lest someone else beat them there — in the belief that the shortest line will reduce their time cost of obtaining their food. They are acting purposefully; time is limited and most people would prefer using it in some way other than standing in line.

All lines in the fast-food establishment normally are of roughly equal lengths. If one line is temporarily shorter than other lines, some people will move towards that line. These movers apparently view the time saving associated with the shorter line to exceed the cost of moving from their present line. Line changing normally results in an equilibrium line length. No further movement of customers between lines will occur once all lines are of equal length.

Fast-food customers face another cost-benefit decision when a clerk opens a new station at the counter. Should customers move to the new station or stay put? Those who do shift to the new line decide that the benefit of the time savings from the move exceeds the extra cost of physically moving. In so deciding, customers must also consider just how quickly they can get to the new station compared to others who may be contemplating the same move. (Those who hesitate in this situation are lost!)

Customers at the fast-food establishment select lines without having perfect information. For example, they do not first survey those in the lines to determine what they are ordering before deciding on which line to enter. There are two reasons. First, most customers would tell them "it is none of your business," and therefore no information would be forthcoming. Second, even if they could obtain the information, the amount of time necessary to get it (cost) would most likely exceed any time saving associated with finding the best line (benefit). Because information is costly to obtain, fast-food patrons select lines on the basis of imperfect information. Thus, not all decisions turn out to be as expected. For example, some people may enter a line in which the person in front of them is ordering hamburgers and fries for the 40 people in the Greyhound bus parked out back! Nevertheless, at the time the customer made the decision, he or she thought that it was optimal.

Imperfect information also explains why some people who arrive at a fast-food restaurant and observe long lines decide to leave. These people conclude that the marginal cost (monetary plus time costs) of obtaining the fast food is too large relative to the marginal benefit. They would not have come to the restaurant in the first place had they known the lines were so long. But, getting that information by, say, employing an advance scout with a cellular phone, would cost more than the perceived benefit.

Finally, customers must decide what to order when they arrive at the counter. In making these choices, they again compare marginal costs and marginal benefits in attempting to obtain the greatest personal well-being.

Economists believe that what is true for the behaviour of customers at fast-food restaurants is true for economic behaviour in general. Faced with an array of choices, consumers, workers, and businesses rationally compare marginal costs and benefits in making decisions.

On the national level, government is continuously making decisions involving marginal benefits and costs. More spending on health care means sacrifices on spending on shelter for the homeless, aid for the poor, or military security. Lesson: In a world of scarcity the marginal benefit derived from a given choice also means you incur the marginal cost of forgoing something else. Unfortunately, there's no free lunch.

One of the implications of marginal analysis in a world pervaded by scarcity is that there can be too much of a "good thing." Although certain goods and services seem inherently desirable — education, health care, a clean environment — we can in fact have too much of them. "Too much" occurs when we push their production to some point where their marginal costs (the value of the forgone options) exceeds their marginal benefit. If we choose to produce health care to the extent that its marginal cost exceeds its marginal benefit, we are providing "too much" health care even though health care is a good thing. If the marginal cost of health care is greater than its marginal benefit, then we are sacrificing alternative products (for example, education and pollution reduction) that are more valuable than health care at the margin. (**Key Question 13**)

QUICK REVIEW 1-3

1. Beware of logical errors such as the fallacy of composition and the post hoc fallacy when engaging in economic reasoning.

2. The economic perspective stresses **a** resource scarcity and the necessity of making choices; **b** the assumption of rational behaviour; and **c** marginal analysis.

CHAPTER SUMMARY

1. Economics deals with the efficient use of scarce resources in the production of goods and services to satisfy material wants.

2. A knowledge of economics contributes to effective citizenship and provides useful insights for consumers and businesspersons.

3. The tasks of descriptive or empirical economics are **a** gathering those economic facts relevant to a particular problem or specific segment of the economy, and **b** testing hypotheses against facts to validate theories.

4. Generalizations stated by economists are called "principles," "theories," "laws," or "models." The derivation of these principles is the task of economic theory.

5. Induction distils theories from facts; deduction uses logic to derive hypotheses that are then tested against facts.

6. Some economic principles deal with macroeconomics (the economy as a whole or major aggregates), while others pertain to microeconomics (specific economic units or institutions).

7. Economic principles are valuable as predictive devices; they are the bases for the formulation of economic policy designed to solve problems and control undesirable events.

8. Economic growth, full employment, price level stability, equity in the distribution of income, and a viable balance of payments are widely accepted economic goals in our society. Some of these goals are complementary; others are mutually exclusive.

9. Positive statements deal with facts ("what is"), while normative statements encompass value judgements ("what ought to be").

10. In studying economics the beginner may encounter numerous pitfalls. Some of the more important are **a** biases and preconceptions, **b** terminological difficulties, **c** the fallacy of composition, and **d** the difficulty of establishing clear cause-effect relationships.

11. The economic perspective envisions individuals and institutions making rational decisions based on costs and benefits.

TERMS AND CONCEPTS

ceteris paribus or "other things being equal" assumption (p. 7)
choices (p. 11)
correlation and causation (p. 11)
descriptive economics (p. 6)
economics (p. 3)
economic goals (p. 9)
economic perspective (p. 11)
economic policy (p. 8)
economic theory (p. 6)
fallacy of composition (p. 10)
hypothesis (p. 5)

induction and deduction (p. 5)
macroeconomics and microeconomics (p. 7, p. 8)
normative economics (p. 9)
policy economics (p. 6)
positive and normative economics (p. 9)
post hoc, ergo propter hoc or "after this, therefore because of this" fallacy (p. 10)
principles or generalizations (p. 7)
scarcity (p. 11)
theory (p. 5)
trade-offs (p. 9)
wants (p. 11)

QUESTIONS AND STUDY SUGGESTIONS

1. **Key Question** *Explain in detail the interrelationships between economic facts, theory, and policy. Critically evaluate: "The trouble with economics is that it is not practical. It has too much to say about theory and not enough to say about facts."*

2. Analyze and explain the following quotation:

    Facts are seldom simple and usually complicated; theoretical analysis is needed to unravel the complications and interpret the facts before we can understand them.... The opposition of facts and theory is a false one; the true relationship is complementary. We cannot in practice consider a fact without relating it to other facts, and the relation is a theory. Facts by themselves are dumb; before they will tell us anything we have to arrange them, and the arrangement is a theory. Theory is simply the unavoidable arrangement and interpretation of facts, which gives us generalizations on which we can argue and act, in the place of a mass of disjointed particulars.[1]

3. Of what significance is the fact that economics is not a laboratory science? What problems may be involved in deriving and applying economic principles?

4. Explain each of the following statements:

    a. "Like all scientific laws, economic laws are established in order to make successful prediction of the outcome of human actions."
    b. "Abstraction... is the inevitable price of generality.... Indeed abstraction and generality are virtually synonyms."
    c. "Numbers serve to discipline rhetoric."

[1] Henry Clay, *Economics for the General Reader* (New York: The Macmillan Company, 1925), pp. 10-11.

5. Key Question   *Indicate whether each of the following statements pertains to microeconomics or macroeconomics:*

   a. The unemployment rate in Canada was 10.3% in 1994.
   b. The Alpo dogfood plant in Bowser, Alberta, laid off 15 workers last month.
   c. An unexpected freeze in central Florida reduced the citrus crop and caused the price of oranges to rise.
   d. Our domestic output, adjusted for inflation, dropped by 1.5% in 1991.
   e. Last week the Bank of Montreal lowered its interest rate on business loans by one-half of a percentage point.
   f. The consumer price index rose by less than 3% in 1994.

6. Key Question   *Identify each of the following as either a positive or a normative statement:*

   a. The high temperature today was 33°C.
   b. It was too hot today.
   c. The general price level rose by 4.4% last year.
   d. Inflation greatly eroded living standards last year and should be reduced by government policies.

7. To what extent would you accept the five economic goals stated and described in this chapter? What priorities would you assign to them? It has been said that we seek simply four goals: progress, stability, justice, and freedom. Is this list of goals compatible with that given in the chapter?

8. Analyze each of the following specific goals in terms of the five general goals stated in this chapter, and note points of conflict and compatibility: a. conservation of natural resources and the lessening of environmental pollution; b. increasing leisure; c. protection of Canadian producers from foreign competition. Indicate which of these specific goals you favour, and justify your position.

9. Key Question   *Explain and give an illustration of a. the fallacy of composition; b. the "after this, therefore because of this" fallacy. Why are cause-and-effect relationships difficult to isolate in the social sciences?*

10. Suppose empirical studies show that students who study more hours receive higher grades, as suggested by the graph accompanying question 4 in this chapter's appendix. Does this relationship guarantee that any particular student who studies longer will get higher grades?

11. A recent psychiatric study found that there is a positive correlation between the amount of time children and youth spend watching television and mental depression. Speculate on possible cause-effect relationships.

12. "Economists should never be popular; men who afflict the comfortable serve equally as those who comfort the afflicted and one cannot suppose that ... capitalism would prosper without the critics its leaders find such a profound source of annoyance."[2] Interpret and evaluate.

13. Key Question   *Use the economic perspective to explain why someone who normally is a light eater at a standard restaurant may become somewhat of a glutton at a buffet-style restaurant that charges a single price for all you can eat.*

14. (Applying the Theory, Box 1-3) Explain how the economic perspective can be used to explain the behaviour of customers in fast-food restaurants.

---

[2] John Kenneth Galbraith, *American Capitalism*, rev. ed. (Boston: Houghton Mifflin Company, 1956), p. 49.

APPENDIX TO CHAPTER 1

GRAPHS AND THEIR MEANING

If you glance quickly through the pages of this text, you will find many graphs. Some seem simple while others appear more formidable. Graphs are employed to help you visualize and understand important economic relationships. They are a way for economists to express their theories or models. Physicists and chemists sometimes illustrate their theories by building arrangements of multicoloured wooden balls that represent protons, neutrons, and so forth, held in proper relation to one another by wires or sticks. Economists often use graphs to illustrate their models. By understanding these "pictures" you can more readily understand what economists are saying.

Most of our models will explain the relationship between just two sets of economic facts, which can be conveniently represented with two-dimensional graphs.

CONSTRUCTING A GRAPH

A graph is a visual representation of the relationship between two variables. Table A1-1 provides a hypothetical illustration that shows the relationship between income and consumption. Without ever having studied economics, you would intuitively expect that high-income people consume more than low-income people. Thus we are not surprised to find in Table A1-1 that consumption increases as income increases.

TABLE A1-1   The relationship between income and consumption

Income (per week)	Consumption (per week)	Point
$ 0	$ 50	a
100	100	b
200	150	c
300	200	d
400	250	e

How can the information in Table A1-1 be expressed graphically? Glance at the graph shown in Figure A1-1. Now look back at the information in Table A1-1 and we will explain how to represent in it a meaningful way by constructing the graph you just examined.

FIGURE A1-1   Graphing the direct relationship between consumption and income

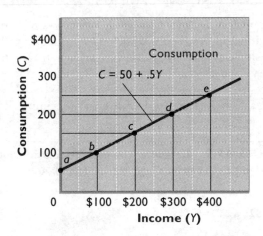

Two sets of data that are positively or directly related, such as consumption and income, graph as an upsloping line. In this case the vertical intercept is $50 and the slope of the line is $+\frac{1}{2}$.

What we are trying to visually show is how consumption changes as income changes. Since income is the determining factor, we represent it on the horizontal axis of the graph as is customary. And, because consumption is dependent on income, we represent it on the vertical axis of the graph, as is also customary. What we are doing is representing the independent variable on the **horizontal axis** and the dependent variable on the **vertical axis**.

Now arrange the vertical and horizontal scales of the graph so that they reflect the range of values of consumption and income. As you can see, the ranges in the graph cover the ranges of values in Table A1-1. The increments on both scales are $100 for each 1 cm.

Next, we locate for each consumption value and the income value a single point that reflects the same information graphically. Our five income–consumption combinations are plotted by drawing perpendiculars from the appropriate points on the two axes. For example, in plotting point c — the $200 income–$150 consumption point — perpendiculars must be drawn up from the horizontal (income) axis at $200 and across from the vertical (consumption) axis at $150. Where these perpendiculars intersect at point c locates this particular income–consumption combination. The other income–consumption combinations shown in Table A1-1 have also been located in Figure A1-1. A line or curve can now be drawn to connect these points.

Using Figure A1-1 as a benchmark, we can make several additional comments.

DIRECT AND INVERSE RELATIONSHIPS

Our upsloping line tells us that there is a **direct relationship** between income and consumption. By a positive or direct relationship, we mean that the two variables change in the *same* direction. An increase in consumption is associated with an increase in income; a decrease in consumption is associated with a decrease in income. When two sets of data are positively or directly related, they will always graph as an *upsloping* line as in Figure A1-1.

In contrast, two sets of data may be inversely related. Consider Table A1-2, which shows the relationship between the price of hockey tickets and game attendance at Informed University (IU). We observe a negative or **inverse relationship** between ticket prices and attendance; these two variables change in *opposite* directions. When ticket prices decrease, attendance increases. When ticket prices increase, attendance decreases. In Figure A1-2 we have plotted the six data points of Table A1-2 following the same procedure outlined above. Observe that an inverse relationship will always graph as a *downsloping* line.

TABLE A1-2   The relationship between ticket prices and attendance

Ticket price	Attendance (thousands)	Point
$25	0	a
20	4	b
15	8	c
10	12	d
5	16	e
0	20	f

DEPENDENT AND INDEPENDENT VARIABLES

Although it is not always easy, economists seek to determine which variable is "cause" and which is "effect," or, more formally, the independent and the dependent variables. By definition, the **dependent variable** is the "effect" or outcome; it changes as a consequence of a change in some other (independent) variable.

The **independent variable** is the "cause"; it causes the change in the dependent variable. In our income–consumption example, income is the independent variable and consumption is the dependent variable. Income causes consumption to be what it is rather than the other way around. Similarly, ticket prices determine attendance at IU

FIGURE A1-2   Graphing the inverse relationship between ticket prices and game attendance

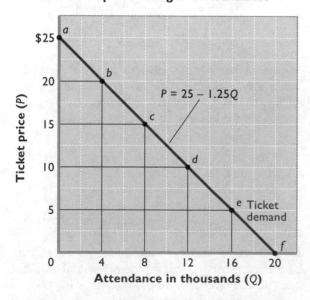

Two sets of data that are negatively or inversely related, such as ticket price and the attendance at basketball games, graph as a downsloping line. The slope of this line is –1¼.

hockey games; attendance does not determine ticket prices. Ticket price is the independent variable, and the quantity purchased is the dependent variable.

You may recall from your high school courses that mathematicians always put the independent variable (cause) on the horizontal axis and the dependent variable (effect) on the vertical axis. Economists are less tidy; their graphing of independent and dependent variables is more arbitrary. Thus their conventional graphing of the income–consumption relationship is consistent with mathematical presentation. But economists put price and cost data on the vertical axis. Hence, the economist's graphing of IU's ticket price–attendance data conflicts with mathematical procedure.

OTHER VARIABLES HELD CONSTANT

Our simple two-variable graphs ignore a variety of other factors that might affect the amount of consumption occurring at each income level or the number of people that attend IU hockey games at each possible ticket price. When we plot the relationship between any two variables, we invoke the *ceteris paribus* or "other things being equal" assumption. Thus in Figure A1-1 all other factors (that is, all factors other than income) that might affect the amount of consumption are presumed to be constant or unchanged. Similarly, in Figure A1-2 all factors other than ticket price that might influence attendance at IU hockey games are assumed constant. In reality, we know "other things" often change, and when they do, the specific relationships presented in our two tables and graphs may change. Specifically, we would expect the lines we have plotted to shift to new locations.

For example, what might happen to the income–consumption relationship if there occurred a stock market crash such as that of October 1987? The expected impact of this dramatic fall in the value of stocks would be to make people feel less wealthy and therefore less willing to consume at each income level. Thus, we would anticipate a downward shift of the consumption line in Figure A1-1. You should plot a new consumption line based on the assumption that consumption is, say, $20 less at each income level. Note that the relationship remains direct, but the line has merely shifted to reflect less consumer spending at each level of income.

Similarly, a variety of factors other than ticket prices might affect IU game attendance. For example, if the provincial government were to abandon its program of student loans, IU enrolment and hence attendance at games might be less at each ticket price. You are urged to redraw Figure A1-2 on the assumption that 2000 fewer students attend IU games at each ticket price. (**Key Appendix Question 2**)

SLOPE OF A LINE

Lines can be described in terms of their slopes. The **slope of a straight line** between any two points is defined as the ratio of the vertical change (the rise or fall) to the horizontal change (the run) involved in moving between those points.

POSITIVE SLOPE In moving from point *b* to point *c* in Figure A1-1 we find that the rise or vertical change (the change in consumption) is +$50 and the run or horizontal change (the change in income) is +$100. Therefore:

$$\text{Slope} = \frac{\text{vertical change}}{\text{horizontal change}} = \frac{+50}{+100} = +\frac{1}{2}$$

Note that our slope of ½ is positive because consumption and income change in the same direction, that is, consumption and income are directly or positively related.

A slope of +½ indicates that there will be a $1 increase in consumption for every $2 increase in income. It also indicates that for every $2 decrease in income there will be a $1 decrease in consumption.

NEGATIVE SLOPE For our ticket price–attendance data, the relationship is negative or inverse, with the result that the slope of Figure A1-2's line is negative. In particular, the vertical change or fall is 5 and the horizontal change or run is 4. Therefore:

$$\text{Slope} = \frac{\text{vertical change}}{\text{horizontal change}} = \frac{-5}{+4} = -1\frac{1}{4}$$

This slope of $\frac{-5}{+4}$ or $-1\frac{1}{4}$ means that lowering the price of a ticket by $5 will increase attendance by 4000 people, which is the same as saying that a $1 price reduction will increase attendance by 800 persons.

THREE ADDENDA Our discussion of line slopes needs three additional comments.

1. MEASUREMENT UNITS The slope of a line will be affected by the choice of units for either variable. For example, if in our ticket price illustration we had chosen to measure prices in dimes rather than dollars, then our vertical change for a price cut would be −50 (dimes) instead of −5 (dollars) and the slope would be $-12\frac{1}{2}$ (= 50 ÷ 4) rather than −1. The measurement of slope depends on the way the relevant variables are denominated.

2. MARGINAL ANALYSIS Economics is largely concerned with *marginal* or incremental changes. Should you work an hour more or an hour less each day on your part-time job? Should you buy one more or one less IU basketball ticket? Should a fast-food restaurant, now employing eight workers, hire an extra or marginal worker?

This is relevant because the slopes of lines measure marginal changes. For example, in Figure A1-1 the slope shows that $50 of extra or marginal consumption is associated with each $100 increase in income. Consumers will spend half of any increase in their income and reduce their consumption by half of any decline in income. The concept of slope is important in economics because it reflects marginal changes.

3. INFINITE AND ZERO SLOPES Many variables are unrelated or independent of one another. We would not expect the price of bananas to be related to the quantity of wristwatches purchased. If we were to put the price of bananas on the vertical axis and the quantity demanded of watches on the horizontal axis, the absence of a relationship between them would be described by a line parallel to the vertical axis, indicating that changes in the price of bananas have no impact on watch purchases. The slope of such a line is *infinite*. Similarly, if aggregate consumption were completely unrelated to, say, the quantity of rainfall and we were to put consumption on the vertical axis and rainfall on the horizontal axis, this unrelatedness would be represented by a line parallel to the horizontal axis. This line has a slope of *zero*.

INTERCEPT

In addition to its slope, the only other information needed in locating a line on a graph is the vertical intercept. The **vertical intercept** is the point where the line meets the vertical axis. For Figure A1-1 the intercept is $50. This means that, if current income were zero, consumers would still spend $50. How might they manage to consume when they have no current income? Answer: By borrowing or by selling some of their assets. Similarly, the vertical intercept in Figure A1-2 shows us that at a $25 ticket price IU's hockey team would be playing in an empty arena.

EQUATION FORM

With a specific intercept and slope, our consumption line can be succinctly described in equation form. In general, a linear equation is written as $y = a + bx$, where y is the dependent variable, a is the vertical intercept, b is the slope of the line, and x is the independent variable. For our income–consumption example, if C represents consumption (the dependent variable) and Y represents income (the independent variable), we can write $C = a + bY$. By substituting the values of the intercept and the slope for our specific data, we have $C = 50 + .5Y$. This equation allows us to determine consumption at *any* level of income. At the $300 income level (point d in Figure A1-1), our equation predicts that consumption will be $200 [= $50 + (.5 × $300)]. You should confirm that at the $250 income level consumption will be $175.

When economists reverse mathematical convention by putting the independent variable on the vertical axis and the dependent variable on the horizontal axis, in a sense the standard linear equation solves for the independent, rather than the dependent, variable. We noted earlier that this case is relevant for IU ticket price–attendance data. If we let P represent the ticket price and Q represent attendance, our relevant equation is $P = 25 - 1.25Q$, where the vertical intercept is 25 and the slope is $-1\frac{1}{4}$ or −1.25. But knowing the value for P enables us to solve for Q, which is actually our dependent variable. For example, if $P = 15$, then the values in our equation become: $15 = 25 - 1.25(Q)$, or $1.25Q = 10$, or $Q = 8$. Check this answer against Figure A1-2, and use this equation to predict IU ticket sales when the price is $7.50. **(Key Appendix Question 3)**

SLOPE OF A NONLINEAR CURVE

We now move from the simple world of linear relationships (straight lines) to the more complex world of nonlinear relationships (curves). By defini-

FIGURE A1-3 Determining the slopes of curves

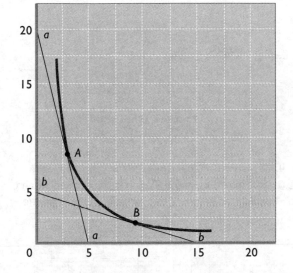

The slope of a nonlinear curve changes as one moves from point to point on the curve. The slope at any point can be determined by drawing a straight line tangent to that point and calculating the slope of that straight line.

tion, the slope of a straight line is constant at every point. The slope of a curve changes as we move from one point to another on the curve.

For example, consider the downsloping curve in Figure A1-3. Although its slope is negative throughout, it diminishes or flattens as we move southeast along the curve. Because the slope is constantly changing, we can measure the slope only at some particular point on the curve.

We begin by drawing a straight line that is tangent to the curve at that point where we want to measure its slope. A line is **tangent** at that point where it touches, but does not intersect, the curve. Thus, line *aa* is tangent to the curve at point A in Figure A1-3. Having done this, we can measure the slope of the curve at point A by measuring the slope of the straight tangent line *aa*. Specifically, in Figure A1-3 the vertical change (fall) in *aa* is –20 and the horizontal change (run) is +5. Thus the slope of the tangent *aa* line is $^{-20}/_{+5}$ or –4 and therefore the slope of the curve at A is also –4.

We can now draw line *bb* tangent to a flatter part of the curve at point *B*. Following the same procedure, we find the negative slope to be smaller, specifically $-^5/_{15}$ or $-^1/_3$. Similar analysis applies to upsloping curves. **(Key Appendix Question 6)**

APPENDIX SUMMARY

1. Graphs are a convenient and revealing means of presenting economic relationships or principles.

2. Two variables are positively or directly related when their values change in the same direction. Two directly related variables will plot as an upsloping line on a graph.

3. Two variables are negatively or inversely related when their values change in opposite directions. Two variables that are inversely related will graph as a downsloping line.

4. The value of the dependent variable ("effect") is determined by the value of the independent variable ("cause").

5. When "other factors" that might affect a two-variable relationship are allowed to change, the plotted relationship will likely shift to a new location.

6. The slope of a straight line is the ratio of the vertical change to the horizontal change in moving between any two points. The slope of an upsloping line is positive; the slope of a downsloping line is negative.

7. The slope of a line depends on the choice of units in denominating the variables. The slope of a line is especially relevant for economics because it measures marginal changes.

8. The slope of a horizontal line is zero; the slope of a vertical line is infinite.

9. The vertical (or horizontal) intercept and the slope of a line establish its location and are used in expressing the relationship between two variables as an equation.

10. The slope of a curve at any point is determined by calculating the slope of a straight line drawn tangent to that point.

APPENDIX TERMS AND CONCEPTS

dependent and independent variables (p. 18)
direct and inverse relationships (p. 18)
slope of a straight line (p. 19)
tangent (p. 21)
vertical and horizontal axes (p. 17)
vertical intercept (p. 20)

APPENDIX QUESTIONS AND STUDY SUGGESTIONS

*1. Briefly explain the use of graphs as a means of pre-senting economic principles. What is an inverse rela-tionship? How does it graph? What is a direct relationship? How does it graph? Graph and explain the relationships one would expect to find between a. the number of centimetres of rainfall per month and the sale of umbrellas; b. the amount of tuition and the level of enrolment at a university; c. the size of an NHL club's budget for player salaries and the number of games won. In each case, cite and explain how considerations other than those specifically mentioned might upset the expected relationship. Is your second generalization consistent with the fact that historically enrolments and tuition have both increased? If not, explain any difference.

2. **Key Appendix Question** *Indicate how each of the following might affect the data shown in Table A1-2 and Figure A1-2 of this appendix: a. IU's athletic direc-tor schedules higher quality opponents; b. IU's Fighting Aardvarks experience three losing seasons; c. IU con-tracts to have all of its home games televised.*

3. **Key Appendix Question** *The following table con-tains data on the relationship between saving and income. Rearrange these data as required, and graph the data on the accompanying grid. What is the slope of the line? The vertical intercept? Interpret the meaning of both the slope and the intercept. Write the equation that rep-resents this line. What would you predict saving to be at the $12,500 level of income?*

Income (per year)	Saving (per year)
$15,000	$1000
0	–500
10,000	500
5,000	0
20,000	1500

* Note to the reader: A floppy disk symbol 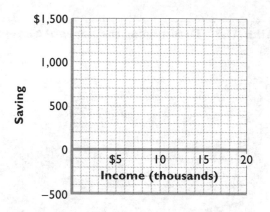 precedes each of the questions in this appendix. This icon is used throughout the text to indicate that a particular question relates to the content of one of the tutorial programs in the student software that accompanies this book. Please refer to the Preface for more detail about this software.

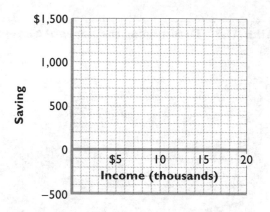

4. Construct a table from the data shown on the accompanying graph. Which is the dependent and which the independent variable? Summarize the data in equation form.

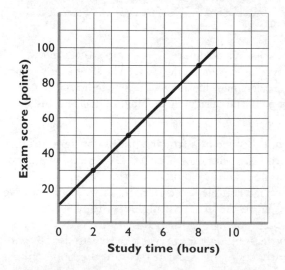

5. Suppose that when the interest rate that must be paid to borrow funds is 16%, businesses find it is unprofitable to invest in machinery and equipment. However, when the interest rate is 14%, $5 billion worth of investment is profitable. At 12%, a total of $10 billion of investment is profitable. Similarly, total investment increases by $5 billion for each succes-sive 2 percentage point decline in the interest rate. Indicate the relevant relationship between the inter-est rate and investment verbally, tabularly, graphical-ly, and as an equation. Put the interest rate on the vertical axis and investment on the horizontal axis. In your equation use the form $i = a - bI$, where i is the interest rate, a is the vertical intercept, b is the slope of the line, and I is the level of investment. Comment on the advantages and disadvantages of each of these four forms of presentation.

6. Key Appendix Question *The accompanying diagram shows curve XX and three tangents at points A, B, and C. Calculate the slope of the curve at these three points.*

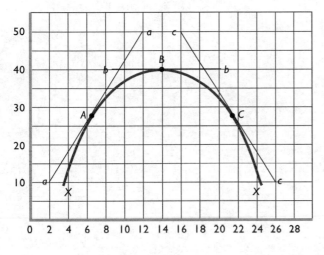

7. In the accompanying diagram is the slope of curve AA' positive or negative? Does the slope increase or decrease as we move from A to A'? Answer the same two questions for curve BB'.

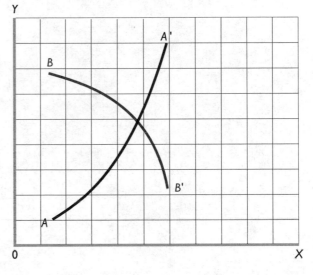

CHAPTER 2

The Economizing Problem: Scarcity, Wants, and Choices

You make decisions every day that capture the essence of economics. Suppose you have $20 and are deciding how to spend it. Should you buy a new pair of blue jeans? A couple of compact discs? A ticket for a rock concert? Similarly, what to do with your time between three and six o'clock on, say, a Thursday afternoon? Should you work extra hours on your part-time job? Do research on a term project? Prepare for an economics quiz? Watch TV? Take a nap? Money and time are both scarce and making decisions in the context of scarcity implies costs. If you choose the jeans, the cost is the forgone CDs or concert. If you nap or watch TV, the cost might be a low grade on your quiz. Scarcity, wants, choices — these are the building blocks of this chapter.

Here we introduce and explore the fundamentals of economic science. We expand on the definition of economics introduced in Chapter I and explore the essence of the economizing problem. We will illustrate, extend, and modify our definition by using production possibilities tables and curves. Next, we will briefly survey different ways by which institutionally and ideologically diverse economies respond to the economizing problem. Finally, we present an overview of the market system in the form of the circular flow model.

BOX 2-1 THE BIG PICTURE

The economizing problem arises from scarcity (or limited) resources and human unlimited wants. As a consequence, individuals and societies must make choices about what they want to produce and consume.

Consider the following scenario. Fall term has just ended and one weekend remains before the Christmas holiday begins. You must study for a final exam but you also need to do your Christmas shopping. Also, it just snowed and you are itching to ski for the first time of the season. Moreover, your friends have invited you to a Christmas party Friday night of the same weekend.

You need to make choices since it would be impossible for you to do all the things you want. And whatever choices you make entails giving something up. That, in short, captures the economizing problem, the result of limited resources and many wants.

As you read this chapter, keep the following points in mind:

- Resources to produce the goods and services we want are limited in relation to our wants.
- Even if a few very wealthy individuals have all the material things they desire, the vast majority of the human race certainly does not.
- In the face of limited resources, choices about what to produce and consume must be made.
- Limited resources imply that choosing more of one good or service means giving up some quantity of another good or service. If you have $50 to spend, a decision to buy a pair of jeans means *not* buying a $50 shirt.

THE FOUNDATION OF ECONOMICS

Two fundamental facts that constitute the **economizing problem** provide a foundation for economics. You must fully understand these two facts, because everything that follows depends directly or indirectly on them:

1. *Society's material wants are virtually unlimited.*
2. *Economic resources — the means for goods and services — are limited or scarce.*

UNLIMITED WANTS

In the first statement, what do we mean by "material wants"? We mean, first, the desires of consumers to obtain and use various *goods and services* that provide **utility**, the economist's term for pleasure or satisfaction.[1] An amazingly wide range of products fills the bill in this respect: houses, automobiles, toothpaste, compact-disc players, pizzas, sweaters, and the like. Innumerable products, sometimes classified as *necessities* (food, shelter, clothing) and *luxuries* (perfumes, yachts, mink coats), are all capable of satisfying human wants. Of course, what is a luxury to Smith may be a

necessity to Jones, and what is a common necessity today may have been a luxury a few short years ago.

Services satisfy our wants as much as products. Repair work on our car, the removal of our appendix, a haircut, and legal advice also satisfy human wants. We buy many goods — such as automobiles and washing machines — for the services they render. The differences between goods and services are often less than they first appear.

Businesses and governments also seek to satisfy material wants. Businesses want factory buildings, machinery, communication systems, and so forth, to assist them in realizing their production goals. Government, reflecting the collective wants of its citizenry or goals of its own, seeks highways, schools, hospitals, and military equipment.

As a group, these material wants are *insatiable,* or *unlimited,* meaning that material wants for goods and services cannot be completely satisfied. Our wants for a *particular* good or service can be satisfied. For example, over a short period of time we can get sufficient amounts of toothpaste or beer. Certainly one appendicitis operation is par for the course.

But goods in *general* are another story. We do not, and presumably cannot, get enough. A simple experiment will help verify this. Suppose all members of society are asked to list those goods and services they want. Chances are this list will be impressive!

---

[1] This definition leaves a variety of wants — recognition, status, love, and so forth — for the other social sciences to worry about.

Furthermore, over time, our wants multiply. As we fill some of the wants on the list, we add new ones. The rapid introduction of new products whets our appetites and extensive advertising persuades us that we need countless items we might not otherwise buy. Not long ago, we didn't want personal computers, light beer, video cassette recorders, fax machines, and compact discs because they didn't exist. Furthermore, we often cannot stop with simple satisfaction: the acquisition of an Escort or Geo has been known to whet the appetite for a Porsche or Mercedes.

The overall objective of all economic activity is the attempt to satisfy all these diverse material wants.

SCARCE RESOURCES

In considering the second fundamental fact — **economic resources are limited or scarce** — what do we mean by **economic resources**? In general, we mean all the natural, human, and manufactured resources that go into the production of goods and services. This covers a lot of ground: factory and farm buildings and all sorts of equipment, tools, and machinery used in the production of manufactured goods and agricultural products; transportation and communication facilities; innumerable types of labour; and land and mineral resources of all kinds.

RESOURCE CATEGORIES We need economic resources to produce goods and services to satisfy human wants. Let's divide these various resources into categories so we can get a better understanding of them.

LAND **Land** refers to all natural resources or raw materials — all "gifts of nature" — that are usable in the productive process. Resources such as arable land, forests, mineral and oil deposits, and water resources come under this general classification.

CAPITAL **Capital**, or investment goods, refers to all manufactured aids to production such as tools, machinery, equipment, and factory storage, transportation, and distribution facilities used in producing goods and services and getting them to the consumer. The process of producing and purchasing capital goods is known as **investment**.

Two other points are pertinent. First, *capital goods* ("tools") differ from *consumer* goods in that the latter satisfy wants directly, whereas capital goods do so indirectly by facilitating the production of consumable goods. Second, the term "capital" does *not* refer to money. Business executives and economists often do talk of "money capital," meaning money that is available for use in the purchase of machinery, equipment, and other productive facilities. But money, as such, produces nothing, and therefore is not an economic resource. To reemphasize, *real capital* — tools, machinery, and other productive equipment — is an economic resource; *money* or *financial capital* is not.

LABOUR **Labour** is a broad term referring to all the physical and mental talents of men and women available and usable in producing goods and services. (This excludes a special set of human talents — entrepreneurial ability — which, because of their special significance in a market economy, we consider separately.) The services of a logger, retail clerk, machinist, teacher, professional football player, and nuclear physicist all fall under the general heading of labour.

ENTREPRENEURIAL ABILITY The final category is **entrepreneurial ability**, or, simply, *enterprise*. The entrepreneur has four related functions:

1. The entrepreneur takes the *initiative* in combining the resources of land, capital, and labour in the production of a good or service. The entrepreneur is at once the driving force behind production and the agent that combines the other resources in what is hoped will be a profitable venture.
2. The entrepreneur undertakes major *business-policy decisions* — that is, those nonroutine decisions that set the course of a business enterprise.
3. The entrepreneur is an *innovator* — the person who attempts to introduce on a commercial basis new products, new productive techniques, or new forms of business organization.
4. The entrepreneur is a *risk taker*. This is apparent from a close examination of the other three entrepreneurial functions. The entrepreneur in a market economy has no guarantee of profit. The reward for his or her time, efforts, and abilities may be profits *or* losses and eventual bankruptcy.

RESOURCE PAYMENTS The income received from supplying property resources — raw materials and capital equipment — is called **rental** and **interest income.** The income to those who supply labour is

BOX 2-2   IN THE MEDIA

DOWN'S TRANSPLANT BID POSES DILEMMA: LUNG RECIPIENTS FACE LONG ODDS

BY ALANNA MITCHELL

CALGARY — Terry Urquhart's request for a new lung has created a moral dilemma for the doctors and ethicists who decide who gets organ transplants.

Mr. Urquhart, 17, who has been placed on a waiting list and who reports for his medical assessment next week, is the first person with Down's syndrome in Canada, perhaps in the world, to be actively considered for a new lung, and the decision to put him on the list has raised an ethical storm that has shaken Alberta.

Some call it a moral victory and others say it is a waste of a scarce resource. To Mr. Urquhart, the medical miracle of a new lung means simply the chance to live out his last few years without gasping for air.

The people who run Canada's transplant programs say that since lung transplants became an option in Canada in the late 1980s, Mr. Urquhart is the first person with Down's to request one, despite the fact that severe lung problems are a common feature of that genetic disorder.

The case poses a problem for those who decide who gets which scarce organs, especially since costly transplant programs need to show success in order to survive. They also have a duty to use the scarce donated lungs in the best way possible.

In all of Canada, just 28 single-lung transplants were performed in 1993, the last year for which statistics are available. Between 20 per cent and 40 per cent of those who await a lung die during the wait.

Those who survive the operation face long odds. Roughly 14 per cent die within 30 days of the operation. About half are alive three years later. Doctors cannot offer recipients a guarantee of longer life, only the possibility of a life of better quality.

SOURCE: *The Globe and Mail*, April 28, 1995, p. A1. Reproduced with permission.

The Story in Brief

Scarcity often causes difficult moral dilemmas. There are not enough human organ donors to satisfy the need for organs. In this story, the issue is whether a person with Down's syndrome should receive one of the "scarce donated lungs."

The Economics Behind the Story

• The number of patients who want a lung transplant is greater than the number of donated lungs.

• A person with Down's syndrome has requested one of the scarce donated lungs. But giving a donated lung to one person necessarily means denying another patient one.

• The "moral" dilemma arises because of scarcity. If there were enough donated lungs to satisfy the demand for them, the "moral" dilemma would be resolved.

• Think of some other examples where "moral dilemmas" could be resolved by having more of any good or service so that painful trade-offs are avoided. Is there a direct relationship between scarcity and moral dilemmas?

called **wages**, which includes salaries and various wage and salary supplements, such as bonuses, commissions, and royalties. Entrepreneurial income is called **profits** (which may be a negative figure — losses).

These four broad categories of economic resources, or **factors of production** as they are often called, leave room for debate when it comes to classifying specific resources. For example, is a dividend on some newly issued Canadian Pacific stock you may own an interest return for the capital equipment the company was able to buy with the money you provided, or a profit that compensates you for the risks involved in purchasing corporate stock? But, although we might quibble about classifying a particular flow of income as wages, rent, interest, or profits, all income can be fitted under one of the general headings.

RELATIVE SCARCITY All economic resources, or factors of production, have one fundamental characteristic in common: *They are scarce or limited in supply given our unlimited wants.* Our "spaceship earth" contains only limited amounts of resources that can be put to use in the production of goods and services. Quantities of arable land, mineral deposits, capital equipment, and labour (time) are all limited. The scarcity of productive resources and the constraint this scarcity puts on productive activity means output will necessarily be limited. Society will *not* be able to produce and consume all the goods and services it wants.

ECONOMICS: GETTING THE MOST FROM AVAILABLE RESOURCES

Let's restate the basic definition of economics: **Economics is the social science concerned with the problem of fulfilling society's unlimited wants with limited, or scarce, resources.** Thus, economics is about "doing the best we can with what we have." If the available resources are scarce, we cannot satisfy all our unlimited material wants. The next best thing is to satisfy as many of the material wants as possible.

The challenge for economics is to satisfy unlimited wants with limited resources and thus it is concerned with *efficiency*: getting the most output with the resources, or inputs, we have available. The more output from a specific quantity of inputs results in an increase in efficiency.

If a society wants to satisfy as many of its material wants as possible, it needs to have full employment of its available resources and must get the most from them — what we term full production.

FULL EMPLOYMENT: USING ALL AVAILABLE RESOURCES

A society has **full employment** when all available resources are used in the production of goods and services. No worker who is willing and able to work is unemployed, all capital equipment, land, and natural resources known to exist and all entrepreneurial talents are utilized. Note we say all *available* resources must be utilized to achieve full employment. Each society has certain customs and practices that determine what particular resources are available for employment. For example, legislation and custom dictate that children and the very old cannot be employed. Also, it is desirable to "conserve" some resources for future generations.

FULL PRODUCTION: USING AVAILABLE RESOURCES EFFICIENTLY

The employment of all available resources is not sufficient to get the maximum output from them. We also require **full production**: the most efficient use of the available resources. If a society fails to achieve full production, at least some resources are *underemployed*; we are not getting the maximum amount of output those resources are capable of contributing.

Full production requires two kinds of efficiency — allocative and productive efficiency.

ALLOCATIVE EFFICIENCY Allocative efficiency means that resources are being devoted to the production of goods and services most wanted by society. It is attained when we produce the best or optimal output-mix: the combination of goods and services society wants most. For example, society now wants resources allocated to compact discs and cassettes, rather than 45 rpm or long-playing records. We now prefer word processors and personal computers to manual typewriters. Photocopiers are desired, not mimeograph machines.

PRODUCTIVE EFFICIENCY Productive efficiency is achieved when the goods and services society wants most are produced in the least costly ways. Producing in the least costly ways automatically ensures producers use more of the relatively abundant resources and less of the relatively scarce resources. For example, if labour is in short supply compared to capital equipment, labour inputs will be costly compared to machinery. Productive efficiency will be achieved if less labour and more capital equipment are used, resulting in the least costly way of producing a good or service.

The relative costs of labour and capital in the 1990s requires that Tauruses and Grand Ams be produced with computerized and robotized assembly techniques rather than the more primitive and labour-intensive assembly lines of the 1920s. Productive efficiency is not achieved today by farmers picking corn by hand when advanced harvesting equipment will do the job at a much lower cost per bushel.

In summary, society's unlimited material wants in a world of limited resources can best be satisfied if we get the most production from our scarce resources. To achieve this desirable end, all available resources have to be fully employed and we must get full production from them. Full production implies producing the "right" good (allocative efficiency) in the "right" way (productive efficiency). Allocative efficiency occurs when resources are apportioned among firms and industries so that the particular product mix society most desires is produced. Productive efficiency occurs when goods and services in this optimal product mix are produced in the least costly fashion. **(Key Question 5)**

QUICK REVIEW 2-1

1. Human material wants are virtually unlimited.

2. Economic resources — land, capital, labour, and entrepreneurial ability — are scarce or limited.

3. Economics is concerned with the efficient management of these scarce resources to achieve the maximum fulfilment of our material wants.

4. Getting the most output from available resources requires both full employment and full production, the latter necessitating both allocative and productive efficiency.

PRODUCTION POSSIBILITIES TABLE

We can clarify the economizing problem through the use of a **production possibilities table**. This device reveals the core of the economizing problem: *Because resources are scarce, even a full-employment, full-production economy cannot have an unlimited output of goods and services. A society must make choices about which goods and services to produce and which to forgo.*

ASSUMPTIONS   In order to better understand the production possibilities table (Table 2-1), we make several assumptions to set the stage.

1. EFFICIENCY   The economy is operating at full employment and achieving productive efficiency. (We will consider allocative efficiency later.)

2. FIXED RESOURCES   The available supplies of the factors of production are fixed in both quantity and quality. But they can be shifted or reallocated, within limits, among different uses; for example, a relatively skilled labourer can work on a farm, at a fast-food restaurant, or as a gas-station attendant.

3. FIXED TECHNOLOGY   Technology does not change during the course of our analysis.

Assumptions 2 and 3 are another way of saying that we are looking at our economy at some specific point in time. Over a relatively long period, technological advances are possible and resource supplies can vary.

4. TWO PRODUCTS   To further simplify, suppose our economy is producing just two products — industrial robots and pizza — instead of the innumerable goods and services actually produced. Pizza is symbolic of **consumer goods**, those goods that directly satisfy our wants; industrial robots are symbolic of **capital goods**, those goods that satisfy our wants *indirectly* by permitting more efficient production of consumer goods.

NECESSITY OF CHOICE   From our assumptions we see a choice must be made among alternatives since the available resources are limited. Thus, the total amounts of robots and pizza that our economy is capable of producing are limited. *Limited resources result in a limited output.* Since resources are limited in supply and fully employed, any increase in the production of robots will require shifting resources away from the production of pizza. And the reverse holds true: if we choose to step up the production of pizza, needed resources must come at the expense of robot production.

Table 2-1 shows alternative combinations of robots and pizza that our economy might choose. Though the data in this and the following production possibility tables are hypothetical, the points illustrated are of great practical significance. At alternative A, our economy would be devoting all its resources to the production of robots (capital goods). At alternative E, all available resources would be devoted to pizza production (consumer goods).

Both these alternatives are unrealistic extremes: any economy typically strikes a balance in dividing its total output between capital and consumer goods. As we move from alternative A to alternative E, we step up the production of consumer goods (pizza) by shifting resources away from capital good production.

Since consumer goods directly satisfy our wants, any movement towards alternative E looks tempting. In making this move, society increases the current satisfaction of its wants. But there is a cost involved. This shift of resources catches up with society over time as its stock of capital goods dwindles — or at least ceases to expand at the current rate — with the result that the potential for greater future production is impaired. In moving from alternative A towards alternative E, society is in effect choosing "more now" at the expense of "much more later."

In moving from E towards A, society is choosing to forgo current consumption. This sacrifice of current consumption frees resources that can now be used to increase the production of capital goods. By building up its stock of capital, society can anticipate greater production and therefore greater consumption in the future. In moving from E towards A, society is choosing "more later" at the cost of "less now."

TABLE 2-1   Production possibilities of pizza and robots with full employment, 1996

Type of product	Production alternatives				
	A	B	C	D	E
Pizza (in hundred thousands)	0	1	2	3	4
Robots (in thousands)	10	9	7	4	0

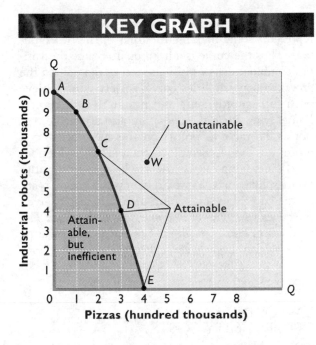

KEY GRAPH

FIGURE 2-1   The production possibilities curve

Each point on the curve represents some maximum combination of any two products that can be achieved if full employment and full production are realized. When operating on the curve, more robots mean less pizza, and vice versa. Limited resources and a fixed technology make any combinations of robots and pizza lying outside the curve, such as W, unattainable. Points inside the curve are attainable, but indicate that full employment and productive efficiency are not being realized.

At any point in time, an economy that is achieving full employment and productive efficiency must sacrifice some of product X *to obtain more of product* Y. *The fact that economic resources are scarce prohibits such an economy from having both* X *and* Y.

PRODUCTION POSSIBILITIES CURVE

To ensure our understanding of the production possibilities table, let's view these data graphically. We employ a two-dimensional graph, arbitrarily putting the output of robots (capital goods) on the vertical axis and the output of pizza (consumer goods) on the horizontal axis, as in **Figure 2-1 (Key Graph)**. Following the plotting procedure in the appendix to Chapter 1, we can locate the "production possibilities" curve, as shown in Figure 2-1.

Each point on the production possibilities curve represents some maximum output of the two products. Thus the curve is a frontier. To realize the various combinations of pizza and robots that fall *on* the production possibilities curve, society must achieve both full employment and productive efficiency. Points lying *inside* the curve are also attainable, but not as desirable as points on the curve because it means less than full employment and full production.

Points lying *outside* the production possibilities frontier, like point W, would be superior to any point on the curve; but such points are unattainable, given the current supplies of resources and technology. The production barrier of limited resources and existing technological knowledge makes it impossible to produce any combination of capital and consumer goods lying outside the production possibilities curve.

LAW OF INCREASING OPPORTUNITY COSTS

The amount of other products that must be forgone or sacrificed to obtain some amount of a specific product is called the opportunity cost of that good. In our case the amount of Y (robots) that must be forgone or given up to get another unit of X (pizza) is the **opportunity cost** of that unit of X.

In moving from possibility A to B in Table 2-1, we find that the cost of 1 additional unit of pizza is 1 less unit of robots. But as we now pursue the concept of cost through the additional production possibilities — B to C, C to D, and D to E — an important economic principle is revealed. The sacrifice or cost of robots involved in getting each additional unit of pizza *increases*. In moving from A to B, just 1 unit of robots is sacrificed for 1 more unit of pizza; but going from B to C sacrifices 2 additional units of robots for 1 more of pizza; then 3 more of robots for 1 more of pizza; and finally 4 to 1. Conversely, you should confirm that in moving from E to A the cost of an additional robot is $\frac{1}{4}$, $\frac{1}{3}$, $\frac{1}{2}$, and 1 unit of pizza respectively for each of the four shifts.

Note two points about this discussion of opportunity costs:

1. The analysis is in *real* or physical terms. We will shift to monetary comparisons in a moment.
2. Our explanation also is in terms of *marginal* (meaning "added" or "extra") cost, rather than cumulative or *total* opportunity cost. For example, the marginal opportunity cost of the third unit of

pizza in Table 2-1 is 3 units of robots (= 7 − 4). But the total opportunity cost of 3 units of pizza is 6 units of robots (= 10 − 4 or 1 + 2 + 3).

CONCAVITY   Graphically, the **law of increasing opportunity costs** is reflected in the shape of the production possibilities curve. The curve is *concave*, or bowed out from the origin. When the economy moves from A towards E, it must give up successively larger amounts of robots (1, 2, 3, 4) to acquire equal increments of pizza (1, 1, 1, 1). The slope of the production possibilities curve becomes steeper as we move from A to E. Such a curve, by definition, is concave as viewed from the origin.

RATIONALE   The rationale for the law of increasing opportunity costs is: *Economic resources are not completely adaptable to alternative uses.* As we attempt to step up pizza production, resources less and less adaptable to making pizza must be induced, or "pushed," into pizza production. As we move from B to C, C to D, and so on, those resources that are highly productive of pizza become increasingly scarce. To get more pizza, resources whose productivity in robots is great in relation to their productivity in pizza will be needed. It will take more and more of such resources — and a greater sacrifice of robots — to achieve each increase of 1 unit in the production of pizza. This lack of perfect interchangeability is behind the law of increasing opportunity costs. (**Key Question 6**)

ALLOCATIVE EFFICIENCY REVISITED

Our analysis has purposely stressed full employment and productive efficiency, both of which allow society to achieve *any point* on its production possibilities curve. We now focus again on allocative efficiency, the question of determining the most-valued or *optimal point* on the production possibilities curve. Of all the attainable combinations of pizza and robots in Figure 2-1, which is optimal or "best"? What quantities of resources should be allocated to pizza and what quantities to robots?

Our discussion of the "economic perspective" in Chapter 1 puts us on the right track. Recall that economic decisions compare marginal benefits and marginal costs. Any economic activity — for example, production or consumption — should be expanded so long as marginal benefits exceed marginal costs.

Consider pizza. We already know from the law of diminishing opportunity costs that the marginal cost (MC) of additional units of pizza will rise as more

FIGURE 2-2 Allocative Efficiency: MB = MC

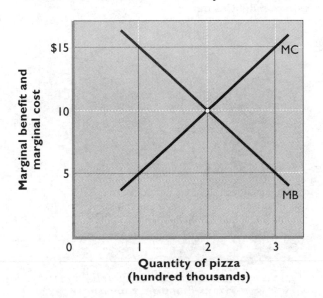

Resources are efficiently allocated to any product when its output is such that marginal benefits equal marginal costs.

units are produced. This is shown by the upsloping MC curve in Figure 2-2. We are also aware that we obtain extra or marginal benefits (MB) from additional units of pizza. However, although material wants *in the aggregate* are insatiable, the consumption of each *particular* product yields less and less extra satisfaction or, in other words, less MB. A consumer can become relatively saturated with a specific product. A second pizza provides less additional utility to you than does the first. And a third will provide even less MB than did the second. So it is for society as a whole. Thus, we can portray the marginal benefits from pizza by the downsloping MB line in Figure 2-2.

The optimal amount of pizza to produce is 200,000 units as indicated by the intersection of the MB and MC curves. Why is this optimal? If only 100,000 pizzas were produced, the MB of pizzas would be greater than their MC. In money terms the MB of a pizza here might be $15 while its MC is only $5. This suggests that society is *underallocating* resources to pizza production.

Why? Because society values an additional pizza at $15, while the alternative products or services the required resources could have produced are valued at $5. Society will benefit — it will be better off in the sense of having a larger total output to enjoy — whenever it can gain something worth $15 by giving up something (alternative goods and services) worth

only $5. A reallocation of resources from other products to pizza means society is using its resources more efficiently. Each additional pizza up to 200,000 provides such gains, indicating that allocative efficiency is improved. But when MB=MC, the value of producing pizza or alternative products with available resources is the same. Allocative efficiency is achieved when MB=MC.

The production of 300,000 pizzas would represent an *overallocation* of resources to their production. Here the MC of pizza is $15 and their MB is only $5. A unit of pizza is worth only $5 to society while the alternative products are valued at $15. By producing 1 less unit, society suffers the loss of a pizza worth $5, but by reallocating the freed resources it gains other products worth $15. Any time society can gain something worth $15 by forgoing something (a pizza) worth only $5, it has realized a net gain. The net gain in this instance is $10 worth of total output. In Figure 2-2 net gains can be realized as long as pizza production is reduced from 300,000 to 200,000. A more valued output from the same aggregate amount of inputs means greater allocative efficiency.

Resources are being efficiently allocated to any product when its output is such that its marginal benefit equals its marginal cost (MB=MC). Suppose that by applying the same analysis to robots we find that 7000 is their optimal or MB=MC output. This means that alternative C on our production possibilities curve — 200,000 pizzas and 7000 robots — results in allocative efficiency for our hypothetical economy. **(Key Question 9)**

QUICK REVIEW 2-2

I. The production possibilities curve illustrates four basic concepts.

   a. Resources are scarce. All combinations of output lying outside the production possibilities curve are unobtainable.

   b. Choices must be made. A society must select among the various attainable combinations of goods lying on (or within) the curve.

   c. The downward slope of the curve implies the notion of opportunity cost — choosing more of one good, an individual or a society has to accept less of another good.

   d. The concavity of the curve reveals increasing opportunity costs.

2. Full employment and productive efficiency must be attained for the economy to operate on its production possibilities curve. A comparison of marginal benefits and marginal costs is needed to determine allocative efficiency — the best or optimal output mix on the curve.

3. A comparison of marginal benefits and marginal costs is needed to determine allocative efficiency — the best or optimal output-mix on the curve.

UNEMPLOYMENT, GROWTH, AND THE FUTURE

Let's now drop the first three assumptions underlying the production possibilities curve to see what happens.

UNEMPLOYMENT AND PRODUCTIVE INEFFICIENCY

The first assumption was that our economy is characterized by full employment and productive efficiency. With unemployment or inefficient production, the economy would be producing less than each alternative shown in the table.

Graphically, a situation of unemployment can be illustrated by a point *inside* the original production possibilities frontier, such as point U in Figure 2-3. Here the economy is falling short of the various maximum combinations of pizza and robots reflected by all the points *on* the production possibilities frontier. The broken arrows in Figure 2-3 indicate three of the possible paths back to full employment and least cost production. A movement towards full employment and productive efficiency will mean a greater output of one or both products.

A GROWING ECONOMY

When we drop the remaining assumptions that the quantity and quality of resources and technology are fixed, the production possibilities curve can shift position and the potential total output of the economy will change. An expanding economy will shift the frontier rightward, while an economy whose potential total output declines will shift the production possibility curve leftward. What are the factors that can increase the potential total output of an economy?

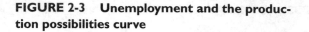

FIGURE 2-3 **Unemployment and the production possibilities curve**

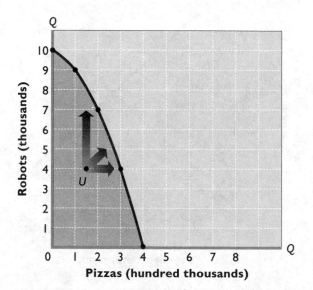

Any point inside the production possibilities curve or frontier, such as U, indicates unemployment or a failure to achieve productive efficiency. By achieving full employment and productive efficiency, the economy can produce more of either or both of the two products, as the arrows indicate.

1. EXPANDING RESOURCE SUPPLIES Let's abandon the assumption that total supplies of land, labour, capital, and entrepreneurial ability are fixed in both quantity and quality. Common sense tells us that over a period of time a nation's growing population will bring about increases in the supplies of labour and entrepreneurial ability.[2] The quality of labour improves over time if the percentage of community college and university graduates rises. Over the long run, a nation with a more skilled and educated labour force and a larger entrepreneurial pool will be able to produce more goods and services.

The stock of capital will affect the capacity of an economy. Those nations that devote a large proportion of their outputs to the production of capital goods achieve high rates of economic growth. The

---

[2] This is not to say that population growth as such is always desirable. Overpopulation can be a constant drag on the living standards of many less-developed countries. In advanced countries, overpopulation can have adverse effects on the environment and the quality of life.

discovery of new sources of energy and mineral resources will also contribute to increasing output of goods and services.

The net result of these increased supplies of the factors of production will be the ability to produce more of both robots and pizza. Thus in, say, the year 2016, the production possibilities of Table 2-1 (for 1996) may be obsolete, having given way to those in Table 2-2. The greater abundance of resources results in a greater potential output of one or both products at each alternative.

But such a favourable shift in the production possibilities frontier does not guarantee that the economy will actually operate at a point on that new frontier. The economy might fail to realize fully its new potentialities.

2. TECHNOLOGICAL ADVANCE Advancing technology translates into new and better goods *and* improved ways of producing them. For now, let's

think of technological advance as improvements in capital facilities — more efficient machinery and equipment. Such technological advance will alleviate the economizing problem by improving productive efficiency, allowing society to produce more goods with a fixed amount of resources. As with increases in resource supplies, technological advance permits the production of more robots *and* more pizza.

When the supplies of resources increase or an improvement in technology occurs, the frontier shifts outward and to the right, as illustrated by the thin curve in Figure 2-4. **Economic growth** — *the ability to produce a larger total output — is reflected in a rightward shift of the production possibilities frontier; it is the result of increases and the improvement in quality of resource supplies and technological progress.* The consequence of growth is that our full-employment economy can enjoy a greater output of both pizza and robots.

Economic growth does *not* typically translate into proportionate increases in a nation's capacity to produce various products. Note in Figure 2-4 that, while the economy is able to produce twice as much pizza, the increase in robot production is only 40%. You should pencil in two new production possibilities curves: one to show the situation where a better technique for producing robots has been developed, the technology for producing pizza being unchanged, and the other to illustrate an improved technology for pizza, the technology for producing robots being constant.

PRESENT CHOICES AND FUTURE POSSIBILITIES *An economy's current choice on its production possibilities frontier is a basic determinant of the future location of that curve.* Let's designate the two axes of the production possibilities frontier as "goods for the future" and "goods for the present," as in Figures 2-5(a) and

FIGURE 2-4 Economic growth and the production possibilities curve

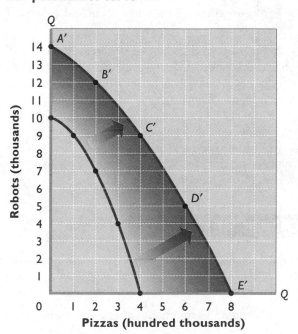

The expanding resource supplies and technological advances that characterize a growing economy move the production possibilities curve or frontier outward and to the right. This permits the economy to enjoy larger quantities of both types of goods.

TABLE 2-2 Production possibilities of pizza and robots with full employment, 2016

Type of product	Production alternatives				
	A'	B'	C'	D'	E'
Pizza (in hundred thousands)	0	2	4	6	8
Robots (in thousands)	14	12	9	5	0

FIGURE 2-5

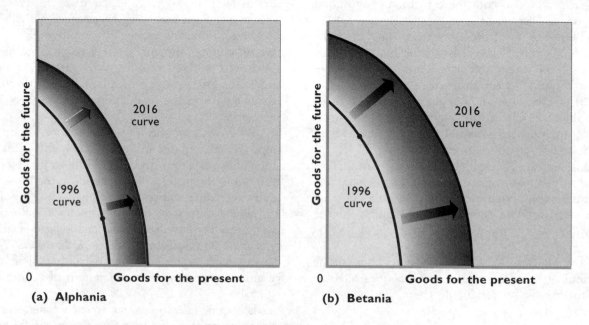

(a) **Alphania**   (b) **Betania**

A current choice favouring "present goods," as made by Alphania in (a), will cause a modest right-ward shift of the frontier. A current choice favouring "future goods," as made by Betania in (b), will result in a greater rightward outward shift of the frontier.

(b). "Goods for the future" are such things as capital goods, research and education, and preventive medicine, which increase the quantity and quality of resources, enlarge the stock of technological information, and improve the quality of human resources. It is "goods for the future" that are the ingredients of economic growth. "Goods for the present" are pure consumer goods in the form of such things as food, clothing, and automobiles.

Now suppose there are two economies, Alphania and Betania, which are initially identical in every respect except that Alphania's current (1996) choice of position on its production possibilities frontier strongly favours "present goods" as opposed to "future goods." The dot in Figure 2-5(a) indicates this choice. Betania, on the other hand, renders a current (1996) choice that stresses large amounts of "future goods" and lesser amounts of "present goods" as shown by the dot in Figure 2-5 (b).

All other things being the same, we can expect the future (2016) production possibilities frontier of Betania to be farther to the right than Alphania's curve. By currently choosing an output that is more conducive to technological advance and to increases in the quantity and quality of resources, Betania will achieve greater economic growth than will Alphania. In terms of capital goods, Betania is choosing to make larger current additions to its "national factory" — to invest more of its current output — than is Alphania. The payoff from this choice is more rapid growth — greater future productivity capacity — for Betania. The opportunity cost is fewer consumer goods in the present. **(Key Questions 10 and 11)**

QUICK REVIEW 2-3

1. Unemployment and the failure to realize productive efficiency cause the economy to operate at a point inside its production possibilities curve.

2. Expanding resource supplies, improvements in resource quality, and technological progress cause economic growth, depicted as an outward shift of the production possibilities curve.

3. An economy's present choice of capital and consumer goods output determines the future location of its production possibilities curve.

BOX 2-2   APPLYING THE THEORY

THE DIMINISHING PRODUCTION POSSIBILITIES OF CASTRO'S CUBA

Inefficiencies associated with its command economy, a 30-year trade embargo with the United States, and the recent loss of Soviet aid are causing the Cuban economy to collapse.

The fortieth anniversary in 1993 of Cuba's communist revolution was overshadowed by a collapsing economy. Shortages of essential goods began to appear on the island by mid-1989 and have since become widespread and severe. Long lines are common as consumers attempt to buy rationed goods such as eggs, fish, meat, and soap. Some 50,000 Cubans have been diagnosed as having optic neuritis, a disease causing gradual blindness because of malnutrition and vitamin deficiencies. Energy shortages have closed factories and disrupted construction projects. Shortages of gasoline and spare parts have idled automobiles, buses, and farm tractors. Ox carts are being substituted for tractors in agriculture and hundreds of thousands of bicycles are being imported from China as substitutes for autos and buses.

There are three reasons for the collapse of Fidel Castro's Cuban economy. First, the Cuban economy has suffered increasingly from the central planning problems that brought about the fall of the command economies of Eastern Europe and the former Soviet Union. Central planning has failed to (a) accurately assess consumer wants, (b) provide the market signals needed to minimize production costs, and (c) provide adequate economic incentives for workers and business managers.

The second factor in Cuba's economic decline is the American trade embargo. Although Cuba is only 144 km from the vast American market, that market has been denied to Cuba for some 30 years, causing a substantial decline in and distortion of Cuba's world trade.

Third, Soviet patronage has ended. For decades the Soviet Union heavily subsidized its communist partner in the Western Hemisphere. The Soviets bought Cuban exports (primarily sugar) at inflated prices and sold oil and other goods to Cuba at low prices. Best estimates suggest Soviet economic and military aid averaged about $5 billion per year. The decline of the Soviet economy and the subsequent political breakup of the Soviet Union has brought an end to these subsidies and dealt a damaging blow to the Cuban economy.

Estimates of the decline in Cuba's production possibilities vary. Some suggest that in recent years the domestic output has fallen by one-half; others indicate a three-quarters decline. In either case this decline in output is not simply a temporary move to a point inside Cuba's production possibilities curve, but rather a significant inward shift of the curve itself.

Castro has attempted to rejuvenate the Cuban economy in several ways. First, an effort is being made to revitalize the tourist industry through joint ventures — for example, hotel and resort construction — with foreign firms. Second, Cuba has invited foreign companies to explore the island for oil. Third, Cuba is making a concerted effort to cultivate trade relations with new trading partners such as China and Japan. Whether such efforts will be successful is doubtful and most experts predict the economic crisis in Cuba to spark either widespread reforms towards a market economy or the overthrow of the Castro regime.

APPLICATIONS

Let's consider several applications of the production possibilities curve that highlight scarcity, choice, and opportunity cost.

1. BUDGETING Individuals have limited money incomes. A limited budget means making choices when buying goods and services. The opportunity cost of buying a pair of blue jeans may be the dinner and a rock concert that must be given up. Many students are faced with the problem of allocating a fixed amount of time between studying and working to finance their education. The trade-off is that more hours spent working mean more income, but also less study time and a probable lower grade average.

2. DISCRIMINATION Discrimination based on race, sex, age, or ethnic background is an obstacle to the efficient employment of labour resources and keeps the economy operating at some point inside the production possibilities curve. Discrimination prevents racial minorities, women, and others from obtaining jobs in which society can efficiently utilize their skills and talents. The elimination of discrimination would help to move the economy from some point inside the production possibilities curve towards a point on the curve.

3. PRODUCTIVITY SLOWDOWN During the 1970s and early 1980s, Canada experienced a decline in the growth of labour productivity, defined as output per worker hour. One cause of this decline is that the rate of increase in the mechanization of labour slowed because of investment in manufacturing. One remedy is an increase in investment as compared with consumption — a D to C type of shift in Figure 2-1. Special tax incentives to make business investment more profitable might be an appropriate policy to facilitate this shift. The restoration of a more rapid rate of productivity growth will accelerate the growth of the economy and shift of the production possibilities curve rightward.

During the mid-1980s the growth of output per hour recovered somewhat. While the reasons for the partial recovery of productivity are complex and controversial, an increase in capital investment contributed to the improvement.

4. LUMBER VERSUS OWLS The trade-offs portrayed in the production possibilities curve occur regularly in environmental issues. An example is the much-publicized conflict between the logging industry of the U.S. Pacific Northwest and environmentalists. Envision a production possibilities curve with "lumber production" on one axis and "environmental quality" or "biodiversity" on the other. The conflict is centred on the spotted owl, which depends on the mature or old-growth trees of the Pacific Northwest for survival. Increasing the output of lumber limits the owl's habitat, destroys the species, and thus reduces environmental quality. Maintaining the old-growth forests preserves the owl, but destroys thousands of jobs in the logging and lumber industries. The production possibilities curve is an informative context within which to grasp the many difficult environmental decisions confronting society.

5. INTERNATIONAL TRADE ASPECTS The message of the production possibilities curve is that a nation cannot live beyond its means or production potential. When the possibility of international trade is taken into account, this statement must be modified in two ways.

TRADE AND GROWTH We will discover in later chapters that a nation can circumvent the output constraint imposed by its domestic production possibilities curve through international specialization and trade. International specialization and trade have the same impact as having more and better resources or discovering improved production techniques. Both have the effect of increasing the quantities of both capital and consumer goods available to society. International specialization and trade are the equivalent of economic growth.

TRADE DEFICITS Within the context of international trade, a nation can consume a combination of goods outside of its domestic production possibilities curve (such as point W in Figure 2-1) by incurring a *trade deficit*. A nation may buy and receive an amount of imported goods from the rest of the world that exceeds the amount of goods exported to the rest of the world.

This looks like a favourable state of affairs. Unfortunately, there is a catch. To finance its deficit — to pay for its excess of imports over exports — a nation must go into debt to its international trading partners *or* it must give up ownership of some of its assets to those other nations. Analogy: How can you live beyond your current income? Answer: Borrow from your parents, the sellers of goods, or a financial institution. Or sell some of the real assets (your car or stereo) or financial assets (stocks or bonds) you own.

We would find that a major consequence of large and persistent trade deficits is that foreign nationals hold larger portions of our private and public debt and own larger amounts of our business corporations, agricultural land, and real estate. To pay for debts and to repurchase those assets would mean living well *within* a nation's means. A *trade surplus* is required to pay off world debts and reacquire ownership of those assets.

6. GROWTH The growth impact of a nation's decision on how to divide its domestic output is vividly illustrated by comparing the growth performance of a few advanced industrialized nations. As Global Perspective 2-1 shows, between 1970 and 1990 Japan invested a yearly average of over 30% of its domestic output in productive machinery and

GLOBAL PERSPECTIVE 2-1

Investment and economic growth, selected countries

Nations that invest large proportions of their national outputs achieve high growth rates, measured here by output per person. Additional capital goods make workers more productive and this means greater output per person.

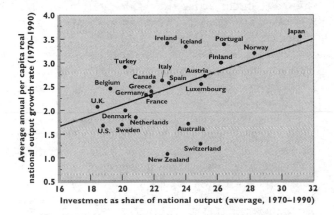

SOURCE: International Monetary Fund data, as reported in the U.S. government publication *Economic Report of the President, 1994*, p. 37.

equipment. Not surprisingly Japan's output growth during the period averaged 3.5% per year. The United States, on the other hand, invested an average of less than 20% of its domestic output and, thus, had a lower growth rate of slightly over 1.5% per year on average. Canada invested an average of slightly over 20% of its domestic output, which translated into an average growth rate of about 2.5% per year.

7. FAMINE IN AFRICA Modern industrial societies take economic growth — more-or-less continuous rightward shifts of the production possibilities curve — for granted. But as the recent catastrophic famines in Somalia and other sub-Saharan nations of Africa indicate, in some circumstances the production possibilities curve may shift leftward. In addition to drought, a cause of African famines is ecological degradation — poor land-use practices. Land has been deforested, overfarmed, and overgrazed, causing the production possibilities of these highly agriculturally oriented countries to diminish. In fact, the per capita domestic output of most of these nations declined in the last decade or so.

THE "ISMS"

A society can use different institutional arrangements and co-ordinating mechanisms to respond to the economizing problem. Generally speaking, the industrially advanced economies of the world differ essentially on two grounds: (1) the ownership of the means of production, and (2) the method of co-ordinating and directing economic activity. Let's examine the main characteristics of the two "polar" types of economic systems.

PURE CAPITALISM

Pure, or **laissez-faire**, **capitalism** is characterized by the private ownership of resources and the use of a system of markets and prices to co-ordinate and direct economic activity. In such a system each participant is motivated by his or her own self-interests. The market system communicates and co-ordinates individual decisions and preferences. Because goods and services are produced and resources are supplied under competitive conditions, there are many independent buyers and sellers of each product and resource. As a result, economic power is widely dispersed. Advocates of pure capitalism argue that such an economy is conducive to efficiency in the use of resources, output and employment stability, and rapid economic growth. Thus there is little or no need for government planning, control, or intervention. The term *laissez-faire* means "let it be": keep the government from interfering with the economy. Interference will disturb the efficient working of the market system. Government's role is therefore limited to the protection of private property and establishing an appropriate legal framework for free markets.

THE COMMAND ECONOMY

The polar alternative to pure capitalism is the **command economy**, characterized by public ownership of virtually all property resources and the rendering of economic decisions through central economic planning. All major decisions concerning the level of resource use, the composition and distribution of output, and the organization of production are determined by a central planning board. Business firms are government-owned and produce according to state directives. Production targets are determined by the planning board for each enterprise and the plan specifies the amounts of resources to be allocated to each enterprise so that it might realize its production goals. The division of output between capital and consumer goods is centrally decided and capital goods are allocated among industries based on the central planning board's long-term priorities.

MIXED SYSTEMS

Most economies fall between the extremes of pure capitalism and the command economy. The Canadian economy leans towards pure capitalism, but with important differences. Government plays an active role in our economy in promoting economic stability and growth, in providing certain goods and services that would be underproduced or not produced at all by the market system, in modifying the distribution of income, and so forth. In contrast to the wide dispersion of economic power among many small units that characterizes pure capitalism, Canadian capitalism has spawned powerful economic organizations in the form of large corporations and labour unions. The ability of these power blocs to manipulate and distort the functioning of the market system to their advantage provides a further reason for governmental involvement in the economy.

While the former Soviet Union historically approximated the command economy, it relied to some extent on market-determined prices and had some vestiges of private ownership. Recent reforms in the former Soviet Union, China, and most of the Eastern European nations are designed to move these command economies towards more market-oriented systems. North Korea and Cuba are the best remaining examples of centrally planned economics.

But private ownership and reliance on the market system do not always go together, nor do public ownership and central planning. For example, the fascism of Hitler's Nazi Germany has been dubbed **authoritarian capitalism** because the economy had a high degree of governmental control and direction, but property was privately owned. In contrast, the former Yugoslavian economy of **market socialism** was characterized by public ownership of resources coupled with considerable reliance on free markets to organize and co-ordinate economic activity. The Swedish economy is also a hybrid system. Although over 90% of business activity is in private hands, government is deeply involved in achieving eco-

nomic stability and in redistributing income. Similarly, the market-oriented Japanese economy entails a great deal of planning and "co-ordination" between government and the business sector.

THE TRADITIONAL ECONOMY

Many of the less developed countries of the world have **traditional** or **customary economies**. Production methods, exchange, and the distribution of income are all sanctioned by custom. Heredity and caste circumscribe the economic roles of individuals and socioeconomic immobility is pronounced. Technological change and innovation may be closely constrained because they clash with tradition and threaten the social fabric. Economic activity is often secondary to religious and cultural values and society's desire to perpetuate the status quo.

The point is that there is no unique or universally accepted way to respond to the economizing problem. Various societies, having different cultural and historical backgrounds, different mores and customs, and contrasting ideological frameworks — not to mention resources that differ both quantitatively and qualitatively — use different institutions in dealing with the reality of relative scarcity. Canada, China, the United States, and Great Britain, for example, are all — in their accepted goals, ideology, technologies, resources, and culture — attempting to achieve efficiency in the use of their resources. The best method for responding to the unlimited wants–scarce resources dilemma in one economy may be inappropriate for another economic system.

THE CIRCULAR FLOW MODEL

Market-oriented systems now dominate the world scene. Thus, our focus in the remainder of this chapter and in the following two chapters is on how nations use markets to respond to the economizing problem. Our goal in this last section is modest; we want to identify the major groups of decision makers and the major markets in the market system. Our point of reference is the circular flow diagram.

RESOURCE AND PRODUCT MARKETS

Figure 2-6 (Key Graph) shows two groups of *decision makers* — households and businesses. (Government will be added as a third decision maker in Chapter

KEY GRAPH

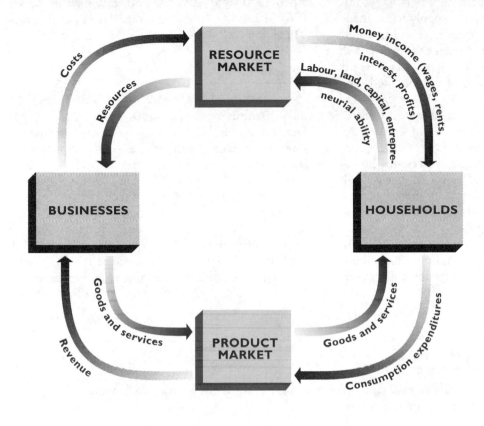

FIGURE 2-6 The circular flow of output and income

The prices paid for the use of land, labour, capital, and entrepreneurial ability are determined in the resource market shown in the upper loop. Businesses are on the demand side and households on the supply side of this market. The prices of finished goods and services are determined in the product market located in the lower loop. Households are on the demand side and businesses are on the supply side of this market.

5.) The *co-ordinating mechanism* that brings the decisions of households and businesses into alignment with one another is the market system, in particular resource and product markets.

The upper half of the diagram portrays the **resource market**. Here, households, which directly or indirectly (through their ownership of business corporations) own all economic resources, *supply* these resources to businesses. Businesses will *demand* resources because they are the means by which firms produce goods and services. The interaction of demand and supply for the immense variety of human and property resources establishes the price of each. The payments that businesses make in obtaining resources are costs to businesses, but simultaneously constitute flows of wage, rent, interest, and profit income to the households supplying these resources.

Now consider the **product market** shown in the bottom half of the diagram. The money income received by households from the sale of resources does not, as such, have real value. Consumers cannot eat or wear coins and paper money. Thus,

through the expenditure of money income, households express their *demand* for a vast array of goods and services. Simultaneously, businesses combine the resources they have obtained to produce and *supply* goods and services in these same markets. The interaction of these demand and supply decisions determines product prices (Chapter 4). Note, too, that the flow of consumer expenditures for goods and services constitutes sales revenues or receipts from the viewpoint of businesses.

The **circular flow model** implies a complex, interrelated web of decision making and economic activity. Note that households and businesses participate in both basic markets, but on different sides of each. Businesses are on the buying or demand side of resource markets, and households, as resource owners and suppliers, are on the selling or supply side. In the product market, these positions are reversed; households, as consumers, are on the buying or demand side, and businesses are on the selling or supply side. Each group of economic units both buys and sells.

Furthermore, the spectre of scarcity haunts these transactions. Because households have only limited amounts of resources to supply to businesses, the money incomes of consumers will be limited. This means that each consumer's income will go only so far. A limited number of dollars clearly will not permit the purchase of all the goods and services the consumer might like to buy. Similarly, because resources are scarce, the output of finished goods and services is also necessarily limited. Scarcity and choice permeate our entire discussion.

To summarize: In a monetary economy, households, as resource owners, sell their resources to businesses and, as consumers, spend the money income received buying goods and services. Businesses must buy resources to produce goods and services; their finished products are then sold to households in exchange for consumption expenditures or, as businesses view it, revenues. The net result is a counter-clockwise *real* flow of economic resources and finished goods and services, and a clockwise *money* flow of income and consumption expenditures. These flows are simultaneous and repetitive.

LIMITATIONS

Our model simplifies in many ways. Intrahousehold and intrabusiness transactions are concealed. Government and the "rest of the world" are ignored as decision makers. The model subtly implies constant flows of output and income, while in fact these flows are unstable over time. Nor is the circular flow a perpetual motion machine; production exhausts human energies and absorbs physical resources, the latter giving rise to problems of environmental pollution. Finally, our model does not explain how product and resource prices are actually determined, which is examined in Chapter 4.

CHAPTER SUMMARY

1. Economics centres on two basic facts: first human material wants are virtually unlimited; second, economic resources are scarce.

2. Economic resources may be classified as land, capital, labour, and entrepreneurial ability.

3. Economics is concerned with the problem of administering scarce resources in the production of goods and services to fulfil the material wants of society. Both full employment and full production of available resources are essential if this administration is to be efficient.

4. Full production requires productive efficiency — producing any output in the least costly way — and allocative efficiency — producing the specific output mix most desired by society.

5. An economy that is achieving full employment and productive efficiency — operating *on* its production possibilities curve — must sacrifice the output of some types of goods and services to achieve increased production of others. Because resources are not equally productive in all possible uses, shifting resources from one use to another yields the law of increasing opportunity costs; the production of additional units of product X requires the sacrifice of increasing amounts of product Y.

6. Allocative efficiency means achieving the optimal or most desired point on the production possibilities curve. It is determined by comparing marginal benefits and marginal cost.

7. Over time, technological advance and increases in the quantity and quality of resources permit the economy to produce more of all goods and services. Society's choice as to the composition of current output is a determinant of the future location of the production possibilities curve.

8. The various economic systems of the world differ in their ideologies and also in their responses to the economizing problem. Critical differences centre on **a** private versus public ownership of resources, and **b** the use of the market system versus central planning as a co-ordinating mechanism.

9. An overview of the operation of the market system can be gained through the circular flow of income. This simplified model locates the product and resource markets and presents the major income-expenditure flows and resources-output flows that constitute the lifeblood of the capitalist economy.

TERMS AND CONCEPTS

allocative efficiency (p. 29)
authoritarian capitalism (p. 40)
capital goods (p. 30)
circular flow model (p. 41)
command economy (p. 39)
consumer goods (p. 30)
economic growth (p. 35)
economizing problem (p. 26)
economic resources (p. 27)
factors of production (p. 29)
full employment (p. 29)
full production (p. 29)
interest income (p. 27)
investment (p. 27)

land, capital, labour, and entrepreneurial ability (p. 27)
law of increasing opportunity costs (p. 32)
market socialism (p. 40)
opportunity cost (p. 32)
production possibilities table (curve) (p. 30)
productive efficiency (p. 29)
product market (p. 41)
profits (p. 29)
pure or laissez-faire capitalism (p. 39)
rental income (p. 27)
resource market (p. 41)
traditional or customary economies (p. 40)
utility (p. 26)
wages (p. 29)

QUESTIONS AND STUDY SUGGESTIONS

1. "Economics is the study of the principles governing the allocation of scarce means among competing ends when the objective of the allocation is to maximize the attainment of the ends." Explain.

2. Comment on the following statement from a newspaper article: "Our junior high school serves a splendid hot meal for $1 without costing the taxpayers anything, thanks in part to a government subsidy."

3. Critically analyze: "Wants aren't insatiable. I can prove it. I get all the coffee I want to drink every morning at breakfast." Explain: "Goods and services are scarce because resources are scarce." Analyze: "It is the nature of all economic problems that absolute solutions are denied us."

4. What are economic resources? What are the major functions of the entrepreneur?

5. Key Question   *Why is the problem of unemployment a part of the subject matter of economics? Distinguish between allocative efficiency and productive efficiency. Give an illustration of achieving productive, but not allocative, efficiency.*

6. Key Question   *The following is a production possibilities table for war goods and civilian goods:*

Type of production	Production alternatives				
	A	B	C	D	E
Automobiles	0	2	4	6	8
Rockets	30	27	21	12	0

a. *Show these data graphically. On what specific assumptions is this production possibilities curve based?*
b. *If the economy is at point C, what is the cost of one more automobile? One more rocket? Explain how this curve reflects the law of increasing opportunity costs.*
c. *What must the economy do to operate at some point on the production possibilities curve?*

7. What is the opportunity cost of attending college or university?

8. Suppose you arrive at a store expecting to pay $100 for an item, but learn that a store three kilometres away is charging $50 for it. Would you drive there and buy it? How does your decision benefit you? What is the opportunity cost of your decision? Now suppose that you arrive at a store expecting to pay $6,000 for an item, but learn that it costs $5,950 at the other store. Do you make the same decision as before? Perhaps surprisingly, you should! Explain why.

9. Key Question   *Specify and explain the shape of the marginal benefit and marginal cost curves and use these curves to determine the optimal allocation of resources to a particular product. If current output is such that marginal cost exceeds marginal benefit, should more or fewer resources be allocated to this product? Explain.*

10. Key Question   *Label point G inside the production possibilities curve you have drawn in question 6. What does it indicate? Label point H outside the curve. What does this point indicate? What must occur before the economy can attain the level of production indicated by point H?*

11. Key Question   *Referring again to question 6, suppose improvement occurs in the technology of producing rockets but not in the production of automobiles. Draw the new production possibilities curve. Now assume that a technological advance occurs in producing automobiles but not in producing rockets. Draw the new production possibilities curve. Finally, draw a production possibilities curve that reflects technological improvement in the production of both products.*

12. Explain how, if at all, each of the following affects the location of the production possibilities curve.

a. standardized examination scores of high school and college and university students decline
b. the unemployment rate falls from 11 to 8% of the labour force
c. defence spending is reduced to allow the government to spend more on education
d. society decides it wants compact discs rather than long-playing records
e. a new technique improves the efficiency of extracting copper from ore
f. a new "baby boom" increases the size of the nation's work force

13. Explain: "Affluence tomorrow requires sacrifice today."

14. Explain how an international trade deficit may permit an economy to acquire a combination of goods in excess of its domestic production potential. Explain why nations try to avoid having trade deficits.

15. Contrast how pure capitalism, market socialism, and a command economy try to cope with economic scarcity.

16. Describe the operation of pure capitalism as portrayed by the circular flow model. Locate resource and product markets and emphasize the fact of scarcity throughout your discussion. Specify the limitations of the circular flow model.

17. (Applying the Theory)   What are the major causes of Cuba's diminishing production possibilities?

CHAPTER 3

OVERVIEW OF THE MARKET SYSTEM

I n the past few years the media have inundated us with stories of how Russian and other centrally planned economies are trying to alter their systems in the direction of capitalism, otherwise referred to as the market system or market economy. Precisely what are the features and institutions of a market system that these nations are trying to emulate?

Our initial task is to describe and explain how a pure market system, or laissez-faire capitalism, functions. Although a pure market system has never existed, a description of such an economy provides a useful first approximation of how the economies of Canada and many other industrially advanced nations function. We will modify our model of a pure market economy in later chapters to correspond more closely to the reality of modern economies.

In explaining the operation of a pure market economy we will discuss: (1) the institutional framework and basic assumptions underlying its dynamics; (2) certain institutions and practices common to all modern economies; and (3) how a market system can co-ordinate economic activity and contribute to the efficient use of scarce resources.

BOX 3-1   THE BIG PICTURE

The scarcity problem is confronted by all societies. Each society much choose a co-ordinating system that will determine how much of each product is produced, how it will be produced, and how output is divided among its population. This chapter offers an overview of one way to co-ordinate production and distribution: the market system — sometimes referred to as the capitalist system. A familiarity with the main features of a market system will greatly help you put the materials of this textbook in their proper perspective.

As you read this chapter, keep the following points in mind:

- A market system does not arise automatically; it needs the proper institutions, such as private property.
- The driving force of the market system is "self-interest," not to be confused with selfishness. In a world of limited resources in relation to wants, competition ensues automatically. In competing for the available resources, all participants in a market system — businesses and households — try to do the best they can for themselves.
- The distinguishing characteristics of the market system are *a.* autonomous decision-making by each participant, and *b.* spontaneous co-ordination of production and consumption.

THE MARKET SYSTEM

There is no neat and universally accepted definition of a market system, or, as it is sometimes referred to, capitalism. We must examine in some detail the basic tenets of the market economy to acquire a comprehensive understanding of how it functions. The framework of the market system has the following institutions and assumptions: (1) private property, (2) freedom of enterprise and choice, (3) self-interest as the dominant motive, (4) competition among firms and consumers, (5) reliance on self-regulating markets, and (6) a limited role for government.

PRIVATE PROPERTY

In a pure market system, resources are owned by private individuals and private institutions, not by government. **Private property**, coupled with the freedom to negotiate binding legal contracts, permits private persons or businesses to obtain, control, employ, and dispose of resources as they see fit. The institution of private property is sustained over time by the right of a property owner to designate the recipient of this property at the time of death.

Property rights — rights to own, use, and dispose of property — are significant because they encourage investment, innovation, exchange, and economic growth. Why would anyone build a house, construct a factory, or clear land for farming if some-

one or some institution (for example, government) could confiscate that property for their own benefit?

Property rights also apply to "intellectual property." Patents and copyrights exist and are enforced to encourage individuals to write books, music, and computer programs and to invent new products and production processes without fear that others will expropriate them along with the associated economic rewards.

Another important role of property rights is that they facilitate exchange. A title to an automobile or a deed to a house assures the buyer that the seller is in fact the legitimate owner. Finally, without property rights, people would have to devote a considerable portion of their energy and resources simply to protect and retain the property they have produced or acquired.

Society often imposes broad legal limits to this right to private ownership if such rights can lead to the harming of oneself or others. For example, the use of resources for the production of illicit drugs is prohibited. Nor is public ownership nonexistent. Even in a pure market system, public ownership of certain utilities may be essential to the achievement of efficiency in the use of resources.

FREEDOM OF ENTERPRISE AND CHOICE

Closely related to private ownership of property is freedom of enterprise and choice. The market system imposes on its participants the responsibility of making certain choices. **Freedom of enterprise** means that private business enterprises are free to obtain economic resources, to organize these resources in the production of a good or service of the firm's own choosing, and to sell it in the markets of their choice. No artificial obstacles or restrictions imposed by government or other producers block an entrepreneur's choice to enter or leave a particular industry.

Freedom of choice means that owners of resources can employ or dispose of them as they see fit. It also means that workers are free to enter any of those lines of work for which they are qualified. Consumers are at liberty, within the limits of their money incomes, to buy goods and services that they feel satisfy their wants.

Freedom of *consumer* choice is perhaps the most profound of these freedoms. Recall that economics is about scarcity of resources and unlimited wants, and how to best satisfy those wants within the scarcity constraint. Thus, the consumer is in a particularly strategic position in a market economy for it is consumers collectively that decide to what use the scarce resources will be allocated. In a sense, the consumer is sovereign. The range of free choices for suppliers of resources is circumscribed by the choices of consumers. The consumer ultimately decides what the economy should produce and resource suppliers must make their choices within the constraints delineated. Resource suppliers and businesses are not "free" to produce goods and services consumers do not desire because their production would be unprofitable.

ROLE OF SELF-INTEREST

The primary driving force of a market economy is **self-interest**; each economic unit attempts to do what is best for itself. Note that the assumption of self-interest follows naturally from the universal problem of scarcity and unlimited wants. If there were no scarcities of resources, there would be no reason to behave in a self-interested way. The existence of scarcity means entrepreneurs aim at the maximization of their firms' profits, and owners of resources attempt to get the highest price or rent from these resources. Those who supply labour resources will try to get the highest possible incomes from their employment. Consumers, in purchasing a product, will seek to get it at the lowest price. Specific consumers apportion their expenditures to maximize their satisfaction; they try to fulfil their many wants as best they can within a given income. That means getting the goods they want at the lowest possible price.

The pursuit of economic self-interest must not be confused with selfishness. A stockholder may invest to receive the best available corporate dividends and then may contribute a portion to the United Way or leave bequests to grandchildren. Similarly, a church official may carefully compare price and quality among various brands in buying new pews for the church.

COMPETITION

Freedom of choice exercised in promoting one's own monetary returns provides the basis for **competition**, or economic rivalry, as a fundamental feature of a market economy. Competition requires:

1. Large numbers of independent buyers and sellers operating in the market for any particular product or resource.
2. The freedom of buyers and sellers to enter or leave particular markets.

LARGE NUMBERS The essence of competition is the widespread diffusion of economic power within the two major groups that make up the economy: businesses and households. When many buyers and sellers are present in a particular market, no one buyer or seller will be able to noticeably influence the price. Let's examine this statement in terms of the selling or supply side of the product market.

When a product becomes unusually scarce, its price will rise. An unseasonable frost in Florida may seriously curtail the supply of citrus crops and sharply increase the price of oranges. Similarly, *if* a single producer, or a small group of producers together, can somehow control or restrict the total supply of a product, then price can be raised to the seller's advantage. By controlling supply, the producer can "rig the market" on his or her own behalf. The essence of competition is that there are so many independent pure sellers that each, *because he or she is contributing an almost negligible fraction of the total supply,* has virtually no influence over the supply nor, therefore, over product price.

Suppose there are 10,000 farmers, each supplying 100 bushels of wheat in the Winnipeg grain market when the price of wheat is $4 per bushel. Could a single farmer who feels dissatisfied with that price cause an artificial scarcity of wheat and thereby boost the price above $4? No, because Farmer Jones, by restricting output from 100 to 75 bushels, exerts virtually no effect on the total supply of wheat. In fact, the total amount supplied is reduced only from 1,000,000 to 999,975 bushels. Not much of a shortage! Supply is virtually unchanged, and, therefore, the $4 price persists.

Competition means that each seller is providing a drop in the bucket of total supply. Individual sellers can make no noticeable dent in total supply; thus, a seller cannot *as an individual producer* manipulate product price. This is what is meant when it is said that an individual competitive seller is "at the mercy of the market."

The same rationale applies to the demand side of the market. Buyers are plentiful and act independently. Thus single buyers cannot manipulate the market to their advantage. *The widespread diffusion of economic power underlying competition controls the use and limits the potential abuse of that power.*

ENTRY AND EXIT   Competition also implies that it is simple for producers to enter or leave a particular industry; there are no artificial legal or institutional obstacles to prohibit expansion or contraction of specific industries. The freedom of an industry to expand or contract provides a competitive economy with the flexibility to remain efficient over time. Freedom of entry and exit is necessary for the economy to adjust appropriately to changes in consumer tastes, technology, or resource supplies.

MARKETS AND PRICES

What co-ordinates production and consumption decisions in a capitalist economy is the market system. *Capitalism is a market economy and markets use price to allocate resources.* Decisions by buyers and sellers of products and resources are made through a system of markets. A **market** is a mechanism or arrangement that brings buyers and sellers of a good or service into contact with one another. A McDonald's, a gas station, a grocery supermarket, a Sotheby's art auction, the Toronto Stock Exchange, and worldwide foreign exchange markets are but a few illustrations. The preferences of sellers and buyers are registered on the supply and demand sides of various markets, and the outcome of these choices is a system of product and resource prices. These prices are guideposts on which resource owners, entrepreneurs, and consumers make and revise their free choices in furthering their self-interests.

Just as competition is the controlling mechanism, so a system of markets and prices is a basic organizing force. Prices relay information about supply and demand conditions in each market. The market system is an elaborate communication system through which innumerable individual free choices are recorded, summarized, and balanced against one another. Those who obey the dictates of the market system are rewarded; those who ignore them are penalized by the system. Through this communication system, society decides what the economy should produce, how it should be produced, and how the fruits of productive endeavour are distributed among the individual economic units that make up a market economy.

Not only is the market system the mechanism through which society decides how it allocates its resources and distributes the resulting output, but it is through the market system that these decisions are carried out.

LIMITED GOVERNMENT

A competitive market economy promotes a high degree of efficiency in the use and allocation of resources. There is allegedly little real need for governmental intervention in the operation of such an economy beyond its role of imposing broad legal limits on the exercise of individual choices and the use of private property. The concept of a pure market system as a self-regulating and self-adjusting economy precludes any extensive economic role for government.

QUICK REVIEW 3-1

1. A pure market economy rests on the private ownership of property and freedom of enterprise and choice.

2. Economic entities — business, resource suppliers, and consumers — seek to further their own self-interests.

3. The co-ordinating mechanism of a market economy is a competitive system of markets that use prices to allocate resources.

4. The efficient functioning of the market system allegedly precludes significant government intervention.

OTHER CHARACTERISTICS

Private property, freedom of enterprise and choice, self-interest as a motivating force, competition, and reliance on a market system are all institutions and assumptions that are associated with a pure market system.

In addition, there are certain institutions and practices characteristic of all modern economies: (1) the use of an advanced technology and large amounts of capital goods, (2) specialization, and (3) the use of money. Specialization and an advanced technology are prerequisites to the efficient employment of any economy's resources. The use of money is a permissive characteristic that allows society more easily to practise and reap the benefits of specialization and of the employment of advanced productive techniques.

EXTENSIVE USE OF CAPITAL GOODS

All modern or "industrially advanced" economies are based on state-of-the-art technology and the extensive use of capital goods. In a market economy it is competition that brings about technological advance. Technological advancement helps a society get more output of goods and services with the same inputs as before, or even fewer inputs, thereby alleviating the scarcity problem. The market is highly effective in harnessing incentives to develop new products and improved techniques of production because the rewards accrue directly to the innovator. A market economy therefore presupposes the extensive use and relatively rapid development of complex capital goods: tools, machinery, large-scale factories, and facilities for storage, transportation, communication, and marketing.

Advanced technology and the use of capital goods is important because the most direct method of producing a product is usually the least efficient. Even Robinson Crusoe avoided the inefficiencies of direct production in favour of **roundabout production**. It would be ridiculous for a farmer — even a backyard farmer — to go at production with bare hands. It pays to create tools of production — capital equipment — to aid in the productive process. There is a better way of getting water out of a well than to dive in after it!

But there is a catch. Recall our discussion of the production possibilities curve and the basic nature of the economizing problem. For any economy operating on its production possibilities curve, resources must be diverted from the production of consumer goods in order to be used in the production of capital goods. We must currently tighten our belts as consumers in order to free resources for the production of capital goods that will allow a greater output of consumer goods at some future date. Greater abundance tomorrow requires sacrifice today. **(Key Question 2)**

SPECIALIZATION AND EFFICIENCY

The extent to which society relies on **specialization** is astounding. The vast majority of consumers produce virtually none of the goods and services they consume. The machine-shop worker who spends a lifetime stamping out parts for jet engines may never "consume" an airline trip. The worker who devotes eight hours a day to the installation of windows in Fords may own a Honda.

Few households seriously consider any extensive production of their own food, shelter, and clothing. Many farmers sell their milk to the local dairy and then buy margarine at the nearest supermarket. Society learned long ago that self-sufficiency breeds inefficiency. The jack-of-all-trades may be a very colourful individual, but is certainly not efficient.

DIVISION OF LABOUR In what ways might specialization — the **division of labour** — enhance a society's output and lessen the economizing problem?

1. **ABILITY DIFFERENCES** Specialization permits individuals to take advantage of existing differences in their abilities and skills. If caveman A is strong, swift afoot, and accurate with a spear, and caveman B is weak and slow, but patient, these talents can be most efficiently used by making A a hunter and B a fisherman.
2. **LEARNING BY DOING** Even if the abilities of A and B are identical, specialization may be advantageous. By devoting all one's time to a single task, it is more likely one will develop the appropriate skills and discover improved techniques than when apportioning time among a number of diverse tasks. A person learns to be a good hunter by hunting!
3. **SAVING TIME** Specialization also avoids the loss of time shifting from one job to another. For all these reasons, the division of labour results in greater productive efficiency in the use of resources.

GEOGRAPHIC SPECIALIZATION Specialization works on a regional and international basis. Apples could be grown in Saskatchewan, but because of the unsuitability of the land, rainfall, and temperature, the cost would be very high. The Okanagan Valley could achieve some success in the production of wheat, but for similar reasons such production would be relatively costly. Saskatchewan produces those products — wheat in particular — for which its resources are best adapted and the Okanagan does the same, producing apples and other fruit.

In so doing, both produce surpluses of their specialties. Then Saskatchewan and the Okanagan swap some of their surpluses. Specialization permits each area to turn out those goods its resources can most efficiently produce. In this way, both Saskatchewan and the Okanagan can enjoy a larger amount of both wheat and apples than would otherwise be the case.

Similarly, on an international basis we find Canada specializing in such items as the Dash-8 aircraft and communication equipment that it sells abroad in exchange for video cassette recorders from Japan, bananas from Honduras, shoes from Italy, and coffee from Brazil. In short, *specialization is essential to achieve efficiency in the use of scarce resources and thus get the most output from those resources.*

USE OF MONEY

Exchange can, and sometimes does, occur on the basis of **bartering**, that is, swapping goods for goods. But bartering as a means of exchange can pose serious problems for the economy. Exchange by barter requires a **coincidence of wants** between the two transactors. In our example, we assume Saskatchewan had excess wheat to trade and wanted to obtain apples. We also assumed the Okanagan had excess apples to swap and that it wanted to acquire wheat. So exchange occurred. But if this coincidence of wants did not exist, trade would not occur. Let us examine this.

Suppose Saskatchewan does not want any of the Okanagan's apples but is interested in buying potatoes from New Brunswick. Ironically, New Brunswick wants the Okanagan's apples but not Saskatchewan's wheat. And to complicate matters, suppose that the Okanagan wants some of Saskatchewan's wheat but none of New Brunswick's potatoes. The situation is summarized in Figure 3-1.

Specialization requires that people exchange the goods and services they produce for others they lack. In our Saskatchewan-Okanagan example, Saskatchewan must trade or exchange wheat for the Okanagan's apples if both regions are to share in the benefits of specialization. Because consumers want a wide variety of products, without trade they would devote their resources to many diverse types of production. If exchange could not occur or was very inconvenient, Saskatchewan and the Okanagan would be forced to be self-sufficient, denying both the advantages of specialization.

In no case do we find a coincidence of wants. Trade by barter would be difficult. *Thus, a convenient means of exchanging goods is a prerequisite of specialization.*

To overcome such a stalemate, economies use a **medium of exchange**, or **money**, which is convenient for facilitating the exchange of goods and services. Historically cattle, cigarettes, skins, liquor,

FIGURE 3-1 Money facilitates trade where wants do not coincide

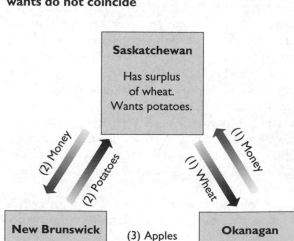

By the use of money as a medium of exchange, trade can be accomplished, as indicated by the arrows, despite a noncoincidence of wants. By facilitating exchange, the use of money permits an economy to realize the efficiencies of specialization.

BOX 3-2 APPLYING THE THEORY

BACK TO BARTER

Despite the advantages of using money, there is evidence that bartering is a "growth industry."

Since money facilitates exchange, it may seem odd that a considerable and growing volume of both domestic and international trade occurs through barter.

Suppose you own a small firm selling equipment to television stations. The economy is in recession; business is slow, your cash flow is down; and your inventories are much higher than desired. What do you do? You approach a local TV station that needs new equipment. But it, too, is feeling the effects of recession. Its advertising revenues are down and it also faces a cash-flow crunch. So a deal is struck. You provide $50,000 worth of equipment in exchange for $50,000 worth of "free" advertising. Advantage to seller: You move unwanted inventory, eliminating warehousing and insurance costs. You also receive valuable advertising time. The TV station gets needed equipment and pays for it with time

slots which would otherwise be unfilled. Both parties gain and no money changes hands.

Internationally, a firm might encounter an obstacle in selling its goods to a nation that does not have "hard" (exchangeable) currencies such as dollars, marks, or yen. Barter circumvents this problem. Example: PepsiCo swaps cola syrup for Russian vodka. Coca-Cola has traded for Egyptian oranges, Turkish tomato paste, Polish beer, and Hungarian soft-drink bottles. Recently, large Canadian companies have negotiated "joint ventures" with Russia based on barter.

Estimates differ on the volume of barter transactions within Canada. One estimate is that 17,500 businesses engaged in barter transactions of almost $100 million in 1990, a fivefold increase in dollar volume since 1980. Other estimates put the dollar value of barter transactions as high as $600 million per year.

---

playing cards, shells, stones, pieces of metal, and many other diverse commodities have been used with varying degrees of success as a medium for facilitating exchange. To be money, an item needs to pass only one test: *it must be generally acceptable by buyers and sellers in exchange.* Money is socially defined; whatever society accepts as a medium of exchange is money.

Most economies, for reasons made clear in macroeconomics, find it convenient to use paper as money. This is the case with the Saskatchewan-Okanagan-New Brunswick economy; they use pieces of paper called "dollars" as money. Can the use of paper dollars as a medium of exchange overcome the stalemate we have posed?

Yes, with trade occurring as shown in Figure 3-1:

1. The Okanagan can exchange money for some of Saskatchewan's wheat.
2. Saskatchewan uses the money from the sale of wheat and exchanges it for some of New Brunswick's potatoes.

3. New Brunswick can then exchange the money received from the sale of potatoes for some of the Okanagan's surplus apples.

The willingness to accept paper money (or any other kind of money) as a medium of exchange has permitted a three-way trade, which allows each region to specialize in one product and obtain the other product(s) its residents desire, despite the absence of a coincidence of wants between any two of the parties. Barter, resting as it does on a coincidence of wants, would impede this exchange, and thus keep the three regions from specializing. The efficiencies of specialization would then have been lost to those regions.

QUICK REVIEW 3-2

1. Advanced economies achieve greater efficiency in production through the use of large quantities of capital goods.

2. Specialization enhances efficiency and brings about surpluses by having individuals, regions, and nations produce those goods and services for which their resources are best suited.

3. The use of money is necessary to facilitate the exchange of goods that specialization brings about.

THE COMPETITIVE MARKET SYSTEM

There are two primary *decision makers* in a market economy: **households** (consumers) and **firms** (businesses). Households are the ultimate suppliers of all economic resources and simultaneously the major spending group in the economy. Firms provide goods and services to the economy.

Consumers are at liberty to buy what they choose; firms to produce and sell what they choose; and resource suppliers to make their resources available in whatever endeavours or occupations they choose. We may wonder why such an economy does not collapse in chaos. If consumers want breakfast cereal, businesses choose to produce aerobic shoes, and resource suppliers want to offer their services in manufacturing computer software, production would seem to be deadlocked because of the apparent inconsistency of these free choices.

In reality, the millions of decisions made by households and firms are highly consistent with one another. Firms do produce those particular goods and services that consumers want. Households provide the kinds of labour that businesses want to hire. What we want to explain is how a competitive market system constitutes a co-ordinating mechanism that overcomes the potential chaos of freedom of enterprise and choice. The competitive market system is a mechanism both for communicating the decisions of consumers, producers, and resource suppliers to one another and for synchronizing those decisions towards consistent production objectives.

THE FIVE FUNDAMENTAL QUESTIONS

To understand the operation of a market economy we must recognize that there are **Five Fundamental Questions** to which *every* economy must respond:

1. *How much* is to be produced? At what level — to what degree — should available resources be employed or utilized in the production process?

2. *What* is to be produced? What collection of goods and services will best satisfy society's material wants?

3. *How* is that output to be produced? How should production be organized? What firms should do the producing and what productive techniques should they use?

4. *Who* is to receive the output? How should the output of the economy be shared by consumers?

5. Can the system *adapt* to change? Can it appropriately adjust to changes in consumer wants, resource supplies, and technology?

Two points are relevant. First, we will defer the "how much" question for the moment. Macroeconomics deals in detail with the complex question of the level of resource employment.

Second, the Five Fundamental Questions are merely an elaboration of the choices underlying Chapter 2's production possibilities curve. These questions would be irrelevant were it not for the economizing problem.

THE MARKET SYSTEM AT WORK

Chapter 2's circular flow diagram (Figure 2-6) provides the setting for our discussion.

DETERMINING WHAT IS TO BE PRODUCED

Given the product and resource prices established by competing buyers and sellers in both the product and resource markets, how would a market economy decide the types and quantities of goods to be produced? Since businesses seek profits and want to avoid losses, we can generalize that those goods and services that can be produced at a profit will be produced and those whose production entails a loss will not. Those industries that are profitable usually expand, those that incur losses usually contract.

ORGANIZING PRODUCTION

How is production to be organized in a market economy? This Fundamental Question is composed of three subquestions:

1. How should resources be allocated among specific industries?
2. What specific firms should do the producing in each industry?
3. What combinations of resources — what technology — should each firm employ?

The market system steers resources to those industries whose products consumers want badly enough to make their production profitable. It simultaneously deprives unprofitable industries of scarce resources. If all firms had sufficient time to enter prosperous industries and to leave unprosperous industries, the output of each industry would be large enough for the firms to make normal profits (Chapter 8).

The second and third subquestions are closely intertwined. In a competitive market economy, the firms that do the producing are those that are willing and able to employ the economically most efficient technique of production. And what determines the most efficient technique? Economic efficiency depends on:

1. Available technology, that is, the alternative combinations of resources or inputs that will produce the desired output.
2. The prices of needed resources.

DISTRIBUTING TOTAL OUTPUT

The market system enters the picture in two ways in solving the problem of distributing total output. Generally speaking, any given product will be distributed to consumers on the basis of their ability and willingness to pay the existing market price for it. This is the rationing function of equilibrium prices.

The size of one's money income determines a consumer's ability to pay the equilibrium price for X and other available products. And money income depends on the quantities of the various resources that the income receiver supplies and the prices that they command in the resource market. Thus, resource prices play a key role in determining the size of each household's income claim against the total output of society. Within the limits of a consumer's money income, his or her willingness to pay the equilibrium price for X determines whether some of this product is distributed to that person. And this willingness to buy X will depend on one's preference for X in comparison with available close substitutes for X and their relative prices. Thus, product prices play a key role in determining the expenditure patterns of consumers.

There is nothing particularly ethical about the market system as a mechanism for distributing output. Households that accumulate large amounts of property by inheritance, through hard work and frugality, through business acumen, or by crook will receive large incomes and thus command large shares of the economy's total output. Others, offering unskilled and relatively unproductive labour resources that elicit low wages, will receive meagre money incomes and small portions of total output.

ACCOMMODATING CHANGE

Industrial societies are dynamic: Consumer preferences, technology, and resource supplies all change. This means that the particular allocation of resources that is *now* the most efficient for a *given* pattern of consumer tastes, for a *given* range of technological alternatives, and for *given* supplies of resources can be expected to become obsolete and inefficient as consumer preferences change, new techniques of production are discovered, and resource supplies change over time. The market economy adjusts to these changes so that resources are still used efficiently.

COMPETITION AND CONTROL

The market mechanism of supply and demand communicates the wants of consumers (society) to businesses and through businesses to resource suppliers. It is competition, however, that forces businesses and resource suppliers to make appropriate responses. But competition does more than guarantee responses appropriate to the wishes of society. It also forces firms to adopt the most efficient productive techniques. In a competitive market, the failure of some firms to use the least costly production technique leads to their eventual elimination by more efficient firms. Finally, competition provides an environment conducive to technological advance.

THE "INVISIBLE HAND"

The operation and the adjustments of a competitive market system create a curious and important identity — the identity of private and social interests. Firms and resource suppliers, seeking to further their own self-interest and operating within the framework of a highly competitive market system, will simultaneously, as though guided by an "**invisible hand**," promote the public or social interest. For example, in a competitive environment, business firms use the least costly combination of resources in producing a given output because it is in their private self-interest to do so. To act otherwise would be to forgo profits or even to risk bankruptcy. But, at the same time, it is clearly also in the social interest to use scarce resources in the least costly, that is, most efficient, manner. Not to do so would be to produce a given output at a greater cost or sacrifice of alternative goods than is necessary. It is self-interest, awakened and guided by the competitive market system, that induces responses appropriate to the assumed change in society's wants. Businesses seeking to make higher profits and to avoid losses, on the one hand, and resource suppliers pursuing greater monetary rewards, on the other, negotiate the changes in the allocation of resources and therefore the composition of output society demands. The force of competition controls or guides the self-interest motive in such a way that it automatically, and quite unintentionally, furthers the best interests of society. The "invisible hand" tells us that when firms maximize their profits, society's domestic output is also maximized.

THE CASE FOR THE MARKET SYSTEM

The virtues of the market system are implicit in our discussion of its operation. Three merit emphasis.

EFFICIENCY The basic economic argument for the market system is that it promotes the efficient use of scarce resources. The competitive market system guides scarce resources into production of those goods and services most wanted by society. It forces use of the most efficient techniques in organizing scarce resources for production and is conducive to the development and adoption of new and more efficient production techniques so that the economizing problem — scarce resources and unlimited human wants — can be alleviated.

INCENTIVES The market system effectively harnesses incentives to alleviate the economizing prob-

lem. Greater work effort is rewarded by higher money incomes that translate into a higher standard of living. Similarly, the assuming of risks by entrepreneurs to provide what consumers want can result in substantial profit incomes. Successful innovations that produce more of what society wants may also generate ample economic rewards.

FREEDOM The major noneconomic argument for the market system is its great emphasis on personal freedom. In contrast to central planning, the market system can co-ordinate economic activity without coercion. The market system permits — indeed, it thrives on — freedom of enterprise and choice. Entrepreneurs and workers are not herded from industry to industry by government directives to meet production targets established by some omnipotent governmental agency. On the contrary, they are free to further their own self-interests, subject to the rewards and penalties imposed by the market system itself.

QUICK REVIEW 3-3

1. The output mix of the competitive market system is determined by profits. Profits cause industries to expand; losses cause them to contract.

2. Competition forces firms to use the least costly (most efficient) production methods.

3. The distribution of output in a market economy is determined by consumer incomes and product prices.

4. Competitive markets reallocate resources in response to changes in consumer tastes, technological progress, and changes in resource supplies.

CHAPTER SUMMARY

1. The capitalist, or market, system is characterized by private ownership of resources and the freedom of individuals to engage in the economic activities of their choice as a means for advancing their material well-being. Self-interest is the driving force of such an economy, and competition functions as a regulatory or control mechanism.

2. Capitalist production is not organized by a central government, but rather features the market system as a means of organizing and making effective the many individual decisions that determine what is produced, the methods of production, and the sharing of output. A pure capitalist system envisions government playing a minor and relatively passive economic role.

3. Specialization and an advanced technology based on the extensive use of capital goods are common to all modern economies.

4. Functioning as a medium of exchange, money circumvents problems of bartering and thereby permits greater specialization both domestically and internationally.

5. Every economy faces Five Fundamental Questions: **a** At what level should available resources be employed? **b** What goods and services are to be produced? **c** How is that output to be produced? **d** To whom should the output be distributed? **e** Can the system adapt to changes in consumer tastes, resource supplies, and technology?

6. Consumer sovereignty means that both businesses and resource suppliers channel their efforts in accordance with the wants of consumers.

7. The competitive market system can communicate changes in consumer tastes to resource suppliers and entrepreneurs, thereby prompting appropriate adjustments in the allocation of the economy's resources. The competitive market system also provides an environment conducive to technological advance and capital accumulation.

8. Competition, the primary mechanism of control in the market economy, will foster an identity of private and social interests; as though directed by an "invisible hand," competition harnesses the self-interest motives of businesses and resource suppliers so as to simultaneously further the social interest in using scarce resources efficiently.

TERMS AND CONCEPTS

bartering (p. 50)
coincidence of wants (p. 50)
competition (p. 47)
firms (p. 52)
Five Fundamental Questions (p. 52)
freedom of choice (p. 47)
freedom of enterprise (p. 47)
households (p. 52)

"invisible hand" (p. 53)
market economy (p. 48)
medium of exchange (p. 50)
money (p. 50)
private property (p. 46)
roundabout production (p. 49)
self-interest (p. 47)
specialization and division of labour (p. 49)

QUESTIONS AND STUDY SUGGESTIONS

1. "Capitalism may be characterized as an automatic self-regulating system motivated by the self-interest of individuals and regulated by competition." Explain and evaluate.

2. **Key Question** *What advantages result from "roundabout" production? What problem is involved in increasing a full-employment, full-production economy's stock of capital goods? Illustrate this problem in terms of the production possibilities curve. Does an economy with unemployed resources face the same problem?*

3. What are the advantages of specialization in the use of resources? Explain: "Exchange is the necessary consequence of specialization."

4. What problems does barter entail? Indicate the economic significance of money as a medium of exchange. "Money is the only commodity that is good for nothing but to be gotten rid of. It will not feed you, clothe you, shelter you, or amuse you unless you spend or invest it. It imparts value only in parting." Explain this statement.

5. Describe in detail how the market system answers the Fundamental Questions. Why must economic choices be made? Explain: "The capitalist system is a profit and loss economy."

6. Evaluate and explain the following statements:

   a. "The most important feature of capitalism is the absence of a central economic plan."
   b. "Competition is the indispensable disciplinarian of the market economy."
   c. "Production methods that are inferior in the engineering sense may be the most efficient methods in the economic sense."

7. Explain fully the meaning and implications of the following quotation.

   The beautiful consequence of the market is that it is its own guardian. If output prices or certain kinds of remuneration stray away from their socially ordained levels, forces are set into motion to bring them back to the fold. It is a curious paradox which thus ensues: the market, which is the acme of individual economic freedom, is the strictest taskmaster of all. One may appeal the ruling of a planning board or win the dispensation of a minister, but there is no appeal, no dispensation, from the anonymous pressures of the market mechanism. Economic freedom is thus more illusory than at first appears. One can do as one pleases in the market. But if one pleases to do what the market disapproves, the price of individual freedom is economic ruination.[1]

8. (Applying the Theory) What considerations have increased the popularity of barter in recent years?

[1] Robert L. Heilbroner, *The Worldly Philosophers*, 3d ed. (New York: Simon & Schuster, Inc., 1967), p. 42.

CHAPTER 4

UNDERSTANDING INDIVIDUAL MARKETS: DEMAND AND SUPPLY

"Teach a parrot to say, 'Demand and supply,' and you have an economist!" There is a strong element of truth in this quip. The tools of demand and supply can take one far in understanding not only specific economic issues, but also how the entire economy works.

The goal of this chapter is to understand the nature of markets and how prices and outputs are determined. Our circular flow model of Chapter 2 identified the participants in both product and resource markets. But we assumed product and resource prices were "given"; here we will explain how prices are determined by discussing more fully the concept of a market.

BOX 4-1 THE BIG PICTURE

In a world of scarcity in relation to unlimited wants, there is constant competition for the available goods and services. The supply and demand curves represent the self-interest of the producers and consumers respectively. Firms are willing to supply *more* of a specific product at successively higher prices, but consumers actually want less at successively higher prices. What quantities of a particular good or service and at what price it is exchanged are determined by the interaction of these two opposing forces. The price mechanism is at the heart of the market system because prices adjust in response to choices made by consumers, suppliers, and other actors in the economy. Price changes mediate the effects of these various choices, leading to a more or less coherent allocation of resources in our society.

As you read this chapter, keep the following points in mind:

- Think of the supply and demand curves as independent of each other. Each of these curves shifts for different reasons. Remember that suppliers of goods and services and the consumers have diverging interests.
- Make sure you understand the distinction between movement along the curves and shifts of the curves.
- The supply and demand curves shift only when certain conditions change. It is imperative that you learn the causes of the demand and supply curve shifts, reproduced in Tables 4-3 and 4-7.
- Supply and demand analysis can appear deceptively easy at first glance. Whenever applying supply and demand analysis, be sure to use graphs; trying to figure out a problem in your head can quickly lead to errors. Supply and demand analysis is mastered by getting "your hands dirty"; you need lots of practice applying it, and graphing is an important part.

MARKETS DEFINED

A **market** *is an institution that brings together buyers and sellers of particular goods and services.* Markets exist in many forms. The corner gas station, the fast-food outlet, the local record shop, a farmer's roadside stand, are all familiar markets. The Toronto Stock Exchange and the Chicago Board of Trade are highly organized markets where buyers and sellers of stocks and bonds and farm commodities, respectively, may communicate with one another. Auctioneers bring together potential buyers and sellers of art, livestock, used farm equipment, and sometimes real estate. The professional hockey player and his agent bargain with the owner of an NHL team. A graduating engineer interviews with Canadian Pacific and Petro-Canada at the university placement office.

All of these situations that link potential buyers with potential sellers constitute markets. Some markets are local while others are national or international in scope. Some are highly personal, involving face-to-face contact between demander and supplier; others are impersonal and buyer and seller never see or know one another.

This chapter looks at *purely competitive markets.* Such markets have large numbers of independently acting buyers and sellers exchanging a standardized product. The kind of market we have in mind is not the record shop or corner gas station, where products have price tags on them, but such competitive markets as a central grain exchange, a stock market, or a market for foreign currencies, where the equilibrium price is "discovered" by the interacting decisions of many buyers and sellers.

DEMAND

D **emand** *refers to the various amounts of a product consumers are willing and able to purchase at each specific price during a specified period of time, all other things being equal.*[1]

A **demand schedule** shows the amounts consumers will buy at various possible prices. Table 4-1 is a hypothetical demand schedule for a single consumer purchasing bushels of oats.

---

[1] In adjusting this definition to the resource market, substitute the word "resource" for "product" and "businesses" for "consumers."

TABLE 4-1 An individual buyer's demand for oats

Price per bushel	Quantity demanded per week
$5	10
4	20
3	35
2	55
1	80

This demand curve reflects the relationship between the price of oats and the quantity that our hypothetical consumer would be willing and able to purchase at each of these prices. We say willing and *able*, because willingness alone will not suffice. I may be willing to buy a Porsche, but if this willingness is not backed by the ability to buy, it will not be effective and therefore not be reflected in the market. In Table 4-1, if the price of oats in the market were $5 per bushel, our consumer would buy 10 bushels per week; if it were $4, the consumer would buy 20 bushels per week, and so forth.

The demand schedule does not tell us which of the five possible prices will actually exist in the oats market. This depends on demand *and supply*. Demand is simply a statement of a buyer's plans or intentions to purchase a product.

To be meaningful the quantities demanded at each price must relate to some specific time period — a day, a week, a month, and so forth. To say "a consumer will buy 10 bushels of oats at $5 per bushel" is vague and meaningless. In the absence of a specific time period we would be unable to tell whether the demand for a product was large or small.

LAW OF DEMAND: A FIRST LOOK

A fundamental characteristic of demand is this: *All else being constant, as price falls, the quantity demanded rises. Or, other things being equal, as price increases, the quantity demanded falls.* There is an inverse relationship between price and quantity demanded. We call this inverse relationship the **law of demand**.

The "other things being constant" assumption is critical. Many factors other than the price of the product under consideration can affect the amount

purchased. The quantity of Nikes purchased will depend not only on the price of Nikes, but also on the prices of such substitutes as Reeboks, Adidas, and L.A. Gear. The law of demand in this case says that fewer Nikes will be purchased if the price of Nikes rises *and the prices of Reeboks, Adidas and L.A. Gear all remain constant.* Thus, if the relative price of Nikes increases, fewer Nikes will be bought.

What is the foundation for the law of demand? Why is it that as price falls, the quantity demanded of a good rises, and vice versa?

1. In any time period, each buyer of a product will derive less satisfaction or utility from each successive unit consumed. The second Big Mac will yield less satisfaction than the first; the third still less than the second, and so forth. Because consumption is subject to **diminishing marginal utility** — successive units of a particular product yield less and less extra satisfaction — consumers will buy additional units only if price is reduced.
2. The law of demand can also be explained in terms of substitution effects and income effects. The **substitution effect** tells us that at a lower price, you have the incentive to substitute the cheaper good for similar goods that are now relatively more expensive.

The **income effect** indicates that at a lower price, you can afford more of the good without giving up other goods. A decline in the price of a product will increase the purchasing power of your money income, allowing you to buy more of the product than before.

For example, at a lower price, beef is relatively more attractive and it is substituted for pork, lamb, chicken, and fish (the substitution effect). A decline in the price of beef will increase the purchasing power of consumer incomes, enabling them to buy more beef (the income effect). The substitution and income effects combine to make consumers able and willing to buy more of a product at a low price than at a high price.

THE DEMAND CURVE

This inverse relationship between product price and quantity demanded can be represented on a simple two-dimensional graph, measuring quantity demanded on the horizontal axis and price on the vertical axis. The process involves locating on the graph those five price-quantity possibilities in Table 4-1.

Assuming the same inverse relationship between price and quantity demanded at all points between the ones graphed, we can generalize on the inverse relationship between price and quantity demanded by drawing a curve to represent *all* price–quantity-demanded possibilities within the limits shown on the graph. The resulting curve is called a **demand curve** and is labelled D in Figure 4-1. It slopes downward and to the right because the relationship it portrays between price and quantity demanded is negative or inverse. The law of demand is reflected in the downward slope of the demand curve.

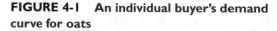

FIGURE 4-1   An individual buyer's demand curve for oats

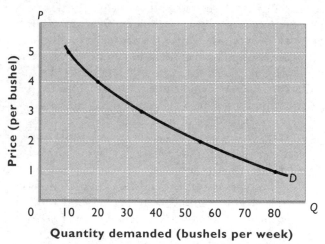

An individual's demand schedule graphs as a downsloping curve such as D, because price and quantity demanded are inversely related. Specifically, the law of demand generalizes that consumers will buy more of a product as its price declines.

The advantage of graphing is that it permits us to represent clearly a given relationship — in this case, the law of demand — in a much simpler way. A single curve on a graph, if understood, is simpler to state *and to manipulate* than tables and lengthy verbal presentations. Graphs are invaluable tools in economic analysis. They permit clear expression and handling of sometimes complex relationships.

INDIVIDUAL AND MARKET DEMAND

Until now we have been dealing with one consumer. We can get from an *individual* to a *market* demand schedule easily by summing the quantities demanded by each consumer at the various possible prices. If there were just three buyers in the market, as in Table 4-2, it would be easy to determine the total quantities demanded at each price. Figure 4-2 shows the same summing procedure graphically, using only the $3 price to illustrate the adding-up process. Note that we are simply summing the three individual demand curves *horizontally* to derive the total demand curve.

Competition requires many more than three buyers of a product. For simplicity, let's suppose there are 200 buyers of oats in the market, each choosing to buy the same amount at each of the various prices as our original consumer. We can determine total or market demand multiplying the quantity demanded data of Table 4-1 by 200, as in Table 4-3. Curve D_0 in Figure 4-3 indicates this market demand curve for the 200 buyers.

DETERMINANTS OF DEMAND

Constructing a demand curve such as D_0 in Figure 4-3 assumes that price is the most important determinant of the amount of any product purchased. But factors other

---

FIGURE 4-2   The market demand curve is the sum of the individual demand curves

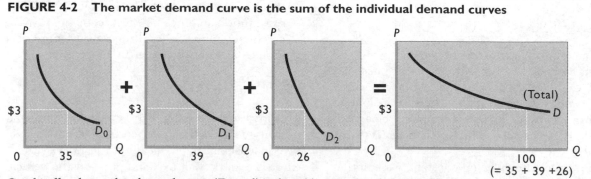

Graphically, the market demand curve (*D* total) is found by summing horizontally the individual demand curves (D_0, D_1, and D_2) of all consumers in the market.

FIGURE 4-3   Change in the demand for oats

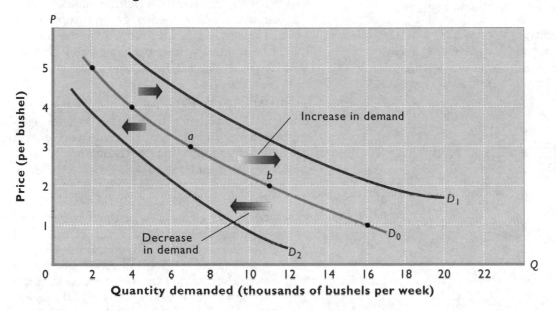

Quantity demanded (thousands of bushels per week)

A change in one or more of the determinants of demand — consumer tastes, the number of buyers in the market, money incomes, the prices of other goods, or consumer expectations — will cause a change in demand. An increase in demand shifts the demand curve to the right, as from D_0 to D_1. A decrease in demand shifts the demand curve to the left, as from D_0 to D_2. A change in the quantity demanded involves a movement, caused by a change in the price of the product under consideration, from one point to another — as from a to b — on a fixed demand curve.

than price can and do affect purchases. In locating a specific demand curve such as D_0, it must be assumed that other *determinants* of the amount demanded are constant. When these determinants of demand do change, the location of the demand curve will shift to some new position to the right or left of D_0. For this reason these determinants are also referred to as "demand shifters."

The determinants of market demand are: (1) the tastes or preferences of consumers, (2) the number of consumers in the market, (3) the money incomes of consumers, (4) the prices of related goods, and (5) consumer expectations with respect to future prices and incomes.

TABLE 4-2   Market demand for oats, three buyers

Price per bushel	Quantity demanded, first buyer		Quantity demanded, second buyer		Quantity demanded, third buyer		Total quantity demanded per week
$5	10	+	12	+	8	=	30
4	20	+	23	+	17	=	60
3	35	+	39	+	26	=	100
2	55	+	60	+	39	=	154
1	80	+	87	+	54	=	221

TABLE 4-3   Market demand for oats, 200 buyers

(1) Price per bushel	(2) Quantity demanded per week, single buyer		(3) Number of buyers in the market		(4) Total quantity demanded per week
$5	10	x	200	=	2,000
4	20	x	200	=	4,000
3	35	x	200	=	7,000
2	55	x	200	=	11,000
1	80	x	200	=	16,000

CHANGES IN DEMAND

A change in one or more of the determinants will change the demand schedule data in Table 4-3, and therefore the location of the demand curve in Figure 4-3. A change in the demand schedule data or, graphically, a shift in the location of the demand curve, is called a **change in demand.**

If consumers buy more oats at each possible price than is reflected in column 4 of Table 4-3, the result will be an *increase in demand*. In Figure 4-3, this increase in demand is reflected in a shift of the demand curve to the right from D_0 to D_1. Conversely, a *decrease in demand* occurs when, because of a change in one or more of the determinants, consumers buy less oats at each possible price than is indicated in column 4 of Table 4-3. Graphically, a decrease in demand is shown as a shift of the demand curve to the left, from D_0 to D_2, in Figure 4-3.

Let's now examine how changes in each of the determinants affects demand.

1. TASTES   A change in consumer tastes or preferences favourable to a product — possibly prompted by advertising or fashion changes — will result in more being demanded at each price; that is, demand will increase. An unfavourable change in consumer preferences will decrease demand, shifting the curve to the left. Technological change in the form of new products may affect consumer tastes. The introduction of compact discs has greatly decreased the demand for long-playing records. Consumer concerns over the health hazards posed by cholesterol and obe-

sity have increased the demands for broccoli, low-calorie sweeteners, and fresh fruits, while decreasing the demands for beef, veal, eggs, and whole milk. Medical studies linking beta carotene to the prevention of heart attacks, strokes, and some types of cancer have greatly boosted the demand for carrots.

2. NUMBER OF BUYERS   An increase in the number of consumers in a market will increase demand. Fewer consumers will result in a decrease in demand. For example, improvements in communications have given financial markets international range, increasing the demand for stocks and bonds. The "baby boom" of the post–World War II period increased the demand for diapers and baby lotion, not to mention the services of obstetricians. When the "baby boomers" reached their twenties in the 1970s, the demand for housing greatly increased. Conversely, the aging of the baby boomers in the late 1980s and 1990s has been a factor in the recent "slump" in housing demand. Increasing life expectancy has increased the demands for medical care, retirement communities, and nursing homes. Note, too, that recent international trade agreements such as the North American Free Trade Agreement (NAFTA) and the General Agreement on Tariffs and Trade (GATT) have reduced foreign trade barriers to Canadian products, increasing the demand for them.

3. INCOME   For most commodities, a rise in income will cause an increase in demand. Consumers typically buy more shoes, steaks, sunscreen, and stereos as their incomes increase. Conversely, the demand for such products will decline as incomes fall. Commodities whose demand varies *directly* with money income are called **superior** or **normal goods.**

Although most products are normal goods, there are a few exceptions. As incomes increase beyond some point, the amounts of bread or potatoes or cabbages purchased at each price may diminish because higher incomes now allow consumers to buy more high-protein foods, such as dairy products and meat. Rising incomes may also decrease the demands for used clothing and third-hand automobiles. Rising incomes may cause the demands for hamburger to decline, as wealthier consumers switch to T-bone steak. Goods whose demand varies *inversely* with a change in money income are called **inferior goods.**

4. PRICES OF RELATED GOODS Whether a particular change in the price of a related good will increase or decrease the demand for the product under consideration will depend on whether the related good is a substitute for, or a complement to, the product. A substitute good is one that can be used in place of another good. A complementary good is one that is used in conjunction with another good.

SUBSTITUTES Butter and margarine are examples of **substitute goods**. When the price of butter rises, consumers buy less butter, increasing the demand for margarine.[2] Conversely, as the price of butter falls, consumers buy more butter, decreasing the demand for margarine. *When two products are substitutes, the price of one good and the demand for the other are directly related.* So it is with sugar and NutraSweet, Toyotas and Hondas, Coke and Pepsi, and tea and coffee.

COMPLEMENTS Other products are **complementary goods**; they "go together" in that they are used in tandem and jointly demanded. If the price of gasoline falls, you drive your car more, and this extra driving will increase your demand for motor oil. Conversely, an increase in the price of gasoline will diminish the demand for motor oil.[3] Thus gas and oil are jointly demanded; they are complements. And so it is with ham and eggs, university courses and textbooks, movies and popcorn, VCRs and video cassettes, golf clubs and golf balls, cameras and film. *When two commodities are complements, the price of one good and the demand for the other are inversely related.*

Many goods are not related to one another — they are *independent* goods. For example, butter and golf balls, potatoes and automobiles, bananas and wristwatches. A change in the price of one would have little or no impact on the demand for the other.

---

[2] Note that the consumer is moving up a stable demand curve for butter. But the demand curve for margarine shifts to the right. Given the supply of margarine, this rightward shift in demand means that more margarine will be purchased and that its price will also rise.

[3] While the buyer is moving up a stable demand curve for gasoline, the demand for motor oil shifts to the left (decreases). Given the supply of motor oil, this decline in demand for motor oil will decrease both the amount purchased and its price.

5. EXPECTATIONS Consumer expectations about future products prices, product availability, and future income can shift demand. Consumer expectations of higher future prices may prompt them to buy now to "beat" the anticipated price rises. The expectation of rising incomes may induce consumers to be less tight-fisted in their current spending. Conversely, expectations of falling prices and income will decrease current demand for products.

For example, if freezing weather destroys a substantial portion of Florida's citrus crop, consumers may reason that forthcoming shortages of frozen orange juice will escalate its price. They may stock up on orange juice by purchasing large quantities now.

A first-round NHL draft choice might splurge on a new Rolls-Royce in anticipation of a lucrative professional hockey contract.

Table 4-4 provides a convenient listing of the determinants of demand along with additional illustrations. (**Key Question 2**)

TABLE 4-4 Determinants of demand: factors that shift the demand curve

1. *Change in buyer tastes* Example: Physical fitness increases in popularity, increasing the demands for jogging shoes and bicycles.

2. *Change in number of buyers* Examples: Japanese reduce import restrictions on Canadian telecommunications equipment, increasing the demand for it; a birthrate decline reduces the demand for education.

3. *Change in income* Examples: An increase in incomes increases the demand for such normal goods as butter, lobster, and filet mignon, while reducing the demand for such inferior goods as cabbage, turnips, retreaded tires, and used clothing.

4. *Change in the prices of related goods* Examples: An increase in air fares because of increased concentration of ownership (mergers) increases the demand for bus transportation (substitute goods); a decline in the price of compact disc players increases the demand for compact discs (complementary goods).

5. *Change in expectations* Example: Inclement weather in South America causes the expectation of higher future coffee prices, thereby increasing the current demand for coffee.

CHANGES IN QUANTITY DEMANDED

A "change in demand" must not be confused with a "change in the quantity demanded." A **change in demand** refers to a shift in the entire demand curve either to the right (an increase in demand) or to the left (a decrease in demand). The term "demand" refers to a schedule or curve; therefore, a "change in demand" must mean that the entire schedule has changed, and that graphically, the curve has shifted its position.

In contrast, a **change in the quantity demanded** designates the movement from one point to another point — from one price combination to another — on a fixed demand curve. The cause of a change in the quantity demanded is a change in the price of the product under consideration. In Table 4-3, a decline in the price asked by suppliers of oats from $5 to $4 will increase the quantity of oats demanded from 2,000 to 4,000 bushels.

In Figure 4-3 the shifts of the demand curve D_0 to either D_1 or D_2 are each a "change in demand." But the movement from point *a* to point *b* on curve D_0 is a "change in the quantity demanded."

Is a change in demand or a change in the quantity demanded illustrated in each of the following?

1. Consumer incomes rise, with the result that more jewellery is purchased.
2. A barber raises the price of haircuts and experiences a decline in volume of business.
3. The price of Toyotas goes up and, as a consequence, the sales of Chevrolets increase.

QUICK REVIEW 4-1

1. A market is any arrangement that facilitates the purchase and sale of goods, services, or resources.

2. The law of demand indicates that, other things being constant, the quantity of a good purchased will vary inversely with its price.

3. The demand curve will shift as a consequence of changes in (a) consumer tastes, (b) the number of buyers in the market, (c) incomes, (d) the prices of substitute or complementary goods, and (e) expectations.

4. A "change in the quantity demanded" refers to a movement from one point to another on a stable demand curve; a "change in demand" designates a shift in the entire demand curve.

SUPPLY

The term supply *refers to the various amounts of a product that a producer is willing and able to produce and make available for sale at each specific price in a series of possible prices during some specified time period.*[4] The **supply schedule** portrays a series of alternative possibilities, such as those shown in Table 4-5 for a single producer.

Suppose in this case that our producer is a farmer producing oats, the demand for which we have just considered. Our definition of supply indicates that supply is viewed from the vantage point of price. That is, we read supply as showing the amounts producers will offer at various prices.

LAW OF SUPPLY

Table 4-5 shows a positive or *direct* relationship between price and quantity supplied. As price rises, the corresponding quantity supplied rises; as price falls, the quantity supplied also falls. This relationship is called the **law of supply**. It tells us that producers are willing to produce and offer for sale more of their product at a high price than they are at a low price.

Price is a deterrent from the consumer's standpoint. The higher the price, the less the consumer buys. To a supplier, price is revenue per unit and therefore an incentive to produce and sell a product. Given production costs, a higher product price will result in larger profits and thus an incentive to increase the quantity supplied.

Consider a farmer who can shift resources among alternative products. As price moves up in Table 4-5, the farmer will find it profitable to take land out of wheat, rye, and barley production and put it into oats. Higher oat prices will make it possible for the farmer to cover the costs associated with more intensive cultivation and the use of larger quantities of fertilizers and pesticides. The result is more output of oats.

Now consider a manufacturer. As output increases manufacturers generally find that costs rise after some point. They rise because certain productive resources — in particular, the firm's plant and machinery — cannot

---

[4] In discussing the resource market, our definition of supply reads: The various amounts of a resource that its owners are willing to supply in the market at each possible price during some specified time, all other things being equal.

be expanded in a short period of time. As the firm increases the amounts of more readily variable resources such as labour, materials, and component parts, the fixed plant will at some point become crowded or congested. Productive efficiency will decline and the cost of successive units of output will increase. Producers must receive a higher price to produce costly units.

TABLE 4-5   An individual producer's supply of oats

Price per bushel	Quantity supplied per week
$5	60
4	50
3	35
2	20
1	5

THE SUPPLY CURVE

As with demand, it is convenient to present graphically the concept of supply. Our axes in Figure 4-4 are the same as in Figure 4-3, except for the change of "quantity demanded" to "quantity supplied" on the horizontal axis. The graphing procedure is the same as that previously explained, but the quantity

TABLE 4-6   Market supply of oats, 200 producers

(1) Price per bushel	(2) Quantity supplied per week, single producer		(3) Number of sellers in the market		(4) Total quantity supplied per week
$5	60	x	200	=	12,000
4	50	x	200	=	10,000
3	35	x	200	=	7,000
2	20	x	200	=	4,000
1	5	x	200	=	1,000

data and relationship are different. The market supply data graphed in Figure 4-4 as S_0 are shown in Table 4-6, which assumes there are 200 suppliers in the market having the same supply schedules as the producer previously portrayed in Table 4-5.

DETERMINANTS OF SUPPLY

In constructing a supply curve, we assume that price is the most significant determinant of the quantity supplied of any product. But, as with the demand curve, the supply curve is anchored on the "other

FIGURE 4-4   Changes in the supply of oats

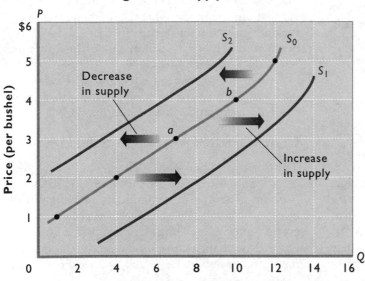

A change in one or more of the determinants of supply — productive techniques, resource prices, taxes and subsidies, the prices of other goods, price expectations, or the number of sellers in the market — will cause a change in supply. An increase in supply shifts the supply curve to the right, as from S_0 to S_1. A decrease in the supply is shown graphically as a movement of the curve to the left, as from S_0 to S_2. A change in the quantity supplied involves a movement, caused by a change in the price of the product under consideration, from one point to another — as from a to b — on a fixed supply curve.

things are equal" assumption. The supply curve is drawn assuming that certain determinants of the amount supplied are given and do not change. If any of these determinants of supply do in fact change, the location of the supply curve will shift.

The basic determinants of supply are (1) the technique of production, (2) resource prices, (3) taxes and subsidies, (4) prices of other goods, (5) price expectations, and (6) the number of sellers in the market.

A change in any one or more of these determinants or "supply shifters" will cause the supply curve for a product to move to either the right or the left. A shift to the *right*, from S_0 to S_1 in Figure 4-4, designates *an increase in supply*: producers will supply larger quantities of the product at each possible price. A shift to the left, S_0 to S_2 in Figure 4-4, indicates a *decrease in supply*: suppliers offer less at each price.

CHANGES IN SUPPLY

Let's consider how changes in each of these determinants affect supply.

1. RESOURCE PRICES The relationship between production costs and supply is a close one. A firm must receive higher prices for additional units of output because those extra units are more costly to produce. It follows that a decrease in resource prices will lower production costs and increase supply (shift the supply curve to the right). If the prices of oat seed and fertilizer decrease, we can expect the supply of oats to increase. Conversely, an increase in input prices will raise production costs and reduce supply (shift the supply curve to the left). Increases in the prices of iron ore and coke will increase the cost of producing steel and reduce its supply.

2. TECHNOLOGY A technological improvement means producing a unit of output with fewer resources. Given the prices of resources, this will lower production costs and increase supply. Example: Currently about 30% of electric power is lost when transmitted by copper cable. Recent breakthroughs in the area of superconductivity point to the possibility of transporting electrical power with little or no loss. The consequence is significant cost reductions and supply increases may occur in a wide range of products where electricity is an important input.

3. TAXES AND SUBSIDIES An increase in taxes on business will increase costs and reduce supply. Conversely, subsidies are "taxes in reverse." If government subsidizes the production of some good, it in effect lowers costs and increases supply.

4. PRICES OF OTHER GOODS Changes in the prices of other goods can also shift the supply curve of a product. A decline in the price of wheat may cause a farmer to produce and offer more oats at each possible price. A firm making sports equipment might reduce its supply of basketballs in response to a rise in the price of soccer balls.

5. EXPECTATIONS Expectations concerning the future price of a product can affect a producer's current willingness to supply that product. It is difficult, however, to generalize about how the expected higher price will affect the present supply. Farmers might withhold some their current harvest of oats from the market, anticipating a higher future price for oats. This will decrease the current supply of oats. On the other hand, in many types of manufacturing, expected price increases may induce firms to expand production facilities, causing supply to increase.

6. NUMBER OF SELLERS Generally, the larger the number of suppliers, the greater will be market supply. As more firms enter an industry, the supply curve will shift to the right. As firms leave an industry, the supply curve shifts to the left. For example, Canada and the United States recently imposed restrictions on haddock fishing to replenish dwindling stocks. The requirement that every haddock fishing boat remain in dock 80 days a year put a number of fishermen out of business and reduced the supply of haddock.

Table 4-7 provides a checklist of the determinants of supply; the accompanying illustrations deserve careful study. **(Key Question 5)**

CHANGES IN QUANTITY SUPPLIED

The distinction between a "change in supply" and a "change in the quantity supplied" parallels that between a change in demand and a change in the quantity demanded. A **change in supply** means the entire supply curve shifts. The cause of a change in supply is a change in one or more of the determinants of supply. The term "supply" refers to a schedule or curve.

A **change in the quantity supplied**, on the other hand, refers to the movement from one point to another point on a supply curve. The cause of such a movement is a change in the price of the product under consideration. In Table 4-6, a decline in the price of oats from $5 to $4 decreases the quantity of oats supplied from 12,000 to 10,000 bushels.

TABLE 4-7   Determinants of supply: factors that shift the supply curve

1. *Change in technology*   Example: The development of a more effective insecticide for corn rootworm increases the supply of corn.

2. *Change in resource prices*   Examples: A decline in the price of bauxite increases the supply of aluminum; an increase in the price of irrigation equipment reduces the supply of corn.

3. *Changes in taxes and subsidies*   Examples: An increase in the excise tax on cigarettes reduces the supply of cigarettes; a decline in provincial grants to universities reduces the supply of higher education.

4. *Changes in prices of other goods*   Example: Declines in the prices of mutton and pork increase the supply of beef cattle.

5. *Change in expectations*   Example: Expectations of substantial declines in future oil prices cause oil companies to increase current supply.

6. *Change in number of suppliers*   Example: An increase in the number of firms producing personal computers increases the supply of personal computers; a new professional football league increases the supply of professional football games on Canadian TV.

Shifting the supply curve from S_0 to S_1 or S_2 in Figure 4-4 each entails a "change in supply." The movement from point *a* to point *b* on S_0, however, is a "change in the quantity supplied."

You should determine which of the following involves a change in supply and which a change in the quantity supplied.

1. Because production costs decline, producers sell more automobiles.
2. The price of wheat declines, causing the number of oats sold per month to increase.
3. Fewer apples are offered for sale because their price has decreased in retail markets.

4. The federal government doubles its excise tax on the production of liquor.

QUICK REVIEW 4-2

1. The law of supply states that, other things being unchanged, the quantity of a good supplied varies directly with its price.

2. The supply curve will shift because of changes in (a) resource prices, (b) technology, (c) taxes or subsidies, (d) expectations regarding future product prices, and (e) the number of suppliers.

3. A "change in supply" means a shift in the supply curve; a "change in the quantity supplied" designates the movement from one point to another point on a given supply curve.

SUPPLY AND DEMAND: MARKET EQUILIBRIUM

Let's now bring supply and demand together to see how the interaction of the buying decisions of households and the selling decisions of producers determines the price of a product and the quantity that is actually bought and sold. In Table 4-8, columns 1 and 2 reproduce the market supply schedule for oats (from Table 4-6), and columns 2 and 3 show the market demand schedule for oats (from Table 4-3). Note in column 2 we are using a common set of prices. We assume competition — a large number of buyers and sellers.

TABLE 4-8   Market supply and demand for oats

(1) Total quantity supplied per week	(2) Price per bushel	(3) Total quantity demanded per week	(4) Surplus (+) or shortage (-) (arrows indicate effect on price)
12,000	$5	2,000	+10,000↓
10,000	4	4,000	+6,000↓
7,000	3	7,000	0
4,000	2	11,000	−7,000↑
1,000	1	16,000	−15,000↑

SURPLUSES

Of the five possible prices at which oats might sell in this market, which will actually prevail as the market price? Could $5 be the prevailing market price for oats? No, because producers are willing to produce and offer in the market some 12,000 bushels of oats, while buyers are willing to take only 2000 bushels at this price. The $5 price encourages farmers to produce lots of oats, but discourages most consumers from buying it. Other products appear as better buys when oats are high-priced. The result, in this case, is a 10,000-bushel **surplus** or *excess quantity supply* of oats. This surplus, shown in column 4, is the excess of quantity supplied over quantity demanded at $5. Oat farmers find themselves with unwanted inventories of output. Thus, the price of $5 could not persist over a period of time.

SHORTAGES

Let's jump to $1 as the possible market price for oats. Observe in column 4 that at this price quantity demanded exceeds quantity supplied by 15,000 units. This price discourages farmers from devoting resources to oats production and encourages consumers to attempt to buy more oats than are available. The result is a 15,000-bushel **shortage** of, or *excess quantity demand* for, oats. This $1 price cannot persist as the market price. Competition among buyers will bid up the price to something greater than $1.

EQUILIBRIUM

At $3, *and only at this price*, the quantity of oats farmers are willing to produce and supply in the market is identical with the amount consumers are willing and able to buy. There is neither a shortage nor a surplus. A surplus causes price to decline and a shortage causes price to rise.

With neither a shortage nor a surplus at $3, there is no reason for the price of oats to change. This price is the *market clearing* or **equilibrium price**, equilibrium meaning "in balance" or "at rest." At $3, quantity supplied and quantity demanded are in balance, and thus **equilibrium quantity** is 7000 bushels. Thus, $3 is the only stable price of oats under the supply and demand conditions shown in Table 4-8.

Figure 4-5 (Key Graph) puts the market supply and market demand curves for oats on the same graph. At any price above the equilibrium price of $3, quantity supplied will exceed quantity demanded. This surplus will bid down the price by sellers eager to rid themselves of their surplus. The falling

KEY GRAPH

FIGURE 4-5 **The equilibrium price and quantity for oats as determined by market demand and supply**

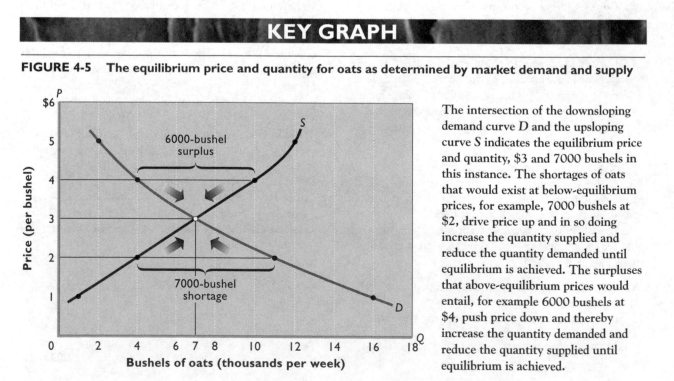

The intersection of the downsloping demand curve *D* and the upsloping curve *S* indicates the equilibrium price and quantity, $3 and 7000 bushels in this instance. The shortages of oats that would exist at below-equilibrium prices, for example, 7000 bushels at $2, drive price up and in so doing increase the quantity supplied and reduce the quantity demanded until equilibrium is achieved. The surpluses that above-equilibrium prices would entail, for example 6000 bushels at $4, push price down and thereby increase the quantity demanded and reduce the quantity supplied until equilibrium is achieved.

BOX 4-2 APPLYING THE THEORY

TICKET SCALPING: A BUM RAP?

Some market transactions get a bad name that is unwarranted.

Tickets to athletic and artistic events are sometimes resold at higher-than-original prices — a market transaction known by the unsavoury term "scalping." For example, a $40 ticket to an NHL hockey game may be resold by the original buyer for $200, $250, or more. The media often denounce scalpers for "ripping off" buyers by charging "exorbitant" prices. Scalping and extortion are synonymous in some people's minds.

But is scalping really sinful? We must first recognize that such ticket resales are voluntary, not coerced, transactions. This correctly implies that both buyer and seller gain from the exchange or it would not occur. The seller must value the $200 more than seeing the game and the buyer must value seeing the game more than the $200. There are no losers or victims here; both buyer and seller benefit from the transaction. The "scalping" market simply redistributes assets (game tickets) from those who value them less to those who value them more.

Does scalping impose losses or injury on other parties — in particular, the sponsors of the event? If the sponsors are injured, it is because they initially priced tickets below the equilibrium level. In so doing they suffer an economic loss in the form of less revenue and profit than they might have otherwise received. But the loss is self-inflicted because of their pricing error. That mistake is quite separate and distinct from the fact that some tickets were later resold at a higher price.

What about spectators? Does scalping somehow impose losses by deteriorating the quality of the game's audience? No! People who most want to see the game — generally those with the greatest interest in and understanding of the game — will pay the scalper's high prices. Ticket scalping will benefit athletic teams and performing artists — they will appear before more understanding and appreciative audiences.

So, is ticket scalping undesirable? Not on economic grounds. Both buyer and seller of a "scalped" ticket benefit and a more interested and appreciative audience results. Game sponsors may sacrifice revenue and profits, but that derives from their own misjudgement of equilibrium price.

price will mean less oats offered and will simultaneously encourage consumers to buy more. These adjustments are shown in Figure 4-5 by the arrows pointing down the supply and demand curves.

Any price below the equilibrium price will produce a shortage; quantity demanded will exceed quantity supplied. Competitive bidding by buyers will push the price up towards equilibrium. This rising price will simultaneously cause producers to increase the quantity supplied and buyers to want less, eliminating the shortage. These adjustments are shown in Figure 4-5 by the arrows pointing up the supply and demand curves. *The intersection of the supply curve and the demand curve for the product indicates the equilibrium point.* In this case, equilibrium price and quantity are $3 and 7000 bushels.

RATIONING FUNCTION OF PRICES

The ability of the competitive forces of supply and demand to establish a price where selling and buying decisions are synchronized is called the **rationing function of prices**. In this case, the equilibrium price of $3 "clears the market," leaving no burdensome surplus for the sellers and no inconvenient shortage for buyers. Freely made individual buying and selling decisions set this price that clears the market. The market mechanism of supply and demand dictates that any buyer who is willing and able to pay $3 for a bushel of oats will be able to acquire one. Similarly, any seller who is willing and able to produce bushels of oats and offer them for sale at a price of $3 will be able to do so. **(Key Question 7)**

CHANGES IN SUPPLY AND DEMAND

We know demand might change because of fluctuations in consumer tastes or incomes, changes in consumer expectations, or variations in the prices of related goods. Supply might vary in response to changes in technology, resource prices, or taxes. Now we are ready to consider the effect of changes in supply and demand on equilibrium price and quantity.

CHANGING DEMAND First we analyze the effects of a change in demand, assuming supply is constant. Suppose that demand *increases*, as shown in Figure 4-6(a). What is the effect on price? The new intersection of the supply and demand curves is at a higher point on both the price and quantity axes, and an increase in demand, other things (supply) being equal, will have a *price-increasing effect* and a *quantity-increasing effect*. A decrease in demand, as illustrated in Figure 4-6(b), reveals a *price-decreasing effect* and a *quantity-decreasing effect*. Price falls and so does quantity. *Thus we find a direct relationship between a change in demand and the resulting changes in both equilibrium price and quantity.*

FIGURE 4-6 Changes in demand and supply and the effects on price and quantity

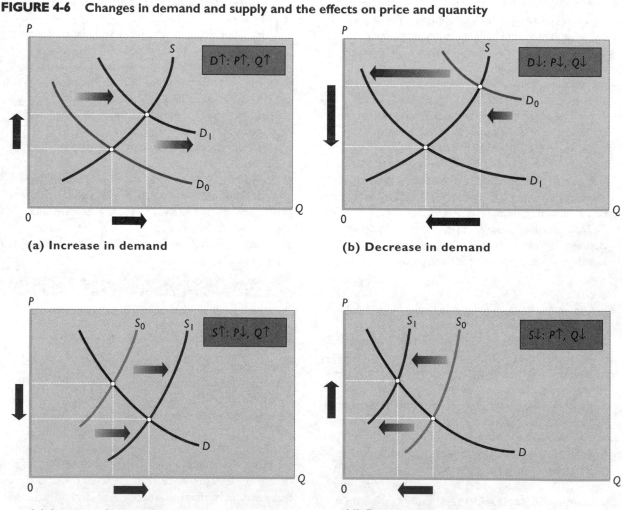

(a) Increase in demand

(b) Decrease in demand

(c) Increase in supply

(d) Decrease in supply

The increase in demand of (a) and the decrease in demand of (b) indicate a direct relationship between a change in demand and the resulting changes in equilibrium price and quantity. The increase in supply of (c) and the decrease in supply of (d) show an inverse relationship between a change in supply and the resulting change in equilibrium price, but a direct relationship between a change in supply and the accompanying change in equilibrium quantity.

CHANGING SUPPLY   Let's analyze the effect of a change in supply on price, assuming that demand is constant. If supply increases, as in Figure 4-6(c), the new intersection of supply and demand is at a lower equilibrium price. Equilibrium quantity, however, increases. If supply decreases, product price will rise. Figure 4-6(d) illustrates this situation. Here, price increases but quantity declines. In short, an increase in supply has a *price-decreasing* and a *quantity-increasing effect*. A decrease in supply has a *price-increasing* and a *quantity-decreasing effect. There is an inverse relationship between a change in supply and the resulting change in equilibrium price, but the relationship between a change in supply and the resulting change in equilibrium quantity is direct.*

SIMULTANEOUS CHANGES IN SUPPLY AND DEMAND

There may be situations in which both supply and demand change at the same time. There are four possibilities: (1) supply increases and demand decreases; (2) supply decreases and demand increases; (3) supply increases and demand increases; and (4) supply decreases and demand decreases. Table 4-9 summarizes these four cases. Draw a supply and demand diagram for each case to determine the effects on equilibrium price and quantity indicated in the table. **(Key Question 8)**

THE RESOURCE MARKET

As in the product market, resource supply curves are typically upsloping and resource demand curves are downsloping because they reflect a *direct* relationship between resource price and quantity supplied. It is in the interests of resource owners to supply more of a resource at a high price than at a low price. High-income payments in a particular occupation or industry encourage households to supply more of their resources. Low-income payments do the opposite.

On the demand side, businesses buy less of a given resource as its price rises and they substitute other, relatively low-priced, resources for it. More of a particular resource will be demanded at a low price than at a high price as entrepreneurs try to minimize costs. The result is a downsloping demand curve for the various resources.

"OTHER THINGS EQUAL" REVISITED

In Chapter 1 we explained that because of the difficulty of conducting controlled experiments, economists assume "other things are equal" in their analyses. We have seen in this chapter that a number of forces bear on both demand and supply. Therefore, in locating specific supply and demand curves such as D_0 and S in Figure 4-6(a), economists are isolating the impact of what they judge to be the most important determinant of the amounts supplied and demanded — that is, the price of the specific product under consideration. In thus representing the laws of demand and supply by downsloping and upsloping curves respectively, we assume that all determinants of demand (incomes, tastes, and so forth) and supply (resource prices, technology, and other factors) are constant. That is, price and quantity demanded are inversely related, *other things being equal*. And price and quantity supplied are directly related, *other things being equal*.

If you forget the "other things equal" assumption you can encounter confusing situations that *seem* to be in conflict with these laws. For example:

TABLE 4-9   Effects of changes in both supply and demand

	Change in supply	Change in demand	Effect on equilibrium price	Effect on equilibrium quantity
(1)	increase	decrease	decrease	indeterminate
(2)	decrease	increase	increase	indeterminate
(3)	increase	increase	indeterminate	increase
(4)	decrease	decrease	indeterminate	decrease

BOX 4-3   IN THE MEDIA

STEEL MAKERS FACE SOFTENING PRICES AND GROWING GLUT

HAMILTON (CP) — Another stormy year awaits steel makers as their market is flooded by production capacity and their profits are eroded by low prices.

Stelco Inc. chairman Fred Telmer offers a blunt forecast.

"I'm looking forward to a very gloomy winter," said Telmer in an interview from his company's downtown Stelco Tower headquarters.

"There's a lot of nervousness in the marketplace and prices are being held down. We're expecting a continuation of difficult conditions in 1992."

Dofasco chairman Paul Phoenix offers a similar assessment from his headquarters in Hamilton's industrialized northeast end.

"There's no pricing relief that we can see," Phoenix said. "And we're looking at ongoing poor market conditions."

Phoenix said a worldwide oversupply of steel and shrinking demand continue to drive down steel prices despite rising production costs.

The Toronto Star, January 2, 1992. By permission of The Canadian Press.

The Story in Brief

Executives at Stelco Inc. and Dofasco Inc. — Canada's two largest steel producers — complain of "ongoing poor market conditions" driving down steel prices.

The Economics Behind the Story

• Demand and supply determine both the market price and quantity transacted in a market.

• The world supply of steel is increasing, while the demand for steel is falling.

• We know that the supply and demand curves shift when certain factors change (see Tables 4-4 and 4-7). There is no indication in the story of why the world supply of steel is increasing while the demand for it is falling.

• We expect the price of steel to drop and the quantity exchanged to fall when the supply of steel shifts right and the demand for steel shifts left.

• Draw a graph that represents the economic analysis behind this story. What are some of the likely factors that caused the demand and supply curves for steel to shift?

Suppose General Motors of Canada sells 100,000 Cutlasses in 1994 at $21,000; 150,000 at $22,000 in 1995; and 200,000 in 1996 at $23,000. Price and the number purchased vary *directly*, and these real-world data seem to be at odds with the law of demand.

These data do *not* refute the law of demand. The catch is that the law of demand's "other things equal" assumption has been violated over the three years in the example. Because of, for example,

growing incomes, population growth, and relatively high gasoline prices, all increasing the attractiveness of intermediate and compact cars, the demand curve for Cutlasses has increased over the years — shifted to the right as from D_0 to D_1 in Figure 4-6(a) — causing price to rise and, simultaneously, a larger quantity to be purchased.

Conversely, consider Figure 4-6(d). Comparing the original S_0D and the new S_1D equilibrium positions, we note that *less* of the product is being sold or supplied at a higher price. Price and quantity supplied seem to be *inversely* related, rather than *directly* related as the law of supply indicates. The catch, again, is that the "other things equal" assumption underlying the upsloping supply curve has been violated. Perhaps production costs have gone up or a specific tax has been levied on this product, shifting the supply curve from S_0 to S_1. These examples also emphasize the importance of our earlier distinction between a "change in the quantity demanded (or supplied)" and a "change in demand (supply)."

QUICK REVIEW 4-3

1. In competitive markets, price adjusts to the equilibrium level at which quantity demanded equals quantity supplied.

2. A change in demand changes both equilibrium price and equilibrium quantity in the same direction as the change in demand.

3. A change in supply causes equilibrium price to change in the opposite direction, but equilibrium quantity to change in the same direction, as the change in supply.

4. Over time, equilibrium price and quantity may change in directions that seem at odds with the laws of demand and supply because the "other things equal" assumption is violated.

CHAPTER SUMMARY

1. A market is any institution or arrangement that brings together buyers and sellers of some product or service.

2. Demand refers to the willingness of buyers to purchase a given product during a specific time period at each of the various prices at which it might be sold. According to the law of demand, consumers will ordinarily buy more of a product at a low price than they will at a high price. Other things being equal, the relationship between price and quantity demanded is negative or inverse and demand graphs as a downsloping curve.

3. Changes in one or more of the basic determinants of demand — consumer tastes, the number of buyers in the market, the money incomes of consumers, the prices of related goods, and consumer expectations — will cause the market demand curve to shift. A shift to the right is an increase in demand; a shift to the left, a decrease in demand. A "change in demand" is distinguished from a "change in the quantity demanded," the latter involving the movement from one point to another point on a fixed demand curve because of a change in the price of the product under consideration.

4. Supply is the amounts of a product producers would be willing to offer in the market during a given time period at each possible price. The law of supply says that producers, other things being equal, will offer more of a product at a higher price than they will at a low price. The relationship between price and quantity supplied is a positive or direct one, and the supply curve is upsloping.

5. A change in resource prices, production techniques, taxes or subsidies, the prices of other goods, price expectations, or the number of sellers in the market will cause the supply curve of a product to shift. A shift to the right is an increase in supply; a shift to the left, a decrease in supply. In contrast, a change in the price of the product under consideration will result in a change in the quantity supplied, a movement from one point to another on a given supply curve.

6. Under competition, the interaction of market demand and market supply will adjust price until the quantity demanded and the quantity supplied are equal. This is the equilibrium price. The corresponding quantity is the equilibrium quantity.

7. The ability of market forces to synchronize selling and buying decisions to eliminate potential surpluses or shortages is termed the "rationing function" of prices.

8. A change in either demand or supply will cause equilibrium price and quantity to change. There is a direct relationship between a change in demand and the resulting changes in equilibrium price and quantity. Though the relationship between a change in supply and the resulting change in equilibrium price is inverse, the relationship between a change in supply and equilibrium quantity is direct.

9. The concepts of supply and demand are also applicable to the resource market.

TERMS AND CONCEPTS

change in demand (supply) versus change in the
    quantity demanded (supplied) (pp. 62, 64, 66, 67)
complementary goods (p. 63)
demand (p. 58)
demand curve (p. 60)
demand schedule (p. 58)
diminishing marginal utility (p. 59)
equilibrium price and quantity (p. 68)
income and substitution effects (p. 59)
inferior goods (p. 62)

law of demand (p. 59)
law of supply (p. 64)
market (p. 58)
normal (superior) goods (p. 62)
rationing function of prices (p. 69)
shortage (p. 68)
substitute goods (p. 63)
supply (p. 64)
supply schedule (curve) (p. 64)
surplus (p. 68)

QUESTIONS AND STUDY SUGGESTIONS

1. Explain the law of demand. Why does a demand curve slope downward? What are the determinants of demand? What happens to the demand curve when each of these determinants changes? Distinguish between a change in demand and a change in the quantity demanded, noting the cause(s) of each.

2. *Key Question   What effect will each of the following have on the demand for product B?*

  a. *Product B becomes more fashionable.*
  b. *The price of substitute product C falls.*
  c. *Incomes decline if B is an inferior good.*
  d. *Consumers anticipate the price of B will be lower in the near future.*
  e. *The price of complementary product D falls.*
  f. *Foreign tariff barriers on B are eliminated.*

3. Explain the following news dispatch from Hull, England: "The fish market here slumped today to what local commentators called 'a disastrous level' — all because of a shortage of potatoes. The potatoes are one of the main ingredients in a dish that figures on almost every café menu — fish and chips."

4. Explain the law of supply. Why does the supply curve slope upward? What are the determinants of supply? What happens to the supply curve when each of these determinants changes? Distinguish between a change in supply and a change in the quantity supplied, noting the cause(s) of each.

5. Key Question *What effect will each of the following have on the supply of product B?*

a. *A technological advance in the methods of producing B.*

b. *A decline in the number of firms in industry B.*

c. *An increase in the prices of resources required in the production of B.*

d. *The expectation that the equilibrium price of B will be lower in the future than it is currently.*

e. *A decline in the price of product A, a good whose production requires substantially the same techniques and resources as does the production of B.*

f. *The levying of a specific sale tax on B.*

g. *The granting of a 50-cent-per-unit subsidy for each unit of B produced.*

6. "In the oats market, demand often exceeds supply and supply sometimes exceeds demand." "The price of oats rises and falls in response to changes in supply and demand." In which of these two statements are the terms "supply" and "demand" used correctly? Explain.

7. Key Question *Suppose the total demand for eggs (Grade A large) and the total supply of eggs (Grade A large) per month in the Halifax market are as follows:*

Thousands of dozens demanded	Price per dozen	Thousands of dozens supplied	Surplus (+) or shortage (-)
85	$1.25	72	_____
80	1.30	73	_____
75	1.35	75	_____
70	1.40	77	_____
65	1.45	79	_____
60	1.50	81	_____

a. *What will be the market or equilibrium price? What is the equilibrium quantity? Using the surplus-shortage column, explain why your answers are correct.*

b. *Using the above data, graph the demand for eggs and the supply of eggs. Be sure to label the axes of your graph correctly. Label equilibrium price "P" and equilibrium quantity "Q".*

c. *Why will $1.25 not be the equilibrium price in this market? Why not $1.50? "Surpluses drive prices up; shortages drive them down." Do you agree?*

d. *Now suppose that the government establishes a ceiling price of, say, $1.30 for these eggs. Explain carefully the effects of this ceiling price. Demonstrate your answers graphically. What might prompt government to establish a ceiling price?*

e. *"Government-fixed prices strip the price mechanism of its rationing function." Explain this statement relating your explanation to your answers to 7d.*

8. Key Question *How will each of the following changes in demand and/or supply affect equilibrium price and equilibrium quantity in a competitive market; that is, do price and quantity rise, fall, remain unchanged, or are the answers indeterminate, depending on the magnitudes of the shifts in supply and demand? You should rely on a supply and demand diagram to verify answers.*

a. *Supply decreases and demand remains constant.*

b. *Demand decreases and supply remains constant.*

c. *Supply increases and demand is constant.*

d. *Demand increases and supply increases.*

   e. *Demand increases and supply is constant.*
   f. *Supply increases and demand decreases.*
   g. *Demand increases and supply decreases.*
   h. *Demand decreases and supply decreases.*

9. "Prices are the automatic regulator that tends to keep production and consumption in line with each other." Explain.

10. Explain: "Even though parking meters may yield little or no net revenue, they should nevertheless be retained because of the rationing function they perform."

11. Critically evaluate: "In comparing the two equilibrium positions in Figure 4-6a, I note that a larger amount is actually purchased at a higher price. This refutes the law of demand."

12. Suppose you go to a recycling centre and are paid 25¢ per kilogram for your aluminum cans. However, the recycler charges you 20¢ per bundle to accept your old newspapers. Use demand and supply diagrams to portray both markets. Can you explain how different government policies with respect to the recycling of aluminum and paper might account for these different market outcomes?

13. **Advanced Analysis**   Assume that the demand for a commodity is represented by the equation $P = 10 - 0.2Q_d$ and supply by the equation $P = 2 + 0.2Q_s$, where Q_d and Q_s are quantity demanded and quantity supplied respectively and P is price. Using the equilibrium condition $Q_s = Q_d$ solve the equations to determine equilibrium price. Then determine equilibrium quantity. Graph the two equations to equations to substantiate your answers.

14. (Applying the Theory) Discuss the economic aspects of ticket scalping, specifying gainers and losers.

CHAPTER 5

THE PUBLIC SECTOR

We noted in Chapter 2 that a society can choose various ways to deal with the economizing problem. A pure market system is one possibility; at the other extreme is a command economy, in which a central government makes the decisions as to what to produce, how much to produce, by what method to produce it, and how that production is distributed.

In fact, all economies are "mixed" to some extent; government and the market system share the responsibility of responding to the Five Fundamental Questions. In Canada, we have an economy dominated by markets, but government has played a significant role in the economic system of this country from the time of Confederation.

In this chapter we investigate the possible economic functions of the public sector in a market economy. Much emphasis is put on the crucial role of government when markets fail to fulfil their function of co-ordinating economic activity. The chapter ends with a discussion of the growth of government in recent decades and the ongoing debate on the extent of government involvement in self-regulating markets.

BOX 5-1   THE BIG PICTURE

Private markets are very good at getting the most out of available resources. Markets also produce those goods and services that people with income to spend want most. But the market system does not arise instantaneously on its own. It requires certain institutions to function well. Among the most important of these is a central government that provides an environment conducive to a market economy.

Sometimes the market system fails to do its job of co-ordinating production and consumption decisions, or does it badly. We call these instances "market failures," and they require government intervention.

As you read this chapter, keep the following points in mind:

- At times market participants have an effect on individuals not involved in market transactions. These effects can be negative, as in the case of a firm polluting the water supply of a village, or positive, as when a neighbour undertakes to beautify her house.
- Sometimes the market system does not produce enough of a specific good that is economically or socially justified. In such instances the government either produces the good itself or gives subsidies to private firms to supply it.

THE ECONOMIC FUNCTIONS OF GOVERNMENT

There is a mistaken view held by some that in an economy dominated by markets, less government is better since government action distorts the efficient function of markets. These critics point out that private markets are regulated by an "invisible hand" that co-ordinates economic activities for the good of both individuals and society.

While economists generally agree that self-regulating markets are efficient at allocating scarce resources, they also hold that governments have crucial roles in a market economy. The following outlines what a government must provide to strengthen and facilitate the operation of the market system.

LEGAL AND SOCIAL FRAMEWORK

Government provides the legal framework and the basic services needed for a market economy to operate effectively. The legal framework provides the legal status of business enterprises, defines the rights of private ownership, and makes it possible to provide for the enforcement of contracts. Government also establishes legal "rules of the game" governing the relationships of businesses, resource suppliers, and consumers with one another. Through legislation, government can referee economic relationships, detect foul play, and impose appropriate penalties.

Services provided by government include police powers to maintain internal order, a system of standards for measuring the weight and quality of products, and a monetary system to facilitate exchange of goods and services.

The Food and Drug Act and Regulations of 1920 is an example of how government has strengthened the market system. This act sets rules of conduct governing producers in their relationships with consumers. It prohibits the sale of adulterated and misbranded foods and drugs, requires net weights and ingredients of products to be specified on their containers, establishes quality standards that must be stated on labels of canned foods, and prohibits deceptive claims on patent-medicine labels. These measures help prevent fraudulent activities by producers and increase the public's confidence in the integrity of the market system. Similar legislation pertains to labour-management relations and relations of business firms to one another.

This type of government activity is presumed to improve resource allocation. Supplying a medium of exchange, ensuring product quality, defining ownership rights, and enforcing contracts all increase the volume of exchange. This widens markets and permits greater specialization in the use of property and human resources. Such specialization means a more efficient allocation of resources. However, some argue that government overregulates interactions of businesses, consumers, and workers, stifling economic incentives and impairing productive efficiency.

MAINTAINING COMPETITION

Competition is the basic regulatory mechanism in a market economy. It is the force that subjects producers and resource suppliers to the dictates of consumer sovereignty. With competition, buyers are the boss, the market is their agent, and businesses are their servants.

It's completely different with **monopoly**. *Monopoly exists if the number of sellers becomes small enough for each seller to influence total supply and therefore the price of the commodity being sold.*

In a monopoly, sellers can influence, or "rig," the market in their own interests, to the detriment of society as a whole. Through their ability to influence total supply, monopolists can restrict the output of products and charge higher prices and, frequently, have substantial economic profits. These above-competitive prices and profits directly conflict with the interests of consumers. Monopolists are not regulated by the will of society as are competitive sellers. Producer sovereignty replaces consumer sovereignty. In a monopoly resources are allocated according to the profit-seeking interests of sellers rather than the wants of society as a whole. Monopoly causes a misallocation of economic resources.

In Canada government has attempted to control monopoly in two ways.

1. REGULATION AND OWNERSHIP In the case of "natural monopolies" — industries in which technological and economic realities rule out competitive markets — government has created public commissions regulating prices and service standards. Transportation, communications, and electric and other utilities are industries that are regulated in varying degrees. At municipal levels of government, public ownership of electric and water utilities is common.

2. ANTI-COMBINES LAWS In nearly all markets, efficient production can be attained with a high degree of competition. The federal government has therefore enacted a series of anti-combines laws, to maintain and strengthen competition as a regulator of business behaviour.

Even if the legal foundation of market institutions is assured and competition is maintained, there is still a need for certain additional economic functions by government. *The market economy has certain biases and shortcomings that make it necessary for government to supplement and modify its operation in certain instances.*

REDISTRIBUTION OF INCOME

The market system is impersonal. It may distribute income with more inequality than society desires. The market system yields very large incomes to those whose labour, by virtue of inherent ability and acquired education and skills, commands high wages. Similarly, those who possess — through hard work or easy inheritance — valuable capital and land receive large incomes.

But others in our society have less ability; have received modest amounts of education and training; and have not accumulated or inherited property resources. Thus, their incomes are very low. Furthermore, many of the aged, the physically and mentally handicapped, and female-headed families earn only very small incomes or, like the unemployed, no incomes at all through the market system. In the market system, there is considerable inequality in the distribution of money income and therefore in the distribution of total output among individual households. Poverty in the midst of overall plenty in our economy persists and is a major economic and political issue.

Government's role in attempting to reduce income inequality is reflected in a variety of policies and programs.

1. TRANSFERS *Transfer payments* provide relief to the destitute, aid to the dependent and handicapped, and unemployment insurance to the unemployed. Social insurance programs provide financial support for the retired and aged sick. These programs transfer income from government to households that would otherwise have little or none.

2. MARKET INTERVENTION Government also alters the distribution of income by *market intervention*, that is, by modifying the prices established by market forces. Price supports for farmers and minimum-wage legislation are examples of government price fixing designed to raise incomes of specific groups.

3. TAXATION The personal income tax is used to take a larger proportion of the incomes of the rich than the poor.

REALLOCATION OF RESOURCES

Economists recognize *market failure* occurs when the competitive market system either (1) produces the "wrong" amounts of certain goods and services, or (2) fails to allocate any resources whatsoever to the production of certain goods and services whose output is economically justified. The first case involves "spillovers" or "externalities," and the second "public" or "social" goods.

SPILLOVERS OR EXTERNALITIES

The idea that competitive markets automatically bring about efficient resources rests on the assumption that *all* the benefits and costs of production and consumption of each product are fully reflected in the market demand and supply curves. It is assumed that there are no *spillovers* or *externalities* associated with the production or consumption of any good or service.

A *spillover* occurs when benefits or costs of production or consumption of a good "spill over" onto parties other than the immediate buyer or seller. Spillovers are also called *externalities* because they are benefits and costs to a third party external to the market transaction.

SPILLOVER COSTS When production or consumption of a commodity inflicts costs on a third party without compensation, these costs are **spillover costs.** Examples of spillover costs include environmental pollution. When a chemical manufacturer or meat-packing plant dumps its wastes into a lake or river, swimmers, fishing enthusiasts, and boaters — not to mention communities' water supplies — suffer spillover costs. Human health hazards may arise and wildlife may be damaged or destroyed. When a petroleum refinery pollutes the air with smoke or a paint factory creates distressing odours, the community bears spillover costs for which it is not compensated. Acid rain and global warming are spillover costs that receive almost daily media attention.

What are the economic effects? Recall that costs underlie the firm's supply curve. When a firm avoids some costs by polluting, its supply curve will lie further to the right than when it bears the full costs of production. This results in a larger output and causes an *overallocation* of resources to the production of this good.

CORRECTING FOR SPILLOVER COSTS Government can do two things to correct this overallocation of resources. Both are designed to *internalize* the external costs, that is, to make the offending firm pay these costs rather than shift them to society.

1. LEGISLATION In our examples of air and water pollution, the most direct action is *legislation* prohibiting or limiting pollution. Such legislation forces potential polluters to bear costs of properly disposing of industrial wastes. Firms must buy and install smoke-abatement equipment or facilities to purify water contaminated by manufacturing processes. The idea is to force potential offenders, under the threat of legal action, to bear *all* costs associated with their production.

2. SPECIFIC TAXES A less direct action is based on the fact that taxes are a cost and therefore a determinant of a firm's supply curve (Chapter 4). Government might levy a *specific tax* that equals or approximates the spillover costs per unit of output. Through this tax, government attempts to shove back onto the offending firm those spillover costs that private industry would otherwise avoid and thus eliminate the overallocation of resources.

SPILLOVER BENEFITS But spillovers may also appear as benefits. Production or consumption of certain goods and services may bring spillover or external benefits on third parties or the community at large for which payment or compensation is not required. Measles and polio immunization shots result in direct benefits to the immediate consumer. But immunization against these contagious diseases brings widespread and substantial spillover benefits to the entire community. Discovery of an AIDS vaccine would benefit society far beyond those vaccinated. Unvaccinated individuals would benefit by the slowing of the spread of the disease.

Education is another example of **spillover benefits.** Education benefits individual consumers: "More educated" people generally earn higher incomes than "less educated" people. But education also provides benefits to society. The economy as a whole benefits

BOX 5-2   IN THE MEDIA

SCALING BACK TO SAVE SALMON

BY MIRO CERNETIG

KINCOLITH, B.C. — Just as they have done for millenniums, salmon are swimming back to the Nass River, triggering familiar sights around this often-forgotten Indian fishing village on the edge of the Alaskan Panhandle.

Bald eagles skim the bay, diving to snag a fish with their talons. Indians fish along the tidal flats for dinner. And 70-year-old Sydney Alexander is out in his yard, tending nets and warning passers-by that the West Coast's greatest fishery is on the edge of ruin.

"There's far too many people fishing," he complains, looking out toward the ice-blue bay that is filled each summer with an armada of Canadian fishing boats. "They're spreading the fish too thin."

That, in a dozen words, is as good as you will get of what ails the West Coast salmon fishery, now into another hot summer, complete with the threat of a fish war with the United States, racial tension between Indians and non-natives, and charges of rampant overfishing.

Standing on a tidal flat, upon which his nine-tonne skiff sits in clumps of windswept elephant grass, Mr. Alexander points out why most Pacific salmon never make it back up into the Nass River's spawning grounds.

To the east, beyond the mouth of the rushing river, Nisga'a Indians are fishing, one of many aboriginal-only fisheries proliferating along the British Columbia coast.

To the west, where the Queen Charlotte Islands are a purple blur on the horizon, sit fishing lodges where thousands of trophy hunters catch the endangered chinook, the largest of the salmon.

To the north, across the U.S. border, floats the Alaskan fishing fleet, a 2,500-vessel flotilla that is accused by Canada of overfishing. And just over the southern horizon is Canada's own commercial fleet, now universally viewed as a killing machine that could obliterate, in a few hours, salmon runs that have taken generations to build.

"If they're not careful," Mr. Alexander laments, "there won't be enough salmon left."

The complexities of managing the province's salmon stocks could — and do — fill volumes. But the major threat to the salmon is that the West Coast fishing fleet has grown in size and efficiency, thanks to new boats and better technology.

The best measure of this is the drastically reduced time it takes to fish, even though the amount of salmon the fleet has been allowed to catch actually has gone up. In 1972, the salmon season in Johnstone Strait, a rich fishing ground, was 51 days for seine boats, the most potent fish-harvesting machines on the ocean. By 1982, that had shrunk to 24 days. Last year, it was 3.25 days.

For fishermen who use gill nets, the season shrank from 125 days in 1972 to 32 days in 1982 and to only 19 days in 1994.

That has caused headaches for Fisheries Department officers charged with regulating the amount of fish taken.

"Such a large number of vessels can put fisheries managers in difficult-if-not-impossible situations, as slight miscalculations of the catch can have severely detrimental effects on salmon stocks," says a new DFO report that looks into the department's attempts to gauge the amount of fish the powerful fleet is harvesting. "There is growing concern that the present management system used to manage the commercial Salmon [fleet] is not sustainable."

None of this is good news. But it finally is forcing fishing companies, fishermen and the Fisheries Department to agree that Canada's salmon fleet must be trimmed, and the system of UI, which keeps marginal players in the industry, overhauled. This fall, industry and the federal government will begin to develop a strategy to reduce the fleet by from 10 to 50 per cent. If no consensus is reached, Ottawa warns, it will cut the fleet unilaterally.

The Story in Brief

The West Coast salmon stocks are dwindling because of overfishing by Canadian and American fishing fleets, as well as thousands of recreational fishing enthusiasts.

The Economics Behind the Story

• Too many people fishing with modern boats and technology are able to wipe out the West Coast salmon stocks. This is an example of market failure; it is the result of the absence of private property rights. A market failure requires government intervention.

• Since fish do not stay in one place, it is impossible to establish private property rights. Thus, the only solution is for the federal government to reduce the salmon taken in each season — to the point where the existing fish stocks will be maintained. The easiest way to cut down on the number of salmon taken each year is to reduce the fishing fleet. Since a licence is already required, the federal government would reduce the number of fishing licences issued.

• In recent years salmon "fish farms" have appeared in Canada. Fish are raised in an enclosed area. Why do you not expect overfishing under such circumstances? Use marginal benefit-cost analysis to help you answer the question.

from a more versatile and more productive labour force, on the one hand, and smaller outlays in crime prevention, law enforcement, and welfare programs, on the other. There is evidence indicating that any worker with a *given* educational or skill level will be more productive if associated workers have more education. In other words, worker X becomes more productive because fellow-workers Y and Z are more educated. Also significant is the fact that political participation increases with the level of education; the percentage of persons who vote increases with the educational level of the population.

Spillover benefits mean the market demand curve, which reflects only private benefits, understates total benefits. The demand curve for the product lies further to the left than if all benefits were taken into account by the market. This means that a smaller amount is produced or, alternatively stated, there is an *underallocation* of resources to the product.

CORRECTING FOR SPILLOVER BENEFITS   How might the underallocation of resources associated with spillover benefits be corrected? The answer is to either subsidize consumers (increase demand) or subsidize producers (increase supply), or, in the extreme, have government produce the product.

1. INCREASE DEMAND   In the care of higher education, government provides low-interest student loans and grants to provide student employment.

2. INCREASE SUPPLY   In some cases, government might find it administratively simpler to subsidize producers. This is also true with higher education where provincial governments provide substantial portions of the budgets of colleges and universities. These subsidies lower costs to students and increase educational supply. Public subsidizing of immunization programs, hospitals, and medical research are additional examples.

3. GOVERNMENT PROVISION   A third policy option arises if spillover benefits are extremely large: Government may choose to finance or, in the extreme, to own and operate such industries. This option leads us into a discussion of public goods and services.

PUBLIC GOODS AND SERVICES

Private goods, which are produced through the market system, are *divisible* in that they come in units small enough to be afforded by individual buyers. Also, private goods are subject to the **exclusion**

principle: those willing and able to pay the equilibrium price get the product but those unable or unwilling to pay are excluded from the benefits provided by that product.

Certain goods and services — **public goods** — would not be produced by the market system because their characteristics are opposite those of private goods. Public goods are *indivisible*, involving such large units that they cannot ordinarily be sold to individual buyers. Individuals can buy hamburgers, computers, and automobiles through the market, but not missiles, highways, space telescopes, and air-traffic control.

More importantly, the exclusion principle does *not* apply to public goods; there is no effective way of excluding individuals from their benefits. Benefits from private goods come from their *purchase*; benefits from public goods accrue to society from their *production*.

ILLUSTRATIONS

The classic public goods example is a lighthouse on a treacherous coast. The construction of a lighthouse would be economically justified if benefits (fewer shipwrecks) exceeded production costs. But the benefit accruing to each individual user would not justify the purchase of such a large and indivisible product. But once in operation, its warning light is a guide to *all* ships. There is no practical way to exclude certain ships from its benefits. Therefore, why should any ship owner voluntarily pay for the benefits received from the light? The light is there for all to see, and a ship captain cannot be excluded from seeing it if the ship owner chooses not to pay. This is called the **free-rider problem**; *people can receive benefits from a good without contributing to its costs.*

Because the exclusion principle does not apply, there is no economic incentive for private enterprises to supply lighthouses. If the services of the lighthouse cannot be priced and sold, it will be unprofitable for private firms to devote resources to lighthouses. Here is a service that brings substantial benefits but for which the market would allocate no resources. National defence, flood control, public health, satellite navigation systems, and insect-abatement programs are other public goods. If society is to enjoy such goods and services, they must be provided by the public sector and financed by compulsory charges in the form of taxes.

LARGE SPILLOVER BENEFITS

While the exclusion principle distinguishes public from private goods, many other goods and services are provided by government even though the exclusion principle *could* be applied. Such goods and services as education, streets and highways, police and fire protection, libraries and museums, preventive medicine, and sewage disposal could be subject to the exclusion principle. All could be priced and provided by private producers through the market system. But, as noted earlier, these are all services with substantial spillover benefits and would be underproduced by the market system. Therefore, government provides them to avoid the underallocation of resources that would otherwise occur. Such goods and services are called *quasi-public goods*.

ALLOCATING RESOURCES TO PUBLIC GOODS

The price system will fail to allocate resources for public goods and will underallocate resources for quasi-public goods. What is the mechanism by which such goods get produced?

Public goods are purchased through the government on the basis of group, or collective, choices, in contrast to private goods, which are purchased from private enterprises on the basis of individual choices. The types and quantities of public goods produced are determined in a democracy by voting. The quantities of the various public goods consumed are a matter of public policy.[1] These group decisions supplement the choices of households and businesses in answering the Five Fundamental Questions.

How are resources reallocated from production of private goods to production of public goods? In a full-employment economy, government must free resources from private employment to make them available for production of public goods. The means of releasing resources from private uses is to reduce private demand

---

[1] There are differences between *dollar voting*, which dictates output in the private sector of the economy, and *political voting*, which determines output in the public sector. The rich person has many more votes to cast in the private sector than does the poor person. In the public sector, each — at least in theory — has an equal say. Furthermore, the children who cast their votes for bubble gum and comic books in the private sector are banned by virtue of their age from the registering of social choices.

for them. This is accomplished by levying taxes on businesses and households, diverting some of their incomes — some of their potential purchasing power — out of the income-expenditure streams. With lower incomes, businesses and households must cut back their investment and consumption spending. *Taxes diminish private demand for goods and services, which in turn prompts a drop in the private demand for resources.* By diverting purchasing power from private spenders to government, taxes free resources from private uses.

Government expenditure of the tax revenues can then reabsorb these resources in the provision of public goods and services. Corporation and personal income taxes release resources from production of investment goods — printing presses, boxcars, warehouses — and consumer goods — food, clothing, and television sets. Government expenditures can reabsorb these resources in production of post offices, military aircraft, and new schools and highways. Government purposely reallocates resources to bring about significant changes in the composition of the economy's total output. **(Key Questions 3 and 4)**

STABILIZATION

Historically, the most recent function of government is that of stabilizing the economy — assisting the private economy to achieve full employment and a stable price level. Here we will only outline (rather than fully explain) how government tries to do this.

The level of output depends directly on total or aggregate expenditures. A high level of total spending will be profitable for industries to produce large outputs. This means that resources be employed at high levels. But aggregate spending may either fall short of, or exceed, that particular level that will provide for full employment and price stability. Two possibilities, unemployment or inflation, may then occur.

1. UNEMPLOYMENT The level of total spending in the private sector may be too low for full employment. Thus, the government may choose to increase private spending so that total spending — private and public — will be sufficient to generate full employment. Government can do this by using the same techniques — government spending and taxes — as

it uses to reallocate resources to production of public goods. Specifically, government might increase its own spending on public goods and services on the one hand, and reduce taxes to stimulate private spending on the other.[2]

2. INFLATION If total expenditures are greater than the economy's capacity to produce, the price level will rise. Excessive aggregate spending is inflationary. Government's obligation here is to eliminate the excess spending. It can do this by cutting its own expenditures and by raising taxes to curtail private spending.

QUICK REVIEW 5-1

1. Government enhances the operation of the market system by providing an appropriate legal foundation and promoting competition.

2. Transfer payments, direct market intervention, and the tax system are ways government can lessen income inequality.

3. Government can correct the overallocation of resources associated with spillover costs through legislation or specific taxes; the underallocation of resources associated with spillover benefits can be offset by government subsidies.

4. Government must provide public goods because they are indivisible and the exclusion principle does not apply to them.

5. Government spending and tax revenues can be manipulated to stabilize the economy.

THE CIRCULAR FLOW REVISITED

Government is thoroughly integrated into the real and monetary flows that make up our economy. Let's re-examine the redistributional, allocative, and stabilization functions of government in terms of Chapter 2's circular flow model. In Figure 5-1 flows (1) through (4) restate Figure 2-6. Flows (1) and (2) show business expenditures for the resources provided by households. These expenditures are costs to businesses, but represent wage, rent, interest, and profit income to households. Flows (3) and (4) portray households making consumer expenditures for the goods and services produced by businesses.

---

[2] In macroeconomics we learn that government can also use monetary policy — changes in the nation's money supply and interest rates — to help achieve economic stability.

FIGURE 5-1 The circular flow and the public sector

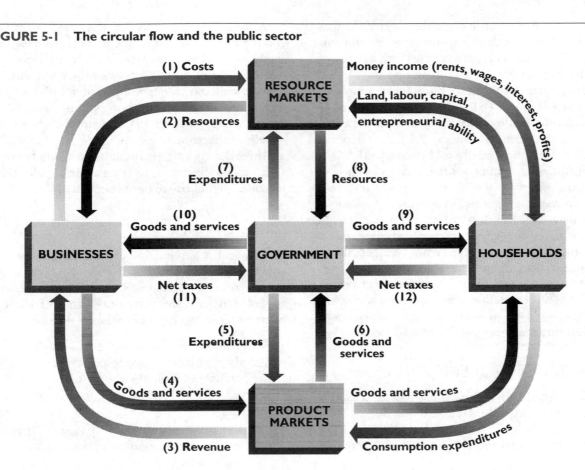

Government expenditures, taxes, and transfer payments affect the distribution of income, the allocation of resources, and the levels of economic activity.

Now consider the numerous modifications that stem from the addition of government. Flows (5) through (8) tell us that government makes purchases in both product and resource markets. Specifically, flows (5) and (6) represent government purchasing such things as paper, computers, and military hardware from private businesses. Flows (7) and (8) reflect government purchases of resources. The federal government employs and pays salaries to members of Parliament, the armed forces, and various other bureaucrats. Provincial and municipal governments hire teachers, bus drivers, police, and firefighters. The federal government might lease or purchase land to expand a military base; a city may buy land to build a new elementary school.

Government then provides public goods and services to both households and businesses as shown by flows (9) and (10). Financing public goods and services requires tax payments by businesses and house-

holds as reflected in flows (11) and (12). We have labelled these flows as *net* taxes to acknowledge that they also include "taxes in reverse" in the form of transfer payments to households and subsidies to businesses. Thus, flow (11) reflects not merely corporate income, sales, and excise taxes flowing from businesses to government but also various subsidies to farmers and some private sector firms. Most business subsidies are "concealed" in the form of low-interest loans, loan guarantees, tax concessions, or the public provision of facilities at prices less than costs. Similarly, government collects taxes (personal income taxes, payroll taxes) directly from households and makes available transfer payments, for example, welfare payments and social insurance benefits as shown by flow (12).

Our circular flow model shows us how government can alter the distribution of income, reallocate resources, and change the level of economic activity. The structure of taxes and transfer payments can have a significant impact on income distribution. In flow (12) a tax structure that draws tax revenues primarily from well-to-do households combined with a system of transfer payments to low-income households will result in greater equality in the distribution of income.

Flows (6) and (8) reflect an allocation of resources different from that of a purely private economy. Government buys goods and labour services that differ from those purchased by households.

Finally, all governmental flows suggest ways government might try to stabilize the economy. If there is unemployment, an increase in government spending, while taxes and transfers are held constant, would increase aggregate spending, output, and employment. Similarly, given the level of government expenditures, a decline in taxes or an increase in transfer payments would increase spendable incomes and boost private spending. With inflation, the opposite government policies would be in order: reduced government spending, increased taxes, and reduced transfers.

THE SIZE OF GOVERNMENT

The size of governments has increased significantly since the end of World War II. Not only have the number of employees of the federal, provincial, and municipal governments increased, but the shares of the total output of goods and services governments take in taxes and spend have also risen significantly. In 1994 the expenditures of all three levels of governments in Canada collectively represented about 45% of the annual production of the country; this is more than double what it was in 1945. Figure 5-2 shows the growth of government expenditures and revenues of all three levels of governments in Canada since 1970. Expenditures have risen more rapidly than revenues, giving rise to persistent deficits.

GROWTH OF GOVERNMENT OUTLAYS

We can get a general impression of the size and growth of government's economic role by examining government purchases of goods and services and government transfer payments. The distinction between these two types of outlays is significant.

1. **Government purchases** are "exhaustive"; they directly absorb or employ resources. For example, the purchase of a car absorbs the labour of engineers along with steel, plastic, and a host of other inputs.
2. **Transfer payments** are "nonexhaustive"; they do not directly absorb resources or account for pro-

---

FIGURE 5-2   The growth of government

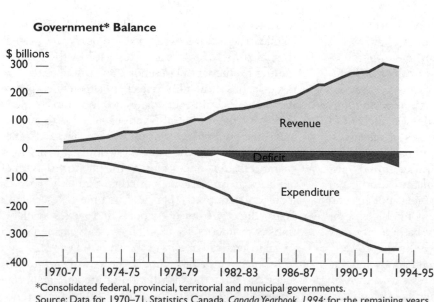

Government* Balance

An indication of the increasing growth of government is the expanding combined expenditures and revenues of the federal, provincial, and municipal governments. Both government revenues and expenditures have increased rapidly since 1970.

*Consolidated federal, provincial, territorial and municipal governments.
Source: Data for 1970–71, Statistics Canada, *Canada Yearbook, 1994*; for the remaining years computed from data in Statistic Canada, *Canadian Economic Observer, Statistical Summary.*

FIGURE 5-3   The trend in government expenditures

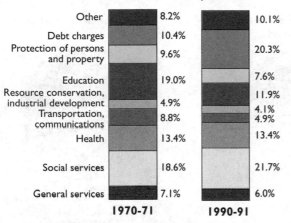

Government* Expenditures

	1970-71	1990-91
Other	8.2%	10.1%
Debt charges	10.4%	20.3%
Protection of persons and property	9.6%	
Education	19.0%	7.6%
Resource conservation, industrial development	4.9%	11.9%
Transportation, communications	8.8%	4.1% / 4.9%
Health	13.4%	13.4%
Social services	18.6%	21.7%
General services	7.1%	6.0%

*Consolidated federal, provincial, territorial and municipal governments.
Source: Statistics Canada, *Canada Yearbook, 1994.*

The two main changes in the pattern of government expenditures have been the increase in debt payment and the significant reduction in education spending.

duction. Social and health benefits, welfare payments, veterans' benefits, and unemployment insurance payments are examples of transfer payments. Their key characteristic is that those who receive them make no current contribution to output in return for these payments.

Figure 5-3 shows the changing pattern of government expenditures in the last quarter of a century. The two areas in which there have been significant changes are debt charges and education. Debt charges have doubled, while expenditure on education has dropped from 19% in 1970–71 to less than 12% in 1990–91.

SOURCES OF GOVERNMENT EXPENDITURES AND REVENUES

Now let's disaggregate the public sector into federal, provincial, and municipal units of government to compare their expenditures. Figure 5-4(a) tells the story for the federal government.

FEDERAL EXPENDITURES AND REVENUES

Figure 5-4 (a) shows that three important areas of federal spending stand out: (1) social services, (2) protection of persons and property, and (3) interest on the public debt. The social services category, representing

a third of total expenditures, reflects the myriad income-maintenance programs for the aged, the disabled, the unemployed, the handicapped, and families with no breadwinner. *Transfers to other governments* constitute about 18% of the federal budget and underscore the fact that provinces and municipalities have constitutional responsibilities but inadequate sources of revenues. *Interest on the public debt* has grown dramatically in recent years because the public debt itself has grown.

On the revenue side, **personal income taxes** continue to contribute the largest share of federal government revenues at about 47%; **corporate income taxes** represent almost 7%, while unemployment insurance contributions account for 13%. The remaining 24% is raised by a variety of taxes, including the Goods and Services Tax (GST), which contributes about 12%.

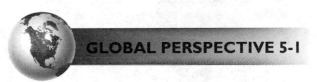

GLOBAL PERSPECTIVE 5-1

The tax burden in selected countries, 1993

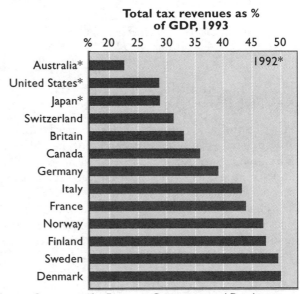

Total tax revenues as % of GDP, 1993

%	20 25 30 35 40 45 50
Australia*	1992*
United States*	
Japan*	
Switzerland	
Britain	
Canada	
Germany	
Italy	
France	
Norway	
Finland	
Sweden	
Denmark	

Source: Organization for Economic Cooperation and Development

Tax burdens in Canada are closer to those in Western European countries such as Italy and Germany, than those of our immediate neighbour to the south, the United States.

FIGURE 5-4   The major components of expenditures and revenues of the three levels of governments in Canada, 1992–93

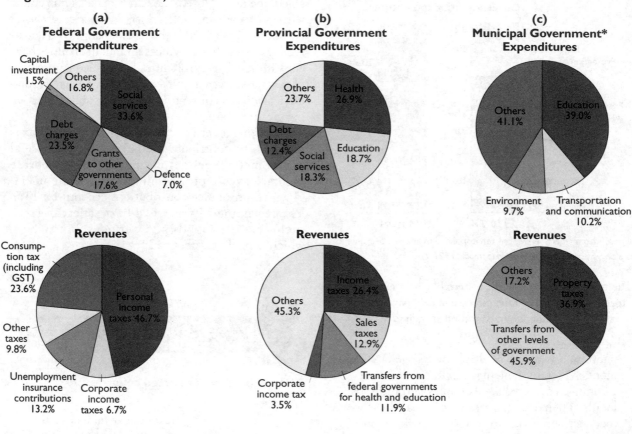

Source: Statistics Canada, *Canada Yearbook, 1994.*
* Municipal government data are for 1991.

PROVINCIAL EXPENDITURES AND REVENUES

Health is the largest provincial and territorial outlay at an estimated 27% of total expenditures in 1992–93. Education was the second largest outlay at about 19%, and social services, the third largest expenditure, accounted for about the same percentage (18.3%).

Figure 5-4(b) shows that income taxes, general sales taxes, and transfers from other levels of governments represented the main generators of revenues at 26.4%, 12.9%, and 11.9% respectively.

MUNICIPAL GOVERNMENT EXPENDITURES AND REVENUES

Education is the largest component of municipal government spending at almost 40% of total expenditures, as Figure 5-4(c) shows. The other main categories of

expenditures are transportation and communications, environmental, person and property protection, and social services outlays.

Municipal government revenues come primarily from **property taxes** (37% of the total); provincial government transfers make up the bulk of the rest.

THE DEBATE OVER THE SIZE OF GOVERNMENT

The debate over the appropriate size of government is a long-standing one, but it has received considerable attention in the last decade as government debt has spiralled upwards.

There are those who argue passionately for reducing government expenditure as a way of bringing down government deficits and reducing the size of government itself. Others maintain the govern-

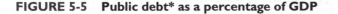

FIGURE 5-5   Public debt* as a percentage of GDP

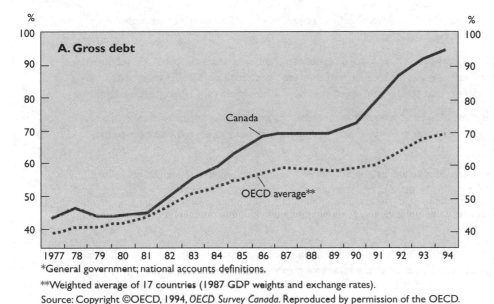

Since 1981, Canada's public debt has grown much more rapidly than the OECD average.

*General government; national accounts definitions.

**Weighted average of 17 countries (1987 GDP weights and exchange rates).

Source: Copyright ©OECD, 1994, *OECD Survey Canada*. Reproduced by permission of the OECD.

ment debt problem has been exaggerated and that if it is, or becomes, a problem the government ought to raise revenues by taxing corporations and well-off Canadians at a higher rate.

These differing views arise because of the different perceptions of the effectiveness of government policies in the past. Those in favour of reducing the size of government argue that instances of government success at alleviating social and economic problems are rare. Those who favour increasing taxes to deal with the mounting debt point out how much worse the social and economic problems would have been and are likely to become if drastic government expenditure cutbacks were implemented.

Whichever side of the debate you are on, there is no dispute over the fact that in the last 20 years the public debt in Canada has risen steeply, and more so than the OECD average. Figure 5-5 shows the steep rise in the Canadian public net debt compared with the OECD average.

CHAPTER SUMMARY

1. Government enhances the operation of the market system by **a** providing an appropriate legal and social framework, and **b** acting to maintain competition.

2. Government alters the distribution of income by direct market intervention and through the tax-transfer system.

3. Spillovers or externalities cause the equilibrium output of certain goods to vary from the optimal output. Spillover costs result in an overallocation of resources that can be corrected by legislation or specific taxes. Spillover benefits are accompanied by an underallocation of resources that can be corrected by subsidies to either consumers or producers.

4. Government must provide public goods because such goods are indivisible and entail benefits from which nonpaying consumers cannot be excluded.

5. The manipulation of taxes and its expenditures is one way government can reduce unemployment and inflation.

6. The circular flow model helps us envision how government performs its redistributional, allocative, and stabilizing functions.

7. Government purchases exhaust or absorb resources; transfer payments do not. Government purchases have been rising as a percentage of domestic output since 1950. Transfers also have grown significantly, so that total government spending is now over 40% of domestic output.

8. The main categories of federal spending are for unemployment insurance, health, and interest on the public debt; revenues come primarily from personal income, payroll, and corporate income taxes.

9. The primary sources of revenue for the provinces are sales and excise taxes; public welfare, education, highways, and health and hospitals are their major expenditures.

10. At the local level, most revenue comes from property tax, and education is the largest expenditure.

11. Under our system of fiscal federalism, provincial and municipal tax revenues are supplemented by sizable revenue transfers from the federal government.

TERMS AND CONCEPTS

corporate income taxes (p. 87)
exclusion principle (p. 82)
free-rider problem (p. 83)
government purchases (p. 86)
monopoly (p. 79)

personal income taxes (p. 87)
property taxes (p. 88)
public goods (p. 83)
spillover costs and spillover benefits (p. 80)
transfer payments (p. 86)

QUESTIONS AND STUDY SUGGESTIONS

1. List and briefly discuss the main economic functions of government.

2. What divergences arise between equilibrium and an efficient output when a. spillover costs and b. spillover benefits are present? How might government correct for these discrepancies? "The presence of spillover costs suggests underallocation of resources to that product and the need for governmental subsidies." Do you agree? Explain how zoning and seat belt laws might be used to deal with a problem of spillover costs.

3. *Key Question   What are the basic characteristics of public goods? Explain the significance of the exclusion principle. By what means does government provide public goods?*

4. *Key Question   Draw a production possibilities curve with public goods on the vertical axis and private goods on the horizontal axis. Assuming the economy is initially operating on the curve, indicate how the production of public goods might be increased. How might the output of public goods be increased if the economy is initially functioning at a point inside the curve?*

5. Use your understanding of the characteristics of private and public goods to determine whether the following should be produced through the market system or provided by government: a. bread; b. street lighting; c. bridges; d. parks; e. swimming pools; f. medical care; g. mail delivery; h. housing; i. air traffic control; j. libraries.

6. Explain how government might manipulate its expenditures and tax revenues to reduce a. unemployment and b. the rate of inflation.

7. "Most governmental actions affect the distribution of income, the allocation of resources, and the levels of unemployment and prices." Use the circular flow model to confirm this assertion for each of the following: a. the construction of a new high school in Huron County; b. a 2% reduction in the corporate income tax; c. an expansion of preschool programs for disadvantaged children; d. a $50 million increase in spending for space research; e. the levying of a tax on air polluters; and f. a $1 increase in the minimum wage.

8. What is the most important source of revenue and the major type of expenditure for the federal government? For provincial governments? For municipal governments?

CHAPTER 6

CANADA IN THE GLOBAL ECONOMY

 ackpackers In the wilderness like to think they are "leaving the world behind." Ironically, like Atlas, they carry the world on their shoulders. Much of their backpacking equipment is imported — knives from Switzerland, rain gear from South Korea, cameras from Japan, aluminum pots made in England, miniature stoves from Sweden, sleeping bags from China, and compasses from Finland. Some backpackers wear hiking boots from Italy, sunglasses made in France, and watches from Japan or Switzerland. Moreover, they may drive to the trailheads in Japanese-made Toyotas or Swedish-made Volvos, sipping coffee from Brazil or snacking on bananas from Honduras.

International trade and the global economy affect all of us daily, whether we are hiking in the wilderness, driving our cars, listening to music, or working at our jobs. We cannot "leave the world behind." We are enmeshed with the rest of the world in a complex web of economic relationships — trade of goods and services, multinational corporations, co-operative ventures among the world's firms, and ties among the world's financial markets. This web is so complex that is difficult to determine just what is — or isn't — a Canadian product! Japanese auto companies have set up factories in Ontario, while many "Canadian" manufacturers have factories or outlets in other countries, particularly in the United States.

The goal of this chapter is to introduce you to the basic principles underlying the global economy. (We defer a more advanced discussion of international economics to Part 5 of this book.)

In this chapter we will first look at the growth of world trade, Canada's role in it, and the factors causing the growth. Next, we will modify Chapter 5's circular flow diagram to account for international trade flows. Third, we will explore the basis for world trade, focusing on the concept of comparative advantage. This discussion is followed by a look at foreign currencies and exchange rates. Then we will examine some restrictive trade practices implemented by nations. That leads us to a discussion of multilateral trade agreements and free-trade regions of the globe. We conclude with some answers to the question: "Can Canadian firms compete?"

BOX 6-1   THE BIG PICTURE

The scarcity problem can be lessened if a society can produce more goods and services from its limited resources. One powerful way for all societies to produce more from the limited resources available to them is to specialize in producing specific goods. If all nations specialized in producing what each was especially good at, each could get its other needs by trading. If all nations specialized, the whole world would be materially better off since we would increase the total goods and services we could produce from available resources. As the twentieth century is coming to a close, this lesson is being followed by more and more nations. Not surprisingly, trade among nations is growing, and Canada is no exception in this trend.

As you read this chapter, keep the following points in mind:

• Opportunity cost plays a central role in specialization, and determines what products a nation

ought to specialize in. Keep asking yourself what a particular good would cost to produce domestically compared to purchasing it from another nation. We could grow bananas in Canada (in greenhouses, of course), but could we purchase bananas at a lower price from a nation better suited to grow bananas?

• Specialization necessarily implies trade. Since nations have different currencies, there is a market for them called the foreign exchange market. As with any market, there are suppliers and those that demand a particular currency. The exchange rate is determined by supply and demand conditions at any given time period.

• Trade is reciprocal in nature: one nation's exports are another's imports, and a nation cannot import unless it also exports.

GROWTH OF WORLD TRADE

The volume of world trade is so large and its characteristics so unique that it requires special consideration.

VOLUME AND PATTERN

Figure 6-1 shows the importance of world trade for several representative countries. Many nations, such as Canada, with limited domestic markets cannot produce with reasonable efficiency the variety of goods they want to consume. For such countries, exports — sales abroad — are the route for obtaining imported goods they desire. In Canada exports make up about 30% of our national output. Other countries, the United States, for example, have rich and diversified resource bases and vast internal markets and are less dependent on world trade.

VOLUME   For Canada and the world, the volume of international trade has been increasing both absolutely and relatively. A comparison of the boxed data within Figure 6-2 reveals the substantial growth in the absolute dollar volume of both Canadian exports and imports over the past several decades. The lines in the figure show the growth of exports and imports as a percent of gross domestic

FIGURE 6-1   Exports of goods and services as a percentage of GDP, selected countries, 1993

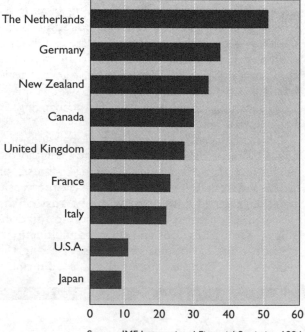

Source: IMF, International Financial Statistics, 1994.

Canada's exports make up almost 30% of domestic output of goods and services.

FIGURE 6-2 Canada's imports and exports as a percentage of GDP

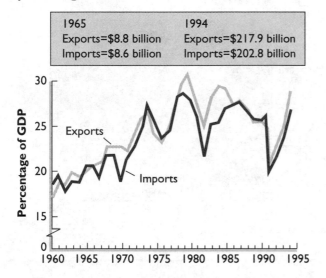

1965	1994
Exports=$8.8 billion	Exports=$217.9 billion
Imports=$8.6 billion	Imports=$202.8 billion

Source: Statistics Canada, *Canadian International Merchandise Trade.*

Canada's imports and exports have expanded since 1960, but have fluctuated over this period.

product (GDP) — the dollar value of all goods and services produced within Canadian borders. Exports and imports currently are 29 and 27% of GDP respectively, up substantially from 1960.

DEPENDENCE   Canada depends heavily on the world economy. We are almost entirely dependent on other countries for bananas, cocoa, coffee, spices, tea, raw silk, and natural rubber. Imported goods compete strongly in many of our domestic markets — for example, French and Italian wines, and Japanese autos. Foreign cars now account for about a third of the total automotive sales in Canada. Even the great Canadian pastime — hockey — relies heavily on imported equipment.

But world trade is a two-way street, and many Canadian industries are highly dependent on foreign markets. Almost all segments of agriculture rely heavily on foreign markets — wheat exports vary from one-fourth to more than one-half of total output. The chemical, aircraft, automobile, machine tool, and forest industries are only a few of many Canadian industries that sell significant portions of their output in

FIGURE 6-3 Canadian exports and imports, 1994

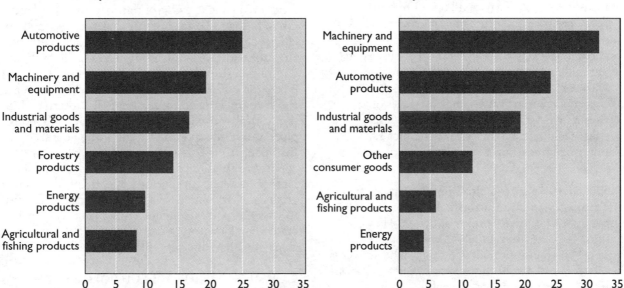

Source: Statistics Canada, *Canadian International Merchandise Trade,* October 1994.

Automotive products (vehicle and parts) are our largest export and second largest import. Machinery and equipment, industrial goods and machinery, and forestry products are Canada's largest export categories.

FIGURE 6-4   Canadian international trade by geographical areas, 1994

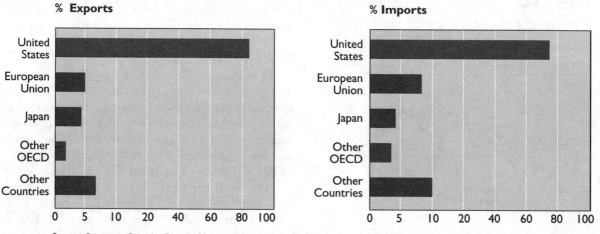

Source: Statistics Canada, *Canadian International Merchandise Trade*, October 1994.

The bulk of our exports and imports are with the United States.

international markets. Figure 6-3 shows some of Canada's major commodity exports and imports.

TRADE PATTERNS   Figure 6-4 provides an overall picture of the pattern of Canada's merchandise trade. Note the following:

1. The bulk of our export and import trade is with other industrially advanced nations, not with the less developed nations or the countries of Eastern Europe.
2. The United States is our most important trading partner quantitatively. Over 80% of our exports are sold to Americans, who in turn provide us with three-quarters of our imports.
3. We import some of the same categories of goods that we export (specifically, automobiles, industrial machinery and materials, chemicals, and telecommunications equipment).

LINKAGES   Figure 6-4 also implies complex financial linkages among nations. A nation can have either an overall trade surplus or deficit. How does a nation — or an individual — obtain more goods from others than it provides to them? The answer is by either borrowing from them or by giving up ownership of some of its assets or wealth.

FACILITATING FACTORS

Several factors have facilitated the rapid growth of international trade since World War II.

TRANSPORTATION TECHNOLOGY   High transportation costs are a barrier to any type of trade, and particularly to trade between distance places. But improvements in transportation have shrunk the globe, fostering world trade. Airplanes now transport low-weight, high-value items such as diamonds and semiconductors quickly from one nation to another. We now routinely transport oil in massive tankers, greatly reducing the cost of transportation per barrel. Grain is loaded onto ocean-going ships at modern, efficient grain silos located at Great Lakes ports and the coastal ports of Vancouver and Halifax. Container ships transport self-contained railroad boxes directly to foreign ports, where cranes place the containers onto railroad cars for internal shipment. Natural gas flows through large diameter pipelines from exporting to importing countries, for instance, from Russia to Germany and from this country to the United States. Workers clean fish on large processing ships located directly on the fishing grounds. Refrigerated vessels then transport the fish to overseas ports. Commercial airplane manufacturers deliver new aircraft in a matter of hours; they simply fly them directly to their foreign customers.

COMMUNICATIONS TECHNOLOGY   Perhaps equally important to the explosion of world trade has been dramatic improvements in communications technology. Telephones, facsimile machines, and computers now directly link traders around the world. These devices have aided exporters in assessing the potential for selling products abroad and in consummating trade deals. The communications revolution has also globalized financial markets and banking industries. People can move money around the world in the blink of an eye. Exchange rates, stock prices, and interest rates flash onto computer screens nearly simultaneously in Vancouver, Toronto, London, and Lisbon.

In short, exporters and importers in today's world can as easily communicate between Sweden and Australia as between Calgary and Winnipeg. A distributor in Montreal can get a price quote on 1000 thatched baskets in Thailand just as quickly as a quotation on 1000 tonnes of steel in Hamilton.

GENERAL DECLINE IN TARIFFS Tariffs — excise taxes or duties on imported products — have had their ups and downs, but since 1940 have generally fallen worldwide. A glance ahead to Figure 6-8 reveals that Canada's tariff duties as a percent of dutiable imports are now about 5%, down substantially from the highs of 1930. Many nations still have barriers to free trades, but on average, tariffs have fallen greatly, increasing international trade.

PEACE World War II matched powerful industrial countries against one another and thus disrupted commercial international trade. Not only has trade been restored since World War II, but it has been greatly bolstered by peaceful relations and by trade-conducive institutions linking most industrial nations. In particular, Japan and Germany — two defeated World War II powers — now are major participants in world trade.

PARTICIPANTS

Nearly all nations of the world participate to some extent in international trade.

CANADA, UNITED STATES, JAPAN, AND WESTERN EUROPE As indicated in Global Perspective 6-1, the top participants in world trade are the United States, Germany, and Japan. In 1993 these three nations had combined exports of U. S. $1.2 trillion. Along with Germany, other Western European nations such as France, Britain, and Italy are major exporters and importers. In fact, Canada, the United States, Japan, and the Western European nations now dominate world trade. These areas also are at the heart of the world's financial system and headquarter most of the world's large **multinational**

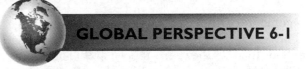

GLOBAL PERSPECTIVE 6-1

Comparative exports in billions of dollars

The United States, Germany, and Japan are the world's largest exporters. Canada ranks seventh.

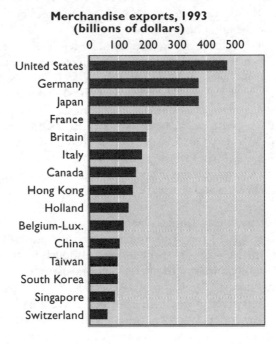

Merchandise exports, 1993 (billions of dollars)

Source: GATT.

corporations, which are firms with sizable foreign production and distribution assets.

NEW PLAYERS New, important participants have arrived on the world trade scene. One such group of nations is the newly industrializing Asian economies of Hong Kong, Singapore, South Korea, and Taiwan. These "**Asian tigers**" have expanded their share of world exports from about 3% in 1972 to more than 9% today. Their combined exports roughly match that of Japan and greatly exceed those of either France, Britain, or Italy. Other countries in southeast Asia, particularly Malaysia and Indonesia, have also expanded their international trade.

China is another emerging trading power. Since initiating market reforms in 1979, its annual growth of output has averaged nearly 10% (compared to 2 to 3% annually in Canada). At this remarkable rate of growth, China's total output nearly doubles every seven years! An upsurge of exports and imports has accompanied this expansion of output. In 1989 Chinese exports and imports each were about $45 billion. In 1993 they each topped $89 billion, with 30% of the exports going to Canada and the United States. Also, China has been a recent magnet for foreign investment. In 1993 alone, it contracted for about $100 billion of foreign-produced capital to be delivered during the next several years. Experts predict that China eventually will become one of the world's leading trade nations.

The collapse of communism in Eastern Europe and the former Soviet Union has also altered world trade patterns. Before this collapse, the Eastern European nations of Poland, Hungary, Czechoslovakia, and East Germany traded mainly with the Soviet Union and its political allies such as North Korea and Cuba. Today, East Germany is reunited with West Germany, and Poland, Hungary, and the Czech Republic have established new trade relationships with Europe and America.

Russia itself has initiated far-reaching market reforms, including widespread privatization of industry, and has consummated major trade deals with firms from across the globe. Although its transition to capitalism has been far from smooth, there is no doubt that Russia has the potential to be a major trading power. Other former Soviet republics — now independent nations — such as Ukraine and Estonia also are opening their economies to international trade and finance.

BACK TO THE CIRCULAR FLOW MODEL

Now that we have an idea of the size and growth of world trade, we need to incorporate it into Chapter 5's circular flow model. Fortunately, this is a rather straightforward matter. In Figure 6-5 we make two adjustments to Figure 5-1:

1. Our previously labelled "Resource Markets" and "Product Markets" now become "Canadian Resource Markets" and "Canadian Product Markets." Similarly, we add the modifier "Canadian" to the "Businesses," "Government," and "Households" sectors.
2. We place the foreign sector — the "Rest of the World" — at the bottom of the circular flow diagram. This sector designates all foreign nations that we deal with and the individuals, businesses, and governments that make them up.

Flow (13) shows that people, businesses, and governments abroad buy Canadian products — our exports — from our product market. This real flow of Canadian exports to foreign nations is accompanied by an opposite monetary revenue flow (14) from the rest of the world to us. In response to these revenues from abroad, Canadian businesses demand more domestic resources to produce the exported goods; they are on the demand side of the resource market. Thus, the domestic flow (1) of money income (rents, wages, interest, and profits) to Canadian households rises.

But our exports are only half the picture. Flow (15) shows that Canadian households, businesses, and government spend some of their income on foreign products. These products, of course, are our imports (flow 16). These purchases of imports, say, autos and electronic equipment, contribute to foreign output and income, which in turn provides the means for foreign households to buy our exports.

Our circular flow model is a simplification that emphasizes product market effects. But a few other Canada-Rest of the World relationships also merit mention. Specifically, there are linkages between the Canadian resource market and the rest of the world.

Canada imports and exports not only products, but resources as well. For example, we import some crude oil and export raw logs. Moreover, some Canadian firms choose to engage in "offshore" production, which diverts spending on capital from our domestic resource market to resource markets in other nations. For instance, Northern Telecom might build an assembly plant in Germany. Or flowing the other direction, Sony might construct a plant for manufacturing CD players in Canada. There are also international flows of labour. About 250,000 immigrants enter Canada each year. These immigrants expand the availability of labour resources in Canada, raising our total output and income. On the other hand, immigration increases labour supply in specific Canadian labour markets, pulling down wage rates for some types of Canadian labour.

The expanded circular flow model also demonstrates that a nation engaged in world trade faces potential sources of instability that would not affect a "closed" nation. For example, recessions and inflation can be highly contagious among nations. Suppose that the nations of Western Europe experienced a rather severe recession. As their income declined, they would curtail purchases of Canadian exports. As a result flows (13) and (14) in Figure 6-5 would decline and inventories of unsold Canadian goods would rise. Canadian firms would respond by limiting their production and employment, reducing the flow of money income to Canadian households (flow 1). Recession in Europe might contribute to a recession in Canada.

Figure 6-5 also helps us to see that the foreign sector alters resource allocation and incomes in the Canadian economy. In the presence of the foreign sector, we produce more of some goods (our exports) and

fewer of others (our imports) than we would otherwise. Thus, Canadian labour and other productive resources are shifted towards export industries and away from import industries. We use more of our resources to manufacture autos and telecommunication equipment. So we ask: "Do these shifts of resources make any economic sense? Do they enhance our total output and thus our standard of living?" We look at some answers next. (Key Question 3)

FIGURE 6-5   The circular flow with the foreign sector

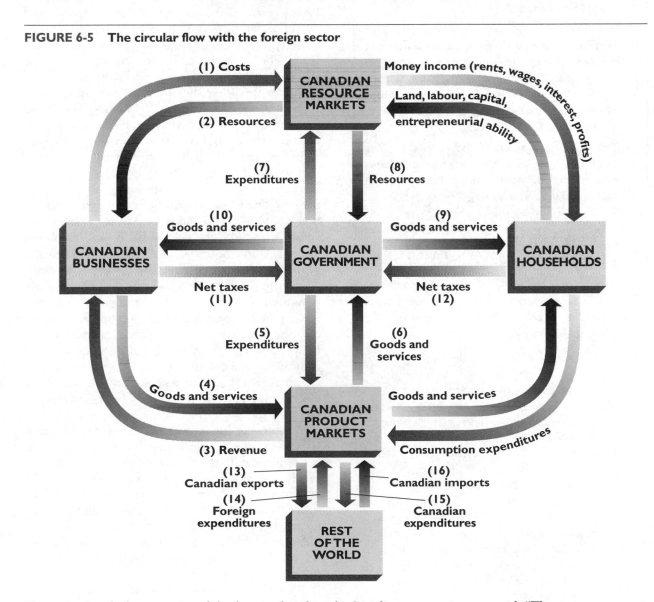

Flows 13-16 in the lower portion of the diagram show how the Canadian economy interacts with "The Rest of the World." People abroad buy Canadian exports, contributing to our business revenue and money income. Canadians, in turn, spend part of their incomes to buy imports from abroad. Income from a nation's exports helps pay for its imports.

QUICK REVIEW 6-1

1. World trade has increased globally and nationally. Canada is a leading international trader, with our exports and imports being about 27 to 29% of our national output.

2. Transportation technology, communications technology, declines in tariffs, and peaceful relations among major industrial countries have all helped to expand world trade.

3. World trade is dominated by Canada, the United States, Japan, and the Western European nations, but has recently been bolstered by new participates such as the "Asian tigers" (Hong Kong, Singapore, South Korea, and Taiwan), China, Eastern European nations, and the newly independent states formerly making up the Soviet Union.

4. The circular flow model now incorporates the foreign sector by adding flows of exports from our domestic product market, imports to our domestic product market, and the corresponding flows of spending.

SPECIALIZATION AND COMPARATIVE ADVANTAGE

Specialization and trade increase the productivity of a nation's resources and allow for larger total output than otherwise. This notion is not new! According to Adam Smith in 1776:

> It is the maxim of every prudent master of a family, never to attempt to make at home what it will cost him more to make than to buy. The taylor does not attempt to make his own shoes, but buys them from the shoemaker. The shoemaker does not attempt to make his own clothes, but employs a taylor. The farmer attempts to make neither the one or the other, but employs those different artificers....
>
> What is prudence in the conduct of every private family, can scarce be folly in that of a great kingdom. If a foreign country can supply us with a commodity cheaper than we can make it, better buy it of them with some part of the produce of our own industry, employed in a way in which we have some advantage.[1]

---

[1] Adam Smith, *The Wealth of Nations* (New York: Modern Library, Inc., 1937), p. 424. [Originally published in 1776.]

Nations specialize and trade for the same reasons as individuals: Specialization and exchange among individuals, regions, and nations results in greater overall output and income.

BASIC PRINCIPLE

In the early 1800s British economist David Ricardo expanded Smith's idea, observing that it pays for a person or a country to specialize and exchange even if that person or nation is more productive than a potential trading partner in *all* economic activities.

Consider an example of a chartered accountant (CA) who is also a skilled house painter. Suppose the CA can paint her house in less time than the professional painter she is thinking of hiring. Also suppose the CA can earn $50 per hour doing her accounting and must pay the painter $15 per hour. Let's say that it will take the accountant 30 hours to paint her house; the painter, 40 hours.

Should the CA take time from her accounting to paint her own house or should she hire the painter? The CA's opportunity cost of painting her house is $1500 (= 30 hours × $50 per hour of sacrificed income). The cost of hiring the painter is only $600 (40 hours × $15 per hour paid to the painter). Although the CA is better at both accounting and painting — she has an **absolute advantage** in both accounting and painting — her relative or comparative advantage lies in accounting. She will *lower the cost of getting her house painted* by specializing in accounting and using some of the earnings from accounting to hire a house painter.

Similarly, the house painter can reduce his cost of obtaining accounting services by specializing in painting and using some of his income to hire the CA to prepare his income tax forms. Suppose that it would take the painter ten hours to prepare his tax return, while the CA could handle this task in two hours. The house painter would sacrifice $150 of income (= 10 hours × $15 per hour of sacrificed time) to accomplish a task that he could hire the CA to do for $100 (= 2 hour × $50 per hour of the CA's time). By using the CA to prepare his tax return, the painter lowers *his cost of getting the tax return completed*.

What is true for our CA and house painter is also true for nations. Countries can reduce their cost of obtaining desirable goods by specializing in production where they have comparative advantages.

COMPARATIVE COSTS

Our simple example clearly shows that specialization is economically desirable because it results in more efficient production. Because it is vital to understanding the global economy, let's tackle an illustration that puts specialization in the context of trading nations. Since you are already familiar with the concept of the production possibilities table, let's use it in our analysis. Suppose production possibilities for Mexico and Canada are as shown in Tables 6-1 and 6-2.

In these production possibilities tables we assume constant costs. Each country must give up a constant amount of one product in securing constant increments of the other product. (This assumption will simplify our discussion without impairing the validity of our conclusions.)

TABLE 6-1 Mexico's production possibilities table (in tonnes)

Product	Production alternatives				
	A	B	C	D	E
Corn	0	20	24	40	60
Soybeans	15	10	9	5	0

Specialization and trade are mutually beneficial or "profitable" to the two nations if the comparative costs of the two products within the two nations differ. What are the domestic comparative costs of corn and soybeans in Mexico? Comparing production alternatives A and B in Table 6-1, we see that 5 tonnes of soybeans (= 15 − 10) must be sacrificed to produce 20 tonnes of corn (= 20 − 0). Or more simply, in Mexico it costs 1 tonne of soybeans to produce 4 tonnes of corn — that is, $1S = 4C$. Because we assumed constant costs, this domestic comparative-cost relationship will not change as Mexico expands the output of either product. This is evident from looking at production possibilities B and C, where we see that 4 more tonnes of corn (= 24 − 20) cost 1 unit of soybeans (= 10 − 9).

Similarly, in Table 6-2, a comparison of production alternatives R and S reveals that at a domestic opportunity cost of 10 tonnes of soybeans (= 30 − 20), Canadians can obtain 30 tonnes of corn (= 30 − 0). That is, the domestic comparative-cost ratio for the

TABLE 6-2 Canada's production possibilities table (in tonnes)

Product	Production alternatives				
	R	S	T	U	V
Corn	0	30	33	60	90
Soybeans	30	20	19	10	0

two products in Canada is $1S = 3C$. A comparison of production alternative S and T demonstrates this. Note that an extra 3 tonnes of corn (= 33 − 30) comes at the direct sacrifice of 1 tonne of soybeans (= 20 − 19).

The comparative cost of the two products within the two nations is clearly different. Economists say that Canada has a domestic comparative-cost advantage, or simply, a **comparative advantage**, in soybeans. Canada must forgo less corn — 3 tonnes — to get 1 tonne of soybeans than in Mexico where 1 tonne of soybeans costs 4 tonnes of corn. In terms of domestic opportunity costs, soybeans are relatively cheaper in Canada. *A nation has a comparative advantage in some product when it can produce that product at a lower domestic opportunity cost than can a potential trading partner.* Mexico, on the other hand, has a comparative advantage in corn. While it costs ⅓ tonne of soybeans to get 1 tonne of corn in Canada, by comparison 1 tonne of soybeans costs only ¼ tonne of soybeans in Mexico. Comparatively speaking, corn is cheaper in Mexico. In summary:

Mexico's domestic cost conditions $1S = 4C$
Canada's domestic cost conditions $1S = 3C$

Because of these differences in domestic opportunity costs, we can show that if both nations specialize, each according to its comparative advantage, then each can achieve a larger total output with the same total input of resources. Together, they will be using their scarce resources more efficiently.

TERMS OF TRADE

Since Canada's cost ratio of $1S$ equals $3C$, it makes sense that Canadians would be pleased to specialize in soybeans, if they could obtain *more than* 3 tonnes of corn for a tonne of soybeans through trade with Mexico. Similarly, recalling Mexico's $1S$ equals $4C$ cost ratio, it will be advantageous to Mexicans to specialize in corn, provided they can get 1 tonne of soybeans *for less than* 4 tonnes of corn.

Suppose through negotiation the two nations agree on an exchange rate of 1 tonne of soybeans for 3 ½ tonnes of corn. These **terms of trade** will be mutually beneficial to both countries since each can "do better" through trade than via domestic production alone. Canadians get 3 ½ tonnes of corn by sending 1 tonne of soybeans to Mexico, while they can get only 3 tonnes of corn by shifting resources domestically from soybeans to corn. It would cost Mexicans 4 tonnes of corn to obtain 1 tonne of soybeans by shifting their domestic resources. Instead they can obtain 1 tonne of soybeans through trade with Canada at the lower cost of 3 ½ tonnes of corn.

GAINS FROM SPECIALIZATION AND TRADE

Let's pinpoint the size of the gains in total output from specialization and trade. Suppose that before specialization and trade, production alternative C in Table 6-1 and alternative T in 6-2 were the optimal product mixes for each country. These outputs are shown in column 1 of Table 6-3. That is, Mexicans preferred 24 tonnes of corn and 9 tonnes of soybeans (Table 6-1) and Canadians preferred 33 tonnes of corn and 19 tonnes of soybeans (Table 6-2) to all other alternatives available within their respective domestic economies.

Now let's assume both nations specialize according to comparative advantage, Mexico producing 60 tonnes of corn and no soybeans (alternative E) and Canada producing no corn and 30 tonnes of soybeans (alternative R) as reflected in

column 2 of Table 6-3. Using our 1S = 3 ½ terms of trade, assume Mexico exchanges 35 tonnes of corn for 10 tonnes of Canadian soybeans. Column 3 of Table 6-3 shows quantities exchanged in this trade. As observed in Column 4, Mexicans will now have 25 tonnes of corn and 10 tonnes of soybeans, while Canadians will obtain 35 tonnes of corn and 20 tonnes of soybeans. Compared with their optimum product mixes before specialization and trade (column 1), *both* nations now enjoy more corn and more soybeans! Specifically, Mexico will gain 1 tonne of corn and 1 tonne of soybeans. Canada will gain 2 tonnes of corn and 1 tonne of soybeans. These gains are shown in column 5 where we have subtracted the *before*-specialization outputs of column (1) from the outputs realized *after* specialization in column (4).

The point germane to our understanding the world economy is that *specialization according to comparative advantage improves resource allocation. The same total inputs of world resources have resulted in a larger global output.* By having Mexico and Canada allocate all their resources to corn and soybeans respectively, the same total inputs of resources have produced more output between them, indicating that resources are being more efficiently used or allocated.

We saw in Chapter 2 that through specialization and international trade a nation can overcome the production constraints imposed by its domestic production possibilities curve. Although the domestic production possibilities frontiers of the two countries have not been pushed outward, specialization and trade have circumvented the constraints of the production possibilities curve. The economic effects of specialization and trade between two

TABLE 6-3   Specialization according to comparative advantage and the gains from trade (in tonnes)

Country	(1) Outputs before specialization	(2) Outputs after specialization	(3) Amounts traded	(4) Outputs available after trade	(5) = (4) – (1) Gains from specialization and trade
Mexico	24 corn	60 corn	-35 corn	25 corn	1 corn
	9 soybeans	0 soybeans	+10 soybeans	10 soybeans	1 soybeans
Canada	33 corn	0 corn	+35 corn	35 corn	2 corn
	19 soybeans	30 soybeans	–10 soybeans	20 soybeans	1 soybeans

nations are tantamount to having more or better resources or to having achieved technological progress. The national self-interests of trading partners is the foundation of the world economy. Such trade provides mutual gains in consumable output and thus higher domestic standards of living. **(Key Question 4)**

FOREIGN EXCHANGE MARKET

People, firms, or nations specializing in the production of specific goods or services exchange those products for money and then use the money to buy other products or to pay for the use of resources. Within an economy — for example, Mexico — prices are stated in pesos and buyers use pesos to purchase domestic products. The buyers possess pesos, exactly the currency sellers want.

International markets are different. How many dollars does it take to buy a truckload of Mexican corn selling for 3000 pesos, a German automobile selling for 90,000 marks, or a Japanese motorcycle priced at 300,000 yen? Producers in Mexico, Germany, and Japan want payment in pesos, marks, and yen, respectively, so they can pay their wages, rent, interest, dividends, and taxes. This need is served by a **foreign exchange market**, *the market where various national currencies are exchanged for one another.* At the outset two points about this market require emphasis.

1. A COMPETITIVE MARKET Real-world foreign exchange markets conform closely to the kinds of markets studied in Chapter 4. These are competitive markets characterized by large numbers of buyers and sellers dealing in a standardized "product" such as the Canadian dollar, the German mark, the British pound, Swedish krona, or the Japanese yen.

2. LINKAGE TO ALL DOMESTIC AND FOREIGN PRICES The price or exchange value of a nation's currency is an unusual price; it links all domestic (say, Canada) prices, with all foreign (say, Japanese or German) prices. Exchange rates enable consumers in one country to translate prices of foreign goods into units of their own currency — just multiply the foreign product price by the exchange rate. If the dollar-yen exchange rate is $.01 (1 cent) per yen, a Sony cassette player priced at 20,000 yen will cost a Canadian $200 (=

20,000 × $.01). If the exchange rate is $.02 per yen, it would cost a Canadian $400 (= 20,000 × $.02). Similarly, all other Japanese products will double in price to Canadian buyers. As we will see, a change in exchange rates has important implications for a nation's levels of domestic production and employment.

DOLLAR-YEN MARKET

Let's look at how the foreign exchange market for dollars and yen works. (We defer technical details until Chapter 21.) When nations trade they need to exchange their currencies. Canadian exporters want to be paid in dollars, not yen; but Japanese importers of Canadian goods possess yen, not dollars. This problem is resolved by Japanese importers who offer to supply their yen in exchange for dollars. Conversely, there are Canadian importers who need to pay Japanese exporters with yen, not dollars. So these Canadians go to the foreign exchange market as demanders of yen.

GLOBAL PERSPECTIVE 6-2

Exchange rates: foreign currency per Canadian dollar

The amount of foreign currency that a dollar will buy varies greatly from nation to nation. These amounts are for February 1995 and fluctuate in response to supply and demand changes in the foreign exchange market.

One Canadian dollar will buy:

1.08 German marks
.45 British pounds
.71 U.S. dollars
3.9 Mexican pesos
.92 Swiss francs
3.8 French francs
71 Japanese yen
562 South Korean won
15,420 Polish zloty

FIGURE 6-6   The market for foreign exchange

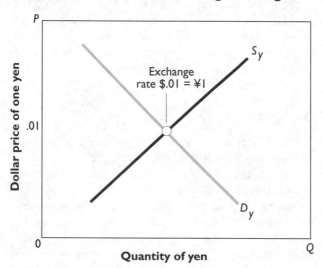

Canadian imports from Japan create a demand for yen, while Canadian exports to Japan create a supply of yen. The dollar price of one yen — the exchange rate — is determined at the intersection of the supply and demand curves. In this case the equilibrium price is $.01, meaning that 1¢ will buy 1 yen (or $1 will buy 100 yen).

Figure 6-6 shows Japanese importers as suppliers of yen and Canadian importers as demanders of yen. The intersection of the demand for yen curve D_y and the supply of yen curve S_y establishes the equilibrium dollar price of yen. Note that the equilibrium dollar price of 1 yen — the dollar-yen exchange rate — is $.01 = 1 yen, or $1 = 100 yen. At this price, the yen market clears; there is neither a shortage nor a surplus of yen. The equilibrium $.01 price of 1 yen means that $1 will buy 100 yen and therefore 100 yen worth of Japanese goods. Conversely, 100 yen will buy $1 worth of Canadian goods.

CHANGING RATES: DEPRECIATION AND APPRECIATION

What might cause the exchange rate to change? The determinants of the demand for and the supply of yen are similar to the determinants of supply and demand discussed in Chapter 4. Looking at it from Canada, several things might take place to increase the demand for — and therefore the dollar price of — yen. Incomes might rise in Canada, enabling Canadians to buy not only more domestic goods, but also more Sony televisions, Nikon cameras, and Nissan automobiles from Japan. So Canadians need more yen and the demand for yen increases. Or, there may be a change in Canadian tastes that enhances our preferences for Japanese goods. For instance, when gas prices soared in the 1970s, many Canadian auto buyers shifted their demands from gas-guzzling domestic cars to gas-efficient Japanese compact cars. The result? An increased demand for yen.

An increase in the Canadian demand for Japanese goods will increase the demand for yen and raise the dollar price of yen. Suppose the dollar price of yen rises from $.01 = ¥1 (or $1 = ¥100) to $.02 = ¥1 (or $2 = ¥100). When the dollar price of yen increases, a **depreciation** of the dollar relative to the yen has occurred. Dollar depreciation means that it takes more dollars (pennies in this case) to buy a single unit of a foreign currency (the yen). A dollar is worth less because it will buy fewer yen and therefore fewer Japanese goods; the yen and therefore all Japanese goods become more expensive to Canadians. Result: Canadian consumers shift their expenditures from Japanese to Canadian goods. The Ford Taurus becomes relatively more attractive than the Honda Accord to Canadian consumers. Conversely, because each yen will buy more dollars, Canadian goods become cheaper to people in Japan and our exports to them rise.

If opposite events occurred — if incomes rise in Japan and Japanese prefer more Canadian goods — then the supply of yen in the foreign exchange market would increase. This increase in the supply of yen relative to demand would decrease the equilibrium dollar price of yen. For example, yen supply might increase, causing the dollar price of yen to decline from $.01 = ¥1 (or $1 = ¥100) to $.005 = ¥1 (or $1 = ¥200). This decrease in the dollar price of yen means there has been an **appreciation** of the dollar relative to the yen. Appreciation of the dollar means that it takes fewer dollars (or pennies) to buy a single yen; the dollar is worth more because it can purchase more yen and therefore more Japanese goods. Each Sony Walkman becomes less expensive in terms of dollars, so Canadians purchase more of them. In general, Canadian imports rise. Meanwhile, because it takes more yen to get a dollar, Canadian exports to Japan fall.

We summarize these currency relationships in Figure 6-7 and you should examine this figure closely. **(Key Question 6)**

FIGURE 6-7 **Currency appreciation and depreciation**

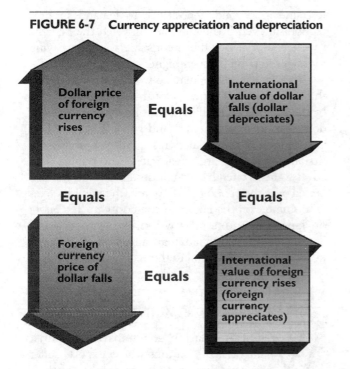

An increase in the dollar price of foreign currency is equivalent to a decline in the international value of the dollar (dollar depreciation). An increase in the dollar price of foreign currency also implies a decline in the foreign currency price of dollars. That is, the international value of foreign currency rises relative to the dollar (foreign currency appreciates).

QUICK REVIEW 6-2

1. A country has a comparative advantage in some product when it can produce it at a lower domestic opportunity cost than can a potential trading partner.

2. Specialization based on comparative advantage increases the total output available for nations that trade with one another.

3. The foreign exchange market is the market where the currency of one nation is exchanged for that of another nation.

4. Appreciation of the dollar is an increase in the international value of the dollar relative to the currency of some other nation; a dollar now buys more units of another currency. Depreciation of the dollar is a decrease in the international value of the dollar relative to other currencies; a dollar now buys fewer units of another currency.

GOVERNMENT AND TRADE

I f people and nations benefit from specialization and international exchange, why do governments sometimes try to restrict the free flow of imports or to subsidize exports? What kinds of world trade barriers exist? And what is the rationale for them?

TRADE IMPEDIMENTS AND SUBSIDIES

The major government interferences with free trade are fourfold:

1. *Protective tariffs* are excise taxes or duties placed on imported goods. Most are designed to shield domestic producers from foreign competition. They impede free trade by increasing the prices of imported goods, shifting demand towards domestic products.

2. *Import quotas* are maximum limits on the quantity or total value of specific imported items. Once the quotas are "filled," they choke off imports that domestic consumers might prefer to domestic goods. Import quotas can be more effective in retarding international commerce than tariffs. A particular product might be imported in large quantities despite high tariffs; low import quotas completely prohibit imports once quotas are filled.

3. *Nontariff barriers* include licensing requirements, unreasonable standards pertaining to product quality, or simply unnecessary bureaucratic red tape in customs procedures. Some nations require their domestic importers of foreign goods to obtain licences. By restricting the issuance of licences, imports can be effectively impeded. Great Britain bars coal importation in this way. Also, some nations impede imports of fruit by insisting that each individual crate of fruit be inspected for worms and insects.

4. *Export subsidies* consist of governmental payments to domestic producers to reduce their production costs. With lower production costs, domestic producers can charge lower prices and thus sell more exports in world markets. Two examples: Participating European governments have heavily subsidized Airbus Industries, which produces commercial aircraft. Canada and other nations have subsidized domestic farmers, boosting domestic food supply. This has reduced the market price of food, artificially decreasing export prices on agricultural produce.

WHY GOVERNMENT TRADE INTERVENTIONS?

Why would a nation want to send more of its output for consumption abroad than it gains as imported output in return? Why the impulse to impede imports or boost exports through government policy when free trade is beneficial to a nation? There are several reasons — some legitimate, most not. We will look at two here, and examine others in a later chapter.

1. MISUNDERSTANDING OF THE GAINS FROM TRADE It is a commonly accepted myth that the fundamental benefit of international trade is larger domestic employment in the export sector. This suggests that exports are "good" because they increase domestic employment, whereas imports are "bad" since they deprive people of jobs at home. In reality, the true benefit from international trade is the *overall* increase in output obtained through specialization and exchange. A nation can fully employ its resources, including labour, with or without international trade. International trade, however, enables society to use its resources in ways that increase its total output and therefore its overall material well-being.

A nation does not need international trade to locate *on* its production possibilities curve. A closed (nontrading) national economy can have full employment without international trade. But through world trade an economy can reach a point *beyond* its domestic production possibilities curve. The gain from trade is the extra output obtained from abroad — the imports got for less cost than if they had to be produced using domestic resources. The only valid reason for exporting part of our domestic output is to obtain imports of greater value to us. Specialization and international exchange make this possible.

2. POLITICAL CONSIDERATIONS While a nation as a whole gains from trade, trade may harm particular domestic industries and groups of resource suppliers. In our example of comparative advantage, specialization and trade adversely affected the Canadian corn industry and the Mexican soybean industry. These industries may seek to preserve or improve their economic positions by persuading their respective governments to impose tariffs or quotas to protect them from harm. The costs of protectionism are hidden because tariffs and quotas are embedded in the prices of goods. Thus policy makers face fewer political restraints in responding positively to demands for protectionism even if the costs far outweigh the benefits to the country. Inevitably, consumers end up paying for the protection through higher prices.

Indeed, the public may be won over, not only by the vigour of the arguments for trade barriers, but also by the apparent plausibility ("Cut imports and prevent domestic unemployment") and patriotic ring ("Buy Canadian!") of the protectionists. Alleged tariff benefits are immediate and clear-cut to the public. The adverse effects cited by economists are obscure and dispersed over the economy. Then, too, the public is likely to stumble on the fallacy of composition: "If a quota on Japanese automobiles will preserve profits and employment in the Canadian automobile industry, how can it be detrimental to the economy as a whole?"

MULTILATERAL AGREEMENTS AND FREE TRADE ZONES

When one nation enacts barriers against imports, the nations whose exports suffer may retaliate with trade barriers of their own. In a "trade war" tariffs escalate, choking off world trade and reducing everyone's economic well-being. The raising of tariffs by many nations in the early 1930s to fight domestic unemployment is a classic example. Rather than reduce imports and stimulate domestic production, high tariffs prompted affected nations to retaliate with equally high tariffs. International trade across the globe fell, lowering the output, income, and employment levels of all nations. Economic historians generally agree that the tariffs were a contributing cause of the Great Depression. In view of this fact, the world's nations have pursued avenues to lower tariffs worldwide. This pursuit of free trade has been aided by the expansion of powerful domestic interest groups. Specifically, exporters of goods and services, importers of foreign components used in "domestic" products, and domestic sellers of imported products all strongly support lower tariffs worldwide.

Figure 6-8 shows that Canada was a high-tariff nation in the past. But it also demonstrates that, in general, Canadian tariffs have declined during the past half century.[2]

---

[2] Average tariff-rate figures understate the importance of tariffs, however, by not accounting for the fact that some goods are excluded from Canadian markets because of existing tariffs. Then, too, average figures conceal the high tariffs on particular items.

BOX 6-2   APPLYING THE THEORY

PETITION OF THE CANDLEMAKERS, 1845

The French economist Frédéric Bastiat (1801–1850) devastated the proponents of protection-ism by satirically extending their reasoning to its logical and absurd conclusions.

Petition of the Manufacturers of Candles, Waxlights, Lamps, Candlesticks, Street Lamps, Snuffers, Extinguishers, and of the Producers of Oil Tallow, Rosin, Alcohol, and, Generally, of Everything Connected with Lighting.

TO MESSIEURS THE MEMBERS OF THE CHAMBER OF DEPUTIES.

Gentlemen — You are on the right road. You reject abstract theories, and have little consideration for cheapness and plenty. Your chief care is the interest of the producer. You desire to emancipate him from external competition, and reserve the *national market* for *national industry*.

We are about to offer you an admirable opportunity of applying your — what shall we call it? your theory? No; nothing is more deceptive than theory; your doctrine? your system? your principle? but you dislike doctrines, you abhor systems, and as for principles, you deny that there are any in social economy: we shall say, then, your prac-tice, your practice without theory and without principle.

We are suffering from the intolerable competition of a foreign rival, placed, it would seem, in a condition so far superior to ours for the production of light, that he absolutely inundates our national market with it at a price fabulously reduced. The moment he shows himself, our trade leaves us — all consumers apply to him; and a branch of native industry, having countless ramifications, is all at once rendered com-pletely stagnant. This rival ... is no other than the Sun.

What we pray for is, that it may please you to pass a law ordering the shutting up of all windows, sky-lights, dormerwindows, outside and inside shutters, curtains, blinds, bull's-eyes; in a word, of all openings, holes, chinks, clefts, and fissures, by or through which the light of the sun has been in use to enter houses, to the prejudice of the meritorious manufactures with which we flatter ourselves we have accommo-dated our country, — a country which, in gratitude, ought not to abandon us now to a strife so unequal.

If you shut up as much as possible all access to natural light, and create a demand for artificial light, which of our French manufactures will not be encouraged by it?

If more tallow is consumed, then there must be more oxen and sheep; and, consequently, we shall behold the multiplication of artificial meadows, meat, wool, hides, and, above all, manure, which is the basis and foundation of all agricultural wealth.

The same remark applies to navigation. Thousands of vessels will proceed to the whale fishery; and, in a short time, we shall possess a navy capable of main-taining the honor of France, and gratifying the patri-otic aspirations of your petitioners, the undersigned candlemakers and others.

Only have the goodness to reflect, Gentlemen, and you will be convinced that there is, perhaps, no Frenchman, from the wealthy coalmaster to the hum-blest vender of lucifer matches, whose lot will not be ameliorated by the success of this our petition.

SOURCE: Frédéric Bastiat, *Economic Sophisms* (Edinburgh: Oliver and Boyd, Tweeddale Court, 1873), pp. 49-53, abridged.

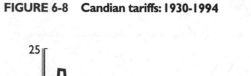

FIGURE 6-8   Candian tariffs: 1930-1994

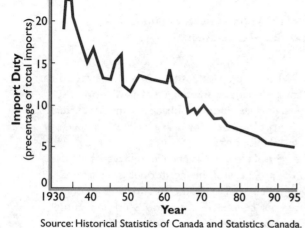

Source: Historical Statistics of Canada and Statistics Canada.

Canadian tariffs have been coming down steadily since 1930.

BILATERAL AGREEMENTS AND GATT

The across-the-board reduction of tariffs has come about because of various bilateral (between two nations) agreements Canada has signed. By incorporating **most-favoured-nation clauses** in these agreements, the reduced tariffs would apply not only to the specific nation negotiating with Canada, but to all nations previously granted most-favoured nation status.

This approach was broadened in 1947 when 23 nations, including Canada, signed a **General Agreement on Tariffs and Trade (GATT)**. GATT is based on three cardinal principles: (1) equal, nondiscriminatory treatment for all member nations; (2) the reduction of tariffs by multilateral negotiations; and (3) the elimination of import quotas.

Basically, GATT is a forum to negotiate reductions in trade barriers on a multilateral basis among nations. More than 100 nations now belong to GATT, and there is little doubt that it has been a positive force in the trend towards liberalized trade. Under its sponsorship, member nations have completed eight "rounds" of negotiations to reduce trade barriers in the post-World War II period.

URUGUAY ROUND   The eighth "round" of GATT negotiations began in Uruguay in 1986. After seven years of wrangling, in 1993 the participant nations reached a new agreement. This new agreement took effect on January 1, 1995, and its provisions will be phased in through 2005.

The major provisions of the new GATT agreement are:

1. TARIFF REDUCTION   Tariffs will be eliminated or reduced on thousands of products, including construction equipment, medical equipment, paper, steel, chemicals, wood, memory chips, and aluminum. Overall, tariffs will drop by about 33%.

2. INCLUSION OF SERVICES   Services are now a $900-billion segment of world trade and GATT will apply to them for the first time. The GATT accord will liberalize governmental rules that in the past have impeded the global market for advertising, insurance, consulting, accounting, legal, tourist, financial, and other services.

3. AGRICULTURAL   All member nations together agree to cut agricultural subsidies they pay to farmers, reducing the collective total subsidy by about 21%, or $300 billion annually.

4. INTELLECTUAL PROPERTY   International protection against piracy is provided for intellectual property such as patents, trademarks, and copyrights. This protection will greatly benefit Canadian book publishers, music producers, and software firms.

5. PHASED REDUCTION OF QUOTAS ON TEXTILES AND APPAREL   Quotas on imported textiles and apparel will be phased out over a ten-year period, to be replaced with tariffs. These quotas have choked off apparel and clothing imports to the industrial nations. Eliminating them will benefit the developing countries having comparative advantages in these areas.

6. WORLD TRADE ORGANIZATION   GATT becomes the World Trade Organization with judicial powers to mediate among members disputing the new rules.

When fully implemented, the GATT agreement will boost the world's GDP by $6 trillion, or 8%! Consumers in Canada will save about $3 billion annually.

BOX 6-3   IN THE MEDIA

CHILE VIEWED AS NAFTA TRAIL BLAZER

BY DREW FAGAN

SANTIAGO — Chile is acting as a prototype for other South American countries by entering into free-trade negotiations with North America, the leaders of Chile and Canada said yesterday.

At the end of a two-day official visit by Prime Minister Jean Chrétien, Chilean President Eduardo Frei said free trade will force Chilean companies to become more productive and the government to help prepare sensitive sectors such as agriculture for open trade.

"Chile is actually blazing a trail ... towards integration of the market of the Americas," Mr. Frei said at a press conference.

"Every day, companies need to be more efficient, their costs have to be lower and they have to train their people more."

Mr. Chrétien said he expects that the talks to add Chile to the North American free-trade agreement will make future negotiations to add other countries easier. "After Chile, others will fall in line."

Mr. Chrétien added that the continuing economic crisis in Mexico has not set back talks with Chile.

Canadian Trade Minister Roy MacLaren said in an interview yesterday that his meetings with Eduardo Aninat, the Chilean minister responsible for NAFTA accession, have reaffirmed his view that the negotiations will be relatively simple. "I don't anticipate any problems."

Indeed, an unreleased report commissioned by the Canadian government concludes that existing Chilean laws and policies make the country virtually ready to enter NAFTA. The study was done by a handful of Chilean legal, economic and trade experts and has not been challenged by the U.S. or Mexican governments.

The main changes Chile will have to make to enter NAFTA include, according to the report: extension of patent protection to 17 from 15 years; elimination of a one-year restriction on repatriation of foreign capital; inclusion of improved trade remedy rules; and harmonized procedures for enforcement of environmental standards.

Chile has an 11-per-cent tariff on goods that would be phased out for its NAFTA partners. It has practically no non-tariff barriers to elimi-

nate, has open government procurement procedures, and has services regulations generally in accordance with NAFTA standards.

"This openness would greatly facilitate the negotiation of a trade agreement," the report concludes....

The Chilean government toughened its environmental regulations late last year in an attempt to address criticism, mentioned in the Canadian government study, that the standards were haphazardly applied.

Mr. Aninat has committed the Chilean government to accepting the NAFTA environmental side deal, according to Canadian officials.

But Mr. Frei also implied yesterday that environmental laws must take a back seat in a developing country like Chile. Lax environmental rules are one reason that Canadian mining companies have invested heavily in countries like Chile and Mexico.

"We must use our natural resources ... to develop our industry," Mr. Frei said.

SOURCE: *Globe and Mail*, January 27, 1995, p. B1. Reprinted with permission.

The Story in Brief

In early 1995 Canada, the United States, and Mexico entered into negotiations with Chile in an effort to reach an agreement that would make the South American country a member of the North American Free Trade Agreement (NAFTA).

The Economics Behind the Story

- Negotiations between Chile and NAFTA members to allow the former into NAFTA stem from the desire of both parties to gain from increased trade. Chile had an 11% duty on goods entering its borders. These would be phased out, forcing domestic producers to become more competitive — producing more output with the same, or fewer, inputs. Likewise, Canada, the United States, and Mexico would reduce tariffs on Chilean goods entering their countries — for example, fresh fruits and wine. Consumers of all four countries would benefit from lower prices.

- Do you agree with the Chilean minister responsible for NAFTA accession that "environmental laws must take a back seat in a developing country like Chile"? Would your answer be different if you lived in Chile and were very poor? Use marginal benefit-cost analysis to help you answer the question.

EUROPEAN UNION

Countries have also sought to reduce tariffs by creating regional free-trade zones or trade blocs. The most dramatic example is the **European Union (EU)**, formerly called the European Economic Community. Initiated as the "Common Market" in 1958, the EU now comprises 15 Western European nations — France, Germany, Italy, Belgium, the Netherlands, Luxembourg, Denmark, Ireland, United Kingdom, Greece, Spain, Portugal, Austria, Finland, and Sweden.

GOALS   The original "Common Market" called for (1) gradual abolition of tariffs and import quotas on all products traded among the 12 participating nations; (2) establishment of a common system of tariffs applicable to all goods received from nations outside the EU; (3) free movement of capital and labour within the common market; and (4) creation of common policies with respect to other economic matters of joint concern, such as agriculture, transportation, and restrictive business practices. The EU has achieved most of these goals and is now a strong **trade bloc**.

RESULTS   Motives for creating the European Union were both political and economic. The main economic motive was freer trade for members. While it is difficult to determine how much of EU prosperity and growth has resulted from economic integration, integration has created the mass markets essential to EU industries. The economies of large-scale production have enabled European industries to achieve the lower costs denied them by small, localized markets.

Effects on nonmember nations, such as Canada, are less certain. On one hand, a peaceful and increasingly prosperous EU makes its member nations better customers for Canadian exports. On the other hand, Canadian and other nonmember firms encounter tariffs that make it difficult to compete against firms within the EU trade bloc. For example, before the establishment of the EU, North American, German, and French automobile manufacturers all faced the same tariff selling their products in, say, Belgium. However, with the establishment of internal trading among EU members, Belgium tariffs on German Volkswagens and French Renaults fell to zero, but an external tariff still applies to North American Chevrolets and Fords. This puts North American automobile firms at a serious disadvantage. Similarly, EU trade restrictions hamper Eastern European exports of metals, textiles, and farm products, goods that the Eastern Europeans produce in abundance.

By giving preferences to other countries within their free-trade zone, trade blocs such as the EU may reduce their trade with nonbloc members. Thus, the world loses some of the benefits of a completely open global trading system. Eliminating this disadvantage has been one of the motivations for promoting freer global trade through GATT.

NORTH AMERICAN FREE TRADE AGREEMENT

In 1993 Canada, Mexico, and the United States formed a trade bloc. The **North American Free Trade Agreement (NAFTA)** established a free-trade zone having about the same combined output as the EU, but a much larger geographical area. A

1989 free-trade agreement between Canada and the United States — the **Canada-U.S. Free Trade Agreement (FTA)** — preceded NAFTA. Through the FTA Canadian producers have gained increased access to a market ten times the size of Canada; Canadian consumers have gained the advantage of lower-price American goods. But eliminating tariffs has also helped American producers and consumers. Because Canada and the United States are each other's largest trade partners, there have been large gains for both countries from the Canadian-United States accord. When fully implemented in 1999, the agreement is expected to generate $1 billion to $3 billion of annual gains for each nation.

Free trade with Mexico is more controversial in Canada than is free trade with the United States. NAFTA will eliminate tariffs and other trade barriers between Mexico and Canada and the United States over a 15-year period. Critics of the agreement fear a loss of Canadian jobs as firms move to Mexico to take advantage of lower wages and less stringent regulations on pollution and workplace safety. These detractors also are concerned that Japan and South Korea will build plants in Mexico to transport goods duty-free to Canada, further hurting Canadian firms and workers.

Defenders of NAFTA reject these concerns and cite several strong arguments in its favour.

1. Specialization according to comparative advantage will enable Canada to obtain more total output from its scarce resources.
2. The reduction of high Mexican tariffs will increase Canadian exports to Mexico.
3. This free-trade zone will encourage worldwide investment in Mexico, enhancing Mexican productivity and national income. Mexican consumers will use some of that increased income to buy Canadian exports.
4. A higher standard of living in Mexico will enable Mexico to afford more pollution-control equipment and to provide safer workplaces.
5. The loss of specific Canadian jobs to Mexico may have occurred anyway to low-wage countries such as South Korea, Taiwan, and Hong Kong. NAFTA will enable and encourage Canadian firms to be more efficient, enhancing their long-term competitiveness with firms in Japan and the European Union.

It may appear that the world's nations are combining into potentially hostile trade blocs. But NAFTA constitutes a vehicle to negotiate reductions in trade barriers with the EU, Japan, and other trading countries. Access to the vast North American market is as important to the EU and Japan as is access to their markets by Canada, the United States, and Mexico. NAFTA gives Canada a lever in future trade negotiations with the EU and Japan. Conceivably, direct negotiations between NAFTA and the EU could eventually link the two free-trade zones. Japan and other major trading nations, not wishing to be left out of the world's wealthiest trade markets, would be forced to eliminate their high trade barriers — to open their domestic markets to additional imports. Nor do other nations and trade blocs want to be excluded from North America. Example:

1. APEC In late 1994 Canada and 17 other members of the Asia-Pacific Economic Cooperation (APEC) nations agreed to establish freer trade and more open investment over the next few decades. APEC nations are Australia, Brunei, Canada, Chile, Hong Kong, Indonesia, Japan, Malaysia, Mexico, New Zealand, the Philippines, Papua New Guinea, Singapore, South Korea, Taiwan, Thailand, and the United States.

2. ADMISSION OF CHILE INTO NAFTA At the invitation of Canada, Mexico, and the United States, Chile has agreed to become the fourth partner in NAFTA (see Box 6-3).

3. MERCOSUR The free-trade area encompassing Brazil, Argentina, Uruguay, and Paraguay — called *Mercosur* — is interested in linking up with NAFTA. So are other South American countries. In late 1994 the Canadian prime minister and 33 other prime ministers and presidents of Western hemisphere nations agreed to begin negotiations on a free-trade area from "Alaska to Argentina."

Economists agree that the *ideal* free-trade area would be the world. **(Key Question 10)**

QUICK REVIEW 6-3

1. Governments promote exports and reduce imports through tariffs, quotas, nontariff barriers, and export subsidies.

2. The various "rounds" of the General Agreement on Tariffs and Trade (GATT) have established multinational reductions in tariffs and import quotas among the more than 120 member nations.

3. The Uruguay Round of GATT that went into effect in 1995: **a** reduced tariffs worldwide; **b** liberalized rules impeding barriers to trade in services; **c** reduced agricultural subsidies; **d** created new protections for intellectual property; **e** phased out quotas on textiles and apparel, and **f** set up the World Trade Organization.

4. The European Union (EU), the Canada-U.S. Free Trade Agreement (FTA), and the North American Free Trade Agreement (NAFTA) have reduced trade barriers by establishing large free-trade zones.

CAN CANADIAN FIRMS COMPETE?

Freer international trade has brought with it intense competition in a number of product markets in Canada and worldwide. Not many decades ago three large domestic producers dominated our automobile industry. Imported autos were an oddity that accounted for a minuscule portion of the market. But General Motors, Ford, and Chrysler now face intense competition as they struggle for market shares with Nissan, Honda, Toyota, Hyundai, BMW, and others. Similarly, imports have gained major market shares in automobile tires, clothing, sporting goods, electronics, motorcycles, outboard motors, and toys.

Nevertheless, thousands of firms — large and small — have thrived and prospered in the global marketplace. Northern Telecom, Bombardier, and MacMillan-Bloedel are just a few cases in point. These and many other firms have continued to retain high market shares at home and have expanded their sales broad. Of course, not all firms have been so successful. Some corporations simply have not been able to compete; their international competitors make better quality products, have lower production costs, or both. Not surprisingly, the Canadian firms that have been most vulnerable to foreign competition are precisely those that have enjoyed long periods of trade protection via tariffs and quotas. These barriers to imports have artificially limited competition, greatly dampening incentives to innovate, reduce costs, and improve products. Also, trade barriers have shielded some domestic firms from the usual consequences of national shifts in comparative advantages over time. As trade protection declines under GATT and NAFTA, some Canadian firms will surely discover that they are producing goods for which Canada clearly has a comparative *dis*advantage (apparel, for example).

Is the greater competition accompanying the global economy a good thing? Although some domestic producers and their workers do not like it, foreign competition benefits consumers. Imports reduce product prices and provide consumers with a greater variety of goods. Foreign competition also forces domestic producers to become more efficient and to improve product quality — precisely the outcome in several Canadian industries, including autos and steel. Evidence shows that most — clearly not all — Canadian firms *can* and *do* compete successfully in the global economy.

What about Canadian firms that cannot successfully compete in open markets? The harsh reality is that they should go out of business, much like an unsuccessful corner boutique. Persistent economic losses mean valuable scarce resources are not being used efficiently. Shifting these resources to alternative, profitable, uses will increase the total value of Canadian output.

CHAPTER SUMMARY

1. International trade is growing in importance globally and for Canada. World trade is vital to Canada in two respects. **a** Canadian imports and exports as a percentage of national output are significant. **b** Canada is completely dependent on trade for certain commodities and materials that cannot be obtained domestically.

2. Our principal exports include automotive products, machinery and equipment, and grain; our major imports are general machinery and equipment, automobiles, and industrial goods and machinery. Quantitatively, the United States is our most important trading partner.

3. Global trade has been greatly facilitated by **a** improvements in transportation technology; **b** improvements in communications technology; **c** general declines in tariffs; and **d** peaceful relations among major industrial nations. Canada and the United States, Japan, and the Western European nations dominate the global economy. But the total volume of trade has been increased by several new trade participants, including the "Asian tigers" (Hong Kong, Singapore, South Korea, and Taiwan), China, the Eastern European countries, and the newly independent countries of the former Soviet Union.

4. The "open economy" circular flow model connects the domestic Canadian economy to the "Rest of the World." Customers from abroad enter our product market to buy some of our output. These Canadian exports create business revenues and generate income in Canada. Canadian households spend some of their money income on products made abroad and imported to Canada.

5. Specialization according to comparative advantage permits nations to achieve higher standards of living through exchange with other countries. A trading partner should specialize in products and services where its domestic opportunity costs are lowest. The terms of trade must be such that both nations can get more of a particular output via trade than they can at home.

6. The foreign exchange market sets exchange rates between nations' currencies. Foreign importers are suppliers of their currencies and Canadian exporters are demanders of foreign currencies. The resulting equilibrium exchange rates link the price levels of all nations. Depreciation of the dollar reduces our imports and increases our exports, dollar appreciation increases our imports and reduces our exports.

7. Governments shape trade flows through **a** protective tariffs; **b** quotas; **c** nontariff barriers; and **d** export subsidies. These are impediments to free trade; they result from misunderstanding about the gains from trade and from political considerations. By driving up product prices, trade barriers cost Canadian consumers billions of dollars annually.

8. The post-World War period has seen a trend towards lower Canadian tariffs. In 1947 the General Agreement on Tariffs and Trade (GATT) was formed to **a** encourage nondiscriminatory treatment for all trading nations; **b** reduce tariffs; and **c** eliminate import quotas.

9. The Uruguay Round of GATT negotiations, completed in 1993: **a** reduced tariffs; **b** liberalized trade in services; **c** reduced agricultural subsidies; **d** reduced pirating of intellectual property; **e** phased out import quotas on textiles and apparel; and **f** established the World Trade Organization, which replaces GATT.

10. Free-trade zones (trade blocs) may liberalize trade within regions but may also impede trade with nonbloc members. Three examples of free-trade arrangements are **a** the European Union (EU), formerly the European Community or "Common Market"; **b** the Canada-U.S. Free Trade Agreement (FTA); and **c** the North American Free Trade Agreement (NAFTA), comprising Canada, Mexico, and the United States, and later, Chile.

11. The global economy has created intense foreign competition in many Canadian product markets.

TERMS AND CONCEPTS

absolute advantage (p. 100)
appreciation (p. 104)
"Asian tigers" (p. 97)
Canada-U.S. Free Trade Agreement (FTA)
　(p. 111)
comparative advantage (p. 101)
depreciation (p. 104)
European Union (EU) (p. 110)
export subsidies (p. 105)
foreign exchange market (p. 103)

General Agreement on Tariffs and Trade (GATT) (p. 108)
import quotas (p. 105)
most-favoured-nation clauses (p. 108)
multinational corporations (p. 97)
nontariff barriers (p. 105)
North American Free Trade Agreement (NAFTA)
　(p. 110)
protective tariffs (p. 105)
terms of trade (p. 102)
trade bloc (p. 110)

QUESTIONS AND STUDY SUGGESTIONS

1. What is the quantitative importance of world trade to Canada? Who is quantitatively Canada's most important trade partner? How can persistent trade deficits be financed? "Trade deficits mean we get more merchandise from the rest of the world than we provide them in return. Therefore, trade deficits are economically desirable." Do you agree?

2. Account for the rapid growth of world trade since World War II. Who are the major players in international trade? Who are the "Asian tigers" and how important are they in world trade?

3. **Key Question**　*Use the circular flow model (Figure 6-5) to explain how an increase in exports would affect revenues of domestic firms, money income of domestic households, and imports from abroad. Use Figure 6-3 to find the amounts (1994) of Canada's exports (flow 13) and imports (flow 16) in the circular flow model. What do these amounts imply for flows 14 and 15?*

4. **Key Question**　*The following are production possibilities tables for South Korea and Canada. Assume that before specialization and trade the optimal product mix for South Korea is alternative B and for Canada alternative D.*

Product	South Korea's production alternatives					
	A	B	C	D	E	F
Radios (in thousands)	30	24	18	12	6	0
Chemicals (in tonnes)	0	6	12	18	24	30

Product	Canada's production alternatives					
	A	B	C	D	E	F
Radios (in thousands)	10	8	6	4	2	0
Chemicals (in tonnes)	0	4	8	12	16	20

　　a. *Are comparative-cost conditions such that the two areas should specialize? If so, what product should each produce?*

　　b. *What is the total gain in radio and chemical output that results from this specialization?*

c. *What are the limits of the terms of trade? Suppose actual terms of trade are 1 unit of radios for 1 1/2 units of chemicals and that 4 units of radios are exchanged for 6 units of chemicals. What are the gains from specialization and trade for each area?*

d. *Can you conclude from this illustration that specialization according to comparative advantage results in more efficient use of world resources? Explain.*

5. Suppose that the comparative-cost ratios of two products — baby formula and tuna fish — are as follows in the hypothetical nations of Canswicki and Tunata.

   Canswicki: 1 can baby formula = 2 cans tuna fish

   Tunata: 1 can baby formula = 4 cans tuna fish

   In what product should each nation specialize? Explain why terms of trade of 1 can baby formula = 2 1/2 cans tuna fish would be acceptable to both nations.

6. **Key Question** *"Our exports create a demand for foreign currencies; foreign imports of our goods generate supplies of foreign currencies." Do you agree? Other things being equal, would a decline in Canadian incomes or a weakening of Canadian preferences for foreign products cause the dollar to depreciate or appreciate? What would be the effects of that depreciation or appreciation on our exports and imports?*

7. If the French franc declines in value (depreciates) in the foreign exchange market, will it be easier or harder for the French to sell their wine in Canada? If you were planning a trip to Paris, how would the depreciation of the franc change the dollar price of this trip?

8. True or false? "An increase in the Canadian dollar price of the German mark implies that the German mark has depreciated in value." Explain.

9. What tools do governments use to promote exports and restrict imports? What are the benefits and the costs of protectionist policies? What is the net outcome for consumers?

10. **Key Question** *What is GATT? How does it affect nearly every person in the world? What were the major outcomes of the Uruguay Round of GATT? How is GATT related to the European Union (EU), the Canada-U.S. Free Trade Agreement (FTA), and the North American Free Trade Agreement (NAFTA)?*

11. Explain: "Free trade zones such as the EU and NAFTA lead a double life: They can promote free trade among members, but pose serious trade obstacles for nonmembers." Do you think the net effects of these trade blocs are good or bad for world trade?

12. Do you think Canadian firms will be able to compete with foreign firms in world trade during the next 20 years? What do you see as the competitive strengths of Canadian firms? Competitive weaknesses? Explain: "Even if Japan captured the entire worldwide auto market, that simply would mean that Japan would have to buy a whole lot of other products from abroad. Thus, Canada and other industrial nations would necessarily experience an increase in exports to Japan."

13. (Applying the Theory) What point is Bastiat trying to make with his petition of the candlemakers?

NATIONAL INCOME, EMPLOYMENT, AND FISCAL POLICY

CHAPTER 7

MEASURING DOMESTIC OUTPUT, NATIONAL INCOME, AND THE PRICE LEVEL

Disposable Income Flat"; "Personal Consumption Surges"; "Domestic Investment Stagnates"; "Japan Suffers GDP Decline"; "GDP Deflator Rises Less Rapidly Than CPI" — typical headlines in the business and economics news, and gibberish unless you know the language of macroeconomics and national income accounting. This chapter will help you learn this language and understand the ideas it communicates.

There are two substantial payoffs from carefully studying this chapter. One is an understanding of how government statisticians and accountants measure and record the levels of domestic output, national income, and prices for an economy. Second, knowledge of the terms and ideas examined in this chapter — for example,

consumption, investment, government purchases, net exports, real GDP, national income, and the price level — will help you comprehend material in subsequent chapters.

In this chapter we will first explain why it is important to measure the performance of the economy. Second, we define the key measure of total output — gross domestic product (GDP) — and show how it is measured. We then derive and explain several other important measures of output and income. Next, measurement of the overall level of prices — the price level — is examined. We then demonstrate how GDP is adjusted for inflation or deflation so that changes in the physical amount of a nation's production are more accurately reflected. Finally, some limitations of the measures of domestic output and national income are listed and explained.

BOX 7-1   THE BIG PICTURE

You are about to embark on the study of macroeconomics — the study of the whole economy (the aggregation of individual markets) and its major components. You would be well advised to review Chapter 2, particularly the production possibility curve and what it represents: the economizing problem, brought about by scarcity of resources in relation to our wants, and thus the necessity of making choices. Macroeconomics in its broadest sense is concerned with understanding how the overall economy works so we can devise effective macroeconomic policies. In the short to medium term these policies aim to get the most out of available resources (getting on the production possibility curve) and in the long run they aim to promote the growth of the economy's productive capacity. These goals should be achieved with stable prices, equitable distribution of income, and a long-run balance in our international trade and financial transactions. This chapter deals with measurement of the output and the price level of the economy.

As you read this chapter, keep the following points in mind:
- We need a way to measure the output performance of the economy to determine how well or badly it is doing. The output of the economy is measured in dollars and the time period is one year.
- We can measure what is produced in a given year either by adding up all the expenditures during that year, or all the income earned by the factors of production (land, labour, capital, and entrepreneurial talent) in producing total output.
- The fluctuation of the value of money makes it necessary to have a measurement for that change. Inflation and disinflation measure, respectively, a general increase and a general decrease in the price level of all goods.
- If we know the amount by which the value of money has changed, it is easier to get a true measure of what is produced in an economy in a given year.

MACROECONOMIC MEASUREMENT

Our first goal is to explain the ways the overall production performance of the economy is measured. This comes under the heading of national income accounting, which does for the economy as a whole what private accounting does for the individual business enterprise or, for that matter, for the household. The business executive must know how well his or her firm is doing, but that is not always immediately discernible.

A firm measures its flows of income and expenditures to assess its operations, usually for a three-month period or for the current year. With this information in hand the firm can gauge its economic health. If things are going well, the accounting data can be used to explain this success. Costs might be down or output or prices up, resulting in large profits. If things are going badly, accounting measures can help discover why. And by examining the accounts over a specific period, the firm can detect growth or decline of profits and what caused the change. All this information helps the firm's managers make intelligent business decisions.

National income accounting operates in much the same way for the economy.

1. It allows us to keep a finger on the economic pulse of the nation. Our national income accounting system permits us to measure the level of production in the economy at some point in time and explain why it is at that level.
2. By comparing national income accounts over a number of years, we can track the long-run course of the economy and see whether it has grown, been steady, or stagnated.
3. Information supplied by national income accounts provides a basis for formulating and applying public policies to improve the performance of the economy. Without national income accounts, economic policy would be based on guesswork. *National income accounting allows us to keep tabs on the health of the economy and formulate policies that will maintain and improve that health.*

What are the accounting measures?

GROSS DOMESTIC PRODUCT

There are many measures of the economic well-being of society. But the best available indicator of an economy's health is its annual total output of goods and services or, as it is sometimes called, the economy's aggregate output. There are two closely related basic national income accounting measures of the total output of goods and services: gross national product and gross domestic product. Both measure *the total market value of all final goods and services produced in the economy in one year.* The difference is in how the "economy" is defined.

Gross national product (GNP) consists of the total output produced by land, labour, capital, and entrepreneurial talent supplied by Canadians, whether these resources are located in Canada or abroad. For example, the share of output (income) produced by a Canadian working in France or Saudi Arabia is included in our GNP. Conversely, the share of output (income) produced in Canada by foreign-owned resources is excluded from our GNP.

Alternatively, **gross domestic product** (GDP) includes the value of the total goods and services produced within the boundaries of Canada whether by Canadians or foreign-supplied resources. For instance, the full value of the autos produced at a Japanese-owned Honda factory in Canada, including profits, is a part of Canadian GDP. Conversely, profits earned by a Canadian-owned IBM plant in France are excluded from our GDP.

Specifically, the difference between GNP and GDP is that the former measures output of Canadians and Canadian-owned firms wherever they may be in the world, whereas GDP measures what is produced within our borders. In Canada many foreign firms, particularly American, have established subsidiaries. And there are many more foreign-owned firms in Canada than Canadian-owned firms abroad. This means that in Canada GDP is usually

larger than GNP. We arrive at this difference by subtracting payments of factor (resource) income to the rest of the world from receipts of factor income earned abroad (*net investment income from non-residents*). As you can see below, in 1994 net investment income from non-residents was –$26.272 billion, meaning foreign-owned firms produced more in Canada than Canadian-owned firms did abroad.

	Billions
Gross domestic product at market prices	$750.053
Net investment income from non-residents	–26.272
Gross national product at market prices	$723.781

Most nations, including Canada, use GDP as the measure of their output. That's why we will focus on GDP. **(Key Question 2)**

A MONETARY MEASURE

If the economy produces 3 pears and 2 plums in year 1 and 2 pears and 3 plums in year 2, in which year is output greater? There is no answer to this question until price tags are attached to the various products as indicators of society's evaluation of their relative worth.

That's what GDP does. It measures the market value of annual output. GDP is a monetary measure. Indeed it must be if we are to compare the various collections of goods and services produced in different years.

In Table 7-1, we assume that the money price of the pears is 20¢ and the price of plums is 30¢. Year 2's output is greater than that of year 1's, because society values year 2's output more highly; it is willing to pay 10¢ more for the collection of goods produced in year 2 than that produced in year 1.

TABLE 7-1 Comparing output of different products using money prices

Year	Annual outputs	Market value
1	3 pears + 2 plums	3 at 20¢ + 2 at 30¢ = $1.20
2	2 pears + 3 plums	2 at 20¢ + 3 at 30¢ = $1.30

AVOIDING DOUBLE COUNTING

To measure total output accurately, all goods and services produced in any specific year must be counted only once. Most products go through a series of production stages before reaching a market. As a result, parts of components of most products are bought and sold many times. Hence, to avoid counting several times the parts of products that are sold and resold, GDP includes only the market value of final goods and ignores transactions involving intermediate goods.

By **final goods** we mean goods and services purchased for final use and not for resale or further processing or manufacturing. They are *"purchases not resold."* Transactions involving **intermediate goods** refer to purchases of goods and services for further processing and manufacturing or for resale.

The sale of *final goods is included* and the sale of *intermediate goods is excluded* from GDP because the value of final goods already includes all the intermediate transactions involved in producing those final goods. To count intermediate transactions separately would be **double counting** and exaggerate the value of GDP.

To clarify this, suppose there are five stages of production in getting a suit manufactured and into the hands of a consumer — the ultimate or final user. As Table 7-2 indicates, firm A, a sheep ranch, provides $120 worth of wool to firm B, a wool processor. Firm A pays out the $120 it receives in wages, rents, interest, and profits. Firm B processes the wool and sells it to firm C, a suit manufacturer, for $180. What does firm B do with this $180? As noted, $120 goes to firm A, and the remaining $60 is used by B to pay wages, rents, interest, and profits for the resources needed in processing the wool. And so it goes. The manufacturer sells the suit to firm D, a clothing wholesaler, who in turn sells it to firm E, a retailer, and then at last it is bought for $350 by a consumer, the final user.

At each stage the difference between what a firm paid for the product and what it receives for its sale is paid out as wages, rent, interest, and profits for the resources used by that firm in helping to produce and distribute the suit.

How much should we include in GDP in accounting for the production of this suit? Just $350, the value of the final product, because this figure includes all the intermediate transactions leading up to the product's final sale. It would be a gross distortion to sum all the intermediate sales figures and the final sales value of the product in column 2 and include the entire amount, $1140, in GDP. This would be double counting — counting the final product *and* the sale and resale of its various parts in the multi-stage production process. The production and sale of the suit has generated $350, *not* $1140, worth of output and income.

TABLE 7-2   Value added in a five-stage production process

(1) Stage of production	(2) Sales value of materials or product	(3) Value-added
	0	
		$120 (= $120 – $ 0)
Firm A, sheep ranch	$120	
		60 (= 180 – 120)
Firm B, wool processor	180	
		40 (= 220 – 180)
Firm C, suit manufacturer	220	
		50 (= 270 – 220)
Firm D, clothing wholesaler	270	
		80 (= 350 – 270)
Firm E, retail clothier	350	
Total sales values	$1140	
Value-added (total income)		$350

To avoid double counting, national income accountants are careful to calculate only the value added by each firm. **Value added** is the market value of a firm's output *less* the value of the inputs that it has purchased from others. In column 3 of Table 7-2 the value added of Firm B is $60, the difference between the $180 value of its output and the $120 it paid for the inputs provided by Firm A. By adding together the values-added by the five firms in Table 7-2, the total value of the suit can be determined. Similarly, by calculating and summing the values added by all firms in the economy, we can determine the GDP — the market value of total output.

GDP EXCLUDES NONPRODUCTION TRANSACTIONS

GDP measures the annual production of the economy. The many nonproduction transactions must be excluded. *Nonproduction transactions* are of two major types: (1) purely financial transactions, and (2) second-hand sales.

FINANCIAL TRANSACTIONS Purely financial transactions are of three general kinds.

1. PUBLIC TRANSFER PAYMENTS These are social insurance payments, welfare payments, and veterans' benefits that government makes to particular households. The basic characteristic of these payments is that recipients make no contributions to *current* production in return for them. To include them in GDP would be to overstate the year's production.

2. PRIVATE TRANSFER PAYMENTS These payments, for example, a university student's monthly subsidy from home or an occasional gift from a wealthy relative, do not entail production but simply the transfer of funds from one private individual to another.

3. SECURITY TRANSACTIONS Buying and selling of stocks and bonds are also excluded from GDP. Stock-market transactions involve merely the swapping of paper assets. As such, these transactions do not directly create current production. Only the services provided by the security broker, represented by a commission, are included in GDP.

SECOND-HAND SALES Second-hand sales are excluded from GDP because they either reflect no current production, or involve double counting. If you sell your used Ford to a friend, this transaction would be excluded in determining GDP because no current production is involved. The inclusion of the sales of goods produced some years ago in this year's GDP would be an exaggeration of this year's output.

TWO SIDES TO GDP: SPENDING AND INCOME

There are two ways of measuring GDP. One is to add up all the expenditures involved in taking that total output off the market. This is called the **expenditure approach**. The other is to add up all the income earned by the factors of production in producing the GDP. This is called the **income approach** to the determination of GDP. *GDP can be calculated either by adding up all that is spent to buy this year's total output or by summing all the incomes from the production of this year's output.* Putting this as an equation, we can say

$$\left. \begin{array}{c} \text{the amount spent} \\ \text{to buy this year's} \\ \text{total output} \end{array} \right\} = \left\{ \begin{array}{c} \text{the money} \\ \text{income earned} \\ \text{from the produc-} \\ \text{tion of this year's} \\ \text{output} \end{array} \right.$$

This is more than an equation; it is an identity. Buying (spending money) and selling (receiving money income) are actually two aspects of the same transaction. **What is spent on a product is income to those who have contributed their resources in getting that product produced and to market.**

For the economy as a whole we can expand our identity to read as in Figure 7-1. Considered as output, all final goods produced in the Canadian economy are purchased by the three domestic sectors — households, government, and business — and by foreign buyers. On the income side of GDP, this figure shows that (aside from two nonincome allocations, discussed later) the total receipts businesses acquire from the sales of total output are allocated among the various resource suppliers as wage, rent, interest, and profit income. Using this diagram as a point of reference, we next examine the types of expenditures and the incomes derived from these expenditures.

FIGURE 7-1 The expenditures and income approaches to GDP

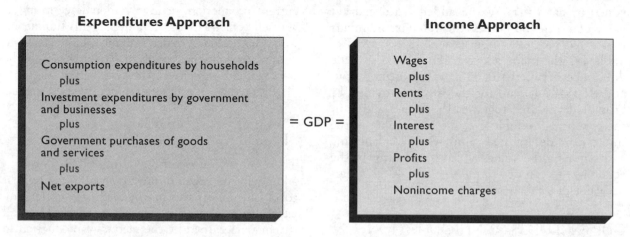

There are two general approaches to measuring gross domestic product. We can determine the value of output by summing the expenditures on that output. Alternatively, with some modifications, we can determine GDP by adding up the components of income arising from the production of that output.

EXPENDITURE APPROACH

To determine GDP through expenditures, we add up all types of spending on finished or final goods and services. But national income accountants have more sophisticated terms for the different types of spending than the ones we have used in Figure 7-1. There are four categories of expenditures.

PERSONAL CONSUMPTION EXPENDITURE (C)

What we have called "consumption expenditure by households" is "**personal expenditure on consumer goods and services**" to the national income accountants. It entails expenditure by households on *durable consumer goods* (automobiles, refrigerators, video cassette recorders, and so forth), *semi-durable consumer goods* (shirts, suits, socks, shoes), *nondurable consumer goods* (bread, milk, vitamins, pencils, toothpaste), and *consumer expenditures for services* (of lawyers, doctors, mechanics, barbers). We will use C to designate the total of this expenditure.

GROSS INVESTMENT (I_g)

This refers to all investment spending by Canadian governments and business firms. It includes:

1. All final purchases of machinery, equipment, and tools by governments and businesses

2. All construction
3. Changes in inventories.

This more than we have meant by "investment" thus far. We therefore must explain why each of these three items is included under the general heading of **gross investment** or, alternatively, **gross capital formation**.

The first group restates our definition of investment spending as the purchase of tools, machinery, and equipment.

The second — all construction such as building a new factory, warehouse, or grain elevator — is also a form of investment. But why include residential construction as investment rather than consumption? Because apartment buildings are investment goods that, like factories and grain elevators, are income-earning assets. Other residential units that are rented are for the same reason investment goods. Owner-occupied houses are investment goods because they could be rented out to yield a money income return, even though the owner does not choose to do so. For these reasons, all residential construction is considered as investment.

Finally, changes in inventories are counted as investment because an increase in inventories is, in effect, "unconsumed output." And that is precisely what investment is!

INVENTORY CHANGES AS INVESTMENT
Since GDP measures total current output, we must include in GDP any products produced this year even though *not sold* this year. To be an accurate measure of total production, GDP must include the market value of any additions to inventories accruing during the year. A tube of lipstick produced in 1996 must be counted as GDP in 1996, even though it remains unsold as of February 1997. If businesses have more goods on their shelves and in their warehouses at the end of the year than they had at the start, the economy has produced more than it has consumed during this particular year. This increase in inventories must be added to GDP as a measure of *current* production.

A decline in inventories must be subtracted in calculating GDP. The economy can sell a total output that exceeds its current production by dipping into and thus reducing its inventories. The tube of lipstick produced in 1996 but sold in 1997 cannot be counted as 1997 GDP. A decline in inventories in any specific year means that the economy has purchased more than it has produced during that year. Society has used up all of this year's output plus some of the inventories inherited from the previous year's production. Since GDP is a measure of the *current* year's output, we must omit any using up of past production, that is, any drawing down of inventories, determining GDP.[1] When referring to gross investment with changes in inventory excluded (that is, net of inventory change), the phrase used is gross *fixed* capital formation.

NONINVESTMENT TRANSACTIONS Investment does *not* refer to the transfer of paper assets or secondhand tangible assets. Economists exclude the buying of stocks and bonds from their definition of investment because such purchases merely transfer the ownership of existing assets. It's the same for the resale of existing assets.

---

[1] Both *planned* and *unplanned* changes in inventories are included as a part of investment. In the former instance firms may intentionally increase their inventories because aggregate sales are growing. In the latter case an unexpected drop in sales may cause firms to have more unsold goods (larger inventories) than they intended.

GROSS VERSUS NET INVESTMENT *Gross capital formation* or *gross investment* includes the production of all investment goods — those that are to replace the machinery, equipment, and buildings used up to produce the current year's output *plus* any net additions to the economy's stock of capital. Gross investment includes both replacement and added investment. **Net investment** refers only to the added investment that has occurred in the current year.

In 1994 our economy produced $125.250 billion of capital goods. However, in producing the GDP in 1994, the economy used up $92.973 billion of machinery and equipment. As a result, our economy added $32.277 billion (125.250 – 92.973) to its stock of capital in 1994. *Gross* investment was $125.250 billion in 1994, *net* investment was only $32.277 billion. The difference is the value of the capital used up or depreciated in the production of 1994's GDP. The capital used up (the **depreciation**) is referred to as the **capital consumption allowances**.

NET INVESTMENT AND ECONOMIC GROWTH
The relationship between gross investment and depreciation — the amount of the nation's capital worn out or used up in a particular year — indicates whether our economy is expanding, static, or declining. Figure 7-2 illustrates these cases.

1. EXPANDING ECONOMY When gross investment exceeds depreciation, as in Figure 7-2(a), the economy is expanding. Its productive capacity — as measured by its stock of capital goods — is growing. Net investment is a positive figure in an expanding economy. For example, in 1994 gross investment was $125.250 billion, and $92.973 billion of capital goods were consumed in producing that year's GDP. This meant that our economy ended 1994 with $32.277 billion more capital goods than it had on hand at the start of the year. We added $32.277 billion to our "national factory" in 1994.

Increasing the supply of capital goods is a basic means of expanding the productive capacity of the economy (Chapter 2).

2. STATIC ECONOMY In a stationary or static economy gross investment and depreciation are equal. This means the economy is standing still. It is producing just enough capital to replace what is consumed in producing the year's output — no more and no less. This happened in 1942, during World War II. Private

FIGURE 7-2

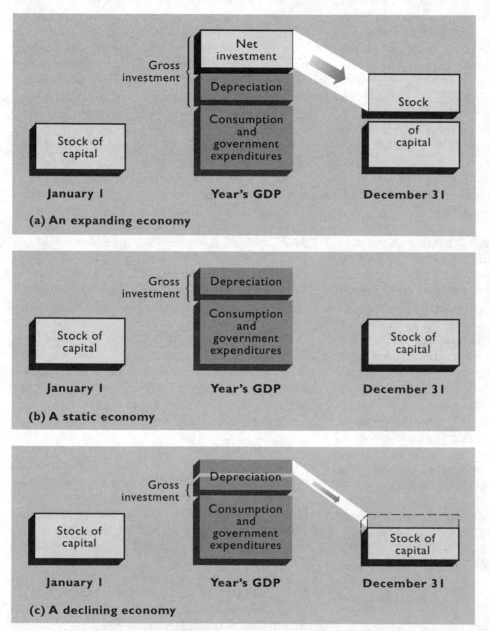

In an expanding economy (a), gross investment exceeds depreciation, which means that the economy is making a net addition to its stock of capital facilities. In a static economy (b), gross investment precisely replaces the capital facilities depreciated in producing the year's output, leaving the stock of capital goods unchanged. In a declining economy (c), gross investment is insufficient to replace the capital goods depreciated by the year's production. As a result, the economy's stock of capital declines.

investment was purposely restricted by governmental action to free resources to produce war goods. These war goods were consumed or used up and thus did not add to the nation's stock of capital. In 1942 gross investment and depreciation were approximately equal to $1.2 billion, thus net investment was almost zero. At the end of 1942 our stock of capital was roughly the same as at the start of that year. Figure 7-2(b) represents the case of a static economy.

3. DECLINING ECONOMY An economy declines when gross investment is less than depreciation. The economy uses up more capital in a year than it produces. When this happens net investment will be negative — the economy will be *disinvesting*. Depressions foster such circumstances. When production and employment are low, the nation has a greater productive capacity than it is currently using. There is no incentive to replace depreciated capital equipment, much less add to the existing stock. Depreciation is likely to exceed gross investment, with the result that the nation's stock of capital is less at the end of the year than it was at the start.

This was the case during the Great Depression. In 1933, for example, gross investment was only $208 million, while the capital consumed during that year was $532 million. Net disinvestment was therefore $324 million, indicating that the size of our "national factory" shrank during that year. Figure 7-2(c) illustrates the case of a disinvesting, or declining, economy.

We will use I to refer to investment spending and attach the subscript g when referring to gross and n when referring to net investment. **(Key Question 5)**

GOVERNMENT CURRENT PURCHASES (G)

Government purchases *include* all current government spending (federal, provincial, and local) on finished products and all direct purchases of resources — labour in particular. It *excludes* (1) all government outlay on new nondefence durable assets (which are included in I) and (2) all government transfer payments, because transfer payments do not reflect any current production. We'll use G to indicate **government purchases**.

NET EXPORTS (X_n)

Spending by people abroad on Canadian goods and services accounts for Canadian output just as does spending by Canadians. Thus we add the value of Canadian exports in calculating GDP by the expenditures approach. However, you should note that a portion of consumption, investment, and government purchases is for imports, meaning goods and services produced abroad. This spending does *not* reflect production in Canada. The value of imports is subtracted to avoid an overstatement of total production in Canada.

Rather than treat Canadian exports and imports separately, our national income accounts take the difference between them. Thus, *net exports of goods and services*, or **net exports**, *is the amount by which foreign spending on Canadian goods and services exceeds Canadian spending on foreign goods and services.*

For example, if people abroad buy $100 billion worth of Canadian exports and Canadians buy $98 billion worth of foreign imports in a year, net exports would be *plus* $2 billion. Net exports might result in a negative figure. If the rest of the world spends $100 billion on Canadian exports and Canadians spend $105 billion on foreign imports, our "excess" of spending on imports over earnings from export sales is $5 billion. Thus, net exports are *minus* $5 billion. Note in

Table 7-3 that in 1994 Canadians spent $5.615 billion less on foreign goods and services than the rest of the world spent on Canadian goods and services.

The letter X_n will designate net exports.

TOTAL EXPENDITURES

These four categories of expenditures — personal consumption expenditure (C), gross capital formation (I_g), government current purchases of goods and services (G), and exports (X_n) — are comprehensive. They include all possible types of spending. Added together, they measure the market value of the year's output or the GDP. That is,

$$C + I_g + G + X_n = GDP$$

For 1994, in billions (Table 7-3):

$$\$452.9 + \$125.3 + \$167.5 + 5.6 + (\$-1.2)^* = 750.1$$

Global Perspective 7-1 compares GDPs for selected nations.

GLOBAL PERSPECTIVE 7-1

Comparative GDPs in trillions of U.S. dollars

Canada has the world's seventh highest GDP. These GDP data have been converted to dollars via international exchange rates.

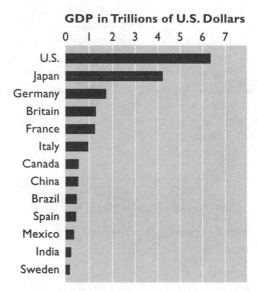

GDP in Trillions of U.S. Dollars

Source: International Monetary Fund data.

_____

* Statistical discrepancy. For an explanation see page 129.

THE INCOME APPROACH[2]

How was this $750.1 billion of expenditures allocated or distributed as income? The second method of measuring GDP — called the **income** or **factor payment** (cost) approach — answers this question. This method divides income flows into wages, rent, interest, and profits.

It would be simple if we could say that the total expenditures made in purchasing the economy's annual output flowed to households as wage, rent, interest, and profit incomes. The picture is complicated by two *nonincome charges* against the value of total output (GDP). These will be dealt with at the end of the section. Let's first turn to the ways in which GDP expenditures are distributed as income.

There are five categories of factor income payments in our national accounts. These are (1) wages, salaries, and supplementary labour income, (2) corporate profits before taxes, (3) interest and miscellaneous investment income, (4) farmers' income, and (5) income of nonfarm unincorporated businesses.

WAGES, SALARIES, AND SUPPLEMENTARY LABOUR INCOME

This largest income category is made up primarily of the wages and salaries paid by businesses and government to suppliers of labour. It also includes wage and salary supplements, in particular payments by employers of unemployment insurance premiums, workers' compensation premiums, and employer contributions to a variety of private and public pension and welfare funds for workers. These wage and salary supplements (or "fringe benefits") are a part of the employer's cost of obtaining labour and therefore are treated as a component of the firm's total wage payments.

CORPORATE PROFITS BEFORE TAXES

Corporate profits are distributed three ways.

1. A part is claimed by government as **corporate income taxes**.

2. A part of the remaining corporate profits is paid out to stockholders as **dividends**. Such payments flow to households, the ultimate owners of all corporations.
3. What remains of corporate profits is **undistributed corporate profits**. These retained corporate earnings, along with capital consumption allowances (see page 129), are invested in new plants and equipment, increasing the real assets and the income-generating capacity of the investing business.

INTEREST AND MISCELLANEOUS INVESTMENT INCOME

Interest refers to money income payments that flow from private businesses to the suppliers of money capital. It is the firm's cost of borrowing funds supplied to it by lenders (either individuals, other businesses, or governments). For reasons to be noted later, interest payments made by government and consumers are excluded from interest income. Miscellaneous investment income includes such smaller categories as royalties received by individuals.

FARMERS' INCOME

The net income of farmers includes the sales of farm products, plus the imputed value of farm output consumed by the farm family, plus the value of the physical change in farm inventories, less farm operating expenses and capital consumption allowances on farm buildings and equipment.

NET INCOME OF NONFARM UNINCORPORATED BUSINESS, INCLUDING RENT

This is the earnings of working proprietors from their own businesses, excluding farms and corporations. Like the previous category, this one represents a mixture of labour income and investment income that is impossible to segregate. Farm and nonfarm proprietors supplying their own capital earn profits (or losses), interest, and rents mixed in with their labour income. Rents cover the net income received by persons, other than farms and corporations, for the rental of property.

The last two categories represent factor of production payment: wages, rent, interest, and profits. A small business with one owner may supply her own labour, capital, and land, therefore it is not

---

[2] Some instructors may choose to omit this section, because the expenditures approach is more relevant for the analysis of Chapters 9 to 12.

easy to divide the income earned into the four conventional categories.

Note that since we want to measure current production, a small adjustment must be made that reflects changes in the price of inventories during the current year. Inventory prices are averaged out during the year rather than using end-of-the-year prices. Suppose a widget was produced in January, its price 1¢ at the time, and became part of inventory. If in December the price of a widget were 3¢, for national accounting purposes the average price, say 1.5¢, is used.

This adjustment is referred to as "inventory valuation adjustment."

When we add wages, salaries and supplementary labour income, corporate profits, interest and miscellaneous investment income, farmers' income, income of nonfarm unincorporated business, and make the appropriate inventory valuation adjustment, we get *net domestic income at factor costs* — all the income earned by Canadian-supplied resources. To arrive at GDP from net domestic income, we need to add two nonincome charges against the value of total output.

INDIRECT TAXES LESS SUBSIDIES

The first complicating nonincome charge arises because government levies certain taxes, **indirect taxes**, which business firms treat as costs of production and therefore add to the prices of the products they sell. Such taxes include the GST, provincial sales taxes, excise and property taxes, licence fees, and customs duties. Assume a firm produces a product priced at $1. Production of this item creates an equal amount of wages, rental, interest, and profit income. But now the federal government imposes a 7% Goods and Services Tax (GST) on most products. Retailers add this 7% to the price of the product, raising its price from $1 to $1.07.

This 7% of total receipts that reflects the tax (and additional provincial sales taxes) must be paid out to government before the remaining $1 can be paid to households as wage, rent, interest, and profit incomes. Furthermore, this flow of indirect taxes to government is not earned income, because government contributes nothing directly to the production of the good in return for these sales tax receipts. For this reason we exclude indirect taxes when calculating the total income earned in each year by the factors of production. Part of the value of the annual output reflects the indirect taxes that are passed along to consumers as higher product prices. This part of the value of the nation's output is *not* available as either wages, rent, interest, or profits.

Subsidies represent amounts contributed by governments toward current costs of production. Since their effect is to reduce prices below costs of production, they must be deducted from factor costs (corporate profits in particular) to arrive at GDP at market prices. Most of the subsidies are federal production and consumption subsidies, to encourage certain types of economic activity (some food production, railway passenger transportation, the CBC), and to lower prices to the consumer.

DEPRECIATION: CAPITAL CONSUMPTION ALLOWANCES

The second nonincome charge against total output is depreciation. The useful life of capital equipment extends far beyond the year of purchase. Actual expenditures for capital goods and their productive life are not synchronized in the same accounting period. In order to avoid a gross understatement of profit and total income in the year of purchase and overstatement of profit and of total income in succeeding years, individual businesses estimate the useful life of their capital goods and allocate the total cost of such goods over the life of the machinery. The annual charge that estimates the amount of capital equipment used up in each year's production is called "depreciation." Depreciation is essentially a bookkeeping entry designed to provide a more accurate statement of profit income, hence total income, provided by a firm in each year.

If profits and total income for the economy are to be stated accurately, a depreciation charge for the economy as a whole must be made against the total receipts of the business sector. This depreciation charge is called **capital consumption allowances**, the allowance for capital goods "consumed" in producing this year's GDP. This depreciation charge constitutes the difference between gross investment and net investment (I_g and I_n).

STATISTICAL DISCREPANCY

Despite their best efforts, when statisticians at Statistics Canada have finished rechecking their estimate of GDP through both approaches, they often find that the figures do not quite add up. Should they find, for example, that their expenditure estimate is

TABLE 7-3   The income statement for the economy, 1994 (in billions of dollars)

Receipts: expenditure approach		Allocations: income approach	
Personal consumption expenditure (C)	$452.859	Wages, salaries, and supplementary labour income	$410.298
Gross investment (I_g)	125.250	Corporation profits before taxes	57.357
Government current purchases of goods and services (G)	167.522	Interest and miscellaneous investment income	56.410
Net exports (X_n)	5.615	Accrued net income of farm operators from farm production	2.030
Statistical discrepancy	−1.193	Net income of nonfarm unincorporated business, including rent	40.970
		Inventory valuation adjustment	−4.840
		Net domestic income at factor cost	$562.225
		Indirect taxes less subsidies	93.662
		Capital consumption allowances	92.973
		Statistical discrepancy	1.193
Gross domestic product at market prices	$750.053	Gross domestic product at market prices	$750.053

Source: Statistics Canada, National Income and Expenditure Accounts, First Quarter 1995.

$2.386 billion less than their income estimate, they will split the difference. They will subtract $1.193 billion from the expenditure estimate and add $1.193 billion to the income estimate. That is what they did in 1994, as shown in Table 7-3.

Table 7-3 summarizes our discussions of both the expenditure and income approaches to GDP. This is a gigantic income statement for the economy. The left-hand side tells us what the economy produced in 1994 and the total receipts derived from that production. The right-hand side indicates how the income derived from the production of 1994's GDP was allocated.

QUICK REVIEW 7-1

1. Gross domestic product (GDP) measures the total market value of all final goods and services produced in the economy in a specific year.

2. The expenditure approach to GDP sums the total spending on final goods and services:

$$C + I_g + G + X_n$$

3. When net investment is positive, the economy's production capacity expands; when net investment is negative, the economy's production capacity erodes.

4. The income approach to GDP sums the total income earned by resource suppliers and adds two nonincome charges: depreciation and indirect taxes less subsidies.

OTHER INCOME MEASUREMENTS

Our discussion thus far has centred on GDP as a measure of the economy's annual output. There are certain related income concepts of equal importance that can be derived from GDP. In identifying these concepts, let's start with GDP and make the adjustments — subtractions and additions — necessary to derive the related income accounts.

NATIONAL INCOME (NI)

In analyzing some problems, it is useful to know how much income is earned by factors of production or resource suppliers for their contributions of land, labour, capital, and entrepreneurial talent. The two components of GNP that do not reflect the current productive contributions of economic resources are indirect taxes and capital consumption allowances. Thus, to get a measure of total wage, rent, interest, and profit incomes earned from the production of the year's output, we must subtract indirect taxes and capital consumption allowances from GNP. The resulting figure is called the *net national income at factor cost* or, more simply, **national income**. From the viewpoint of resource suppliers, it measures the incomes they have earned for their current contributions to production. From the viewpoint of firms, national income measures factor or resource costs; national income reflects the market costs of the economic resources that have gone into the creation of this year's output. In 1994:

	Billions
Gross national product	$723.781
Indirect taxes less subsidies	− 93.662
Capital consumption allowances	− 92.973
Statistical discrepancy (reversed)	− 1.193
National Income	$535.953

A glance ahead at Table 7-4 shows that national income can also be obtained through the income approach by adding up all the allocations, with the exception of capital consumption allowances and indirect taxes. The six allocations of GDP that remain after the two nonincome charges have been subtracted constitute the **net domestic income**. Adding the (negative) net investment income from nonresidents to this gives us the national income; that is, $562.225 billion − $26.272 billion = $535.953 billion.

PERSONAL INCOME (PI)

Personal income (income *received*) and national income (income *earned*) are likely to differ because some income that is earned — corporation income taxes, undistributed corporation profits, government investment income, and social insurance contributions — is not actually received by households, and conversely, some income that is received — transfer payments — is not currently earned. Transfer payments, you may recall, are made up of such items as (1) Canada and Quebec Pension Plan

payments, old age security pension payments, and unemployment insurance benefits; (2) welfare payments; (3) a variety of veterans' payments.

In moving from national income as a measure of income earned to personal income as an indicator of income actually received, we must subtract from national income those four types of income that are earned but not received and add in income received but not currently earned. This is done as follows for 1994:

	Billions
National income (income earned)	$535.953
Government transfer payments*	+ 113.346
Transfers from nonresidents*	+ 1.426
Interest on the public debt*	+ 40.126
Interest on consumer debt (transfer portion*)	+ 4.432
Corporate income taxes	− 16.890
Undistributed corporation profits	− 20.120
Government investment income	− 13.179
Other earnings not paid out to persons†	+ 2.098
Personal income (income received)	$647.192

* Since national income excludes transfer payments and personal income includes them, these four items are added back here.
† This comprises current transfers to nonresidents (withholding taxes), adjustment on grain transactions, and inventory valuation adjustment. The plus sign comes about because the negative inventory valuation adjustment outweighs the other two elements (a double negative becomes a plus).

DISPOSABLE INCOME (DI)

Disposable income is personal income less personal taxes and other personal transfers to government. *Personal taxes* comprise personal income taxes and personal property taxes, the first of which is the most important. The other personal transfers to government include contributions to unemployment insurance, Canada and Quebec Pension Plans, and public service pensions.

Households apportion their disposable income in two ways. The bulk of it is spent, the other portion is saved. However, relatively small amounts are also paid out as interest or consumer debt or in transfers to nonresidents (mostly recent immigrants sending money to their families still abroad).

Personal saving is the amount of disposable income that remains after consumption, interest, and immigrant outlays have been made out of disposable income. The difference between personal income and disposable income and the division of the latter for 1994 are as follows:

	Billions
Personal income (income received before personal taxes)	$647.192
Personal taxes and other personal transfers to government	−149.835
Disposable income (income received after personal taxes)	497.357
Personal consumption expenditure	−452.859
Interest paid by consumers to corporations	−4.432
Current transfers to nonresidents	−1.048
Personal saving	$39.018

It is worth noting that just as GDP and NI can be derived by adding up their component parts, so can PI and DI. DI is the sum of personal saving, personal consumption expenditures, personal interest payments, and current transfers to nonresidents. PI is the sum of personal saving, personal consumption expenditures, personal taxes, personal interest payments, and current transfers to nonresidents. You should employ the figures used in the above calculation of personal saving to verify these points.

QUICK REVIEW 7-2

We have derived three additional national accounting concepts from GDP:

1. National income (NI) is income *earned* by the factors of production for their current contributions to production, or the factor costs of getting the year's total output produced;

2. Personal income (PI) is income *received* by households before personal taxes;

3. Disposable income (DI) is income received by households less personal taxes.

The relationships between GDP, NI, PI, and DI are summarized in Table 7-4. (**Key Question 7**)

TABLE 7-4 The relationships between GDP, GNP, NI, PI, and DI in 1994

	Billions
GDP at market prices	$750.053
Net investment income from nonresidents	− 26.272
GNP at market prices	$723.781
Indirect taxes less subsidies	− 96.662
Capital consumption allowances	− 92.973
Statistical discrepancy	− 1.864
Net national income (NI)	$535.953
Government transfer payments	+ 113.346
Transfers from nonresidents	+ 1.426
Interest on the public debt	+ 40.126
Interest on consumer debt (transfer portion)	+ 4.432
Corporation income taxes	− 16.890
Undistributed corporation profits	− 20.120
Government investment income	− 13.179
Other earnings not paid out to persons	+ 2.098
Personal income (PI)	$647.192
Personal taxes	− 149.835
Personal disposable income (DI)	$497.357
Personal consumption expenditure (C)	− 452.859
Interest paid by consumers to corporations	− 4.432
Current transfers to nonresidents	− 1.048
Personal saving (S)	$39.018

THE CIRCULAR FLOW REVISITED

Figure 7-3 combines the expenditure and income approaches to GDP. As a more realistic and more complex expression of the circular flow model of the economy (discussed in Chapters 2 and 5), this figure merits your careful study.

Starting at the GDP rectangle in the upper left, the expenditure side of GDP is shown by the large arrow. Immediately to the right of the GDP rectangle are the nine components of GDP and the additions and subtractions needed to derive NI and PI. All allocations or income flows are depicted by arrows. Note the flow of personal taxes out of PI and the division of DI between consumption and personal saving in the household sector. In the government sector the flows of revenue in the form of four basic types of taxes are denoted on the right; on the left, government disbursements take the form of purchases of goods and services and transfers. The position of the business sector emphasizes, on the left, investment expenditures and, on the right, the three major sources of funds for business investment.

Observe the role of the rest of the world in Figure 7-3. Spending by people abroad on our exports adds to our GDP, but our consumption, government, and investment expenditures buy imported products as well as domestically produced goods. The flow emanating from "Rest of the World" shows that we handle this complication by calculating *net* exports (exports minus imports). This may be a positive or negative amount.

The major virtue of Figure 7-3 is that it simultaneously portrays the expenditure and income aspects of GDP, fitting the two approaches to one another. These flows of expenditure and income are part of a continuous, repetitive process. Cause and effect are intermingled: expenditures create income, and out of this income arise expenditures that again flow to resource owners as income.

The table at the back of this book contains a useful historical summary of the national income accounts and related statistics since 1926.

MEASURING THE PRICE LEVEL

Measurement of the price level is significant for two reasons.

1. MEASURING INFLATION AND DEFLATION

It is useful for us to know how much the price level has changed, if at all, from one period to another. We need to be aware of whether and to what extent inflation (a rising price level) or deflation (a falling price level) has occurred.

2. COMPARING GDPs

Since GDP is the market value, or total money value, of all final goods and services produced in a year, money values are used as the common measure when adding up various outputs. The value of different years' output

(GDPs) can be compared only if we account for changes in the value of the money.

PRICE INDEXES

The price level is stated as an index number. A **price index** measures the combined price of a particular collection of goods and services called a "market basket" in a *specific* period relative to the combined price of identical or similar collection of goods and services in a *reference* period. This point of reference, or bench mark, is called the **base year**. More formally,

$$\text{Price index in a given year} = \frac{\text{Price of market basket in a specific year}}{\text{Price of the same market basket in the base year}} \times 100$$

By convention, the price ratio between the specific year and the base year is multiplied by 100. For example, a price ratio of 2/1 (= 2) is expressed as an index number of 200. Similarly a price ratio of 1/3 (= 0.33), is expressed as 33.

Statistics Canada computes indexes of the prices of several different collections or market baskets of goods and services. The best-known of these indexes is the **Consumer Price Index** (CPI), which measures the prices of a fixed market basket of over 300 consumer goods and services purchased by a "typical" urban consumer. In the CPI the items in the market basket are determined in a base year and their relative importance — their so-called "weights" — remain fixed in subsequent years. Neither the items nor their composition change from year to year. Because the CPI is an important measure of inflation, we will consider it in detail in Box 7-3.

Another price index — the **GDP deflator** — is more relevant than the CPI for measuring the price level for all the goods making up the GDP. The GDP deflator is broader than the CPI. The GDP deflator includes not only the prices of consumer goods and services, but also the prices of investment goods, goods and services purchased by government, and goods and services entering into world trade. For this reason, the GDP deflator is the price index used to account for inflation or deflation when comparing GDP from year to year.

The GDP deflator differs from the CPI in another respect. While the CPI employs a historic,

FIGURE 7-3   Domestic output and the flows of expenditure and income

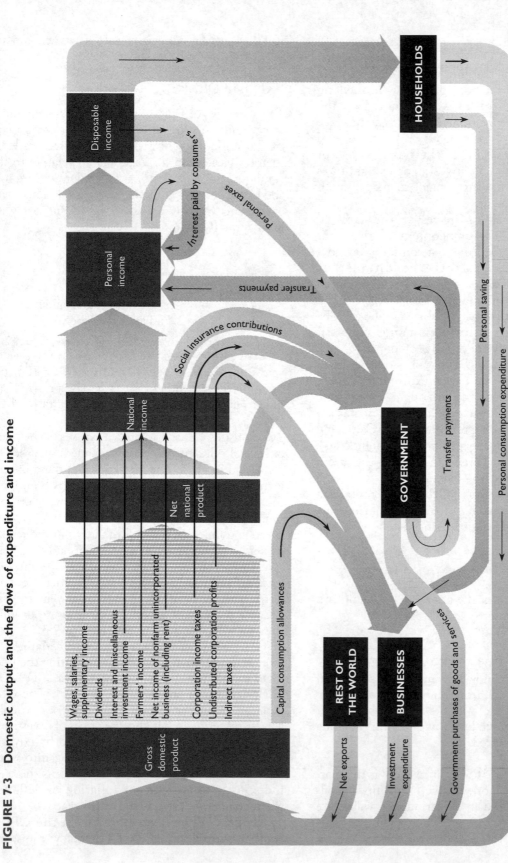

This figure is an elaborate circular-flow diagram that fits the expenditure and income sides of GDP to one another. You should trace through the income and expenditure flows, relating them to the five basic national income accounting measures. Note that net exports are assumed to be zero (imports = exports) and that net foreign investment income is also assumed to be zero. Thus, in this case, GDP = GNP.

fixed-composition market basket to calculate the CPI, the GDP deflator uses the *current* composition of output to determine the relative importance of the items in the market basket for the base year. This fact will become evident in the discussion that follows.

COMPUTING A GDP PRICE INDEX

Table 7-5 provides a simple example of how a GDP deflator can be computed in a particular year for a hypothetical economy. Observe from column 1 that in 1996 this economy produces only four goods: pizzas (a consumption good); industrial robots (a capital good); paper clips (a good purchased by government); and computer disks (an export good). Suppose that in 1996 the output of the four goods are 2, 1, 1, and 1 units, respectively, as shown in column 2. Also, assume that the per unit prices of these four products in 1996 are those shown in column 3. The total price (cost) of the 1996 output therefore is $64, an amount found by summing the expenditures on each of the four goods (column 4).

Let's arbitrarily select 1986 as our reference or base year so that we can establish a price index for 1996. The 1986 prices of the components of the 1996 output are listed in column 5 of Table 7-5. From columns 5 and 3, we observe that the prices of pizza and paper clips were lower in 1986 than in 1996, the price of robots was higher, and the price of computer disks did not change. Most impor-

tantly, the total price (cost) of the 1996 output — shown at the bottom of column 6 — was $50 in 1986 rather than $64 as in 1993. This fact tells us that the 1996 output would have cost $50 if 1986 prices had persisted. To determine the 1996 price index, we divide the 1996 price of the market basket ($64) by the 1986 price of that same collection of goods ($50). The quotient is then multiplied by 100 to express the price index in its conventional form.

$$\text{GDP price index}_{1996} = \frac{\text{Price of market basket}_{1996}}{\text{Price of 1996 market basket in the base year}_{1986}} \times 100$$

More concretely, GDP price index$_{1996}$

$$= \frac{\$64}{\$50} \times 100 = 128$$

The price index for 1996 is 128. This index value may be thought of as the price level for 1996.

These same steps can be used to calculate the price level for all years in a series of years. For example, the price index in the 1986 base year is found by finding the price of the particular collection of goods and services produced in 1986 and comparing this price to the price of that same market basket in the base year. However, in this special

TABLE 7-5   Computing a GDP price index for 1996

(1) Product	(2) Quantities in market basket in 1996	(3) Prices of 1996 market basket in 1996	(4) Expenditures on 1996 market basket in 1996 (3) x (2)	(5) Prices of 1996 market basket in 1986 prices (base year)	(6) Expenditures on 1996 market basket in 1986 prices (5) x (2)
Pizzas	2	$12	$24	$ 5	$10
Robots	1	18	18	20	20
Paper clips	1	8	8	6	6
Computer disks	1	14	14	14	14
Total Price (Cost)			$64		$50
GDP Price Index 1996			$128 \left(\dfrac{\$64}{\$50} \times 100 \right)$		

case, the "specific year" and the "reference year" are both the same. That is,

$$\text{GDP price index}_{1986} = \frac{\text{Price of market basket}_{1986}}{\text{Price of market basket}_{1986}} \times 100$$

The GDP price index for the 1986 base year therefore is 100. In effect, we automatically set the price index at 100 in the base year.

Likewise, if we wanted to know the GDP price index for 1950, we would determine 1950 output and then estimate what that same or a similar collection of goods and services would have cost in the 1986 base year. For example, if prices on the 1950 output had quadrupled between 1950 and 1986, the price ratio of the market basket would be 1/4 (= 0.25) and the 1950 GDP price index would be 25 (= 0.25 × 100).

Once a GDP price index has been constructed for each year in a series of years, comparisons of price levels between years is possible. Examples:

(1) If the price indexes for 1996 and 1986 are 128 and 100 respectively, we can calculate that the price level increased by 28% [= (128 − 100)/100] between the two years.

(2) If the price index for 1950 is 25, we can say that the price level rose by 412% [(128 − 25)/25] between 1950 and 1996.

(3) If the price index fell from 100 in 1986 to 98 in 1987, we would know that the price level declined by 2% [= (98 − 100)/100].

In summary, the GDP price index or deflator compares the price of each year's output to the price of that same output in the base year or reference year. A series of price indexes for various years enables us to compare price levels among years. An increase in the GDP price index from one year to the next constitutes *inflation*; a decrease in the price index indicates *deflation*. **(Key Question 10)**

BOX 7-2   APPLYING THE THEORY

THE CPI: DOES IT OVERSTATE INFLATION?

The consumer price index is the most widely reported measure of inflation; therefore, we should become familiar with its characteristics and limitations.

The consumer price index (CPI) measures changes in the prices of a "market basket" of some 300 goods and services purchased by urban consumers. The present composition of the market basket was determined from a survey of the spending patterns of urban consumers in 1986. Unlike the GDP deflator, the CPI is a historical, fixed-weight price index. In each year, the composition or "weight" of the items in the market basket remains the same as in the base period (1986). If 20% of consumer spending was on housing in 1986, it is assumed that 20% of consumer spending is still spent on housing in 1988 and 1995. The base period is changed roughly every ten years — a new CPI index appeared in 1995. The idea behind the historical, fixed-weight approach is to measure changes in the cost of a constant standard of living. These changes supposedly measure the rate of inflation facing consumers.

But here are four problems with the CPI that cause it to overstate the true rate of inflation, according to critics.

1. CHANGED SPENDING PATTERNS.   Although the composition of the market basket is assumed to remain unchanged, in fact, consumers do change their spending patterns, particularly in response to changes in relative prices. When the price of beef rises while fish and chicken prices are steady, consumers move away from beef and buy fish or chicken instead. Over time consumers are buying a market basket that contains more of the relatively low-priced and less of the relatively high-priced goods and services. The fixed-weight CPI assumes that these substitutions have not occurred. Therefore the index overstates the actual cost of living.

2. NEW PRODUCTS.   Many new consumer goods and services such as fax machines, multimedia computers, and cellular phone service either are not included or are severely underweighted in the market basket used to construct the CPI. Often prices of new products drop following their introductions. The CPI, with its historical, fixed-weight market basket, fails to pick up these price changes and thus overstates inflation.

3. QUALITY IMPROVEMENTS.   The CPI does not take quality improvements into account. To the extent that product quality has improved since the base year, prices should be higher. We ought to pay more for televisions today than a decade ago because they are generally of higher quality. In general, it's the same for automobiles, automobile tires, electronic equipment, and many other items. But the CPI assumes that all the increases in the nominal value of the market basket arise solely from inflation, not quality improvements. Again the CPI overstates the rate of inflation.

4. PRICE DISCOUNTING.   In calculating the CPI, Statistics Canada continually rotates the stores it checks for prices. But once a set of stores is selected, the price survey picks up price changes only on a same-store basis. If Hudson Bay department stores raise their price on footwear, then this price increase is picked up in the CPI. But the CPI survey does not fully account for price discounts on footwear that The Bay may have offered during a particular period. If people increasingly shop for discounts and special sales to buy footwear — and other products — the CPI will overstate the true increase in the cost of living.

In general, economists conclude that the CPI overstates the rate of inflation, perhaps by as much as 0.5 percentage points a year. So what? The problem is that the CPI affects nearly everyone. Examples abound: Government payments to social insurance receivers are indexed to the CPI; when the CPI rises, social security payments automatically rise in lockstep. Millions of unionized workers have cost-of-living adjustment clauses (COLAs) in their labour contracts. Moreover, the wage demands of virtually all workers — union or nonunion, blue- or white-collar — are linked to the rate of inflation as measured by the CPI. Also, interest rates are often linked to the rate of inflation, as measured by the CPI. When the CPI rises, lenders raise their nominal interest rates to keep their real interest rates constant.

Another consequence of an overstated CPI stems from the indexing of personal income tax brackets. This adjusting of tax brackets upward to account for the rate of inflation was begun in the mid-1970s to resolve an inequity in the personal income tax. The intent of indexing is to prevent inflation from pushing households into higher tax brackets even though their real incomes have not increased. For example, a 10% increase in your *nominal* income might put you in a higher marginal tax bracket and increase the proportion of your income paid in taxes. But if product prices are also rising by 10%, your *real* or inflation-adjusted income has remained constant. The result would be an unintended redistribution of real income from taxpayers to the federal government. The purpose of indexing tax brackets was to prevent this redistribution. However, to the extent that the CPI *overstates* inflation, indexing will reduce government's tax share. The federal government will be deprived of substantial tax revenues and real income will be redistributed from government to taxpayers.

NOMINAL AND REAL GDP

Inflation or deflation complicates GDP because GDP is a prices-times-quantity figure. The data from which the national income accountants estimate GDP are the total sales figures of business firms; however, these revenue figures obviously embody changes in *both* the quantity of output *and* the level of prices. This means that a change in either the quantity of total physical output or the price level will affect the size of GDP. However, it is the quantity of goods and services produced and distributed to households that affects their standard of living, and not the size of the price tags these goods bear. The hamburger of 1970 that sold for 65¢ yielded the same satisfaction as will an identical hamburger selling for $2 in 1996.

The situation facing government accountants is this: In gathering statistics from the financial reports of business and deriving GDP in various years, they get nominal GDP figures. They do *not* know directly to what extent changes in price and changes in quantity of output have accounted for changes in nominal GDP. For example, they would not know directly if a 4% increase in nominal GDP resulted from a 4% rise in output and zero inflation, from a zero percent change in output and 4% inflation, or some other combination of changes in output and the price level, say, a 2% increase and 2% inflation. The problem is adjusting a price-times-quantity figure so it will accurately reflect changes in the quantity of physical output, not changes in prices.

As we will see soon, this problem is resolved by *deflating* GDP for rising prices and *inflating* it when prices are falling. These adjustments give us a picture of GDP for various years as *though* prices and the value of the dollar were constant. A GDP figure that reflects current prices — that is, *not* adjusted for changes in the price level — is called *unadjusted, current dollar, money,* or **nominal GDP**. Similarly, GDP figures that are inflated or deflated for price level changes measure *adjusted, constant dollar,* or **real GDP**.

THE ADJUSTMENT PROCESS

The process for adjusting current dollar or nominal GDP for inflation or deflation is straightforward. The GDP deflator for a specific year, remember, tells us the ratio of that year's prices to the prices of the same goods in the base year. The GDP deflator or GDP price index therefore can be used to inflate or deflate nominal GDP figures for each year to express in real terms — in other words, *as though* base year prices prevailed. *The simplest and most direct method of deflating or inflating a year's nominal GDP is to express that year's index number in hundredths, and divide it into the nominal GDP.* This yields the same result as the more complex procedure of dividing nominal GDP by the corresponding index number and multiplying the quotient by 100. In equation form:

$$\frac{\text{Nominal GDP}}{\text{Price index (in hundredths)}} = \text{Real GDP}$$

To illustrate in Table 7-5, nominal GDP in 1996 is $64, the price index for that year is 128 (= 1.28 times one hundred); and real GDP is:

$$\frac{\$64}{1.28} = \$50$$

In summary, the real GDP figures measure the value of the total output *as if* the prices of the products had been constant from the reference or base year throughout all the years being considered. Real GDP thus shows the market value of each year's output measured in dollars of the same value, or purchasing power, as the base year.

Real GDP is clearly superior to nominal GDP as an indicator of the economy's productive performance.

INFLATING AND DEFLATING

Table 7-6 illustrates the **inflating** and **deflating** process. Here we are taking actual nominal GDP

figures for selected years and adjusting them with the GDP deflator for these years to obtain real GDP. Note the base year is 1986.

Since the long-run trend has been for the price level to rise, we need to increase or *inflate* the pre-1986 figures. This upward revision of nominal GDP acknowledges that prices were lower in years before 1986 and, as a result, nominal GDP figures understated the real output of these years. Column 4 reveals what GDP would have been in these four selected years had the 1986 price level prevailed.

The rising price level has caused the nominal GDP figures for the post-1986 years to overstate real output. These figures must be reduced, or *deflated*, as in column 4, in order for us to gauge what GDP would have been in 1988 and 1991, and so on, if 1986 prices had prevailed.

In short, while the *nominal* GDP figures reflect both output and price changes, the *real* GDP figures allow us to make a better estimate of changes in real output, because the real GDP figures, in effect, hold the price level constant.

Example: For 1994, nominal GDP was $750.053 billion and the implicit GDP price index was 125.4 or 25.4 higher than in 1986. To compare 1994's GDP with 1986's we express the 1994 index in hundredths (1.254) and divide it into the nominal GDP of $750.053 billion, as shown in column 4. The resulting real GDP of $597.936 billion is directly comparable to the 1986 base year's GDP because both reflect only changes in output and *not* price-level changes. You should trace through the computations involved in deriving the real GDP figures given in Table 7-6 and also determine real GDP for years 1964, 1968, and 1991, for which the figures have been purposely omitted. **(Key Question 11)**

QUICK REVIEW 7-3

1. A price index compares the price of a specific market basket of goods and services in a particular year to the price in a base year.

2. Nominal GDP is output valued at current prices; real GDP is output valued at constant prices (base year prices).

3. A year's nominal GDP can be adjusted to real GDP by dividing nominal GDP by the GDP price index (expressed in hundredths).

TABLE 7-6   Adjusting GDP for changes in the price level (selected years, in billions of dollars)

(1) Year	(2) Nominal or unadjusted GDP	(3) Price level index,* percent (1986 = 100)	(4) Real, or adjusted, GDP (1986 dollars)
1961	$ 40.886	24.1541	$169.271 (= $40.886 ÷ 0.241541)
1964	52.191	25.6615	
1968	75.418	30.0393	
1971	97.290	33.8991	286.998 (= $97.290 ÷ 0.338991)
1981	355.994	80.8843	440.127 (= $355.994 ÷ 0.80884)
1986	504.631	100.000	
1988	605.906	121.1785	552.928 (= $605.90 ÷ 1.211785)
1991	673.388	121.7567	
1994	750.053	125.4403	597.936 (= 750.053 ÷ 1.254403)

* Statistics Canada, implicit price indexes, GDP.

Source: Statistics Canada, *National Income and Expenditure Accounts.*

GDP AND SOCIAL WELFARE

GDP is a reasonably accurate and useful measure of national economic performance. It is not, and was never intended to be, an index of social welfare. GDP is merely a measure of the annual volume of market-oriented activity. And, while GDP may yield a workable impression of material well-being, it is a far cry from being a precise indicator of social welfare.

Nevertheless, it is widely held that there is a positive correlation between real GDP and social welfare. Hence it is important to understand some of the shortcomings of GDP — why GDP might understate or overstate real output and why more output will not necessarily make society better off.

NONMARKET TRANSACTIONS

Certain production transactions do not appear in the market. Thus, GDP as a measure of the market value of output fails to include them. Examples include the productive services of the homemaker, the work of the carpenter who repairs his or her own home, or the work of the professor who writes a scholarly article. Such transactions are *not* reflected in the profit and loss statements of business firms and therefore are deliberately excluded by the national income accountants, causing GDP to be understated.

LEISURE

Over a long period of time, leisure has increased significantly. The current average work week is about 38 hours in manufacturing, as compared with 50 hours in 1926. The expanded availability of paid vacations and holidays, particularly since World War II, has significantly reduced work time. This increased leisure has had a positive effect on our well-being. Our system of social accounting understates our well-being by not directly taking cognizance of this. Nor do the accounts reflect the satisfaction — the "psychic income" — people derive from their work.

IMPROVED PRODUCT QUALITY

GDP is a quantitative not a qualitative measure. It does not accurately reflect improvements in the

BOX 7-3   IN THE MEDIA

AMAZING FACTS

BACK WHERE WE ONCE BELONGED

BRUCE LITTLE

Economists have been saying for at least two years that the recession is over. And yet many Canadians continue to be skeptical — surly about the taxes they pay and more obsessed than ever with bargain hunting.

There's a good reason for this.

For their yardstick, the economists look to Canada's gross domestic product. The sum total of the goods and services we produce did indeed claw its way back to prerecession levels by the middle of 1993.

But there's another way of looking at the GDP that better reflects what most Canadians experience in their daily lives. You simply account for the fact that the population has kept growing all along.

When you divide the total economic output by the population to obtain a measure of GDP per person, a very different profile emerges. Not only did the recession begin earlier than commonly thought (1989

rather than 1990), but the recovery has taken much longer.

And now the good news: After a full six years, we're finally there. At some point during the first quarter of the current year (which ended on Friday), Canada's output per person returned to where it was in the first quarter of 1989.

As milestones go, it may not seem like much, but it is certainly worth marking: Canadians have escaped their longest economic slump since the Great Depression.

The accompanying chart traces the evolution of the two "recessions." From top to bottom, judged by GDP alone, the tumble lasted one year and reduced the national output 3.6 per cent. With population taken into account, however, it ran almost four years and reduced output 6.3 per cent.

In the third quarter of 1993, when total GDP surpassed its 1990 peak

(after coming within a whisker of the mark in the second quarter), the per-person rate still lingered more than 5 per cent below its 1989 benchmark.

In the summer of 1993, Amazing Facts highlighted that gap and linked it to the mental state of the nation. Preoccupied with high unemployment, lower incomes and higher taxes, most Canadians still believed they were in the grip of a recession. The federal election campaign — then under way — gave them a chance to act on that belief.

Since then, both measures of output have chugged steadily upward, with last year's gain particularly strong — the biggest since 1988.

The overall GDP expanded 5.6 per cent, while the population grew only 1.1 per cent, to produce a 4.5-per-cent increase in GDP per person. By the end, economic output per person had reached $26,104. In constant 1986 dollars — the kind Statistics Canada uses to compensate for inflation — that translated to $20,748 — very close to the $20,808 recorded in the first quarter of 1989....

In some ways, it's surprising that economists don't make more frequent use of GDP per person as a measure of Canada's economic well-being. After all, a country whose population is growing faster than its economy is getting poorer, not richer.

Consider the things that it helps to explain:

- Why, when adjusted for inflation, the average personal income fell in 1991, 1992 and 1993. It rose

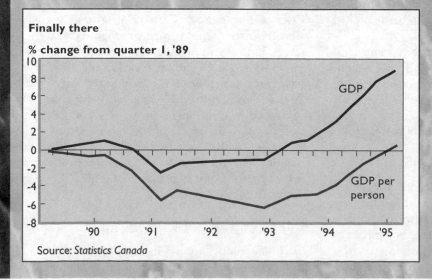

Finally there

% change from quarter 1, '89

Source: *Statistics Canada*

slightly in 1994, but was still down 3.6 per cent from 1990. If the country isn't producing more goods and services per person, it's impossible to earn more income per person.

- Why consumers have become so cost-conscious, relentlessly seeking out bargains and laying the foundation for the success of discount retailers.
- Why people are so surly about tax increases. Between 1989 and

1994, income taxes and other government deductions (such as unemployment insurance and Canada Pension Plan premiums) climbed 5.1 per cent, while take-home pay fell 5 per cent.

These conditions are hardly going to disappear overnight, but the fact that Canada is once again producing what it did in 1989 is worth at least a passing nod.

For one thing it may have a psychological impact. Every travelling parent has heard that plaintive wail from the back seat: Are we there yet? Put that in economic terms, and we can finally answer: Yes, kids, it's been a long tough ride, but we're finally back where we started.

Source: *Globe and Mail.* April 3, 1995, p. A9. Reproduced with permission.

The Story in Brief

The author of the story reminds us GDP per capita is the most important measure of a nation's material well-being.
In Canada, GDP was back to its pre-recession (1990) level by 1993.
But GDP per capita did not reach its pre-recession level until the first quarter of 1995.

The Economics Behind the Story

- GDP measures the total output of goods and services of an economy in a year. A far better measure of a nation's material well-being is GDP per capita (per person).

- To understand this, consider two families each with an income of $50,000. If family A has a total of four members and family B has eight members, family A is materially better off; each member of family A has more goods and services available to satisfy his or her wants. Note that we are implicitly assuming an equal distribution of the $50,000 income. An unequal distribution of income means some family member would get a disproportionately large share of the family income.

- Is the assertion "Economic growth is desirable," a positive or normative statement (see Chapter 1 for the distinction)? Will economic growth — particularly an increase in GDP per capita — bring about a rise in the well-being of a nation's citizens?

quality of products. For example, there is a fundamental qualitative difference between a $3000 personal computer purchased today and a computer for that same amount bought just a few years ago. Today's $3000 computer has far more speed and storage capacity, as well as a clearer monitor and improved multimedia capabilities.

Failure to account for quality improvement is a shortcoming of GDP accounting: quality improvement clearly affects economic well-being as much as does the quantity of goods. Because product quality has improved over time, GDP understates improvements in our material well-being.

COMPOSITION AND DISTRIBUTION OF OUTPUT

Changes in the composition and the allocation of total output among specific households may influence economic welfare. GDP, however, reflects only the size of output and does not tell us anything about whether this collection of goods is "right" for society. A switchblade knife and a Beethoven compact disc, both selling for $18.95, are weighted equally in the GDP.

Some economists believe that a more equal distribution of total output would increase national economic well-being. If they are correct, a future trend towards a less unequal distribution of GDP would enhance the economic welfare of society. A more unequal distribution would have the reverse effect.

Conclusion: GDP measures the size of total output but does not reflect changes in the composition and distribution of output that might also affect the economic well-being of society.

PER CAPITA OUTPUT

For many purposes the most meaningful measure of economic well-being is per capita output. Since GDP measures the size of total output, it may conceal or misrepresent changes in the standard of living of individual households in the economy. For example, GDP may rise significantly, but if population is also growing rapidly, the per capita standard of living may be relatively constant or may even be declining.

This is the plight of many of the less-developed countries. Ethiopia's domestic output grew at 1.2% a year over the 1980–1992 period. But annual population growth exceeded 3%, resulting in a yearly decrease in per capita output of 1.9%.

GDP AND THE ENVIRONMENT

There are undesirable and much-publicized "gross national by-products" that may accompany the production and growth of the GDP. These take the form of dirty air and water, automobile junkyards, congestion, noise, and various other forms of environmental pollution. The costs of pollution reduce our economic well-being. These spillover costs associated with the production of the GDP are not deducted from total output and thus, GDP overstates our national economic welfare.

Ironically, the final physical product of economic production and consumption is garbage. A rising GDP means more garbage and may mean more pollution and a greater divergence between GDP and economic well-being. In fact, under existing accounting procedures, when a manufacturer pollutes a river and government spends to clean it up, the cleanup expense is added to the GDP while the pollution is not subtracted!

THE UNDERGROUND ECONOMY

Economists agree there is a large underground or subterranean sector in our economy. Some partici-

pants in this sector engage in illegal activities such as gambling, loan-sharking, prostitution, and the narcotics trade. These may well be "growth industries." Obviously, persons receiving income from illegal businesses choose to conceal their incomes.

Most participants in the underground economy are in legal activities, but do not fully report their incomes to Revenue Canada. A waiter or waitress may underreport tips from customers. A businessperson may record only a portion of sales receipts for the tax collector. A worker who wants to retain unemployment insurance or welfare benefits may obtain an "off the books" or "cash only" job so there is no record of his or her work activities. A nanny who is an illegal immigrant may wish to be

GLOBAL PERSPECTIVE 7-2

The underground economy as a percentage of GDP, selected nations

Several nations have relatively larger underground economies than Canada. In general, the higher the tax rates and the greater the number of regulations, the larger is the underground economy.

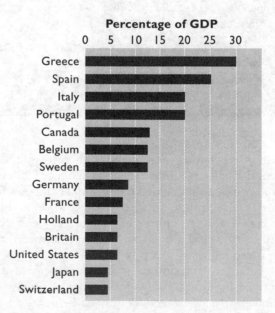

Source: *The Economist* estimates based on various studies. Estimate for Canada reported in "Tax Revolt," *Globe and Mail*, Report on Business, January 28, 1995, p. B19.

paid in cash, so as not to be detected by the immigration service, and her employer may acquiesce, as a way to avoid paying social security taxes.

Although there is no consensus on the size of the underground economy, estimates suggest it is between 5 and 15% of the recorded GDP. In 1994, that meant GDP was understated by between $37 and $112 billion. If this additional income had been taxed at a 30% average tax rate, the federal budget deficit for 1994 would have declined from $29 billion to between an $18-billion deficit and a surplus of almost $4 billion.

Global Perspective 7-2 indicates the relative sizes of underground economies of selected nations.

CHAPTER SUMMARY

1. Gross domestic product (GDP) is the market value of all final goods and services produced within Canada in a year. GDP in Canada is usually larger than GNP because of the large number of foreign-owned firms operating in this country.

2. Intermediate goods, nonproduction transactions, and second-hand sales are purposely excluded in calculating GDP.

3. GDP may be calculated by summing total expenditures on all final output or by summing the income earned from the production of that output.

4. By the expenditure approach, GDP is determined by adding consumer purchases of goods and services, gross investment spending by government and business, government current purchases of goods and services, and net exports; $GDP = C + I_g + G + X_n$.

5. Gross investment can be divided into **a** replacement investment (required to maintain the nation's stock of capital at its existing level) and **b** net investment (the net increase in the stock of capital). Positive net investment is associated with a growing economy; negative net investment with a declining economy.

6. By the income approach, GDP is calculated as the sum of wages and salaries, dividends, interest, net income of farmers, net income of nonfarm unincorporated business (including rent), corporation income taxes, undistributed corporation profits, and the two nonincome charges (indirect taxes less subsidies and capital consumption allowances).

7. Other national income accounting measures are derived from the GDP. National income (NI) is total income earned by resource suppliers; it is found by subtracting indirect taxes and capital consumption allowances from GNP. Personal income (PI) is the total income paid to households prior to any allowance for personal taxes. Disposable income (DI) is personal income after personal taxes have been paid. DI measures the amount of income households have available to consume or save.

8. Price indexes are computed by comparing the price of a specific collection or "market basket" or output in a particular period with the price (cost) of the same market basket in a base period and multiplying the outcome (quotient) by 100. The GDP deflator is the price index associated with adjusting nominal GDP to account for inflation and thereby to obtain real GDP.

9. Nominal (current dollar) GDP measures each year's output valued in terms of the prices prevailing in that year. Real (constant dollar) GDP measures each year's output in terms of the prices that prevailed in a selected base year. Because it is adjusted for price level changes, real GDP measures the level of productive activity.

10. National income accounting measures exclude nonmarket and illegal transactions, changes in leisure and product quality, the composition and distribution of output, and the environmental effects of production. Nevertheless, these measures are reasonably accurate and very useful indicators of the nation's economic performance.

TERMS AND CONCEPTS

base year (p. 133)
capital consumption allowances
    (depreciation) (pp. 125, 129)
corporate income taxes (p. 128)
Consumer Price Index (p. 133)
depreciation (p. 125)
disposable income (p. 131)
dividends (p. 128)
double counting (p. 122)
expenditure and income approaches (p. 123)
final and intermediate goods (p. 122)
GDP deflator (p. 133)
government current purchases of goods
    and services (p. 127)
gross and net investment (pp. 124-125)
gross domestic product (GDP) (p. 121)

gross national product (GNP) (p. 121)
income or factor payment (p. 128)
indirect taxes (p. 129)
inflating and deflating (p. 138)
national income (p. 131)
national income accounting (p. 120)
net domestic income (p. 131)
net exports (p. 127)
nominal GDP (p. 138)
personal consumption expenditure (p. 124)
personal income (p. 131)
personal saving (p. 132)
price index (p. 133)
real GDP (p. 138)
undistributed corporate profits (p. 128)
value added (p. 123)

QUESTIONS AND STUDY SUGGESTIONS

1. "National income statistics are a powerful tool of economic understanding and analysis." Explain. "An economy's output is its income." Do you agree?

2. *Key Question*   *Why do national income accountants include only final goods in measuring total output? How do GDP and GNP differ?*

3. What is the difference between gross investment and net investment?

4. Why are changes in inventories included as part of investment spending? Suppose inventories declined by $1 billion during 1996. How would this affect the size of gross investment and gross domestic product in 1996? Explain.

5. *Key Question*   *Use the concepts of gross and net investment to distinguish between an expanding, a static, and a declining economy. "In 1933 net investment was minus $324 million. This means in that particular year the economy produced no capital goods at all." Do you agree? Explain: "Though net investment can be positive, negative, or zero, it is quite impossible for gross investment to be less than zero."*

6. Define net exports. Explain how Canadian exports and imports each affect domestic production. Suppose foreigners spend $117 billion on Canadian exports in a given year and Canadians spend $105 billion on imports from abroad in the same year. What is the amount of Canada's net exports? Explain how net exports might be a negative amount.

7. Key Question *Following is a list of national income figures for a given year. All figures are in billions. Determine the major national income measures by both the expenditure and income methods. The answers derived by each approach should be the same.*

Personal consumption expenditures	$120
Government transfer payments	29
Accrued net income of farmers	5
Capital consumption allowances (depreciation)	20
Interest and miscellaneous investment income	10
Net income of nonfarm unincorporated business (including rent)	12
Net exports	+5
Corporate profits before taxes	34
Wages, salaries, and supplementary labour income	113
Indirect taxes (less subsidies)	21
Undistributed corporate profits	8
Personal taxes	30
Corporate income taxes	9
Government current purchases of goods and services	40
Net investment (net capital formation)	30
Personal saving	17
Other earnings not paid out to persons	9
Net investment income from nonresidents	−10

a. Using the above data, determine GDP by both the expenditure and income methods.

b. Determine GNP by making the required subtractions from GDP.

c. Determine NI by making the required subtractions from GNP.

d. Make those adjustments for NI required to arrive at PI.

e. Make the required adjustments from PI (as determined in 7e) to obtain DI.

8. Given the following national income accounting data, compute a. GDP, b. GNP, and c. NI. All figures are in billions.

Wages, salaries, and supplementary labour income	$194.2
Canadian exports of goods and services	13.4
Capital consumption allowances	11.8
Government current purchases of goods and services	59.4
Indirect taxes	12.2
Net investment (net capital formation)	52.1
Government transfer payments	13.9
Canadian imports of goods and services	7.5
Personal taxes	40.5
Personal consumption expenditures	219.1
Net investment income from nonresidents	−9.0

9. Why do national income accountants compare the market value of the total outputs in various years rather than actual physical volumes of production? Explain. What problem is posed by any comparison, over time, of the market values of various total outputs? How is this problem resolved?

10. **Key Question**   *Suppose that in 1974 the total output of a hypothetical economy consisted of three goods — X, Y, and Z — produced in the following quantities: X = 4, Y = 1, Z = 3. Also suppose that in 1974 the prices of X, Y, and Z were as follows: X = $3, Y = $12, and Z = $5. Finally, assume that in 1986 the prices of these goods were X = $5, Y = $10, and Z = $10. Determine the GDP price index for 1974, using 1986 as the base year. By what percent did the price level rise between 1974 and 1988?*

11. **Key Question**   *The table below shows nominal GDP and an appropriate price index group of selected years. Compute real GDP. Indicate in each calculation whether you are inflating or deflating the nominal GDP data.*

Year	Nominal GDP (billions)	Price level index (percent) (1986 = 100)	Real GDP (billions)
1929	$6.400	15.2	$_____
1933	3.723	12.4	$_____
1962	44.408	30.3	$_____
1974	152.111	55.1	$_____
1984	444.735	92.4	$_____
1988	605.906	108.6	$_____

12. Which of the following are actually included in deriving this year's GDP? Explain your answer in each case.

  a. Interest on a Bell Canada bond.

  b. Canada Pension payments received by a retired factory worker.

  c. The services of a painter in painting the family home.

  d. The income of a dentist.

  e. The money received by Smith in selling a 1983 Chevrolet to Jones.

  f. The monthly allowance a college student receives from home.

  g. Rent received on a two-bedroom apartment.

  h. The money received by Wilson in reselling this year's model Plymouth to Wilcox.

  i. Interest received on government bonds.

  j. A two-hour decline in the length of the work week.

  k. The purchase of a Quebec Hydro bond.

  l. A $2 billion increase in business inventories.

  m. The purchase of 100 shares of CP Ltd. common stock.

  n. The purchase of an insurance policy.

  o. Wages paid to a domestic servant.

  p. The market value of a homemaker's services.

  q. The purchase of a Renaissance painting by a public art museum.

13. Explain: "A woman diminishes the national income by marrying her chauffeur."

14. What would be the most likely effect on real GDP of each of the following: a. a law mandating an increase in the work week from 40 hours to 50 hours for every able-bodied adult; b. the legalization of all the activities at present undertaken in the underground economy; and c. a $1-million increase in the production of burglar alarms offset by a $1-million decline in the provision of pre-natal health care services? Would society's well-being in each of these situations change in the same direction as the change in real GDP? Explain.

15. (Applying the Theory) What is the CPI? How does it differ from the GDP deflator? What are the shortcomings of the CPI in accurately measuring inflation?

CHAPTER 8

MACROECONOMIC INSTABILITY: UNEMPLOYMENT AND INFLATION

In an ideal economy, real GDP would expand over time at a brisk, steady pace and the price level, as measured by the GDP deflator or the consumer price index, would remain constant or only rise slowly. The result would be neither significant unemployment nor inflation. Several periods of Canadian history fit this pattern. But experience shows that steady economic growth, full employment, and a stable price level cannot be taken for granted. Recent examples: (1) The inflation rate skyrocketed to 10.2% in 1980. (2) During 1982, real GDP fell by 3.2%. (3) Over half a million more people were unemployed in 1983 than in 1980. (4) In 1990, output in the Canadian economy turned downward for its fifth time since

1945 and unemployment has remained stubbornly high right into the mid-1990s.

In this and the next several chapters we explore the problem of achieving macroeconomic stability, which means steady economic growth, full employment, and price stability. The present chapter proceeds as follows: First, we establish an overview of the business cycle — the periodic fluctuations in output, employment, and price levels characterizing our economy. Second, we look in more detail at unemployment: What are the various types of unemployment? How is unemployment measured? Why is unemployment an economic problem? Third, our attention turns to inflation — a problem that plagued us throughout the 1970s and into the early 1980s. What are inflation's causes? And consequences?

BOX 8-1   THE BIG PICTURE

In a perfect world everyone would have as many goods and services as he or she desired. In an imperfect world not only are there limited resources, but these limited resources (land, labour, capital, and entrepreneurial talent) are often not fully employed; we fail to get the most out of the limited resources we do have. The one resource we are particularly interested in is labour. Quite often in Canada we have had unacceptably high unemployment. People want to work but can't find a job. Moreover, the economy can build inflationary pressures that can, if not checked, impede the efficient functioning of a market economy. In recent decades there have been periods when the Canadian economy has suffered from both high unemployment and inflation at the same time.

Market economies are prone to a certain amount of instability — unemployment and inflation. In this chapter we take a first glance at this instability — also referred to as the business cycle — and its causes. Understanding the nature of economic instability will allow us to devise better macroeconomic policies to maintain healthy economic growth, and low levels of unemployment and inflation.

As you read this chapter, keep the following points in mind:

- In a market economy "full employment" does not mean zero unemployment.
- There is a difference between what the economy could produce if all its available resources were utilized and what the economy actually produces. Applying this to the production possibility curve, it means the economy is functioning inside the curve. In a world of scarcity, this is a paradox. This is a major challenge for macroeconomists to explain and attempt to rectify.
- Inflation is an increase in the general price level. High inflation can potentially diminish a nation's output as household and firms become preoccupied with minimizing the negative effect of inflation or profiting from inflation rather than striving to improve their economic positions by producing more output.

THE BUSINESS CYCLE

Our society seeks economic growth *and* full employment *and* price-level stability, along with other less quantifiable goals (Chapter 1). Canadian economic history reflects quite remarkable economic growth. Technological progress, rapid increases in productive capacity, and a standard of living among the highest in the world are major facets of the dynamic character of our economy.

THE HISTORICAL RECORD

But our long-run economic growth has not been steady. As Figure 8-1 reveals, it has been interrupted by periods of economic instability. Periods of rapid economic expansion have sometimes been marred by inflation. Altogether, we have had eight recessions since 1945. Table 8-1 looks at the calendar years during which GDP dropped. At other times, expansion has given way to recession and depression — low levels of employment and output. On a few occasions — in the 1970s and 1980s — we have experienced a rising price level and abnormally high unemployment simultaneously. Both unemployment and inflation have interrupted and complicated the long-term trend of economic growth.

TABLE 8-1   Canadian recessions since 1945

Year	Depth (decline in real GDP)
1945	−2.4%
1946	−2.2
1954	−1.1
1982	−3.2
1991	−1.7

Source: Statistics Canada

FIGURE 8-1 Canadian business-cycle experience

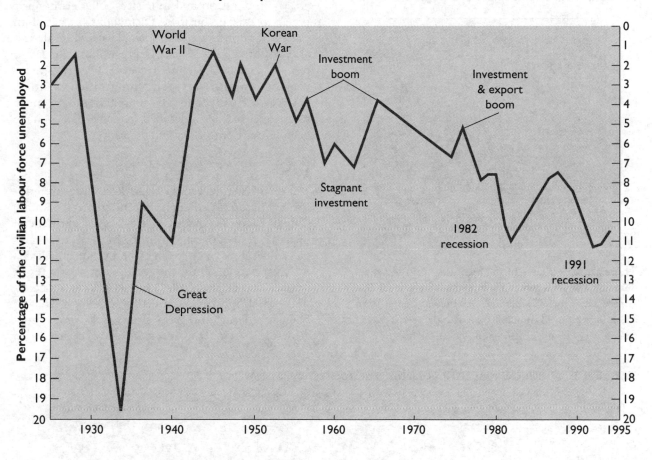

The Canadian economy has encountered periods of prosperity and recession. Until 1981, only minor slowdowns had occurred since World War II.

PHASES OF THE CYCLE

The term **business cycle** refers to the ups and downs in the level of economic activity. Individual business cycles vary substantially in duration and intensity, yet all have common phases. Figure 8-2 shows the phases of a stylized business cycle.

1. PEAK We begin with a **peak** at which business activity has reached a temporary maximum. Here the economy is at full employment and domestic output is also at or very close to capacity. The price level is likely to rise during this phase.

2. RECESSION The peak is followed by a **recession** — a period of decline in total output, income, and employment, lasting six months or longer. This downturn is marked by widespread contractions of business in many sectors of the economy. But, because many prices and wages are downwardly inflexible, the price level is likely to fall only if the recession is severe and prolonged.

3. TROUGH The **trough** of the recession or depression is where output and employment "bottom out" at their lowest levels. The trough may be short-lived or quite long.

4. RECOVERY In the **recovery** phase output and employment expand towards full employment. As recovery intensifies, the price level may begin to rise before there is full employment and full capacity production.

FIGURE 8-2   The business cycle

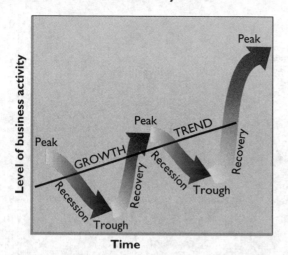

There are four phases of the business cycle and the duration and strength of each phase is highly variable. A recession, for example, need not always entail serious and prolonged unemployment. Nor need a cyclical peak always result in full employment or inflation.

Despite common phases, business cycles vary greatly in duration and intensity. Some economists prefer to talk of business *fluctuations*, rather than cycles, because cycles imply regularity while fluctuations do not. The Great Depression of the 1930s resulted in a 40% decline in real GDP over a three-year period and seriously undermined business activity for a decade. By comparison, our more recent recessions — detailed in Table 8-1 — have been minor in intensity and duration.

PROVINCIAL VARIATIONS

National GDP data for Canada do not reveal significant differences in economic fluctuations among Canada's ten provinces. Table 8-2 gives a provincial breakdown of economic growth. In 1994, for example, GDP grew by 5.7% in Alberta, but only 1.3% in Nova Scotia. Thus, the national growth rates in Canada can be misleading; in 1994 Alberta's economy was booming, while that of Nova Scotia, Newfoundland, and New Brunswick were barely growing. Notice the five-year growth rates also

TABLE 8-2   Provincial real GDP at factor cost   (per cent change)

	1992	1993	1994	Compound Annual Growth Rates (%) 1984-89	1989-94
CANADA	0.8	2.2	4.6	3.8	1.1
Newfoundland	−1.2	0.7	1.3	2.2	−0.6
P.E.I.	1.2	1.8	5.0	3.3	1.5
Nova Scotia	0.8	1.8	1.3	2.8	0.8
New Brunswick	−0.3	2.4	1.7	3.9	0.4
Quebec	−0.1	2.3	3.6	3.6	0.7
Ontario	0.4	1.8	4.5	4.9	0.3
Manitoba	1.9	−0.9	2.6	2.3	0.1
Saskatchewan	−1.7	4.1	4.5	1.4	2.2
Alberta	1.5	6.3	5.7	2.6	3.4
British Columbia	2.9	3.7	4.6	4.3	2.6

Real GDP: Real Gross Domestic Product in 1986 dollars
Source: Toronto-Dominion Bank and Statistics Canada

show significant differences, for the 1989–94 period ranging from –0.6% for Newfoundland to 3.4% for Alberta. More detailed provincial GDP data, broken down by industry, can be found in the appendix to this chapter.

CAUSATION: A FIRST GLANCE

Historically, economists have suggested many theories to explain fluctuations in business activity. Some contend that major innovations, such as the railroad, the automobile, or synthetic fibres have great impact on investment and consumption spending and therefore on output, employment, and the price level. But these major innovations occur irregularly and thus contribute to the variability of economic activity.

Other economists have explained the business cycle in terms of political and random events, as suggested by some of the labelling in Figure 8-1. Wars, for example, can be economically disruptive. A virtually insatiable demand for war goods during hostility can generate a period of overfull employment and sharp inflation, followed by an economic slump when peace returns and military spending plummets.

Still other economists view the cycle as a purely monetary phenomenon. When government creates too much money, an inflationary boom is generated; too little money will precipitate a declining output and unemployment.

Despite a diversity of opinion, most economists agree that the immediate determinant of the levels of domestic output and employment is the level of total or aggregate expenditures. In a market economy, businesses produce goods and services only if they can be sold profitably. If total spending is low most businesses will not find it profitable to produce a large volume of goods and services. As a result, output, employment, and the level of incomes will all be low. A higher level of total spending will mean that more production will be profitable; thus output, employment, and incomes will all be higher also. Once the economy approaches full employment, further real output gains become more difficult to achieve and added spending will pull up the price level.

NONCYCLICAL FLUCTUATIONS

Not all changes in business activity are due to the business cycle. There are **seasonal variations** in

business activity. The pre-Christmas and pre-Easter buying rushes cause fluctuations each year in the tempo of business activity, particularly in the retail industry. Agriculture, the automobile industry, and construction — indeed, virtually all industries — are subject to some degree of seasonality.

Business activity also displays a **secular trend** — expansion or contraction over a long period of years, for example, 25, 50, or 100 years. The long-run secular trend for the Canadian economy has been remarkable expansion. For present purposes, the importance of this long-run expansion is that the business cycle involves fluctuations in activity around a long-run growth trend. In Figure 8-1, cyclical fluctuations are measured as deviations from the secular growth trend and are revealed by changes in the unemployment rate. The stylized cycle in Figure 8-2 is drawn against a trend of growth.

CYCLICAL IMPACT: DURABLES AND NONDURABLES

The business cycle is felt in virtually every sector of the economy. The interdependence of sectors of the economy allows few to escape the negative effects of recession or surging inflation. Yet we must keep in mind that the business cycle affects various individuals and segments of the economy in different ways and in different degrees.

Insofar as production and employment are concerned, those industries producing capital goods are hit hardest by recession. The construction industry is particularly vulnerable. Consumer durables are

"Well, we tried to come up with a name that would really scare people"

Alan King, The Ottawa Citizen

BOX 8-2   IN THE MEDIA

CONSUMER CHILL HITS ECONOMY

Job worries blamed for Conference Board confidence index plummeting to 18-month low

BY ALAN FREEMAN
Parliamentary Bureau

OTTAWA — Consumer confidence dropped in the first quarter to its lowest level in 18 months as Canadians became more pessimistic about job prospects and increasingly hesitant to purchase large-ticket items.

The Conference Board of Canada said its quarterly index of consumer attitudes fell to 96.2 in March, the first time it has dropped below 100 in more than a year. "Consumers are reeling from anxiety over job prospects," said Paul Darby, the board's director of forecasting and analysis.

The drop in confidence adds to a string of statistics that suggest a slow-down in economic activity, including sluggish car, home and retail sales.

Statistics Canada reported yesterday that the value of residential building permits fell 17.5 per cent in the first quarter from the fourth quarter of 1994 to $3.6-billion — the lowest level in four years. The non-residential sector fared much better, with building permits up 11.1 per cent over the previous quarter to $3-billion....

Bad news bearers

- Building permits issued in the first quarter were at the lowest level in four years.
- First quarter sales of cars and trucks were down 11.3%.
- Consumer confidence at lowest level in 18 months.
- Canadian GDP fell 0.1% in February, first time since July, '93.
- Inflation at highest rate since February, '93.
- First quarter personal and business bankruptcies up 10% in first quarter.

Source: *Globe and Mail*, May 4, 1995, p. B1. Reproduced with permission.

The Story in Brief

Consumer confidence fell, implying retail, car, and home sales all suffered setbacks. Data are given that show lower car and truck sales and lower residential building permits. GDP actually declined in February 1995.

The Economics Behind the Story

- All economies are subject to cyclical fluctuations. The immediate cause of changes in output and employment is the level of aggregate expenditures.

- As consumers have become less optimistic about job prospects, they are expected to cut back on purchases in general, and big ticket items in particular. Durable goods purchases, such as cars and homes, are the first items to be cut back by consumers, because, within limits, the purchases of durable goods can be delayed.

- If Canadian consumers continue to cut back on their purchases, the economy could go into recession. The recession would be prevented if the drop in domestic consumer expenditures were replaced by higher expenditures by business, governments, or foreign buyers of Canadian products.

- Which of the expenditure categories that you studied in Chapter 7 are affected according to this news story? How do expenditures affect GDP and employment?

also hit hard. Output and employment in non-durable consumer goods industries are less sensitive to the cycle. Industries and workers producing housing and commercial buildings, heavy capital goods, farm implements, automobiles, refrigerators, microwave ovens, and similar products bear the brunt of bad times. But these durable goods industries are also stimulated most by expansion.

Two facts go far to explain the vulnerability of these industries to the business cycle.

1. POSTPONABILITY Within limits, the purchase of durable goods can be delayed. As the economy slips into recession, producers therefore forestall the acquisition of more modern productive facilities and the construction of new plants. The business outlook does not warrant increases in the stock of capital goods. The firm's present capital facilities and buildings will probably still be usable. In good times, capital goods are usually replaced before they are completely depreciated. When recession strikes, however, business firms will patch up their outmoded equipment. As a result, investment in capital goods will decline sharply. Some firms will not even bother to replace all the capital they are currently consuming. Net investment for them may be negative.

It's the same for consumer durables. During recessions the family budget must be trimmed, and it is likely that purchases of durables such as major appliances and automobiles will feel the axe. People repair their old appliances and cars rather than buy new models.

Food and clothing — consumer nondurables and semi-durables — are a different story. A family must eat and clothe itself. These purchases are much less postponable. To some extent the quantity and quality of these purchases will decline, but not so much as is the case with durables.

2. MONOPOLY POWER Most industries producing capital goods and consumer durables are industries of high concentration, where a relatively small number of large firms dominates the market. These firms have sufficient monopoly power to resist lowering prices temporarily by restricting output in the face of a declining demand. Therefore, the impact of a fall in demand centres primarily on production and employment.

The reverse holds true in nondurable and semi-durable goods industries, which are highly competitive and have low concentration. Firms are unable to resist price declines in such industries, and the impact of a declining demand reduces prices more than levels of production.

During the Great Depression this was especially serious for Canada, for we exported mostly raw materials, including agricultural commodities, whose prices fell considerably, while we imported mostly manufactured and highly processed goods, whose prices dropped very little. **(Key Question 1)**

QUICK REVIEW 8-1

1. The long-term secular trend of real domestic output has been upward in Canada.

2. The typical business cycle has four phases: peak, recession, trough, and recovery.

3. Industries producing capital goods and consumer durables normally suffer greater output and employment declines during recession than do service and nondurable consumer goods industries.

UNEMPLOYMENT

"Full employment" is hard to define. A person might think it means that everyone in the labour market — 100% of the labour force — is employed. But that's not so; some unemployment is normal.

TYPES OF UNEMPLOYMENT

Before defining full employment, we need to know about unemployment. There are several different types.

FRICTIONAL UNEMPLOYMENT With the freedom to choose occupations and jobs, at any time some workers will be between jobs. Some workers will be voluntarily switching jobs. Others will have been fired and are seeking re-employment. Still others will have been temporarily laid off from their jobs because of seasonal unemployment, for example, bad weather in the construction industry. There will be some, particularly young workers, searching for their first jobs.

As these unemployed people find jobs or are called back from temporary layoffs, other job seekers and temporarily laid-off workers will replace them in the unemployment pool. Therefore, even though the individuals who are unemployed for these reasons change from month to month, this type of unemployment persists.

Economists use the term **frictional unemployment** — consisting of *search unemployment* and *wait unemployment* — for workers who are either searching for jobs or waiting to take jobs in the near future. "Frictional" implies that the labour market does not operate perfectly nor instantaneously — without friction — in matching workers and jobs.

Frictional unemployment is inevitable and, at least in part, desirable. Many workers who are voluntarily "between jobs" are moving from low-paying, low-productivity jobs to higher-paying, higher-productivity positions. This means more income for workers and a better allocation of labour resources — and therefore a larger real output — for the economy as a whole.

STRUCTURAL UNEMPLOYMENT Frictional unemployment blurs into a category called **structural unemployment**. Economists use the term "structural" in the sense of "compositional." Changes occur over time in the structure of consumer demand and in technology, which alter the "structure" of the total demand for labour. Because of such changes, some particular skills will be in less demand or may even become obsolete. Demand for other skills will be expanding, including skills that did not exist before. Unemployment results because the labour force does not respond quickly or completely to the new structure of job opportunities. Some workers, therefore, find that they have no readily marketable talents since their skills and experience became obsolete by changes in technology and consumer demand. Similarly, the geographic distribution of jobs constantly changes.

We can cite many illustrations of structural unemployment.

1. Many years ago, highly skilled glass blowers were thrown out of work by the invention of bottle-making machines.
2. Historically, mechanization of agriculture dislodged thousands of low-skilled, poorly educated rural workers from their jobs. Many migrated to cities and suffered prolonged unemployment because of insufficient skills.
3. Many oil-field workers in Alberta found themselves structurally unemployed when the world price of oil nose-dived in the 1980s. Less drilling

and oil-related activity took place, resulting in widespread layoffs.
4. Recently, "corporate downsizing" has occurred in several major Canadian manufacturing industries. Many people losing their jobs have been corporate managers, who have had difficulty finding new work.
5. Recent closures of military bases and other defence cutbacks have displaced many workers, adding them to the rolls of the structurally unemployed.
6. The depletion of the cod stock off Canada's eastern seaboard has put thousands of fishermen without other skills out of work.
7. The decline of coal-mining and steel-making in Cape Breton has resulted in endemic unemployment there, already higher than the national average.

The distinction between frictional and structural unemployment is hazy. However, the key difference is that frictionally unemployed workers have saleable skills, while structurally unemployed workers are not readily re-employable without retraining, additional education, and possible geographic relocation. Frictional unemployment is short-term; structural unemployment is more long-term and therefore regarded as more serious.

CYCLICAL UNEMPLOYMENT Cyclical unemployment is caused by the recession phase of the business cycle. As the overall level of demand for goods and services decreases, employment falls and unemployment rises. For this reason, cyclical unemployment is sometimes called *deficient-demand unemployment*. During the recession year 1983, for example, the unemployment rate averaged 11.9%. Cyclical unemployment at the depth of the Great Depression in 1933 reached just under 20% of the labour force.

DEFINING "FULL EMPLOYMENT"

Full employment does *not* mean zero unemployment. Economists regard frictional and structural unemployment as essentially unavoidable. Thus, "full employment" is defined as something less than 100% employment of the labour force. Specifically, the **full-employment unemployment rate** is equal to the total of frictional and structural unemployment. Stated differently, the full-employment unemployment rate is achieved when cyclical unemployment is zero. The full-employment rate of unemployment is also referred to as the **natural rate of unemployment**. The real level of domestic output associated with the natural rate of unemployment is called the economy's **potential output**, the real output forthcoming when the economy is "fully employed."

The full or natural rate of unemployment results when labour markets are in balance in the sense that the number of job seekers equals the number of job vacancies. The natural rate of unemployment is always more than zero because it takes time for frictional unemployed job seekers to find open jobs they can fill. Also, regarding the structurally unemployed, it takes time to achieve the skills and geographic relocation needed for reemployment. If the number of job seekers exceeds available vacancies, labour markets are not in balance; there is a deficiency of aggregate demand and cyclical unemployment is present. But if aggregate demand is excessive a "shortage" of labour will arise; the number of job vacancies will exceed the number of workers seeking employment. In this situation the actual rate of unemployment is below the natural rate. Unusually "tight" labour markets such as this are associated with inflation.

The concept of the natural rate of unemployment merits elaboration in two respects.

1. NOT AUTOMATIC "Natural" does *not* mean the economy will always operate at the natural rate and realize its potential output. Our brief discussion of the business cycle demonstrated that the economy frequently operates at an unemployment rate higher than the natural rate. On the other hand, the economy may on some occasions achieve an unemployment rate lower than the natural rate. For example, during World War II, when the natural rate was about 4%, the pressure of wartime production resulted in an almost unlimited demand for labour. Overtime work was common as was "moonlighting" (holding more than one job). The government also froze some people working in "essential" industries in their jobs, reducing frictional unemployment. The actual rate of unemployment was below 2% in 1944 and 1945. The economy was producing beyond its potential output, but incurred considerable inflationary pressure in the process.

2. NOT IMMUTABLE The natural rate of unemployment itself is *not* immutable. It is subject to periodic revision because of the shifting demo-

graphics of the labour force or institutional changes (changes in society's laws and customs). In the 1960s this unavoidable minimum of frictional and structural unemployment was about 4% of the labour force. That is, full employment meant 96% of the labour force was employed. But today, economists generally agree that the natural rate of unemployment in Canada is between 7 and 8%.

Why is the natural rate of unemployment higher today than in the 1960s? First, the demographic makeup of the labour force has changed. Young workers — who traditionally have high unemployment rates — have become relatively more important in the labour force. Second, laws and custom have changed. For example, our unemployment insurance program has been expanded both in numbers of workers covered and size of benefits. By cushioning the economic impact of unemployment, unemployment insurance permits unemployed workers to engage in a more deliberate, lengthy job search, increasing frictional unemployment and the overall unemployment rate.

MEASURING UNEMPLOYMENT

Defining the full-employment unemployment rate — or natural rate of unemployment — is complicated by problems in measuring unemployment. Figure 8-3 is a helpful starting point. The **labour force population** consists of all persons 15 years old and older living in Canada, with the exception of the following: residents of Yukon and the Northwest Territories, persons living on Native reserves, inmates of institutions, and full-time members of the armed forces. The **civilian labour force** is the portion of the labour force population that is employed or unemployed. The **participation rate** is the labour force expressed as a percentage of the labour force population. In 1994 this rate was 65.2% — a significant 10-percentage-point increase since 1972.

The *employed* includes all persons who did any work at all or had a job but did not work because of illness, vacation, labour dispute, personal or family responsibilities, or bad weather. The *unemployed* includes all persons available for work who were without work but either had actively looked for work in the past four weeks or had not actively looked for work because of layoff for 26 weeks or less, or because they had a new job starting in four weeks or less. The *unemployment rate* is the percentage of the labour force that is unemployed:

TABLE 8-3   The civilian labour force, employment, and unemployment, 1994

(1) Total population	29,409,000
(2) Labour force population	22,714,000
(3) Civilian labour force	14,817,000
(4) Employed	13,276,000
(5) Unemployed	1,541,000

$$\text{Participation rate} = \frac{\text{Labour force}}{\text{Labour force population}}$$

$$= \frac{14,817,000}{22,714,000} \times 100 = 65.2\%$$

$$\text{Unemployment rate} = \frac{\text{Unemployed}}{\text{Labour force}}$$

$$= \frac{1,541,000}{14,817,000} \times 100 = 10.4\%$$

Source: Statistics Canada, *Canadian Economic Observer*, July, 1995.

FIGURE 8-3   The labour force, employment, and unemployment, 1994

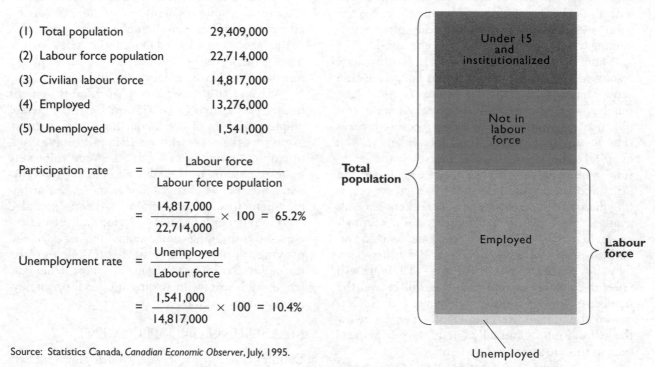

The labour force consists of persons 15 years of age or older who are not in institutions or the armed forces, and who are employed or unemployed.

$$\text{Unemployment rate} = \frac{\text{unemployed}}{\text{labour force}} \times 100$$

In 1994 the rate was

$$10.4\% = \frac{1,541,000}{14,817,000} \times 100$$

Unemployment rates for selected years between 1926 and 1994 are provided at the end of this book.

Statistics Canada (StatsCan) determines who is employed and who is not by conducting its nationwide random Labour Force Survey of some 55,000 representative households each month. A series of questions is asked regarding what members of the household are working, unemployed and looking for work, not looking for work, and so on. Despite the very sophisticated sampling and interview techniques used, the data collected from this survey are subject to three criticisms.

1. PART-TIME EMPLOYMENT The official data include all part-time workers as fully employed. Many part-timers want to work full-time, but can't find suitable full-time work or worked fewer hours because of a temporary lapse in consumer demand. These workers are really partially employed and partially unemployed. By counting them as fully employed, the official StatsCan data tend to *understate* the unemployment rate.

2. DISCOURAGED WORKERS You must be actively seeking work to be counted as unemployed. An unemployed individual who is not actively seeking employment and is not on layoff or starting a new job in four weeks or less is classified as "not in the labour force." There are numerous workers who, after unsuccessfully seeking employment for a time, become discouraged by their efforts and drop out of the labour force. Although the number of **discouraged workers** is larger during recession than during prosperity, estimates suggest that several hundred thousands may fall into this category. By not counting discouraged workers as unemployed, official data *understate* the employment rate.

3. FALSE INFORMATION But the unemployment rate may be *overstated*. Some respondents who are not working may claim they are looking for work, even though they are not. These individuals will be classified as "unemployed" rather than "not in the labour force." The motivation for giving this false information is that an individual's unemployment insurance benefits or welfare benefits may be contingent on professed job pursuit. The underground economy may also cause the official unemployment rate to be overstated. Individuals fully employed in drug trafficking are likely to identify themselves as being "unemployed."

The point is that although the unemployment rate is a basic consideration in policy-making, it is subject to certain shortcomings. While the unemployment rate is one of the best measures of the economic condition of the nation, it is not an infallible barometer. **(Key Question 5)**

ECONOMIC COST OF UNEMPLOYMENT

Problems in measuring the unemployment rate and defining the full-employment unemployment rate do not disguise an important fact: above-normal unemployment brings about great economic and social costs.

GDP GAP AND OKUN'S LAW The basic economic cost of unemployment is forgone output. *When the economy fails to generate enough jobs for all who are able and willing to work, potential production of goods and services is irretrievably lost.* In Chapter 2's analysis, unemployment keeps society from moving all the way to its production possibilities frontier. This sacrificed output is measured by the **GDP gap**. This gap is the amount by which the *actual GDP* falls short of *potential GDP*.

Potential GDP is determined by assuming that the natural rate of unemployment exists and projecting the economy's "normal" growth rate. Figure 8-4 shows the GDP gap for recent years and the close correlation between (a) the GDP gap and (b) the actual unemployment rate. The higher the unemployment rate, the larger the GDP gap.

The GDP gap, in constant dollars, can be determined from Figure 8-4. It can also be calculated by assuming that the relationship between the unemployment rate and the GDP gap that the macroeconomist Arthur Okun derived for the American economy is also applicable in Canada. **Okun's Law** indicates that *for every 1% that the actual unem-*

ployment rate exceeds the natural rate, a 2.5% GDP gap occurs. With this 1:2.5 unemployment rate–GDP gap link we can calculate the absolute loss of output associated with any unemployment rate. For example, in 1993 the unemployment rate was 11.2%, or 3.7% in excess of the assumed 7.5% natural rate. Multiplying this 3.7% by Okun's 2.5 figure indicates that the 1993 GDP gap was 9.25%. Stated differently, 1993's GDP would have been 9.25% larger had the natural rate of unemployment been realized. Applying this 9.25% loss to 1993's $712.855 billion real GDP, we find that the economy sacrificed $65.939 billion (= $712.855 billion × 9.25%) of output because the natural rate of unemployment was not achieved. **(Key Question 3)**

You should note that sometimes the economy's actual output can exceed its potential output. We have already mentioned that this happened during World War II, when unemployment rates fell below 2%. Extra shifts of workers were employed, capital equipment was used beyond its designed capacity, and overtime work and moonlighting were common. The late 1960s was also a period when the actual GDP exceeded potential GDP — a case where a "negative" GDP was created. When actual GDP exceeds potential GDP a "negative" GDP gap is created. Potential GDP can occasionally be exceeded, but the excess of actual over potential GDP cannot be sustained indefinitely.

UNEQUAL BURDENS Aggregate figures conceal that the cost of unemployment is unequally distributed. An increase in the unemployment rate from 7% to, say, 12% might be more tolerable to society if every worker's hours of work and wage income were reduced proportionately. But this is not the case.

Table 8-4 contrasts unemployment rates for various labour market groups for the same month, March, in 1989 and 1992, where unemployment for the month increased from 7.5% to 11.1%. The large variance in the rates of unemployment between the categories of workers *within each year* and comparison of the rates *between* the two years yields several generalizations.

1. OCCUPATION White-collar workers enjoy lower unemployment rates than blue-collar workers. White-collar workers generally are employed in less cyclically vulnerable industries (services and non-durable goods) or are self-employed. Also, white-collar workers are usually less subject to unemployment

FIGURE 8-4   (a) Potential and actual GDP and (b) the unemployment rate

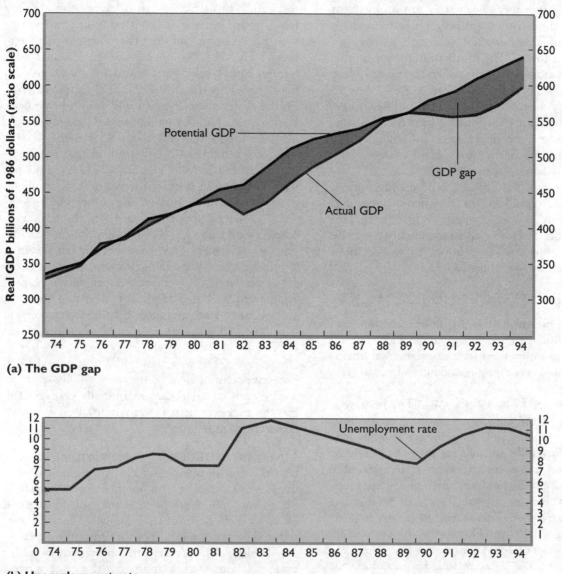

(a) The GDP gap

(b) Unemployment rate

The difference between potential and actual GDP is the GDP gap. The GDP gap measures the output that the economy sacrifices because it fails to utilize fully its productive potential. A high employment rate means a large GDP gap.

during recession than blue-collar workers. Businesses want to retain their more-skilled white-collar workers in whom they have invested the expense of training. But it's not always this way. During the 1990–1991 recession, many firms "downsized" their management structures, discharging more white-collar workers than ever before. The unemployment rate of white-collar workers increased more rapidly than for blue-collar labourers. Nevertheless, the unemployment rate of white-collar workers remained far below that of blue-collar workers.

2. AGE   Teenagers incur much higher unemployment rates than adults. Teenagers have lower skill levels, more frequently quit their jobs, are more frequently discharged from jobs, and have little geo-

TABLE 8-4 Unemployment by demographic group and duration as unemployment increases

Demographic group	Unemployment rate, March 1989	Unemployment rate, March 1992
Overall	7.5%	11.1%
Occupation		
Manufacturing	7.2	12.7
Services	6.8	9.2
Age		
15-24 years	10.6	19.1
25 years and over	6.7	11.1
Sex		
Male	7.2	13.9
Female	7.9	10.8
Duration		
14 weeks +	4.0	6.6

Source: Statistics Canada, *The Labour Force, March 1989* and *March 1992*.

graphic mobility. Many unemployed teenagers are new in the labour-market, searching for their first job.

3. GENDER Male and female unemployment rates are generally comparable. The lower unemployment rates for women in March 1992, when the Canadian economy just began to recover from a recession, reflect the fact there are more male than female workers in such cyclically vulnerable durable and capital goods industries as automobiles, steel, and construction.

4. DURATION The number of persons unemployed for long periods — 14 weeks or more — as a percentage of the labour force is often much less than the overall unemployment rate. This figure rises significantly during recessions. The "long-term" unemployed were only 4.0% of the labour force in 1989 as compared with the overall 7.5% unemployment rate. A large proportion of unemployment is of relatively short duration. The "long-term" unemployment rose to 6.6% of the labour force by March 1992, after a period of recession.

5. REGIONAL VARIATIONS The national unemployment rate in Canada does not reveal the significant diversity in regional unemployment. Table 8-5 gives both the national unemployment

TABLE 8-5 Provincial breakdown of the unemployment rate (per cent)

	1992	1993	1994
CANADA	11.3	11.2	10.4
Newfoundland	20.2	20.1	20.4
Prince Edward Island	17.9	18.1	17.1
Nova Scotia	13.2	14.7	13.3
New Brunswick	12.8	12.6	12.4
Quebec	12.8	13.2	12.2
Ontario	10.9	10.6	9.6
Manitoba	9.7	9.3	9.2
Saskatchewan	8.2	8.0	7.0
Alberta	9.5	9.7	8.6
British Columbia	10.5	9.7	9.4

Data are seasonally adjusted.
Source: Statistics Canada

BOX 8-3 APPLYING THE THEORY

THE STOCK MARKET AND MACROECONOMIC INSTABILITY

How, if at all, do changes in stock prices relate to the macroeconomy?

Financial investors daily buy and sell the stock certificates of hundreds of corporations. These corporations pay dividends — a portion of their profits — to the owners of their stock shares. The price of a particular company's stock is determined by supply and demand. Individual stock prices generally rise and fall in concert with the collective expectations for each firm's profits. Greater profits normally result in higher dividends to the owners of the stock and, in anticipation of these higher dividends, financial investors are willing to pay more for the stock.

Stock market averages such as the Toronto Stock Exchange industrial average — the average price of the stocks of a selected list of major Canadian industrial firms — are closely watched and reported. It is common for these price averages to change over periods of time, and even to rise or fall sharply during a single day. On "Black Monday," October 19, 1987, the TSE industrial average experienced a record one-day fall of 20%.

The volatility of the stock market raises this question: Do changes in stock price averages *cause* macroeconomic instability? There are linkages between the stock market and the economy that might lead us to think the answer is "Yes." Consider a sharp decline in stock prices. Feeling poorer, owners of stock may respond by reducing their spending on goods and services. Because it is less attractive to raise funds by issuing new shares of stock, firms may react by cutting back on their purchases of new capital goods.

Research studies find, however, that the consumption and investment impacts of stock price changes are relatively mild. Therefore, although stock price averages do influence total spending, the stock market is *not* a major cause of recession or inflation.

A related question emerges: Even though changes in stock prices do not *cause* significant changes in domestic output and the price level, might they *predict* such changes? That is, if stock market values are based on expected profits, wouldn't we expect rapid changes in stock price averages to forecast changes in future business conditions? Indeed, stock prices often *do* fall prior to recessions and rise prior to expansions. For this reason stock prices are among a group of ten variables that constitute an index of leading indicators. This index often provides a useful clue as to the future direction of the economy. But taken alone, stock market prices are not a reliable predictor of changes of domestic output. Stock prices have fallen rapidly in some instances with no recession following. Black Monday itself did not produce a recession during the following two years. In other instances, recessions have occurred with no prior decline in stock market prices.

In summary, the relationship between stock market prices and the macroeconomy is quite loose. Changes in stock prices are not a major source of macroeconomic instability nor are they reliable in forecasting business recessions or expansions.

rate and a provincial breakdown for the years 1992–94. For 1994 the national rate was 10.4% but as high as 20.4% in Newfoundland and as low as 7% in Saskatchewan.

NONECONOMIC COSTS

Severe cyclical unemployment is much more than an economic malady; it is a social catastrophe. Depression means idleness. And idleness means loss

of skills, loss of self-respect, a plummeting of morale, family disintegration, and sociopolitical unrest.

History demonstrates that severe unemployment is conducive to rapid and sometimes violent social and political change. Witness Hitler's ascent to power against a background of unemployment. At a more mundane level, recent research links increases in suicides, homicides, cardiovascular mortality, and mental illness to high unemployment.

4. Blue-collar workers and teenagers bear a dispro-portionate burden of unemployment.

INFLATION: DEFINED AND MEASURED

Now let's turn to inflation as an aspect of macroeconomic instability. The problems posed by inflation are more subtle than those of unemployment.

THE MEANING OF INFLATION

What is inflation? *Inflation is a rising general level of prices.* This does not mean that all prices are rising. Even during periods of rapid inflation, some specific prices may be relatively constant and others falling. For example, although Canada experienced high rates of inflation in the 1970s and early 1980s, the prices of such products as video cassette recorders and personal computers declined. One of the troublesome aspects of inflation is that prices rise unevenly. Some streak upward; others rise leisurely; others do not rise.

MEASURING INFLATION

Inflation is measured by price index numbers introduced in Chapter 7. Recall that a price index measures the general level of prices with reference to a base year.

The so-called **rule of 70** provides a quantitative appreciation of inflation. The rule allows us to calculate quickly the number of years required for a doubling of the price level. All we need do is divide the number 70 by the annual rate of inflation:

$$\text{Approximate number of years required to double} = \frac{70}{\text{percentage annual rate of inflation}}$$

For instance, a 3% annual rate of inflation will double the price level in about 23 (70 ÷ 3) years. Inflation of 8% per year will double the price level in about 9 (70 ÷ 8) years. Inflation at 12% will double the price level in only about six years. The rule of 70 will allow you, for example, to estimate how long it will take for real GDP or your savings account to double, or for your (or your country's) debts to double and then double again and again if the interest is not paid. **(Key Question 7)**

GLOBAL PERSPECTIVE 8-1

Unemployment rates in five industrial nations, 1984–1994

The unemployment rate in Canada has been above average compared with that in the United States, the United Kingdom, Japan, and Germany in the past 11 years.

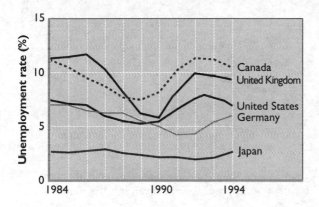

Source: OECD

INTERNATIONAL COMPARISONS

Unemployment rates vary greatly among nations of the world over specific periods. The major reason for these differences is that nations have different natural rates of unemployment and also may find themselves in different phases of their business cycle. Global Perspective 8-1 shows average unemployment rates for five industrialized nations for recent years. Within this group our record is mediocre. In the late 1980s our unemployment rate fell, but it had reached double digits again by 1994.

QUICK REVIEW 8-2

1. Unemployment is of three general types: frictional, structural, and cyclical.

2. The natural unemployment rate is estimated to be between 7 and 8%.

3. Society loses domestic output — goods and services — when cyclical unemployment occurs.

FIGURE 8-5   Price level in Canada since 1926

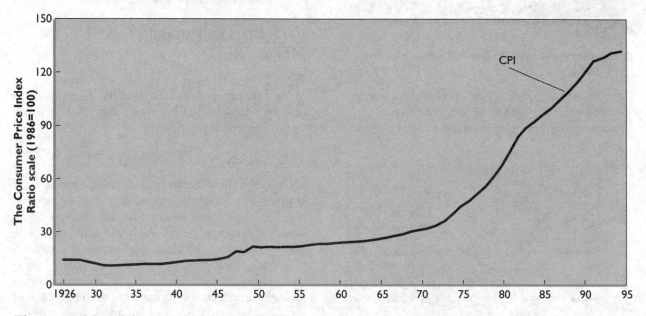

The price stability of the 1920s and the deflation of the 1930s gave way to sharp inflation in the immediate post-World War II period. The 1951–65 period was characterized by a reasonably stable price level, but the period since 1965 has been an age of inflation.

Sources: Statistics Canada, *National Income and Expenditures Accounts 1926–1986* (Ottawa, 1988) and Statistics Canada, *Canadian Economic Observer,* June 1992.

THE FACTS OF INFLATION

Figure 8-5 surveys inflation in Canada since 1926. The CPI curve represents annual increases in the consumer price index, which is constructed using the base year 1986. That is, the CPI for 1986 is arbitrarily set at 100.

Although most of you have grown up in an "age of inflation," our economy has not always been inflation-prone. The price level declined — *deflation* occurred — during the late 1920s and during the early years of the Great Depression of the 1930s. Prices then rose sharply in the immediate post–World War II period (1945–48) and in 1950. Overall price stability characterized the 1951–65 period, when the average annual increase in the price levels was less than 1.5%. But the inflation of the late 1960s, which then surged in the 1970s, introduced Canadians to double-digit inflation. In 1981 and 1982 the price level rose at 11% to 12% annual rates. By the middle of 1995, the rate of inflation had fallen to about a 2% annual rate. Specific national annual rates can be found in the tables at the back of this textbook.

TABLE 8-6   Consumer Price Index (Per cent change)

	1991	1992	1993	1994
CANADA	5.6	1.5	1.8	0.2
Newfoundland	6.2	1.1	1.6	1.3
Prince Edward Island	7.5	0.8	1.9	–0.2
Nova Scotia	6.1	0.6	1.2	1.2
New Brunswick	6.5	0.6	1.3	0.6
Quebec	7.4	1.8	1.4	–1.4
Ontario	4.6	1.1	1.7	0.1
Manitoba	5.1	1.4	2.7	1.4
Saskatchewan	5.2	1.0	3.0	1.8
Alberta	5.9	1.4	1.2	1.4
British Columbia	5.3	2.7	3.5	2.0

Source: Statistics Canada

REGIONAL VARIATIONS

Just as there are significant differences in unemployment rates among the provinces, there are also differences in the rates of inflation. Table 8-6 shows both the national and provincial annual percentage change in the CPI. In 1994, for example, the national rate was 0.2% but provincial rates varied from a low of –1.4% in Quebec to 2% in British Columbia.

But inflation is not distinctly Canadian. All the industrial nations have experienced this problem. Global Perspectives 8-2 traces the post-1981 inflation rates of Canada, the United States, the United Kingdom, Japan, and Germany. Observe that inflation in Canada has been neither unusually high nor low relative to inflation in these other industrial countries.

Some nations have had double-digit, triple-digit, or still higher annual rates of inflation in recent years. In 1983, for example, the inflation rate in Hungary was 23%; in Turkey, 23%; and in Romania, 256%. A few nations experienced astronomical rates of inflation in 1993: Zaire, 1,987%; and Brazil, 2,148%! Such rates of inflation are often referred to as **hyperinflation**.

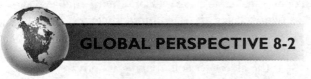

GLOBAL PERSPECTIVE 8-2

Inflation rates in five industrial nations, 1984–1994

Inflation rates in Canada over the past ten years have neither been extraordinarily high nor low relative to rates in other industrial nations.

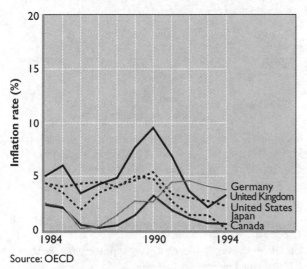

Source: OECD

CAUSES OF INFLATION: A FIRST GLANCE

Economists distinguish between two types of inflation.

1. DEMAND-PULL INFLATION   Traditionally, changes in the price level have been attributed to an excess of total demand. If in an economy spending rises beyond its capacity to produce, it represents a point beyond its production possibilities curve. The business sector cannot respond to this excess demand by expanding real output because all available resources are already fully employed. This excess demand will bid up the prices of the fixed real output, causing **demand-pull inflation**. The essence of demand-pull inflation is "too much money chasing too few goods."

2. COST-PUSH OR SUPPLY-SIDE INFLATION   Inflation may also arise on the supply or cost side of the market. During several periods in our recent economic history the price level has risen even though aggregate demand was not excessive. These were periods when output and employment were both *declining* (evidence of a deficiency of total demand), while at the same time the general price level was *increasing*.

The theory of **cost-push inflation** explains rising prices in terms of factors that raise **per unit production cost**. Per unit production cost is the average cost of a particular level of output. This average cost is found by dividing the total cost of resource inputs by the amount of output produced. That is,

$$\text{Per unit production cost} = \frac{\text{total input cost}}{\text{units of output}}$$

Rising per unit production costs squeeze profits and reduce the amount of output firms are willing to supply at the existing price level. As a result, the economy-wide supply of goods and services declines. This decline in supply drives up the price level. Under this scenario, costs are *pushing* the price level upward, rather than demand *pulling* it upward, as with demand-pull inflation.

Two sources of cost-push inflation are increases in nominal wages and increases in the prices of nonwage inputs such as raw materials and energy.

We leave until Chapter 16 a more detailed analysis of demand-pull and cost-push inflation.

REDISTRIBUTIVE EFFECTS OF INFLATION

Shifting from what causes inflation, we now look at its effects. We first consider how inflation redistributes income. We then examine possible effects on domestic output.

The relationship between the price level and the domestic output is ambiguous. Historically, real output and the price level have risen and fallen together. In the past two decades, however, there have been times when real output has fallen while prices have continued to rise. We will dodge this matter for a moment by assuming that the real output is constant and at the full employment level. By holding real output and income constant, we can isolate the effects of inflation on the distribution of that income. Assuming a fixed size of the national income pie, how does inflation affect the size of the slices going to different income receivers?

NOMINAL AND REAL INCOME To answer this question, it is essential to understand the difference between money income or nominal income and real income.[1] Money income or **nominal income** is the number of dollars received as wages, rent, interest, or profits. **Real income** measures the amount of goods and services your money income can buy.

If your nominal income increases faster than does the price level, your real income will rise. If the price level increases faster than your nominal income, your real income will decline. We can approximate the change in real income through this formula:

Percentage change in real income	=	Percentage change in nominal income	−	Percentage change in price level

If your nominal income rises by 10% and the price level rises by 5% in the same period, your real income will *increase* by about 5%. Conversely, a 5%

increase in nominal income accompanied by 10% inflation will *decrease* your real income by approximately 5%.[2]

The point to remember is this: while inflation reduces the purchasing power of the dollar — the amount of goods and services each dollar will buy — it does not necessarily follow that a person's real income will fall. The purchasing power of the dollar declines whenever inflation occurs, but a decline in your real income or standard of living occurs only when your nominal income fails to keep pace with inflation.

ANTICIPATIONS The redistributive effects of inflation depend on whether or not it is expected. In the case of **anticipated inflation**, an income receiver *may* be able to take steps to avoid or lessen the adverse effects inflation would otherwise have on real income. The generalizations that follow assume **unanticipated inflation**. We will then modify our generalizations to reflect the anticipation of inflation.

FIXED-NOMINAL-INCOME RECEIVERS

Our prior distinction between nominal and real incomes makes it clear that *inflation penalizes people who receive fixed nominal incomes*. Inflation redistributes income away from fixed-income receivers towards others in the economy. The classic case is the elderly couple living on a private pension or annuity providing a fixed amount of money income each month. The pensioner who retired in 1980 on what appeared to be an adequate pension would have found by 1995 that the purchasing power of that pension had been cut by over one-half.

---

[1] Chapter 7's distinction between nominal and real GDP is pertinent, and you may want to refresh your memory on the "inflating" and "deflating" process involved in converting nominal GDP to real GDP (Table 7-6).

[2] A more precise calculation follows Chapter 7's process for changing nominal GDP to real GDP. Thus

$$\text{Real income} = \frac{\text{nominal income}}{\text{price index (in hundredths)}}$$

In our first illustration, if nominal income rises by 10% from $100 to $110 and the price level (index) increases from 5% from 100 to 105, then real income has increased as follows:

$$\frac{\$110}{1.05} = \$104.76$$

The 5% increase in real income shown by the simple formula in the text is clearly a good approximation of the 4.76% yielded by our precise formula.

Similarly, landlords who receive rental payments of fixed dollar amounts will be hurt by inflation as they receive dollars of declining value over time. Families living on welfare payments that remain fixed over extended periods of time will also be victims of inflation. Note, however, that the adverse redistribution effect of inflation on old-age security pensioners has been offset in recent years by substantial increases in the size of benefits. The old-age security pension is now partially *indexed* — tied to the Consumer Price Index — to prevent erosion by inflation.

Some people living on flexible incomes *may* benefit from inflation. The nominal incomes of such households may spurt ahead of the price level, increasing their real incomes. Workers employed in expanding industries and represented by aggressive unions may keep their nominal wages apace with, or ahead of, the rate of inflation.

Some wage earners are hurt by inflation. Those situated in declining industries or without the benefit of strong unions may find that the price level races ahead of their money incomes.

Business executives and other profit receivers might benefit from inflation. If product prices rise faster than resource prices, business receipts will grow at a faster rate than will costs. Thus some — but not necessarily all — profit incomes will outdistance the rising tide of inflation.

SAVERS

Inflation hurts savers. **As prices rise, the real value, or purchasing power, of a nest egg of savings will deteriorate.** Savings accounts, insurance policies, annuities, and other fixed-value paper assets that were once adequate to meet rainy-day contingencies or to provide for a comfortable retirement, decline in real value during inflation. The simplest case is the individual who hoards money as a cash balance. A $1000 cash balance would have lost about half of its real value between 1978 and 1990. Most forms of savings, however, earn interest. But the value of savings will still decline if the rate of inflation exceeds the rate of interest.

Example: A household may save $1000 in a chartered bank or a credit union at 6% annual interest. But if inflation is 12.5% (as in 1981), the purchasing power of that $1000 will be cut to about $942 at the end of the year. The saver will receive $1060 (equal to $1000 plus $60 of interest), but

deflating that $1060 for 12.5% inflation means that the real value of that $1060 is only about $942 (equal to $1060 divided by 1.125).

DEBTORS AND CREDITORS

Inflation redistributes income by changing the relationship between debtors and creditors. **Unanticipated inflation benefits debtors (borrowers) at the expense of the creditors (lenders).** Suppose you borrow $1000 from a bank and you are to repay it in two years. If in that period of time the general level of prices were to double, the $1000 you repay will have only half the purchasing power of the $1000 originally borrowed. If we ignore interest charges, the same number of dollars is repaid as was borrowed. But because of inflation, each of these dollars will now buy only half as much as it did when the loan was negotiated. As prices go up, the value of the dollar comes down. Thus, because of inflation, the borrower is given "expensive" dollars but pays back "cheap" dollars.

The inflation of the past several decades has been a particular windfall to those who purchased homes in, say, the mid-1960s with fixed-interest-rate mortgages. Inflation has greatly reduced the real burden of their mortgage indebtedness, and the nominal value of housing has increased more rapidly than the overall price level.

ANTICIPATED INFLATION

The redistributive effects of inflation will be less severe or eliminated if people (1) anticipate inflation and (2) can adjust their nominal incomes to reflect expected price-level changes. The prolonged inflation that began in the late 1960s prompted many unions in the 1970s to insist on labour contracts that contain **cost-of-living adjustment (COLA)** clauses to adjust workers' incomes automatically to inflation.

Similarly, the redistribution of income from lender to borrower might be altered if inflation is anticipated. Suppose that a lender (perhaps a chartered bank or a credit union) and a borrower (a household) both agree that 5% is a fair rate of interest on a one-year loan, *provided* the price level is stable. But assume inflation has been occurring and is expected to be 6% over the next year. If the bank lends the household $100 at 5%, the bank will be paid back $105 at the end of the year. But if 6%

inflation does occur during the year, the purchasing power of that $105 will have been reduced to about $99. The *lender* will in effect have paid the *borrower* $1 to use the lender's money for a year.

The lender can avoid this subsidy by charging an **inflation premium** which means increasing the amount of the 6% anticipated inflation. Specifically, by charging 11%, the lender will receive back $111 at the end of the year which, adjusted for the 6% inflation, has the real value or purchasing power of about $105. In this instance, there is a mutually agreeable transfer of purchasing power, from borrower to lender, of $5 or 5% for the use of $100 for one year.

Our illustration points out the difference between the real rate of interest and the money or nominal rate of interest. The **real interest rate** *is the percentage increase in purchasing power that the lender receives from the borrower*. In our example, the real interest rate is 5%. The **nominal interest rate** *is the percentage increase in money that the lender receives*. The nominal rate of interest is 11% in our example. The difference in these

two concepts is that the real interest rate is adjusted or "deflated" for the rate of inflation while the nominal interest rate is not. The nominal interest rate is the sum of the real interest rate plus the premium paid to offset the anticipated rate of inflation. These distinctions are illustrated in Figure 8-6.

ADDENDA

Three final points must be mentioned.

1. DEFLATION The effects of unanticipated deflation are substantially the reverse of those of inflation. *Assuming no change in total output*, people with fixed money incomes will find their real incomes enhanced. Creditors will benefit at the expense of debtors. And savers will discover the purchasing power of their savings has grown because of falling prices.

2. MIXED EFFECTS The fact that any family may be an income earner, a holder of financial assets, and an owner of real assets simultaneously will likely cushion the redistributive impact of inflation. If the family owns fixed-value monetary assets (savings accounts, bonds, and insurance policies), inflation will lessen their real value. But that same inflation may increase the real value of any property assets (a house, land) that the family owns.

In short, many families simultaneously are hurt and benefit by inflation. All these effects must be considered before we can conclude that the family's net position is better or worse because of inflation.

3. ARBITRARINESS The redistributive effects of inflation are *arbitrary*; they occur regardless of society's goals and values. Inflation lacks a social conscience and takes from some and gives to others, whether they be rich, poor, young, old, healthy, or infirm.

FIGURE 8-6 The inflation premium and nominal and real interest rates

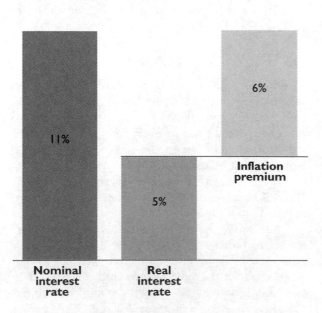

The inflation premium — the expected rate of inflation — gets built into the nominal interest rate. Here, the real interest rate of 5% plus the inflation premium of 6% equals the nominal interest rate of 11%.

QUICK REVIEW 8-3

1. Inflation arbitrarily "taxes" those who receive relatively fixed money incomes and "subsidizes" some people who receive flexible money incomes.

2. Unanticipated inflation arbitrarily penalizes savers and it benefits debtors at the expense of creditors.

3. The nominal interest rate exceeds the real interest rate by the expected rate of inflation.

CHAPTER SUMMARY

1. Our economy has been characterized by fluctuations in domestic output, employment, and the price level. Although having common phases — peak, recession, trough, recovery — business cycles vary greatly in duration and intensity.

2. Although economists explain the business cycle in terms of such ultimate causal factors as innovations, political events, and money creation, they generally agree that the level of total spending is the immediate determinant of domestic output and employment.

3. The business cycle affects all sectors of the economy, but in varying ways and degrees. The cycle has greater output and employment ramifications in the capital goods and durable consumer goods industries than it does in nondurable goods industries. Over the cycle, price fluctuations are greater in competitive than in monopolistic industries.

4. Economists distinguish between frictional, structural, and cyclical unemployment. The full-employment or natural rate of unemployment is currently between 7 and 8%. Part-time and discouraged workers complicate the accurate measurement of unemployment.

5. The economic cost of unemployment, as measured by the GDP gap, consists of the goods and services society forgoes when its resources are involuntarily idle. Okun's Law suggests that every 1% increase in unemployment above the natural rate causes a 2.5% GDP gap.

6. Unemployment rates and inflation rates vary greatly between nations. Unemployment rates differ because nations have different natural rates of unemployment and often are in different phases of their business cycles. Inflation and unemployment in Canada have been in the middle range over the last decade in comparison with that of a number of the other industrial nations.

7. Economists distinguish between demand-pull and cost-push (supply-side) inflation.

8. Unanticipated inflation arbitrarily redistributes income at the expense of fixed-income receivers, creditors, and savers. If inflation is anticipated, individuals and businesses may be able to take steps to lessen or eliminate adverse redistributive effects.

TERMS AND CONCEPTS

anticipated versus unanticipated inflation (p. 166)

business cycle (p. 151)

civilian labour force (p. 157)

cost-of-living adjustment (COLA) (p. 167)

demand-pull and cost-push inflation (p. 165)

discouraged workers (p. 158)

frictional, structural, and cyclical unemployment (p. 156)

full-employment unemployment rate (p. 156)

GDP gap (p. 159)

hyperinflation (p. 165)

inflation premium (p. 167)

labour force population (p. 157)

natural rate of unemployment (p. 157)

nominal and real income (p. 166)

nominal and real interest rates (p. 168)

Okun's Law (p. 159)

participation rate (p. 157)

peak, recession, trough, and recovery phases (p. 151)

per unit production cost (p. 165)

potential output (p. 157)

rule of 70 (p. 163)

seasonal variations (p. 153)

secular trend (p. 153)

QUESTIONS AND STUDY SUGGESTIONS

1. *Key Question*   *What are the major phases of the business cycle? How long do business cycles last? How long do seasonal variations and secular trends complicate measurement of the business cycle? Why does the business cycle affect output and employment in durable goods industries more severely than in industries producing nondurables?*

2. Why is it difficult to determine the full-employment unemployment rate? Why is it difficult to distinguish between frictional, structural, and cyclical unemployment? Why is unemployment an economic problem? What are the consequences of the "GDP gap"? What are the noneconomic effects of unemployment?

3. *Key Question*   *Assume that in a given year the natural rate of unemployment is 5% and the actual rate of unemployment is 9%. Use Okun's Law to determine the size of the GDP gap in percentage point terms. If the nominal GDP is $500 billion in that year, how much output is being forgone because of unemployment?*

4. Given that there exists an unemployment compensation program which provides income for those out of work, why worry about unemployment?

5. *Key Question*   *Use the following data to calculate a. the size of the labour force and b. the official unemployment rate. Total population, 500; population under 15 years of age and institutionalized, 120; not in labour force, 150; unemployed, 23; part-time workers looking for full-time jobs, 10.*

6. Explain how an *increase* in your nominal income and a *decrease* in your real income might occur simultaneously. Who loses from inflation? From unemployment? If you had to choose between a. full employment with a 6% annual rate of inflation or b. price stability with an 8 percent unemployment rate, which would you select? Why?

7. *Key Question*   *If the price index was 110 last year and is 121 this year, what was this year's rate of inflation? What is the "rule of 70"? How long would it take for the price level to double if inflation persisted at a. 2%, b. 5%, and c. 10% per year?*

8. Carefully describe the relationship between total spending and the levels of output and employment. Explain the relationship between the price level and increases in total spending as the economy moves from substantial unemployment to moderate unemployment, to full employment, and, finally, to absolute capacity.

9. Evaluate as accurately as you can how each of the following individuals would be affected by unanticipated inflation of 10% per year.
   a. a pensioned railroad worker
   b. a department-store clerk
   c. a unionized assembly-line worker
   d. a heavily indebted farmer
   e. a retired business executive whose current income comes entirely from interest on government bonds
   f. the owner of an independent, small-town department store

10. A noted television comedian once defined inflation as follows: "Inflation? That means your money today won't buy as much as it would have during the depression when you didn't have any." Is his definition accurate?

11. (Applying the Theory) Suppose that stock prices fall by 10% in the stock market. All else being equal, are these lower stock prices likely to cause a decrease in real GDP? How might these lower prices forecast a decline in real GDP? Are stock prices always reliable predictors of recessions?

APPENDIX TO CHAPTER 8

NEWFOUNDLAND: REAL GDP BY INDUSTRY

	Level: (Billions of 1986 dollars) 1994	Share of total 1994	Per cent change: year/year					Compound annual growth rates (%)		Index* (1989 = 100)
			1990	1991	1992	1993	1994	1984-89	1989-94	as at 1994
TOTAL ECONOMY	**6.52**	**100.0%**	**−0.8**	**−3.2**	**−0.8**	**0.7**	**1.3**	**2.2**	**−0.6**	**97.2**
GOODS	**1.65**	**25.3%**	**−5.2**	**−10.1**	**−7.8**	**0.4**	**2.4**	**0.7**	**−4.2**	**80.8**
Industrial production**	1.04	15.9%	−8.3	−8.7	−6.8	−0.6	0.4	1.2	−4.9	77.8
Manufacturing	0.47	7.2%	−8.4	−7.5	−11.4	−4.5	−3.5	3.8	−7.1	69.2
Mining	0.25	3.8%	−13.9	−19.3	−4.2	2.7	12.6	−3.3	−5.1	77.0
Utilities	0.33	5.0%	−2.9	−2.3	−0.6	3.3	−1.9	1.2	−0.9	95.7
Agriculture	0.02	0.3%	−10.1	5.7	−10.6	−6.6	7.2	3.0	−3.2	85.1
Fishing	0.08	1.2%	8.3	−20.9	−17.2	−17.9	−6.7	−0.2	−11.5	54.3
Logging	0.05	0.7%	−2.5	−8.7	−8.1	4.6	−0.9	−0.9	−3.3	84.7
Construction	0.47	7.2%	−0.8	−10.8	−7.6	7.5	8.8	0.8	−0.9	95.6
Residential construction	0.10	1.5%	−3.7	−15.9	−14.0	1.4	−2.4	9.0	−7.2	68.9
Non-res. bldg. construction	0.05	0.8%	6.9	−8.3	−10.0	−10.2	−4.9	4.2	−8.1	65.7
Engineering construction	0.32	4.9%	2.5	−8.9	−3.9	14.4	15.6	−3.2	3.5	118.7
SERVICES	**4.87**	**74.7%**	**1.1**	**−0.4**	**1.8**	**0.9**	**1.0**	**3.0**	**0.9**	**104.5**
Transportation & storage	0.22	3.4%	−16.2	−6.4	5.0	3.0	3.7	−2.5	−2.5	88.0
Communications	0.42	6.5%	4.4	7.9	6.3	4.6	6.6	8.8	5.9	133.5
Finance, insurance & real estate	1.02	15.6%	1.9	0.6	0.8	2.3	3.0	2.4	1.7	108.9
Community, business & personal	1.66	25.5%	1.3	0.2	1.5	0.6	0.3	2.7	0.8	104.1
Wholesale & retail trade	0.72	11.1%	6.1	−7.7	−0.3	−0.9	1.1	4.8	−0.5	97.8
Wholesale trade	0.24	3.6%	14.4	−15.1	2.4	−0.2	−2.9	6.8	−0.7	96.4
Retail trade	0.49	7.5%	2.0	3.6	−1.7	−1.3	3.1	4.0	−0.3	98.4
Government & other services	0.82	12.6%	−0.7	2.6	2.8	−1.0	−3.4	2.7	0.0	100.0

*An index greater than 100 means that industry has surpassed its pre-recession level of output.

** Industrial production includes manufacturing, mining and utilities.

GDP: Gross Domestic Product at factor cost in 1986 dollars; Source: Statistics Canada and the Toronto Dominion Bank

PRINCE EDWARD ISLAND: REAL GDP BY INDUSTRY

	Level: (Billions of 1986 dollars) 1994	Share of total 1994	Per cent change: year/year					Compound annual growth rates (%)		Index* (1989 = 100)
			1990	1991	1992	1993	1994	1984-89	1989-94	as at 1994
TOTAL ECONOMY	**1.78**	**100.0%**	**−0.2**	**−0.4**	**1.6**	**1.8**	**5.0**	**3.3**	**1.5**	**107.8**
GOODS	**0.54**	**30.1%**	**−3.8**	**1.6**	**6.7**	**0.6**	**10.3**	**3.1**	**2.9**	**115.6**
Industrial production**	0.22	12.5%	1.6	−1.9	5.0	10.9	12.1	7.3	5.4	130.0
Manufacturing	0.17	9.5%	3.2	−2.2	7.9	13.3	17.0	7.1	7.6	144.4
Mining	0.00	0.0%	—	—	—	—	—	—	—	—
Utilities	0.05	3.0%	−1.7	−1.5	−1.7	5.1	−1.0	7.7	−0.2	98.9
Agriculture	0.14	8.1%	−10.0	2.6	19.0	−1.9	−2.2	−1.6	1.1	105.4
Fishing	0.04	2.1%	10.2	0.8	9.5	−15.7	−4.6	2.8	−0.4	98.0
Logging	0.00	0.2%	−4.1	2.8	14.1	2.3	−0.5	0.2	2.7	114.5
Construction	0.13	7.1%	−9.4	6.6	−6.3	−6.4	32.5	7.4	2.3	112.2
Residential construction	0.03	1.6%	−11.4	0.9	−10.4	5.2	3.9	7.0	−2.6	87.6
Non–res. bldg. construction	0.02	0.9%	−16.1	20.1	−11.6	−7.5	−27.5	13.9	−9.8	59.8
Engineering construction	0.08	4.6%	−4.7	3.5	−1.2	−11.7	79.8	5.0	9.1	154.6
SERVICES	**1.25**	**69.9%**	**1.2**	**−1.2**	**−0.4**	**2.3**	**2.8**	**3.4**	**0.9**	**104.7**
Transportation & storage	0.05	3.0%	−1.5	0.9	−6.4	4.6	−0.8	0.5	−0.7	96.5
Communications	0.08	4.5%	7.5	7.9	6.0	3.7	6.1	9.0	6.2	135.4
Finance, insurance & real estate	0.27	14.9%	1.2	0.5	0.6	2.1	3.4	4.1	1.6	108.2
Community, business & personal	0.42	23.3%	0.5	−0.6	0.7	1.5	0.8	3.8	0.5	102.8
Wholesale & retail trade	0.21	11.6%	1.7	−4.3	3.8	3.5	3.3	4.2	1.5	107.9
Wholesale trade	0.08	4.3%	9.4	−0.6	3.7	2.4	5.1	9.3	3.9	121.3
Retail trade	0.13	7.3%	−2.2	−6.3	3.9	4.2	2.2	2.1	0.3	101.3
Government & other services	0.22	12.5%	1.0	−4.3	−7.3	1.7	5.1	1.1	−0.8	95.9

* An index greater than 100 means that industry has surpassed its pre-recession level of output.
** Industrial production includes manufacturing, mining and utilities.
GDP: Gross Domestic Product at factor cost in 1986 dollars; Source: Statistics Canada and the Toronto Dominion Bank

NOVA SCOTIA: REAL GDP BY INDUSTRY

	Level: (Billions of 1986 dollars) 1994	Share of total 1994	Per cent change: year/year					Compound annual growth rates (%)		Index* (1989 = 100)
			1990	1991	1992	1993	1994	1984-89	1989-94	as at 1994
TOTAL ECONOMY	13.29	100.0%	0.1	−0.6	1.3	1.7	1.3	2.8	0.8	103.9
GOODS	3.39	25.5%	0.7	−1.8	0.0	−1.8	0.5	1.8	−0.5	97.5
Industrial production**	2.21	16.6%	−2.0	4.8	3.0	0.4	2.3	0.3	1.7	108.6
Manufacturing	1.71	12.9%	−3.0	6.6	2.6	−0.7	1.2	0.6	1.3	106.6
Mining	0.17	1.3%	3.4	2.4	11.9	18.0	20.7	−11.1	11.0	168.7
Utilities	0.32	2.4%	1.6	−3.0	2.0	−0.3	0.1	4.3	0.1	100.4
Agriculture	0.15	1.1%	−8.0	2.8	−4.5	−0.7	6.4	5.2	−0.9	95.4
Fishing	0.25	1.9%	5.3	1.0	−2.6	−9.1	−3.9	4.1	−2.0	90.5
Logging	0.10	0.7%	−2.0	−8.4	2.6	−8.9	11.5	6.9	−1.3	93.6
Construction	0.68	5.1%	7.0	−16.3	−6.2	−4.6	−5.8	3.7	−5.5	75.6
Residential construction	0.24	1.8%	13.7	−17.7	4.2	−1.4	7.3	2.9	0.6	103.2
Non-res. bldg. construction	0.13	1.0%	−5.7	−26.5	−19.2	14.8	−12.5	9.7	−10.9	56.3
Engineering construction	0.31	2.3%	10.5	−10.8	−6.3	−12.8	−11.1	1.5	−6.5	71.6
SERVICES	9.90	74.5%	−0.1	−0.1	1.7	2.9	1.6	3.1	1.2	106.2
Transportation & storage	0.45	3.4%	−5.6	−7.5	0.2	7.2	7.1	3.6	0.1	100.4
Communications	0.73	5.5%	9.7	7.1	2.8	5.7	7.1	9.2	6.5	136.8
Finance, insurance & real estate	2.22	16.7%	2.1	1.5	2.1	2.5	2.4	4.0	2.1	110.9
Community, business & personal	3.13	23.6%	0.0	−0.3	1.8	1.5	1.5	2.4	0.9	104.6
Wholesale & retail trade	1.68	12.7%	1.4	−3.4	2.8	4.6	1.6	5.0	1.4	107.1
Wholesale trade	0.66	4.9%	12.2	−2.9	1.7	5.0	1.5	6.8	3.4	118.1
Retail trade	1.02	7.7%	−4.4	−3.8	3.5	4.4	1.7	4.1	0.2	101.1
Government & other services	1.70	12.8%	−5.6	1.0	0.2	2.3	−2.7	0.1	−1.0	95.2

* An index greater than 100 means that industry has surpassed its pre-recession level of output.
** Industrial production includes manufacturing, mining and utilities.
GDP: Gross Domestic Product at factor cost in 1986 dollars; Source: Statistics Canada and the Toronto Dominion Bank

NEW BRUNSWICK: REAL GDP BY INDUSTRY

	Level: (Billions of 1986 dollars) 1994	Share of total 1994	Per cent change: year/year					Compound annual growth rates (%)		Index* (1989 = 100)
			1990	1991	1992	1993	1994	1984-89	1989-94	as at 1994
TOTAL ECONOMY	**10.22**	**100.0%**	**–0.5**	**–0.9**	**–0.5**	**2.3**	**1.7**	**3.9**	**0.4**	**102.0**
GOODS	**3.07**	**30.1%**	**–3.5**	**–1.3**	**–4.9**	**1.7**	**1.6**	**4.6**	**–1.3**	**93.5**
Industrial production**	2.12	20.7%	–7.1	0.6	–0.6	3.3	1.8	5.3	–0.5	97.8
Manufacturing	1.41	13.8%	–9.5	3.3	–2.1	7.6	2.4	5.2	0.2	100.8
Mining	0.17	1.6%	0.3	12.6	13.9	–8.8	–2.4	4.0	2.7	114.5
Utilities	0.54	5.3%	–3.3	–7.8	–1.5	–2.5	1.6	5.7	–2.7	87.0
Agriculture	0.14	1.3%	–13.7	0.4	18.6	–4.0	–0.4	4.9	–0.4	98.2
Fishing	0.09	0.9%	25.2	–12.3	9.4	–2.4	0.4	8.8	3.3	117.6
Logging	0.19	1.9%	–8.5	–21.2	2.3	–2.2	13.9	3.2	–3.9	82.1
Construction	0.53	5.2%	8.6	0.3	–24.1	–0.8	–2.6	3.2	–4.4	80.0
Residential construction	0.15	1.4%	–12.3	–8.0	6.8	–2.8	5.1	4.8	–2.5	87.9
Non-res. bldg. construction	0.10	1.0%	–6.3	–10.2	–26.8	–4.1	–0.6	5.5	–10.1	58.7
Engineering construction	0.28	2.8%	27.2	7.4	–32.5	1.4	–6.8	1.4	–2.7	87.1
SERVICES	**7.14**	**69.9%**	**1.0**	**–0.8**	**1.5**	**2.5**	**1.7**	**3.5**	**1.2**	**106.1**
Transportation & storage	0.43	4.2%	–0.9	–8.9	–6.6	7.5	6.0	4.1	–0.8	96.0
Communications	0.54	5.2%	10.1	3.4	6.5	9.4	8.9	7.1	7.6	144.5
Finance, insurance & real estate	1.49	14.6%	–0.7	2.1	0.9	1.9	2.3	3.8	1.3	106.7
Community, business & personal	2.39	23.4%	4.2	1.1	1.7	2.3	1.2	2.7	2.1	110.8
Wholesale & retail trade	1.19	11.7%	–4.3	–5.8	2.8	0.5	1.3	5.0	–1.2	94.3
Wholesale trade	0.48	4.7%	–10.3	–5.8	3.0	–3.4	3.7	7.8	–2.7	87.2
Retail trade	0.72	7.0%	0.3	–5.8	2.7	3.2	–0.3	3.1	–0.0	99.8
Government & other services	1.10	10.8%	0.5	–0.9	1.9	1.4	–2.1	2.2	0.1	100.7

* An index greater than 100 means that industry has surpassed its pre-recession level of output.

** Industrial production includes manufacturing, mining and utilities.

GDP: Gross Domestic Product at factor cost in 1986 dollars; Source: Statistics Canada and the Toronto Dominion Bank

QUEBEC: REAL GDP BY INDUSTRY

	Level: (Billions of 1986 dollars) 1994	Share of total 1994	Per cent change: year/year					Compound annual growth rates (%)		Index* (1989 = 100)
			1990	1991	1992	1993	1994	1984-89	1989-94	as at 1994
TOTAL ECONOMY	116.86	100.0%	0.2	−2.9	0.3	2.4	3.6	3.6	0.7	103.5
GOODS	39.42	33.7%	0.1	−6.8	−2.4	3.2	4.6	3.7	−0.3	98.3
Industrial production**	30.60	26.2%	−0.3	−6.2	−0.7	4.3	4.1	3.4	0.2	100.8
Manufacturing	24.88	21.3%	0.3	−7.9	−1.0	4.8	4.1	3.4	−0.0	99.8
Mining	1.13	1.0%	4.4	6.4	−9.5	−3.9	4.9	6.1	0.3	101.3
Utilities	4.59	3.9%	−4.6	0.7	3.7	3.5	3.6	2.4	1.3	106.7
Agriculture	1.80	1.5%	−9.8	−1.0	−1.6	1.4	7.2	1.6	−0.9	95.5
Fishing	0.06	0.1%	16.1	−14.3	8.7	−4.7	−5.7	1.4	−0.6	97.1
Logging	0.83	0.7%	−11.1	−11.5	−9.9	26.9	22.4	8.2	1.9	110.1
Construction	6.14	5.3%	5.4	−10.0	−9.4	−3.1	4.6	5.3	−2.7	87.1
Residential construction	1.62	1.4%	3.2	−19.1	−2.8	−10.9	9.6	4.1	−4.5	79.2
Non-res. bldg. construction	1.20	1.0%	9.2	−17.9	−14.8	0.7	−0.4	9.7	−5.2	76.6
Engineering construction	3.31	2.8%	4.9	−0.9	−10.5	−0.4	4.2	4.2	−0.7	96.6
SERVICES	77.44	66.3%	0.2	−0.8	1.6	2.0	3.1	3.6	1.2	106.3
Transportation & storage	4.40	3.8%	−4.1	−2.9	3.5	1.3	6.9	2.1	0.9	104.4
Communications	4.89	4.2%	5.9	3.4	0.7	3.8	6.9	6.2	4.1	122.3
Finance, insurance & real estate	15.96	13.7%	0.4	2.0	1.4	2.0	2.7	4.9	1.7	108.7
Community, business & personal	27.99	24.0%	0.4	−1.0	1.0	1.7	2.3	3.1	0.9	104.4
Wholesale & retail trade	15.05	12.9%	−2.2	−4.8	3.5	3.4	5.6	5.1	1.0	105.3
Wholesale trade	7.27	6.2%	−1.0	−3.6	6.9	1.9	5.4	6.3	1.8	109.4
Retail trade	7.78	6.7%	−3.2	−5.8	0.4	4.9	5.7	4.0	0.3	101.6
Government & other services	9.15	7.8%	2.4	0.4	0.9	0.6	−0.9	0.9	0.7	103.4

*An index greater than 100 means that industry has surpassed its pre-recession level of output.

** Industrial production includes manufacturing, mining and utilities.

GDP: Gross Domestic Product at factor cost in 1986 dollars; Source: Statistics Canada and the Toronto Dominion Bank

ONTARIO: REAL GDP BY INDUSTRY

	Level: (Billions of 1986 dollars) 1994	Share of total 1994	Per cent change: year/year 1990	1991	1992	1993	1994	Compound annual growth rates (%) 1984-89	1989-94	Index* (1989 = 100) as at 1994
TOTAL ECONOMY	208.31	100.0%	-2.6	-2.7	0.4	1.9	4.5	4.9	0.3	101.4
GOODS	70.46	33.8%	-6.8	-6.6	-1.0	2.2	6.7	3.8	-1.3	93.9
Industrial production**	58.33	28.0%	-7.0	-6.1	0.8	4.7	7.5	3.1	-0.2	98.9
Manufacturing	50.92	24.4%	-6.7	-8.0	1.2	5.5	8.5	3.3	-0.1	99.5
Mining	2.02	1.0%	-5.8	-5.9	-3.0	-2.9	-5.9	2.0	-4.7	78.6
Utilities	5.40	2.6%	-10.8	12.8	-1.5	0.8	3.3	1.4	0.6	103.1
Agriculture	2.57	1.2%	-6.1	-5.1	-0.9	5.9	1.6	1.0	-1.0	95.0
Fishing	0.04	0.0%	—	—	—	—	—	—	—	—
Logging	0.43	0.2%	-11.7	-13.5	17.3	2.1	-0.6	-0.4	-1.9	90.9
Construction	9.08	4.4%	-6.1	-8.7	-10.1	-11.7	3.7	8.7	-6.7	70.6
Residential construction	3.15	1.5%	-18.8	-19.0	3.0	-3.1	6.1	11.0	-7.0	69.6
Non-res. bldg. construction	2.08	1.0%	-3.7	-9.1	-22.7	-17.2	7.7	12.4	-9.6	60.4
Engineering construction	3.85	1.8%	4.0	-1.0	-10.3	-14.6	-0.3	4.8	-4.7	78.7
SERVICES	137.85	66.2%	-0.2	-0.6	1.2	1.8	3.4	5.5	1.1	105.7
Transportation & storage	7.13	3.4%	-1.9	-9.1	-0.4	1.3	4.3	4.4	-1.3	93.8
Communications	7.73	3.7%	7.8	3.1	1.1	0.7	5.9	7.9	3.7	119.8
Finance, insurance & real estate	33.74	16.2%	0.0	2.1	1.6	2.6	2.7	5.9	1.8	109.3
Community, business & personal	47.99	23.0%	-0.9	-0.5	-0.9	1.2	1.9	5.3	0.1	100.7
Wholesale & retail trade	27.65	13.3%	-1.4	-4.1	5.1	3.9	8.5	7.2	2.3	112.1
Wholesale trade	15.14	7.3%	0.6	-2.8	8.0	5.5	10.5	10.3	4.3	123.2
Retail trade	12.51	6.0%	-3.3	-5.4	2.1	2.0	6.2	4.6	0.2	101.1
Government & other services	13.62	6.5%	1.3	2.3	1.2	-0.8	-0.6	2.0	0.7	103.5

* An index greater than 100 means that industry has surpassed its pre-recession level of output.

** Industrial production includes manufacturing, mining and utilities.

GDP: Gross Domestic Product at factor cost in 1986 dollars; Source: Statistics Canada and the Toronto Dominion Bank

MANITOBA: REAL GDP BY INDUSTRY

	Level: (Billions of 1986 dollars) 1994	Share of total 1994	Per cent change: year/year					Compound annual growth rates (%)		Index* (1989 = 100)
			1990	1991	1992	1993	1994	1984-89	1989-94	as at 1994
TOTAL ECONOMY	17.51	100.0%	1.4	−4.2	1.0	−0.2	2.6	2.3	0.1	100.6
GOODS	4.85	27.7%	6.4	−9.7	0.6	−5.7	4.0	2.6	−1.1	94.7
Industrial production**	3.18	18.2%	−1.6	−5.2	2.0	1.6	0.9	2.6	−0.5	97.6
Manufacturing	2.13	12.1%	−0.9	−9.4	0.8	0.4	2.2	3.4	−1.5	92.8
Mining	0.26	1.5%	−10.2	4.1	2.4	−9.5	−21.2	0.7	−7.3	68.3
Utilities	0.79	4.5%	1.1	5.3	6.0	11.8	7.3	1.0	6.2	135.4
Agriculture	0.76	4.3%	49.3	−15.2	6.6	−29.5	12.4	−1.3	1.4	107.0
Fishing	0.01	0.1%	−16.4	−0.0	8.2	−23.0	−10.2	0.2	−9.0	62.6
Logging	0.02	0.1%	10.7	−26.5	9.1	9.7	5.3	−1.4	0.5	102.6
Construction	0.88	5.0%	2.8	−17.1	−10.2	−5.5	9.2	6.0	−4.6	79.0
Residential construction	0.19	1.1%	−5.3	−31.2	1.9	13.7	13.5	0.2	−3.0	85.7
Non-res. bldg. construction	0.16	0.9%	−7.4	−15.6	−2.0	−13.1	16.5	2.8	−5.0	77.5
Engineering construction	0.52	3.0%	8.7	−13.4	−15.1	−8.5	5.6	9.6	−5.0	77.3
SERVICES	12.66	72.3%	−0.6	−1.7	1.2	2.0	2.1	2.1	0.6	103.0
Transportation & storage	1.28	7.3%	−2.2	−6.4	−3.9	7.1	6.5	1.1	0.1	100.4
Communications	0.77	4.4%	6.5	−0.3	2.2	5.2	5.8	8.6	3.9	120.8
Finance, insurance & real estate	2.77	15.8%	−0.2	0.8	2.6	0.1	1.6	2.6	1.0	105.0
Community, business & personal	4.00	22.8%	−1.3	−1.1	0.6	1.6	−0.6	1.9	−0.1	99.3
Wholesale & retail trade	2.23	12.7%	−1.9	−5.1	4.9	4.5	6.6	1.4	1.7	108.8
Wholesale trade	1.15	6.6%	−1.9	−6.6	8.3	5.6	9.1	1.1	2.7	114.4
Retail trade	1.08	6.2%	−1.9	−3.6	1.7	3.3	4.0	1.8	0.7	103.3
Government & other services	1.62	9.3%	0.2	−0.1	−0.5	−1.7	−0.9	1.5	−0.6	97.1

* An index greater than 100 means that industry has surpassed its pre-recession level of output.
** Industrial production includes manufacturing, mining and utilities.
GDP: Gross Domestic Product at factor cost in 1986 dollars; Source: Statistics Canada and the Toronto Dominion Bank

SASKATCHEWAN: REAL GDP BY INDUSTRY

	Level: (Billions of 1986 dollars) 1994	Share of total 1994	Per cent change: year/year					Compound annual growth rates (%)		Index* (1989 = 100)
			1990	1991	1992	1993	1994	1984-89	1989-94	as at 1994
TOTAL ECONOMY	**18.07**	**100.0%**	**6.5**	**−0.5**	**−3.3**	**4.2**	**4.5**	**1.4**	**2.2**	**111.7**
GOODS	**6.88**	**38.1%**	**17.6**	**−1.4**	**−10.0**	**9.4**	**7.0**	**1.2**	**4.1**	**122.1**
Industrial production**	3.94	21.8%	2.1	−1.8	4.4	7.5	11.8	0.9	4.7	125.7
Manufacturing	1.18	6.5%	9.3	−8.1	2.3	8.4	8.1	2.3	3.8	120.4
Mining	2.24	12.4%	−0.9	1.7	5.7	7.0	16.1	0.1	5.7	132.2
Utilities	0.53	2.9%	−2.0	0.4	4.1	7.3	3.1	0.9	2.5	113.3
Agriculture	1.89	10.5%	67.6	3.1	−26.6	15.4	−2.3	0.1	7.4	143.0
Fishing	0.01	0.0%	—	—	—	—	—	—	—	—
Logging	0.03	0.2%	−18.2	−29.4	−0.6	4.9	12.6	5.3	−7.5	67.8
Construction	1.01	5.6%	3.4	−8.1	−17.3	5.3	8.4	0.6	−2.2	89.6
Residential construction	0.12	0.7%	−23.9	−31.7	27.7	−8.6	2.7	−2.4	−9.0	62.3
Non-res. bldg. construction	0.13	0.7%	12.7	−24.9	−24.8	3.7	4.1	−1.5	−7.2	68.7
Engineering construction	0.76	4.2%	8.1	0.5	−21.4	8.4	10.1	2.1	0.4	101.8
SERVICES	**11.19**	**61.9%**	**0.6**	**0.1**	**0.9**	**1.3**	**3.0**	**1.1**	**1.2**	**106.1**
Transportation & storage	1.10	6.1%	−0.1	3.1	3.5	2.7	8.5	0.3	3.5	118.8
Communications	0.81	4.5%	5.5	−0.0	4.1	4.3	9.4	7.4	4.6	125.3
Finance, insurance & real estate	2.75	15.2%	−1.2	−2.0	0.7	1.0	3.0	0.6	0.3	101.4
Community, business & personal	3.37	18.6%	1.7	1.2	0.7	−0.8	−1.4	1.8	0.3	101.4
Wholesale & retail trade	1.91	10.6%	−0.5	0.3	0.3	5.8	9.8	−0.2	3.0	116.2
Wholesale trade	0.90	5.0%	2.4	2.7	−1.6	8.5	11.6	0.1	4.6	125.4
Retail trade	1.01	5.6%	−2.8	−1.7	1.8	3.6	8.2	−0.4	1.7	109.0
Government & other services	1.26	7.0%	1.0	−0.5	−1.1	−0.8	−2.3	0.2	−0.8	96.3

* An index greater than 100 means that industry has surpassed its pre-recession level of output.

** Industrial production includes manufacturing, mining and utilities.

GDP: Gross Domestic Product at factor cost in 1986 dollars; Source: Statistics Canada and the Toronto Dominion Bank

ALBERTA: REAL GDP BY INDUSTRY

	Level: (Billions of 1986 dollars) 1994	Share of total 1994	Per cent change: year/year					Compound annual growth rates (%)		Index* (1989 = 100)
			1990	1991	1992	1993	1994	1984-89	1989-94	as at 1994
TOTAL ECONOMY	70.56	100.0%	3.3	0.5	1.3	6.1	5.7	2.5	3.4	117.9
GOODS	30.54	43.3%	3.8	1.4	0.3	10.0	8.9	2.3	4.8	126.5
Industrial production**	23.83	33.8%	3.5	2.2	3.0	9.9	9.9	2.4	5.6	131.6
Manufacturing	6.46	9.2%	8.5	0.9	–0.9	8.2	12.4	3.1	5.7	131.7
Mining	14.80	21.0%	2.2	2.5	5.1	12.3	9.7	1.5	6.3	135.6
Utilities	2.56	3.6%	–1.4	3.9	2.0	1.6	5.7	5.3	2.3	112.2
Agriculture	2.64	3.7%	11.8	4.8	–9.4	21.5	1.7	7.0	5.6	131.2
Fishing	0.01	0.0%	—	—	—	—	—	—	—	—
Logging	0.16	0.2%	1.6	26.6	–0.1	–1.4	18.9	14.8	8.6	150.7
Construction	3.91	5.5%	1.2	–5.2	–7.3	4.3	7.7	0.1	–0.0	99.9
Residential construction	0.69	1.0%	16.8	–17.0	25.2	–8.1	0.9	10.8	2.4	112.6
Non-res. bldg. construction	0.44	0.6%	1.1	–11.0	–2.4	–8.5	–21.7	–0.3	–8.8	63.0
Engineering construction	2.78	3.9%	–2.4	–0.4	–16.1	12.3	16.6	–1.6	1.3	106.7
SERVICES	40.03	56.7%	3.0	–0.1	1.9	3.4	3.4	2.6	2.3	112.2
Transportation & storage	3.72	5.3%	0.8	1.4	6.5	6.1	6.1	2.7	4.1	122.5
Communications	2.18	3.1%	3.7	1.3	4.9	6.0	9.0	4.6	4.9	127.3
Finance, insurance & real estate	12.16	17.2%	4.1	1.3	3.3	3.9	4.2	1.9	3.4	117.9
Community, business & personal	11.66	16.5%	3.5	0.3	–1.1	2.0	–0.2	2.4	0.9	104.4
Wholesale & retail trade	6.82	9.7%	1.1	–4.2	2.8	6.5	9.2	4.7	3.0	115.8
Wholesale trade	3.34	4.7%	4.5	–6.1	2.5	7.6	12.4	6.9	4.0	121.5
Retail trade	3.48	4.9%	–1.8	–2.5	3.1	5.5	6.4	3.0	2.1	110.8
Government & other services	3.49	4.9%	3.4	–0.9	0.4	–1.7	–3.3	1.6	–0.5	97.7

*An index greater than 100 means that industry has surpassed its pre-recession level of output.

** Industrial production includes manufacturing, mining and utilities.

GDP: Gross Domestic Product at factor cost in 1986 dollars; Source: Statistics Canada and the Toronto Dominion Bank

BRITISH COLUMBIA: REAL GDP BY INDUSTRY

	Level: (Billions of 1986 dollars) 1994	Share of total 1994	Per cent change: year/year					Compound annual growth rates (%)		Index* (1989 = 100)
			1990	1991	1992	1993	1994	1984-89	1989-94	as at 1994
TOTAL ECONOMY	**66.92**	**100.0%**	**1.8**	**0.8**	**2.8**	**3.2**	**4.6**	**4.3**	**2.6**	**114.0**
GOODS	**18.70**	**27.9%**	**-2.6**	**-2.2**	**1.6**	**2.4**	**4.9**	**4.2**	**0.8**	**103.9**
Industrial production**	11.67	17.4%	-4.4	-2.1	1.6	2.2	3.1	4.2	0.0	100.1
Manufacturing	8.21	12.3%	-6.0	-5.3	4.5	2.5	2.8	4.6	-0.4	98.0
Mining	1.87	2.8%	-2.2	7.0	-9.9	5.0	3.9	3.2	0.6	102.9
Utilities	1.59	2.4%	2.2	4.0	2.0	-2.6	3.6	3.4	1.8	109.4
Agriculture	0.80	1.2%	-4.0	-0.2	-0.4	13.9	6.5	6.4	3.0	115.7
Fishing	0.43	0.6%	13.1	-0.0	-1.8	26.0	-9.9	12.3	4.7	125.9
Logging	1.17	1.8%	-7.3	-12.1	5.9	5.6	-3.3	0.9	-2.5	88.1
Construction	4.62	6.9%	3.1	-0.1	0.9	-1.9	14.1	4.8	3.1	116.4
Residential construction	1.28	1.9%	13.4	-10.8	19.6	1.2	1.9	10.1	4.5	124.6
Non-res. bldg. construction	1.00	1.5%	-0.5	4.4	4.6	-10.3	15.3	3.7	2.4	112.5
Engineering construction	2.35	3.5%	-0.5	4.0	-9.7	0.4	21.5	3.1	2.6	113.9
SERVICES	**48.23**	**72.1%**	**3.7**	**2.1**	**3.3**	**3.6**	**4.5**	**4.4**	**3.4**	**118.4**
Transportation & storage	4.13	6.2%	-2.4	-2.9	-2.7	2.9	8.0	2.9	0.5	102.5
Communications	2.69	4.0%	10.5	3.8	4.7	2.9	8.1	7.1	6.0	133.6
Finance, insurance & real estate	13.14	19.6%	2.4	7.0	4.6	3.8	3.4	5.1	4.2	123.0
Community, business & personal	14.86	22.2%	6.1	0.9	1.6	1.7	2.3	4.2	2.5	113.0
Wholesale & retail trade	9.47	14.1%	2.8	-0.1	7.4	7.9	9.0	5.9	5.3	129.8
Wholesale trade	4.74	7.1%	4.3	2.8	12.4	10.4	9.5	7.2	7.8	145.6
Retail trade	4.73	7.1%	1.5	-2.6	3.1	5.6	8.5	5.0	3.2	117.0
Government & other services	3.94	5.9%	4.3	0.9	3.0	1.9	0.3	1.2	2.1	110.7

*An index greater than 100 means that industry has surpassed its pre-recession level of output.

** Industrial production includes manufacturing, mining and utilities.

GDP: Gross Domestic Product at factor cost in 1986 dollars; Source: Statistics Canada and the Toronto Dominion Bank

Source: Statistics Canada and the Toronto Dominion Bank. Reproduced by authority of the Minister of Industry 1995, Statistics Canada, adapted from *Provincial Gross Domestic Product by Industry*, Cat. 15–203, 1995.

CHAPTER 9

BUILDING THE AGGREGATE EXPENDITURES MODEL: THE CLOSED ECONOMY

Sometime during your lifetime you or a member of your family may be permanently discharged or temporarily laid off from work during a recession — total spending will not be sufficient to buy all the goods produced and services offered. You may also live through "boom" periods in which total spending surges, sharply increasing employment, real GDP, and national income.

In this chapter and Chapter 10, we shift from description to analysis by building on the definitions and facts of Chapter 7 (national income accounting) and Chapter 8 (macroeconomic instability). We will construct an aggregate expenditures model to explain how the economy's equilibrium real GDP relates to total spending and how a change in total spending affects the level of real GDP.

We intend to accomplish these goals in the following way. First, we set out the historical backdrop of the aggregate expenditures model. Next, we focus on the consumption-income and saving-income relationships that are part of the model. Third, we shift to investment — specifically, how firms choose the amounts of capital goods to buy. Finally, we combine the consumption, saving, and investment concepts to explain the equilibrium levels of output, income, and employment in a private (no government), closed (no foreign sector) economy.

In this chapter and the next we develop a *model* of the economy to clarify the basic determinants of the levels of output and employment. The specific numbers employed are not intended to measure the real world. Also, be forewarned that, while the aggregate expenditures model provides valuable insights about the macroeconomy, it assumes a constant price level. In Chapter 11 we develop a complementary model allowing for changes in real GDP *and* the price level.

BOX 9-1 THE BIG PICTURE

We noted in the last chapter that a market economy is prone to a certain amount of instability, also referred to as the business cycle. We need to understand how GDP and the price level are determined so that we can devise the appropriate macroeconomic policies to counteract macroeconomic fluctuations. Remember, the goal is to employ all of the economy's available factors of production — particularly labour — and get the most output out of them. We put aside the issue of the price level until Chapter 11, to concentrate on how GDP is determined.

We already know that the main immediate determinant of GDP in an economy is the level of expenditures. From Chapter 7 we also learned there are four expenditure categories: consumption, investment, government, and net export. Here we begin with the simplest expenditure model of an economy: one with only two categories of expenditure: consumption and investment. In doing so, we also investigate the main determinants of consumption and investments.

As you read this chapter, keep the following points in mind:

- Our simple expenditure model has no foreign sector (thus, a closed economy), and no government sector. These will be added in the next chapter.
- The main determinant of the level of consumption is disposable income; the main determinant of investments are interest rates.
- The expenditure model assumes a fixed price level. The price level will be considered in another model (the aggregate supply-aggregate demand model) to be introduced in Chapter 11.

HISTORICAL BACKDROP

L et's gain some historical perspective on the aggregate expenditures model.

CLASSICAL ECONOMICS AND SAY'S LAW

Until the Great Depression of the 1930s, many economists of the nineteenth and early twentieth centuries — now called classical economists — believed the market system would ensure full employment of the economy's resources. They acknowledged that now and then abnormal circumstances such as wars, political upheavals, droughts, speculative crises, and gold rushes would occur, deflecting the economy from the path of full employment (review Figure 8-1). But when these deviations occurred, automatic adjustments in prices, wages, and interest rates within the market would soon restore the economy to the full-employment level of output. A slump in output and employment would reduce prices, wages, and interest rates. The lower prices would increase consumer spending, the lower wages would increase employment, and the lower interest rates would boost investment spending. Any excess supply of goods and workers would be soon be eliminated.

Classical economists denied the possibility of long-term underspending — a level of spending insufficient to purchase a full-employment output. This denial was based in part on **Say's Law**, attributed to the nineteenth-century French economist J. B. Say. Say's Law is the disarming notion that the very act of producing goods generates an amount of income equal to the value of the goods produced. The production of any output automatically provides the income needed to take that output off the market — the income needed to buy what's produced. *Supply creates its own demand.*

Say's Law can be understood in terms of a barter economy. A shoemaker, for example, produces (*supplies*) shoes as a means of buying (*demanding*) goods and services produced by other craft workers. The shoemaker's supply of shoes is his demand for other goods. And so it allegedly is for other producers and for the entire economy. Demand must be the same as supply! The circular flow model of the economy and national income accounting both suggest something of this sort. Income generated from the production of any level of output would, when spent, be just sufficient to provide a matching total demand. Assuming the composition of output is in accord with consumer preferences, all markets would be cleared of their outputs. It would seem that all business owners need to do to sell a full-employment output is to produce that output; Say's Law guarantees there will be sufficient consumption spending to buy it all.

Say's Law and classical economics are not simply historical curiosities. A few modern economists have reformulated, revitalized, and extended the work of these nineteenth- and twentieth-century economists to generate a "new" classical economics. We will examine classical economics and its modern reincarnation in more detail in later chapters.

THE GREAT DEPRESSION AND KEYNES

Two events undermined the theory that supply creates its own demand (Say's Law) and led to the emergence of the theory that underspending or overspending can occur (aggregate expenditure theory).

1. THE GREAT DEPRESSION The depression of the 1930s was worldwide. In Canada, this depression plummeted real GDP by about a third and skyrocketed the unemployment rate to nearly 20%. Much the same occurred in other industrial nations. The negative effects of the depression lasted for a decade. Some economists noted the inconsistency between a theory that concludes that unemployment is virtually impossible and the actual occurrence of a ten-year seige of very substantial unemployment.

2. KEYNES AND KEYNESIAN ECONOMICS In 1936 the English economist John Maynard Keynes (pronounced "Caines") set forth a new explanation of the levels of employment in market economies. In his *The General Theory of Employment, Interest and Money*, Keynes attacked the foundations of classical theory and touched off a major revolution in economic thinking on macroeconomic questions. Keynes disputed Say's Law, pointing out that in some periods not all income will necessarily get spent on the output produced. When widespread underspending occurs, unsold goods will accumulate in producers' warehouses. Producers will respond to rising inventories by reducing their output and cutting their employment. Thus, a recession or depression will follow.

Keynes initiated modern employment theory, but many others have since refined and extended his work. That's why the modern aggregate expenditures model reflects **Keynesian economics**, not just the economics of Keynes. In the aggregate expenditures model, the macroeconomy is inherently unstable; it is subject to periods of recession and inflation. A market economy is not a self-regulating system capable of uninterrupted prosperity. While capitalism is an excellent engine of long-term economic growth, we cannot always depend on it to "run itself."

Furthermore, economic fluctuations are not associated exclusively with external forces such as wars, droughts, and similar abnormalities. Rather, the Keynesian view sees the causes of unemployment and inflation as the failure of certain fundamental economic decisions — in particular saving and investment decisions — to be completely synchronized. In addition, product prices and wages are downwardly inflexible, meaning that extended and costly periods of recession or depression will prevail before significant declines in prices and wages occur. Internal factors, in addition to external forces (wars and droughts), contribute to economic instability.

SIMPLIFICATION

Four assumptions will help us build the aggregate expenditures model.

1. Initially we will assume a "closed economy" where there are no international trade transactions. Discussion of the complications arising from exports and imports in the "open economy" will be deferred to Chapter 10.
2. We will also ignore government until Chapter 10, permitting us first to demonstrate that at times a market economy may not achieve and maintain full employment. For now we will be dealing with a "private" closed economy.
3. Although both businesses and households save, we will for convenience speak as if all saving were personal saving.
4. To keep things simple, we will assume that depreciation and *net* Canadian income earned abroad are zero.

We should tell you about two implications of these assumptions. First recall from Chapter 7 that there are four components of aggregate spending: consumption, investment, government purchases, and net exports. Assumptions 1 and 2 mean that, for now, we are concerned only with consumption and investment.

BOX 9-2 APPLYING THE THEORY

JOHN MAYNARD KEYNES (1883–1946)

The English economist John Maynard Keynes is regarded as the originator of modern macroeconomics.

In 1935 George Bernard Shaw received a letter from John Maynard Keynes in which Keynes asserted, "I believe myself to be writing a book on economic theory which will largely revolutionize ... the way the world thinks about economic problems." And, in fact, Keynes's *The General Theory of Employment, Interest, and Money* did revolutionize economic analysis and established Keynes as one of the most influential economists of all time.

The son of an eminent English economist, Keynes was educated at Eton and Cambridge. While his early interests were in mathematics and probability theory, Keynes ultimately turned to economics.

Keynes was far more than an economist: He was an incredibly active, many-sided man who also played such diverse roles as principal representative of the Treasury at the World War I Paris Peace Conference, deputy for the Chancellor of the Exchequer, a director of the Bank of England, trustee of the National Gallery, chairman of the Council for the Encouragement of Music and the Arts, bursar of King's College, Cambridge, editor of the *Economic Journal*, chairman of the *Nation* and later the *New Statesman* magazines, and chairman of the National Mutual Life Assurance Society. He also ran an investment company, organized the Camargo Ballet (his wife, Lydia Lopokova, was a renowned star of the Russian Imperial Ballet), and built (profitably) the Arts Theatre at Cambridge.*

*E. Ray Canterbery, *The Making of Economics*, 3d ed. (Belmont, Calif.: Wadsworth Publishing Company, 1987), p. 126.

In addition, Keynes found time to amass a $2-million personal fortune by speculating in stocks, international currencies, and commodities. He was also a leading figure in the "Bloomsbury group," an *avant-garde* group of intellectual luminaries who greatly influenced the artistic and literary standards of England.

Most importantly, Keynes was a prolific scholar. His books encompassed such widely ranging topics as probability theory, monetary economics, and the economic consequences of the World War I peace treaty. His *magnum opus*, however, was the *General Theory*, which has been described by John Kenneth Galbraith as "a work of profound obscurity, badly written and prematurely published." Yet the *General Theory* attacked the classical economists' contention that recession will automatically cure itself. Keynes's analysis suggested that recession could easily spiral downward into a depression. Keynes claimed that modern capitalism contained no automatic mechanism that would propel the economy back towards full employment. The economy might languish for many years in depression. Indeed, the massive unemployment of the worldwide depression of the 1930s seemed to provide sufficient evidence that Keynes was right. His basic policy recommendation — a startling one in view of the balanced-budget sentiment at the time — was for government in these circumstances to increase its spending to induce more production and put the unemployed back to work.

Second, assumptions 2 through 4 permit us to treat gross domestic product (GDP), national income (NI), personal income (PI), and disposable income (DI) as being equal to one another. All the items that in practice distinguish them from one another result from depreciation, net Canadian income earned abroad, government (taxes and transfer payments), and business saving (see Table 7-4). Our assumptions mean if $500 billion of goods and services is produced as GDP, exactly $500 bil-

lion of DI is received by households to use as either consumption or saving.

TOOLS OF THE AGGREGATE EXPENDITURES THEORY

How are the levels of output and employment determined? *The amount of goods and services produced, and therefore the level of employment, depends directly on the level of total, or aggregate, expenditures.* Businesses will produce a level of output that they can profitably sell. Workers and machinery are idled when there are no markets for the goods and services they are capable of producing. Total output and employment vary directly with aggregate expenditures.

Our strategy in this chapter is to analyze the consumption and investment components of aggregate expenditures and derive a private sector model of equilibrium GDP and employment. Chapter 10 examines changes in real GDP and adds net exports and government expenditures (along with taxes) to the model.

Be sure you understand as we begin our discussion that unless specified otherwise we assume the economy has substantial excess productive capacity and unemployed labour. An increase in aggregate expenditures thus will increase real output and employment but *not* the price level.

QUICK REVIEW 9-1

1. Classical economics was grounded in Say's Law, which asserted that supply creates its own demand and thus that underspending leading to recessions was highly unlikely.

2. The Great Depression and Keynes's development of an alternative model of the macroeconomy created doubt about the validity of classical economics and led to the emergence of the modern aggregate expenditures theory.

3. In the aggregate expenditures model, the level of total or aggregate expenditures determines the amount of goods and services produced and thus the level of employment.

CONSUMPTION AND SAVING

Consumption is the largest component of aggregate expenditures (Chapter 7). We therefore need to understand the determinants of consumption spending. Recall that economists define personal saving as "not spending" or "that part of disposable income (DI) not consumed"; in other words, disposable income equals consumption plus saving. Thus, in examining the determinants of consumption, we are also simultaneously exploring the determinants of saving.

INCOME-CONSUMPTION AND INCOME-SAVING RELATIONSHIPS

Many considerations influence the level of consumer spending. But the most significant determinant of consumer spending is income — in particular, disposable income. And since saving is that part of disposable income that is not consumed, DI is also the basic determinant of personal saving.

Consider some recent historical data. In Figure 9-1, each dot indicates the consumption-disposable income relationship for each year since 1970; the C line is fitted to these points. Note that consumption is directly related to disposable income and, indeed, households spend most of their income.

But we can say more. The **45° line** is added to the diagram for reference purposes. Because the 90° angle formed by the vertical and horizontal axes of the graph is bisected by this 45° line, each point must be equidistant from the two axes. We can therefore regard the vertical distance from any point on the horizontal axis to the 45° line as either consumption or disposable income. If we regard it as disposable income, then the amount (the vertical distance) by which the actual amount consumed in any year falls short of the 45° guideline indicates the amount of saving in that year. For example, in 1994 consumption (including interest paid and transfers to nonresidents) was $458.339 billion and disposable income was $497.357 billion; thus saving in 1994 was $39.018 billion. Disposable income less consumption equals saving. As we move to the right on Figure 9-1, we see that saving also varies directly with the level of disposable income.

Figure 9-1 suggests (1) households consume most of their disposable income, and (2) both consumption and saving are directly related to the income level.

THE CONSUMPTION SCHEDULE

The dots in Figure 9-1 represent historical data — how much households *actually did consume* (and save) at various levels of DI over a period of years. To analyze what the data can tell us, we need an income-consumption relationship — a consumption schedule — showing the various amounts households *plan* to consume at various levels of disposable income that might conceivably prevail at some specific *point in time.* A hypothetical **consumption schedule** of the

FIGURE 9-1   Consumption and disposable income, 1970–1994

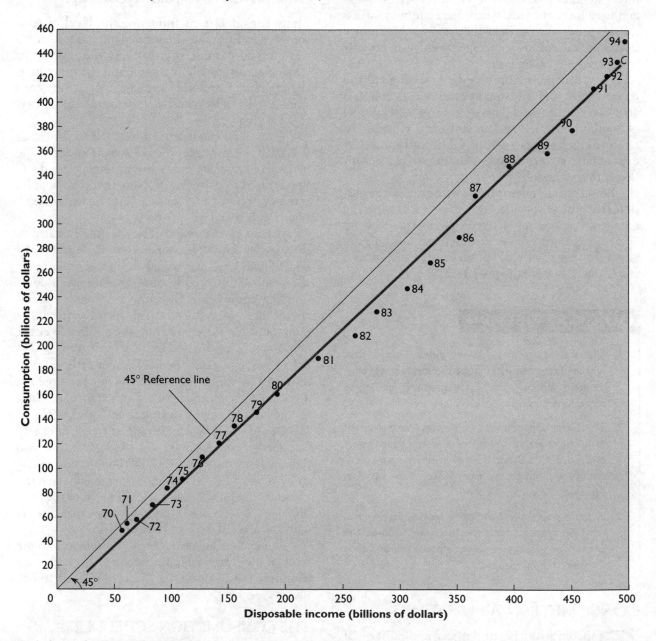

Each dot in this figure shows consumption and disposable income in a given year. The C line generalizes on the relationship between consumption and disposable income. It indicates a direct relationship and that households consume the bulk of their incomes.

Source: Statistics Canada, *National Income and Expenditure Accounts.*

KEY GRAPH

FIGURE 9-2   Building the aggregate expenditure model

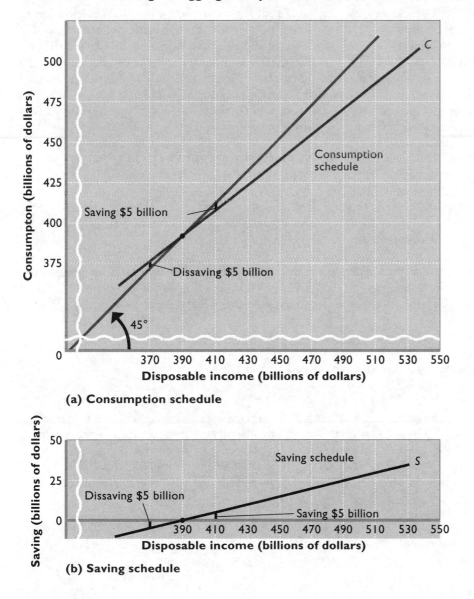

(a) Consumption schedule

(b) Saving schedule

The two parts of this figure show the income-consumption and income-saving relationships graphically. Each point on the 45° line in (a) indicates a point where DI equals consumption. Therefore, because saving equals DI minus consumption, the saving schedule in (b) is found by subtracting the consumption schedule from the 45° line. Consumers "break even" — that is, consumption equals DI (and saving therefore equals zero) at $390 billion for these hypothetical data.

type we require for analysis is shown in columns 1 and 2 of Table 9-1. It is plotted in **Figure 9-2(a) (Key Graph)**. This consumption schedule reflects the consumption-disposable income relationship suggested by the empirical data of Figure 9-1, and it is consistent with a variety of empirical family-budget studies. The relationship is direct, and we note that households will spend a *larger proportion* of a small disposable income than of a large disposable income.

THE SAVING SCHEDULE

It is simple to derive a **saving schedule**. Because disposable income equals consumption plus saving (DI = C + S), we need only subtract consumption (Table 9-1, column 2) from disposable income (column 1) to find the amount saved (column 3) at each level of DI: that is, DI − C = S. Thus, columns 1 and 3 of Table 9-1 constitute the saving schedule. This schedule is plotted in Figure 9-2(b). Note there is a direct relationship between saving and DI but that saving is a smaller proportion (fraction) of a small DI than of a large DI. If households consume a smaller and smaller proportion of DI as DI goes up, they must save a larger and larger proportion.

Since at each point on the 45° line DI equals consumption, we see that dissaving would occur at the relatively low DI of $370 billion, where consumption is actually $375 billion. Households will consume in excess of their current incomes by liquidating (selling for cash) accumulated wealth or by borrowing. Graphically, the vertical distance of the consumption schedule *above* the 45° line is equal to the vertical distance of the saving schedule *below* the horizontal axis at the $370 billion level of output and income [see Figures 9-2(a) and (b)]. In this instance, each of these two vertical distances measures the $5 billion of *dissaving* that occurs at the $370 billion income level.

The **break-even income** is at the $390 billion level (row 2). This is the level where households consume their entire incomes. Graphically, the

consumption schedule cuts the 45° line, and the saving schedule cuts the horizontal axis (saving is zero) at the break-even income level.

At all higher incomes, households will plan to save a portion of their income. The vertical distance of the consumption schedule *below* the 45° line measures this saving, as does the vertical distance of the saving schedule *above* the horizontal axis. For example, at the $410 billion level of income, both these distances indicate $5 billion worth of saving [see Figures 9-2(a) and (b)].

AVERAGE AND MARGINAL PROPENSITIES

Columns 4 to 7 of Table 9-1 point out additional characteristics of the consumption and saving schedules.

APC AND APS That fraction, or percentage, of any given total income that is consumed is called the **average propensity to consume (APC)**. That

TABLE 9-1 Consumption and savings schedules (columns 1 to 3 in billions)

(1) Level of output and income (GDP = DI)	(2) Consumption (C)	(3) Saving (1) – (2) (S)	(4) Average propensity to consume (APC) (2)/(1)	(5) Average propensity to save (APS) (3)/(1)	(6) Marginal propensity to consume (MPC) Δ(2)/Δ(1)*	(7) Marginal propensity to save (MPS) Δ(3)/Δ(1)
(1) $370	$375	$ –5	1.01	–0.01		
					0.75	0.25
(2) 390	390	0	1.00	0.00		
					0.75	0.25
(3) 410	405	5	0.99	0.01		
					0.75	0.25
(4) 430	420	10	0.98	0.02		
					0.75	0.25
(5) 450	435	15	0.97	0.03		
					0.75	0.25
(6) 470	450	20	0.96	0.04		
					0.75	0.25
(7) 490	465	25	0.95	0.05		
					0.75	0.25
(8) 510	480	30	0.94	0.06		
					0.75	0.25
(9) 530	495	35	0.93	0.07		
					0.75	0.25
(10) 550	510	40	0.93	0.07		

*The Greek capital letter Δ, delta, means "difference" or "a change in."

fraction of any total income that is saved is the **average propensity to save (APS)**. That is,

$$APC = \frac{consumption}{income}$$

and

$$APS = \frac{saving}{income}$$

For example, at the $470 billion level of income (row 6) in Table 9-1, the APC is $^{450}/_{470} = {}^{45}/_{47}$, or about 96%, while the APS is $^{20}/_{470} = {}^{2}/_{47}$, or about 4%. By calculating the APC and APS at each of the ten levels of DI shown in Table 9-1, we find that the APC falls and the APS rises as DI increases. This quantifies a point made a moment ago: the fraction of total DI that is consumed declines as DI rises, and the fraction of DI that is saved rises as DI rises.

Because disposable income is either consumed or saved, the sum of the fraction of any level of DI consumed plus the fraction saved (not consumed) must exhaust that level of income. Mathematically,

$$APC + APS = 1$$

Columns 4 and 5 of Table 9-1 illustrate this point.

Global Perspective 9-1 shows APCs for several countries.

MPC AND MPS The fact that households consume a certain portion of some total income — for example, $^{45}/_{47}$ of a $470 billion disposable income — does not guarantee they will consume the same proportion of any *change* in income they might receive. The proportion, or fraction, of any change in income consumed is called the **marginal propensity to consume (MPC)**, marginal meaning "extra" or "a change in." Or the MPC is the ratio of a *change* in consumption to the *change* in income that caused that change in consumption:

$$MPC = \frac{change\ in\ consumption}{change\ in\ income}$$

Similarly, the fraction of any change in income saved is called the **marginal propensity to save (MPS)**. The MPS is the ratio of a *change* in saving to the change in income bringing it about:

$$MPS = \frac{change\ in\ saving}{change\ in\ income}$$

Average propensities to consume, selected nations

There are surprisingly large differences in average propensities to consume (APCs) among nations. Canada in particular has a substantially higher APC — and thus a lower APS — than many other advanced economies.

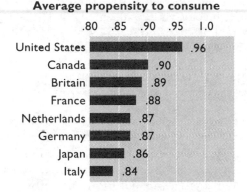

Average propensity to consume

Source: *Statistical Abstract of the United States 1994*, p. 863.

If disposable income is $470 billion (row 6) and household incomes rise by $20 billion to $490 billion (row 7), they will consume $^{15}/_{20}$ or $^{3}/_{4}$ and save $^{5}/_{20}$ or $^{1}/_{4}$ of that increase in income (see columns 6 and 7 of Table 9-1). In other words, the MPC is $^{3}/_{4}$, or 0.75, and the MPS is $^{1}/_{4}$, or 0.25.

The sum of the MPC and the MPS for any change in disposable income must always be 1. Consuming and saving out of extra income is an either-or proposition; that fraction of any change in income that is not consumed is, by definition, saved. Therefore the fraction consumed (MPC) plus the fraction saved (MPS) must exhaust the whole increase in income:

$$MPC + MPS = 1$$

In our example, 0.75 plus 0.25 equals 100%, or 1.

MPC AND MPS AS SLOPES The MPC is the numerical value of the slope of the consumption schedule and the MPS is the numerical value of the slope of the saving schedule. We know from the Appendix to Chapter 1 that the slope of any line can be measured by the ratio of the vertical change to horizontal change involved in moving from one point to another on that line.

In Figure 9-3 we highlight the slopes of the consumption and saving lines derived from Table 9-1 by enlarging relevant portions of Figures 9-2(a) and 9-2(b). Observe that consumption changes by $15 billion (vertical change) for each $20 billion change in disposable income (horizontal change); the slope of the consumption line is .75 (= $15/$20) — the value of the MPC. Saving changes by $5 billion (vertical change) for every $20 billion change in disposable income (horizontal change). The slope of the saving line therefore is .25 (= $5/$20), which is the value of the MPS. **(Key Question 6)**

NONINCOME DETERMINANTS OF CONSUMPTION AND SAVING

The level of disposable income is the basic determinant of the amounts households will consume and save, just as price is the basic determinant of the quantity demanded of any product. You will recall that changes in determinants other than price, such as consumer tastes, incomes, and so forth (Chapter 4), will shift the demand curve for a given product. Similarly, certain determinants might cause households to consume more or less at each possible level of DI and shift the consumption and saving schedules.

1. WEALTH   Generally, the greater the amount of wealth households have accumulated, the larger will be the amount of consumption and the smaller the amount of saving out of any level of current income. By *wealth* we mean both real assets (a house, automobiles, television sets, and other durables) and financial assets (cash, savings accounts, stocks, bonds, insurance policies, pensions) that households own. Households save — refrain from consumption — in order to accumulate wealth. The more wealth households have accumulated, the weaker the incentive to save in order to accumulate additional wealth. Stated differently, an increase in wealth shifts the saving schedule downward and the consumption schedule upward.

Examples: The dramatic stock-market crash of 1929 had the effect of significantly decreasing the financial wealth of many families almost overnight and was undoubtedly a factor in the low levels of consumption in the depressed 1930s. More recently, the general decline in real estate values chipped

FIGURE 9-3   The marginal propensity to consume and the marginal propensity to save

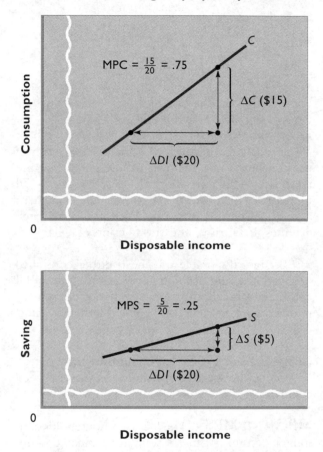

The MPC is the slope of the consumption schedule and the MPS is the slope of the saving schedule.

away household wealth and contributed to a retrenchment of consumer spending.

For the most part, however, the amount of wealth held by households changes only modestly from year to year and therefore does not account for large shifts in the consumption and saving schedules.

2. EXPECTATIONS   Household expectations about future prices, money incomes, and the availability of goods may significantly affect current spending and saving. Expectations of rising prices and product shortages trigger more spending and less saving currently. This shifts the consumption schedule upward and the saving schedule downward.

It is natural for consumers to seek to avoid paying higher prices or to avoid having to do without. Expected inflation and expected shortages induce people to buy now to escape higher future prices and bare shelves. The expectation of rising money incomes in the future also makes consumers more willing to increase their current spending. Conversely, expected dollar declines, anticipations of shrinking incomes, and the feeling that goods will be abundantly available may induce consumers to cut back on their consumption and build up their savings.

3. CONSUMER INDEBTEDNESS The level of consumer debt can also be expected to affect the willingness of households to consume and save out of current income. If households are in debt to the degree that, say, 20% or 25% of their current incomes are committed to instalment payments on previous purchases, consumers may well be obliged to cut back on current consumption in order to reduce their indebtedness. Conversely, if consumer indebtedness is relatively low, households may consume at an unusually high rate by increasing this indebtedness.

4. TAXATION In Chapter 10, we will find that changes in taxes will shift the consumption and saving schedules. Taxes are paid partly at the expense of consumption *and* partly at the expense of saving. Therefore, an *increase* in taxes will shift *both* the consumption and saving schedules *downward*. Conversely, a tax reduction will be partly consumed and partly saved by households. A tax *decrease* will shift *both* the consumption and saving schedules *upward*.

SHIFTS AND STABILITY

Three final, related points are relevant to our discussion of the consumption and saving schedules.

1. TERMINOLOGY The movement from one point to another on a specific stable consumption schedule [for example, a to b on C_0 in Figure 9-4(a)] is called a *change in the amount consumed*. The sole cause of the change in consumption is a change in disposable income. On the other hand, *a change in the consumption schedule* refers to an upward or downward shift of the entire schedule as viewed from the horizontal axis — for example, a shift from C_0 to C_1 or C_2 in Figure 9-4(a). A relocation of the consumption schedule is caused by changes in any one or more of the four nonincome determinants just discussed.

A similar distinction in terminology applies to the saving schedule in Figure 9-4(b).

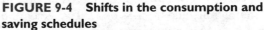

FIGURE 9-4 Shifts in the consumption and saving schedules

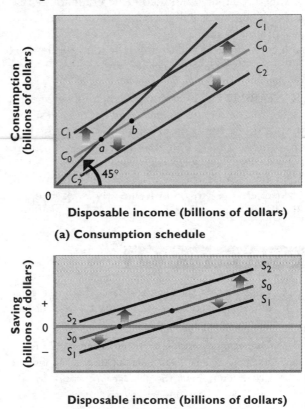

Disposable income (billions of dollars)

(a) Consumption schedule

Disposable income (billions of dollars)

(b) Saving schedule

A change in any one or more of the nonincome determinants will cause the consumption and saving schedules to shift. If households consume more at each level of DI, they are necessarily saving less. Graphically, this means that an upshift in the consumption schedule (C_0 to C_1) entails a downshift in the saving schedule (S_0 to S_1). Conversely, if households consume less at each level of DI, they are saving more. A downshift in the consumption schedule (C_0 to C_2) is reflected in an upshift of the saving schedule (S_0 to S_2).

2. SCHEDULE SHIFTS The first three nonincome determinants of consumption will shift the consumption and saving schedules in opposite directions. If households decide to consume *more* at each possible level of disposable income, they want to save *less*, and vice versa. Graphically, if the consumption schedule shifts upward from C_0 to C_1 in Figure 9-4, the saving schedule will shift downward from S_0 to S_1. Similarly, a downshift in the consumption schedule from C_0 to C_2 means an upshift in the saving schedule from S_0 to S_2. The exception to this is the fourth nonincome determinant — taxation. Households will consume less *and* save less to pay higher taxes. Thus, a tax increase will lower *both* consumption and saving schedules, while a tax cut will shift *both* schedules upward.

3. STABILITY Economists generally agree that, aside from deliberate governmental actions designed to shift them, the consumption and saving schedules are usually stable. This may be because consumption-saving decisions are strongly influenced by habit or because the nonincome determinants are diverse; changes in them frequently work in opposite directions and therefore may be self-cancelling.

QUICK REVIEW 9-2

1. Consumption spending and saving both rise when disposable income increases; they fall when disposable income decreases.

2. The average propensity to consume (APC) is the fraction of any given level of disposable income that is consumed; the average propensity to save (APS) is the fraction of any given level of disposable income that is saved. The APC falls and the APS rises as disposable income increases.

3. The marginal propensity to consume (MPC) is the fraction of any change in disposable income that is spent for consumer goods and is the slope of the consumption schedule; the marginal propensity to save (MPS) is the fraction of any change in disposable income that is saved and is the slope of the saving schedule.

4. Changes in consumer wealth, consumer expectations, consumer indebtedness, and taxes shift the consumption and saving schedules.

INVESTMENT

We now turn to investment, the second component of private spending. Recall that investment consists of expenditures on new plants, capital equipment, machinery, and so on. The investment decision is a marginal benefit-marginal cost decision (Chapters 1 and 2). The marginal benefit from investment is the expected rate of net profits businesses hope to realize. The marginal cost is the interest rate — the cost of borrowing. We will see that businesses will invest in all projects for which expected net profits exceed the interest rate. Expected net profits and the interest rate therefore are the two basic determinants of investment spending.

EXPECTED RATE OF NET PROFIT, r

Investment spending is guided by the profit motive; businesses buy capital goods only when they expect such purchases to be profitable. Suppose the owner of a small cabinetmaking shop is considering investing in a new sanding machine costing $1000 and having a useful life of only one year. The new machine will presumably increase the firm's output and sales revenue. Suppose the *net* expected revenue (that is, net of such operating costs as power, lumber, labour, certain taxes, and so forth) from the machine is $1100. In other words, after operating costs have been accounted for, the remaining expected net revenue is sufficient to cover the $1000 cost of the machine and leave a profit of $100. Comparing this $100 profit with the $1000 cost of the machine, we find that the expected *rate* of net profit, r, on the machine is 10% (= $100/$1000). Instead of "profit," businesses sometimes refer to the "return" on the investment, meaning the profits that resulted from the investment, thus, our use of r for this "return" or "profit."

THE REAL INTEREST RATE, i

One important cost associated with investing that our example has ignored is the interest rate — the financial cost the firm must pay to borrow the *money* capital required to purchase the *real* capital (the sanding machine).

We can consider the interest rate in the context of an investment and its expected return with the following generalization: If the expected rate of net profits (10%) exceeds the interest rate (say, 7%), it will be profitable to invest. But if the interest (say, 12%) exceeds the expected rate of net profits (10%), it will be unprofitable to invest.

But what if the firm does *not* borrow, instead financing the investment internally out of funds saved from past profits? The role of the interest rate as a cost in investing in real capital doesn't change. By using money from savings to invest in the sander, the firm incurs an opportunity cost (Chapter 2) because it forgoes the interest income it could have realized by lending the funds to someone else.

The *real* rate of interest, rather than the nominal rate, is crucial in making investment decisions. Recall from Chapter 8 that the nominal interest rate is expressed in dollars of current value, while the real interest rate is stated in dollars of constant or inflation-adjusted value. The real interest rate is the nominal rate less the rate of inflation. In our sanding machine illustration, we implicitly assumed a constant price level so that all our data, including the interest rate, were in real terms.

But what if inflation is occurring? Suppose a $1000 investment is estimated to yield a real (inflation-adjusted) expected rate of net profits of 10% and the nominal interest rate is 15%. At first we would say the investment will be unprofitable. But assume there is ongoing inflation of 10% per year. This means the investor will pay back dollars with approximately 10% less in purchasing power. While the nominal interest rate is 15%, the real rate is only 5% (= 15% – 10%). Comparing this 5% real interest rate with the 10% expected real rate of net profits, we find that the investment is profitable and should be undertaken.

INVESTMENT-DEMAND CURVE

We now move from a single firm's investment decision to total demand for investment goods by the entire business sector. Assume every firm has estimated the expected rate of net profits from all investment projects and these data have been collected. These estimates can be *cumulated* — successively summed — by asking: How many dollars' worth of investment projects have an expected rate of net profit of, say, 16% or more? Of 14% or more? Of 12% or more? And so on.

Suppose there are no prospective investments yielding an expected net profit of 16% or more. But there are $5 billion of investment opportunities with an expected rate of net profits between 14 and 16%; an *additional* $5 billion yielding between 12 and 14%; still an *additional* $5 billion yielding between 10 and 12%; and an *additional* $5 billion in each successive 2% range of yield down to and including the 0 to 2% range.

By *cumulating* these figures we obtain the data of Table 9-2, shown graphically by the economy's **investment-demand curve** in Figure 9-5. In Table 9-2 the number opposite 12%, for example, tells us there are $10 billion of investment opportunities, which will yield an expected net profit of 12% *or more*; the $10 billion includes the $5 billion of investment yielding an expected return of 14% or

FIGURE 9-5   The investment-demand curve

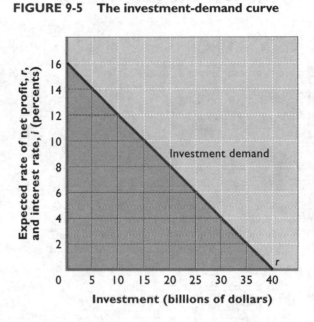

The investment-demand curve for the economy is derived by arraying all relevant investment projects in descending order of their expected rate of net profitability and applying the rule that investment should be undertaken up to the point at which the interest rate is equal to the expected rate of net profit. The investment-demand curve is downsloping, reflecting an inverse relationship between the interest rate (the financial price of investing) and the aggregate quantity of capital goods demanded.

TABLE 9-2   Profit expectations and investment

Expected rate of net profit, r (in %)	Amount of investment (billions of dollars per year)
16%	$ 0
14	5
12	10
10	15
8	20
6	25
4	30
2	35
0	40

BOX 9-3 IN THE MEDIA

FLOOR DROPS OUT OF HOUSING SALES

Higher interest rates, buyers' job concerns factors in fall, LePage chairman says

BY LEONARD ZEHR
Real Estate Reporter

TORONTO — Housing sales have collapsed dramatically across the country, and the head of a major real-estate company says that for people trying to sell their houses, the outlook is bleak.

Colum Bastable, president and chief executive officer of real-estate brokerage Royal LePage Ltd., told the company's annual meeting yesterday that housing sales fell 20 per cent nationally in January and 38 per cent in February, and "we expect March unit sales to show an equally depressing drop.

"And the end is still not in sight," he said, citing dampening consumer confidence because of concerns over interest rates — both current and anticipated. "With the threat of further hikes looming, the immediate outlook for residential real-estate sales appears to be bleak."

Mr. Bastable said that while last year's overall sales were down only 1 per cent from 1993, this was on the strength of a rise in sales in the first half of 1994. The numbers have been falling ever since, and the last half of 1994 was "the most brutal on record,"

with sales plummeting like "an elevator with its cables snapped."

Mr. Bastable's bleak forecast matched the latest survey from Canada Mortgage and Housing Corp., which predicts that high interest rates will keep the real-estate market in the doldrums in 1995.

Statistics Canada also says the declining number of building permits being issued signals "that further contraction will occur in residential construction in coming months." ...

Source: *Globe and Mail*, April 5, 1995, p. A1. Reproduced with permission.

The Story in Brief

The sale of houses dropped precipitously as rising interest rates pushed up mortgage rates. The number of building permits also declined.

The Economics Behind the Story

- A house is an investment good. Demand for investment goods is inversely related to the rate of interest.

- As interest rates go up, so do mortgage rates. With higher mortgage rates, a purchaser's monthly mortgage payment increases. Thus, the number of people buying houses falls.

- Since builders are selling fewer new houses, the number of additional houses they plan to build in the near future has also dropped.

- Why is a house considered an investment good? Describe how a fall in the number of houses built and sold will affect the level of output and income.

more *plus* the $5 billion which is expected to yield between 12 and 14%.

With this cumulated information on expected net profit rates of all possible investment projects, we introduce the real interest rate or financial cost of investing. We know from our sanding machine example that an

investment project will be undertaken if its expected net profit rate *r* exceeds the real interest rate, *i*.

Let's apply this reasoning to Figure 9-5. If we assume that rate of interest is 12%, we find that $10 billion of investment spending will be profitable, that is, $10 billion worth of investment projects have an expected net profit rate of 12% or more. At a financial "price" of 12%, $10 billion of investment goods will be demanded. If the interest rate were lower, say, 10%, an additional $5 billion of investment projects would become profitable and the total amount of investment goods demanded would be $15 billion (= $10 + $5). At 8%, a further $5 billion of investment would become profitable and the total demand for investment goods would be $20 billion. At 6%, investment would be $25 billion.

By applying the marginal benefit-marginal cost rule that all investment projects should be undertaken up to the point where the expected rate of net profit equals the interest rate (r = i), we discover that the curve of Figure 9-5 is the investment-demand curve. Various possible financial prices of investing (various real interest rates) are shown on the vertical axis and the corresponding quantities of investment goods demanded are revealed on the horizontal axis. Any line or curve embodying such data is the investment-demand curve. Consistent with our product and resource demand curves of Chapter 4, observe the *inverse* relationship between the interest rate (price) and the amount of spending on investment goods (quantity demanded). **(Key Question 8)**

SHIFTS IN INVESTMENT DEMAND

In discussing the consumption schedule, we noted that although disposable income is the key determinant of the amount consumed, other factors affect consumption. These "nonincome determinants" shift the consumption schedule. So it also is with the investment-demand schedule. In view of the expected rates of net profit of various possible investments, Figure 9-5 portrays the interest rate as the main determinant of investment.

But other factors determine the location of the investment-demand curve. Any factor that increases the expected net profitability of investment will shift the investment-demand curve to the right. Anything decreasing the expected net profitability of investment will shift the investment-demand curve to the left.

1. ACQUISITION, MAINTENANCE, AND OPERATING COSTS   As our sanding machine example revealed, the initial costs of capital goods, along with the estimated costs of operating and maintaining those goods, must be considered in

gauging the expected rate of net profitability of any investment. When these costs rise, the expected rate of *net* profit from prospective investment projects will fall, shifting the investment-demand curve to the left. Conversely, when these costs decline, expected net profit rates will rise, shifting the investment-demand curve to the right. Example: Higher wages or electricity costs would shift the investment demand curve to the left.

2. BUSINESS TAXES   Business owners look to expected profits *after taxes* in making their investment decisions. An increase in business taxes will lower profitability and shift the investment-demand curve to the left; a tax reduction will shift it to the right.

3. TECHNOLOGICAL CHANGE   Technological progress — the development of new products, improvements in existing products, the creation of new machinery and production processes — stimulates investment. The development of a more efficient machine, for example, will lower production costs or improve product quality, increasing the expected rate of net profit from investing in the machine. Profitable new products — mountain bikes, sports utility vehicles, high-resolution television, legal drugs, and so on — induce a flurry of investment as firms tool up for expanded production. A rapid rate of technological progress shifts the investment-demand curve to the right.

4. THE STOCK OF CAPITAL GOODS ON HAND   Just as the stock of consumer goods on hand affects household consumption-saving decisions, so the stock of capital goods on hand influences the expected profit rate from additional investment in industry. When a specific industry is well stocked with productive facilities and inventories of finished goods, investment will be retarded in that industry. Such an industry will be amply equipped to fulfil present and future market demand at prices that yield mediocre profits. If an industry has enough, or even excessive, production capacity, the expected rate of profit from further investment in the industry will be low, and therefore little or no investment will occur. Excess production capacity shifts the investment-demand curve to the left; a relative scarcity of capital goods shifts it to the right.

5. EXPECTATIONS   We noted earlier that business investment is based on *expected* profits. Capital

goods are durable — they may have a life expectancy of 10 or 20 years — and thus the profitability of any capital investment will depend on business planners' expectations of the *future* sales and *future* profitability of the product that the capital helps produce. Business expectations may be based on elaborate forecasts of future business conditions. In addition, such elusive and difficult-to-predict factors as changes in the domestic political climate, the thrust of foreign affairs, population growth, and stock market conditions must be taken into account on a subjective or intuitive basis. If business executives become more optimistic about future business conditions, the investment-demand curve will shift to the right; a pessimistic outlook will shift it to the left.

The amount of investment spending in the world economy is enormous. The seven leading industrial nations alone invest more than $3 trillion annually (Global Perspective 9-2).

QUICK REVIEW 9-3

1. A specific investment will be undertaken if the expected rate of net profit, *r*, exceeds the real interest rate, *r*.

2. The investment demand curve shows the expected rates of net profit for various levels of total investment.

3. Total investment is established where the real interest rate and the expected rate of net profit on investment are equal.

4. The investment demand curve shifts when changes occur in the costs of capital goods, business taxes, technology, the stock of capital goods on hand, and business expectations.

INVESTMENT AND INCOME

To add the investment decisions of businesses to the consumption plans of households, we must express investment plans in terms of the level of disposable income (DI), or GDP. That is, we need to construct an **investment schedule** showing the amounts business firms as a group plan or intend to invest at each possible level of income or output. Such a schedule will mirror the investment plans or intentions of business owners and managers in the same way the consumption and saving schedules reflect the consumption and saving plans of households.

GLOBAL PERSPECTIVE 9-2

Private investment expenditures, G-7 nations

Private investment spending in the Group of Seven (G-7) nations — the world's major industrial powers — was $3.1 trillion in 1992. Here's how the total amount was divided:

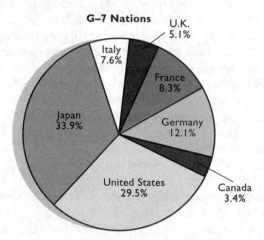

G–7 Nations

- U.K. 5.1%
- Italy 7.6%
- France 8.3%
- Germany 12.1%
- Japan 33.9%
- United States 29.5%
- Canada 3.4%

Total investment = $3.115 trillion

Source: World Bank, *World Tables*, 1994.

We assume that business investment is geared to long-term profit expectations as influenced by technological progress, population growth, and so forth, and therefore is *autonomous* or independent of the level of current disposable income or real output. Suppose the investment-demand curve is as shown in Figure 9-5 *and* the current rate of interest is 8%. This means that the business sector will find it profitable to spend $20 billion on investment goods. In Table 9-3, columns 1 and 2, we are assuming that this level of investment will occur at every level of income. The I_g line in Figure 9-6 shows this graphically.

This assumed independence of investment and income is admittedly simplified. A higher level of business activity may *induce* additional spending on capital facilities, as suggested by columns 1 and 3 of Table 9-3 and I'_g in Figure 9-6. There are at least two reasons why investment might vary directly with income.

1. Investment is related to profits; much investment is financed internally out of business profits. Therefore, it is plausible that as disposable income and GDP rise, so will business profits and therefore the level of investment.

TABLE 9-3   The investment schedule (in billions)

(1) Level of real output and income	(2) Investment, I_g	(3) Investment, I'_g
$370	$20	$10
390	20	12
410	20	14
430	20	16
450	20	18
470	20	20
490	20	22
510	20	24
530	20	26
550	20	28

2. At low levels of income and output, the business sector will have excess production capacity; many industries will have idle machinery and equipment and therefore little incentive to purchase additional capital goods. But, as the level of income rises, this excess capacity disappears and firms are inclined to add to their stock of capital goods.

Our simplification, however, is not too unrealistic and will help later analysis.

INSTABILITY OF INVESTMENT

In contrast to the consumption schedule, the investment schedule is unstable; it shifts significantly upward or downward quite often. Proportionately, investment is the most volatile component of total spending. Figure 9-7 shows the volatility of investment and that its swings are greater than GDP. These data also suggest that our simplified treatment of investment as being independent of GDP (Figure 9-6) is essentially realistic; investment does not closely follow GDP.

Factors explaining the variability of investment are:

1. DURABILITY   Because of their durability, capital goods have an indefinite useful life. Within limits, purchases of capital goods are discretionary and therefore postponable. Older equipment or buildings can be scrapped and entirely replaced or patched up and used for a few more years. Optimism about the future may prompt business planners to replace their older facilities; modernizing their plants will call for a high level of investment. A less optimistic view, however, may lead to very small amounts of investment as older facilities are repaired and kept in use.

2. IRREGULARITY OF INNOVATION   We know that technological progress is a major determinant of investment. New products and processes provide a stimulus to investment. But history suggests that major innovations — railroads, electricity, auto-

FIGURE 9-6   The investment schedule: two possibilities

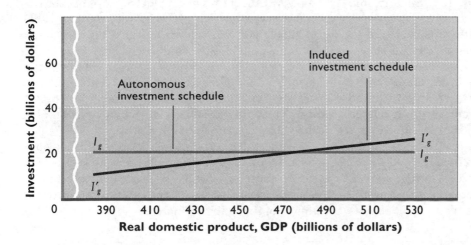

Our discussion will be facilitated by employing the investment schedule I_g which assumes that the investment plans of businesses are independent or autonomous of the current level of income. Actually, the investment schedule may be slightly upsloping, as suggested by I'_g.

FIGURE 9-7 **The volatility of investment**

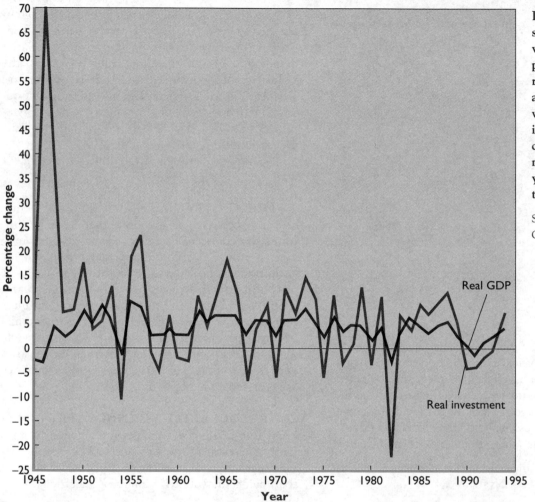

Investment spending is highly volatile. In comparing changes in real investment and real GDP, we observe that investment changes much more year-to-year than does the GDP.

Source: Statistics Canada.

mobiles, computers — occur quite irregularly, and when they do occur, they induce a vast upsurge or "wave" of investment spending that in time recedes.

A classic illustration is the widespread acceptance of the automobile in the 1920s. This event not only substantially increased investment in the automobile industry itself, but also induced tremendous amounts of investment in such related industries as steel, petroleum, glass, and rubber, not to mention public investment in streets and highways. But when investment in these related industries was ultimately "completed" — when enough capital facilities had been created to meet the needs of the automobile industry — total investment levelled off.

3. VARIABILITY OF PROFITS   Business owners and managers invest only when they think it will be profitable and, to a significant degree, the expectation of future profitability is influenced by the size of current profits. Current profits, however, are themselves highly variable (line 18 of the table at the back provides information on undistributed corporate profits). Thus, the variability of profits contributes to the volatile nature of the incentive to invest.

Furthermore, the instability of profits may also cause investment fluctuations, because profits are a major source of funds for business investment. Canadian businesses often prefer this internal source of financing to increases in external debt or stock issue.

In short, expanding profits give business planners both greater *incentives* and greater *means* to invest; declining profits have the reverse effects. The fact that actual profits are variable adds to the instability of investment.

4. VARIABILITY OF EXPECTATIONS While business firms often project current business conditions into the future, it is equally true that expectations are sometimes subject to radical revision when some event suggests a significant change in future business conditions. Changes in the domestic political climate, changes in exchange rates, changes in population growth and therefore in anticipated market demand, court decisions in key labour or antitrust cases, legislative actions, changes in trade barriers, changes in governmental economic policies, and a host of similar considerations may cause substantial shifts in business optimism or pessimism.

The stock market requires specific comment in this regard. Business planners frequently look to the stock market as an index or barometer of the overall confidence of society in future business conditions; a rising "bull" market signifies public confidence in the business future, while a falling "bear" market implies a lack of confidence. The stock market, however, is a highly speculative market and initially modest changes in stock prices can be seriously intensified by participants who jump in by buying when prices begin to rise and by selling when stock prices start to fall. Also, by affecting the amount of proceeds gained through offerings of new stock, upsurges and slumps in stock values affect the level of investment — the amount of capital goods purchased.

For these and similar reasons, changes in investment cause most fluctuations in output and employments. In Figure 9-6, we can think of this volatility as being reflected in frequent and substantial upward and downward shifts in the investment schedule.

EQUILIBRIUM GDP: EXPENDITURES-OUTPUT APPROACH

Now let's use the consumption, saving, and investment schedules to explain the equilibrium levels of output, income, and employment. We'll begin with the **aggregate expenditures-domestic output** (or $C + I_g$ = GDP) **approach**.

TABULAR ANALYSIS

Table 9-4 combines the income-consumption and income-saving data of Table 9-1 and the simplified income-investment data of columns 1 and 2 in Table 9-3.

REAL DOMESTIC OUTPUT Column 2 of Table 9-4 is the total or real output schedule for the economy. It indicates the various possible levels of total output — the various possible real GDPs — which the business sector might produce. *Producers are willing to offer each of these ten levels of output in the expectation that they will receive an identical amount of receipts of income from its sale.* For example, the business sector will produce $370 billion of output, incurring $370 billion of costs (wages, rents, interest, and profit), only if businesses believe this output can be sold for $370 billion of receipts. Some $390 billion of output will be offered if businesses think this output can be sold for $390 billion. And so it is for all the other possible levels of output.

AGGREGATE EXPENDITURES The total, or aggregate, expenditures schedule is shown in column 6 of Table 9-4. It shows the total amount that will be spent at each possible output-income level. In the closed private sector of the economy, the aggregate expenditures schedule shows the amount of consumption and planned gross investment spending $(C + I_g)$ forthcoming at each output-income level. Aggregate expenditures are the sum of columns 3 and 5 at each level of GDP.

We'll start by focusing on *planned* or intended investment in column 5 of Table 9-4. Later we'll see that imbalances in aggregate expenditures and real output will result in unplanned or unintended investment in the form of inventory changes (Column 7).

EQUILIBRIUM GDP Of the ten possible levels of GDP in Table 9-4, which will be the equilibrium level? Which level of total output will the economy be capable of sustaining?

The equilibrium level of output is that output whose production will create total spending just sufficient to purchase that output. The equilibrium level of GDP is where the total quantity of goods produced (GDP) equals the total quantity of goods purchased $(C + I_g)$. Look at the domestic output schedule of column 2 and the aggregate expenditures schedule of column 6 and you see that this equality exists only at $470 billion of GDP (row 6). This is the only output at which the economy is willing to spend precisely the amount necessary to take that output off the market. Here the annual rates of production and spending are in balance. There is no overproduction, which would result in a piling up of unsold goods and therefore cutbacks in the production rate. Nor is there an excess of total spending, which would draw down inventories and prompt increases in the rate of production. In short there is no reason for businesses to alter this rate of production; $470 billion is therefore the **equilibrium GDP**.

DISEQUILIBRIUM To understand better the meaning of the equilibrium level of GDP, let's examine other levels of GDP to see why they cannot be sustained.

At the $410 billion level of GDP (row 3), businesses would find that if they produced this output,

the income created would produce $405 billion in consumer spending. Supplemented by $20 billion of planned investment, total expenditures $(C + I_g)$ would be $425 billion, as shown in column 6. The economy provides an annual rate of spending more than sufficient to purchase the current $410 billion rate of production. Because businesses are producing at a lower rate than buyers are taking goods off the shelves, an unintended decline in business inventories of $15 billion would occur (column 7) if this situation were sustained. But businesses will adjust to this imbalance between aggregate expenditures and real output by stepping up production. A higher rate of output will mean more jobs and a higher level of total income. In brief, if aggregate expenditures exceed the domestic output, those expenditures will drive domestic output upward.

By making the same comparisons of GDP (column 2) and $C + I_g$ (column 6) at all other levels of

TABLE 9-4 Determination of the equilibrium levels of employment, output, and income: the closed private sector

(1) Possible levels of employment, millions	(2) Real domestic output (and income) (GDP = DI),* billions	(3) Consumption, C, (GDP =	(4) Saving, S, billions	(5) Investment, I_g, billions	(6) Aggregate expenditures $(C + I_g)$, billions	(7) Unintended investment (+) or disinvestment (−) in inventories	(8) Tendency of employment, output, and incomes
(1) 40	$370	$375	$−5	$20	$395	$−25	Increase
(2) 45	390	390	0	20	410	−20	Increase
(3) 50	410	405	5	20	425	−15	Increase
(4) 55	430	420	10	20	440	−10	Increase
(5) 60	450	435	15	20	455	−5	Increase
(6) 65	470	450	20	20	470	0	Equilibrium
(7) 70	490	465	25	20	485	+5	Decrease
(8) 75	510	480	30	20	500	+10	Decrease
(9) 80	530	495	35	20	515	+15	Decrease
(10) 85	550	510	40	20	530	+20	Decrease

* If depreciation and net Canadian income earned abroad are zero, government is ignored, and it is assumed that all saving occurs in the household sector of the economy, GDP as a measure of domestic output is equal to NI, PI, and DI. This means that households receive a DI equal to the value output.

GDP below the $470 billion equilibrium level, we find that the economy wants to spend in excess of the level at which businesses are willing to produce. The excess of total spending at all these levels of GDP will drive GDP upward to the $470 billion level.

The reverse is true at all levels of GDP above the $470 billion equilibrium level. Businesses will find that the production of these total outputs fails to generate the levels of spending needed to take them off the market. Being unable to recover their costs, businesses will cut back on production.

To illustrate: At the $510 billion level of output (row 8), business managers will find there is insufficient spending to permit the sale of that output. Of the $510 billion of income that this output creates, $480 billion is received back by businesses as consumption spending. Though supplemented by $20 billion of planned investment spending, total expenditures ($500 billion) fall $10 billion short of the $510 billion quantity produced. If this imbalance persisted, $10 billion of inventories would pile up (column 7). But businesses will react to this unintended accumulation of unsold goods by cutting back on the rate of production. This decline in GDP will mean fewer jobs and a decline in total income. You should verify that deficiencies of total spending exist at all other levels of GDP above the $470 billion level.

The equilibrium level of GDP occurs where the total output, measured by GDP, and aggregate expenditures, C + I_g, are equal. Any excess of total spending over total output will drive GDP upward. Any deficiency of total spending will pull GDP downward.

GRAPHIC ANALYSIS

The same analysis can be shown in a graph. In **Figure 9-8 (Key Graph)** the 45° line now takes on increased significance. Recall that the special property of this line is that at any point on it, the value of what is being measured on the horizontal axis (in this case GDP) is equal to the value of what is being measured on the vertical axis (here, aggregate expenditures or C + I_g). Having discovered in our tabular analysis that the equilibrium level of domestic output is determined where C + I_g equals GDP, we can say that the 45° line in Figure 9-8 is a graphical statement of this equilibrium condition.

Next, we must add the aggregate expenditures schedule to Figure 9-8. To do this we graph the consumption schedule of Figure 9-2(a) and add to it *ver-*

tically the constant $20 billion amount I_g from Figure 9-6, which, we assume, businesses plan to invest at each possible level of GDP. More directly, we can plot the C + I_g data of column 6 in Table 9-4.

Observe that the aggregate expenditures line C + I_g shows total spending rising with output and income, but not as much as income rises. This is because the marginal propensity to consume — the slope of line C — is less than 1. Because the aggregate expenditures line C + I_g is parallel to the consumption line, the slope of the aggregate expenditures line equals the MPC and is also less than 1. A part of any increase in disposable income will *not* be spent; it will be saved. For our particular data, aggregate expenditures rise by $15 billion for every $20 billion increase in real output and income because $5 billion of each $20 billion income increment is saved.

The equilibrium level of GDP is that GDP level corresponding to the intersection of the aggregate expenditures schedule and the 45° line. This intersection locates the only point at which aggregate expenditures (on the vertical axis) are equal to GDP (on the horizontal axis). Because our aggregate expenditures schedule is based on the data of Table 9-4, we once again find that equilibrium output is $470 billion. Observe that consumption at this output is $450 billion and investment is $20 billion.

It is evident from Figure 9-8 that no levels of GDP above the equilibrium level are sustainable, because C + I_g falls short of GDP. Graphically, the aggregate expenditures schedule lies *below* the 45° line. At the $510 billion GDP level, C + I_g is only $500 billion. Inventories of unsold goods rise to undesired levels, prompting businesses to readjust production sights downward in the direction of the $470 billion output level.

Conversely, at all possible levels of GDP less than $470 billion, the economy wants to spend in excess of what businesses are producing. C + I_g exceeds the value of the corresponding output. Graphically, the aggregate expenditures schedule lies *above* the 45° line. At the $410 billion GDP, for example, C + I_g totals $425 billion. Inventories decline as the rate of spending exceeds the rate of production, prompting businesses to raise production towards the $470 billion GDP. Unless there is some change in the location of the aggregate expenditures line, the $470 billion level of GDP will be sustained indefinitely.

KEY GRAPH

FIGURE 9-8 **The aggregate expenditures-domestic output approach to the equilibrium GDP**

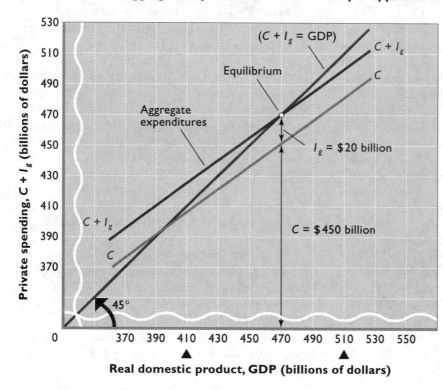

The aggregate expenditures schedule, $C + I_g$, is determined by adding investment (in this case a fixed amount) to the upsloping consumption schedule. The equilibrium level of GDP is determined where the aggregate expenditures schedule intersects the 45° line, in this case at $470 billion.

EQUILIBRIUM GDP: LEAKAGES-INJECTIONS APPROACH

The expenditures-output approach to determining GDP spotlights total spending as the immediate determinant of the levels of output employment and income. Though the **leakages-injections** ($S = I_g$) **approach** is less direct, it does have the advantage of underscoring the reason $C + I_g$ and GDP are unequal at all levels of output except the equilibrium level.

The idea of the leakages-injections approach is this: Under our simplifying assumptions we know that the production of any level of output will generate an identical amount of disposable income. But we also know a part of that income may be saved — *not* consumed — by households. Saving therefore represents a *leakage* or withdrawal of spending from the income-expenditures stream. Saving is what keeps consumption short of total output or GDP; thus, by itself consumption is insufficient to take

the domestic output off the market, setting the stage, it would seem, for a decline in total output.

However, the business sector does not intend to sell its entire output to consumers; some domestic output will consist of capital or investment goods sold within the business sector. Investment can therefore be thought of as an *injection* of spending into the income-expenditures stream that supplements consumption. Investment is a potential offset to, or replacement for, the leakage of saving.

If the leakage of saving exceeds the injection of investment, then $C + I_g$ will fall short of GDP and this level of GDP will be too high to be sustained. Any GDP where saving exceeds investment will be an above-equilibrium GDP. Conversely, if the injection of investment exceeds the leakage of saving, then $C + I_g$ will be greater than GDP and GDP will be driven upward. Any GDP where investment exceeds saving will be a below-equilibrium GDP.

Only where $S = I_g$ — where the leakage of saving is exactly offset by the injection of investment — will aggregate expenditures equal real output. And we know this equality defines the equilibrium GDP.

In the simple closed economy assumed here, there are only one leakage (saving) and one injection (investment). In general terms, a *leakage* is any use of income other than its expenditure on domestically produced output. In the more realistic models that follow (in Chapter 10), we will need to incorporate the additional leakages of imports and taxes into our analysis.

Similarly, an *injection* is any supplement to consumer spending on domestic production. In later models we must add injections of exports and government purchases to our discussion. But for now we need only compare the single leakage of saving with the sole injection of investment to assess the impact on GDP.

TABULAR ANALYSIS

Our $C + I_g$ = GDP approach has led us to conclude that all levels of GDP less than $470 billion are unstable because the corresponding $C + I_g$ exceeds these GDPs, driving upward. Now let's look at the saving schedule (columns 2 and 4) and the investment schedule (columns 2 and 5) of Table 9-4. Comparing the amounts households and businesses want to save and invest at each of the below-equilibrium GDP levels explains the excesses of total spending. At each of these lower GDP levels, businesses plan to invest more than households want to save.

For example, at the $410 billion level of GDP (row 3), households will save only $5 billion, spending $405 of their $410 billion incomes. Supplemented by $20 billion of business investment, aggregate expenditures ($C + I_g$) are $425 billion. Aggregate expenditures exceed GDP by $15 billion (=$425 – $410) *because* the amount businesses plan to invest at this level of GDP exceeds the amounts households save by $15 billion. The fact is that a very small leakage of saving at this relatively low income level will be more than compensated for by the relatively large injection of investment spending, which causes $C + I_g$ to exceed GDP and induce GDP upward.

Similarly, all levels of GDP above the $470 billion level are also unstable, because they exceed $C + I_g$. The reason for this insufficiency of aggregate expenditures is that at all GDP levels above $470 billion, households will want to save more than

businesses plan to invest. The saving leakage is not compensated for by the injection of investment.

For example, households will choose to save at the high rate of $30 billion at the $510 billion GDP (row 8). Businesses, however, will plan to invest only $20 billion. This $10 billion excess of saving over planned investment will reduce total spending to $10 billion below the value of total output. Specifically, aggregate expenditures are $500 billion and real GDP is $510 billion. This spending deficiency will reduce GDP.

Again we verify that the equilibrium GDP is $470 billion. Only at this level are the saving desires of households and the investment plans of businesses equal. Only when businesses and households attempt to invest and save at the same rate — where the leakages and injections are equal — will $C + I_g$ = GDP. Only here will the annual rates of production and spending be in balance; only here will there be no unplanned changes in inventories.

Think of it in this way: If savings were zero, consumer spending would always be sufficient to clear the market of any GDP; consumption would equal GDP. But saving can and does occur, causing consumption to fall short of GDP. Only when businesses are willing to invest at the same rate at which households save will the amount by which consumption falls short of GDP be precisely counterbalanced.

GRAPHIC ANALYSIS

The leakages-injections approach to determining the equilibrium GDP can be demonstrated graphically, as in Figure 9-9. Here we have combined the saving schedule of Figure 9-2(b) and the investment schedule of Figure 9-6. The numerical data for these schedules are in columns 2, 4, and 5 of Table 9-4. We see the equilibrium level of GDP is at $470 billion, where the saving and investment schedules intersect. Only here do businesses and households invest and save at the same rates; therefore, only here will GDP and $C + I_g$ be equal.

At all higher levels of GDP, households will save at a higher rate than businesses plan to invest. The saving leakage exceeds the investment injection, which causes $C + I_g$ to fall short of GDP, driving GDP downward. At the $510 billion GDP, for example, saving of $30 billion will exceed investment of $20 billion by $10 billion, with the result that $C + I_g$ is $500 billion, $10 billion short of GDP.

At all levels of GDP below the $470 billion equilibrium level, businesses will plan to invest more than households save. Here the injection of investment exceeds the leakage of saving so that C + I_g exceeds GDP, driving GDP upward. To illustrate: At the $410 billion level of GDP the $5 billion leakage of saving is more than compensated for by the $20 billion that businesses plan to invest. The result is that C + I_g exceeds GDP by $15 billion, inducing businesses to produce a larger GDP. **(Key Question 10)**

PLANNED VERSUS ACTUAL INVESTMENT

We have emphasized that discrepancies in saving and investment can occur and bring about changes in the equilibrium GDP. Now we must recognize that in another sense, saving and investment must always be equal! This apparent contradiction concerning the equality of saving and investment is resolved when we distinguish between **planned investment** and saving (which need not be equal) and **actual investment** and saving (which by definition must be equal). The catch is that *actual investment consists of both planned and unplanned investment (unplanned changes in inventory investment), and unplanned investment acts as a balancing item that always equates the actual amounts saved and invested in any period of time.*

DISEQUILIBRIUM AND INVENTORIES

Consider, for example, the $490 billion above-equilibrium GDP (row 7 of Table 9-4). What would happen if businesses produced this output thinking they could sell it? At this level, households save $25 billion of their $490 billion DI, so consumption is only $465 billion. Planned investment (column 5) is $20 billion; businesses plan or desire to buy $20 billion worth of capital goods. This means aggregate expenditures (C + I_g) are $485 billion, and sales therefore fall short of production by $5 billion. This extra $5 billion of goods is retained by businesses as an *unintended* or *unplanned* increase in inventories (column 7). It is unintended because it results from the failure of total spending to take total output off the market. Remembering that by definition, changes in inventories are a part of investment, we note the *actual* investment of $25 billion ($20 planned plus $5 unintended or unplanned) equals saving of $25 billion, even though saving exceeds *planned* investment by $5 billion. Businesses, being unwilling to accumulate unwanted inventories at this annual rate, will cut back production.

Now look at the below-equilibrium $450 billion output (row 5 of Table 9-4). Because households save only $15 billion of their $450 billion DI, consumption is $435 billion. Planned investment by businesses is $20 billion, so aggregate expenditures are $455 billion. Sales exceed production by $5 billion. This is so because an

---

FIGURE 9-9   The leakages-injection approach to equilibrium GDP

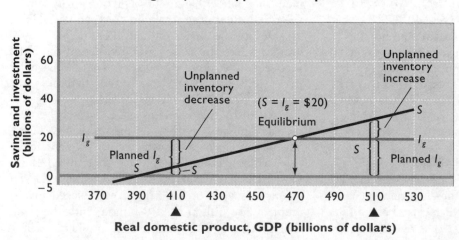

A second approach is to view the equilibrium GDP as determined by the intersection of the saving (S) and investment (I_g) schedules. Only at the point of equilibrium will households plan to save the amount businesses want to invest. It is the consistency of these plans that causes GDP and C + I_g to be equal.

unplanned decline in business inventories has occurred. Businesses have unintentionally *disinvested* $5 billion in inventories (column 7). Note once again that *actual* investment is $15 billion ($20 planned *minus* $5 unintended or unplanned) and equal to saving of $15 billion, even though *planned* investment exceeds saving by $5 billion. This unplanned decline in investment in inventories due to the excess of sales over production will induce businesses to increase the GDP by expanding production.

To summarize: At all *above-equilibrium* levels of GDP (where saving exceeds planned investment), actual investment and saving are equal because of unintended increases in inventories, which are a part of actual investment. Graphically (Figure 9-9), the unintended inventory increase is measured by the vertical distance by which the saving schedule lies above the (planned) investment schedule.

At all *below-equilibrium* levels of GDP (where planned investment exceeds saving), actual investment will be equal to saving because of unintended decreases in inventories, which must be subtracted from planned investment to determine actual investment. These unintended inventory declines are shown graphically as the vertical distance by which the (planned) investment schedule lies above the saving schedule.

ACHIEVING EQUILIBRIUM

These distinctions are important because they mean that *it is the equality of planned investment and saving that determines the equilibrium level of GDP.* We can think of the process by which equilibrium is achieved as follows:

1. A difference between saving and planned investment causes a difference between the production and spending plans of the economy as a whole.

2. This difference between aggregate production and spending plans results in unintended investment or disinvestment in inventories.

3. As long as unintended investment in inventories persists, businesses will revise their production plans downward and reduce GDP. Conversely, as long as unintended disinvestment in inventories exists, firms will revise their production plans upward and increase GDP. Both movements in GDP are towards equilibrium because they bring about the equality of planned investment and saving.

4. Only where planned investment and saving are equal will the level of GDP be in equilibrium. Only where planned investment equals saving will there be no unintended investment or disinvestment in inventories to drive the GDP downward or upward. Note in column 7 of Table 9-4 that only at the $470 billion equilibrium GDP is there no unintended investment or disinvestment in inventories. **(Key Question 11)**

QUICK REVIEW 9-4

1. In a closed economy, equilibrium GDP occurs where aggregate expenditures equal real domestic output ($C + I_g$ = GDP).

2. Alternatively, equilibrium GDP is established where planned investment equals saving ($I_g = S$).

3. Actual investment consists of planned investment plus unplanned changes in inventories and is always equal to saving.

4. At equilibrium GDP, changes in inventories are zero; no unintended investment or disinvestment occurs.

CHAPTER SUMMARY

1. Classical economists argued that because supply creates its own demand (Say's Law), general underspending was improbable. Thus the economy would provide virtually continuous full employment. Even if temporary declines in total spending occurred, these declines would be compensated for by downward price-wage adjustments that would boost spending and employment, restoring the economy to its full-employment level of output. The Great Depression challenged the classical precept that full employment was the norm in a market economy.

2. The basic tools of the aggregate expenditures model are the consumption, saving, and investment schedules, which show the various amounts households intend to consume and save and businesses plan to invest at the various income-output levels, assuming a fixed price level.

3. The locations of the consumption and saving schedules are determined by **a** the amount of wealth owned by households; **b** expectations of future income, future prices, and product availability; **c** the relative size of consumer indebtedness; and **d** taxation. The consumption and saving schedules are relatively stable.

4. The *average* propensities to consume and save show the fraction of any level of *total* income consumed and saved. The *marginal* propensities to consume and save show the fraction of any *change* in total income consumed or saved.

5. The locations of the consumption and saving schedules are determined by **a** the amounts of wealth owned by households; **b** expectations of future income, future prices, and product availability; **c** the relative size of consumer indebtedness; and **d** taxation. The consumption and saving schedules are relatively stable.

6. The immediate determinants of investment are **a** the expected rate of net profit and **b** the real rate of interest. The economy's investment-demand curve can be determined by cumulating investment projects and arraying them in descending order according to their expected net profitability and applying the rule that investment will be profitable up to the point at which the real interest rate, i, equals the expected rate of net profit, r. The investment-demand curve reveals an inverse relationship between the interest rate and the level of aggregate investment.

7. Shifts in the investment-demand curve can occur as the result of changes in **a** the acquisition, maintenance, and operating costs of capital goods; **b** business taxes; **c** technology; **d** the stocks of capital goods on hand; and **e** expectations.

8. For simplicity we assume the level of investment determined by the current interest rate and the investment-demand curve does not vary with the level of real GDP.

9. The durability of capital goods, the irregular occurrence of major innovations, profit volatility, and the variability of expectations all contribute to the instability of investment spending.

10. For a closed economy the equilibrium level of GDP is where aggregate expenditures and real output are equal or, graphically, where the $C + I_g$ line intersects the 45° line. At any GDP greater than equilibrium GDP, real output will exceed aggregate spending, resulting in unintended investment in inventories, depressed profits, and eventual declines in output, employment, and income. At any below-equilibrium GDP, aggregate expenditures will exceed real output, resulting in unintended disinvestment in inventories, substantial profits, and eventual increases in GDP.

11. The leakages-injections approach determines equilibrium GDP at the point where the amount households save and the amount businesses plan to invest are equal. This is at the point where the saving and planned investment schedules intersect. Any excess of saving over planned investment will cause a shortage of total spending, forcing GDP to fall. Any excess of planned investment over saving will cause an excess of total spending, inducing GDP to rise. These changes in GDP will in both cases correct the indicated discrepancies in saving and planned investment.

TERMS AND CONCEPTS

aggregate expenditures-domestic output
   approach (p. 199)
average propensities to consume and
   save (pp. 188, 189)
break-even income (p. 188)
consumption and saving schedules
   (pp. 185, 187)
equilibrium GDP (p. 200)
45° line (p. 185)

investment-demand curve (p. 193)
investment schedule (p. 196)
Keynesian economics (p. 183)
leakages-injections approach (p. 202)
marginal propensities to consume and
   save (p. 189)
planned versus actual investment (p. 204)
Say's Law (p. 182)

QUESTIONS AND STUDY SUGGESTIONS

1. Relate Say's Law to the perspective held by classical economists that the economy generally will operate at a position *on* its production possibilities curve (Chapter 2). Use production possibilities analysis to demonstrate the Keynesian perspective on this matter.

2. Explain what relationships are shown by a. the consumption schedule, b. the saving schedule, c. the investment-demand curve, and d. the investment schedule.

3. Precisely how are the APC and the MPC different? Why must the sum of the MPC and the MPS equal 1? What are the basic determinants of the consumption and saving schedules? Of your own level of consumption?

4. Explain how each of the following will affect the consumption and saving schedules or the investment schedule:

   a. A decline in the amount of government bonds that consumers are holding

   b. The threat of limited, nonnuclear war, leading the public to expect future shortages of consumer durables

   c. A decline in the real interest rate

   d. A sharp decline in stock prices

   e. An increase in the rate of population growth

   f. The development of a cheaper method of manufacturing pig iron from ore

   g. The announcement that the social insurance program is to be restricted in size of benefits

   h. The expectation that mild inflation will persist in the next decade

   i. An increase in the federal personal income tax

5. Explain why an upshift in the consumption schedule typically involves an equal downshift in the saving schedule. What is the exception?

6. *Key Question   Complete the table at the top of page 208.*

   a. *Show the consumption and saving schedules graphically.*

   b. *Locate the break-even level of income. How is it possible for households to dissave at very low income levels?*

Level of output and income (GDP = DI)	Consumption	Saving	APC	APS	MPC	MPS
$240	$_____	$–4	____	____		
260	_____	0	____	____	____	____
280	_____	4	____	____	____	____
300	_____	8	____	____	____	____
320	_____	12	____	____	____	____
340	_____	16	____	____	____	____
360	_____	20	____	____	____	____
380	_____	24	____	____	____	____
400	_____	28	____	____	____	____

c.   *If the proportion of total income consumed decreases and the proportion saved increases as income rises, explain both verbally and graphically how the MPC and MPS can be constant at various levels of income.*

7. What are the basic determinants of investment? Explain the relationship between the real interest rate and the level of investment. Why is the investment schedule less stable than the consumption and saving schedules?

8. **Key Question**   *Assume there are no investment projects in the economy that yield an expected rate of net profit of 25% or more. But suppose there are $10 billion of investment projects yielding expected net profit of between 20 and 25%; another $10 billion yielding between 15 and 20%; another $10 billion between 10 and 15%; and so forth. Cumulate these data and present them graphically, putting the expected rate of net profit on the vertical axis and the amount of investment on the horizontal axis. What will be the equilibrium level of aggregate investment if the real interest rate is a. 15%, b. 10%, and c. 5%? Explain why this curve is the investment-demand curve.*

9. Explain graphically the determination of the equilibrium GDP by a. the aggregate expenditures-domestic output approach and b. the leakages-injections approach for a private closed economy. Why must these two approaches always yield the same equilibrium GDP? Explain why the intersection of the aggregate expenditures schedule and the 45° line determines the equilibrium GDP.

10. **Key Question**   *Assuming the level of investment is $16 billion and independent of the level of total output, complete the table at the top of page 209 and determine the equilibrium levels of output and employment that this private closed economy would provide. What are the sizes of the MPC and MPS?*

11. **Key Question**   *Using the consumption and saving data given in question 10 and assuming the level of investment is $16 billion, what are the levels of saving and planned investment at the $380 billion level of domestic output? What are the levels of saving and actual investment? What are saving and planned investment at the $300 billion level of domestic output? What are the levels of saving and actual investment? Use the concept of unintended investment to explain adjustments towards equilibrium from both the $380 and $300 billion levels of domestic output.*

Possible levels of employment, millions	Real domestic output (GDP = DI), billions	Consumption, billions	Saving, billions
40	$240	$244	$_____
45	260	260	_____
50	280	276	_____
55	300	292	_____
60	320	308	_____
65	340	324	_____
70	360	340	_____
75	380	356	_____
80	400	372	_____

12. "Planned investment is equal to saving at all levels of GDP: actual investment equals saving only at the equilibrium GDP." Do you agree? Explain. Critically evaluate: "The fact that households may save more than businesses want to invest is of no consequence, because events will in time force households and businesses to save and invest at the same rates."

13. **Advanced Analysis** Linear equations (see Appendix to Chapter 1) for the consumption and saving schedules take the general form $C = a + bY$ and $S = -a + (1 - b)Y$, where C, S, and Y are consumption, saving, and national income, respectively. The constant a represents the vertical intercept and b is the slope of the consumption schedule.

   a. Use the following data to substitute specific numerical values into the consumption and saving equations.

National income (Y)	Consumption (C)
$ 0	$80
100	140
200	200
300	260
400	320

   b. What is the economic meaning of b? Of $(1 - b)$?

   c. Suppose the amount of saving that occurs at each level of national income falls by $20, but the values for b and $(1 - b)$ remain unchanged. Restate the saving and consumption equations for the new numerical values and cite a factor that might have caused the change.

14. **Advanced Analysis** Suppose that the linear equation for consumption in a hypothetical economy is $C = 40 + .8Y$. Also suppose that income (Y) is $400. Determine a. the marginal propensity to consume, b. the marginal propensity to save, c. the level of consumption, d. the average propensity to consume, e. the level of saving, and f. the average propensity to save.

15. **Advance Analysis** Assume that the linear equation for consumption in a hypothetical private closed economy is $C = 10 + .9Y$, where Y is total real income (output). Also suppose that the equation for investment is $I_g = I_{g0} = 40$, meaning that I_g is 40 at all levels of real income (output). Using the equation $Y = C + I_g$, determine the equilibrium level of Y. What are the total amounts of consumption, saving, and investment at equilibrium Y?

16. (Applying the Theory) What is the significance of John Maynard Keynes's book, *The General Theory*, published in 1936?

CHAPTER 10

AGGREGATE EXPENDITURES: THE MULTIPLIER, NET EXPORTS, AND GOVERNMENT

Y ou have just learned, with the help of a simple model, how a particular level of real GDP is arrived at in a private closed economy. Now we want to see why and how that level might change, as it often does in the real economy. Then we add the foreign sector and government to our aggregate expenditures model.

We analyze changes in investment spending and how they affect real GDP, income, and employment. We will find that a change in invest-

ment creates a multiple change in output and income. Then we "open" our simplified "closed" economy to show how exports and imports affect it. Government — with its expenditures and taxes — is next brought into the model; the "private" economy becomes the "mixed" economy. Finally, we apply our model to two historical periods and consider some of its deficiencies. We continue to assume the price level remains constant unless explicitly stated otherwise. Our focus therefore remains on real GDP.

BOX 10-1   THE BIG PICTURE

We now complete the expenditure model with the addition of the government and foreign sectors. You are reminded that we are trying to understand how GDP is determined to help us devise macroeconomic policies that lessen fluctuations and attain full employment and price stability — to keep us on the production possibility curve. We will see that government expenditures can be used to stabilize the economy in the short to medium term.

As you read through this chapter, keep the following points in mind:

- Imports take away from aggregate expenditures and exports add to them. The volume of imports into

Canada depends primarily on domestic economic growth; exports depend primarily on economic growth in the economies of our major trading partners.

- Full employment is not zero unemployment. A market economy will always have some frictional and structural unemployment.
- Think of government as both reducing consumer expenditures by levying taxes, and adding to expenditures through its own purchases of goods and services.
- An economy can be at equilibrium at either above or below the economy's potential (full employment) output.

CHANGES IN EQUILIBRIUM GDP AND THE MULTIPLIER

Thus far, we have been concerned with using the aggregate expenditure model to explain the equilibrium levels of total output and income. But we saw in Chapter 8 that actually Canada's GDP is seldom stable. Rather, it is characterized by long-run growth and punctuated by cyclical fluctuations. Let's see *why* and *how* the equilibrium level of real GDP fluctuates.

The equilibrium level of GDP will change in response to changes in the investment schedule or the consumption-saving schedules. Because investment spending generally is less stable than the consumption-saving schedules, we assume the investment schedule changes.

The impact of changes in investment can be envisioned through Figures 10-1(a) and (b). Suppose the expected rate of net profit on investment rises (shifting the investment-demand curve of Figure 9-5 to the right) *or* the interest rate falls (the investment-demand curve in Figure 9-5 doesn't shift; we move down the stable curve). As a result, investment spending increases by, say, $5 billion. This is indicated in Figure 10-1(a) by an upward shift in the aggregate expenditures schedule from $(C + I_g)_0$ to $(C + I_g)_1$, and in Figure 10-1(b) by an upward shift in the investment schedule from I_{g0}

to I_{g1}. In each graph the consequence is a rise in the equilibrium GDP from $470 to $490 billion.

If the expected rate of net profit from investment decreases *or* the interest rate rises, the result is a decline in investment spending of, say, $5 billion. This is shown by the downward shift of the investment schedule from I_{g0} to I_{g2} in Figure 10-1(b) and the aggregate expenditures schedule from $(C + I_g)_0$ to $(C + I_g)_2$ in Figure 10-1(a). In each case, these shifts reduce the equilibrium GDP from the original $470 billion level to $450 billion.

You should verify these conclusions in terms of Table 9-4 by substituting $25 billion and then $15 billion for the $20 billion planned investment figure in column 5 of the table.

THE MULTIPLIER EFFECT

You may have noticed in these examples that a $5 billion change in investment spending has given rise to a $20 billion change in the output-income level. This surprising result is called the **multiplier effect** or, simply, the *multiplier*. The multiplier is the ratio of a change in equilibrium GDP to the change in (investment) spending that caused that change in real GDP. Stated generally,

$$\text{Multiplier} = \frac{\text{change in real GDP}}{\text{initial change in spending}}$$

**FIGURE 10-1   Changes in the equilibrium GDP caused by shifts in
(a) the aggregate expenditures schedule and (b) the investment schedule**

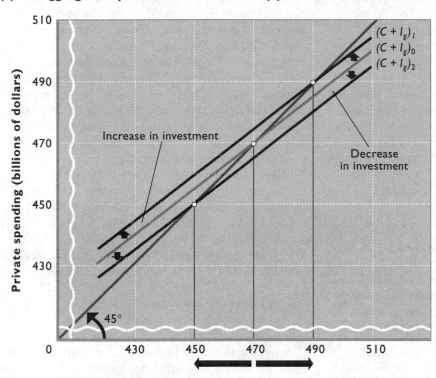

(a) Change in aggregate expenditures schedule

An upshift in the aggregate expenditures schedule from $(C + I_g)_0$ to $(C + I_g)_1$ will increase the equilibrium GDP. Conversely, a downshift in the aggregate expenditures schedule from $(C + I_g)_0$ to $(C + I_g)_2$ will lower the equilibrium GDP. In the saving–investment figure an upshift in the investment schedule (I_{g0} to I_{g1}) will raise, and downshift (I_{g0} to I_{g2}) will lower, the equilibrium GDP.

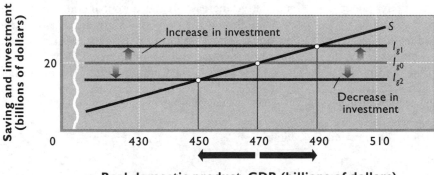

(b) Change in investment schedule

Here the multiplier is 4 (change of GDP of 20/change in investment of 5). Or, by rearranging our equation, we can say that:

$$\text{Change in real GDP} = \text{multiplier} \times \begin{array}{l}\text{initial change}\\\text{in spending}\end{array}$$

Three points about the multiplier must be made here.

1. The "initial change in spending" is usually associated with investment spending because investment is the most volatile component of aggregate expenditures (Figure 9-7). But changes in consumption, exports, or government purchases also are subject to the multiplier effect.

2. The "initial change in spending" refers to an upshift or downshift in the aggregate expenditures schedule due to an upshift or downshift in one of its components. In Figure 10-1(b) we find that real GDP has increased by $20 billion because the investment schedule has shifted upward by $5 billion from I_{g0} to I_{g1}.
3. Implicit in our second point is that the multiplier works in both directions. A small increase in spending can be multiplied into a much larger increase in GDP, or a small decrease in spending can be magnified into a much larger decrease in GDP. Note carefully the effects of the shift in $(C + I_g)_0$ to $(C + I_g)_1$ or to $(C + I_g)_2$ and I_{g0} to I_{g1} or to I_{g2} in Figure 10-1(a) and (b).

RATIONALE   The multiplier is based on two facts.

1. The economy has repetitive, continuous flows of expenditures and income in which the dollars spent by Smith are received as income by Jones.
2. Any change in income will cause both consumption and saving to vary in the same direction as, and by a fraction of, the change in income.

It follows from these two facts that an initial change in the rate of spending will cause a spending chain reaction that, although of diminishing importance at each successive step, will cumulate to a multiple change in GDP.

The rationale underlying the multiplier effect is illustrated numerically in Table 10-1. Suppose a $5 billion increase in investment spending occurs. This is the upshift of the aggregate expenditures schedule by $5 billion in Figure 10-1(a) and the upshift of the investment schedule from $20 to $25 billion in Figure 10-1(b). We continue to assume that the MPC is .75 and the MPS is .25. Also, we suppose that the economy is in equilibrium at $470 billion.

The initial increase in investment spending generates an equal amount of wage, rent, interest, and profit income because spending and receiving of income are two sides of the same transaction. How much consumption will be induced by this $5 billion increase in the incomes of households? The answer is found by applying the marginal propensity to consume of .75 to this change in income. Thus, the $5 billion increase in income raises consumption by $3.75 (= .75 × $5) billion and saving by $1.25 (= .25 × $5) billion, as shown in columns (2) and (3) of Table 10-1.

The $3.75 billion that is spent is received by other households as income (second round). These households consume .75 of this $3.75 billion or $2.81 billion, and save .25 of it, or $0.94 billion. The $2.81 billion that is consumed flows to still other households as income (third round). This process continues.

Figure 10-2, which is derived from Table 10-1, shows the cumulative effects of the various rounds of the multiplier process. Each round *adds* the coloured blocks to domestic income and GDP. The cumulation of the additional income in each round — the sum of all the lightly shaded blocks — is the total change in income or GDP. Though the spending and respending effects of the increase in investment diminish with each successive round of spending, the cumulative increase in the output-income level will be $20 billion if the process is carried through to the last dollar. The $5 billion increase in investment will therefore increase the equilibrium GDP by $20 billion, from $470 to $490 billion. Thus, the multiplier is 4 (= $20 billion ÷ $5 billion).

TABLE 10-1   The multiplier: a tabular illustration (*in billions*)

	(1) Change in income	(2) Change in consumption (MPC = .75)	(3) Change in saving (MPS = .25)
Assumed increase in investment	$ 5.00	$ 3.75	$1.25
Second round	3.75	2.81	0.94
Third round	2.81	2.11	0.70
Fourth round	2.11	1.58	0.53
Fifth round	1.58	1.19	0.39
All other rounds	4.75	3.56	1.19
Totals	$20.00	$15.00	$5.00

FIGURE 10-2   The multiplier process (MPC = .75)

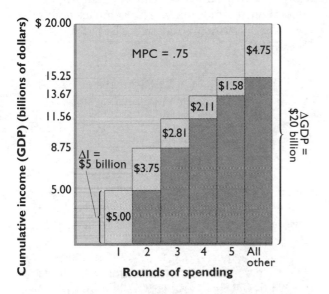

An initial change in investment spending of $5 billion creates an equal $5 billion of new income in round 1. Households spend $3.75 (= .75 × $5) billion of this new income, creating $3.75 of added income in round 2. Of this $3.75 of new income, households spend $2.81 (= .75 × $3.75) billion and income rises by that amount in round 3. The cumulation of such income increments over the entire process eventually results in a total change of income and GDP of $20 billion. The multiplier therefore is 4 (= $20 billion/$5 billion).

The multiplier effect ends at the point where exactly enough saving has been generated to offset the initial $5 billion increase in investment spending. Only then will the disequilibrium created by the investment increase be corrected. GDP and total incomes must rise by $20 billion to create $5 billion in additional saving to match the $5 billion increase in investment spending. Income must increase by four times the initial excess of investment over saving, because households save one-fourth of any increase in their incomes (that is, the MPS is one-fourth). In this example the multiplier — the number of times the ultimate increase in income exceeds the initial increase in investment spending — is 4.

THE MULTIPLIER AND THE MARGINAL PROPENSITIES   You may have sensed from Table 10-1 that a relationship of some sort must exist between the MPS and the size of the multiplier.

The fraction of an increase in income that is saved — the MPS — determines the cumulative respending effects of any initial change in I_g, G, X_n, or C, and therefore the multiplier. *The size of the MPS and the size of the multiplier are inversely related.* The smaller the fraction of any change in income that is saved, the greater the respending at each round and, therefore, the greater the multiplier. If the MPS is .25, as in our example, the simple multiplier is 4. If the MPS were .33, the multiplier would be 3. If the MPS were .2, the multiplier would be 5.

Look again at Table 9-4 and Figure 10-1(b). Initially the economy is in equilibrium at the $470 billion level of GDP. Now businesses increase investment by $5 billion so that planned investment of $25 billion exceeds saving of $20 billion at the $470 billion GDP level. This means $470 billion is no longer the equilibrium GDP. By how much must GDP rise to restore equilibrium? By enough to generate $5 billion of additional saving to offset the $5 billion increase in investment. Because households save $1 out of every $4 of additional income they receive (MPS = .25), GDP must rise by $20 billion — four times the increase in investment — to create the $5 billion of extra saving necessary to restore equilibrium. Thus, the multiplier is 4.

We can summarize by saying *the simple multiplier is equal to the reciprocal of the MPS*:

$$\text{The multiplier} = \frac{1}{\text{MPS}}$$

This formula provides us with a shorthand way to determine the multiplier. All you need to know is the MPS to calculate the size of the multiplier.

Recall that since MPC + MPS = 1, it follows that MPS = 1 – MPC. Therefore, we can also write our multiplier formulas as

$$\text{The multiplier} = \frac{1}{1 - \text{MPC}}$$

SIGNIFICANCE OF THE MULTIPLIER   The significance of the multiplier is that a small change in the investment plans of businesses or the consumption-saving plans of households can trigger a larger change in the equilibrium level of GDP. The multiplier magnifies the fluctuations in business activity initiated by changes in spending.

As illustrated in Figure 10-3, the larger the MPC (the smaller the MPS), the greater will be the multiplier. For example, if the MPC is .75, the

FIGURE 10-3   The MPC and the multiplier

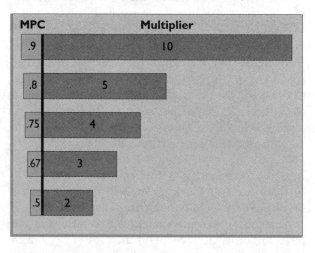

The larger the MPC (the smaller the MPS), the greater
is the size of the multiplier.

multiplier is 4; whereas, if the MPC is only .67,
the multiplier is 3. A large MPC means the chain
of induced consumption shown in Figure 10-2
dampens down slowly and thereby cumulates to a
large change in income. Conversely, a small MPC
(a large MPS) causes induced consumption to
decline quickly so the cumulative change in
income is small.

GENERALIZING THE MULTIPLIER   The multiplier we have presented here is called the **simple
multiplier** because it is based on a simple model of
the economy. In terms of $\dfrac{1}{\text{MPS}}$, the simple multiplier reflects only the leakage of saving. But successive rounds of income and spending can also be
dampened down by other leakages of imports and
taxes. As with the leakage into savings, some part
of income at each round would be used to purchase
additional goods from abroad and another part
would be siphoned off as additional taxes. The
result of these added leakages is that $\dfrac{1}{\text{MPS}}$ statement of the multiplier can be generalized by
changing the denominator to read "fraction of the
change in income that is not spent on domestic
output." The more realistic multiplier that results
when all leakages — saving, imports, and taxes —

are included is called the **complex multiplier**.
More will be said below about the impact of
imports on the multiplier. The complex multiplier
for Canada is estimated to be about 1.2. **(Key
Question 2)**

EQUILIBRIUM OUTPUT IN AN OPEN ECONOMY

Our aggregate expenditures model has
ignored international trade by assuming a
closed economy. We now acknowledge
exports and imports and **net exports** (exports minus
imports), which may be either positive or negative.
Line 4 in the table at the back of this book reveals
that net exports in some years have been positive
(exports > imports) and in other years negative
(imports > exports). Observe that net exports in
1994 were a *positive* $5.6 billion, for example, while
in 1993 they were a *negative* $3.2 billion.

How do net exports — exports minus imports
— relate to aggregate expenditures?

NET EXPORTS AND AGGREGATE EXPENDITURES

Like consumption and investment, exports (X) create domestic production, income, and employment.
Even though the goods and services produced in
response to such spending flow abroad, foreign
spending on Canadian goods and services increases
production and creates jobs and incomes in
Canada. Exports must therefore be added as a component of aggregate expenditures.

Conversely, when an economy is open to international trade, a portion of its consumption, investment, and government purchases will be for imports
(M) — for goods and services that were produced
abroad. So as not to overstate the value of domestic
production, we must reduce the sum of consumption and investment expenditures by the amount
spent on imported goods. In measuring aggregate
spending for domestic goods and services, we must
subtract expenditures on imports.

In short, for a closed economy aggregate
expenditures are $C + I_g$. But for an open economy
with international trade, aggregate expenditure is
$C + I_g + (X - M)$. Or, recalling from Chapter 7 that
net exports (X_n) equals $(X - M)$, we can say that
aggregate spending for a private open economy is $C
+ I_g + X_n$.

BOX 10-2   APPLYING THE THEORY

SQUARING THE ECONOMIC CIRCLE

American humorist Art Buchwald examines the multiplier.

WASHINGTON — The recession hit so fast that nobody knows exactly how it happened. One day we were the land of milk and honey and the next day we were the land of sour cream and food stamps.

This is one explanation.

Hofberger, the Chevy salesman in Tomcat, Va., a suburb of Washington, called up Littleton, of Littleton Menswear & Haberdashery, and said, "Good news, the new Novas have just come in and I've put one aside for you and your wife."

Littleton said, "I can't, Hofberger, my wife and I are getting a divorce.

"I'm sorry," Littleton said, "but I can't afford a new car this year. After I settle with my wife, I'll be lucky to buy a bicycle."

Hofberger hung up. His phone rang a few minutes later.

"This is Bedcheck the painter," the voice on the other end said. "When do you want us to start painting your house?"

"I changed my mind," said Hofberger. "I'm not going to paint the house."

"But I ordered the paint," Bedcheck said. "Why did you change your mind?"

"Because Littleton is getting a divorce and he can't afford a new car."

That evening when Bedcheck came home his wife said, "The new color television set arrived from Gladstone's TV Shop."

"Take it back," Bedcheck told his wife.

"Why?" she demanded.

"Because Hofberger isn't going to have his house painted now that the Littletons are getting a divorce."

The next day Mrs. Bedcheck dragged the TV set in its carton back to Gladstone. "We don't want it."

Gladstone's face dropped. He immediately called his travel agent, Sandstorm. "You know that trip you had scheduled for me to the Virgin Islands?"

"Right, the tickets are all written up."

"Cancel it. I can't go. Bedcheck just sent back the color TV set because Hofberger didn't sell a car to Littleton because they're going to get a divorce and she wants all his money."

Sandstorm tore up the airline tickets and went over to see his banker, Gripsholm. "I can't pay back the loan this month because Gladstone isn't going to the Virgin Islands."

Gripsholm was furious. When Rudemaker came in to borrow money for a new kitchen he needed for his restaurant, Gripsholm turned him down cold. "How can I loan you money when Sandstorm hasn't repaid the money he borrowed?"

Rudemaker called up the contractor, Eagleton, and said he couldn't put in a new kitchen. Eagleton laid off eight men.

Meanwhile, General Motors announced it was giving a rebate on its new models. Hofberger called up Littleton immediately. "Good news," he said, "even if you are getting a divorce, you can afford a new car."

"I'm not getting a divorce," Littleton said. "It was all a misunderstanding and we've made up."

"That's great," Hofberger said. "Now you can buy the Nova."

"No way," said Littleton. "My business has been so lousy I don't know why I keep the doors open."

"I didn't realize that," Hofberger said.

"Do you realize I haven't seen Bedcheck, Gladstone, Sandstorm, Gripsholm, Rudemaker or Eagleton for more than a month? How can I stay in business if they won't patronize my store?"

SOURCE: Art Buchwald, "Squaring the Economic Circle," *Cleveland Plain Dealer*, February 22, 1975. Reprinted by permission.

TABLE 10-2   Net export schedule

(1) Domestic output (and income) (GDP = NI = DI) (billions)	(2) Exports (billions) (X)	(3) Imports (billions) (M)	(4) Net exports (billions) (X_n) (2) – (3)	(5) Marginal propensity to import (MPM) $\Delta(3)/\Delta(1)$
$370	$40	$15	$25	0.25
390	40	20	20	0.25
410	40	25	15	0.25
430	40	30	10	0.25
450	40	35	5	0.25
470	40	40	0	0.25
490	40	45	–5	0.25
510	40	50	–10	0.25
530	40	55	–15	0.25
550	40	60	–20	0.25

THE DETERMINANTS OF IMPORTS AND EXPORTS AND THE NET EXPORT SCHEDULE

What are the determinants of exports and imports? Note that in Table 10-2 exports are constant at all levels of GDP. This is because the GDP in other countries is the main determinant of our exports. **If the GDP in other countries is growing, we can expect the demand for our exports to increase.** If GDP in the United States increases, we can expect that it will purchase more goods and services from Canada. Usually, housing construction expands with the economy and, thus, if that sector were to expand in the United States, it would translate into higher sales of Canadian lumber, for example. If the United States experiences a recession, we can expect our exports to decrease.

Our imports are dependent on our own GDP. When the Canadian economy expands, imports also rise. For example, as the business sector expands and GDP rises, it will require machines and materials from abroad. Likewise, as consumer spending rises, some of it will go to imports.

Another determinant of imports and exports is the exchange rate, the rate at which the Canadian dollar can be exchanged for other currencies. A **depreciation** of the Canadian dollar occurs when our currency buys fewer units of another currency or currencies. An **appreciation** of the Canadian dollar is the opposite: when the value of the Canadian dollar rises against other currencies, fewer Canadian dollars are required to purchase a unit of a foreign currency.

Generally, an appreciation of the Canadian dollar will lead to a rise of imports and a decrease in exports,[1] thus a decrease of net exports and aggregate expenditure. A depreciation of the Canadian dollar will have the opposite result.

A hypothetical **net export schedule** is shown in columns 1 to 4 of Table 10-2. Note that while exports are constant at all levels of GDP, imports, and therefore *net* exports (X – M), change by $5 billion for every $20 billion change in GDP. The change in imports to a given change in GDP is called the **marginal propensity to import** (MPM). In our example the marginal propensity to import is 0.25 (= $5 billion/$20 billion). Just as the marginal

[1] As well, price and income elasticity of demand for particular imports and exports will influence their demand.

TABLE 10-3   Determination of the equilibrium levels of output and income: private and foreign sectors

(1) Domestic output (and income) (GDP = NI = DI) (billions)	(2) Aggregate expenditures for closed economy, without government (C + I_g) (billions)	(3) Exports (billions) (X)	(4) Imports (billions) (M)	(5) Net exports (billions) (3) − (4) (X_n)	(6) Aggregate expenditures for open economy, without government (C + I_g + X_n) (billions) (2) + (5)
$370	$395	$40	$15	$25	$420
390	410	40	20	20	430
410	425	40	25	15	440
430	440	40	30	10	450
450	455	40	35	5	460
470	470	40	40	0	470
490	485	40	45	−5	480
510	500	40	50	−10	490
530	515	40	55	−15	500
550	530	40	60	−20	510

propensity to consume was the slope of the consumption schedule, so the marginal propensity to import is the slope of the net export schedule.

NET EXPORTS AND EQUILIBRIUM GDP

Let's now add exports and imports to our discussion of income determination. Columns 1 and 2 of Table 10-3 repeat columns 2 and 6 from Table 9-4, where the equilibrium GDP for a closed economy was $470 billion. Columns 3 to 5 of Table 10-3 repeat columns 2 to 4 of Table 10-2. In column 6, we have adjusted the domestic aggregate expenditures of column 2 for net exports, giving us aggregate expenditures for an open economy.

The particular export and import figures we have selected are such that foreign trade leaves the equilibrium GDP unchanged. Net exports are zero at the closed economy's equilibrium GDP of $470 billion, so aggregate expenditures for the open economy (column 6) equal domestic output (column 1) at $470 billion.

Figure 10-4 portrays these results. The C + I_g schedule is aggregate expenditures for the closed economy, plotted from column 2 of Table 10-2. The (C + I_g + X_n)$_0$ schedule is aggregate expenditures for the open economy and reflects the figures of column 6. Observe that, *in this case*, aggregate expenditures for the open economy intersect domestic output at the same point as do aggregate expenditures for the closed economy, and therefore the $470 billion equilibrium GDP is unchanged by world trade.

NEGATIVE NET EXPORTS   But there is no reason why net exports will have a neutral effect on equilibrium GDP. For example, by *either* reducing exports by $10 billion (from $40 to $30 billion) or increasing imports by $10 billion at each level of GDP, we find that net exports would be *minus* $10 billion at the $470 billion GDP. Recalculating aggregate expenditures in column 6 of Table 10-3, the resulting net equilibrium GDP will be $450 billion.

Graphically, the new open-economy aggregate expenditures schedule is shown by $(C + I_g + X_n)_1$ in Figure 10-4(a). This schedule lies $10 billion below $(C + I_g + X_n)_0$, reflecting the assumed $10 billion decline in net exports. Thus, at the original $470 billion equilibrium GDP, a spending gap of $10 billion exists, which causes the equilibrium GDP to *decline* to $450 billion.

Figure 10-4(b) shows the same result. Note that the $I_g + X_0$ schedule intersects the "leakages," S + M, schedule at the equilibrium GDP of $470 billion. The new $I_g + X_1$ schedule (denoting a $10 billion drop in exports: $I_g + X$ decreases from $60 to $50 billion) intersects the S + M schedule at the new equilibrium GDP of $450 billion. The same result would be obtained by raising the S + M schedule a vertical distance of $10 billion, indicating an increase in imports of $10 billion at all income levels.

FIGURE 10-4   Net exports and the equilibrium GDP

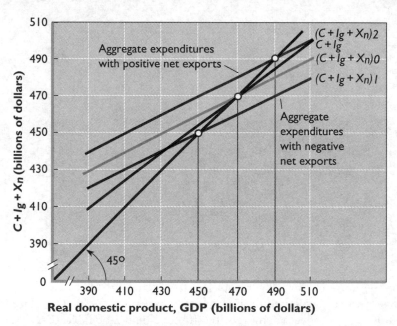

(a) Aggregate expenditures schedule

An increase in net exports raises the aggregate expenditures schedule as from $(C + I_g + X_n)_0$ to $(C + I_g + X_n)_2$ and increases the equilibrium GDP. Conversely, a decrease in net exports shifts the aggregate expenditures schedule downward as from $(C + I_g + X_n)_0$ to $(C + I_g + X_n)_1$ and lowers the equilibrium GDP. Note also that net exports in (a) reduce the slope of the aggregate expenditures schedule and that in (b) imports increase the slope of the "leakages" (S + M) schedule.

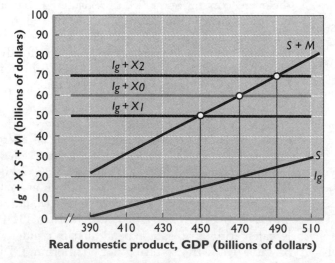

(b) Investment/export schedule

POSITIVE NET EXPORTS   Conversely, by *either* increasing exports by $10 billion (from $40 to $50 billion) or decreasing imports by $10 billion at each GDP level, we discover that net exports are now *plus* $10 billion at the original $470 billion GDP. Again, the recalculation of aggregate expenditures in column 6 of Table 10-3 reveals that the equilibrium GDP will shift from $470 to $490 billion.

In Figure 10-4(a), the new open-economy aggregate expenditures line is $(C + I_g + X_n)_2$, which lies $10 billion above $(C + I_g + X_n)_0$ because of the assumed $10 billion increase in net exports. This creates a $10 billion gap at the original $470 equilibrium GDP, and as a result the equilibrium GDP *increases* to $490 billion.

Figure 10-4(b) shows the same result. The new $I_g + X_2$ schedule (denoting a $10 billion increase in exports: $I_g + X$ increases from $60 to $70 billion) intersects the $S + M$ schedule at the new equilibrium GDP of $490 billion. The same result would be obtained by dropping the $S + M$ schedule a vertical distance of $10 billion, indicating a decrease in imports of $10 billion at all income levels.

The generalizations that follow from these examples are these: *a decline in net exports decreases aggregate expenditures and has a contractionary effect on domestic GDP; conversely, an increase in net exports increases aggregate expenditures and has an expansionary effect on domestic GDP*.

Net exports vary greatly among the major industrial nations, as shown in Global Perspective 10-1. **(Key Question 5)**

INTERNATIONAL ECONOMIC LINKAGES

Our analysis of net exports and real GDP reveals how circumstances or policies abroad can affect our GDP.

PROSPERITY ABROAD   A rising level of national income among our trading partners permits us to sell more goods abroad, thus raising our net exports and increasing our GDP. We should be interested in the prosperity of our trading partners because their good fortune enables them to buy more of our exports and transfer some of their prosperity to us.

TARIFFS   Suppose our trading partners impose high tariffs on Canadian goods to reduce their imports and stimulate production in their economies. But their imports are our exports. When they restrict their imports to stimulate *their*

GLOBAL PERSPECTIVE 10-1

Merchandise net exports, selected nations

Some nations, such as Canada, Japan, and Germany, have positive net exports; other countries, such as the United States and the United Kingdom, have negative net exports.

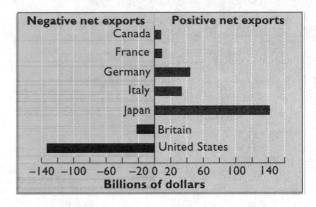

Source: *Organization for Economic Cooperation and Development.* Data are for 1993.

economies, they are reducing our exports and depressing *our* economy. We may retaliate by imposing trade barriers on their products. If so, their exports will decline and their net exports may be unchanged or even fall. In the Great Depression of the 1930s various nations, including Canada, imposed trade barriers as a way to reduce domestic unemployment. But rounds of retaliation simply throttled world trade, worsened the depression, and increased unemployment.

EXCHANGE RATES   Depreciation of the dollar relative to other currencies will permit people abroad to obtain more dollars per unit of their currencies. The price of Canadian goods in terms of these currencies will fall, stimulating purchases of our exports. Also Canadian consumers will find they need more dollars to buy foreign goods and consequently will reduce their spending on imports. Higher Canadian exports and lower imports will result, increasing our net exports and expanding our GDP.

Whether depreciation of the dollar raises real GDP or produces inflation depends on the initial position of the economy relative to its full-employment level of output. If the economy is operating below its production capacity, the depreciation of

BOX 10-3   IN THE MEDIA

"SPECTACULAR" CANADIAN EXPORTS SURGE TO RECORD HIGHS

BY ALAN FREEMAN
Parliamentary Bureau

OTTAWA — Propelled by a strong U.S. economy, soaring commodity prices and a weak currency, Canadian exports surged 21 per cent in 1994 to a record total of $219.4-billion.

The performance beat the 16-percent export growth recorded in 1993.

"Spectacular," is the word used by David Rosenberg, senior economist at Nesbitt Burns Inc., to describe the merchandise trade figures reported yesterday by Statistics Canada.

"What has most impressed me is the broad-based nature of the robust export expansion," Mr. Rosenberg said. "Of all the major export categories surveyed, not one showed sales growth of less than 12 per cent in 1994."

Some examples: forestry products jumped 20.7 per cent; machinery and equipment soared 27.3 per cent;

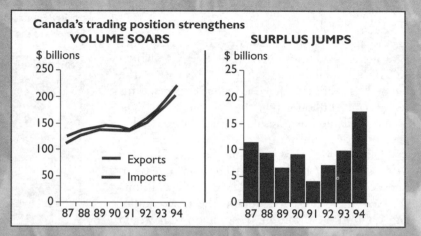

and automotive produces rose 20.5 per cent.

Imports also grew, rising 18 per cent to $202.3-billion, also a record, after growing 16 per cent in 1993. Canada's merchandise trade surplus for 1994 totalled $17.1-billion, compared with $9.5-billion for 1993. All figures are seasonally adjusted.

"It's a tale of two economies. It's an extremely strong sales market and an extremely weak domestic market," said Jayson Myers, chief economist at the Canadian Manufacturers Association....

Source: *Globe and Mail*, February 18, 1995, p. B1. Reproduced with permission.

The Story in Brief

Canadian exports surged to a record total in 1994, increasing by 21%. Canadian imports also grew but, at 18%, slightly lower than exports.

The Economics Behind the Story

- The demand for Canadian exports is dependent primarily on economic growth in our major trading partners and the value of the Canadian dollar on international exchange markets.
- Rapid economic growth in the United States, our largest trading partner, and a weaker Canadian dollar against the U.S. dollar were responsible for the strong growth of Canadian exports.
- Since exports rose at a faster rate than imports, net exports increased, pushing up GDP.
- How do you explain the old adage "When the U.S. economy sneezes, the Canadian economy gets pneumonia"?

the dollar and the resulting rise in net exports will increase real GDP. If the economy is fully-employed, the depreciation of the dollar and higher level of net exports will cause domestic inflation.

Finally, while this last example has been cast in terms of a depreciation of the dollar, you should think through the impact that an *appreciation* of the dollar will have on net exports and equilibrium GDP.

OPEN-ECONOMY MULTIPLIER

The slope of the aggregate expenditures schedule in Figure 10-4 is reduced by the introduction of international trade. The lower slope implies a smaller multiplier. Expressed differently, note in Figure 10-4(b) that the leakages, S + M, schedule has an *increased* slope. In the above illustrations we noted that a $10 billion change in net exports would cause a $20 billion change in equilibrium GDP, indicating a multiplier of 2 (= $20/$10). Why does this new **open-economy multiplier** differ from the multiplier of 4 in the closed economy?

Recall that for the closed economy the multiplier is 1/MPS or, for our data, 1/0.25 or 4. The multiplier is the reciprocal of the MPS, where we define the MPS as the fraction of any change in national income that "leaks" into saving. Moving to an open economy we add a second leakage — expenditures on imports. Saving and imports are similar because both are ways of disposing of income other than spending it on *domestically* produced goods. Since the *marginal propensity to import* (MPM) is the fraction of any change in disposable income spent on imports, we must add the MPM to the MPS in the denominator of the multiplier formula. The multiplier for an open economy becomes

$$\frac{1}{MPS + MPM}$$

For the data of Table 10-1, the MPM is 5/20, or 0.25, and the open-economy multiplier is

$$\frac{1}{MPS + MPM} = \frac{1}{0.25 + 0.25} = \frac{1}{0.5} = 2$$

QUICK REVIEW 10-1

1. The multiplier is the principle that initial changes in spending can cause magnified changes in national income and GDP.

2. The higher the marginal propensity to consume (the lower the marginal propensity to save), the larger is the simple multiplier.

3. The main determinant of exports is the GDP in other countries, particularly our trading partners.

4. The main determinant of imports is our own GDP.

5. An appreciation of the Canadian dollar will decrease net exports, while a depreciation will increase net exports.

6. Positive net exports increase aggregate expenditures on domestic output and increase equilibrium GDP; negative net exports decrease aggregate expenditures on domestic output and reduce equilibrium GDP.

7. The open economy multiplier is smaller than the multiplier for a closed economy. The higher the marginal propensity to import, the smaller is the open economy multiplier.

ADDING THE PUBLIC SECTOR

Our final step in constructing the aggregate expenditures model is to move the analysis from that of a private (no government) open economy to a mixed open economy that has a public sector. Unlike private expenditures, government expenditures and taxes are subject to direct public control. Government can manipulate them to counter private underspending or overspending and thereby promote economic stability.

SIMPLIFYING ASSUMPTIONS

For clarity and simplicity, the following simple assumptions are made.

1. We continue to use the simplified investment schedule, where the level of investment is independent of the level of GDP.
2. We suppose government purchases neither depress nor stimulate private spending. They do not cause any upward or downward shifts in the consumption, investment, and net export schedules.
3. We assume the government's net tax revenues — total tax revenues less "negative taxes" in the form of transfer payments — are derived entirely from personal taxes. Although DI will fall short of PI by the amount of government's tax revenues, GDP, NI, and PI will remain equal.
4. We assume that a fixed amount of taxes is collected regardless of the level of GDP.
5. We continue to suppose that, unless otherwise indicated, the price level is constant.

These assumptions will give us a simple and uncluttered view of how government spending and taxes fit within the aggregate expenditures model. Most of these assumptions will be dropped in Chapter 12 when we discuss how government uses changes in its expenditures and taxes to alter equilibrium GDP and the rate of inflation.

GOVERNMENT PURCHASES AND EQUILIBRIUM GDP

Suppose that government decides to purchase $40 billion of goods and services regardless of the level of GDP.

TABULAR EXAMPLE   Table 10-4 shows the impact on the equilibrium GDP. Columns 1 to 7 are carried over from Tables 9-4 and 10-3 for the private, open economy in which the equilibrium GDP was $470 billion. The only new wrinkle is the addition of government purchases in column 8. By adding government purchases to private spending $(C + I_g + X_n)$, we get a new, higher level of aggregate expenditures, as shown in column 9. Comparing columns 1 and 9, we find that aggregate expenditures and real output are equal at a higher level of GDP. Without government spending, equilibrium GDP was $470 (row 6); with government spending, aggregate expenditures and real output are equal at $550 billion (row 10). *Increases in public spending, like increases in private spending, will boost the aggregate expenditures schedule and result in a higher equilibrium GDP.*

Note, too, that government spending is subject to the open-economy multiplier. A $40 billion increase in government purchases has increased equilibrium GDP by $80 billion (from $470 billion to $550 billion). We have implicitly assumed the $40 billion dollar in government expenditure has all gone to purchase domestic output.

In the leakages-injections approach, government expenditures — like investment and exports — are an injection of spending. Leakages of saving and imports cause consumption of real output to fall short of disposable income, creating a potential spending gap. This gap may be filled by injections of any or all of investment, exports, and government purchases. In Table 10-4, the $550 billion equilibrium level of GDP (row 10) occurs where $S + M = I_g + X + G$. That is, when taxes are zero, $40 + 60 = 20 + 40 + 40$.

TABLE 10-4   The impact of government purchases on equilibrium GDP

(1) Domestic output (and income) (GDP = DI) (billions)	(2) Consumption (billions) (C)	(3) Savings (billions) (S)	(4) Investment (billions) (I_g)	(5) Exports (billions) (X)	(6) Imports (billions) (M)	(7) Net exports (billions) (5) – (6) (X_n)	(8) Government purchases (billions) (G)	(9) Aggregate expenditures ($C + I_g + X_n + G$) (billions) (2) + (4) + (7) + (8)
(1) $370	$375	$–5	$20	$40	$15	$ 25	$40	$460
(2) 390	390	0	20	40	20	20	40	470
(3) 410	405	5	20	40	25	15	40	480
(4) 430	420	10	20	40	30	10	40	490
(5) 450	435	15	20	40	35	5	40	500
(6) 470	450	20	20	40	40	0	40	510
(7) 490	465	25	20	40	45	–5	40	520
(8) 510	480	30	20	40	50	–10	40	530
(9) 530	495	35	20	40	55	–15	40	540
(10) 550	510	40	20	40	60	–20	40	550

GRAPHIC ANALYSIS   In Figure 10-5(a) we add government purchases, G, vertically to the level of private spending, $C + I_g + X_n$. That increases the aggregate expenditures schedule (private plus public) to $C + I_g + X_n + G$, resulting in the $80 billion increase in equilibrium GDP shown on the horizontal axis.

Figure 10-5(b) shows the same change in the equilibrium GDP in the leakages-injections approach. Like investment and exports, government spending is an offset to the leakage of saving and imports. With G added to our economy, the equilibrium level of GDP is determined where the amount households save and the economy imports is offset exactly by the amount businesses both export and plan to invest *plus* the amount government spends on domestic goods and services. Assuming no taxes, the equilibrium GDP is determined by the intersection of the S + M schedule and the $I_g + X + G$ schedule.

FIGURE 10-5   Government spending and the equilibrium GDP

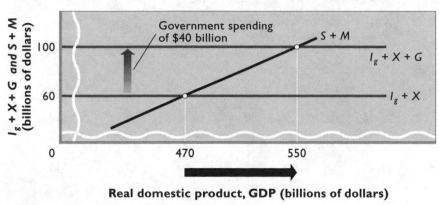

(a) *The aggregate expenditures–domestic output approach.*
The addition of government purchases, G, raises the aggregate expenditures ($C + I_g + X_n + G$) schedule and increases the equilibrium level of GDP as would an increase in C, I_g or X_n. Note that changes in government spending are subject to the multiplier effect.

(b) *Leakages–injections approach.*
In the leakages–injections approach, government spending supplements investment spending and exports ($I_g + X + G$), increasing the equilibrium GDP.

(a) Aggregate expenditures-domestic output approach

(b) Leakages-injections approach

Both the aggregate expenditures and leakages-injections approaches indicate the same new $550 billion equilibrium GDP.

A *decline* in government spending G will cause the aggregate expenditures schedule to fall in Figure 10-5(a), and the $I_g + X + G$ schedule to fall in Figure 10-5(b). In either case, the result is a multiple *decline* in the equilibrium GDP. You should verify that, if government spending were to decline from $40 billion to $20 billion, the equilibrium GDP would fall by $40 billion, that is, from $550 billion to $510 billion.

TAXATION AND EQUILIBRIUM GDP

But government also collects tax revenues. Suppose that government imposes a **lump-sum tax**, which is *a tax yielding the same amount of tax revenue at each level of GDP*. Also, assume the lump-sum tax is $40 billion so that government obtains $40 billion of tax revenue at each level of GDP. What is the impact?

TABULAR EXAMPLE In Table 10-5 we find in column 2 and in column 3 that disposable (after-tax) income is reduced by $40 billion — the

Adrian Raeside — Victoria Times-Colonist

amount of the taxes — at each level of GDP. Because DI consists of consumer spending and saving, a decline in DI will lower both consumption and saving. But by how much will each decline as a result of taxes? The MPC, MPS, and MPM hold the answer: the MPC tells us the portion of the decline in DI that will be at the expense of consumption, and the MPS indicates what fraction of the drop in DI will be at the expense of saving. Since the MPC

TABLE 10-5 Determination of the equilibrium levels of employment, output, and income: private and public sectors (in billions)

(1) Real domestic output (GDP)	(2) T	(3) Possible levels of disposable incomes, (DI) (1) − (2)	(4) C_a	(5) S_a (3) − (4)	(6) I_g	(7) X	(8) M_a	(9) X_{n_a} (7) − (8)	(10) G	(11) Aggregate expenditures $(C_a + I_g + X_{n_a} + G)$ (4) + (6) + (9) + (10)
(1) $370	$40	$330	$345	$ −15	$20	$40	$5	$35	$40	$440
(2) 390	40	350	360	−10	20	40	10	30	40	450
(3) 410	40	370	375	−5	20	40	15	25	40	460
(4) 430	40	390	390	0	20	40	20	20	40	470
(5) 450	40	410	405	5	20	40	25	15	40	480
(6) 470	40	430	420	10	20	40	30	10	40	490
(7) 490	40	450	435	15	20	40	35	5	40	500
(8) 510	40	470	450	20	20	40	40	0	40	510
(9) 530	40	490	465	25	20	40	45	−5	40	520
(10) 550	40	510	480	30	20	40	50	−10	40	530

equals $3/4$ (.75) and the MPS equals $1/4$ (.25), if government collects $40 billion in taxes at each possible level of GDP, the amount of consumption at each level of GDP will drop by $30 billion ($3/4$ of $40 billion), and the amount of saving at each level of GDP will fall by 10 billion ($1/4$ of 40 billion).

But there is one more refinement we must make to the new lower consumption level brought about by the tax increase. In an open economy such as Canada's, consumption consists of both domestic and imported commodities. Of the $30 billion drop in total consumption, there will be a $10 billion decrease in M since the MPM equals $1/4$. The remaining $20 billion, therefore, comes out of domestic consumption.

In columns 4 and 5 of Table 10-5, the amounts of consumption, saving, and imports *at each level of GDP* are $30, $20 and $10 billion smaller, respectively, than in Table 10-4. Before the taxes, where GDP equalled DI, for example, consumption was $435 billion, saving $15 billion, and imports $35 billion at the $450 billion level of GDP (row 5 of Table 10-4). After taxes are imposed, DI is $410 billion, $40 billion short of the $450 billion GDP, with the result that consumption is only $405 billion, saving is $5 billion, and imports $25 billion (row 5 of Table 10-5).

Taxes cause DI to fall short of GDP by the amount of the taxes. This decline in DI reduces consumption, saving, and imports at each level of GDP. The sizes of the declines in C, S, and M are determined by the MPC, the MPS, and the MPM, respectively.

What is the effect of taxes on equilibrium GDP? We calculate aggregate expenditures once again, as shown in column 11 of Table 10-5. Note that aggregate spending is $20 billion less at each level of real output than it was in Table 10-4. The reason is that after-tax consumption, C_a, is $30 billion less, and M_a is $10 billion less (therefore, X_{n_a} is $10 billion more) at each level of GDP. Comparing real output and aggregate expenditures, in columns 1 and 11, we see that the aggregate amounts produced and purchased are equal only at the $510 billion level of GDP (row 8). The imposition of a $40 billion lump-sum tax has caused equilibrium GDP to fall from $550 billion (row 10 in Table 10-4) to $510 billion (row 8).

Our alternative leakages–injections approach confirms this result. Taxes, like saving and imports, are a leakage from the domestic income–expenditures stream. Consumption will now fall short of domestic output — creating a potential spending gap — in the amount of imports and after-tax saving *plus* taxes. This gap may be filled by planned investment, government purchases, and exports.

Thus, our new equilibrium condition for the leakages–injections approach is: after-tax saving, S_a, plus imports, M_a, plus taxes equal planned investment plus exports plus government purchases. Symbolically,

$$S_a + M_a + T = I_g + X + G$$

$$(20 + 40 + 40 = 20 + 40 + 40)$$

You should verify, in Table 10-5, that this equality of leakages and injections is fulfilled only at the $510 billion level of GDP (row 8).

GRAPHIC ANALYSIS In Figure 10-6(a) the $40 billion *increase* in taxes shows up as a $20 (*not* $40) billion *decline* in the aggregate expenditures ($C_a + I_g + X_{n_a} + G$) schedule. Under our continuing assumption that all taxes are personal income taxes, this decline in aggregate spending results from a decline in the consumption component of the aggregate expenditures schedule = $(MPC)(\Delta T)$ = ($3/4$) ($40 billion) = $30 billion, of which $20 billion is domestic consumption and $10 billion is import consumption. The equilibrium GDP shifts from $550 billion to $510 billion because of this tax-induced drop in total consumption.

Increases in taxes will lower the aggregate expenditures schedule relative to the 45° line and reduce the equilibrium GDP.

Consider the leakages-injections approach. The analysis here is slightly more complex because the $40 billion in taxes has a twofold effect in Figure 10-6(b).

1. The taxes reduce DI by $40 billion and, with the MPS at $1/4$, cause saving to fall by $10 billion at each level of GDP. Also, the import component of consumption falls by $10 billion. In Figure 10-6(b), this is shown as a shift from S + M (saving before taxes and imports) to $S_a + M_a$ (saving after taxes and reduction in import consumption).
2. The $40 billion in taxes is a $40 billion additional leakage at each GDP level, which must be added to $S_a + M_a$ (not S + M), giving us $S_a + M_a + T$.

Equilibrium now exists at the $510 billion GDP, where the total amount that households save and the economy imports, plus the amount of taxes government intends to collect, are equal to the total amount businesses both export and plan to invest plus the amount of government purchases. The equilibrium condition for the leakages-injection approach now is $S_a + M_a + T = I_g + X + G$. Graphically, it is the

FIGURE 10-6 **Taxes and the equilibrium GDP**

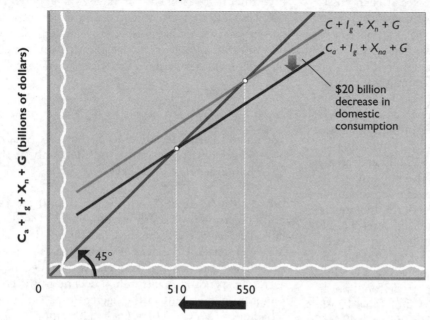

Real domestic product, GDP (billions of dollars)

(a) Aggregate expenditures–domestic output approach

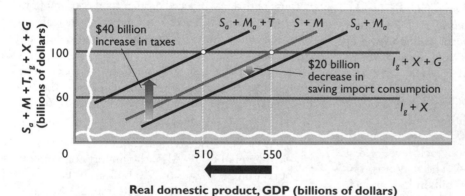

Real domestic product, GDP (billions of dollars)

(b) Leakages–injections approach

(a) *The aggregate expenditures–domestic output approach.* If the MPC is $3/4$, the imposition of $40 billion of taxes will lower the aggregate domestic expenditures schedule by $20 billion and cause a decline in the equilibrium GDP.

(b) *The leakages–injections approach.* Here, taxes have a twofold effect. First, with an MPS of $1/4$, the imposition of taxes of $40 billion will reduce disposable income by $40 billion and saving by $10 billion at each level of GDP. Also imports fall by $10 billion because some of the reduction of aggregate consumption reduces the consumption good component of imports. This is shown by a shift from $(S + M)$ (savings before taxes plus imports) to $(S_a + M_a)$ (savings after taxes plus imports). Second, the $40 billion of taxes constitute an additional $40 billion leakage at each GDP level, giving us $S_a + M_a + T$. By adding government, the equilibrium condition changes from $S + M = I_g + X$ to $S_a + M_a + T = I_g + X + G$.

intersection of the $S_a + M_a + T$ and the $I_g + X + G$ schedules that determines the equilibrium GDP.

A *decrease* in existing taxes will cause the aggregate expenditures schedule $[C_a + I_g + X_{n_a} + G$ in Figure 10-6(a)], to rise as a result of an upward shift in the consumption schedule. In Figure 10-6(b), a tax cut will cause a decline in the $S_a + M_a + T$ schedule. The result in either case is a multiple *increase* in the equilibrium GDP.

You should use both the expenditures-output and the leakages–injections approaches to confirm that a

tax reduction of $20 billion (from the present $40 billion to $20 billion) will increase the equilibrium GDP from $510 billion to $530 billion. **(Key Question 8)**

BALANCED-BUDGET MULTIPLIER

There is an important and curious thing about our tabular and graphical illustrations. *Equal increases in government spending and taxation increase the equilibrium GDP. If G and T are each increased by a particular amount, the equilibrium level of domestic output will rise by that same amount.*

In our example the $40 billion increases in G and T increase the equilibrium GDP by $40 billion (from $470 to $510 billion).

The rationale for this **balanced-budget multiplier** is revealed in our example. A change in government spending has a more powerful effect on aggregate expenditures than does a tax change of the same size.

Government spending has a *direct* impact on aggregate expenditures. Government spending is a component of aggregate expenditures and, when government purchases increase by 40 billion as in our example, the aggregate expenditures schedule shifts upward by the entire $40 billion.

But a change in taxes affects aggregate expenditures *indirectly* by changing disposable income and thereby changing both the domestic and import components of consumption. Specifically, our $40 billion lump-sum tax increase shifts the domestic aggregate expenditures schedule downward by $20 billion. While there has been a $30 billion decrease in total consumption (since MPC = $3/4$), $10 billion of it represents the decrease in the consumption of imported goods. Thus, there is an overall $20 billion decrease in domestic consumption.

The overall result is a *net* upward shift of the domestic aggregate expenditures schedule of $20 billion (i.e., $40 billion *more* government spending, but $20 billion *less* spending on domestic consumption), which, subject to a multiplier of 2, boosts GDP by $40 billion. This $40 billion increase in GDP is equal to the size of the initial increase in government expenditures and taxes. *The balanced budget multiplier is 1.*

The fact that the balanced budget multiplier is 1 is shown in Figure 10-7. With an MPC of .75, the tax increase of $40 billion reduces disposable income by $40 billion and decreases total consumption expenditures by $30 billion. The $30 billion decline in consumption results in a $20 billion drop in domestic consumption, and $10 billion in import consumption and the fall in domestic expenditures *reduces* GDP by $40 billion (= $20 billion × the multiplier of 2). However, observe in Figure 10-7 that the increase in government expenditures of $40 billion *increases* GDP by $80 billion (= $40 billion × the multiplier of 2). The equal increases of taxes and government expenditures of $40 billion thus yield a net increase of GDP of $40 billion (= $80 billion –

FIGURE 10-7 The balanced-budget multiplier

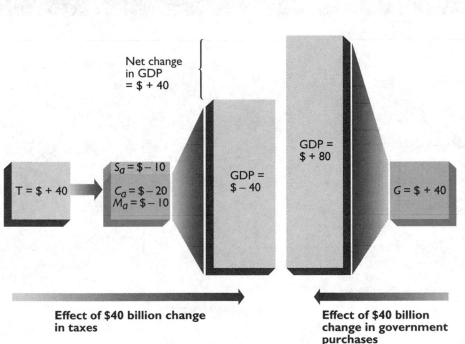

Net change
in GDP
= $ + 40

$S_a = \$ - 10$
$C_a = \$ - 20$
$M_a = \$ - 10$

T = $ + 40

GDP =
$ – 40

GDP =
$ + 80

G = $ + 40

Effect of $40 billion change in taxes

Effect of $40 billion change in government purchases

The balanced-budget multiplier is 1. An equal increase in taxes and government expenditures will increase GDP by an amount equal to the increase in the amount of government expenditures and taxes. Given an MPC of .75, a tax increase of $40 billion will reduce disposable income by $40 billion and lower consumption expenditures by $20 billion. Because the multiplier is 2, GDP will therefore decline by $40 billion. The $40 billion increase in government expenditures, however, will produce a more than offsetting increase in GDP of $80 billion. The net increase in GDP will be $20 billion, which equals the amount of the increase in government expenditures and taxes.

$40 billion). *Equal increases in G and T increase real GDP by an amount equal to the increase in G and T.* You should experiment to verify that the balanced-budget multiplier is valid regardless of the sizes of the marginal propensities to consume and save. Note that the balanced budget multiplier also works in the reverse: equal decreases in G and T cause real GDP to fall by the same amount.

EQUILIBRIUM VERSUS FULL-EMPLOYMENT GDP

Now that we have the full aggregate expenditures model at our disposal, we can turn from the task of explaining to evaluating the equilibrium GDP.

The $510 billion equilibrium GDP in our complete analysis (Table 10-5 and Figure 10-6) may or may not entail full employment. The aggregate expenditures schedule might well lie above or below that which would intersect the 45° line at the full-employment level of output. Indeed, our assumption thus far has been that the economy is operating at less than full employment.

RECESSIONARY GAP

Assume in **Figure 10-8(a) (Key Graph)** that the full-employment noninflationary level of domestic output is $530 billion and the aggregate expenditures schedule is at $(C + I_g + X_n + G)_1$. This schedule intersects the 45° line to the left of the full-employment output, causing the economy's aggregate production to fall $20 billion short of its capacity production. The economy is failing to employ all of its available workers and, as a result, is sacrificing $20 billion of output.

The amount by which GDP falls short of the full-employment level of GDP (also called potential GDP) is called the **recessionary gap**. In Table 10-5, assuming the full-employment GDP to be $530 billion, the corresponding recessionary gap is $20 billion. The aggregate expenditures schedule would have to shift upward to realize the full-employment GDP. Because the multiplier is 2, the expenditure shortfall is $10 billion; an increase in any of the expenditure components by $10 billion would raise GDP by $20 billion to the full-employment GDP.

KEY GRAPH

FIGURE 10-8   Recessionary and inflationary gaps

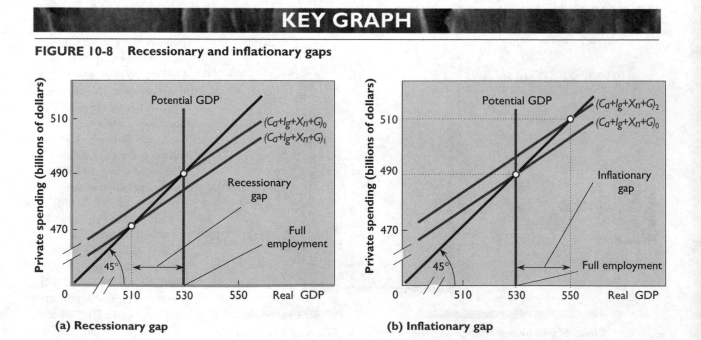

(a) Recessionary gap

(b) Inflationary gap

The equilibrium and full-employment GDPs may not coincide. A recessionary gap, shown in (a), is the amount by which equilibrium GDP falls short of full-employment GDP. The inflationary gap in (b) is the amount by which equilibrium GDP exceeds full-employment GDP.

INFLATIONARY GAP

If aggregate expenditures are at $(C_a + I_g + X_n + G)_2$ in Figure 10-8(b), a demand-pull inflationary gap will exist. The amount by which GDP exceeds the full-employment level of GDP is called an **inflationary gap**. In this case, there is a $20 billion inflationary gap. The effect of this inflationary gap — an excess aggregate demand of $10 billion — will be to pull up the prices of the economy's output. **(Key Question 10)**

HISTORICAL APPLICATIONS

Let's see how these concepts of recessionary and inflationary gaps apply to two economic events.

GREAT DEPRESSION

In October of 1929 the stock market collapsed, marking the beginning of the most severe and prolonged depression of modern times. Real GDP (1986 dollars) plummeted from $53 billion in 1929 to a low of $38.3 billion in 1933. The unemployment rate rose from 2.9% in 1929 to 19.1% in the same period. As late as 1939, real GDP was only 6% above its level of ten years earlier and the unemployment rate still was 11.4%!

A sagging level of investment spending was the major weight that pulled the Canadian economy to the economic chaos of the 1930s. In real terms, gross investment spending contracted from $1.24 billion in 1929 to $.187 billion in 1933 — an 85% decline. In Figure 10-8, we would depict this decline in investment as a dramatic downward shift in the nation's aggregate expenditure schedule, causing a severe recessionary (depressionary) gap and an historic decline in real GDP.

What factors caused this precipitous decline in investment?

1. OVERCAPACITY AND BUSINESS INDEBTEDNESS
Flush with the prosperity of the 1920s, businesses overexpanded their productive capacity. In particular, the tremendous expansion of the automobile industry — and the related petroleum, rubber, steel, glass, and textile industries — came to a halt as the market for new autos became saturated. Business indebtedness also increased rapidly during the twenties. Furthermore, by the late 1920s much of the income of businesses was committed

GLOBAL PERSPECTIVE 10-2

Changes in industrial production, selected countries, 1929–1930 and 1937–1938

The Great Depression of the 1930s was global, with large declines in industrial output occurring in most countries. The Depression began in 1929–1930 for many countries. Between 1933 and 1937 industrial output partially recovered. Precipitous declines in industrial output again occurred in some nations in 1937–1938.

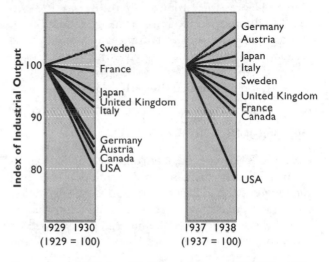

Source: League of Nations, *World Economic Survey, 1938–1939*, p. 107.

for the payment of interest and principal on past purchases, and thus not available for current expenditures on new capital.

2. DECLINE IN RESIDENTIAL CONSTRUCTION
The 1920s experienced a boom in residential construction in response to population growth and housing demand deferred because of World War I. This investment spending began to level off as early as 1926, and by the late 1920s the construction industry had virtually collapsed.

3. STOCK MARKET CRASH
The most dramatic facet of the Great Depression was the stock market crash of October 1929. The optimism of the prosperous 1920s had elevated stock market speculation to something of a national pastime. This speculation had bid up stock prices to the point where they did not reflect financial reality — stock prices were far beyond the profit-making potentials of the

firms they represented. A downward adjustment was necessary and it came suddenly and quickly in 1929.

The stock market crash had significant secondary effects. Most important was the psychological repercussions. The buoyant optimism of the 1920s gave way to a wave of crippling pessimism, and the crashing of stock prices created highly unfavourable conditions for acquiring additional money for investment.

4. SHRINKING MONEY SUPPLY   The nation's money supply plummeted in the early years of the Great Depression, from $2.27 billion in 1929 to $1.99 billion by 1933. This shrinkage resulted from forces operating both at home and abroad. The reduction of the money supply contributed to the sharp decline in the volume of aggregate expenditures that characterized the early 1930s.

IMPACT OF AMERICAN ECONOMIC GROWTH

The 1960s was a period of prolonged economic expansion, fuelled by increases in consumption spending and investment. A major factor in this long expansion was the rapid economic growth in our main trading partner, the United States. American policy called for government to manipulate its tax collections and expenditures in such a way as to increase aggregate demand, increasing employment and real GDP. For example, in 1962 legislation was enacted that provided for a 7% tax credit on investment in new machinery and equipment, thus strengthening the incentives of businesses to invest. In 1964 the government cut personal and corporate income taxes, boosting consumption spending and further increasing investment spending. The American unemployment rate fell from 5.2% in 1964 to 4.5% in 1965.

At this time another expansionary force came into play. The escalation of American participation in the Vietnam war resulted in a 40% increase in U.S. government spending on national defence between 1965 and 1967. Another 15% increase in war-related spending occurred in 1968. Remarkably, the American unemployment rate fell below 4% during the entire 1966–1969 period. But the increased government expenditures, imposed on an already booming economy, also brought about the worst inflation in two decades. Inflation jumped from 1.6% in 1965 to 5.7% by 1970. In terms of Figure 10-8, the booming investment expenditures and the added

government expenditures shifted the aggregate expenditures schedule sharply upward, creating an inflationary gap. The rapid economic growth in the United States spilled over into Canada through our increased exports to them, creating an inflationary gap in Canada as well. Real GDP expanded at almost 7% per annum in a number of years during the 1960s, reaching a high of 7.7% in 1971. Inflation also rose, but did not become serious until 1973.

QUICK REVIEW 10-2

1. Government purchases shift the aggregate expenditures schedule upward and raise equilibrium GDP.

2. Taxes reduce disposable income, lower consumption spending on domestically produced goods and saving, shift the imported and aggregate expenditures schedules downward, and reduce equilibrium GDP.

3. The balanced budget multiplier is 1. If G and T are each increased by a particular amount, the equilibrium level of domestic output will rise by the same amount, and vice versa.

4. A recessionary gap is the amount by which GDP must increase for the economy to realize full employment; the inflationary gap is the amount by which GDP must decrease for the economy to eliminate inflationary pressures.

5. The Great Depression of the 1930s is a good example of a period characterized by a large recessionary (depressionary) gap; the late 1960s and early 1970s represent a period having an inflationary gap.

CRITIQUE AND PREVIEW

Our analysis and examples demonstrate the power of the aggregate expenditures model to help us understand how the economy works, how recessions or depressions can occur, and how demand-pull inflation can arise. But all models are approximations of what really happens. So they have their shortcomings. The aggregate expenditures theory has two limitations.

1. PRICE LEVEL CHANGES   This model can account for demand-pull inflation, as in Figure 10-8(b), but it does not indicate how *much* the price level will rise when aggregate expenditures are excessive relative to the economy's capacity. Will the $10 billion inflationary gap of Figure 10-8(b) cause a 3%, 5%, 10%, or some other rate of inflation? By how much will the GDP price deflator of Chapter 7 rise where there is a particular inflationary gap? The aggregate expenditures model has no price level axis; it has no way of measuring the rate of inflation.

2. COST-PUSH INFLATION   We know from Chapter 8 there are two general types of inflation: demand-pull inflation and cost-push inflation. The aggregate expenditures model does not address cost-push inflation.

In Chapter 11 we remedy these deficiencies, while preserving the insights of the aggregate expenditures model. We use the model to derive aggregate demand — a schedule or curve relating various price levels to corresponding amounts of real GDP that will be demanded. When this aggregate demand curve is combined with an aggregate supply curve, we obtain an aggregate expenditures-based model that overcomes the shortcomings just discussed. The better you understand the aggregate expenditures model, the easier it will be for you to grasp Chapter 11's aggregate demand–aggregate supply model.

CHAPTER SUMMARY

1. Shifts in the saving-consumption schedules or in the investment schedule will change the equilibrium output-income level by several times the amount of the initial change in spending. This multiplier effect accompanies both increases and decreases in aggregate expenditures.

2. The simple multiplier is equal to the reciprocal of the marginal propensity to save. The higher the marginal propensity to save, the lower is the size of the simple multiplier. The higher the marginal propensity to consume, the greater is the simple multiplier. The complex multiplier includes all the leakages — saving, imports, and taxes.

3. The net export schedule relates net exports (exports minus imports) to levels of GDP.

4. Positive net exports increase aggregate expenditures above their level in a closed economy, raising Canadian real GDP by a multiple amount; negative net exports decrease aggregate expenditures below their level, decreasing Canadian real GDP by a multiple amount. Increases in exports or decreases in imports have an expansionary effect on real GDP, while decreases in exports or increases in imports have a contractionary effect. The open economy multiplier is smaller than the simple multiplier for a closed economy.

5. Government purchases shift the aggregate expenditures schedule upward and raise equilibrium GDP.

6. Taxation reduces disposable income; reduces consumption spending, imports, and saving; shifts the aggregate expenditures schedule downward; and reduces equilibrium GDP.

7. The balanced budget multiplier is 1, meaning that equal increases in government spending and taxation will increase the equilibrium real GDP by the amount of the increases in government expenditures and taxes (and vice versa).

8. The equilibrium level of real GDP and the full-employment GDP need not coincide. The amount by which equilibrium GDP falls short of the full-employment GDP (potential GDP) is called the recessionary gap. The amount by which equilibrium GDP exceeds full-employment GDP (potential GDP) is the inflationary gap; it causes demand–pull inflation.

9. The Great Depression of the 1930s resulted from a precipitous decline in aggregate expenditures that produced a severe and long-lasting recessionary gap. The late 1960s and early 1970s provides a good example of an inflationary gap with its accompanying demand-pull inflation.

10. The aggregate expenditures model provides many insights about the macroeconomy, but does not show price level changes or account for cost-push inflation. The aggregate demand-aggregate supply model — the subject of Chapter 11 — addresses these shortcomings.

TERMS AND CONCEPTS

appreciation (p. 218)
balanced-budget multiplier (p. 229)
complex multiplier (p. 216)
depreciation (p. 218)
inflationary gap (p. 231)
lump-sum tax (p. 226)
marginal propensity to import (p. 218)

multiplier effect (p. 212)
net export schedule (p. 218)
net exports (p. 216)
open-economy multiplier (p. 223)
recessionary gap (p. 230)
simple multiplier (p. 216)

QUESTIONS AND STUDY SUGGESTIONS

1. What effect will each of the changes designated in question 4 at the end of Chapter 9 have on the equilibrium level of GDP? Explain your answers.

2. *Key Question   What is the multiplier effect? What relationship does the MPC bear to the size of the simple multiplier? The MPS? What will the multiplier be when the MPS is 0, .4, .6, and 1? When the MPC is 1, .90, .67, .50, and 0? How much of a change in GDP will result if businesses increase their level of investment by $8 billion and the MPC in the economy is .80? If the MPC is .67? Explain the difference between the simple and the complex multiplier.*

3. Graphically depict the aggregate expenditures model for a private closed economy. Next, show a decrease in the aggregate expenditures schedule and explain why the decrease in real GDP in your diagram is greater than the initial decline in aggregate expenditures. What would be the ratio of the decline in real GDP to the initial drop in aggregate expenditures if the slope of your aggregate expenditures schedule were .8?

4. Speculate on why a planned increase in saving by households, unaccompanied by an increase in investment spending by businesses, might instead result in a decline in real GDP and *no* increase in actual saving. Demonstrate this point graphically using the leakage-injection approach to equilibrium real GDP. Now assume in your diagram that investment instead increases to match the initial increase in desired saving. Using your knowledge from Chapter 2, explain why these joint increases in saving and investment might be desirable for a society.

5. *Key Question   The data in columns 1 and 2 of the table below are for a private closed economy.*

(1) Real domestic output (GDP = DI), billions	(2) Aggregate expenditures, private closed economy, billions	(3) Exports, billions	(4) Imports, billions	(5) Net exports, billions	(6) Aggregate expenditures, private open economy (billions)
$200	$240	$20	$18	$____	$____
250	280	20	22	____	____
300	320	20	26	____	____
350	360	20	30	____	____
400	400	20	34	____	____
450	440	20	38	____	____
500	480	20	42	____	____
550	520	20	46	____	____

  a. *Use columns 1 and 2 to determine the equilibrium GDP for this hypothetical economy.*

  b. *Now open this economy for international trade by including the export and import figures of columns 3 and 4. Calculate the net exports and determine the equilibrium GDP for the open economy. Explain why equilibrium GDP differs from the closed economy.*

  c. *Given the original $20 billion level of exports, what would be the equilibrium GDP if imports were $14 billion larger at each level of GDP? Or $14 billion smaller at each level of GDP? What generalizations concerning the level of imports and the equilibrium GDP is illustrated by these examples?*

  d. *What is the size of the open economy multiplier in these examples?*

6. Assume that, without taxes, the consumption schedule for an economy is as shown below:

GDP, billions	Consumption, billions
$100	$120
200	200
300	280
400	360
500	440
600	520
700	600

  a. Graph this consumption schedule and note the size of the MPC.

  b. Assume now a lump-sum tax system is imposed such that the government collects $10 billion in taxes at all levels of GDP. Graph the resulting consumption schedule and compare the MPC and the multiplier with that of the pretax consumption schedule.

  c. Now suppose a proportional tax system with a 10% tax rate is imposed instead. Calculate the new consumption schedule, graph it, and note the MPC and the multiplier.

  d. Finally, impose a progressive tax system such that the tax rate is 0% when GDP is $100, 5% at $200, 10% at $300, 15% at $400, and so forth. Determine and graph the new consumption schedule, noting the effect of this tax system on the MPC and the multiplier.

7. Explain graphically the determination of equilibrium GDP through both the aggregate expenditures–domestic output approach and the leakages–injections approach for the private sector. Now add government spending and taxation, showing the impact of each on the equilibrium GDP.

8. *Key Question*   *Refer to columns 1 and 6 of the tabular data for question 5. Incorporate government into the table by assuming that it plans to tax and spend $100 billion at each possible level of GDP. Also assume that all taxes are personal taxes and that government spending does not induce a shift in the private aggregate expenditures schedule. Explain the changes in the equilibrium GDP that the addition of government entails.*

9. What is the balanced-budget multiplier? Demonstrate the balanced-budget multiplier in terms of your answer to question 8. Explain: "Equal increases in government spending and tax revenues of n dollars will increase the equilibrium GDP by n dollars." Does this hold true regardless of the size of the MPS?

10. *Key Question*   *Refer to the accompanying table in answering the questions that follow.*

(1) Possible levels of employment, millions	(2) Real domestic output, billions	(3) Aggregate expenditures, $C + I_g + X_n + G$, billions
9	$500	$520
10	550	560
11	600	600
12	650	640
13	700	680

a. *If full employment in this economy is $13 million, will there be an inflationary or a recessionary gap? What will be the consequences of this gap? By how much would aggregate expenditures in column 3 have to change to eliminate the inflationary or recessionary gap? Explain.*

b. *Will there be an inflationary or recessionary gap if the full-employment level of output is $500 billion? Explain the consequences. By how much would aggregate expenditures in column 3 have to change to eliminate the inflationary or recessionary gap? Explain.*

c. *Assuming that investment, net exports, and government expenditures do not change with changes in real GDP, what are the sizes of the MPC, the MPS, and the multiplier?*

11. Which of the two situations in Question 10 — the one described in part **a** or part **b** — is consistent with the realities of the Great Depression? With the late 1960s and early 1970s? Explain your answers.

12. Advanced Analysis Assume the consumption schedule for a private open economy is such that $C = 50 + 0.8Y$. Assume further that investment and net exports are autonomous (indicated by I_{g0} and X_{n0}); that is, planned investment and net exports are independent of the level of real GDP and in the amount $I_g = I_{g0} = 30$ and $X_n = X_{n0} = 10$. Recall also that in equilibrium the amount of domestic output produced (Y) is equal to the aggregate expenditures ($C + I_g + X_n$), or $Y = C + I_g + X_n$.

a. Calculate the equilibrium level of income or real GDP for this economy. Check your work by putting the consumption, investment, and net export schedules in tabular form and determining the equilibrium GDP.

b. What will happen to equilibrium Y if $I_g = I_{g0} = 10$? What does this tell you about the size of the multiplier?

13. Advanced Analysis We can add the public sector to the private economy of question 12 as follows. Assume $G = G_0 = 28$ and $T = T_0 = 30$. Because of the taxes, the consumption schedule, $C = 50 + 0.8Y$, must be modified to read $C_a = 50 + 0.8(Y - T)$, where the term $(Y - T)$ is disposable (after-tax) income. Assuming all taxes are on personal income, investment remains $I_g = I_{g0} = 30$. Net exports are again independent of the level of income, that is, $X_n = X_{n0} = 10$. Using the equilibrium condition $Y = C_a + I_g + X_n + G$, determine the equilibrium level of income. Explain why the addition of the public budget with a slight surplus increases the equilibrium income.

14. (Applying the Theory) What is the central economic idea humorously illustrated in Art Buchwald's piece, "Squaring the Economic Circle"?

CHAPTER 11

AGGREGATE DEMAND
AND AGGREGATE SUPPLY

he aggregate expenditures model developed in Chapters 9 and 10 is a *fixed-price-level model* — its focus is on changes in real GDP, not on changes in the price level. We now develop a *variable-price-level model* so that we can simultaneously analyze changes in real GDP and the price level. To do this we need to combine — or aggregate — all individual markets in the economy into a single market. We must combine the thousands of individual equilibrium prices — of pizzas, robots, corn, computers, crankshafts, doughnuts, diamonds, oil, perfume, and lipstick — into an aggregate price level. Similarly, we must merge the equilibrium quantities of individual products and services into real GDP, which is already familiar to us. Thus, our new graphical model measures the price level on the vertical

axis and real domestic output, or "real GDP" or "real output" on the horizontal axis.

What you learn in this chapter will help organize your thinking about equilibrium GDP, the price level, and government macroeconomic policies. The tools learned here will also help you in later chapters, where we contrast differing views on macroeconomic theory and policy.

In the present chapter we introduce the concepts of aggregate demand and aggregate supply, explaining the shapes of the aggregate demand and aggregate supply curves and the forces causing them to shift. Next, we consider the equilibrium levels of prices and real GDP. Finally, we explore the effects of shifts in the aggregate demand and aggregate supply curves on the price level and the size of real GDP.

BOX 11-1   THE BIG PICTURE

Those of you who have studied the expenditure model will recall that it assumed a fixed price level. Also, the expenditure model deals only with aggregate demand; the aggregate supply in an economy is ignored. In this chapter you will study a model of the macroeconomy that explains both the price level and GDP — the aggregate demand and aggregate supply model. If you have previously studied demand and supply analysis, you will discern similarities. But there are many differences. For those who have covered the aggregate expenditure model, there is a section that links it to the aggregate demand curve.

The purpose of studying the aggregate demand-aggregate supply model is the same as for the aggregate expenditure model. We aim to understand how the macroeconomy functions, so we can devise policies that will stabilize the economy and promote growth. The aggregate demand–aggregate supply model is a powerful theoretical model that allows us to better understand the main macroeconomic issues: economic growth, inflation, and unemployment.

As you read this chapter, keep the following points in mind:

- Distinguish between factors that *shift* the aggregate demand and aggregate supply curves and movements *along* each curve. Each of the curves is independent of the other; each shifts for different reasons.
- We are still focusing on the short run. For the most part, the short-run aggregate supply curve is upward-sloping.
- In short to medium term, the economy may be at equilibrium at a level of GDP below full employment (potential GDP). This means the economy is not fully employing all its available resources, particularly its labour force. If such is the case, the economy is in a recession. If equilibrium GDP is above full-employment GDP, inflationary pressures appear.

AGGREGATE DEMAND

Aggregate demand *is a schedule, graphically represented as a curve, showing the various amounts of goods and services — the amounts of real output — that domestic consumers, businesses, government, and foreign buyers collectively desire to purchase at each possible price level.* Other things being equal, the lower the price level, the larger will be the real GDP these buyers will purchase. Conversely, the higher the price level, the smaller will be the real output they buy. Thus, the relationship between the price level and the amount of real GDP demanded is inverse or negative.

AGGREGATE DEMAND CURVE

The inverse relationship between the price level and real output is shown in Figure 11-1 where the aggregate demand curve slopes downward, as does the demand curve for an individual product.

FIGURE 11-1   The aggregate demand curve

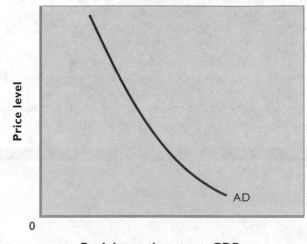

Real domestic output, GDP

The downsloping aggregate demand curve indicates an inverse relationship between the price level and the amount of real domestic output purchased.

Why? The rationale is *not* the same as it is for the demand for a single product. That explanation centred on income and substitution effects. When the price of an individual product falls, the consumer's (constant) nominal income will enable him or her to purchase more of the product (the income effect). And, as price falls, the consumer wants to buy more of the product because it becomes relatively less expensive than other goods (the substitution effect).

But these explanations do not work for aggregates. In Figure 11-1 prices in general are falling as we move down the aggregate demand curve so the rationale for the substitution effect (a product becoming cheaper relative to all other products) is not applicable. Similarly, while an individual's demand curve for a specific product assumes the consumer's nominal income is fixed, the aggregate demand curve implies differing levels of aggregate incomes. As we move up the aggregate demand curve, we move to higher price levels. But, recalling our circular flow model, higher prices paid for goods and services will flow to resources suppliers as expanded wage, rent, interest, and profit incomes. As a result, an increase in the price level does *not* necessarily mean a decline in the nominal income of the economy as a whole.

If substitution and income effects do not explain the downsloping aggregate demand curve, what does? The rationale rests on three factors:

1. WEALTH EFFECT

The first reason the aggregate demand curve is downsloping is the **wealth** or **real-balances effect**. A higher price level reduces the real value or purchasing power of the public's accumulated financial assets. In particular, the real value of assets with fixed money values such as savings accounts or bonds diminishes. Because of the erosion of purchasing power of such assets, the public is poorer in real terms and will retrench on its spending. A household might buy a new car or a sailboat if the purchasing power of their financial asset balances is, say, $50,000. But if inflation erodes the purchasing power of these asset balances to $30,000, the family may defer its purchase.

Conversely, a decline in the price level will increase the real value or purchasing power of a person's wealth and increase spending.

2. INTEREST-RATE EFFECT

The **interest-rate effect** tells us that as the price level rises so do real interest rates, and rising real interest rates reduce certain kinds of consumption and investment spending.

Elaboration: *The aggregate demand curve assumes the supply of money in the economy is fixed.* When the price level increases, consumers need more money for purchases, and businesses similarly require more money to meet their payrolls and to buy other needed inputs. In short, a higher price level increases the demand for money.

With a fixed supply of money, this increase in demand for money drives up the price paid for its use. That price is the interest rate. Higher real interest rates curtail interest-sensitive expenditures by businesses and households. A firm expecting a 10% return on a potential purchase of capital will find that purchase profitable when the real interest rate is, say, only 7%. But the purchase is unprofitable and will not be made when the interest rate has risen to, say, 12%. Similarly, some consumers will decide *not* to purchase houses or automobiles because of the rise in the interest rate.

Conclusion: A higher price level — by increasing the demand for money and the real interest rate — reduces the amount of real output demanded.

3. FOREIGN-TRADE EFFECT

We found in Chapter 7's discussion of national income accounting that imports and exports are components of total spending. The volumes of our imports and exports depend on, among other things, relative price levels here and abroad. If the price level rises in Canada relative to foreign countries, Canadian buyers will purchase more imports and fewer Canadian goods. Similarly, the rest of the world will buy fewer Canadian goods, reducing Canadian exports. A rise in our price level will increase our imports and reduce our exports, reducing the amount of net export (export minus import) spending on Canadian-produced products.

Conclusion: The **foreign-trade effect** of a price-level increase results in a decline in the aggregate amount of Canadian output demanded. Conversely, a relative decline in our price level reduces our imports and increases our exports, increasing the net exports component of Canadian aggregate demand.

DERIVING THE AGGREGATE DEMAND CURVE FROM THE AGGREGATE EXPENDITURES MODEL[1]

We can directly derive the downsloping aggregate demand curve shown in Figure 11-1 from the aggregate expenditures model developed in Chapters 9 and 10. The aggregate demand curve in Figure 11-1 merely relates the various possible price levels to corresponding GDPs. Note in **Figure 11-2 (Key Graph)** that we can stack the aggregate expenditures model of Figure 11-2(a) and the aggregate demand curve of Figure 11-2(b) vertically because real output is measured on the horizontal axis of both models. Now we can start at the top with the aggregate expenditures schedule $(C_a + I_g + X_n + G)_2$. The price level relevant to this schedule is P_2 as shown in the graph to remind us of that fact. From this information we can plot the equilibrium real output, GDP_2, and the corresponding price level P_2. This gives us one point — namely $2'$ — on Figure 11-2(b)'s aggregate demand curve.

Let's now assume the price level is P_1. Other things being equal, this lower price level will: (a) increase the value of wealth, boosting consumption expenditures; (2) reduce the real interest rate, promoting investment expenditures; and (3) reduce imports and increase exports, increasing net export expenditures. The aggregate expenditures schedule will rise from $(C_a + I_g + X_n + G)_2$ to, say, $(C_a + I_g + X_n + G)_1$, giving us equilibrium at GDP_1. In Figure 11-2(b) we locate this new price level-real output combination, P_1, and GDP_1, at point $1'$.

Now suppose the price level increases from the original P_2 level to P_3. The real value of wealth falls, the real interest rate rises, exports fall, and imports rise. Consequently, the consumption, investment and net export schedules fall, shifting the aggregate expenditures schedule downward from $(C_a + I_g + X_n + G)_2$ to $(C_a + I_g + X_n + G)_3$ where real output is GDP_3. This lets us locate a third point on Figure 11-2(b)'s aggregate demand curve, namely point $3'$ where the price level is P_3 and real output is GDP_3.

In summary, a decrease in the price level shifts the aggregate expenditures schedule upward and increases

[1] This section presumes knowledge of the aggregate expenditures model in Chapters 9 and 10 and can be skipped by readers who are not assigned those chapters.

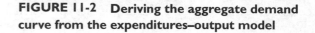

KEY GRAPH

FIGURE 11-2 Deriving the aggregate demand curve from the expenditures–output model

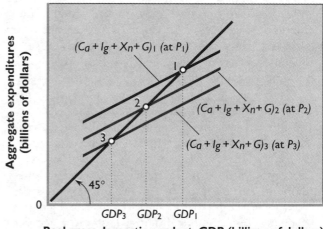

(a) Expenditures – output model

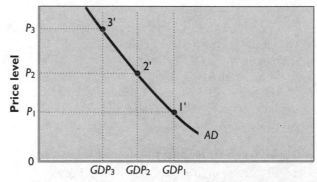

(b) Aggregate demand – aggregate supply model

Through the wealth, interest-rate, and foreign-trade effects, the consumption, investment, and net exports schedules and therefore the aggregate expenditures schedule will rise (fall) when the price level declines (increases). If the aggregate expenditure schedule is at $(C_a + I_g + X_n + G)_2$ when the price level is P_2, we can combine that price level and the equilibrium output, GDP_2, to determine one point ($2'$) on the aggregate demand curve. A lower price level such as P_1 shifts aggregate expenditures to $(C_a + I_g + X_n + G)_1$, providing us with point $1'$ on the aggregate demand curve. Similarly, a higher price level at P_3 shifts aggregate expenditures down to $(C_a + I_g + X_n + G)_3$ so P_3 and GDP_3 yield another point on the aggregate demand curve at $3'$.

real GDP. An increase in the price level shifts the aggregate expenditures schedule downward, reducing real GDP. The resulting price level-real GDP combinations yield various points such as 1′, 2′, and 3′, which locate a downsloping aggregate demand curve.

DETERMINANTS OF AGGREGATE DEMAND

Thus far we have found that changes in the price level change the level of spending by domestic consumers, businesses, government, and foreign buyers such that we can predict changes in the amount of real GDP. That is, an increase in the price level, *other things equal*, will decrease the quantity of real GDP demanded; a decrease in the price level will increase the amount of real GDP desired. This relationship is represented graphically as movements along a stable aggregate demand curve. However, if one or more of those "other things" change, the entire aggregate demand curve shifts. We refer to those "other things" as **determinants of aggregate demand**; they "determine" the location of the aggregate demand curve.

To understand what causes changes in real output, you must distinguish between *changes in the quantity of real output demanded* caused by changes in the price level and *changes in aggregate demand* caused by changes in one or more of the determinants of aggregate demand. We made a similar distinction when discussing single-product demand curves in Chapter 3.

As shown in Figure 11-3, an increase in aggregate demand is depicted by the rightward movement of the curve from AD_0 to AD_1. This shift indicates that, at each price level, the desired amount of real goods and services is larger than before.

A decrease in aggregate demand is shown as the leftward shift of the curve from AD_0 to AD_2, indicating that people desire to buy less real output at each price level.

To emphasize: The changes in aggregate demand shown in the graph occur when changes happen in one or more of the factors previously assumed to be constant. These determinants of aggregate demand, or *aggregate demand shifters*, are listed in Table 11-1. Let's examine each element of the table.

CONSUMER SPENDING Independent of changes in the price level, domestic consumers collectively may alter their purchases of Canadian-produced real output. When this happens the entire aggregate demand curve shifts. It shifts leftward as

FIGURE 11-3 Changes in aggregate demand

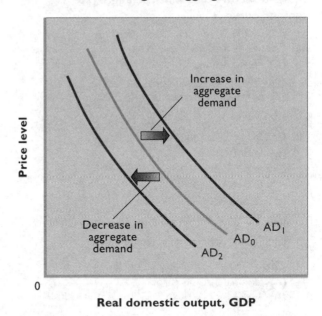

Real domestic output, GDP

A change in one or more of the determinants of aggregate demand listed in Table 11-1 will change aggregate demand. An increase in aggregate demand is shown as the rightward shift of the AD curve from AD_0 to AD_1; a decrease in aggregate demand, as a leftward shift from AD_0 to AD_2.

from AD_0 to AD_2 in Figure 11-3 when consumers buy less output than before at each possible price level; it moves rightward as from AD_0 to AD_1 when they buy more at each possible price level.

Changes in one or more of several non–price-level factors may change consumer spending, shifting the aggregate demand curve. As indicated in Table 11-1, these factors are real consumer wealth, consumer expectations, consumer indebtedness, and taxes.

CONSUMER WEALTH Consumer wealth comprises all consumer assets, including financial assets such as stocks and bonds and physical assets such as houses and land. A sharp decline in the real value of consumer assets encourages people to save more (buy fewer products) to restore their wealth. The resulting decline in consumer spending will decrease aggregate demand — shift the aggregate demand curve leftward. An increase in the real value of consumer wealth will increase consumption spending at each price level; the aggregate demand curve will shift rightward.

TABLE 11-1   Determinants of aggregate demand: factors that shift the aggregate demand curve

1. Change in consumer spending
   (a) consumer wealth
   (b) consumer expectations
   (c) consumer indebtedness
   (d) taxes

2. Change in investment spending
   (a) interest rates
   (b) profit expectations
   (c) business taxes
   (d) technology
   (e) degree of excess capacity

3. Change in government spending

4. Change in net export spending
   (a) national income abroad
   (b) exchange rates

Warning: We are *not* referring here to the previously discussed "wealth effect" or "real balances effect." It assumes a fixed aggregate demand curve and results from a change in the price level. In contrast, the change in real wealth addressed here is independent of a change in the price level; it is a *non–price-level-factor* that shifts the entire aggregate demand curve. An example would be a sharp increase in stock prices that increases consumer wealth, even though the price level has not changed. Similarly, a sharp decline in the real value of houses and land reduces consumer wealth, independent of changes in the general price level.

CONSUMER EXPECTATIONS   Changes in expectations about the future may alter consumer spending. When people expect their future real income to rise, they spend more of their current income. Present consumption spending increases (present saving falls), and the aggregate demand curve shifts rightward. An expectation that real income will decline in the future reduces present consumption spending and therefore reduces aggregate demand.

Similarly, a widely held expectation of surging future inflation increases aggregate demand today, because consumers buy products before prices escalate. Just the opposite, expectations of lower price levels in the near future, may reduce present consumption since people may postpone some of their present consumption to take advantage of the future lower prices.

CONSUMER INDEBTEDNESS   Consumers with high levels of indebtedness from past buying financed by instalment loans may be forced to cut present spending to pay off their existing debt. The result is a decline in consumption spending and a leftward shift of the aggregate demand curve. When consumers' indebtedness falls, their present consumption spending increases. This produces an increase in aggregate demand.

TAXES   A reduction in personal income tax rates raises take-home income and increases consumer purchases at each possible price level. Tax cuts shift the aggregate demand curve rightward. Tax increases reduce consumption spending and shift the aggregate demand curve to the left.

INVESTMENT SPENDING   Investment spending — the purchase of capital goods — is a second determinant of aggregate demand. A decline in the amount of new capital goods desired by firms at each price level will shift the aggregate demand curve leftward. An increase in the desired amount of investment goods will increase aggregate demand. Let's consider the factors that can alter the level of investment spending as listed in Table 11-1.

INTEREST RATES   All else being equal, an increase in the real interest rate caused by a factor other than a change in the price level will lower investment spending and reduce aggregate demand. We are *not* referring here to the so-called "interest-rate effect" occurring due to a change in the price level. Instead, we are referring to a change in the interest rate resulting from, say, a change in the nation's money supply. A detailed discussion of the money supply will be covered in Chapters 13 to 15. For now let's accept that an increase in the money supply reduces the interest rate, increasing investment. A decrease in the supply of money increases the interest rate and reduces investment.

PROFIT EXPECTATIONS ON INVESTMENT PROJECTS   Improved profit expectations on investment projects will increase the demand for capital goods and shift the aggregate demand curve rightward. For example, if consumers are expected to begin buying new cars at a faster rate, an automaker would expect higher profits from an investment in a new factory. Alternatively, if the profit outlook on possible investment projects dims because of an expected decline in consumer spending, investment spending will decline. Consequently, aggregate demand will also decline.

BUSINESS TAXES   An increase in business taxes reduces after-tax profits from corporate investment and reduces investment spending and aggregate demand. Conversely, tax reductions increase after-tax profits from corporate investment, boost investment spending, and push the aggregate demand curve rightward.

TECHNOLOGY   New and improved technologies stimulate investment spending and increase aggregate demand. Example: Recent advances in microbiology and electronics have spawned new labs and production facilities to exploit the new technologies.

DEGREE OF EXCESS CAPACITY   A rise in excess capacity — unused existing capital — will retard the demand for new capital goods and reduce aggregate demand. Firms operating factories at well below capacity have little incentive to build new factories. But when firms collectively discover their excess capacity is dwindling, they build new factories and buy more equipment. Thus, investment spending rises and the aggregate demand curve shifts to the right.

GOVERNMENT SPENDING   Government's purchases of goods and services is a third determinant of aggregate demand. An increase in government purchases of output at each price level will increase aggregate demand so long as tax collections and interest rates do not change as a result. An example would be a decision by government to expand the nation's highway system. A reduction in government spending, such as a cutback in military hardware, will reduce aggregate demand.

NET EXPORT SPENDING   The final determinant of aggregate demand is net export spending. When foreign consumers change their purchases of Canadian goods independently of changes in our price level, the Canadian aggregate demand curve shifts as well. We again specify "independent of changes in our price level" to distinguish clearly

from changes in spending associated with the foreign trade effect. That effect helps explain why a change in the Canadian price level produces a change in real Canadian output.

In discussing aggregate demand shifters we instead address changes in net exports caused by factors other than changes in the price level. Increases in net exports (exports minus imports) caused by these other factors push our aggregate demand curve rightward. The logic is as follows. First, a higher level of Canadian exports constitutes an increased *foreign demand* for Canadian goods. Second, a reduction of our imports implies an increased *domestic demand* for Canadian-produced products.

The non–price-level factors that alter net exports are primarily domestic income abroad and exchange rates.

NATIONAL INCOME ABROAD   Rising national income in a foreign nation increases the foreign demand for Canadian goods, increasing aggregate demand in Canada. As income levels rise in a foreign nation, its citizens can afford to buy both more products made at home *and* made in Canada. Our exports therefore rise in step with increases in the domestic income levels of our trading partners. Declines in national income abroad have the opposite effect: Our net exports decline, shifting the aggregate demand curve leftward.

EXCHANGE RATES   A change in the exchange rate (Chapter 6) between the dollar and other currencies also affects net exports and hence aggregate demand. Suppose the dollar price of the yen rises, meaning the *dollar depreciates* in terms of the yen. This is the same as saying the yen price of dollars falls — the *yen appreciates*. The new relative values of dollars and yen means consumers in Japan can obtain *more* dollars with any particular number of yen and that consumers in Canada will obtain *fewer* yen for each dollar. Japanese consumers will therefore discover that Canadian goods are cheaper in terms of yen. Canadian consumers will find that fewer Japanese products can be purchased with a set number of dollars.

With respect to our *exports*, a $30 pair of Canadian-made blue jeans now might be bought for 2880 yen compared to 3600 yen. And in terms of our *imports*, a Japanese watch might now cost $225 rather than $180. In these circumstances our exports will rise and imports will fall. This increase in net exports translates into an increase in Canadian aggregate demand.

You are urged to think through the opposite scenario in which the dollar appreciates (yen depreciates).

QUICK REVIEW 11-1

1. Aggregate demand reflects an inverse relationship between the price level and the amount of real domestic output demanded.

2. Changes in the price level produce wealth, interest-rate, and foreign trade effects that explain the downward slope of the aggregate demand curve.

3. Changes in one or more of the determinants of aggregate demand (Table 11-1) alter the amounts of real GDP demanded at each price level; they shift the aggregate demand curve.

4. An increase in aggregate demand is shown as a rightward shift of the aggregate demand curve; a decrease entails a leftward shift of the curve.

AGGREGATE DEMAND SHIFTS AND THE AGGREGATE EXPENDITURES MODEL[2]

The determinants of aggregate demand in Table 11-1 are the components of Chapter 10's aggregate expenditures model. When one of these determinants changes, so does the location of the aggregate expenditures schedule. We can easily link shifts in the aggregate expenditures schedule to shifts in the aggregate demand curve.

Let's suppose that the price level is constant. In Figure 11-4 we begin with the aggregate expenditures schedule at $(C_a + I_g + X_n + G)_0$ in the top diagram, yielding real output of GDP_0. Assume now that more optimistic business expectations increase investment so the aggregate expenditures schedule rises from $(C_a + I_g + X_n + G)_0$ to $(C_a + I_g + X_n + G)_1$. (The P_1 labels remind us that the price level is assumed to be constant.) The result will be a multiplied increase in real output from GDP_0 to GDP_1.

---

[2] This section presumes knowledge of the aggregate expenditures model (Chapters 9 and 10). It may be skipped by instructors who wish to rely exclusively on the aggregate demand-aggregate supply framework.

FIGURE 11-4   Shifts in the aggregate expenditures schedule and in the aggregate demand curve

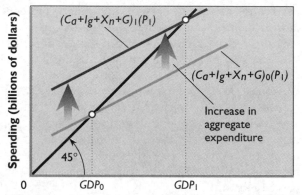

(a) Expenditures–output model

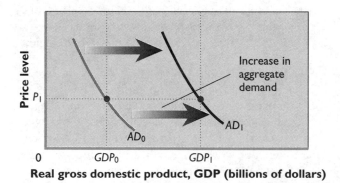

(b) Aggregate demand–aggregate supply model

In (a) we assume that some determinant of consumption, investment, or net exports other than the price level shifts the aggregate expenditures schedule from $(C_a + I_g + X_n + G)_0$ to $(C_a + I_g + X_n + G)_1$, increasing real GDP from GDP_0 to GDP_1. In (b) we find that the aggregate demand counterpart of this is a rightward shift of the aggregate demand curve from AD_0 to AD_1 that is just sufficient to show the same increase in real output as in the expenditures–output model. The "aggregate demand shifters" are summarized in Table 11-1.

In the lower graph the initial increase in investment spending is reflected in the horizontal distance between AD_0 and the broken line to its right. The immediate effect of the increase in investment is to increase aggregate demand by the amount of this new spending. The multiplier process then magnifies the initial change in investment into successive rounds of consumption spending and an ultimate increase in aggregate demand from AD_0 to AD_1. Equilibrium real output rises from GDP_0 to GDP_1, the same multiplied increase in real GDP as in the top graph. *The initial increase in investment in the top graph has shifted the AD curve in the lower graph by a horizontal distance equal to the change in investment times the multiplier.* In this case, the change in real GDP is associated with the constant price level P_1. To generalize,

$$\text{Shift in AD curve} = \frac{\text{change in initial}}{\text{spending} \times \text{multiplier}}$$

AGGREGATE SUPPLY

Aggregate supply *is a schedule, graphically represented by a curve, showing the level of real domestic output which will be produced at each price level.* Higher price levels create an incentive to produce and sell more output. Lower price levels reduce output. As a result, the relationship between the price level and the amount of real output businesses offer for sale is direct or positive.

THE SHAPE OF THE AGGREGATE SUPPLY CURVE: THE SHORT RUN

Figure 11-5 is a portrayal of the aggregate supply curve. Note that there is a positive relationship between the price level and output. This is in fact a *short-run* aggregate supply curve. We define the short run as a period in which input prices — particularly nominal wages — remain fixed. If input prices are fixed and the price level rises, there is an incentive for producers to increase supply.

Moreover, the aggregate economy is made up of many product and resource markets; full employment is not reached at the same time in the various sectors or industries. Thus, as the economy expands from Q_0 to Q_1, some industries may encounter shortages of skilled workers while other industries are still faced with substantial unemployment. In certain industries raw-material shortages or similar production bottlenecks may begin to appear. Expansion will force some firms to use older and less efficient machinery as they approach capacity production. Also, less capable workers may be hired as output expands. For all of these reasons, per unit production costs rise and firms must receive higher prices for additional production to be profitable.

FIGURE 11-5   The aggregate supply curve

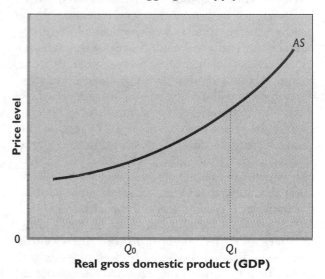

The aggregate supply curve shows the level of real domestic output that will be produced at various price levels. The flatter it is, the more slack there is in the economy. The steeper it is, the closer the economy is to capacity utilization.

Therefore, a rising real output is accompanied by a higher price level.

The steepness of the aggregate supply in the short run will depend on **capacity utilization**, the extent to which present productive capacity is being utilized. If all resources are utilized close to their maximum, the aggregate supply curve will be steep, since a small increase in output would require a relatively large increase in the price level, for the reason stated above. The more slack in the economy, the flatter the aggregate supply curve.

In the long run — a period long enough for all input prices to become fully responsive to the price level — the aggregate supply curve is vertical. The long-run aggregate supply curve will be analyzed in Chapter 16.

Conceptually you can think of the short-run aggregate supply curve as having three potential segments or ranges, depending on capacity utilization. In the **horizontal range** the aggregate supply curve is completely flat, meaning there is much slack in the economy; the economy is either in a severe recession or depression. Large amounts of unused machinery and equipment and unemployed workers are available for production. These idle resources can be put back to work with no upward pressure on the price level. As output expands over the horizontal range, no shortages or production bottlenecks will be incurred to raise prices. Workers unemployed for a number of months will hardly expect wage increases when recalled to their jobs. Because producers can acquire labour and other inputs at stable prices, production costs will not rise as output is expanded, so there is no reason to raise product prices.

At the other extreme a **vertical range** of the aggregate supply curve is possible; the economy reaches its short-run full-capacity level of real output. Any further increase in the price level will not bring about a further increase in real output because the economy is operating at full capacity. Individual firms may try to expand production by bidding resources away from other firms. But the resources and the additional production one firm gains will be lost by some other firm. This will raise resources prices (costs) and ultimately product prices, but real output will remain unchanged.

In most instances, the aggregate supply curve will be its **intermediate range**; an expansion of real output is accompanied by a rising price level for the reasons stated earlier. The economy is neither in a severe recession or depression, nor at full capacity level. Since the intermediate range of the short run is the one in which the economy functions most of the time, it will be the range on which we will focus.

DETERMINANTS OF AGGREGATE SUPPLY

Changes in output resulting from *movements along* the aggregate supply curve need to be distinguished from shifts in the aggregate supply curve itself. An existing aggregate supply curve identifies the relationship between the price level and real domestic output, *other things being equal.* But when one or more of these "other things" change, the aggregate supply curve itself shifts.

The shift of the curve from AS_0 to AS_2 in Figure 11-6 shows an *increase* in aggregate supply. This shift is rightward, indicating that businesses collectively will produce more output at each price level. A leftward shift of the curve from AS_0 to AS_1 indicates a *decrease* in aggregate supply. Businesses now will produce less output at each price level than before (or charge higher prices at each level of output).

Table 11-2 lists the "other things" that shift the aggregate supply curve when they change. These factors are called the **determinants of aggregate**

FIGURE 11-6   Changes in aggregate supply

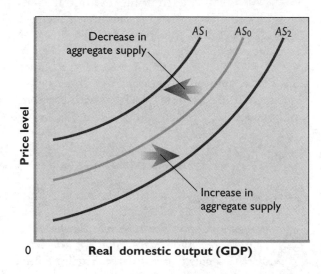

A change in one or more of the determinants of aggregate supply listed in Table 11-4 will cause a change in aggregate supply. An increase in aggregate supply is shown as a "rightward" shift of the AS curve from AS_0 to AS_2; a decrease in aggregate supply, as a "leftward" shift from AS_0 to AS_1.

supply because they collectively establish the location of the aggregate supply curve. When they change, per unit production costs also change. We saw earlier that supply decisions of firms are based on production costs and revenues. Firms are profit seekers, and profits arise from the difference between product prices and per unit production costs. Producers respond to higher prices for their products — higher price levels — by increasing their real output. And production bottlenecks mean that per unit production costs rise as output expands towards — and beyond — full employment. For this reason the aggregate supply curve slopes upward.

But, there are factors *other than changes in real output* that alter per unit production costs. These factors are those listed in Table 11-2. When one or more of them change, per unit production costs change *at each price level.* The aggregate supply curve shifts. Decreases in per unit production costs of this type shift the aggregate supply rightward; increases in per unit production costs shift it leftward. **When per unit production costs change for reasons other than a change in real output, firms collectively alter the amount of real output they produce at each price level.**

TABLE 11-2 Determinants of aggregate supply: factors that shift the aggregate supply curve

1. Change in input prices
   (a) domestic resource availability of:
       land
       labour
       capital
       entrepreneurial ability
   (b) price of imported resources
   (c) market power
2. Change in productivity
3. Change in legal-institutional environment
   (a) business taxes and subsidies
   (b) government regulation

Let's examine how changes in the "*aggregate supply shifters*" listed in Table 11-2 affect per unit production costs and shift the aggregate supply curve.

INPUT PRICES   Input or resource prices are a major determinant of aggregate supply. All else equal, higher input prices increase per unit production costs and reduce aggregate supply. Lower input prices do the opposite. A number of factors influence input prices.

DOMESTIC RESOURCE AVAILABILITY   We noted in Chapter 2 that a society's production possibility frontier shifts outward when the resources available to it increase. Rightward shifts in the production possibilities frontier translate to rightward shifts of our aggregate supply curve. Increases in the supply of domestic resources lower input prices, and decrease per unit production costs. At any specific price level, firms collectively will produce and offer for sale more real output than before.

How might changes in the availability of land, labour, capital, and entrepreneurial resources work to shift the aggregate supply curve? Let's look at several examples.

LAND   Land resources might expand through discoveries of mineral deposits, irrigation of land, or technical innovations permitting us to transform what was previously non-productive land into valuable factors of production. An increase in the supply of land resources lowers the price of land inputs, lowering per unit production costs.

Examples of reductions in the availability of land resources may also be cited. Two such examples are (1) the widespread depletion of a nation's underground water through irrigation, and (2) a nation's loss of topsoil through intensive farming. Eventually, these problems may increase input prices and shift aggregate supply leftward.

LABOUR   Nearly 75% of all business costs are wages or salaries. Therefore, all else equal, changes in wages have a significant impact on per unit production costs and on the location of the aggregate supply curve. An increase in the availability of labour resources reduces the price of labour; a decrease raises labour's price. Examples: The influx of women into the labour force during the past three decades placed a downward pressure on wages and thereby tended to expand Canadian aggregate supply. The immigration of employable workers from abroad has also historically increased the availability of labour in Canada.

CAPITAL   Aggregate supply usually increases when society adds to its stock of capital. Such an addition would happen, for example, if society decided to save more of its income and to direct the savings towards purchase of capital goods. In much the same way, an improvement in the quality of capital tends to reduce production costs and increase aggregate supply. For example, businesses over the years have replaced equipment of poorer quality with new, superior equipment.

On the other hand, aggregate supply declines when the quantity and quality of the nation's stock of capital diminishes. Example: In the depths of the Great Depression of the 1930s, our capital stock deteriorated because new purchases of capital were insufficient to offset the normal wearing-out and obsolescence of plant and equipment.

ENTREPRENEURIAL ABILITY   Finally, the amount of entrepreneurial ability available to the economy can occasionally change and shift the aggregate supply curve. For instance, the recent media focus on individuals who have amassed fortunes through entrepreneurial efforts might increase the number of people who have entrepreneurial aspirations. If so, the aggregate supply curve might shift rightward.

PRICES OF IMPORTED RESOURCES   Just as foreign demand for Canadian goods contributes to our aggregate demand, resources imported from abroad add to our aggregate supply. Resources, whether domestic or imported, boost our productive capacity. Imported resources can reduce input prices and decrease the per unit cost of producing Canadian real output. Generally, a decrease in the prices of imported resources expands our aggregate supply; an increase in the prices of these resources reduces it.

Exchange-rate fluctuations alter the price of imported resources. Suppose the Canadian dollar appreciates, enabling Canadian firms to obtain more foreign currency with each Canadian dollar. Under these conditions, Canadian firms would expand their imports of foreign resources and realize reductions in per unit production costs at each level of output. Falling per unit production costs of this type shift the Canadian aggregate supply curve to the right.

Also, an increase in the dollar price of foreign currencies — dollar depreciation — raises the prices of imported resources. Our imports of these resources fall, our per unit production costs jump upward, and our aggregate supply curve moves leftward.

MARKET POWER   A change in the degree of market power, or monopoly power, held by sellers of resources can also affect input prices and aggregate supply. *Market power* is the ability to set a price above the price that would occur in a competitive situation. The rise and fall of market power held by the Organization of Petroleum Exporting Countries (OPEC) during the past three decades is a good illustration. The tenfold increase in the price of oil OPEC was able to achieve during the 1970s permeated our economy, drove up per unit production costs, and jolted the Canadian aggregate supply curve leftward. But then a steep reduction in OPEC's market power during the mid-1980s reduced the cost of manufacturing and transporting products, and as a direct result, increased Canadian aggregate supply.

A change in labour union market power also can affect the location of the aggregate supply curve. Some observers believe that unions experienced growing market power in the 1970s, resulting in union wage increases. This higher pay may have increased per unit production costs and produced leftward shifts of aggregate supply.

PRODUCTIVITY   Productivity relates a nation's level of real output to the quantity of input used to produce that output. In other words, **productivity** is a measure of average output, or of real output per unit of input.

$$\text{Productivity} = \frac{\text{real output}}{\text{input}}$$

An increase in productivity means the economy can obtain more real output from its resources — or inputs. Generally, productivity increases are caused by technological advances.

How does an increase in productivity affect the aggregate supply curve? We first need to see how a change in productivity alters per unit production costs. Suppose real output is $10, the input quantity needed to produce that quantity is 5, and the price of each input unit is $2. Productivity — output per input — is $2 (= $10/5). The per unit cost of output would be found as follows.

$$\text{Per unit production cost} = \frac{\text{total input cost}}{\text{units of output}}$$

Per unit cost is $1, found by dividing $10 of input cost (= $2 × 5 units of input) by $10 of output.

Now suppose real output doubles to $20, while the input price and quantity remain constant at $2 and 5 units. That means productivity rises from $2 (= $10/5) to $4 (= $20/5). Because the total cost of the inputs stays at $10 (= $2 × 5 units of input), the per unit cost of the output falls from $1 to 50¢ (= $10 of input cost/$20 of output).

By reducing per unit production costs, an increase in productivity shifts the aggregate supply curve rightward; a decline in productivity increases per unit production costs and shifts the aggregate supply curve leftward.

LEGAL–INSTITUTIONAL ENVIRONMENT
Changes in the legal-institutional setting in which businesses collectively operate may alter per unit costs of output and shift the aggregate supply curve. Two changes of this type are (1) changes in taxes and subsidies, and (2) changes in the extent of regulation.

BUSINESS TAXES AND SUBSIDIES   Higher business taxes, such as sales, excise, and social insurance taxes, increase per unit costs and reduce aggregate supply in much the same way that a wage increase does. Example: An increase in the social insurance taxes paid by businesses will increase production costs and reduce aggregate supply. Similarly, a business subsidy — a payment or tax break by government to a firm — reduces production costs and increases aggregate supply.

GOVERNMENT REGULATION Under most circumstances, it is costly for businesses to comply with government regulations. Thus, regulation increases per unit production costs and shifts the aggregate supply curve leftward. "Supply-side" proponents of deregulation of the economy have argued forcefully that, by increasing efficiency and reducing the paperwork associated with complex regulations, deregulation will reduce per unit costs. In this way, the aggregate supply curve purportedly will shift rightward. Conversely, it is argued that increases in regulation raise production costs and reduce aggregate supply. **(Key Question 5)**

QUICK REVIEW 11-2

1. The aggregate supply curve is upward sloping in the short run — a period defined as one during which input prices do not change.

2. The shape of the short-run aggregate supply curve is determined by the extent of resource utilization; it can have a horizontal range, an upsloping intermediate range, and a vertical range.

3. By altering per unit production costs independent of changes in the level of output, changes in one or more of the determinants of aggregate supply (Table 11-2) shift the location of the aggregate supply curve.

4. An increase in aggregate supply is shown as a rightward shift of the aggregate supply curve; a decrease by a leftward shift of the curve.

EQUILIBRIUM: REAL OUTPUT AND THE PRICE LEVEL

We found in Chapter 4 that the intersection of the demand for and supply of a particular product determines its equilibrium price and output. Similarly, as we see here in Figure 11-7, the intersection of the aggregate demand and aggregate supply curves determines the **equilibrium price level** and **equilibrium real domestic output**.

In **Figure 11-7 (Key Graph)**, where aggregate demand crosses aggregate supply, the equilibrium price level and level of real domestic output are P_0 and Q_0, respectively. To illustrate why P_0 is the equilibrium price level and Q_0 is the equilibrium level of

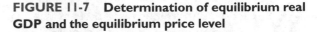

KEY GRAPH

FIGURE 11-7   Determination of equilibrium real GDP and the equilibrium price level

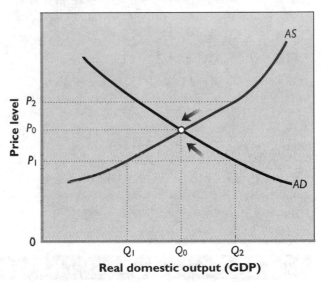

If the price level were below the equilibrium P_0, aggregate demand would be greater than aggregate supply (at P_1). Thus there would be upward pressure on the price level toward the equilibrium level P_0. The opposite would be the case at P_2.

output, suppose the price level were P_1 rather than P_0. We observe from the aggregate supply curve that price level P_1 would entice businesses to produce (at most) real output level Q_1. How much real output would domestic consumers, businesses, government, and foreign buyers want to purchase at P_1? The aggregate demand curve tells us the answer is Q_2. The competition among buyers to purchase the available real output of Q_1 will drive up the price level to P_0.

As our arrows in Figure 11-7 indicate, the rise in the price level from P_1 to P_0 encourages *producers* to increase their real output from Q_1 to Q_0 and simultaneously causes *buyers* to scale back their purchases from Q_2 to Q_0. When equality occurs between the amount of real output produced and the amount purchased, as it does at P_0, the economy has achieved equilibrium.

At a price level above equilibrium, the story just told would be reversed. At P_2 aggregate supply would be greater than aggregate demand, creating forces that would lead to price level P_0 and a GDP of Q_0. **(Key Questions 4 and 7)**

EQUILIBRIUM VERSUS FULL EMPLOYMENT GDP

We now turn from explaining to evaluating equilibrium GDP. Q_0 in Figure 11-7 may or may not be full employment GDP, also referred to as potential GDP.

RECESSIONARY GAP

Assume in **Figure 11-8(a) (Key Graph)** the full employment non-inflationary level of output, or potential GDP is $510 billion. AD_0 intersects the aggregate supply curve at $490 billion. The equilibrium level of GDP is thus $20 billion short of full-employment GDP. The **recessionary gap** is the amount by which equilibrium GDP is below full employment GDP. A resolution of a recessionary gap requires a rightward shift of the aggregate demand curve, from AD_0 to AD_1, or a rightward shift of the

aggregate supply curve, from AS_0 to AS_1, or some combination of the two. Note that the larger the recessionary gap becomes, the more slack there is in the economy and the flatter will be the relevant range of the aggregate supply curve. In a severe recession, the aggregate supply curve would be almost horizontal; any shift of the aggregate demand curve would have little or no effect on the price level.

INFLATIONARY GAP

If equilibrium GDP is above full employment GDP, the economy has an **inflationary gap**, shown in Figure 11-8(b). Note that as the economy approaches its short-run full-capacity level of real output, the AS curve becomes increasingly steep. At $530 equilibrium GDP is $20 billion above full-employment GDP, generating inflationary pressures in the economy. A resolution of an inflationary gap requires either a leftward

KEY GRAPH

FIGURE 11-8   Recessionary and inflationary gaps

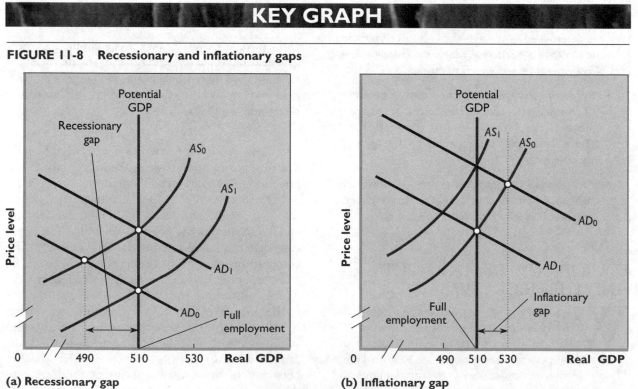

(a) Recessionary gap

(b) Inflationary gap

The equilibrium and full-employment GDPs may not coincide. A recessionary gap, shown in (a), is the amount by which equilibrium GDP falls short of full-employment GDP. The inflationary gap in (b) is the amount by which equilibrium GDP exceeds full-employment GDP. As the economy approaches its short-run full-capacity level of real output, the AS curve becomes increasingly steeper. The elimination of a recessionary gap requires an increase of aggregate demand from AD_0 to AD_1. A rightward shift of the aggregate supply curve would also close a recessionary gap. The elimination of an inflationary gap requires either a decrease in aggregate demand or a decrease in aggregate supply, or some combination of the two.

BOX 11-2 APPLYING THE THEORY
WHY IS UNEMPLOYMENT IN EUROPE SO HIGH?

Are the high unemployment rates in Europe the result of structural problems or deficient aggregate demand?

Several European economies have had high rates of unemployment in the past several years. For example, in 1994 France had an unemployment rate of 12.3%; Great Britain, 10.0%; Italy, 11.2%; and Germany, 10.2%.

There is little dispute that recessions in Europe in the early 1990s contributed to these high rates. Declines in aggregate demand reduced real GDP and increased unemployment. Nevertheless, a mystery remains: Why were unemployment rates in many European nations so high even *before* their recessions? In 1990 the unemployment rate in France was 9.1%; in Great Britain, 6.9%; and in Italy, 7.0%. And why have European unemployment rates remained far higher than in other countries during economic recovery? There are two views on these questions:

1. High Natural Rates of Unemployment Many economists believe the high unemployment rates in Europe largely reflect high natural rates of unemployment. They envision a situation where aggregate demand and aggregate supply have produced the full-employment level of real output. But high levels of frictional and structural unemployment accompany this level of output. In this view, the recent extensive unemployment in Europe has resulted from a high natural rate of unemployment, not from deficient aggregate demand. An increase in aggregate demand would push these economies beyond their full-employment levels of output, causing demand–pull inflation.

The alleged sources of the high natural rates of unemployment are government policies and union contracts that have increased the costs of hiring workers and reduced the cost of being unemployed. Example: High minimum wages have discouraged employers from hiring low-skilled workers; generous welfare benefits have weakened incentives for people to take available jobs; restrictions against firings have discouraged firms from employing workers; 30 to 40 days per year of paid vacations and holidays have boosted the cost of

hiring workers; high worker absenteeism has reduced productivity; and high employer costs of health, pension, disability, and other benefits have discouraged hiring.

2. Deficient Aggregate Demand Not all economists agree that government and union policies have ratcheted up Europe's natural rate of unemployment. Instead, they point to insufficient aggregate demand as the culprit. They see the European economies in terms of Figure 11-8(a), where real output is less than it would be if aggregate demand were stronger — Europe suffers from a recessionary gap. The argument is that the European governments have been so fearful of inflation that they have not undertaken appropriate fiscal and monetary policies (Chapters 12 and 15) to increase aggregate demand. In this view, increases in aggregate demand would not be inflationary, since these economies have considerable excess capacity. A rightward shift in aggregate demand curves would expand output and employment, even if it would create inflationary pressures.

Conclusion: The debate over high unemployment in Europe reflects disagreement on where European aggregate demand curves lie relative to full-employment levels of output. If these curves are *at* the full-employment real GDP, then the high levels of unemployment are "natural." Public policies should focus on lowering minimum wages, reducing vacation time, reducing welfare benefits, easing restrictions on layoffs, and so on. But if the aggregate demand curves in the European nations lie to the left of their full-employment levels of output, as in Figure 11-8(a), then expansionary government policies such as reduced interest rates or tax cuts may be in order. The debate over the cause of high rates of unemployment in Europe extends to Canada. We have also experienced relatively high rates of unemployment compared with the United States, but much discussion still continues about the reason(s).

shift of the aggregate demand curve, from AD_0 to AD_1 or a leftward shift of the aggregate supply curve, from AS_0 to AS_1, or some combination of the two.

MULTIPLIER WITH PRICE LEVEL CHANGES[3]

The assumption in the aggregate expenditures model is that prices are constant — a perfectly horizontal aggregate supply curve. Any change in aggregate demand leads to a change in real GDP and employment while the price level remains constant.

But with an upward sloping supply curve, a part or all of any initial increase in aggregate demand will be dissipated in inflation and *not* be reflected in increased real output and employment. In Figure 11-9 the multiplier induced shift of aggregate demand from AD_0 to AD_1 is partly offset since a portion of the increase in aggregate demand is absorbed as inflation as the price level rises from P_0 to P_1. Real GDP rises to only GDP_1. If the aggregate supply curve were horizontal, the shift would have increased real domestic output to GDP_2. But inflation has reduced the multiplier so that the actual increase is to GDP_1, which is only about half as much.

Our conclusion is that, *for an increase in aggregate demand, the resulting increase in real GDP will be smaller the larger the increase in the*

---

[3] Instructors who do not assign Chapters 9 and 10 may want to use this section as a springboard for introducing MPC, MPS, and multiplier concepts.

FIGURE 11-9   Inflation and the multiplier

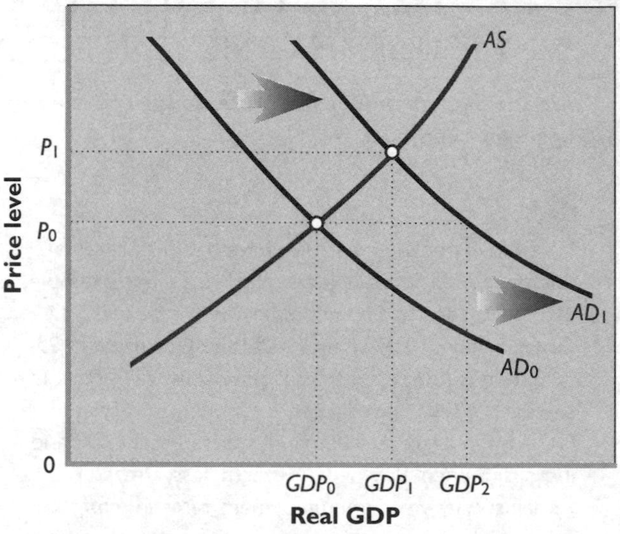

The aggregate demand–aggregate supply model allows us to see how inflation reduces the size of the multiplier. The increase in aggregate demand from AD_0 to AD_1 is partly dissipated in inflation (P_0 to P_1) and real output therefore only increases from GDP_0 to GDP_1.

price level. Price level increases weaken the multiplier. You should sketch an increase in demand with a steeper aggregate supply curve to confirm that this increase in spending would be almost entirely absorbed as inflation; the steeper the aggregate supply curve the smaller the multiplier.

CHAPTER SUMMARY

1. For purposes of analysis we consolidate — or aggregate — the large number of individual product markets into a composite market in which there are two variables — the price level and the level of real output. This is accomplished through an aggregate demand–aggregate supply model.

2. The aggregate demand curve shows the level of real output that the economy will purchase at each price level.

3. The rationale for the downsloping aggregate demand curve is based on the wealth or real balances effect, the interest-rate effect, and the foreign trade effect. The wealth or real balances effect indicates that inflation will reduce the real value or purchasing power of fixed-value financial assets held by households, causing them to retrench on their consumer spending. The interest-rate effect means that, with a specific supply of money, a higher price level will increase the demand for money, raising the interest rate and reducing consumption and investment purchases. The foreign trade effect suggests that an increase in Canada's price level relative to other countries will reduce the net exports component of Canadian aggregate demand.

*4. A change in the price level alters the location of the aggregate expenditures schedule through the wealth, interest rate, and foreign trade effects. The aggregate demand curve is derived from the aggregate expenditures model by allowing the price level to change and observing the effect on the aggregate expenditures schedule and thus on equilibrium GDP.

5. The determinants of aggregate demand are spending by domestic consumers, businesses, government, and foreign buyers. Changes in the factors listed in Table 11-1 cause changes in spending by these groups and shift the aggregate demand curve.

*6. Holding the price level constant, increases in consumption, investment, and net export expenditures shift the aggregate expenditures schedule upward and the aggregate demand curve to the right.

7. The aggregate supply curve shows the levels of the real output that businesses produce at various possible price levels. The aggregate supply curve is upward sloping in the short run — a period during which input prices remain fixed.

8. The shape of the short-run aggregate supply curve depends on capacity utilization. The closer the economy is to maximum capacity utilization, the steeper the aggregate supply curve. The more slack in the economy the flatter the aggregate supply curve becomes. There are three potential ranges to the short-run aggregate supply curve. In the horizontal range of aggregate supply, there is substantial unemployment and thus production can be increased without raising per unit cost or prices. In the intermediate range, per unit costs increase as production bottlenecks appear and less efficient equipment and workers are employed. Prices must therefore rise as real output is expanded. The vertical range coincides with absolute short-run full capacity; real output is at a maximum and cannot be increased, but the price level will rise in response to an increase in aggregate demand.

9. As indicated in Table 11-2, the determinants of aggregate supply are input prices, productivity, and the legal-institutional environment. A change in one of these factors will change per unit production costs at each level of output and therefore alter the location of the aggregate supply curve.

10. The intersection of the aggregate demand and aggregate supply curves determines the equilibrium price level and real GDP.

11. Given an upward-sloping aggregate supply, rightward shifts of aggregate demand will increase both real domestic output and the level of prices.

12. Leftward shifts of aggregate supply lead to real output declines and the price level rises; rightward shifts increase real output and lower the price level.

  * This summary point presumes knowledge of the aggregate expenditures model presented in Chapters 9 and 10.

TERMS AND CONCEPTS

aggregate demand (p. 238)

aggregate supply (p. 245)

capacity utilization (p. 245)

determinants of aggregate demand (p. 241)

determinants of aggregate supply (p. 246)

equilibrium price level (p. 249)

equilibrium real domestic output (p. 249)

foreign-trade effect (p. 239)

horizontal range (p. 245)

interest-rate effect (p. 239)

intermediate range (p. 246)

productivity (p. 248)

recessionary and inflationary gaps (p. 250)

vertical range (p. 246)

wealth or real-balances effect (p. 239)

QUESTIONS AND STUDY SUGGESTIONS

1. Why is the aggregate demand curve downsloping? Specify how your explanation differs from the rationale for the downsloping demand curve for a single product.

2. Explain the shape of the aggregate supply curve, accounting for the differences between the horizontal, intermediate, and vertical ranges of the curve.

*3. Explain carefully: "A change in the price level shifts the aggregate expenditures curve, but not the aggregate demand curve."

4. **Key Question** *Suppose that the aggregate demand and supply schedules for a hypothetical economy are as shown below:*

Amount of real domestic output demanded, billions	Price level (price index)	Amount of real domestic output supplied, billions
$100	300	$400
200	250	400
300	200	300
400	150	200
500	150	100

a. *Use these sets of data to graph the aggregate demand and supply curves. What is the equilibrium price level and level of real output in this hypothetical economy? Is the equilibrium real output also the absolute full-capacity output? Explain.*

b. *Why will a price level of 150 not be an equilibrium price level in this economy? Why not 250?*

c. *Suppose that buyers desire to purchase $200 billion of extra real output at each price level. What factors might cause this change in aggregate demand? What is the new equilibrium price level and level of real output?*

5. **Key Question** *Suppose that the hypothetical economy in question 4 had the following relationship between its real output and the input quantities necessary for producing that output:*

Input quantity	Real domestic output
150.0	400
112.5	300
75.0	200

a. *What is the level of productivity in this economy?*

b. *What is the per unit cost of production if the price of each input is $2?*

* Questions designated with an asterisk presume knowledge of the aggregate expenditures model (Chapters 9 and 10).

c. Assume that the input price increases from $2 to $3 with no accompanying change in productivity. What is the new per unit cost of production? In what direction would the $1 increase in input price push the aggregate supply curve? What effect would this shift in aggregate supply have on the price level and the level of real output?

d. Suppose that the increase in input price had not occurred but instead that productivity had increased by 100%. What would be the new per unit cost of production? What effect would this change in per unit production cost have on the aggregate supply curve? What effect would this shift in aggregate supply have on the price level and the level of real output?

6. Will an increase in the Canadian price level relative to price levels in other nations shift our aggregate demand curve? If so, in what direction? Explain. Will a decline in the Canadian dollar price of foreign currencies shift our aggregate supply curve rightward or simply move the economy along an existing aggregate supply curve? Explain.

7. Key Question *What effects would each of the following have on aggregate demand or aggregate supply? In each case use a diagram to show the expected effects on the equilibrium price level and level of real output. Assume all other things remain constant.*

    a. A widespread fear of depression among consumers

    b. A large purchase of wheat by Russia

    c. A $1 increase in the excise tax on cigarettes

    d. A reduction in interest rates at each price level

    e. A cut in federal spending for higher education

    f. The expectation of a rapid rise in the price level

    g. The complete disintegration of OPEC, causing oil prices to fall by one-half

    h. A 10% reduction in personal income tax rates

    i. An increase in labour productivity

    j. A 12% increase in nominal wages

    k. Depreciation in the international value of the dollar

    l. A sharp decline in the national incomes of our main trading partners

    m. A decline in the percentage of the Canadian labour force that is unionized

8. What is the relationship between the production possibilities curve discussed in Chapter 2 and the aggregate supply curve discussed in this chapter?

9. Other things equal, what effect will each of the following have on the equilibrium price level and level of real output:

    a. An increase in aggregate demand in an economy close to capacity utilization

    b. An increase in aggregate supply

    c. An equal increase in both aggregate demand and aggregate supply

    d. A reduction in aggregate demand in an economy with much slack in it

    e. An increase in aggregate demand and a decrease in aggregate supply

    f. A decrease in aggregate demand

*10. Suppose that the price level is constant and investment spending increases sharply. How would you show this increase in the aggregate expenditures model? What would be the outcome? How would you show this rise in investment in the aggregate demand–aggregate supply model?

*11. Explain how an upsloping aggregate supply curve might weaken the multiplier.

12. "Unemployment can be caused by a leftward shift of aggregate demand or a leftward shift of aggregate supply." Do you agree? Explain. In each case, specify price level effects.

13. (Applying the Theory) What are the alternative views on why unemployment in Europe has recently been so high? Discuss the policy implication of each view.

CHAPTER 12

FISCAL POLICY

ecall that the consumption, investment, and import-export decisions of households and businesses are based on private self-interest and that the outcomes of these decisions may be either recession or inflation. In contrast, government is an instrument of society as a whole. Within limits (and admitting several complications), government's decisions on spending and taxing can be altered to influence the equilibrium real GDP in terms of the general welfare. We saw in Chapter 5 that a fundamental function of government is to stabilize the economy. Stabilization is achieved in part through the manipulation of the public budget — government spending and tax collections — for the expressed purpose of increasing output and employment or reducing the rate of inflation.

This chapter briefly looks at the legislative mandates given government to pursue stabilization, then explores the tools of government stabilization policy in terms of the aggregate demand-aggregate supply model. Next, some factors that automatically adjust government expenditures and tax revenues in appropriate ways as the economy moves through the business cycle are examined. Finally, problems, criticisms, and complications of government stabilization policy are addressed.

BOX 12-1   THE BIG PICTURE

One of the major issues in macroeconomics is how to avoid or to smooth out fluctuations in economic activity that cause recessions or inflation. Fluctuations can originate either on the aggregate demand or the aggregate supply side of the economy. For example, an economy can get "stuck" at an equilibrium GDP below full employment GDP (a recessionary gap), and possibly remain there for an unacceptably long period of time. Governments can influence the level of GDP through their spending and taxation — together referred to as fiscal policy. Fiscal policy will affect aggregate demand, if it primarily has an impact on one of the expenditure categories, or affects aggregate supply if it primarily has an impact on the cost of production.

As you read this chapter, keep the following points in mind:

- A recessionary gap requires an increase in government spending and/or cut in taxes. Such policies will help close the gap by shifting the demand curve to the right. An inflationary gap requires a decrease and/or an increase in taxes, which will shift the aggregate demand curve to the left.
- Discretionary fiscal policy is implemented by governments whenever there is a perceived need for stabilization; in contrast, fiscal stabilizers are automatically implemented according to the needs of the macroeconomy.
- The implementation of discretionary fiscal policy is subject to limitations, including difficulties encountered by governments in collecting up-to-date information about the economy, and problems associated with quickly implementing the right fiscal policy as soon as it is necessary.
- In recent years Canada has experienced large structural annual deficits and a mounting national debt, leaving the federal government little leeway for expansionary fiscal policy during recessions.

LEGISLATIVE MANDATES

The idea that government fiscal actions can exert an important stabilizing influence on the economy began to gain widespread acceptance during the Great Depression of the 1930s. Macroeconomic employment theory played a major role in emphasizing the importance of remedial fiscal measures. The federal government brought in unemployment insurance during World War II, and in 1945 Mackenzie King won his last election on the promise of full employment and social security. Since then, no party contending for office has promised less. Parties out of office have never failed to blame the government for whatever level of unemployment currently exists. And governments, while blaming current unemployment on a recession in the United States, have always insisted that their policies, either in place or to be unveiled in the next budget, will bring the country back to full — or at least "fuller" — employment.

Since 1945 one of the main tools used by governments in stabilization policy is fiscal policy.

Fiscal policy can be one of two varieties: (1) discretionary and (2) nondiscretionary.

DISCRETIONARY FISCAL POLICY

Discretionary fiscal policy is the deliberate manipulation of taxes and government spending by Parliament to alter real GDP and employment, control inflation, and stimulate economic growth. "Discretionary" means changes in taxes and government spending *at the option* of the federal government. These changes do not occur automatically, independent of specific parliamentary action.

To keep our discussion of fiscal policy clear, we assume government purchases neither depress nor stimulate private spending. Also, we assume for now that fiscal policy affects only the aggregate demand side of the macroeconomy; it has no intended or unintended effects on aggregate supply. Both assumptions will be dropped as we examine the complications and shortcomings of fiscal policy in the real world.

Let's start by examining fiscal policy in two situations: (1) a recessionary gap and (2) an inflationary gap caused by demand-pull — a rightward shift of the aggregate demand curve beyond full employment GDP.

EXPANSIONARY FISCAL POLICY

When recession occurs, an **expansionary fiscal policy** may be in order. Consider Figure 12-1 where we suppose a sharp decline in investment spending has shifted the economy's aggregate demand curve leftward from AD_1 to AD_0. Perhaps profit expectations on investment projects have dimmed, curtailing much investment spending and reducing aggregate demand. Consequently, real GDP has fallen to GDP_0 from its full-employment level of GDP_f. Accompanying this decline in real output is an increase in unemployment, since fewer workers are needed to produce the diminished output. This economy is experiencing recession and cyclical unemployment — the economy is not fully utilizing all its available resources.

What should the federal government do? It has three main fiscal policy options: (1) increase government spending; (2) reduce taxes; or (3) some combination of the two. If the federal budget is balanced at the outset, fiscal policy during a recession or depression should create a government **budget deficit** — government spending exceeding tax revenues.

INCREASED GOVERNMENT SPENDING All else equal, an increase in government spending will shift an economy's aggregate demand curve to the right, as from AD_0 to AD_1 in Figure 12-1. To see why, let's suppose that in response to the recession government initiates new spending on highways, satellite communications systems, and federal prisons. At *each* price level the amount of real output demanded is greater than before the increase in government spending. Real output increases to GDP_f, closing the recessionary gap, therefore unemployment will fall as firms call back workers laid off during the recession.

TAX REDUCTIONS Alternatively, government could reduce taxes to shift the aggregate demand curve rightward, as from AD_0 to AD_1. Suppose government cuts personal income taxes, which increases disposable income by the same amount. Consumption will rise by a fraction of the increase in disposable income — the other fraction goes to increased saving. The aggregate demand will shift rightward because of the increase in consumption produced by the tax cut. Real GDP will rise and employment will also increase accordingly.

COMBINED GOVERNMENT SPENDING INCREASES AND TAX REDUCTIONS Government can combine spending increases and tax cuts to produce the desired initial increase in spending and the eventual increase in aggregate demand and real GDP.

If you were assigned Chapters 9 and 10, you should think through these three fiscal policy options in terms of the aggregate expenditures model (Figure 10-7). Recall from Chapter 11 that rightward shifts of the aggregate demand curve relate directly to upshifts in the aggregate expenditures schedule.

CONTRACTIONARY FISCAL POLICY

When the economy has an inflationary gap caused by excessive growth of aggregate demand, demand-pull inflation occurs, and a restrictive or **contractionary fiscal policy** may help control it. Look at Figure 12-2. First, suppose that an AD_2 to AD_3 shift in the aggregate demand curve above the full employment level increases the price level from P_2

FIGURE 12-1 Expansionary fiscal policy

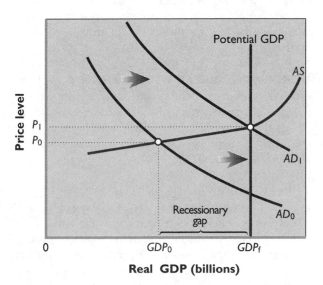

The effect of an expansionary policy is to close a recessionary gap caused by insufficient aggregate demand.

to P_3. This increase in aggregate demand might have resulted from a sharp increase in, say, investment or net export spending. If government looks to fiscal policy to control this inflation, its options are opposite those used to combat recession. It can (1) decrease government spending, (2) raise taxes, or (3) use some combination of these two policies. When the economy faces demand-pull inflation, fiscal policy should move towards a government **budget surplus** — tax revenues in excess of government spending.

FIGURE 12-2   Contractionary fiscal policy

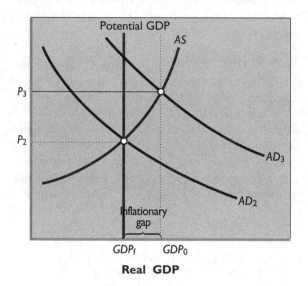

The effect of a contractionary policy is to close an inflationary gap caused by increases of aggregate demand beyond full employment GDP.

DECREASED GOVERNMENT SPENDING

Government can reduce its spending to eliminate the inflationary gap. This spending cut will shift the aggregate demand curve leftward from AD_3 to AD_2. Real output returns at its full employment level of GDP_f.

In the real world prices are often "sticky" downward so stopping inflation is a matter of halting the rise in the price level, not reducing it to some previous level. Demand-pull inflation usually is a continuously shifting aggregate demand curve to the right. Fiscal policy is designed to stop these shifts, not to restore a lower previous price level. Nevertheless,

Figure 12-2 displays the basic principle: reductions in government expenditures can help close an inflationary gap caused by excessive growth of aggregate demand, and causing demand-pull inflation.

INCREASED TAXES   Just as government can use tax cuts to increase consumption spending, it can use tax increases to reduce it. A tax increase reduces consumption (if it is borne by households) reducing aggregate demand from AD_3 to AD_2. The inflationary gap will have been closed and inflationary pressures alleviated.

COMBINED GOVERNMENT SPENDING DE-CREASES AND TAX INCREASES   Government can combine spending decreases and tax increases to reduce aggregate demand from AD_3 to AD_2 and check inflation.

If you were assigned Chapters 9 and 10, you should be able to explain the three fiscal policy options for fighting inflation in terms of the aggregate expenditures model (Figure 10-8). Recall from Chapter 11 that leftward shifts in the aggregate demand curve are associated with downshifts in the aggregate expenditures schedule. **(Key Question 1)**

FINANCING DEFICITS AND DISPOSING OF SURPLUSES

The expansionary effect of a specific budget deficit on the economy will depend on the method used to finance it. Similarly, the deflationary impact of a particular budget surplus will depend on what is done with it.

BORROWING VERSUS NEW MONEY   There are two ways the federal government can finance a deficit: borrowing from (selling interest-bearing bonds to) the public, or issuing new money to its creditors. The impact on aggregate demand will be different in each case.

1. BORROWING   If the government enters the money market and borrows, it will be competing with private business borrowers for funds. This added demand for funds may drive up the equilibrium interest rate. Investment spending is inversely related to the interest rate. Government borrowing therefore may increase the interest rate and "crowd out" some private investment spending and interest-sensitive consumer spending.

2. MONEY CREATION If deficit spending is financed by issuing new money, crowding-out of private expenditures can be avoided. Federal spending can increase without any adverse effect on investment or consumption. *The creation of new money is a more expansionary way of financing deficit spending than is borrowing.* However, there is a limit to how much money can be created before inflationary pressures set in.

DEBT RETIREMENT VERSUS IDLE SURPLUS

Demand-pull inflation calls for fiscal action that will result in a budget surplus. But the anti-inflationary effect of this surplus depends on what government does with it.

1. DEBT REDUCTION Since the federal government had an outstanding debt of some $435 billion by the end of 1994, it is logical that government should use a surplus to retire outstanding debt. The anti-inflationary impact of a surplus, however, may be reduced by paying off debt. In retiring debt held by the general public, the government transfers its surplus tax revenues back into the money market. This may cause the interest rate to fall, stimulating investment and consumption.

2. IMPOUNDING On the other hand, government can realize a greater anti-inflationary impact from its budgetary surplus by impounding the surplus funds, meaning allowing them to stand idle. An impounded surplus means that the government is extracting and withholding purchasing power from the economy. If surplus revenues are not reinjected into the economy, there is no possibility of some portion of that surplus being spent. There is no chance that the funds will create inflationary pressure to offset the deflationary impact of the surplus itself. We conclude that *the impounding of a budgetary surplus is more contractionary than the use of the surplus to retire public debt.*

POLICY OPTIONS: G OR *T*?

Is it preferable to use government spending or taxes to eliminate recessionary and inflationary gaps? The answer depends on one's view as to whether the public sector is too large or too small.

"Liberal" economists, who think the public sector needs to be enlarged to meet various failures of the market system (Chapter 5), can recommend that aggregate demand be expanded during recessions by increasing government purchases *and* that aggregate demand should be constrained during inflationary periods by increasing taxes. Both actions either expand or preserve the absolute size of government.

"Conservative" economists, who think the public sector is too large and inefficient, can advocate that aggregate demand be increased during recessions by cutting taxes *and* that aggregate demand be reduced during inflation by cutting government spending.

An active fiscal policy designed to stabilize the economy can be associated with either an expanding or a contracting public sector.

QUICK REVIEW 12-1

1. Fiscal policy is the purposeful manipulation of government expenditures and tax collections by Parliament to promote full employment, price stability, and economic growth.

2. Government uses expansionary fiscal policy — shown as a rightward shift of the aggregate demand curve — to stimulate spending and expand real output. It involves increases in government spending, reduction in taxes, or some combination of the two.

3. Contractionary fiscal policy — shown as a leftward shift of the aggregate demand curve — is aimed at demand-pull inflation brought about by an inflationary gap. It entails reductions in government expenditures, tax increases, or some combination of each.

4. The expansionary effect of fiscal policy will depend on how the budget deficit is financed; the contractionary effect of fiscal policy depends on the disposition of the budget surplus.

NONDISCRETIONARY FISCAL POLICY: BUILT-IN STABILIZERS

To some degree, appropriate changes in government expenditures and taxes occur automatically. This is an automatic or *built-in stabilizer.* Built-in stabilizers arise because our net tax system (net taxes equal taxes minus transfers and subsidies) is such that *net tax revenues*[1] *vary directly with GDP.*

---

[1] From now on, we will use the term "taxes" in referring to net taxes.

BOX 12-2   APPLYING THE THEORY

THE LEADING INDICATORS

One tool policy makers use to forecast the future direction of real GDP is a monthly index of a group of variables that in the past have provided advanced notice of changes in GDP.

"Index of Leading Indicators Falls for Third Month — Recession Feared"; "Index of Leading Indicators Surges Again"; "Decline in Stock Market Drags Down Index of Leading Indicators." Headlines such as these appear regularly in newspapers. The focus of the articles are Statistics Canada's weighted average — or composite index — of ten economic variables that has historically reached its peak or trough in advance of the corresponding turns in the business cycle. Hence, changes in the index of leading indicators provide a clue to the future direction of the economy and thus may shorten the length of the recognition lag associated with the implementation of macroeconomic policy.

Let us examine the ten components of the index of leading indicators in terms of a predicted *decline* in GDP, keeping in mind that the opposite changes forecast a rise in GDP.

1. Furniture and appliance sales   A slump in these retail trade sales portends reduced future production — that is, a decline in GDP.

2. Other durable goods sales   This part of retail trade is four times greater than the first. It includes sales of automobiles, which are more sensitive to interest rates than are purchases of other goods. A decline in sales here may be more a result of rising consumer loan rates than an impending downturn in the economy — though rising interest rates themselves often do precede a downturn.

3. House spending index   This is a composite index of housing starts (units) and house sales. Decreases in the number of housing starts and in house sales forecast declines in investment and therefore the distinct possibility that GDP will decline or at least grow more slowly.

4. New orders for durable goods   A decline in the number of orders received for durable goods indicates reduced future production — a decline in GDP.

5. Shipment to inventory ratio of finished goods   A decline in the ratio — a decline in shipments and/or an increase in inventory — indicates that sales are declining and, probably, that undesired investment in inventories is occurring. In either case, a decline in production is probable.

6. Average work week (hours)   Decreases in the length of the average work week in manufacturing foretell declines in future manufacturing output and GDP.

7. Business and personal service employment   A decline in employment, especially in view of the continuing growth of our labour force of some 250,000 a year, indicates a serious slowdown in the economy and therefore GDP.

8. United States composite leading index   With 70% of our trade with the United States — approximately 18% of our GDP — a slowdown in the United States is quickly transmitted to Canada. If the U.S. composite leading index is sharply down, Canada's GDP will almost certainly decline.

9. TSE 300 stock price index   The Toronto Stock Exchange (TSE) is the country's largest, and the price movements of the 300 stocks that make up its index are a good indication of market sentiment in Canada. If the index is dropping sharply, this is a strong indication that financial investors are pessimistic about the economy and expect GDP to decline. This can become a self-fulfilling prophecy, because lower stock market prices diminish consumer wealth, leading consumers to cut back on their spending. Lower stock market values also make it less attractive for firms to issue new shares of stock as a way to raise funds for investment. Hence, declines in the stock market can bring forth declines in aggregate demand and GDP.

10. Money supply   Decreases in the money supply are associated with falling GDP. The components of the money supply and its role in the macroeconomy are the subjects of Chapters 13 to 15.

None of these factors *alone* consistently predicts the future course of the economy. It is not unusual in any month, for example, for one or two of the indicators to be decreasing while the other is increasing. Rather, changes in the *weighted average* — or composite index — of the ten components in the past have provided advance notice of a change in the direction of GDP. The rule of thumb is that three successive monthly declines or increases in the index indicate that the economy will soon turn in that same direction.

Although the composite index has correctly signalled business fluctuations on numerous occasions, it has not been infallible. At times the index has provided false warnings of recessions that have never occurred. In other instances, recessions have so closely followed the downturn in the index that policy makers have not had sufficient time to make use of the "early" warning. Moreover, changing structural features of the economy have on occasion rendered the existing index obsolete and necessitated its revision.

Given these caveats, the index of leading indicators can best be thought of as a useful but not totally reliable signalling device that authorities must employ with considerable caution in formulating macroeconomic policy.

Virtually all taxes will yield more tax revenue as GDP rises. In particular, personal income taxes have progressive rates and result in more than proportionate increases in tax collection as GDP expands. Furthermore, as GDP increases and more goods and services are purchased, revenues from corporate income taxes and sales taxes will increase. Conversely, when GDP declines, tax receipts from all these sources will decline.

Transfer payments (or "negative taxes") behave in precisely the opposite way as tax collections. Unemployment insurance benefits, welfare payments, and subsidies to farmers all *decrease* during economic expansion and *increase* during contraction.

AUTOMATIC OR BUILT-IN STABILIZERS

Figure 12-3 helps us understand how the tax system creates built-in stability. Government expenditures G are fixed and assumed to be independent of the level of GDP; expenditures are decided on at some specific level by Parliament. But Parliament does *not* determine the *level* of tax revenues; rather, it establishes tax *rates*. Tax revenues then vary directly with the level of GDP that the economy actually realizes. The direct relationship between tax revenues and GDP is shown in the upsloping T line.

FIGURE 12-3   Built-in stability

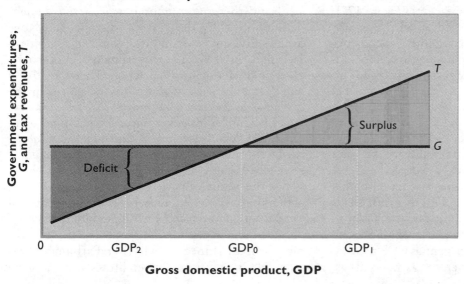

If tax revenues vary directly with GDP, then the deficits that will tend to occur automatically during recession will help alleviate that recession. Conversely, the surpluses that tend to occur automatically during expansion will assist in offsetting possible inflation.

ECONOMIC IMPORTANCE The economic importance of this direct relationship between tax receipts and GDP comes into focus when we consider two things.

1. Taxes reduce spending and aggregate demand.
2. It is desirable from the standpoint of stability to reduce spending when the economy is moving towards inflation and to increase spending when the economy is slumping.

In other words, the tax system portrayed in Figure 12-3 builds some stability into the economy. It automatically brings about changes in tax revenues, and therefore in the public budget, that counter both inflation and unemployment. A **built-in stabilizer** is *anything that increases the government's deficit (or reduces its surplus) during a recession and increases its surplus (or reduces its deficit) during inflation without requiring explicit action by policy makers*. As Figure 12-3 reveals, this is precisely what our tax system does.

As GDP rises during prosperity, tax revenues *automatically* increase and, because they reduce spending, they restrain the economic expansion. Conversely, as GDP falls during recession, tax revenues *automatically* decline, increasing spending and cushioning the economic contraction. With a falling GDP, tax receipts decline and move the public budget from a surplus towards a deficit. In Figure 12-3, the low level of income GDP_1 will automatically yield to an expansionary budget deficit; the high and perhaps inflationary income level, GDP_3, will automatically generate a contractionary budget surplus.

PROGRESSIVE TAX It is clear from Figure 12-3 that the size of the automatic budget deficits or surpluses, and therefore built-in stability, depends on the responsiveness of changes in taxes to changes in GDP. If tax revenues change sharply as GDP changes, the slope of line T in the figure will be steep and the vertical distances between T and G — the deficits or surpluses — will be large. If tax revenues change very little when GDP changes, the slope will be gentle and built-in stability will be low.

The steepness of T in Figure 12-3 depends on the tax system in place. If it is **progressive**, meaning the average tax rate (= tax revenue/GDP) rises with GDP, the T line will be steeper than if the tax system is **proportional** or **regressive**. In a proportional tax system the average tax rate remains constant as GDP rises; in a regressive tax system the average tax rate falls as

GDP rises. Tax revenues will rise with GDP under progressive and proportional tax systems and may either rise, fall, or remain the same when GDP increases under a regressive system. But what you should realize is this: *The more progressive the tax system, the greater is the economy's built-in stability.*

Changes in public policies or laws that change the progressivity of the net tax system (taxes minus transfers and subsidies) affect the degree of built-in stability. The federal government's "indexing" of the personal income tax and lowering of marginal tax rates in the mid-1970s flattened the slope of T in Figure 12-3. Prior to the mid-1970s inflation would push taxpayers into higher marginal tax brackets and thus increase government's tax revenues. Since then, income tax brackets have been "indexed," or widened, to adjust for inflation. As a result, changes in GDP do not produce as large automatic changes in tax revenue as previously and the economy's degree of built-in stability is less than it was.

The built-in stability provided by our tax system has reduced the severity of business fluctuation. But the built-in stabilizers can only diminish, *not* correct major changes in the equilibrium GDP. Discretionary fiscal policy may be needed to correct inflation or recession of any appreciable magnitude.

THE CYCLICALLY ADJUSTED BUDGET

Built-in stability — the fact that tax revenues vary directly with GDP — means the **actual budget** surplus or deficit in any specific year is not a good measure of the status of fiscal policy. Suppose the economy is at full employment at GDP_f in Figure 12-4 and the government has an actual budget deficit shown by the vertical distance *ab*. Now, assume investment spending plummets, causing a recession to GDP_r. The government, let's assume, takes no discretionary fiscal action. Therefore, the G and T lines remain in the positions shown in the diagram. As the economy moves to GDP_r, tax revenues fall, and with government expenditures unaltered, the deficit rises to *ec*, expanding from *ab* (= *ed*) by the amount *dc*. This **cyclical deficit** of *dc* — so named because it relates to the business cycle — is not the result of positive countercyclical fiscal actions by government; rather it is the by-product of fiscal inaction as the economy slides into recession.

We cannot gain a true picture of the government's fiscal stance — whether Parliament was manipulating taxes and expenditures — by looking

FIGURE 12-4 Full-employment (structural) deficits and cyclical deficits

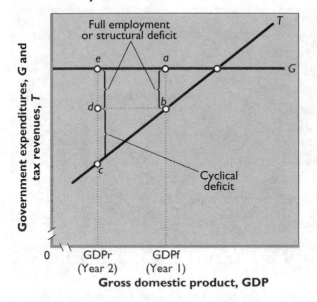

The actual budget deficit for any specific year consists of the cyclically adjusted deficit (or structural deficit) and the cyclical deficit. The *cyclically adjusted deficit* is the difference between government expenditures and tax collections that would occur if there were full employment output (GDP_f). Here, this deficit is positive, since government spending exceeds tax collections at GDP_f. The *cyclical deficit* results from a below-full-employment output (GDP_r). At GDP_f the structural deficit is *ab*, while the cyclical budget is zero. The structural deficit at GDP_r is *ab*; the cyclical deficit, *de*.

at the historical record of budget deficits or surpluses. The actual budget deficit or surplus reflects not only possible discretionary fiscal decisions about spending and taxes (as shown by the locations of the G and T lines in Figure 12-4), but also the level of GDP (where the economy is operating on the horizontal axis of Figure 12-4). Because tax revenues vary with GDP, the problem of comparing deficits or surpluses in any two years is that the level of GDP may be different in each year. In Figure 12-4, the actual budget deficit in year 2 (GDP_r) differs from that in year 1 (GDP_f) only because GDP is lower in year 2 than in year 1.

RESOLVING THE PROBLEM Economists have resolved the problem of comparing budget deficits for different years in the business cycle by using the

cyclically adjusted budget. The **cyclically adjusted budget**, also called *the full-employment budget, measures what the federal budget deficit or surplus would be with existing tax and government spending structures, if the economy were at full employment throughout the year.* In Figure 12-4 the full-employment deficit or **structural deficit** is the same in year 1 and year 2 (*ab = ed*). This is the budget deficit that would have existed in year 2 even if there were no recession. It is called "structural" because it reflects the configuration of G and T, independent of the state of the economy.

In year 2 the actual budget deficit exceeds the cyclically adjusted or structural budget by *dc*. This is the amount of the cyclical budget deficit. To eliminate the *dc* cyclical deficit, government must move the economy back to full-employment output at GDP_f. Ironically, this may require a temporary increase in the full-employment deficit, or structural deficit, via expansionary discretionary fiscal policy. That is, government must cut taxes (shift T downward) or increase government spending (shift G upward) to move the economy from GDP_r to GDP_f. Once prosperity is restored, government can, if it wishes, eliminate the structural deficit by increasing tax rates (shift the T line upward) or reducing government spending (shift the G line downward).

To emphasize: Discretionary fiscal policy is reflected in deliberate *changes* in the cyclically adjusted or structural deficit, not in changes in the cyclical deficit. Since the actual budget deficit includes both the structural and cyclical deficits, the actual budget deficit is an unreliable measure of the government's fiscal policy stance.

Figure 12-5 compares the cyclically adjusted budget and the actual budget as percentages of GDP since 1961. In many years the sizes of the actual budget deficits or surpluses differ from the sizes of the deficits or surpluses of the cyclically adjusted budget. The key to assessing discretionary fiscal policy is to disregard the actual budget and instead observe the change in the *cyclically adjusted budget* in a particular year or period. For example, fiscal policy was restrictive between 1964 and 1970, reflected in the increase in cyclically adjusted deficit below the actual budget. Fiscal policy was also contractionary between 1972 and 1974.

Also observe in Figure 12-5 that cyclically adjusted or structural deficits have been particularly large since 1981. A large part of the actual deficits during the 1980s and early 1990s were not cyclical

FIGURE 12-5   The cyclically adjusted budget and the actual budget

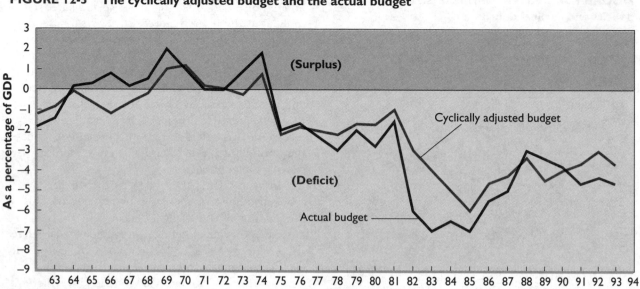

The cyclically adjusted budget surplus or deficit is a better indicator of the government's fiscal posture than is the actual surplus or deficit. The actual budget was below the cyclically adjusted budget in the 1980s because of high unemployment. The fact that the cyclically adjusted budget was in deficit in the 1980s shows that the actual budget had a stimulatory effect on the economy.

Source: Department of Finance, Economic and Fiscal Reference Tables, September, 1994.

deficits resulting from automatic deficiencies in tax revenue brought forth from below-full employment GDP. Rather, much of the actual deficits reflected structural imbalances between government spending and tax collections. The year 1989 is an example. Although the economy had achieved full employment, a sizable cyclically adjusted deficit remained.

Large cyclically adjusted budget deficits have persisted into the 1990s. During the 1990s the Canadian government has largely abandoned countercyclical fiscal policy in its attempt to reduce the large structural deficits. Some maintain these deficits were so massive that financing them increased real interest rates and may have crowded out much private investment, a scenario we will discuss shortly. Thus, in the 1990s the role of stabilizing the economy has fallen nearly exclusively to the nation's central bank, the Bank of Canada. This institution and its policies are the subject of Chapters 13 to 15, while budget deficits and the public debt are the subject of Chapter 18.

QUICK REVIEW 12-2

1. Tax revenues automatically increase in economic expansions and decrease in recessions; transfers automatically decrease in expansions and increase in recessions.

2. Automatic changes in taxes and transfers add a degree of built-in stability to the economy.

3. The cyclically adjusted budget compares government spending to the tax revenues that would accrue if there were full employment; it is more useful than the actual budget in revealing the status of fiscal policy.

4. Cyclically adjusted budget deficits are also called structural deficits.

GLOBAL PERSPECTIVE 12-1

Budget deficits as a percentage of GDP, selected nations

In 1994 all the major industrial nations had budget deficits, but these deficits varied greatly as a percentage of GDP. In some cases the deficits were largely cyclical; in other instances they were mainly cyclically adjusted or structural deficits.

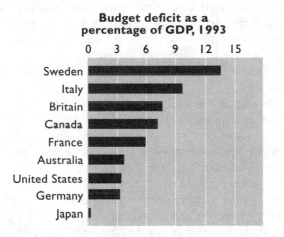

Budget deficit as a percentage of GDP, 1993

Source: *Organization for Economic Cooperation and Development.*

PROBLEMS, CRITICISMS, AND COMPLICATIONS

Unfortunately, there is much difference between fiscal policy on paper and fiscal policy in practice. Let's examine specific problems government may encounter in enacting and applying fiscal policy.

PROBLEMS OF TIMING

Several problems of timing may arise in connection with fiscal policy.

1. RECOGNITION LAG The recognition lag refers to the time between the beginning of a recession or inflation and the certain awareness that it is actually happening. It is difficult to predict accurately the future course of economic activity. Although forecasting tools such as the index of leading indicators (see this chapter's Applying the Theory box) provide clues to the direction of the economy, the economy may be four or six months into a recession or inflation before that fact appears in relevant statistics and is acknowledged.

2. ADMINISTRATIVE LAG The wheels of democratic government turn slowly. There will typically be a significant lag between the time the need for fiscal action is recognized and the time action is actually taken. Parliament has on occasion taken so much time in adjusting fiscal policy that the economic situation has turned around in the interim, rendering the policy action inappropriate.

3. OPERATIONAL LAG There will also be a lag between the time that fiscal action is taken by Parliament and the time that action affects output, employment, or the price level. Although changes in tax rates can be put into effect quickly, government spending on public works — the construction of dams, highways, and so on — requires long planning periods and even longer periods of construction. Such spending is of questionable usefulness in offsetting short — for example, six- to eighteen-month — periods of recession. Because of these problems, discretionary fiscal policy has increasingly relied on tax changes.

POLITICAL PROBLEMS

Fiscal policy is created in the political arena, and this greatly complicates its use in stabilizing the economy.

1. OTHER GOALS Economic stability is *not* the sole objective of government spending and taxing policies. Government is also concerned with providing public goods and services and redistributing income. During World War II, government spending for military goods rose dramatically, causing strong and persistent inflationary pressures in the early 1940s. The defeat of Nazi Germany and Japan was a higher priority goal than achieving price level stability.

2. PROVINCIAL AND MUNICIPAL FINANCE Fiscal policies of provincial and local governments are frequently pro-cyclical — they do not counter recession or inflation. Like households and private businesses, provincial and local governments increase expenditures during prosperity and cut them during recession. During the Great Depression of the 1930s, some of the increase in federal spending was offset by decreases in provincial and local spending.

3. EXPANSIONARY BIAS?   Rhetoric to the contrary, deficits may be politically attractive and surpluses politically painful. Fiscal policy may have an expansionary-inflationary bias. Tax reductions are politically popular. And so are increases in government spending, provided the constituents share in the benefits. But higher taxes upset voters, and reducing government expenditures can be politically precarious.

4. POLITICAL BUSINESS CYCLE?   A few economists have suggested the notion of a **political business cycle**. They have argued that politicians might manipulate fiscal policy to maximize voter support, even though their fiscal decisions *destabilize* the economy. In this view, fiscal policy as we have described it may be corrupted for political purposes and thereby be a cause of economic fluctuations.

The populace, it is assumed, take economic conditions into account in voting. Incumbents are penalized at the polls if economic conditions are depressed; they are rewarded if the economy is prosperous. As an election approaches, the government will invoke tax cuts and increases in government spending. Not only will these actions be popular, but the resulting stimulus to the economy will push all the critical economic indicators in proper directions. Output and real incomes will rise, and unemployment will fall. As a result, the government will enjoy a cordial economic environment in which to stand for re-election.

But after the election, continued expansion of the economy is reflected increasingly in a rising price level and less in growing real incomes. Growing public concern over inflation will prompt politicians to invoke a contractionary fiscal policy. A "made-in-Ottawa" recession will be engineered by trimming government spending and increasing taxes in order to restrain inflation. Such a recession would not hurt the government because the next election would still be three or four years away and the critical consideration for most voters is the performance of the economy in the year or so prior to the election. Indeed, the recession provides a new starting point from which fiscal policy can again be used to generate another expansion in time for the next election campaign.

This possible perversion of fiscal policy is disturbing but difficult to document. Although empirical evidence is mixed and inconclusive, there is some evidence in support of this political theory of the business cycle.

CROWDING-OUT EFFECT

We now move from practical problems in the application of fiscal policy to a basic criticism of fiscal policy. The essence of the **crowding-out effect** is that an expansionary (deficit) fiscal policy will increase the interest rate and reduce investment spending, weakening or cancelling the stimulus of the fiscal policy.

Suppose the economy is in a recession and government invokes discretionary fiscal policy in the form of an increase in government spending. To do so, government goes into the money market to finance the deficit. The resulting increase in the demand for money raises the interest rate. Because investment spending varies inversely with the interest rate, some investment will be choked off or crowded out.[2]

While few would question this logic, there is disagreement as to the size of the crowding-out effect. Some economists argue there will be little crowding-out when there is considerable unemployment. The rationale for this contention is that, given a recession, the stimulus provided by an increase in government spending will likely improve business profit expectations, which are an important determinant of investment. Thus, investment spending need not fall — it may even increase — even though interest rates are higher.

OFFSETTING SAVING

A few economists theorize that deficit spending is offset by an equal increase in private saving. Supposedly, people recognize that today's deficit spending will eventually require higher taxes for themselves or their heirs. People therefore increase their present saving (reduce their current consumption) in anticipation of these higher taxes. A budget deficit — *public dissaving* — produces an increase in *private saving*. This concept is termed the **Ricardian equivalence theorem**, named after British economist David Ricardo, who first suggested it in the early 1800s. More formally, the theorem states that financing a deficit by borrowing has the same limited effect on GDP as financing it through a present tax increase.

---

[2] Some interest-sensitive consumption spending — for example, automobile purchases — may also be crowded out.

In Figure 12-1, the increase in spending from the rise in government spending or decline in taxes is partially or fully offset by a decline in consumption caused by the increase in saving. Aggregate demand and real GDP therefore do not expand as predicted. Fiscal policy is either rendered totally ineffective or is severely weakened.

Although research continues on this theory, mainstream economists reject it as unrealistic and contrary to historical evidence. They point out that the large budget deficits of the 1980s were accompanied by *declines* — not increases — in the national saving rate.

AGGREGATE SUPPLY AND INFLATION

Our discussion of complications and criticisms of fiscal policy has thus far concentrated entirely on aggregate demand. We now consider a supply-side complication. With an upsloping aggregate supply curve, some portion of the potential effect of an expansionary fiscal policy on real output and employment may be dissipated in the form of inflation.

GRAPHIC PORTRAYAL: CROWDING-OUT AND INFLATION

An upsloping aggregate supply curve causes a part of the increase in aggregate demand, as in Figure 12-6, to be dissipated in higher prices with the result that the increase in real GDP is diminished. The price level rises from P_0 to P_1 and real domestic output increases to only $\$GDP_1$, rather than GDP_f.

With a rise in the price level, the increase in government expenditures will be partially offset by declines in consumption, investment, and net exports expenditures. These declines result respectively from the wealth, interest-rate, and foreign-trade effects created by the higher domestic price level. Demand-side fiscal policy does not escape the realities imposed by the aggregate supply curve. **(Key Question 7)**

FISCAL POLICY IN THE OPEN ECONOMY: A FIRST GLANCE

Additional complications arise when we recognize our economy is a component of the world economy.

SHOCKS ORIGINATING FROM ABROAD

Events and policies abroad that affect our net exports have an impact on our economy. Economies are susceptible to unforeseen international *aggregate demand shocks* that can alter domestic GDP and render domestic fiscal actions inappropriate.

FIGURE 12-6   Fiscal policy: the effects of inflation

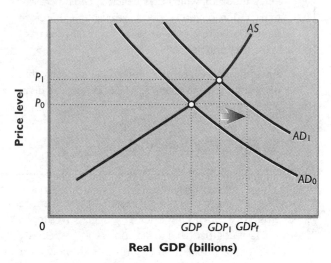

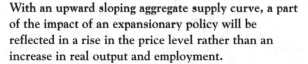

Real GDP (billions)

With an upward sloping aggregate supply curve, a part of the impact of an expansionary policy will be reflected in a rise in the price level rather than an increase in real output and employment.

Suppose we are experiencing a recession and have changed government expenditures and taxes to bolster aggregate demand and GDP without igniting inflation (as from AD_0 to AD_1 in Figure 12-6). Now suppose the economies of our major partners unexpectedly expand rapidly. Greater employment and rising incomes in those nations translate into more purchases of Canadian goods and services. Our net exports rise, aggregate demand increases too rapidly, and we experience an inflationary gap. Had we known in advance that our net exports would rise significantly, we would have enacted a less expansionary fiscal policy. The point is that our growing participation in the world economy brings with it the *complications* of mutual interdependence along with *gains* from specialization and trade.

A more detailed discussion of fiscal policy in an open economy is treated in Chapter 22.

QUICK REVIEW 12-3

1. Time lags and political problems complicate fiscal policy.

2. The crowding-out effect indicates that an expansionary fiscal policy may increase the interest rate and reduce investment spending.

3. A few economists believe in the Ricardian equivalency theorem, which says deficit spending creates expectation of future tax increases and therefore people privately save a dollar for each dollar of taxes they anticipate.

4. An upsloping aggregate supply curve means that part of an expansionary fiscal policy may be dissipated in inflation.

SUPPLY-SIDE FISCAL POLICY

We have seen how movements along the aggregate supply curve can complicate the operation of fiscal policy. Let's now turn to the possibility of a more direct link between fiscal policy and aggregate supply. Economists recognize that fiscal policy — especially tax changes that affect production costs — *may* alter aggregate supply and thereby affect the price level-real output outcomes of a change in fiscal policy.

Suppose in Figure 12-7 that aggregate demand and aggregate supply are AD_0 and AS_0 so that the equilibrium level of real GDP is Q_0 and the price level is P_0. Assume the government concludes the level of unemployment associated with Q_0 is too high and that an expansionary fiscal policy is therefore implemented in the form of a tax cut. The demand-side effect is to increase aggregate demand from AD_0 to, say, AD_1. This shift increases real GDP to Q_1, but also boosts the price level to P_1.

How might tax cuts affect aggregate supply? Some economists — labelled "supply-side" economists — insist that tax reductions will shift the aggregate supply curve to the right.

1. SAVING AND INVESTMENT
Lower taxes will increase disposable incomes, increasing household saving. Similarly, tax reductions on businesses will increase the profitability of investment. In brief, lower taxes will increase the volumes of both saving and investment, thereby increasing the rate of capital accumulation. The size of our "national factory" — our productive capacity — will grow more rapidly.

2. WORK INCENTIVES
Lower personal income tax rates also increase after-tax wages and thereby stimulate work incentives. Many people not already in the labour force will offer their services because after-tax wages are higher. Those already in the labour force will want to work more hours and take fewer vacations.

3. RISK TAKING
Lower tax rates also mean individuals and businesses will be more willing to risk their energies and financial capital on new production methods and new products if there is a larger potential after-tax reward. Through all these avenues, lower taxes will shift aggregate supply to the right as from AS_0 to AS_1 in Figure 12-7, thereby reducing inflation and further increasing real GDP.

Supply-siders also contend that lower tax *rates* need not result in lower tax *revenues*. In fact, lower tax rates that cause a substantial expansion of domestic output and income may generate increases in tax revenues. This enlarged tax base may enhance total tax revenues even though tax rates are lower.

MAINSTREAM SCEPTICISM
Most economists are sceptical concerning the supply-side effects of tax cuts. First, these critics contend that the hoped-for positive effects of a tax reduction on incentives to work, save and invest, and bear risks are not nearly as strong as supply-siders believe. Second, any rightward shifts of the aggregate supply curve will occur over an extended period of time, while the demand-side impact will be more immediate.

FIGURE 12-7   Supply-side effects of fiscal policy

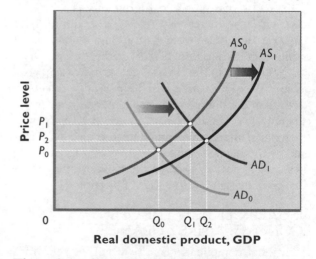

The traditional view is that tax cuts will increase aggregate demand as from AD_0 to AD_1, increasing both real domestic output (Q_0 to Q_1) and the price level (P_0 to P_1). If the tax reductions induce favourable supply-side effects, aggregate supply will shift rightward as from AS_0 to AS_1. This allows the economy to realize an even larger output (Q_2 as compared to Q_1) and a lower price level (P_2 as compared to P_1).

CHAPTER SUMMARY

1. Increases in government spending expand, and decreases contract, aggregate demand and equilibrium GDP. Increases in taxes reduce, and decreases expand, aggregate demand and equilibrium GDP. Fiscal policy therefore calls for increases in government spending and decreases in taxes — a budget deficit — to correct for a recessionary gap. Decreases in government spending and increases in taxes — a budget surplus — are appropriate fiscal policy for correcting an inflationary gap.

2. Built-in stability refers to net tax revenues that vary directly with the level of GDP. During a recession, the public budget automatically moves towards a stabilizing deficit; during expansion, the budget automatically moves towards an anti-inflationary surplus. Built-in stability lessens, but does not correct, undesired changes in the GDP.

3. The cyclically adjusted budget or structural budget indicates what the budgetary surplus or deficit would be *if* the economy operated at full employment throughout the year. The cyclically adjusted budget is a meaningful indicator of the government's fiscal posture, while their actual budgetary surplus or deficit is not.

4. The enactment and application of appropriate fiscal policy are subject to certain problems and questions. The most important ones are **a** Can the enactment and application of fiscal policy be better timed so as to maximize its effectiveness in heading off economic fluctuations? **b** Can the economy rely on Parliament to enact appropriate fiscal policy? **c** An expansionary fiscal policy may be weakened if it crowds out some private investment spending. **d** Do people increase their saving in anticipation of the future higher taxes that they think deficit spending will entail? **e** Some of the effect of an expansionary fiscal policy may be dissipated in inflation. **f** Fiscal policy may be rendered ineffective or inappropriate by unforeseen events occurring in the world economy. Also, fiscal policy may precipitate changes in exchange rates that may weaken its effects. **g** Supply-side economists contend that traditional fiscal policy fails to consider the effects of a tax change on aggregate supply.

TERMS AND CONCEPTS

actual budget surplus or deficit (p. 264)
budget deficit (p. 259)
budget surplus (p. 260)
built-in stabilizers (p. 264)
crowding-out effect (p. 268)
cyclical deficit (p. 264)
cyclically adjusted budget (p. 265)
discretionary fiscal policy (p. 258)

expansionary and contractionary fiscal policy (p. 259)
political business cycle (p. 268)
progressive, proportional, and regressive tax systems (p. 264)
Ricardian equivalence theorem (p. 268)
structural deficit (p. 265)
supply-side fiscal policy (p. 270)

QUESTIONS AND STUDY SUGGESTIONS

1. *Key Question   What are government's fiscal policy options for an inflationary gap caused by demand-pull inflation? Use the aggregate demand-aggregate supply model to show the impact of these policies on the price level. Which of these fiscal policy options do you think a "conservative" economist might favour? A "liberal" economist?*

2. (Optional for students assigned Chapters 9 and 10) Use the aggregate expenditures model to show how government fiscal policy could eliminate either a recessionary gap or an inflationary gap (Figure 10-8). Use the concept of the balanced budget multiplier to explain how equal increases in *G* and *T* could eliminate a recessionary gap and how equal decreases in *G* and *T* could eliminate an inflationary gap.

3. Designate each statement true or false and justify your answer.

   a. Expansionary fiscal policy during a recession will have a greater positive effect on real GDP if government borrows the money to finance the budget deficit than if it creates new money to finance the deficit.

   b. Contractionary fiscal policy will be more effective if government impounds the budget surplus than using the surplus to pay off some of its past debt.

4. Explain how the built-in (or automatic) stabilizers work. What are the differences between a proportional, progressive, and regressive tax system as they relate to an economy's built-in stability?

5. **Key Question**   *Define the "cyclically adjusted budget" and explain its significance. How does it differ from the "actual budget"? What is the difference between a structural deficit and a cyclical deficit? Suppose the economy depicted in Figure 12-4 is operating at full-employment real output, GDP$_f$. What is the size of its structural deficit? Its cyclical deficit? Should government raise taxes or reduce government spending to eliminate this structural deficit? What are the risks of so doing?*

6. The actual budget deficit increased significantly in 1990 and 1991, but the cyclically adjusted budget deficit remained relatively constant. Can you think of a logical explanation?

7. **Key Question**   *Briefly state and evaluate the problems in enacting and applying fiscal policy. Explain the notion of a political business cycle. What is the crowding-out effect and why is it relevant to fiscal policy? Do you think people increase their saving in anticipation of the future higher taxes they believe will follow?*

8. In view of your answers to question 7, explain the following statement: "While fiscal policy clearly is useful in combating severe recession and demand-pull inflation, it is impossible to use fiscal policy to 'fine tune' the economy to the full-employment, noninflationary level of real GDP and keep the economy there indefinitely."

9. Discuss: "Mainstream economists tend to focus on the aggregate demand effects of tax-rate reductions; supply-side economists emphasize the aggregate supply effects." What are the routes through which a tax cut might increase aggregate supply? If tax cuts are so good for the economy, why don't we cut taxes to zero?

10. Using Figure 12-3 as a basis for your response, explain the stabilizing or destabilizing impacts of fiscal policy if a constitutional amendment requiring an annually balanced budget were passed.

11. Use Figure 12-4 to explain why a deliberate increase in the full-employment or structural deficit that causes the economy to expand from GDP$_r$ to GDP$_f$ might reduce the size of the actual deficit.

12. **Advanced Analysis** (Optional for students assigned Chapters 9 and 10) Assume that, without taxes, the consumption schedule for an economy is as shown below:

GDP, billions	Consumption, billions
$100	$120
200	200
300	280
400	360
500	440
600	520
700	600

a. Graph this consumption schedule and determine the size of the MPC.

b. Assume a lump-sum (regressive) tax is imposed such that the government collects $10 billion in taxes at all levels of GDP. Calculate the tax rate at each level of GDP. Graph the resulting consumption schedule and compare the MPC and the multiplier with that of the pretax consumption schedule.

c. Now suppose a proportional tax system with a 10% tax rate is imposed instead of the regressive system. Calculate the new consumption schedule, graph it, and note the MPC and the multiplier.

d. Finally, impose a progressive tax system such that the tax rate is zero % when GDP is $100, 5% at $200, 10% at $300, 15% at $400, and so forth. Determine and graph the new consumption schedule, noting the effect of this tax system on the MPC and the multiplier.

e. Explain why the proportional and progressive tax systems contribute to greater economic stability, while the regressive system does not. Demonstrate using a graph similar to Figure 12-3.

13. (Applying the Theory) What is the composite index of leading economic indicators and how does it relate to discretionary fiscal policy?

MONEY, BANKING, AND MONETARY POLICY

CHAPTER 13

MONEY AND BANKING IN CANADA

Money bewitches people. They fret for it, and they sweat for it. They devise most ingenious ways to get it, and most ingenious ways to get rid of it. Money is the only commodity that is good for nothing but to be got rid of. It will not feed you, clothe you, shelter you, or amuse you unless you spend it or invest it. It imparts value only in parting. People will do almost anything for money, and money will do almost anything for people. Money is a captivating, circulating, masquerading puzzle."[1]

Money. A fascinating aspect of the economy. And a crucial element of an economy. Money is more than a tool to facilitate the functioning of the economy. Operating properly, the monetary system is the lifeblood of the circular flows of income and expenditure that typify all economies. A smoothly operating money system is conducive to both full employment and efficient resource use. A malfunctioning monetary system can lead to severe fluctuations in the economy's levels of output, employment, and prices, *and* can distort the allocation of resources.

In this chapter, we are concerned with the nature and functions of money and the basic institutions of the Canadian banking system. Chapter 14 looks into the ways individual chartered banks and the banking system as a whole can vary the money supply. In Chapter 15 we discuss how the Bank of Canada regulates the supply of money to promote full employment and price-level stability.

We begin with a review of the functions of money. Next, we shift to the supply of money and pose the question: What constitutes money in our economy? Third, we consider what "backs" the supply of money in Canada. Finally, the institutional structure of the Canadian financial system will be investigated.

[1] Federal Reserve Bank of Philadelphia, "Creeping Inflation," *Business Review*, August 1957, p. 3.

BOX 13-1   THE BIG PICTURE

We now leave the topic of how equilibrium GDP and the price level are determined to focus on the often misunderstood concept of money and the role of the financial system in a market economy. While most people maintain that they desire more money, you should note that what they really want is more of what money can buy. Consider a world in which everyone could have whatever his or her heart desired; money in such a world would be literally worthless!

A market economy could function without money or a financial system, but it would certainly function much, much less efficiently. Money makes exchange and saving infinitely easier. You will better understand the role and importance of money and a financial system in the efficient functioning of a modern market economy if you imagine an economy without them. The cost of buying and selling goods and services, and borrowing and lending funds, would go way up. Thus, understand-

ing what money is and how the financial system functions in Canada is important to comprehend the monetary side of this macroeconomy.

As you read this chapter, keep the following points in mind:

- Money makes exchange in any economy much easier compared to barter. Money is desired for the goods and services it can purchase. Money also makes it easier to save and put a value on goods and services.
- While money comes in many different forms, its functions are always the same.
- An economy can function, albeit with some difficulties, with only the use of cheque money.
- Chartered banks are profit-maximizing firms. The Bank of Canada is the "bankers' bank" and is responsible for the supply of money.

THE FUNCTIONS OF MONEY

Money has three functions:

1. MEDIUM OF EXCHANGE   You will recall from Chapter 3 that first and foremost, money is a **medium of exchange**; it is used to buy and sell goods and services. A worker in a bagel bakery does not want to be paid 300 bagels per week. Nor does the bagel bakery wish to receive, say, fresh fish, for its bagels. However, money is readily acceptable as payment. It is a social invention allowing resource suppliers and producers to be paid with a "good" (money) that can be used to buy a full range of items available in the marketplace.

Money allows society to escape the complications of **barter** — the direct exchange of goods and services. Barter requires a *double coincidence of wants*. In the above example, if the worker in the bagel shop were paid in bagels and wanted to purchase fresh fish, the worker would have to find someone who wanted to sell fresh fish *and* wanted bagels in return — not an easy task. And because it provides a convenient way of exchanging goods, money allows society to gain the advantages of specialization.

2. MEASURE OF VALUE   Money is also a **measure of value**. Society uses the monetary unit as a yardstick to measure the relative worth of a variety of goods and resources. Just as we measure distance in kilometres, we gauge the value of goods and services in dollars. With a money system, we need not state the price of each product in terms of all other products for which it can be exchanged; we need not specify the price of cows in terms of corn, crayons, cigars, Chevrolets, and croissants.

The use of money as a common denominator means that the price of each product need be stated *only* in terms of the monetary unit. It permits buyers and sellers to compare readily the relative worth of various commodities and resources.

3. STORE OF VALUE   Finally, money serves as a **store of value**. Because money is the most liquid — the most spendable — of all assets, it is a very easy way to store wealth. The money you place in a safe or chequing account will still be available to you months or years later when you wish to use it to make purchases. Though most methods of holding money do not yield monetary returns such as one gets by storing wealth in the form of real assets (property) or paper assets (stocks, bonds, and so forth), money does have the advantage of being immediately usable by a firm or a household in meeting financial obligations.

THE SUPPLY OF MONEY

Conceptually, anything generally acceptable as a medium of exchange *is* money. Historically, playing cards, whales' teeth, elephant tail bristles, circular stones, nails, slaves (yes, human beings), cattle, beer, cigarettes, and pieces of metal have functioned as media of exchange. In our economy the debts of governments and of commercial banks and other financial institutions are used as money, as we will see.

DEFINING MONEY: M1

Narrowly defined — and designated **M1** — the money supply is composed of two items:

1. Currency (coins and paper money) outside chartered banks.
2. All **demand deposits**, meaning chequing account deposits in the chartered banks.

Coins and paper money are issued by the Bank of Canada, and demand deposits — personal chequing accounts — are a debt of the chartered banks. Let's comment briefly on the components of the M1 money supply (Table 13-1).

CURRENCY: COINS + PAPER MONEY From copper pennies to "loonies," coins are the "small change" of our money supply. Coins are a small portion of M1. They are convenience money that permits us to make very small purchases.

All coins in circulation in Canada are **token money**. This means the **intrinsic value** — the value of the bullion (metal) contained in the coin itself — is less than the face value of the coin. This is to avoid the melting down of token money for profitable sale as bullion. If our 25¢ pieces each contained 50¢ worth of silver bullion, it would be profitable to melt them and sell the metal. Although it is illegal to do this, 25¢ pieces would disappear from circulation. This is one of the potential defects of commodity money: its worth as a commodity may come to exceed its worth as money, ending its function as a medium of exchange. This

happened with our *then* silver coins in the late 1960s and early 1970s. An 80% silver pre-1967 quarter is now worth several dollars.

Paper money constitutes over 40% of the economy's narrowly defined (M1) money supply. Paper currency is in the form of **Bank of Canada notes** — the paper notes you carry in your wallet — issued by our government-owned central bank.

Together coins and paper money amounted to $25,805 million in mid-1995, almost 45% of M1.

DEMAND DEPOSITS The safety and convenience of using cheques, or bank money, have made chequing accounts the most important money in Canada. You would not think of stuffing $4,896.47 in bills and coins in an envelope and dropping it in a mailbox to pay a debt. But to write and mail a cheque for a large sum is commonplace. A cheque must be endorsed (signed on the reverse) by the person cashing it. Similarly, because the writing of a cheque requires endorsement by the one who cashes the cheque, the theft or loss of a chequebook is not nearly so bad as losing an identical amount of currency. Furthermore, it is more convenient to write a cheque than it is to transport and count out a large sum of currency. For all these reasons, *chequebook money*, or demand deposit, is the dominant form of money in the Canadian economy. Even Table 13-1 understates the significance of bank money. In dollar volume, about 90% of all transactions are carried out by the use of cheques.

It might seem strange that chequing accounts are part of the money supply. But it's clear why: Cheques, which are nothing more than a way to transfer the ownership of deposits in chartered banks and other financial institutions, are generally acceptable as a medium of exchange. True, as a stop at most gas stations will verify, cheques are less generally accepted than currency for small purchases. But, for major purchases, sellers willingly accept cheques as payment. Moreover, people can convert these deposits immediately into paper money and coins on demand; cheques drawn on these deposits are thus the equivalent of currency.

To summarize:

Money, M1 = currency + demand deposits

INSTITUTIONS OFFERING DEMAND DEPOSITS Table 13-1 shows that **demand deposits** (= chequable deposits) are over half the M1 money

TABLE 13-1 Money in Canada, May 1995†

Money	Millions of dollars	Percent of M1	Percent of M2	Percent of M3	Percent of M2+
Currency outside banks	$ 25,805	44.0	6.9	5.7	4.3
+ Demand deposits (current and personal chequing)	32,466	56.0	8.8	7.2	5.4
Total M1	58,271	100.0	15.7	12.9	9.7
+ Personal savings deposits and nonpersonal notice deposits	312,167		84.3	69.4	52.3
Total M2	370,438		100.0	82.3	62.0
+ Nonpersonal fixed-term deposits plus foreign currency deposits of residents booked in Canada	79,370			17.7	13.3
Total M3	449,808			100.0	75.3
+ Deposits at trust and mortgage companies, credit unions, and caisses populaires	147,548				24.7
Total M2+	$597,356				100.0

† Seasonally adjusted average monthly data
Source: Bank of Canada Review, Summer, 1995.

supply. Many financial institutions offer chequable deposits in Canada.

1. CHARTERED BANKS These are the mainstays of the system. They accept the deposits of households and businesses and use these financial resources to make available a wide variety of loans. Chartered bank loans provide short-term working capital to businesses and farmers, finance consumer purchases of automobiles and other durable goods, and so on.

2. OTHER DEPOSITORY INSTITUTIONS The chartered banks are supplemented by other financial institutions — trust companies, caisse populaires, and credit unions. They marshal the savings of households and businesses that are then used, among other things, to finance housing mortgages. Credit unions accept the deposits of "members" — usually a group of individuals who work for the same company — and lend these funds to finance instalment purchases.

QUALIFICATION We must qualify our definition of money: Currency owned by the chartered banks,

other depository institutions, and Government of Canada deposits are excluded.

A five-dollar bill in the hands of Jane Doe constitutes just $5 of the money supply. But, if we count dollars held by banks as a part of the money supply, that same $5 would count for $10 when deposited in a chartered bank. It would count for a $5 demand deposit owned by Doe and also for $5 worth of currency resting in the bank's vault. This problem of double-counting is avoided by excluding currency resting in the chartered banks and currency redeposited in the Bank of Canada in determining the total money supply.

Excluding deposits owned by the Government of Canada is somewhat more arbitrary. This exclusion permits us to better gauge the money supply and rate of spending in the private sector of the economy, apart from spending initiated by government policy.

NEAR-MONIES: M2, M3, AND M2+

Near-monies are highly liquid financial assets such as nonchequable savings accounts, term deposits, and short-term government securities. Although they do not directly function as a medium of exchange, they can be readily and without risk of financial loss converted into currency or chequable deposits. Thus, on demand you may withdraw currency from a **nonchequable savings account** at a chartered bank or trust and mortgage loan company, credit union, or *caisse populaire*. Or you may request that funds be transferred from a nonchequable savings account to a chequable account.

As the term implies, **term deposits** become available to a depositor only at maturity. For example, a 90-day or six-month term deposit is available without penalty only when the designated period expires. Although term deposits are less liquid (spendable) than nonchequable savings accounts, they can be taken as currency or shifted into chequable accounts when they mature.

MONEY DEFINITION M2 The chartered banks' portion of these "personal savings deposits and nonpersonal notice deposits" are added to M1 to give us a yet broader definition of money **M2**, as shown in Table 13-1.

MONEY DEFINITION M3 A third "official" definition, M3, recognizes that large term deposits — which are usually owned by businesses in the form of certificates of deposit — are also easily convertible into chequable deposits. In fact, there is a going market for these certificates and they can therefore be sold (liquidated) at any time. The addition of these large term deposits to M2 yields the still broader definition of money, **M3**, as shown in Table 13-1.

M2+ The broadest monetary aggregate is **M2+**, which is M2 plus deposits at trust and mortgage loan companies, and deposits at *caisses populaires* and credit unions.

Which definition shall we use? The simple M1 includes only items *directly* and *immediately* usable as a medium of exchange. For this reason it is an oft-cited statistic in discussions of the money supply. However, for some purposes economists prefer the broader M2 definition. And what of M3 and M2+? These definitions are so inclusive that many economists question their usefulness.

We will use the narrow M1 definition of money in our discussion and analysis, unless stated otherwise. The important principles that apply to M1 are also applicable to M2 and M3 and M2+ because M1 is a base component in these broader measures.

NEAR-MONIES: IMPLICATIONS

Near-monies are important for several related reasons.

1. SPENDING HABITS These highly liquid assets affect people's consuming-saving habits. Usually, the greater the amount of financial wealth people hold as near-monies, the greater is their willingness to spend out of their money incomes.

2. STABILITY Conversion of near-monies into money or vice versa can affect the economy's stability. For example, during the prosperity-inflationary phase of the business cycle, nonchequable deposits converted into chequable deposits or currency adds to the money supply, which could increase inflation. Such conversions can complicate the task of the monetary authorities in controlling the money supply and the level of economic activity.

3. POLICY The specific definition of money used is important for monetary policy. For example, the money supply as measured by M1 might be constant, while money defined as M2 might be increasing. If the monetary authorities believe it is appropriate to have an expanding supply of money, the narrow M1 definition would call for specific actions to increase currency and chequable deposits. But the broader M2 definition would suggest that the desired expansion of the money supply is already taking place and that no specific policy action is required. (**Key Question 5**)

CREDIT CARDS

You may have wondered why we have ignored credit cards — Visa, MasterCard, American Express — in our discussion of how money is defined. After all, credit cards are a convenient means of making purchases. The answer is that credit cards are *not* really money, but rather a means of obtaining a short-term loan from the chartered bank or other financial institution that has issued the card.

When you purchase a sweatshirt with a credit card, the issuing bank will reimburse the store. Later, you reimburse the bank. You will pay an annual fee for the services provided, and if you choose to repay the bank in instalments, you will pay a sizable interest charge. Credit cards are merely a means of deferring or postponing payment for a short period. Your purchase of the sweatshirt is not complete until you have paid your credit-card bill.

BOX 13-2   APPLYING THE THEORY

THE GLOBAL GREENBACK*

Two-thirds of the $350 billion of American currency is circulating abroad.

Russians use them. So do Argentinians, Brazilians, Poles, Vietnamese, Chinese — and even Cubans. They are American dollars. Like blue jeans, computer software, and movie videos, the U.S. dollar has become a major American "export." About $200 billion of American currency is circulating overseas. Russians hold more than $20 billion in American cash, while another $5 billion to $7 billion is circulating freely in Argentina. The Polish government estimates that $5 billion of American dollars is circulating in Poland.

American currency leaves the United States when Americans buy imports, travel in other countries, or send dollars to relatives living abroad. The United States profits when American dollars stay in other countries. It costs the government about 4¢ to print a dollar. For someone abroad to obtain this new dollar, $1 worth of resources, goods, or services must be sold to Americans. These items are American gains. The dollar goes abroad, and assuming it stays there, it presents no claim on American resources or goods or services. Americans in effect make 96¢ on the dollar (= $1 gain in resources, goods, or services *minus* the 4¢ printing cost). It's like American Express selling traveller's cheques that never get cashed.

Black markets and other illegal activity undoubtedly fuel some of the demand for American cash abroad. The American dollar is king in covert trading in diamonds, weapons, and pirated software. Billions of dollars of cash are involved in the narcotics trade. But the illegal use of dollars is only a small part of the story. The massive volume of American dollars in other

nations reflects a global search for monetary stability. Based on past experience, foreign citizens are confident the dollar's purchasing power will remain relatively steady.

Argentina has pegged its peso directly to the American dollar, with the central bank issuing new pesos only when it has more dollars, gold, or other convertible reserves on hand. The result has been a remarkable decline in inflation. In Russia and the newly independent countries of Eastern Europe, the dollar has retained its buying power while that of domestic currencies has plummeted. As a result, many Russian workers demand to be paid at least partially in American dollars. In Brazil, where the inflation rate is more than 300% annually, people have long sought the stability of American dollars. In the shopping districts of Beijing and Shanghai, Chinese consumers trade their renminbi for American dollars. In Bolivia half of all bank accounts are denominated in American dollars. There is a thriving "dollar economy" in Vietnam, and even Cuba has partially legalized the use of the American currency. The American dollar is the official currency in Panama and Liberia.

There is little risk to the United States in satisfying the world's demand for dollars. If all the dollars came rushing back to the United States at once, the nation's money supply would surge, possibly causing demand-pull inflation. But there is not much chance of that happening. Overall, the global greenback is a positive economic force. It is a reliable medium of exchange, measure of value, and store of value facilitating transactions that might not otherwise occur. Dollar holdings have helped buyers and sellers abroad overcome special monetary problems. The result has been increased output in those countries and thus greater output and income globally.

* Based partly on "The Global Greenback," *Business Week*, August 9, 1993, and "Dollar Drain: Most Greenbacks Are Overseas," *Lincoln-Star*, March 15, 1994.

However, credit cards — and all other forms of credit — allow individuals and businesses to "economize" in the use of money. Credit cards permit you to have less currency and chequable deposits on hand for transactions. Credit cards help you synchronize your expenditures and your receipt of income, reducing the cash and chequable deposits you must hold.

WHAT "BACKS" THE MONEY SUPPLY?

This is a slippery question. A complete answer is likely to be at odds with preconceptions about money.

MONEY AS DEBT

The major components of the money supply — paper money and demand deposits — are debts, or promises to pay. *Paper money is the circulating debt of the Bank of Canada, while demand deposits are the debts of the chartered banks.*

Paper currency and demand deposits have no intrinsic value. A $5 bill is just a piece of paper. A demand deposit is merely a bookkeeping entry. And coins, we know, have less intrinsic value than their face value. Nor will the Bank of Canada redeem that paper money you hold for anything tangible, such as gold. In effect, we have chosen to "manage" our money supply. The Bank of Canada attempts to provide the amount of money needed for a particular volume of business activity that will foster full employment, price level stability, and economic growth.

Most economists believe that managing the money supply is more sensible than linking it to gold or any other commodity, whose supply might arbitrarily and capriciously change. A large increase in the nation's gold stock, as the result of a new gold discovery, might increase the money supply far beyond the amount needed for a full-employment level of business activity and cause rapid inflation.

The point is that paper money cannot be converted into a fixed amount of gold or some other precious metal. The Bank of Canada will swap one paper $5 bill for another bearing a different serial number. That is all you can get should you ask the Bank of Canada to redeem some of your paper money. Similarly, cheque money cannot be exchanged for gold but only for paper money.

VALUE OF MONEY

If currency and chequable deposits have no intrinsic characteristics giving them value *and* they are not backed by gold or other precious metals, what gives a $20 bill or a $100 chequing account entry its value? A reasonably complete answer to these questions involves three points.

1. ACCEPTABILITY Currency and demand deposits are money because they are accepted as money. By virtue of long-standing business practice, currency and demand deposits perform the basic function of money: they are acceptable as a medium of exchange. Suppose you swap a $20 bill for a shirt or blouse at a clothing store. Why does the merchant accept this piece of paper in exchange for that product? The merchant accepts paper money because he or she is confident that others will also accept it in exchange for goods and services.

2. LEGAL TENDER Our confidence in the acceptability of paper money is partly a matter of law; currency has been designated as **legal tender** by government. This means paper currency must be accepted in the payment of a debt or the creditor forfeits the privilege of charging interest and the right to sue the debtor for nonpayment. Thus, paper dollars are accepted because the government says they are money. The paper money in our economy is **fiat money**; it is money because the government says it is, not because it can be redeemed as precious metal.

BOX 13-3 IN THE MEDIA

ANGOLA'S REAL CURRENCY IS BEER

LUANDA, ANGOLA — Forget about the gold standard and welcome to Angola, where everyone has a little something going on the side and where monetary stability, such as it is, comes packed under pressure in a can — a beer can.

"Beer is the national currency here," said a Portuguese teacher working in Luanda.

As they earnestly seek a more solid footing for the world's wobbly monetary system, economists could perhaps do worse than to take a careful look at the sturdy Angolan model, where the black-market price of a case of 24 cans of imported European beer stands unshaken at 28,000 Angolan kwanzas.

At the official rate of exchange, this works out to $931 — equivalent to a monthly salary for a mid-level government official — suggesting that beer is an unaffordable luxury for all but the most affluent Angolans.

In fact, however, almost nobody in Angola could survive by relying exclusively on his or her salary. Besides, the official rate of exchange carries very little weight in Angola. What carries weight is imported beer.

"Everything is more or less related to that," said an Argentine technician employed by the Angolan government. "For the past year, beer has stayed at about the same price."

Imported beer enters the economy by several means. European and U.S. petroleum companies with operations in Angola, for example, all run company stores where their employees can buy imported goods — including beer — for hard currency. And the Angolan government itself runs a huge duty-free retail emporium for diplomats and others with foreign currency.

Known as the Jumbo, the store sprawls near the inland edge of Luanda, filled with imported foods and consumer goods, including 10 brands of Scotch whiskey and seven kinds of imported beer.

It's the beer that catches the eye — the stacked cases of West German, Danish, and Belgian ales and lagers seem to stretch forever.

Sold at the official exchange rate, a case of 24 cans of beer here costs 395 kwanzas, or about $13. The lines at the Jumbo's 15 cash registers are dotted with people pushing shopping carts piled high with seven or eight cases.

Outside, the beer is promptly resold on the black market — called the "candongua" — for 28,000 kwanzas a case. It is then broken up and bartered or resold at 1,500 kwanzas a can.

Typically, foreign residents in Luanda pay their household staff in beer. An Angolan family can live, albeit frugally, on two cases a month, bartering or reselling the beer one can at a time.

This eccentric monetary system has developed largely because of the almost complete collapse of Angola's centrally planned official economy.

That collapse is immediately apparent from a visit to almost any state-run store in Luanda — places where ordinary Angolans theoretically buy their monthly rations. The shelves are almost utterly bare — always.

In fact, of 10 basic rationed commodities provided by one such store in central Luanda, only two — beans and sugar — were ever in stock last month.

War and the remarkable inefficiencies of the Angolan productive apparatus are to blame for these shortages. But even when basic goods are produced, they are liable to be purloined and sold on the black market long before they reach the official retailer's shelves.

The reason is simple. Official prices in Angola are tied to the official exchange rate and reflect a wholly artificial world that has not existed in Angola since the early 1970s, when the Portuguese were in power and the official monetary unit was the escudo.

Black market prices, on the other hand, are tied to the value of beer, which means they are between 60 and 70 times higher than official prices. They represent the world in which most urban Angolans dwell, or at least those with access to money or beer.

At the Roque Santeró, the largest of Luanda's sprawling, circuslike black markets, they may pay 10,000 kwanzas — or about six cans of beer — for a liter of vegetable oil prominently stamped with the information that it was "furnished by the people of the United States of America," who presumably did not expect it to be sold for profit.

Products shipped as international aid often end up being sold in this manner. In fact, most of the goods for sale at the condonguas probably have been pilfered from somewhere.

Angolans refer to such theft as "*fazer desvio*" — making detours — and it is the most common means by which people supplement their low official incomes, enabling them to live on the beer economy.

This heady economic activity — quietly tolerated by the government — may explain why the government-run Jumbo is never out of stock.

"They run out of milk," the Argentine technician said. "But beer? They never run out of beer."

Oakland Ross, "Angolan Economy Tied to Beer," *Lincoln Sunday Journal-Star*, December 13, 1987.

The Story in Brief

In the mid-1980s, beer became one of the main mediums of exchange in Angola. Official prices were tied to the official exchange rate, which did not reflect the international market value of the kwanza, Angola's currency. Black market prices were unofficially tied to the value of beer, between 60 and 70 times higher than official prices.

The Economics Behind the Story

- In the mid-1980s, Angola's economy was centralized and highly regulated. Prices were set by government authorities, as was the official exchange rate. The centrally planned economy collapsed, leading to severe shortages.

- A sizable black market arose, in which prices better reflected supply and demand conditions. Moreover, the dominant medium of exchange became beer since prices and wage in kwanzas, the official currency, were completely divorced from free market realities. For example, a mid-level government official earned enough to buy one case of beer in a month, but a family needed at least two cases of beer per month to live frugally!

- Market participants turned to a medium of exchange — beer — that better reflected relative scarcities of goods and services in the economy.

- What difficulties can a country expect to encounter using beer as money?

3. RELATIVE SCARCITY The value of money, like the economic value of anything else, is a supply and demand phenomenon. Money derives its value from its scarcity relative to its utility (want-satisfying power). The utility of money lies in its unique capacity to be exchanged for goods and services, now or in the future. Thus, demand for money comes from people's desire to buy goods and services. The supply of money is regulated by the Bank of Canada. As will be discussed in Chapter 15, the value of our money will depend critically on the Bank of Canada supply of money in relation to demand. The latter is determined by the total dollar volume of transactions in any specific time period and the amount of money individuals want to hold for possible future transactions.

MONEY AND PRICES

The real value or purchasing power of money is the amount of goods and services a unit of money will buy. When money rapidly loses its purchasing power, it quickly loses its role as money.

VALUE OF THE DOLLAR The amount a dollar will buy varies inversely with the price level; *a reciprocal relationship exists between the general price level and the value of the dollar*. Figure 13-1 shows this inverse relationship. When the consumer price index or "cost-of-living" index goes up, the purchasing power of the dollar goes down, and vice versa. Higher prices lower the value of the dollar because more dollars will be needed to buy a particular amount of goods and services.

Lower prices increase the purchasing power of the dollar. If the price level doubles, the value of the dollar will decline by one-half, or 50%. If the price level falls by one-half, or 50%, the purchasing power of the dollar will double.

If we let P equal the price level expressed as an index number and D equal the value of the dollar, then the reciprocal relationship between them is

$$D = \frac{1}{P}$$

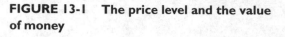

FIGURE 13-1 **The price level and the value of money**

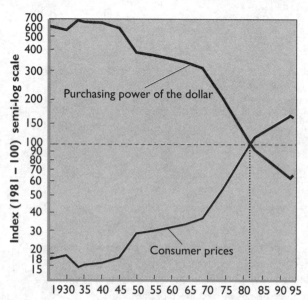

A reciprocal or inverse relationship exists between the general price level and the purchasing power of the dollar. (This figure is called a "ratio" or "semi-log" chart, because equal vertical distances measure equal percentage changes rather than equal absolute changes.)

If the price level P equals 1.00, then the value of the dollar D is 1.00. But, if P rises from 1.00 to 1.20, D will be .833, meaning a 20% increase in the price level will reduce the value of the dollar by 16.67%. You should check your understanding of this reciprocal relationship by determining the value of D and its percentage rise when P falls by 20% to .80. (Key Question 7)

INFLATION AND ACCEPTABILITY   There are situations in which a nation's currency can become worthless and unacceptable in exchange. These are circumstances where government issues so many pieces of paper currency that the value of each of these units of money is almost totally undermined. The infamous post-World War I inflation in Germany is an example. In December of 1919 there were about 50 billion marks in circulation. Four years later this figure had expanded to 496,585,345,900 billion marks! The result? The

German mark in 1923 was worth an infinitesimal fraction of its 1919 value.[2]

How might inflation and the accompanying decreases in the value of a nation's currency affect the acceptability of paper currency as money? Households and businesses will accept paper currency as a medium of exchange so long as they know they can spend it without any noticeable loss in its purchasing power. But, with spiralling inflation, this is not the case. Runaway inflation, such as in Germany in the early 1920s and in several Latin American nations in the 1980s, may significantly depreciate the value of money between the time of its receipt and its expenditure. Money will be "hot" money. It is as though the government were constantly taxing away the purchasing power of its currency. Rapid depreciation of the value of a currency may cause it to cease functioning as a medium of exchange. Businesses and households may refuse to accept paper money in exchange fearing a large loss in its value while it is in their possession. Without an acceptable domestically provided medium of exchange, the economy may try to substitute a more stable currency from another nation. Example: Many transactions in Russia and South America now occur in American dollars rather than highly unstable rubles or pesos. At the extreme, the economy may simply revert to inefficient barter.

Similarly, people will use money as a store of value so long as there is no sizable deterioration in the value of those stored dollars because of inflation. And the economy can effectively employ the monetary unit as a measure of value only when its purchasing power is relatively stable. A yardstick of value subject to drastic shrinkage no longer permits buyers and sellers to establish the terms of trade clearly. When the value of the dollar is declining rapidly, sellers will not know what to charge and buyers will not know what to pay for various goods and services.

MAINTAINING MONEY'S VALUE

What "backs" paper money is the government's ability to keep the value of money reasonably stable. Stability entails (1) appropriate fiscal policy, as explained in Chapter 12 and (2) intelligent

[2] Frank G. Graham, *Exchange, Prices and Production in Hyperinflation Germany*, 1920-1923 (Princeton, N.J.: Princeton University Press, 1930), p. 13.

management or regulation of the money supply, as will be explained in Chapter 15. Businesses and households accept paper money in exchange for goods and services so long as they expect it to command a roughly equivalent amount of goods and services when they spend it. In our economy a blending of legislation, government policy, and social practice inhibits imprudent expansion of the money supply that might seriously jeopardize money's value in exchange.

What we have said with respect to paper currency also applies to chequing account money — the debt of chartered banks and other depository institutions. Your chequing account of $200 means your bank is indebted to you for that number of dollars. You can collect this debt in one of two ways. You can go to the bank and demand paper currency for your chequable deposit; this amounts to changing the debts you hold from the debts of a bank to government-issued debts. Or, and this is more likely, you can "collect" the debt the bank or savings institution owes you by transferring this claim by cheque to someone else.

For example, if you buy a $200 coat from a store, you can pay for it by writing a cheque, which transfers your bank's indebtedness from you to the store. Your bank now owes the store the $200 it previously owed to you. The store accepts this transfer of indebtedness (the cheque) as a medium of exchange because it can convert it into currency on demand or can transfer the debt to others in making purchases of its choice. Thus, cheques, as means of transferring the debts of banks, are acceptable as money because banks will honour these claims.

The ability of chartered banks to honour claims against them depends on their not creating too many of these claims. We will see that a decentralized system of private, profit-seeking banks does not contain sufficient safeguards against the creation of too much cheque money. Thus, the banking and financial system has substantial centralization and governmental control to guard against the imprudent creation of chequable deposits.

Caution: This does not mean that in practice the monetary authorities have always judiciously controlled the supplies of currency and chequable-deposit money to achieve economic stability. Indeed, many economists allege that most of the inflationary woes we have encountered in the past are the consequence of imprudent increases in the money supply.

QUICK REVIEW 13-2

1. In Canada and other advance economies, all money is essentially issued by the government or is the debts of chartered banks.

2. These instruments efficiently perform the functions of money so long as their value, or purchasing power, is relatively stable.

3. The value of money does not come from carefully defined quantities of precious metals (as in the past), but rather in the amount of goods and services money will purchase in the marketplace.

4. Government's responsibility in stabilizing the value of the monetary unit involves (1) appropriate fiscal policies, and (2) effective control over the supply of money.

THE CANADIAN BANKING SYSTEM

The main component of the money supply — demand deposits — is created by chartered banks, and the Bank of Canada-created money — coins and paper currency — comes into circulation through the chartered banks. We now take a look at the framework of the Canadian banking system.

Under the Constitution Act, money and banking are federal responsibilities. Under the Bank Act, each bank is incorporated under a separate Act of Parliament and granted a charter. Thus our commercial banks are called **chartered banks**.

In 1867, there were twenty-eight chartered banks; this number grew in the following years to forty-one, before failures and mergers brought the number to eight in the 1960s. The late 1960s and 1970s brought the formation of new banks, and after six more amalgamations and two failures, by 1994 there were eight domestically owned banks. With the 1980 Bank Act revisions, foreign banks were allowed to establish Canadian subsidiaries, and there are now 55 foreign-owned banks.

The size of the Canadian-owned banks varies widely, from the large Royal Bank of Canada to the relatively small Canadian Western Bank.

All the foreign-owned banks are destined to remain small: foreign bank loans *in total* may not exceed 16% of the total domestic assets of the Canadian-owned banks. Thus entry of the foreign banks has had little effect on competition.

The largest of the Canadian chartered banks control the lion's share of banking activity. About 90% of total banking assets and deposits and more than 75% of payments volume are accounted for by the big five chartered banks: the Royal Bank, the Bank of Montreal, the Bank of Nova Scotia, the Toronto-Dominion Bank, and the Canadian Imperial Bank of Commerce. This constitutes a concentrated banking system compared to the United States, where such coverage would require more than 3000 institutions.

Table 13-2 sets out the balance sheet of the Canadian chartered banks. Its reserves are only a small percentage of deposits. As will be discussed in the next chapter, our banking system is a *fractional reserve system* — chartered banks loan out most of their deposit, keeping only a small percentage to meet everyday cash withdrawals. If depositors in the chartered banks were to come all at once to withdraw their money, there would not be enough cash reserves to meet their requests. In such an unlikely event, chartered banks borrow from the Bank of Canada, the bankers' bank.

PROFIT MAXIMIZING

Chartered banks have shareholders who seek a competitive return on their investments. Thus, the primary goal of chartered banks is to try to maximize profits. They loan out as much of their deposits that is prudently possible in order to increase profits. Those funds that cannot be safely loaned out are used to buy Government of Canada securities. The rate charged by banks on loans to their best corporate customers is referred to as the **prime rate**.

FINANCIAL INTERMEDIARIES

Although the present analysis focuses on chartered banks, the banking system is supplemented by other **financial intermediaries**. These include trust companies, loan companies, credit unions, and *caisses populaires* — savings institutions — that accept the funds of small savers and make them available to investors, by extending mortgage loans or by purchasing marketable securities. Insurance companies accept huge volumes of savings in the form of premiums on insurance policies and annuities and use these funds to buy a variety of private, corporate, and government securities.

The Canadian financial system is presently undergoing restructuring aimed at permitting more competition between the former "Four Pillars": the banking, insurance, trust, and securities industries.

Chartered banks and savings institutions have two basic functions: they hold the money deposits of businesses and households; and they make loans to the public in an effort to make profits. We will see in Chapter 15 that in doing so the intermediaries increase the economy's supply of money.

CHEQUE CLEARING

As previously noted, a cheque is a written order the drawer may use to make a purchase or pay a debt. A cheque is collected, or "cleared," when one or more banks or near-banks negotiates a transfer of part of the drawer's chequing account to the chequing account of the recipient of the cheque. If Jones and Smith have chequing accounts in the same bank and Jones gives Smith a $10 cheque, Smith can collect this cheque by taking it to the bank, where his

TABLE 13-2   The balance sheet of Canadian chartered banks, December 31, 1994 (*billions of dollars*)

Assets		Liabilities	
Reserves (currency and deposits with Bank of Canada)	5.0	Demand deposits	37.9
Loans (determined in Canadian dollars)	393.0	Savings deposits	242.4
Government of Canada securities	36.0	Time deposits	90.9
Foreign-currency assets	268.3	Foreign-currency liabilities	289.4
Other assets	138.7	Other liabilities	180.4
Total	841.0	Total	841.0

Source: *Bank of Canada Review*, Summer, 1995.

account will be increased by $10 and Jones's reduced by $10. In many cases, however, the drawer and the receiver of a cheque will be located in different towns or provinces and more likely than not, in different banks. Under federal law the **Canadian Payments Association** was set up in 1982 to take over the inter-bank cheque clearing system, which had been run by the Canadian Bankers' Association. The mechanics of cheque collecting, and its effect on the financial position of chartered banks, will be outlined in the next chapter.

GLOBALIZATION   The world's financial markets have become increasingly integrated. Major Canadian financial institutions have off-shore operations and foreign financial institutions have operations in Canada. Moreover, investment companies now offer a variety of international stock and bond funds. Financial capital increasingly flows globally in search of the highest risk-adjusted returns.

We must take care not to overstate this extent of international financial integration, however. Studies show that the bulk of investment in the major nations still is financed via domestic saving in those countries. But there is no doubt that money and banking have increasingly become a global activity.

Global Perspective 13-1 lists the world's largest commercial banks. The Royal Bank of Canada ranks as the forty-seventh largest bank in the world, as measured by the amount of financial capital.

GLOBAL PERSPECTIVE 13-1

The world's largest commercial banks (billions of dollars of financial capital)

Japanese firms dominate the list of the world's largest banks, as measured by their financial capital. Royal Bank, Canada's largest chartered bank, ranks as the forty-seventh largest bank in the world.

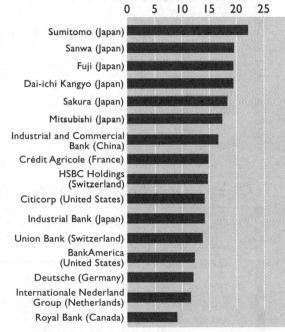

Source: *The Banker*, as reported in *The Economist*, July 23, 1994, p. 103.

CHAPTER SUMMARY

1. Anything that functions as **a** a medium of exchange, **b** a measure of value, and **c** a store of value is money.

2. Money is generally defined as demand deposits plus currency (coins and paper money) in circulation (M1). Demand deposits, the largest component of the money supply, are money because they can be spent by writing cheques against them. Savings, term, and notice deposits — some chequable and some not — are also money and are added to more broadly defined monetary aggregates (M2, M3, and M2+). In our analysis we concentrate on M1 since its components are immediately spendable.

3. Money, which either is issued by the Bank of Canada or is the debts of the chartered banks, has value because of the goods and services it will command in the market. Maintaining the purchasing power of money depends on the effectiveness with which the Bank of Canada manages the money supply.

4. The Canadian banking system is composed of **a** the Bank of Canada and **b** eight Canadian-owned and fifty-five foreign-owned chartered banks. The chartered banks of the economy accept money deposits and make loans. In lending, chartered banks create demand deposits and are therefore money-creating institutions.

TERMS AND CONCEPTS

Bank of Canada notes (p. 279)
barter (p. 278)
Canadian Payments Association (p. 289)
chartered banks (p. 287)
credit unions (p. 280)
demand deposits (p. 279)
fiat money (p. 283)
financial intermediaries (p. 288)
intrinsic value (p. 279)
legal tender (p. 283)

M1, M2, M3, and M2+ (pp. 279-281)
measure of value (p. 278)
medium of exchange (p. 278)
near-monies (p. 280)
nonchequable savings account (p. 281)
prime rate (p. 288)
store of value (p. 278)
term deposits (p. 281)
token money (p. 279)

QUESTIONS AND STUDY SUGGESTIONS

1. Describe how rapid inflation can undermine money's ability to perform its three basic functions.

2. What are the disadvantages of commodity money? What are the advantages of a. paper money and b. cheque money compared with commodity money?

3. "Money is only a bit of paper or a bit of metal that gives its owner a lawful claim to so much bread or beer or diamonds or motorcars or what not. We cannot eat money, nor drink money, nor wear money. it is the goods that money can buy that are being divided up when money is divided up."[3] Evaluate and explain.

4. Fully evaluate and explain the following statements:

    a. "The invention of money is one of the great achievements of the human race, for without it the enrichment that comes from broadening trade would have been impossible."

    b. "Money is whatever society says it is."

    c. "When prices of everything are going up, it is not because everything is worth more, but because the dollar is worth less."

    d. "The difficult questions concerning paper [money] are ... not about its economy, convenience or ready circulation, but about the amount of the paper which can be wisely issued or created, and the possibilities of violent convulsions when it gets beyond bounds."[4]

---

[3] George Bernard Shaw, *The Intelligent Woman's Guide to Socialism and Capitalism* (New York: Brentano's, Inc., 1928), p. 9. Used by permission of the Public Trustee and the Society of Authors.

[4] F.W. Taussig, *Principles of Economics*, 4th ed. (New York: The Macmillan Company, 1946), pp. 247-248.

e. "In most modern industrial economies of the world the debts of government and of commercial banks are used as money."

5. *Key Question* *What items constitute the M1 money supply? What is the most important component of the M1 money supply? Why is the face value of a coin greater than its intrinsic value? Distinguish between M1, M2, M3, and M2+. What are near-monies? Of what significance are they? What arguments can you make for including term and notice deposits in a definition of money?*

6. What "backs" the money supply in Canada? What determines the value of money? Who is responsible for maintaining the value of money? Why is it important to be able to alter the money supply? What is meant by a. "sound money" and b. a "52¢ dollar"?

7. *Key Question* *Suppose the price level and the value of the dollar in year 1 are 1.0 and $1.00, respectively. If the price level rises to 1.25 in year 2, what is the new value of the dollar? If instead the price level had fallen to .50, what would have been the value of the dollar? What generalization can you draw from your answers?*

8. What are the two basic functions of our chartered banks? How do chartered banks differ from other financial intermediaries?

9. (Applying the Theory) Over the years, the Federal Reserve Banks in the United States have printed about $235 billion more in American dollars than American households, businesses, and financial institutions now hold. Where is this "missing" money? Why is it there?

CHAPTER 14

HOW BANKS CREATE MONEY

 e are all fascinated by large sums of currency. Nevertheless, we use the demand (or chequable) deposits of chartered banks, trust companies, and credit unions, not currency, for most transactions. The amount of these deposits far exceeds the amount of currency banks hold. Who creates these extra demand deposits? Loan officers at chartered banks! Their tools? Computers and computer printers. Sounds like something "The Fifth Estate" or a Parliamentary committee should investigate. But, banking authorities are well aware that banks create demand deposit money. In fact, the Bank of Canada *relies* on banks to create most of the nation's money supply.

Because the bulk of demand deposits are deposits of chartered banks, this chapter will explain how they can *create* demand deposit money. We explain and compare the money-creating abilities of (1) a *single* chartered bank that is part of a multi-bank system, and (2) the chartered banking *system* as a whole. Keep in mind throughout our discussion that near-banks also provide demand deposits. Therefore, when we say "chartered bank" we also mean the other "depository institutions."

BOX 14-1 THE BIG PICTURE

After reading Chapter 13, you now know more about the nature of money and the financial system, particularly the banking system, in Canada. The main question addressed in this chapter is: How does the Bank of Canada "create" new money to accommodate the need of a growing economy? You may have thought that "creating" money is the simple act of printing paper money and stamping coins. The printing of money and stamping coins actually comes after the chartered banking system creates money out of "thin air." If money creation began by printing money, how would the authorities know to whom to distribute it?

As you read this chapter, keep the following points in mind:

- The creation of money begins through the chartered banking system's ability to lend out more than it has on deposit — fractionally backed reserves. Households and firms borrow money from the banking system as their need arises. To pay these loans back to chartered banks, households and firms work at producing goods and services and earn the "money" to pay back the loans.
- For every new deposit received, a chartered bank will keep part of it as vault cash and lend out the rest. It is through lending (or borrowing by households and firms) that money is created.
- The process of money creation works in reverse: if the banking system loses deposits (reserves), money is "destroyed."
- Chartered banks are profit-maximizing firms. It is the pursuit of profit that leads them to lend out money; they charge a higher interest rate on loans than they pay out on their deposits.
- Distinguish between a single chartered bank and the chartered banks as a group.

THE BALANCE SHEET OF A CHARTERED BANK

An understanding of the basic items on a bank's balance sheet, and how various transactions change these items, will give us the tools for analyzing the workings of our monetary and banking systems.

A **balance sheet** is a statement of assets and claims that summarizes the financial position of a firm — in this case a chartered bank — at some point in time. Every balance sheet must balance because each and every known *asset* will be claimed by someone. The claims shown on a balance sheet are divided into two groups: the claims of the owners of a firm against the firm's assets, called *net worth*, and the claims of nonowners, called *liabilities*. Thus, a balance sheet balances because:

Assets = liabilities + net worth

A balance-sheet approach to our study of the money-creating ability of chartered banks is invaluable in two respects.

1. A bank's balance sheet provides us with a convenient point of reference from which we can introduce new terms and concepts in an orderly manner.
2. The use of balance sheets allows us to quantify certain concepts and relationships that would defy comprehension if discussed in verbal terms alone.

PROLOGUE: THE GOLDSMITHS

Using balance sheets, let's see how a **fractional reserve system of banking** operates. The characteristics and working of such a system can be understood by considering a bit of stylized economic history.

When the ancients began to use gold in making transactions, it became apparent that it was both unsafe and inconvenient for consumers and merchants to carry gold and have it weighed and assessed for purity every time a transaction was negotiated. It therefore became commonplace to deposit one's gold with goldsmiths whose vaults or strong-rooms could be used for a fee. On receiving a gold deposit, the goldsmith issued a receipt — an IOU — to the depositor. Soon goods were traded for the goldsmith's receipts, and the receipts became the first kind of paper money.

At this point the goldsmiths — embryonic bankers — used a 100% reserve system; *their circulating paper money receipts, or IOUs, were fully backed by gold*. But given the public's acceptance of the goldsmiths' IOUs as paper money, the goldsmiths became aware that the gold they stored was rarely redeemed. Usually, the amount of gold deposited in any week or month was likely to exceed the amount of gold withdrawn.

Then some adroit goldsmith hit on the idea that paper money could be issued *in excess* of the amount of gold held. Goldsmiths would put this additional paper money — redeemable in gold — into circulation by making interest-earning loans to merchants, producers, and consumers. Borrowers were willing to accept loans in this form because gold receipts were accepted as a medium of exchange.

This was the beginning of the *fractional reserve system* of banking. Fractional reserve banking — the system we have today — has two significant characteristics.

1. Money Creation and Reserves Banks in such a system can *create money*. When our goldsmith made loans by giving borrowers paper money not fully backed by gold reserves, money was being created. The quantity of such money the goldsmith could create would depend on the amount of gold reserves deemed prudent to keep on hand. The smaller the amount of reserves, the larger the amount of paper money the goldsmith could create. For example, if our goldsmith made loans equal to the amount of gold stored, the total value of paper money in circulation would be twice the value of gold. Gold reserves would be 50% of outstanding paper money. If the goldsmith made loans equal to twice the amount of gold stored, the total value of paper money would be three times the value of gold, and gold reserves would be 33% ($1/3$) of outstanding paper money.

Although gold is no longer used to "back" our money supply, bank lending (money creation) today is — as with the goldsmiths — constrained by the amount of cash reserves banks feel obligated to keep.

2. Bank Panics and Regulation Banks that operate on the basis of fractional reserves are vulnerable to bank "panics" or "runs." Our goldsmith could not convert all that paper money into gold in the event all the holders of that paper money appeared at the same time to redeem gold. In fact, many European and American banks were once ruined by this unfortunate circumstance. But a bank panic is highly unlikely *if* the banker's reserve and lending policies are prudent. Indeed, a basic reason why banking systems are highly regulated industries is to prevent bank runs. (See Box 14-2.) This is also the reason Canada has a system of deposit insurance.

A SINGLE CHARTERED BANK

We now explore how money can be created by a single bank that is part of a multibank banking system. What accounts make up a chartered bank's balance sheet? How does a single chartered bank create money? If it can create money, can it destroy it? What factors govern how a bank creates money?

FORMATION OF A CHARTERED BANK

To answer these questions we must understand what's on a chartered bank's balance sheet, and how certain transactions affect it. We start with the organization of a local chartered bank.

Transaction 1: The Birth of a Bank Suppose some citizens of Vancouver decide Canada in general, and their province in particular, is in need of a new chartered bank. Assuming they are able to get the Parliament of Canada to pass an Act granting a charter for their bank, they then sell, say, $250,000 worth of capital stock (equity shares) to buyers, both in and out of the province. The Bank of Vancouver now exists. How does the bank's balance statement appear at its birth?

The bank now has $250,000 in cash on hand and $250,000 worth of capital stock outstanding. The cash is an asset to the bank. Cash held by a bank is sometimes dubbed **vault cash** or *till money*. The outstanding shares of stock constitute an equal amount of claims the owners of the stock have against the bank's assets. The bank's balance sheet reads:

BOX 14-2 APPLYING THE THEORY

THE BANK PANICS OF 1930-1933

A series of bank panics in 1930-1933 in the U.S.A. resulted in a multiple contraction of the money supply.

In the early months of the Great Depression, several financially weak banks became insolvent in the United States. As word spread that customers of these banks had lost their uninsured deposits, a general concern arose that something similar could happen at other banks. Depositors therefore began to withdraw funds — "cash out" their accounts — at local banks, most of which had been financially healthy. In economic terminology, the initial failures of weak banks created negative externalities or spillover costs affecting healthy banks. More than 9000 banks failed within three years.

The massive conversion of chequable deposits to currency during the U.S. banking crisis of 1930-1933 reduced the nation's money supply. The outflow of currency from banks meant the loss of bank reserves and a multiple decline of loans and chequable deposits. Also, banks "scrambled for liquidity" to meet anticipated further withdrawals by calling in loans and selling government securities to the public. Both actions enabled banks to increase their excess reserves — reserves *not* lent out. The lost deposits (reserves) and the scramble for liquidity collapsed the money supply. The 1930-1933 period also saw a precipitous drop in the Canadian money supply, but fortunately no bank failures.

In 1933 U.S. President Franklin Roosevelt ended the bank panics by declaring a "national bank holiday," which closed all banks for a week and resulted in the federally insured deposit program, later also implemented in

Canada. Meanwhile, the nation's money supply had plummeted by some 25%, contributing to the worst and longest depression in U.S. history. The steep decline in the Canadian money supply also contributed to the severity of the depression in this country.

Today, a multiple contraction of the money supply of the 1930-1933 magnitude is unthinkable. Deposit insurance has kept individual bank failures from becoming general bank panics. For example, the failures of two Canadian-owned chartered banks in 1985 had no significant repercussion on the rest of the banking sector. Also, while the Federal Reserve stood idly by during the American bank panics of 1930-1933, today the U.S. central bank would take immediate actions (as would any central bank) to maintain the banking system's reserves and the nation's money supply.

BIRTH OF A BANK

BALANCE SHEET 1: BANK OF VANCOUVER

Assets		Liabilities and net worth	
Cash	$250,000	Capital stock	$250,000

TRANSACTION 2: BECOMING A GOING CONCERN   The first step for the new bank will be

to acquire property and equipment. The bank purchases buildings for $220,000 and $20,000 of office equipment. This transaction changes the composition of the bank's assets. The bank now has $240,000 less in cash and $240,000 of new property assets. Using colour type and an asterisk (*) to denote those accounts affected by each transaction, we find that the bank's balance sheet at the conclusion of Transaction 2 appears as follows:

ACQUIRING PROPERTY AND EQUIPMENT

BALANCE SHEET 2: BANK OF VANCOUVER

Assets		Liabilities and net worth	
Cash*	$10,000	Capital stock	$250,000
Property*	240,000		

TRANSACTION 3: ACCEPTING DEPOSITS

Chartered banks have two basic functions: to accept deposits of money and to make loans. Now that our bank is in operation, suppose that the citizens and businesses of Vancouver decide to deposit $100,000 in the Bank of Vancouver. What happens to the bank's balance sheet?

The bank receives cash, an asset to the bank. Suppose this money is placed in the bank as demand deposits (chequing accounts). These newly created demand deposits are claims that depositors have against the assets of the Bank of Vancouver. Thus the depositing of money in the bank creates a new liability account — demand deposits. The bank's balance sheet now looks like this:

ACCEPTING DEPOSITS

BALANCE SHEET 3: BANK OF VANCOUVER

Assets		Liabilities and net worth	
Cash*	$110,000	Demand deposits*	$100,000
Property	240,000	Capital stock	250,000

Although there is no direct change in the total supply of money, a change in the composition of the economy's money supply has occurred as a result of Transaction 3. Demand deposits have *increased* by $100,000 and currency in circulation has *decreased* by $100,000. Currency held by a bank is *not* part of the economy's money supply.

DEPOSITS IN THE BANK OF CANADA The Bank of Vancouver has to have sufficient **cash reserves** to keep a minimum ratio between those assets and its deposit liabilities. These reserves are partly vault cash to serve the daily cash needs of the chartered bank's customers, and partly deposits in the Bank of Canada. Prior to 1995 chartered banks were required by law to keep a specified percentage of their deposit liabilities as reserves —

referred to as *required reserves*. In 1991 changes to the Bank Act did away with required reserves so that chartered banks keep their reserves mostly as vault cash, with just enough deposited in the Bank of Canada for cheque clearing (see Transaction 4).[1] For simplicity, from now on we will refer only to vault cash.

Since banks will still need to keep vault (till) cash to meet withdrawals in excess of deposits from day to day, this chapter's analysis will remain relevant even if reserves are no longer *required*. The "specified percentage" of deposit liabilities the chartered bank chooses to keep as vault cash can be referred to as the **desired reserve ratio**. The ratio can be calculated as follows:

$$\frac{\text{Reserve}}{\text{ratio}} = \frac{\text{chartered bank's desired reserves}}{\text{chartered bank's deposit liabilities}}$$

If the desired reserve ratio were 10%, our bank, having accepted $100,000 in deposits from the public, would keep $10,000 as reserves to meet its daily cash needs.

There are two additional points to be made about reserves:

1. EXCESS RESERVES Some terminology: The amount by which the bank's **actual reserves** exceed its **desired reserves** is the bank's **excess reserves**. In this case,

Actual reserves	$110,000
Desired reserves	−10,000
Excess reserves	$100,000

To understand this, you should compute excess reserves for the bank's balance sheet as it stands at the end of Transaction 3 on the assumption that the desired reserve ratio is (a) 5%, (b) 20%, and (c) 50%.

Because the ability of a chartered bank to make loans depends on the existence of excess reserves, this concept is essential in seeing how money is created by the banking system.

---

[1] The Bank Act was changed in 1991, but the elimination of required reserves was spread over four years, to the end of 1994. One of the main reasons the Bank of Canada did away with required reserves was the chartered banks' complaint that these reserves paid no interest while the chartered banks had to pay interest to their depositors.

2. INFLUENCE   Excess reserves are a means by which the Bank of Canada can influence the lending ability of chartered banks. The next chapter will explain in detail how the Bank of Canada can implement certain policies that either increase or decrease chartered bank reserves and affect the ability of banks to grant credit. To the degree that these policies are successful in influencing the volume of chartered bank credit, the Bank of Canada can help the economy smooth out business fluctuations.

As we will see in a moment, another function of reserves is to facilitate the collection or "clearing" of cheques. (**Key Question 2**)

TRANSACTION 4: A CHEQUE IS DRAWN AGAINST THE BANK

Suppose that James Bradshaw, a Vancouver lumberyard owner who deposited a substantial portion of the $100,000 in deposits that the Bank of Vancouver received in Transaction 3, purchases $10,000 worth of lumber from the Ajax Forest Products Company of Chilliwack. Bradshaw pays for this lumber by writing a $10,000 cheque against his deposit in the Bank of Vancouver. We want to determine (1) how this cheque is collected or cleared, and (2) the effect that the collection of the cheque has on the balance sheets of the banks involved in the transaction.

To learn this, we must consider the Bank of Vancouver, the Chilliwack bank (a branch, say, of the Bank of Manitoba), the Vancouver clearing house of the Canadian Payments Association, and, finally, the Bank of Canada office in Vancouver. To keep our illustration simple, we deal only with the changes that occur in those specific accounts affected by this transaction.

(**a**) Mr. Bradshaw gives his $10,000 cheque, drawn against the Bank of Vancouver, to the Ajax Company. Ajax deposits the cheque in its account with the Bank of Manitoba branch in Chilliwack, which increases the Ajax Company's deposit by $10,000 when it deposits the cheque. The Ajax Company is now paid off. Bradshaw receives his lumber.

(**b**) Now the Bank of Manitoba in Chilliwack has Bradshaw's cheque. This cheque is a claim against the assets of the Bank of Vancouver. The Bank of Manitoba collects this claim by sending the cheque to its main Vancouver branch (there being as yet no branch of the Bank of Vancouver in Chilliwack). The Vancouver branch of the Bank of Manitoba takes the cheque to the Vancouver clearing house of the Canadian Payments Association

(CPA), which is operated by the chartered banks and the near-banks. At the clearing house, representatives of the financial institution meet every banking day. They bring with them all the cheques drawn on each other that have been presented to them for payment. Assuming, for simplicity, that on this day the only transaction involving the Banks of Vancouver and Manitoba is Mr. Bradshaw's cheque, the Bank of Canada will, on being informed by the clearing house, *reduce* the Bank of Vancouver's cash deposit by $10,000 and *increase* that of the Bank of Manitoba by the same amount.

(**c**) Finally, the cleared cheque is sent back to the Bank of Vancouver's main branch, which learns for the first time that one of its depositors has drawn a cheque for $10,000 against his deposit. Accordingly, the Bank of Vancouver reduces Mr. Bradshaw's deposit by $10,000 and recognizes that the collection of this cheque has reduced its cash deposit at the Bank of Canada by $10,000.

Note that the balance statements of all three banks will balance. The Bank of Vancouver will have reduced both its assets and its liabilities by $10,000. The Bank of Manitoba will have $10,000 more in cash and in deposits. The ownership of deposits at the Bank of Canada will have changed, but total deposits will stay the same.

Whenever a cheque is drawn against a bank and deposited in another bank, collection of that cheque will reduce both cash and deposits by the bank on which the cheque is drawn. In our example, the Bank of Vancouver loses $10,000 in both reserves and deposits to the Bank of Manitoba. But there is no loss of cash or deposits for the banking system as a whole. What one bank loses another bank gains.

Bringing all the other assets and liabilities back into the picture, the Bank of Vancouver's balance sheet looks like this at the end of Transaction 4:

CLEARING A CHEQUE

BALANCE SHEET 4: BANK OF VANCOUVER

Assets		Liabilities and net worth	
Reserves*	$100,000	Demand deposits*	$90,000
Property	240,000	Capital stock	250,000

You should verify that with a 10% desired reserve ratio, the bank's *excess* reserves now stand at $91,000.

QUICK REVIEW 14-1

1. When a bank accepts deposits of cash, the composition of the money supply is changed, but the total supply of money is not directly altered.

2. Chartered banks keep reserves (cash) equal to a desired percentage of their own deposit liabilities.

3. The amount by which a bank's actual cash reserves exceed its desired reserves is called "excess reserves."

4. A bank that has a cheque drawn and collected against it will lose to the recipient bank both cash and deposits equal to the value of the cheque.

MONEY-CREATING TRANSACTIONS OF A CHARTERED BANK

The next two transactions are crucial, because they explain (1) how a chartered bank can create money by making loans, (2) how money is destroyed when loans are repaid, and (3) how banks create money by purchasing government bonds from the public.

TRANSACTION 5: GRANTING A LOAN

Suppose the Grisley Meat Packing Company of Vancouver decides to expand. Suppose, too, that the company needs exactly $91,000 — which, by coincidence, just happens to be equal to the Bank of Vancouver's excess reserves — to finance this project.

Grisley requests a loan for this amount from the Bank of Vancouver. Convinced of Grisley's ability to repay, the bank grants the loan. Grisley hands a promissory note — a high-class IOU — to the bank. Grisley wants the convenience and safety of paying its obligations by cheque. So, instead of receiving a bushel basket full of currency from the bank, Grisley will get a $91,000 increase in its demand deposit in the bank. The bank has acquired an interest-earning asset (the promissory note) and has created a deposit (a liability) to pay for this asset.

At the moment the loan is negotiated, the bank's position is shown by balance sheet 5.

A close examination of the bank's balance statement will reveal a startling fact: **When a bank makes loans, it creates money.** The president of Grisley went to the bank with something that is not money — her IOU — and walked out with something that *is* money — a demand deposit.

WHEN A LOAN IS NEGOTIATED

BALANCE SHEET 5A: BANK OF VANCOUVER

Assets		Liabilities and net worth	
Reserves	$100,000	Demand deposits*	$181,000
Loans*	91,000	Capital stock	250,000
Property	240,000		

When banks lend, they create demand deposits that *are* money. By extending credit, the Bank of Vancouver has "monetized" an IOU. Grisley and the bank have created and then swapped claims. The claim created by the bank and given to the Grisley Company is money; cheques drawn against a deposit are acceptable as a medium of exchange. It is through the extension of credit by chartered banks that the bulk of the money used in our economy is created.

Assume that Grisley awards a $91,000 contract to the Quickbuck Construction Company of Kamloops. Quickbuck completes the expansion job and is paid with a cheque for $91,000 drawn by Grisley against its demand deposit in the Bank of Vancouver. Quickbuck, having its headquarters in Kamloops, does not deposit this cheque back in the Bank of Vancouver but instead deposits it in a Kamloops branch of the Bank of Manitoba, which now has a $91,000 claim against the Bank of Vancouver. This cheque is collected in the manner described in Transaction 4. As a result, the Bank of Vancouver *loses* both reserves and deposits equal to the amount of the cheque; the Bank of Manitoba *acquires* $91,000 of reserves and deposits.

In summary, assuming a cheque is drawn by the borrower for the entire amount of the loan ($91,000) and given to a firm that deposits it in another bank, the Bank of Vancouver's balance sheet will read as follows *after the cheque has been cleared against it*:

AFTER A CHEQUE IS DRAWN ON THE LOAN

BALANCE SHEET 5B: BANK OF VANCOUVER

Assets		Liabilities and net worth	
Reserves*	$9,000	Demand deposits*	$90,000
Loans	91,000	Capital stock	250,000
Property	240,000		

After the cheque has been collected, the Bank of Vancouver is just barely meeting its desired reserve ratio of 10%. The bank has *no excess reserves*.

TRANSACTION 6: REPAYING A LOAN

If chartered banks create demand deposits — money — when they make loans, is money destroyed when the loans are repaid? Yes. Using Balance Sheet 6, we see what happens when the Grisley Company repays the $91,000 it borrowed.

To simplify, we will (1) suppose that the loan is repaid not in instalments but in one lump sum two years after the date of negotiation, and (2) ignore interest charges on the loan. Grisley will simply write a cheque for $91,000 against its deposit. As a result, the Bank of Vancouver's deposit liabilities decline by $91,000; Grisley has given up $91,000 worth of its claim against the bank's assets. In turn, the bank will surrender Grisley's IOU. The bank and the company have reswapped claims.

But the claim given up by Grisley is money; the claim it is repurchasing — its IOU — is not. The supply of money has therefore been reduced by $91,000; that amount of deposits has been destroyed, unaccompanied by any increase in the money supply elsewhere in the economy. This fact is shown in Balance Sheet 6, where we note that the Bank of Vancouver's loans return to zero and its cash has increased by $91,000. In short, the bank has reverted to Balance Sheet 4, the situation that existed before the Grisley loan was negotiated.

REPAYING THE LOAN
BALANCE SHEET 6: BANK OF VANCOUVER

Assets		Liabilities and net worth	
Reserves	$100,000	Demand deposits*	$90,000
Loans*	0	Capital stock	250,000
Property	240,000		

The decline in demand deposits increases the bank's holdings of excess reserves; this provides the basis for new loans to be made. **(Key Questions 4 and 8)**

TRANSACTION 7: BUYING GOVERNMENT SECURITIES

When a chartered bank buys government bonds from the public, the effect is substantially the same as lending. New money is created.

Assume that the Bank of Vancouver's balance sheet initially stands as it did at the end of Transaction 6. Now suppose that instead of making a $91,000 loan, the bank buys $91,000 of government securities from a securities dealer. The bank receives the interest-bearing bonds, which appear on its balance statement as the asset "Securities" and gives the dealer an increase in its deposit account. The bank's balance sheet would appear as follows:

BUYING GOVERNMENT SECURITIES
BALANCE SHEET 7: BANK OF VANCOUVER

Assets		Liabilities and net worth	
Reserves	$100,000	Demand deposits*	$181,000
Securities*	91,000	Capital stock	250,000
Property	240,000		

Demand deposits — that is, the supply of money — have been increased by a total of $91,000, as in Transaction 5. *Chartered bank bond purchases from the public increase the supply of money in the same way as does lending to the public.*

Finally, the selling of government bonds to the public by a chartered bank — like the repayment of a loan — will reduce the supply of money. The securities buyer will pay by cheque and both "Securities" and "Demand deposits" (the latter being money) will decline by the amount of the sale.

PROFITS AND LIQUIDITY

The asset items on a chartered bank's balance sheet reflect the banker's pursuit of two conflicting goals.

1. PROFITS One goal is profits. Chartered banks, like any other business, seek profits. This is why the bank makes loans and buys securities — the two major earning assets of chartered banks.

2. LIQUIDITY The other goal is safety. For a chartered bank, safety lies in liquidity — specifically, such liquid assets as cash. Banks must be on guard for depositors transforming their demand deposits into cash. Similarly, more cheques will be cleared against a bank than are cleared in its favour, causing a net outflow of cash. Bankers seek a proper balance between prudence and profits. The compromise is between earning assets and highly liquid assets.

QUICK REVIEW 14-2

1. Banks create money when they make loans; money vanishes when bank loans are repaid.

2. New money is created when banks buy government bonds from the public; money disappears when banks sell government bonds to the public.

3. Banks balance profitability and safety in determining their mix of earning assets and highly liquid assets.

THE BANKING SYSTEM: MULTIPLE-DEPOSIT EXPANSION

Thus far we have seen that a single bank in a banking system can lend one dollar for each dollar of excess reserves. The situation is different for chartered banks taken as a group. We will find that *the chartered banking system can lend — can create money — by a multiple of its excess reserves. This multiple lending is accomplished despite the fact that each bank in the system can only lend dollar for dollar with its excess reserves.* How do these seemingly paradoxical conclusions come about?

To do this we must keep our analysis uncluttered. Therefore, we will rely on three simplifying assumptions.

1. The desired reserve ratio for all chartered banks is 5%.
2. Initially all banks are meeting this 5% desired reserve ratio. No excess reserves exist; all banks are "loaned up" (or "loaned out").
3. If any bank can increase its loans as a result of acquiring excess reserves, an amount equal to these excess reserves will be loaned to one borrower, who will write a cheque for the entire amount of the loan and give it to someone else who deposits the cheque in another bank.

THE BANKING SYSTEM'S LENDING POTENTIAL

Suppose a junkyard owner finds a $100 bill while dismantling a car that has been on the lot for years. He deposits the $100 in Bank A, which adds the $100 to its reserves. Since we are recording only *changes* in the balance sheets of the various chartered banks, Bank A's balance sheet now appears as shown by the entries designated as (a_1):

MULTIPLE DEPOSIT EXPANSION PROCESS

BALANCE SHEET: CHARTERED BANK A

Assets		Liabilities and net worth	
Reserves	$+100 ($a_1$)	Demand deposits	$+100 ($a_1$)
	−95 (a_3)		+95 (a_2)
Loans	+95 (a_2)		−95 (a_3)

Bank A has acquired *excess reserves* of $95. Of the newly acquired $100 in reserves, 5%, or $5, is earmarked to offset the new $100 deposit and the remaining $95 is excess reserves that can be lent out. When a loan for this amount is negotiated, Bank A's loans will increase by $95, and the borrower will get a $95 deposit. We add these figures designated as (a_2) to Bank A's balance sheet.

But now we use our third assumption: the borrower draws a cheque for $95 — the entire amount of the loan — and gives it to someone who deposits it in another bank, Bank B. As we saw in Transaction 5, Bank A *loses* both reserves and deposits equal to the amount of the loan (a_3). The net result of the transaction is that Bank A's reserves now stands at $5 (= $100 − $95), loans at $95, and deposits at $100 (= $100 + $95 − $95). When the dust has settled, Bank A is just meeting its 5% desired reserve ratio.

Recalling Transaction 4, Bank B acquires both the reserves and the deposits that Bank A has lost. Bank B's balance sheet looks like this (b_1):

MULTIPLE DEPOSIT EXPANSION PROCESS

BALANCE SHEET: CHARTERED BANK B

Assets		Liabilities and net worth	
Reserves	$+95 ($b_1$)	Demand deposits	$+95 ($b_1$)
	−90.25 (b_3)		+90.25 (b_2)
Loans	+90.25 (b_2)		−90.25 (b_3)

When the cheque is drawn and cleared, Bank A *loses* $95 in reserves and deposits and Bank B *gains* $95 in reserves and deposits. But 5%, or $4.75, of Bank B's new reserves is kept as reserves against the new $95 in deposits. This means that Bank B has $90.25 (= $95 − $4.75) excess reserves. It can therefore lend $90.25 ($b_2$). When the borrower draws a cheque for the entire amount and deposits it in Bank C, the reserves and deposits of Bank B each fall by the $90.25 ($b_3$). As a result of these transactions, Bank B's reserves will now stand at $4.75 (= $95 – $90.25), loans at $90.25, and deposits at $95 (= $95 + $90.25 – $90.25). After all this, Bank B is just meeting its 5% desired reserve ratio.

We are off and running again. Bank C has acquired the $90.25 in reserves and deposits lost by Bank B. Its balance statement appears as follows (c_1):

MULTIPLE DEPOSIT EXPANSION PROCESS

BALANCE SHEET: CHARTERED BANK C

Assets		Liabilities and net worth	
Reserves	$+90.25 ($c_1$)	Demand deposits	$+90.25 ($c_1$)
	–85.74 (c_3)		+85.74 (c_2)
Loans	+85.74 (c_2)		–85.74 (c_3)

Exactly 5%, or $4.51, of this new reserve will be set aside, the remaining $85.74 being excess reserves. Thus, Bank C can lend a maximum of $85.74. Suppose it does ($c_2$). And suppose the borrower draws a cheque for the entire amount and gives it to someone who deposits it in another bank (c_3).

Bank D — the bank receiving the $85.74 in reserves and deposits — now notes these changes on its balance sheet (d_1):

MULTIPLE DEPOSIT EXPANSION PROCESS

BALANCE SHEET: CHARTERED BANK D

Assets		Liabilities and net worth	
Reserves	$+85.74 ($d_1$)	Demand deposits	$+85.74 ($d_1$)
	–81.45 (d_3)		+81.45 (d_2)
Loans	+81.45 (d_2)		–81.45 (d_3)

It can now lend $81.45 ($d_2$). The borrower draws a cheque for the full amount and deposits it in another bank (d_3).

Now, if we wanted to be particularly obnoxious, we could go ahead with this procedure by bringing banks E, F, G, H ... N into the picture. Instead, we suggest that you check through computations for banks E, F, and G, to ensure that you understand the procedure.

This analysis is summarized in Table 14-1. Data for banks E through N are supplied, so you can check your computations. Our conclusion is that on the basis of the $95 in excess reserves (acquired by the banking system when someone deposited the $100 of currency in Bank A), the entire *chartered banking system* is able to lend $1,900, the sum of the amounts in column (4). The banking system can lend by a multiple of 20 when the desired reserve ratio is 5%. Yet each single bank in the banking system is lending an amount equal only to its excess reserves. How do we explain this?

The answer to these seemingly conflicting conclusions is that the cash lost by a single bank is not lost to the banking system as a whole. The reserves lost by Bank A are acquired by Bank B. Those lost by B are gained by C. Bank C loses to D, D to E, E to F, and so forth.

THE MONEY MULTIPLIER

This *demand-deposit multiplier*, or **money multiplier**, is similar to the income multiplier of Chapter 10. The income multiplier occurs because the expenditures of one household are received as income by another; the deposit multiplier occurs because the reserves and deposits lost by one bank are received by another bank. And, just as the size of the income multiplier is determined by the reciprocal of the MPS (the leakage into saving that occurs at each round of spending) so the deposit multiplier m is the reciprocal of the desired reserve ratio R (the leakage into desired reserves that occurs at each step in the lending process). In short,

$$\text{Money multiplier} = \frac{1}{\text{desired reserve ratio}}$$

or, using symbols,

$$m = \frac{1}{R}$$

In this formula, m is the maximum number of new deposit dollars that can be created by a *single dollar* of excess reserves, given the value of R. We determine the maximum amount of new deposit money, D, that can be created by the banking system on the basis of any amount of excess reserves,

$$\text{Maximum deposit expansion} = \frac{\text{excess}}{\text{reserves}} \times \text{money multiplier}$$

or, more simply,

$$D = E \times m$$

TABLE 14-1 Expansion of the money supply by the chartered banking system

Bank	(1) Acquired reserves and deposits	(2) Desired reserves	(3) Excess reserves, or (1) − (2)	(4) Amount that the bank can lend; new money created = (3)
Bank A	$100.00 ($a_1$)	$5.00	$95.00	$ 95.00 (a_2)
Bank B	95.00 (a_3, b_1)	4.75	90.25	90.25 (b_2)
Bank C	90.25 (b_3, c_1)	4.51	85.74	85.74 (c_2)
Bank D	85.74 (c_3, d_1)	4.29	81.45	81.45 (d_2)
Bank E	81.45	4.07	77.38	77.38
Bank F	77.38	3.87	73.51	73.51
Bank G	73.51	3.68	69.83	69.83
Bank H	69.83	3.49	66.34	66.34
Bank I	66.34	3.32	63.02	63.02
Bank J	63.02	3.15	59.87	59.87
Bank K	59.87	2.99	56.88	56.88
Bank L	56.88	2.84	54.04	54.04
Bank M	54.04	2.71	51.33	51.33
Bank N	51.33	2.56	48.77	48.77
Other banks	975.36	48.77	926.59	926.59
Totals	$2000.00	$100.00	$1900.00	$1900.00

In our example of Table 14-1:

$$\$1900 = \$95 \times 20$$

DIAGRAMMATIC SUMMARY   Figure 14-1 depicts the final outcome from our example of a multiple-deposit expansion of the money supply. The initial deposit of $100 of currency into the bank (lower right box) creates an initial demand deposit of an equal amount (upper box). Given our assumption of a 5% desired reserve ratio, however, only $5 reserves are need to "back up" this $100 demand deposit. The excess reserves of $95 permit the creation of $1900 of new demand deposits via the making of loans, making the money multiplier 20. The $100 of new reserves thus supports a total supply of money of $2000, made up of the $100 of initial demand deposit plus $1900 of demand deposits created through lending. You might experiment with these teasers in testing your understanding of multiple credit expansion by the banking system:

1. Rework the analysis of Table 14-1 (at least three or four steps of it) on the assumption that the desired reserve ratio is 10%. What is the maximum amount of money the banking system could create upon acquiring $100 in new reserves and deposits? (No, the answer is not $950!)

2. Explain how a banking system that is loaned up and with a 5% desired reserve ratio will *reduce* its outstanding loans by $1900 as a result of a $100 cash withdrawal from a demand deposit that forces the bank to draw down its reserves by $100. (**Key Question 13**)

SOME MODIFICATIONS

There are complications that will make our simple money multiplier smaller.

OTHER LEAKAGES   Aside from the **leakage** of desired reserves, two other leakages of money from the chartered banks might occur, dampening the money-creating potential of the banking system.

1. **CURRENCY DRAINS**   A borrower may request that a part of his or her loan be paid in cash. Or the recipient of a cheque drawn by a borrower may present it at the bank to be redeemed partially or wholly in cash rather than added to the borrower's account. If

FIGURE 14-1   The outcome of the money expansion process

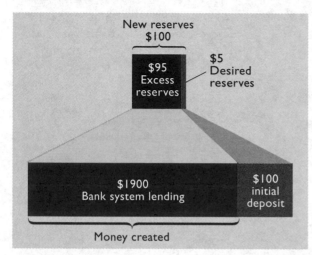

A deposit of $100 of currency into a chequing account creates an initial demand deposit of $100. If the desired reserve ratio is 5%, only $5 of reserves are needed to support the $100 demand deposit. The $5 of excess reserves allows the banking system to create $95 of demand deposits through making loans. The $100 of reserves supports a total of $2000 of money ($100 + $1900).

the person who borrowed the $95 from Bank A in our illustration asked for $15 of it in cash and the remaining $80 as a deposit, Bank B would receive only $80 in new reserves (of which only $76 would be excess) rather than $95 (of which $90.25 was excess). This decline in excess reserves reduces the lending potential of the banking system accordingly. If the first borrower had taken the entire $95 in cash and if this currency remained in circulation, the multiple expansion process would have stopped then and there. But the convenience and safety of deposits make this unlikely.

2. EXCESS RESERVES   Our analysis is based on the assumption that chartered banks are willing to hold a specific desired reserve ratio. To the extent that bankers hold excess reserves, the overall credit expansion potential of the banking system will be reduced. For example, suppose Bank A, on receiving $100 in new cash, decided to add $10, rather than $5, to its reserves. Then it would lend only $90, rather than $95, and the money multiplier would be diminished accordingly.

In fact, the amount of excess reserves that banks have held in recent years has been very small. The

explanation is simple: Excess reserves earn no interest income for a bank; loans and investments do. Our assumption that a bank will lend an amount equal to its excess reserves is reasonable and generally accurate.

QUICK REVIEW 14-3

1. Whereas a single bank in a multibank system can lend (create money) by an amount equal to its excess reserves, the banking system can lend (create money) by a multiple of its excess reserves.

2. The simple money multiplier is the reciprocal of the desired reserve ratio and indicates the multiple by which the banking system can expand the money supply for each dollar of excess reserves.

3. Currency drains and a desire by banks to hold excess reserves reduce the size of the simple money multiplier.

NEED FOR MONETARY CONTROL

Our illustration of the banking system's ability to create money rests on the assumption that chartered banks are willing to create money by lending and that households and businesses are willing to borrow. In reality the willingness of banks to lend on the basis of excess reserves varies cyclically, and here lies the rationale for governmental control of the money supply to promote economic stability.

In times of prosperity, banks expand credit to the maximum of their ability. Loans are interest-earning assets, and in good economic times there is little fear of borrowers' defaulting. But, as we will find in the next two chapters, the money supply has an effect on aggregate demand. By lending and thereby creating money to the maximum of their ability during prosperity, chartered banks may contribute to excessive aggregate demand and thus to an inflationary gap.

If a recession appears on the economic horizon, bankers may withdraw their invitations to borrow, seeking the safety of liquidity (excess reserves) even if it means sacrificing potential interest income.

We can conclude that profit-motivated bankers can be expected to vary the money supply so as to reinforce cyclical fluctuations. For this reason the Bank of Canada has at its disposal certain policy instruments designed to control the money supply in an anti-cyclical, rather than pro-cyclical, fashion. We turn to these policy tools in Chapter 15.

CHAPTER SUMMARY

1. The operation of a chartered bank can be understood through its balance sheet, wherein assets are equal to liabilities plus net worth.

2. Modern banking systems are based on fractional reserves.

3. Chartered banks keep reserves as vault cash and a small amount in the Bank of Canada for cheque-clearing purposes. This reserve is equal to a desired percentage of the chartered bank's deposit liabilities. Excess reserves are equal to actual reserves minus desired reserves.

4. Banks lose reserves and deposits when cheques are drawn against them.

5. Chartered banks create money — create demand deposits, or bank money — when they make loans. The creation of demand deposits by bank lending is the most important source of money in the Canadian economy. Money is destroyed when loans are repaid.

6. The ability of a single chartered bank to create money by lending depends on the size of its excess reserves. Generally speaking, a chartered bank lends only an amount equal to the amount of its excess reserves.

7. Rather than making loans, chartered banks may decide to use excess reserves to buy bonds from the public. In doing so, banks merely credit the demand-deposit accounts of the bond sellers, thus creating demand-deposit money. Money vanishes when banks sell bonds to the public because bond buyers must draw down their demand-deposit balances to pay for the bonds.

8. The chartered banking system as a whole can lend by a multiple of its excess reserves because the banking *system* cannot lose reserves, although individual banks can lose reserves to other banks in the system. The multiple by which the banking system could lend on the basis of each dollar of excess reserves is the reciprocal of the desired reserve ratio. This multiple credit expansion process is reversible.

9. The fact that profit-seeking banks would tend to alter the money supply in a pro-cyclical fashion underlies the need for the Bank of Canada to control the money supply.

TERMS AND CONCEPTS

actual, desired and excess cash reserves (p. 297)

balance sheet (p. 294)

cash reserves (p. 297)

desired reserve ratio (p. 297)

fractional reserve system of banking (p. 294)

leakage (p. 303)

money multiplier (p. 302)

vault cash (p. 295)

QUESTIONS AND STUDY SUGGESTIONS

1. Why must a balance sheet always balance? What are the major assets and claims on a chartered bank's balance sheet?

2. *Key Question* Why do chartered banks have reserves? What are excess reserves? How do you calculate the amount of excess reserves held by a bank? What is their significance?

3. "Whenever currency is deposited in a chartered bank, cash goes out of circulation and, as a result, the supply of money is reduced." Do you agree? Explain.

4. **Key Question**   *"When a chartered bank makes loans, it creates money; when loans are repaid, money is destroyed." Explain.*

5. Explain why a single chartered bank could lend an amount equal only to its excess reserves, but the chartered banking system could lend by a multiple of its excess reserves. Why is the multiple by which the banking system could lend equal to the reciprocal of its desired reserve ratio?

6. Assume that Jones deposits $500 in currency in the Bank of Vancouver. A half-hour later, Smith negotiates a loan for $750 at this bank. By how much and in what direction has the money supply changed? Explain.

7. Suppose the Bank of Newfoundland has excess reserves of $8000 and outstanding deposits of $150,000. If the desired reserve ratio is 10%, what is the size of the bank's actual reserves?

8. **Key Question**   *Suppose the Yukon Bank has the following simplified balance sheet. The desired reserve ratio is 6.25%.*

Assets		(1)	(2)	Liabilities and net worth		(1)	(2)
Reserves	$22,000	____	____	Deposits	$100,000	____	____
Securities	38,000	____	____				
Loans	40,000	____	____				

a. *What is the maximum amount of new loans this bank can make? Show in column 1 how the bank's balance sheet will appear after the bank has loaned this additional amount.*

b. *By how much has the supply of money changed? Explain.*

c. *How will the bank's balance sheet appear after cheques drawn for the entire amount of the new loans have been cleared against this bank? Show this new balance sheet in column 2.*

d. *Answer questions a, b, and c on the assumption that the desired reserve ratio is 10%.*

9. The Bank of Manitoba has reserves of $10,000 and deposits of $100,000. The desired reserve ratio is 10%. Households deposit $5000 in currency in the bank, which is added to reserves. How much excess reserves does the bank now have?

10. Suppose again that the Bank of Manitoba has reserves of $10,000 and deposits of $100,000. The desired reserve ratio is 10%. The bank now sells $5000 in securities to the Bank of Canada, receiving a $5000 increase in its deposit there in return. How much excess reserves does the bank now have? Why does your answer differ (yes, it does!) from the answer to question 9?

11. Suppose a chartered bank discovers its reserves will temporarily fall slightly short of those it desires to hold. How might it remedy this situation? Next, assume the bank finds that its reserves will be substantially and permanently deficient. What remedy is available to this bank? Hint: Recall your answer to question 4.

12. Suppose that Bob withdraws $100 of cash from his chequing account at Calgary Chartered Bank and uses it to buy a camera from Joe, who deposits the $100 in his chequing account in Annapolis Valley Chartered Bank. Assuming a desired reserve ratio of 10% and no initial excess reserves, determine the extent to which **a** Calgary Chartered Bank must reduce its loans and demand deposits because of the cash withdrawal and **b** Annapolis Valley Chartered Bank can safely increase its loans and demand deposits because of the cash deposit. Have the cash withdrawal and deposit changed the money supply?

13. Key Question *Suppose the following is a simplified consolidated balance sheet for the chartered banking system. All figures are in billions. The desired reserve ratio is 4%.*

Assets		(1)	Liabilities and net worth		(1)
Reserves	$ 6.1	_____	Deposits	$150	_____
Securities	20	_____			
Loans	123.9	_____			

a. *How much excess reserves does the chartered banking system have? What is the maximum amount the banking system might lend? Show in column 1 how the consolidated balance sheet would look after this amount has been lent. What is the money multiplier?*

b. *Answer question 13a assuming that the desired reserve ratio is 5%. Explain the resulting difference in the lending ability of the chartered banking system. What is the new money multiplier?*

14. What are banking "leakages"? How might they affect the money-creating potential of the banking system? Be specific.

15. Explain why there is a need for the Bank of Canada to control the money supply.

16. (Applying the Theory) Can bank panics produce a decline in the nation's money supply? Why are such panics unlikely today?

CHAPTER 15

THE BANK OF CANADA AND MONETARY POLICY

We focused on the money-creating ability of individual banks and the chartered banking system in Chapter 14. Our discussion ended on a disturbing note: As chartered banks pursue their goal of profit maximization, they could contribute to cyclical fluctuations of business activity. Chartered banks will find it profitable to expand the supply of money during periods of economic expansion and restrict the money supply in seeking liquidity during recessions. In this chapter we will see how Canada's monetary authorities attempt to reverse the pro-cyclical tendencies of the chartered banking system through a variety of techniques.

In this chapter, we first discuss the objectives of monetary policy and the roles of participating institutions. Next, we survey the balance sheet of the Bank of Canada through which monetary policy is implemented. Third, techniques of monetary control are analyzed in detail. What are the key instruments of monetary control and how do they function? Fourth, the transmission mechanism through which monetary policy affects aggregate demand is detailed and the effectiveness of monetary policy is evaluated. Finally, we present a summary of mainstream macroeconomic theory and policy.

A detailed discussion of monetary policy in an open economy is postponed until Chapter 22.

BOX 15-1   THE BIG PICTURE

In the last two chapters you have become acquainted with the function of money in a market economy and how money is created (and destroyed). But what is the connection between the total money supply and the output performance and price level in a macroeconomy?

Recall from Chapter 8 that market economies are subject to instability, often experiencing substantial unemployment and sometimes inflationary pressures. In this chapter you will learn that a change in money supply affects interest rates, which influence the level of investment and real GDP. Thus the Bank of Canada, within limits, can help smooth out the fluctuation in the Canadian economy by influencing interest rates through its control of the money supply. The main aim of the Bank of Canada policies is price stability, but it would also like to achieve full employment. Price stability facilitates the ultimate aim of ensuring a nation is employing all its resources — particularly its labour force — to their fullest extent. Note that monetary policy is in broad measure a substitute for fiscal policy, but there are situations where they both need to be used in unison.

As you read through this chapter, keep the following points in mind:

- The Bank of Canada is the "bankers' bank," overseeing the operation of Canada's banking system and its money supply. The Bank of Canada is not motivated by profits, as is the case with the chartered banks.
- Given that a market economy is prone to instability, one of the main roles of the Bank of Canada is to pursue policies that smooth out the fluctuation of the Canadian economy. The transmission mechanism between the monetary side of the economy and the "real" side of the economy is through interest rates, which affect investments, thereby influencing aggregate demand.
- If the economy is experiencing a recessionary gap, the Bank of Canada embarks on policies to lower interest rates, thereby stimulating investments and increasing aggregate demand. If the economy is experiencing an inflationary gap, the Bank of Canada embarks on policies to increase interest rates, thereby dampening investments and lowering aggregate demand.

GOALS OF MONETARY POLICY

As was discussed in the last chapter, the Bank of Canada has the responsibility of supervising and controlling the operation of our monetary and banking systems. The bank formulates the basic policies that the banking system follows. Because it is a public body, its decisions are made in what it perceives to be the public interest.

The *objective of* **monetary policy** *is to help assist the economy to achieve and maintain a full-employment, noninflationary level of total output*. Monetary policy consists of altering the economy's money supply for the purpose of stabilizing aggregate output, employment, and the price level. It entails increasing the money supply during a recession to stimulate spending and restricting it during inflation to constrain spending.

The Bank of Canada alters the size of the nation's money supply by manipulating the amount of excess reserves held by chartered banks. Excess reserves, you will recall, are critical to the money-creating ability of the banking system. Once we see how the Bank of Canada controls excess reserves and the money supply, we will explain how changes in the stock of money affect interest rates and aggregate demand.

FUNCTIONS OF THE BANK OF CANADA

The functions of the Bank of Canada — the bankers' bank — can be divided into five categories. The most important will be discussed last.

1. THE "BANKERS' BANK"   Although you head for the nearest chartered bank if you either want to deposit, withdraw, or borrow money, the chartered banks turn to the Bank of Canada as their "bank." There are times when the chartered banks need to borrow from the central bank. As well, chartered banks keep minimal reserves with the Bank of Canada to settle bilateral payment balances among themselves.

2. SUPPLYING THE ECONOMY WITH PAPER CURRENCY
It is the responsibility of the Bank of Canada to supply the economy with needed paper currency — Bank of Canada notes.

3. FISCAL AGENT FOR THE FEDERAL GOVERNMENT
The Bank of Canada acts as the main banker and fiscal agent for the federal government. The federal government collects funds through taxation, spends these funds on a variety of goods and services, and sells and redeems bonds. The Bank of Canada holds a part of the federal government's chequing accounts, aids the government in collecting various tax revenues, and administers the sale and redemption of government bonds.

4. SUPERVISING THE CHARTERED BANKS
The Department of Finance and the Bank of Canada *supervise* the operations of chartered banks. A banking system stands or falls on the financial soundness of the individual chartered banks. Unsound banking practices can have widespread repercussions, to the point of threatening the financial structure of the entire economy. Since chartered banking is "vested with a public interest," it is subject to government supervision.

5. REGULATING THE SUPPLY OF MONEY
Finally — and most important of all — the Bank of Canada has ultimate responsibility for regulating the supply of money. *The major task of the central bank is to manage the money supply in accordance with the needs of the economy.* It makes an amount of money available that is consistent with high and steadily rising levels of output and employment and a relatively constant price level. While all the other functions of the bank are of a more or less routine or service nature, the goal of correctly managing the money supply entails the making of basic and unique policy decisions.

STATEMENT OF ASSETS AND LIABILITIES OF THE BANK OF CANADA

Because monetary policy is implemented by the Bank of Canada, we need to consider the nature of its balance sheet. Some of its assets and liabilities differ from those found on the balance sheet of a chartered bank. Table 15-1 is a simplified balance sheet showing all the pertinent assets and liabilities of the Bank of Canada.

ASSETS

The two Bank of Canada assets we need to consider are:

1. SECURITIES
Securities are Government of Canada bonds and Treasury bills (government bonds with terms of three months to a year) issued by the Government of Canada to finance past and present budget deficits. These securities are part of the

TABLE 15-1 Bank of Canada statement of assets and liabilities, December 31, 1994 (*in millions*)

Assets		Liabilities	
Treasury bills of Canada	$19,147	Notes in circulation	$28,329
Other securities issued or guaranteed by Canada	5,929	Government of Canada deposits	26
Foreign currency deposits	525	Chartered bank deposits	586
Other assets	4,449	Other deposits	141
		Other liabilities	968
Total	$30,050	Total	$30,050

Source: Bank of Canada, *Bank of Canada Review*, Summer, 1995.

national debt (Chapter 18). Some were bought directly from the government, most from the public (through investment dealers) and the chartered banks. Although the interest on these bonds represents the Bank of Canada's income, they are not bought and sold purposely to make a profit. Rather, they are bought and sold primarily to influence the amount of reserves held by the chartered bank and therefore their ability to create money by lending.

2. ADVANCES TO CHARTERED BANKS   For reasons we will soon discuss, chartered banks occasionally borrow from the Bank of Canada. The IOUs the chartered banks give to the Bank of Canada in negotiating advances are listed as advances to chartered banks. From the Bank of Canada's point of view, these IOUs are assets — they are claims against the chartered banks that have borrowed from it. To the chartered banks, these IOUs are liabilities. By borrowing, the chartered banks obtain increases in their reserves in exchange for their IOUs.

LIABILITIES

On the liability side we find three items.

1. CHARTERED BANK DEPOSITS   These deposits are assets from the viewpoint of the chartered banks but a liability to the Bank of Canada.

With the abolition of required reserves, these deposits will be considerably reduced, since their only function will be to permit cheque-clearing.

2. GOVERNMENT OF CANADA DEPOSITS   Just as businesses and private individuals find it convenient and desirable to pay their obligations by cheque, so does the Government of Canada. By far, the major part of the government's funds — mostly tax receipts — are transferred by the Bank of Canada to government deposit accounts with the various chartered banks. To the government, all such deposits are assets, while to the banks, including the central bank, they are liabilities.

3. NOTES IN CIRCULATION   Our paper money supply consists of bank notes issued by the Bank of Canada. In circulation, Bank of Canada notes are claims against the assets of the Bank of Canada and are therefore treated as liabilities. These notes, which come into circulation through chartered banks, are not a part of the money supply until they are in the hands of the public.

QUICK REVIEW 15-1

1. The major functions of the Bank of Canada are: **a** to hold deposits of the chartered banks; **b** to supply the economy's needs for paper currency; **c** to act as fiscal agent for the federal government; **d** to supervise the operations of chartered banks; and **e** to regulate the money supply.

2. The Bank of Canada's two major assets are Government of Canada securities and advances to chartered banks. Its three major liabilities are chartered bank deposits, Government of Canada deposits, and notes in circulation.

TOOLS OF MONETARY POLICY

There are two main instruments of monetary control at the disposal of the Bank of Canada to influence chartered bank reserves: (1) open-market operations and (2) switching Government of Canada deposits.

OPEN-MARKET OPERATIONS

The term **open-market operations** refers to *buying and selling of government bonds and Treasury bills by the Bank of Canada in the open market* — the buying and selling of bonds from or to chartered banks and the public (through investment dealers). How do these purchases and sales of government securities affect the excess reserves of chartered banks?

BUYING SECURITIES   Suppose the Bank of Canada decides to buy government bonds in the open market, that is, from chartered banks and the public. In either case, the overall effect is the same — chartered bank reserves are increased.

FROM CHARTERED BANKS   Let's trace the process the Bank of Canada uses when buying government bonds *from chartered banks*.

(a) The chartered banks give up a part of their holdings of securities to the Bank of Canada.

(b) The Bank of Canada pays for these securities by increasing the deposits of the chartered banks by the amount of the purchase.

The balance sheets of the chartered banks and the Bank of Canada will change as follows:

BANK OF CANADA BUYS BONDS FROM CHARTERED BANKS

BANK OF CANADA	
Assets	**Liabilities**
+ Securities (*a*)	+ Deposits of chartered banks (*b*)
↑ (*a*) Securities	(*b*) + Reserves ↓

CHARTERED BANKS	
Assets	**Liabilities**
– Securities (*a*) + Reserves (*b*)	

The upward arrow shows that securities have moved from the chartered banks to the Bank of Canada. Therefore, we place a *minus* sign in front of "Securities" in the asset column of the balance sheet of the chartered banks. For the same reason, we place a *plus* sign in front of "Securities" in the asset column of the balance sheet of the Bank of Canada.

The downward arrow indicates that the Bank of Canada has provided reserves to the chartered banks. Therefore we place a *plus* sign in front of "Reserves" in the balance sheet for the chartered banks. The *plus* sign in the liability column of the balance sheet of the Bank of Canada indicates that chartered bank deposits have increased; they are a liability to the Bank of Canada.

The important aspect of this transaction is that when the Bank of Canada purchases securities from chartered banks, the reserves — and therefore the lending ability — of the chartered banks are increased.

FROM THE PUBLIC If the Bank of Canada purchases securities *from the public* (through investment dealers), the effect on chartered bank deposits in the central bank would be much the same. Suppose Mariposa Investments Limited (a large Toronto dealer representing the public) possesses Government of Canada bonds that it sells in the open market to the Bank of Canada. The transaction goes like this:

(a) Mariposa Investments gives up securities to the Bank of Canada and gets in payment a cheque drawn by the Bank of Canada on itself.

(b) Mariposa Investments promptly deposits this cheque in its account with the Bank of York.

(c) The Bank of York collects against the Bank of Canada by sending the cheque to the Toronto clearing house for collection. As a result, the Bank of York receives an increase in its reserves.

Balance sheet changes are as follows.

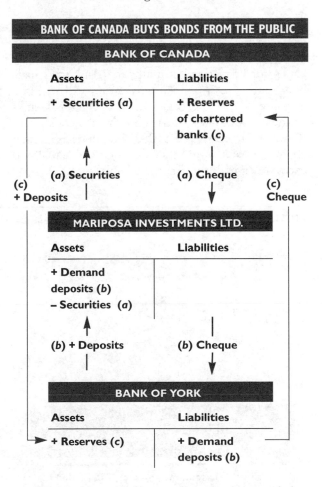

We need to understand two aspects of this transaction.

1. As with Bank of Canada purchases of securities directly from chartered banks, the reserves and lending ability of the chartered banking system have been increased. This is indicated by the *plus* sign in front of "Reserves," indicating an increase in assets of the Bank of York.

2. The supply of money is directly increased by the central bank's purchase of government bonds

(aside from any expansion of the money supply that may occur from the increase in chartered bank reserves). This direct money supply has taken the form of an increased amount of chequing account money in the economy, thus the plus sign in front of demand deposits in the Bank of York. Because these demand deposits are an asset as viewed by Mariposa Investments, demand deposits have increased (plus sign) on Mariposa Investments' balance sheet.

There is a slight difference between the Bank of Canada's purchases of securities from the chartered banks and from the public. Assuming all chartered banks are "loaned up" initially, the Bank of Canada bond purchases *from chartered banks* will increase actual reserves and excess reserves of chartered banks by the entire amount of the bond purchases. Thus, as shown in Figure 15-1, a $1000 bond purchase from a chartered bank would increase both the actual and excess reserves of the chartered bank by $1000.

On the other hand, Bank of Canada purchases of bonds *from the public* increase actual reserves but also increase demand deposits. Thus, a $1000 bond purchase from the public would increase actual reserves of the "loaned up" banking system by $1000. But with a 10% desired reserve ratio, the excess reserves of the banking system would amount only to $900. In the case of bond purchases from the public, it is *as if* the chartered banking system had already used 10% of its new reserves to support $1000 worth of new demand-deposit money.

However, in each transaction the basic conclusion is the same: **When the Bank of Canada buys securities (bonds) in the open market, chartered banks' reserves will be increased.** Assuming that the chartered banks lend out their excess reserves, the nation's money supply will rise. Observe in Figure 15-1 that a $1000 purchase of bonds by the Bank of Canada will result in $10,000 of additional money, regardless of whether the purchase was made from the banks or the general public.

FIGURE 15-1   The Bank of Canada's purchase of bonds and the expansion of the money supply

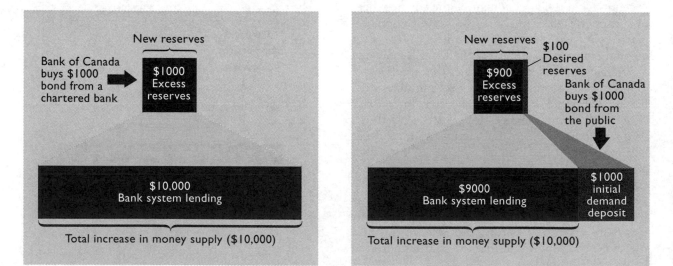

Assuming all chartered banks are "loaned up" initially, a Bank of Canada purchase of a $1000 bond from either a chartered bank or the public can increase the money supply by $10,000 when the desired reserve ratio is 10%. In the left portion of the diagram, the purchase of a $1000 bond from a chartered bank creates $1000 of excess reserves that support an expansion of demand deposits of $10,000 through making loans. In the right portion, the purchase of a $1000 bond from the public creates only $900 of excess reserves, because $100 of reserves are needed to "back up" the $1000 new demand deposit in the banking system. The chartered banks can therefore expand the money supply by $9000 by making loans. This $9000 of chequing account money *plus* the initial new demand deposit of $1000 together equal $10,000 of new money.

SELLING SECURITIES   You should now suspect that Bank of Canada sales of government bonds reduce chartered bank reserves. Let's see why.

TO CHARTERED BANKS Suppose the Bank of Canada sells securities in the open market to *chartered banks*:

(a) The Bank of Canada gives up securities, which the chartered banks acquire.

(b) Chartered banks pay for these securities by drawing cheques against their deposits — that is, against their reserves — in the Bank of Canada. The Bank of Canada collects these cheques by reducing the chartered banks' reserves accordingly.

The balance sheet changes appear as follows.

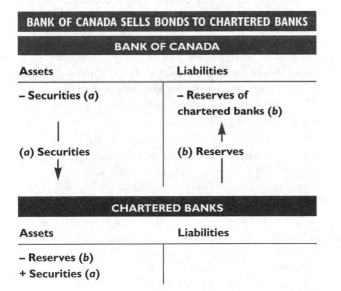

The reduction in chartered bank deposits in the Bank of Canada is indicated by the minus signs before these entries.

TO THE PUBLIC   If the Bank of Canada sells securities *to the public* (which goes through investment dealers) the final outcome will be the same. Suppose Mariposa Investments Ltd. buys government bonds from the Bank of Canada.

(a) The Bank of Canada sells Government of Canada bonds to Mariposa Investments, who pays for these securities by a cheque drawn on the Bank of York.

(b) The Bank of Canada clears this cheque against the Bank of York by reducing its reserves.

(c) The Bank of York returns the cheque to Mariposa Investment, reducing the company's demand deposit accordingly.

The balance sheets change as follows:

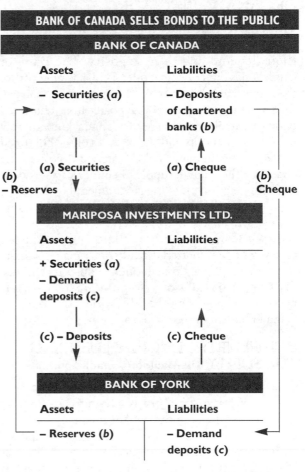

The Bank of Canada bond sales of $1000 to the chartered banking system reduce the system's actual and excess reserves by $1000. But a $1000 bond sale to the public reduces excess reserves by $900, because demand deposit money is also reduced by $1000 in the sale. Since the chartered banking system has reduced its outstanding deposits by $1000 it need only keep $100 less in reserves.

Whether the Bank of Canada sells securities to the public or to chartered banks, the conclusion is identical: **When the Bank of Canada sells securities in the open market, chartered bank reserves are reduced.**

If all excess reserves are already lent out, this decline in chartered bank reserves will translate into a decline in the nation's money supply. In our example, a $1000 sale of government securities will result in a $10,000 decline in the money supply, irrespective of whether the sale was made to chartered banks or the public.

SWITCHING GOVERNMENT OF CANADA DEPOSITS

The chartered banks' lending power (and thus money-creating power) is restricted to given ratios of their demand and term deposits. The Bank of Canada has direct control over a considerable part of these deposits: those of the Government of Canada. By **switching government deposits** from chartered banks to itself, the Bank of Canada immediately reduces the deposits and the reserves of the chartered banks by the amount of the switched deposits. The effect on the money supply is similar to the open-market operation of selling government bonds.

Alternatively, by switching government deposits from itself to the chartered banks, the Bank of Canada increases the deposits and the reserves of the chartered banks, making it possible to increase the nation's money supply. In the last decade, switching of government deposit has become the main method by which the Bank of Canada has tried to control the money supply.

OTHER METHODS OF INFLUENCING THE SUPPLY OF MONEY

One of the functions of a central bank is to be a "lender of last resort." Just as chartered banks may lend to the public, so the bankers' bank may lend to the chartered banks [and to a select group of money market (investment) dealers]. The rate of interest charged by the Bank of Canada on these loans is called the **bank rate**.

These Bank of Canada loans are called "advances," implying they are *normally* very short-term loans. The chartered banks rarely borrow from the central bank. A chartered bank will call in "day-to-day" and "call" loans it has made to money market dealers before it asks the Bank of Canada for an advance. Occasionally, however, a chartered bank will need to get an advance from the Bank of Canada, since chartered banks do their best to keep their excess reserves as low as they can, as vault cash and any deposits with the Bank of Canada earn the banks no interest.

A chartered bank covers advances from the Bank of Canada by giving a promissory note. The promissory note is an asset to the Bank of Canada. To the chartered bank, the note is a liability. The changes will be as shown at the top of the next column.

How do these operations help the Bank of Canada to control interest rates? *The bank rate's*

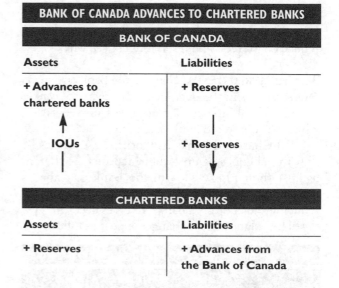

main function is psychological, for changes in the bank rate are signals to the chartered banks to change their own borrowing and lending rates in the same direction. The chartered banks obey the central bank's signals because they know the Bank of Canada can affect their reserves — through buying and selling bonds on the open market — if they fail to comply. The bank rate is a means by which the Bank of Canada can communicate the overall direction of monetary policy to banks and the public. The Bank of Canada rate is set each Tuesday afternoon at $1/4$ of a percentage point above the average rate paid by the government on its three-month Treasury bills at that day's weekly auction.

MORAL SUASION The Bank of Canada sometimes uses the less tangible technique of moral suasion to influence the lending policies of the chartered banks. **Moral suasion** means the use by the central bank of "friendly persuasion" — private discussions, policy statements, public pronouncements, or outright appeals — warning that excessive expansion or contraction of bank credit might involve serious consequences for the banking system and the economy as a whole. **(Key Question 2)**

QUICK REVIEW 15-2

1. The objective of monetary policy is to help the economy achieve a full-employment, noninflationary level of output.

2. The Bank of Canada has two main instruments of monetary control, each of which works by changing the amount of reserves in the banking system. The two mechanisms are: **a** open-market operations and **b** switching government of Canada deposits.

THE DEMAND FOR MONEY

Now that we know what constitutes the supply of money and how the supply of money is "backed," let's turn to the demand for money. There are two reasons that the public wants to hold money.

TRANSACTIONS DEMAND, D_t

People want money as a medium of exchange — to conveniently negotiate the purchase of goods and services. Households must have enough money on hand to buy groceries and pay mortgage and utility bills until the next paycheque. Businesses need money to pay for labour, materials, power, and so on. Money demanded for all such purposes is called the **transactions demand** for money.

The basic determinant of the amount of money demanded for transactions purposes is the level of nominal GDP. The larger the total money value of all

goods and services exchanged in the economy, the larger will be the amount of money needed to negotiate these transactions. *The transactions demand for money varies directly with nominal GDP.* We specify *nominal* GDP because households and firms will want more money for transactions if *either* prices rise or real output increases. In both instances, there will be a larger dollar volume of transactions to accomplish.

In Figure 15-2(a) (Key Graph) we show the relationship between the transactions demand for money, D_t, and the interest rate. Because the transactions demand for money depends on the level of nominal GDP and is independent of the interest rate, we draw the transactions demand as a vertical line. For simplicity we assume the amount of money der for transactions is unrelated to changes in interest rate. That is, higher interest rates will not reduce the amount of money demanded for transactions.[1]

---

[1] This is a simplification. We would also expect the amount of money held by businesses and households to negotiate transactions to vary inversely with the interest rate. When real interest rates are high, consumers and businesses will make an effort to reduce the amount of money held for transactions purposes in order to have more funds to put into interest-earning assets.

KEY GRAPH

FIGURE 15-2   The demand for money (M1) and the money market

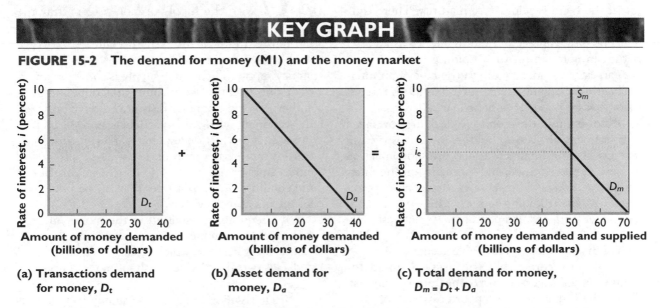

(a) Transactions demand for money, D_t

(b) Asset demand for money, D_a

(c) Total demand for money, $D_m = D_t + D_a$

The total demand for money, D_m, is determined by horizontally adding the asset demand for money, D_a, to the transactions demand, D_t. The transactions demand is vertical because it is assumed to depend on nominal GDP rather than the real interest rate. The asset demand varies inversely with the real interest rate because of the opportunity cost involved in holding currency and chequable deposits that do not pay interest. Combining the money supply (stock), S_m, with total money demand, D_m, portrays the money market and determines the equilibrium real interest rate, i_e.

The transactions demand at $30 billion is arbitrary, but a rationale can be easily provided. For example, if each dollar held for transactions purposes is spent, on the average, 15 times per year *and* nominal GDP is assumed to be $450 billion, then the public would need $30 billion of money to purchase that GDP.

ASSET DEMAND, D_a

The second reason for holding money is that money functions as a store of value. People may hold their financial assets in many forms — for example, as corporate stocks, private or government bonds, or as M1 money. Thus, there is an **asset demand** for money.

What determines the asset demand for money? We must first recognize that each of the various forms of holding our financial assets has advantages and disadvantages. To simplify, let's compare holding bonds as an asset with holding money as an asset. The advantages of holding money are its liquidity and lack of risk. Money is the most liquid of all assets; it is immediately usable in the making of purchases. Money is an attractive asset to be holding when the prices of goods, services, and other financial assets are expected to decline. When the price of a bond falls, the bondholder will suffer a loss if the bond is sold before maturity. There is no such risk with holding money.

The disadvantage of holding money as an asset is that in comparison with holding bonds, it does *not* earn interest income, or, in the case of an interest-bearing chequing account, earn as much interest income as on bonds or nonchequable deposits.

Knowing this, the problem is deciding how much of your financial assets to hold as, say, bonds (i.e., all interest-bearing financial assets) and how much as money. The solution depends primarily on the interest rate. A household or business incurs an opportunity cost when holding money; interest income is forgone or sacrificed. If a bond pays 9% interest, then it costs $9 per year of forgone income to hold $100 as cash or in a noninterest chequable account.

It is no surprise that **the asset demand for money varies inversely with the rate of interest**. When the interest rate or opportunity cost of holding money as an asset is low, the public will choose to hold a large amount of money as assets. When the interest rate is high, it is costly to "be liquid," and the amount of assets held in the form of money will be small. This inverse relationship between the interest rate and the amount of money people will want to hold as an asset is shown by D_a in Figure 15-2(b).

TOTAL MONEY DEMAND, D_m

As shown in Figure 15-2(c), the **total demand** for money, D_m, is found by adding the asset demand horizontally to the transactions demand. [The vertical dashed line in Figure 15-2(c) represents the transactions demand to which Figure 15-2(b)'s asset demand has been added.] The resulting downsloping line in Figure 15-2(c) represents the total amount of money the public will want to hold for transactions and as an asset at each possible interest rate.

Also note that a change in the nominal GDP — working through the transactions demand for money — will shift the total money demand curve. An increase in nominal GDP will mean that the public will want to hold a larger amount of money for transactions purposes, and this will shift the total money demand curve to the right. A decline in nominal GDP will shift the total money demand curve to the left.

THE MONEY MARKET

We can combine the demand for money with the supply of money to portray the **money market** and determine the equilibrium real rate of interest. In Figure 15-2(c) we have drawn a vertical line, S_m, to represent the money supply. The money supply is shown as a vertical line because we assume that our monetary authorities and financial institutions have provided the economy with some particular *stock* of money. Just as in a product or resource market, the intersection of money demand and money supply determines equilibrium price. The "price" in this case is the equilibrium interest rate, that is, the price paid for the use of money.

If disequilibrium existed in the money market, how would the money market achieve equilibrium? Consider Figure 15-3, which replicates Figure 15-2(c) and adds two alternative supply-of-money curves.

1. SHORTAGE Suppose the supply of money is reduced from $50 billion, S_{m0}, to $38 billion, S_{m1}. Note the quantity of money demanded exceeds the quantity supplied by $12 billion at the previous equilibrium interest rate of 5%. People will attempt to make up for this shortage of money by selling

FIGURE 15-3   Restoring equilibrium in the money market

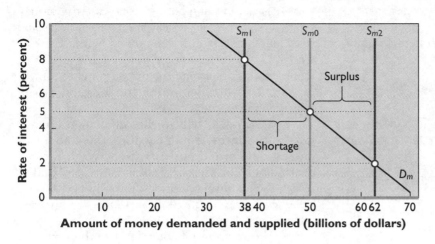

A decrease in the supply of money creates a temporary shortage of money in the money market. People and institutions attempt to gain more money by selling bonds. The supply of bonds therefore increases, which reduces bond prices and raises interest rates. At higher interest rates, people reduce the amount of money they wish to hold. As a result, the amount of money supplied and demanded once again are equal at the higher interest rate. An increase in the supply of money creates a temporary surplus of money, resulting in an increase in the demand for bonds and higher bond prices. Interest rates fall and equilibrium is re-established in the money market.

some of the financial assets they own (we assume for simplicity that these assets are bonds). But one person's receipt of money through the sale of a bond is another person's loss of money through the purchase of that bond. Overall, there is only $38 billion of money available. The collective attempt to get more money by selling bonds will increase the supply of bonds relative to demand in the bond market and drive down bond prices.

Generalization: **Lower bond prices increase interest rates.** To clarify this point, suppose a bond with no expiration date pays a fixed $50 annual interest and is selling for its face value of $1000.

$$\frac{\$50}{\$1000} = 5\%$$

Now suppose that the price of this bond drops to $625 because of the increased supply of bonds. The $50 fixed annual interest payment will now yield 8% to whoever buys the bond:

$$\frac{\$50}{\$625} = 8\%$$

Because all borrowers must compete by offering to pay lenders interest rates similar to those available on bonds, a higher general interest rate thus emerges. In Figure 15-3 the interest rate rises from 5% at the money supply of $50 billion to 8% when the money supply is $38 billion. This higher interest

rate raises the opportunity cost of holding money and reduces the amount of money firms and households want to hold. Specifically, the amount of money demanded declines from $50 billion at the 5% interest rate to $38 billion at the 8% interest rate. The money market is back into equilibrium: the quantity of money demanded and supplied are each $38 billion at the 8% interest rate.

2. SURPLUS   An increase in the supply of money from $50 billion, Sm_0, to $62 billion, Sm_2, will result in a surplus of $12 billion at the initial 5% interest rate. People will try to rid themselves of money by purchasing more bonds. The collective attempt to buy more bonds therefore will increase the demand for bonds and pull bond prices upward.

Corollary: **Higher bond prices reduce interest rates.** In terms of our example, the $50 interest payment on a bond now priced at, say, $2500, will yield a bond buyer only a 2% interest rate:

$$\frac{\$50}{\$2500} = 2\%$$

The point is that interest rates in general will fall as people unsuccessfully attempt to reduce their money holding below $62 billion by buying bonds. In this case, the interest rate will fall to a new equilibrium at 2%. Because the opportunity cost of holding money now is lower — being liquid is less expensive — consumers and businesses will increase the amount of currency and chequable deposits they are willing to hold from $50 billion to $62 billion. Once again equilibrium in the money market is restored: the quantity of money demanded and supplied are each $62 billion at an interest rate of 2%. **(Key Question 3)**

QUICK REVIEW 15-3

1. People hold money for transaction and asset purposes.

2. The total demand for money is the sum of the transaction and asset demands; it is drawn as an inverse relationship between the interest rate and the quantity of money demanded.

3. The equilibrium interest rate is determined by money demand and supply; it occurs when people are willing to hold the exact amount of money being supplied by the monetary authorities.

4. Bond prices and interest rates are inversely related.

MONETARY POLICY, REAL GDP, AND THE PRICE LEVEL

CAUSE-EFFECT CHAIN: THE TRANSMISSION MECHANISM

How does monetary policy work towards the goal of full employment with price-level stability? The central factors and relationships are illustrated in **Figure 15-4 (Key Graph)**.

MONEY MARKET   Figure 15-4(a) shows the money market, where the demand for money curve and the supply of money curve are brought together. Recall that the total demand for money is the sum of the transactions and asset demands. The transactions demand is directly related to level of economic transactions as reflected in the size of the nominal GDP. The asset demand is inversely related to the interest rate. The interest rate is the opportunity cost of holding money as an asset; the higher the cost, the smaller the amount of money the public wants to hold. In Figure 15-4(a) the total demand for money is inversely related to the interest rate. Also, recall that an increase in nominal GDP would shift D_m to the right and a decline in nominal GDP would shift D_m to the left.

We complete our portrayal of the money market by showing three potential money supply curves, Sm_0, Sm_1, and Sm_2. In each case the money supply is shown as a vertical line representing some fixed amount of money determined by the Bank of Canada. While monetary policy (the supply of money) helps determine the interest rate, the interest rate does not determine the location of the money supply curve.

Figure 15-4(a) tells us the equilibrium interest rate — the interest rate equating the amount of money demanded and supplied. With money demand of D_m, if the supply of money is $50 billion ($Sm_0$), the equilibrium interest rate will be 10%. At a money supply of $75 billion ($Sm_1$), the interest rate will be 8%; at $100 billion ($Sm_2$), 6%.

We know from Chapter 10 that the real, not the nominal, rate of interest is critical for investment decisions. So here we assume Figure 15-4(a) portrays real interest rates.

INVESTMENT   These 10, 8, and 6% interest rates are carried rightward to the investment demand curve of Figure 15-4(b). This curve shows the inverse relationship between the interest rate — the cost of borrowing to invest — and amount of the nation's investment spending. At the 10% interest rate it will be profitable for businesses to invest $15 billion; at 8%, $20 billion; and at 6%, $25 billion.

The investment component of total spending is more likely to be affected by changes in the interest rate than is consumer spending. Of course, consumer purchases of automobiles — which depend heavily on instalment credit — are sensitive to interest rates. But overall the interest rate is *not* a very crucial factor in determining how households divide their disposable income between consumption and saving.

The impact of changing interest rates on investment spending is great because of the large cost and long-term nature of such purchases. Capital equipment, factory buildings, and warehouses are tremendously expensive. In absolute terms, interest charges on funds borrowed for these purchases are considerable.

Similarly, the interest cost on a house purchased on a long-term contract will be very large: A one-half percentage point change in the interest rate could amount to thousands of dollars on the total cost of a home.

KEY GRAPH

FIGURE 15-4   Monetary policy and equilibrium GDP

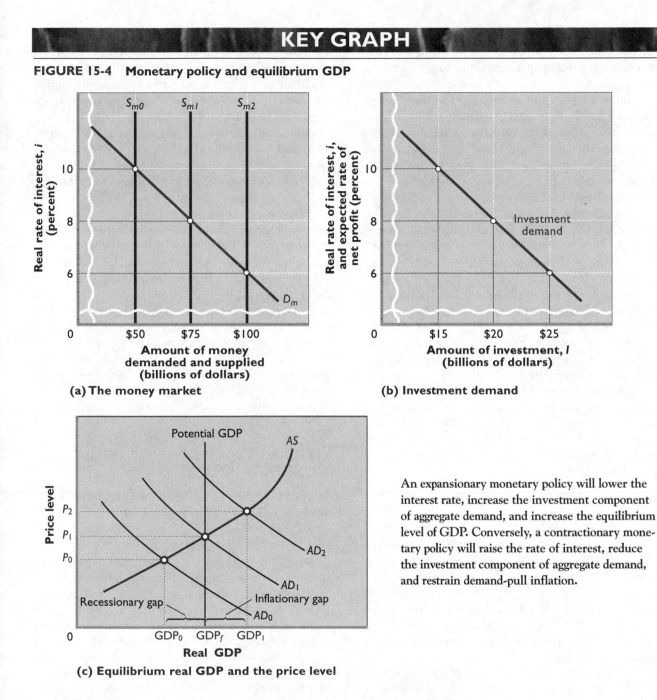

(a) The money market

(b) Investment demand

(c) Equilibrium real GDP and the price level

An expansionary monetary policy will lower the interest rate, increase the investment component of aggregate demand, and increase the equilibrium level of GDP. Conversely, a contractionary monetary policy will raise the rate of interest, reduce the investment component of aggregate demand, and restrain demand-pull inflation.

Also, changes in the interest rate may affect investment spending by changing the attractiveness of capital equipment purchases versus bond purchases. If the interest rate rises on bonds, then, given the profit expectations on capital goods purchases, businesses will be more inclined to use business savings to purchase securities than to buy capital equipment. Conversely, given profit expectations on investment spending, a fall in the interest rate makes capital goods purchases more attractive than bond ownership.

In brief, the impact of changing interest rates will be primarily on investment spending and, through this channel, on aggregate demand, output, employment, and the level of prices. More specifically, as Figure 15-4(b) indicates, investment spending varies inversely with the interest rate.

EQUILIBRIUM GDP Figure 15-4(c) shows the impact of our three interest rates and corresponding levels of investment spending on aggregate demand. Aggregate demand curve AD_0 is associated with the $15 billion level of investment, AD_1, with investment of $20 billion, and AD_2 with investment of $25 billion. That is, investment spending is one of the determinants of aggregate demand (Chapter 11). All else being equal, the greater this investment spending, the further to the right lies the aggregate demand curve.

Suppose the money supply in Figure 15-4(a) is $50 billion ($S_{m_0}$), producing an equilibrium interest rate of 10%. In Figure 15-4(b) we see this 10% interest rate will bring forth $15 billion of investment spending. This $15 billion of investment spending joins with consumption spending, net exports, and government spending to yield aggregate demand curve AD_0 in Figure 15-4(c). The equilibrium levels of real output and prices are GDP_0 and P_0, as determined by the intersection of AD_0 and the aggregate supply curve AS.

To test your understanding of these relationships, you should explain why each of the other two levels of money supply shown in Figure 15-4(a) results in a different interest rate, level of investment, aggregate demand curve, and real output-price level combination.

EFFECTS OF AN EXPANSIONARY MONETARY POLICY

We have assumed the money supply is $50 billion ($S_{m_0}$) in Figure 15-4(a). Because the resulting real output GDP_0 in Figure 15-4(c) is far below the full-employment output, GDP_f, the economy must be experiencing substantial unemployment, or a recessionary gap. The Bank of Canada therefore should institute an **expansionary monetary policy** (Column 1 of Table 15-2).

To increase the money supply the Bank of Canada will take one or both of the following actions: (1) buy government securities from chartered banks and the public in the open market; (2) switch government deposits to the chartered banks. (The Bank of Canada will also attempt to decrease the bank rate, but as previously mentioned, the bank rate's main function is psychological; it is a signal to the chartered banks as to the direction of the Bank of Canada's monetary policy.) The result will be an increase in excess reserves in the chartered banking system. Because excess reserves are the basis on which chartered banks can expand the money supply by lending, the nation's money supply likely will rise. An increase in the money supply will lower the interest rate, increasing investment, aggregate demand, and equilibrium GDP.

For example, an increase in the money supply from $50 to $75 billion will reduce the interest rate from 10 to 8%, as indicated in Figure 15-4(a), and increase investment from $15 billion to $20 billion, as shown in Figure 15-4(b). This $5 billion increase in investment spending will shift the aggregate demand curve rightward by more than the increase in investment because of the multiplier effect. Assuming the open economy multiplier is 2, the $5 billion increase in investment will shift the AD curve rightward by $10 billion (= 2 × $5) at each price level. Specifically, aggregate demand will shift from AD_0 to AD_1, as shown in Figure 15-4(c). This rightward shift in aggregate demand moves the economy from GDP_0 to the desired full-employment output at GDP_f, thereby closing the recessionary gap.

Column (1) in Table 15-2 summarizes the chain of events associated with an expansionary monetary policy.

EFFECTS OF A CONTRACTIONARY MONETARY POLICY

Now let's assume the money supply and interest rate are $100 billion ($S_{m_2}$) in Figure 15-4(a). This results in an interest rate of 6%, investment spending of $25 billion, and aggregate demand of AD_2. As observed in Figure 15-4(c) we have depicted an inflationary gap. Aggregate demand AD_2 is excessive relative to the economy's full-employment level of real output GDP_f. To rein in spending, the Bank of Canada will institute a **contractionary monetary policy** (Column 2 of Table 15-2).

The Bank of Canada will undertake one or both of the following actions: (1) sell government bonds to chartered banks and to the public in the open market; (2) switch government deposits out of the chartered banks. Banks then will discover their reserves are too low to meet possible cash withdrawals and therefore will need to reduce their demand deposits by refraining from issuing new loans as old loans are paid back. This will shrink the money supply and increase the interest rate. The higher interest rate will reduce investment, decreasing aggregate demand, and closing the inflationary gap.

TABLE 15-2   Monetary policy: the transmission mechanism

(1) Expansionary monetary policy	(2) Contractionary monetary policy
Problem: recessionary gap	*Problem:* Inflationary gap
Bank of Canada buys bonds, switches government deposits into the chartered banks, or both	Bank of Canada sells bonds, switches government deposits out of the chartered banks, or both
↓	↓
Money supply rises	Money supply falls
↓	↓
Interest rate falls	Interest rate rises
↓	↓
Investment spending increases	Investment spending decreases
↓	↓
Aggregate demand increases	Aggregate demand decreases
↓	↓
Real GDP rises by a multiple of the increase in investment	Inflation declines

If the Bank of Canada reduces the money supply from \$100 billion (S_{m_2}) to \$75 billion (S_{m_1}), as shown in Figure 15-4(a), the interest rate will increase from 6 to 8% and reduce investment from \$25 to \$20 billion [Figure 15-4(b)]. The consequent \$5 billion decrease in investment, bolstered by the multiplier process, will shift the aggregate demand curve leftward from AD_2 to AD_1. For example, with an open economy multiplier of 2, the aggregate demand curve will shift leftward by \$10 billion (= 2 × \$5 billion of investment) at each price level. This leftward shift of the aggregate demand curve will eliminate the excessive spending and thus the inflationary gap.

Column (2) of Table 15-2 summarizes the cause-effect chain of contractionary monetary policy on an inflationary gap. **(Key Question 6)**

REFINEMENTS AND FEEDBACKS

The components of Figure 15-4 allow us to (1) appreciate some of the factors determining the effectiveness of monetary policy and (2) note the existence of a "feedback" or "circularity" problem complicating monetary policy.

POLICY EFFECTIVENESS   Figure 15-4 reveals the magnitudes by which an expansionary or contractionary monetary policy will change the interest rate, investment, and aggregate demand. These magnitudes are determined by the particular shapes of the demand for money and investment-demand curves. Pencil in other curves to see that *the steeper the D_m curve, the larger will be the effect of any given change in the money supply on the equilibrium rate of interest. Furthermore, any given change in the interest rate will have a larger impact on investment — and hence on aggregate demand and GDP — the flatter the investment-demand curve.* A specific change in quantity of money will be most effective when the demand for money curve is relatively steep and the investment-demand curve is relatively flat.

A particular change in the quantity of money will be relatively ineffective when the money-demand curve is flat and the investment-demand curve is steep. As we will find in Chapter 17, there is controversy as to the precise shapes of these curves and therefore the effectiveness of monetary policy.

FEEDBACK EFFECTS   You may have sensed in Figure 15-4 a feedback or circularity problem that complicates monetary policy. The problem is this: By reading Figure 15-4(a) to 15-4(c), we discover that the interest rate, working through the investment-demand curve, is a determinant of the equilibrium GDP. Now we must recognize that causation also runs the other way. The level of GDP is a determinant of the equilibrium interest rate. This link comes about because the transactions component of the money-demand curve depends directly on the level of nominal GDP.

How does this feedback from Figure 15-4(c) to 15-4(a) affect monetary policy? It means that the increase in the GDP that an expansionary monetary policy brings about will *increase* the demand for money, partially offsetting the interest-reducing effect of the expansionary monetary policy. A contractionary monetary policy will reduce the nominal GDP. But this will decrease the demand for money and dampen the initial interest-increasing effect of the contractionary monetary policy. This feedback is also at the core of a policy dilemma, as we will see later. (**Key Question 7**)

MONETARY POLICY AND AGGREGATE SUPPLY

As with fiscal policy (Chapter 12), monetary policy is subject to the constraints implicit in the aggregate supply curve. The cause-effect chain represented in Figure 15-3 and Table 15-2 indicates that monetary policy primarily affects investment spending and, therefore, aggregate demand, real output, and the price level. The aggregate supply curve explains how the change in investment and aggregate demand *is divided* between changes in real output and changes in the price level.

As we noted in Chapter 11, in the short run the more slack there is in an economy the flatter (more horizontal) the aggregate supply curve will be. In such a situation, a rightward shift of the aggregate demand curve will increase real GDP, but the impact on the price level will be small. Indeed if the economy were in a depression — the aggregate supply curve would be completely flat (horizontal) — a rightward shift in the aggregate demand curve would not affect the price level at all.

Similarly, if in the short run the economy is close to its capacity utilization, the aggregate supply curve would be very steep (vertical). In such a situation, a rightward shift of the aggregate demand curve would have little effect on real GDP but would greatly increase the price level.

EFFECTIVENESS OF MONETARY POLICY

Let's evaluate how well monetary policy works.

STRENGTHS OF MONETARY POLICY

Most economists regard monetary policy as an essential component of our national stabilization policy, especially in the following respects:

1. **SPEED AND FLEXIBILITY**   Compared with fiscal policy, monetary policy can be quickly altered. We have seen (Chapter 12) that the application of fiscal policy may be delayed by parliamentary deliberations. In contrast, the Bank of Canada can buy or sell securities on a daily basis and affect the money supply and interest rates.

2. **ISOLATION FROM POLITICAL PRESSURE** Since the governor and deputy governor of the Bank of Canada are appointed for seven-year terms and may be removed from office only by an Act of Parliament, they are not often subject to lobbying and pressure to remain elected. Thus, the Bank of Canada can engage in politically unpopular policies that it thinks might be necessary for the long-term health of the economy.

But while the governor can be removed only by Parliament, the Bank Act allows the Minister of Finance to issue an instruction to the governor to undertake policy changes. It is understood by convention that any such instruction would cause the governor of the Bank of Canada to resign because his or her judgement has been questioned.

Monetary policy is a more subtle and more politically conservative measure than is fiscal policy. Changes in government spending directly affect the allocation of resources, and tax changes can have extensive political ramifications. By contrast, monetary policy works more subtly and therefore is more politically palatable.

3. **RECENT SUCCESSES**   The case for monetary policy has been greatly bolstered by its successful use during the 1980s and 1990s. A contractionary monetary policy helped bring down the inflation rate from 12.5% in 1981 to 4.4% three years later.

Recently, monetary policy was successfully used to help move the economy — at first very slowly,

BOX 15-2   IN THE MEDIA

CENTRAL BANK COULD EASE MONETARY POLICY: STUDY

But cutting rates to lower government payments might backfire

BY BRUCE LITTLE

The Bank of Canada could ease monetary policy slightly without jeopardizing its inflation control targets, thus stimulating more growth and bringing down interest rates, the C. D. Howe Institute says in a new study.

But it warns that any major attempt to reduce rates for the sole purpose of cutting the federal government's huge interest payments on the public debt would likely backfire and drive rates higher.

Economists David Laidler and William Robson argue in a commentary released today that the Bank of Canada "inadvertently" tightened its money policy too much during the second half of 1994 and could well afford to ease back now without risking an outburst of inflation.

They say the money supply expanded rapidly from late 1992 to early 1994, a burst of growth that was needed to keep the economy growing at a time of low inflation and falling interest rates. Although the growth of new money should have been moderately reined in last year, the central bank abruptly halted its growth, the study says.

"Between April and the end of the year, M1 [the narrowest measure of the money supply] scarcely grew," Mr. Laidler and Mr. Robson say. If that pattern persists, "monetary policy will begin to exert downward pressure on output and on prices, and CPI [consumer price index] inflation will likely remain at, or even fall below, the bottom of the

bank's target band" of an inflation rate between 1 and 3 per cent.

Although lower interest rates would save Ottawa money because it is the country's single biggest debtor, the report says any overt or overdone attempt by the government or the Bank of Canada to reduce rates would simply trigger an increase in interest costs.

"An explicit effort to reduce Ottawa's financing costs by the Bank of Canada would signal an abandonment of the inflation-control targets. As recognition of that fact spread through financial markets — likely very rapidly — all interest rates ... would move upward." ...

SOURCE: *Globe and Mail*, February 21, 1995, p. B7. Reproduced with permission.

The Story in Brief

The conduct of monetary policy is a combination of art and science. While the Bank of Canada knows its policy aims, they are not so easily realized. According to a C.D. Howe Institute study, monetary policy was tightened too much during the second half of 1994 and could subsequently be eased somewhat without risking an outburst of inflation.

The Economics Behind the Story

- The Bank of Canada has a mandate to design monetary policy so as to achieve price stability, full employment GDP, and external balance with the rest of the world.

- In the first half of 1994, the Bank of Canada embarked on a tight monetary policy; between April and December of 1994 M1 expanded very little, and interest rates rose. Unless the tight monetary policy is loosened, the C.D. Howe Institute report argues that the Canadian economy will experience downward pressure on output and prices.

- To tighten monetary policy and raise short-term interest rates, the Bank of Canada resorted to switching of government deposit and open market operations.

- What is the likely effect of a tight monetary policy on the growth of GDP? Explain how monetary policy accomplishes this.

and then briskly — from the 1990–1991 recession. This success is noteworthy because the huge budget deficits of the 1980s and early 1990s had put fiscal policy on the shelf. The federal government budgeting was mainly aimed at reducing the budget deficit, not at stimulating the economy. From a fiscal policy perspective, the tax hikes and government spending reductions during this period were mildly contractionary. But the Bank of Canada's expansionary monetary policy dropped the prime rate on chartered banks' loans from 13% in 1990 to 8% in 1993. Eventually, these low interest rates had their intended effects: investment spending and interest-sensitive consumer spending rose rapidly, increasing the economy's real GDP.

In view of Canada's budget deficits and these successes, monetary policy — at least for now — appears to be Canada's primary antirecession tool.

SHORTCOMINGS AND PROBLEMS

However, monetary policy has certain limitations and encounters real-world complications.

1. LESS CONTROL?   Some economist fear that changes in banking practices may reduce — or make less predictable — the Bank of Canada's control of the money supply. Financial innovations have allowed people quickly to move near-monies from mutual funds and other investment accounts to chequing accounts, and vice versa. A particular monetary policy aimed at changing chartered bank reserves therefore might be rendered less effective by movements of funds within the financial system. For example, people might respond to a contractionary monetary policy by quickly converting near-monies in their mutual funds accounts or other liquid financial investments to money in their chequing accounts. Thus, bank reserves may not fall as intended, the interest rate may not rise, and aggregate demand may not change. Also, banking and finance are increasingly global. Flows of funds to or from Canada might undermine or render inappropriate a particular domestic monetary policy.

How legitimate are these concerns? These financial developments make the Bank of Canada's task of monetary policy more difficult. But recent studies and Bank of Canada experience confirm that the traditional central bank tools of monetary policy remain effective in changing the money supply and interest rates.

2. CYCLICAL ASYMMETRY   If pursued vigorously enough, tight or contractionary monetary policy can lower chartered bank reserves to the point where banks are *forced* to contract the volume of loans. This means a contraction of the money supply. But an easy or expansionary monetary policy suffers from a "You can lead a horse to water, but you can't make it drink" kind of problem. An easy monetary policy can see to it only that chartered banks have the excess reserves needed to make loans. It cannot guarantee that the bank will provide the loans and thus that the supply of money will increase. If chartered banks, seeking liquidity, are unwilling to lend, the efforts of the Bank of Canada will be of little avail. The public can frustrate the intentions of the Bank of Canada by deciding not to borrow excess reserves. Or, the money the central bank injects into the system through the open market buying of bonds from the public could be used by the public to pay off existing loans.

This cyclical asymmetry has not created a major difficulty for monetary policy except during depression. During normal times, higher excess cash reserves translate into added lending and therefore to an increase in the money supply.

Some economists would add to the shortcomings of monetary policy. These supposed shortcomings are reviewed in Chapter 17, where controversies in macroeconomics are discussed.

3. CHANGES IN VELOCITY   Total expenditures may be regarded as the money supply multiplied by the **velocity of money** — the number of times per year the average dollar is spent on goods and services. If the money supply is $50 billion, total spending will be $600 billion if velocity is 12, but only $450 billion if velocity is 9.

Some economists feel that velocity changes in the opposite direction from the money supply, offsetting or frustrating policy-instigated changes in the money supply. During inflation, when the money supply is restrained by policy, velocity may increase. Conversely, when policy measures are taken to increase the money supply during recession, velocity may well fall.

Velocity might behave this way because of the asset demand for money. An expansionary monetary policy, for example, means an increase in the supply of money relative to the demand for it and therefore a reduction in the interest rate [Figure 15-3(a)]. But when the interest rate — the opportunity cost of holding money as an asset — is lower, the public will hold larger money balances. This means dollars move from hand to hand — from households to businesses and back again — less rapidly. That is, the velocity of money has declined. A reverse sequence of events may cause a contractionary monetary policy to induce an increase in velocity.

4. THE INVESTMENT IMPACT Some economists doubt that monetary policy has as much impact on investment as Figure 15-4 implies. A combination of a relatively flat money-demand curve and a relatively steep investment-demand curve will mean that a particular change in the money supply will not elicit a very large change in investment and, thus, not a large change in the equilibrium GDP (Figure 15-4).

Furthermore, the operation of monetary policy as portrayed may be complicated, or temporarily offset, by unfavourable changes in the location of the investment-demand curve. For example, a contractionary monetary policy designed to drive up interest rates may have little impact on investment spending if the investment demand curve in Figure 15-4(b) at the same time shifts to the right because of business optimism, technological progress, or expectations of higher future prices of capital. Monetary policy will have to raise interest rates extraordinarily high under these circumstances to be effective in reducing aggregate demand. Conversely, a severe recession may undermine business confidence, collapse the investment-demand curve to the left and frustrate an easy money policy.

5. INTEREST AS INCOME We have seen that monetary policy is predicated on the idea that interest rates and expenditures on capital goods and interest-sensitive consumer goods are *inversely* related. We must now acknowledge that businesses and households are also recipients of interest income and that the size of such income and the spending that flows from it vary *directly* with the level of interest rates.

Suppose inflation is intensifying and the Bank of Canada increases interest rates to increase the cost of capital goods, housing, and automobiles. The complication is that higher interest rates on a wide range of financial instruments (for example, bonds, certificates of deposits, chequing accounts) will increase the incomes and spending of the households and businesses who own them. Such added spending is obviously at odds with the Bank of Canada's effort to restrict aggregate demand. Example: In 1991 and 1992 the Bank of Canada repeatedly lowered interest rates to stimulate a sluggish economy. One possible reason this strategy took so long to become effective was that households who were receiving 8 or 10% on their bonds and GICs in the late 1980s received only 4 or 5% in the early 1990s. This diminished interest income undoubtedly lowered their spending.

The point is that, although interest rate changes viewed as an *expense* change spending in the *opposite* direction as the interest rate changes, these rate changes when viewed as *income* change spending in the *same* direction as the interest rate changes. The change in spending by interest income receivers partly offsets and weakens the change in spending by purchasers of capital goods, homes, and autos.

THE TARGET DILEMMA

This brings us to one of the most difficult problems of monetary policy. Should the Bank of Canada attempt to control the money supply *or* the interest rate? This **target dilemma** arises because monetary authorities cannot simultaneously stabilize both.

THE POLICY DILEMMA To understand this dilemma, review the money market diagram of Figure 15-4(a).

INTEREST RATE Assume the Bank of Canada's policy target is to stabilize the interest because interest rate fluctuations destabilize investment spending and, working through the income multiplier, destabilize aggregate demand and the economy. Now suppose expansion of the economy increases nominal GDP and increases the transactions demand, and therefore the total demand, for money. As a result the equilibrium interest rate will rise. To stabilize the interest rate — to bring it down to its original level — the Bank of Canada would have to increase the supply of money. But this may turn a healthy recovery into an inflationary boom — exactly what the Bank of Canada wants to prevent.

A similar scenario can be applied to recession. As GDP falls, so will money demand and interest rates, provided the money supply is unchanged. But to prevent interest rates from declining, the Bank of Canada would have to reduce the money supply.

This decline in the supply of money would contribute to a further contraction of aggregate expenditures and intensify the recession.

MONEY SUPPLY   What if the Bank of Canada's policy target is the money supply, not the interest rate? Then the Bank of Canada must tolerate interest rate fluctuations that will contribute to instability in the economy. Explanation: Assume in Figure 15-4(a) that the Bank of Canada achieves its desired money supply target of $75 billion. Any expansion of GDP will increase the demand for money and raise the interest rate. This higher interest rate may lower investment spending and choke off an otherwise healthy expansion. The point again is that the monetary authorities cannot simultaneously stabilize both the money supply and the interest rate.

RECENT FOCUS: INTEREST RATES

Because an interest rate target and a money supply target cannot be realized simultaneously, which target, if either, is preferable? In the early-to-mid 1980s the Bank of Canada focused its policy mainly on controlling the rate of growth of the money supply, letting markets determine interest rates accordingly. But innovations in the financial industry made reliance on the M1 or M2 money supply targets unreliable. The expansion of highly liquid non-chequing accounts, money market mutual funds, and mutual fund investment accounts distorted the M1 and M2 data. People switched some of their money holdings from M1 accounts to M2 and M3 accounts. Also, velocity — historically rising at a stable rate — began to decline. The Bank of Canada therefore could no longer depend on the traditional relationships among M1, M2, and nominal GDP.

In view of these developments the Bank of Canada has turned to targeting the interest rate rather than the money supply. The goal is to peg the interest rate at the level appropriate for the state of the economy. Specifically, aiming to increase aggregate demand to lift the economy from recession, the Bank of Canada sharply reduced the bank rate in 1991. The Bank of Canada reduced this interest rate by aggressively buying government securities in the open market.

Interest rates in general, including the **prime interest rate** — the rate banks charge to their most credit-worthy loan customers — rise and fall with the bank rate. When the Bank of Canada buys bonds from chartered banks and the public, total reserves and excess reserves in the banking system rise, making it less expensive for banks to borrow reserves from one another. That is, the bank rate falls because of the greater supply of reserves in the banking system. We know that increases in reserves also increase bank lending to the public and therefore raise the money supply. As the money supply rises, the prime interest rate falls, increasing investment spending, aggregate demand, and GDP.

At first the economy only slowly expanded from the recession of 1990-1991, but in late 1993 real GDP began to surge upward. Fearing the expansionary monetary policy and low interest rates might eventually fuel renewed inflation, the Bank of Canada began to tighten monetary policy in 1994. It used open-market operations and switching of government of Canada deposits to increase the bank rate, and thereby boost the prime interest rate.

In summary: The Bank of Canada's recent policies have been both activist and consistent with Figure 15-3. It has determined what it thinks to be the desirable interest rate for the state of the economy and then changed the money supply to achieve these interest rate targets. The Bank of Canada has recently focused less attention on the money aggregates themselves — M1 and M2 — and more on the bank rate and prime interest rates. (**Key Question 10**)

QUICK REVIEW 15-4

1. The Bank of Canada is engaging in an expansionary monetary policy when it increases the money supply to reduce interest rates; it is engaging in a contractionary monetary policy when it reduces the money supply to increase interest rates.

2. The transmission mechanism by which monetary policy affects aggregate demand is primarily through investment spending.

3. The steeper the money demand curve and the flatter the investment demand curve, the larger is the impact of a change in the money supply on the economy.

4. The main strengths of monetary policy are **a** speed and flexibility and **b** political acceptability. Its main weaknesses are (1) potential impotence during recession and (2) offsetting changes in velocity.

5. The Bank of Canada faces a target dilemma because it cannot simultaneously stabilize both the money supply and interest rates.

MONETARY POLICY AND THE INTERNATIONAL ECONOMY: A FIRST GLANCE

In Chapter 12 we established that linkages among economies of the world complicate domestic fiscal policy. These linkages also relate to monetary policy.

Suppose we are experiencing a recession and the Bank of Canada pursues an expansionary monetary policy to reduce interest rates and thereby stimulate aggregate demand. Lower interest rates compared to other nations will lead to decreased foreign demand for dollars, and thus a lower Canadian dollar. A lower exchange rate will help increase our exports abroad and reduce our imports, thereby increasing net exports and aggregate demand.

In this instance an expansionary policy has repercussions on the exchange rate that reinforce the initial goal of eliminating a recessionary gap. But there are instances where the policy needs of the domestic economy may be at odds with the policy aim of achieving external balance. This issue is taken up more fully in Chapter 22 after we have a better grasp of international trade and the foreign exchange markets, covered in Chapters 20 and 21, respectively.

THE "BIG PICTURE"

Figure 15-5 (Key Graph) brings together the many analytical and policy aspects of macroeconomics discussed in this and the eight preceding chapters. This "big picture" shows how the many concepts and principles discussed relate to one another and how they constitute a coherent theory of what determines the level of resource use in a market economy.

Study this diagram and you will see that the levels of output, employment, income, and prices all result from the interaction of aggregate supply and aggregate demand. In particular, note those items — shown in green — that constitute, or are strongly influenced by, public policy.

Self-test: Suppose the economy represented by this diagram was experiencing a severe, long-lasting recession. What specific stabilization policies would you recommend? Use the linkages in this diagram to explain how your policies would work.

CHAPTER SUMMARY

1. The major functions of the Bank of Canada are **a** to hold deposits of the chartered banks, **b** to supply the economy's needs for paper currency, **c** to act as fiscal agent for the federal government, **d** to supervise the operations of chartered banks (together with the Department of Finance), and **e** to regulate the supply of money in terms of the best interests of the economy as a whole.

2. The Bank of Canada's two major assets are Government of Canada securities and advances to chartered banks. Its three major liabilities are chartered bank reserves, Government of Canada deposits, and notes in circulation.

3. The goal of monetary policy is to assist the economy in achieving a full-employment, noninflationary level of total output.

4. For a consideration of monetary policy, the most important assets of the Bank of Canada are Government of Canada bonds and Treasury bills.

5. The major instruments of monetary control are **a** open-market operations; and **b** switching of government deposits.

6. The total demand for money is made up of the transactions and asset demands for money. The transactions demand varies directly with nominal GDP; the asset demand varies inversely with the interest rate. The money market combines the demand for money with the money supply to determine the equilibrium interest rate.

KEY GRAPH

FIGURE 15-5   The theory of employment and stabilization policies

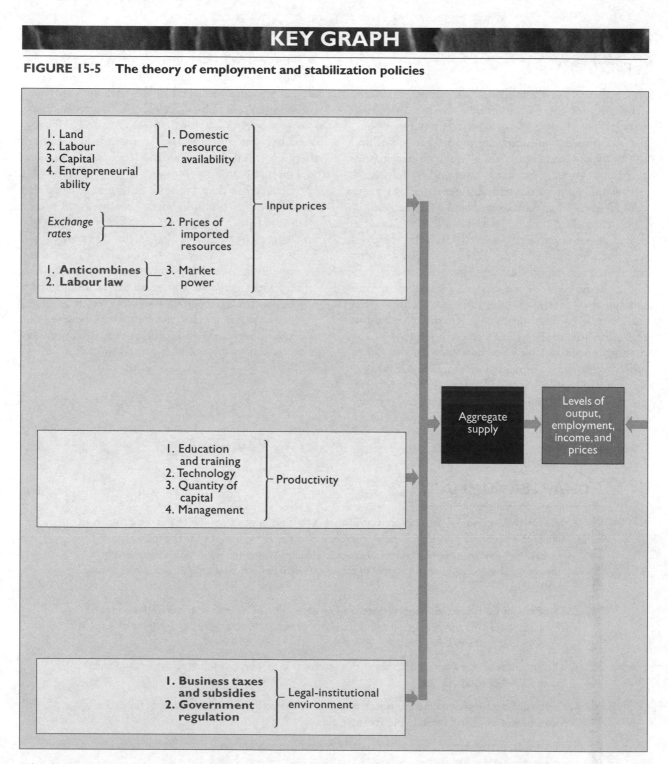

This figure integrates the various components of macroeconomic theory and stabilization policy. Determinants that constitute, or are strongly influenced by, public policy are shown in bold green.

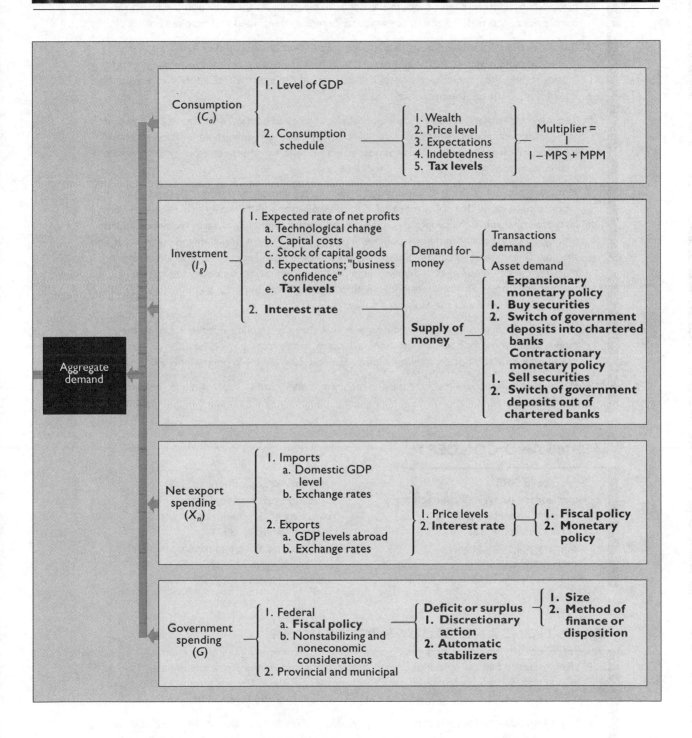

Consumption (C_a)
1. Level of GDP
2. Consumption schedule

1. Wealth
2. Price level
3. Expectations
4. Indebtedness
5. **Tax levels**

$$\text{Multiplier} = \frac{1}{1 - MPS + MPM}$$

Investment (I_g)
1. Expected rate of net profits
   a. Technological change
   b. Capital costs
   c. Stock of capital goods
   d. Expectations; "business confidence"
   e. **Tax levels**
2. **Interest rate**

Demand for money
Transactions demand
Asset demand

Supply of money

Expansionary monetary policy
1. **Buy securities**
2. **Switch of government deposits into chartered banks**
Contractionary monetary policy
1. **Sell securities**
2. **Switch of government deposits out of chartered banks**

Aggregate demand

Net export spending (X_n)
1. Imports
   a. Domestic GDP level
   b. Exchange rates
2. Exports
   a. GDP levels abroad
   b. Exchange rates

1. Price levels
2. **Interest rate**

1. **Fiscal policy**
2. **Monetary policy**

Government spending (G)
1. Federal
   a. **Fiscal policy**
   b. Nonstabilizing and noneconomic considerations
2. Provincial and municipal

Deficit or surplus
1. **Discretionary action**
2. **Automatic stabilizers**

1. **Size**
2. **Method of finance or disposition**

7. Disequilibriums in the money market are corrected through changes in bond prices. As bond prices change, interest rates move in the opposite direction. At the equilibrium interest rate, bond prices tend to stabilize and the amounts of money demanded and supplied are equal.

8. Monetary policy operates through a complex cause-effect chain: **a.** policy decisions affect chartered bank reserves; **b.** changes in reserves affect the supply of money; **c.** changes in the money supply alter the interest rate; and **d.** changes in the interest rate affect investment, the equilibrium GDP, and the price level.

9. The advantages of monetary policy include its flexibility and political acceptability. In the past 15 years monetary policy has been used successfully both to reduce rapid inflation and push the economy from recession. Today, almost all economists view monetary policy as a significant stabilization tool.

10. Monetary policy has some limitations and problems. **a** Financial innovations and global considerations have made this policy more difficult to administer and its impact less certain. **b** Policy-instigated changes in the supply of money may be partially offset by changes in the velocity of money. **c** The impact of monetary policy will be lessened if the money-demand curve is flat and the investment-demand curve is steep. The investment-demand curve may also shift, negating monetary policy. **d** Changes in interest rates resulting from monetary policy change the amount of interest income received by lenders, altering some people's spending in a way counter to the intent of the monetary policy.

11. Monetary authorities face a policy dilemma in that they can stabilize interest rates or the money supply, but not both. Recent monetary policy has been pragmatic, focusing on the health of the economy and not on stabilizing either interest rates or the money supply exclusively.

12. Figure 15-4 summarizes macroeconomic theory and policy in the short run and deserves your careful study.

TERMS AND CONCEPTS

bank rate (p. 316)
expansionary (easy) and contractionary
   (tight) monetary policies (p. 322)
feedback effects (p. 323)
monetary policy (p. 310)
money market (p. 318)
moral suasion (p. 316)

open-market operations (p. 312)
prime interest rate (p. 328)
switching government deposits (p. 316)
target dilemma (p. 327)
transactions, asset, and total demand for
   money (pp. 317–318)
velocity of money (p. 326)

QUESTIONS AND STUDY SUGGESTIONS

1. Use chartered bank and Bank of Canada balance sheets to demonstrate the impact of the following transactions on chartered bank reserves: a. The Bank of Canada purchases securities from dealers. b. The Bank of Canada makes an advance to a chartered bank.

2. *Key Question   In the table at the top of page 333 you will find simplified consolidated balance sheets for the chartered banking system and the Bank of Canada. In columns 1 and 2, indicate how the balance sheets would read after each of the two transactions described in a. and b. is completed. Do not accumulate your answers; analyze each transaction separately, starting in each case from the given figures. All accounts are in billions of dollars.*

Consolidated Balance Sheet: All Chartered Banks (*billions of dollars*)	(1)	(2)
Assets:		
Reserves .... $ 4.8	_____	_____
Securities 20.0	_____	_____
Loans 71.2	_____	_____
Liabilities:		
Demand deposits .. $96.0	_____	_____

Advances from
  Bank of
  Canada 0.0
	_____	_____

Balance Sheet: Bank of Canada (*billions of dollars*)	(1)	(2)
Assets:		
Securities $15.8	_____	_____
Advances to chartered banks 0.0	_____	_____
Liabilities:		

Reserves of
  chartered
  banks .... $ 4.8
	_____	_____

Government of
  Canada
  deposits 0.1
	_____	_____

Notes in circulation 10.9	_____	_____

a. *The Bank of Canada sells $100 million in securities to the public, who pay for the bonds with cheques. Show the new balance sheet figures in column 1.*

b. *The Bank of Canada buys $200 million of securities from chartered banks. Show the new balance sheet figures in column 2.*

c. *Now review both of these transactions, asking yourself these three questions:*

   (1) What change, if any, took place in the money supply as a direct and immediate result of each transaction? (2) What increase or decrease in chartered banks' reserves took place in each transaction? (3) Assuming a desired reserve ratio of 5%, what change in the money-creating potential of the chartered banking system occurred as a result of each transaction?

3. **Key Question**   *What is the basic determinant of a. the transactions demand and b. the asset demand for money? Explain how these two demands might be combined graphically to determine total money demand. How is the equilibrium interest rate determined in the money market? How might a. the expanded use of credit cards; b. a shortening of worker pay periods; and c. an increase in nominal GDP affect the transactions demand for money and the equilibrium interest rate?*

4. Suppose that a bond has a face value of $10,000 and annually pays a fixed amount of interest of $800. Compute and enter in the space provided either the interest rate that a bond buyer could secure at each of the bond prices listed or the bond price at each of the interest rates shown. State the generalization that can be drawn from the completed table.

Bond price	Interest rate(s)
$ 8,000	_____
_____	8.9
$10,000	_____
$11,000	_____
_____	6.2

5. Assume the money market is initially in equilibrium and that the money supply is now increased. Explain the adjustments towards a new equilibrium interest rate. What effects would you expect this interest rate change to have on the levels of output, employment, and prices? Answer the same questions for a decrease in the money supply.

6. *Key Question   Suppose you are the governor of the Bank of Canada. The economy is experiencing a sharp and prolonged inflationary trend. What changes in a. open-market operations and b. switching government deposits would you consider? Explain in each case how the change you advocate would affect chartered bank cash reserves and influence the money supply.*

7. *Key Question   What is the basic objective of monetary policy? Describe the cause-effect chain through which monetary policy is made effective. Discuss how a. the shapes of the demand-for-money and investment-demand curves, and b. the size of the MPS and MPM influence the effectiveness of monetary policy. How do feedback effects influence the effectiveness of monetary policy?*

8. Evaluate the overall effectiveness of monetary policy. Why have open-market operations evolved as the primary means of controlling chartered bank reserves? Discuss the specific limitations of monetary policy.

9. Explain why the Bank of Canada cannot simultaneously stabilize interest rates and the money supply. Explain why the target of stable interest rates might contribute to ongoing inflation.

10. *Key Question   Suppose the Bank of Canada decides to engage in a contractionary monetary policy as a way to close an inflationary gap. Use the aggregate demand-aggregate supply model to show the intent of this policy for a closed economy.*

11. Design an anti-recession stabilization policy, involving both fiscal and monetary policies, that is consistent with a. a relative decline in the public sector, b. greater income equality, and c. a high rate of economic growth. Explain: "Truly effective stabilization policy presumes the co-ordination of fiscal and monetary policy."

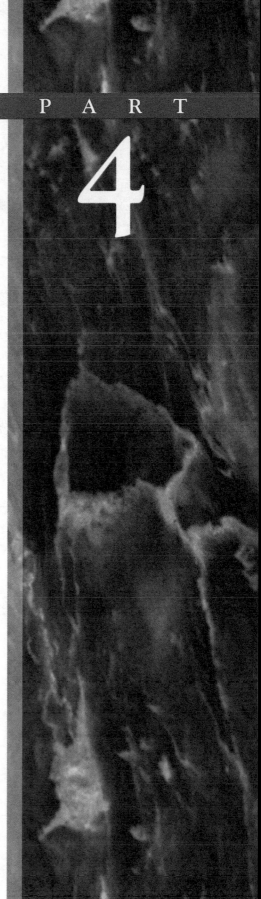

THE LONG RUN AND PROBLEMS AND CONTROVERSIES IN MACROECONOMICS

CHAPTER 16

LONG-RUN MACROECONOMIC ADJUSTMENTS

I n the last two decades there has been much work done by economists in the area of expectations and long-run analysis. New insights have arisen as to how expectations are formed and their effects on the aggregate supply curve in particular. These new developments have also helped us understand the nature of inflation and the relationship between inflation and unemployment.

This chapter's specific goals are as follows.

First, we examine the Phillips curve, which was used by economists to explain the apparent trade-off between unemployment and inflation. Next, the *natural-rate hypothesis* is introduced, and we explore the distinction between short-run and long-run aggregate supply. This distinction will permit us to understand better the nature and causes of inflation. Finally, we discuss policy proposals designed to deal with stagflation.

BOX 16-1   THE BIG PICTURE

Up to this chapter we have stressed the short- to medium-term dynamics of the economy. The aim in the short to medium term is to get the economy operating at a level that employs all the economy's available resources, particularly its labour force. In terms of Chapter 2's production possibility curve, macroeconomic policies in the short to medium term attempt to keep the economy on the curve and to do so with stable prices.

We have stressed the pivotal role aggregate demand plays in achieving and maintaining full employment and price stability. But the pivotal role of aggregate demand in achieving full employment ceases when the economy is at a long-run full-employment GDP. At such a point, further aggregate demand increases (shifts to the right) will only put upward pressure on the price level since all the economy's resources are being utilized.

In the long run, the aggregate supply curve is verti-cal. The economy could temporarily go beyond what is referred to as the natural rate of unemployment, but it is not a level of GDP that can be sustained.

As you read this chapter, keep the following points in mind:

- The discussion of the trade-off between unemployment and inflation (the Phillips curve) is meant to shed light on the evolution of macroeconomic theory with regard to long-run adjustment in the last three decades.

- The incorporation of expectations in the macro model has led to the conclusions that some trade-off may exist between inflation and unemployment in the short run, but not in the long run. In particular, in the long run nominal wages are fully responsive to changes in the price level.

- In the long run, economic growth will occur only if the aggregate supply expands (shifts right).

THE EVOLUTION OF LONG-RUN ANALYSIS

In the last 25 years there has been a change in how economists perceive the long-run adjustment of the macroeconomy. Let's first examine the conventional wisdom up to the early 1970s.

ANALYTICAL AND HISTORICAL BACKGROUND

Our analysis of Chapters 9 and 10 focused on aggregate expenditures as the determinant of real output and employment. The simplest expenditure model implies that the economy may realize *either* unemployment (a recessionary gap) *or* inflation (an inflationary gap), but *not both simultaneously*.

This expenditure model did provide a satisfactory explanation of the economy's macro behaviour over the four decades preceding the 1970s. But this situation changed in the 1970s. The coexistence of inflation and unemployment — indeed, the simultaneous occurrence of *increasing* unemployment and a *rising* price level — became common and the central macroeconomic problem of the 1970s and early 1980s. There were two serious stagflationary episodes — 1971–75 and 1980–82 — that were not readily explainable by the aggregate expenditures model.

THE PHILLIPS CURVE: CONCEPT AND DATA

In Figure 16-1 we perform a simple mental experiment. Suppose that in some specific period aggregate demand expands from AD_0 to AD_2. This shift might result from a change in any one of the determinants of aggregate demand. For example, businesses may decide to buy more investment goods or government may decide to increase its expenditures in order to provide more public goods. Whatever the cause of the aggregate demand increase, we observe that the price level rises from P_0 to P_2, while real output expands from Q_0 to Q_2.

Now let's compare what would have happened if the increase in aggregate demand had been larger, say from AD_0 to AD_3. The new equilibrium tells us that both the amount of inflation and the growth of real output would have been greater (and

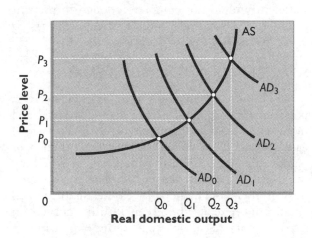

Comparing the effects of various possible increases in aggregate demand yields the conclusion that the larger the increase in aggregate demand, the greater will be the resulting inflation and the greater the increase in real output. Because real output and the unemployment rate are inversely related, we can generalize that given aggregate supply, high rates of inflation should be accompanied by low rates of unemployment.

the unemployment rate smaller). Similarly, suppose aggregate demand in our specific year had increased only modestly from AD_0 to AD_1. Compared with our original AD_0 to AD_2 shift, the amount of inflation and the growth of real output would have been smaller (and the unemployment rate larger). The generalization from this mental experiment is this: *the greater the rate of growth of aggregate demand, the higher will be the resulting inflation and the larger the growth of real output (and the lower the unemployment rate).* Conversely, if aggregate demand grows more slowly, the smaller will be the resulting inflation and the slower the growth of real output (and the higher the unemployment rate). More simply, *high rates of inflation are accompanied by low rates of unemployment and vice versa.* Figure 16-2(a) generalizes how the expected relationship should look.

Do the facts fit the theory? Empirical work by economists in the late 1950s and 1960s verified this inverse relationship. It came to be known as the **Phillips curve**, named after A. W. Phillips, who developed this concept in Great Britain. For example, Figure 16-2(b) shows the relationship between the unemployment rate and the rate of inflation in Canada for 1959–69. The coloured line generalizing

FIGURE 16-2 The Phillips curve: concept and empirical data

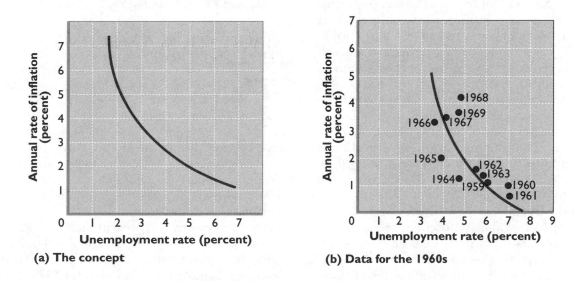

(a) The concept

(b) Data for the 1960s

(a) The Phillips curve purported to show a stable relationship between the unemployment rate and the rate of inflation. Because this relationship is inverse, there is presumably a trade-off between unemployment and inflation.
(b) Data for the 1960s seemed to confirm the Phillips curve concept.

on the data portrays the expected inverse relationship. Based on this kind of empirical evidence, economists believed that a stable, predictable trade-off existed between unemployment and inflation. Furthermore, national economic policy was based on this supposed trade-off.

LOGIC OF THE PHILLIPS CURVE

How can the Phillips curve be explained? What causes the apparent trade-off between full employment and price level stability?

The factors underlying the Phillips curve are the same as those previously used to explain the upward sloping aggregate supply curve. Certain imbalances — "bottlenecks" and structural problems — arise in labour markets as the economy expands towards full employment. The labour market in Canada is composed of a large number of individual labour markets that are stratified and distinct both occupationally and geographically. This labour market diversity suggests that as the economy expands, full employment will *not* be realized simultaneously in each individual labour market. While full employment and labour shortages may exist for some occupations and areas, unemployment will persist for other occupations and regions. This disparity means that in an expanding economy, even though the overall unemployment rate may be 7% or 8%, scarcities will develop for specific kinds of labour and for labour in certain geographic areas. Wage rates of such workers will rise. Rising wage rates mean higher costs and necessitate higher prices. The net result is rising prices, even though the economy as a whole is still operating short of full employment.

Labour market adjustments do not eliminate these bottleneck problems because labourers cannot quickly shift from one occupation, sector, or region to another. The training for a new occupation is costly in both time and money. Also, even if an unemployed labourer has the ability, time, and money to acquire new skills and relocate, what should they be and where are these skills needed?

Then, too, artificial restrictions on the shiftability of workers sustain structural imbalances. For example, discrimination based on ethnic background or gender can keep qualified workers from available positions. Similarly, licensing requirements — especially interprovincially — and union restrictions on the number of available apprentice-

ships inhibit the levelling out of imbalances between specific labour markets.

In brief, labour market adjustments are neither sufficiently rapid nor complete enough to prevent production costs and product prices from rising *before* overall full employment is achieved.

STABILIZATION POLICY DILEMMA

If the Phillips curve remains fixed, as in Figure 16-2, policy-makers are faced with a dilemma. Fiscal and monetary policies are intended merely to alter aggregate demand. They do nothing to correct the labour market imbalances and the market power fuelling inflation. The manipulation of aggregate demand through fiscal and monetary measures simply moves the economy *along* the given Phillips curve. An expansionary fiscal policy and the expansionary monetary policy that combine to shift the aggregate demand to the right and achieve a lower rate of unemployment will simultaneously produce a higher rate of inflation. A restrictive fiscal policy and a contractionary monetary policy can be used to reduce the rate of inflation, but only at the cost of a higher unemployment rate and more forgone production.

Policies to manage aggregate demand can be used to choose a point on the Phillips curve, but such policies do not improve the "unemployment rate–inflation rate" trade-off embodied in the curve. Because of the Phillips curve, it is impossible to achieve "full employment without inflation."

STAGFLATION: A SHIFTING PHILLIPS CURVE?

The concept of a stable Phillips curve broke down during the 1970s and 1980. Events of the 1970s on into the 1980s were clearly at odds with the inflation rate–unemployment rate trade-off embodied in the Phillips curve. Figure 16-3 enlarges on Figure 16-2(b) by adding data for the 1970–94 period. The relatively clear-cut inverse relationship of the 1959–69 period now becomes obscure and highly questionable.

Note in Figure 16-3 that in many years of the 1970s the economy experienced *rising* inflation and *rising* unemployment — in a word, **stagflation**. Trace, for example, the data points for 1973–75. At best, these data suggest that the Phillips curve has been shifting to the right, that is, to a less desirable position, where any level of unemployment is

FIGURE 16-3   Inflation rates and unemployment rate, 1959–1994

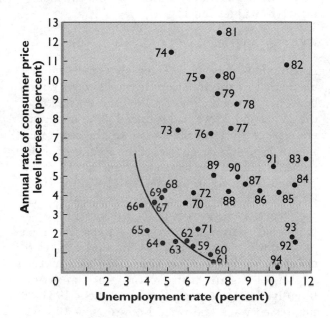

Data points for the 1959–94 period suggest no clear relationship between unemployment rates and rates of inflation. This raises questions as to the stability or existence of the Phillips curve.

FIGURE 16-4   Aggregate supply shocks and stagflation

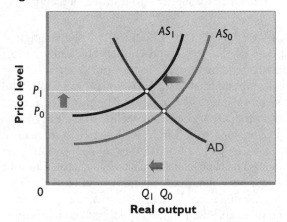

In the mainstream interpretation, in 1974–75 a series of supply shocks, including sharply increased energy costs, higher agricultural commodity prices, higher import prices, diminishing productivity growth, and inflationary expectations, shifted the aggregate supply curve leftward. The result was stagflation — a higher price level accompanied by a decline in real output.

accompanied by more inflation. At worst, the data imply that there is no dependable trade-off between unemployment and inflation.

AGGREGATE SUPPLY SHOCKS

What caused stagflation in the 1970s and early 1980s? One answer is that a series of cost or **aggregate supply shocks** occurred. And the fact that these disturbances arose on the cost or supply side makes a difference. Remember that we derived the inverse relationship between the rate of inflation and the unemployment rate shown in Figure 16-2(a) by changing the level of *aggregate demand* along the upward sloping section of the aggregate supply curve in Figure 16-1.

Now look at our cost-push inflation model in Figure 16-4. Here a decrease (leftward shift) of *aggregate supply* causes the unemployment rate and the price level to increase to give us stagflation.

Let's consider the series of more or less random adverse shocks that raised unit production costs and shifted the aggregate supply curve leftward, as from AS_0 to AS_1 in Figure 16-4, to generate the stagfla-

tion that started in 1974. We want to examine how changes in one or more of the determinants of aggregate supply contributed to inflation.

1. OPEC AND ENERGY PRICES   First and foremost, the Organization of Petroleum Exporting Countries (OPEC) oil cartel resulted in a dramatic quadrupling of oil prices. The cost of producing and distributing virtually every good and service rose sharply.

2. AGRICULTURAL SHORTFALLS   Severe worldwide agricultural shortfalls occurred in 1972 and 1973, particularly in Asia and the Soviet Union. In response, North American agricultural exports expanded sharply, reducing domestic supplies of agricultural commodities. The resulting higher prices for raw agricultural products in North America translated into higher costs to the industrial sectors producing food and fibre products. These higher costs were passed on to consumers as higher prices.

3. DEPRECIATED DOLLAR   In the 1971–73 period, the Canadian dollar (along with the U.S. dollar) fell relative to other foreign currencies. Depreciation of the dollar caused the prices of some of our imports to rise. Because many Canadian imports are production inputs, unit production costs increased and the aggregate supply curve shifted leftward.

4. PRODUCTIVITY DECLINE The stagflation episodes of the 1970s and early 1980s were not due solely to the three supply shocks just discussed. More subtle considerations involving productivity and expectations were also at work. The rate of growth of labour productivity began to decline in the early 1970s and continued to fall more or less persistently until 1982. This decline in the output per worker hour increased unit production costs. An increase in unit labour costs (labour cost per unit of output) approximates the difference between the increase in nominal-wage rates and the increase in labour productivity.

5. INFLATIONARY EXPECTATIONS AND WAGES The inflation of the 1970s had its birth in the inflation of the late 1960s, caused, at least in part, by increased government expenditures. By the early 1970s, workers had been exposed to a period of accelerating inflation. As a result, the nominal-wage demands of labour began to include the expectation of an increasing rate of inflation. Most employers, expecting to pass on higher wage costs in this context of mounting inflation, did not resist labour's demands for larger and larger increases in nominal wages. (Recall from Chapter 15 that a reciprocal relationship exists between the general price level and the purchasing power of money. The nominal wage refers simply to the money wage, whereas the real wage refers to the purchasing power of that wage.) These nominal-wage increases raised unit production costs and tend to shift aggregate supply from AS_0 to AS_1 in Figure 16-4.

We can incorporate both **inflationary expectations** *and* declining labour productivity as causes of stagflation. If nominal wages are being pushed up at an accelerating rate and the growth rate of labour productivity is simultaneously falling, there will be a double impetus for unit labour costs — and ultimately product prices — to rise.

Regardless of the causes of stagflation, it was clear in the 1970s that the Phillips curve did not represent a stable relationship. Adverse (leftward) shifts in aggregate supply were at work that seemed to explain those occasions when the inflation rate and the unemployment rate increased simultaneously. To many economists the experience of the

1970s and early 1980s suggested the Phillips curve was shifting to the right and confronting the economy with higher rates of inflation and unemployment. **(Key Question 1)**

STAGFLATION'S DEMISE: 1983–1989

A return look at Figure 16-3 reveals a modest inward movement of the inflation-unemployment points between 1983 and 1989. By 1989 the stagflation of the 1970s and 1980s had subsided. One important precursor of this favourable trend was the deep recession of 1982–83, largely caused by a contractionary monetary policy. The recession propelled the unemployment rate to an average of 11.9% for 1983. Under conditions of labour market slack, workers accepted smaller increases in their nominal wages — or in some cases wage reductions — to preserve their jobs. Firms, in turn, had to restrain price hikes to maintain their relative shares of a diminished market.

Other significant factors were at work. Intensive foreign competition throughout 1983–89 suppressed wage and price hikes in several basic industries such as automobiles and steel. A decline in OPEC's monopoly power produced a stunning fall in the price of oil and its derivative products.

All these factors combined to reduce unit production costs and to shift the aggregate supply curve rightward (as from AS_1 to AS_0 in Figure 16-4). Meanwhile, a record-long peacetime economic expansion created 1.7 million new jobs between 1983 and 1988. The previously very high unemployment rate therefore fell from 11.9% in 1983 to 7.6% by the end of 1989. Figure 16-3 reveals that the inflation-unemployment points represented for 1987-89 are closer to the points associated with the Phillips curve for the 1960s than the points in the late 1970s and early 1980s.

During the stagflation of 1980–82, inflation and unemployment simultaneously *increased*; during several of the years of the economic expansion of 1983–89, inflation and unemployment simultaneously *declined*. Global Perspective 16-1 is relevant to this latter point.

THE NATURAL-RATE HYPOTHESIS

The standard explanation for the scattering of inflation rate-unemployment points to the right of the 1960s Phillips curve is that a

GLOBAL PERSPECTIVE 16-1

The misery index, selected nations, 1984–1994

The so-called "misery index" adds together a nation's unemployment rate and its inflation rate to get a measure of national economic discomfort. For example, a nation with a 5% rate of unemployment and 5% inflation rate would have a misery index number of 10, as would a nation with an 8% unemployment rate and 2% inflation.

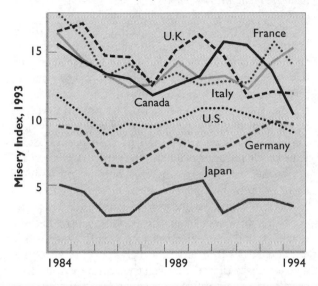

Source: U.S. Government, *Economic Report of the President*, 1995.

series of supply shocks shifted the aggregate supply curve *leftward* moving the Phillips curve rightward and upward as suggested in Figure 16-3. The inward collapse of inflation rate-unemployment points in the 1980s came about because of *rightward* shifts of the aggregate supply curve. Thus, a trade-off between the inflation rate and the unemployment rate still may exist in the short run, but changes in aggregate supply may change the menu of inflation and unemployment choices — they may shift the Phillips curve itself — during some abnormal periods.

A second explanation of simultaneously higher rates of unemployment and inflation is associated with the **natural-rate hypothesis**. It questions the very existence of the downsloping Phillips curve as portrayed in Figure 16-3. This view concludes that the economy is stable in the long run at the natural rate of unemployment. We know from Chapter 8 that the natural rate of unemployment is the rate of unem-

ployment that exists when cyclical unemployment is zero; it is the full-employment rate of unemployment.

According to the natural-rate hypothesis, misguided full-employment policies, based on the incorrect assumption of a stable Phillips curve will result in an increasing rate of inflation. The natural-rate hypothesis has its empirical roots in Figure 16-3, where one can argue that a vertical line located at a presumed 7% or 8% natural rate of unemployment summarizes the inflation-unemployment "relationship" better than the traditional downsloping Phillips curve. According to the natural-rate hypothesis, any particular rate of inflation is compatible with the economy's natural rate of unemployment.

There are two variants of the natural-rate interpretation of the inflation-unemployment data points shown in Figure 16-3: the adaptive expectations and rational expectations theories.

ADAPTIVE EXPECTATIONS THEORY

The **theory of adaptive expectations** assumes people form their expectations of future inflation on the basis of previous and present rates of inflation, and only gradually change their expectations as experience unfolds. The adaptive expectations theory was advanced and popularized by Milton Friedman, a Nobel prize winner in economics.

The adaptive expectations theory suggests there may be a short-run trade-off between inflation and unemployment, but in the long run no such trade-off exists. Any attempt to reduce the unemployment rate below the natural rate sets in motion forces that destabilize the Phillips curve and shift it rightward. Thus, the adaptive expectations view distinguishes between a "short-run" and a "long-run" Phillips curve.

SHORT-RUN PHILLIPS CURVE Consider Phillips curve PC_0 in Figure 16-5. Suppose the economy initially is experiencing a mild 3% rate of inflation and a 6% natural rate of unemployment. In the adaptive expectations theory, such short-run curves as PC_0 (drawn as straight lines for simplicity) exist because the actual rate of inflation is not always the same as the expected rate.

Establishing an additional point on Phillips curve PC_0 will clarify. We begin at a_0, where we assume nominal wages are set on the expectation that the 3% rate of inflation will continue. But now suppose that government mistakenly judges

FIGURE 16-5   The adaptive expectations theory

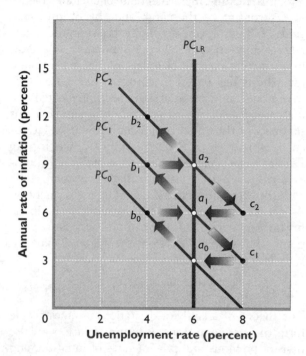

The expansion of aggregate demand may temporarily increase profits and therefore output and employment (a_0 to b_0). But nominal wages will soon rise, reducing profits and thereby negating the short-run stimulus to production and employment (b_0 to a_1). Consequently, in the long run there is no trade-off between the rates of inflation and unemployment; the long-run Phillips curve is vertical. This suggests expansionary policies will generate accelerating inflation rather than a lower rate of unemployment. On a more positive note, it also implies restrictive stabilization policies can reduce inflation without creating long-lived increases in unemployment.

the full-employment unemployment rate to be 4% instead of 6%. This misjudgement might occur because the economy temporarily achieved a 4% rate of unemployment in an earlier period. To achieve the targeted 4% rate of unemployment, suppose the government invokes expansionary fiscal and monetary policy.

The resulting increase in aggregate demand boosts the rate of inflation to 6%. With a specific level of nominal wages, *set on the expectation that the rate of inflation would continue to be 3%*, the higher product prices raise business profits. Firms respond to expanded profits by increasing output and therefore hiring workers. In the short run, the economy moves to point b_0, which

in contrast with a_0, entails a lower rate of unemployment (4%) and a higher rate of inflation (6%).

This movement from a_0 to b_0 is generally consistent with our earlier interpretation of the Phillips curve. Presumably, the economy has accepted some inflation as the "cost" of achieving a reduced level of unemployment. But the natural-rate theorists interpret the movement from a_0 to b_0 quite differently. They see it as only a manifestation of the following principle: *When the actual rate of inflation is higher than expected, profits temporarily rise and the unemployment rate temporarily falls.*

LONG-RUN VERTICAL PHILLIPS CURVE

Point b_0 is *not* a stable equilibrium position in this theory. Workers recognize their nominal wages have not been rising as fast as inflation. They therefore demand and receive nominal wage increases to restore purchasing power. But, as nominal wages rise to restore the previous level of real wages existing at a_0, business profits fall to their earlier level. This profit reduction means that the original motivation of businesses to increase output and employ more workers disappears.

Unemployment returns to its natural level at point a_1. Note, however, that the economy now faces a higher actual *and* expected rate of inflation — 6% rather than 3%. Because the higher level of aggregate demand that originally moved the economy from a_0 to b_0 still exists, the inflation it engendered still persists.

In view of the now-higher 6% expected rate of inflation, the short-run Phillips curve shifts upward from PC_0 to PC_1. In brief, an "along the Phillips curve" kind of movement from a_0 to b_0 on PC_0 is merely a short-run or transient phenomenon. In the long run — after nominal wages catch up with price level increases — unemployment will return to the natural rate at a_1 and a new short-run Phillips curve PC_1 exists at the higher expected rate of inflation.

If we conceive of a_0b_0, a_1b_1, a_2b_2 as a series of short-run Phillips curves, the adaptive expectations theory can be interpreted as saying that, ironically, government attempts through policy initiatives to move along the short-run Phillips curve (a_0 to b_0 on PC_0) *cause* the curve to shift to a *less* favourable position (PC_1, then PC_2, and so on). A stable Phillips curve with the dependable series of unemployment rate-inflation rate trade-offs does not exist.

There is in fact no *higher* rate of inflation (such as 6% at b_0) that can be accepted as the "cost" of reduced unemployment *in the long run*. The *long-run relationship* between unemployment and inflation is shown by the vertical line through a_0, a_1, a_2. Any rate of inflation is consistent with the 6% natural rate of unemployment. The Phillips curve trade-off, portrayed in Figure 16-2, does not exist.

DISINFLATION   We can also employ the adaptive expectations theory to explain **disinflation** — reductions in the rate of inflation. Suppose in Figure 16-5 the economy is at point a_2 where the inflation rate is 9% and the unemployment rate is 6%. A significant decline in aggregate demand such as that associated with the 1982–83 recession will reduce inflation below the 9% expected rate, say, to 6%. Business profits will fall because product prices are rising less rapidly than wages. The nominal wage increases, remember, were set on the assumption that the 9% rate of inflation would continue. In response to the profit decline, firms will reduce their employment and consequently the unemployment rate will rise. The economy will temporarily slide downward from point a_2 to c_2 along short-run Phillips curve PC_2. According to the natural rate theorists, *when the actual rate of inflation is lower than the expected rate, profits temporarily fall and the unemployment rate temporarily rises.*

Firms and workers will eventually adjust their expectations to the new 6% rate of inflation and thus newly negotiated wage increases will decline. Profits will be restored, employment will rise, and the unemployment rate will return to its natural rate of 6% at point a_1. Because the expected rate of inflation is now 6%, the short-run Phillips curve PC_2 will shift leftward to PC_1.

If aggregate demand falls further, the scenario will continue. Inflation will decline from 6%, to say, 3%, moving the economy from a_1 to c_1 along PC_1. The reason once again is that the lower-than-expected rate of inflation (lower prices) has squeezed profits and reduced employment. But, in the long run, firms can be expected to respond to the lower profits by reducing their nominal wage increases. Profits will therefore be restored and unemployment will return to its natural rate at a_0 as the short-run Phillips curve moves from PC_1 to PC_0. Once again, the long-run Phillips curve is vertical at the natural rate of unemployment. **(Key Question 2)**

RATIONAL EXPECTATIONS THEORY

The adaptive expectations theory assumes that changes in nominal wages lag behind changes in the price level. This lag gives rise to *temporary* increases in profits, which in turn *temporarily* stimulate employment.

Rational expectations theory is the second variant of the natural-rate hypothesis. This theory contends that businesses, consumers, and workers generally understand how the economy functions and effectively use available information to protect or further their own self-interests. In particular, people understand how government policies will affect the economy and anticipate these impacts in their own decision-making.

This supposes that, when government invokes expansionary policies, workers anticipate inflation and a subsequent decline in real wages. They therefore immediately incorporate this expected inflation into their nominal wage demands. If workers correctly and fully anticipate the amount of price inflation and adjust their current nominal-wage demands accordingly so as to maintain their real wages, then even the temporary increases in profits, output, and employment will *not* occur. Instead of the temporary increase in employment shown by the movement from a_0 to b_0 in Figure 16-5, the movement will be directly from a_0 to a_1. Fully anticipated inflation by labour means there will be no short-run decline in unemployment. Price inflation, fully anticipated in the money wage demands of workers, will generate a vertical line through a_0, a_1, a_2 in Figure 16-5.

The policy implication is that fiscal and monetary policy measures to achieve a mis-specified full-employment rate of unemployment will generate an increasing rate of inflation, not a lower rate of unemployment. Note that the adaptive and rational expectations theories are consistent with the conservative philosophy that government's attempts to do good deeds typically fail and at considerable cost to society. In this instance, the "cost" is accelerating inflation.

CHANGING INTERPRETATIONS

Interpretations of the Phillips curve have changed dramatically over the past three decades. The original idea of a stable trade-off between unemployment and inflation has given way to the adaptive expectations view that, while a short-run trade-off existed, no such trade-off is available in the long run.

The more controversial rational expectations theory stresses that macroeconomic policy is ineffective because it is anticipated by workers. Not even a short-run trade-off between unemployment and inflation exists.

BOX 16-2   IN THE MEDIA

INFLATION SPECTRE HAUNTS FINANCIAL MARKETS

Investors worry despite growth in big economies

BY PETER COOK
Economics Editor

As the world enters 1995, all its big economies are growing with almost no inflation. But this good news, celebrated by those who run governments, is going uncelebrated in one important place — financial markets.

Markets for capital take a critical, some would say jaundiced, view of the world because they focus not on the known present, for which politicians take credit, but on the uncertain future.

At the moment, there is a marked difference between present and future. Take the world's biggest economy, the United States, as an example. Its strong performance in 1994 is not going to be duplicated in 1995 because there is insufficient spare capacity in its factories and its labour market and, if it did, inflation would soar. Instead, interest rates have been rising to ensure that growth is kept down.

As of now, the Clinton administration can say it has achieved a wonderful combination of strong growth and low inflation and, even, that it is solvent enough to offer Americans tax cuts.

But U.S. financial markets spent the tail end of the year as they had spent most of the rest of it — worrying about the imminence of another rise in official interest rates, worrying about whether the inflation genie would slip out of the bottle

soon, and worrying about whether the economy would be hit by a slowdown later in 1995 or even a recession early in 1996.

To ward off all this, investors in the bond market continued to demand, and receive, a high premium. Inflation may be down. But to look at borrowing costs in the United States — and, still more, in high-debtor countries like Canada, Sweden and Italy — it appears no battle has been won.

Interest rates across the maturity spectrum in Canada are roughly where they were in 1989; then, inflation was 5 per cent, now it is 1 per cent.

The consequence of high interest rates, and a rapid climb in those rates, casts a pall over the future. Linked to it is concern not only about inflation but also about what governments must do to cut their deficits and make their debt-servicing costs more manageable.

In the opinion of financial markets — which have made their opinion clearer as 1994 has unfolded — there is an opportunity for the major economies to benefit from global growth and recovery. But seizing that opportunity requires two things, that prices remain stable and that public borrowing shrinks....

SOURCE: *Globe and Mail*, January 3, 1995, p. B1. Reproduced by permission.

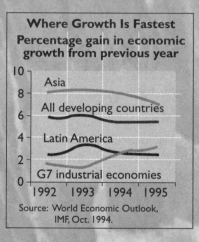

Where Growth Is Fastest
Percentage gain in economic growth from previous year

Source: World Economic Outlook, IMF, Oct. 1994.

DEBTORS' LEAGUE

Gross government debt and current-year deficit as a percentage of GDP for major industrial countries, 1995

	Debt	Deficit
Italy	126%	9.1%
Sweden	103	10.2
CANADA	**96**	**4.7**
Japan	83	1.8
Spain	67	6.1
United States	65	1.8
France	59	5.0
Britain	54	4.7

Source: OECD Economic Outlook, Dec. 1994

The Story in Brief

Despite a low rate of current inflation in early 1995, investors in the bond market continued to demand a high premium because of the expectation of higher future inflation. Investors were concerned not only about strong economic growth in 1994, but the high debt loads of many countries.

The Economics Behind the Story

- Investors look at the real return on their financial investment.

- Fearing that rapid economic growth and high demand for funds by heavily indebted governments might spur inflation, investors worried that their real returns on investments would fall.

- Such expectations of inflation led investors to demand a higher interest rate premium, even if the current inflation rate was low.

- If workers expect the inflation rate will rise, they will attempt to compensate for the higher expected inflation by higher wage demands. What factors could impede higher wage demands in a small open economy such as Canada's?

Taken together, the natural-rate hypotheses (adaptive and rational expectations theories) conclude that, in the long run, demand-management policies cannot influence real output and employment but only the price level.

Which view is correct? Most economists accept the notion of a short-run trade-off while recognizing that in the long run such a trade-off is much less likely. They also believe aggregate supply shocks can cause stagflation. The episodes of rising unemployment and inflation during the 1970s and early 1980s were *not* exclusively the products of misguided stabilization policies.

QUICK REVIEW 16-1

1. The original Phillips curve showed an apparent stable, inverse relationship between annual unemployment rates and inflation rates over a period of years.

2. Stagflation occurred in 1973–75 and 1980–82 and produced Phillips curve data points above and to the right of the Phillips curve for the 1960s.

3. The following aggregate supply shocks contributed to stagflation during the 1970s and early 1980s: **a** OPEC oil price hikes, **b** poor agricultural harvests, **c** dollar depreciation, **d** a productivity decline, and **e** inflationary expectations.

4. The natural rate hypothesis holds that the economy automatically gravitates to its natural rate of unemployment; therefore the Phillips curve is vertical in the long run.

AGGREGATE SUPPLY REVISITED

The distinction between short-run Phillips curves and the long-run vertical Phillips curve has stimulated new thinking about aggregate supply.

In Figures 16-1 and 16-2(a) the Phillips curve was derived by shifting aggregate demand rightward along a *stable* short-run aggregate supply curve. Firms responded to the increasing price level by producing more and increasing their employment. Thus, the unemployment rate fell as the price level rose.

The natural-rate theory suggests, however, that the short-run aggregate supply curve in Figure 16-1 is stable only so long as nominal wages remain constant. Once workers alter their expectations in response to a higher price level, they will demand and receive higher money wages so as to restore their real wages. An increase in nominal wages, other things equal, will *shift* the short-run aggregate supply curve leftward. That is, a change in nominal wages is one of the determinants of short-run aggregate supply.

These short-run aggregate supply-curve shifts imply a long-run aggregate supply curve. Thus, we must distinguish between the short-run and long-run aggregate supply.

DEFINITIONS: SHORT RUN AND LONG RUN

Here *the short run is a period in which input prices — particularly nominal wages — remain fixed in the presence of a change in the price level*. There are two basic reasons that input prices may remain constant for a time even though the price level has changed.

1. Workers may not immediately be aware of the existence of a higher or a lower price level. So, they will have no knowledge that their real wages have changed and will not adjust their wage demands accordingly.
2. Many employees are hired under conditions of fixed-wage contracts. Unionized employees, for example, receive nominal wages based on the terms of their collective bargaining agreements. Also, most managers and many professionals receive set salaries established in annual contracts.

The upshot of the lack of information about the price level and the existence of labour contracts is that changes in the price level normally do not immediately change nominal wages.

The long run is a period in which input prices (wages) are fully responsive to changes in the price level. With sufficient time, workers can gain full information about price-level changes and can ascertain the effects on their real wage. Workers will be aware that a price-level increase has reduced their real wage and that a price-level decline has increased their real wage. More importantly, workers and employers in the long run are freed from their existing labour contracts and can negotiate changes in nominal wages and salaries.

With these definitions in mind, let's add further details to our previous discussion of aggregate supply.

SHORT-RUN AGGREGATE SUPPLY

Consider the **short-run aggregate supply curve** AS_0 in **Figure 16-6(a) (Key Graph)**. This curve is constructed on the basis of two assumptions: (1) the initial price level is P_0, and (2) nominal wages have been established on the expectation that the price

level P_0 will persist. Observe from point a_0 and the vertical dotted line intersecting it, the economy is operating at its full-employment level of real output Q_f at price level P_0. This real output is the real production forthcoming when the economy is operating at its natural rate of unemployment.

Now let's determine the consequence of changes in the price level by initially examining an *increase* in the price level from P_0 to P_1. Because nominal wages are fixed in the short run, it is apparent that the higher product prices associated with P_1 will enhance profits. In response to the higher profits, producers will increase their output from Q_f to Q_1, as indicated by the movement from a_0 to a_1 on AS_0. Observe that at Q_1 the economy is operating beyond its full-employment output. This is made possible by extending work hours of part-time and full-time workers, enticing new workers such as homemakers and retirees into the labour force, and hiring and training the structurally unemployed. Thus, the nation's unemployment rate will decline below its natural rate.

How will producers respond when there is a *decrease* in the price level from P_1 to P_2 in Figure 16-6(a)? Firms will discover that their profits have diminished or disappeared. After all, product prices have dropped while nominal wages have not. Producers therefore will reduce employment and production and, as revealed by point a_2, real output will fall to Q_2. This decline in real output will be accompanied by an unemployment rate greater than the natural rate.

LONG-RUN AGGREGATE SUPPLY

By definition, nominal wages are fully responsive in the long run to changes in the price level. What are the implications of this assumption for aggregate supply?

In Figure 16-6(b) again, suppose the economy initially is at point a_0 (P_0 and Q_f). Our previous discussion indicated that an *increase* in the price level from P_0 to P_1 will move the economy from point a_0 to a_1 along short-run aggregate supply curve AS_0. In the long run, workers will discover their real wages have fallen as a result of this increase in the price level. They will therefore demand and presumably receive higher nominal wages to restore their previous level of real wages. The short-run aggregate supply curve will shift leftward from AS_0 to AS_1. This short-run AS curve will now reflect the *higher* price

KEY GRAPH

FIGURE 16-6   Short-run and long-run aggregate supply

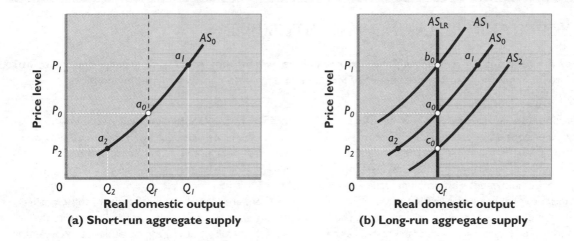

In the short run (a), input prices such as nominal wages are assumed to be fixed based on price level P_0. Hence, an increase in the price level will bolster profits and entice firms to expand real output. Alternatively, a decrease in the price level will reduce profits and real output. The short-run AS curve therefore slopes upward. In the long run (b), a price level rise will result in an increase in nominal wages and thus a leftward shift of the short-run AS curve. Conversely, a decrease in the price level will produce a decline in nominal wages and a rightward shift of the short-run AS curve. The long-run AS curve therefore is vertical.

level P_1 and the expectation that P_1 will continue. Figure 16-6(b) shows that the leftward shift in the short-run aggregate supply to AS_1 curve will move the economy from a_1 to b_0. Real output will fall to its full-employment level and the unemployment rate will return to its natural rate.

A *decrease* in the price level from P_0 to P_2 in Figure 16-6(b) will produce an opposite scenario. The economy will initially move from point a_0 to point a_2, where profits will be squeezed or eliminated because prices have fallen and nominal wages have not. But this is simply the short-run response. With enough time, the lower price level P_2, which has increased the real wage, together with the higher unemployment associated with the reduction in real output, will diminish nominal wages. We know that sufficiently lower nominal wages will shift the short-run aggregate supply curve rightward to AS_2 and real output will return to Q_f at point c_0.

By tracing a line between the long-run equilibrium points b_0, a_0, and c_0, a **long-run aggregate supply curve** appears. Observe that it is vertical at the full-employment level of real output, Q_f.

POLICY IMPLICATIONS

You may well ask at this point what is the use of aggregate demand management policy in the face of a vertical long-run aggregate supply curve. If the economy will eventually settle at the full-employment level of GDP, why tinker with it?

THE NATURE OF THE SELF-CORRECTING MECHANISM

If the economy's self-correcting mechanism functioned quickly there would be no need for corrective anti-cyclical policies. Let's examine the economy's self-correcting mechanism using inflationary and recessionary gaps.

INFLATIONARY GAP   **Figure 16-7(a) (Key Graph)** shows the economy with an inflationary gap. What would occur if the authorities did nothing? You will recall from Chapter 11 that if input prices increase, the short-run aggregate supply curve will shift left. With an inflationary gap, there will be upward pressure on the price of inputs. Even if the authorities did nothing, the short-run aggregate

BOX 16-3   APPLYING THE THEORY

PROFIT SHARING: MAKING WAGES FLEXIBLE

One of the problems of reducing inflation is that unemployment may result. Can greater downward wage flexibility be achieved to soften the impact of a decline in aggregate demand on employment?

Most economists recognize that labour contracts, among other considerations, make wages downwardly inflexible, at least in the short run. The declines in labour demand accompanying recessions, therefore primarily affect employment. This problem has led some economists to propose profit sharing as a way to increase the downward flexibility of wage rates. The idea is to make labour markets operate more like the new classical model, with its vertical aggregate supply curve, by creating greater employment stability.*

The essence of these profit-sharing proposals is to tie some portion of wages directly to the firm's profitability, making profit-sharing payments a part of workers' pay. Instead of paying workers a guaranteed wage rate of, say, $10 per hour, workers might be guaranteed $5 per hour (the base wage) and additional compensation equal to some predetermined percentage of the firm's profits (the profit-share wage). Total compensation (base wage + profit-share wage) may exceed or fall short of $10 per hour, depending on the firm's economic fortunes.

How would such a plan affect employment? Initially assume workers are receiving $10 per hour — $5 as a guaranteed wage and another $5 as profit-sharing compensation. Now suppose a recession occurs and the employer's sales and profits plummet. The $5 of profit-sharing income will fall and might decline to zero so that the actual wages paid by the firm fall from $10

---

*This idea is developed in detail in Martin L. Weitzman, *The Share Economy* (Cambridge, Mass.: Harvard University Press, 1984).

to $5 an hour. With the new depressed demand for labour, the firm would clearly choose to employ more workers under this wage system than the standard system. Hourly wages will have automatically fallen from $10 to $5.

There are a number of criticisms of these profit-sharing wage plans. The plans might jeopardize the wage uniformity and wage gains achieved by organized labour. A further criticism is that employers might respond to the low base wage by adopting production techniques that use relatively more labour and less capital. Because the amount of capital equipment per worker is critical to productivity and economic growth, this pay scheme might impair the long-run expansion of real GDP. At the pragmatic level, critics point out that wage plans linked to profits eliminate the present certainty that workers have as to whether their employers have properly fulfilled the labour contract. With profit sharing, employers might use accounting and other techniques to hide profits and therefore evade paying share wages.

Finally, there is the fundamental question as to whether workers will accept more jobs and greater employment stability in exchange for a reduced hourly wage guarantee and higher variability of earnings. But it should be noted that in the past decade a growing number of union and nonunion contracts have contained profit-sharing arrangements. Although a full-blown profit-sharing economy seems improbable, limited profit-sharing appears to be spreading.

---

supply curve would shift to the left until the inflationary gap was eliminated.

RECESSIONARY GAP   Similarly, a recessionary gap would resolve itself over the long run as real input prices — particularly wages — would fall, and

the aggregate supply curve would shift to the right towards the natural rate of unemployment. Such an adjustment is shown in Figure 16-7(b).

MONETARY AND FISCAL POLICIES   As Chapter 17 will show, there is still debate about the speed with

FIGURE 16-7 The economy's self-adjusting mechanism in the long run

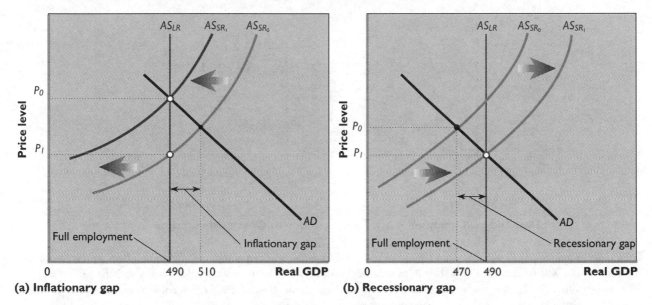

(a) Inflationary gap

(b) Recessionary gap

The long-run aggregate supply curve implies that inflationary and recessionary gaps will resolve themselves in the long run. With an inflationary gap (a), the bidding up of input prices will shift the short-run aggregate supply curve to the left, from AS_{SR_0} to AS_{SR_1}. With a recessionary gap (b), input prices will eventually fall, particularly real wages — and shift the short-run aggregate supply to the right, from AS_{SR_0} to AS_{SR_1}.

which the economy's self-adjusting mechanism works. Many believe that in the case of a recessionary gap in particular, the economy's self-adjusting mechanism is unacceptably slow because wages are "sticky" downward. The economy will eventually get back to the full-employment level GDP, but only after enduring a long period of recession. A sizable majority of economists believe that there is still an important role for both monetary and fiscal policy to speed the economy along to its full-employment GDP.

DEMAND-PULL AND COST-PUSH INFLATION

Let's now apply our new tools of short-run and long-run aggregate supply to demand-pull and cost-push inflation.

DEMAND-PULL INFLATION

Demand-pull inflation occurs when an increase in aggregate demand pulls up the price level. In our more complete version of aggregate supply, an increase in the price level will eventually produce

an increase in nominal wages and thus a leftward *shift* of the short-run aggregate supply curve itself. This is shown in **Figure 16-8(a) (Key Graph)**.

Suppose the price level is P_0, at the intersection of aggregate demand curve AD_0 and aggregate supply curve AS_0. The aggregate supply curve AS_0 is a short-run curve based on the nominal wages associated with the price level P_0. These nominal wages were set on the expectation P_0 would persist. Observe that at *a* the economy is achieving its full employment real output Q_f.

Now consider the effects of an increase in aggregate demand such as shown by the rightward shift from AD_0 to AD_1 in Figure 16-8(a). This shift can result from any one of a number of factors, including an increase in the money supply, an increase in investment spending, and so forth. Whatever its cause, the increase in aggregate demand boosts the price level from P_0 to P_1 and expands output to Q_1 at point *b*.

So far, nothing new has been said. But now we must ask, what will happen to the short-run aggregate supply curve once workers realize their real

KEY GRAPH

FIGURE 16-8   Demand-pull and cost-push inflation

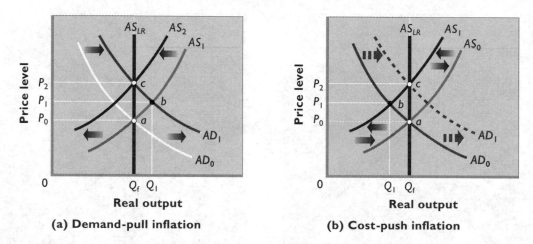

(a) Demand-pull inflation   **(b) Cost-push inflation**

In (a), an increase in AD will drive up the price level and increase real output in the short run. But, in the long run, nominal wages will rise and AS will shift leftward. Real output will return to its previous level and the price level will rise still further. In (b), cost-push inflation occurs when AS shifts leftward. If government counters the decline in real output by increasing AD to the broken line, the price level will rise even further. On the other hand, if government allows a recession to occur, nominal wages eventually will fall and the AS curve will shift back rightward to its original location. Observe that the long-run AS curves are vertical in both (a) and (b).

wages have fallen and once their existing contracts have expired? Our answer is that nominal wages will rise, and as they do, the short-run aggregate supply curve will shift leftward, as from AS_0 to AS_1. Consequently, the price level will further increase to P_2 at point c and the equilibrium level of output will return to its full-employment level Q_f.

In the short run, demand-pull inflation will drive up the price level and increase real output; in the long run, only the price level will rise. In the long run, the increase in aggregate demand has only moved the economy along its vertical aggregate supply curve AS_{LR}.

COST-PUSH INFLATION

Cost-push inflation arises from increases in the cost of production at each price level — factors that shift the aggregate supply curve leftward — and therefore increases the price level. But our previous analysis considered only the short-run aggregate supply. Let's now examine the cost-push theory in the long-run context.

ANALYSIS   Look at Figure 16-8(b), in which the economy is initially assumed to be operating at the

P_0 and Q_f levels of price and output at point a. Suppose that, by exerting monopoly power, labour unions secure nominal wage gains exceeding advances in labour productivity. Moreover, suppose that many nonunion employers, wishing to deter unionism in their own enterprises, respond by increasing the nominal wages they pay to keep them proportionate to union wage scales. As wages and unit production costs rise, the short-run aggregate supply curve shifts leftward, as depicted by the movement from AS_0 to AS_1.

The price level rises from P_0 to P_1, as shown by point b. In this case, aggregate supply curve AS_1 has resulted from a wage-rate hike and therefore is the *cause* of the price-level rising from P_0 to P_1. The shift of the aggregate supply curve from AS_0 to AS_1 is not a *response* to a price-level increase, as was the case in our previous discussions of short- versus long-run aggregate supply.

POLICY DILEMMA   Cost-push inflation creates a major dilemma for policy-makers. If aggregate demand in Figure 16-8(b) remains at AD_0 real output will decline from Q_f to Q_1. Government can counter this recession and its attendant unemployment by using stabilization policies to increase aggregate demand to AD_1. But there is a potential policy trap. An increase in aggregate demand to AD_1 will further aggravate inflation by increasing the price level from P_1 to P_2 at point c.

And the P_1 to P_2 increase in the price level is not likely to be a one-time boost because wage earners will respond to a decline in their real wages by seeking and receiving increases in nominal wages. If they are successful, the higher nominal wages will cause a further increase in per-unit production costs. This will shift the short-run aggregate supply curve (not shown) to a position left of AS_1. This leftward shift of the short-run aggregate supply curve is in *response* to the higher price level P_2 that was caused by the rightward shift of aggregate demand to AD_1. You may wish to draw in this leftward shift of AS to convince yourself that such a shift of aggregate supply will regenerate the stagflation problem.

In brief, government will have to increase aggregate demand once again to restore the Q_f level of real output. But if government does so, the scenario may simply repeat itself.

The point is that shifts in the short-run aggregate supply curve may be induced when government applies expansionary demand-management policy to alleviate output reductions resulting from cost-push inflation. These shifts in short-run aggregate supply frustrate the attainment of the natural rate of unemployment and increase the price level.

Suppose that government recognizes the policy trap and decides *not* to increase aggregate demand from AD_0 to AD_1. Instead the government decides to allow a cost-push induced recession to run its course. Widespread layoffs, plant shutdowns, and business failures will eventually occur. At some point there will be sufficient slack in labour markets to undo the initial leftward shift of short-run aggregate supply — a severe recession will shift the short-run aggregate supply from AS_1 back to AS_0. The price level will return to P_0 and the full-employment level of output will be restored along long-run aggregate supply AS_{LR}.

Two generalizations emerge:

1. *If government attempts to maintain full employment under conditions of cost-push inflation, an inflationary spiral is likely to occur.*
2. *If government takes a "hands-off" approach to cost-push inflation, a recession will occur.*

Although the recession eventually will undo the initial rise in production costs, the economy meanwhile will experience high unemployment and a loss of real output. **(Key Question 7)**

QUICK REVIEW 16-2

1. The short-run aggregate supply curve has a positive slope because nominal wages are assumed to be fixed as the price level changes.

2. The long-run aggregate supply curve is vertical because wages and other input prices eventually respond fully to changes in the price level.

3. In the short run, demand-pull inflation will increase the price level and domestic output; in the long run, only the price level will rise.

4. Cost-push inflation creates a policy dilemma for government: If it engages in an expansionary stabilization policy to increase output, an inflationary spiral may ensue; if it does nothing, a recession may occur.

OTHER OPTIONS

Experiences with cost-push inflation and the difficulties in using demand-management policies to deal with it have led government to seek out additional policy options. In Figure 16-8(b) these policies are designed to prevent the aggregate supply curve from shifting leftward. Or if the economy is experiencing stagflation, the goal would be to shift the aggregate supply curve rightward towards AS_0.

Generally speaking, three categories of policies have been used: (1) employment and retraining policy; (2) wage–price, or incomes, policy; and (3) the set of policies known as "supply-side economics."

EMPLOYMENT AND TRAINING POLICY

The goal of **employment and training policy** is to improve the efficiency of labour markets so that any given level of aggregate demand will be associated with a lower level of unemployment. The purpose of this policy is to achieve a better matching of workers to jobs, reducing labour market imbalances or bottlenecks. Several different kinds of programs provide a better matching of workers to jobs.

VOCATIONAL TRAINING

Programs of vocationally oriented education and training permit marginal and displaced workers to be more quickly reemployed. The federal government, while carefully avoiding *direct* involvement in education, which is under provincial jurisdiction, provides for both institutional and on-the-job training for the unemployed, for disadvantaged youth, and for older workers whose skills are meagre or obsolete. New government programs emphasize apprenticeship training to ease the transition from high school to work, thus reducing the high unemployment rates for youth who do not attend college or university.

JOB INFORMATION

A second type of employment and training policy is concerned with improving the flow of job information between unemployed workers and potential employers, and with enhancing the geographic mobility of workers. Federal legislation has experimented with subsidies to help defray the relocation costs of workers who are willing to move from high-unemployment areas to more prosperous regions.

NONDISCRIMINATION

Another facet of employment and training policy tries to reduce or eliminate artificial obstacles to employment. The rate of unemployment among native Canadians — often at 50% and more — is related, at least in part, to discrimination. Equal-opportunity legislation enacted by all the provinces is designed to combat discrimination in hiring, promotion, and conditions of employment.

WAGE–PRICE (INCOMES) POLICIES

A second approach to stagflation views monopoly power and labour market imbalances as inevitable facts of economic life. This approach seeks to alter the behaviour of labour and product-market monopolists to make their wage and price decisions more compatible with the twin goals of full employment and price level stability. Although they differ primarily in degree, it is useful to distinguish between **wage–price guideposts** and **wage–price controls**. Both guideposts and controls establish standards of noninflationary wage and price increases. But guideposts rely on voluntary compliance by labour and business, whereas under controls the standards are enforced by law.

Wage–price guideposts and wage–price controls are also referred to as **incomes policies**. That's because they are designed to constrain excessive rises in nominal income payments (wages, rents, interest, profits), which presumably are contributing to inflation. By limiting the increases in nominal income and prices, incomes policies affect real income — the amount of goods and services obtained with one's nominal income. Real income depends on the two targets of wage–price guideposts or controls: the size of the nominal income and the prices of the goods and services bought.

Canada opted for income controls on October 13, 1975, in circumstances worse than those facing the United States more than four years earlier. Canada's consumer price index was rising at a rate of more than 10% a year and wage settlements at a rate of 10% — both rates greatly exceeding those then prevailing in the United States. Though Canada was also faced with high unemployment — 7.1% for 1975 — the government did not adopt an expansionary fiscal policy through tax cuts, as President Nixon had done in 1971. While the 1975 federal deficit was more than $4 billion, it was a "passive" deficit, not one deliberately engineered by the government to stimulate aggregate demand.

THE WAGE–PRICE POLICY DEBATES

Incomes policy has evoked heated and prolonged debate in both Canada and the United States. The debate centres on two points.

1. WORKABILITY AND COMPLIANCE Critics argue that voluntary *guideposts* fail because they ask business and labour leaders to abandon their primary functions and to forgo the goals of maximum profits and higher wages. A union leader will not gain favour with members by reducing demands; nor is a corporate official endeared to stockholders by by-passing profitable price increases. For these reasons, little voluntary co-operation can be expected from labour and management.

Wage and price *controls* have the force of law, and therefore government can force labour and management to obey. Nevertheless, problems of enforcement and compliance can be severe, particularly if wage and price controls are comprehensive and if they are maintained for an extended time. *Black markets* — illegal markets where prices exceed legal maximums — become commonplace under these circumstances. Furthermore, firms can circumvent price controls by lowering the quality or size of their product. If the price of a candy bar is frozen at 40¢, its price can be effectively doubled by reducing its size by one-half.

Proponents of incomes policies point out that inflation is frequently fuelled by *inflations expectations*. Workers demand unusually large money wage increases because they expect future inflation to diminish their real incomes. Employers give in to these demands because they too anticipate an inflationary environment where higher costs can be easily passed along to consumers. A strong wage-price control program can quell inflationary expectations by convincing labour and management that the government does not intend to allow inflation to continue. Therefore workers do not need anticipatory wage increases. And firms are put on notice that they may not be able to shift higher costs to consumers via price increases. Expectations of inflation can generate inflation; wage–price controls can undermine those expectations.

2. ALLOCATIVE EFFICIENCY AND RATIONING

Opponents of incomes policies say effective guideposts or controls interfere with the allocative function of the market system. Effective price controls prohibit the market system from making necessary adjustments. If an increase in the demand for some product should increase, its price could *not* rise to signal society's wish for more output and therefore more resources to produce it.

Also, controls strip the market mechanism of its rationing function, that is, of its ability to equate quantity demanded and quantity supplied. Product shortages thus result. Which buyers are to obtain the product and which are to do without? One possibility is that the product can be rationed on a first-come-first-served basis or by favouritism. But both are highly arbitrary and inequitable; those who are first in the line or those able to cultivate a friendship with the seller get as much of the product as they want, while others get none at all. In the interest of equity, government may have to undertake the task of impartially rationing the product to all consumers.

Defenders of incomes policies respond as follows: if effective guideposts or controls are imposed on a competitive economy, then in time the resulting rigidities will impair allocative efficiency. But it is *not* correct to assume that resource allocation will

be efficient in the absence of a wage–price policy. Cost-push inflation allegedly arises *because* large unions and corporations possess monopoly power and consequently have the capacity to distort the allocation of resources.

EFFECTIVENESS

How effective have incomes policies been? The use of direct wage–price controls during World War II did contain — or at least defer — the serious inflation that would otherwise have occurred. On the other hand, the wage and price guideposts of the early 1970s did little to arrest the growing demand-pull inflation of the period. The wage and price controls of 1974–77 not only failed to achieve their purposes, but worsened stagflation by causing inefficiencies in the allocation of resources.

In view of the historical record, there remains little support for incomes policies among Canadian macroeconomists. Nevertheless, wage and price controls are still occasionally tried in other nations, particularly those facing hyperinflation. Normally, these controls are part of a larger set of policies — including a tight money policy — designed to break the price-wage inflationary spiral. (Key Question 8)

SUPPLY-SIDE ECONOMICS

In the past two decades some economists have stressed the low growth of productivity and real output as basic causes of stagflation and the relatively weak performance of our economy. These **supply-side economists** assert that mainstream economics does not come to grips with stagflation because its focal point is aggregate demand.

Supply-side economists contend that shifts in the short-run and long-run aggregate supply curve must be recognized as an "active" force in determining the levels of both inflation *and* unemployment. Economic disturbances can be generated on the supply side as well as on the demand side. Most important for our present purposes, by emphasizing the demand side, mainstream economics has neglected certain supply-side policies that might alleviate stagflation.

TAX-TRANSFER DISINCENTIVES

Supply-side economists argue that the spectacular growth of our tax-transfer system has negatively affected incentives to work, save, invest, innovate and assume entrepreneurial risks. The tax-transfer system has eroded the productivity of our economy, and this decline in efficiency has meant higher production costs and stagflation. The argument is that higher taxes reduce the after-tax rewards of workers and producers thereby making work, innovations, saving, investing, and risk-bearing less financially attractive. Supply-side economists stress the importance of *marginal tax rates* because these rates are most relevant to decisions to undertake *additional* work and *additional* savings and investing.

INCENTIVES TO WORK   Supply-siders argue that how long and how hard individuals work depends upon how much additional *after-tax* earnings they derive from this extra work. To induce more work — to increase aggregate inputs of labour — marginal tax rates on earned incomes should be reduced. Lower marginal tax rates increase the attractiveness of work and simultaneously increase the opportunity cost of leisure. Thus, individuals will choose to substitute work for leisure. This increase in productive effort can occur in many ways: by increasing the number of hours worked per day or per week; by encouraging workers to postpone retirement; by inducing more people to enter the labour force; by making people willing to work harder; and by discouraging long periods of employment.

TRANSFER DISINCENTIVES   Supply-side economists also believe the existence of a wide variety of public transfer programs has eroded incentives to work. Unemployment insurance benefits and welfare programs have made the loss of one's job less of an economic crisis than formerly. Indeed, most transfer programs discourage work, in that payments are reduced sharply or even eliminated entirely if recipients earn income. These programs encourage recipients *not* to be productive by imposing a "tax" in the form of a loss of transfer benefits on those who work.

INCENTIVES TO SAVE AND INVEST   The rewards of saving and investing have also been reduced by high marginal tax rates. Saving, remember, is the prerequisite of investment. Thus supply-side economists recommend lower marginal tax rates on saving. They also call for lower taxes on investment income to ensure there are ready investment outlets for the economy's enhanced

pool of saving. Lower marginal tax rates encourage saving and investing so that workers will find themselves equipped with more and technologically superior machinery and equipment. Therefore, labour productivity will rise and the price level be held down.

LAFFER CURVE

In the supply-side view, reductions of marginal tax rates will shift Figure 16-4's aggregate supply curve from AS_1 towards AS_0, alleviating inflation, increasing real output, and reducing the unemployment rate. Moreover, according to supply-side economist Arthur Laffer, lower tax *rates* are compatible with constant or even enlarged tax *revenues*. Supply-side tax cuts need not cause federal budget deficits.

This position is based on the **Laffer curve**. As shown in Figure 16-9, it depicts the relationship between tax rates and tax revenues. The idea is that as tax rates increase from zero to 100%, tax revenues will increase from zero to some maximum level (at m) and then decline to zero. Tax revenues decline beyond some point because higher tax rates discourage economic activity, diminishing the tax base (domestic output and income). This is easiest to see at the extreme where tax rates are 100%. Tax revenues here are reduced to zero because the 100% confiscatory tax rate has halted production. A 100% tax rate applied to a tax base of zero yields no revenue.

In the early 1980s Laffer suggested that we were now at some point such as n, where tax rates were so high that production had been discouraged to the extent that tax revenues were below the maximum at m. If the economy is at n, then lower tax *rates* are quite compatible with constant tax *revenues*. In Figure 16-9 we simply lower tax rates, moving from point n to point l, and government will collect an unaltered amount of tax revenue. Laffer's reasoning was that lower tax rates would stimulate incentives to work, save and invest, innovate, and accept business risks, thereby triggering a substantial expansion of domestic output and income. This enlarged tax base would sustain tax revenues even though tax rates were lower. Indeed, between n and m, lower tax rates will result in increased tax revenues.

Supply-side economists think tax rates can be lowered without incurring budget deficits for two additional reasons.

FIGURE 16-9   The Laffer curve

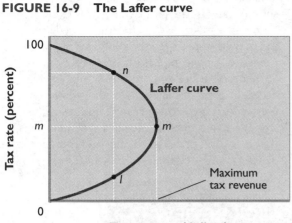

The Laffer curve suggests that up to point *m*, higher tax rates will result in larger tax revenues. But still higher rates will have adverse effects on incentives to produce, reducing the size of the national income tax base to the extent that tax revenues decline. It follows that if tax rates are above 0_m, tax reductions will produce increases in tax revenues. The controversial empirical question is to determine at what actual tax rates tax revenues will begin to fall.

1. LESS TAX EVASION   Tax avoidance and evasion will decline. High marginal tax rates prompt taxpayers to avoid taxes through the use of various tax shelters (for example, buying rental properties to be able to claim mortgage payments, taxes, insurance, and so on, as deductions against other income) or to conceal income from Revenue Canada. Lower tax rates reduce the inclination to engage in such activities.

2. REDUCED TRANSFERS   The stimulus to production and employment that a tax cut provides reduces government transfer payments. For example, more job opportunities lower unemployment insurance payments and thereby tend to reduce a budget deficit.

CRITICISMS OF THE LAFFER CURVE

The Laffer curve and its supply-side policy implications have been subject to severe criticism.

1. TAXES: INCENTIVES AND TIME   A fundamental criticism has to do with the sensitivity of economic incentives to changes in tax rates.

Sceptics point out there is ample empirical evidence that the impact of a tax reduction on incentives is small, of uncertain direction, and relatively slow to emerge. With respect to work incentives, studies indicate that decreases in tax rates lead some people to work more, but others to work less. Those who work more are enticed by the higher after-tax pay; they substitute work for leisure because the opportunity cost of leisure has increased. Those who work less do so because the higher after-tax pay increases their ability to "buy leisure." They can meet their after-tax income goals while working fewer hours.

2. REINFORCING INFLATION   Most economists think demand-side effects of a tax cut exceed supply-side effects. Thus, tax cuts undertaken when the economy is expanding or at its full-employment output will produce large increases in aggregate demand that will overwhelm any increase in aggregate supply. Large budget deficits and inflation will result.

3. POSITION ON CURVE   Sceptics note that the Laffer curve is merely a logical proposition asserting that there must be some level of tax rates between zero and 100% where tax revenues will be maximized. Economists of all persuasions can agree with this statement. But the issue of where a particular economy is located on the Laffer curve is an empirical question. If we assume — as Laffer did in the early 1980s — that we are at *n* in Figure 16-9, then tax rate cuts will increase tax revenues. But critics contend that the economy's location on the Laffer curve is undocumented and unknown. If the economy is actually at any point southwest of *m*, then tax reduction will reduce tax revenues and create budget deficits.

OTHER SUPPLY-SIDE TENETS

Although removing tax-transfer disincentives is the main idea of supply-side economics, there are two other tenets.

1. THE TAX "WEDGE"   Supply-side economists note that the historical growth of the public sector has increased the nation's tax bill both absolutely and as a percentage of the national income. In the mainstream view, higher taxes represent a withdrawal of purchasing power from the economy and therefore have a contractionary or anti-inflationary effect. Supply-siders argue to the contrary: They contend that sooner or later most taxes are incorporated into business costs and shifted forward to consumers as higher prices. Taxes, in short, entail a cost-push effect.

Supply-side economists point out that in the 1970s, 1980s, and the early 1990s local and provincial governments increased municipal and sales taxes and that the federal government boosted compulsory social insurance contributions. These are precisely the kinds of taxes incorporated in business costs and reflected in higher prices. Many taxes constitute a "wedge" between the costs of resources and the price of a product. As government has grown, this **tax wedge** has increased, shifting the aggregate supply curve leftward.

2. OVERREGULATION Supply-siders also claim that government involvement in the economy has adversely affected productivity and costs. Two points should be noted here.

1. "Industrial" regulation — government regulation of specific industries such as transportation or communications — frequently provides firms in the regulated industry with a legal monopoly or cartel. Governmental regulation protects such firms from competition, with the result that these firms are less efficient and incur higher costs of production.

2. The "social" regulation of industry has increased substantially in the past two decades. New government regulations have been imposed on industry in response to the problems of pollution, product safety, worker health and safety, and equal access to job opportunities. Supply-side economists point out that social regulation has greatly increased costs of doing business. The overall impact of both varieties of regulation is that costs and prices are higher and there is a tendency towards stagflation. **(Key Question 10)**

QUICK REVIEW 16-3

1. Policy options for stagflation include: employment and training policies; incomes policies (wage–price guideposts and controls); and supply-side economics (tax cuts, deregulation).

2. The Laffer curve contends that, when tax rates are higher than optimal, tax reductions can expand real output and simultaneously increase tax revenue.

3. The supply-side policies (tax cuts, deregulation) did not increase aggregate supply more rapidly than otherwise would have been expected.

CHAPTER SUMMARY

1. Using the aggregate demand-aggregate supply model to compare the impacts of different size increases in aggregate demand on the price level and real output yields the generalization that high rates of inflation are associated with low rates of unemployment, and vice versa. This relationship is known as the Phillips curve, and the empirical data before the 1970s were generally consistent with this inverse relationship. Labour market imbalances and monopoly power are used to explain the Phillips curve trade-off.

2. In the 1970s the Phillips curve seems to have shifted rightward — a shift that is consistent with stagflation. A series of supply shocks, in the form of higher energy and food prices and depreciated Canadian and American dollars, were involved in the stagflation that started in 1975. More subtle factors such as inflationary expectations and a decline in productivity growth also contributed to stagflation tendencies. By the mid-1980s the Phillips curve had started shifting inward towards its original position. By 1988 stagflation had largely subsided.

3. The adaptive expectations variant of the natural rate hypothesis argues that in the long run the traditional Phillips curve trade-off does not exist. Expansionary demand-management policies will shift the short-run Phillips curve upward, resulting in increasing inflation with no permanent decline in unemployment.

4. The rational expectations variant of the natural-rate hypothesis contends that the inflationary effects of expansionary policies will be anticipated and reflected in nominal wage demands. As a result, there will be no short-run increase in employment and thus no short-run Phillips curve.

5. In the short run — where nominal wages are fixed — an increase in the price level will bolster profits and result in greater real output. A decrease in the price level will reduce profits and real output. Thus, the short-run aggregate supply curve is upward sloping. In the long run — where nominal wages are variable — price-level increases will cause increases in nominal wages and thus leftward shifts of the short-run aggregate supply curve. Conversely, price-level declines will shift the short-run aggregate supply curve rightward. The long-run aggregate supply curve therefore tends to be vertical at the full employment level of output.

6. The long-run aggregate supply curve implies that the economy has a self-adjusting mechanism that will bring it back to full-employment GDP (the natural rate of unemployment) if there exists either a recessionary or inflationary gap. However, the adjusting mechanism is slow, particularly in the case of a recessionary gap. Thus, there is still a place for monetary and fiscal policy to quicken the speed with which the economy moves back to full-employment GDP.

7. In the short run, demand-pull inflation will tend to increase the price level *and* real output. Once nominal wages have increased, however, the temporary increase in real output will dissipate.

8. In the short run, cost-push inflation increases the price level and reduces real output. Unless government expands aggregate demand, nominal wages eventually will decline under conditions of recession and the short-run aggregate supply curve will shift back to its initial location. Hence, prices and real output will return to their original levels.

9. Employment and training policies, wage-price (incomes) policies, and supply-side policies to shift the aggregate supply curve rightward have been used as antistagflation measures.

10. Employment and training programs are designed to reduce labour market imbalances; they include vocational training, job information, and nondiscrimination programs.

11. Incomes policies comprise wage–price guideposts or controls. Economists have debated the desirability of such policies because of their workability and their impact on resource allocations. Presently, there is little support among economists for these policies.

12. Supply-side economists trace stagflation to the growth of the public sector and, more specifically, to the growing tax "wedge" between production costs and product prices, the adverse effects of the tax-transfer system on incentives, and government over-regulation of businesses. Relying on the Laffer curve, supply-side adherents advocated sizable tax cuts such as the United States' Economic Recovery Tax Act of 1981 as a remedy for stagflation. Evidence has cast considerable doubt on the validity of the supply-side view.

TERMS AND CONCEPTS

adaptive expectations theory (p. 343)
aggregate supply shocks (p. 341)
cost-push inflation (p. 352)
demand-pull inflation (p. 351)
disinflation (p. 345)
employment and training policy (p. 353)
incomes policies (p. 354)
inflationary expectations (p. 342)
Laffer curve (p. 356)
long-run aggregate supply curve (p. 349)

natural-rate hypothesis (p. 343)
Phillips curve (p. 339)
rational expectations theory (p. 345)
short-run aggregate supply curve (p. 348)
stagflation (p. 340)
supply-side economics (p. 355)
tax-transfer disincentives (p. 355)
tax wedge (p. 358)
wage–price guideposts and controls (p. 354)

QUESTIONS AND STUDY SUGGESTIONS

1. **Key Question** *Employ the aggregate demand-aggregate supply model to derive the Phillips curve. What events occurred in the 1970s to cast doubt upon the stability and existence of the Phillips curve?*

2. **Key Question** *Use an appropriate diagram to explain the adaptive expectations rationale for concluding that the Phillips curve is a vertical line.*

3. Explain rational expectations theory and its relevance to analysis of the Phillips curve.

4. Assume the following information is relevant for an industrially advanced economy in the 1996–98 period:

Year	Price level index	Rate of increase in labour productivity	Index of industrial production	Unemployment rate	Average hourly wage rates
1996	167	4%	212	4.5%	$12.00
1997	174	3	208	5.2	13.00
1998	181	2.5	205	5.8	14.20

Describe in detail the macroeconomic situation faced by this economy. Is cost-push inflation in evidence? What policy proposals would you recommend?

5. Evaluate or explain the following statements:

   a. "Taken together, the adaptive expectations and rational expectations theories imply that demand-management policies cannot influence the real level of economic activity in the long run."

   b. "The essential difference between the adaptive expectations and rational expectations theory is that inflation is unanticipated in the former and anticipated in the latter."

6. Suppose that the full-employment level of real domestic output (Q) for a hypothetical economy is $250 and that the price level (P) initially is 100. Use the short-run aggregate supply schedules shown below to answer the questions that follow.

$AS(P_{100})$		$AS(P_{125})$		$AS(P_{75})$	
P	Q	P	Q	P	Q
125	280	125	250	125	310
100	250	100	220	100	280
75	220	75	190	75	250

   a. What will be the level of real domestic output in the *short run* if the price level (1) rises unexpectedly from 100 to 125 because of an increase in aggregate demand? (2) falls unexpectedly from 100 to 75 because of a decrease in aggregate demand? Explain each situation.

   b. What will be the level of real domestic output in the *long run* when the price level (1) rises from 100 to 125? (2) falls from 100 to 75? Explain each situation.

    c. Show the circumstances described in *a* and *b* on graph paper and derive the long-run aggregate supply curve.

7. **Key Question**   *Use graphical analysis to show (1) demand-pull inflation in the short run and long run, and (2) cost-push inflation in the short run and long run. Assume in the second case that government does not increase aggregate demand to offset the real output effect of the cost-push inflation.*

8. **Key Question**   *How do wage and price guideposts differ from wage and price controls? What specific problems are associated with the use of wage and price controls? Evaluate these problems and note the arguments in favour of controls. What has been the Canadian experience with wage and price guideposts and controls? Have they been largely successful or unsuccessful?*

9. "Controlling prices to halt inflation is like breaking a thermometer to control the heat. In both instances you are treating symptoms rather than causes." Do you agree? Does the correctness of the statement vary when applied to demand-pull and to cost-push inflation? Explain.

10. **Key Question**   *What are the major tenets of supply-side economics? How do these tenets relate to leftward shifts of the aggregate supply curve and stagflation? Using the Laffer curve, explain why supply-siders recommend deep tax cuts to remedy stagflation.*

11. You have just been elected prime minister of Canada and the present governor of the Bank of Canada has resigned. You need to appoint a new person to this position. Using your knowledge of macroeconomics, identify the perspectives on macroeconomic theories and policies that you would want your candidate to hold. Remember, the economic health of the entire nation — and your chances for re-election — may depend on these selections.

12. (Applying the Theory) How would profit sharing by labour increase downward "wage" flexibility? Why is greater downward wage flexibility desirable?

CHAPTER 17

THE EVOLUTION OF MACROECONOMICS AND RECENT CONTROVERSIES

acroeconomic theory and stabilization policy, as represented in Figure 15-4, have dominated the thinking of most economists in all market-oriented industrial economies since World War II. In Canada, Liberal and Progressive Conservative governments alike have accepted these precepts, at least as evidenced by policy actions. Presently, the stabilization policies of nearly all the major industrial nations can be understood through Figure 15-4.

But it would be misleading to suggest there is common agreement on all aspects of macroeconomic theory and stabilization policy. Both historically and currently, macroeconomics is the subject of much dispute. In this chapter we want to explore points of disagreement among "camps" of macroeconomists. Keep in mind that the differences in perspectives of individual economists rarely are as extreme as suggested by these polar comparisons.

We start by contrasting the crude, simplified forms of classical and Keynesian macroeconomic theories. Then we move closer to the present by looking at the *monetarist school*, whose intellectual leader is Milton Friedman, winner of the 1976 Nobel Prize in economics. Friedman asserted that the role of money in determining the level of economic activity and the price level was much greater than suggested by early Keynesian theory. Next, we turn to the *rational expectations theory* (RET), which asserts that expectations created by traditional stabilization policies will largely render these policies ineffective. Finally, we point out that some aspects of monetarism and RET have been absorbed into mainstream macroeconomic thinking.

BOX 17-1 THE BIG PICTURE

While in many areas of macroeconomics something resembling a consensus has emerged in the last 25 years, many disagreements remain. This chapter serves two purposes. The first is to look at the evolution of macroeconomics; the second, to make you aware of the main controversies that still rage and those that have been at least partially resolved.

At the heart of all controversies in macroeconomics has been the issue of how quickly markets clear — the elimination of any excess supply or excess demand, particularly labour markets. In order for markets to clear you need flexible prices. Many economists do not believe prices are fully flexible, particularly the price of labour — wages. If markets do not clear quickly, the economy can get "stuck" in a recession for a considerable period of time.

As you read this chapter, keep the following points in mind:

- Economists of the nineteenth and early twentieth centuries believed the economy had self-correcting powers and that recessions and inflationary periods would work themselves out and the economy would return to full employment.

- Keynes argued in the 1930s that although economics would eventually return to full employment, the adjustment mechanism worked much too slowly, particularly in the case of a recession. The stimulation of aggregate demand through government spending could quicken the resolution of a recession. Keynesian economics enlarged the scope of government initiatives in stabilizing the economy.

- The monetarist school emphasized the important role of money and argued that markets cleared more rapidly than the Keynesian school proposed.

- The rational expectation school proposed nearly instant market clearing, making government macroeconomic policy unnecessary.

- The mainstream has adopted some of the monetarist and rational expectation schools' arguments.

CLASSICS AND KEYNES: AD-AS INTERPRETATION

Recall from Chapter 9 that **classical economics** suggests that full employment is the norm of a market economy and that a *laissez faire* ("let it be") policy by government is best. Yet Keynes contended that recurring recessions or depressions with widespread unemployment are characteristic of laissez faire capitalism, and activist government policies are required to avoid wastes of idle resources.

These two views of the macroeconomic world — classical and Keynesian — can be restated and compared in their simple forms through aggregate demand and aggregate supply curves.

CLASSICAL VIEW

The classical view is that the aggregate supply curve is vertical and exclusively determines the level of real domestic output. The downsloping aggregate demand curve is stable and solely establishes the price level.

VERTICAL AGGREGATE SUPPLY CURVE In the classical perspective, the aggregate supply curve is a vertical line as shown in Figure 17-1(a). This line is located at the full-employment level of real output, which in this particular designation is also the absolute full-capacity level of real output. According to the classical economists, the economy will operate at its full-employment level of output, Q_f, because of Say's Law (Chapter 9) and responsive, flexible prices and wages.

We stress that classical economists believed that Q_f does *not* change in response to changes in the price level. Observe that as the price level falls from P_0 to P_1 in Figure 17-1(a), real domestic output remains firmly anchored at Q_f.

But this stability of output might seem at odds with Chapter 4's upsloping supply curves for individual products. There we found that lower prices would make production less profitable and cause producers to offer *less* output and employ *fewer* workers. The classical response to this view is that input costs would fall along with product prices to leave *real* profits and output unchanged.

FIGURE 17-1 Classical and Keynesian views of the macroeconomy

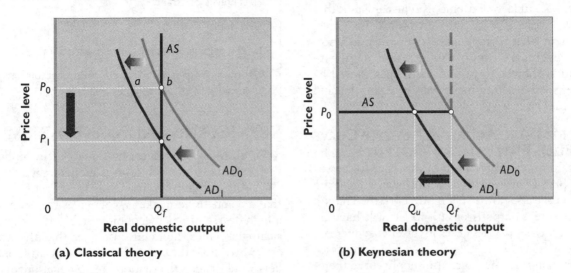

(a) Classical theory **(b) Keynesian theory**

According to classical theory (a), aggregate supply will determine the full employment level of real domestic output while aggregate demand will establish the price level. Aggregate demand normally is stable, but if it should decline, say as shown from AD_0 to AD_1, the price level will quickly fall from P_0 to P_1 to eliminate the temporary excess supply of ab and to restore full employment at c. The Keynesian view (b) is that aggregate demand is unstable and that price and wages are downwardly inflexible. An AD_0 to AD_1 decline in aggregate demand has no effect on the price level. Rather, real output falls from Q_f to Q_u and can remain at this equilibrium indefinitely.

STABLE AGGREGATE DEMAND   The classical economists theorized that money underlies aggregate demand. The amount of real output that can be purchased depends on (1) the quantity of money households and businesses possess and (2) the purchasing power or real value of that money as determined by the price level. The purchasing power of the dollar refers to the real quantity of goods and services a dollar will buy. Thus as we move down the vertical axis of Figure 17-1(a), the price level is falling. This means the purchasing power of each dollar increases and therefore the quantity of money can buy a larger quantity of real output. If the price level declined by one-half, a particular quantity of money would now purchase a real output twice as large. With a fixed money supply, the price level and real output are inversely related.

And what of the *location* of the aggregate demand curve? According to the classical economists, aggregate demand will be stable if the nation's monetary authorities maintain a constant supply of money. With a fixed aggregate supply, increases in the supply of money will shift the aggregate demand curve rightward and spark demand-pull inflation. Reductions in the supply of money will shift the curve leftward and trigger deflation. The key to price-level stability then, said the classical economists, is to control the nation's money supply to prevent unwarranted shifts in aggregate demand.

A final observation: Even if there are declines in the money supply and therefore in aggregate demand, the economy depicted in Figure 17-1(a) will *not* experience unemployment. Admittedly, the immediate effect of a decline in aggregate demand from AD_0 to AD_1 is an excess supply of output since the aggregate output of goods and services exceeds aggregate spending by the amount ab. But, with the presumed downward flexibility of product and resource prices, this excess supply will reduce product prices along with workers' wages and the prices of other inputs. As a result, the price level will quickly decline from P_0 to P_1 until the amounts of output demanded and supplied are brought once again into equilibrium, this time at c. While the real price level has fallen from P_0 to P_1, real output remains at the full-employment level.

KEYNESIAN VIEW

The core of crude, or extreme, **Keynesianism** is that product prices and wages are downwardly inflexible, resulting in what is graphically represented as a horizontal aggregate supply curve. Also, aggregate demand is subject to periodic changes caused by changes in the determinants of aggregate demand (Table 11-1).

1. HORIZONTAL AGGREGATE SUPPLY CURVE (TO FULL-EMPLOYMENT OUTPUT)
The downward inflexibility of prices and wages discussed in Chapter 11 translates to a horizontal aggregate supply curve as shown in Figure 17-1(b). Here, a decline in real output from Q_f to Q_u will have no impact on the price level. Conversely, an increase in output from Q_u to Q_f will also leave the price level unchanged. The aggregate supply curve therefore extends from zero real output rightward to the full-employment output Q_f. Once full employment is reached, in this simplified view, the aggregate supply curve becomes vertical. This is shown by the vertical (dashed) line extending upward from the horizontal aggregate supply curve at Q_f.

2. UNSTABLE AGGREGATE DEMAND
Keynesian economists view aggregate demand as unstable from one period to the next, even without changes in the money supply. In particular, the investment component of aggregate demand fluctuates, altering the location of the aggregate demand curve. Suppose that aggregate demand in Figure 17-1(b) declines from AD_0 to AD_1. The sole impact of this decline in aggregate demand will be on output and employment because real output falls from Q_f to Q_u while the price level remains constant at P_0. Moreover, Keynesians believe that unless there is a fortuitous offsetting increase in aggregate demand, real output may remain at Q_u, which is below the full-employment level Q_f. Active macroeconomic policies of aggregate demand management by government are essential to avoid the wastes of recession and depression. (**Key Question 1**)

QUICK REVIEW 17-1

Classical Theory

1. The aggregate supply curve is vertical at the full-employment level of output.

2. The aggregate demand curve is stable if the money supply is constant.

Keynesian Theory

3. The aggregate supply curve is horizontal.

4. The aggregate demand curve is unstable largely because of the volatility of investment.

KEYNESIANS AND MONETARISM

Classical economics has emerged in modern forms. One such form is **monetarism**, which holds that markets are highly competitive and that a competitive market system gives the economy a high degree of macroeconomic stability. Like classical economics, monetarism argues that the price and wage flexibility provided by competitive markets would cause fluctuations in aggregate demand to alter product and resource prices rather than output and employment. Thus, the market system would provide substantial macroeconomic stability *were it not for governmental interference in the economy.*

The problem, as the monetarists see it, is that government has fostered and promoted downward wage-price inflexibility through the minimum-wage law, pro-union legislation, farm price supports, pro-business monopoly legislation, and so forth. The free-market system could provide macroeconomic stability, but, despite good intentions, government interference has undermined this capability. Furthermore, monetarists argue that government has contributed to the instability of the system — to the business cycle — through its clumsy and mistaken attempts to achieve greater stability through *discretionary* fiscal and monetary policies.

In view of the preceding comments, it is no surprise that monetarists have a strong laissez faire or free-market orientation. Governmental decision making is held to be bureaucratic, inefficient, harmful to individual incentives, and frequently characterized by policy mistakes that destabilize the economy. Furthermore, as emphasized by Friedman, centralized decision making by government inevitably erodes individual freedoms.[1] The public sector should be kept to the smallest possible size.

---

[1] Friedman's philosophy is effectively expounded in two of his books: *Capitalism and Freedom* (Chicago: The University of Chicago Press, 1962); and with Rose Friedman, *Free to Choose* (New York: Harcourt Brace Jovanovich, 1980).

Keynesians and monetarists therefore are opposed in their conceptions of the private and public sectors.

To the Keynesian, the instability of private investment causes the economy to be unstable. Government plays a positive role by applying appropriate stabilization medicine.

To the monetarist, government has harmful effects on the economy. Government creates rigidities that weaken the capacity of the market system to provide stability. It also embarks on monetary and fiscal measures that although well intentioned, aggravate the instability they are designed to cure.

THE BASIC EQUATIONS

Keynesian economics and monetarism each build their analysis on specific equations.

AGGREGATE EXPENDITURES EQUATION As indicated in Chapters 9 and 10, Keynesian economics focuses on aggregate spending and its components. The basic Keynesian equation is:

$$C_a + I_g + X_n + G = GDP \qquad (1)$$

This theory says that the aggregate amount of after-tax consumption, gross investment net exports, and government spending determines the total value of the goods and services sold. In equilibrium, $C_a + I_g + X_n + G$ (aggregate expenditures) is equal to GDP (real output).

EQUATION OF EXCHANGE Monetarism focuses on money. The fundamental equation of monetarism is the **equation of exchange**:

$$MV = PQ \qquad (2)$$

where M is the supply of money; V is the **velocity of money**, that is, *the number of times per year the average dollar is spent on final goods and services*; P is the price level or, more specifically, *the average price at which each unit of physical output is sold*; and Q is the physical volume of all goods and services produced.

The label "equation of exchange" is easily understood. The left side, MV, represents the total amount *spent* by purchasers of output while the right side, PQ, represents the total amount *received* by sellers of that output.

Both the Keynesian and monetarist approaches are helpful in understanding macroeconomics. In fact, the Keynesian equation can be readily "trans-lated" into monetarist terms. In the monetarist approach, total spending is the supply of money multiplied by its velocity. In short, MV is the monetarist counterpart of equilibrium $C_a + I_g + X_n + G$. Because MV is the total amount spent on final goods in one year, it is equal to nominal GDP. Furthermore, nominal GDP is the sum of the physical outputs of various goods and services (Q) multiplied by their respective prices (P). That is, GDP = PQ. We can therefore restate the Keynesian $C_a + I_g + X_n + G$ = GDP equation in nominal terms as the monetarist equation of exchange, $MV = PQ$.[2]

The two approaches are two ways of looking at much the same thing. But the critical question remains: Which theory more accurately portrays macroeconomics and therefore is the better basis for economic policy?

SPOTLIGHT ON MONEY The Keynesian equation puts money in a secondary role. Indeed, the Keynesian conception of monetary policy entails a rather lengthy transmission mechanism, as shown in Figure 17-2(a). A change in monetary policy alters the nation's supply of money. The change in the money supply affects the interest rate, which changes the level of investment. When the economy is operating at less than capacity, changes in investment affect nominal GDP (= PQ) by changing real output (Q) through the income multiplier effect. Alternatively, when the economy is achieving full employment, changes in investment affect nominal GDP by altering the price level (P).

Keynesians contend there are many loose links in this cause-effect chain with the result that monetary policy is an uncertain and weak stabilization tool compared with fiscal policy. For example, recall from Figure 15-2 that monetary policy will be relatively ineffective if the demand for money curve is flat and the investment-demand curve is steep. Also, the investment-demand curve may shift adversely so that the impact of a change in the interest rate on investment spending is muted or offset. Nor will an expansionary monetary policy be very effective if banks and other depository institutions are not anxious to lend or the public eager to borrow.

[2] Technical footnote: There is an important conceptual difference between the Keynesian $C_a + I_g + X_n + G$ and the MV component of the equation of exchange. The former indicates planned or *intended* expenditures, which equal actual expenditures only in equilibrium. MV reflects *actual spending*.

FIGURE 17-2 Alternative views of the monetary transmission mechanism

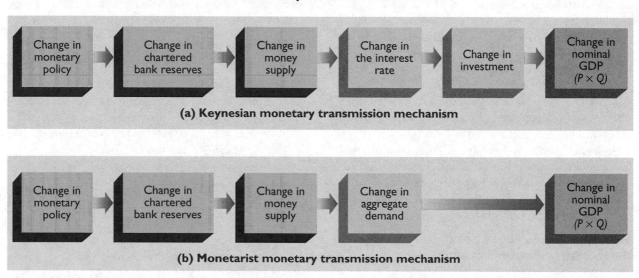

Keynesians (a) emphasize the roles of interest rates and investment spending in how changes in the money supply affect nominal GDP. On the other hand, monetarists (b) contend that changes in the money supply cause direct changes in aggregate demand and thereby changes in nominal GDP.

Monetarists believe that money and monetary policy are more important in determining the level of economic activity than do the Keynesians. *Monetarists hold that changes in the money supply are the single most important factor in determining the levels of output, employment, and prices.* They see a different cause-effect chain between the supply of money and the level of economic activity than the Keynesian model suggests. Rather than limiting the effect of an increase in money to bond purchases and consequent declines in the interest rate, monetarists theorize that an increase in the money supply drives up the demand for all assets — real or financial — as well as for current output. Under conditions of full employment the prices of all these items will rise. Monetarists also say the velocity of money is stable — meaning it does not fluctuate wildly and does not change in response to a change in the money supply itself. Thus, changes in the money supply will have a predictable effect on the level of nominal GDP (= PQ). More precisely, an increase in M will increase P or Q, or some combination of both P and Q; a decrease in M will do the opposite.

Monetarists believe that, although a change in M may cause short-run changes in real output and employment as market adjustments occur, the long-run impact of a change in M will be on the price level. Monetarists think the private economy is inherently stable and usually operates at the full-employment level of output. The exact level of that full-employment output depends on such "real" factors as the quantity and quality of labour, capital, and land and on technology (Chapter 19). The point is that if Q is constant at the economy's capacity output, then changes in M will lead to changes in P.

Monetarism implies a more direct transmission mechanism than does the Keynesian model. Observe in Figure 17-2(b) that monetarists view changes in the money supply as producing direct changes in aggregate demand that alter nominal GDP. Monetarists contend that changes in the money supply affect all components of aggregate demand, not just investment. Furthermore, changes in aggregate demand allegedly affect nominal GDP in the long run primarily through changes in the price level, not through changes in real output.

VELOCITY: STABLE OR UNSTABLE?

A critical theoretical issue in the Keynesian-monetarist debate centres on whether the velocity of money, V, is stable. As used here, "stable" is *not* synonymous with "constant." Monetarists are aware that velocity is higher today than in 1945. Shorter pay periods, greater use of credit cards, and faster means of making payments have increased velocity since 1945. These factors have enabled people to reduce their cash and chequebook holdings relative to the size of the nominal GDP.

What monetarists mean when they say velocity is stable is that the factors altering velocity change gradually and predictably. Changes in velocity from one year to the next can be easily anticipated. Moreover, velocity does *not* change in response to changes in the supply of money itself.

If velocity is stable, the equation of exchange tells us that monetarists are correct in claiming that a direct predictable relationship exists between the money supply and nominal GDP (= PQ).

Suppose M is 100, V is 1, and nominal GDP is 100. Also assume velocity increases annually at a stable rate of 2%. Using the equation of exchange, we can predict that a 5% annual growth rate of the money supply will result in about a 7% increase in nominal GDP. M will increase from 100 to 105, V will rise from 1 to 1.02, and nominal GDP will increase from 100 to about 107 (= 105 × 1.02).

But if V is not stable, then the strict Keynesians are correct that money plays only a secondary role in macroeconomics. If V is variable and unpredictable from one period to another, the link between M and PQ will be loose and uncertain. A steady growth of M will not necessarily translate into a steady growth of nominal GDP.

MONETARISTS: V IS STABLE   What rationale do monetarists offer for their contention that V is stable? They argue that people have a stable desire to hold money relative to holding other financial and real assets and buying current output. The factors determining the amount of money people and businesses wish to hold at any specific time are independent of the supply of money. Most importantly, the amount of money the public will want to hold will depend on the level of nominal GDP.

Example: Suppose that when the level of nominal GDP is $500 billion, the amount of money the public wants or *desires* to hold to buy this output is $50 billion. (V is 10.) If we further assume that the *actual* supply of money is $50 billion, we can say the economy is in equilibrium with respect to money; the *actual* amount of money supplied equals the amount the public *desires* to hold.

In the monetarist view an increase in the money supply of, say, $5 billion will upset this equi-

librium since the public will find itself holding more money or liquidity than it wants; the actual amount of money held exceeds the amount of holdings desired. The reaction of the public (households and businesses) is to restore its desired balance of money relative to other items such as stocks and bonds, factories and equipment houses and automobiles, and clothing and toys. The public has more money than it wants; the way to get rid of it is to buy things. But one person's spending of money leaves more cash in someone else's chequable deposit or wallet. That person, too, tries to "spend down" excess cash balances.

The collective attempt to reduce cash balances will increase aggregate demand, boosting the nominal GDP. Because velocity is 10 — the typical dollar is spent ten times per year — nominal GDP must rise by $50 billion. When nominal GDP reaches $550 billion, the *actual* money supply of $55 billion again will be the amount the public *desires* to hold, and equilibrium will be re-established. Spending on goods and services will increase until nominal GDP has increased to restore the original equilibrium relationship between nominal GDP and the money supply.

The relationship GDP/M defines V. A stable relationship between GDP and M means a stable V.

KEYNESIANS: V IS UNSTABLE   In the Keynesian view the velocity of money is variable and unpredictable. This position can be understood through the Keynesian conception of the demand for money (Chapter 15). Money is demanded, not only to use in negotiating transactions, but also to hold as an asset. Money demanded for *transactions* purposes will be "active" money — money changing hands and circulating through the income-expenditures stream. Transactions dollars have some positive velocity; the average transactions dollar may be spent say, six times per year and buy $6 of output. In this case V is 6 for each transactions dollar.

But money demanded and held as an *asset* is "idle" money; these dollars do *not* flow through the income expenditures stream. So their velocity is zero. Therefore, the overall velocity of the entire money supply will depend on how it is divided between transactions and asset balances. The greater the relative importance of "active" transactions balances, the larger will be V. The greater the relative significance of "idle" asset balances, the smaller will be V.

Using this framework, Keynesians discredit the monetarist transmission mechanism — the allegedly dependable relationship between changes in M and changes in GDP — arguing that a significant portion of any increase in the money supply may go into asset balances, *causing V to fall*. In the extreme, assume *all* the increase in the money supply is held by the public as additional asset balances. The public simply hoards the additional money and uses none of it for transactions. The money supply will have increased, but velocity will decline by an offsetting amount so that there will be no effect on the amount of aggregate demand and the size of nominal GDP.

We can consider the Keynesian position on a more advanced level by referring to Figure 15-1. There, the relative importance of the asset demand for money varies inversely with the rate of interest. An *increase* in the money supply will *lower* the interest rate. That will make it less expensive to hold money as an asset, so the public will hold larger zero-velocity asset balances. Therefore, the overall velocity of the money supply will fall. A *reduction* in the money supply will *raise* the interest rate, increasing the cost of holding money as an asset. The resulting decline in asset balances will increase the overall velocity of money.

In the Keynesian view velocity varies (1) directly with the rate of interest and (2) inversely with the supply of money. If this is correct, the stable relationship between M and nominal GDP in the monetarist's transmission mechanism does *not* exist because V will vary whenever M changes.

EMPIRICAL EVIDENCE   The stability of V is an empirical question and an appeal to "the facts" would seem to settle the issue. But the facts are not easy to discern or interpret.

Monetarists think the empirical evidence supports their position. In Figure 17-3 the money supply and the nominal domestic output (PQ) are both plotted. Since $MV = PQ$, the close correlation between M and PQ suggests that V is stable. Monetarists reason that the money supply is the causal force in determining nominal GDP; causation runs from M to nominal GDP.

But Keynesians offer two rebuttals.

1. By simple manipulation of $MV = PQ$, we find that $V = PQ/M = GDP/M$. That is, we can empirically calculate the value of V by dividing each year's nominal output (GDP) by the money

supply. Keynesians contend that the resulting data, shown in Figure 17-4 repudiate the monetarist contention that V is stable.

Keynesians also point out that the close correlation between the velocity of money and the interest rate shown in Figure 17-4 supports their analysis that velocity varies directly with the rate of interest. The short-term interest rate used here is the rate on three-month Treasury bills. Velocity, in the Keynesian view, is variable and these variations downgrade the role of money as a determinant of output, employment, and the price level.

Keynesians add this reminder: Given the large size of the money supply, a small variation in velocity can have a substantial impact on nominal GDP. Assume M is $25 billion and V is 10. A modest 10% increase in V will increase nominal GDP by $25 billion. That is, MV — and therefore PQ — are initially $250 billion (= $25 × 10). Now, if V increases by 10% to 11, PQ will be $275 billion (= MV = $25 × 11). *A very small variation in V can offset a large change in M.*

2. Keynesians respond to Figure 17-3 by noting that *correlation* and *causation* are different. Changes in money GDP in Figure 17-3 were in fact caused by changes in aggregate expenditures — that is, in $C_a + I_g + X_n + G$ — as suggested by the Keynesian model. Perhaps a favourable change in business expectations increased investment. Also, the indicated growth in the nominal domestic output prompted — indeed, necessitated — businesses and consumers to borrow more money from chartered banks to finance this rising volume of economic activity.

Keynesians claim that causation may in fact run from aggregate expenditures *to* output *to* the money supply, rather than from the money supply *to* aggregate demand *to* output, as monetarists contend. The point, argue Keynesians, is that the data of Figure 17-3 are as consistent with the Keynesian view as they are with the monetarist position.

The question of the stability of V remains a crucial point of conflict between Keynesians and monetarists. For example, the great instability of M1 velocity in the 1980s led many monetarists to change their focus to the seemingly more stable M2. But in the past few years, the relationship between M2 and nominal GDP and the price level has also become unpredictable. Acknowledging these difficulties, some monetarists have looked to still broader measures of the money supply; others have narrowed their focus to the *monetary base* — currency in circulation plus bank reserves.

FIGURE 17-3   The money supply and the GDP, 1926–1994

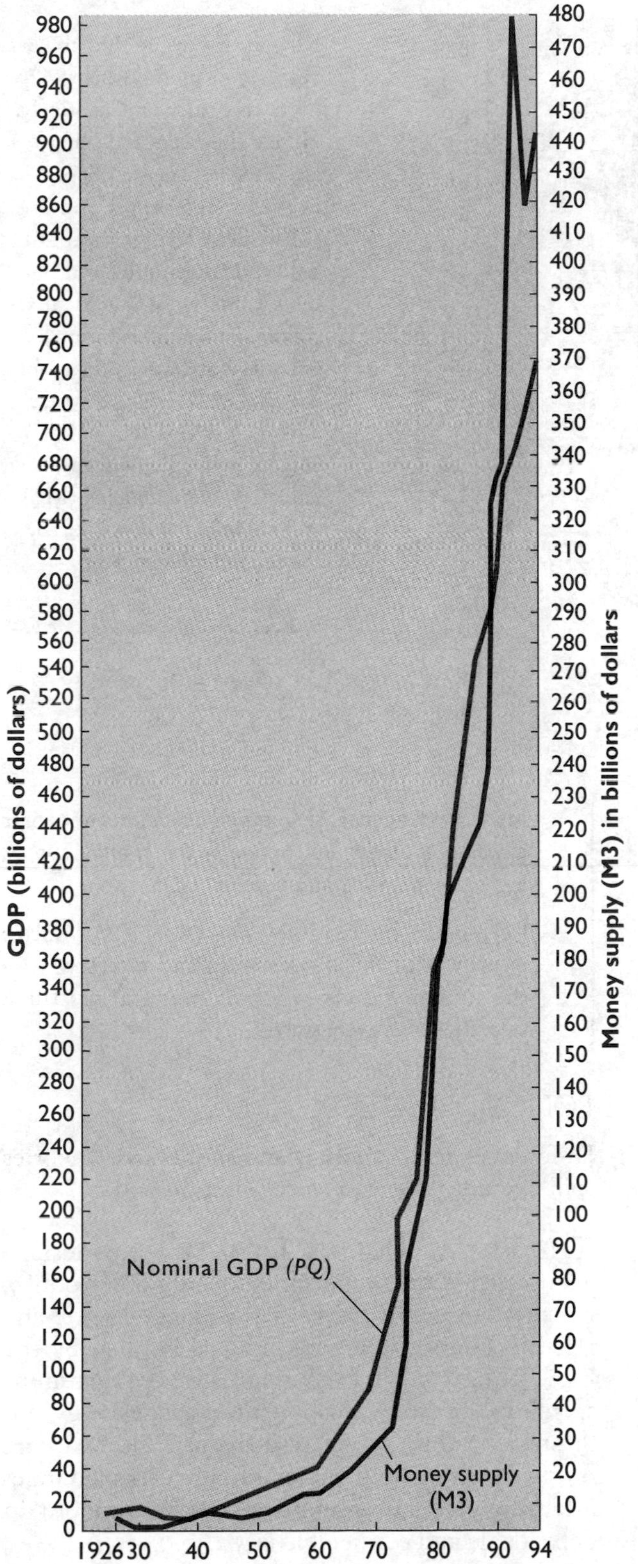

Monetarists cite the close positive correlation between the money supply and nominal GDP as evidence in support of their position that money is the critical determinant of economic activity and the price level. They assume that the money supply is the "cause" and the GDP is the "effect," an assumption that Keynesians question. Monetarists also believe that the close correlation between M and nominal GDP indicates that the velocity of money is stable.

Source: *Bank of Canada Review*, Summer 1995.

FIGURE 17-4   The velocity of money and the interest rate, 1936–1994

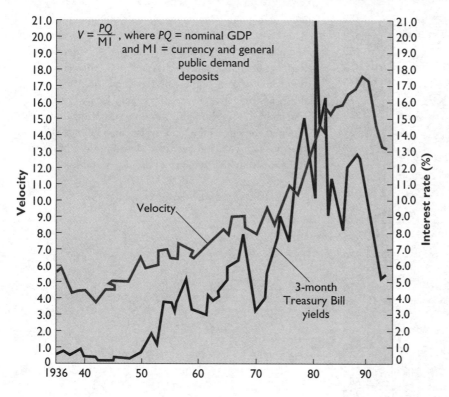

$V = \dfrac{PQ}{M1}$, where PQ = nominal GDP and M1 = currency and general public demand deposits

Velocity

3-month Treasury Bill yields

Keynesians argue that the velocity of money varies both cyclically and secularly. Hence they conclude that any link between a change in the money supply and the subsequent change in nominal GDP is tenuous and uncertain. More specifically, Keynesians contend that velocity varies directly with the rate of interest, because a lower interest rate will increase the size of zero-velocity asset balances (M1) and therefore will lower the overall velocity of money.

Source: *Bank of Canada Review,* Summer 1995.

However, the experience of the last decade has been unkind to the strict monetarist view that M1 or M2 velocity is stable and predictable. Keynesians are quick to point out that a theory without a clearly defined key variable — the money supply — does not offer solid ground for establishing macroeconomic policy.

ment, and aggregate expenditures; monetarists envision a direct link between the money supply, aggregate demand, and nominal GDP.

4. Keynesians contend velocity ($V = PQ/M$) varies directly with the interest rate and inversely with the money supply, whereas monetarists think velocity is relatively stable.

QUICK REVIEW 17-2

1. Keynesians view the economy as inherently unstable and therefore requiring stabilization through active fiscal and monetary policies; monetarists see the economy as relatively stable in the absence of government interference.

2. Keynesians focus on the aggregate expenditures equation ($C_a + I_g + X_n + G$ = GDP) while monetarists base their analysis on the equation of exchange ($MV = PQ$).

3. Keynesians see changes in the money supply as working through changes in interest rates, invest-

POLICY DEBATES

Differences in Keynesian and monetarist theories spill over into the area of stabilization policy.

THE FISCAL POLICY DEBATE   Keynesians acknowledge the importance of monetary policy, but they believe fiscal policy is a more powerful and reliable stabilization tool. This is implied by the basic equation of Keynesianism. Government spending is a direct component of aggregate expenditures and thus aggregate demand. And taxes are only one short step removed, since tax changes allegedly affect consumption and investment in dependable and predictable ways.

Monetarists downgrade or reject fiscal policy as a stabilization tool. They believe that fiscal policy is weak and ineffectual because of the **crowding-out effect** (Chapter 12). Suppose government runs a budgetary deficit by selling bonds, which means borrowing from the public. By borrowing, government competes with private businesses for funds. Government borrowing will increase the demand for money, raise the interest rate, and crowd out a substantial amount of private investment that otherwise would have been profitable. Thus, the net effect of a budget deficit on aggregate expenditures is unpredictable and, at best, modest.

The workings of the crowding-out effect can be seen from a more analytical perspective by referring to Figure 15-2. Financing the government's deficit will increase the demand for money, shifting the D_m curve of Figure 15-2(a) to the right. With a fixed money supply, S_m, the equilibrium interest rate will rise. This interest rate increase will be large, according to the monetarists, because the D_m curve is relatively steep.

Furthermore, monetarists believe that the investment-demand curve of Figure 15-2(b) is relatively flat, meaning investment spending is very sensitive to changes in the interest rate. The initial increase in the demand for money causes a relatively large rise in the interest rate, which, projected off an interest-sensitive investment-demand curve, causes a large decline in the investment component of aggregate expenditures. The resulting large contractionary effect offsets the expansionary impact of the fiscal deficit and, on balance, the equilibrium GDP is unaffected.

If a deficit was financed by issuing new money, the crowding-out effect could be avoided and the deficit would be followed by economic expansion. *But*, the monetarists point out, the expansion would be due, *not* to the fiscal deficit per se, but rather, to the creation of additional money.

Keynesians, for the most part, do not deny that some investment may be crowded out. But they perceive the amount as small and conclude that the net impact of an expansionary fiscal policy on equilibrium GDP will be substantial. In Figure 15-2, the extreme Keynesian view is that the demand for money curve is relatively flat and the investment-demand curve is steep. (You may recall that this combination makes monetary policy relatively weak and ineffective.) An increase in D_m will cause a very modest increase in the interest rate, which, when projected off a steep investment-demand curve, will result in a very small decrease in the investment component of aggregate expenditures. Little investment will be crowded out.

Keynesians *do* acknowledge that a deficit financed by creating new money will have a greater stimulus than one financed by borrowing. In Figure 15-2(a), for any given increase in D_m there is some increase in S_m that will leave the interest rate, and therefore the volume of investment, unchanged.

MONETARY POLICY: DISCRETION OR RULES?

We portray the Keynesian conception of monetary policy in Figure 15-2. Keynesians believe that the demand for money curve is relatively flat and the investment-demand curve relatively steep, weakening monetary policy as a stabilization tool. We have also seen that in contrast, monetarists contend that the money demand curve is very steep and the investment-demand curve quite flat, a combination meaning a change in the money supply has a powerful effect on the equilibrium level of nominal GDP. This is monetarism's fundamental contention — the money supply is the critical determinant of the level of economic activity and the price level.

However, strict monetarists do *not* advise use of expansionary and contractionary monetary policies to modify "downs" and "ups" of the business cycle. Friedman contends that, historically, *discretionary* changes in the money supply made by monetary authorities have *destabilized* the economy.

Examining the monetary history of the United States from the Civil War up to the establishment of the Federal Reserve System (the central bank of the United States) in 1913 and comparing this with the post-1913 record, Friedman concludes that even if the economically disruptive World War II period is ignored, the latter (post-1913) period was clearly more unstable. Much of this decline in economic stability after the Federal Reserve System became effective is attributed to faulty decisions by the monetary authorities. *In the monetarist view economic instability is more a product of monetary mismanagement than it is of any inherent destabilizers in the economy.* There are two sources of monetary mismanagement.

1. IRREGULAR TIME LAGS Although the monetary transmission mechanism is direct, changes in the money supply affect nominal GDP only after a long and variable time period. Friedman's empirical work suggests that a change in the money supply may significantly change GDP in as short a period as six to eight months or in as long a period as two years. Because it is virtually impossible to predict the time lag of a policy action, there is little chance of determining accurately when specific policies should be invoked or which policy — easy or tight money — is appropriate.

In view of the uncertain duration of this time lag, the use of discretionary monetary policy to "fine-tune" the economy for cyclical "ups" and "downs" may backfire and intensify these cyclical changes.

2. INTEREST RATE: WRONG TARGET   Monetarists argue that monetary authorities have typically tried to control interest rates to stabilize investment and therefore the economy. Recalling Chapter 15's discussion of the targeting dilemma, the problem is the Bank of Canada cannot simultaneously stabilize both the money supply and interest rates. In trying to stabilize interest rates, the Bank of Canada might *destabilize* the economy.

THE MONETARY RULE   Monetarist moral: Monetary authorities should stabilize, not the interest rate, but the rate of growth of the money supply. Specifically, Friedman advocates legislating the **monetary rule** that the money supply be expanded each year at the same annual rate as the potential growth of our real GDP, meaning the supply of money should be increased steadily at 3 to 5% per year.

Despite a somewhat spotty record, Keynesians argue it would be foolish to replace discretionary monetary policy with a monetary rule. Arguing that V is variable both cyclically and secularly, Keynesians contend that a constant annual rate of increase in the money supply could contribute to substantial fluctuations in aggregate expenditures and promote economic instability. (**Key Question 5**)

AD-AS ANALYSIS

Let's now contrast monetarist and Keynesian views in terms of the aggregate demand-aggregate supply model. By bringing aggregate supply into the picture we can see more clearly the implications of each model for real output and the price level. We can also further our understanding of policy differences.

CONTRASTING PORTRAYALS   Figure 17-5(a) portrays the monetarist perspective and Figure 17-5(b), the crude Keynesian conception. The difference on the demand side concerns the factors that will shift the aggregate demand curve. To mone-

tarists the aggregate demand curve will shift rightward or leftward because of an increase or decrease, respectively, in the money supply. Keynesians are more general, recognizing that in addition to changes in private spending both fiscal and monetary policy can shift the aggregate demand curve.

On the supply side we find that monetarists view the aggregate supply curve as very steep or, in the long run, vertical, while Keynesians see it as quite flat or in the extreme case, horizontal. The flat range reflects the belief that the economy can operate short of the full-employment or capacity level, while a vertical range reflects the classical heritage of monetarism and the belief that flexible prices and wages continuously move the economy towards full employment.

POLICY IMPLICATIONS   These different conceptions of the aggregate supply curve relate to stabilization policy. In the monetarist view a change in aggregate demand affects primarily the price level and has little impact on real GDP. This conclusion derives from the assumption that, if the Bank of Canada adheres to a monetary rule, the economy will be operating near or at its full-employment output at all times. If policy makers try to use stabilization policy to increase real output and employment, their efforts will be largely in vain. As aggregate demand shifts from AD_0 to AD_1 in Figure 17-5(a), we get a very modest increase in real output (Q_0 to Q_1) but a large increase in the price level (P_0 to P_1). The economy will pay a high "price" in terms of inflation to realize very modest increases in output and employment.

In comparison, the Keynesian conception indicates that an expansionary policy will have large effects on production and employment and little impact on the price level. This conclusion derives from the assumption that, because of its inherent instability, the private economy may be operating far below its productive potential. Thus in Figure 17-5(b) we find that the AD'_0 to AD'_1 increase in aggregate demand will entail a large increase in real output (Q'_0 to Q'_1) while eliciting only a small price level increase (P'_0 to P'_1). To Keynesians, when the economy operates at less than its capacity, large gains in real output and employment can be obtained at a small inflationary cost.

Once the economy has reached full-employment output, the debate between Keynesians and monetarists ends. Both agree that expansionary stabilization policies will produce demand-pull inflation in the vertical range of aggregate supply.

FIGURE 17-5   Monetarism, Keynesianism, and the aggregate demand–aggregate supply model

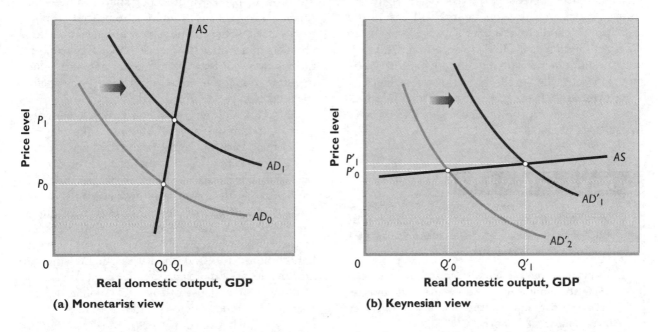

(a) Monetarist view

(b) Keynesian view

The monetarist view (a) is that the aggregate supply curve is relatively steep, which means that a change in aggregate demand will have a large effect on the price level but cause only a small change in real output and employment. The Keynesian conception (b) envisions a relatively flat aggregate supply curve, which implies that a change in aggregate demand will cause large changes in real output and employment and small changes in the price level.

DEBATE OVER THE MONETARY RULE   The aggregate demand-aggregate supply model also can help clarify the debate over the monetarists' call for a monetary rule. In Figure 17-6 suppose for simplicity that the aggregate supply curve is vertical, rather than near-vertical as in Figure 17-5(a). Also assume the economy is operating at the Q_1 full-employment level of GDP. The aggregate supply curve shifts rightward from AS to AS', depicting a typical or average annual

Monetarists favour a monetary rule that would fix the increase in the money supply over time to the average increase in real output. An increase in aggregate demand (AD_0 to AD_1) thus would match an increase in aggregate supply (AS_0 to AS_1) and the price level would remain constant. Keynesians counter that the monetary rule will not guarantee that aggregate demand will shift from AD_0 to AD_1. Because of instability within the private economy, aggregate demand may either shift to the right of AD_1, creating demand–pull inflation, or fail to shift all the way to AD_1, resulting in deflation. Hence, Keynesians argue that the discretionary use of stabilization policies is more likely to maintain price stability than is a monetary rule.

increase in full-employment real output. Such increases in aggregate supply result from real factors such as added resources and improved technology.

FIGURE 17-6   The monetary rule and the aggregate demand–aggregate supply model

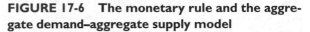

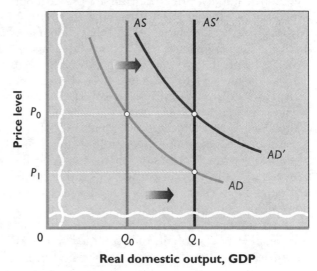

Real domestic output, GDP

Monetarists argue that a monetary rule tying increases in the money supply to the typical rightward shift of the aggregate supply curve will ensure the aggregate demand curve shifts rightward from AD to AD'. As a result, real GDP will rise from Q_0 to Q_1 and the price level will remain constant at P_0. A monetary rule will allegedly promote price stability.

Keynesians dispute the close predictable link between changes in the money supply and changes in aggregate demand.

QUICK REVIEW 17-3

1. In contrast to Keynesians, monetarists believe fiscal policy is weak and ineffectual because of a severe crowding-out effect.

2. Monetarists see the money demand curve as relatively steep and the investment-demand curve as relatively flat, implying that monetary policy has strong impacts on nominal GDP.

3. Strict monetarists advocate that the Bank of Canada adhere to a monetary rule whereby it expands the money supply at a fixed annual rate approximating the growth of potential output.

RATIONAL EXPECTATIONS THEORY

Keynesian economics and monetarism are not alone in the battle for the minds of economists, policy makers, and students. Developed largely since the mid-1970s, **rational expectations theory** (RET) has entered the fray. Although several variants of RET have emerged, including Keynesian ones, we will discuss the version associated with the *new classical economics*. Our goal here is to relate RET to the debate over whether stabilization policy should be discretionary, as Keynesians argue, or based on rules, as monetarists contend. First some relevant background on RET.

Rational expectations theory follows the thrust of economic theory in suggesting that people behave rationally. Market participants gather information and process it intelligently to form expectations about things in which they have a monetary stake. If financial investors, for instance, expect stock market prices to fall, they sell their shares in anticipation of that decline. The increased avail-

ability of stock in the market results in an immediate drop in prices offered per share. When consumers learn that a drought is expected to boost food prices, some of them purchase storable food products in advance of the price hike. These expectations cause an increase in market demand, which in turn produces an increase in food prices before the food crop is even harvested.

But RET contains a second basic element that gives it its "new classical" flavour. Like classical economics, rational expectations theory assumes that all markets — both product and resource — are highly competitive. Therefore, wages and prices are flexible both upward and downward. RET goes further, assuming that new information is quickly (in some cases instantaneously) taken into account in the demand and supply curves of such markets. Equilibrium prices and quantities quickly adjust to new events (technological change), market shocks (a drought or collapse of the OPEC oil cartel), or changes in public policies (a shift from fight to easy money). Both product and resource prices are highly flexible and change quickly as consumers, businesses, and resource suppliers change their economic behaviour as they get new information.

POLICY FRUSTRATION

RET adherents contend that *the aggregate responses of the public to its expectations will render anticipated discretionary stabilization policies ineffective.* Consider monetary policy. Suppose monetary authorities announce an easy money policy is in the offing. Purpose: To increase real output and employment. But based on past experience, the public anticipates that this expansionary policy will be inflationary and takes self-protective actions. Workers will press for higher nominal wages. Businesses will increase the prices of products. Lenders will raise interest rates.

All these responses are designed to prevent inflation from having anticipated adverse effects on the *real* incomes of workers, businesses, and lenders. But collectively this behaviour raises wage and price levels, and the increase in aggregate demand brought about by the easy money policy is completely dissipated in higher prices and wages. Real output and employment do *not* expand.

In Keynesian terms, the increase in real investment spending that the easy money policy was designed to generate never materializes. The expected rate of net profit on investment remains unchanged since the price of capital rises in lockstep with the prices of the extra production that the capital allows. Also, the nominal interest rate rises proportionately to the price level, leaving the real interest rate unchanged. No increase in real investment spending happens and no expansion of real GDP occurs.

In the monetarists' equation of exchange, an expansionary monetary policy increases M and thus aggregate expenditures, MV. But the public's expectation of inflation elicits an increase in P by a percentage equal to the increase in MV. Despite the increased MV, real output, Q, and employment are therefore unchanged.

Note carefully what has occurred here. The decision to increase M was made to increase output and employment. But the public, acting on the expected effects of an expansionary monetary policy, has taken actions that have frustrated the policy's goal. An expansionary monetary policy has been translated into inflation, rather than into desired increases in real output and employment.

AD-AS INTERPRETATION

We can better understand the RET view of policy ineffectiveness by examining Figure 17-7. This diagram restates the classical model from Figure 17-1(a). Here we show the aggregate supply curve as being *vertical*.

Once again, assume an expansionary monetary policy shifts the aggregate demand curve rightward from AD_0 to AD_1. Why doesn't this increase in aggregate demand increase real output significantly (as in the Keynesian model of Figure 17-5[b]) or at least slightly (as in the monetarist model of Figure 17-5[a])? According to RET, the answer is that consumers, businesses, and workers will anticipate that an expansionary policy means rising prices and will have built the expected effects into their market decisions concerning product prices, nominal wage rates, nominal interest rates, and so forth. Markets will instantaneously adjust, bringing the price level upward from P_0 to P_1. The economy does not move beyond output Q_0 because the price level rises by precisely the amount required to cancel any impact the expansionary policy might have had on real output and employment. The *combination of rational expectations and instantaneous market adjustments* — in this case upward wage, price, and interest rate flexibility — dooms the policy change to ineffectiveness. As aggregate demand expands from AD_0

to AD_1, the economy moves upward along the vertical aggregate supply curve directly from point a to point b. The only result is a higher price level; the *real* incomes of workers, businesses, lenders, and others are all unchanged because they have rationally anticipated the effects of public policy and have incorporated their expectations into market decisions to cause the resulting upshift of nominal wages, nominal profits, and nominal interest rates.

Presumably a decline in aggregate demand from AD_1 to AD_0 would do precisely the opposite. Instead of causing unemployment, the economy would move directly along the aggregate supply curve from b to a.

In the "old" classical theory, there would be a period when a decline in aggregate demand would cause a temporary "lapse" from full employment until market adjustments were completed. The economy would first move from b to c in Figure 17-7, but then in time falling prices and wages would

FIGURE 17-7 Rational expectations and the aggregate demand–aggregate supply model

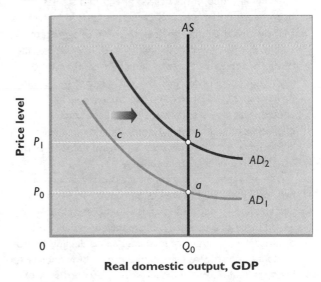

Real domestic output, GDP

Rational expectations theory implies that the aggregate supply curve is vertical. Strictly interpreted, the theory suggests that an increase in aggregate demand from, say, AD_0 to AD_1 will immediately result in an offsetting increase in the price level (P_0 to P_1) so that real domestic output will remain unchanged at Q_0. Conversely, a decline in aggregate demand from AD_1 to AD_0 will instantaneously reduce the price level from P_1 to P_0, leaving real domestic output and employment unchanged.

BOX 17-2   APPLYING THE THEORY

REAL BUSINESS CYCLE THEORY

A handful of proponents of rational expectations theory (RET) stand traditional economic theory on its head by arguing that business cycles are caused by real factors affecting aggregate supply rather than by fluctuations in aggregate demand.

Keynesians and monetarists conclude that business cycles largely result from changes in aggregate demand. But RET (new classical) theorists rule out aggregate demand changes as likely causes of long-lasting changes in real output. They contend the economy adjusts quickly — if not instantaneously — to changes in aggregate demand through rapid changes in nominal wages and other input prices (Figure 17-7).

But history shows that long-lasting business recessions and expansions have occurred. If changes in aggregate demand are not the reason, what are the causes?

A small group of new classical economists has hypothesized that business cycles are caused by factors that disturb the long-run growth trend of aggregate supply. In this view, recessions begin on the supply side of the economy, not on the demand side as tradition-ally assumed. In other words, "real" factors — technol-ogy, resource availability, and productivity — all affecting aggregate supply, are the alleged causes of business cycles. In contrast, traditional theory sees "monetary" factors that alter aggregate demand as the usual source of cyclical instability.

An example focusing on a recession will clarify this new classical thinking. Suppose productivity — output per worker — declines because an increase in the world price of oil makes it prohibitively expensive to operate certain types of machinery. This decline in pro-ductivity implies a reduction in the economy's ability to produce real output and therefore a leftward shift of its (vertical) aggregate supply curve. As real output falls in response to the decline in aggregate supply, peo-ple need less money to buy the reduced volume of goods and services. That is, the decline in output reduces the demand for money. Moreover, the slow-

down in business activity lessens business borrowing from banks, reducing the supply of money.

In this scenario, changes in the supply of money respond passively to changes in the demand for money. The decline in the money supply in turn reduces aggregate demand (shifts the *AD* curve leftward) to the same extent as the initial decline in aggregate supply. The result is that real equilibrium output is lower, while the price level remains unchanged. Like the simple Keynesian model (Figure 17-1[b]), the real business cycle theory allows for a decline in real output in the presence of a constant price level. (You are urged to test your comprehension of the real business cycle theory by using the AD-AS model in Figure 17-7 to diagram it.)

The policy implications of the real business cycle theory are as unusual and controversial as the theory itself. 1. Demand-management policies are inappro-priate and doomed to fail. Expansionary stabilization policy in this situation will not increase real output; instead, it will cause inflation. 2. Deviations of aggre-gate supply from its long-term growth trend should not be the source of social concern. In real business cycle theory, gains from "real" business booms roughly match the output losses arising from "real" downturns. The *net* long-run costs of business cycles therefore are allegedly modest. The emphasis of pub-lic policy should be on stimulating long-term eco-nomic growth rather than on trying to stabilize the economy.

Many economists reject the real business cycle the-ory, claiming it does not square with the facts of past business cycles. But, at a minimum, the theory shows that conventional macroeconomic theory is not the only analytical game in town.

move the economy down AD_0 to full employment at point a. But in the RET version of the "new" classical economics, prices would adjust instantaneously to the anticipated policy so that the real output and employment would not deviate from Q_0.

In the "old" classical economics, changes in aggregate demand could cause short-run changes in output and employment But the decision-making process and instantaneous market adjustments of the strict RET form of "new" classical economics preclude this.

While RET supports monetarism in arguing for policy rules rather than discretion their rationales are quite different. In the rational expectations theory, policy is ineffective, not because of policy errors or inability to time decisions properly, but because of public reaction to the expected effects of these policies. Monetarists are saying that discretionary policy doesn't work because monetary authorities do not have enough information about time lags and such. RET supporters claim that discretionary policy is ineffective because the public has considerable knowledge concerning policy decisions and their effects.

EVALUATION

RET has stirred macroeconomics in the past two decades. Anyone exposed to RET thinking looks at the macroeconomy from a somewhat different perspective. The appeal of RET stems from at least two considerations.

1. As with monetarism, RET is an option that might fill the void left by Keynesian economics' alleged inability to explain and correct by policy the simultaneous inflation and unemployment of the 1970s and early 1980s.
2. RET is strongly rooted in the theory of markets or, in other words, in microeconomics (defined in Chapter 1). Therefore, RET purports to provide linkages between macro- and microeconomics that economists have long sought.

But criticisms of RET are manifold and persuasive enough so that at this point most economists do *not* subscribe to strict interpretations of RET. Here are three basic criticisms.

1. BEHAVIOUR Many economists question whether people are, or can be, as well-informed as RET assumes. Can we expect households, businesses, and workers to understand how the economy works and what the impact will be of, say, the Bank of Canada's announced decision to increase its annual M2 money target growth rate from $3^{1}/2$ to 5%? After all, economists who specialize in forecasting frequently mispredict the *direction* of changes in output, employment, and prices, much less correctly indicate the *amounts* by which such variables will change.

RET proponents argue they are not suggesting that people always make *perfect* forecasts, but rather that they do not make consistent forecasting errors that can be exploited by policy makers. Furthermore, RET theorists point out that key decision-making institutions — large corporations, major financial institutions, and labour organizations — employ full-time economists to help anticipate effects of newly implemented public policies. It allegedly is impossible to fool important decision-making institutions in the economy on a consistent basis. But the issue of whether people and institutions behave as RET suggests is highly controversial.

2. STICKY PRICES A second criticism of RET is that most markets are *not* sufficiently competitive to adjust instantaneously (or even rapidly) to changing market conditions. While the stock market and certain commodity markets experience day-to-day or minute-to-minute price changes, many sellers can control within limits the prices they charge. When demand falls, for example, these sellers resist price cuts so that the impact is on output and employment (see Figure 11-10). This is particularly true of labour markets where union and individual contracts keep wages unresponsive to changing market conditions for extended periods. If markets adjust quickly and completely as RET suggests, how do we explain the decade of severe unemployment of the 1930s or the high 9% to 12% unemployment rates that persisted over the 1981–1984 period?

3. POLICY AND STABILITY There is substantial domestic and international evidence to indicate that, contrary to RET predictions, economic policy has affected real GDP and employment. Thus in the post-World War II period, when government has more actively invoked stabilization policies, fluctuations in real output have been less than in earlier periods. (**Key Question 12**)

ABSORPTION INTO THE MAINSTREAM

George Stigler, a Nobel Prize winning econo-mist and historian of economic theory, once stated: "New ideas [in economics] do not lead to the abandonment of the previous heritage; the new ideas are swallowed up by the existing cor-pus, which is thereafter a little different. And some-times a little better."[3] As revolutionary as they were, Keynesian ideas themselves did not supplant the existing, micro-based economic heritage. Instead, economics simply incorporated the new macroeconomics within its expanded domain.

The controversies discussed in this chapter have forced economists to rethink some of the fundamen-tal aspects of macroeconomics. And as is true of many debates, much compromise and revision of positions have occurred. Although considerable dis-agreement remains — for example, the "rules" versus "discretion" debate — contemporary macroeconom-ics has absorbed several of the fundamental ideas of monetarism and RET. Three examples:

1. MONEY MATTERS There are few econo-mists today who embrace the extreme Keynesian view that "money isn't important." Mainstream economics now incorporates the monetarist view that "money matters" in the economy. This is demonstrated by the emphasis we have given mone-tary policy in this book (Chapters 13–15). Changes in the money supply and interest rates are main-stream tools for pushing the economy towards full employment or pulling it back from expansionary booms and attendant inflation.

In the last half of the 1980s and thus far in the 1990s, government has largely abandoned discre-tionary fiscal policy because of large full-employ-ment, or structural, deficits. Elected officials have deemed tax cuts or increases in government expen-diture to be economically undesirable under these conditions. Tax increases and reductions in govern-ment expenditures have been aimed at reducing the deficit, largely independently of the state of the economy. Thus, Bank of Canada monetary policy, not countercyclical fiscal policy, has recently been the tool for stabilizing the economy.

---

[3] George J. Stigler, *Five Lectures on Economic Problems* (London: Longmans, Green, 1949), p. 24.

Also, macroeconomics has incorporated the monetarist precept that excessive growth of the money supply over long periods is a source of rapid inflation. (See Global Perspective 17-1.)

In summary, mainstream macroeconomics has accepted one part of monetarism — the impor-tance of the money supply and monetary policy — while rejecting another — the monetary rule expounded by strict monetarism.

GLOBAL PERSPECTIVE 17-1

Money supply growth and inflation in selected high-inflation economies, 1980–1992

Nations with high average annual rates of inflation typi-cally have high average annual rates of money growth.

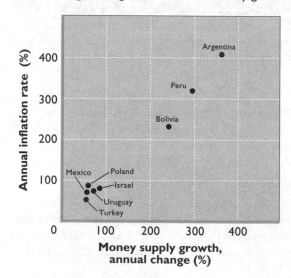

Source: World Bank data, 1980–1992.

2. CROWDING OUT AND CO-ORDINATION Thanks to the monetarists' emphasis on the crowd-ing-out effect, mainstream economists now incorpo-rate this idea within their analysis and are more fully aware of the wisdom of co-ordinating fiscal and monetary policy. If fiscal policy generates a siz-able crowding-out effect that diminishes the effec-tiveness of fiscal policy, then it is imperative that an appropriate monetary policy be applied simultane-ously to negate any potential crowding out of pri-vate investment.

3. EXPECTATIONS AND MARKET Mainstream economists and policy makers are now more aware of expectations and how they might affect the economy and the outcome of a policy change. We have seen in previous chapters that expectations can shift the aggregate expenditures schedule in the Keynesian model (Chapter 10) and the aggregate demand curve in the AD-AS model.

Thanks to RET, mainstream economics increasingly searches for the links between microeconomics and macroeconomics. We are increasingly aware that what happens to the aggregate levels of output, employment, and prices depends on how individual product and resource markets work. Some Keynesians incorporate rational expectation assumptions directly into their macro analysis. Unlike the new classical-based RET, however, this analysis also assumes imperfect product and resource markets. Even with rational expectations, downward price and wage inflexibility lead to Keynesian conclusions: Instability *can* occur in the economy and fiscal and monetary policies *can* work.

Thus, monetarism and RET have both had a discernible impact on macro theory and policy. Disagreements in this case have led to new insights. An expanded and altered body of widely accepted macroeconomic principles has emerged and is a new base of agreement among professionals and policy makers. The modern macroeconomics we have studied in previous chapters descends from Keynesian macroeconomics, but it is different and better than it was before the monetarist and rational expectations critiques. (**Key Question 13**)

RECAP: ALTERNATIVE MACROECONOMIC PERSPECTIVES

We have seen that a number of theories purport to explain how the national economy operates. We have presented the central ideas and policy implications of Keynesianism, monetarism, rational expectations theory, and supply-side economics.

Table 17-1 summarizes major aspects of these theories and policy perspectives. In reviewing the table, you will see there is no direct reference to "new classical economics." This viewpoint is simply that associated with the natural rate hypothesis, which asserts that the economy tends automatically to achieve equilibrium at its full potential level of output — at its natural rate of unemployment. The natural rate hypothesis is supported by economists of the monetarist and rational expectations persuasions.

CHAPTER SUMMARY

1. Classical economists see **a** a vertical aggregate supply curve that establishes the level of output, and **b** a stable aggregate demand curve that establishes the price level.

   Keynesians see **a** a horizontal aggregate supply curve at less-than-full-employment levels of output and **b** an inherently unstable aggregate demand curve.

   The following four statements contrast the polar Keynesian and monetarist positions on a number of critical points.

2. **Basic differences:** The *Keynesian* view is that the market system is not sufficiently competitive and flexible to ensure macroeconomic stability. An activist stabilization policy, centred on fiscal policy, is required to remedy this shortcoming.

   The *monetarist* view is that markets are highly competitive and conducive to macroeconomic stability. Monetarists favour a *laissez faire* policy.

3. **Analytical framework:** To *Keynesians* the basic determinant of real output, employment, and the price level is the level of aggregate expenditures. Their basic equation is $C_a + I_g + X_n + G =$ GDP. Components of aggregate expenditures are determined by a wide variety of factors that, for the most part, are unrelated to the supply of money.

   Monetarism focuses on the equation of exchange: $MV = PQ$. Because velocity V is basically stable, the critical determinant of real output and employment (Q) and the price level (P) is the supply of money (M).

TABLE 17-1 **Alternative macroeconomic theories and policies**

| Issue | Keynesianism | Natural rate hypothesis | | Supply-side economics |
		Monetarism	Rational expectations	
View of the private economy	Inherently unstable	Stable in long run at natural rate of unemployment	Stable in long run at natural rate of unemployment	May stagnate without proper work, saving, and investment incentives
Cause of the observed instability of the private economy	Investment plans unequal to saving plans (changes in AD); AS shocks	Inappropriate monetary policy	Unanticipated AD and AS shocks in the short run	Changes in AS
Appropriate macro policies	Active fiscal and monetary policy; occasional use of incomes policies	Monetary rule	Monetary rule	Policies to increase AS
How changes in the money supply affect the economy	By changing the interest rate, which changes investment, and real GDP	By directly changing AD which changes GDP	No effect on output because price-level changes are anticipated	By influencing investment and thus AS
View of the velocity of money	Unstable	Stable	No consensus	No consensus
How fiscal policy affects the economy	Changes AD and GDP via the multiplier process	No effect unless money supply changes	No effect on output because price-level changes are anticipated	Affects GDP and price level via changes in AS
View of cost-push inflation	Possible (wage-push, AS shock)	Impossible in the long run in the absence of excessive money supply growth	Impossible in the long run in the absence of excessive money supply growth	Possible (productivity decline, higher costs due to regulation, etc.)

4. **Fiscal policy:** The *Keynesian* position is that because **a** government spending is a component of aggregate expenditures and **b** tax changes have direct and dependable effects on consumption and investment, fiscal policy is a powerful stabilization tool.

Monetarists argue that fiscal policy is weak and uncertain in its effects. Unless financed by an increase in the money supply, deficit spending will raise the interest rate and crowd out private investment spending.

5. **Monetary policy:** *Keynesians* argue that monetary policy entails a lengthy transmission mechanism, involving monetary policy decisions, bank reserves, the interest rate, investment, and finally the nominal GDP. Uncertainties at each step in the mechanism limit the effectiveness and dependability of monetary policy. Money matters, but its manipulation through monetary policy is not as powerful a stabilization device as fiscal policy. Specifically, the combination of a

relatively flat demand for money curve and a relatively steep investment-demand curve makes monetary policy relatively ineffective.

Monetarists believe that the relative stability of *V* indicates a rather dependable link between the money supply and nominal GDP. However, monetarists think that because of **a** variable time lags in becoming effective and **b** the incorrect use of the interest rate as a guide to policy, the application of discretionary monetary policy to "fine-tune" the economy is likely to fail. In practice, monetary policy has tended to destabilize the economy. Monetarists therefore recommend a monetary rule whereby the money supply is increased in accordance with the long-term growth of real GDP.

Statements 6 and 7 contain the essence of rational expectations theory (RET).

6. RET is based on two assumptions: **a** consumers, businesses, and workers understand how the economy works; are able to assess the future effects of policy and other changes; do not make consistent forecasting errors; and adjust their decisions to further their own self-interests; **b** markets are highly competitive and prices and wages adjust quickly to changes in demand and supply.

7. RET holds that, when the public reacts to the expected effects of stabilization policy, the effectiveness of such policy will be negated. This theory therefore supports policy rules as opposed to discretionary policy.

8. Several aspects of monetarism and rational expectations have been incorporated into mainstream macroeconomic analysis, including the ideas that **a** "money matters," in the macroeconomy; **b** excessive growth of money over long periods is inflationary; **c** fiscal policy may crowd out some private investment, and **d** expectations play an important role in the economy.

TERMS AND CONCEPTS

classical economics (p. 364)
crowding-out effect (p. 373)
equation of exchange (p. 367)
Keynesianism (p. 366)

monetarism (p. 366)
monetary rule (p. 374)
rational expectations theory (p. 376)
velocity of money (p. 367)

QUESTIONS AND STUDY SUGGESTIONS

1. *Key Question*   *Use the aggregate demand-aggregate supply model to compare classical and Keynesian interpretations of a. the aggregate supply curve, and b. the stability of the aggregate demand curve. Which model do you think is more realistic?*

2. Explain: "The debate between Keynesians and monetarists is an important facet of the larger controversy over the role of government in our lives."

3. State and explain the basic equations of Keynesianism and monetarism. "Translate" the Keynesian equation into the monetarist equation.

4. In 1994 the money supply (M1) was approximately $57.3 billion and the nominal GDP was about $750.1 billion. What was the velocity of money in 1994? Figure 17-4 indicates that velocity increased steadily between the mid-1940s and 1982 and then levelled off or declined. Can you think of reasons to explain these trends?

5. **Key Question** *What is the transmission mechanism for monetary policy according to* a. *Keynesians and* b. *monetarists? What significance do the two schools of thought apply to money and monetary policy as a determinant of economic activity? According to monetarism, what happens when the actual supply of money exceeds the amount of money that the public wants to hold?*

6. Why do monetarists recommend that a "monetary rule" be substituted for discretionary monetary policy? Explain: "One cannot assess what monetary policy is doing by just looking at interest rates." Indicate how an attempt to stabilize interest rates can be destabilizing to the economy.

7. Answer the ensuing questions on the basis of the following information for a hypothetical economy in year 1: money supply = $50 billion; long-term annual growth of real GDP = 4%; velocity = 12. Assume that the banking system initially has no excess reserves and that the desired cash reserve ratio is 5%. Also, suppose that velocity is constant and that the economy initially is operating at its full employment level of output.

    a. What is the level of nominal GDP in year 1 in this economy?

    b. Suppose that the Bank of Canada adheres to the monetarist's rule through open-market operations. What amount of bonds will it have to sell to, or buy from, chartered banks and investment dealers between years 1 and 2 to meet its monetary rule?

8. Explain why monetarists assert fiscal policy is weak and ineffective. What specific assumptions do a. monetarists and b. strict Keynesians make with respect to the shapes of the demand for money and investment-demand curves? Why are the differences significant?

9. Indicate the precise relationship between the demand for money and the velocity of money. Discuss in detail: "The crucial issue separating Keynesians from monetarists is whether the demand for money is sensitive to changes in the rate of interest." Explain the Keynesian contention that a change in M is likely to be accompanied by a change in V in the opposite direction.

10. Explain and evaluate these statements in the context of the Keynesian-monetarist controversy:

    a. "If the national goal is to raise income, it can be achieved only by raising the money supply."

    b. "The size of the federal budget deficit is not important. What is important is how the deficit is financed."

    c. "There is no reason in the world why, in an equation like $MV = PQ$, the V should be thought to be independent of the rate of interest. There is every plausible reason for the velocity of circulation to be a systematic and increasing function of the rate of interest."

    d. "Monetarists assume that the PQ side of the equation of exchange is 'passive'; Keynesians assume it is 'active.'"

    e. "If expectations are rational, then monetary policy cannot be used to stabilize production and employment. It only determines the price level."

11. Explain how rational expectations might impede discretionary stabilization policies. Relate Chapter 12's Ricardian equivalence theorem to the idea of RET. Do you favour discretionary policies or rules? Justify your position.

12. **Key Question** *Use the aggregate demand-aggregate supply model to sketch graphically the* a. *monetarist,* b. *Keynesian, and* c. *rational expectations theories of the macroeconomy. Carefully compare the implications of each for public policy. In what respect, if any, does your RET portrayal differ from the "old" classical model of Figure 17-1(a)?*

13. *Key Question* *Which of the following tenets of monetarism and RET have been absorbed into mainstream macroeconomics:*

   a. *The Bank of Canada should increase the money supply at a fixed annual rate.*

   b. *Money matters; it is an important factor in determining GDP and the price level.*

   c. *Excessive growth of the money supply over long periods will cause inflation.*

   d. *Fiscal policy may cause a crowding-out effect.*

   e. *Expectations are important; they can influence the locations of the aggregate demand and supply curves.*

   f. *Changes in expectations created by traditional fiscal and monetary policy will render these policies completely ineffective.*

CHAPTER 18

BUDGET DEFICITS AND THE PUBLIC DEBT

Federal deficits and our rapidly expanding public debt have received much publicity in the past few years. That is because both have been expanding at a rapid rate. In 1973 the federal public debt stood at about $30 billion; by 1994 it had reached $435 billion.

In this chapter we examine the persistent federal deficits and the mounting public debt these deficits have produced. We will then compare different budget philosophies. Next, we examine the quantitative dimensions of the public debt. How large is the debt? How can it be most meaningfully measured? We then consider the problems associated with the public debt and will find that some are false or bogus problems, while others are real. Next, we assess the upsurge in the size of deficits and in the public debt that have occurred in the past two decades. We seek to understand why most economists see these deficits as adversely affecting domestic investment and international trade.

BOX 18-1   THE BIG PICTURE

Governments raise revenues through taxes and spend the revenues on all sorts of goods, services, and capital projects. In the last 20 years the federal government has consistently spent more than it has taken in. Just as a family's debt rises if every week it spends more than it takes in, so the federal government's debt level has soared.

The analogy with a family is slightly misleading; governments live on indefinitely and can increase their revenues by raising taxes. Still, the federal government's debt load — and that of a few provinces — has become worrisome to some economists because of its potential effects on interest rates and the value of our dollar.

As you read this chapter, keep the following points in mind:

- Government debt must be measured against the government's — and indirectly, the nation's — ability to repay it.
- If the growth of the public debt outpaces the economy's growth rate over long periods, there will be significant implications.
- The primary implication of very large public debt in relation to a nation's ability to pay it is through higher interest rates, which lead to other implications. Among the most important ones in Canada are cutbacks in social programs and the inability to embark on expansionary fiscal policy to avert recession.

DEFICITS AND DEBT: DEFINITIONS

A budget deficit is the amount by which a government's expenditures exceed its revenues during a particular year. For example, during 1994–95 the federal government spent $152 billion and its receipts were only $122 billion, producing a $30 billion deficit.

The national or **public debt** is the total accumulation of the federal government's total deficits and surpluses that have occurred through time. At the end of 1994 the public debt was about $435 billion.

Note that "public debt" does *not* include the entire public sector; provincial and local finance is omitted.

BUDGET PHILOSOPHIES

Is it good or bad to incur deficits and let the public debt grow? Should the budget be balanced annually, if necessary by legislation or constitutional amendment? We saw in Chapter 12 that counter-cyclical fiscal policy should move the federal budget towards a deficit during recession and towards a surplus during inflation. This means an activist fiscal policy is unlikely to result in a balanced budget in any particular year. Is this a matter for concern?

Let's approach this question by examining the economic implications of several contrasting budget philosophies.

ANNUALLY BALANCED BUDGET

Until the Great Depression of the 1930s, the **annually balanced budget** was accepted as a desirable goal of public finance. However, an annually balanced budget largely is not compatible with government fiscal activity as a counter-cyclical, stabilizing force. Indeed, an annually balanced budget intensifies the business cycle.

Illustration: Suppose the economy encounters unemployment and falling incomes. As Figure 12-3 shows, in such circumstances tax receipts will automatically decline. To balance its budget, government must either (1) increase tax rates, (2) reduce government expenditures, or do both. All these policies are contractionary; each further dampens, rather than stimulates, aggregate demand.

Similarly, an annually balanced budget will intensify inflation. Again, Figure 12-3 tells us that as nominal incomes rise during the course of inflation, tax collections will automatically increase. To avoid the impending surplus, government must either (1) cut tax rates, (2) increase government expenditures, or do both. But any of these policies will add to inflationary pressures.

An annually balanced budget is not neutral; the pursuit of such a policy is pro-cyclical, not counter-cyclical.

Some economists have advocated an annually balanced budget, not because of a fear of deficits and a mounting public debt, but because they believe an annually balanced budget is essential in constraining an undesirable expansion of the public sector. Budget deficits, they argue, are a manifestation of political irresponsibility. Deficits allow politicians to give the public the benefits of government spending programs while *currently* avoiding raising taxes to pay for them.

These economists believe government has a tendency to grow larger than it should because there is less popular opposition to this growth when it is financed by deficits rather than taxes. Wasteful governmental expenditures are likely to creep into the federal budget when deficit financing is readily available. Deficits are viewed as a symptom of a more fundamental problem — government encroachment on the vitality of the private sector.

CYCLICALLY BALANCED BUDGET

The idea of a **cyclically balanced budget** is that government exerts a counter-cyclical influence and at the same time balances its budget. However, this budget would not be balanced annually — there is nothing sacred about 12 months as an accounting period — but rather over the course of the business cycle.

The rationale is simple, plausible, and appealing. To offset recession, government should lower taxes and increase spending, purposely incurring a deficit. During the ensuing inflationary upswing, taxes would be raised and government spending slashed. The resulting surplus could be used to retire the federal debt incurred in offsetting the recession. Government fiscal operations would therefore exert a positive, counter-cyclical force, and the government could still balance its budget — not annually, but over a period of years.

The problem with this budget philosophy is that the upswings and downswings of the business cycle may not be of equal magnitude and duration. The goal of stabilization may therefore conflict with balancing the budget over the cycle. A long and severe slump followed by a modest and short period of prosperity would mean a large deficit during the slump, little or no surplus during prosperity, and a cyclical deficit in the budget.

FUNCTIONAL FINANCE

With **functional finance**, a balanced budget — annually or cyclically — is secondary. The primary purpose of federal finance is to provide for noninflationary full employment to balance the economy, not the budget. If this objective causes either persistent surpluses or a large and growing public debt, so be it. In this philosophy, the problems of government deficits or surpluses are minor compared with the undesirable alternatives of prolonged recession or persistent inflation. The federal budget is first and foremost an instrument for achieving and maintaining macroeconomic stability. How best to finance government spending — through taxation or borrowing — depends on existing economic conditions. Government should not hesitate to incur any deficits and surpluses required to achieve macroeconomic stability and growth.

To those who express concern about the large federal debt that the pursuit of functional finance might entail, proponents of this budget philosophy offer three arguments.

1. Our tax system is such that tax revenues automatically increase as the economy expands. Assuming constant government expenditures, a deficit that is successful in stimulating equilibrium GDP will be partially self-liquidating.
2. Because of its taxing powers and the ability to create money, the government's capacity to finance deficits is virtually unlimited.
3. Those who support functional finance contend the problems of a large federal debt are less burdensome than most people think. (**Key Question 1**)

THE PUBLIC DEBT: FACTS AND FIGURES

Because modern fiscal policy endorses unbalanced budgets to stabilize the economy, its application may lead to a growing public debt. Let's consider the public debt — its causes, characteristics, size, and its burdens and benefits.

The public debt, as column 5 in Table 18-1 shows, has grown considerably since 1926. As noted, the public debt is the accumulation of all past deficits, minus surpluses, of the federal budget.

TABLE 18-1 Quantitative significance of the Government of Canada public debt and interest payments in relation to GDP, selected years, 1926–1994*

(1) End of year	(2) Public debt held by Bank of Canada (billions)	(3) Public debt held by Canadian banks and general public (billions)	(4) Public debt held by non-residents (billions)	(5) Total federal public debt (billions) (2)+(3)+(4)	(6) Gross domestic product (billions)	(7) Interest payments (billions)	(8) Public debt as per cent of GDP (5)÷(6)	(9) Interest payments as per cent of GDP (7)÷(6)	(10) Per capita public debt
1926	–	–	–	$ 2.481	$ 5.354	$ 0.130	46.3%	2.4%	$ 263
1929	–	–	–	2.284	6.400	0.122	35.6	1.9	228
1940	$ 0.572	$ 3.302	$ 1.276	5.150	6.987	0.137	73.7	2.0	453
1946	1.909	12.999	1.091	15.998	12.167	0.444	131.5	3.6	1,301
1954	2.267	11.203	0.792	14.262	26.531	0.482	55.7	1.8	933
1958	2.670	11.857	0.632	15.159	35.689	0.568	42.5	1.6	888
1960	2.744	13.329	0.808	16.881	39.448	0.753	42.8	1.9	945
1966	3.473	15.980	0.810	20.263	64.388	1.151	31.5	1.8	1,012
1969	4.112	17.798	0.959	22.869	83.026	1.589	27.5	1.9	1,089
1973	6.025	22.971	0.741	29.737	127.372	2.518	23.3	2.0	1,349
1975	7.880	29.073	0.967	37.920	171.540	3.705	22.1	2.2	1,671
1979	13.754	49.861	6.985	70.600	276.096	8.080	25.6	2.9	2,973
1983	17.184	109.254	12.256	138.694	405.717	17.420	34.2	4.3	5,571
1988	20.653	201.049	52.778	273.856	605.906	31.882	45.2	5.3	10,574
1991	22.404	246.610	78.877	347.820	676,477	41.815	51.6	6.2	12,770
1994	30.317	298.212	106.856	435.385	750.053	40.142	58.0	5.4	14,886

* In current dollars.

Sources: Columns (2) to (5): *Bank of Canada Review*, Summer, 1995

CAUSES

Why has our public debt increased? What has caused us to incur these large and persistent deficits? The answer is threefold: wars, recessions, and the lack of political will.

WARS Some of the public debt has resulted from the deficit financing of wars. The public debt increased substantially during World War I and grew almost fourfold during World War II.

Consider World War II and the options it posed. The task was to reallocate a substantial portion of the economy's resources from civilian to war goods production. Government expenditures for armaments and military personnel soared. There were three financing options: increase taxes, print the needed money, or use deficit financing. Government feared that tax financing would require tax rates so high that they would diminish incentives to work. The national interest required attracting more people into the labour force and encouraging those already participating to work longer hours. Very high tax rates would interfere with these goals. Printing and spending additional money would be inflationary. Thus, much of World War II was financed by selling bonds to the public, draining off spendable income and freeing resources from civilian production so they would be available for defence industries.

RECESSIONS Another cause of the public debt is recessions, and, more specifically, the built-in stability characterizing our fiscal system. In periods when the income declines, tax collections automatically fall and deficits arise. Thus the public debt rose during the Great Depression of the 1930s and, more recently, during the recessions of 1981–82 and 1990–91.

LACK OF POLITICAL WILL Without being too cynical, one might also assert that deficits and a growing public debt are the result of lack of political will and determination: spending tends to gain votes; tax increases precipitate political disfavour. While opposition to deficits is widely expressed both by politicians and by their constituencies, *specific* proposals to raise taxes or cut programs typically encounter more opposition than support. University students may favour smaller deficits so long as funds for student loans are not eliminated in the process.

Similarly, new taxes or tax increases to reduce budget deficits may be acceptable in the abstract, but far less popular when specific tax changes are proposed. The popular view of taxation seems to be "Don't tax me, don't tax thee, tax the person behind the tree." The problem is there are not a sufficient number of taxpayers "behind the tree" to raise the amounts of new revenue needed to close the budget deficit.

QUANTITATIVE ASPECTS

The public debt was approximately $435 billion at the beginning of 1995. That's more than twice what it was a mere eight years ago.

But we must not fear large numbers. You'll see why when we put the size of the public debt in better perspective.

DEBT AND GDP A statement of the absolute size of the debt ignores the fact that the wealth and productive ability of our economy have also increased tremendously. A wealthy nation can more easily incur and carry a large public debt than can a poor nation. It is more meaningful to measure changes in the public debt *in relation* to changes in the economy's GDP, as shown in column 8 in Table 18-1. Instead of the large increase in the debt between 1940 and 1995 shown in column 5, we now find that the *relative* size of the debt has *declined* since 1946. However, our data also show that the relative size of the debt and the resulting interest payments have increased significantly since 1975.

INTERNATIONAL COMPARISONS As shown in Global Perspectives 18-1, in the last 15 years Canada's public debt compared with other industrial nations has grown rapidly. From having the lowest net debt (as a percentage of GDP) in 1980, it had the third highest by the mid-1990s.

INTEREST CHARGES Many economists think the primary burden of the debt is the annual interest charge accruing as a result. The absolute size of these interest payments is shown in column 7. Interest payments have increased sharply beginning in the mid-1970s. This reflects not only increases in the debt, but also periods of very high interest rates. Interest on the debt is now the largest item of expenditures in the federal budget. Interest charges as a percentage of the GDP are shown in column 9 of Table 18-1. Interest payments as a proportion of GDP have increased significantly in recent years and now stand at an all-time high. This ratio reflects the level of taxation (the average tax rate) required to service the public debt. In 1994 government had to collect taxes equal to 6.2% of GDP to pay interest on its debt.

OWNERSHIP Figure 18-1 reveals that about 7% of the total public debt is held by the Bank of Canada, the remaining 93% by private individuals, chartered banks, insurance companies, and corporations. About 25% of the total debt is held by foreigners. This is significant because, as we will see shortly, the implications of internally and externally held debt are different.

ACCOUNTING AND INFLATION The data on budget deficits and public debt may not be as straightforward as they appear. Governmental accounting procedures may not reflect the govern-

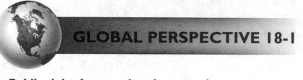

GLOBAL PERSPECTIVE 18-1

Public debt: International comparisons

Canada has the third largest public debt as a percentage of GDP. Only Belgium and Italy have larger debts as a percentage of their GDPs.

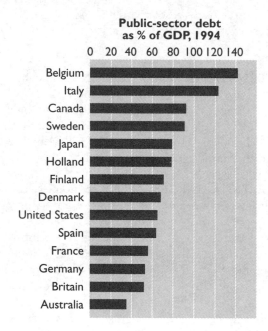

Public-sector debt as % of GDP, 1994

Source: Organization for Economic Cooperation and Development.

ment's actual financial position. Private firms have a separate capital budget because, in contrast to current expenses on labour and raw materials, expenditures for capital equipment represent tangible money-making assets. The federal government treats expenditures for highways, harbours, and public buildings in the same fashion as it does welfare payments, while in fact the former outlays are investments in physical assets. The federal government holds more than $100 billion in such tangible assets.

Also, inflation works to the benefit of debtors. A rising price level reduces the real value or purchasing power of the dollars paid back by borrowers. Taking this "inflationary tax" into account further reduces the sizes of deficits and public debt.

The point is that there are different ways of measuring the public debt and government's overall financial position. Some of these alternative measures differ greatly from the data presented in Table 18-1.

FIGURE 18-1   Ownership of Canada's public debt

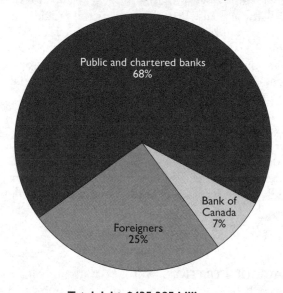

Total debt: $435.385 billion

Almost 70% of the federal government debt is held by the public and the chartered banks. The Bank of Canada holds 7% of the federal debt, while a quarter of it is foreign owned.

QUICK REVIEW 18-1

1. A budget deficit is an excess of government expenditures above tax revenues in a particular year; the public debt is the total accumulation of budget deficits and surpluses through time.

2. The three major budget philosophies are: **a** an annually balanced budget; **b** a budget balanced over the business cycle; and **c** functional finance.

3. The $435 billion public debt has resulted mainly from wartime financing, recessions, and lack of political will to address the issue.

4. Canada's public debt as a percent of GDP has been growing rapidly in the last 20 years.

ECONOMIC IMPLICATIONS: FALSE ISSUES

How does the public debt and its growth affect the economy? Can a mounting public debt bankrupt the nation? Does the debt place a burden on our children and grandchildren?

These are false issues. The debt is not about to bankrupt the government or the nation. Nor, except under certain specific circumstances, does the debt place a burden on future generations.

GOING BANKRUPT?

Can a large public debt bankrupt the government, making it unable to meet its financial obligations? No, for the following three points.

1. REFINANCING   There is no reason why the public debt need be reduced, much less eliminated. As portions of the debt fall due each month, government does not cut expenditures or raise taxes to provide funds to *retire* the maturing bonds. (We know that with depressed economic conditions, this would be unwise fiscal policy.) Rather, the government *refinances* the debt by selling new bonds and using the proceeds to pay off holders of the maturing bonds.

2. TAXATION   Government has the constitutional authority to levy and collect taxes. A tax increase is an option for gaining sufficient revenue to pay interest and principal on the public debt. Financially distressed private households and corporations *cannot* raise revenue via taxes, but government *can*. Private households and corporations *can* go bankrupt; the federal government *cannot*.

3. CREATING MONEY   Bankruptcy is also difficult to imagine because the federal government can print money to pay both principal and interest on the debt. A government bond obligates the government to redeem that bond for some specific amount of money on its maturity date. Government can use the proceeds from the sale of other bonds *or* it can create the needed money to retire the maturing bonds. The creation of new money to pay interest on or to retire debt, however, will be inflationary. But it is difficult to conceive of governmental bankruptcy when government has the power to create new money by running the printing presses. However, it *is* possible for lower-level governments to bankrupt themselves; they do not have the federal government's unlimited power of taxation, nor do they have a central bank ready to buy their bonds.

SHIFTING BURDENS

Does the public debt impose a burden upon future generations? We noted earlier that per capita debt at the beginning of 1994 was $14,886. Did each newborn child in 1994 enter the world with a $14,886 bill from Ottawa? Not really!

To whom do we owe the public debt? For the most part, we owe it to ourselves. About 75% of Government of Canada bonds are held by citizens and institutions — banks, businesses, insurance companies, government agencies, and pensions and trust funds — within Canada. Thus the *federal public debt is also a public credit*. While the public debt is a liability to the Canadian people (as taxpayers), part of the same debt is simultaneously an asset to Canadians (as bondholders).

To retire the public debt would call for a gigantic transfer payment where Canadians would pay higher taxes and the government, in turn, would pay out most of those tax revenues to those same taxpaying individuals and institutions in the aggregate, to redeem the Canadian bonds they hold. Although a redistribution of wealth would result from this huge financial transfer, it need not result in any immediate decline in the economy's aggregate wealth or standard of living. Repayment of an internally held public debt entails no leakage of purchasing power from the economy as a whole. Still, the redistribution of income means some Canadians would have much more wealth and income, while others would have much less. We know that large disparities of income lead to conflict between those Canadian citizens that have a great deal of wealth and those that have very little.

We noted earlier that the public debt increased sharply during World War II. Was some of the economic burden of World War II, for example, shifted to future generations by the decision to finance military purchases through the sale of government bonds? The answer is no. The burden of the war was borne almost entirely by the people who lived during the war; they were the ones who did without a multitude of consumer goods to permit Canada to arm itself and help arm its allies.

Also, wartime production may cause a nation's stock of capital to cease to grow or to dwindle as precious resources are shifted from the production of capital goods to the production of war goods. As a result, future generations inherit a smaller stock of capital goods. This occurred in Canada during World War II. But, again, this shifting of costs is independent of how a war is financed.

IMPLICATIONS AND ISSUES

We must be careful not to leave the impression that the public debt is of no concern among economists. The large debt *does* pose some real and potential problems, although economists attach varying degrees of importance to them.

INCOME DISTRIBUTION

The distribution of government bond ownership is uneven. Some people own much more than their per capita share; others less or none at all. Although our knowledge of the owners of the public debt by income class is limited, we presume that ownership is concentrated among wealthier groups. Because the tax system is mildly progressive, payment of interest on the public debt probably increases income inequality. If greater income equality is one of our social goals, then this redistributive effect is clearly undesirable.

INCENTIVES

Table 18-1 indicates that the 1994 federal public debt necessitated an annual interest payment of over $40 billion. Adding in the lower-level governments, interest charges on the total public debt amounted to over $50 billion. With no increase in the size of the debt, this annual interest charge must be paid out of tax revenues. These added taxes dampen incentives to bear risk, to innovate, to invest, and to work. Indirectly, the existence of a large debt can impair economic growth. As noted earlier, the ratio of interest payments to the GDP indicates the level of taxation needed to pay interest on the debt. Thus, many economists are concerned by the fact that this ratio has increased sharply in recent years (column 6 of Table 18-1).

EXTERNAL DEBT

A part of the public debt — **external debt** — is *not* "owed to ourselves," and in real terms the payment of interest and principal requires the transfer of some of our real output to other nations. Our federal public debt held by foreigners has risen rapidly since 1973, rising from about 2% to 25% in 1994. Starting in 1975, the provinces, local governments, and provincial Crown corporations reacted to the Bank of Canada's high-interest-rate policy by borrowing abroad, thus increasing the burden of the total public debt on Canadians. (**Key Question 3**)

CURB ON FISCAL POLICY

A large and growing public debt makes it politically difficult to use fiscal policy during a recession. For example, in 1991 and 1992 the Bank of Canada substantially reduced interest rates to stimulate a sluggish economy. But this expansionary monetary policy was slow to expand output and reduce unemployment. Had the public debt not been at an historic high and increasing due to the aforementioned structural deficit, it would have been politically feasible to reduce taxes or increase government spending to generate the stimulus of a deficit. But the growing "debt problem" ruled out this stimulus on political grounds. In general, a large and growing public debt creates political impediments to the use of antirecessionary fiscal policy.

CROWDING OUT AND THE STOCK OF CAPITAL

There is a potentially more serious problem. One way the public debt can transfer a real economic burden to future generations is by causing future generations to inherit a smaller stock of capital goods — a smaller "national factory." This possibility involves the **crowding-out effect**, which you will recall, is the notion that deficit financing will increase interest rates and reduce private investment spending. If this happens, future generations would inherit an economy with a smaller productive capacity and, other things being equal, the standard of living would be lower than otherwise.

Suppose the economy is operating at its full-employment level of output and the federal budget is initially in balance. Now for some reason government increases its level of spending. The impact of this increase in government spending will fall on

BOX 18-2   APPLYING THE THEORY

LOTTERIES: FACTS AND CONTROVERSIES AS A WAY OF RAISING GOVERNMENT REVENUES

Lotteries, which began in the 1970s, are a potentially important source of public revenue. What are the characteristics of lotteries? And what are the arguments for and against this means of enhancing provincial government revenues?

The average lottery returns about 46% of its gross revenues to ticket purchasers as prizes and 36% goes to the provincial treasury. The remaining 18% is for designing and promoting the lottery and for commissions to retail outlets that sell tickets. Although provinces sponsoring lotteries currently obtain only a small share of their total revenues in this way, per capita sales of lottery tickets increased substantially in the 1975-1989 period.

Lotteries have been controversial. Critics make the following arguments. First, the 40% of gross revenues from lotteries that goes to the provincial governments is in effect a 40% tax on ticket purchases. This tax is higher than the taxes on cigarettes and liquor. Furthermore, research indicates that the "lottery tax" is highly regressive in that there is little relationship between ticket purchases and household incomes. This means that low-income families spend a larger proportion of their incomes on lotteries than do high-income families. The 10% of the adults who patronize lotteries most heavily account for one-half of total ticket sales. Second, critics argue that it is ethically wrong for the government to sponsor gambling. Gambling is generally regarded as immoral and, in other forms, is illegal in most provinces. It is also held that lotteries may whet the appetite for gambling and generate compulsive gamblers who will impoverish themselves and their families. Third, lotteries may be sending the message that luck and fate — rather than education, hard work, and saving and investing — are the route to success and wealth in Canada.

But there are counterarguments. It is contended, in the first place, that lottery revenue should not be regarded as a tax. Tax collections are compulsory and involve coercion; the purchase of a lottery ticket is voluntary and entails free consumer choice. A second and related argument is that within wide limits it is not appropriate to make moral judgements about how people should spend their incomes. Individuals allegedly achieve the maximum satisfaction from their incomes by spending without interference. If some people derive satisfaction from participating in lotteries, they should be free to do so. Third, faced with tax revenue shortfalls and intense pressure not to raise taxes, lotteries are a relatively painless source of revenue to finance important services such as education and welfare programs. Finally, lotteries are competitive with illegal gambling and thereby may be socially beneficial in curtailing the power of organized crime.

Two observations seem certain at the moment. One is that total lottery revenue will continue to increase. More and more provinces are establishing lotteries and people seem to enjoy gambling, particularly when they feel their losses are being used for "good causes." The other point is that this source of revenue will remain controversial.

SOURCE: Adapted from Charles T. Clotfelter and Philip J. Cook, "On the Economics of State Lotteries," *Journal of Economic Perspectives*, Fall, 1990, pp. 105-119.

those living at the time it occurs. Think of Chapter 2's production possibilities curve with "government goods" on one axis and "private goods" on the other. In a full-employment economy an increase in government spending will move the economy *along*

the curve in the direction of the government-goods axis, meaning fewer private goods.

But private goods may be consumer or investment goods. If the increased government goods are provided at the expense of *consumer goods*, then the present generation bears the entire burden as a lower current standard of living. The current investment level is *not* affected and therefore neither is the size of the national factory inherited by future generations. But if the increase in government goods entails a reduction in production of *capital goods*, then the present generation's level of consumption (standard of living) will be unimpaired. In the future our children and grandchildren will inherit a smaller stock of capital goods and will have lower income levels.

TWO SCENARIOS
Let's sketch two scenarios yielding these different results.

FIRST SCENARIO   Suppose the presumed increase in government spending is financed by an increase in personal income taxes. We know most income is consumed. Therefore, consumer spending will fall by almost as much as the increase in taxes. Here, the burden of the increase in government spending falls primarily on today's generation; it has fewer consumer goods.

SECOND SCENARIO   Assume the increase in government spending is financed by increasing the public debt, meaning the government enters the money market and competes with private borrowers for funds. With the supply of money fixed, this increase in money demand will increase the interest rate — the "price" paid for the use of money.

In Figure 18-2, the curve I_{d0} reproduces the investment-demand curve of Figure 9-5. (Ignore curve I_{d1} for now.) The investment-demand curve is downsloping, indicating investment spending varies inversely with the interest rate. Here, government deficit financing drives up the interest rate, reducing private investment. If government borrowing increases the interest rate from 6% to 10%, investment spending would fall from $25 billion to $15 billion; thus, $10 billion of private investment would be crowded out.

Conclusion: An assumed increase in public goods production is more likely to come at the expense of private investment goods when financed by deficits. In comparison with tax financing, the future generation inherits a smaller national factory and therefore has a lower standard of living with deficit financing.

TWO QUALIFICATIONS
But there are two loose ends to our discussion that might mitigate or

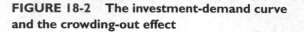

FIGURE 18-2   The investment-demand curve and the crowding-out effect

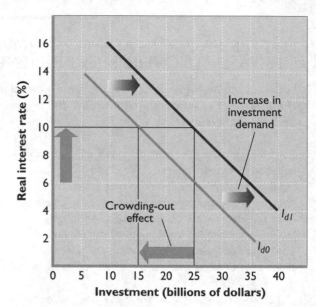

The crowding-out effect suggests that, with a fixed investment-demand curve (I_{d0}), an increase in the interest rate caused by a government deficit will reduce private investment spending and thereby decrease the size of the "national factory" inherited by future generations. In this case an increase in the interest rate from 6% to 10% crowds out $10 billion of private investment. However, if the economy is initially in a recession, the government deficit may improve business profit expectations and shift the investment-demand curve rightward as from I_{d0} to I_{d1}. This shift may offset the crowding-out effect wholly or in part.

even eliminate the size of the economic burden shifted to future generations.

1. PUBLIC INVESTMENT   Our discussion has neglected the character of the increase in government spending. Just as private goods may involve consumption or investment, so it is with public goods. If the increase in government spending consists of consumption-type outlays — subsidies for school lunches or the provision of limousines for government officials — then our second scenario's conclusion that the debt increase has shifted a burden to future generations is correct. But what if the government spending is investment-type outlays, for example, for construction of highways, harbours, and flood-control projects?

Similarly, what if they are "human capital" invest-ments in education, job training, and health?

Like private expenditures on machine and equipment, **public investments** increase the econ-omy's future production capacity. The capital stock of future generations need not be diminished, but rather its composition is changed so there is more public capital and less private capital.

2. UNEMPLOYMENT The other qualification relates to our assumption that the initial increase in government expenditures occurs when the economy is at full employment. Again the production possi-bilities curve reminds us that, *if* the economy is at less than full employment or, graphically, at a point inside the production possibilities curve, then an increase in government expenditures can move the economy *to* the curve without any sacrifice of either current consumption or capital accumulation. If unemployment exists initially, deficit spending by government need *not* mean a burden for future gen-erations in the form of a smaller national factory.

Look at Figure 18-2 once again. If deficit financing increases the interest rate from 6% to 10%, a crowding-out effect of $10 billion will occur. But the increase in government spending will stim-ulate a recession economy via the multiplier effect, improving profit expectations and shifting invest-ment demand rightward to I_{d1}. In the case shown, investment spending remains at $25 billion despite the higher 10% interest rate. Of course, the increase in investment demand might be smaller or larger than that in Figure 18-2. In the former case, the crowding-out effect would not be fully offset; in the latter, it would be more than offset. The point? An increase in investment demand counters the crowding-out effect. (**Key Question 7**)

RECENT FEDERAL DEFICITS

Federal deficits and the growing public debt have been in the economic spotlight in the last decade.

1. ENORMOUS SIZE As Figure 18-3 makes clear, the absolute size of the annual federal deficits increased enormously in the 1980s and 1990s. The average annual deficit for the 1970s was under $10 billion. In the 1980s annual deficits averaged between $20 and $30 billion. Consequently the public debt increased more than four fold during the 1980s.

The federal deficit jumped to $30 billion in 1991 mainly because of the 1990–91 recession and a weak recovery, which slowed the inflow of tax revenues. The deficit peaked at $35 billion in 1993, but began to come down in 1994 as the economy's expansion quickened and Parliament's efforts to reduce the deficit took hold.

2. RISING INTEREST COSTS Interest costs associated with the debt have risen sharply. By 1989, the annual interest costs exceeded the *total* federal debt that existed in 1973 (Table 18-1, columns 7 and 5). Since the mid-1980s the massive federal budget deficits have been entirely caused by the interest costs of past deficits. If it were not for the interest payments, the federal budget would be in surplus. Because interest payments are part of government expenditures, the debt feeds on itself through interest charges.

3. INAPPROPRIATE POLICY A further point of concern is that our current large annual deficits occurred in an economy operating at or close to full employment.

Large deficits during times of economic pros-perity raise the concern of fuelling demand-pull inflation. To counteract potentially rising prices, the Bank of Canada is forced to employ a tighter monetary policy. Along with the strong demand for money in the private sector, the tight money policy raises real interest rates and reduces investment spending. The greatest potential for budget deficits to produce a crowding-out effect occurs when the economy is near or at full employment.

4. BALANCE OF TRADE PROBLEMS Large budget deficits make it difficult for the nation to achieve a balance in its international trade. Large annual budget deficits promote imports and stifle exports.

DEFICIT-RELATED PROBLEMS

Let's trace out the manifold effects of these large recent deficits. The cause-effect chain is quite lengthy, but it yields important insights. Figure 18-4 is a helpful guide for our discussion.

HIGHER INTEREST RATES

Beginning with boxes 1 and 2, we note again that in financing its deficits government must go into

FIGURE 18-3   Annual federal budget deficits, 1973–1994 (fiscal year in billions of dollars)

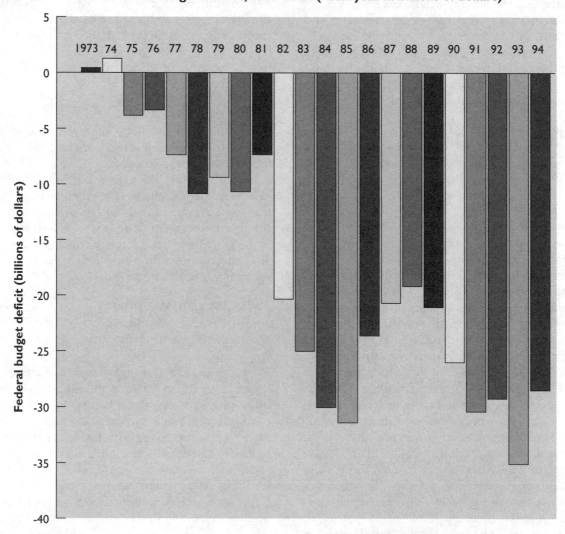

Compared to the 1970s, annual budget deficits in the 1980s and first half of the 1990s are strikingly high.

Source: Statistics Canada

the money market to compete with the private sector funds. We know this drives up real interest rates. High real interest rates have two important effects. First, as shown in box 3, they discourage private investment spending; this is the crowding-out effect. When the economy is closer to full employment, the crowding-out effect is likely to be large. Therefore, although they are willing to admit that the short-run impact of deficits is expansionary, some economists express concern that the long-run effect of structural deficits will retard the economy's growth rate. They envision deficits being used to finance consumption-type government goods at the

expense of investment in modernized factories and equipment. Deficits, it is contended, are forcing the economy on to a slower long-run growth path.

DOLLAR APPRECIATION

The second effect, shown by box 4, is that high interest rates on both Canadian government and corporation bonds make financial investment in Canada more attractive for foreigners. While the resulting inflow of foreign funds is helpful in financing both the deficit and private investment, box 5 reminds us that this inflow represents an increase in our external debt. Paying interest on and retiring debts to the rest

FIGURE 18-4   Possible effects of recent large budget deficits

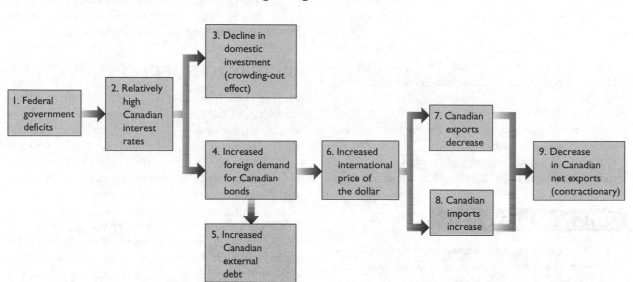

Many economists contend that large budget deficits have the effects shown above. Deficits increase domestic interest rates, resulting in both the crowding out of private investment and an increase in the demand for Canadian bonds. The latter increases our externally held debt and increases the demand for dollars. The strong demand for dollars raises the international value of the dollar, making our exports more expensive to foreigners and imports cheaper to Canadians. The consequent decline in our net exports has a contractionary effect on our economy.

of the world will reduce domestic output available to our domestic economy in the future.

Box 6 indicates that in order to purchase high-yielding Canadian bonds, foreigners must first buy Canadian dollars with their own currencies. This increases the worldwide demand for dollars and increases the international price or exchange value of the dollar.

DECREASED NET EXPORTS

This appreciation of the dollar will eventually depress our exports (box 7) and increase our imports (box 8), giving rise to an "unfavourable" balance of trade. Net exports are a component of aggregate demand. When net exports decline, this has a contractionary effect on the economy, as shown in box 9. As our exports fall, unemployment will rise in Canadian exporting industries such as agriculture, wood, and paper. Canadian import-competing industries such as automobiles and textiles will also be adversely affected. The increase in the value of the dollar makes foreign exports of these products less expensive and the Canadian

auto and textile industries find themselves with excess productive capacity and redundant labour.

INCREASED CANADIAN INDEBTEDNESS

Since we have increasingly been selling bonds abroad to finance at least part of the federal and provincial deficits this may create problems in the future, particularly for the external value of the Canadian dollar, our interest rates, and balance of payments.

CONTRARY VIEW: RICARDIAN EQUIVALENCE THEOREM

A few economists disagree with the analysis just outlined. They adhere to the **Ricardian equivalence theorem** (Chapter 12), which says financing a deficit by borrowing has the same effect on GDP as financing it through an explicit tax increase. People are supposedly aware that deficits today will require higher future taxes on them or their children to pay the added interest expense resulting from the increase in the public debt. Households therefore spend less today — saving more — in anticipation of having less future after-tax income available for consumption. Because the increase in private saving perfectly offsets the increase in government borrowing, the interest rate does not change. Thus neither a crowding-out effect nor a trade deficit necessarily emerges from a budget deficit. In Figure 18-4 the Ricardian equivalence theorem breaks the chain between box 1 and box 2, negating all of the effects purportedly following (boxes 3 through 9).

But most economists reject this unusual perspective. They claim instead that the 1980s and early 1990s provide ample evidence of negative foreign-sector effects of large budget deficits. (**Key Question 8**)

QUICK REVIEW 18-3

1. The borrowing and interest payments associated with the public debt may **a** increase income inequality, **b** require higher taxes, which dampen incentives, **c** curb the use of antirecessionary fiscal policy, and **d** impede the growth of the nation's capital stock *if* public borrowing significantly crowds out private investment.

2. Recent federal deficits are of concern because of **a** their enormous size, **b** rising total interest costs, and **c** their inappropriateness when the economy is near, or at, full-employment output.

3. Budget deficits can be linked to trade deficits as follows: budget deficits increase domestic real interest rates; the dollar appreciates; Canadian exports fall; and Canadian imports rise.

POSITIVE ROLE OF DEBT

Having completed this survey of imagined and real problems of deficits and the public debt, we conclude our discussion on a more positive note. We must not forget that debt — both public and private — plays a positive role in a prosperous and growing economy. As income expands, so does saving. Macroeconomic theory and fiscal policy tell us that if aggregate demand is to be sustained at the full-employment level, this expanding volume of saving or its equivalent must be obtained and spent by consumers, businesses, or government. The process by which saving is transferred to spenders is *debt creation*. Consumers and businesses do borrow and spend a great amount of saving.

But if households and businesses are not willing to borrow, and thereby to increase private debt sufficiently quickly to absorb the growing volume of saving, an increase in public debt must absorb the remainder. If this doesn't happen, the economy will falter from full employment and fail to realize its growth potential.

CHAPTER SUMMARY

1. A budget deficit is the excess of government expenditures over its receipts; the public debt is the total accumulation of its deficits and surpluses over time.

2. Budget philosophies include the annually balanced budget, the cyclically balanced budget, and functional finance. The basic problem with an annually balanced budget is that it is procyclical rather than counter-cyclical. Similarly, it may be difficult to balance the budget over the course of the business cycle if upswings and downswings are not of roughly comparable magnitude. Functional finance is the view that the primary purpose of federal finance is to stabilize the economy, and the problems associated with consequent deficits or surpluses are of secondary importance.

3. Historically, growth of the public debt has been caused by the deficit financing of wars, recessions, and lack of political will. The large structural deficits in recent years are primarily the result of recession and increased transfer payments.

4. The federal public debt was about $435 billion at the end of 1994. Since the 1970s the debt and associated interest charges have both been increasing as a percentage of the GDP. The debt has also been rising on a per capita basis.

5. The argument that a large public debt may bankrupt the government is false because **a** the debt need only be refinanced rather than refunded and **b** the federal government has the power to levy taxes and create money.

6. The crowding-out effect aside, the public debt is not a vehicle for shifting economic burdens to future generations.

7. More substantive problems associated with the public debt include the following: **a** Payment of interest on the debt probably increases income inequality. **b** Interest payments on the debt require higher taxes that may impair incentives. **c** A large and growing public debt creates political impediments to the use of antirecessionary fiscal policy. **d** Paying interest or principal on the portion of the debt held by foreigners entails a transfer of real output abroad. **e** Government borrowing to refinance or pay interest on a debt may increase interest rates and crowd out private investment spending.

8. Federal budget deficits have been much larger in the 1980s and 1990s than earlier. Some economists think these large deficits have increased real interest rates in Canada that have then **a** crowded out private investment and **b** increased foreign demand for Canadian bonds. Increased demand for Canadian bonds, some economists argue, has increased the international price of the dollar, causing Canadian exports to fall and Canadian imports to rise. Declining net exports have a contractionary effect on our domestic economy.

TERMS AND CONCEPTS

annually balanced budget (p. 388)
budget deficit (p. 388)
crowding-out effect (p. 394)
cyclically balanced budget (p. 389)
external debt (p. 394)

functional finance (p. 389)
public debt (p. 388)
public investments (p. 397)
Ricardian equivalence theorem (p. 399)

QUESTIONS AND STUDY SUGGESTIONS

1. *Key Question*   *Assess the potential for using fiscal policy as a stabilization tool under a. an annually balanced budget, b. a cyclically balanced budget, and c. functional finance.*

2. What have been the major sources of the public debt historically? Why have deficits been so large since the mid-1970s? Why did the deficits rise in 1991 and 1992?

3. *Key Question*   *Discuss the two ways of measuring the size of the public debt. How does an internally held public debt differ from an externally held public debt? What would be the effects of retiring an internally held public debt? Distinguish between refinancing and retiring the debt.*

4. Explain or evaluate each of the following statements:

   a. "A national debt is like a debt of the left hand to the right hand."

   b. "The least likely problem arising from a large public debt is that the federal government will go bankrupt."

   c. "The basic cause of our growing public debt is a lack of political courage."

5. Is the crowding-out effect likely to be larger during recession or when the economy is near full employment? Explain.

6. Some economists argue that the quantitative importance of the public debt can best be measured by interest payments on the debt as a percentage of the GDP. Can you explain why?

7. *Key Question* *Is our $435 billion public debt (at the end of 1994) a burden to future generations? If so, in what sense? Why might deficit financing be more likely to reduce the future size of our "national factory" than tax financing of government expenditures?*

8. *Key Question* *Trace the cause-and-effect chain through which large deficits might affect domestic real interest rates, domestic investment, the international price of the dollar, and our international trade. Comment: "There is too little recognition that the deterioration of Canada's position in world trade is more the result of our own policies than the harm wrought by foreigners." Provide a critique of this position, using the idea of Ricardian equivalence.*

9. Explain how a significant decline in the federal budget deficit could be expected to reduce a. the size of a trade deficit, b. the total debt Canadians owe to foreigners, and c. foreign purchases of Canadian assets such as factories and real estate.

10. Would you favour a constitutional amendment requiring the federal budget to be balanced annually? Why or why not?

CHAPTER 19

ECONOMIC GROWTH

Despite periods of cyclical instability, economic growth in Canada has been impressive during this century. Real output has increased twentyfold while population has only tripled, making seven times more goods and services available to the average Canadian than in 1900. And the quality of today's output is far superior. Economic growth has created material abundance, lifted the standard of living, and eased the unlimited wants-scarce resource dilemma.

But the Canadian growth story is not all upbeat. Since 1970 economic growth in Canada has slowed relative to earlier periods. There are indications that economic growth is picking up again, but there is no consensus on whether economic growth in the 1990s will return to levels seen between 1945 and 1975.

We begin by defining economic growth. Next, we develop an analytical perspective on economic growth. How can we depict growth within our graphical models? Then, we assess the long-term growth record of Canada and explore the relative importance of the various factors contributing to growth. This enables us to examine the causes of the slowdown in Canadian productivity beginning in the 1970s. We next present and critique so-called "doomsday" models of economic collapse. Finally, government policies designed to boost the rate of growth are briefly considered.

BOX 19-1   THE BIG PICTURE

In Chapter 7 we pointed out that there are two main themes in macroeconomics: In the short to medium term, to attempt to keep an economy on its production possibility curve with stable prices through the appropriate policies; and to bring about economic growth in the long run to very long run (an outward shift of the production possibility curve). This chapter is concerned with the second of these objectives.

As you read this chapter, keep the following points in mind:

- Both aggregate demand and aggregate supply factors can affect long-term economic growth, but aggregate supply factors are more important.

- There are two ways to achieve economic growth: (a) by increasing the amounts of factor inputs, and (b) getting more output from available factor inputs — an increase in productivity.
- There are those who believe economic growth cannot be sustained forever; resources of natural resources are fixed, and there is a limit to the pollutants that the environment can absorb. Others disagree, claiming that technological advancement will save us.

GROWTH ECONOMICS

Growth economics examines why production capacity increases over time. It also deals with the policy question of how to increase the economy's full employment level of real GDP.

TWO DEFINITIONS

Economic growth can be defined and measured in two ways:

1. An increase in real GDP occurring over a period
2. An increase in real GDP *per capita* occurring over time

In measuring military potential or political pre-eminence, the first definition is more relevant. But per capita output is superior for comparing living standards. While India's GDP is $215 billion compared to Denmark's $124 billion, per capita GDP is $26,000 in Denmark and only $310 in India.

Economic growth by either definition is usually calculated as annual percentage *rates* of growth. If real GDP was $200 billion last year and $210 billion this year, we can calculate the rate of growth by subtracting last year's real GDP from this year's real GDP and comparing the difference to last year's real GDP. The growth rate in this example is ($210 – $200)/$200, or 5%.

GROWTH AS A GOAL

Growth is a widely held economic goal. The growth of total output relative to population means a higher standard of living. An expanding real output means greater material abundance and implies a more satisfactory answer to the economizing problem. *A growing economy is in a better position to meet people's wants and resolve socioeconomic problems both domestically and internationally.* A growing economy enjoys an increment in its annual real output that it can use to satisfy new or existing wants more effectively.

An expanding real wage or salary income makes new opportunities available to individuals and families — a vacation trip, a home computer, a university or college education for each child — without sacrificing other opportunities and enjoyments. A growing economy can take on new programs to alleviate poverty and clean up the environment *without* impairing existing levels of consumption, investment, and public goods production. *Growth lessens the burden of scarcity.* A growing economy, unlike a static one, can consume more while increasing its capacity to produce more in the future. By easing the burden of scarcity — by relaxing society's production constraints — economic growth allows a nation to attain economic goals more fully and to undertake new endeavours that require output.

ARITHMETIC OF GROWTH

Why do economists get excited about small changes in the rate of growth? Because it really matters whether an economy grows at 4% or 3%. For Canada, with a current real GDP of about $750 billion, the difference between a 3 and a 4% growth rate is about $7.5 billion of output per year. For a very poor country, a 0.5% change in the growth rate may mean the difference between starvation and mere hunger.

When viewed over a period of years, an apparently small difference in the rate of growth becomes highly significant because of compounding. Suppose Alphania and Betania have identical GDPs, but Alphania grows at a 4% annual rate, while Betania grows at 2%. Based on the "rule of 70" (Chapter 8), Alphania's GDP would double in about 18 years (= 70 ÷ 4); Betania's would take 35 years (= 70 ÷ 2) to double.

Some argue that growth is more important than achieving economic stability. Eliminating a gap between actual GDP and potential GDP might increase the national income by, say, 6% on a one-time basis. But a 3% annual growth rate will increase the national income by 6% in two years and will provide that 6% biannual increment indefinitely.

INGREDIENTS OF GROWTH

There are six ingredients in the growth of any economy.

SUPPLY FACTORS

Four factors relate to the physical ability of an economy to grow. They are (1) the quantity and quality of its natural resources, (2) the quantity and quality of its human resources, (3) the supply or stock of capital goods, and (4) technology. These are the **supply factors** in economic growth — the physical agents of greater production. The availability of more and better resources, including the stock of technological knowledge, is what permits an economy to produce a greater real output.

DEMAND AND EFFICIENCY FACTORS

Two other considerations contribute to growth.

1. There is a **demand factor**. To realize its growing production potential, a nation must achieve full employment of its expanding supplies of resources. This requires a growing level of aggregate demand.

2. There is the **efficiency factor**. To achieve its production potential, a nation must obtain not only full employment of its resources, but also full production from them. We must use additional resources in the least-costly way ("productive efficiency") in producing those goods and services most valued by society ("allocative efficiency"). The ability to expand production is not sufficient for the maximum expansion of total output. Also required are the actual employment of expanded resource supplies *and* the efficient use of those resources to get the maximum amount of useful goods produced.

The supply and demand factors in growth are related. Unemployment can retard the rate of capital accumulation and slow expenditures for research. Conversely, a low rate of innovation and investment can cause unemployment.

GRAPHIC ANALYSIS

The six factors underlying economic growth are placed in proper perspective through Chapter 2's production possibilities curves and Chapter 11's aggregate demand and aggregate supply analysis.

GROWTH AND PRODUCTION POSSIBILITIES

Recall that a curve such as *AB* in Figure 19-1 is a best-performance curve. It indicates the various *maximum* combinations of products the economy can produce with its fixed quantity and quality of natural, human, and capital resources, and its stock of technological knowledge. An improvement in any of the supply factors will push the production possibilities curve outward, as shown by the shift from *AB* to *CD* in Figure 19-1. Increases in the quantity or quality of resources and technological progress will accomplish this.

But the demand and efficiency factors remind us the economy need not attain its maximum production potential. The curve may shift outward but leave the economy behind at some level of operation such as *a* on *AB*. Because *a* is inside the new curve *CD*, the economy has not achieved its growth potential. This enhanced production potential will not be realized unless (1) aggregate demand

FIGURE 19-1   Economic growth and the production possibilities curve

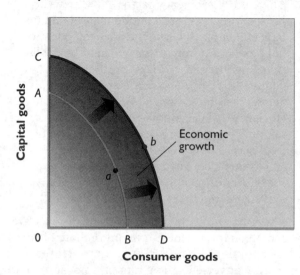

Economic growth is indicated by an outward shift of the production possibilities curve, as from *AB* to *CD*. Increases in the quantity and quality of resources and technological advance permit this shift; full employment and economic efficiency are essential to its realization.

increases sufficiently to sustain full employment, and (2) the additional resources are employed efficiently so they make the maximum possible dollar contribution to output.

An increase in aggregate demand must move the economy from *a* to a point on *CD*. And, to realize the greatest increase in the monetary value of its output — its greatest real GDP growth — this location on *CD* must be optimal. We know from Chapter 2 that this "best allocation" is determined by expanding production of each good until its marginal benefit equals its marginal cost (Figure 2-2). Here, we assume this optimal combination of capital and consumer goods is *b*.

Example: The net increase in the labour force of Canada is roughly 200,000 workers per year. This increment raises the production capacity of the economy. But obtaining the extra output these added workers can produce presumes they can find jobs and that these jobs are in firms and industries where their talents are fully and optimally used. Society doesn't want new labour force entrants to be unemployed. Nor does it want pediatricians working as plumbers, or workers producing goods that have higher marginal costs than marginal benefits. **(Key Question 2)**

LABOUR AND PRODUCTIVITY   Although demand and efficiency considerations are important, discussions of growth focus primarily on the supply side. Figure 19-2 provides a framework for discussing the supply factors in growth. It indicates two fundamental ways society can increase its real output and income: (1) by increasing its inputs of resources, and (2) by increasing the productivity of those inputs. Let's focus on inputs of labour. We can say *our real GDP in any year depends on the input of labour (measured in worker-hours) multiplied by* **labour productivity** *(measured as real output per worker per hour).*

Total output = worker-hours × labour productivity

FIGURE 19-2   The determinants of real output

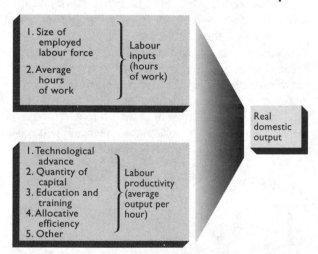

Real GDP can be usefully viewed as the product of the quantity of labour inputs multiplied by labour productivity.

Illustration: Assume an economy has 10 workers, each working 2000 hours per year (50 weeks at 40 hours per week). The total input of worker-hours therefore is 20,000 hours. If productivity — average real output per worker-hour — is $5, then total output or real GDP will be $100,000 (= 20,000 × $5).

What determines the number of hours worked each year? And what determines labour productivity? Figure 19-2 provides some answers. The hours of labour input depend on the size of the employed labour force and the length of the average work week. Labour force size depends on the size of the working age population and the **labour force participation rate** — *the percentage of the working age* *population actually in the labour force*. The average work week is governed by legal and institutional considerations and by collective bargaining.

Productivity is determined by technological progress, the quantity of capital goods available to workers, the quality of labour itself, and the efficiency with which inputs are allocated, combined, and managed. Productivity increases when the health, training, education, and motivation of workers are improved; when workers have more and better machinery and natural resources with which to work; when production is better organized and managed; and when labour is reallocated from less efficient industries to more efficient industries.

AD-AS FRAMEWORK

We can also view economic growth through the long-run aggregate supply and aggregate demand analysis developed in Figures 16-6 and 16-7. Suppose aggregate demand is AD_0 and long-run and short-run aggregate supply curves are AS_0 and AS_0' as shown in Figure 19-3. The initial equilibrium price level is P_0 and the level of real output is Q_0.

Recall that the upward slope of short-run aggregate supply curve AS_0' shows that a change in the price level will alter the level of real output. In the long run, however, wages and other input prices will fully adjust to the new price level, making the aggregate supply curve vertical at the economy's full-employment or potential level of real output. As with the location of the production possibilities curve, real supply factors — the quantity and quality of resources and technology — determine the long-run level of full-employment real output. Price level changes do not alter the location of the production possibilities curve; neither do they change the location of the long-run aggregate supply curve.

AGGREGATE SUPPLY SHIFTS Now assume changes in the supply factors listed in Figure 19-2 shift the long-run aggregate supply curve rightward from AS_0 to AS_1. This means the production possibilities curve in Figure 19-1 has been pushed outward and the long-run aggregate supply curve in Figure 19-3 has shifted to the right.

AGGREGATE DEMAND SHIFTS If aggregate demand remains at AD_0, the increase in long-run aggregate supply from AS_0 to AS_1 eventually will overcome downward price and wage rigidity and reduce the price level. But in recent decades a rising, not a falling, price level has accompanied economic growth. This suggests that aggregate demand has increased more rapidly than long-run aggregate supply. We show this in Figure 19-3 by shifting aggregate demand from AD_0 to AD_1, which results from changes in one or more of the determinants of aggregate demand (Table 11-1).

FIGURE 19-3 Economic growth and aggregate demand-aggregate supply analysis

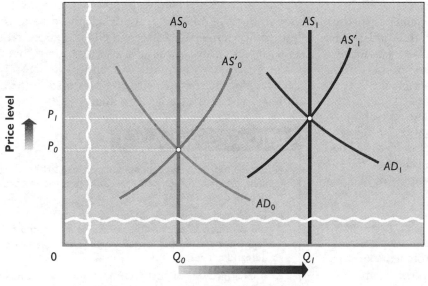

Long-run and short-run aggregate supply curves have shifted rightward over time, as from AS_0 and AS_0' to AS_1 and AS_1'. Meanwhile, aggregate demand has shifted rightward even more rapidly. The outcome of these combined shifts has been economic growth, shown as the increase in real output from Q_0 to Q_1, accompanied by inflation, shown as the rise in the price level from P_0 to P_1.

The combined increases in aggregate supply and aggregate demand in Figure 19-3 have produced economic growth of Q_0Q_1 and a rise in the price level from P_0 to P_1. At price level P_1, the economy confronts a new short-run aggregate supply curve AS_1'. (If not clear why, review Figure 16-6.)

Also, nominal GDP ($= P \times Q$) has increased more rapidly than real GDP ($= Q$) because of inflation. This diagram describes the secular trend of nominal GDP, real GDP, and the price level in Canada, a fact you can confirm by examining the tables at the back of this book. (**Key Question 3**)

CANADIAN GROWTH

Table 19-1 provides an overview of economic growth in Canada over past decades as viewed through our two definitions of growth. Column 2 shows the economy's growth as measured by increases in real GDP. Although not steady, the growth of real GDP has been strong. *Real GDP has increased over tenfold since 1946.* But our population has also grown significantly. Using our second definition of growth, we find in column 4 that *real per capita GDP has increased almost fivefold since 1946.*

What about our *rate* of growth? Global Perspective 19-1 shows that the post-1948 growth rate of Canada's real GDP has been 4.1% per year, while real GDP per capita has grown at more than 2% per year.

These numbers must be modified.

1. IMPROVED PRODUCTS AND SERVICES The figures of Table 19-1 and Global Perspective 19-1 do *not* fully take into account improvements in the quality of products and services, and thus understate the growth of economic well-being. Purely quantitative data do not accurately compare an era of ice-boxes and LPs and one of refrigerators and CDs.

2. ADDED LEISURE The increases in real GDP and per capita GDP shown in Table 19-1 were accomplished despite large increases in leisure. The standard work week, once 70 hours, is now about 40 hours. The result again is an understatement of economic well-being.

3. ENVIRONMENTAL EFFECTS But these measures of growth do *not* take into account adverse effects that growth may have on the environment and the quality of life. If growth debases the physical environment, our data will overstate the benefits of growth.

GLOBAL PERSPECTIVE 19-1

Average annual growth rates since 1948, selected nations

Real GDP in Canada has grown at a respectable rate compared to several other advanced industrial countries since 1948. Japan and Germany have had the highest average annual growth rates in this period.

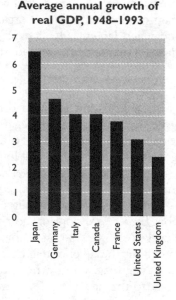

Average annual growth of real GDP, 1948–1993

Source: Organization for Economic Cooperation and Development data.

4. INTERNATIONAL COMPARISONS While Canada's growth record is impressive, economic growth in some other industrially advanced nations has been even more so. As seen in Global Perspective 19-1, Japan's growth rate has averaged more than 50% of Canada's growth over the past several decades. Germany's growth rate was also better, although by a much less wider margin.

QUICK REVIEW 19-1

1. Economic growth can be viewed as either the increase in real GDP or real GDP per capita that occurs over time.

2. Graphically, growth is shown as outward shifts of the production possibilities curve or as combined rightward shifts of aggregate supply and aggregate demand curves.

3. Annual growth of real GDP in Canada has averaged more than 4% since World War II.

TABLE 19-1   Real GDP and per capita GDP, 1900-1994

(1) Year	(2) GDP (billions of 1986 dollars)	(3) Population (millions)	(4) Per capita GDP (1986 dollars) (2) ÷ (3)
1900	$ 11.2	5.3	$ 2,109
1910	18.7	7.0	2,676
1920	23.3	8.6	2,705
1926	26.7	9.5	2,806
1929	31.9	10.0	3,195
1931	26.7	10.4	2,567
1933	22.3	10.6	2,102
1936	28.2	11.0	2,561
1941	43.8	11.5	3,809
1946	53.5	12.3	4,348
1951	67.1	14.0	4,791
1956	89.9	16.1	5,583
1961	103.4	18.2	5,681
1966	141.5	20.0	7,073
1971	175.3	21.6	8,116
1976	227.0	23.0	9,871
1981	268.9	24.3	11,065
1986	307.9	25.4	12,123
1991	555.0	27.0	20,555
1994	598.0	29.2	20,479

Sources: (1) 1900-1920: Derived from O.J. Firestone, *Canada's Economic Development, 1867-1953* (London: Bowes and Bowes, 1958), p. 66; (b) 1926-1983: Statistics Canada, *National Income and Expenditure Accounts, 1926-1986* (1988); (c) 1984-1988; *ibid., First Quarter*, 1995.

ACCOUNTING FOR GROWTH

Postwar output growth has been considerably greater than that which can be attributed solely to increase in the inputs of labour and capital. There are two other factors involved. The first is interindustry shifts from lower to higher productivity occupations. The best-known example is the shift of workers out of relatively low-productivity farming to higher-productivity urban industry. The second factor is **total factor productivity (TFP)**, the efficiency with which factors are used together in the production process. It encompasses technological progress, organizational structure, economies of scale, regulation, entrepreneurship and risk-taking, labour-management relations, capacity utilization, and the efficiency with which resources are allocated. TFP is output growth less input growth.

Table 19-2 details the sources of the growth of real GDP from 1961 to 1994.

INPUTS VERSUS PRODUCTIVITY

There are two fundamental ways in which a society can increase its real income: (1) by increasing its inputs of resources and (2) by increasing the productivity of those inputs. We find that about 75% of our growth between 1961 and 1994 was due to the use of more inputs and about 25% was the consequence of rising productivity — getting more output per unit of labour and capital input. These data underscore the fact that *productivity growth has been a significant force underlying the growth of our real GDP.* However, the rate of growth of productivity has greatly diminished since 1975, as will be discussed below.

QUANTITY OF LABOUR

Figure 19-4 indicates that our population and labour force have both expanded through time. Until recently, a high birth rate, a declining death rate, and continuous (and at times heavy) immigration have combined to provide Canada with substantial population growth throughout much of its history. From New France's 65,000 in 1759, the population of Canada grew to almost 2 1/2 million by 1851. Today there are more than ten times as many Canadians.

By the beginning of 1995, the population and civilian labour force were 29.2 million and 14.9 million respectively; they continue to grow. Historical declines in the length of the average work week have reduced labour inputs, but the

TABLE 19-2   Sources of growth of real GDP, 1961–1994

Growth in	Average annual rates of growth (as percent)				Contribution to total growth (as percent)		
	1961-75	1975-82	1982-91	1961-94	1961-75	1975-82	1961-94
GDP	5.2	2.5	2.8	3.8			
Labour productivity*	3.3	1.5	1.3	2.2			
Capital/labour ratio	2.9	4.5	1.8	2.8			
Input of labour**	2.3	1.2	1.6	1.7	28.0	33.9	29
Input of capital	5.3	5.7	3.4	4.6	38.4	63.0	44.5
Aggregate TFP†	1.7	–0.4	0.5	1.0	33.5	3.2	26.7

Source: Statistics Canada, *The Daily*, April 21, 1995.

* Real GDP per person hour.   ** Measured in person hours.   † Also referred to as Multifactor Productivity (MFP).

FIGURE 19-4   Population and civilian labour force growth, 1900–1994

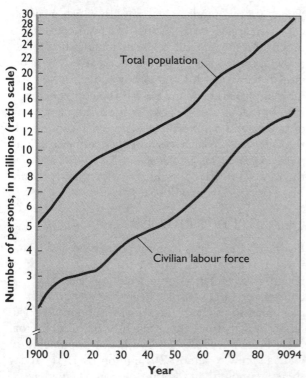

The Canadian civilian labour force as a percentage of the total population has averaged about 40% since 1900, but has been rising in the 1970s and 1980s to reach almost 50% in 1994. *Source: Historical Statistics of Canada and Statistics Canada.*

work week has declined very modestly since World War II. Declining birth rates in the past 30 years have brought about a decline in the rate of population growth. However, largely because of immigration and increased participation of women in labour markets, our civilian labour force continues to grow by about 200,000 workers a year. As Table 19-2 shows, the input of labour, measured in person hours, has grown at about 1.7% per annum in the last 30 years.

TECHNOLOGICAL ADVANCE

Technological advance is broadly defined so as to include not only new production techniques and product innovation but also new managerial techniques and new forms of business organization. Generally, technological advance is linked with the discovery of new knowledge that permits the combining of given resources in ways to achieve a larger output.

Technological advance and capital formation (investment) are closely related; technological advance often requires investment in new machinery and equipment. The sense there was a more efficient way to catch a rabbit than by running it down led to investment in the bow and arrow. The purchase of new computers not only means more of these computers, but quicker, more powerful computers embodying new technology. And it is necessary to construct new nuclear power plants to apply improved nuclear power technology. However, modern crop-rotation practices and contour ploughing are ideas that contribute to output, although they do not necessarily use new kinds or increased amounts of capital equipment.

Technological advance has been both rapid and profound. Gas and diesel engines, conveyor belts, and assembly lines are examples of significant developments of the past. More recently, technology has produced automation and the push-button factory. Bigger, faster, and more fuel-efficient commercial aircraft; integrated microcircuits, computers, xerography, containerized shipping, and nuclear power — not to mention biotechnology, lasers, and superconductivity — are technological achievements that were in the realm of fantasy a generation or two ago.

QUANTITY OF CAPITAL

Almost 45% of the annual growth of real national income between 1961 and 1994 was attributable to increases in the quantity of capital. A worker will be more productive when equipped with a larger amount of capital goods. And how does a nation acquire more capital? Capital accumulation results from saving and the investment in plant and equipment these savings make possible. A recent estimate suggests that total output will increase by about one-fourth of a percentage point for each extra percentage of GDP invested in machinery and equipment.

The critical consideration for labour productivity is the amount of capital goods *per worker*. The aggregate stock of capital might expand in a specific period, but if the labour force also increases rapidly, labour productivity need not rise because each worker will not necessarily be better equipped. This happened in the 1970s and 1980s when the labour force surged, contributing to a slowing of Canadian productivity growth.

EDUCATION AND TRAINING

Education and training improve a worker's productivity and result in higher earnings. Like investment in physical capital, investment in human capital is an important means of increasing labour productivity. Perhaps the simplest measure of labour quality is the level of educational attainment. Figure 19-5 reflects the educational gains in the past two decades. University is now being attended by almost 20% of those aged 18 to 24 years, as opposed to about 12% in the early 1970s; those attending community colleges have increased during the same period from 12% to almost 23% in the 1992-93 school year. Education has become accessible to more and more people, which means our labour force is more educated than it was in the early 1970s.

But there are concerns about the quality of Canadian education. Scores on standardized achievement tests have declined relative to scores of a few decades ago. Furthermore, Canadian students in science and mathematics do not do as well as students in many other industrialized nations. Japanese children have a longer school day and

---

FIGURE 19-5   Full-time post-secondary enrolment by level, relevant population, 1973–74 to 1992–93

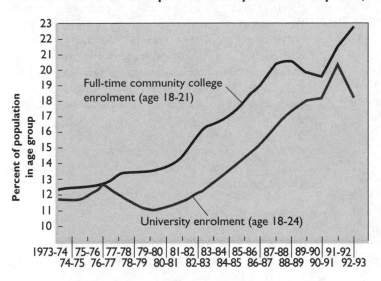

Young Canadians seem to be reacting to high unemployment by taking programs of study that lead most quickly to jobs.

Source: Statistics Canada, *Education in Canada, A Statistical Review for 1992–93* (Ottawa, 1994), cat. no. 81-229, Table 21.

attend school 240 days per year compared to 180 in Canada. Also, we have been producing fewer engineers and scientists, a problem that may be a result of inadequate training in math and science in elementary and high schools. And it is argued that on-the-job training (apprenticeship programs) in Japan and Germany — nations with fast rates of productivity growth — are more available and far superior to those in Canada.

RESOURCE ALLOCATION AND SCALE ECONOMIES

Labour productivity in Canada has increased in part because of economies of scale and improved resource allocation. Let's consider resource allocation first.

IMPROVED RESOURCE ALLOCATION Improved resource allocation means that workers over time have reallocated themselves from low-productivity employment to high-productivity employment. Historically, much labour has been shifted from agriculture — where labour productivity is low — to manufacturing, where it is quite high. More recently, labour has shifted away from some manufacturing industries to even higher productivity industries such as legal, health, consulting, and financial services. As a result of such shifts, the average productivity of Canadian workers in the aggregate has increased.

Also, labour market discrimination has historically denied women and minorities access to high-productivity jobs. The decline of such discrimination over time has shifted these groups from low-productivity jobs to higher-productivity jobs, increasing overall labour productivity and raising real GDP.

Tariffs, import quotas, and other barriers to international trade (Chapter 6) often keep resources in relatively unproductive employments. The long-run movement towards freer international trade has therefore improved the allocation of resources and expanded real output.

ECONOMIES OF SCALE Economies of scale are production advantages deriving from increased market and firm size. A large corporation often can select more efficient production techniques than can a small-scale firm. A large manufacturer of autos can use elaborate assembly lines, with

computerization and robotics, while smaller producers must settle for less advanced technologies. Markets have increased in scope over time and firms have increased in size, allowing more efficient production methods to be used. Accordingly, labour productivity has increased and economic growth has occurred.

DETRIMENTS TO GROWTH

Some developments detract from the growth of real output and income. There have been several changes in the regulation of industry, environmental pollution, and worker health and safety since World War II that have negatively affected growth. The expansion of government regulation in such areas as pollution control, worker health and safety, and access for the disabled has diverted investment spending away from growth-increasing capital goods and towards expenditures providing cleaner air and water, greater worker protection, and improved access for disabled workers and consumers. A firm required to spend $1 million on a new scrubber to meet government standards for air pollution or to make its stores accessible to the disabled will not have that $1 million to spend on machinery and equipment that would expand real output. The diversion of resources to deal with dishonesty and crime, the effects of work stoppages because of labour disputes, and the impact of bad weather on agricultural output are also factors that impede economic growth.

While worker safety, clean air and water, equal access for the disabled, and the overall quality of life may come at the expense of economic growth, the reverse is also true. Economic growth does not automatically enhance society's welfare. Growth of real output may involve opportunity costs of other things (a clean environment, a fair society) we value more highly. Productivity measures output per hour of work, *not* overall well-being per hour of work. Increases in real GDP are not necessarily matched with equal increases in well-being. Thus, society may rationally decide to "trade off" some economic growth to achieve other desirable ends. **(Key Question 5)**

OTHER FACTORS

There are other difficult-to-quantify considerations that affect an economy's growth rate. For example,

Canada's generous and varied supplies of natural resources have been an important contributor to our economic growth. We enjoy an abundance of fertile soil, desirable climatic and weather conditions, large quantities of most mineral resources, and generous sources of power. Canada has a larger variety and greater quantity of natural resources than the vast majority of other nations.

While an abundant natural resource base is helpful to growth, a meagre resource base does not doom a nation to slow growth. Although Japan's natural resources are severely constrained, its post-World War II growth has been remarkable (Global Perspective 19-1). In contrast, some of the impoverished countries of Africa and South America have substantial amounts of natural resources.

There are additional unmeasurable factors affecting a nation's growth rate. In particular, the overall social-cultural-political environment of Canada generally has promoted economic growth. Several factors contribute to this favourable environment.

1. Unlike many other nations, there are virtually no social or moral taboos on production and material progress. Canadian social philosophy has embraced material advance as an attainable and desirable economic goal. The inventor, the innovator, and the business executive are accorded high degrees of prestige and respect in Canadian society.
2. Canadians have traditionally possessed healthy attitudes towards work and risk taking; our society has benefited from a willing labour force and an ample supply of entrepreneurs.
3. Our market system has many personal and corporate incentives encouraging growth; our economy rewards actions that increase output.
4. Our economy is founded on a stable political system characterized by democratic principles, internal order, the right of property ownership, the legal status of enterprise, and the enforcement of contracts. One recent study has shown that politically open societies grow much more rapidly on average than those where freedom is limited.

Though difficult to quantify, these characteristics have provided an excellent foundation for Canadian economic growth.

AGGREGATE DEMAND, INSTABILITY, AND GROWTH

The data in Table 19-2 explain the growth of actual, not potential or full-employment, real national income. The annual growth rate the table attempts to explain includes changes in real GDP caused by fluctuations in aggregate demand. Our annual growth rate would have been approximately 0.4 to 0.5 percentage points higher over this period if the economy's full-employment output had been obtained year after year. Deviations from full employment arising from deficiencies of aggregate demand cause the actual rate of growth to fall short of the potential rate.

A glance back at Figure 8-4 reminds us that the actual performance of our economy occasionally falls short of its potential output. The Great Depression of the 1930s in particular was a serious blow to Canada's long-run growth record. Between 1929 and 1933 our real GDP (measured in 1986 prices) actually *declined* from $53 to $38 billion. In 1939 the real GDP was only slightly higher than in 1929. More recently, the severe 1980–82 recessions cost Canada more than $60 billion in lost output and income.

But this is only part of the picture. Cyclical unemployment can have harmful "carry-over" effects on the growth rate in subsequent years of full employment through the adverse effects it may have on other growth factors. Unemployment depresses investment and capital accumulation. Furthermore, the expansion of research budgets may be slowed by recession so that technological progress diminishes; union resistance to technological change may stiffen; and so forth. Though it is difficult to quantify the impact of these considerations on the growth rate, they undoubtedly have had an effect.

QUICK REVIEW 19-2

1. Since 1961 increases in total factor productivity have accounted for about one-quarter of the increases in real output; the use of more labour and capital inputs accounted for the remainder.

2. Improved technology, more capital, more education and training, economies of scale, and improved resource allocation are the main contributors to growth.

3. Growth rates in Canada have sometimes been erratic, particularly because of fluctuations in aggregate demand.

THE CANADIAN PRODUCTIVITY SLOWDOWN

As shown in Table 19-2, total factor productivity growth has slowed down considerably since 1975. Labour productivity growth has also markedly diminished since 1975, particularly during the 1980s when it grew at just 1.3% per annum, almost a third of the growth rate in the 1961–75 period. While there are indications that both total factor productivity and labour productivity growth improved during the early 1990s, both are still well below the growth rates achieved during the 1961–75 period.

Although labour productivity growth has been slowing worldwide, Canadian productivity growth has been slower than most other major industrialized nations. Canada still enjoys one of the highest absolute levels of output per worker, but the productivity advantage is diminishing.

SIGNIFICANCE

Our productivity slowdown has many implications.

1. STANDARD OF LIVING   Productivity growth is the basic source of improvements in real wage rates and the standard of living. Real income per worker-hour can increase only at the same rate as real output per worker-hour. More output per hour means more real income to distribute for each hour worked. The simplest case is of Robinson Crusoe on his deserted island. The number of fish he can catch or coconuts he can pick per hour *is* his real income or wage per hour.

The broadest measure of living standards — the growth of real per capita GDP — follows the path of labour productivity.

2. INFLATION   Productivity increases partly or fully offset increases in nominal-wage rates, lessening cost-push inflationary pressures. Other things equal, a decline in the rate of productivity growth contributes to rising unit labour costs and a higher rate of inflation. Many economists believe that productivity stagnation contributed to the unusually high inflation rates of the 1970s.

3. WORLD MARKETS   Other things equal, our slow rate of productivity growth compared to some of our major international trading partners increases relative prices of Canadian goods in world markets.

The result is a decline in our competitiveness and a loss of international markets for Canadian producers.

CAUSES OF THE SLOWDOWN

There is no consensus among experts as to why Canadian productivity growth has slowed and fallen behind the rate of other industrialized nations. Because so many factors affect a country's productivity performance, there may be no simple explanation. However, let's survey some of the possible causes that analysts have put forward.

INVESTMENT   Investment — the amount of machinery and equipment each worker uses — is a critical determinant of productivity growth. A worker using a bulldozer can move more landfill per hour than can that same worker equipped with an ordinary shovel. There is a correlation between the percentage of a nation's GDP devoted to investment goods and its realized increase in productivity. Canada achieves remarkably lower productivity increases than Belgium, Italy, and France, despite investing approximately the same percentage of GDP. It is also noteworthy that our productivity performance has been relatively poor over several decades. Why is this so?

1. LOW SAVING RATE   Canada has seen its saving rate fall, which coupled with strong private and public demands for credit, has resulted in high real interest rates relative to historical standards. High interest rates discourage investment spending.

2. IMPORT COMPETITION   Growing import competition may have made some Canadian producers reluctant to invest in new capital equipment. They may have shifted more investment overseas towards nations with low-wage workers.

3. REGULATION   The expansion of government regulations in the areas of pollution control, worker health and safety, and access for the disabled diverted some investment spending away from output-increasing capital goods. This investment spending may have increased total utility to society, but did not directly increase output itself. The composition of investment may have shifted towards uses that do not increase productivity.

ENERGY PRICES   The sharp increases in energy princes in the 1970s made energy-intensive capital stock uncompetitive. The direct impact of higher oil prices was to increase the cost of operating capital equipment, in effect raising the "price" of capital relative to labour. Producers were more inclined to use less-productive labour-intensive techniques.

The indirect macroeconomic effects of higher energy prices may have been even more important in reducing productivity growth. The two episodes of soaring energy prices precipitated stagflation — inflationary recessions. Government's use of restrictive macroeconomic policies to control inflation worsened and prolonged the periods of recession and slow economic growth. Recessions diminish productivity — output per worker — in that output tends to decline more rapidly than employment. The prolonged periods of underuse of productive capacity in many industries contributed to the productivity slowdown.

TECHNOLOGICAL PROGRESS Technological advance — usually reflected in improvements in the quality of capital goods and the efficiency with which inputs are combined — may also have faltered. Technological progress is fuelled by expenditures for formal research and development (R & D) programs. R & D spending in Canada declined as a percent of GDP from a peak of 3% of GDP in the mid-1960s to about 1% by the late 1970s, before rising once again in the early 1990s to about 1.5% of GDP.

But some economists discount the importance of the R & D decline in explaining the productivity slowdown. R & D *spending* alone tells us little about R & D *accomplishments*. There is clear evidence of continuing technological advance during the past two decades.

LABOUR QUALITY One possibility is that slower improvements in labour quality may have dampened productivity growth. The following factors may have been at work.

1. DECLINE IN EXPERIENCE LEVEL The experience level of the labour force may have declined. The large number of baby-boom workers who entered the labour force had little experience and training and were therefore less productive. The labour force participation of women increased significantly over the past two decades. Many were married women with little or no prior labour force experience who therefore had low productivity.

2. LESS ABLE WORKERS The declining test scores of sample students on international standardized examinations during the 1970s and 1980s perhaps indicates a decline in worker capabilities. Some claim that fewer of our graduates from secondary and post-secondary institutions have the sophisticated analytical training required in an increasingly technologically driven economy. If so, this decline may have contributed to the productivity slowdown.

However, one study in the mid-1980s[1] casts doubt on the role of education in the productivity growth slowdown. This study claimed that education made a slightly greater contribution to TFP in 1973–79 than it did in 1960–73.

A RESURGENCE?

The 1982–91 data in Table 19-2 suggest a modest improvement in productivity growth; the 0.5% annual increase of total factor productivity for this period compares favourably with the actual decline in the 1975–82 period. It is evident that many of the factors that may have depressed productivity growth have dissipated or been reversed.

Energy prices are stable and the stagflation problem overcome. Since 1977 research and development spending has been increasing as a percentage of GDP. Innovations involving computers, telecommunications, robotics, genetic engineering, and superconductors may finally be providing a big stimulus to productivity. Although higher than a few years earlier, interest rates are still low, promoting purchases of new plant and equipment. Wages of college and university graduates have risen relative to wages of high school graduates and this wage premium should soon attract more students to universities.

The inexperienced baby-boom workers who flooded labour markets in the 1960s and 1970s are now rapidly moving into the 25- to 54-year-old prime labour force as more mature, more productive workers.

Nevertheless, it is unclear at this point whether the recent revival of productivity is transitory or permanent. **(Key Question 8)**

---

[1] *Cf.* M.J. Daly and P.S. Rao, "Some Myths and Realities Concerning Canada's Recent Productivity Slowdown, and Their Policy Implications," in *Canadian Public Policy*, Vol. XI, No. 2 (Guelph: University of Guelph, June 1985), pp. 209-10.

DOOMSDAY MODELS

Annual 2 to 7% rates of economic growth in the industrial nations — compounded year after year — raise the questions: Can economic growth in the industrially advanced nations continue over the next few decades? Can it continue over the next century? Forever?

Computer modellers[2] have developed complex simulation models, called **doomsday models**, indicating that the world economy is using resources and dumping wastes at rates that the planet cannot sustain. Population and industrial production, it is argued, are expanding at exponential (2, 4, 16, 256, ...) rates. Modern industrial production depends heavily on exhaustible natural resources that allegedly are fixed in supply. Industrial economies also employ the environment — which has a limited absorptive capacity — for waste disposal. In this view, we must ultimately run out of certain natural resources — oil, coal, copper, arable land — critical to the production process. Also, the increased waste inevitably resulting from economic growth will overwhelm the absorptive capacity of the world's ecological system. Air, water, and solid waste pollution will worsen.

THE "STANDARD RUN" MODEL

Figure 19-6 shows one computer simulation. In this scenario it is assumed the world proceeds along its historical paths of production and population growth with no policy changes and that technological advances occur "according to established patterns." In Figure 19-6(a), population, industrial output, and food production all grow significantly in the 1900–90 period. But then in the early twenty-first century the economy stops growing and, in effect, collapses. Why?

After 2000, pollution reaches a level at which the fertility of land is seriously reduced and food production begins to fall. Nonrenewable resources become increasingly scarce and more costly to obtain. As a result, the world economy must shift more investment to the agricultural sector and to the discovery, extraction, and refining of raw materi-

---

[2] Donella H. Meadows, Dennis L. Meadows, and Jorgen Randers, *Beyond the Limits* (Post Mills, Vermont: Chelsea Green Publishers, 1992). Also see Dennis L. Meadows, et al., *The Limits To Growth* (Washington, D.C.: Potomac Associates, 1972).

als. In time this reallocation of investment means that industrial capital declines as depreciation exceeds new industrial investment spending. As the stock of industrial capital declines, the agricultural and service (including health) sectors also falter because they have become dependent on industrial outputs such as hospital laboratories and equipment, fertilizers, and pesticides. We find in Figure 19-6(b) that, as food and health services per capita decline, life expectancy falls and population declines.

Other computer simulations use more optimistic assumptions on industrial and population growth and the rate of technological progress. But, although the timing and magnitude of the changes are different, the basic conclusion is the same — population and production growth will tip the world's economic and life-support systems into collapse.

DOOMSDAY EVIDENCE

The "doomsday" modellers see evidence of economic and environmental collapse. Desperate people in the poorest nations chop down forests for firewood, altering local and perhaps global weather patterns. Land is overcultivated and overgrazed to the extent that it reverts to desert and the planet's ability to feed its population is diminished. In the last half of the 1980s, food production per capita declined in more than 90 nations. Fisheries have been exploited beyond sustainable rates; fish are being taken from the world's oceans at rates beyond which they are being regenerated.

TOWARDS A SUSTAINABLE SOCIETY

The world must make the hard decisions to achieve a sustainable society — "one that can persist over generations, one that is far-seeing enough, flexible enough, and wise enough not to undermine either its physical or its social systems of support." Specific recommendations include: (1) slowing and eventually stopping the exponential growth of population and industrial output; (2) minimizing the use of nonrenewable resources such as fossil fuels and minerals; (3) limiting the rates of use of renewable resources such as forests and fisheries to their rates of regeneration; and (4) restricting pollution emissions to the amounts that can be assimilated by the environment.

CRITICISMS

Doomsday modelling has been controversial and has prompted a number of rebuttals.

FIGURE 19-6   Growth and collapse: a doomsday model

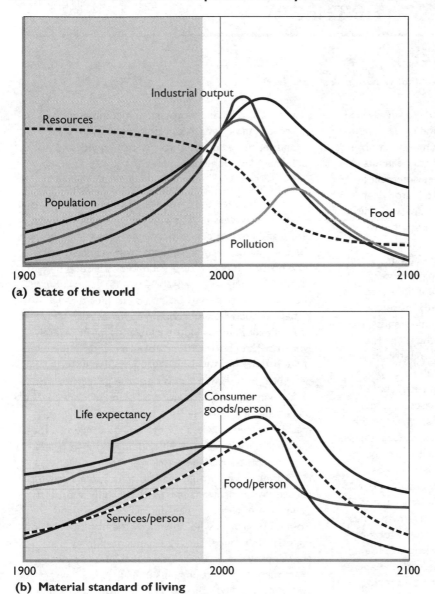

(a) State of the world

(b) Material standard of living

This computer model assumes that "the world society proceeds along its historical path as long as possible without major policy change. Population and industry output grow until a combination of environmental and natural resource constraints eliminate the capacity of the capital sector to sustain investment. Industrial capital begins to depreciate faster than the new investment can rebuild it. As it falls, food and health services also fall, decreasing life expectancy and raising the death rate."

(Meadows, Meadows, and Randers, *op. cit.*, pp. 132–133.)

1. FUN AND GAMES WITH NUMBERS   The doomsdayers have *assumed* continuing exponential growth of population and output growth, while *assuming* absolute limits on natural resources and technological capabilities. The outcome of the resulting computer simulations is merely the inevitable consequence of these assumptions. But are these assumptions realistic? To paraphrase an old joke, one can project the reproduction rate of alligators and conclude that in 50 years we will be up to our eyeballs, or thereabouts, in alligators. The point is that a different — and equally or more plausible — set of assumptions would yield a much happier portrayal of humanity's future.

2. TECHNOLOGY AND EXPANDING RESOURCES Another rebuttal to the doomsday models is that technological advance expands the supplies of existing resources and creates new resources. Technological progress permits us to use existing resources more efficiently, effectively increasing their supplies. In 1900 the lowest grade copper ore

BOX 19-2   APPLYING THE THEORY

IS GROWTH DESIRABLE?

Economists usually take for granted that growth is desirable. Is it?

THE ANTIGROWTH VIEW   Critics of growth say industrialization and growth result in pollution, global warming, ozone depletion, and other environmental problems. These adverse spillover costs occur because inputs in the production process re-enter the environment as some form of waste. The more rapid our growth and the higher our standard of living, the more waste there is for the environment to absorb — or attempt to absorb. In an already wealthy society, further growth usually means satisfying increasingly trivial wants at the cost of mounting threats to our ecological system.

Critics of growth also argue there is little compelling evidence that economic growth has solved sociological problems such as poverty, homelessness, and discrimination. Consider poverty. In the antigrowth view, Canadian poverty is a problem of distribution, not production. The requisite for solving the problem is commitment and political courage to redistribute wealth and income, not further increases in output.

Antigrowth sentiment also says that while growth may permit us to "make a better living," it does not give us "the good life." We may be producing more and enjoying it less. Growth means assembly line jobs, worker burnout, and alienated employees who have little or no control over the decisions affecting their lives. The changing technology at the core of growth poses new anxieties and new sources of insecurity for workers. Both high-level and low-level workers face the prospect of having their hard-earned skills and experience rendered obsolete by an onrushing technology. High-growth economies are high-stress economies, which may impair our physical and mental health.

IN DEFENCE OF GROWTH   The primary defence of growth is that it is the path to greater material abundance and rising living standards. Rising output and incomes allow us to buy:

> more education, recreation, and travel, more medical care, closer communications, more skilled personal and professional services, and better-designed as well as more numerous products. It also means more art, music, and poetry, theater, and drama. It can even mean more time and resources devoted to spiritual growth and human development.*

Growth also enables us to improve the nation's infrastructure, enhance the care of the sick and elderly, provide greater access for the disabled, and provide more police and fire protection. Economic growth may be the only realistic way to reduce poverty, since there is little political support for greater redistribution of income. The way to improve the economic position of the poor is to increase household incomes through higher productivity and economic growth. Also, a no-growth policy among industrial nations might severely limit growth in poor nations. Foreign investment in these nations — as well as development assistance — would fall, keeping the world's poor in poverty longer.

Economic growth has not made labour more unpleasant or hazardous, as critics suggest. New machinery is usually less taxing and less dangerous than the machinery it replaces. Air-conditioned workplaces are more pleasant than steamy workshops. Furthermore, why would the end to economic growth reduce materialism or alienation? The loudest protests against materialism are heard in those nations and from those groups who now enjoy the highest levels of material abundance! The high standard of living that growth provides has increased our leisure and given us more time for reflection and self-fulfilment.

But does growth threaten the environment? The connection between growth and environment is tenuous, say growth proponents. Increases in economic growth need not mean increases in pollution. Pollution is not so much a by-product of growth as it is a "problem of the commons." Much of the environment — streams, lakes, oceans, and the air — are treated as "common property" and we have not placed adequate charges and restrictions on their use. The commons

---

* Alice M. Rivlin, *Reviving the American Dream* (Washington, D. C.: Brookings Institution, 1992), p. 36.

have become our dumping grounds; we have overused and debased them. Environmental pollution is a case of spillover or external costs, and correcting this problem involves regulatory legislation or specific taxes ("effluent charges") to remedy the misuse of the environment.

There *are* serious pollution problems. But limiting growth is the wrong solution. Growth has allowed economies to reduce pollution, be more sensitive to environmental considerations, set aside wilderness, and clean up hazardous waste, while still enabling rising household incomes.

that was economically mineable was about 3%; technological advance now makes 0.35% ore mineable. Similarly, thanks to improvements in search and extraction techniques, the world's known oil reserves are several times larger than they were thought to be just a few decades ago.

Technology also allows us to discover or develop substitutes for existing resources and therefore to expand our resource base. The development of fibre optics, for example, has meant that a single ultrathin fibre can replace over 600 copper wires, making it less likely (and perhaps irrelevant) if we "run out" of copper. Similarly, future developments in solar, geothermal, or hydrogen power may add to our resource base so that it becomes unnecessary to worry over our supplies of oil, coal, and natural gas.

In general, technological progress makes it erroneous to assume natural resource supplies are fixed. Rather, such supplies depend on our technological knowledge and because that knowledge has been expanding, so also have our stocks of resources. Resource supplies, it is argued, are limited only by human ingenuity. Doomsday critics point out that the relative prices of practically all mineral resources have in fact been *declining*, indicating they are *less* scarce.

3. Market Signals Changes in market prices generate signals that work to offset the economic collapse indicated by the doomsday models. If reserves of, say, copper or aluminum or oil become increasingly scarce, their prices will rise and two responses automatically occur. First, users of the resource will be more strongly motivated to conserve such resources either by employing substitutes (for example, plastic for copper pipes in new housing) or by developing new resource-saving techniques (more fuel-efficient autos and machinery in the case of oil). Second, higher resource prices also

provide an incentive for resource producers to expand output by mining lower-grade ores or by recycling, both of which may have been economically unfeasible at lower prices. The point is the price mechanism automatically induces responses that alleviate resource shortages.

RECAP

Whether you agree with the doomsday pessimists or with the critics of the doomsday models, certain messages and questions emerge from the limits-to-growth debate. For example, the fundamental question of scarcity has a time dimension. Absolutely exhaustible resources that are used today will not be available tomorrow. What is the optimal way to allocate such resources through time?

The debate also emphasizes that growth is not an unmitigated good. The impact of an ever-expanding output on the environment and on lifestyles must be taken into account in any evaluation of future growth.

Finally, the debate points out that factors that fall partially outside the realm of economics — in particular, population growth — have a critical bearing on our economic well-being. (**Key Question 12**)

QUICK REVIEW 19-3

1. Economists have cited the following reasons for Canada's slowdown in productivity in the past 25 years: **a** declines in labour quality, **b** a slowing of technological progress, **c** decreasing investment spending as a percentage of GDP, **d** higher energy prices, and **e** growth-impeding labour relations.

2. Computer modellers have developed simulation models indicating the world is using resources and dumping wastes at unsustainable rates.

3. To prevent complete economic collapse, "dooms-day" modellers recommend slowing and eventually stopping the exponential growth of population and industrial output.

4. Critics of the "doomsday" models argue that **a** technological advance expands the supplies of existing resources and creates new resources, making it erroneous to assume that natural resource supplies are fixed; and **b** the price mechanism automatically reduces the use of increasingly scarce resources and encourages the development and use of new resources.

GROWTH POLICIES

If we accept the view that economic growth is desirable and sustainable, then the question arises as to what public policies might best stimulate growth. Several policies are either in use or have been suggested.

DEMAND-SIDE POLICIES

Low growth is often the consequence of inadequate aggregate demand and resulting GDP gaps. The purpose of demand-side policies is to eliminate or reduce the severity of recessions through active fiscal and monetary policy. The idea is to use government tools to increase aggregate demand at an appropriate, noninflationary pace. Adequate aggregate demand not only keeps present resources fully employed, it also creates an incentive for firms to expand their operations. In particular, low real interest rates (easy money policy) promote high levels of investment spending. This spending leads to capital accumulation, which expands the economy's capacity to produce.

SUPPLY-SIDE POLICIES

These policies emphasize factors that will directly increase the potential or full-capacity output of the economy over time. The goal is to shift Figure 19-3's long-run and short-run aggregate supply curves rightward. Policies fitting this category include tax policies designed to stimulate saving, investment, and entrepreneurship. For example, by lowering or eliminating the tax on income placed in saving accounts, the return on saving will increase and so will the amount of saving. Likewise, by lowering or eliminating the deduction of interest expenses on your personal income tax, consumption will be discouraged and saving encouraged.

On the investment side, some economists propose eliminating the corporate income tax or allowing generous tax credits for business investment spending. If effective, this proposal would increase both aggregate demand and aggregate supply.

INDUSTRIAL AND OTHER POLICIES

There are other potential growth-stimulating policies that economists of various persuasions recommend. Some advocate an **industrial policy** whereby government would take a direct, active role in shaping the structure and composition of industry to promote growth. Thus government might take steps to hasten expansion of high-productivity industries and speed the movement of resources out of low-productivity industries. Government might also increase its expenditures on basic research and development to stimulate technological progress. Also, increased expenditures on basic education and apprenticeship skill training may help increase the quality and productivity of labour.

While the litany of potential growth-enhancing policies is long and involved, most economists agree it is not easy to increase a nation's growth rate.

CHAPTER SUMMARY

1. Economic growth may be defined either in terms of **a** an expanding real domestic output (income) or **b** an expanding per capita real output (income). Growth lessens the burden of scarcity and provides increases in real output that can be used to resolve domestic and international socioeconomic problems.

2. The supply factors in economic growth are **a** the quantity and quality of a country's natural resources, **b** the quantity and quality of its human resources, **c** its stock of capital facilities, and **d** its technology. Two other factors — a sufficient level of aggregate demand and economic efficiency — are essential for the economy to realize its growth potential.

3. Economic growth can be shown graphically as an outward shift of a nation's production possibility curve or as a rightward shift of its long-run aggregate supply curve.

4. The post-World War II growth rate of real GDP for Canada has been around 4%; real GDP per capita has grown at slightly more than 2%.

5. Real GDP of Canada has grown partly because of increased inputs of labour, but primarily because of increases in the productivity of labour. Technological progress, increases in the quantity of capital per worker, improvements in the quality of labour, and improved allocation of labour are among the more important factors that increase labour productivity.

6. The rate of productivity growth declined in the 1970s and early 1980s, causing a slowdown in the rise of our living standards and contributing to inflation. Although productivity growth increased in the 1980s and early 1990s, it remains substantially below the rates attained in the three decades following World War II.

7. Suspected causes of the decline in productivity growth include: decreases in labour quality; slowing of technological progress; declining investment spending as a percentage of GDP; higher energy prices; and adversarial labour relations.

8. Computer simulations called "doomsday models" indicate the world is using resources and dumping waste at rates that will result in the collapse of industrial output and food production somewhere near the year 2025. To stop this collapse, say the "doomsdayers," the world must quickly slow and eventually stop the exponential growth of population and industrial output.

9. Critics challenge the assumption of absolute limits on the supply of natural resources in the doomsday models, pointing out that technological advance expands the supplies of existing resources and creates new resources. Critics also argue these models overlook the role of the price mechanism in offsetting the predicted economic collapse. Declining resource supplies result in higher resource prices, which automatically reduces the use of the higher-price inputs while expanding the development and use of new resources.

10. Growth-promoting policies include both demand-side and supply-side policies, along with efforts to shape the composition of industry.

TERMS AND CONCEPTS

doomsday models (p. 416)
economic growth (p. 404)
industrial policy (p. 420)
labour force participation rate (p. 406)

labour productivity (p. 406)
supply, demand, and efficiency factors in
   growth (p. 405)
total factor productivity (TFP) (p. 409)

QUESTIONS AND STUDY SUGGESTIONS

1. Why is economic growth important? Explain why the difference between a 2.5% and a 3.0% annual growth rate might be of great importance.

2. *Key Question   What are the major causes of economic growth? "There is both a demand and a supply side to economic growth." Explain. Illustrate the operation of both sets of factors in terms of the production possibilities curve.*

3. **Key Question** Suppose an economy's real GDP is $30,000 in year 1 and $31,200 in year 2. What is the growth rate of its real GDP? Assume that population was 100 in year 1 and 102 in year 2. What is the growth rate of GDP per capita? Between 1949 and 1994, Canada's price level rose by 606%, while its real output has increased by 515%. Use the aggregate demand–aggregate supply model to show these outcomes graphically.

4. Briefly describe the growth record of Canada in this century. Compare the rates of growth in real GDP and real GDP per capita, explaining any differences. How does the Canadian growth rate compare to the rates of Japan and Germany since World War II? To what extent might growth rates understate or overstate economic well-being?

5. **Key Question** To what extent have increases in our real GDP been the result of more capital and labour inputs? Of increasing productivity? Discuss the factors that contribute to productivity growth in order of their quantitative importance.

6. Using examples, explain how changes in the allocation of labour can affect labour productivity.

7. How do you explain the close correlation between changes in the rate of productivity growth and changes in real wage rates? Discuss the relationship between productivity growth and inflation.

8. **Key Question** Account for the recent slowdown in Canada's rate of productivity growth. What are the consequences of this slowdown? What is the nature of a low-productivity trap? "Most of the factors that have contributed to poor productivity in the past two decades are now behind us and are unlikely to recur in future." Do you agree?

9. "If you want economic growth in a free society, we may have to accept a measure of instability." Evaluate. The philosopher Alfred North Whitehead once remarked that "the art of progress is to preserve order amid change and to preserve change amid order." What did he mean? Is this contention relevant for economic growth? What implications might this have for public policy? Explain.

10. Comment on the following statements:

    a. "Technological advance is destined to play a more important role in economic growth in the future than it has in the past."

    b. "Nations headed by dictators have faster growth rates than democratic nations on average."

    c. "Many public capital goods are complementary to private capital goods."

    d. "Racial and gender discrimination are impediments to productivity growth."

11. What is the world's economic future as predicted by recent computer simulation models? What is the basis for this outcome, according to the models?

12. **Key Question** Explain the following, and cite examples to illustrate: "Some of our present economic resources were not viewed as resources a century ago. Likewise, many things not now thought of as resources may become resources in the future." What role does the price mechanism play in this matter? How does this relate to the doomsday models?

13. Suppose you are the chief economic adviser to the federal government and have been asked to prepare a set of proposals for increasing the productivity of Canadian workers as a way to raise our rate of economic growth. What would you put on your list? What impediments would you envision in accomplishing your policies?

14. (Applying the Theory) Do you think economic growth is desirable? Explain your position on this issue.

INTERNATIONAL ECONOMICS AND THE WORLD ECONOMY

CHAPTER 20

INTERNATIONAL TRADE

 **N**AFTA, GATT, the Canada–U.S. Free Trade Agreement. Exchange rates, dumping, the European Union. The IMF, nontariff trade barriers, exchange rates. Official international reserves, the G-7 nations, currency interventions. Capital flight, brain drains, the ruble.

People across the globe are speaking the language of international economics — on television, in the newspapers, in corporate offices, in stores, and in union halls. A "foreign" language? Not if you have read Chapter 6 and now master the materials in Part 5.

This chapter builds on Chapter 6, providing a more focused analysis of international trade and protectionism. First we review some salient facts about world trade. Second, we take a more advanced look at how international specialization based on comparative advantage can mutually benefit participating nations. Third, we use supply and demand analysis to examine equilibrium prices and quantities of imports and exports. Fourth, the economic impact of trade barriers such as tariffs and import quotas is examined. Fifth, we evaluate the arguments for protectionism. Finally, we discuss the costs of protectionism and some continuing controversies in international trade.

BOX 20-1 THE BIG PICTURE

The economizing problem consists of limited resources, unlimited wants, and thus the need for choices. In a world of limited resources, if we can somehow get more output of goods and services from those resources, the constraints an individual or a society faces are less severe. One of the ways to get more output from the limited resources available is specialization. Adam Smith, the so-called father of economics, noticed the beneficial effect of specialization in the celebrated pin factory he talks about in *The Wealth of Nations.* Just as a factory can greatly increase its output if each person specializes, the world output of goods and services would increase if each nation specialized in those pursuits to which it is best suited. In technical terms, it should specialize in the line of production in which it enjoys a comparative advantage. Each nation would then import goods to satisfy its other needs. In this manner, each nation would be materially better off than if each tried to produce all the goods and services it consumes. These beneficial effects are the driving force behind the globalization of trade, such as manifested by the Canada–U.S. Free Trade

Agreement (FTA), and the North American Free Trade Agreement (NAFTA).

As you read this chapter, keep the following points in mind:

- It may be helpful for you to think of trading between two nations as similar to trading between two individuals. Each specializes in what he or she does best and then trades.
- The purpose of tariffs is to protect domestic industries from international competition. Tariff protection implies an inability to successfully compete with imports. Firms in the protected industries enjoy a level of profit higher than would be the case if they had to compete. Consumers lose because they have to pay higher prices for goods produced by the protected industries.
- Protecting domestic industry has an intuitive appeal, particularly in regards to "saving jobs." But ultimately, consumers and society at large will pay for the tariff protection through higher prices. Each of the jobs saved will be very costly.

FACTS OF INTERNATIONAL TRADE

In Chapter 6 we presented a number of facts about international trade. Let's quickly review them and add a few others.

1. Exports of goods and services are almost 30% of Canadian GDP. The percentage is even greater in a number of other nations. Examples: Netherlands, 37%; Germany, 36%, New Zealand, 34%. (Table 6-1.)
2. Canadian exports and imports have increased in volume and risen by more than a third as a percentage of GDP since 1965 (Figure 6-2).
3. In 1994 Canada had a $15.0 billion trade surplus, meaning that the export of goods exceeded the import of goods by this amount. But in that year Canada's imports of services exceeded its exports of services by $9.4 billion. Thus, the goods and services surplus was $5.6 billion.

4. Canada's principal commodity exports are automotive products, machinery and equipment, and forestry products. Its main imports are machinery and equipment and automotive products.
5. Like other advanced industrial nations, Canada imports some of the same categories of goods that it exports (Figure 6-3).
6. The bulk of Canadian export and import trade is with other industrially advanced nations, specifically the United States, nations of Western Europe, and Japan (Figure 6-4).
7. Improved transportation and communications technologies, declines in tariffs, and peaceful relations among major industrial nations have all helped expand world trade since World War II.
8. Although trade is still dominated by industrially advanced nations, several new "players" have greatly increased their roles (Global Perspective 20-1). The four "Asian tigers" of Hong Kong,

Shares of world exports, selected nations

The United States has the largest share of world exports, followed closely by Germany and Japan. Canada, a much smaller economy, represents over 4% of the world's exports. The seven largest export nations account for nearly 50% of world exports.

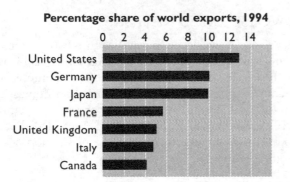

Percentage share of world exports, 1994

Source: *OECD.*

Singapore, South Korea, and Taiwan have expanded their share of world trade from 3% in 1972 to nearly 10% today. China has emerged as a major new international trader, and the collapse of communism has led Eastern European nations and Russia to look globally for new trade partners.

9. International trade has recently been at the centre stage of international policy. Examples: The North American Free Trade Agreement (NAFTA), and the conclusion of negotiations on the General Agreement on Tariffs and Trade (GATT).

Keeping these facts in mind, let's take a closer look at the economics of international trade.

THE ECONOMIC BASIS FOR TRADE

In Chapter 6 we found that international trade is a way nations can specialize, increase the productivity of their resources, and realize a larger total output than otherwise. Sovereign nations, like individuals and regions of a nation, can gain by specializing in products they can produce with the greatest relative efficiency and by trading for goods they cannot produce efficiently.

This rationale for trade is correct, but a more detailed understanding is needed. The more complete answer to the question, "Why do nations trade?" hinges on two points.

1. The distribution of economic resources — natural, human, and capital goods — among nations is uneven; nations are different in their endowments of economic resources.
2. Efficient production of various goods requires different technologies or combinations of resources.

The character and interaction of these two points is readily illustrated. Japan, for example, has a large and well-educated labour force; skilled labour is abundant and therefore relatively inexpensive compared to other inputs, such as land. Thus, Japan can produce efficiently (at low cost) a variety of goods whose production requires much skilled labour: cameras, transistor radios, and video recorders are examples of such **labour-intensive** commodities.

In contrast, Australia has vast amounts of land compared to its human and capital resources and can inexpensively produce such **land-intensive** commodities as wheat, wool, and meat, compared to labour-intensive commodities. Brazil has the soil, tropical climate, rainfall, and lots of unskilled labour needed for efficient low-cost production of coffee.

Industrially advanced nations are in a position to produce inexpensively a variety of **capital-intensive** goods, such as automobiles, agricultural equipment, machinery, and chemicals.

The economic efficiency with which nations produce various goods can change. The distribution of both resources and technology can change so as to alter the relative efficiency with which goods can be produced by various countries.

For example, in the last few decades South Korea has upgraded the quality of its labour force and has expanded its stock of capital. Although South Korea was primarily an exporter of agricultural products and raw materials a half century ago, it now exports manufactured goods. Similarly, the new technologies that gave us synthetic fibres and synthetic rubber drastically altered the resource mix needed to produce these goods and changed the relative efficiency of countries in manufacturing them.

As national economies evolve, the size and quality of their labour forces may change, the volume and composition of their capital stocks may shift, new technologies will develop, and even the quality of land and quantity of natural resources may be altered. As these changes occur, the efficiency with which a nation can produce goods will also change.

SPECIALIZATION AND COMPARATIVE ADVANTAGE

Let's now use the concept of comparative advantage to analyze the basis for international specialization and trade.

THE BASIC PRINCIPLE

The central concept underlying comparative advantage can be illustrated by posing a problem. Consider the case of a chartered accountant (CA) who, we will assume, is also a skilled house painter. Suppose the CA can paint her house in less time than the professional painter she is thinking of hiring. Also suppose the CA can earn $50 per hour doing her accounting and must pay the painter $15 per hour. It will take the accountant 30 hours to paint her house; the painter, 40 hours. Finally, assume the CA receives no special pleasure from painting.

Should the CA take time off from her accounting to paint her own house or should she hire the painter? The CA should hire the painter. Her opportunity cost of painting her house is $1500 (= 30 hours × $50 per hour of sacrificed income). The cost of hiring the painter is only $600 (= 40 hours × $15 per hour paid to the painter). Although the CA is better at both accounting and painting, the CA's relative or comparative advantage lies in accounting. She will *lower her cost of getting her house painted* by specializing in accounting and using some of the proceeds to hire the house painter.

Note that the CA has **absolute advantage** in both accounting and painting; she can do accounting and paint more efficiently than our hypothetical house painter. Despite this, the CA has a comparative advantage in accounting, and thus should hire the house painter to paint her house.

Similarly, the house painter perhaps can reduce his cost of obtaining accounting services by specializing in painting and using some of his income to hire the CA. Suppose it would take the painter 10 hours to prepare his income tax, while the CA could handle this task in 2 hours. The house painter would sacrifice $150 of income (= 10 hours × $15 per hour of sacrificed time) to get a task done that he could hire

out for $100 (= 2 hours × $50 per hour of the CA's time). By using the CA to prepare his tax return, the painter *lowers his cost of getting the tax return completed.*

What is true for our hypothetical CA and house painter is also true for two nations. Countries can reduce their cost of obtaining desirable goods by specializing where they have comparative advantages.

With this simple example in mind, let's turn to an international trade model to acquire an understanding of the gains from international specialization and trade.

TWO ISOLATED NATIONS

Suppose the world economy has just two nations, Canada and Brazil. Each can produce both steel and soybeans, but at differing levels of economic efficiency. Suppose Canadian and Brazilian domestic production possibilities curves for soybeans and steel are as shown in Figure 20-1(a) and (b). Let's look at two characteristics of these production possibilities curves.

1. CONSTANT COSTS We have purposely drawn the "curves" as straight lines, in contrast to the concave-from-the-origin type of production possibilities boundaries introduced in Chapter 2. This means the law of increasing costs has been replaced with the assumption of constant costs. This simplification will make it easier for you to follow our discussion and will not impair the validity of our analysis and conclusions. We will consider later the effect of the more realistic increasing costs.

2. DIFFERENT COSTS The production possibilities lines of Canada and Brazil are different, reflecting different resource mixes and differing levels of technological progress. Specifically, the opportunity costs of producing steel and soybeans differ between the two nations.

CANADA In Figure 20-1(a), with full employment, Canada can increase its output of steel 30 tonnes by forgoing an output of 30 tonnes of soybeans. That means the slope of the production possibilities curve is –1 (= –1/1), implying that 1 tonne of steel can be obtained for every tonne of soybeans sacrificed. In Canada the domestic exchange ratio or **cost ratio** for the two products is 1 tonne of steel for 1 tonne of soybean, or

$$1 \, S_t = 1 \, S_{oy}$$

FIGURE 20-1 Production possibilities for Canada and Brazil

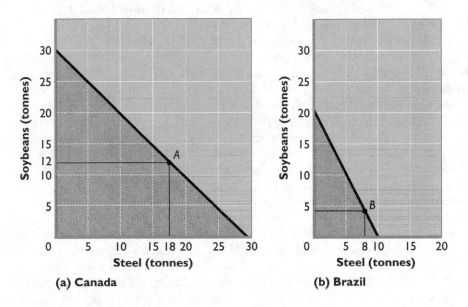

(a) Canada

(b) Brazil

The two production possibilities lines show the amounts of soybeans and steel (a) Canada and (b) Brazil can produce domestically. The production possibilities for both countries are straight lines because we are assuming constant costs. The different cost ratios — $1S_t = 1S_{oy}$ for Canada and $1S_t = 2S_{oy}$ for Brazil — are reflected in the different slopes of the two lines.

Canada can "exchange" a tonne of steel for a tonne of soybeans domestically by shifting resources from steel to soybeans. Our constant-cost assumption means this exchange or cost ratio prevails for all possible moves on Canada's production possibilities curve.

BRAZIL Brazil's production possibilities line in Figure 20-1(b) represents a different exchange or cost ratio. In Brazil 20 tonnes of soybeans must be given up to get 10 tonnes of steel. The slope of the production possibilities curve is –2 (= –²/1). This means that in Brazil the domestic cost ratio for the two goods is 1 tonne of steel for 2 tonnes of soybeans, or

$$1 S_t = 2 S_{oy}$$

3. SELF-SUFFICIENCY If Canada and Brazil are isolated and self-sufficient, each must choose some output mix on its production possibilities line. Assume point A in Figure 20-1(a) is the optimum output mix in Canada. The choice of this combination of 18 tonnes of steel and 12 tonnes of soybeans is presumably made through the market system. Suppose Brazil's optimum product mix is 8 tonnes of steel and 4 tonnes of soybeans, as indicated by point B in Figure 20-1(b). These choices are also reflected in column 1 of Table 20-1.

TABLE 20-1 International specialization according to comparative advantage and the gains from trade (in tonnes)

Country	(1) Outputs before specialization	(2) Outputs after specialization	(3) Amounts exported (–) and imported (+)	(4) Outputs available after trade	(5) = (4) – (1) Gains from specialization and trade
Canada	18 steel	30 steel	–10 steel	20 steel	2 steel
	12 soybeans	0 soybeans	+15 soybeans	15 soybeans	3 soybeans
Brazil	8 steel	0 steel	+10 steel	10 steel	2 steel
	4 soybeans	20 soybeans	–15 soybeans	5 soybeans	1 soybeans

SPECIALIZATION ACCORDING TO COMPARATIVE ADVANTAGE

With these different cost ratios, the way to determine the product in which Canada and Brazil should specialize is as follows: The **principle of comparative advantage** says *that total output will be greatest when each good is produced by that nation that has the lower domestic opportunity cost.* For our illustration, Canada's domestic opportunity cost is lower for steel. Canada need only forgo 1 tonne of soybeans to produce 1 tonne of steel, while Brazil must forgo 2 tonnes of soybeans for 1 tonne of steel. **Canada has a comparative (cost) advantage in steel and should specialize in steel production.** The "world" (Canada and Brazil) is *not* economizing in the use of its resources if a specific product (steel) is produced by a high-cost producer (Brazil) when it could have been produced by a low-cost producer (Canada). To have Brazil produce steel would mean that the world economy would have to give up more soybeans than is necessary to obtain a tonne of steel.

Brazil's domestic opportunity cost is lower for soybeans. Brazil must sacrifice only $1/2$ tonne of steel in producing 1 tonne of soybeans, whereas Canada must forgo 1 tonne of steel in producing a tonne of soybeans. **Brazil has a comparative advantage in soybeans and should specialize in soybean production.**

Economizing — using fixed quantities of scarce resources so as to obtain the greatest total output — requires that any particular good be produced by that nation having the lower domestic opportunity cost, or a comparative advantage. Canada should produce steel and Brazil soybeans. Note that this holds even though Canada has an absolute advantage in both steel and soybeans.

In column 2 of Table 20-1 we can verify that specialized production in accordance with the principle of comparative advantage allows the world to get more output from given amounts of resources. By specializing completely in steel, Canada can produce 30 tonnes of steel and no soybeans: Brazil, specializing completely in soybeans, produces 20 tonnes of soybeans and no steel. The world has more steel — 30 tonnes, compared with 26 (= 18 + 8) tonnes — *and* more soybeans — 20 tonnes, compared with 16 (= 12 + 4) tonnes — than where there is self-sufficiency or unspecialized production.

TERMS OF TRADE

But consumers of each nation will want *both* steel and soybeans. Specialization implies the need to trade or exchange the two products. What will be the **terms of trade**? At what exchange ratio will Canada and Brazil trade steel and soybeans?

Because $1\ S_t = 1\ S_{oy}$ in Canada, Canada must get *more than* 1 tonne of soybeans for each tonne of steel exported or it will not pay Canada to export steel in exchange for Brazilian soybeans. Canada must get a better "price" (more soybeans) for its steel in the world market than it can get domestically, or else there is no gain from trade and it won't occur.

Similarly, because $1\ S_t = 2\ S_{oy}$ in Brazil, Brazil must get 1 tonne of steel by exporting some amount *less than* 2 tonnes of soybeans. Brazil must pay a lower "price" for steel in the world market than it must pay domestically, or it will not want to trade. We can be certain that the international exchange ratio or *terms of trade* must lie somewhere between

$$1\ S_t = 1\ S_{oy} \text{ (Canada's cost conditions)}$$

and

$$1\ S_t = 2\ S_{oy} \text{ (Brazil's cost conditions)}$$

But where will the world exchange ratio fall between these limits? The exchange ratio or terms of trade determines how the gains from international specialization and trade are divided between the two nations. Canada will prefer a ratio close to $1\ S_t = 2\ S_{oy}$, say, $1\ S_t = 1^3/4\ S_{oy}$. Canadians want to get a great deal of soybeans for each tonne of steel they export. Similarly, Brazil wants a rate near $1\ S_t = 1\ S_{oy}$, say $1\ S_t = 1^1/4\ S_{oy}$. Brazil wants to export as little soybean as possible for each tonne of steel it receives in exchange.

The exchange ratio between the two limits depends on world supply and demand for the two products. If overall world demand for soybeans is weak relative to its supply and the demand for steel is strong relative to its supply, the price of soybeans will be low and the price of steel high. The exchange ratio will settle near the $1\ S_t = 2\ S_{oy}$ figure preferred by Canada. Under the opposite world supply and demand conditions, the ratio will settle near the $1\ S_t = 1\ S_{oy}$ level most favourable to Brazil. We will take up the topic of equilibrium world prices later in this chapter.

GAINS FROM TRADE

Suppose the international exchange ratio or terms of trades is $1\,S_t = 1^1/_2\,S_{oy}$. The possibility of trading on these terms permits each nation to supplement its domestic production possibilities line with a **trading possibilities line**. This can be seen in **Figure 20-2(a) and (b) (Key Graph)**. A trading possibilities line shows the options that a nation has by specializing in one product and trading (exporting) its specialty to obtain the other product. The trading possibilities lines in Figure 20-2 are drawn on the assumption that both nations specialize based on comparative advantage — Canada specializes completely in steel [point S in Figure 20-2(a)] and Brazil completely in soybeans [point c in Figure 20-2(b)].

IMPROVED OPTIONS Now, instead of being constrained by its domestic production possibilities line and having to give up 1 tonne of steel for every tonne of soybeans it wants as it moves up its domestic production possibilities line from point S, Canada, through trade with Brazil, can get $1^1/_2$ tonnes of soybeans for every tonne of steel it exports

to Brazil, so long as Brazil has soybeans to export. Line SC' demonstrates the $1\,S_t$ - $1^1/_2\,S_{oy}$ trading ratio.

Similarly, we can think of Brazil as starting at point c and, instead of having to move down its domestic production possibilities line, giving up 2 tonnes of soybeans for each tonne of steel it wants; it can now export just $1^1/_2$ tonnes of soybeans for each tonne of steel it wants by moving along its cs' trading possibilities line.

Specialization and trade create a new exchange ratio between steel and soybeans, reflected in a nation's trading possibilities line. This exchange ratio is superior for both nations to the self-sufficiency exchange ratio embodied in the production possibilities line of each. By specializing in steel and trading for Brazil's soybeans, Canada can obtain *more than* 1 tonne of soybeans for 1 tonne of steel. By specializing in soybeans and trading for Canada's steel, Brazil can get 1 tonne of steel for *less than* 2 tonnes of soybeans.

ADDED OUTPUT By specializing according to comparative advantage and trading for those goods produced with the lowest efficiency domestically,

KEY GRAPH

FIGURE 20-2 Trading possibilities lines and the gains from trade

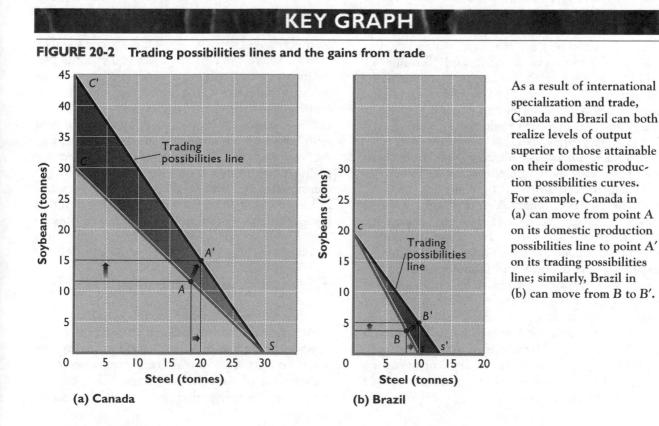

As a result of international specialization and trade, Canada and Brazil can both realize levels of output superior to those attainable on their domestic production possibilities curves. For example, Canada in (a) can move from point A on its domestic production possibilities line to point A' on its trading possibilities line; similarly, Brazil in (b) can move from B to B'.

(a) Canada

(b) Brazil

both Canada and Brazil can realize combinations of steel and soybeans beyond their production possibilities boundaries. *Specialization according to comparative advantage results in a more efficient allocation of world resources, and larger outputs of both steel and soybeans are therefore available to Canada and Brazil.*

Suppose that at the $1 S_t = 1^1/_2 S_{oy}$ terms of trade, Canada exports 10 tonnes of steel to Brazil and Brazil in return exports 15 tonnes of soybeans to Canada. How do the new quantities of steel and soybeans available to the two nations compare with the optimum product mixes that existed before specialization and trade? Point A in Figure 20-2(a) reminds us that Canada chose 18 tonnes of steel and 12 tonnes of soybeans originally. Now, by producing 30 tonnes of steel and no soybeans, and by trading 10 tonnes of steel for 15 tonnes of soybeans, Canada can enjoy 20 tonnes of steel and 15 tonnes of soybeans. This new, superior combination of steel and soybeans is shown by point A' in Figure 20-2(a). Compared with the nontrading figures of 18 tonnes of steel and 12 tonnes of soybeans, Canada's **gains from trade** are 2 tonnes of steel and 3 tonnes of soybeans.

Similarly, we assumed Brazil's optimum product mix was 4 tonnes of soybeans and 8 tonnes of steel (point B) before specialization and trade. Now, by specializing in soybeans and producing 20 tonnes of soybeans and no steel, Brazil can realize a combination of 5 tonnes of soybeans and 10 tonnes of steel by exporting 15 tonnes of its soybeans in exchange for 10 tonnes of Canadian steel. This new position is shown by point B' in Figure 20-2(b). Brazil's gains from trade are 1 tonne of soybeans and 2 tonnes of steel.

As a result of specialization and trade, both countries have more of both products. Table 20-1 is a summary statement of these figures.

The fact that points A' and B' are economic positions superior to A and B is very important. Recall, from Chapter 2, that a nation can go beyond its production possibilities boundary by (1) expanding the quantity and improving the quality of its resources or (2) realizing technological progress. We have now explained another way — international trade — for a nation to circumvent the output constraint imposed by its production possibilities curve. The effects of international specialization and trade are the equivalent of having more and better resources or discovering improved production techniques.

INCREASING COSTS

Suppose, as in our previous constant-cost illustration, that Canada and Brazil are at positions on their production possibilities curves where their cost ratios are initially $1 S_t = 1 S_{oy}$ and $1 S_t = 2 S_{oy}$ respectively. As before, comparative advantage indicates that Canada should specialize in steel and Brazil in soybeans. But now, as Canada begins to expand steel production, its $1 S_t = 1 S_{oy}$ cost ratio will *rise*, it will have to sacrifice *more than* 1 tonne of soybeans to get 1 additional tonne of steel. Resources are no longer perfectly shiftable between alternative uses, as the constant-cost assumption implied. Resources less and less suited to steel production must be allocated to the Canadian steel industry in expanding steel output, and this means increasing costs — the sacrifice of larger and larger amounts of soybeans for each additional tonne of steel.

Similarly, Brazil, starting from its $1 S_t = 2 S_{oy}$ cost ratio position, expands soybean production. But as it does, it will find that its $1 S_t = 2 S_{oy}$ cost ratio begins to *fall*. Sacrificing a tonne of steel will free resources that are capable of producing only something *less than* 2 tonnes of soybeans, because these transferred resources are less suitable to soybean production.

As the Canadian cost ratio rises from $1 S_t = 1 S_{oy}$ and Brazil's falls from $1 S_t = 2 S_{oy}$, a point will be reached where the cost ratios are equal in the two nations, for example, at $1 S_t = 1^1/_2 S_{oy}$. At this point, the underlying basis for further specialization and trade — differing cost ratios — has disappeared. Most important, this point of equal cost ratios may be realized where Canada is still producing *some* soybeans along with its steel and Brazil is producing *some* steel along with its soybeans. *The primary effect of increasing costs is to make specialization less than complete.* For this reason we often find domestically produced products competing directly against identical or similar imported products within a particular economy. **(Key Question 4)**

THE CASE FOR FREE TRADE RESTATED

The case for free trade reduces to this one potent argument. *Through free trade based on the principle of comparative advantage, the world economy can achieve a more efficient allocation of resources and a higher level of material well-being.* The resource mixes and technological knowledge of each country are different. Therefore each nation can produce particular commodities at different real costs. Each nation should produce goods for which its domestic opportunity costs are lower than the domestic opportunity cost of other nations, and exchange these specialties for products for which its domestic opportunity costs are high relative to those of other nations. If each nation does this, the world can realize the advantages of geographic and human specialization.

A side benefit of free trade is that it promotes competition and deters monopoly. The increased competition from foreign firms forces domestic firms to adopt the lowest-cost production techniques. It also compels them to be innovative and progressive with respect to both product quality and production methods, thereby contributing to economic growth. And free trade provides consumers with a wider range of product choices. The reasons to favour free trade are essentially the same reasons that endorse competition. That's why most economists embrace free trade.

QUICK REVIEW 20-1

1. International trade has always been important to Canada, and it is becoming increasingly so.

2. International trade enables nations to specialize, enhance the productivity of their resources, and achieve a larger global output.

3. Comparative advantage means total world output will be greatest when each good is produced by that nation having the lowest domestic opportunity cost.

4. Specialization is less than complete among nations because opportunity costs normally rise as more of a particular good is produced.

SUPPLY AND DEMAND ANALYSIS OF EXPORTS AND IMPORTS

Supply and demand analysis provides useful insights on the equilibrium prices and quantities of exports and imports. The amount of a good or service that a nation will export or import depends on differences between equilibrium world and domestic prices. The equilibrium **world price** derives from the interaction of *world* supply and demand; it is the price that equates quantity supplied and demanded globally. The equilibrium **domestic price** is determined by *domestic* supply and demand; it is the price that would prevail in a closed economy — one having no international trade. At this price there will be neither a domestic surplus nor shortage of the good or service.

Because of comparative advantages and disadvantages, no-trade domestic prices *may* or *may not* equal world equilibrium prices. When economies are opened for international trade, differences between world and domestic prices form the basis for exports or imports. Let's look at the international effects of these price differences in a simple two-nation world.

SUPPLY AND DEMAND IN CANADA

Suppose the world consists of just Canada and the United States, the product involved is aluminum, and there are no trade barriers such as tariffs and quotas. Let's also ignore international transportation costs to keep things simple.

Figure 20-3(a) shows the domestic supply and demand curves for aluminum in Canada. The intersection of S_d and D_d determines the equilibrium domestic price is $1.25 per kilogram and the equilibrium domestic quantity is 100 million kilograms. The market clears at $1.25 — there are no domestic surpluses nor shortages of aluminum.

But what if the economy is opened to world trade and the *world price* of aluminum is above or below this $1.25 domestic price?

CANADIAN EXPORT SUPPLY   If the world aluminum price exceeds $1.25, Canadian firms will produce more than 100 million kilograms and export the excess domestic output to the rest of the world (United States). First consider a world price of $1.50. We see from the supply curve S_d that Canadian aluminum firms will produce 125 million kilograms of aluminum. The demand curve D_d tells us that Canadians will purchase only 75 million kilograms at $1.50. A domestic surplus or excess supply of 50 million kilograms of aluminum results. Canadian producers will export these 50 million kilograms at the $1.50 world price.

What if the world price is $1.75? The supply curve shows that Canadian firms will produce 150 million kilograms of aluminum, while the demand curve tells us that Canadian consumers will buy only 50 million kilograms. The domestic surplus or excess supply of 100 million kilograms will be exported.

FIGURE 20-3 **Canadian export supply and import demand**

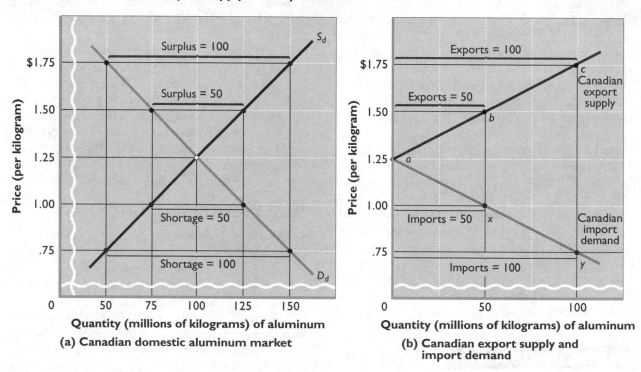

(a) Canadian domestic aluminum market

(b) Canadian export supply and import demand

In (a) world prices above the $1.25 domestic price create domestic surpluses of aluminum. As shown by the export supply curve in (b), these surpluses are exported. Domestic shortages occur when the world price is below $1.25 (a). These shortages are met by importing aluminum (b). The export supply curve shows the direct relationship between world prices and Canadian exports; the import supply curve portrays the inverse relationship between world prices and Canadian imports.

In Figure 20-3(b) we plot on the horizontal scale the domestic surpluses — Canadian exports — occurring at world prices above the $1.25 domestic equilibrium price. When the world and domestic prices are equal (= $1.25), the quantity of exports supplied is zero (point *a*). There is *no* surplus of domestic output to export. But when the world price is $1.50, Canadian firms export 50 million kilograms of surplus aluminum, as shown by point *b*. At a $1.75 world price, the domestic surplus of 100 million kilograms is exported (point *c*).

The upsloping Canadian **export supply curve** — found by connecting points such as *a*, *b*, and *c* — shows the amount of aluminum that Canadian producers will export at each world price above $1.25. This curve slopes upward, revealing a direct or positive relationship between the world price and amount of Canadian exports. *When world prices rise relative to domestic prices, Canadian exports increase.*

CANADIAN IMPORT DEMAND   World prices below $1.25 in Figure 20-3(a) result in Canadian imports. Consider a $1.00 world price. The supply curve reveals Canadian firms can profitably produce and domestically sell 75 million kilograms of aluminum. But we see from the demand curve that Canadians want to buy 125 million kilograms at this price. The result? A domestic shortage of 50 million kilograms. To satisfy this shortage, 50 million kilograms of aluminum imports will enter Canada.

At the lower $.75 world price, Canadian producers supply only 50 million kilograms. Because Canadian consumers want to buy 150 million kilograms, there is a domestic shortage of 100 million kilograms. Imports flow into Canada to make up the 100 million kilogram difference. That is, at a $.75 world price Canadian firms supply 50 million kilograms and foreign firms supply 100 million kilograms.

FIGURE 20-4   American export supply and import demand

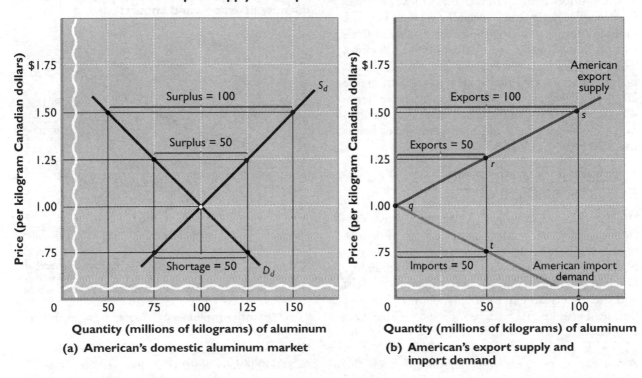

In (a) domestic production of aluminum in the United States exceeds domestic consumption at all world prices above the $1.00 domestic price. These domestic surpluses result in American exports (b). When the domestic price falls below $1.00, domestic shortages occur (a) and imports flow to the United States (b). The American export supply curve and import demand curve depict these relationships.

In Figure 20-3(b) we derive the Canadian **import demand curve.** This downsloping curve shows the amount of aluminum imported at world prices below the $1.25 Canadian domestic price. The relationship between world prices and imports is inverse or negative. Domestic output will satisfy Canadian demand at a world price of $1.25; imports will be zero (point *a*). But at $1.00 Canadians will import 50 million kilograms of aluminum (point *x*); at $.75, they will import 100 million kilograms (point *y*). Connecting points such as *a*, *x*, and *y* yields a downsloping Canadian import demand curve. *When world prices fall relative to domestic prices, Canadian imports increase.*

SUPPLY AND DEMAND IN THE UNITED STATES

Now we repeat our analysis in Figure 20-4, this time for the United States. (We have converted

American dollar prices to Canadian dollar prices via the exchange rate [Chapters 6 and 21]). To begin, be sure to note that the domestic supply and demand curves for aluminum in the United States yield a domestic price of $1.00, which is $.25 lower than the $1.25 Canadian domestic price.

The analysis is identical. If the world price is $1.00, Americans will neither export nor import aluminum (point *q* in Figure 20-4[b]). At prices above $1.00, American firms will produce more aluminum than American consumers will buy. The surplus or excess supply of aluminum represents the United States' supply of exports. At a $1.25 world price, the United States will export a domestic surplus of 50 million kilograms (point *r*). At $1.50 it will export a domestic surplus of 100 million kilograms (point *s*). The upsloping American *export supply curve* reflects the domestic surpluses and thus exports occurring when the world price exceeds the $1.00 American domestic price.

Domestic shortages occur in the United States at world prices below $1.00. At a $.75 world price, for example, American consumers want to buy 125 million kilograms of aluminum but American firms can profitably produce only 75 million kilograms. The shortage or excess demand invokes 50 million kilograms of imports to Canada (point *t* in Figure 20-4[b]). The American *import demand curve* represents the domestic shortages and thus American imports occurring at world aluminum prices below the $1.00 American domestic price.

EQUILIBRIUM WORLD PRICE, EXPORTS, AND IMPORTS

We now have the tools to determine the equilibrium world price of aluminum and ascertain the equilibrium world levels of exports and imports. Figure 20-5 combines the Canadian export supply curve and import demand curve of Figure 20-3(b) and the American export supply curve and import demand curve of Figure 20-4(b). The two Canadian curves emanate rightward from the $1.25 Canadian domestic price; the two American curves emanate rightward from the $1.00 American domestic price. *International equilibrium occurs in this two-nation model where one nation's import demand curve intersects another nation's export supply curve.* In this case Canada's import demand curve intersects America's export supply curve at *e*. There, the world price of aluminum is $1.12. Observe from the American export supply curve that the United States will export 25 million kilograms of aluminum at this price. Said differently, Canada will import 25 million kilograms from the United States, as seen from the Canadian import demand curve. The $1.12 world price equates the quantity of imports demanded and the quantity of exports supplied (= 25 million kilograms). This price reflects world demand and supply (the United States and Canada).

Note that after trade, the single $1.12 world price will prevail in both Canada and the United States. *Only one price for a standardized commodity can persist in a highly competitive market.* With trade, all consumers can buy a kilogram of aluminum for $1.12 and all producers can sell it for that price. This world price means that Americans will pay more for aluminum with trade (= $1.12) than without it (= $1.00). The increased American output

FIGURE 20-5   Equilibrium world price and quantity of exports and imports

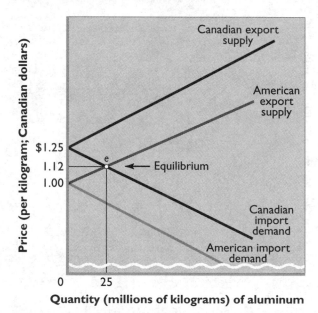

Quantity (millions of kilograms) of aluminum

In a two-nation world, the equilibrium world price (= $1.12) is determined at the intersection of one nation's export supply curve and another nation's import demand curve. This intersection also decides the equilibrium volume of exports and imports. Here, the United States exports 25 million pounds of aluminum to Canada.

caused by trade raises American production costs and therefore the price of aluminum in the United States. Canadians, however, pay less for aluminum with trade (= $1.12) than without it (= $1.25). The Canadian gain comes from America's competitive cost advantage in producing aluminum.

Why would the United States willingly send 50 million kilograms of its aluminum output to Canada for consumption? Producing this output uses up scarce American resources and drives up the price of aluminum for Americans. Americans are willing to export aluminum to Canada because they can gain the means — the earnings of Canadian dollars — to import other goods, say, computer software, from Canada. American exports enable Americans to acquire imports that have greater value to Americans than the exported aluminum. American exports to Canada finance Canadian exports to the United States. **(Key Question 6)**

TRADE BARRIERS

No matter how compelling the logic for free trade, barriers to free trade do exist. Let's look again at Chapter 6's list of trade impediments and see what we can add to our understanding of them.

1. TARIFFS Tariffs are excise taxes on imported goods; they may be imposed for purposes of revenue or protection.

Revenue tariffs are usually applied to products that are not produced domestically, for example, coffee and bananas. Rates on revenue tariffs are modest and their purpose is to provide the federal government with tax revenues.

Protective tariffs are designed to shield domestic producers from foreign competition. Although protective tariffs are usually not high enough to prohibit importation of foreign goods, they put foreign producers at a competitive disadvantage in selling in domestic markets.

2. IMPORT QUOTAS Import quotas specify the maximum amounts of specific commodities that may be imported in any period. Import quotas can more effectively retard international commerce than tariffs. A product might be imported in large quantities despite high tariffs; low import quotas completely prohibit imports once the quotas are filled.

3. NONTARIFF BARRIERS Nontariff barriers (NTBs) refer to licensing requirements, unreasonable standards for product quality and safety, or unnecessary red tape in customs procedures. Japan and the European countries frequently require their domestic importers of foreign goods to obtain licences. By restricting the issuance of licences, imports can be restricted. Great Britain bars coal in this way.

4. VOLUNTARY EXPORT RESTRICTIONS Voluntary export restrictions (VERs) are a trade barrier by which foreign firms "voluntarily" limit the amount of their exports to a particular country. VERs, which have the effect of import quotas, are agreed to by exporters in the hope of avoiding more stringent trade barriers. Japanese auto manufacturers agreed to a VER on exports to Canada under the threat of the imposition of low import quotas.

Later in this chapter we will consider the specific arguments and appeals made to justify protection.

ECONOMIC IMPACT OF TARIFFS

Once again we use supply and demand analysis — now to examine the economic effects of protective tariffs. The D_d and S_d curves in Figure 20-6 show domestic demand and supply for a product in which Canada has a comparative *dis*advantage, for example, video cassette recorders (VCRs). (Disregard $S_d + Q$ for now.) Without world trade, the domestic price and output would be P_d and q respectively.

Assume now that the domestic economy is opened to world trade and that the Japanese, who have a comparative advantage in VCRs, begin to sell their recorders in Canada. We assume that with free trade the domestic price cannot differ from the world price, which here is P_w. At P_w domestic consumption is d and domestic production is a. The horizontal distance between the domestic supply and demand curves at P_w reflects imports of ad. Thus far, our analysis is similar to the analysis of world prices in Figure 20-3.

FIGURE 20-6 The economic effects of a protective tariff or an import quota

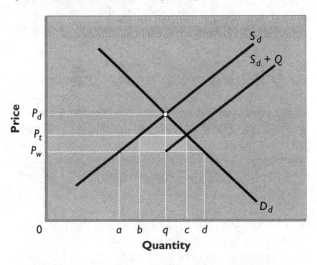

A tariff of P_wP_t will reduce domestic consumption from d to c. Domestic producers will be able to sell more output (b rather than a) at a higher price (P_t rather than P_w). Foreign exporters are injured because they are able to sell less output (bc rather than ad) in Canada. The shaded area represents the amount of tariffs paid by Canadian consumers. An import quota of bc units will have the same effects as the tariff, with one exception: the shaded area will go to foreign producers rather than to the Canadian government.

DIRECT EFFECTS Suppose now that Canada imposes a tariff of P_wP_t per unit on the imported VCRs. This will raise the domestic price from P_w to P_t and will have several effects.

1. DECLINE IN CONSUMPTION Consumption of video recorders in Canada will decline from d to c as the higher price moves buyers up their demand curve. The tariff prompts consumers to buy fewer recorders and to reallocate a portion of their expenditures to less-desired substitute products. Canadian consumers are injured by the tariff, since they pay P_wP_t more for each of the c units they now buy at price P_t.

2. INCREASED DOMESTIC PRODUCTION Canadian producers — who are *not* subject to the tariff — will receive a higher price of P_t per unit. Because this new price is higher than the pre-tariff or world price of P_w, the domestic VCR industry will move up its supply curve S_d, increasing domestic output from a to b. Domestic producers will enjoy both a higher price and expanded sales. This explains why domestic producers lobby for protective tariffs. But from a social point of view, the expanded domestic production of ab reflects the fact that the tariff permits domestic producers of recorders to bid resources away from other, more efficient, industries.

3. DECLINE IN IMPORTS Japanese producers will be hurt. Although the sale price of recorders is higher by P_wP_t, that increase accrues to the Canadian government, not to Japanese producers. The after-tariff world price — and thus the per unit revenue to Japanese producers — remains at P_w, while the volume of Canadian imports (Japanese exports) falls from ad to bc.

4. TARIFF REVENUE The shaded rectangle indicates the amount of revenue that the tariff yields. Total revenue from the tariff is determined by multiplying the tariff, P_wP_t per unit, by the number of imported recorders, bc. This tariff revenue is a transfer of income from consumers to government and does *not* represent any net change in the nation's economic well-being. The result is that government gains a portion of what consumers lose.

INDIRECT EFFECTS There are subtle effects of tariffs, beyond what our simple supply and demand

diagram indicates. Because of diminished sales of VCRs in Canada, Japan will earn fewer dollars with which to buy Canadian exports. Canadian export industries — industries in which Canada has a comparative advantage — will cut production and release resources. These are highly efficient industries, as evidenced by their comparative advantage and ability to sell goods in world markets.

Tariffs directly promote expansion of inefficient industries that do not have a comparative advantage and indirectly cause contraction of relatively efficient industries that do have a comparative advantage. This means tariffs cause resources to be shifted in the wrong direction. Not surprising. We know that specialization and unfettered world trade based on comparative advantage would lead to the efficient use of world resources and an expansion of the world's real output. The purpose and effect of protective tariffs are to reduce world trade. Therefore, aside from their specific effects on consumers and foreign and domestic producers, tariffs diminish the world's real output.

ECONOMIC IMPACT OF QUOTAS

We noted previously that an import quota is a legal limit placed on the amount of some product that can be imported each year. The economic impact of quotas is similar to that of a tariff with one salient difference: While tariffs generate revenue for the Canadian government, a quota transfers that revenue to foreign producers.

Suppose in Figure 20-6 that, instead of imposing a tariff of P_wP_t per unit, Canada prohibits any Japanese imports of VCRs in excess of bc units. In other words, an import quota of bc VCRs is imposed on Japan. We have deliberately chosen the size of this quota to be the same amount as imports would be under a P_wP_t tariff so we are comparing "equivalent" situations. As a consequence of the quota, the supply of recorders is $S_d + Q$ in Canada. This consists of the domestic supply plus the constant amount bc ($= Q$) that importers will provide at each domestic price. The $S_d + Q$ supply curve does not exist below price P_w because Japanese producers would not export VCRs to Canada at any price below P_w when they can sell them to other countries at the world market price of P_w.

Most of the economic results are the same as with a tariff. VCR prices are higher (P_t instead of P_w)

because imports have been reduced from ad to bc. Domestic consumption of VCRs is down from ad to bc. Canadian producers enjoy both a higher price (P_t rather than P_w) and increased sales (b rather than a).

The difference is that the price increase of P_wP_t paid by Canadian consumers on imports of bc — the shaded area — no longer goes to the Canadian government as tariff (tax) revenue, but flows to those Japanese firms that have acquired the rights to sell VCRs in Canada. Other things being the same, the economic effects of a tariff are better for Canadians than are those of a quota. A tariff generates government revenue that can be used to cut other taxes or to finance public goods and services that benefit Canadians. In contrast, the higher price created by quotas results in additional revenue for foreign producers.

In the early 1980s the Canadian automobile industry, with the support of its workers, successfully lobbied for an import quota on Japanese autos. The Japanese government in turn apportioned this quota among its various auto producers. The restricted supply of Japanese cars in the Canadian market allowed Japanese manufacturers to increase their prices and, hence, their profits. The Canadian import quotas in effect provided Japanese auto manufacturers with a cartel-like arrangement that enhanced their profits. When Canadian import quotas were dropped in the mid-1980s, the Japanese government replaced them with its own system of production quotas for Japanese automakers. **(Key Question 7)**

THE CASE FOR PROTECTION: A CRITICAL REVIEW

Although free-trade advocates prevail in the classroom, protectionists regularly reside on Parliament Hill. What arguments do protectionists make to justify trade barriers? How valid are these arguments?

MILITARY SELF-SUFFICIENCY ARGUMENT

The argument here is not economic — it's political-military. Protective tariffs are needed to preserve or strengthen industries producing goods and materials essential for defence or war. It contends that in an uncertain world, political-military objectives (self-

sufficiency) must take precedence over economic goals (efficiency in the use of world resources).

Unfortunately, there is no objective criterion for weighing the worth of the increase in national security relative to the decrease in efficiency accompanying reallocation of resources towards strategic industries when such tariffs are imposed. The economist can only point out there are economic costs when tariffs are levied to enhance military self-sufficiency.

The self-sufficiency argument is open to serious abuse. Nearly every industry can directly or indirectly claim a contribution to national security.

Aside from the problem of abuses, are there not better ways than tariffs to provide the strength required in strategic industries? When achieved through tariffs, self-sufficiency creates costs in the form of higher domestic prices on the output of the shielded industry. The cost of enhanced military security is apportioned arbitrarily among those consumers who buy the industry's product. A direct subsidy to strategic industries, financed out of general tax revenues, would more equitably distribute these costs.

INCREASE DOMESTIC EMPLOYMENT

Arguing for tariffs to "save Canadian jobs" becomes increasingly fashionable as an economy encounters a recession. It is rooted in macro analysis. Aggregate demand in an open economy is made up of consumption expenditures (C) plus investment expenditures (I_g) plus government expenditures (G) plus net export expenditures (X_n). Net export expenditures consist of exports (X) minus imports (M). By reducing imports, M, aggregate demand will rise, stimulating the domestic economy by boosting income and employment. But there are shortcomings associated with this policy.

1. JOB CREATION FROM IMPORTS While imports may eliminate some Canadian jobs, they create others. Imports may have eliminated jobs of Canadian automobile and textile workers in recent years, but others have gained jobs selling Toyotas and imported electronics equipment. While import restrictions alter the composition of employment, they may have little or no effect on the volume of employment.

2. FALLACY OF COMPOSITION All nations cannot simultaneously succeed in import restriction; what is true for *one* nation is not true for *all* nations. The exports of one nation must be the imports of another. To the extent that one country is able to stimulate its economy through an excess of exports over imports, some other economy's unemployment problem is worsened by the resulting excess of imports over exports. It is no wonder that tariffs and import quotas for the purposes of achieving domestic full employment are termed "beggar my neighbour" policies. They achieve short-run domestic goals by making trading partners poorer.

3. RETALIATION   Countries adversely affected by tariffs and quotas are likely to retaliate, causing a competitive raising of trade barriers that will choke off trade, to the end that all countries are worse off. For example, when the United States, under the *Smoot-Hawley Tariff Act of 1930*, imposed the highest tariffs ever enacted, the action backfired miserably. Rather than stimulate the American economy, this tariff act only induced a series of retaliatory restrictions by adversely affected nations, including Canada. This "trade war" caused a further contraction of international trade and lowered the income and employment levels of all nations. As Paul Krugman, one of the world's foremost international trade experts, has written:

> A trade war in which countries restrict each other's exports in pursuit of some illusory advantage is not much like a real war. On the one hand, nobody gets killed. On the other, unlike real wars, it is almost impossible for anyone to win, since the main losers when a country imposes barriers to trade are not foreign exporters but domestic residents. In effect, a trade war is a conflict in which each country uses most of its ammunition to shoot itself in the foot.[1]

4. LONG-RUN FEEDBACK   In the long run an excess of exports over imports is doomed to fail as a device for stimulating domestic employment. It is through Canadian imports that foreign nations earn dollars for buying Canadian exports. In the long run, a nation must import to export. The long-run impact of tariffs is not to increase domestic employment but at best to reallocate workers away from

export industries and towards protected domestic industries. This shift implies a less efficient allocation of resources.

DIVERSIFICATION FOR STABILITY

Highly specialized economies — for example, Kuwait's oil economy or Cuba's sugar economy — are very dependent on international markets for their incomes. Wars, cyclical fluctuations, and adverse changes in the structure of industry will force large and painful readjustments on such economies. Tariff and quota protection is allegedly needed in such nations to promote greater industrial diversification, and less dependence on world markets for just one or two products. This will help insulate the domestic economy from international political developments and depressions abroad, and from random fluctuations in world supply and demand for one or two particular commodities, thereby providing greater domestic stability.

There is some truth in this diversification for stability argument, but there are also serious qualifications and shortcomings.

1. The argument has little or no relevance to Canada and other advanced economies that are already highly diversified.
2. The economic costs of diversification may be great; one-crop economies may be highly inefficient in manufacturing.

INFANT-INDUSTRY ARGUMENT

The infant-industry argument contends that protective tariffs are needed to allow new domestic industries to establish themselves. Temporarily shielding young domestic firms from the severe competition of more mature and more efficient foreign firms will give infant industries a chance to develop and become efficient producers.

This argument for protection rests on an alleged exception to the case for free trade. The exception is that all industries have not had — and facing mature foreign competition will never have — the chance to make long-run adjustments in the direction of larger scale and greater efficiency in production. Tariff protection for infant industries will correct a misallocation of world resources perpetuated by historically different levels of economic development between domestic and foreign industries.

---

[1] Paul Krugman, *Peddling Prosperity* (New York: W. W. Norton & Co., 1994), p. 287.

COUNTERARGUMENTS   Consider these qualifying points to the logical validity of the infant-industry argument.

1. In the less-developed nations it is very difficult to determine which industries are the infants capable of achieving economic maturity and therefore deserving of protection.
2. Protective tariffs may not fade away, but rather persist even after industrial maturity has been realized.
3. Most economists believe that if infant industries are to be subsidized, there are better means than tariffs for doing it. Direct subsidies, for example, have the advantage of making explicit what industries are being aided and to what degree.

STRATEGIC TRADE POLICY   In recent years the infant-industry argument has taken a modified form in advanced economies. The contention is that government should use trade barriers to reduce the risk of product development borne by domestic firms, particularly those involving advanced technology. Firms protected from foreign competition can grow more rapidly and achieve greater economies of scale than unprotected foreign competitors. The "protected" firms can eventually dominate world markets because of lower costs. Supposedly, dominance of world markets will enable the domestic firms to return profits to the home nation that exceed the sacrifices caused by trade barriers. Also, specialization in high-technology industries is deemed beneficial because technology advances often can be transferred to other domestic industries.

Japan and South Korea, in particular, have been accused of using this form of **strategic trade policy**. The problem with this strategy and argument for trade barriers is that nations put at a disadvantage by these trade policies invariably retaliate with tariffs and similar strategies of their own. The outcome may be higher tariffs worldwide, reductions in world trade, and the loss of the gains from specialization and exchange.

PROTECTION AGAINST "DUMPING"

The protection-against-dumping argument for tariffs contends that tariffs are needed to protect Canadian firms from foreign producers that "dump" their excess goods onto the Canadian market at less than the cost to the foreign producers. Two reasons have been suggested as to why foreign firms might wish to sell in Canada at below costs.

1. **DRIVING OUT COMPETITORS**   Firms may use **dumping** to drive out Canadian competitors, obtain monopoly power, and then raise prices. The long-term economic profits resulting from this strategy may more than offset the earlier losses that accompany the dumping.

2. **PRICE DISCRIMINATION**   Dumping may be a form of price discrimination — charging different prices to different customers. The foreign seller may find it can maximize its profits by charging a high price in its monopolized domestic market while unloading its surplus output at a lower price in Canada. The surplus output may be needed to obtain the overall per unit costs saving associated with large-scale production.

Dumping is prohibited under Canadian trade law, as it is in most other countries. Where dumping occurs and is shown to injure Canadian firms, the federal government imposes tariffs called "anti-dumping duties" on the specific goods. But relative to the number of goods exported to Canada, documented cases of dumping are few. Dumping therefore does *not* justify widespread, permanent tariffs. Furthermore, allegations of dumping require careful investigation to determine their validity.

Foreign producers argue that dumping allegations and anti-dumping duties are Canada's efforts to restrict legitimate trade. The fact is that some foreign firms can produce certain goods at substantially less cost than can Canadian competitors. What on the surface may seem to be dumping often is simply comparative advantage at work. If abused, the anti-dumping law can increase the price of imports and reduce competition in the Canadian market. This reduced competition allows Canadian firms to raise prices at consumers' expense. And even where true dumping does occur, Canadian consumers gain from the lower-priced product — at least in the short term — much as they gain from a price war among Canadian producers.

CHEAP FOREIGN LABOUR

The cheap-foreign-labour argument says domestic firms and workers must be shielded from the ruinous competition of countries in which wages are low. If protection is not provided, cheap imports will flood Canadian markets and the prices of Canadian goods —

along with the wages of Canadian workers — will be pulled down and our domestic living standard reduced.

This argument can be rebutted at several levels. The logic of the argument suggests it is *not* mutually beneficial for rich and poor persons to trade with one another. But that is not the case. A low-income farm worker may pick lettuce or tomatoes for a rich landowner, and both may benefit from the transaction. And don't Canadian consumers gain when they buy a Taiwanese pocket radio for $12 instead of a similar Canadian-made radio selling for $20?

Also, recall that the gains from trade are based on comparative advantage. Looking back at Figure 20-1, suppose that Canada and Brazil have approximately the same total population and their labour forces are exactly the same size. Noting the positions of the production possibilities curves, we observe that Canadian labour is absolutely more productive because Canada's labour force can produce more of either good. Because of this greater productivity, we can expect wages and the standard of living to be higher for Canadian labour. Brazil's less-productive labour will receive lower wages.

The cheap-foreign-labour argument suggests that to maintain our standard of living, Canada should not trade with low-wage Brazil. Suppose we don't. Will wages and living standards rise in Canada as a result? No. To obtain soybeans, Canada will have to reallocate a portion of its labour from its efficient steel industry to its inefficient soybean industry. The average productivity of Canadian labour will fall as will real wages and the standard of living. The labour forces of *both* countries will have diminished standards of living because without specialization and trade they will have less output available to them. Compare column 4 with column 1 in Table 20-1 or points A′ and B′ with A and B in Figure 20-2 to confirm this point. **(Key Question 8)**

QUICK REVIEW 20-2

1. A nation will export a particular product if the world price exceeds the domestic price; it will import the product if the world price is less than the domestic price.

2. In a two-country model, equilibrium world prices and quantities of exports and imports occur where one nation's export supply curve intersects the other nation's import demand curve.

---

3. Trade barriers include tariffs, import quotas, non-tariff barriers, and voluntary export restrictions.

4. A tariff on a product increases price, reduces consumption, increases domestic production, reduces imports, and generates tariff revenue for government; an import quota does the same, except that a quota generates revenue for foreign producers rather than the government imposing the quota.

5. Most arguments for trade protection are special-interest pleas that, if followed, would create gains for protected industries and their workers at the expense of greater losses for the economy.

COSTS OF PROTECTIONISM

How costly are existing Canadian trade protections such as tariffs, quotas, and voluntary export restraints to Canadians?

COST TO SOCIETY

In Figure 20-6 we showed that tariffs and quotas impose costs on domestic consumers, but confer gains to domestic producers, and in the case of tariffs, revenue to the federal government. The consumer cost of trade restrictions can be calculated by determining the effect they have on prices of protected goods. Protection will raise the price of a product in three ways.

1. The price of the imported product goes up (Figure 20-6).
2. The higher price of imports will cause some consumers to shift their purchases to higher-priced domestically produced goods.
3. The price of domestically produced goods will rise because import competition has declined.

Studies indicate the costs to consumers of protected products substantially exceed the gains to producers and government. There is a sizable net cost or efficiency loss to society from trade protection. Furthermore, net losses from trade barriers are greater than the losses reported in most studies. Tariffs and quotas produce myriad costly, difficult-to-quantify secondary effects. For example, the import restraints on steel in the 1980s drove up the price of steel to all Canadian buyers of steel — including the Canadian automobile industry. Therefore Canadian automakers had higher costs than otherwise and were less competitive in world markets.

BOX 20-2 APPLYING THE THEORY

PETITION OF THE CANDLEMAKERS, 1845

The French economist Frédéric Bastiat (1801–1850) devastated the proponents of protectionism by satirically extending their reasoning to its logical and absurd conclusions.

Petition of the Manufacturers of Candles, Wax-lights, Lamps, Candlesticks, Street Lamps, Snuffers, Extinguishers, and of the Producers of Oil Tallow, Rosin, Alcohol, and, Generally, of Everything Connected with Lighting.

TO MESSIEURS THE MEMBERS
OF THE CHAMBER
OF DEPUTIES.

GENTLEMEN — You are on the right road. You reject abstract theories, and have little consideration for cheapness and plenty. Your chief care is the interest of the producer. You desire to emancipate him from external competition, and reserve the *national market for national industry*.

We are about to offer you an admirable opportunity of applying your — what shall we call it? your theory? No; nothing is more deceptive than theory; your doctrine? your system? your principle? but you dislike doctrines, you abhor systems, and as for principles, you deny that there are any in social economy: we shall say, then, your practice, your practice without theory and without principle.

We are suffering from the intolerable competition of a foreign rival, placed, it would seem, in a condition so far superior to ours for the production of light, that he absolutely *inundates* our *national market* with it at a price fabulously reduced. The moment he shows himself, our trade leaves us — all consumers apply to him; and a branch of native industry, having countless ramifications, is all at once rendered completely stagnant. This rival ... is no other than the Sun.

What we pray for is, that it may please you to pass a law ordering the shutting up of all windows, skylights, dormerwindows, outside and inside shutters, curtains, blinds, bull's-eyes; in a word, of all openings, holes, chinks, clefts, and fissures, by or through which the light of the sun has been in use to enter houses, to the prejudice of the meritorious manufactures with which we flatter ourselves we have accommodated our country, — a country which, in gratitude, ought not to abandon us now to a strife so unequal.

If you shut up as much as possible all access to natural light, and create a demand for artificial light, which of our French manufactures will not be encouraged by it?

If more tallow is consumed, then there must be more oxen and sheep; and, consequently, we shall behold the multiplication of artificial meadows, meat, wool, hides, and, above all, manure, which is the basis and foundation of all agricultural wealth.

The same remark applies to navigation. Thousands of vessels will proceed to the whale fishery; and, in a short time, we shall possess a navy capable of maintaining the honour of France, and gratifying the patriotic aspirations of your petitioners, the undersigned candlemakers and others.

Only have the goodness to reflect, Gentlemen, and you will be convinced that there is, perhaps, no Frenchman, from the wealthy coalmaster to the humblest vendor of lucifer matches, whose lot will not be ameliorated by the success of this our petition.

SOURCE: Frédéric Bastiat, *Economic Sophisms* (Edinburgh: Oliver and Boyd, Tweeddale Court, 1873) pp.49-53, abridged.

Finally, industries employ large amounts of economic resources to influence Parliament to pass and retain protectionist laws. To the extent that these rent-seeking efforts divert resources away from more socially desirable purposes, trade restrictions impose another cost on society.

Conclusion: The gains that Canada's trade barriers create for protected industries and their

GLOBAL PERSPECTIVE 20-2

Growth per capita and level of trade protection

Higher levels of trade protection in less developed nations are generally associated with lower levels of economic growth, as measured by average annual increases in output per person.

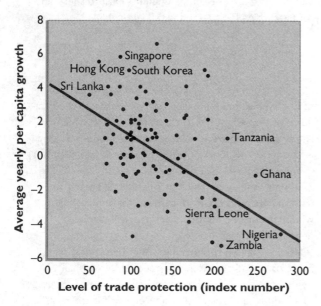

Level of trade protection (index number)

Source: David M. Gould, Graeme L. Woodbridge, and Roy J. Ruffin, "The Theory and Practice of International Trade," *Economic Review*, Federal Reserve Bank of Dallas, 4th Quarter, 1993, p. 3. Data are for 1976–1985.

workers come at the expense of much greater losses for the entire economy. The result is economic inefficiency.

IMPACT ON INCOME DISTRIBUTION

Studies also show that import restrictions affect low-income families proportionately more than high-income families. Because tariffs and quotas act much like sales or excise taxes, these trade restrictions are highly regressive. That is, the "overcharge" associated with trade protection falls *as a percentage of income* as income increases. Example: Households pay more per year for clothing because of trade restrictions. Relative to their incomes, the burden of this protectionism is heavier for poorer households than for wealthier ones. **(Key Question 11)**

CANADIAN INTERNATIONAL TRADE POLICIES

Having explored some general principles in international trade, we turn to a consideration of major trade policies affecting Canada, the results of these policies, and proposed alternatives. We look first at domestic policy.

THE NATIONAL POLICY

The general policy on which the present tariff structure of Canada has been built was adopted shortly after Confederation. The **National Policy**, introduced in 1879, included, among other things, high tariffs to protect Canada's manufacturing sector. Canada's manufacturing remained highly protected up to 1945. Tariffs on our manufactured goods have been falling ever since, but until very recently our manufacturing sector was highly protected.

If tariffs are economically undesirable, why has Parliament been willing to employ them? The answer lies in the political realities of tariff making and the special-interest effect. A small group of domestic producers who will receive large economic gains from tariffs and quotas will press vigorously for protection through well-financed and well-informed political lobbyists. The large number of consumers who individually will have small losses imposed on them will be generally uninformed, indifferent, and unorganized.

The public may be won over, not only by the vigour, but also by the apparent plausibility ("Cut imports and prevent domestic unemployment") and the patriotic ring ("Buy Canadian!") of the protectionists. Alleged tariff benefits are immediate and clear-cut to the public. The costs are obscure and widely dispersed over the economy. Moreover, the public is likely to stumble on the fallacy of composition: "If a quota on Japanese automobiles will preserve profits and employment in the Canadian automobile industry, how can it be detrimental to the economy as a whole?"

BILATERAL AGREEMENTS AND GATT

The across-the-board reduction of tariffs has come about because of various bilateral agreements Canada signed. By incorporating **most-favoured-nation clauses** in these agreements, the resulting tariff reductions not only apply to the specific nation negotiating with Canada, but would apply to all nations.

But bilateral (two-nation) negotiations were slow and cumbersome. This approach was broadened in 1947 when 23 nations, including Canada, signed the **General Agreement on Tariffs and Trade (GATT)**. GATT is based on three principles: (1) equal, nondiscriminatory treatment for all member nations; (2) the reduction of tariffs by *multilateral* negotiations; and (3) the elimination of import quotas. GATT is a forum for the negotiation of reductions in tariff barriers on a multilateral basis. One hundred nations now belong to GATT, and there is little doubt that it has been an important force in the trend towards liberalized trade. Under its sponsorship, seven "rounds" of negotiations to reduce trade barriers have been completed in the post-World War II period.

In 1994 more than 100 of the world's nations successfully completed the eighth "round" of negotiation, known as the Uruguay Round of the GATT. Provisions to be implemented between 1995 and 2005 include:

1. reduction of tariffs worldwide;
2. liberalization of rules that have impeded trade in services;
3. reduction of agricultural subsidies that have distorted the global pattern of trade in agricultural goods;
4. new protections for intellectual property (copyrights, patents, trademarks);
5. a phasing out of quotas on textiles and apparel, to be replaced with gradually declining tariffs;
6. establishment of the **World Trade Organization** to oversee the provisions of the agreement and to resolve any disputes under the new rules.

When completed in 2005, GATT will boost the world's GDP by an estimated $6 trillion, or 8%.

ECONOMIC INTEGRATION

Another development in trade liberalization has taken the form of **economic integration** — the joining of the markets of two or more nations into a free-trade zone. Three illustrations of economic integration are the European Union (EU) — also called the Common Market — the Canada–United States Free Trade Agreement (FTA), and the North American Free-Trade Agreement (NAFTA).

THE COMMON MARKET   The best example is the **European Union (EU)** — formerly called the European Economic Community. Begun in 1958

with six nations, the EU is now made up of 15 Western European nations — France, Germany, Italy, Belgium, the Netherlands, Luxembourg, Denmark, Ireland, United Kingdom, Greece, Spain, Portugal, Austria, Finland, and Sweden.

GOALS   The original Common Market calls for (1) the gradual abolition of tariffs and import quotas on all products traded among the participating nations, (2) establishment of a common system of tariffs applicable to all goods received from nations outside the EU, (3) free movement of capital and labour within the Common Market, (4) the creation of common policies with respect to other economic matters of joint concern, such as agriculture, transportation, and restrictive business practices. The EU has achieved most of these goals and is now a strong **trade bloc.**

RESULTS   Motives for creating the European Union were both political and economic. The economic motive was to gain the advantages of freer trade for members. While it is difficult to determine how much EU prosperity and growth have resulted from integration, integration has created mass markets essential to EU industries. The economies of large-scale production have permitted European industries to achieve the lower costs that small, localized markets have historically denied them.

Effects on nonmember nations such as Canada are less certain. A peaceful and increasingly prosperous EU makes member nations better potential customers for Canadian exports. But Canadian firms encounter tariffs that make it difficult to compete in EU markets. For example, before the establishment of the EU, Canadian, German, and French manufacturers all faced the same tariff in selling their products to, say, Belgium. However, with the establishment of internal free trade among EU members, Belgian tariffs on German Volkswagens and French Renaults fell to zero, but an external tariff still applies to all nonmember nations such as Canada. This puts Canadian firms and those of other nonmember nations at a competitive disadvantage. Similarly, EU trade restrictions hamper Eastern European exports of metals, textiles and farm products, goods the Eastern Europeans produce in abundance.

By giving preferences to other countries within their free-trade zone, trade blocs such as the EU may reduce their trade with nonbloc members. Thus, the world loses some of the benefits of a completely open global trading system. Eliminating this disadvantage has been one of the motivations for promoting freer global trade through GATT.

THE CANADA–U.S. FREE TRADE AGREEMENT

Other examples of economic integration are the **Canada–U.S. Free Trade Agreement (FTA)** enacted in 1989 and the North American Free Trade Agreement (NAFTA), which came into effect in 1995. More will be said about NAFTA below.

Although three-fourths of the trade between Canada and the United States was already free in 1988, the FTA accord is highly significant: It created the largest free-trade area in the world. Under terms of the agreement, all trade restrictions such as tariffs, quotas, and nontariff barriers will be eliminated by 1999. Canadian producers will gain increased access to a market ten times the size of Canada, while U.S. consumers will gain the advantage of lower-priced Canadian goods. In return, Canada will cut its tariffs by more than the United States because Canadian tariffs are higher.

WHY FREE TRADE?

If we agree that free trade is desirable, it makes sense to achieve it first with our overwhelmingly most important trading partner. With the increasingly protectionist climate in the United States in the late 1980s, Canada needed to protect its access to this market. Let's take a closer look at some of the more important provisions of the agreement.

TARIFFS Opponents of the FTA often point out that three-quarters of our trade with the United States is already duty-free and that tariff rates have been dropping continuously for over 40 years. This argument ignores two important facts: (1) *average* tariffs have indeed been dropping, but many articles are not traded at all because *individual* tariffs remain very high, for example, on petrochemicals and woven fabrics; (2) it is mostly Canada's raw materials that are imported duty-free into the United States. As we stressed earlier, foreign (including American) tariffs on our goods increase with the degree of processing done in Canada.

Under the FTA, some tariffs between Canada and the United States were eliminated entirely on January 2, 1989; another group was eliminated by 1994; and all the rest by 1999, with 10% of the original tariff being removed each year. Those industries thought to require the most adjustment to free trade — such as agriculture — are given the full ten years before losing all tariff protection.

IMPACT In effect, after more than 100 years, the FTA finally rids us of the remnants of the National Policy, which included high tariff protection.

But this does not mean that all the American branch plants that have been established to get around our tariff will now pack up and go home. Had we never had the National Policy, many of the foreign firms would have set up anyway because of the growing Canadian market.

However, while the theory of comparative advantage tells us that eventually both Canada and the United States will be better off because of the agreement, in the short to medium term there will be significant adjustment cost. As those industries that cannot compete shrink, and thus shed employees, structural unemployment will rise since many of the displaced workers in shrinking industries will lack the skills needed in expanding industries. Retraining programs will be crucial to minimize the short- to medium-term restructuring costs.

NONTARIFF BARRIERS (NTBS) Under the FTA, Canada and the United States have agreed to reduce trade obstacles by endeavouring to standardize their product standards, testing, and approval processes. Moreover, to the extent that such standardization does not exist, this must not be used as an NTB to prevent the import of goods from the other country. There is plenty of ground for disagreement between the two countries in this area.

SERVICES The FTA imposes a "standstill" on services trade restrictions. Generally, the FTA imposes an obligation on both countries to accord national treatment to foreign service providers, including the right to establish a commercial presence, except where it is necessary to do otherwise for reasons relating to "prudential, fiduciary, health and safety, or consumer protection" concerns. But even here differential treatment must not involve implicit protection for domestic firms.

ENERGY Under the FTA, Canada can no longer restrict oil and natural gas exports to the United

States unless it at the same time restricts supply by the same proportion in Canada. Canada may not impose export taxes and thus charge Americans higher prices than those existing in Canada.

THE AUTO SECTOR   The whole idea of negotiating an FTA was much criticized on the basis that it would destroy the 1965 Automotive Products Trade Agreement between Canada and the United States (the Auto Pact). It seems instead that the FTA simply made marginal changes in the Auto Pact and thus induced the Americans not to end it outright.

What the Americans had been objecting to was that, until the FTA came into effect at the beginning of 1989, Japanese firms operating in Canada could get Canadian duties on their imports from Japan remitted by exporting from Canada to the United States. The Americans looked on this as an export subsidy. The issue of whether Japanese company-made cars in Canada should be treated as those produced by the "Big Three" auto companies has been the source of some disagreement between Canada and the United States.

EXCLUSIONS FROM THE FTA   The following areas are excluded:

1. *Agricultural marketing boards*
2. *Cultural industries*
3. *Social insurance programs* (Medicare, pensions, unemployment insurance, welfare)
4. *Regional development programs*

1. AGRICULTURAL MARKETING BOARDS   Those opposed to the FTA claimed that trade in agricultural commodities would bring prices down to levels below those set by the marketing boards, making their supply management (restriction) ineffective. Farmers would end up selling directly to the market and getting whatever price they could. However, the FTA specifically allows the Americans to maintain only their market share during the five years prior to the agreement in poultry, eggs, and products thereof. The dairy industry, too, has been protected from American competition.

Despite the agreement to remove all tariffs within ten years, either country may apply a temporary tariff on fresh fruit and vegetables for a period of twenty years.

Both countries agreed to work towards the removal of all agricultural subsidies that distort agri-cultural trade, including participation in multilateral trade negotiations. Canada and the United States were not so much working to reduce their own bilateral subsidies as expressing their partnership in working to bring down the high agricultural subsidies of the EU and of Japan. These subsidies have led to massive surpluses and low prices and have forced Canada and the United States to match them with their own subsidies to prevent the bankruptcy of many of their farmers. The success of the Uruguay Round will reduce agricultural subsidies between 1995 and 2005.

2. CULTURAL INDUSTRIES   Although cultural industries are specifically exempt from the FTA, each country has the right to retaliate against action taken by the other country that would have violated the terms of the trade deal had cultural industries been included. Thus, if the Canadian or a provincial government were to subsidize the writing of better Canadian economics textbooks and restrict the subsidy to Canadians, the American government would be justified in restricting, say, the sale of Canadian beef in the United States until the loss to Canadian ranchers equalled the subsidy to Canadian authors.

3. SOCIAL INSURANCE PROGRAMS   There is no reference to Canada's social programs in the FTA. Critics insist that the Americans will at one point claim that our social programs are a subsidy to Canadian business and retaliate by putting countervailing duties on our exports to the extent of the assumed subsidies. The government's answer has been that such general subsidies as social programs cannot lead to countervailing action under international law.

4. REGIONAL DEVELOPMENT PROGRAMS   The arguments on both sides here are similar to those relating to social programs: the government claims that such general subsidies cannot lead to countervailing duties. Although the government may well be right on social programs, it may find that the Americans will be harder to convince on regional-development programs — unless the Americans can be made to acknowledge that they have very extensive regional-development programs of their own, even though they call them by different names.

SUBSIDIES   What constitutes a subsidy is not easy to define, and there has been disagreement between Canada and the United States on this point. In 1992 the United States imposed a 6.51% duty on softwood lumber, maintaining that the industry was being subsidized. Although the duty was subsequently removed, Canadian and American negotiators will have to resolve the issue.

COMPLIANCE BY THE PROVINCES Article 103 of the FTA obliges both governments to ensure that "all necessary steps are taken in order to give effect to its provisions, including the observance, except as otherwise provided in this Agreement, by state, provincial, and local governments." Thus, the FTA is binding or must be made binding by the federal government on the junior governments.

DISPUTE SETTLEMENT

Under the FTA, a binational panel is established to settle disputes. This panel is a final court of appeal, *but* it can only determine whether each country's regulators are correctly applying their own trade laws — laws that may have been legislated *after* the coming into force of the FTA. The panel is *not* entitled to judge the merits of any particular case.

ENDING THE FTA

Either country may end the FTA with six months' notice. However, since U.S. exports to Canada account for only 1.3% of U.S. GDP while Canadian exports to the United States account for over 20% of Canadian GDP, the United States can end the agreement and hardly feel it. Canada could not end the FTA without at least being deeply concerned about the effects on Canadians' living standards.

THE RESULTS OF THE FTA

The consensus among economists is that the FTA has been beneficial for Canada once all costs and benefits are considered. In the first six years of its operation, exports to the United States have grown significantly, particularly in those goods on which tariffs were lowered. While imports have also increased, they have not done so to the same extent as exports. In 1994 exports to the United States totalled $177.9 billion, while imports totalled $151.6 billion, for a net surplus trade balance of $26.3 billion. It must be stressed the growth of exports to the United States is a reversal of the trend in the years leading to the FTA.

On the cost side, it is indisputable that the FTA has brought about much rationalization of industries in Canada, with negative consequence to structural unemployment. This outcome was foreseen, but government promises of mass retraining programs have only partly been fulfilled and with mixed results. For some individuals, the FTA has indeed been costly, but when we consider the fact that our exports to the United States have increased significantly, we can also see that for many other Canadians the FTA so far has been a success. We also have to consider the counterfactual: what would have been the economic outcome had Canada not signed the FTA? Seen in this light, the growing protectionist trend in the United States prior to the FTA could have resulted in a much worse outcome than the one we have seen.

THE NORTH AMERICAN FREE-TRADE ZONE

In 1993 Canada, Mexico, and the United States formed a trade bloc. The **North American Free Trade Agreement (NAFTA)** established a free-trade zone having about the same combined output as the EU, but a much larger geographical area. The agreement went into effect January 1, 1995. When fully implemented in 1999, the agreement is expected to generate $1 billion to $3 billion of annual gains for each nation.

Free trade with Mexico is even more controversial in Canada than is free trade with the United States. Critics fear a loss of Canadian jobs as firms move to Mexico to take advantage of lower wages and less stringent pollution and workplace safety regulations. Critics also are concerned that Japan and South Korea will build plants in Mexico to ship goods tariff-free through the United States and into Canada, further hurting domestic firms and workers.

Defenders of NAFTA reject these concerns and cite several strong arguments in its favour.

1. Specialization according to comparative advantage will enable Canada to obtain more total output from its scarce resources.
2. The reduction of high Mexican tariffs will increase Canadian exports to Mexico.
3. This free-trade zone will encourage worldwide investment in Mexico, enhancing Mexican productivity and national income. Mexican consumers will use some of that increased income to buy Canadian exports.

4. The higher standard of living in Mexico will enable Mexico to afford more pollution-control equipment and to provide safer workplaces.

5. The loss of specific Canadian jobs to Mexico may have occurred anyway to low-wage countries such as South Korea, Taiwan, and Hong Kong. NAFTA will enable and encourage Canadian firms to be more efficient, enhancing their long-term competitiveness with firms in Japan and the European Union.

REASONS FOR JOINING NAFTA

It may appear that the world's nations are combining into potentially hostile trade blocs. But NAFTA constitutes a vehicle to negotiate reductions in trade barriers with the EU, Japan, and other trading countries. Access to the vast North American market is as important to the EU and Japan as is access to their markets by Canada, the United States, and Mexico. NAFTA gives Canada a lever in future trade negotiations with the EU and Japan. Conceivably, direct negotiations between NAFTA and the EU could eventually link the two free-trade zones. Japan and other major trading nations, not wishing to be left out of the world's wealthiest trade markets, would be forced to eliminate their high trade barriers — to open their domestic markets to additional imports. Nor do other nations and trade blocs want to be excluded from North America. Example:

1. APEC In late 1994 Canada and 17 other members of the Asia-Pacific Economic Cooperation (APEC) nations agreed to establish freer trade and more open investment over the next few decades. APEC nations are Australia, Brunei, Canada, Chile, Hong Kong, Indonesia, Japan, Malaysia, Mexico, New Zealand, the Philippines, Papua New Guinea, Singapore, South Korea, Taiwan, Thailand, and the United States.

2. ADMISSION OF CHILE INTO NAFTA At the invitation of Canada, Mexico, and the United States, Chile has agreed to become the fourth partner in NAFTA.

3. MERCOSUR The free-trade area encompassing Brazil, Argentina, Uruguay, and Paraguay — called Mercosur — is interested in linking up with NAFTA. So are other South American Countries. In late 1994 the Canadian prime minister and 33 other prime ministers and presidents of Western hemisphere nations agree to begin negotiations on a free-trade area from "Alaska to Argentina."

Canada had defensive reasons to join in NAFTA. If it had chosen to exclude itself from the agreement, it would have been excluded from bilateral agreements between the United States and Mexico, to the detriment of Canadian exporters seeking access to the Mexican market. Even in the U.S. market, Canada could have ended up at a competitive disadvantage vis à vis Mexico in the American market.

Subsequent events to the signing of NAFTA have also pointed to another reason for joining NAFTA — trade liberalization that may eventually include the Western hemisphere. If, as it is likely, Chile officially joins NAFTA, there will undoubtedly be demands from other nations in the Western hemisphere to join in; many of these claims will probably be defensive actions in a bid not to be excluded.

NAFTA'S STRENGTHENING OF THE RULES OF ORIGIN

NAFTA has strengthened the rules of origin to ensure a certain amount of North American content in goods produced and traded among Canada, United States, and Mexico. For example, a car built by Toyota in Ontario must have a specified minimum percentage of its parts produced in North America. This will in effect protect some producers against foreign competition.

Already disputes have arisen between the Canadian and U.S. governments over whether the Honda plant in Canada was meeting the content requirements on its automobiles shipped to the United States. While the rules of origin are clearer in NAFTA compared to the FTA, they will likely continue to be a source of dispute.

NAFTA AND CONCERNS ABOUT ENVIRONMENTAL AND LABOUR LAWS

Critics of NAFTA were particularly vocal against Canada joining because of concern over the perceived less stringent regulations of Mexico's environmental and workplace safety regulations, which would put producers there at a huge competitive advantage when added to the lower wages in Mexico. These concerns were expressed equally strongly in both Canada and the United States over the course of negotiations.

Proponents of NAFTA pointed out that Mexico has adequate laws to protect the environment and workplace safety but these laws are not strongly enforced. Provisions in the agreement make it possible for Canada and the United States to demand Mexico enforce its own environmental and labour laws. Thus NAFTA ensures a higher compliance by its three members to laws that protect the environment and make the workplace safer for workers than in its absence.

Both critics and defenders of NAFTA agree on one point: It constitutes a powerful trade bloc to counter the European Common Market. Access to the vast North American market is as important to Common Market nations as is access to the European market by Canada, the United States, and Mexico. Observers believe negotiations between the North American trade bloc and the Common Market will follow, eventually resulting in a free-trade agreement between the two blocs.

Economists agree that the ideal free-trade area would be the world. **(Key Question 10)**

QUICK REVIEW 20-3

1. The various "rounds" of the General Agreement on Tariffs and Trade (GATT) have established multinational reductions in tariffs and import quotas among the more than 120 member nations.

2. The Uruguay Round of GATT that went into effect in 1995: **a** reduced tariffs worldwide; **b** liberalized rules impeding barriers to trade in services; **c** reduced agricultural subsidies; **d** created new protections for intellectual property; **e** phased out quotas on textiles and apparel, and **f** set up the World Trade Organization.

3. The European Union (EU), the Canada-U.S. Free Trade Agreement (FTA), and the North American Free Trade Agreement (NAFTA) have reduced trade barriers by establishing large free-trade zones.

CHAPTER SUMMARY

1. International trade is important to most nations, including Canada. Since 1965 our exports and imports have more than doubled as a percentage of GDP. Our major trading partner is the United States. Other major trading nations are Germany, Japan, the Western European nations, and the newly industrialized Asia tigers (Hong Kong, Singapore, South Korea, and Taiwan).

2. World trade is based on two considerations: the uneven distribution of economic resources among nations, and the fact that efficient production of various goods requires particular techniques or combinations of resources.

3. Mutually advantageous specification and trade are possible between any two nations so long as the domestic opportunity cost ratios for any two products differ. By specializing according to comparative advantage, nations can realize larger real incomes with fixed amounts of resources. The terms of trade determine how this increase in world output is shared by the trading nations. Increasing costs impose limits on gains from specialization and trade.

4. A nation's export supply curve shows the quantity of exports it will supply when world prices exceed the domestic price — the price in a closed, no-international-trade economy. The import demand curve reveals the quantity of imports demanded at world prices below the domestic price. In a two-nation model, the equilibrium world price and the equilibrium quantities of exports and imports occur where one nation's import supply curve intersects another nation's export demand curve.

5. Trade barriers take the form of protective tariffs, quotas, nontariff barriers, and "voluntary" export restrictions. Supply and demand analysis reveals that protective tariffs and quotas increase the prices and reduce the quantities demanded of affected goods. Foreign exporters find their sales diminish. Domestic producers, however, enjoy higher prices and enlarged sales. Tariffs and quotas promote a less efficient allocation of domestic and world resources.

6. The strongest arguments for protection are the infant-industry and military self-sufficiency arguments. Most of the other arguments for protection are half-truths, emotional appeals, or fallacies that emphasize the immediate effects of trade barriers while ignoring long-run consequences. Numerous historical examples suggest that free trade promotes economic growth; protectionism does not.

7. Protectionism costs Canadian consumers large amounts annually. The cost to consumers for each job saved is far greater than the average salary paid. Consumer losses from trade restrictions greatly exceed producer and government gains, creating an efficiency loss to society.

8. Recent Canadian international trade policy entails: **a** general liberalization of trade through NAFTA and GATT; and **b** bilateral negotiations over specific trade disputes.

9. The Uruguay Round of GATT negotiations, completed in 1993: **a** reduced tariffs; **b** liberalized trade in services; **c** reduced agricultural subsidies; **d** reduced pirating of intellectual property; **e** phased out import quotas on textiles and apparel; and **f** established the World Trade Organization, which replaces GATT.

10. Free-trade zones (trade blocs) may liberalize trade within regions but may also impede trade with nonbloc members. Three examples of free-trade arrangements are **a** the European Union (EU), formerly the European Community or "Common Market"; **b** the Canada-U.S. Free Trade Agreement (FTA); and **c** the North American Free Trade Agreement (NAFTA), comprising Canada, Mexico, and the United States, and later, Chile.

TERMS AND CONCEPTS

absolute advantage (p. 428)
Canada–U.S. Free Trade Agreement (FTA) (p. 446)
comparative advantage (p. 430)
cost ratio (p. 428)
domestic price (p. 433)
dumping (p. 441)
economic integration (p. 445)
European Union (EU or Common Market) (p. 445)
export supply curve (p. 434)
gains from trade (p. 432)
General Agreement on Tariffs and Trade (GATT) (p. 445)
import demand curve (p. 435)
import quotas (p. 437)

labour- (land-, capital-) intensive commodity (p. 427)
most-favoured-nation clause (p. 444)
National Policy (p. 444)
nontariff barriers (NTBs) (p. 437)
North American Free Trade Agreement (NAFTA) (p. 448)
revenue and protective tariffs (p. 437)
strategic trade policy (p. 441)
terms of trade (p. 430)
trade bloc (p. 445)
trading possibilities line (p. 431)
voluntary export restrictions (VERs) (p. 437)
world price (p. 433)
World Trade Organization (p. 445)

QUESTIONS AND STUDY SUGGESTIONS

1. Quantitatively, how important is international trade to Canada relative to other nations?

2. Distinguish among land-, labour- and capital-intensive commodities, citing an example of each. What role do these distinctions play in explaining international trade?

3. Suppose nation A can produce 80 units of X by using all its resources to produce X and 60 units of Y by devoting all its resource to Y. Comparative figures for nation B are 60 of X and

60 of Y. Assuming constant costs, in which product should each nation specialize? Why? Indicate the limits of the terms of trade.

4. **Key Question**   *The following are hypothetical production possibilities tables for New Zealand and Spain.*

New Zealand's production possibilities table (millions of bushels)

Product	Production alternatives			
	A	B	C	D
Apples	0	20	40	60
Plums	15	10	5	0

Spain's production possibilities table (millions of bushels)

Product	Production alternatives			
	R	S	T	U
Apples	0	20	40	60
Plums	60	40	20	0

Using a graph, plot the production possibilities data for each of the two countries. Referring to your graphs, determine:

a. *Each country's domestic opportunity cost of producing plums and apples;*

b. *Which nation should specialize in which product;*

c. *The trading possibilities lines for each nation if the actual terms of trade are 1 plum for 2 apples.*

d. *Suppose the optimum product mixes before specialization and trade were B in New Zealand and S in Spain. What are the gains from specialization and trade?*

5. "Canada can produce product X more efficiently than can Great Britain. Yet we import X from Great Britain." Explain.

6. **Key Question**   *Refer to Figure 4-5. Assume the graph depicts Canada's domestic market for oats. How many bushels of oats, if any, will Canada export or import at a world price of $1, $2, $3, $4, and $5? Use this information to construct Canada's export supply curve and import demand curve for oats. Suppose the only other oats-producing nation is France, where the domestic price is $4. Why will the equilibrium world price be between $3 and $4? Who will export oats at this world price; who will import it?*

7. **Key Question**   *Draw a domestic supply and demand diagram for a product in which Canada does not have a comparative advantage. Indicate the impact of foreign imports on domestic price and quantity. Now show a protective tariff that eliminates approximately one-half the assumed imports. Indicate the price-quantity effects of this tariff to a. domestic consumers, b. domestic producers, and c. foreign exporters. How would the effects of a quota that creates the same amount of imports differ?*

8. "The most valid arguments for tariff protection are also the most easily abused." What are these arguments? Why are they susceptible to abuse? Evaluate the use of artificial trade barriers, such as tariffs and import quotas, as a means of achieving and maintaining full employment.

9. Evaluate the following statements:

   a. "Protective tariffs limit both the imports and the exports of the nation levying tariffs."

   b. "The extensive application of protective tariffs destroys the ability of the international market system to allocate resources efficiently."

   c. "Unemployment can often be reduced through tariff protection, but by the same token inefficiency typically increases."

   d. "Foreign firms that 'dump' their products onto the Canadian market are in effect presenting the Canadian people with gifts."

   e. "In view of the rapidity with which technological advance is dispersed around the world, free trade will inevitably yield structural maladjustments, unemployment and balance of payments problems for industrially advanced nations."

   f. "Free trade can improve the composition and efficiency of domestic output. Only the Volkswagen forced Detroit to make a compact car, and only foreign success with the oxygen process forced Canadian steel firms to modernize."

   g. "In the long run foreign trade is neutral with respect to total employment."

10. From 1981 to 1985 the Japanese agreed to a voluntary export restriction that reduced Canadian imports of Japanese automobiles by about 10%. What would you expect the short-run effects to have been on the Canadian and Japanese automobile industries? If this restriction were permanent, what would be its long-run effects on a. the allocation of resources, b. the volume of employment, c. the price level, and d. the standard of living in the two nations?

11. *Key Question* *What are the benefits and the costs of protectionist policies? Which are larger, benefits or costs?*

12. What are NAFTA and GATT and how do they relate to international trade? What policies has the Canadian government recently used to promote our exports?

13. (Applying the Theory) What point is Bastiat trying to make with his petition of the candlemakers?

CHAPTER 21

EXCHANGE RATES AND THE BALANCE OF PAYMENTS

If you take a Canadian dollar to the bank and ask to exchange it for Canadian currency, you will get a puzzled look and, if you are persistent enough, perhaps another dollar. One Canadian dollar can buy exactly one Canadian dollar. But, as of mid-June 1995, one Canadian dollar could buy .84 Swiss francs, 1.13 Dutch guilders, .45 British pounds, .73 U.S. dollars, 3.5 French francs, 1.0 German mark, 61 Japanese yen, and 1190 Italian lire. What explains this seemingly haphazard array of exchange rates?

In Chapter 20 we examined comparative advantage as the underlying economic basis of world trade and discussed the effects of barriers to free trade. In this chapter we want to introduce the monetary or financial aspects of international trade. How are the currencies of various nations exchanged when import and export transactions occur? We also analyze and interpret a nation's balance of international payments. What is meant by a "favourable" or "unfavourable" balance of trade? Finally, the kinds of exchange-rate systems that trading nations have used are explained and evaluated. In this discussion we examine the polar extremes of freely flexible and fixed exchange rates and then survey systems that have been employed in the recent past.

BOX 21-1   THE BIG PICTURE

Nations trade with one another, but each has a different currency. Moreover, as they trade with one another, in any given year some nations import more than they export, or export more than they import. To complicate matters, financial capital moves across international markets seeking the highest returns. This chapter looks at how nations keep a record of these international transactions and how the value of the Canadian dollar against other currencies is determined.

As you read this chapter, keep the following points in mind:

- If nations did not trade and there were no capital movements across national boundaries, there would be no need for a balance of payment account or an exchange-rate market.

- Think of transactions between nations as roughly similar to exchange between individuals. It will help you to better understand trade and financial transactions between nations.
- The value of any currency is determined by the demand and supply for that currency.
- In order for Canada to purchase goods and services from other nations, it needs to earn foreign exchange by exporting goods or services, otherwise it will have to either borrow foreign exchange or draw down its reserves (savings) of foreign exchange.
- There is a trade-off between rate stability and the desire for autonomy in domestic macroeconomic policy making. Exchange-rate volatility is an ongoing political issue.

FINANCING INTERNATIONAL TRADE

One thing that makes international trade different from domestic trade is the use of two different national currencies. When Canadian firms export goods to British firms, the Canadian exporter wants to be paid in dollars; but the British importers have pounds sterling. They must exchange pounds for dollars to permit the Canadian export transaction to occur.

This problem is resolved by **foreign-exchange markets** in which Canadian dollars can purchase American dollars, British pounds, Japanese yen, German marks, Italian lire, and other currencies and vice versa. Sponsored by major banks in Toronto, Montreal, New York, London, Zurich, Tokyo, and elsewhere, foreign-exchange markets facilitate Canadian exports and imports.

CANADIAN EXPORT TRANSACTION

Suppose a Canadian exporter agrees to sell $30,000 worth of lumber to a British firm. Assume that the **rate of exchange** — the rate or price at which pounds can be exchanged for, or converted into, dollars, and vice versa — is $2 for £1. This means

the British importer must pay £15,000 to the Canadian exporter. Let's track what occurs by using simple bank balance sheets (Figure 21-1).

(a) To pay for the Canadian lumber, the British importing firm draws a cheque on its demand deposit (chequing account entry) in a London bank for £15,000. This is shown by the –£15,000 demand deposit entry in the right-hand side of the balance sheet of the London bank.

(b) The British firm sends this £15,000 cheque to the Canadian exporter. But the Canadian exporting firm must pay its employees, materials suppliers, and taxes, in dollars, not pounds. So the exporter sells the £15,000 cheque or draft on the London bank to a Canadian bank that is a dealer in foreign exchange and is located, say, in Vancouver. The Canadian firm is given a $30,000 demand deposit in the Vancouver bank in exchange for the £15,000 cheque. Note the new demand deposit entry of +$30,000 in the Vancouver bank.

(c) What does the Vancouver bank do with the £15,000? It deposits it in a correspondent London bank for future sale. Thus, +£15,000 of demand deposits appear in the liabilities column of the balance sheet of the London bank. At the same time this +£15,000 ($30,000) is an asset, as viewed by

FIGURE 21-1   Financing a Canadian export transaction

LONDON BANK		VANCOUVER BANK	
Assets	Liabilities and net worth	Assets	Liabilities and net worth
	Demand deposit of British importer − £15,000 *(a)*	Deposit in London bank + £15,000 *(c)* ($30,000)	Demand deposit of Canadian exporter + $30,000 *(b)*
	Deposit of Vancouver bank + £15,000 *(c)*		

Canadian export transactions create a foreign demand for dollars. The satisfaction of this demand increases the supplies of foreign monies held by Canadian banks.

the Vancouver bank. To simplify, we assume this correspondent bank is the same bank from which the British firm obtained the £15,000 draft.

Note these points.

1. *Canadian exports create a foreign demand for dollars, and the satisfaction of this demand generates a supply of foreign monies — pounds, in this case — held by Canadian banks and available to Canadian buyers.*
2. The financing of a Canadian export (British import) reduces the supply of money (demand deposits) in Britain and increases the supply of money in Canada by the amount of the purchase.

CANADIAN IMPORT TRANSACTION

Let's now suppose that a Canadian retail business wants to import £15,000 worth of woollens from a British mill. Again, simple bank balance sheets track what goes on (Figure 21-2).

(a) Because the British exporting firm must pay its obligations in pounds rather than dollars, the Canadian importing firm must exchange dollars for pounds. It does this by going to the Vancouver bank and purchasing £15,000 for $30,000 — perhaps the Canadian importer purchases the very same £15,000 that the Vancouver bank acquired in the previous Canadian export transaction. In Figure 21-2, this purchase reduces the Canadian importer's demand deposit in the Vancouver bank by $30,000, and the Vancouver bank gives up its £15,000 deposit in the London bank.

(b) The Canadian importer sends its newly purchased cheque for £15,000 to the British firm, which deposits it in the London bank where it is recorded as a +£15,000 deposit in the liabilities and net worth column of its balance sheet.

Here, you see that:

1. *Canadian imports create a domestic demand for foreign monies (pounds sterling, in this*

FIGURE 21-2   Financing a Canadian import transaction

LONDON BANK		VANCOUVER BANK	
Assets	Liabilities and net worth	Assets	Liabilities and net worth
	Demand deposit of British exporter + £15,000 *(b)*	Deposit in London bank − £15,000 *(a)* ($30,000)	Demand deposit of Canadian importer − $30,000 *(a)*
	Deposit of Vancouver bank − £15,000 *(a)*		

Canadian import transactions create a Canadian demand for foreign monies. Fulfilling that demand reduces the supplies of foreign monies held by Canadian banks.

case) and that the fulfilment of this demand reduces the supplies of foreign monies held by Canadian banks.

2. A Canadian import transaction increases the supply of money in Britain and reduces the supply of money in Canada.

By combining export and import transactions, a further point comes into focus. Canadian exports (lumber) make available, or "earn," a supply of foreign monies for Canadian banks, and Canadian imports (British woollens) create a demand for these monies. *In a broad sense, any nation's exports finance or "pay for" its imports.* Exports provide the foreign currencies needed to pay for imports. From Britain's point of view, its exports of woollens earn a supply of dollars that are then used to meet the demand for dollars associated with Britain's imports of lumber.

Although our examples are confined to the exporting and importing of goods, demands for and supplies of pounds also arise from transactions involving services and the payment of interest and dividends on foreign investments. Canadians demand pounds not only to finance imports, but also to purchase insurance and transportation services from the British, to vacation in England, to pay dividends and interest on British investments in Canada, and to make new financial and real investments in Britain. **(Key Question 2)**

THE INTERNATIONAL BALANCE OF PAYMENTS

We now explore the variety of international transactions that create a demand for and generate a supply of a specific currency. This spectrum of international trade and financial transactions is reflected in Canada's **international balance of payments**. A nation's balance of payments statement records *all* of the transactions that take place between its residents (including individuals, businesses, and governmental units) and the residents of all foreign nations. These transactions include merchandise exports and imports, imports and exports of services, interest and dividends received or paid abroad, purchases and sales of financial or real assets abroad, and so on. *Canada's balance of payments shows the balance between all the payments Canada receives from other countries and all the payments that we make to them.* Canada's balance of payments for 1994 is presented in Table 21-1.

Note the two-part division: **current account** and **capital account**, the latter including change in **official international reserves**. Let's analyze this accounting statement to see what it reveals about Canadian international trade and finance.

CURRENT ACCOUNT

The top portion of Table 21-1 summarizes Canada's trade in currently produced goods and services and is called the **current account**. Item 1 shows Canadian exports and imports of merchandise (goods) respectively in 1994. We designate Canadian exports with a *plus* sign because Canadian merchandise exports (and other export-type transactions) are **credits**. They create or earn supplies of foreign exchange. As we saw in our discussion of how international trade is financed, any export-type transaction obligating foreigners to make "inpayments" to Canada generates supplies of foreign monies in Canadian banks.

We designate Canadian imports with a minus sign. Canadian imports (and other import-type transactions) are **debits**; they use up foreign exchange. Our earlier discussion of trade financing indicated that Canadian imports obligate Canadians to make "outpayments" to the rest of the world that draw down available supplies of foreign currencies held by Canadian banks.

MERCHANDISE TRADE BALANCE Item 1 in Table 21-1 tells us that in 1994 our merchandise exports of $217,854 million was more than the merchandise imports of $202,807 million. The **merchandise trade balance** refers to the difference between a country's merchandise exports and merchandise imports. If exports exceed imports, the result is a *merchandise trade surplus* or "favourable balance of trade." If imports exceed exports, then there is a *merchandise trade deficit* or "unfavourable balance of trade" occurring. In 1994 Canada incurred a trade surplus of $15,047 million. The Canadian trade balance is broken down by country or region in Global Perspective 21-1.

BALANCE OF TRADE Item 2 reveals that Canada not only exports autos and computers, but also sells transportation services, insurance, and tourist and brokerage services to residents of foreign countries. These service sales or "exports" totalled $31,519 million in 1994. Canadians also buy or

TABLE 21-1 Canada's balance of payments, 1994 (*in millions of dollars*)

Current Account	Receipts (exports) + (inpayments)	Payments (imports) − (outpayments)	Balance
1. Merchandise (Goods)	$217,854	$202,807	$+15,047
2. Services ("Invisibles") (a) travel (tourism)	10,194	15,949	−5,759
(b) freight and shipping	7,635	7,234	+401
(c) business services	11,689	15,409	−3,720
(d) government transactions	830	1,393	−563
(e) other services	1,171	964	+207
(f) Total services	$ 31,519	$ 40,949	$ −9,430
3. Total goods and services (balance of trade)(X_n)	$249,373	$243,756	$ +5,617
4. Investment income (interest, dividends, miscellaneous)	$ 11,824	$ 40,719	$−28,895
5. Transfers (a) inheritances and immigrants' funds	$ 1,752	$ 362	$ +1,390
(b) personal and institutional remittances	1,428	1,361	+67
(c) official contributions		1,871	−1,871
(d) withholding tax	1,690	296	+1,394
(e) Total transfers	$4,869	$ 3,890	$ +979
6. Total current account (= current account balance) [1 + 2(f) + 4 + 5(e)]	$266,066	$288,365	$−22,299
Capital Account			
7. Direct investment (*excluding* reinvested earnings)			$ +1,713
8. Portfolio securities (a) bonds			+14,625
(b) stocks			−3,163
9. Government of Canada assets (a) official international reserves			+1,630
(b) loans & subscriptions			−1,893
10. Allocation of Special Drawing Rights (SDRs)			0
11. Other capital movements			+5,429
12. Total capital account, net flow			$+18,341
13. Statistical Discrepancy (6) + (12) (with sign reversed)			$ +3,958

Source: Statistics Canada, *Canada's Balance of International Payments, First Quarter,* 1995, Tables 1 and 9, cat. no. 67-001.

"import" similar services from foreigners. These service imports were $40,949 million in 1994. The **balance of trade** or net exports, shown in item 3, is the difference between our imports and exports of goods and services. In 1994, the balance was +$5,617 million, meaning we exported more than we imported.

INVESTMENT INCOME Note that one of the services Canadians get from nonresidents consists of the services of foreign money capital that has been invested in Canada. Line 4 indicates that the interest, dividends, and miscellaneous payments made for the use of foreign capital invested in Canada are a payment for Canada's "import" of the services of this capital. Canada also receives interest and dividends for the "export" of the services of our capital invested abroad. A glance at the last column of line 4 shows that we have a negative balance.

TRANSFERS A third component of Canada's current account is **transfers** — lines 5(a) to (e) in Table 21-1. Note that Canada has a surplus of over $1 billion annually in inheritances and immigrants' funds (line 5[a]). Immigrants as a whole bring more money with them than they send back to their relatives. Personal and institutional remittances, line 5(b), was at a slight surplus in 1994.

Official contributions, line 5(c), shows that the Canadian government makes substantial loans and grants to other countries, mostly through the United Nations. These loans and grants are for economic aid, which the government calls "official development assistance," totalling about $1.9 billion in the 1994 fiscal year. Of this amount, a substantial portion is channelled through the government's Canadian International Development Agency (CIDA).

Note that adding the balances on goods (merchandise) and services together gives us our balance of trade, while adding the balances on services, investment income, and transfers together gives us our **nonmerchandise trade balance**, which was minus 37,346 million in 1994.

CURRENT ACCOUNT BALANCE By taking all the transactions in the current account into consideration, we obtain the **current-account balance** shown by item 6 in Table 21-1. In 1994, Canada had a current-account deficit of $22,299 million. Our current-account import transactions created a demand for a larger quantity of foreign currencies than our export transactions supplied.

CAPITAL ACCOUNT

The **capital account** reflects capital flows in the purchase or sale of real and financial assets. Canadians — both individuals and businesses — make investments in, and extend loans to, other countries. For example, some Canadian corporations have become multinational by purchasing or constructing plants or outlets in foreign countries. Or Canadians may buy the securities — stocks and bonds — of foreign firms, or buy back our own foreign-held securities. Or Canadian individuals or

firms may make deposits in foreign banks or hold foreign currency deposits in our own banks.

All such transactions involve capital outflows. Just like Canadian imports of goods, these Canadian investing and lending transactions provide foreigners with Canadian dollars. Canadian investors and lenders abroad *import* securities — claims of ownership to foreign assets, claims against foreign banks.

Foreigners engage in similar capital transactions in Canada. They may purchase real assets in Canada, buy Canadian stocks and bonds, make deposits in Canadian banks, and so forth. In these instances, Canada is, in effect, *exporting* securities and claims and, as with merchandise or service exports, getting inflows or inpayments of foreign money — overwhelmingly U.S. dollars — in return.

In the capital account section of Table 21-1 an *export* (outflow) of capital is shown with a minus sign and an *import* (inflow) of capital with a *plus* sign. The outflow of liquid capital pays for the *import* of bonds, shares, and titles of property, while the inflow of liquid capital pays for their *export*.

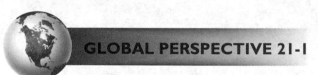

Canada's trade balance with selected nations, 1994

Canada has a net export surplus with the United States and Japan, but a net export deficit with the European Union, and other countries.

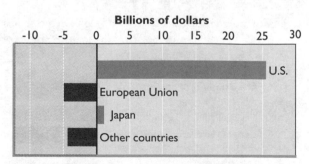

Source: Statistics Canada

DIRECT AND PORTFOLIO INVESTMENT This category in Lines 7 and 8(a) and (b) of Table 21-1 reveals the amount of net *new* long-term foreign investment that occurred in Canada in 1994. There is a distinction between **direct** and **portfolio investment**. Direct investment occurs when a nonresident owns enough of an enterprise in Canada to control it, while portfolio investment is the buying of bonds and company shares for the sake of the return in the form of interest, dividends, and possibly capital gains should the bond or share price appreciate.

OFFICIAL INTERNATIONAL RESERVES Our **official international reserves** are the federal government's and the Bank of Canada's holdings of gold, foreign currencies, and Special Drawing Rights (SDRs) at the International Monetary Fund. SDRs are explained later in this chapter. As will be discussed below, the official international reserves act as the item that assures the current and capital account "balance" to be zero.

CAPITAL ACCOUNT BALANCE The sum of all the items in the capital account (lines 7 to 11) of Table 21-1 gives us the **capital account balance** (line 12). In 1994, Canada realized a capital account surplus of $18,341 million; we exported more stocks and bonds and titles to property in Canada than we imported.

STATISTICAL DISCREPANCY Adding the balance on the current account (line 6) to the balance on the capital account (line 12) in Table 21-1 should result in zero. As a glance at line 13 will show, the balance in 1994 was not zero; it was plus $3,958 million. This is the **statistical discrepancy**, which StatsCan describes as an "indicator of errors and unrecorded transactions." Examples would be investments made by Canadians in foreign real estate markets that did not pass through Canadian intermediaries. In 1994, some $3,958 million flowed into Canada for which StatsCan cannot account.

BALANCE OF PAYMENT SURPLUSES AND DEFICITS AND THE OFFICIAL INTERNATIONAL RESERVES

Although the overall balance of payments will always balance at zero (item 13), as will be seen shortly, the balancing item is in fact the official international reserves. To help you understand the following discussion, you should think of the official international reserves as separate from the capital account.

The central banks of nations hold quantities of gold and foreign currencies. They are added to or drawn on to settle any *net* differences between the current and capital account balances. As can be seen in Table 21-2, a simplified version of Table 21-1, in 1994 the official international reserves were drawn down by $1.630 billion. That is, Canada had a **balance of payment deficit**; our country earned less foreign monies in all financial trade and financial transactions than it used. This deficit of earnings of foreign currencies was subtracted from the existing stock of foreign monies held by our central bank. The *plus* $1,630 million of official reserves shown in item 10 of Table 21-2 represents a decrease of our stock of foreign currencies.

The relationship between the current and capital account can be just the opposite in the case of **balance of payment surplus**. If the capital accounts surplus were larger than the current account deficit, the Bank of Canada would increase its holding of foreign currencies. This would show as a *minus* item in the balance of payment.

To summarize:

1. A balance of payments surplus occurs when line 10 in Table 21-2 is negative — when the Bank of Canada increases the international reserves it holds in the Exchange Fund Account by buying them in the foreign-exchange market with Canadian dollars.
2. A balance of payment deficit occurs when line 10 in Table 21-2 is positive — when the Bank of Canada decreases the international reserves it holds in the Exchange Fund Account by selling them on the foreign exchange market for Canadian dollars.

Thus, the official international reserves are the balancing item in our international balance of payments.

The detail in Table 21-1 is too great to allow a quick grasp of Canada's current balance of payments. Table 21-2 reduces the data of Table 21-1 to the minimum.

INTERRELATIONSHIPS

The current and capital accounts are interrelated; they are reflections of one another. A current-account *deficit* tells us that Canadian exports of goods and services were not sufficient to pay for our imports of goods and services. How did we finance the difference? The answer is that Canada must either borrow from abroad or give up ownership of some of its assets to foreigners as reflected in the capital account.

TABLE 21-2 Simplified balance of payments, Canada, 1994 (*millions of dollars*)

	Exports (receipts) (+)	Imports (payments) (–)	Balance ("net")
Current Account			
1. Merchandise (goods)	$217,854	$202,807	$+15,047
2. Services	31,519	40,949	–9,430
3. Balance of trade (X_n)			$+5,617
4. Investment income	11,824	40,719	–28,895
5. Transfers	4,869	3,890	+979
6. Total current account (3 + 4 + 5)			$–22,299
Capital Account			
7. Net direct investment			$+1,713
8. Net portfolio investment			+11,462
9. Other capital flows			+3,536
10. Official international reserves			+1,630
11. Statistical discrepancy			+3,958
12. Total capital account (7 + 8 + 9 + 10 + 11)			+22,299
13. Overall balance of payments			0

A simple analogy is useful in explaining this notion. Suppose in some year your expenditures exceed your earnings. How will you finance your "deficit"? You might sell some of your assets or borrow. You might sell some real assets (your car or stereo) or perhaps some financial assets (stocks or bonds) that you own. Or you might obtain a loan from your family or a bank.

Similarly, when a nation incurs a deficit in its current account, its expenditures for foreign goods and services (its imports) exceed the income received from the international sales of its own goods and services (its exports). It must finance that current-account deficit by either drawing down its official international reserves, selling foreign assets, or borrowing, that is, by going into debt.

Figure 21-3 shows the trend in Canada's current, capital, and the official international reserves since 1975. What stands out is that after 1985 Canada's current account has been in a persistent and growing deficit, while the capital account has been in a surplus. The cause of the current account deficit is not a deficit on the merchandise balance but the persistent deficit in services and investment income. We have been net borrowers of capital and our usual surplus in our merchandise balance is not enough to cover the capital outflows associated with repaying our debts to nonresidents. Indeed, foreign ownership of Canadian assets has been climbing to record levels, led by rising sales of bonds to foreign investors.

Borrowing from foreigners is not inherently bad. If we use the borrowed capital to invest in plant and equipment that will increase our productive capacity, we can easily repay the borrowed capital. But capital borrowed abroad to finance consumption will mean a lower standard of living for Canadians in the future since part of the country's output must go to repay the loan, along with interest payments on the borrowed funds. (**Key Question 3**)

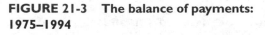

FIGURE 21-3   The balance of payments: 1975–1994

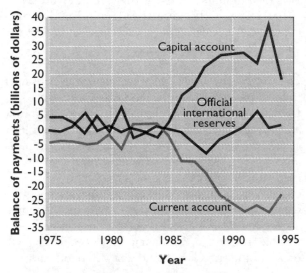

Source: *Bank of Canada Review,* Summer 1995.

After the mid-1980s, a large current account developed along with a capital account surplus.

QUICK REVIEW 21-1

1. Canadian *exports* create a supply of foreign currencies; Canadian *imports* create a demand for foreign currencies.

2. The current account balance is a nation's exports of goods and services less its imports of goods and services plus its net investment income and net transfers.

3. The capital account balance is a nation's capital inflows less its capital outflows.

4. A balance of payments deficit occurs when the official international reserves are drawn down; a balance of payments surplus arises when the official international reserves rise.

FLEXIBLE EXCHANGE RATES

Both the size and persistence of a nation's balance of payments deficits and surpluses and the kinds of adjustments it must make to correct these imbalances depend on the system of exchange

rates being used. There are two polar options: (1) a system of **flexible** or **floating exchange rates**, where the rates at which national currencies exchange for one another are determined by demand and supply; and (2) a system of **fixed exchange rates**, by which government intervention in foreign-exchange markets or some other mechanism offsets the changes in exchange rates that fluctuations in demand and supply would otherwise cause.

Freely floating exchange rates are determined by the unimpeded forces of demand and supply. Let's examine the rate, or price, at which Canadian dollars might be exchanged for American dollars. **Figure 21-4 (Key Graph)** shows the demand for U.S. dollars as downsloping; the supply of American dollars as upsloping.

The downsloping *demand for U.S. dollars* shown by *D* indicates that, if the U.S. dollar becomes less expensive to Canadians, American goods will become cheaper to Canadians. Canadians will demand

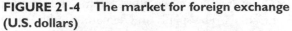

KEY GRAPH

FIGURE 21-4   The market for foreign exchange (U.S. dollars)

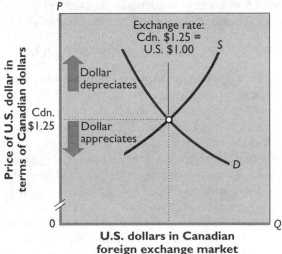

The demand for U.S. dollars is downsloping because, as U.S. dollars become less expensive, all American goods and services become cheaper, therefore Canadians will increase their purchases of both U.S. dollars and goods and services. The supply of U.S. dollars is upsloping because at higher Canadian dollar prices for U.S. dollars, Americans will want to purchase larger quantities of our goods and services. The intersection of the demand and supply curves will determine the equilibrium rate of exchange.

larger quantities of American goods and therefore larger amounts of U.S. dollars to buy those goods.

The *supply of U.S. dollars S* is upsloping, because as the Canadian dollar price of a U.S. dollar *rises*, Americans will purchase more Canadian goods. When Americans buy Canadian goods, they supply U.S. dollars to the foreign exchange market because they must exchange their dollars for ours to purchase Canadian goods.

The intersection of the supply and demand for U.S. dollars will determine the dollar price of U.S. dollars. Here, the equilibrium rate of exchange is U.S. \$1 = Cdn \$1.25.

We have chosen to analyze the determination of the exchange rate vis-à-vis the U.S. dollar. The same analysis would hold for any other currency. We could have pursued the analysis via the supply and demand for Canadian dollars on the international market. For reasons that will become apparent in the next chapter, our chosen method will more clearly reveal the impact of the exchange rate market on Canada's money supply. It is important you note that in our analysis the exchange rate market is *in* Canada. The supply and demand conditions for a given currency *in* Canada will determine its exchange rate vis-à-vis the Canadian dollar.

DEPRECIATION AND APPRECIATION

An exchange rate determined by free-market forces can and does change frequently. When the Canadian dollar price of a U.S. dollar increases, for example, from \$1.25 to \$1.37, the value of the dollar has **depreciated** relative to the U.S. dollar. Currency depreciation means that it takes more units of a country's currency to buy a single unit of some foreign currency.

When the dollar price of U.S. dollars decreases — from \$1.25 to \$1.15 — the value of the Canadian dollar has **appreciated** relative to the U.S. dollar. Currency appreciation means that it takes fewer units of a country's currency to buy a single unit of some foreign currency.

In our illustrations, when the Canadian dollar depreciates, the U.S. dollar appreciates, and vice versa. When the exchange rate between Canadian dollars and U.S. dollars changes from \$1.25 to \$1.37, it takes *more* Canadian dollars to buy one U.S. dollar and thus the Canadian dollar has depreciated. These relationships are shown in Figure 21-4.

DETERMINANTS OF EXCHANGE RATES

Why are the demand for and the supply of American dollars located as they are in Figure 21-4? What forces will cause the demand and supply curves or American dollars to change and cause the Canadian dollar to appreciate or depreciate?

CHANGES IN TASTES   Any change in consumer tastes or preferences for the products of a foreign country will alter the demand for that nation's currency and change its exchange rate. If Canadian technological advances in telecommunications make them more attractive to American consumers and businesses, then American consumers will supply more American dollars in exchange markets in purchasing more Canadian equipment and the Canadian dollar will appreciate. If American beer becomes more fashionable in Canada, our demand for U.S. dollars will increase and the Canadian dollar will depreciate.

RELATIVE INCOME CHANGES   If the growth of a country's national income is more rapid than that of other countries, its currency is likely to depreciate. As incomes rise in Canada, Canadians buy more domestically produced goods *and* more foreign goods. If the Canadian economy is expanding rapidly and the American economy is stagnant, Canadian imports of American goods — and therefore Canadian demand for U.S. dollars — will increase. The U.S. dollar will rise in terms of the Canadian dollar, meaning the Canadian dollar has depreciated.

RELATIVE PRICE CHANGES   If the domestic price level rises rapidly in Canada and remains constant in the United States, Canadian consumers will seek out low-priced American goods, increasing the demand for U.S. dollars. Americans will be less inclined to purchase Canadian goods, reducing the supply of U.S. dollars. This combination of an increase in the demand for, and a reduction in the supply of, U.S. dollars will cause the Canadian dollar to depreciate.

Differences in price levels among nations — which reflect changes in price levels over time — help explain persistent differences in exchange rates. In mid-1995, a Canadian dollar could buy .45 British pounds and 73 Japanese yen. One reason for these differences is that the price level in pounds in Great Britain was far lower than the price level in Japan.

Generally, the higher a nation's price level in terms of its own currency, the greater is the amount of that currency that can be obtained by a unit of another nation's currency.

Taken to extreme, this **purchasing power parity theory** holds that differences in exchange rates *equate* the purchasing power of various currencies; they adjust to match the ratios of the nations' price levels. Thus, a dollar spent on goods sold in Britain, Japan, Argentina, and other nations supposedly will have equal purchasing power. In practice, however, exchange rates depart significantly from purchasing power parity, even over long periods. Nevertheless, relative price levels are a determinant of exchange rates.

RELATIVE REAL INTEREST RATES What if Canada restricts the growth of its money supply (tight monetary policy), as was the case in the late 1970s, early 1980s, and in 1994 to control inflation? As a result, *real* interest rates — money interest rates adjusted for the rate of inflation — were high in Canada in comparison with the United States. Consequently, Americans found Canada to be an attractive place to make financial investments. This increase in the demand for Canadian financial assets increased the supply of U.S. dollars and the Canadian dollar therefore appreciated in value.

SPECULATION Suppose it is widely anticipated that the Canadian economy will (a) grow faster than the American economy, (b) experience more rapid inflation than the United States, and (c) have lower future real interest rates than the United States. All of these expectations would lead us to believe that in the future the Canadian dollar will depreciate and the U.S. dollar will appreciate. Holders of Canadian dollars will attempt to convert them into U.S. dollars, increasing the demand for U.S. dollars. This conversion causes the Canadian dollar to depreciate and the U.S. dollar to appreciate. Note that the exchange rate consequences occur now, not when the forecast events are expected to occur.

Table 21-3 provides additional illustrations to reinforce your understanding of the determinants of exchange rates.

FLEXIBLE RATES AND THE BALANCE OF PAYMENTS

Proponents argue flexible exchange rates have a compelling virtue: *they automatically adjust so as eventually to eliminate current-account deficits or surpluses.* We can explain this by looking at S_0 and D_0 in **Figure 21-5 (Key Graph)**, which restate two of the demand for, and supply of, U.S. dollar curves from Figure 21-4. The equilibrium exchange rate of Cdn $1.25 = U.S. $1 means there is no current-account deficit or surplus. With the U.S. dollar at Cdn $1.25, the quantity of U.S. dollars demanded by Canadians in order to import American goods, buy American transportation and insurance services, and to pay interest and dividends on American investments in Canada are equal to the amount of U.S. dollars supplied by Americans in buying Canadian exports, purchasing services from Canadians, and

TABLE 21-3 **Determinants of exchange rates: factors that change demand or supply of a particular currency and thus alter the exchange rate**

1. Changes in tastes Examples: Japanese autos decline in popularity in Canada (Japanese yen depreciates, Canadian dollar appreciates); German tourists flock to Canada for vacations (Canadian dollar appreciates, German mark depreciates).

2. Changes in relative incomes Example: England encounters a recession, reducing its imports, while Canadian real output and real income surge, increasing Canadian imports (British pound appreciates, Canadian dollar depreciates).

3. Changes in relative prices Example: Germany experiences a 3% inflation rate compared to the United States' 10% rate (German mark appreciates, American dollar depreciates).

4. Changes in relative real interest rates Example: The Bank of Canada drives up interest rates in Canada, while the Bank of England takes no such action (Canadian dollar appreciates, British pound depreciates).

5. Speculation Examples: Currency traders believe France will have much more rapid inflation than Sweden (French franc depreciates; Swedish krona appreciates); currency traders think German interest rates will plummet relative to Canadian rates (German mark depreciates, Canadian dollar appreciates).

KEY GRAPH

FIGURE 21-5   Adjustments under flexible exchange rates, fixed exchange rates, and the gold standard

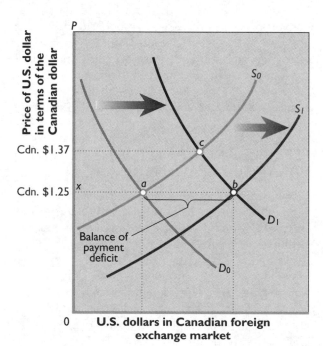

Under flexible rates, a Canadian current-account deficit at the Cdn $1.25 for U.S. $1 rate would be corrected by an increase in the rate to Cdn $1.37 for U.S. $1. Under fixed rates, the *ab* shortage of U.S. dollars would be met out of official international reserves. Under the gold standard, the deficit would cause changes in domestic price and income levels that would shift the demand for U.S. dollars (D_1) to the left and the supply (S_0) to the right, re-establishing equilibrium at the Cdn $1.25 for U.S. $1 rate.

making interest and dividend payments on Canadian investments in the United States.

Suppose tastes change and Canadians buy more American automobiles. Or the Canadian price level has increased relative to the United States, or real interest rates have fallen in Canada as compared to the United States. Any or all of these changes will cause the Canadian demand for U.S. dollars to increase from D_0 to D_1 in Figure 21-5.

We observe that *at the initial Cdn $1.25 = U.S. $1 exchange rate* a Canadian balance of payment

deficit has been created in the amount *ab*. At the Cdn $1.25 = U.S. $1 rate there is a shortage of U.S. dollars for Canadians in the amount of *ab*. Canadian export-type transactions will earn *xa* U.S. dollars, but Canadians will want *xb* U.S. dollars to finance import-type transactions. Because this is a free competitive market, the shortage will change the exchange rate (the price of the U.S. dollar in terms of the Canadian dollar) from Cdn $1.25 = U.S. $1 to, say, Cdn $1.37 = U.S. $1. The Canadian dollar has *depreciated*.

At this point, it must be emphasized that *the exchange rate is a special price that links all domestic (Canadian) prices with all foreign (American) prices*. A change in the exchange rate alters the prices of all American goods to Canadians and all Canadian goods to potential American buyers. The change in the exchange rate from Cdn $1.25 = U.S. $1 to Cdn $1.37 = U.S. $1 will alter the relative attractiveness of Canadian imports and exports so as to restore equilibrium in the Canadian balance of payments. From the Canadian point of view, as the Canadian dollar price of U.S. dollars changes from Cdn $1.25 to Cdn $1.37, the automobile priced at U.S. $10,000 that formerly cost a Canadian Cdn $12,500 now costs Cdn $13,700 ($1.37 × $10,000). Other American goods will also cost more to Canadians, and Canadian imports of American goods and services will decline. Graphically, this is shown as a move from point *b* towards point *c* in Figure 21-5.

From the U.S. standpoint, the exchange rate — the price of the Canadian dollar — has fallen (from U.S. $0.80 to U.S. $0.73). The value of the U.S. dollar has *appreciated* in Canada. Americans previously got only Cdn $1.25 for U.S. $1; now they get Cdn $1.37 for U.S. $1. Canadian goods are therefore less expensive to Americans, and as a result Canadian exports to the United States will rise. In Figure 21-5 this is indicated by the move from point *a* towards point *c*.

The two adjustments described — a decrease in Canadian imports from the United States and an increase in Canadian exports to the United States — are precisely those needed to correct the Canadian current-account deficit. (You should reason through the operation of freely fluctuating exchange rates in correcting an initial Canadian current-account surplus in its trade with the United States.) **(Key Question 6)**

DISADVANTAGES OF FLEXIBLE RATES

Though freely fluctuating exchange rates automatically work to eventually eliminate balance of payments imbalances, they may cause several significant problems.

1. UNCERTAINTY AND DIMINISHED TRADE The risks and uncertainties associated with flexible exchange rates may discourage the flow of trade.

2. TERMS OF TRADE A nation's terms of trade will worsen by a decline in the international value of its currency. For example, a decrease in the price of the Canadian dollar in U.S. terms will mean that Canada must export a larger volume of goods and services to finance a given level of imports from the United States.

3. INSTABILITY Freely fluctuating exchange rates may have destabilizing effects on the domestic economy as wide fluctuations stimulate and then depress industries producing internationally traded goods. If the Canadian economy is operating at full employment and the international value of its currency depreciates, as in our illustration, the results will be inflationary for two reasons. Foreign demand for Canadian goods will increase — the net exports component of aggregate expenditures will increase and cause demand-pull inflation. Also, the price of all Canadian imports will increase. Conversely, appreciation of the dollar could lower exports and increase imports, causing unemployment.

FIXED EXCHANGE RATES

At the other extreme, nations have often fixed or "pegged" their exchange rates in an effort to circumvent the disadvantages associated with floating rates. To analyze the implications and problems associated with **fixed exchange rates**, assume Canada has decided to maintain an exchange rate of Cdn $1.25 = U.S. $1.

The problem is a government proclamation that a Canadian dollar worth so much in terms of the U.S. dollar does *not* enforce stability of the demand for and the supply of U.S. dollars. As demand and supply shift over time, government must intervene directly or indirectly in the foreign-exchange market if the exchange rate is to be stabilized.

In Figure 21-5 suppose the Canadian demand for U.S. dollars increases from D_0 to D_1 and a Canadian balance of payments deficit of *ab* arises. This means the Canadian government is committed to an exchange rate (Cdn $1.25 = U.S. $1) that is below the equilibrium rate (Cdn $1.37 = U.S. $1). How can Canada prevent the shortage of U.S. dollars — reflecting a Canadian balance of payments deficit — from driving the exchange rate up to the equilibrium level? The answer is to alter market demand or supply or both, so that they continue to intersect at the Cdn $1.25 = U.S. $1 rate of exchange. There are several ways to do this.

USE OF RESERVES

The most desirable means of pegging an exchange rate is to manipulate the market through the use of foreign-exchange reserves. Let's assume that in the past the Canadian government had acquired a surplus in the Exchange Fund Account. By selling a part of its reserves of U.S. dollars, the Canadian government could shift the supply of U.S. dollars curve to the right so that S_1 intersects D_1 at *b* in Figure 21-5, thereby maintaining the exchange rate at Cdn $1.25 = U.S. $1.

It is critical that the amount of reserves be enough to accomplish the required increase in the supply of U.S. dollars. This is *not* a problem if deficits and surpluses occur more or less randomly and are about the same size. But if Canada encounters persistent and sizable deficits for an extended period, then the reserves problem can become critical and force the abandonment of a system of fixed exchange rates. Another way of looking at the depletion problem is to consider the supply and demand for American dollars, and therefore the balance of payments as representing flows. An ongoing outflow of reserves will eventually deplete the stock of foreign-exchange reserves.

A nation whose reserves are inadequate must resort to less appealing options if it hopes to maintain exchange-rate stability. Let's consider these options.

TRADE POLICIES

One set of policy options entails measures designed to control directly the flows of trade and finance. Canada might try to maintain the Cdn $1.25 = U.S. $1 exchange rate in the face of a shortage of U.S. dollars by discouraging imports and by encouraging exports. Imports can be reduced by tariff or import quotas. Special taxes may be levied on the interest and dividends that Canadians receive for foreign investments. Also, the Canadian govern-

BOX 21-2   APPLYING THE THEORY

SPECULATION IN CURRENCY MARKETS

Contrary to popular belief, speculators often play a positive role in currency markets.

Most people buy foreign currency to facilitate buying goods or services produced in another country. A Canadian importer buys Japanese yen to purchase Japanese-made automobiles. A British investor purchases marks to buy shares in the German stock market. But there is another group of participants in the currency market — speculators — who buy foreign currencies solely to resell for profit. A British pound bought for $2.00 earns a 10% return when sold for $2.20.

Speculators sometimes contribute to exchange-rate volatility. The expectation of currency appreciation or depreciation can be self-fulfilling. If speculators expect the Japanese yen to appreciate, they sell other currencies to buy yen. The sharp increase in demand for yen boosts its value, which may attract other speculators — people expecting the yen to rise further. Eventually, the yen's value may soar too high relative to economic realities such as tastes, real interest rates, price levels, and trade balances. The "speculative bubble" bursts and the yen plummets.

But speculative bubbles are not the norm in currency markets. Changed economic realities, not speculation, usually are the cause of changing currency values. Anticipating these changes, speculators simply hasten the adjustment process. Most major adjustments in currency values persist long after the speculators have sold their currency and made their profits.

Speculation, in fact, has two positive effects in foreign exchange markets.

1. LESSENING RATE FLUCTUATIONS   Speculation smooths out fluctuations in currency prices. When temporarily slack demand or excess supply reduces a currency's value, speculators quickly buy it, adding to the demand and strengthening its value. When temporarily strong demand or weak supply increases a currency's value, speculators sell the currency. This selling increases the supply of the currency and reduces its value. In this way speculators smooth out supply and demand — and thus exchange rates — from period to period. We know that exchange rate stability facilitates international trade.

2. ABSORBING RISK   Speculators aid international trade in another way: *They absorb risk that others do not want to bear.* International transactions are riskier than domestic transactions because of potential adverse changes in exchange rates. Suppose AnyTime, a hypothetical Canadian retailer, signs a contract with a German manufacturer to buy 10,000 German clocks to be delivered in three months. The stipulated price is 75 marks per clock, which in dollars is $50 per clock at an exchange rate of $1 = 1.5 mark. AnyTime's total bill will be $500,000 (= 750,000 marks).

But if the German mark would appreciate, say, to $1 = 1 mark, the dollar price per clock would rise from $50 to $75 and AnyTime would owe $750,000 for the clocks (= 750,000 marks). AnyTime may reduce part of the risk of unfavourable exchange-rate fluctuations by hedging in the futures market. *Hedging is an action by a buyer or a seller to protect against a change in future prices. The futures market is a market where items are bought and sold at prices fixed now, for delivery at a specified date in the future.*

AnyTime can purchase the needed 750,000 marks at the current $1 for 1.5 mark exchange rate to be made available in three months when the German clocks are delivered. And here is where speculators arrive on the scene. For a price determined in the futures market, they agree to deliver the 750,000 marks to AnyTime in three months at the $1 = 1.5 mark exchange rate, regardless of the exchange rate then. The seller of the futures contract need not own marks at the time the contract is made. If the German mark *depreciates* to, say, $1 = 2 marks in this period, the speculator makes a profit. He or she can buy the 750,000 marks stipulated in the contract for $375,000, pocketing the difference between that amount and the $500,000 AnyTime has agreed to pay for the 750,000 marks.

If the German mark *appreciates*, the speculator — but not AnyTime — suffers a loss. The amount AnyTime will have to pay for this futures contract will depend on how the market views the likelihood of the mark depreciating, appreciating, or staying constant over the three-month period. As in all highly competitive markets, supply and demand determine the price of the futures contract.

Unfortunately, the futures market does not entirely eliminate exchange-rate risks. Suppose the mark depreciates in the three-month delivery period and a competing importing firm did *not* hedge its foreign-exchange purchase. This means the competitive retailer will obtain its shipment of clocks at less than $50 per

clock and can underprice AnyTime. But the futures market *does* eliminate much of the exchange-rate risk associated with buying foreign goods for future delivery. With the full exchange-rate risk, AnyTime might have decided against importing German clocks. The futures market and currency speculators greatly reduce that risk, increasing the likelihood the transaction will occur. *Operating through the futures market, speculation promotes international trade.*

ment might subsidize certain Canadian exports and increase the supply of U.S. dollars.

The fundamental problem with these policies is they reduce the volume of world trade and distort its composition, or pattern, away from that which is economically desirable. Tariffs, quotas, and the like can be imposed only at the sacrifice of some portion of the economic gains or benefits attainable from a free flow of world trade based on comparative advantage. These effects should not be underestimated; the imposition of trade barriers can elicit retaliatory responses from other countries that are adversely affected.

EXCHANGE CONTROLS: RATIONING

Another option is **exchange controls**, or rationing. Under exchange controls, the Canadian government would handle the problem of a U.S. dollar shortage by requiring all U.S. dollars obtained by Canadian exporters be sold to the government. Then the government would allocate this short supply of U.S. dollars (*xa* in Figure 21-5) among various Canadian importers, who demand the quantity *xb*. In this way, the Canadian government would restrict Canadian imports to the amount of foreign exchange earned by Canadian exports. Canadian demand for U.S. dollars in the amount *ab* would be unfulfilled. Government eliminates a balance of payments deficit by restricting imports to the value of exports.

There are many objections to exchange controls.

DISTORTED TRADE Like trade policies — tariffs, quotas, and export subsidies — exchange controls distort the pattern of international trade away from comparative advantage.

DISCRIMINATION The process of rationing scarce foreign exchange means discrimination among importers. Serious problems of equity and favouritism are implicit in the rationing process.

RESTRICTED CHOICE Controls impinge on freedom of consumer choice. Canadians who prefer Toyotas may be forced to buy Fords. The business opportunities of some Canadian importers will be impaired because imports are constrained by government.

BLACK MARKETS There are likely to be enforcement problems. The market forces of demand and supply indicate there are Canadian importers who want foreign exchange badly enough to pay more than the Cdn $1.25 = U.S. $1 official rate; this sets the stage for extra-legal or "black market" foreign-exchange dealings.

DOMESTIC MACRO ADJUSTMENTS

A final means of maintaining a stable exchange rate is to use restrictive fiscal and monetary measures that will reduce Canada's national income relative to the United States' and restrain our demand for American goods — and, therefore, for U.S. dollars.

To the extent that these contractionary policies reduce Canada's price level relative to that of the United States, Canadian buyers of consumption and investment goods will divert their demands from American to Canadian goods, also restricting the demand for U.S. dollars.

Finally, a restrictive (tight) monetary policy will increase Canadian interest rates as compared to American rates, reducing Canadian demand for U.S. dollars to make financial investments in the United States.

BOX 21-3 IN THE MEDIA

CENTRAL BANK DEFENDS DOLLAR

Intervention eases decline; rate rise signals prime jump

BY MARIAN STINSON
Money Markets Reporter

The Bank of Canada jumped to the defence of the embattled dollar yesterday — a move that threatens another prime rate hike — as market watchers criticized the central bank for causing the currency turmoil by not acting weeks ago.

At one point yesterday, the dollar fell by one-third of a cent — changing hands at 70.70 cents (U.S.) for the first time since March, 1986. By late in the day, it bounced back to 70.92 cents, down 0.07 cents from Monday, when it lost half a cent.

The bank's key signal to financial markets yesterday was the "reverses" at 5.75 per cent — selling treasury bills for repurchase later — which sent a clear and long-awaited sign that the cost of overnight loans would be half a percentage point higher, in the range of 5.75 to 6.25 per cent. More expensive short-term financing increases the cost of speculative selling of the dollar.

"[The reverses] should have happened five weeks ago," said Andrew Pyle, economist with MMS International. Such action would have taken pressure off the dollar at a time when worries about the Mexican peso have put North American currencies under scrutiny, he added.

Continuing upward pressure on short-term rates is likely to cause a half-percentage-point increase in prime and higher mortgage rates, Mr. Pyle said. Prime is currently 8 per cent.

The Bank of Canada bought the currency yesterday at 70.90 cents to moderate the fall.

The rebound in the dollar came after the bank rate rose 12 basis points to 7.24 per cent in its regular weekly setting. However, treasury bill rates continued to climb after the setting, pointing to a further increase next week of as much as 25 basis points. The bank rate is pegged at one-quarter of a percentage point, above the average yield on three-month treasury bills. (A basis point is 1/100th of a percentage point.)

The Bank of Canada has been trying to raise interest rates slowly in order to insulate Canadian borrowers from the impact of rising U.S. rates, said Jeffrey Rubin, chief economist at Wood Gundy Inc. He believes the Canadian central bank should match or exceed rate increases by the U.S. Federal Reserve Board.

"I'm not a fan of how the Bank of Canada has been managing the currency," he added. He believes aggressive interest rates hikes are needed in order to protect the currency from selling by speculators that would drive it down to new lows....

SOURCE: *Globe and Mail*, January 11, 1995, p. B1. Reproduced by permission.

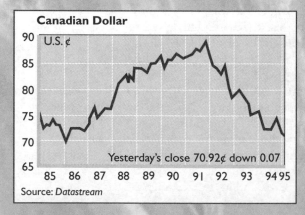

Canadian Dollar

Yesterday's close 70.92¢ down 0.07

Source: *Datastream*

The Story in Brief

In late 1994 and early 1995, the Canadian dollar came under considerable downward pressure against the U.S. dollar. This was due to a number of reasons, including an almost 40% plunge of the Mexican peso against the U.S. dollar.

The Economics Behind the Story

- The exchange rate for a currency is determined by the supply and demand for it on international markets.

- In late 1994 the Mexican peso plunged against most of the world's currencies. Many international investors holding any of the North American currencies — the Canadian dollar, the U.S. dollar, or Mexican peso — sold off these currencies (increased their supply), causing our Canadian dollar to fall against many other currencies.

- While the American dollar was also experiencing downward pressure, our dollar was falling against the U.S. dollar.

- The Bank of Canada intervened in the exchange rate market in Canada to moderate the fall of the Canadian dollar. The Bank of Canada also raised short-term interest rates to attract foreign investors. When foreign investors invest in Canadian securities, they require Canadian dollars, which helps raise its value.

- Explain how the value of the Canadian dollar against the U.S. dollar is determined by the demand and supply of the American dollars in the Canadian foreign exchange market.

This means of maintaining pegged exchange rates is hardly appealing. The "price" of exchange-rate stability for Canada is a recession. Achieving a balance of payments equilibrium and realizing domestic stability are both important national economic objectives; but to sacrifice the latter for the former is to let the tail wag the dog.

QUICK REVIEW 21-2

1. Under a system of freely floating exchange rates, exchange rates are determined by the demand for, and supply of, individual national currencies.

2. Determinants of freely floating exchange rates — factors that shift currency supply and demand curves — include changes in tastes, changes in relative national incomes, relative price level changes, relative real interest rate changes, and speculation.

3. Under a system of fixed exchange rates, nations set their exchange rates and then maintain them by buying or selling reserves of foreign currencies, establishing trade barriers, employing exchange controls, or incurring inflation or recession.

INTERNATIONAL EXCHANGE-RATE SYSTEMS

There have been three different exchange-rate systems that nations have employed in recent history.

THE GOLD STANDARD: FIXED EXCHANGE RATES

During the 1879–1934 period — with the exception of the World War I years — an international monetary system known as the *gold standard* prevailed. The **gold standard** provided for fixed exchange rates. A look at its operation and ultimate downfall helps us see the functioning and some of the advantages and problems with fixed-rate systems. Currently a number of economists advocate fixed exchange rates and a few even call for a return to the international gold standard.

CONDITIONS   A nation is on the gold standard when it fulfils three conditions. It must:

1. define its monetary unit in terms of a certain quantity of gold;
2. maintain a fixed relationship between its stock of gold and its domestic money supply;
3. allow gold to be freely exported and imported.

If each nation defines its monetary unit in terms of gold, the various currencies will have a fixed relationship to one another. Suppose Canada defines its dollar as worth 23.22 grains of gold, the United States having already defined its dollar as worth the same amount. This means that the United States and Canadian dollar are equal in value. This, indeed, was the situation that existed while both countries were on the gold standard: either dollar could be exchanged for 23.22 grains of gold.

GOLD FLOWS Now, if we ignore the costs of packing, insuring, and shipping gold between countries, under the gold standard the rate of exchange would not vary from this $1 for $1 rate. And the reason is clear: no one in Canada would pay more than Cdn $1 for U.S. $1, because one could always buy 23.22 grains of gold for Cdn $1 in Canada, ship it to the United States, and sell it for U.S. $1.

In practice the costs of packing, insuring, and shipping gold must be taken into account. But these costs would only amount to a few cents per 23.22 grains of gold. If these costs were 3¢ for 23.22 grains of gold, Canadians wanting U.S. dollars would pay up to Cdn $1.03 for a U.S. dollar rather than buy and export 23.22 grains of gold to get that U.S. dollar. Why? Because it would cost them $1 for the 23.22 grains of gold plus 3¢ to send it to the United States to be exchanged for U.S. $1. This Cdn $1.03 exchange rate, above which gold would begin to flow out of Canada, is called the **gold export point**.

The exchange rate would fall to Cdn $0.97 before gold would flow into Canada. Americans wanting Canadian dollars would accept as little as Cdn $0.97 in exchange for U.S. $1, because from the Cdn $1 they could get by buying 23.22 grains of gold in the United States and reselling it in Canada, 3¢ must be subtracted to pay shipping and related costs. This Cdn $0.97 exchange rate, below which gold would flow into Canada, is called the **gold import point**.

Under the gold standard, the flow of gold between nations would result in exchange rates that for all practical purposes are fixed.

DOMESTIC MACRO ADJUSTMENTS Figure 21-5 explains the kinds of adjustments that the gold standard would produce. Initially the demand for and the supply of U.S. dollars are D_0 and S_0 and their intersection point at a coincides with the fixed exchange rate that results from the "in gold" definitions of the Canadian and U.S. dollars. Now suppose that for some reason Canadian preferences for American goods increase, shifting the demand for U.S. dollars to D_1. In Figure 21-5 there is now a shortage of U.S. dollars equal to ab, implying a Canadian balance of payments deficit.

What will happen? Remember that the rules of the gold standard game prohibit the exchange rate from moving from the fixed U.S. $1 = Cdn $1.25 relationship; the rate *cannot* move up to a new equilibrium of U.S. $1 = Cdn $1.37 at point c, as it would under freely floating rates. The exchange rate would rise by a few cents to the Canadian gold export point at which gold would flow from Canada to the United States.

Recall that the gold standard requires participants to maintain a fixed relationship between their domestic money supplies and their quantities of gold. The flow of gold from Canada to the United States would bring about a contraction of the money supply in Canada and an expansion of the money supply in the United States. Other things equal, this will reduce aggregate demand and, therefore, lower real domestic output, employment, and the price level in Canada. Also, the reduced money supply will boost Canadian interest rates.

The opposite occurs in the United States. The inflow of gold boosts the money supply, increasing aggregate demand, real domestic output, employment, and the price level. The increased money supply will also lower interest rates in the United States.

In Figure 21-5 declining Canadian incomes and prices will reduce our demand for American goods and services and therefore reduce the Canadian demand for U.S. dollars. Lower interest rates in the United States will make it less attractive for Canadians to buy U.S. bonds, also lessening the demand for U.S. dollars. For all these reasons the D_1 curve will shift to the left.

Similarly, increased incomes and prices in the United States will increase American demand for Canadian goods and services and higher Canadian interest rates will encourage the Americans to buy more Canadian bonds. These developments all increase the supply of U.S. dollars available to Canadians, shifting the S_0 curve of Figure 21-5 to the right.

Note the critical difference in the adjustment mechanisms associated with freely floating exchange rates and the fixed rates of the gold standard. With floating rates the burden of the adjustment is on the exchange rate itself. In contrast, the gold standard involves changes in the domestic money supplies of participating nations that precipitate changes in price levels, real output and employment, and interest rates.

The drawback of the gold standard is that nations must accept domestic adjustments in such distasteful forms as unemployment and falling incomes on the one hand, or inflation, on the other. In using the gold-standard (fixed-exchange-rate) game, countries must be willing to submit their domestic economies to painful macroeconomic adjustments. A nation's monetary policy would be determined largely by changes in the demand for and supply of foreign exchange. If Canada, for example, was already moving towards recession, the loss of gold under the gold standard would reduce its money supply and intensify the problem. Under the international gold standard, nations forgo independent monetary policies.

DEMISE The worldwide Great Depression of the 1930s signalled the end of the gold standard. As domestic outputs and employment plummeted worldwide, the restoration of prosperity became the primary goal of afflicted nations. Protectionist measures were enacted as nations sought to increase net exports and stimulate their domestic economies. And each country was fearful that its economic recovery would be aborted by a balance of payments deficit that would lead to an outflow of gold and consequent contractionary effects. Indeed, nations attempted to devalue their currencies in terms of gold so as to make their exports more attractive and imports less attractive. These devaluations undermined a basic condition of the gold standard, and the system broke down.

THE BRETTON WOODS SYSTEM

Not only did the Great Depression of the 1930s lead to the downfall of the gold standard, it also prompted the erection of trade barriers that greatly impaired international trade. World War II was similarly disruptive to world trade and finance. As World War II drew to a close in the mid-1940s, the world trading and monetary systems were in shambles.

To lay the groundwork for a new international monetary system, an international conference of nations was held at Bretton Woods, New Hampshire, in 1944. This conference produced a commitment to an *adjustable-peg system* of exchange rates, called the **Bretton Woods system**. The new system sought to capture the advantages of the old gold standard (fixed exchange rates), while avoiding its disadvantages (painful domestic macroeconomic adjustments).

Furthermore, the conference created the **International Monetary Fund (IMF)** to make the new exchange-rate system feasible and workable. This international monetary system, emphasizing relatively fixed exchange rates and managed through the IMF, prevailed with modifications until

1971. The IMF continues to play a basic role in international finance and in recent years has performed a major role in ameliorating the debt problems of the less-developed countries.

IMF AND PEGGED EXCHANGE RATES Why did the Bretton Woods adjustable-peg system evolve? We have noted that during the depressed 1930s, various countries resorted to **devaluation** — devaluing[1] their currencies in the hope of stimulating domestic employment. For example, if Canada was faced with growing unemployment, it might devalue the dollar by *increasing* the Canadian dollar price of U.S. dollars from Cdn $1.25 for U.S. $1 to, say, Cdn $1.37 for U.S. $1. This action would make Canadian goods cheaper to the Americans and U.S. goods dearer to Canadians, increasing Canadian exports and reducing Canadian imports. This increase in net exports, abetted by the multiplier effect, would stimulate output and employment in Canada.

But every nation can play the devaluation game, and most did. The resulting rounds of competitive devaluation benefited no one; on the contrary, they actually contributed to further demoralization of world trade. Nations at Bretton Woods therefore agreed that the postwar monetary system must provide for an overall exchange-rate stability in which disruptive currency devaluations could be avoided.

Under the adjustable-peg system of exchange rates, as with the gold standard, each IMF member was obligated to define its monetary unit in terms of gold (or U.S. dollars), thus establishing par rates of exchange between its currency and the currencies of all other members. Each nation was further obligated to keep its exchange rate stable with respect to any other currency.

This obligation was fulfilled by governments using official international reserves to intervene in foreign-exchange markets. Assume that under the Bretton Woods system the Canadian dollar was "pegged" to the U.S. dollar at Cdn $1.25 = U.S. $1. Now suppose in Figure 21-5 the Canadian demand for U.S. dollars temporarily increases from D_0 to D_1 so that a shortage

---

[1] A note on terminology: we noted earlier in this chapter that the dollar has *appreciated* (*depreciated*) when its international value has increased (decreased) as the result of changes in the demand for, or supply of, dollars in foreign-exchange markets. The terms *revalue* and *devalue* are used to describe an increase or decrease, respectively, in the international value of a currency that occurs as the result of governmental, rather than market, action.

of U.S. dollars of *ab* arises at the pegged rate. Canada could supply additional U.S. dollars in the exchange market, shifting the supply of U.S. dollars curve to the right so that it intersects D_1 at *b* and maintains the Cdn $1.25 = U.S. $1 rate of exchange.

Where could Canada obtain the needed U.S. dollars? Under the Bretton Woods system there were three main sources.

1. RESERVES Canada might currently possess U.S. dollars in a "stabilization fund" — the Exchange Fund Account — accumulated in the past.

2. GOLD SALES The Canadian government might sell some of the gold it holds in the Exchange Fund Account to the United States for U.S. dollars. The proceeds would then be offered in the exchange market to augment the supply of U.S. dollars.

3. IMF BORROWING The needed U.S. dollars might be borrowed from the IMF. Nations participating in the Bretton Woods system were required to make contributions to the IMF on the basis of the size of their national income, population, and volume of trade.[2] If necessary, Canada could borrow U.S. dollars on a short-term basis from the IMF by supplying its own currency as collateral.

FUNDAMENTAL IMBALANCES: ADJUSTING THE PEG A fixed-rate system such as Bretton Woods functions well so long as a nation's payments deficits and surpluses occur more or less randomly and are approximately equal in size. If a nation's payments surplus last year allows it to add a sufficient amount to its official international reserves to finance this year's payments deficit, no problems would arise. But if Canada were to encounter a "fundamental imbalance" in its international trade and finance so that it was confronted with persistent and sizable payments deficits, it would eventually run out of reserves and be unable to maintain its fixed exchange rate.

---

[2] In addition, the IMF endorsed, in 1967, a plan providing for a new international money called Special Drawing Rights or, simply, SDRs. Popularly referred to as "paper gold," SDRs are created at the initiative of the directors of the IMF, but only with the approval of an 85% majority of the voting power of its participants. SDRs are made available to IMF members in proportion to their IMF quotas and can be used, as gold was once used, to settle payments deficits or satisfy reserve needs.

Under the Bretton Woods system, a fundamental payments deficit was corrected by an "orderly" reduction in the nation's pegged exchange rate (devaluation). Under the Bretton Woods system, the IMF allowed each member nation to alter the value of its currency by 10% without permission to correct a "fundamental" balance of payments deficit. Larger exchange-rate changes required the sanction of the IMF's board of directors. By requiring approval of significant rate changes, the IMF guarded against arbitrary and competitive currency devaluation prompted by nations seeking a temporary stimulus to their domestic economies.

The objective of the adjustable-peg system was a world monetary system that embraced the best features of both a fixed exchange-rate system (such as the old international gold standard) and a system of freely fluctuating exchange rates.

DEMISE OF THE BRETTON WOODS SYSTEM Under the Bretton Woods system, gold and the U.S. dollar came to be accepted as international reserves. The acceptability of gold as an international medium of exchange was derived from its role under the international gold standard of an earlier era. The U.S. dollar became acceptable as international money for two reasons.

1. The United States emerged from World War II as the world's strongest economy.
2. The United States had accumulated large quantities of gold and between 1934 and 1971 maintained a policy of buying gold from, and selling gold to, foreign monetary authorities at a fixed price of $35 per ounce. The dollar was convertible into gold on demand; the dollar came to be regarded as a substitute for gold, or "as good as gold."

But the role of the U.S. dollar as a component of official international reserves contained the seeds of a dilemma. Consider the situation as it developed in the 1950s and 1960s. The problem with gold as international money was a quantitative one. The growth of the world's money stock depends on the amount of newly mined gold, less any amount hoarded for speculative purposes or used for industrial and artistic purposes. Unfortunately, the growth of the gold stock lagged behind the rapidly expanding volume of international trade and finance. Thus the U.S. dollar came to occupy an increasingly important role as an international monetary reserve.

Economies of the world acquire U.S. dollars as reserves as the result of U.S. balance of payments deficits. With the exception of some three or four years, the United States incurred persistent payments deficits throughout the 1950s and 1960s. These deficits were financed in part by drawing-down American gold reserves. But, mostly, U.S. deficits were financed by growing foreign holdings of U.S. dollars that were "as good as gold" until 1971.

As the amount of U.S. dollars held by foreigners soared and as American gold reserves dwindled, other nations began to question whether the U.S. dollar really was "as good as gold." The ability of the United States to maintain the convertibility of the U.S. dollar into gold became increasingly doubtful, and so did the role of the U.S. dollar as generally accepted official international reserves. The United States had to reduce or eliminate its payments deficits to preserve the dollar's status as an international medium of exchange. But success in this endeavour would limit the expansion of international reserves or liquidity and therefore restrict the growth of international trade and finance.

This problem came to a head in the early 1970s. Faced with persistent and growing U.S. payments deficits, President Nixon suspended the U.S. dollar's convertibility into gold on August 15, 1971. This suspension ended the 37-year policy to exchange gold for U.S. dollars at $35 per ounce. The new policy severed the link between gold and the international value of the U.S. dollar, thereby "floating" the dollar and allowing its value to be determined by market forces. The floating of the U.S. dollar withdrew American support from the old Bretton Woods system of fixed exchange rates and sounded its death knell.

THE MANAGED FLOAT

The present exchange-rate system might best be labelled a system of **managed floating exchange rates** — floating exchange rates, accompanied by occasional currency interventions by central banks to stabilize or alter rates. It is recognized that changing economic conditions among nations require continuing changes in exchange rates to avoid persistent payment deficits or surpluses. Normally, the major trading nations allow their exchange rates to float to equilibrium levels based on supply and demand in the foreign-exchange market. The result has been considerably more volatility in exchange rates than in the Bretton Woods era (see Global Perspective 21-2).

But nations also recognize that short-term changes in exchange rates — perhaps accentuated by purchases and sales by speculators — can disrupt and discourage the flow of trade and finance. Moreover, some longer-term moves in exchange may not be desirable. Thus, at times the central banks of the various nations intervene in the foreign-exchange market by buying or selling large amounts of specific currencies. They "manage" or stabilize exchange rates by influencing currency demand and supply. Two examples:

1. THE 1987 G-7 INTERVENTION In 1987 the "Group of Seven" industrial nations (**G-7 nations**) — Canada, the United States, Germany, Japan, Britain, France, and Italy — agreed to stabilize the value of the U.S. dollar. In the previous two years the U.S. dollar had declined rapidly because of sizable American trade deficits. Although the U.S. trade deficit remained large, these nations concluded that further dollar depreciation might disrupt economic growth in the G-7 economies. The G-7 nations therefore purchased large amounts of U.S. dollars to prop up the dollar's value. Since 1987 the G-7 has periodically intervened in foreign-exchange markets to stabilize currency values.

2. THE 1995 BANK OF CANADA INTERVENTION In early 1995 the Canadian dollar eroded in value relative to the U.S. dollar. The downward pressure on the Canadian dollar was mostly the result of rising short-term interest rates in the United States. The Bank of Canada intervened in the foreign-exchange market to slow down the fall of the Canadian dollar. The Bank of Canada achieved this by selling U.S. dollars it holds in its Exchange Fund Account. By increasing the supply of U.S. dollars, the Bank of Canada tried to slow down its rise against the Canadian dollar.

Actually, the current exchange-rate system is more complicated than we just described. While the major currencies — German marks, American and Canadian dollars, Japanese yen, and the British pound — fluctuate in response to changing demand and supply conditions, some of the European Union nations attempt to peg their currencies to one another. Also, many less-developed nations peg their currencies to the U.S. dollar and allow their currencies to fluctuate with it. And some nations

GLOBAL PERSPECTIVE 21-2

Exchange rates in terms of dollars

The floating exchange rate system (managed float) has produced far more volatile exchange rates than in the earlier Bretton Woods era.

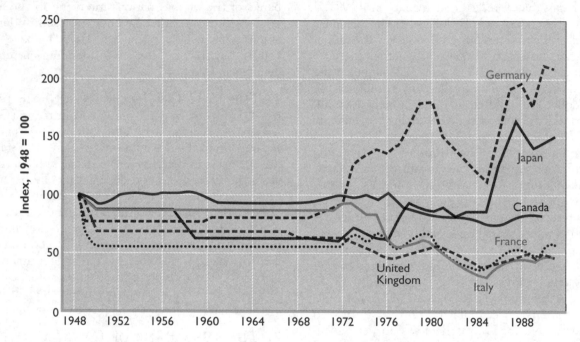

Source: U.S. Government, *Economic Report of the President*, 1993, p. 287.

peg the value of their currencies to a "basket" or group of other currencies.

How well has the managed floating system worked?

PROS Proponents argue the system has functioned well — far better than anticipated.

1. TRADE GROWTH In the first place, fluctuating exchange rates have not reduced world trade and finance as sceptics had predicted. In real terms world trade has grown at approximately the same rate under the managed float as during the decade of the 1960s under the fixed exchange rates of the Bretton Woods system.

2. MANAGING TURBULENCE Proponents argue the managed float has weathered severe economic turbulence that might have caused a fixed-

exchange regime to have broken down. Such events as worldwide agricultural shortfalls in 1972–74, extraordinary oil-price increases in 1973–74 and again in 1979–80, worldwide stagflation in 1974–76 and 1981–83, and large U.S. budget deficits in the 1980s and 1990s, all generated substantial international trade and financial imbalances. Flexible rates facilitated international adjustments to these developments, whereas the same events would have put unbearable pressures on a fixed-rate system.

CONS But there is still much sentiment in favour of greater exchange-rate stability. Those favouring stable rates see problems with the current system.

1. VOLATILITY AND ADJUSTMENT Critics argue that exchange rates have been excessively volatile under the managed float (Global Perspective 21-2). This volatility, it is argued, has occurred even when underlying economic and financial conditions of particular nations have been quite stable. Perhaps more importantly, the managed float has not readily resolved balance of payments imbalances, as flexible rates are supposed to. Thus, the United States has run persistent trade deficits in recent years, while Germany and Japan have had persistent surpluses. Changes in the international values of the U.S. dollar, the mark, and the yen have not yet corrected these imbalances.

2. A "NONSYSTEM"? Sceptics contend the managed float is basically a "nonsystem"; the rules and guidelines circumscribing the behaviour of each nation vis-à-vis its exchange rate are not sufficiently clear or constraining to make the system viable in the long run. Nations will inevitably be tempted to intervene in foreign-exchange markets, not merely to smooth out short-term or speculative fluctuations in the value of their currencies, but to prop up their currency if it is chronically weak or to manipulate the value of their currency to achieve domestic stabilization goals. There is fear that in time there may be more "managing" and less "floating" of exchange rates, and this may be fatal to the present loosely defined system.

The jury is still out on floating exchange rates in general and the managed float in particular.

Floating exchange rates have neither worked perfectly nor failed miserably. But this can be said for them: They *have* survived — and no doubt eased — several shocks to the international trading system. Meanwhile, the "managed" part of the float has given nations some sense of control over their collective economic destiny.

QUICK REVIEW 21-3

1. Under the gold standard (1879–34), nations fixed exchange rates by valuing their currencies in terms of gold, by tying their stocks of money to gold, and by allowing gold to flow between nations when balance of payment deficits and surpluses occurred.

2. The Bretton Woods, or adjustable-peg, system of exchange rates (1944–71) fixed or pegged short-run exchange rates, but permitted orderly long-run adjustments of the pegs.

3. The managed floating system of exchange rates (1971–present) relies on foreign-exchange markets to establish equilibrium exchange rates. But it also permits central banks to buy and sell foreign currencies to stabilize short-term changes in exchange rates caused by speculation, or to correct exchange rate imbalances negatively affecting the world economy.

CHAPTER SUMMARY

1. Canadian exports create a foreign demand for dollars and make a supply of foreign exchange available to Canadians. Conversely, Canadian imports simultaneously create a demand for foreign exchange and make a supply of dollars available to foreigners. Generally, a nation's exports earn the foreign currencies needed to pay for its imports.

2. The balance of payments records the international trade and financial transactions that take place between a given nation and the rest of the world. The balance on goods and services compares exports and imports of both goods and services and constitutes the balance of trade; it is the net-exports component of aggregate expenditures. The current-account balance considers not only goods and services transactions, but also net investment income from nonresidents and transfers.

3. The Bank of Canada records the official international reserves as part of the capital account. The official international reserves are, in fact, a balancing item in the overall balance of payments. A balance of payment deficit occurs when the official international reserves are drawn down. A balance of payment surplus arises when the official international reserves rise. The desirability of a balance of payments deficit or surplus depends on its causes and its persistence.

4. Flexible or floating exchange rates are determined by the demand for and supply of foreign currencies. Under floating rates, a currency will depreciate or appreciate as a result of changes in tastes, relative income changes, relative price changes, relative changes in real interest rates, and because of speculation.

5. Maintenance of fixed exchange rates requires adequate international reserves to accommodate periodic payments deficits. If international reserves are inadequate, nations must invoke protectionist trade policies, engage in exchanging controls, or endure domestic macroeconomic adjustments.

6. The gold standard provided exchange-rate stability until its disintegration during the Great Depression of the 1930s. Under this system, gold flows between nations precipitated sometimes painful changes in price, income, and employment levels in bringing about international equilibrium.

7. Under the Bretton Woods system, exchange rates were pegged to one another and were stable. Participating nations were obligated to maintain these rates by using stabilization funds, gold, or borrowings from the IMF. Persistent or "fundamental" payments deficits could be met by IMF-sanctioned currency devaluations.

8. Since 1971 a system of managed floating exchange rates has been in use. Rates are generally set by market forces, although governments intervene with varying frequency to alter their exchange rates.

TERMS AND CONCEPTS

balance of payments deficit and surplus (p. 461)
balance of trade (p. 459)
Bretton Woods System (p. 473)
capital account (p. 460)
capital account balance (p. 461)
credits (p. 458)
currency depreciation and appreciation (p. 464)
current account (p. 458)
current-account balance (p. 460)
debits (p. 458)
devaluation (p. 473)
direct investment (p. 460)
exchange controls (p. 469)
fixed exchange rates (pp. 463, 467)
flexible (floating) exchange rates (p. 463)

foreign-exchange markets (p. 456)
G-7 nations (p. 475)
gold export and import points (p. 472)
gold standard (p. 471)
international balance of payments (p. 458)
International Monetary Fund (IMF) (p. 473)
managed floating exchange rates (p. 475)
merchandise trade balance (p. 458)
nonmerchandise trade balance (p. 460)
official international (foreign-exchange) reserves (p. 461)
portfolio investment (p. 460)
purchasing power parity (p. 465)
rate of exchange (p. 456)
statistical discrepancy (p. 461)
transfers (p. 460)

QUESTIONS AND STUDY SUGGESTIONS

1. Explain how a Canadian automobile importer might finance a shipment of Fiats from Italy. Demonstrate how a Canadian export of wheat to China might be financed. Explain: "Canadian exports earn supplies of foreign monies, which Canadians can use to finance imports."

2. *Key Question* *Indicate whether each of the following creates a demand for, or a supply of, French francs in foreign-exchange markets:*

a. *A Canadian importer purchases a shipload of Bordeaux wine.*

b. *A French automobile firm builds an assembly plant in Halifax.*

c. *A Canadian university student spends a year studying at the Sorbonne.*

d. *A French manufacturer exports machinery to Morocco on a Canadian freighter.*

e. *Canada incurs a current account deficit in its transactions with France.*

f. *A Government of Canada bond held by a French citizen matures.*

g. *It is widely believed that the international price of the franc will fall in the near future.*

3. Key Question   *Answer the following questions on the basis of the balance of payments of Alpha for 1996. All figures are in billions of dollars.*

What is the balance of trade? The balance on current account? The balance on capital account? Does Alpha have a balance of payments deficit or surplus? Explain how the official international reserves, which appear in the capital account, act as a balancing item that brings the balance on the current and capital account to zero.

Merchandise exports	+$40	Net transfers	+$10
Merchandise imports	−30	Capital inflows*	+ 10
Service exports	+ 15	Capital outflows*	−40
Service imports	−10	Official reserves	+ 10
Investment income	−5		

* Net of balance of official reserves; that is, with official reserves balance shown separately.

4. "A rise in the dollar price of yen necessarily means a fall in the yen price of dollars." Do you agree? Illustrate and elaborate: "The critical thing about exchange rates is that they provide a direct link between the prices of good and services produced in all trading nations of the world." Explain the purchasing power parity theory of exchange rates.

5. The Swedish auto company Saab imports car components from Germany and exports autos to Canada. In 1990 the dollar depreciated, and the German mark appreciated, relative to the Swedish krona. Speculate as to how this hurt Saab — twice.

6. Key Question   *Explain why the Canadian demand for Mexican pesos is downsloping and the supply of pesos to Canadians is upsloping. Assuming a system of floating exchange rates between Mexico and Canada, indicate whether each of the following would cause the Mexican peso to appreciate or depreciate:*

a. *Canada unilaterally reduces tariffs on Mexican products.*

b. *Mexico encounters severe inflation.*

c. *Deteriorating political relations reduce Canadian tourism in Mexico.*

d. *The Canadian economy moves into a severe recession.*

e. *The Bank of Canada embarks on a tight money policy.*

f. *Mexican products become more appealing to Canadians.*

g. *The Mexican government invites Petro-Canada to invest in Mexican oil fields.*

h. *The rate of productivity growth in Canada diminishes sharply.*

7. Explain whether or not you agree with the following statements:

   a. "A country that grows faster than its major trading partners can expect the international price of its currency to depreciate."

   b. "A nation whose interest rate is rising more rapidly than in other nations can expect the international price of its currency to appreciate."

   c. "A country's currency will appreciate if its inflation rate is less than that of the rest of the world."

8. "Exports pay for imports. Yet in 1975, the rest of the world imported about $2.4 billion less worth of goods and services from Canada than were exported to Canada." Resolve the apparent inconsistency of these two statements.

9. Explain in detail how a balance of payments deficit would be resolved under a. the gold standard, b. the Bretton Woods system, and c. floating exchange rates. What are the advantages and shortcomings of each system?

10. Outline the major costs and benefits associated with a large trade or current-account deficit. Explain: "A current-account deficit means we are receiving more goods and services from abroad than we are sending abroad. How can that be called 'unfavourable'?"

11. (Applying the Theory) Suppose Winter Sports — a French retailer of snowboards — wants to order 5000 snowboards made in Canada. The price per board is $200, the current exchange rate is 6 francs = 1 dollar, and payment is due in dollars when the boards are delivered in three months. Use a numerical example to explain why exchange rate risk might make the French retailer hesitant to place the order. How might speculators absorb some of Winter Sports' risk?

MACROECONOMIC POLICY IN AN OPEN ECONOMY

 National economies have become interdependent. Economic policies in one of the major economic powers — the U.S.A., Japan, Germany — will, in a short time, be felt around the world. During the recession of 1990–91 Japan and Germany were urged by the other G-7 countries to stimulate their economies so as to pull the rest of the world economy, particularly the United States, out of recession.

We have so far examined macroeconomic policy — both fiscal and monetary policies — without much reference to international trade and finance. Our task now is to understand some of the complications and macro **policy conflicts** that may arise in an economy open to international trade.

In this chapter we investigate how there may be a conflict between internal and external policy goals, and analyze how monetary and fiscal policies affect our exchange rate, thus our imports, exports, and our balance of payments.

BOX 22-1   THE BIG PICTURE

Macroeconomic policy in an open economy is more difficult to design because of potential conflict between internal and external policy objectives. The conflict arises because both monetary and fiscal policies will influence interest rates, which in turn can influence the value of the Canadian dollar. As was noted in Chapter 10, the value of the Canadian dollar against other currencies will influence both imports into and exports from Canada.

As you read this chapter, keep the following points in mind:

• It would be a good idea to review fiscal and monetary policy, covered in Chapters 12 and 15 respectively.

• The main domestic goals are full employment GDP and price stability. These goals may or may not be compatible with the external policy goal, which is to achieve a balance of zero in our current account.

• Depending where the economy is in respect to domestic and external policy objectives, monetary and fiscal policy can be in harmony with respect to domestic and external goals, or in conflict.

• Monetary and fiscal policy can affect the aggregate supply curve.

GOALS AND ASSUMPTIONS

To make our investigation easier, let's list a nation's policy goals.

1. DOMESTIC OR INTERNAL GOAL   Let's assume that the goal of the domestic economy is to achieve full employment with price stability.

2. INTERNATIONAL OR EXTERNAL GOAL   We will also suppose our international or external economic objective is to achieve a balance of zero in our current account. We want our exports of goods and services to pay for our imports of goods and services as well as our deficit in investment income.

These two goals are portrayed in Figure 22-1, in which the horizontal axis shows the state of the domestic economy and the vertical axis reflects the current-account balance. The heavy dot at the point of intersection indicates the ideal situation where both our internal and external goals are being simultaneously achieved. Here the economy is realizing noninflationary full employment, and the values of its exports and imports are equal. In contrast, domestic inflation accompanied by a current-account deficit would be represented by a point in the southeast quadrant, while a recession accompanied by a trade surplus would place the economy at some point in the northwest quadrant.

FIGURE 22-1   Internal and external balance

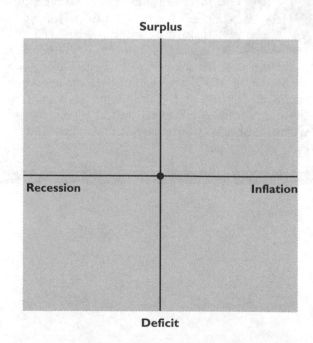

The horizontal axis shows the state of the domestic economy, and the vertical axis shows the nation's current-account position. Only at the intersection are the economy's domestic or internal goal (noninflationary full employment) and its international or external goal (balance in its current account) both attained.

In addition to specifying our internal and external goals, we make two further assumptions. First, we will suppose that exchange rates are fixed. We will drop this assumption later to consider the implications of flexible rates. Second, we make the assumption that our internal goal of noninflationary full employment is considered to be of higher priority than the external goal of balance in the current account. This latter assumption means that we will examine the impact of domestic stabilization policy on international trade, rather than the other way around.

COMPATIBILITY OF GOALS

Policies designed to achieve noninflationary full employment will affect the current-account balance, and vice versa. Let's consider various combinations of domestic and international conditions to determine whether appropriate domestic policy is consistent with our international economic objectives.

In the following analysis it is important to keep in mind that our exports are independent of changes in our domestic national income; our exports are dependent on the incomes of the nations with which we trade, while our imports vary directly with our national income. As our incomes rise, we buy more domestic *and* more foreign goods and services.

1. INFLATION AND A TRADE DEFICIT: COMPATIBLE
Suppose the economy is in the southeast quadrant of Figure 22-1, where it is experiencing domestic inflation and a current-account deficit. There is no conflict between our domestic and international goals. Using restrictive fiscal and monetary policies to reduce inflation will lower our national income, precipitate a decline in imports, and reduce the current-account or trade deficit.

2. UNEMPLOYMENT AND A TRADE DEFICIT: CONFLICT
If the economy is initially in the southwest quadrant of Figure 22-1, our domestic and international goals will be in conflict. The use of macro policies to achieve our domestic goal will take us further from the fulfilment of our international goal. Expansionary monetary and fiscal policies to restore full employment will raise the national income, which, in turn, will increase our purchases of imports and enlarge the existing trade deficit.

3. INFLATION AND A TRADE SURPLUS: CONFLICT
In the northeast quadrant of Figure 22-1 the economy is simultaneously experiencing inflation and a current-account surplus. Using contractionary fiscal and monetary policies to restrain inflation will reduce the national income, diminish our imports, and increase the trade surplus.

4. UNEMPLOYMENT AND A TRADE SURPLUS: COMPATIBLE
Finally, if the economy is initially in the northwest quadrant of Figure 22-1, expansionary fiscal and monetary policies to reduce unemployment will also help eliminate the current-account surplus. As the expansionary policies increase our national income, Canadians will purchase more imports and move the current account from a surplus towards a balance of zero.

Table 22-1 summarizes all these cases and merits careful study.

EXTENSIONS AND MODIFICATIONS

Cases 2 and 3 — a recessionary gap accompanied by a trade deficit, and an inflationary gap with a trade surplus — are of special interest because they entail conflicts in goals. In case 2, recession calls for an

TABLE 22-1 Compatibility and conflict between domestic and international economic policies

Case	Domestic problem	International (current account) problem	Appropriate domestic policy	Appropriate international policy	Relationship between domestic and international policies
(1)	Inflation	Deficit	Contractionary	Contractionary	Compatible
(2)	Unemployment	Deficit	Expansionary	Contractionary	Conflicting
(3)	Inflation	Surplus	Contractionary	Expansionary	Conflicting
(4)	Unemployment	Surplus	Expansionary	Expansionary	Compatible

expansion of domestic national income, while the trade deficit would be alleviated by a reduction in our national income. Similarly, in case 3, inflation necessitates a decrease in national income, but the trade surplus calls for an income increase. These conflict cases raise the question whether there are additional policy measures that might ameliorate the trade-offs between domestic and international goals in these two cases.

TARIFFS AND CURRENCY DEVALUATION

One possibility is to attempt to alter the *composition*, rather than the *level*, of aggregate expenditures. The usefulness of such a policy can best be envisioned in terms of case 2, in which domestic unemployment is accompanied by a trade deficit. If the composition of expenditures can somehow be shifted away from imports to domestically produced goods, we can simultaneously reduce our current-account deficit and stimulate domestic production and employment. We know from Chapters 20 and 21 how this might be accomplished. A tariff on imports will make imports more expensive and deflect domestic demand from those imports to domestically produced goods (see Figure 20-3). A currency devaluation has the same effect. If government takes action to reduce the international price of its currency, that nation's imports will become more expensive and expenditures will be shifted from foreign to domestic goods. This shift simultaneously reduces its trade deficit and boosts domestic output and employment. Try to reason through the problem of how tariff reductions and a currency revaluation might change the composition of expenditures to alleviate simultaneously the inflation and current-account surplus of case 3.

Although using tariffs and currency devaluation to reduce the trade-off between domestic and international goals is tempting, we should recall that such policies are likely to induce retaliatory steps by our trading partners. These are "beggar-my-neighbour" policies, and one's neighbours are not likely to stand by and quietly accept the costs that these actions impose upon them. During the 1930s, nations did respond in kind to the trade barriers and currency devaluations of other nations; as a result, the worldwide Great Depression intensified. Also, in Chapter 20 we documented the high costs of tariffs and other trade barriers to consumers in the country imposing them. Changing the composition of expenditures to lessen conflicts between domestic and international economic goals entails dangerous and expensive policies. **(Key Questions 2 and 3)**

FLEXIBLE EXCHANGE RATES

In our analysis of the four cases, we explicitly assumed that a system of fixed exchange rates prevailed, as was the case under the Bretton Woods system. Let's now extend our discussion to see how a system of floating or flexible exchange rates would function so as to dampen the conflict between a nation's domestic and international goals.

This can be best understood through an example. Suppose Canada initially finds itself at the ideal intersection (heavy dot) position of Figure 22-1, where it is realizing both its domestic and international economic objectives. Now assume that our major trading partners — the United States, Japan, Western Europe — all simultaneously slip into a recession. As a consequence, their purchases of Canadian goods and services decline; our exports fall. This means that we move away from our zero balance in our current account to a deficit position. Furthermore, other things being the same, this decline in our net exports would have a recessionary impact on our economy. Canada would now find itself in the southwest quadrant of Figure 22-1. (We implicitly assume the drop in exports is greater than the drop in imports as a result of our recession.) We have already noted in our discussion of case 2 that expansionary fiscal and monetary policies to counter the recession would further worsen our trade deficit.

But now, with flexible exchange rates, a series of additional adjustments takes place that ameliorate the twin problems of a recession and a trade deficit. The decline in the demand for Canadian exports will reduce the demand for our dollar and, hence, our dollar will depreciate in value. The decline in the international price of our dollar will have two effects. First, now that foreigners can buy more Canadian dollars with each unit of their currency, Canadian goods will be less expensive to foreigners and our exports will rise. Second, now that it takes more Canadian dollars to buy specific amounts of foreign currencies, Canadians will import less and shift their expenditures to domestically produced goods. Thus, the depreciation of the dollar that occurs under flexible exchange rates will automatically stimulate Canada's net exports and expand our domestic economy. The recession and the deficit that our trading partners have transmitted to Canada have been cushioned somewhat by flexible exchange rates. The point locating the position of the Canadian economy in the southwest quadrant of Figure 22-1 will be closer to the desired intersection dot with flexible exchange rates than it is with fixed rates.

FISCAL VERSUS MONETARY POLICY IN AN OPEN ECONOMY

The conflict between domestic and international goals depends in part on whether monetary or fiscal policy is used in seeking the objective of noninflationary full employment. The reason is that, other things equal, an expansionary fiscal policy leads to *higher* domestic interest rates, while an expansionary monetary policy translates into *lower* domestic interest rates.

FISCAL POLICY AND THE NET EXPORTS EFFECT

The **net exports effect** — the impact on net exports — may work through international trade to reduce the effectiveness of fiscal policy. We concluded in our discussion of the crowding-out effect that an expansionary fiscal policy might boost interest rates, reducing *investment* and weakening fiscal policy. Now we want to know what effect interest rate increases might have on our *net exports* (exports minus imports).

Suppose the government embarks on an expansionary fiscal policy that causes a higher interest rate. The higher interest rate will attract financial capital from abroad, assuming interest rates abroad are unchanged. But foreign financial investors must acquire Canadian dollars before buying the desired Canadian bonds. This will increase the supply of foreign currencies in Canada, therefore the Canadian dollar will appreciate.

The impact of this dollar appreciation on our net exports will be that the rest of the world will find our exports more expensive and our exports will decline. Canadians, who can now exchange their dollars for more units of foreign currencies, will buy more imports.

Aggregate demand and supply analysis in Figure 22-2 will help clarify this point. An expansionary fiscal policy aimed at increasing aggregate demand from AD_0 to AD_1 may hike the domestic interest rate and ultimately reduce our net exports through

FIGURE 22-2 Fiscal policy and the net export effect

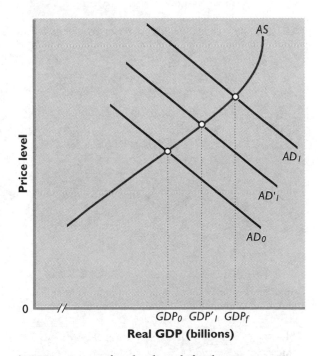

An expansionary fiscal policy shifts the aggregate demand to AD_1. But this raises the interest rate, which attracts foreign financial capital to Canada, and thus the Canadian dollar rises and our net exports fall, weakening the original fiscal stimulus.

the process just described. The decline in the net export component of aggregate demand will partially offset the expansionary fiscal policy. The aggregate demand curve will shift rightward from AD_0 to AD'_1 *not* to AD_1, and equilibrium GDP will increase from GDP_0 to GDP'_1 *not* to GDP_f, the full employment GDP. Thus, the net export effect of fiscal policy joins the problem of timing, politics, crowding-out, Ricardian effects, and inflation in complicating the "management" of aggregate demand.

Table 22-2 summarizes the net export effect resulting from fiscal policy. Column 1 reviews the analysis just discussed. But the net export effect works in both directions. By reducing the domestic interest rate, a *contractionary* fiscal policy tends to *increase* net exports. You should follow through the analysis in column 2 of Table 22-2 and relate it to the aggregate demand-aggregate supply model.

MONETARY POLICY AND THE NET EXPORTS EFFECT

NET EXPORTS EFFECT An expansionary monetary policy designed to alleviate recession will also produce a net exports effect, but its direction will be opposite to that of an expansionary fiscal policy. An expansionary monetary policy will reduce the domestic interest rate. The lower interest rate will discourage the inflow of financial capital to Canada and the Canadian dollar will depreciate in value. This means that all foreign goods are more expensive to Canadians and, conversely, Canadian goods are less expensive to foreigners. Our imports will fall and our exports will rise (net exports will increase). As a result, aggregate expenditures and equilibrium GDP will expand in Canada.[1]

Conclusion: Unlike an expansionary fiscal policy, which *reduces* net exports, an expansionary monetary policy *increases* net exports. **Exchange rate changes in response to interest rate changes in Canada strengthen domestic monetary policy.** This conclusion holds equally for a tight monetary

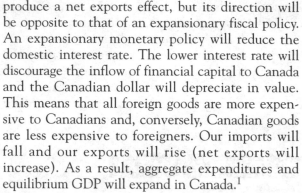

---

[1] The depreciation of the dollar will also increase the price of foreign resources imported to Canada. Aggregate supply in Canada therefore will decline and part of the expansionary effect described here may be offset.

TABLE 22-2 Fiscal policy and net exports

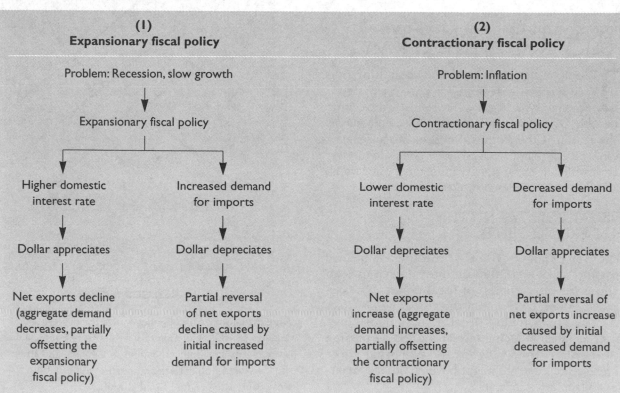

(1) **Expansionary fiscal policy**	(2) **Contractionary fiscal policy**
Problem: Recession, slow growth	Problem: Inflation
↓	↓
Expansionary fiscal policy	Contractionary fiscal policy
Higher domestic interest rate / Increased demand for imports	Lower domestic interest rate / Decreased demand for imports
Dollar appreciates / Dollar depreciates	Dollar depreciates / Dollar appreciates
Net exports decline (aggregate demand decreases, partially offsetting the expansionary fiscal policy) / Partial reversal of net exports decline caused by initial increased demand for imports	Net exports increase (aggregate demand increases, partially offsetting the contractionary fiscal policy) / Partial reversal of net exports increase caused by initial decreased demand for imports

policy, which we know increases the domestic interest rates. To see how this happens, follow through the analysis in column 2 of Table 22-3.

MACRO STABILITY AND THE TRADE BALANCE

Assume in Table 22-3 that, in addition to domestic macroeconomic stability, a widely held economic goal is that Canada should balance its exports and imports. In simple terms, we want to "pay our way" in international trade in that the earnings from our exports are sufficient to finance our imports.

Consider column 1 of Table 22-3 once again, but now suppose that initially Canada has a very large current-account *deficit*, which means our imports substantially exceed our exports, so we are *not* paying our way in world trade. By following through our cause-effect chain in column 1 we find that an expansionary monetary policy lowers the international price of the dollar so that our exports increase and our imports decline. This increase in net exports corrects the assumed initial current-account deficit.

Conclusion: *The expansionary monetary policy that is appropriate for the alleviation of unemployment and sluggish growth is compatible with the goal of correcting a balance of trade deficit.* If initially Canada had a large balance of trade surplus, an easy or expansionary monetary policy would increase the surplus.

Now consider column 2 of Table 22-3 and assume again that at the outset Canada has a large balance of trade deficit. A tight monetary policy to restrain inflation would cause our exports to fall and imports to rise. This means the trade deficit would be enlarged.

Conclusion: *A contractionary monetary policy to alleviate inflation conflicts with the goal of correcting a balance of trade deficit.* If our initial problem was a trade surplus, a tight monetary policy would resolve that surplus.

Overall we find that an expansionary monetary policy reduces a trade deficit and increases a trade surplus. A tight monetary policy reduces a trade surplus and increases a trade deficit. The point is that certain combinations of circumstances create conflicts or trade-offs between the use of monetary policy to achieve domestic stability and the realization of balance in the nation's international trade. (**Key Questions 4 and 5**)

AN OPEN ECONOMY AND AGGREGATE SUPPLY

The discussion to this point has been exclusively in terms of the potential policy conflicts in an open economy with regards to aggregate demand. What about the potential impact of an open economy on the aggregate supply curve?

Recall from Table 11-2 in Chapter 11 that factors shifting the aggregate supply curve include changes in the price of capital and the price of imported resources. Both monetary and fiscal policy can affect interest rates, and thus the price of capital. Moreover, domestic interest rates affect the value of the Canadian dollar, which will influence the price of imported resources.

TABLE 22-3   Monetary policy and net exports

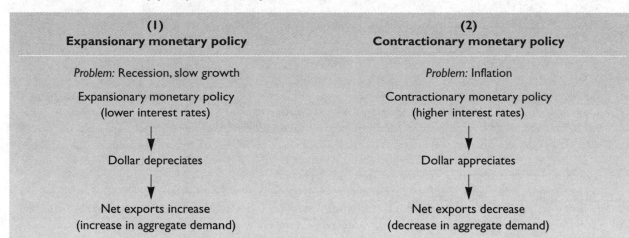

(1) **Expansionary monetary policy**	(2) **Contractionary monetary policy**
Problem: Recession, slow growth	*Problem:* Inflation
Expansionary monetary policy (lower interest rates) ↓	Contractionary monetary policy (higher interest rates) ↓
Dollar depreciates ↓	Dollar appreciates ↓
Net exports increase (increase in aggregate demand)	Net exports decrease (decrease in aggregate demand)

An expansionary monetary policy that results in lower interest rates will have two opposing effects on the aggregate supply curve. Falling interest rates will shift the aggregate supply curve to the right, but if the lower interest rates result in a lower Canadian dollar, it will tend to shift the aggregate supply curve to the left. The net result will depend on the relative magnitude of the two opposing forces. A contractionary monetary policy will produce the opposite results. Note, too, that an expansionary monetary policy will also affect the aggregate demand curve.

As just discussed, an expansionary fiscal policy can put upward pressure on interest rates and also possibly affect the value of the Canadian dollar. The two opposing forces will have an ambiguous impact on the aggregate supply curve — higher interest rates tending to shift it to the left, a higher Canadian dollar to the right. Which of the two opposing forces dominates depends on their relative magnitude. A contractionary fiscal policy will have the opposite effects on the aggregate supply curve.

In an open economy, the impact of both monetary and fiscal policy is more complicated and uncertain. To appreciate this point, consider Figure 22-2 once again. The rise in the interest rate will tend to shift the aggregate supply curve left, possibly negating completely the expansionary effect of the fiscal policy. But a rise in the Canadian dollar will tend to shift the aggregate supply curve to the right, possibly strengthening the expansionary effect of the fiscal policy. Which of these scenarios materializes depends on the relative magnitude of the two opposing forces.

QUICK REVIEW 22-2

1. Fiscal policy may be weakened by an accompanying net export effect that works through changes in **a** the interest rate, **b** the international value of the dollar, and **c** exports and imports.

2. Monetary policy strengthens the accompanying export effect.

3. An expansionary monetary policy is compatible with correcting a balance of trade deficit. A contractionary monetary policy conflicts with correcting a balance of trade deficit.

4. A change in the price of imported resources will shift the aggregate supply curve.

BOX 22-2   IN THE MEDIA

RATES JUMP AS DOLLAR HITS 9-YEAR LOW

Prime hits 8.5 per cent and bank rate increase hints at more

BY MARIAN STINSON
Money Markets Reporter

Chartered banks raised their prime lending rate by half a percentage point to 8.5 per cent yesterday — the highest level in two years — as the Canadian dollar tumbled to a nine-year low.

Most of the banks also raised mortgage rates across the board half a point — a move that threatens the fragile housing market in many cities.

In spite of the hefty increases, investors continued to sell Canadian treasury bills yesterday, indicating another sharp jump in the Bank of Canada rate next week and possibly another hike in the prime rate if the dollar continues to fall, analysts warn. Currently, an increase of 63 basis points in the bank rate (63-100ths of a percentage point) is in the cards for next week.

At the moment, the situation "looks dreadful," said Katharine Beatty, a technical analyst with MMS International, a financial-market information service.

The Bank of Canada rate, 7.24 per cent this week, is set each Tuesday at one-quarter of a percentage point above the average yield on three-month treasury bills.

The jump in prime, which is the rate charged on loans to the banks' best customers, was announced after the Bank of Canada raised its overnight financing rate for banks and stockbrokers by half a point for the second time this week, moving the target range to 6.25 to 6.75 per cent.

Both Canadian and U.S. bonds fell sharply as well, driving the 30- year Government of Canada bond down $8 for each $1,000 in face value, making the effective yield 9.5 per cent.

By late yesterday, the dollar was trading at 70.55 U.S. cents — its low- est since March 4, 1986, down one- third of a cent from Wednesday....

SOURCE: *Globe and Mail*, January 13, 1995, p. A1. Reproduced by permission.

The Story in Brief

The downward pressure on the Canadian dollar leads the Bank of Canada to raise short-term interest rates in an effort to stem its fall. But a rise in short-term interest rates will affect the housing market through higher mortgage rates.

The Economics Behind the Story

- There can be a conflict between domestic and external policy objectives. In this instance, monetary policy appropriate to stabilize the value of the Canadian dollar may end up further damaging what the article refers to as "the fragile housing market" in many cities.

- The Bank of Canada pushes up short-term interest rates to defend the Canadian dollar. The rise in the Bank of Canada rate signals the chartered banks to raise the prime lending rate. The chartered banks also raised mortgage rates.

- Higher interest rates affect aggregate demand primarily through investments goods, whose demand is inversely related to interest rates. Housing is an investment good. Higher interest rates will decrease the number of houses sold. We infer from the article that the housing market is already "threatened," suggesting the rising interest rates will make the situation worse.

- What effect will a depreciation of the Canadian dollar have on the aggregate supply curve? Will such an effect increase or decrease the conflict between the domestic and external policy objectives?

CHAPTER SUMMARY

1. Achieving the internal goal of full employment and the external goal of a current-account or trade balance are sometimes compatible and sometimes in conflict. Anti-inflationary macro policies are compatible with correcting a trade deficit, *and* expansionary macro policies are compatible with eliminating a trade surplus. However, expansionary macro policies are in conflict with correcting a trade deficit, *and* an anti-inflationary policy is in conflict with eliminating a trade surplus.

2. It is possible to lessen the conflict between internal and external economic goals by altering the composition rather than the level of aggregate expenditures. Such policies require tariff increases and currency devaluations that are costly and susceptible to retaliation.

3. Flexible exchange rates are helpful in lessening the conflict involved in correcting a recession- ary gap in the presence of a trade deficit.

4. Flexible exchange rates weaken the effectiveness of an expansionary fiscal policy, but strengthen an easy monetary policy.

5. Fiscal policy may precipitate changes in exchange rates and weaken its effects on GDP.

6. The impact of an expansionary monetary policy on GDP is strengthened by an accompanying increase in net exports precipitated by a lower domestic interest rate. Likewise, a contractionary monetary policy is strengthened by a decline in net exports. In some circumstances, there may be a trade-off between the use of monetary policy to affect the value of the dollar and thus to correct a trade imbalance and that appropriate to achieve domestic stability.

7. In an open economy, changes in the prices of imported resources will shift the aggregate supply curve, complicating the domestic impact of fiscal and monetary policy.

TERMS AND CONCEPTS

net exports effect (p. 485)   policy conflict (p. 481)

QUESTIONS AND STUDY SUGGESTIONS

1. Assume an economy that seeks the internal goal of noninflationary full employment and the external goal of a zero balance in its current account. Indicate in which of the following sets of circumstances would appropriate macroeconomic policies to achieve its internal goal be a. compatible with and b. in conflict with its external goal:

   a. Recession and a current-account deficit.

   b. Inflation and a current-account surplus.

   c. Recession and a current-account surplus.

   d. Inflation and a current-account deficit.

   Explain the reasoning underlying your responses.

2. *Key Question   Carefully explain and evaluate:*

   a. *"Policies that stimulate the domestic economy tend to create a trade deficit."*

   b. *"A trade deficit imposes severe constraints on domestic economic policies."*

3. *Key Question   "When internal and external economic goals are in conflict, policies that change the composition rather than the level of aggregate expenditures can alleviate this conflict." What are such policies? Explain how they might work. Comment on the desirability of such policies.*

4. *Key Question   Explain how recessions in the economies of our major trading partners would tend to push Canada into the southwest quadrant of Figure 22-1. How might flexible exchange rates function so as to counteract recession and a trade deficit in Canada?*

5. *Key Question   Assuming flexible exchange rates, explain how the appreciation or depreciation of a nation's currency might influence the effectiveness of a. an expansionary fiscal policy and b. an easy monetary policy in alleviating a recession.*

6. Assuming flexible exchange rates, use the aggregate demand–aggregate supply model to explain how an expansionary fiscal policy will affect GDP in an open economy compared to a closed economy.

7. Assuming flexible exchange rates, use the aggregate demand–aggregate supply model to discuss the impact of a contractionary monetary policy on the value of the Canadian dollar vis-à-vis other currencies. Also discuss the impact on Canada's balance of payments.

CHAPTER 23

GROWTH AND THE LESS-DEVELOPED COUNTRIES

I t is difficult for the typical Canadian family, whose 1993 average income was $53,454, to grasp the fact that two-thirds of the world's population lives at, or perilously close to, the subsistence level. Hunger, squalor, and disease are common in many nations of the world. The World Bank estimates that over one billion people — approximately 20% of the world's population — lives on less than $1 per day!

In this chapter we identify the poor or less-developed nations. Second, we seek to determine why they are poor. What are the obstacles to growth? Third, the potential role of government in economic development is considered. Fourth, international trade, private capital flows, and foreign aid are examined as vehicles of growth. Fifth, the external debt problems faced by many of the poor nations are analyzed. Finally, we present the demands of the poor nations to establish a "new global contract" to improve their economies.

THE RICH AND THE POOR

Just as there is considerable income disparity among individual families within a nation, so there also is great economic inequality among the family of nations. Table 23-1 shows the remarkable degree of income disparity in the world. The richest one-fifth of the world's population receives almost 83% of world income, the poorest one-fifth obtains less than 1.5%. The poorest 60% of the world population gets less than 6% of the world's income.

TABLE 23-1 Global income disparity

World population	Percentage of world income
Richest 20%	82.7
Second 20%	11.7
Third 20%	2.3
Fourth 20%	1.9
Poorest 20%	1.4

Source: United Nations Development Program, *Human Development Report 1992* (New York: Oxford University Press, 1992), p. 36.

Table 23-2 helps to sort out rich and poor by identifying the following groups of nations.

1. INDUSTRIALLY ADVANCED COUNTRIES

The **industrially advanced countries (IACs)** include Canada, the United States, Australia, New Zealand, Japan, and most of the nations of western Europe. These nations have developed market economies based on large stocks of capital goods, advanced production technologies, and well-educated labour forces. As column 1 of Table 23-2 indicates, these economies have a high per capita (per person) GDP or GNP.

2. LESS DEVELOPED COUNTRIES

Most of the remaining nations of the world — located in Africa, Asia, and Latin America — are underdeveloped or **less-developed countries (LDCs)**. These 97 nations have few industries, and a high share of the labour force still works in agriculture. Literacy rates are low, unemployment is high, population growth is rapid, and exports consist largely of agricultural commodities (cocoa, bananas, sugar, raw cotton) and raw materials (copper, iron ore, natural rubber). Capital equipment is scarce, production technologies are typically primitive, and labour force productivity is low. About three-fourths of the world's population lives in these

TABLE 23-2 GNP per capita, population, and growth rates

	GNP per capita		Population	
	(1) U.S. Dollars, 1992	**(2) Annual growth rate, 1980-1992**	**(3) Millions, mid-1992**	**(4) Average annual growth, 1980-92**
Industrially advanced countries (IACs) (23 nations)	$22,160	2.3%	828	0.7%
Less-developed countries: (LDCs) (109 nations)				
Middle-income LDCs (67 nations)	2,490	−0.1	1,419	1.8
Low-income LDCs (42 nations)	390	3.9	3,191	2.0

Source: World Bank, *World Development Report,* 1994 (New York: Oxford University Press, 1994).

nations, which share the characteristic of widespread poverty.

In Table 23-2 the poor nations are divided into two groups. The first group is made up of 66 "middle-income" LDCs with an average annual per capita GNP of U.S. $2490. The range of per capita GNPs of this diverse group is from U.S. $670 to $7510. The other group is 42 "low income" LDCs with per capita GNPs ranging from U.S. $60 to $670 and averaging only $390. This group is dominated by India, China, and the sub-Saharan nations of Africa.

GROWTH, DECLINE, AND INCOME GAPS

Two other points must be added to our discussion of Table 23-2.

1. MIRACLES AND DISASTERS There have been considerable differences in the ability of the various LDCs to improve their circumstances over time. A group of so-called newly industrialized economies (NICs) — consisting of Singapore, Hong Kong, Taiwan, and South Korea — have achieved very high annual growth rates of real GNP of 6% to 7% in the 1960–89 period. As a consequence, real per capita GNPs rose fivefold in these nations. In vivid contrast, many of the highly indebted LDCs and the very poor sub-Saharan nations of Africa have had *declining* real per capita GNPs in the 1980s.

2. GROWING ABSOLUTE GAPS The income gap between rich and poor nations has been widening. To demonstrate this point, let's assume the per capita GNPs of the advanced and less-developed countries have both been growing at about 2% per year. Because the income base in the advanced countries is initially much higher, the income gap grows. If per capita income is $400 a year, a 2% growth rate means an $8 increase in income. Where per capita income is $4000 per year, the same 2% growth rate translates into an $80 increase in income. The absolute income gap will have increased from $3600 (= $4000 – $400) to $3672 (= $4080 – $408). The LDCs must grow faster than the IACs to catch up.

In fact, the absolute income gap between rich and poor nations has widened significantly. The absolute difference in per capita income between the richest 20% and the poorest 20% of the world's population increased from $1854 in 1960 to $15,149 in 1989. **(Key Question 3)**

IMPLICATIONS

Mere statistics conceal the human implications of the extreme poverty that characterizes so much of our planet and the suffering that accompanies it. In Table 23-3, various socioeconomic indicators for selected Third World nations are contrasted with those for Canada, the United States, and Japan. These data portray the enormous material extremes that human beings suffer.

BREAKING THE POVERTY BARRIER

The avenues of economic growth are essentially the same for industrially advanced and less-developed nations:

1. GREATER EFFICIENCY Existing supplies of resources must be used more efficiently. This means not only eliminating unemployment but also achieving greater efficiency in the utilization of resources.

2. RESOURCE ENHANCEMENT Supplies of productive resources must be altered — typically increased. By expanding supplies of raw materials, capital equipment, effective labour supply, and technological knowledge, a nation can push its production possibilities curve to the right.

Why have some nations been successful in pursuing these avenues of growth while others have lagged far behind? The difference is in the physical, human, and sociocultural environments of the various nations.

NATURAL RESOURCES

There is no simple generalization as to the role of natural resources in the economic development of the LDCs. This is because the distribution of natural resources among these nations is very uneven. Some less-developed nations encompass valuable deposits of bauxite, tin, copper, tungsten, nitrates, and petroleum. Some LDCs have been able to use their natural resource endowments to achieve rapid growth and a significant redistribution of income from the rich to the poor nations. The Organization of Petroleum Exporting Countries (OPEC) is a standard example. On the other hand, in many cases natural resources are owned or controlled by multinational corporations of the industrially advanced countries — with the economic benefits from the resources being largely diverted abroad. World markets for many of the farm products and

TABLE 23-3   Selected socioeconomic indicators of development

Country	(1) Per capita GNP, 1992 ($U.S.)	(2) Life expectancy at birth, 1989	(3) Infant mortality per 1000 live births, 1992	(4) Adult illiteracy, 1990	(5) Daily per capita calorie supply, 1990	(6) Per capita energy consumption, 1992†
1 Japan	$28,190	79 years	5	under 5	2,848	3,586
2 United States	23,240	77	9	under 5	3,666	7,662
3 Canada	20,710	78	7	under 5	3,671	7,912
4 Brazil	2,770	66	57	19	2,730	681
5 Mauritania	530	48	117	66	2,450	108
6 China	470	69	31	27	2,640	600
7 India	310	61	79	52	2,230	235
8 Bangladesh	220	55	91	65	2,040	59
9 Ethiopia	110	49	122	–	1,700	21
10 Mozambique	60	44	162	67	1,810	32

†Kilograms of oil equivalent.
Source: World Bank, *World Development Report, 1994.*

raw materials that the LDCs export are subject to great price fluctuations that contribute to instability in their economies.

Other LDCs lack mineral deposits, have little arable land, and have few sources of power. But while resources could aid growth, we must be careful in generalizing: Switzerland and Japan, for example, have achieved relatively high levels of living *despite* restrictive natural resource bases.

HUMAN RESOURCES

Three statements describe many of the LDCs' circumstances with respect to human resources:

1. They are overpopulated.
2. Unemployment and underemployment are widespread.
3. Labour productivity is low.

OVERPOPULATION   As column 3 of Table 23-2 makes clear, many of the nations with the most meagre natural and capital resources have the largest populations to support. Table 23-4 compares population and population growth rates of a few selected nations with those of Canada, the United States, and the world as a whole.

Most important for the long run is the vivid contrast of population growth rates. The middle- and low-income LDCs of Table 23-2 are now experiencing a 2% annual increase in population, as compared with a 0.7% annual rate for advanced countries. Recalling the "rule of 70," the current rate suggests that the total population of the LDCs will double in about 35 years.

These statistics indicate why the per capita income gap between the LDCs and the IACs has widened. In some of the less-developed countries, rapid population growth actually presses on the food supply to the extent that per capita food consumption is pulled down to the subsistence level or below.

At first glance it would seem that since

$$\text{Per capita standard of living} = \frac{\text{consumer goods (food) production}}{\text{population}}$$

TABLE 23-4 Population statistics for selected countries

Country	Population per square mile 1993	Annual rate of population increase, 1980–92
Canada	7	1.1%
United States	74	1.0
Pakistan	429	3.1
Bangladesh	2,421	2.3
Venezuela	60	2.6
India	801	2.1
China	331	1.4
Kenya	128	3.6
Philippines	606	2.4
World	**112**	**1.7%**

Source: *Statistical Abstract of the United States,* 1993

the standard of living could be raised by boosting consumer goods — particularly food — production. But the problem is more complex than this, because any increase in consumer goods production that initially raises the standard of living is likely to induce a population increase. This increase, if too large, will dissipate the improvements in living standards, and subsistence living levels will again prevail.

By why does population growth in LDCs accompany increases in output? First, the nation's *death* or *mortality rate* will decline with initial increases in production. This decline is the result of (1) a higher level of per capita food consumption, and (2) the basic medical and sanitation programs that accompany the initial phases of economic development.

Second, the *birth rate* will remain high or may increase, particularly as the medical and sanitation programs cut infant mortality. The cliché that "the rich get richer and the poor get children" is uncomfortably accurate for many LDCs. An increase in the per capita standard of living may lead in the short term to a population upsurge that will cease only when the standard of living has again been reduced to the level of bare subsistence.

GLOBAL PERSPECTIVE 23-1

Population growth in rich and poor countries

World population is expected to double over the next century, with the poorest nations accounting for most of the increase.

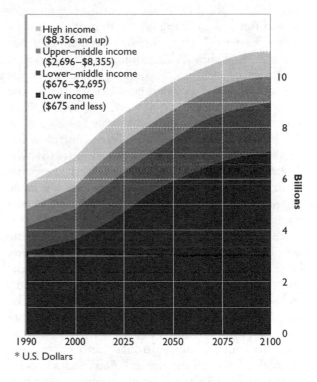

* U.S. Dollars

Source: World Bank data.

In addition to the fact that rapid population growth can translate an expanding GDP into a stagnant or slow-growing GDP per capita, there are other reasons why population expansion is an obstacle to development.

1. SAVING AND INVESTMENT Large families reduce the capacity of households to save, restricting the economy's capacity to accumulate capital.

2. PRODUCTIVITY As population grows, more investment is required to maintain the amount of real capital per person. If investment fails to keep pace, each worker will have fewer tools and equipment, which will cause worker productivity (output per worker) to fall. Declining productivity implies stagnating or declining per capita incomes.

3. RESOURCE EXPLOITATION Because most LDCs are heavily dependent on agriculture, rapid population growth may result in overuse of limited natural resources such as land. The much-publicized African famines are partially the result of past overgrazing and overplanting of land caused by the pressing need to feed the growing population.

4. URBAN PROBLEMS Rapid population growth in the cities of the LDCs, accompanied by unprecedented flows of rural migrants, are generating massive urban problems. Substandard housing in impoverished slums, deteriorating public services, congestion, pollution, and crime are all problems that are worsened by rapid population growth. The resolution of these difficulties necessitates a diversion of resources from growth-oriented uses.

Most authorities advocate birth control as the most effective means for breaking out of this dilemma. And breakthroughs in contraceptive technology in the recent past decades have made this solution increasingly relevant. But obstacles to population control are great. Low literacy rates make it difficult to disseminate information on the use of contraceptive devices. In peasant agriculture, large families are a major source of labour. Adults may regard having many children as a kind of informal social security system; the more children, the greater the probability of having a relative to care for you during old age. Finally, many nations that stand to gain the most through birth control are often the least willing, for religious and sociocultural reasons, to embrace contraception programs. Population growth in Latin America, for example, is among the most rapid in the world.

China — with about one-fifth of the world's population — adopted a harsh "one-child" program in 1980. The government advocated late marriages and one child per family. Couples having more than one child are fined or lose various social benefits. Even though the rate of population growth has diminished under this program, China's population continues to expand at about 100 million per decade. India, the world's second most populous nation, had a 103 million or 13% population increase in the 1986–92 period. With a total population of 884 million, India has 16% of the world's population but less than 2.5% of its land mass.

THREE ADDENDA But three additional points are worthy of note.

1. As with natural resources, the relationship between population and economic growth is less clear than one might expect. A high population density and rapid population growth do not necessarily mean poverty. China and India have immense populations and are poor; but Japan and Hong King are densely populated and relatively wealthy.

2. Population growth rates for the LDCs as a group have declined somewhat in recent decades. In the mid-1960s the annual population growth rate was about 2.35%. Currently it is about 2% and projections suggest further future declines.

3. The traditional view is that the reduction of population growth through the more widespread use of birth control techniques is the basic means for increasing per capita incomes in the LDCs. Reduce population growth in the denominator of our earlier equation, and the standard of living will rise.

But there is a contrary view — known as the **demographic transition** — which reverses causation by arguing that rising incomes must first be achieved and only then will slower population growth follow. The demographic transition view observes that in low-income countries children are viewed as economic assets; they are a cheap source of labour and potentially provide financial support and security for their parents in their old age. Thus people in poor countries have high birth rates. But in wealthy IAC nations children are economic liabilities. In particular, their care requires the sacrifice of high earnings or the need to purchase expensive child care. Also, children require extended and expensive education for the highly skilled jobs characteristic of IAC economies. Finally, the wealth of the IACs results in "social safety nets" that protect adults from the insecurity associated with old age and the inability to work. Thus people in the IACs recognize that high birth rates are neither necessary nor desirable, so they choose to have fewer children.

Note the differences in causation implied by the two views. The traditional view says reduced birth rates must come first and higher per capita incomes will follow; lower birth rates cause per capita income growth. The demographic transition view says higher incomes must first be achieved and lower rates of population growth will be the result; higher incomes are the cause of slower population growth. **(Key Question 6)**

UNEMPLOYMENT AND UNDEREMPLOYMENT
Reliable unemployment statistics for the LDCs are
not readily available, but observation suggests that
unemployment and underemployment are both
quite high. **Unemployment** occurs when someone
who is willing and able to work cannot find a job.
Underemployment refers to the situation wherein
workers are employed fewer hours or days a week
than they desire, work at jobs that do not fully use
their skills, or spend much of the time on their job
unproductively.

Most less-developed countries have experienced substantial migration of population from
rural to urban areas. This migration is motivated by
the *expectation* of finding jobs with higher wage
rates than are available in agricultural and other
rural employments. But this huge migration makes
it very unlikely that a migrant will in fact obtain a
job. Migration to the cities has greatly exceeded the
growth of urban job opportunities, resulting in very
high urban unemployment rates. Thus, rapid
rural–urban migration has given rise to urban
unemployment rates that are two or three times as
great as rural rates.

Underemployment is widespread and characteristic of most LDCs. In many LDCs rural agricultural
labour may be so abundant relative to capital and
natural resources that a significant percentage of this
labour contributes little or nothing to agricultural
output. Similarly, many LDC workers are self-
employed as proprietors of small shops, in handi-
crafts, or as street vendors. A lack of demand means
that small-shop owners and vendors spend more
time in idleness in the shop or on the street. While
they are not without a job, they are underemployed.

LOW LABOUR PRODUCTIVITY Labour productivity tends to be very low in most LDCs. The
LDCs have found it difficult to invest in *physical
capital*. As a result, their workers are underequipped
with machinery and tools and are relatively unproductive. Keep in mind that rapid population growth
tends to reduce the amount of physical capital
available per worker, which decreases labour productivity and real incomes.

In addition, most poor countries have not been
able to invest sufficiently in their *human capital*
(Table 23-2, columns 4 and 5); that is, expenditures
on health and education have been meagre. Low
levels of literacy, malnutrition, absence of proper
medical care, and insufficient educational facilities

all contribute to populations ill-equipped for economic development and industrialization. Attitudes
may also play a role. In some countries hard work is
associated with slavery, servitude, and inferiority. It
is therefore to be avoided.

Particularly important is the absence of a vigorous entrepreneurial class willing to bear risks, accumulate capital, and provide the organizational
requisites essential to economic growth. Closely
related is the dearth of labour to handle the super-
visory functions basic to any program of development. Some LDCs are characterized by an
authoritarian view of human relations — often fostered by repressive governments — which generates
an environment hostile to independent thinking,
taking initiatives, and assuming economic risks.
Authoritarianism discourages experimentation and
change — the essence of entrepreneurship.

An additional irony is that, while migration
from the LDCs has modestly offset rapid population
growth, it has also deprived some LDCs of highly
productive workers. It is often the best-trained and
most highly motivated workers — physicians, engineers, teachers, and nurses — who leave the LDCs
to seek their fortunes in the IACs. This so-called
brain drain deteriorates the overall skill level and
productivity of the labour force.

CAPITAL ACCUMULATION

An important focal point of economic development
is the accumulation of capital goods. There are several reasons for this:

1. All LDCs suffer from shortages of capital
goods — factories, machinery and equipment, public
utilities, and so forth. Better-equipped labour forces
would greatly enhance their productivity and help to
boost the per capita standard of living. There is a
close relationship between output per worker (labour
productivity) and real income per worker. A nation
must produce more goods and services per worker to
enjoy more goods and services per worker as income.
One way of increasing labour productivity is to provide each worker with more tools and equipment.

2. Increasing the stock of capital goods is crucial because of the very limited possibility of
increasing the supply of arable land. If there is little
likelihood of increasing agricultural output by
increasing the supply of land, an alternative is to
use more and better capital equipment with the
available agricultural work force.

3. Once initiated, the process of capital accumulation may be cumulative. If capital accumulation can increase output faster than population grows, a margin of saving may arise that permits further capital formation. In a sense, capital accumulation can feed on itself.

Let's first consider the prospects for less-developed nations to accumulate capital domestically. Later we will examine the possibility of foreign capital flowing into them.

DOMESTIC CAPITAL FORMATION   A less-developed nation — or any nation — accumulates capital through saving and investing. A nation must save (refrain from consumption) to release resources from consumer goods production. Investment spending must then absorb these released resources in the production of capital goods. But impediments to saving and investing are much greater in a low-income nation than in an advanced economy.

THE SAVINGS POTENTIAL   Consider first the savings side of the picture. The situation here is mixed and varies greatly among countries. Some of the very poor countries such as Ethiopia, Bangladesh, Uganda, Haiti, and Madagascar save only from 2% to 5% of their domestic outputs. They are too poor to save a significant portion of their incomes. Interestingly, however, other LDCs save as large a percentage of their domestic outputs as do the advanced industrial countries. For example, in 1992 India and China saved 22% and 36% of their domestic outputs, respectively, as compared with 34% for Japan, 28% for West Germany, and 19% for Canada. The problem is that the domestic outputs of the LDCs are so low that, even when saving rates are comparable to those of the advanced nations, the total absolute volume of saving is not large. As we will see, foreign capital inflows and foreign aid are means of supplementing domestic saving.

CAPITAL FLIGHT   Many of the LDCs have suffered **capital flight**. Citizens of the LDCs have transferred their savings to, or invested their savings in, the IACs. Citizens of many LDCs regard the risks of investing at home to be higher than the risk of investing in the industrially advanced nations. These risks include loss of savings or real capital due to government expropriation, taxation, higher rates of inflation, or fluctuations in exchange rates.

If an LDC's political climate is volatile, savers may shift their funds overseas to a "safe haven" in fear that a new government might confiscate their wealth. Likewise, rapid or galloping inflation in an LDC would have similar confiscatory effects. Transferring savings overseas may also be a means of evading domestic taxes on interest income or capital gains. Finally, financial capital may flow to the IACs where there are higher interest rates or a greater variety of investment opportunities.

Whatever the motivation, studies suggest the amount of capital flight from the LDCs is significant. One estimate suggested that the five largest Latin American debtors had capital outflows of $101 billion of private assets between 1979 and 1984. At the end of 1987 Mexicans are estimated to have held some $84 billion in assets abroad. Foreign asset holdings for Venezuelans, Argentinians, and Brazilians were $58, $46, and $31 billion respectively. It is estimated that $6 to $10 billion flees Brazil every year. Brazilians are sending more money abroad as interest on foreign debt and capital flight than they receive as foreign investment and foreign aid. The critical point is that a significant portion of capital lending by the IACs to the LDCs is offset by LDC capital flights to the IACs. The World Bank estimates that the inflows of foreign aid and loans to Latin America were essentially negated by their capital flight in the 1980s.

INVESTMENT OBSTACLES   The investment side of capital formation abounds with equally serious obstacles. These obstacles undermine the rate of capital formation even when a sufficient volume of savings is available to finance the needed investment. Obstacles to investment fall into two categories: lack of investors and lack of incentives to invest.

Oddly, in some less-developed countries the major obstacle to investment is the lack of business executives willing to assume the risks associated with investment. This is a special case of qualitative deficiencies of the labour force previously discussed.

But even if substantial savings and a vigorous entrepreneurial class are present, an essential ingredient in capital formation — the incentive to invest — may be weak. A host of factors may combine in an LDC to cripple investment incentives. We have just mentioned such factors as political instability and higher rates of inflation in our discussion of capital flight. Similarly, very low incomes mean a limited domestic market — a lack of demand — for most nonagricultural goods. This factor is crucial when the chances of successfully competing with mature industries of advanced nations in international markets are meagre. Then too, lack of trained administrative and operating personnel may be a factor in retarding investment. Finally, many of the LDCs simply do not have an adequate **infrastructure**, that is, the public capital goods that are prerequisite to private investment of a productive nature. Poor roads and bridges, inadequate railways, little gas and electricity production, antiquated communications, unsatisfactory housing, and meagre educational and public health facilities scarcely provide an inviting environment for investment spending. It is significant to note that approximately four-fifths of the investment of multinational companies goes to IACs.

The absence of an adequate infrastructure presents more of a problem than you might first surmise. The dearth of public capital goods means that much investment spending that does not *directly* result in the production of goods, and that may not be capable of bearing profits, must take place before and simultaneously with productive investment in manufacturing machinery and equipment. Statistics for advanced nations indicate that about 60% of gross investment goes for housing, public works, and public utilities, leaving about 40% for directly productive investment in manufacturing, agriculture, and commerce. These figures probably understate the percentage of total investment that must be devoted to infrastructure in emerging nations. The volume of investment required to initiate economic development may be much greater than it first appears.

One bright spot is the possibility of accumulating capital through in-kind or **nonfinancial investment**. With leadership and willingness to co-operate, capital can be accumulated by transferring surplus agricultural labour to improvement of agricultural facilities or the infrastructure. If each agricultural village allocated its surplus manpower to the construction of irrigation canals, wells, schools, sanitary facilities, and roads, significant amounts of capital might be accumulated at no significant sacrifice of consumer goods production. Nonfinancial investment bypasses the problems inherent in the financial aspects of the capital accumulation process. Such investment does not require consumers to save portions of their money income, nor does it presume the presence of an entrepre-

neurial class anxious to invest. When the leadership and co-operative spirit are present, nonfinancial investment is a promising avenue for accumulation of basic capital goods. **(Key Question 8)**

TECHNOLOGICAL ADVANCE

Technological advance and capital formation are frequently part of the same process. Yet there are advantages in treating technological advance — or the discovery and application of new methods of production — and capital formation as separate processes.

The rudimentary state of technology in the LDCs puts them far from the frontiers of technological advance. There already exists an enormous body of technological knowledge accumulated by the advanced nations that the underdeveloped countries *might* adopt and apply without expensive research. Crop rotation and contour ploughing require no additional capital equipment and may contribute significantly to productivity. By raising grain storage bins a few centimetres above the ground, a large amount of grain spoilage can be avoided. Such changes may sound trivial to people of advanced nations. However, resulting gains in productivity can mean the difference between subsistence living and starvation in some poverty-ridden nations.

In most instances, application of either existing or new technological knowledge involves new and different capital goods. But within limits, this capital can be obtained without an increase in the rate of capital formation. If the annual flow of replacement investment is rechannelled from technologically inferior to technologically superior capital equipment, productivity can be increased out of a constant level of investment spending. Actually, some technological advances may be **capital-saving** rather than **capital-using**. A new fertilizer, better adapted to a nation's topography and climate, might be cheaper than one currently employed. A seemingly high-priced metal plough that will last ten years may be cheaper in the long run than an inexpensive but technologically inferior wooden plough that requires annual replacement.

To what extent have LDCs transferred and effectively used available IAC technological knowledge? The picture is mixed. There can be no doubt that such technological borrowing has been instrumental in the rapid growth of such Pacific Rim countries as Japan, South Korea, Taiwan, and Singapore. Similarly, the OPEC nations benefited greatly from IAC knowledge with respect to oil exploration, production, and refining. Recently the former Soviet Union and other Eastern European nations have been seeking western technology to hasten their conversions to viable market-based economies.

But at the same time we must be realistic about the transferability of advanced technologies to less-developed countries. In industrially advanced nations, technologies are based on relatively scarce, highly skilled labour and relatively abundant capital. Such technologies tend to be capital-using or, alternatively stated, labour-saving. In contrast, less-developed economies require technologies appropriate to *their* resource endowments — abundant unskilled labour and very limited quantities of capital goods. Labour-using and capital-saving technologies are appropriate to LDCs. Much of the highly advanced technology of the advanced nations is appropriate in the less-developed countries, which must, therefore, develop their own technologies. But many of the less-developed nations have "traditional economies" and are not highly receptive to change. This is particularly true in the peasant agriculture that dominates the economies of most LDCs. A potential technological advance that fails can mean hunger and malnutrition. It is thus not surprising that there is a strong propensity to retain traditional production techniques.

SOCIOCULTURAL AND INSTITUTIONAL FACTORS

Economic considerations alone do not explain why an economy does or does not grow. Substantial social and institutional readjustments are usually an integral part of the growth process. Economic development means not only changes in a nation's physical environment (new transportation and communications facilities, new schools, new housing, new plants and equipment) but also changes in the ways in which people think, behave, and associate with one another.

Emancipation from custom and tradition is frequently the prerequisite of economic development. A critical but intangible ingredient in economic development is **the will to develop**. Economic growth may hinge on "what individuals and social groups *want*, and *whether they want it badly enough to change their old ways of doing things* and to work hard at installing the new."[1]

---

[1] Eugene Staley, *The Future of Underdeveloped Countries*, rev. ed. (New York: Frederick A. Praeger, 1961), p. 218.

SOCIOCULTURAL OBSTACLES   Sociocultural impediments to growth are numerous and varied.

1. Some of the least developed countries have failed to achieve the preconditions for a national economic entity. Tribal and ethnic allegiances take precedence over national identity. Warring tribes confine all economic activity within the tribe, eliminating any possibility for production-increasing specialization and trade. The pathetic economic circumstances in Somalia, Sudan, Liberia, Zaire, and other sub-Saharan nations of Africa are due in no small measure to martial and political conflicts among rival clans.

2. The existence of a caste system — formal or informal — causes labour to be allocated to occupations on the basis of caste or tradition rather than on the basis of skill or merit. The result is a misallocation of human resources.

3. Religious beliefs and observances may seriously restrict the length of the work day and divert resources that might otherwise have been used for investment to ceremonial uses. In rural India, total ceremonial expenditures are estimated at about 7% of per capita income.[2] Generally, religious and philosophical beliefs may be dominated by the fatalistic **capricious universe view**, the belief that there is little or no correlation between an individual's activities and endeavours, and the outcome or experiences that person encounters.

Other attitudes and cultural factors may impede economic activity and growth: emphasis on the performance of duties rather than the exertion of individual initiative; the focus on group rather than individual achievement; the notion of a preordained and unalterable universe; the belief in reincarnation, which reduces the importance of one's present life.

INSTITUTIONAL OBSTACLES   Political corruption and bribery are common in many LDCs. School systems and public service agencies are often ineptly administered, and their functioning is often impaired by petty politics. Tax systems are frequently arbitrary, unjust, cumbersome, and detri-

---

[2] Inder P. Nijhawan, "Socio-Political Institutions, Cultural Values, and Attitudes: Their Impact on Indian Economic Development," in J.S. Uppal (ed.), *India's Economic Problems* (New Delhi: Tata McGraw-Hill Publishing Company, Ltd., 1975), p. 31.

mental to incentives to work and invest. Political decisions are often motivated by a desire to enhance the nation's international prestige rather than to foster development.

Because of the predominance of farming in the LDCs, the problem of achieving that institutional environment in agriculture most conducive to increasing production must be a vital consideration in any growth program. Specifically, the institutional problem of **land reform** demands attention in virtually all LDCs. But the needed reform may vary tremendously between specific nations.

BOX 23-1 APPLYING THE THEORY

FAMINE IN AFRICA

The roots of Africa's persistent famines include both natural and human causes.

The recent famine in Somalia — documented by shocking photos of fly-tormented, emaciated children with bloated bellies — is not uncommon in sub-Saharan Africa. Before U.S. armed forces and U.N. aid arrived in Somalia in late 1992, severe famine had caused an estimated 2000 deaths each day. One out of four Somali children under the age of five — about 300,000 — are believed to have died.

Similarly, despite an outpouring of aid from the rich nations, the 1983–84 Ethiopian famine caused 1 million deaths. A number of African nations — including Ethiopia, Sudan, Angola, Liberia, Zaire, Mozambique, and Malawi — are persistently threatened by famine. Estimates put from 5 to 20 million Africans at risk. This tragedy is ironic because most African countries were self-sufficient in food at the time they became independent nations; they are now heavily dependent on imported foodstuffs for survival.

The immediate cause of this catastrophe is drought. But the ultimate causes of Africa's declining ability to feed itself are more complex, an interplay of natural and human conditions. Lack of rainfall, chronic civil strife, rapid population growth, widespread soil erosion, and counterproductive public policies, all contribute to Africa's famines.

1. CIVIL STRIFE   Regional rebellions and prolonged civil wars have devastated some African nations. Both Ethiopia and the Sudan, for example, have been plagued by decades of civil strife. Not only do these conflicts divert precious resources from civilian uses, they also greatly complicate the ability of wealthy nations to provide famine and developmental aid. In the 1983–84 famine the Ethiopian government denied food aid to areas occupied by rebel forces. Donated food is frequently diverted to the army and denied to starving civilians. During Ethiopia's 1973–74 famine, Haile Selassie sold much of the donated food on world markets to enrich his regime! In Somalia factional feuding has destroyed most institutions — schools, factories, and government ministries — and reduced the country to anarchy. Armed gangs steal water pumps, tractors, and livestock from farms and loot ports of donated foodstuffs.

2. POPULATION GROWTH   In Africa, population is growing more rapidly than is food production. Population is increasing at about 3% per year while food output is growing at only 2% per year. This grim arithmetic suggests declining living standards, hunger, and malnutrition. The World Bank reports that during the 1980s the per capita incomes of the sub-Saharan nations fell to about three-quarters of the level reached by the end of the 1970s.

3. ECOLOGICAL DEGRADATION   But apart from the simple numbers involved, population growth has contributed to the ecological degradation of Africa. With population pressures and the increasing need for food, marginal land has been deforested and put into crop production. In many cases, trees that have served as a barrier to the encroachment of the desert have been cut for fuel, allowing the fragile topsoil to be blown away by desert winds. The scarcity of wood that has accompanied deforestation has forced the use of animal dung for fuel, thereby denying its traditional use as fertilizer. Furthermore, traditional fallow periods have been shortened, resulting in overplanting, overgrazing and a wearing out of the soil. Deforestation and land overuse have reduced the capacity of the land to absorb moisture, diminishing its productivity and its ability to resist drought. Some authorities feel that the diminished ability of the land to absorb water reduces the amount of moisture that evaporates into the clouds to return ultimately as rainfall. All of this is complicated by the fact that there are few facilities for crop storage. Even when crops are good, it is difficult to accumulate a surplus for future lean years. A large percentage of domestic farm output in some parts of Africa is lost to rats, insects, and spoilage.

4. PUBLIC POLICIES AND DEBT   Ill-advised public policies have contributed to Africa's famines. In the first place, African governments have generally neglected investment in agriculture in favour of industrial development and military strength. It is estimated that African governments on the average spend four times as much on armaments as they do on agriculture. Over 40% of Ethiopia's budget is for the support of an oppressive military. Second, many African governments have followed the policy of establishing the prices of

agricultural commodities at low levels to provide cheap food for growing urban populations. This low-price policy has diminished the incentives of farmers to increase productivity. While foreign aid has helped to ease the effects of Africa's food-population problems, most experts reject aid as a long-term solution. Experience suggests that aid in the form of food can provide only temporary relief and may undermine the realization of long-run local self-sufficiency. Foreign food aid, it is contended, treats symptoms and not causes.

All of this is made more complex by the fact that the sub-Saharan nations are burdened with large and growing external debts. The IMF reports that the aggregate debt of these nations rose from $21 billion in 1976 to $127 billion in 1990. As a condition of further aid, these nations have had to invoke austerity programs that have contributed to declines in their per capita incomes. One tragic consequence is that many of these nations have cut back on social service programs for children.

To summarize: the famine confronting much of Africa is partly a phenomenon of nature and in part self-inflicted. Drought, civil strife, overpopulation, ecological deterioration, and errant public policies have all been contributing factors. This complex of causes implies that hunger and malnutrition in Africa may persist long after the rains return.

In some LDCs, the problem is excessive concentration of land ownership in the hands of a few wealthy families. This situation is demoralizing for tenants; it weakens their incentive to produce and is typically not conducive to capital improvements. At the other extreme is the arrangement where each family owns and farms a minute fragment of land far too small for the application of modern agricultural technology. An important complication to the problem of land reform lies in the fact that political considerations sometimes push reform in that direction that is least defensible on economic grounds. For many nations, land reform may well be the most acute institutional problem to be resolved in initiating the process of economic development.

Examples: Land reform in South Korea undermined the political control of the landed aristocracy and made way for the development of strong commercial and industrial middle classes, all to the benefit of the country's economic development. In

contrast, the prolonged dominance of the landed aristocracy in the Philippines has helped stifle the development of that economy.[3]

QUICK REVIEW 23-1

1. About three-fourths of the world's population lives in the LDCs of Africa, Asia, and Latin America.

2. Natural resource scarcities and inhospitable climates restrict growth in many LDCs.

3. The LDCs are characterized by overpopulation, high unemployment rates, underemployment, and low productivity.

[3] Mrinal Datta-Chaudhuri, "Market Failure and Government Failure," *Journal of Economic Perspectives*, Summer, 1990, p. 36.

4. Low saving rates, capital flight, weak infrastructures, and the lack of investors impair capital accumulation.

5. Sociocultural, political, and institutional factors are often serious impediments to growth.

THE VICIOUS CIRCLE

Many of the characteristics of LDCs just described are simultaneously causes and consequences of their poverty. These countries are caught in a **vicious circle of poverty**. They *stay* poor because they *are* poor! Consider Figure 23-1. The fundamental feature of an LDC is low per capita income. Being poor, a family has little ability or incentive to save. Furthermore, low incomes mean low levels of demand. Thus, there are few available resources, on the one hand, and no strong incentives, on the other, for investment in physical or human capital. This means labour productivity is low. And since output per person is real income per person, it follows that per capita income is low.

Many experts believe that the key to breaking out of this vicious circle is to increase the rate of capital accumulation, to achieve a level of investment of, say, 10% of the national income. But Figure 23-1 reminds us that the real villain for many LDCs — rapid population growth — may be waiting in the wings to undo the potentially beneficial effects of this higher rate of capital accumulation. (**Key Question 14**)

ROLE OF GOVERNMENT

Economists do not agree on the appropriate role of government in seeking economic growth.

A POSITIVE ROLE

One view is that, at least during initial stages of development, government needs to play a major role. The reasons for this stem from the nature of the obstacles facing the LDCs.

1. LAW AND ORDER   Some of the poorest countries are plagued by banditry and intertribal warfare, which divert both attention and resources from the task of development. A strong and stable national government is needed to establish domestic law and order and to achieve peace and unity. Not surprisingly, research demonstrates that political instability (as measured by the number of revolutions and coups per year) is associated with slow growth.

FIGURE 23-1   The vicious circle of poverty

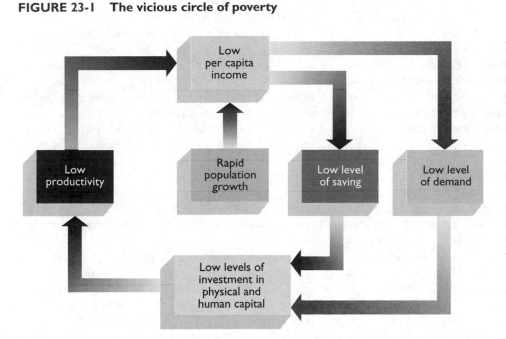

Low per capita incomes make it extremely difficult for poor nations to save and invest, a condition that perpetuates low productivity and low incomes. Furthermore, rapid population growth may quickly absorb increases in per capita real income and thereby negate the possibility of breaking out of the poverty circle.

2. LACK OF ENTREPRENEURSHIP The absence of a sizable and vigorous entrepreneurial class ready and willing to accumulate capital and initiate production indicates that in many cases private enterprise is not capable of spearheading the growth process.

3. INFRASTRUCTURE Many obstacles to economic growth centre on an inadequate infrastructure. Sanitation and basic medical programs, education, irrigation and soil conservation projects, and construction of highways and transportation-communication facilities are all essentially nonmarketable goods and services yielding widespread spillover benefits. Government is the sole institution in a position to provide these goods and services in required quantities.

4. FORCED SAVING AND INVESTMENT Government action may also be required to break through the saving-investment dilemma that impedes capital formation in the LDCs.

It may be that only governmental fiscal action can provide a solution by forcing the economy to accumulate capital. There are two options here. One is to force the economy to save by increasing taxes. These tax revenues can then be channelled into priority investment projects. The problems of honestly and efficiently administering the tax system and achieving a high degree of compliance with tax laws can be great.

The alternative is to force the economy to save through inflation. The government can finance capital accumulation by creating and spending new money or by selling bonds to banks and spending the proceeds. The resulting inflation is the equivalent of an arbitrary tax on the economy.

There are serious arguments against the advisability of saving through inflation. In the first place, inflation often distorts the composition of investment away from productive facilities to such items as luxury housing, precious metals and jewels, or foreign securities, which provide a better hedge against rising prices. Furthermore, significant inflation may reduce voluntary private saving as potential savers become less willing to accumulate depreciating money or securities payable in money of declining value. Inflation also induces "capital flight." Inflation may also boost the nation's imports and retard its flow of exports, creating balance of payments difficulties.

5. SOCIAL-INSTITUTIONAL PROBLEMS Government is in the key position to deal effectively with the social-institutional obstacles to growth. Controlling population growth and land reform are problems that call for the broad approach that only government can provide. And government is in a position to stimulate the will to develop, to change a philosophy of "Heaven and faith will determine the course of events" to one of "God helps those who help themselves."

PUBLIC SECTOR PROBLEMS

But serious problems and disadvantages may exist with a government-directed development program. If entrepreneurial talent is lacking in the private sector, can we expect leaders of high quality to be present in the ranks of government? Is there not a real danger that government bureaucracy will impede, not stimulate, much-needed social and economic change? And what of the tendency of some political leaders to favour the spectacular showpiece projects at the expense of less showy but more productive programs? Might not political projects take precedence over the economic goals of a government-directed development program?

Development experts are less enthusiastic about the role of government in the growth process than they were 30 years ago. Government maladministration and corruption are common in many LDCs. Government officials often line their own pockets with foreign-aid funds. Similarly, political leaders frequently confer monopoly privileges on relatives, friends, and political supporters. A political leader may grant exclusive rights to relatives or friends to produce, import, or export certain products. These monopoly privileges lead to higher domestic prices for the relevant products and diminish the LDCs' ability to compete in world markets. In a similar fashion, the managers of state-owned enterprises are often appointed on the basis of cronyism rather than competence. Many LDC governments, particularly in Africa, have created "marketing boards" as the sole purchaser of agricultural products from local farmers. The boards buy farm products at artificially low prices, sell the output at higher world prices, and the "profit" ends up in the pockets of government officials. In recent years the perception of government has shifted from that of catalyst and promoter of growth to that of a potential impediment to development.

A MIXED BAG

It is possible to muster casual evidence on both sides of this question. Positive government contributions to development are evident in the cases of Japan, South Korea, and Taiwan. In comparison, Mobutu's Zaire, Somoza's Nicaragua, Marcos's Philippines, and Haiti under the Duvaliers are recognized examples of corrupt and inept governments that functioned as impediments to economic progress. Certainly the revolutionary transformations of the former Soviet Union and other Eastern European nations away from communism and towards market-oriented economies make clear that central planning is no longer recognized as an effective mechanism for development. Many LDCs are belatedly coming to recognize that competition and individual economic incentives are important ingredients in the development process. LDCs increasingly recognize that their citizens need to see direct personal gains from their efforts to motivate them to take actions that will expand production.

ROLE OF ADVANCED NATIONS

What are the ways by which industrially advanced nations can help the less-developed countries in their quest for growth? To what degree have these avenues of assistance been pursued?

Generally, less-developed nations can benefit from (1) an expanding volume of trade with advanced nations; (2) foreign aid in the form of grants and loans from the governments of advanced nations; and (3) flows of private capital from the more affluent nations.

EXPANDING TRADE

Some authorities maintain that the simplest and most effective way that Canada and other industrially advanced nations can aid less-developed nations is by lowering international trade barriers, thereby enabling the LDCs to expand their national incomes through increased trade.

Though there is some truth in this view, lowered trade barriers are not a panacea. It is true that some of the poor nations need large foreign markets for their raw materials to stimulate growth. But the problem for many is not obtaining markets for the utilization of existing productive capacity or the sale of relatively abundant raw materials, but rather

getting the capital and technical assistance needed to produce something for export.

Furthermore, close trade ties with advanced nations are not without disadvantages. A recession among the IACs can have disastrous consequences for the prices of raw materials and the export earnings of the LDCs. Stability and growth in industrially advanced nations are important to progress in the less-developed countries.

FOREIGN AID: PUBLIC LOANS AND GRANTS

Foreign capital — both public and private — can supplement an emerging country's saving and investment and play a crucial role in breaking the circle of poverty.

Most LDCs are sadly lacking in infrastructure — irrigation and public health programs and educational, transportation, and communications systems — prerequisites to attracting either domestic or foreign private capital. Foreign public aid is needed to tear down this roadblock to the flow of private capital to the LDCs.

DIRECT AID   Canada and other IACs have assisted the LDCs directly through a variety of programs and through participation in international institutions designed to stimulate economic development. Canadian official development assistance, mostly through the Canadian International Development Agency, cost, in grants, loans and advances, a total of $2.6 billion in 1991. On a per capita basis, Canadian aid is higher than the American. Other advanced nations have also embarked on sizable foreign aid programs. In recent years foreign aid from all IACs was about U.S. $60 billion per year.

The aid programs of the IACs merit several additional comments. First, aid is sometimes distributed on the basis of political and military, rather than economic, considerations. Israel, Turkey, and Greece are major recipients of American aid at the expense of Asian, Latin American, and African nations with much lower standards of living. Second, aid from the IACs only amounts to about one-third of 1% of the IACs' collective GDPs. (Global Perspective 23-2.) Finally, LDCs are increasingly concerned that the shift of the former Soviet Union and Eastern Europe towards more democratic, market-oriented systems will make these nations "new players" as foreign aid recipients.

The LDCs worry that IAC aid that formerly flowed to Latin America, Asia, and Africa may be redirected to, say, Poland, Hungary, and Russia. Similarly, there is the prospect of a substantially larger aid flow to the Middle East if the PLO-Israeli peace accord is durable.

GLOBAL PERSPECTIVE 23-2

Development assistance as a percentage of GDP, selected nations

Canada is a leading provider of development assistance to the LDCs. But other industrialized nations contribute a larger percentage of their GNPs as foreign aid.

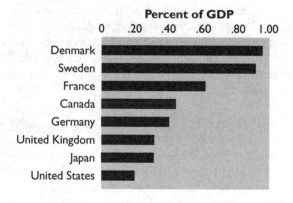

Source: World Bank data.

THE WORLD BANK GROUP   Canada is a participant in the **World Bank**, whose major objective is to assist the LDCs in achieving growth. Supported by nearly 180 member nations, the Bank not only lends out of its capital funds, but also (1) sells bonds and lends the proceeds, and (2) guarantees and insures private loans.

Several characteristics of the World Bank are noteworthy.

1. The World Bank is a "last resort" lending agency; its loans are limited to productive projects, for which private funds are not readily available.

2. Because many World Bank loans have been for basic development projects — dams, irrigation projects, health and sanitation programs, communications and transportation facilities — it has been hoped that the Bank's activities will provide the infrastructure needed to encourage flows of private capital.

3. The Bank has played a role in providing technical assistance to LDCs by helping them discover the avenues of growth that seem appropriate for their economic development.

Two World Bank affiliates function in areas where the World Bank has not had a strong presence. The *International Finance Corporation (IFC)* has the primary function of investing in *private* enterprises in LDCs. The *International Development Association (IDA)* makes "soft loans" — loans that may not be self-liquidating — to the very poorest of the LDCs on more liberal terms than does the World Bank.

FOREIGN HARM?   But foreign aid to the LDCs has been subject to criticism.

1. DEPENDENCY AND INCENTIVES   A basic criticism is that, like domestic welfare programs, foreign aid may generate dependency rather than self-sustaining growth. It is argued that transfers of wealth from the IACs allow the LDCs to avoid the painful economic decisions, the institutional and cultural changes, and the alterations in attitudes regarding thrift, industry, hard work, and self-reliance that are needed for growth. Critics say that, after some five decades of foreign aid, the LDCs' demand for foreign aid has increased; if aid programs had been successful in promoting sustainable growth, demand should have fallen.

2. BUREAUCRACY AND CENTRALIZED GOVERNMENT IAC aid is given, not directly to the residents and businesses of the LDCs, but rather to their governments. The dire consequence is that aid generates massive, relatively unproductive government bureaucracies and centralizes government power over the economy. The recent stagnation and collapse of the centralized economies of the Soviet Union and Eastern Europe provide evidence that market-oriented economies are much more conducive to growth and development. Furthermore, not only does the bureaucratization of the LDCs divert valuable human resources from the private to the public sector, but it shifts the nation's focus from the *production* of output and income to its *redistribution*.

3. CORRUPTION AND MISUSE   Critics also allege that foreign aid is ineffectively used. Corruption is rampant in many LDCs and some estimates suggest 10 to 20% of aid is diverted into the pockets of government officials. Some of the wealthiest individuals in the world — for example, Zaire's Mobutu, the Duvaliers in Haiti, the Philippines' Marcos — are (or were) rulers of LDCs. Foreign aid may create an ironic and perverse incentive for LDC leaders to keep their populations poor so they continue to qualify for aid.

Also, IAC-based aid consultants and multinational corporations are major beneficiaries of aid programs. Some economists contend that as much as one-fourth or more of each year's aid is spent on expert consultants. Furthermore, because IAC corporations carry out most aid projects, they are major beneficiaries of, and lobbyists for, foreign aid.

PRIVATE CAPITAL FLOWS

The LDCs have also received substantial flows of private capital from the IACs. For the most part, these private investors are large corporations and commercial banks. General Motors or Chrysler might finance construction of a plant in Mexico or Brazil to assemble autos or produce auto parts. Or the Royal Bank of Canada or Bank of America may make loans to the governments of Argentina or the Philippines.

Although these private capital flows were modest in the 1950s and 1960s — ranging from $2 billion to $4 billion per year — they grew in the 1970s, averaging $28 billion. Then in the early 1980s an LDC debt crisis developed, which caused private capital flows to the poor nations to fall precipitously.

THE LDC DEBT CRISIS

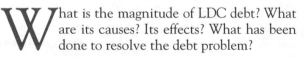What is the magnitude of LDC debt? What are its causes? Its effects? What has been done to resolve the debt problem?

THE DEBT AND ITS GROWTH

The external debt (debts owed to foreign governments, businesses, individuals, and financial institutions) of the LDCs increased thirteenfold in the past two decades, from $100 billion in 1970 to about $1350 billion in 1990.

CAUSES OF THE CRISIS

We have noted that private capital flows — particularly from large IAC commercial banks — increased greatly in the 1970s. But in the 1970s and early 1980s a series of world economic events converged to have serious adverse effects on the LDCs and created a debt crisis.

1. SOARING OIL PRICES The dramatic run-up of oil prices by OPEC in 1973–74 and again in 1979–80 (raising the price of a barrel of oil from about U.S. $2.50 to $35) greatly increased the energy bills of the oil-importing LDCs. These nations faced growing current-account deficits in their balance of payments, which were financed largely by increased borrowing. Hence, the external debt of the oil-importing LDCs grew from $130 billion in 1972 to $700 billion by 1982. Borrowed funds that could have been used for development were instead used to pay higher energy costs.

2. TIGHT MONETARY POLICY In the early 1980s the IACs — particularly the United States and Canada — invoked strong anti-inflationary monetary policies. These tight monetary policies triggered two adverse effects for the LDCs. On the one hand, the growth of IAC national incomes slowed; in 1980–82 both Canada and the United States suffered their most serious postwar recessions. As a result, IAC demands for the raw material and farm product exports of LDCs declined. This translated into sharp reductions in the export earnings that the LDCs needed to pay interest and principal on their debts. On the other hand, tight monetary policies in the IACs resulted in much higher interest rates. This greatly increased the cost to the LDCs of servicing their debts.

3. APPRECIATING DOLLAR The burden of LDC debt arose for still another reason. In the 1981–84 period the international price of the U.S. and Canadian dollars appreciated. The LDCs now had to pay more for their imports of North American manufactured goods. And, because much LDC debt is denominated in U.S. dollars, LDCs had to export a larger amount of goods to acquire each dollar needed to pay interest and principal on their debts.

4. UNPRODUCTIVE INVESTMENTS In a number of LDCs the poor use of borrowed funds contributed to the debt crisis. Because of political corruption and economic mismanagement, LDC investment of loan funds was frequently unproductive. Returns on such investments were not sufficient to cover interest and principal payments, thereby generating loan defaults.

5. MEXICAN CRISIS In 1982 Mexico was on the verge of defaulting on its debt. Creditors were forced to reschedule that debt and make further loans to Mexico. This Mexican debt crisis precipitated an abrupt loss of confidence in the credit-worthiness of many highly indebted LDCs. As a result, private voluntary lending to the LDCs declined sharply.

ECONOMIC CONSEQUENCES

There has followed a period of "muddling through," during which the creditor nations in co-operation with the international Monetary Fund have attempted to deal with the LDC debt crisis on a nation-by-nation basis. The debts of many LDCs were rescheduled (stretched out over a longer period of time) to reduce the burden of annual interest and principal payments. In return for these concessions LDCs had to agree to domestic austerity programs to improve their prospects for debt repayment. This meant that LDCs had to reduce their imports and increase their exports to realize more international trade earnings for debt repayment. But increased exports and reduced imports imply a further impairment of living standards in the LDCs. Similarly, with net export earnings being used primarily for debt retirement, little or nothing is left to invest in development projects. It is not by chance that, while the growth of real GNP for the LDCs as a group was 3.8% per year in the 1980–89 period, the rate for highly indebted LDCs was only 1.9%.

REFORM AND REVIVAL

The 1980s was characterized by intensive negotiations between the IACs and the IMF, on the one hand, and the highly indebted LDCs, on the other, to resolve the debt crisis. The results included (1) restructuring of debt, that is, increasing the period of repayment and reducing interest rates; (2) writing-off or forgiving some of the debt; (3) making additional loans to the LDCs to help them make payments on existing debt; and (4) debt-equity swaps. **Debt-equity swaps** occur when LDC governments and businesses pay off debt by giving shares of stock (ownership claims to government-owned or private enterprises) to foreign creditors. The advantage of such swaps to LDCs is that no fixed interest or principal payments must be made to stockholders. The disadvantage to LDCs is that partial ownership of their businesses is transferred to foreigners. The advantage to lending IACs is that stock ownership is better than default.

Although private capital flows to the LDCs virtually ceased in the 1980s, there has been a modest revival in the 1990s. Two interrelated factors are involved.

LDC ECONOMIC REFORMS   As part of the debt negotiations, heavily indebted LDCs agree to reform their economies so as to promote growth and avert future debt crises. At the macro level, greater efforts are being made to reduce budget deficits and control chronically high levels of inflation. At the micro level, many governments have privatized state-owned businesses and deregulated industry. Tariffs and other trade barriers, along with exchange rate controls, have been reduced. In general, the economic role of government has been lessened and that of free markets enhanced. These reforms have made the LDCs more attractive to foreign lenders.

REVIVED INVESTMENT   The 1990s has witnessed a modest revival in private capital flows to the LDCs, particularly to those that have reformed their economies. However, the makeup of this revived investment flow is now different. First, private IAC firms and individuals, rather than commercial banks, are the primary lenders. Second, the loans are largely direct investments in LDC enterprises, rather than loans to LDC governments. The potential advantage of directly investing in LDC enterprises is that management skills and technological knowledge often accompany such capital flows.

Two words of caution: The revived flow of capital is highly selective. Most of the flow is directed towards the more affluent, reformed countries of Latin America and not towards the extremely impoverished sub-Saharan nations of Africa. And it is premature to say that the LDC debt crisis has been resolved. Some LDC nations still face staggering debt burdens and there is no assurance that some combinations of circumstances will not bring about future defaults. The debt crisis has been alleviated, not solved.

QUICK REVIEW 23-2

I. LDC governments may encourage growth by **a** providing law and order; **b** engaging in entrepreneurial activities; **c** improving the infrastructure; **d** forcing higher levels of saving and investing; and **e** resolving social-institutional problems.

2. The IACs can assist the LDCs through expanded trade, foreign aid, and private capital flows.

3. Many LDCs have huge external debts that have become an additional obstacle to growth.

TOWARDS A NEW GLOBAL COMPACT[4]

As the income gap between the rich and the poor nations widens, spokespersons for the LDCs have put forth an agenda for reform, which includes:

1. SHARING THE PEACE DIVIDEND With the end of the Cold War, LDC leaders argue that IACs' military spending can be reduced and the released resources shared with the poor nations. Specifically, all countries should reduce their military expenditures by at least 3% per year, making available a "peace dividend" of about U.S. $1.2 trillion in the IACs by the year 2000.

2. REFORM OF FOREIGN AID The LDCs say foreign aid is (a) deficient quantitatively; (b) borne inequitably by donor nations; and (c) not allocated to the poorest nations.

QUANTITY While the governments of IACs "recycle" from 15 to 25% of their GDPs to alleviate income inequality internally, they provide only 0.35% of their GDPs in foreign aid to impoverished peoples around the world. The LDCs advocate that this figure should be doubled to the 0.7% level recommended by the United Nations.

EQUITY The LDCs would like to see foreign aid restructured to resemble a progressive tax so that the percentage of aid donated by each nation would increase the larger its GDP. Currently we find that super-rich United States and Japan donate only 0.20 and 0.32% of their GDPs respectively as aid, while less-affluent Sweden and the Netherlands give 0.90% or more. If the United States and Japan were to pay recommended progressive rates of approximately 0.80%, most of the aid shortfall

between the current 0.35 and the recommended 0.70% of GDP would disappear.

ALLOCATION Foreign aid is strongly influenced by political and military — not economic — considerations. The consequence is that LDCs do *not* receive aid in accordance with their needs or degree of destitution. Only a quarter of foreign aid goes to those ten countries whose populations constitute 70% of the world's poorest people. The most affluent 40% of the LDC world population receives over twice as much aid as the poorest 40%.

3. DEBT RELIEF The LDCs have also sought debt relief. They say their present debt is so large that it constitutes a severe obstacle to LDC growth. Arguing that the prosperity of the IACs depends on the prosperity of the LDCs, LDCs feel that forgiving some portion of the debt would be mutually beneficial. One proposal suggests that as much as two-thirds of all existing LDC external debt be cancelled and the remainder be rescheduled for payment over a 25-year period.

4. IMPROVING GLOBAL MARKETS The LDCs complain that their export earnings have been impaired because of deteriorating terms of trade and trade barriers.

TERMS OF TRADE The long-term price trend of LDC commodity exports (such as coffee, sugar, cocoa, bauxite, tin, and copper) has been downward. For example, in the 1980s the price index for a group of 33 primary commodities (excluding oil) fell by almost one-half. Part of this decline is explained by the slow growth of demand relative to supply. Ironically, many LDCs stepped up production of their commodity exports to increase their foreign-exchange earnings to meet interest and principal payments on their external debts. But these attempts were largely frustrated by the price declines that resulted from the increased commodity supplies. Product substitution has also contributed to failing commodity prices. Synthetic fibres have been substituted for cotton and jute; glass fibres have supplanted copper in communications; corn syrup and other sweeteners have tended to reduce the demand for sugar.

In contrast, the LDCs import manufactured goods produced by the corporate giants of the advanced nations that have the market power to

---

[4] This section is based primarily on the United Nations Development Program, *Human Development Report 1992* (New York: Oxford University Press, 1992).

charge high prices. The LDCs argue that the **terms of trade** have shifted against them; the prices of their exports tend to be depressed while the prices of their imports tend to rise. Thus, it takes more of the LDCs' exports to purchase a given quantity of imports.

TRADE BARRIERS   The LDCs lament that trade barriers are highest for the labour-intensive kinds of manufactured goods — textiles, clothing, footwear, and processed agricultural products — in which the LDCs have a comparative advantage. Some 20 of the 24 most industrialized nations are more protectionist than they were a decade ago. And, ironically, many tariffs increase with the degree of product processing — for example, tariffs on chocolate are higher than on cocoa — which effectively denies the LDCs the opportunity to develop processing industries. One estimate suggests that trade barriers reduce the gross domestic products of the LDCs by 3%, causing an annual loss of U.S. $75 billion in income.

5. IMMIGRATION   There are both quantitative and qualitative aspects to the LDC's immigration complaints. Too few people are allowed to move from the LDCs to the IACs and IAC policies tend to favour movement of the most productive LDC workers.

LDC spokespersons believe that the IACs should liberalize their immigration laws to enlarge the flow of unemployed and underemployed workers from the LDCs. While some nations — Canada and the United States, for example — have abolished discrimination by country of origin, several European nations are moving towards more restrictive stances with respect to potential LDC immigrants. Some pressure is building to repatriate unemployed migrants. Not only is migration an outlet for surplus LDC labour, but it is also a source of income in the form of migrant remittances. Currently aggregate remittances from emigrants back to the LDCs is about $25 billion per year.

Canada, the United States, and other IACs have rewritten their immigration laws to favour workers with high skill levels such as researchers,

physicians, engineers, and scientists. This, of course, encourages the "brain drain" where LDCs lose human capital in which they have made substantial investments. Estimates indicate that Africa as a whole lost some 60,000 middle- and high-level managers to migration in the 1985–90 period.

6. NEOCOLONIALISM   A more general grievance is that, despite the realization of political independence, many LDCs feel an economic-based **neocolonialism** persists. Over four-fifths of the world's direct investment by multinational companies is received by IACs and the remaining one-fifth goes largely to those LDCs that are already better off. And most of the contracts, leases, and concessions that multinational corporations of advance countries have negotiated with the LDCs have benefited the multinationals at the expense of the host countries. The poor countries argue that most benefits from the exploitation of their natural resources accrues to others. Furthermore, LDCs seek to achieve greater diversification and therefore greater stability in their economies. Foreign private capital, however, seeks out those industries that are currently the most profitable, that is, the ones now producing for the export market. In brief, while LDCs strive for less dependence on world markets, flows of foreign private capital enhance that dependence. Multinational corporations are after profits and allegedly have no particular interest in either the economic independence, diversification, or overall progress of the LDCs.

Whether the IACs will address these grievances, creating a "new global compact" with the LDCs is problematic. While the poor countries feel their proposals are egalitarian and just, many advanced nations see them as a demand for a massive redistribution of world income and wealth that is simply not in the cards. Many industrialized nations feel there is no "quick fix" for underdevelopment and that the LDCs must undergo the same process of patient hard work and gradual capital formation as did the advanced nations over the past two centuries.

CHAPTER SUMMARY

1. Most nations are less developed (low per capita income) nations. While some LDCs have been achieving quite rapid growth rates in recent years, others have little or no growth.

2. Initial scarcities of natural resources and the limited possibility of augmenting existing supplies may limit a nation's capacity to develop.

3. The large and rapidly growing populations in most LDCs contribute to low per capita incomes. Increases in per capita incomes frequently induce rapid population growth, again reducing per capita incomes to near subsistence levels. The "demographic transition" concept suggests that rising living standards must precede declining birth rates.

4. Most LDCs suffer from unemployment and underemployment. Labour productivity is low because of insufficient investment in physical and human capital.

5. In many LDCs both the saving and investment aspects of capital formation are impeded by formidable obstacles. In some of the poorest LDCs the savings potential is very low. Many LDC savers transfer their funds to the IACs rather than invest domestically. The absence of a vigorous entrepreneurial class and the weakness of investment incentives are also impediments to capital accumulation.

6. Appropriate social and institutional changes and, in particular, the presence of "the will to develop" are essential ingredients in economic development.

7. The vicious circle of poverty brings together many of the obstacles to growth, saying in effect that "poor countries stay poor because of their poverty." Low incomes inhibit saving and accumulation of physical and human capital, making it difficult to increase productivity and incomes. Rapid population growth can offset otherwise promising attempts to break the vicious circle.

8. The nature of the obstacles to growth — the absence of an entrepreneurial class, the dearth of infrastructure, the saving-investment dilemma, and the presence of social-institutional obstacles to growth — suggests the need for government action in initiating growth. However, the corruption and maladministration that are quite common to the public sectors of the LDCs suggest that government may be ineffective as an instigator of growth.

9. Advanced nations can assist in development by reducing trade barriers and by providing both public and private capital. Critics of foreign aid say it **a** creates LDC dependency; **b** contributes to the growth of bureaucracies and centralized economic control; and **c** is ineffective because of corruption and mismanagement.

10. Rising energy prices, declining export prices, depreciation of the dollar, the unproductive use of borrowed funds, and concern about LDCs' creditworthiness combined to create an LDC debt crisis in the early 1980s. External debt problems of many LDCs remain serious and inhibit their growth.

11. The LDCs seek a "new global compact" with the IACs that entails **a** a larger and better allocated flow of aid; **b** debt relief; **c** greater LDC access to world markets; **d** liberalized immigration policies; and **e** an end to neocolonialism.

TERMS AND CONCEPTS

brain drain (p. 497)
capital flight (p. 498)

capital-saving and capital-using
technological advance (p. 499)

capricious universe view (p. 500)
debt-equity swaps (p. 508)
demographic transition (p. 496)
industrially advanced countries (IACs) (p. 492)
infrastructure (p. 499)
land reform (p. 501)
less-developed countries (LDCs) (p. 492)

neocolonialism (p. 510)
New Global Compact (p. 509)
nonfinancial investment (p. 499)
terms of trade (p. 510)
the will to develop (p. 500)
unemployment and underemployment (p. 497)
vicious circle of poverty (p. 503)
World Bank (p. 506)

QUESTIONS AND STUDY SUGGESTIONS

1. What are the characteristics of an LDC? List the avenues of economic development available to such a nation. State and explain obstacles that face LDCs in breaking the poverty barrier. Use the "vicious circle of poverty" to outline in detail steps an LDC might take to initiate economic development.

2. Explain how the absolute per capita income gap between rich and poor nations might increase, even though per capita GDP is growing faster in LDCs than it is in IACs.

3. *Key Question   Assume an LDC and an IAC currently have real per capita outputs of $500 and $5000 respectively. If both nations realize a 3% increase in their real per capita outputs, by how much will the per capita output gap change?*

4. Discuss and evaluate:

   a. "The path to economic development has been clearly blazed by capitalism. It is only for the LDCs to follow this trail."

   b. "Economic inequality is conducive to saving, and saving is the prerequisite of investment. Therefore, greater inequality in the income distribution of the LDCs would be a spur to capital accumulation and growth."

   c. "The IACs fear the complications from oversaving; the LDCs bear the yoke of undersaving."

   d. "The core of development involves changing human beings more than it does altering a nation's physical environment."

   e. "The western world's 'foreign aid' program is a sham. In reality it represents neocolonialism — a means by which the LDCs can be nominally free in a political sense but remain totally subservient in an economic sense."

   f. "Poverty and freedom cannot persist side by side; one must triumph over the other."

   g. "The biggest obstacle facing poor nations in their quest for development is the lack of capital goods."

   h. "A high per capita GDP does not necessarily identify an industrially advanced nation."

5. Explain how population growth might be an impediment to economic growth. How would you define the optimal population of a country?

6. *Key Question   Contrast the "demographic transition" view of population with the traditional view that slower population growth is a prerequisite for rising living standards in the LDCs.*

7. Much of the initial investment in an LDC must be devoted to infrastructure that does not directly or immediately lead to a greater production of goods and services. What bearing might this have on the degree of inflation that results as government finances capital accumulation through the creating and spending of new money?

8. *Key Question*   *Since real capital is supposed to earn a higher return where it is scarce, how do you explain the fact that most international investment flows to the IACs (where capital is relatively abundant) rather than to the LDCs (where capital is very scarce)?*

9. "The nature of the problems faced by the LDCs creates a bias in favour of governmentally directed as opposed to a decentralized development process." Do you agree? Why or why not?

10. What is the LDC debt crisis? How did it come about? What solutions can you offer?

11. What types of products do the LDCs export? Use the law of comparative advantage to explain the character of these exports.

12. Outline the main components of the "New Global Compact" proposed by the LDCs. Which of these demands do you feel are justified?

13. What would be the implications of a worldwide policy of unrestricted immigration between nations for economic efficiency and the global distribution of income?

14. *Key Question*   *Use Figure 23-1 (changing box labels as necessary) to explain rapid economic growth in a country such as Japan or South Korea. What factors other than those contained in the figure might contribute to growth?*

15. (Applying the Theory) Explain how civil wars, population growth, and public policy decisions have contributed to periodic famines in Africa.

CHAPTER 24

ALTERNATIVE ECONOMIC SYSTEMS IN TRANSITION

Arguably the most profound event of the past decade was the collapse of the Soviet Union in late 1991 and the decision by Russia and the other successor republics to transform themselves from centrally directed to market economies.

In this final chapter, we examine the breakup of the Soviet Union and the problems the new republics now face. Specific questions are: What were the main characteristics and goals of the Soviet planned economy? Why did Soviet communism fail? What must be accomplished to achieve the transition to a market or capitalist system? What role, if any, might other western nations play in this transition? What progress has been realized thus far? What problems remain?

The transition from planning to markets has been widespread. Such Eastern European nations as Poland, East Germany, Czechoslovakia, and Hungary, among others, preceded the former Soviet Union on this path. Our focus will be on Russia because of its economic, political, and military importance. Russia encompasses about three-fourths of the territory of the former Soviet Union, and is $2^1/_2$ times larger than Canada, the world's second largest nation. Russia has about 150 million people, over half as many as were in the former Soviet Union. It also encompasses vast natural resources, including oil and gas, precious metals, diamonds, and timber.

IDEOLOGY AND INSTITUTIONS

To understand the planned economy of the former Soviet Union, we must look back at its ideology and institutions.

MARXIAN IDEOLOGY

The Communist Party was the dominant force in Soviet political and economic life. It viewed itself as a dictatorship of the proletariat or working class. Based on Marxism-Leninism, the Communists envisioned their system as the inevitable successor to capitalism, the latter being plagued by internal contradictions stemming from the exploitation, injustice, and insecurity which it was thought to generate. To Communists, the market system was chaotic, unstable, and inequitable. Markets bred inflation, unemployment, and an unfair distribution of income. In contrast, central planning was viewed as a means for rationally organizing the economy's resources, achieving macroeconomic stability, and providing greater equality.

Especially important for our purposes is the Marxian concept of a **labour theory of value** — the idea that the economic or exchange value of any commodity is determined solely by the amount of labour time required for its production. Thanks to the capitalistic institution of private property, capitalists own the machinery and equipment necessary for production in an industrial society. The property-less working class is therefore dependent on the capitalists for employment and for its livelihood. Because of the worker's inferior bargaining position and the capitalist's pursuit of profits, the capitalist will exploit labour by paying a daily wage far below the value of the worker's daily production. The capitalist can and will pay workers a subsistence wage and expropriate the remaining fruits of their labour as profits, or what Marx termed **surplus value**. In the Soviet system, surplus value was to be extracted by the state as an agency of the working class and distributed in large part through subsidies to what we would call public or quasi-public goods, for example, education, transportation, health care, and housing.

The function of communism was to overthrow capitalism and replace it with a classless society void of human exploitation. The Communist Party viewed itself as the vanguard of the working class, and its actions were held to be in keeping with the goals of the working class. In fact, it was a strong dictatorship. Many westerners characterized Soviet government as a dictatorship *over* the proletariat, not *of* the proletariat.

INSTITUTIONS

The two outstanding institutional characteristics of the Soviet economy were: (1) state ownership of property resources, and (2) authoritarian central economic planning.

STATE OWNERSHIP   State ownership meant the Soviet state owned all land, natural resources, transportation and communication facilities, the banking system, and virtually all industry. Most retail and wholesale enterprises and most urban housing were governmentally owned. In agriculture many farms were state-owned; most, however, were government-organized collective farms — essentially co-operatives to which the state assigned land "for free use for an unlimited time."

CENTRAL ECONOMIC PLANNING   Central economic planning meant that the Soviet Union had a centralized "command" economy functioning in a detailed economic plan. The Soviet economy was government-directed rather than market-directed. Choices made through the market in Canada's economy were made by bureaucratic decision in the Soviet Union. Through the plan "all the manifold activities of the Soviet economy are coordinated as if they were parts of one incredibly enormous enterprise directed from the central headquarters in Moscow."[1]

CENTRAL PLANNING AND ITS PROBLEMS

The Soviet system of central planning was put in place in the late 1920s and early 1930s. Despite occasional reforms, the system remained fundamentally unchanged for almost seven decades.

ENDS AND MEANS

The following generalizations describe how Soviet planning functioned historically.

---

[1] Harry Schwartz, *Russia's Soviet Economy*, 2d ed. (Englewood Cliffs, N.J.: Prentice-Hall, Inc., 1954), p. 146.

1. INDUSTRIALIZATION AND MILITARY STRENGTH

The economy of the former Soviet Union was a system of "totalitarianism harnessed to the task of rapid industrialization and economic growth." Planning goals stressed rapid industrialization and military strength. This was achieved through extensive investment in heavy industries — steel, chemicals, and machine tools — and the allocation of a large percentage of domestic output to the military. As a consequence, development of consumer goods industries, the distribution and service sectors, and the infrastructure were neglected.

2. RESOURCE OVERCOMMITMENT

Production increases sought in the various plans were ambitious; they overcommitted the economy's available resources. As a result, not all planning targets could be achieved. And planning priorities were to achieve those goals associated with heavy industry and the military at the expense of consumption.

3. RESOURCE MOBILIZATION

Industrialization and rapid economic growth were initially achieved through mobilization of labour, capital, and raw materials. In the early years of planning there was substantial surplus labour in agriculture that the plans reallocated to industrial production. Similarly, a larger proportion of the population was induced or coerced into the labour force. Early Soviet growth was achieved through more inputs rather than using fixed amounts of inputs more productively. In the 1930s and again in the early post-World War II era, this strategy produced growth rates greater than the United States and other industrialized nations.

4. ALLOCATION BY DIRECTIVES

Soviet central planners directed the allocation of inputs among industries and firms, thereby determining the composition of output. Planning directives were substituted for the market or price system as an allocational mechanism.

5. GOVERNMENT PRICE FIXING

Prices were set by government direction rather than by the forces of demand and supply. Consumer good prices were changed infrequently and, as a matter of social policy, the prices of "necessities" — for example, housing and basic foodstuffs — were established at low levels. Rents on Soviet housing averaged only about 3% of income and did not change between 1928 and 1992! Input prices and the price of an enterprise's output were also government determined and were used primarily as accounting devices to gauge a firm's progress in meeting its production target.

6. SELF-SUFFICIENCY

The Soviet Union viewed itself as a single socialist nation surrounded by hostile capitalistic countries. Therefore, the central plans stressed economic self-sufficiency. Trade with western nations was greatly restricted because the ruble was not convertible into other currencies. Soviet trade was largely with the other communist nations of eastern Europe.

7. PASSIVE MACROECONOMIC POLICIES

The Soviet economy was a quantity-directed system with money and prices playing only a limited role in resource allocation. Unlike most market economies, monetary and fiscal policies were passive rather than active in the Soviet Union. In market systems, monetary and fiscal policies are used to manipulate the aggregate levels of output, employment, and prices. Historically, unemployment in the Soviet Union was very low, perhaps 1 or 2% of the labour force. This was partly the result of ambitious planning targets and various admonitions to work. Low unemployment was also due to overstaffing (managers could not fire redundant workers), a disinterest in cost-minimization (gross output was the overriding objective), and a population whose growth rate was steadily diminishing. Similarly, government price determination was the primary device used to control the price level.

THE CO-ORDINATION PROBLEM

The market system is a powerful organizing force that co-ordinates millions of individual decisions by consumers, resources suppliers, and businesses, and fosters a reasonably efficient use of scarce resources. It is not easy to substitute central planning as a co-ordinating mechanism.

Example: Suppose an enterprise in Minsk is producing men's shoes. Planners must establish a realistic production target for that enterprise and then see that all the necessary inputs — labour, electric power, leather, rubber, thread, nails, appropriate machinery, transportation — for production and delivery of that product are made available. When we move from a simple product such as shoes to more complex products such as television sets and farm tractors, planners' allocational problems are greatly compounded.

Because the outputs of many industries are inputs to other industries, the failure of any single industry to fulfil its output target will cause a chain of adverse repercussions. If iron mines — for want of machinery or labour or transportation inputs — fail to supply the steel industry with the required inputs of iron ore, the steel industry will be unable to fulfil the input needs of the many industries dependent on steel. All these steel-using industries — automobiles, tractors, and transportation — will be unable to fulfil their planned production goals. And so the bottleneck chain reaction goes on to all firms using steel parts or components as inputs. Bottlenecks and production stoppages occurred with alarming regularity in the 1980s and early 1990s.

QUICK REVIEW 24-1

1. Marxian ideology is based on the labour theory of value and views capitalism as a system for expropriating profits or surplus value from workers.

2. The primary institutional features of the former Soviet economy were state ownership of property resources and central economic planning.

3. Soviet plans were characterized by **a** an emphasis on rapid industrialization and military power, **b** resource overcommitment; **c** growth through the use of more inputs rather than greater efficiency; **d** resource allocation by government directives rather than markets; **e** government price determination; **f** an emphasis on economic self-sufficiency; and **g** passive monetary and fiscal policies.

4. The basic planning problem is to direct needed resources to each enterprise so that production targets can be achieved and bottlenecks avoided.

COMMUNISM'S FAILURES

Diminishing economic growth, shoddy product quality, and the inability to meet consumer expectations all contributed to the Soviet system's collapse.

DECLINING GROWTH

Soviet economic growth in the 1950s and 1960s was impressive. In the 1950s Soviet real domestic output expanded at roughly 6% per year compared to about 3% for Canada. The Soviet economy continued to grow at about 5% per year in the 1960s. But growth fell to an annual rate of about 2.5 or 3% in the 1970s and further declined to 2% by the mid-1980s. In the last year or two before the system's breakdown, real output was falling sharply.

POOR PRODUCT QUALITY

Further evidence of economic failure was reflected in the quality of goods. In such vital manufacturing sectors as computers and machine tools, Soviet technology lagged some seven to twelve years behind advanced industrial nations. Overall, the quality of most Soviet manufactured goods was far short of international standards. Consumer goods were of notoriously poor quality and product assortment was greatly limited. Durable goods — automobiles, refrigerators, and consumer electronics products — were primitive by world standards. Furthermore, widespread shortages of basic goods, interminable shopper queues, black markets, and corruption in the distribution of products characterized the consumer sector.

CONSUMER NEEDS

The major contributing factor to the downfall of Soviet communism was its inability to efficiently supply the goods and services consumers wanted to buy. In the early decades of Soviet communism, the government established a "social contract" with its citizenry to the effect that, by enduring the consumer sacrifices with the high rates of saving and investment necessary for rapid industrialization and growth, the population would be rewarded with consumer abundance in the future (Figure 2-5). The failure of the system to meet consumer expectations contributed to frustration and deteriorating morale among consumers and workers.

CAUSES OF THE COLLAPSE

Having chronicled the deteriorating performance of the economy of the former Soviet Union, we now consider the causes of its collapse.

1. MILITARY BURDEN Large Soviet military expenditures of 15 to 20% of domestic output absorbed great quantities of resources that would otherwise have been available for the development and production of consumer and investment goods. During the cold war era it was the government's policy to channel superior management and the best scientists and engineers to defence and space research, which adversely affected technological progress and the quality (productivity) of investment in the civilian sector.

2. AGRICULTURAL DRAG By western standards, agriculture in the former Soviet Union was something of a monument to inefficiency and a drag on economic growth, engulfing some 30% of the labour force and roughly one-fourth of annual investment. Furthermore, output per worker was only 10 to 25% of Canada's level. The low productivity of Soviet agriculture was attributable to many factors: relative scarcity of good land; vagaries in rainfall and length of growing season; serious errors in planning and administration; and, perhaps most important the failure to construct an effective incentive system.

Once a major exporter of grain and other agricultural products, the Soviet Union became one of the world's largest importers of agricultural commodities. Agricultural imports were a serious drain on foreign currency reserves, which its leadership wanted for financing of western capital goods and technology.

3. MORE INPUTS VERSUS INCREASED EFFICIENCY Much of the Soviet Union's rapid growth in the early decades of central planning resulted from using more labour, capital, and land in the production process — taking up "slack" in the economy. But in time this means of increasing real output was exhausted. Soviet labour force participation rates were among the highest in the world so there was little or no opportunity to recruit more workers. Furthermore, population and labour force growth slowed significantly. While the annual average increase in the labour force was about 1.5% in the 1970s, it slowed to about 0.6% in the 1980s. Similarly, the percentage of domestic output devoted to investment was comparatively high and could be increased only by reducing output devoted to consumption. Because of the low standard of living in the Soviet Union, it was unpopular and politically difficult to further increase the input of capital goods at the expense of consumption. Also, natural conditions limit the availability of additional farmland. Occasional attempts to bring more

land of marginal quality into crop production were counterproductive in that yields were minimal and the land lost to grazing.

The alternative to growth through the use of more inputs is to increase the productivity or efficiency of available inputs. But this is a more complex and difficult way of achieving economic growth. Productivity growth requires modern capital equipment, innovation and technological progress, and strong material incentives for workers and managers — none of which characterized the traditional Soviet planning system. Indeed, labour productivity in the Soviet Union was estimated to be only 35 to 40% that of workers in industrially advanced countries.

4. PLANNING PROBLEMS The problem of centrally co-ordinating economic activity becomes much more difficult as an economy grows and develops. Early planning under Stalin in the 1930s and 1940s resembled the simple World War II planning of western capitalist nations. A few key production goals were established and resources were centrally directed towards fulfilling those goals regardless of costs or consumer welfare. But the past success of such "campaign planning" resulted in a more complex, industrially advanced economy. Products became more sophisticated and complex and there were more industries for which to plan. Planning techniques workable in the Stalinist era became inadequate and inefficient in the more advanced Soviet economy of the 1970s and 1980s. The Soviet economy outgrew its planning mechanisms.

5. INADEQUATE SUCCESS INDICATORS Market economies have a single, comprehensive success indicator — profits. Each firm's success or failure is measured by its profit or losses. Profits depend on consumer demand, production efficiency, and product quality.

In contrast, the major success indicator of a Soviet enterprise was its fulfilment of a quantitative production target assigned by the central planners. This generated inefficient practices because production costs, product quality, and product mix became secondary considerations at best. Achieving least-cost production is nearly impossible without a system of genuine market prices accurately reflecting the relative scarcity or economic value of various resources. Product quality was frequently sacrificed by managers and workers who were awarded bonuses for fulfilling quantitative, not qualitative, targets. If meeting production goals of a television or automobile manufacturing plan meant sloppy assembly work, so be it.

Finally, it is difficult for planners to assign quantitative production targets without unintentionally producing ridiculous distortions in output. If the production target for an enterprise manufacturing nails is specified in terms of weight (tonnes of nails), it will tend to produce all large nails. But if its target is a quantity (thousands of nails), it will be motivated to use available inputs to produce all small nails. The problem is that the economy needs both large and small nails.

6. INCENTIVE PROBLEMS   Perhaps the main deficiency of central planning was the lack of economic incentives. The market systems of western economies have built-in signals resulting in the efficient use of resources. Profits and losses generate incentives for firms and industries to increase or decrease production. If a product is in short supply, its price and profitability will increase and producers will be motivated to expand production. Conversely, surplus supply means falling prices and profits and a reduction in output. Successful innovations in the form of either product quality or production techniques are sought because of their profitability. Greater work effort by labour means higher money incomes, which can be translated into a higher real standard of living.

These actions and adjustments do not occur under central planning. The output-mix of the former Soviet economy was determined by the central planners. If their judgements as to the quantities of automobiles, razor blades, underwear, and vodka wanted by the populace at governmentally determined prices were incorrect, there would be *persistent* shortages and surpluses of products. But the managers who oversaw the production of these goods were rewarded for fulfilling their production goals; they had no incentive to adjust production in response to product shortages or surpluses. And they did not have changes in prices and profitability to signal that more or less of each product was desired. Thus in the former Soviet Union many products were unavailable or in short supply, while other unwanted goods languished in warehouses.

Incentives to innovate were almost entirely absent; indeed, innovation was often resisted. Soviet enterprises were essentially government owned monopolies. As a result there was no private gain to managers or workers for improving product quality or developing more efficient production techniques. Historically, government-imposed innovations were resisted by enterprise managers and workers. The reason was that new production processes were usually accompanied by higher and unrealistic production targets, underfulfilment, and loss of bonuses.

Innovation also lagged because there was no competition. New firms could not come into being to introduce better products, superior managerial techniques, or more efficient productive methods. Similarly, the Soviet goal of economic self-sufficiency isolated its enterprises from the competitive pressures of international markets. In general over an extended period Soviet enterprises produced the same products with the same techniques, with both goods and techniques becoming increasingly obsolete by world standards.

Nor were individual workers motivated to work hard, because of a lack of material incentives. Because of the low priority assigned to consumer goods in the plans, there was only a limited array of low-quality goods and services available to Soviet workers–consumers. (The price of an automobile was far beyond the means of average factory workers, and for those able to buy, the waiting period was one to five years.) While hard work might result in promotions and bonuses, the increase in *money* income did not translate into a proportionate increase in *real* income. Why work hard for additional income if there is nothing to buy with the money you earn? As a Soviet worker once lamented to a western journalist: "The government pretends to pay us and we pretend to work."

THE GORBACHEV REFORMS

The deteriorating Soviet economy of the 1970s and early 1980s prompted President Mikhail Gorbachev to introduce in 1986 a reform program described as **perestroika**, a restructuring of the economy. This economic restructuring was accompanied by **glasnost**, a campaign for greater openness and democratization in both political and economic affairs. Under *glasnost*, workers, consumers, enterprise managers, political leaders, and others were provided greater opportunity to voice complaints and make suggestions for improving the economy.

The **Gorbachev reforms** involved six interrelated elements: (1) the modernization of industry; (2) greater decentralization of decision making; (3) provision for a limited private enterprise sector; (4) improved worker discipline and incentives; (5) a more rational price system; (6) an enlarged role in the international economy.

While *perestroika* had some initial success, it did not comprehensively address the systemic economic problems facing the Soviet Union. In retrospect, *perestroika* was more in the nature of traditional Soviet "campaigns" to elicit better performance within the general framework of the planned economy. It was *not* an overall program of institutional change such as those adopted by Poland and Hungary. Thus, in the late 1980s the Soviet economy was stagnating; some estimates put its growth rate at only 2% per year, while others indicated it did not grow at all. In late 1991 Gorbachev's successor, Boris Yeltsin, outlined a program of radical or "shock therapy" reform to move the economy from planning to a market system.

QUICK REVIEW 24-2

1. The failure of central planning in the former Soviet Union was evidenced by diminished growth rates, low-quality goods, and the failure to provide a rising standard of living.

2. The recent collapse of the Soviet economy is attributable to **a** a large military burden; **b** chronic inefficiencies in agriculture, **c** the need to expand real output by increasing the quantity of inputs; **d** the inability of traditional planning techniques to deal with the growing complexity of the Soviet economy; **e** inadequate success indicators; and **f** ineffectual incentives to produce, innovate, and work.

3. The Gorbachev reforms of the late 1980s centred on *perestroika* ("restructuring") and *glasnost* ("openness") but failed to provide major systemic change.

TRANSITION TO A MARKET SYSTEM

The former Soviet republics — particularly Russia — have committed themselves to the transition to a market economy. What are the components of such a dramatic reform program?

PRIVATIZATION

If entrepreneurship is to come into existence, private property rights must be established and protected by law. This means that existing government property — farmland, housing, factories, machinery and equipment stores — must be transferred to private owners. It also means that new private firms must be allowed to form and develop.

PROMOTION OF COMPETITION

The industrial sector of the former Soviet Union consisted of large state-owned enterprises in which average employment exceeded 800 workers. Thirty to 40% of total industrial production was produced by single-firm "industries." When several enterprises produced a product, their actions were coordinated by the planning process to create a cartel. In short, most production took place under monopoly or near-monopoly conditions.

Realization of an efficient market economy requires the dismantling of these public monopolies and the creation of antitrust laws to sustain competition. Privatization without "demonopolization" will be of limited benefit to the economy. Existing monopolies must be restructured or split apart as separate, competing firms. For example, a tractor manufacturing enterprise with four plants could be separated into four independent and competing firms. The establishment and guarantee of property rights are prerequisite to the creation and entry of new firms into previously monopolized industries. Joint ventures between Russia and foreign companies provide a further avenue for increasing competition, as does opening the economy to international trade. Recent legislation has opened the door for foreign firms to invest directly in Russia.

LIMITED AND REORIENTED ROLE FOR GOVERNMENT

The transition to a market economy will curtail government's economic role. The government must reduce its involvement to those tasks associated with a market economy: providing an appropriate legal framework; maintaining competition; reducing excessive inequality in the distribution of income and wealth; making market adjustments where spillover costs or benefits are large; providing public goods and services; and stabilizing the economy (Chapter 5).

Many of these functions will be new to the Russian government, at least in the environment of a market system. Unemployment and overt inflation were controlled by central planning. Historically, ambitious production plans and overstaffing of enterprises yielded low unemployment rates while government price-setting controlled the price level. The task will be to develop monetary and fiscal policies — and institutional arrangements appropriate to their implementation — to indirectly provide macroeconomic stability. Restructuring will likely result in substantial short-run unemployment as inefficient public enterprises are closed or fail to be viable under private ownership. Thus, a priority goal will be to establish a social safety net for Russian citizens. In particular, a program of unemployment insurance must be established, not only on equity grounds but also to reduce worker resistance to the transition. Similarly, antitrust legislation of some sort will be needed to maintain competitive markets.

PRICE REFORM: REMOVING CONTROLS

Unlike competitive market prices, the prices established by the Soviet government bore no relationship to the economic value of either products or resources. In an effectively functioning competitive market system, the price of a product equates, at the margin, the value consumers place on that good ("benefits") and the value of the resources used in its production ("costs"). When free markets achieve this equality for all goods and services, the economy's scarce resources are being used efficiently to satisfy consumer wants.

But in the Soviet Union, both input and output prices were fixed by government and in many instances were not changed for long periods of time. Because input prices did not measure the relative scarcities of resources, it was impossible for a firm to minimize real production costs. With fixed prices it is impossible to produce a unit of X in such a way as to minimize sacrifice of alternative goods.

Example: High energy prices have caused firms in market economies to curtail its use. But energy was underpriced in the Soviet Union (the world's largest producer of energy) and its industries used two to three times as much energy per unit of output as leading industrial countries.

A difficult problem arises in making the transition from government- to market-determined prices because historically the prices of many basic

consumer goods were fixed at low levels. The Soviet rationale for this was that low prices would ensure everyone access to such goods. As Figure 24-1 shows, this pricing policy helps explain the chronic product shortages and long lines that frustrated consumers in the Soviet Union. The perfectly inelastic supply curve S reflects the fixed output of, say, shoes for which the plan provided. (Disregard supply curve S′ for the moment.) The demand curve slopes downward as it would in a market economy. Given S, the equilibrium price would be P_a. But in an effort to make shoes accessible to those with lower incomes, the government fixes the price at P_f.

But not everyone who wanted shoes at price P_f could obtain them. At P_f quantity demanded was substantially greater than quantity supplied, so there was excess demand or, in other words, a shortage. This explains the long, impatient lines of consumers and the empty shelves we saw in television

FIGURE 24-1 The effects of government price fixing

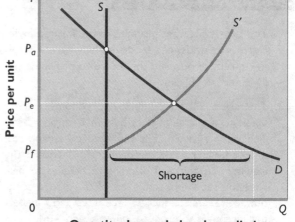

Central planners establish below equilibrium prices such as P_f on many basic consumer goods to make them widely available to everyone. But in fact at such low prices quantity demanded exceeds quantity supplied and this shortage means that many consumers cannot obtain such goods. Assuming no privatization, abandonment of government price fixing would raise price from P_f to P_a. With privatization and an accompanying increase in output as price rises, price would increase from P_f to P_a. In either event, the decontrol of prices can be expected to be inflationary.

news clips of Soviet shoppers. Black markets — illegal markets where goods are sold at much higher prices than those fixed by the government — were widespread. **(Key Question 7)**

JOINING THE WORLD ECONOMY

The Soviet Union was largely isolated from the world economy for almost three-quarters of a century. A key aspect of transition is to open the economy to international trade and finance.

One basic task is to make the ruble a stable convertible currency, meaning that it is acceptable in exchange for other currencies. Convertibility and stability are necessary for Russia to achieve an enlarged role in international trade and finance. Firms cannot buy from or sell to Russia unless a realistic exchange rate is established for the ruble. Nor can western firms be expected to invest in the former Soviet Union unless they are certain that rubles can be exchanged for "hard" currencies. Western firms want their profit in dollars, yen, pounds, and marks, not rubles.

Opening the Russian economy to world trade will be beneficial because world markets are sources of competition and a means of acquiring much-needed superior technologies from industrially advanced capitalist nations. Liberalized international trade will put pressure on privatized Russian forms to produce efficiently products that meet world quality standards. Also, free world trade will allow Russia to realize the benefits from production based on comparative advantage — income gains that its isolation has long denied it.

MACROECONOMIC STABILITY

The transition to free markets poses the possibility of high rates of inflation. Figure 24-1 is again relevant. As government price controls are eliminated, prices will rise from P_f to P_a. With privatization, this runup of prices will be dampened somewhat by the extra output induced by the rising prices. As shown by supply curve S' in Figure 24-1, private producers will respond to higher prices by increasing quantity supplied. Nevertheless, prices will rise substantially, as from P_f to P_e. Similarly, prices will rise for butter, soap, meat, housing, vodka, and all other goods and services whose prices have been liberalized. An important need during the transition is to control inflationary pressures.

The worst scenario is hyperinflation, where there is a "flight from the currency" and the ruble ceases to function as an effective medium of exchange because businesses and consumers find it unacceptable. In these circumstances, hoarding and speculation supplant production and the economy grinds to a halt. Rapidly and unevenly rising prices also provide a hostile environment for macroeconomic decision making. Achieving both least-cost production (productive efficiency) and production of the most desired output-mix (allocative efficiency) is predicated on a reasonable measure of price stability.

Finally, an environment of high and volatile inflation greatly complicates achieving other components of transition. The purchase of formerly public enterprises by private buyers, the establishing of a convertible ruble, and the encouragement of both domestic and foreign investment to modernize the economy are all more difficult with the uncertainties posed by a rapidly rising price level.

PUBLIC SUPPORT: ATTITUDES AND VALUES

The reforms that lead to the transition from planning to markets must have wide public support. Consider some of the difficulties.

1. BUREAUCRATIC RESISTANCE The reforms threaten the jobs and status of many former party members and bureaucrats. These individuals continue in many instances to have positions of power and prestige and want to maintain the status quo. Ironically, those most likely to have access to formerly state-owned enterprises and other assets are those very same bureaucrats who formerly administered the failed system of central planning.

2. WORKER INCENTIVES Under a system of market incentives most workers and managers will be required to be more disciplined and to work harder and more productively. This may be difficult to accept in an economy that historically has served consumers–workers poorly. Money wage increases do not provide incentives without corresponding improvements in the quantity and quality of housing, food, and other consumer goods and services.

Some observers say that many citizens in the former Soviet Union and other communist nations have acquired work habits and personality traits that will only change slowly. These include working at a leisurely pace, avoiding responsibility, resistance to innovation and change, stressing output quantity over quality, and promotion based on connections and party affiliation rather than productive efficiency. It may be wishful thinking to assume that the populace possesses a strong work ethic and a latent entrepreneurial spirit, and that these attributes will emerge as the heavy hand of central planning is removed. The citizenry has been indoctrinated for some 70 years regarding the evils of private property, profits, and capitalist enterprise. The "mental residue" of communism may not be easily removed.

THE SIMULTANEITY PROBLEM

A more subtle problem is that the reform components are interlinked. Not to move forward on all fronts may enhance the prospects for failure. Examples: Private ownership will do little to increase productive efficiency unless prices are reformed to accurately measure relative scarcities. Privatization — the selling off of state enterprises — may be helpful in reducing budget deficits. When market prices for inputs and output are unknown, it is difficult to determine the value of an enterprise when it is being privatized. The creation of a more competitive environment depends on the economy being opened to world trade and foreign investment. **(Key Question 8)**

ROLE OF ADVANCED NATIONS

The world's industrialized capitalist nations can facilitate Russia's reforms in three ways: providing foreign aid; private investment in Russia by western firms; and helping to integrate Russia into the world economy.

FOREIGN AID

Foreign aid can ease the painful transition process when planning is being abandoned and free enterprise has not yet been firmly established. In particular, foreign aid can help the Russian government avoid financing its deficits by money creation and thereby reduce the rate of inflation.

Market democracies have a great economic stake in Russia's transition to democracy and capitalism. If the transition fails, the peace dividend associated with the end of the cold war may not be

realized and the possibility of accelerated economic growth through expanded international trade with a free-market Russia will also be sacrificed. The political benefit is that a democratic Russia will isolate the last strongholds of communism — China, Cuba, and North Korea — and perhaps force their leaders towards political and economic reform.

But there are serious reservations concerning aid to Russia. One is that aid is likely to be ineffectual and wasteful until the transition to market capitalism has been accomplished. Aside from humanitarian aid in the form of foodstuffs and medicine, economic aid is not likely to be of much help until capitalistic institutions are firmly in place.

A second contention is that the Soviet Union has not yet exploited the opportunity it now has to divert vast amounts of resources from the military to the civilian sector.

Finally, there is the hard political fact that foreign aid for a long-time cold war foe may not be popular among the voters of industrialized nations who see in their own countries unemployment, poor education, crime, poverty, and drug abuse.

The foreign aid issue involves a kind of chicken-or-egg problem. The West wants aid to be contingent upon a firm commitment to, or completion of, the reforms; Russia contends that aid is necessary for the reforms to be realized. Similarly, rapid inflation in Russia makes potential aid donors cautious and hesitant; but the lack of aid forces Russia to finance its deficits with money creation, which fuels further inflation.

How much aid has been forthcoming? And in what forms? Table 24-1 shows that in 1992-93 the West has provided $23 billion in aid to Russia. International financial institutions made $3 billion available — $2.5 billion from the International Monetary Fund and $0.5 billion from the World Bank. The remaining $20 billion was bilateral or nation-to-nation aid. About $18 billion of this was in the form of export credits — government subsidized credit that allows Russia to buy a nation's exports via low-interest loans rather than paying cash. The remaining $2 billion is in the form of grants.

PRIVATE INVESTMENT

As Russia moves towards a capitalistic system, will it be able to attract foreign investment to shore up its economy? In view of the vast potential market provided by some 150 million citizens,

TABLE 24-1   Foreign aid to Russia, 1992-1993

Type of aid		Amount (billions of dollars)
International financial institutions		$3
IMF	$2.5	
World Bank	0.5	
Bilateral aid		20
Export credits	$18	
Grants	2	
Total		$23

Source: International Monetary Fund

we would expect the answer to be yes. These flows of private investment could be extremely helpful to the Soviet economy, perhaps more so than public aid. In addition to providing real capital, profit-seeking private investors will bring in managerial skills, entrepreneurial behaviour, and marketing connections.

But there are substantial obstacles to foreign firms doing business in Russia. One problem is determining who is in charge. Should you deal with the Trade Ministry in Moscow or regional officials or both? To whom does a foreign firm pay taxes, and with whom does one sign contracts? Who issues the necessary permits and licences? Furthermore, the legislative underpinnings of commercial activities are often cumbersome, ambiguous, or simply nonexistent. In many cases reliable sources of inputs are not available. And the infrastructure — for example, communication and transportation systems — is primitive by western standards. Business taxes are among the world's highest. Racketeers regularly extort protection money from businesses and scam artists bilk investors. Bouts of hyper-inflation create uncertainty and make private investors hesitant.

MEMBERSHIP IN INTERNATIONAL INSTITUTIONS

Historically the Soviet Union distanced itself from the major international trade and financial institutions such as the International Monetary Fund (IMF), the World Bank, and the General Agreement on Tariffs and Trade (GATT). Membership in these institutions could benefit the former Soviet Union. Russia was admitted to the IMF and World Bank in 1992 and, as we saw in Table 24-1, has received $2 billion in aid from those institutions. Membership in GATT would result in lower tariff barriers for Russian exports.

A PROGRESS REPORT

What's the current status of Russia's reforms?

ACCOMPLISHMENTS

On the positive side, several aspects of Russian economic reform have gone quite well.

1. PRIVATIZATION   By late 1994 about 70% of the entire economy was privately held. About two-thirds of former state-owned enterprises have been privatized; 90% of small companies are privately owned; and 80% of service-sector companies are private.

The privatization process involved two phases. In the first phase the government gave vouchers, each with a designated monetary value, to 40 million Soviet citizens. Recipients could then pool these vouchers to purchase enterprises. The second phase, begun in 1994, allows state enterprises to be purchased for cash. This makes it possible for foreign investors to buy Russian enterprises and also provides much-needed capital to the enterprises.

Land reform, however, has progressed more slowly. Farmers fear the uncertainties and potential problems that might accompany privatization and free markets.

2. PRICE REFORM   With some exceptions, government price fixing has been abandoned. In January of 1992, the government decontrolled approximately 90% of all prices. The international value of the ruble was devalued to the current black market level and was allowed to float, that is, its value was determined by demand and supply.

3. LOW UNEMPLOYMENT   Despite vast structural changes and other dislocations associated with the transition to markets, massive unemployment has not yet occurred. In the spring of 1994, unemployment was slightly under 6%, close to full employment by international standards.

BOX 24-1   APPLYING THE THEORY

CHINA: EMERGING ECONOMIC SUPERPOWER?

The characteristics and consequences of China's reforms are quite different from those of Russia.

China has achieved a remarkable 8 to 9% growth of real output over the last decade. In 1992 its growth rate was a spectacular 12.8%! In terms of real GDP, China has emerged as the world's third largest economy, behind only the United States and Japan. If the current 6 or $6^1/_2$ percentage point differential in the growth rates of China and America persist, China would become the world's largest economy shortly after 2010 (even though its per capita output will remain far below that of the major industrial nations because of its huge population).

The direction of reform in both China and Russia is the same — from planning to markets. Why, then, has China done so well compared to Russia? While there is considerable disagreement among experts, the answer might lie in the different characteristics of China's reforms.

1. "SHOCK THERAPY" VERSUS GRADUALISM   Russia pursued a rapid and radical "shock therapy" approach to reform, seeking to institute privatization, price liberalization, competition, macroeconomic stability and other elements of reform in a short period of time. China's reforms, begun in 1978, have been piecemeal and gradual.

2. POLITICAL AND ECONOMIC REFORM   Russia believed its political apparatus — the Communist Party in particular — was an obstacle to economic reform. Political reform or democratization preceded economic reform. China has sought economic reform under the strong guidance of its Communist Party. China's view is that the upsetting of the political system would generate endless debate, competition for power, and the ultimate stagnation and failure of economic reforms. China feels Communist dictatorship and markets are compatible; Russia does not.

3. ROLE OF SOEs   Russia focused most of its institutional reform on privatizing its state-owned enterprises (SOEs), which produce most of its GDP. China has protected the existence and development of its SOEs, while simultaneously encouraging the creation of competing private enterprises.

4. TIES TO THE WORLD ECONOMY   Russia has sought to integrate itself into the world economy by floating the ruble, lowering international trade barriers, and seeking membership in international institutions such as the IMF. China established "special economic zones" along its coast that eliminate the government's monopoly on foreign trade and finance. The purpose was to attract foreign capital and foreign companies, along with their advanced technologies and business expertise. The result has been burgeoning growth in the zones, spearheaded by ethnic Chinese businesspersons located in Hong Kong, Taiwan, and elsewhere in Asia.

The key question is whether China can sustain its economic surge. Many experts are optimistic. The economy is highly competitive; saving rates are very high, permitting the financing of industrial investment; rising agricultural productivity permits the transfer of redundant farm labour to industry; the labour force has sufficient education and skills to support further industrialization; and its current low level of technology creates the potential for substantial efficiency gains by adopting superior world technology.

Perhaps the main reason for pessimism is the widening gap between economic reform and political control. China remains a politically repressive society. As a rising standard of living permits its citizenry to make more economic choices, it may also decide it wants to choose the kind of government it wants and who will run that government. China's authoritarian capitalism may contain the seeds of upheaval, chaos, and even civil war, which bodes ill for continued economic progress.

The downside of this is that many Russian workers have been forced to accept substantial wage cuts to save their jobs. The consequences have been sharply reduced living standards for such workers and growing wage inequality.

PROBLEMS

The problems Russia has encountered in its economic transition are substantial.

1. INFLATION As column 2 of Table 24-2 shows, inflation in Russia has been enormous. The sources of this inflation are several.

First, prices were decontrolled in January of 1992 and, as expected, prices on many products tripled or quadrupled almost overnight (Figure 24-1).

Second, Russian households stored massive amounts of currency and deposits at savings banks during years of waiting for scarce consumer goods to become more abundant. This **ruble overhang** helped fuel inflation once prices were decontrolled.

The third and most important source of inflation has been large government deficits financed by increases in the money supply. The deficits in turn have many roots. First, the privatization of state enterprises has caused the government to lose an important source of revenue — firm profits. Second, the uncertainties inherent in the transition have given rise to widespread tax avoidance. Many local governments have withheld tax payments to the central government. Large numbers of privatized businesses have avoided the new 28% value-added (sales) tax. And, ironically, the government's anti-alcohol campaign has led to a loss of vodka-tax revenues. Third, the government has extended massive subsidy credits to both industry and agriculture and has increased welfare benefits to ease transition problems.

One dramatic side effect of Russia's inflation has been the plunging international value of the ruble. When the ruble was floated in early 1992, the exchange rate was 90 rubles (R) for 1 dollar (R90 = $1). By January of 1994 the ruble had fallen to R1607=$1 and plunged to R3926=$1 in the fall of 1994 before recovering somewhat as the result of Russian Central Bank Intervention. Such drastic changes in the ruble's international value are obviously detrimental to Russia's world trade.

TABLE 24-2 Consumer prices and real GDP in Russia, 1991-1994

(1) Year	(2) Consumer price index	(3) Growth of real GDP (percent)
1991	93	−13
1992	1353	−19
1993	896	−12
1994*	292	−12

* Estimate

Source: International Monetary Fund and Russian authorities.

2. FALLING OUTPUT AND LIVING STANDARDS Real output began to fall in the 1980s, but its decline has accelerated during the reforms. Column 3 of Table 24-2 documents recent declines. Note that the fall in real GDP bottomed out in 1992 at 19% and the government's program hopes to limit the drop to 10% in 1994.

Causes of these declines include: (1) rapid inflation, which created an uncertain environment for borrowing and investing; (2) the unravelling of Russia's international trade relationships with former communist bloc nations of Eastern Europe; (3) the bankruptcy and closing of many former state-owned enterprises that could not survive in a market environment; and (4) the massive reallocation of resources required by the reforms and the downgrading of the military.

We know that output is income. Declining real output has meant declines in Russian living standards. Farmers, government employees, and pensioners have been hard hit. And we have already noted that many workers have had to accept deep wage cuts to keep their jobs.

3. INEQUALITY AND SOCIAL COSTS Economic inequality has increased during the transition. As noted, many farmers, pensioners, and state employees have been impoverished. A small enriched élite — some associated with honest entrepreneurship and others with corruption, illegal activities, and speculation — is also emerging. There is considerable friction between gainers and losers, which is fuelling public doubts as to the desirability of a market economy. Also, greater economic insecurity exists; medical and educational services have deteriorated and school enrolments have declined. So has life expectancy. In 1988 the life expectancy of Russian men was 65 years. It is currently 59 years, 19 less than Canadian males.

1. Russia has made the commitment to become a capitalist system. Ingredients in the transition from planning to markets include: **a** creating private property and property rights; **b** promoting competition; **c** limiting and reformulating government's role; **d** removing domestic price controls; **e** opening the economy to international market forces; **f** establishing monetary and fiscal policies to stabilize the economy; and **g** sustaining public support for the reforms.

2. Russia's reform effort may be assisted by foreign aid, private investment by foreign firms, and membership in international trade and lending institutions.

3. Substantial progress has been made in privatization and price decontrol; unemployment has not yet been a serious problem. However, inflation has been severe; real output and living standards have fallen; and economic inequality has increased.

FUTURE PROSPECTS

There is widespread disagreement among experts as to the prospects for the success of Russia's transition to a market economy.

DESTABILIZATION AND COLLAPSE

The pessimistic view is that Russia is now plagued by highly volatile economic and political conditions that could deteriorate, undermining both economic reforms and democratization. In particular, the Russian government's persistent deficits, financed by money creation, pose the possibility of hyperinflation and collapse. The perceived dynamics centre on inflation and government weaknesses feeding upon one another. A weak and indecisive central government will find it difficult to impose and collect taxes. Businesses and political subdivisions evade or withhold tax payments because they sense the central government cannot effectively enforce collection. Widespread tax evasion means declining tax revenues, enlarged budget deficits, and therefore more inflation and financial instability. Declining tax revenues further weaken the government's ability to enforce the tax laws, so a kind of vicious circle continues until political and economic collapse results. Declining revenues also cripple the central government's ability to perform other basic functions, such as maintaining law and order and providing a social safety net for its citizens. A "nostalgia trap" may be generated wherein a longing for the political order and economic security of communism leads to the abandonment of economic reforms and democracy.

MUDDLING THROUGH

A more optimistic view is that Russia's reform process is relatively new and that the most severe economic dislocations in the form of inflation and a declining real output may be behind it. As Table 24-2 suggests, while inflation and real GDP declines are still at serious levels, the rate of inflation is falling and production declines may be bottoming out.

More positively, the private sector is developing quite rapidly. Some 70,000 state enterprises have been at least partly privatized and about 18,000 new private firms have come into being. Financial and securities markets are beginning to emerge, posing the possibility that some of the estimated $40 billion that Russians hold abroad will return to fuel investment and growth. While Russia's plan-to-markets transition might span another decade or so and entail further hardships, the collapse of its economic and political reforms and a return to socialism is unlikely.

CHAPTER SUMMARY

1. The labour theory of value is a central principle of Marxian ideology. Capitalists, as property owners, allegedly expropriate most of labour's value as profits or surplus value.

2. Virtually complete state ownership of property resources and central planning historically were the major institutional features of the Soviet economy.

3. Characteristics of Soviet planning included **a** emphasis on industrialization and military strength; **b** overcommitment of resources; **c** economic growth based on additional inputs rather than increased productivity; **d** allocation of resources by bureaucratic rather than market decisions; **e** economic self-sufficiency; and **f** passive macroeconomic policies.

4. The basic problem Soviet central planners faced was achieving co-ordination or internal consistency in their plans to avoid bottlenecks and the chain reaction of production failures that they cause.

5. Diminishing growth rates, shoddy consumer goods, and the inability to provide a promised high standard of living were all outcomes of the failure of Soviet central planning.

6. Stagnation of the agricultural sector, a growing labour shortage, and the burden of a large military establishment contributed to the failure of the Soviet economy. However, the primary causes of failure were the inability of central planning to co-ordinate a more complex economy, the absence of rational success indicators, and the lack of adequate economic incentives.

7. The Gorbachev reforms attempted to restructure the economy and introduce greater political "openness," but did not address fundamental systemic deficiencies.

8. To change from central planning to a market economy, Russia must move from public to private ownership of property; establish a competitive environment for businesses; restructure government's role to activities appropriate to capitalism; abandon state-determined prices in favour of market-determined prices; integrate its system into the world economy; provide price level and employment stability; and sustain public support for the reforms.

9. Industrialized capitalist nations may assist Russia's transition by **a** providing foreign aid; **b** encouraging private firms to invest in Russia; and **c** facilitating Russian membership in international financial and tariff-determining institutions.

10. While progress has been made in privatization and price decontrol, Russia has experienced severe inflation and significant declines in real output and living standards.

TERMS AND CONCEPTS

central economic planning (p. 516)
glasnost (p. 520)
Gorbachev reforms (p. 521)
labour theory of value (p. 516)

perestroika (p. 520)
ruble overhang (p. 527)
state ownership (p. 516)
surplus value (p. 516)

QUESTIONS AND STUDY SUGGESTIONS

1. Compare the ideology and institutional framework of the former Soviet economy with that of capitalism. Contrast the manner in which production was motivated in the Soviet Union compared to how it is motivated in market economies.

2. Discuss the problem of co-ordination that face central planners in the Soviet Union. Explain how a planning failure can cause a chain reaction of additional failures.

3. How was the number of automobiles to be produced determined in the Soviet Union? In Canada? How are the decisions implemented in the two different types of economies?

4. What were the major characteristics and goals of Soviet central planning?

5. What is the evidence of the failure of Soviet planning? Explain why Soviet economic growth diminished after 1970.

6. Explain why the use of quantitative output targets as the major success indicator for Soviet enterprises contributed to economic inefficiency.

7. *Key Question*   *Use a supply and demand diagram to explain why persistent shortages of many consumer goods occurred in the Soviet Union. Why has the transformation to a market economy been accompanied by inflation? Why were black markets so common in the Soviet Union?*

8. *Key Question*   *What specific changes must be made to transform the Soviet economy to a market system? Why is it important that these changes be introduced simultaneously?*

9. What progress has Russia achieved in its transition to a market economy? What problems has it encountered?

10. Briefly assess the quantity and types of foreign aid that have been made available to Russia.

11. (Applying the Theory) In what specific respects have Chinese economic reforms differed from Russia's? Do you believe these differences account for China's superior growth?

ANSWERS TO KEY QUESTIONS

CHAPTER 1

1-1 Effective policy must be based on sound theory — factually supported generalizations about behaviour. Two methods are used to obtain sound economic theory: deduction and induction.

In *deduction*, the economist starts directly with an untested hypothesis. The hypothesis or theory is tested for accuracy by gathering and examining all relevant facts. If the facts support the hypothesis, the theory can be used for policy. The other approach is *induction*, in which the economist starts by gathering facts and then notes their relationship to each other. Eventually, the data may reveal a cause and effect pattern from which a theory results. From this theory, economic policy relevant to the real world can be formulated. Deduction and induction are complementary and often used simultaneously.

As for the quotation, the opposite is true; any theory not supported by facts is not a good theory. Good economics is empirically grounded; it is based on facts and highly practical.

1-5 (a), (d), and (f) are macro; (b), (c), and (e) are micro.

1-6 (a) and (c) are positive; (b) and (d) are normative.

1-9 (a) The fallacy of composition is the mistake of believing that something true for an individual part is necessarily true for the whole. Example: A single auto producer can increase its profits by lowering its price and taking business away from its competitors. But matched price cuts by all auto manufacturers will not necessarily yield higher industry profits.

(b) The "after this, therefore because of this" fallacy is incorrectly reasoning that when one event precedes another, the first event *necessarily* caused the second. Example: Interest rates rise, followed by an increase in the rate of inflation, leading to the erroneous conclusion the rise in interest rates caused the inflation. Higher interest rates slow inflation.

Cause and effect relationships are difficult to isolate because "other things" are continually changing.

1-13 This behaviour can be explained in terms of marginal costs and marginal benefits. At a standard restaurant, items are priced individually — they have a positive marginal cost. If you order more, it will cost you more. You order until the marginal benefit from the extra food no longer exceeds the positive marginal cost. At a buffet you pay a flat fee no matter how much you eat. Once the fee is paid, additional food items have a zero marginal cost. You therefore continue to eat until your marginal benefit is also zero.

Appendix 1-2 (a) More tickets are bought at each price; the line plots to the right of the previous line. (b) and (c) Fewer tickets are bought at each price; the line plots to the left of the previous line.

Appendix 1-3 Income column: $0; $5,000; $10,000, $15,000; $20,000. Saving column: $–500; 0; $500; $1,000; $1,500. Slope = 0.1 (= ($1,000 – $500)/($15,000 – $10,000)). Vertical intercept = $–500. The slope shows how much saving will go up for every $1 increase in income; the intercept shows the amount of saving (dissaving) occurring when income is zero. Equation: $S = \$–500 + 0.1Y$ (where S is saving and Y is income). Saving will be $750 at the $12,500 income level.

Appendix 1-6 Slopes: at $A = +4$; at $B = 0$; at $C = –4$.

CHAPTER 2

2-5 Economics deals with the "limited resources-unlimited wants" problem. Unemployment represents valuable resources that could have been used to produce more goods and services — to meet more wants and ease the economizing problem.

Allocative efficiency means that resources are being used to produce the goods and services most wanted by society. Society is located at the optimal point on its production possibilities curve where marginal benefit equals marginal cost for each good. *Productive efficiency* means the least costly production techniques are being used to produce wanted goods and services.

Example: manual typewriters produced using the least-cost techniques but for which there is no demand.

2-6 (a) See curve *EDCBA* in the accompanying figure. The assumptions are full employment and productive efficiency, fixed supplies of resources, and fixed technology.

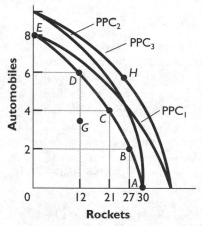

(b) 4.5 rockets [=(21–12)/(6–4)]; .33 automobiles [=(4–2)/(27–21)], as determined from the table. Increasing opportunity costs are reflected in the concave-from-the-origin shape of the curve. This means the economy must give up larger and larger amounts of rockets to get constant added amounts of automobiles — and vice versa.

(c) It must obtain full employment and productive efficiency.

2-9 The marginal benefit (MB) curve is downsloping; MB falls as more of a product is consumed. The first units of a good consumed yield greater additional satisfaction than subsequent units. The marginal cost (MC) curve is upsloping; MC increases as more of a product is produced. The opportunity cost of producing good A rises as resources increasingly better suited to other uses are used to produce A. The optimal amount of a particular product occurs where MB equals MC. If MC exceeds MB, fewer resources should be allocated to this use. The resources have more value in some alternative use (as reflected in MC) than in this use (as reflected in MB).

2-10 See the figure accompanying the answer to question 2-6. G indicates unemployment, productive inefficiency, or both. *H* is at present unattainable. Economic growth — through more inputs, better inputs, improved technology — must be achieved to attain *H*.

2-11 See question 2-6 figure. PPC₁ shows improved rocket technology. PPC₂ shows improved auto technology. PPC₃ shows improved technology in producing both products.

CHAPTER 3

3-2 "Roundabout" production means using capital goods in the production process, enabling producers to obtain more output than through direct production. The direct way to produce a corn crop is to scatter seed about in an unploughed field. The roundabout way is to plough, fertilize, harrow, and till the field using machinery and then use a seed drill to sow the seeds in rows at the correct depth. The higher yield per acre will more than compensate the farmer for the cost of using the roundabout techniques.

To increase the capital stock at full employment, the current production of consumer goods must decrease. Moving along the production possibilities curve towards more capital goods comes at the expense of current consumption.

No, it can use its previously unemployed resources to produce more capital goods, without sacrificing consumption goods. It can move from a point inside to a point on the curve, thus obtaining more capital goods.

CHAPTER 4

4-2 Demand increases in (a), (c), (e), and (f); decreases in (b) and (d).

4-5 Supply increases in (a), (d), (e), and (g); decreases in (b), (c), and (f).

4-7 Data, from top to bottom: –13; –7; 0; +7; +14; and +21.

(a) P_e = $1.35; Q_e = 75,000. Equilibrium occurs where there is neither a shortage nor surplus of eggs. At the immediately lower price of $1.30, there is a shortage of 7000 dozen. At the immediately higher price of $1.40, there is a surplus of 7000 dozen.

(b)

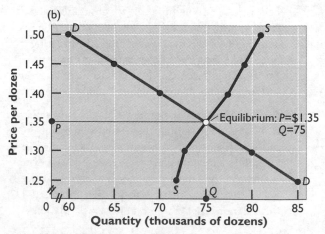

(c) Because at $1.25 there will be a 13,000 dozen eggs shortage, which will drive price up. Because at $1.50

there will be a 21,000 surplus, which will drive the price down. Quotation is incorrect; just the opposite is true.

(d) A $1.30 ceiling causes a persistent shortage. Also, a black market (illegal sales above $1.30) might occur. Government might want to suppress inflation.

(e) Once the government sets the price, that price cannot move towards an equilibrium where quantity demanded equals quantity supplied. The ceiling price removes any inducement for farmers to produce more, and the excess demand of buyers at this ceiling price remains unmet. Thus, there is no price movement upward to ration some buyers out of the market so that the quantity the remaining buyers want equals the quantity farmers bring to market.

4-8 (a) Price up; quantity down; (b) Price down; quantity down; (c) Price down; quantity up; (d) Price indeterminate; quantity up; (e) Price up; quantity up; (f) Price down; quantity indeterminate; (g) Price up; quantity indeterminate; (h) Price indeterminate and quantity down.

CHAPTER 5

5-3 Public goods (a) are indivisible — they are produced in such large units that they cannot be sold to individuals and (b) the exclusion principle does not apply; once the goods are produced nobody — including free riders — can be excluded from the goods' benefits. The free-rider problem explains the significance of the exclusion principle. The government must provide public goods such as the judicial system, national defence, police protection, and weather warning systems since people can obtain the benefits without paying. Government must levy taxes to get revenues to pay for public goods.

5-4 If on the curve, the only way to obtain more public goods is to reduce the production of private goods (from C to B).

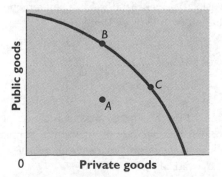

If operating inside the curve, it can expand the production of public goods without sacrificing private goods (from A to B).

CHAPTER 6

6-3 An export increases domestic output and revenues to domestic export firms. Because these firms would employ more resources, household income would rise. Households would then use part of their greater income to buy more imported goods.

Canadian exports in 1994 were $219.4 billion (flow 13) and imports were $202.3 billion (flow 16).

Flow 14 must equal flow 13. Flow 15 must equal flow 16.

6-4 (a) Yes, because the opportunity cost of radios is less (1R = 1C) in South Korea than in Canada (1R = 2C). South Korea should produce radios and Canada, chemicals.

(b) If they specialize, Canada can produce 20 tonnes of chemicals and South Korea can produce 30,000 radios. Before specialization South Korea produced alternative B and Canada alternative D for a total of 28,000 radios (24,000 + 4,000) and 18 tonnes of chemicals (6 tonnes + 12 tonnes). The gain is 2,000 radios and 2 tonnes of chemicals.

(c) The limits of the terms of trade are determined by the comparative cost conditions in each country before trade: 1R = 1C in South Korea and 1R = 2C in Canada. The terms of trade must be somewhere between these two ratios for trade to occur.

If the terms of trade are 1R = 1 1/2 C, South Korea would end up with 26,000 radios (= 30,000 – 4,000) and 6 tonnes of chemicals. Canada would have 4,000 radios and 14 tonnes of chemicals (= 20 – 6). South Korea has gained 2,000 radios. Canada has gained 2 tonnes of chemicals.

(d) Yes, the world is obtaining more output from its fixed resources.

6-6 The first part of this statement is incorrect. Our exports create a domestic *supply* of foreign currencies, not a domestic demand for them. The second part of the statement is accurate. The foreign demand for dollars (from our exports) generates a supply of foreign currencies to Canadians.

A decline in Canadian incomes or a weakening of Canadian preferences for foreign goods would reduce our imports, reducing our demand for foreign currencies. These currencies would depreciate (the dollar would appreciate). Dollar appreciation means our exports will decline and our imports will rise.

6-10 GATT is the General Agreement on Tariffs and Trade. Its provisions apply to more than 120 nations, affecting people around the globe. The Uruguay Round of GATT negotiations produced an agreement that will reduce tariffs, liberalize trade in services, cut agricultural subsidies, protect intellectual property, reduce import quotas, and create the World Trade Organization.

The EU and NAFTA are free-trade blocs. GATT reduces tariffs and liberalizes trade for nearly *all* nations, not just countries in these blocs. The ascendancy of the EU and the passage of NAFTA encouraged nations to reach a new GATT agreement. No nation wanted to be disadvantaged by the formation of the trade blocs.

CHAPTER 7

7-2 Because the dollar value of final goods includes the dollar value of the intermediate goods. If intermediate goods were counted, then double (or triple or quadruple, etc.) counting would occur. The value of the steel used in autos is included in the price of the auto (the final product).

GNP is the dollar value of final goods and services produced by Canadians within Canada and abroad. GDP is the value of final goods and services produced by Canadians and others within the geographical borders of Canada.

GNP is thus GDP plus net investment income from non-residents (often negative in Canada).

7-5 When gross investment exceeds depreciation, net investment is positive and the economy is said to be expanding; it ends the year with more physical capital. When gross investment equals depreciation, net investment is zero and the economy is said to be static; it ends the year with the same amount of physical capital. When depreciation is greater than gross investment, net investment is negative and the economy is said to be declining; it ends the year with less physical capital.

The first statement is wrong. Just because *net* investment was a minus $324 million in 1933 doesn't mean the economy produced no new capital in that year. It simply means depreciation exceeded gross investment by $324 million. Although gross investment was positive, the economy ended the year with $324 million less capital.

The second statement is correct. If only one $20 spade is bought by a construction firm in the entire economy in a year and no other physical capital is bought, then gross investment is $20. This is true even though *net* investment will be highly negative, equalling the whole of depreciation less the $20 spade. If not even this $20 spade had been bought, then gross investment would have been zero. But "gross investment can never be *less* than zero."

7-7 (a) GDP = $215; (b) GNP = $205; (c) NI = $164; (d) PI = $167; (e) DI = $137.

7-10 In this hypothetical case, the GDP price index for 1974 was 0.65 (= $39/$60). Between 1974 and 1986, the price level rose by 53.85 percent [= (($60 − $39)/$39) × 100].

7-11 Values for real GDP, top to bottom of the column: $42.105 (inflating); $30.024 (inflating); $146.51 (inflating); $276.064 (inflating); $481.315 (inflating); $557.924 (deflating).

CHAPTER 8

8-1 The four phases of a typical business cycle, starting at the bottom, are: trough, recovery, peak, and recession. The length of a cycle varies from two to three years to as much as six or seven years or even longer.

Normally there will be a pre-Christmas spurt, followed by a slackening in January after post-Christmas sales. This normal seasonal variation must not be viewed as signalling a boom in the first case nor a recession in the second. From decade to decade the long-term, or secular, trend of the Canadian economy has been upward. If there is no growth of GDP over a period, this does not signal all is normal but rather the economy is functioning below its trend rate of output growth.

Because durable goods last, consumers can postpone buying replacements. This happens when people are worried about a recession and whether there will be a paycheque next month. And firms will soon quit producing what people are not buying. Durable goods industries therefore suffer large output declines during recessions.

In contrast, consumers cannot long postpone the buying of many nondurables such as food and therefore recessions only slightly reduce output.

8-3 GDP gap 10 percent [= (9 − 5) × 2.5]; forgone output = $50 billion (= 10% of $500 billion).

8-5 Labour force = 230 [= 500 − (120 + 150)]; unemployment rate = 10% [= (23/230) × 100].

8-7 This year's rate of inflation = 10% [(121 − 110)/110] × 100.

Dividing 70 by the annual rate of increase of any variable (for instance, the rate of inflation or population growth) will give the approximate number of years for doubling of the variable.

(a) 35 years (= 70/2); (b) 14 years (= 70/5); (c) 7 years (= 70/10).

CHAPTER 9

9-6 Data for completing the table (top to bottom). Consumption: $244; $260; $276; $292; $308; $324; $340; $356; $372. APC: 1.02; 1.00; .99; .97; .96; .95; .94; .94; .93. APS: –.02; .00; .01; .03; .04; .05; .06; .06; .07. MPC: .80, throughout. MPS: .20, throughout.

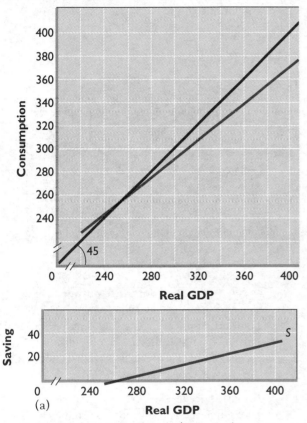

(a)

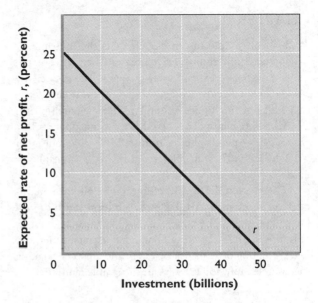

(b) Break-even income = $260. By borrowing or using past savings.

(c) Technically, the APC diminishes and the APS increases because these schedules have positive and negative vertical intercepts (Appendix to Chapter 1). MPC and MPS are measured by the *slopes* of the consumption and saving schedules; they relate to *changes* in consumption and saving as income changes. With straight-line consumption and saving schedules, these slopes do not change as the level of income changes; the slopes and thus the MPC and MPS are unrelated to the intercepts.

9-8 Aggregate investment: (a) $20 billion; (b) $30 billion; (c) $40 billion. This is the investment-demand curve because we have applied the rule of undertaking all investment up to the point where the expected rate of net profit, *r*, equals the interest rate, *i*.

9-10 Saving data for completing the table (top to bottom): $–4; $0; $4; $8; $12; $16; $20; $24; $28.

Equilibrium GDP = $340 billion, determined where (1) aggregate expenditures equal GDP (C of $324 billion + I of $16 billion = GDP of $340 billion); or (2) where planned I = planned S (I of $16 billion = S of $16 billion). Equilibrium level of employment = 65 million; MPC = .8; MPS = .2.

9-11 At the $380 billion level of GDP, planned saving = $24 billion; planned investment = $16 billion (from the question). This deficiency of $8 billion of planned investment causes an unintended $8 billion *increase* in inventories — inventory investment. Actual investment is $24 billion (= $16 billion of planned investment *plus* $8 billion of unplanned inventory investment), matching the $24 billion of actual saving.

At the $300 billion level of GDP, planned saving = $8 billion, planned investment = $16 billion (from the question). This excess of $8 billion of planned investment causes an unintended $8 billion *decline* in inventories — inventory disinvestment. Actual investment is $8 billion (= $16 billion of planned investment *minus* $8 billion of an unplanned inventory disinvestment). Actual saving is also $8 billion.

When unintended investment in inventories occurs, as at the $380 billion level of GDP, businesses revise their production plans downward and GDP falls. When unintended disinvestment in inventories occurs, as at the $300 billion level of GDP, businesses revise their production plans upward and GDP rises. Equilibrium GDP — in this case, $340 billion — occurs where planned investment equals planned saving.

CHAPTER 10

10-2 The simple multiplier effect is the multiple by which the equilibrium GDP increases when any component of aggregate expenditures changes. The greater the MPC (the smaller the MPS), the greater the multiplier.

MPS = 0, multiplier = infinity; MPS = .4, multiplier = 2.5; MPS = .6, multiplier = 1.67; MPS = 1; multiplier = 1.

MPC = 1; multiplier = infinity; MPC = .9, multiplier = 10; MPC = .67; multiplier = 3; MPC = .5, multiplier = 2; MPC = 0, multiplier = 1.

Change in GDP = $40 billion (= $8 billion × multiplier of 5); change in GDP = $24 billion ($8 billion × multiplier of 3). The simple multiplier takes account of only the leakage of saving. The complex multiplier also takes account of leakages of taxes and imports, making the complex multiplier less than the simple multiplier.

10-5 (a) $400

(b) Net exports: $2, –$2, –$6, –$10, –$14, –$18, –$22, –$26. Aggregate expenditures, open economy: $242, $278, $314, $350, $386, $422, $458, $494. Equilibrium GDP: $350. Equilibrium GDP is lower because of imports.

(c) $300; $400; level of imports and equilibrium GDP are inversely related.

(d) Open economy multiplier = 1/(MPS + MPM) = 1/(0.2 + 0.08) = 3.57.

10-8 The addition of government through equal increases of G and T of $100 billion increases equilibrium GDP from $340 billion to $440 billion. This is the balanced-budget multiplier at work. It comes about because the effect of an increase in taxes on AE is not direct, as is an increase in G. Increased taxes work through their effect on C. When MPC is 0.8, increased T of $100 billion results in a decreased C of $80 billion [= 0.8($100 billion)] (with the balance of the tax increase being paid through a $20 billion decrease in saving [= 0.2($100 billion)]).

With a multiplier of 5 = 1/(1 – 0.8), an $80 billion decrease in C causes a $400 billion decline in equilibrium GDP. But the $100 billion increase in G causes a $500 billion increase in equilibrium GDP, which therefore, with the two effects at work, increases by $100 billion (= $500 – $400 billion).

10-10 (a) Recessionary gap. Equilibrium GDP is $600 billion, while full employment GDP is $700 billion. Employment will be 2 million less than at full employment. Aggregate expenditures will have to increase by $20 billion at each level of GDP to eliminate the recessionary gap.

(b) Inflationary gap. Aggregate expenditures are excessive, causing demand-pull inflation. Aggregate expenditures will have to fall by $20 billion at each level of GDP to eliminate the inflationary gap.

CHAPTER 11

11-4 (a)

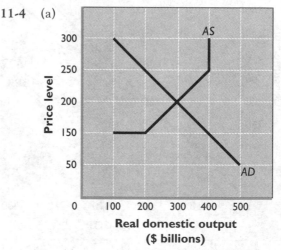

Real domestic output
($ billions)

Equilibrium price level = 200. Equilibrium real output = $300 billion. No, the absolute full-capacity level of GDP is $400 billion, where the AS curve becomes vertical.

(b) At a price level of 150, real GDP supplied is a maximum of $200 billion, less than real GDP demanded of $400 billion. The shortage of real output will drive the price level up. At a price level of 250, real GDP supplied is $400 billion, which is more than real GDP demanded of $200 billion. The surplus of real output will drive down the price level. Equilibrium occurs at the price level where AS and AD intersect.

(c) Increases in consumer, investment, government, or net export spending shift the AD curve rightward. New equilibrium price level = 250. New equilibrium GDP = $400 billion.

11-5 (a) Productivity level = 2.67; (b) Per unit cost of production = $.75; (c) New per unit production cost = $1.13. The AS curve would shift leftward. The price level would rise and real output would decrease; (d) New per unit cost of production = $0.375 [($2 × 150)/800]. AS curve shifts to the right; price level declines and real output increases.

11-7 (a) AD curve left; (b) AD curve right; (c) AS curve left; (d) AD curve right; (e) AD curve left; (f) AD curve right; (g) AS curve right; (h) AD curve right; (i) AS curve right; (j) AS curve left; (k) AD curve right; AS curve left; (l) AD curve left; (m) AS curve right.

CHAPTER 12

12-1 Reduce government spending, increase taxes, or some combination of both. In the real world, the goal is to reduce *inflation* — to keep prices from rising so rapidly — not to reduce the *price level*. A "conservative" economist might favour cuts in government spending, since this would reduce the size of government. A "liberal" economist might favour a tax hike; it would preserve government spending programs.

12-5 The *cyclically adjusted budget* indicates what the federal budgetary deficit or surplus would be if the economy were to achieve full employment throughout the year. This budget is a useful measure of fiscal policy. If the cyclically adjusted budget or full-employment budget is moving towards deficit, fiscal policy is expansionary. If the full-employment budget is moving towards surplus, fiscal policy is contractionary. The *actual budget* simply compares G and T for the year and is an unreliable indicator of the government's fiscal policy. It does not account for shortfalls of tax revenues arising from less than full-employment output. A *structural deficit* — or a full-employment budget deficit — is the difference between G and T when the economy is at full employment. A *cyclical deficit* is the difference between G and T caused by tax revenues being below those accruing when the economy is at full employment.

At GDP_f, the structural deficit is *ab* and the cyclical deficit is zero. Government should raise *T* or reduce G to eliminate this deficit but it may want to take this action over several years to avoid pushing the economy into recession.

12-7 It takes time to ascertain the direction the economy is moving (recognition lag), to get a fiscal policy enacted into law (administrative lag); and for the policy to have its full effect on the economy (operational lag). Meanwhile, other factors may change, rendering inappropriate a particular fiscal policy. Nevertheless, discretionary fiscal policy is a valuable tool in preventing severe recession or severe demand-pull inflation.

A political business cycle is the concept that politicians are more interested in re-election than in stabilizing the economy. Before the election, they enact tax cuts and spending increases even though this may fuel inflation. After the election, they apply the brakes to restrain inflation. The economy will slow and unemployment will rise. In this view the political process creates economic instability.

The crowding-out effect is the reduction in investment spending caused by the increase in interest rates arising from an increase in government spending, financed by borrowing. The increase in G was designed to increase AD but the resulting increase in interest rates may decrease I, thus reducing the impact of the expansionary fiscal policy.

It seems improbable to us that people respond to government budget deficits by reducing consumption and increasing saving in anticipation of a future tax increase tied to current budget deficits.

CHAPTER 13

13-5 The M1 money supply consists of currency — that is, banknotes and coins — and chequable deposits in chartered banks and other financial institutions. The most important component of the M1 money supply is chequable deposits.

If the face value of a coin were not greater than its intrinsic value — that is, the value of the metal in the coin — people would take them out of circulation and sell them for the value of their metal content on the bullion market. That this practice might be illegal would not prevent it from occurring, as several countries found out during the late 1960s and early 1970s, when the price of silver shot up, making their then mostly silver coins (80 to 90% silver) full-bodied — that is, worth more as silver than as coins.

M2 consists of M1 plus personal saving deposits and non-personal notice deposits. M3 consists of M2 plus non-personal fixed-term deposits of residents booked in Canada. M2+ is made up of M2 plus deposits at trust and mortgage loan companies, and deposits and shares of credit unions and caisses populaires.

Near-monies include, first, M2, M2+, and M3, and second, other somewhat less liquid assets that can easily be converted into M1 money. Their significance is that they represent wealth: the more of them people have, the more those people are likely to spend out of current income. The fact that near-monies are liquid adds to potential economic instability, for people may cash in their Treasury bills, for example, and spend the proceeds while the monetary authorities are trying to stem inflation by cutting back on money supply increases. Also, it can happen that M1 is increasing at what the monetary authorities consider an undesirable rate while M2 is decreasing. If the monetary authorities act to stem M1 while disregarding what is happening in M2, the result may be an excessive tightening in purchasing power, leading to a recession.

The argument for including term and notice deposits in a definition of money is that such deposits can quickly be transferred to a chequing account and spent. Also, savings can be withdrawn as cash from non-chequable savings accounts.

13-7 In the first case, the value of the dollar (year 2, relative to year 1) is $.80 (= 1/1.25); in the second case, $2 (= 1/.50). Generalization: The price level and the value of the dollar are inversely related.

CHAPTER 14

14-2 Reserves are assets to chartered banks in that they are cash that belongs to these banks: either cash with which the bank started operations, or profits, or money deposited in the bank by its customers and for which the bank has created in exchange a deposit liability. Excess reserves are cash owned by a chartered bank over and above what it desires to hold as its cash reserves to meet its customers' demand. Excess reserves may safely be lent by the chartered bank; when they are, the money supply increases by the amount of the loan.

14-4 Banks create or add to chequing, or demand, account balances when they make loans; these demand deposits are part of the money supply. People pay off loans by writing cheques. Demand deposits fall, meaning the money supply drops. Money is "destroyed."

14-8

Assets		(1)	(2)	Liabilities and net worth		(1)	(2)
Reserves	$22,000	$22,000	$ 6,250	Demand deposits	$100,000	$115,750	$100,000
Securities	$38,000	$38,000	$38,000				
Loans	$40,000	$55,750	$55,750				

Desired reserves are 6.25% of $100,000 = $6,250

Actual reserves = $22,000

Desired reserves = $ 6,250

Excess reserves = $15,750

(a) The maximum amount of new loans the bank may make is $15,750. The new balance sheet is shown in column 1 above.

(b) The money supply has increased by $15,750, since this is the amount by which demand deposits have increased, and demand deposits are part of the money supply.

(c) After cheques are drawn for the entire amount of the loan and cleared against this bank, its balance sheet will appear as in Column 2 above.

(d) Desired reserves are now $10,000 (–$10% of $100,000). Excess reserves are now $12,000 (–$22,000 – $10,000), which this bank may safely lend. When it does so, the money supply increases by $12,000. Questions (a) and (b) are answered below, with the change in the desired reserve ratio factored in.

Assets		(1)	(2)	Liabilities and net worth		(1)	(2)
Reserves	$22,000	$22,000	$10,000	Demand deposits	$100,000	$112,000	$100,000
Securities	$38,000	$38,000	$38,000				
Loans	$40,000	$52,000	$52,000				

14-13

Assets		(1)	Liabilities and net worth		(1)
Reserves	$ 6.1	$ 6.1	Demand deposits	$150	$152.5
Securities	20	20			
Loans	123.9	126.4			

(a) Desired reserves are $6 billion (= 4% of $150 billion). Excess reserves are $0.1 billion (= $6.1 – $6.0 billion). The maximum amount the banking system might lend is $2.5 billion (= 0.1 × 25 billion), as shown on the balance sheet above.

(b) Desired reserves are $7.5 billion (= 5% of $150 billion). Excess reserves are $–1.4 billion (= $6.1 – $7.5 billion). The banking system must recall loans of $28 billion ($–1.4 × $20 billion).

Assets		(1)	Liabilities and net worth		(1)
Reserves	$ 6.1	$ 6.1	Demand deposits	$150	$122
Securities	20	20			
Loans	123.9	95.9			

The increase in the desired reserve ratio increases the banking system's excess reserves from $0.1 billion to $1.4 billion and decreases the money multiplier from 25 to 20.

CHAPTER 15

15-2   (a)

Consolidated Balance Sheet:
All Chartered Banks (*billions of dollars*)

		(1)	(2)
Assets:			
Reserves	$ 4.8	$ 4.7	$ 5.0
Securities	20.0	20	19.8
Loans	71.2	71.2	71.2
Liabilities:			
Deposits	$96.0	$95.9	$96.0
Advances from Bank of Canada	0.0	0.0	0.0

(b)

Balance Sheet:
Bank of Canada (*billions of dollars*)

		(1)	(2)
Assets:			
Securities	$15.8	$15.7	$16.0
Advances to chartered banks	0.0	0.0	0.0
Liabilities:			
Reserves of chartered banks	$ 4.8	$ 4.7	$ 5.0
Government of Canada deposits	0.1	0.1	0.1
Notes in circulation	10.9	10.9	10.9

(c) (1) Money supply (deposits) *directly* changes only in (a); in this case, it decreases by $0.1.

(2) See balance sheets.

(3) Money-creating potential of the banking system decreases by $2 in (a), and increases by $4 in (b).

15-3 The basic determinant of the transactions demand for money is the level of nominal GDP: the higher the level, the greater the transactions demand. The basic determinant of the asset demand is the rate of interest: the higher the rate of interest, the lower the asset demand, for at high rates of interest people would rather hold bonds. On a graph that has the interest rate on the vertical axis and the amount of money demanded on the horizontal axis, the transactions demand, being dependent on nominal GDP and independent of the interest rate, appears as a vertical line; the asset demand appears as a line sloping down from the vertical axis, starting at the highest rate of interest at which any money at all is held as an asset down to the point on the horizontal axis where people will hold as much of their financial assets as cash as possible. The two demands are combined by drawing the asset demand as starting from the vertical transactions demand rather than from the same interest rate level on the vertical axis. The equilibrium interest rate is the point of intersection of the down-sloping total demand-for-money curve and the vertical supply-of-money curve (this supply having been set by the monetary authorities).

The expanded use of credit cards would reduce the transactions demand for money. This would shift the vertical transactions-demand curve to the left and cause the down-sloping total demand curve to intersect the money supply curve at a lower interest rate level.

A shortening of worker pay periods would have the same effect as expanded credit card use: it would mean that a household's income receipts and expenditures were more closely synchronized. The average household would thus have a smaller amount of money on hand to negotiate a given volume of transactions.

An increase in nominal GDP would have the opposite effect: the vertical transactions-demand curve would shift to the right and cause the down-sloping total-demand curve to intersect the money supply curve at a higher interest rate level.

15-6 (a) Sell government securities in the open market. This would immediately decrease the money supply by the amount of the securities sales. If the banks had been fully loaned up, they would now have to decrease their loans by a multiple (because of the money multiplier) of the bond sales. This would force up interest rates (this, added to the immediate effect of the bond sales, would tend to drive down their prices, that is, drive interest rates up), and decrease aggregate expenditures.

(b) Switching government deposits from the chartered banks will reduce excess reserves, thus banks could loan out fewer funds, thereby decreasing the money supply.

15-7 The basic objective of economic policy is to foster a full-employment, non-inflationary level of total economic output.

An easy-money policy (i.e., increasing the money supply) lowers the interest rate, which increases investment spending and the interest-sensitive component of consumer spending; this in turn increases the equilibrium level of GDP. A tight-money policy is intended to do the reverse.

(a) A steep demand-for-money curve makes monetary policy more effective, since it means that a relatively small increase in the money supply will be sufficient to bring interest rates down sharply. A relatively flat investment-demand curve means that only a small decline in the interest rate will increase investment sharply.

(b) A low MPS (a high MPC) and MPM means a large income multiplier, and a large income multiplier means that a relatively small initial increase in spending will multiply into a large increase in GDP.

When an easy-money policy increases the equilibrium GDP, there will be a feedback effect resulting from the fact that the increase in GDP will increase the transactions demand for money. This will partially offset the reduction in the interest rate associated with the initial increase in the money supply.

15-10 If the closed economy has an inflationary gap, a tight money policy will be wholly beneficial: the price level will drop and output and employment will not be affected.

If the AD curve intersects the AS curve to the left of full employment, the tight money policy will certainly depress output and increase unemployment, by shifting the AD curve to the left.

CHAPTER 16

16-1 To derive the Phillips Curve from the AD-AS model we accept that the AS curve has three ranges: horizontal (or near so), upsloping, and vertical. When the economy moves from its horizontal to upsloping range, there is a tradeoff between more output (or employment) and the price level. The economy can have more output (and employment) only if it is willing to accept a higher price level.

The 1970s saw a succession of supply shocks that destabilized the Phillips Curve and cast doubts on its existence. These included: the quadrupling of world oil prices; decreased agricultural production; depreciation of the dollar; the ending of wage-price controls; and a decline in productivity growth. All these factors shifted the AS curve to the left, causing stagflation — rising unemployment and inflation.

16-2 Check your answer against Figure 16-5 and its legend.

16-7 Check your answer against Figure 16-7(a) and (b) and its legend.

16-8 Guideposts are voluntary; controls have the force of law. Controls (1) cause product shortages, resulting in black markets; (2) lead to lowering of product quality to circumvent the controls; (3) result in an inefficient allocation of society's scarce resources.

The few economists who do favour controls see them as useful in ending the inflationary expectations that often propel rapid inflation. A highly credible wage-price control program can convince businesses and labour that large price and wage hikes are not warranted to keep up with inflation since "inflation is under control." Wage and price controls held down — or at least postponed — inflation during World War II. But guideposts and controls applied since then have been largely ineffective.

16-10 The major tenets of supply side economics are: (1) the tax-transfer system negatively affects incentives to work, invest, innovate, and assume entrepreneurial risks; (2) tax cuts can occur without loss of tax revenues; (3) business taxes such as payroll taxes cause higher business costs, reduced employment, and reduced GDP; (4) government regulation of business is excessive.

According to supply side economists, the basic cause of stagflation — leftward shifts of the AS curve — is rising costs and stagnating productivity. High taxes and excessive regulation reduce economic incentives and lower productivity. The AS curve shifts to the left, causing stagnation.

Refer to Figure 16-8. In the graph, the advocates of tax cuts contend the economy is somewhere above m (where tax revenues would be at their maximum). By lowering the tax rate from, say, n to m, the government would increase tax revenues. This increase would occur because the lower tax rate would increase incentives to produce output and earn income. Example: Suppose GDP in an economy is initially $100 billion. At an average tax rate of 30 percent, tax revenues will be $30 billion (= 30% of $100 billion). Now suppose government drops the tax rate to 20% and, as a result, the economy expands to $200 billion. The new tax revenue rises to $40 billion (= 20% of $200 billion). Aggregate supply would rise, simultaneously decreasing unemployment and prices. In two words: remedy stagflation.

CHAPTER 17

17-1 (a) Classical economists envision the AS curve as being perfectly vertical. When prices fall, real profits would not decrease because wage rates will fall in the same proportion. With constant real profits, firms would have no reason to change the quantities of output they supplied. Keynesians view the AS curve as being horizontal at outputs less than the full-employment output. Declines in aggregate demand in this range do not change the price level because wages and prices are assumed to be inflexible downward.

(b) Classical economists view AD as stable so long as the monetary authorities hold the money supply constant. Therefore inflation and deflation are unlikely. Keynesians view the AD curve as unstable — even if the money supply is constant — since investment spending is volatile. Decreases in AD can cause a recession; rapid increases in AD can cause demand-pull inflation.

Neither model — in these simple forms — is realistic. Wage rates and prices are not perfectly *flexible* downward as the classical vertical AS curve suggests; nor are they completely *inflexible* downward as implied by the Keynesian horizontal AS curve. A more realistic view of the economy would incorporate an AS curve having a horizontal, intermediate, and vertical range.

The Keynesian view of AD seems more realistic than the monetarist's view. Aggregate demand appears to be unstable, sometimes causing recession and other times causing demand-pull inflation.

17-5 (a) Keynesian mechanism: Change in monetary policy; change in commercial bank reserves; change in the money supply; change in the interest rate; change in investment; change in aggregate demand; change in nominal GDP (= PQ).

(b) Monetarists' mechanism: Change in monetary policy; change in commercial bank reserves; change in the money supply; change in aggregate demand; change in nominal GDP (= PQ).

Because of the longer and more problematic chain in their transmission mechanism, Keynesians view monetary policy as less reliable than fiscal policy in achieving full-employment, noninflationary GDP. Monetarists believe there is a dependable link between the money supply and nominal GDP. The preferred monetary policy therefore is for the Bank of Canada to adhere to a monetary rule: increase the money supply at a constant 3% to 5% annual rate.

17-12 Refer to Figures 17-5(a) (Keynesian) and 17-5(b) (monetarism) and Figure 17-6 (rational expectations). Stabilization policy — in this case, to increase AD — is highly effective in the Keynesian model; highly inflationary in the monetarist model; and totally ineffective in the rational expectations model.

In the RET model there is never any deviation from full-employment output — all changes in AD are fully anticipated. In the old classical model, there are temporary "lapses" from full employment until market adjustments are complete.

17-13 (b), (c), (d), and (e).

CHAPTER 18

18-1 (a) There is practically no potential for using fiscal policy as a stabilization tool under an annually balanced budget. In an economic downturn, tax revenues fall. To keep the budget in balance, fiscal policy would require the government to reduce its spending or increase its tax rates, adding to the deficiency in spending and accelerating the downturn. If the economy were booming and tax revenues were mounting, to keep the budget balanced fiscal policy would have to increase government spending or reduce taxes, thus adding to the already excessive demand and accelerating the inflationary pressures. An annually balanced budget would intensify cyclical ups and downs.

(b) A cyclically balanced budget would be countercyclical, as it should be, since it would bolster demand by lowering taxes and increasing government spending during a recession and restrain demand by raising taxes and reducing government spending during an inflationary boom. However, because boom and bust are not always of equal intensity and duration, budget surpluses during the upswing need not automatically match budget deficits during the downswing. Requiring the budget to be balanced over the cycle may necessitate inappropriate changes in tax rates or levels of government expenditures.

(c) Functional finance pays no attention to the balance of deficits and surpluses annually or over the cycle. What counts is the maintenance of a noninflationary full-employment level of spending. Balancing the economy is what counts, not the budget.

18-3   Two ways of measuring the public debt: (1) measure its absolute size; (2) measure its size as a percentage of GDP.

An internally held debt is one where the bondholders live in the nation having the debt; an externally held debt is one where the bondholders are citizens of other nations. Paying off an internally held debt would involve boosting taxes or reducing other government spending and using the proceeds to buy the government bonds. This would present a problem of income distribution, because holders of the government bonds generally have higher incomes than the average taxpayer. But paying off an internally held debt would not burden the economy as a whole — the money used to pay off the debt would stay within the domestic economy.

In paying off an externally held debt, people abroad would use the proceeds of the bonds sales to buy goods from the country paying off its external debt. That nation would have to send some of its output abroad to be consumed by others (with no imported goods in exchange).

Refinancing the public debt simply means rolling over outstanding debt — selling "new" bonds to retire maturing bonds.

18-7   Economists do not view the large public debt as a burden for future generations. Future generations not only inherit the public debt, but they inherit the bonds that constitute the public debt. They also inherit public capital goods, some of which were financed by the debt.

There is one way the debt can be a burden to future generations. Unlike tax financing, debt financing may drive up interest rates, since government must compete with private firms for funds in the bond market. Higher interest rates will crowd out some private investment, resulting in a smaller stock of future capital goods and thus a less productive economy for future generations to inherit.

18-8   Cause and effect chain: Government borrowing to finance the debt competes with private borrowing and drives up the interest rate; the higher interest rate induces an inflow of foreign money to buy the now higher-return Canadian bonds; to buy the bonds, the foreign financiers must first buy dollars; the demand for dollars rises and the dollar appreciates; Canadian exports fall and Canadian imports rise; a Canadian trade deficit results.

The public often blames our large trade deficits on the trade policies of other countries — particularly Japan. But as noted in the scenario just described, a substantial portion of our large *trade* deficits may have resulted from our policy of running large *debt* deficits for the past decade or more.

The controversial Ricardian equivalence idea contradicts this view. People supposedly anticipate that debt-financed increases in government spending will require higher future taxes. In response, they reduce their present consumption and increase their saving. Because this increase in saving perfectly offsets the increase in government borrowing, the interest rate does not rise and crowding out does not occur. Because interest rates do not change, exchange rates are not affected, and the link between budget deficits and trade deficits is broken.

CHAPTER 19

19-2   There are four supply factors, a demand factor, and an efficiency factor in explaining economic growth. (1) Supply factors: the quantity and quality of natural resources; the quantity and quality of human resources; the stock of capital goods; and technology. (2) Demand factor: full employment. (3) Efficiency factor: productive and allocative efficiency.

In the long run, a nation must expand its production capacity in order to grow (supply side). But aggregate demand must also expand (demand side) or else the extra capacity will stand idle. Economic growth depends on an enhanced ability to produce and a greater willingness to buy.

The supply side of economic growth is illustrated by the outward expansion of the production possibilities curve, as from *AB* to *CD* in Figure 19-1. The demand side of economic growth is shown by the movement from a point on *AB* to an optimal point on *CD*, as from *a* to, say, *b* in the figure.

19-3   Growth rate of real GDP = 4% (= $31,200 – $30,000)/$30,000). GDP per capita in year 1 = $300 (= $30,000/100). GDP per capita in year 2 = $305.88 (= $31,200/102). Growth rate of GDP per capita is 1.96% = ($305.88 – $300)/300).

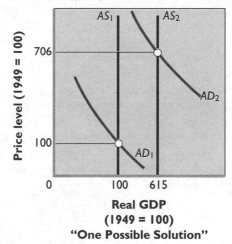

**Real GDP
(1949 = 100)
"One Possible Solution"**

In the graph, AD_1 and AS_1 intersect for 1949 at a price level of 100 and GDP of 100. The 1994 AD_2 and AS_2 intersect at a price level of 706 (an increase of 606%) and at a real GDP of 615 (an increase of 515%).

19-5 Increase in labour inputs: 29%; increase in growth of capital inputs: 44%.

Refer to Table 19-2. Productivity increasing factors are: (1) Technological advance — the discovery of new knowledge that results in the combining of resources in more productive ways. (2) The quantity of capital. (3) Education and training. Since 1940 the proportion of those in the labour force with a high school education has doubled from 40 to 80%. And those with a college or university education have more than doubled from under 10% to 20%. (4) Economies of scale and (5) improved resource allocation. Workers have been moving out of lower productivity jobs to higher productivity jobs. Part of this is associated with the increased efficiency often derived from production in larger plants where specialization of labour and productivity-increasing methods are possible.

19-8 (1) Investment as percentage of GDP has been relatively weak. (2) A rapid increase in the labour force caused by the surge of women workers enabled firms to expand output without raising output per worker. (3) Average labour quality declined as more inexperienced workers moved into the labour force and as the rate of increase of educational attainment slowed. (4) Expenditures on research and development as a percentage of GDP dropped, slowing technological progress. (5) Adversarial relationships between workers and firms impeded advances in labour productivity.

Consequences of the slowdown: (1) a slower rise in the standard of living; (2) higher inflation; and (3) a decline in Canadian competitiveness overseas.

There are several reasons for optimism about future productivity growth: (1) the most recent productivity growth rates are double the averages of the slowdown years; (2) inflation is now more under control than in the 1970s and stagflation and its investment-depressing effect have not returned; (3) some business taxes have been reduced and some regulatory controls relaxed; (4) R&D has increased as a percentage of GDP; (5) the baby boom flood of labour-force entrants is over and the boomers themselves are now well integrated into the labour force; and (6) labour relations have profit sharing and improved wages through training.

19-12 Through technology we have discovered ways to transform once "useless" substances into productive resources. Examples: oil is used to produce gasoline; uranium ore is used to produce nuclear reactions that power electric plants; silicon is used to create microcircuits; petroleum products are used to produce synthetic fibres; and nitrogen is used to produce fertilizers. Future technologies — for example, solar power becoming practical — are likely to transform into economic resources some of the earth's substances not now used in production.

The price mechanism plays an important role in directing technological inquiry and development. Prices of increasingly scarce resources rise, motivating a search for new technologies for producing the output with less use of the higher-priced inputs, or with more abundant alternative inputs. Examples: synthetic rubber replaces natural rubber; "composites" made of plastic replace metals.

Doomsday scenarios — which assume fixed supplies of resources — are highly suspect.

CHAPTER 20

20-4 (a) New Zealand's domestic opportunity cost of 1 plum = 4 apples (or 1 apple = $1/4$ plum). Spain's domestic opportunity cost of 1 plum = 1 apple (or 1 apple = 1 plum).

(b) New Zealand should specialize in apples; Spain in plums.

(c)

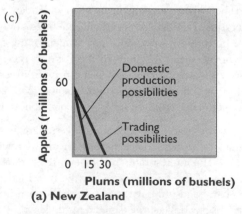

(a) New Zealand

(d) Before specialization and trade: 40 apples (20 + 20) and 50 plums (10 + 40). After specialization and trade: 60 apples and 60 plums. Gain = 20 apples and 10 plums.

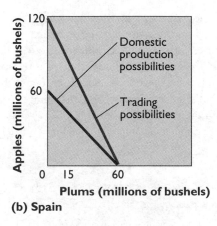

(b) Spain

20-6 At $1: import 15,000. At $2: import 7,000. At $3: no imports or exports. At $4: export 6,000. At $5: export 10,000.

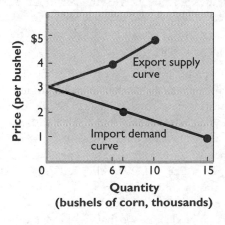

The world price must be between the $3 Canadian domestic price and the $4 French domestic price. Canada will export corn to France.

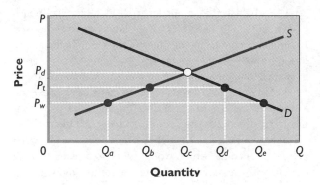

20-7 The world price P_w is below the domestic price P_d. Imports will reduce the price to P_w, increasing consumption from Q_c to Q_e and decreasing domestic production from Q_c to Q_a. A tariff of $P_w P_t$ (a) harms domestic consumers by increasing price from P_w to P_t and decreasing consumption from Q_e to Q_d; (b) aids domestic producers through the increase in price from P_w to P_t and the expansion of domestic production from Q_a to Q_b; (c) harms foreign exporters by decreasing exports from $Q_a Q_e$ to $Q_b Q_d$.

An import quota of $Q_b Q_d$ would have the same effects as the tariff, but there would be no tariff revenues to government from these imports; this revenue is in effect transferred to foreign producers.

20-11 The major portion of the costs of trade protection is borne by consumers through price increases. Prices of imported goods rise, decreasing levels of competition for domestic firms producing similar goods and allowing them to increase their prices. Prices of products using these goods as inputs also rise. Prices of all other goods increase as consumer spending patterns change. Also, resources are reallocated from more-efficient to less-efficient domestic industries.

The main benefit of protectionist policies is greater profits for the protected firms. Government also benefits from the tariff revenues. But empirical studies find that costs of protectionism greatly exceed benefits, resulting in a large net cost — or efficiency loss — to society.

CHAPTER 21

21-2 A demand for francs is created in (a), (c), and (f). A supply of francs is created in (b), (d), (e), and (g).

21-3 Alpha's balance of trade is a surplus of $15 billion, which is the difference between its merchandise exports ($40 billion) and its merchandise imports ($30 billion). Its balance on goods and services is $15 billion, which is the difference between its exports of goods and services ($40 billion + $15 billion = $55 billion) and its imports of goods and services ($30 billion + $10 billion = $40 billion). The balance on its current account is the difference between total current-account credits ($40 billion + $15 billion + $10 billion = $65 billion) and debits ($30 billion + $10 billion + $5 billion = $45 billion) — that is, a surplus of $20 billion. The balance on its capital account is the difference between capital inflows ($10 billion) and outflows ($40 billion) — that is, a deficit of $20 billion (recall official reserves r+10). Alpha has a balance-of-payments deficit of $10 billion. This figure is equal to the $10 billion decrease in official international reserves and can also be arrived at by computing the total current and capital balance ($20 billion – $30 billion).

21-6 The Canadian demand for pesos is downsloping when the dollar price of pesos is used as the relevant exchange rate. As the peso depreciates relative to the dollar, Canadians find that Mexican goods and services are less expensive in dollar terms and purchase more of them, demanding a greater quantity of pesos in the process. The supply of pesos to Canadians is upsloping because as the peso appreciates relative to the dollar, Canadian goods and services become cheaper to Mexicans in peso terms. Mexicans buy more dollars, supplying a larger quantity of pesos.

The peso appreciates in (a), (f), (g), and (h) and depreciates in (b), (c), (d), and (e).

CHAPTER 22

22-2 (a) True. Expansionary macro policies will stimulate the domestic economy and therefore increase imports. Unless offset by an exogenous increase in exports, a trade deficit will result.

(b) True, if a trade deficit is accompanied by a recession. If accompanied by an inflationary gap, a trade deficit need not be a constraint on the domestic economy.

22-3 Tariffs and devaluations alter the composition rather than the level of aggregate expenditures. A tariff on imports makes imports more expensive and deflects domestic demand towards goods produced at home. A currency devaluation has essentially the same effect.

Both tariffs and currency devaluations simultaneously reduce a trade deficit and boost domestic output and employment — at least until one's competitors retaliate. The high probability of retaliation makes such policies of doubtful worth.

22-4 When our major trading partners go into recession, our exports fall, which slows down our own economy and creates a trade deficit. When exchange rates are flexible, the fall in our exports will be accompanied, *ceteris paribus*, by a falling exchange rate. This means that our imports will fall less, and our trade balance will suffer less, than would have been the case if exchange rates were fixed.

22-5 In times of recession, an expansionary *fiscal* policy will put upward pressure on the exchange rate. This will hurt our exports and reduce the effect of the policy. An expansionary *monetary* policy will drive interest rates down and thus bring downward pressure on our exchange rate. This will stimulate our exports, discourage imports, and heighten the effect of the policy.

CHAPTER 23

23-3 Rise in per capita output gap = $135 (= 3% × $5000 – 3% × $500).

23-6 Demographic transition view: Expanded output and income in LDCs will result in lower birth rates and slower growth of population. As incomes of primary family members expand, they begin to see extra children as "liabilities," not "assets." The policy emphasis should therefore be on economic growth. Traditional view: Less developed nations should reduce population growth as a first priority. Slow population growth enables the growth of per capita income.

23-8 Capital earns a higher return where it is scarce, *other things equal*. But, when comparing investment opportunities between IACs and LDCs, other things aren't equal. Advanced factories filled with specialized equipment require a productive work force. IACs have an abundance of educated, experienced workers; these workers are scarce in LDCs. Also, IACs have extensive public infrastructures that increase the returns on private capital. Example: a network of highways makes it more profitable to produce goods that need to be widely transported. Finally, investment returns must be adjusted for risk. IACs have stable governments and "law and order," reducing the risk of capital being "nationalized" or pilfered by organized crime.

23-14 To describe countries such as Japan and South Korea, we would need to change labels on three boxes, leading to a change in the "results" boxes. "Rapid" population growth would change to "low" rate of population growth; "low" level of saving would change to "high" level of saving; "low" levels of investment in physical and human capital would change to "high" levels of investment in physical and human capital. These three changes would result in higher productivity and higher per capita income, which would produce a rising level of demand. Other factors: stable national government; homogeneous population; extensive investment in infrastructure; "will to develop"; strong private incentives.

CHAPTER 24

24-7   See Figure 24-1 in the text. Because prices were set by government and not allowed to change as supply or demand shifted, prices were below the market equilibrium for most goods and services. When the fixed price, P_f, is below the equilibrium price, P_e, there will be a shortage since the quantity demanded will exceed the quantity supplied. As fixed prices are abolished, they will rise to their significantly higher equilibrium levels, contributing to rapid inflation. Black markets are common where prices are fixed below equilibrium levels. People can buy goods at the fixed government prices (or pay off clerks to save such goods to sell to them), and because of the shortages at the low fixed price, resell these goods at a much higher price to those unable to find the goods in the government stores at controlled prices. Official attempts to interfere with the market mechanism often lead to an unofficial market system, which is called the black market.

24-8   Privatization of state-owned property and enterprises; promotion of competition by "demonopolizing" the huge state-run enterprises; reduction of the government's role as owner, manager, price-setter, and production planner; removal of price controls; joining the global economy; achieving macroeconomic stability; and altering entrenched anticapitalist attitudes. Because these changes are interlinked, they need to be accomplished more or less simultaneously. Example: If price controls are lifted without competition or privatization, there is no incentive for producers to expand output. Rather there is incentive to behave like monopolists and take the higher price without expanding supply. Second example: Greater competition requires opening the economy to world trade and foreign investment.

GLOSSARY

Ability-to-pay principle — The belief that those who have the greater income (or wealth) should be taxed absolutely and relatively more than those who have less.

Abstraction — Elimination of irrelevant and non-economic facts to obtain an economic principle.

Actual budget — The amount spent by the federal government (to purchase goods and services and for transfer payments) less the amount of tax revenue collected by it in any (fiscal) year; and which can *not* reliably be used to determine whether it is pursuing an expansionary or contractionary fiscal policy. Compare with the Cyclically adjusted budget (*see*).

Actual deficit — The size of the federal government's Budget deficit (*see*) actually measured or recorded in any given year.

Actual investment — The amount that business Firms do invest; equal to Planned investment plus Unplanned investment.

Actual reserve — The amount a bank has as Vault cash and on deposit at the Bank of Canada.

Adaptive expectations theory — The idea that people determine their expectations about future events (for example, inflation) on the basis of past and present events (rates of inflation) and only change their expectations as events unfold.

Adjustable pegs — The device utilized in the Bretton Woods system (*see*) to change Exchange rates in an orderly way to eliminate persistent Payments deficits and surpluses; each nation defined its monetary unit in terms of (pegged it to) gold or the U.S. dollar, kept the Rate of exchange for its money stable in the short run, and changed (adjusted) it in the long run when faced with international disequilibrium.

Adverse selection problem — A problem arising when information known to one party to a contract is not known to the other party, causing the latter to incur major costs. Example: individuals who have the poorest health are more likely to buy health insurance.

Aggregate demand — A schedule or curve that shows the total quantity of goods and services demanded (purchased) at different price levels.

Aggregate demand–aggregate supply model — The macroeconomic model that uses Aggregate demand and Aggregate supply (*see both*) to determine and explain the Price level and the real Domestic output.

Aggregate expenditures — The total amount spent for final goods and services in the economy.

Aggregate expenditures–domestic output approach — Determination of the Equilibrium gross domestic product (*see*) by finding the real GDP at which Aggregate expenditures are equal to the real Domestic output.

Aggregate expenditures schedule — A schedule or curve showing the total amount spent for final goods and services at different levels of real GDP.

Aggregate supply — A schedule or curve showing the total quantity of goods and services supplied (produced) at different Price levels.

Aggregation — Treating individual units or data as one unit or number. For example, all prices of individual goods and services are combined into a Price level, or all units of output are aggregated into Real GDP.

Agricultural Stabilization Board — The federal agency established in 1958 to support the following commodities at not less than 90% of their average price over the previous five years, with adjustments according to production costs: cattle, hogs, and sheep; industrial milk and cream; and oats and barley not produced on the Prairies [where the Canadian Wheat Board (*see*) has jurisdiction].

Allocative efficiency — The apportionment of resources among firms and industries to obtain the production of the products most wanted by society (consumers): the output of each product at which its Marginal cost and Price are equal.

Allocative factor — The ability of an economy to reallocate resources to achieve the Economic growth that the Supply factors (*see*) make possible.

American Federation of Labor (AFL) — The American organization of affiliated Craft unions formed in 1886.

Annually balanced budget — The equality of government expenditures and tax collections during a year.

Anticipated inflation — Inflation (*see*) at a rate that was equal to the rate expected in that period of time.

Anti-combines — (*See* Combines Investigation Act.)

Anti-Inflation Board — The federal agency established in 1975 (and disbanded in 1979) to administer the government's inflation control program.

Applied economics — (*See* Policy economics.)

Appreciation — An increase in the international price of a currency caused by market forces; not caused by the central bank; the opposite of Depreciation.

Arbitration — The designation of a neutral third to render a decision in a dispute by which both parties (the employer and the labour union) agree in advance to abide.

Asian tigers — The newly industrialized and rapidly growing nations of Hong Kong, Singapore, South Korea, and Taiwan.

Asset — Anything with a monetary value owned by a firm or an individual.

Asset demand for money — The amount of money people want to hold as a Store of value (the amount of their financial assets they wish to have in the form of Money); and which varies inversely with the Rate of interest.

Authoritarian capitalism — An economic system in which property resources are privately owned and government extensively directs and controls the economy.

Authoritarian socialism — (*See* Command economy.)

Average fixed cost — The total Fixed cost (*see*) of a Firm divided by output (the quantity of product produced).

Average product — The total output produced per unit of a resource employed (total product divided by the quantity of a resource employed).

Average propensity to consume — Fraction of Disposable income that households spend for consumer goods and services; consumption divided by Disposable income.

Average propensity to save — Fraction of Disposable income that households save; Saving divided by Disposable income.

Average revenue — Total revenue from the sale of a product divided by the quantity of the product sold (demanded); equal to the price at which the product is sold so long as all units of the product are sold at the same price.

Average tax rate — Total tax paid divided by total (taxable) income; the tax rate on total (taxable) income.

Average total cost — The Total cost of a Firm divided by its output (the quantity of product produced); equal to Average fixed cost (*see*) plus Average variable cost (*see*).

Average variable cost — The total Variable cost (*see*) of a Firm divided by output (the quantity of product produced).

Balanced budget multiplier — The effect of equal increases (decreases) in government spending for goods and services and in taxes is to increase (decrease) the Equilibrium gross domestic product.

Balance of (international) payments — The annual statement of a nation's international economic dealings showing the Current account (*see*) balance and the Capital account (*see*) balance, the latter including the balance in Official international reserves (*see*).

Balance of payments deficit — When the balance in Official international reserves (*see*) is *positive*.

Balance of payments surplus — When the balance in Official international reserves (*see*) is *negative*.

Balance of trade — The addition of the balances on goods (merchandise) and services in the Current account (*see*) of the Balance of payments (*see*).

Balance on the capital account — The Capital inflows (*see*) of a nation less its Capital outflows (*see*), both of which include Official international reserves (*see*).

Balance on current account — The exports of goods (merchandise) and services of a nation less its imports of goods (merchandise) and services plus its Net investment income from nonresidents (*see*) and its Net transfers.

Balance on goods and services — The Balance of trade (*see*).

Balance sheet — A statement of the Assets (*see*), Liabilities (*see*), and Net worth (*see*) of a Firm or individual at some given time.

Bank rate — The interest rate that the Bank of Canada charges on advances (*normally* very short-term loans) made to the chartered banks.

Bankers' bank — The bank that accepts the deposits of and makes loans to chartered banks: the Bank of Canada.

Barrier to entry — Anything that artificially prevents the entry of Firms into an industry.

Barter — The exchange of one good or service for another good or service.

Base year — The year with which prices in other years are compared when a Price index (*see*) is constructed.

Benefit-cost analysis — Deciding whether to employ resources and the quantity of resources to employ for a project or program (for the production of a good or service) by comparing the marginal benefits with the marginal costs.

Benefit-reduction rate — The percentage of any increase in earned income by which subsidy benefits in a Negative income tax (*see*) plan are reduced.

Benefits-received principle — The belief that those who receive the benefits of goods and services provided by government should pay the taxes required to finance them.

Bid rigging — The illegal action of oligopolists who agree either that one or more will not bid on a request for bids or tenders or, alternatively, agree on what bids they will make, and forbidden under the Competition Act (*see*).

Big business — A business Firm that either produces a large percentage of the total output of an industry, is large (measured by number of employees or stockholders, sales, assets, or profits) compared with other Firms in the economy, or both.

Bilateral monopoly — A market in which there is a single seller (Monopoly) and a single buyer (Monopsony).

Brain drain — The emigration of highly educated, highly skilled workers from a country.

Break-even income — The level of Disposable income at which Households plan to consume (spend) all of their income (for consumer goods and services) and to save none of it; also denotes that level of earned income at which subsidy payments become zero in an income-maintenance program.

Break-even point — Any output that a (competitive) Firm might produce at which its Total cost and Total revenue would be equal; an output at which it has neither a profit nor a loss.

Bretton Woods system — The international monetary system developed after World War II in which Adjustable pegs (*see*) were employed, the International Monetary Fund (*see*) helped to stabilize exchange rates, and gold and the major currencies were used as Official international reserves (*see*).

Budget deficit — The amount by which the expenditures of the federal government exceed its revenues in any year.

Budget line — A curve that shows the different combinations of two products a consumer can purchase with a given money income.

Budget restraint — The limit imposed on the ability of an individual consumer to obtain goods and services by the size of the consumer's income (and by the prices that must be paid for the goods and services).

Budget surplus — The amount by which the revenues of the federal government exceed its expenditures in any year.

Built-in stability — The effect of Nondiscretionary fiscal policy (*see*) upon the economy; when Net taxes vary directly with the Gross domestic product, the fall (rise) in Net taxes during a recession (inflation) helps to eliminate unemployment (inflationary pressures).

Business cycle — Recurrent ups and downs over a period of years in the level of economic activity.

Canada Assistance Plan — The federal Act under which the federal government makes funds available to the provinces for their programs of assistance to disabled, handicapped, unemployed who are not entitled to unemployment insurance benefits, and other needy persons.

Canada Deposit Insurance Corporation — Federal Crown Corporation that, for a fee payable by the chartered banks and federally chartered trust companies, insures their customers' deposits up to a limit of $60,000 per customer per bank or trust company.

Canada Labour Code — The federal law of 1970 that consolidated previous legislation regulating employment practices, labour standards, and so on, in the federal jurisdiction.

Canada Pension Plan — The compulsory, contributory, earnings-related federal pension plan that covers most employed members of the labour force between the ages of 18 and 65, and payable at the latter age; it came into effect in 1965; there is transferability between the Plan and the Quebec Pension Plan, which applies to the people of that province.

Canada-United States Free Trade Agreement (FTA) — An accord that came into effect on January 1, 1989, to eliminate all Tariffs (*see*) between the two countries over the following ten years.

Canadian Congress of Labour (CCL) — The federation of Industrial unions (*see*) formed in 1940 and affiliated with the Congress of Industrial Organizations (*see*); amalgamated into Canadian Labour Congress (*see*) in 1956.

Canadian International Development Agency (CIDA) — The federal agency responsible for the operation and administration of Canada's international development assistance programs of approximately $2.5 billion a year.

Canadian Labour Congress (CLC) — The largest federation of Labour unions (*see*) in Canada, with 3 million members in international and national unions; founded in 1956 on the amalgamation of the Canadian Congress of Labour (*see*) and the Trades and Labour Congress of Canada (*see*).

Canadian Payments Association — The federal agency set up in 1982 to provide for Cheque clearing (*see*).

Canadian Wheat Board — Federal Crown Corporation established in 1935, which does not own or operate grain-handling facilities but has complete control over the way western wheat is marketed and the price at which it is sold. The Board also acquired complete control of the supplies of all Prairie coarse grains in 1949.

Capacity-creating aspect of investment — The effect of investment spending on the productive capacity (the ability to produce goods and services) of an economy.

Capital — Human-made resources (machinery and equipment) used to produce goods and services; goods that do not directly satisfy human wants; capital goods.

Capital account — That part of the Balance of payments (*see*) that records the net inflows and outflows of liquid capital (money) for direct and portfolio investments at home and abroad, and includes the balance in Official international reserves (*see*).

Capital account deficit — A negative Balance on the capital account (*see*).

Capital account surplus — A positive Balance on the capital account (*see*).

Capital consumption allowances — Estimate of the amount of Capital worn out or used up (consumed) in producing the Gross domestic product; Depreciation.

Capital flight — The transfer of Savings from less developed to industrially advanced countries to avoid government expropriation, taxation, and high rates of inflation or to realize better investment opportunities.

Capital gain — The gain realized when securities or properties are sold for a price greater than the price paid for them.

Capital goods — (*See* Capital.)

Capital inflow — The expenditures made by the residents of foreign nations to purchase equity, shares, and bonds from the residents of a nation.

Capital-intensive commodity — A product that requires a relatively large amount of Capital to produce.

Capital outflow — The expenditures made by the residents of a nation to purchase equity, shares, and bonds from the residents of foreign nations.

Capital-output ratio — The ratio of the stock of Capital to the productive (output) capacity of the economy; and the ratio of a change in the stock of Capital (net investment) to the resulting change in productive capacity.

Capital-saving technological advance — An improvement in technology that permits a greater quantity of a product to be produced with a specific amount of Capital (or the same amount of the product to be produced with a smaller amount of Capital).

Capital-using technological advance — An improvement in technology that requires the use of a greater amount of Capital to produce a specific quantity of a product.

Cartel — A formal written or oral agreement among Firms to set the price of the product and the outputs of the individual firms or to divide the market for the product geographically.

Causation — A cause-and-effect relationship; one or several events bring about or result in another event.

Ceiling price — (*See* Price ceiling.)

Central bank — The bank whose chief function is the control of the nation's money supply: the Bank of Canada.

Central economic planning — Determination of the objectives of the economy and the direction of its resources to the attainment of these objectives by the national government.

***Ceteris paribus* assumption** — (*See* "Other things being equal" assumption.)

Change in amount consumed — increase or decrease in consumption spending that results from an increase or decrease in Disposable income, the Consumption schedule (curve) remaining unchanged; movement from one line (point) to another on the same Consumption schedule (curve).

Change in amount saved — Increase or decrease in Saving that results from an increase or decrease in Disposable income, the Saving schedule (curve) remaining unchanged; movement from one line (point) to another on the same Saving schedule (curve).

Change in the consumption schedule — An increase or decrease in consumption at each level of Disposable income caused by changes in the Nonincome determinants of consumption and saving (*see*); an upward or downward movement of the Consumption schedule.

Change in the saving schedule — An increase or decrease in Saving at each level of Disposable income caused by changes in the Nonincome determinants of consumption and saving (*see*); an upward or downward movement of the Saving schedule.

Chartered bank — One of the 66 multibranched, privately owned, commercial, financial intermediaries that have received charters by Act of Parliament and that alone, with Quebec Savings Banks, may call themselves "banks"; and which accept Demand deposits (*see*).

Chartered banking system — All Chartered banks as a group.

Checkoff — The deduction by an employer of union dues from the pay of workers and the transfer of the amount deducted to a Labour union.

Chequable deposit — Any deposit in a Chartered bank or other financial intermediary (trust company, credit union, etc.) against which a cheque may be written and which deposit, if it is in a bank, is thus part of the M1 (*see*) money supply.

Cheque clearing — The process by which funds are transferred from the Chequing accounts of the writers of cheques to the Chequing accounts of the recipients of the cheques; also called the "collection" of cheques.

Chequing account — A Demand deposit (*see*) in a chartered bank.

Circular flow of income — The flow of resources from Households to Firms and of products from Firms to Households accompanied in an economy using money by flows of money from Households to Firms and from Firms to Households.

Civilian labour force — Persons 15 years of age and older who are not residents of the Yukon or the Northwest Territories, who are not in institutions or the armed forces, and who are employed for a wage or salary, seeking such employment, or self-employed for gain.

Classical economics — The Macroeconomic generalizations accepted by most economists before the 1930s that led to the conclusion that a capitalistic economy would employ its resources fully.

Closed economy — An economy that neither exports nor imports goods and services.

Close-down case — The circumstance in which a Firm would experience a loss greater than its total fixed cost if it were to produce any output greater than zero; alternatively, a situation in which a firm would cease to operate when the price at which it can sell its product is less than its Average variable cost.

Coase theorem — The idea that Externality problems may be resolved through private negotiations of the affected parties.

Coincidence of wants — The item (good or service) that one trader wishes to obtain is the same as another trader desires to give up and the item the second trader wishes to acquire is the same as the first trader desires to surrender.

COLA — (*See* Cost-of-living adjustment.)

Collection of cheques — (*See* Cheque clearing.)

Collective bargaining — The negotiation of work agreements between Labour unions (*see*) and their employers.

Collective voice — The function a union performs for its members as a group when it communicates their problems and grievances to management and presses management for a satisfactory resolution.

Collusion — A situation in which Firms act together and in agreement (collude) to set the price of the product and the output each firm will produce or to determine the geographic area in which each firm will sell.

Collusive oligopoly — Occurs when the few firms composing an oligopolistic industry reach an explicit or unspoken agreement to fix prices, divide a market, or otherwise restrict competition; may be a Cartel (*see*), Gentleman's agreement (*see*), or Price leadership (*see*).

Combined tax-transfer system — The percentage of income collected as taxes less the percentage of income received as transfer payments in different income classes.

Combines Investigation Act — The federal Act, first passed in 1910, whose avowed aim is to prevent agreements to lessen competition unduly; amended and renamed the Competition Act in June 1986.

Command economy — An economic system (method of organization) in which property resources are publicly owned and Central economic planning (*see*) is used to direct and co-ordinate economic activities.

Commercial bank — (*See* Chartered bank.)

Communism — (*See* Command economy.)

Company union — An organization of employees that is dominated by the employer (the company) and does not engage in genuine collective bargaining with the employer.

Comparable worth doctrine — The belief that women should receive the same salaries (wages) as men when the levels of skill, effort, and responsibility in their different jobs are the same.

Comparative advantage — A lower relative or Comparative cost (*see*) than another producer.

Comparative cost — The amount the production of one product must be reduced to increase the production of another product; Opportunity cost (*see*).

Compensating differences — The differences in the Wages received by workers in different jobs which compensate for nonmonetary differences in the jobs.

Competing goods — (*See* Substitute goods.)

Competition — The presence in a market of a large number of independent buyers and sellers and the freedom of buyers and sellers to enter and to leave the market.

Competition Act — The Act that amended the Combines Investigation Act (*see*) in June 1986 and, in so doing, renamed it the Competition Act.

Competitive industry's short-run supply curve — The horizontal summation of the short-run supply curves of the Firms in a purely competitive industry (*see* Pure competition); a curve that shows the total quantities offered for sale at various prices by the Firms in an industry in the Short run (*see*).

Competitive industry's short-run supply schedule — The summation of the short-run supply schedules of the Firms in a purely competitive industry (*see* Pure competition); a schedule that shows the total quantities that will be offered for sale at various prices by the Firms in an industry in the Short run (*see*).

Competitive labour market — A market in which a large number of (noncolluding) firms demand a particular type of labour from a large number of nonunionized workers.

Complementary goods — Goods or services for which there is an inverse relationship between the price of one and the demand for the other; when the price of one falls (rises) the demand for the other increases (decreases).

Complex multiplier — The Multiplier (*see*) when changes in the Gross domestic product change Net taxes and Imports, as well as Saving.

Concentration ratio — The percentage of the total sales of an industry made by the four (or some other number) largest sellers (Firms) in the industry.

Conditional grant — A transfer to a province by the federal government for a Shared-cost program whereby the federal government undertakes to pay part of the costs (usually half) of programs run by the provinces in accordance with federally set standards; such grants are mostly for health, post-secondary education, and general welfare [mostly under the Canada Assistance Plan (*see*)].

Confederation of National Trade Unions (CNTU) — The Labour union (*see*) federation that represents approximately 20% of Quebec's union members; established in 1921 as the Federation of Catholic Workers of Canada, it was later renamed the Canadian and Catholic Confederation of Labour; it adopted its present name and became nonconfessional in 1956.

Conglomerate combination — A group of Plants (*see*) owned by a single Firm and engaged at one or more stages in the production of different products (of products that do not compete with each other).

Conglomerate merger — The merger of a Firm in one Industry with a Firm in another industry (with a Firm that is neither supplier, customer, nor competitor).

Congress of Industrial Organizations (CIO) — The organization of affiliated Industrial unions formed in the United States in 1936.

Constant-cost industry — An Industry in which the expansion of the Industry by the entry of new Firms has no effect upon the prices the Firms in the Industry pay for resources and no effect, therefore, on their cost curves.

Consumer goods — Goods and services that satisfy human wants directly.

Consumer price index (CPI) — An index that measures the prices of a fixed "market basket" of some 300 consumer goods bought by a "typical" consumer.

Consumer sovereignty — Determination by consumers of the types and quantities of goods and services produced from the scarce resources of the economy.

Consumption schedule — A schedule showing the amounts Households plan to spend for Consumer goods at different levels of Disposable income.

Contractionary fiscal policy — A decrease in Aggregate demand brought about by a decrease in government expenditures for goods and services, an increase in Net taxes, or some combination of the two.

Contractionary monetary policy — Contracting, or restricting the growth of, the nation's Money supply (*see*).

Corporate income tax — A tax levied on the net income (profit) of Corporations.

Corporation — A legal entity ("person") chartered by the federal or a provincial government, which is distinct and separate from the individuals who own it.

Correlation — Systematic and dependable association between two sets of data (two kinds of events); does not necessarily indicate causation.

Cost-of-living adjustment (COLA) — An increase in the incomes (wages) of workers that is automatically received by them when there is inflation and guaranteed by a clause in their labour contracts with their employer.

Cost-plus pricing — A procedure used by (oligopolistic) firms to determine the price they will charge for a product and in which a percentage markup is added to the estimated average total cost of producing the product.

Cost-push inflation — Inflation resulting from a decrease in Aggregate supply (from higher wage rates and raw material prices) and accompanied by decreases in real output and employment (by increases in the Unemployment rate).

Cost ratio — The ratio of the decrease in the production of one product to the increase in the production of another product when resources are shifted from the production of the first to the second product; the amount the production of one product decreases when the production of a second increases by one unit.

Craft union — A Labour union that limits its membership to workers with a particular skill (craft).

Credit — An accounting notation that the value of an asset (such as the foreign money owned by the residents of a nation) has increased.

Credit union — An association of persons who often have a common tie (such as being employees of the same Firm or members of the same Labour union) that sells shares to (accepts deposits from) its members and makes loans to them.

Creeping inflation — A slow rate of inflation; a 2 to 4% annual rise in the price level.

Crop restriction — A method of increasing farm revenue when demand for the product is inelastic. Usually done through a Farm products marketing board (*see*) allotting quotas.

Cross elasticity of demand — The ratio of the percentage change in Quantity demanded of one good to the percentage change in the price of some other good. A positive coefficient indicates the two products are Substitute goods; a negative coefficient indicates Complementary goods.

Crowding model of occupational discrimination — A model of labour markets that assumes Occupational discrimination (*see*) against women and minorities has kept them out of many occupations and forced them into a limited number of other occupations in which the large Supply of labour (relative to the Demand) results in lower wages and incomes.

Crowding-out effect — The rise in interest rates and the resulting decrease in planned investment spending in the economy caused by increased borrowing in the money market by the federal government.

Currency — Coins and Paper money.

Currency appreciation — (*See* Exchange rate appreciation.)

Currency depreciation — (*See* Exchange rate depreciation.)

Current account — That part of the Balance of payments (*see*) that records the total current receipts for merchandise exports, services, investment income from nonresidents, and transfers and the total current payments for merchandise imports, services, investment income to nonresidents, and transfers.

Current account deficit — A negative Balance on current account (*see*).

Current account surplus — A positive Balance on current account (*see*).

Customary economy — (*See* Traditional economy.)

Cyclical unemployment — Unemployment caused by insufficient Aggregate expenditures (or by insufficient Aggregate demand).

Cyclically adjusted budget — What the budget balance would be for the total government sector if the economy were operating at an average or cyclically adjusted level of activity.

Cyclically adjusted deficit — The budget deficit that would have occurred even though the economy was operating at an average or cyclically adjusted level of activity.

Cyclically balanced budget — The equality of Government expenditures for goods and services and Net taxes collections over the course of a Business cycle; deficits incurred during periods of recession are offset by surpluses obtained during periods of prosperity (inflation).

Debit — An accounting notation that the value of an asset (such as the foreign money owned by the residents of a nation) has decreased.

Debt-equity swaps — The transfer of stock in private or government-owned enterprises of Less developed countries (*see*) to foreign creditors.

Declining economy — An economy in which Net investment (*see*) is less than zero (Gross private domestic investment is less than Depreciation).

Declining industry — An industry in which Economic profits are negative (losses are incurred) and which will, therefore, decrease its output as Firms leave the industry.

Decrease in demand — A decrease in the Quantity demanded of a good or service at every price; a shift of the Demand curve to the left.

Decrease in supply — A decrease in the Quantity supplied of a good or service at every price; a shift of the Supply curve to the left.

Deduction — Reasoning from assumption to conclusions; a method of reasoning that tests a hypothesis (an assumption) by comparing the conclusions to which it leads with economic facts.

Deficiency payments — A method of Price support (*see*) whereby the government pays a subsidy to producers when the market price is below the minimum price demand suitable by the government.

Deflating — Finding the Real gross domestic product (*see*) by decreasing the dollar value of the Gross domestic product produced in a year in which prices were higher than in the Base year (*see*).

Deflation — A fall in the general (average) level of prices in the economy.

Demand — A Demand schedule or a Demand curve (*see* both).

Demand curve — A curve showing the amounts of a good or service buyers wish to purchase at various prices during some period of time.

Demand deposit — A deposit in a Chartered bank against which cheques may be written for immediate payment; bank-created money.

Demand factor — The increase in the level of Aggregate expenditures that brings about the Economic growth made possible by an increase in the productive potential of the economy.

Demand management — The use of Fiscal policy (*see*) and Monetary policy (*see*) to increase or decrease Aggregate expenditures.

Demand-pull inflation — Inflation resulting from an increase in Aggregate demand.

Demand schedule — A schedule showing the amounts of a good or service buyers will purchase at various prices during some period of time.

Dependent variable — A variable that changes as a consequence of a change in some other (independent) variable; the "effect" or outcome.

Deposit multiplier — (*See* Monetary multiplier.)

Depository institution — A Firm that accepts the deposits of Money of the public (businesses and persons); Chartered banks and other Financial intermediaries (*see*).

Depreciation (1) — (*See* Capital consumption allowances.)

Depreciation (2) — A decrease in the international price of a currency caused by market forces; not caused by the Central bank; the opposite of Appreciation.

Derived demand — The demand for a good or service that is dependent on or related to the demand for some other good or service; the demand for a resource that depends on the demand for the products it can be used to produce.

Descriptive economics — The gathering or collection of relevant economic facts (data).

Desired reserves — The amount of vault cash each chartered bank chooses to keep on hand for daily transaction. This amount includes reserves held at the Bank of Canada for cheque settlements among the chartered banks.

Determinants of aggregate demand — Factors such as consumption, investment, government, and net export spending that, if they change, will shift the Aggregate demand curve.

Determinants of aggregate supply — Factors such as input prices, productivity, and the legal-institutional environment that, if they change, will shift the Aggregate supply curve.

Determinants of demand — Factors other than its price that determine the quantities demanded of a good or service.

Determinants of supply — Factors other than its price that determine the quantities supplied of a good or service.

Devaluation — A decrease in the government-defined value of a currency brought about by the Central bank; the opposite of Revaluation.

DI — (See Disposable income.)

Differentiated oligopoly — An Oligopoly in which the firms produce a Differentiated product (see).

Differentiated product — A product that differs physically or in some other way from the similar products produced by other Firms; a product such that buyers are *not* indifferent to the seller from whom they purchase it when the price charged by all sellers is the same.

Dilemma of regulation — When a Regulatory agency (see) must establish the maximum price a monopolist may charge, it finds that if it sets the price at the Optimal social price (see), this price is below Average total cost (and either bankrupts the Firm or requires that it be subsidized); and if it sets the price at the Fair-return price (see), it has failed to eliminate the underallocation of resources that is the consequence of unregulated monopoly.

Direct investment — Investment by nonresidents in a firm they thereby establish or control or come to control through the investment. (See also Portfolio investment.)

Directing function of prices — (See Guiding function of prices.)

Directly related — Two sets of economic data that change in the same direction; when one variable increases (decreases) the other increases (decreases).

Direct relationship — The relationship between two variables that change in the same direction, for example, product price and quantity supplied.

Discouraged workers — Workers who have left the Civilian labour force (see) because they have not been able to find employment.

Discretionary fiscal policy — Deliberate changes in taxes (tax rates) and government spending (spending for goods and services and transfer payment programs) by Parliament for the purpose of achieving a full-employment, noninflationary Gross domestic product and economic growth.

Diseconomies of scale — The forces that increase the Average total cost of producing a product as the Firm expands the size of its Plant (its output) in the Long run (see).

Disinflation — A reduction in the rate of Inflation (see).

Disposable income — Personal income (see) less Personal taxes (see); income available for Personal consumption expenditures (see) and Personal saving (see).

Dissaving — Spending for consumer goods and services in excess of Disposable income; the amount by which Personal consumption expenditures (see) exceed Disposable income.

Dividend tax credit — A federal government method of reducing the Double taxation (see) of corporation income.

Division of labour — Dividing the work required to produce a product into a number of different tasks that are performed by different workers; Specialization (see) of workers.

Dollar votes — The "votes" consumers and entrepreneurs in effect cast for the production of the different kinds of consumer and capital goods, respectively, when they purchase them in the markets of the economy.

Domestic economic goal — Assumed to be full employment with little or no Inflation.

Domestic income — (See Net domestic income.)

Domestic output — Gross domestic product (see).

Domestic price — The price of a good or service within a country, determined by domestic demand and supply.

Doomsday models — Computer-based models that predict that continued growth of population and production will exhaust available resources and the environment, causing an economic collapse.

Double counting — Including the value of Intermediate goods (see) in the Gross domestic product; counting the same good or service more than once.

Double taxation — Taxation of both corporation net income (profits) and the dividends paid from this net income when they become the Personal income of households.

Dumping — The sale of products below cost in a foreign country.

Duopoly — A Market in which there are only two sellers; an industry in which there are two firms.

Durable good — A consumer good with an expected life (use) of three years or more.

Dynamic progress — The development over time of more efficient (less costly) techniques of producing existing products and of improved products; technological progress.

Earnings — The Money income received by a worker; equal to the Wage (rate) multiplied by the quantity of labour supplied (the amount of time worked) by the worker.

Easy money policy — Central bank expanding the Money supply in an effort to decrease interest rates.

EC — European Economic Community (*See* European Union).

Economic analysis — Deriving Economic principles (*see*) from relevant economic facts.

Economic cost — A payment that must be made to obtain and retain the services of a resource; the income a Firm must provide to a resource supplier to attract the resource away from an alternative use; equal to the quantity of other products that cannot be produced when resources are employed to produce a particular product.

Economic efficiency — The relationship between the input of scarce resources and the resulting output of a good or service; production of an output with a specific dollar-and-cents value with the smallest total expenditure for resources; obtaining the largest total production of a good or service with resources of a specific dollar-and-cents value.

Economic growth — (1) An increase in the Production possibilities schedule or curve that results from an increase in resource supplies or an improvement in Technology; (2) an increase either in real output (Gross domestic product) or in real output per capita.

Economic integration — Co-operation among and the complete or partial unification of the economies of different nations; the elimination of the barriers to trade among these nations; the bringing together of the markets in each of the separate economies to form one large (a common) market.

Economic law — (*See* Economic principle.)

Economic model — A simplified picture of reality; an abstract generalization.

Economic perspective — A viewpoint that sees individuals and institutions making rational or purposeful decisions based on a consideration of the Marginal benefits and Marginal costs associated with one's actions.

Economic policy — Course of action that will correct or avoid a problem.

Economic principle — Generalization of the economic behaviour of individuals and institutions.

Economic profit — The total receipts (revenue) of a firm less all its Economic costs; also called "pure profit" and "above normal profit."

Economic regulation — (*See* Industrial regulation.)

Economic rent — The price paid for the use of land and other natural resources, the supply of which is fixed (perfectly inelastic).

Economic resources — Land, labour, capital, and entrepreneurial ability, which are used in the production of goods and services.

Economics — Social science concerned with using scarce resources to obtain the maximum satisfaction of the unlimited human wants of society.

Economic theory — Deriving Economic principles (*see*) from relevant economic facts; an Economic principle (*see*).

Economies of scale — The forces that reduce the Average total cost of producing a product as the Firm expands the size of its Plant (its output) in the Long run (*see*); the economies of mass production.

Economizing problem — Society's material wants are unlimited but the resources available to produce the goods and services that satisfy wants are limited (scarce); the inability to produce unlimited quantities of goods and services.

Efficiency factors in growth — The capacity of an economy to combine resources effectively to achieve the growth of real output that the Supply factors (*see*) make possible.

Efficiency loss of a tax — The loss of net benefits to society because a tax reduces the production and consumption of a taxed good below the economically efficient level.

Efficiency wage — A wage that minimizes wage costs per unit of output.

Efficient allocation of resources — The allocation of the resources of an economy among the production of different products that leads to the maximum satisfaction of the wants of consumers; producing the optimal mix of output.

Elastic demand — The Elasticity coefficient (*see*) is greater than one; the percentage change in Quantity demanded is greater than the percentage change in price.

Elasticity coefficient — The number obtained when the percentage change in quantity demanded (or supplied) is divided by the percentage change in the price of the commodity.

Elasticity formula — The price elasticity of demand (supply) is equal to

$$\frac{\text{Percentage change in quantity demanded (supplied)}}{\text{percentage change in price}}$$

Elastic supply — The Elasticity coefficient (*see*) is greater than one; the percentage change in Quantity supplied is greater than the percentage change in price.

Emission fees — Special fees that might be levied against those who discharge pollutants into the environment.

Employment and training policy — Policies and programs involving vocational training, job information, and anti-discrimination that are designed to improve labour market efficiency and lower unemployment at any level of aggregate demand.

Employment rate — The percentage of the Civilian labour force (*see*) employed at any time.

End products — Finished commodities that have attained their final degree of processing, such as commodities used directly for consumption, and machinery.

Entrepreneurial ability — The human resource that combines the other resources to produce a product, makes nonroutine decisions, innovates, and bears risks.

Equality vs. efficiency trade-off — The decrease in Economic efficiency (*see*) that may accompany a decrease in Income inequality (*see*); the presumption that an increase in Income inequality is required to increase Economic efficiency.

Equalization payment — An Unconditional grant (*see*) made by the federal government to the seven less wealthy provinces in an attempt to equalize incomes and opportunities across Canada.

Equalizing differences — The differences in the Wages received by workers in different jobs that compensate for nonmonetary differences in the jobs.

Equation of exchange — $MV = PQ$; in which M is the Money supply (*see*), V is the Velocity of money (*see*), P is the Price level, and Q is the physical volume of final goods and services produced.

Equilibrium GDP — The Gross domestic product at which the total quantity of final goods and services produced (the Domestic output) is equal to the total quantity of final goods and services purchased (Aggregate expenditures); the real Domestic output at which the Aggregate demand curve intersects the Aggregate supply curve.

Equilibrium position — The point at which the Budget line (*see*) is tangent to an Indifference curve (*see*) in the indifference curve approach to the theory of consumer behaviour.

Equilibrium price — The price in a competitive market where the Quantity demanded (*see*) and the Quantity supplied (*see*) are equal; where there is neither a shortage nor a surplus; and where there is no tendency for price to rise or fall.

Equilibrium price level — The Price level at which the Aggregate demand curve intersects the Aggregate supply curve.

Equilibrium quantity — The Quantity demanded (*see*) and Quantity supplied (*see*) at the Equilibrium price (*see*) in a competitive market.

European Common Market — (*See* European Union.)

European Union (EU) — The association of European nations initiated in 1958 to abolish gradually the Tariffs and Import quotas that exist among them, to establish common Tariffs for goods imported from outside the member nations, to allow the eventual free movement of labour and capital among them, and to create other common economic policies. (Earlier known as "European Economic Community" and the "Common Market.")

Excess capacity — A situation where an imperfectly competitive firm produces an output less than the minimum Average total cost output, thereby necessitating a higher product price than a purely competitive firm would charge.

Excess reserve — The amount by which a Chartered bank's Actual reserves (*see*) exceeds its Desired cash reserve (*see*); Actual reserves minus Desired reserves.

Exchange control — (*See* Foreign exchange control.)

Exchange Fund Account — The account operated by the Bank of Canada on the government's behalf wherein are held Canada's Official international reserves (*see*).

Exchange rate — The Rate of exchange (*see*).

Exchange rate appreciation — An increase in the value of a nation's money in foreign exchange markets caused by free market forces; a decrease in the Rates of exchange for foreign monies.

Exchange rate depreciation — A decrease in the value of a nation's money in foreign exchange markets caused by free market forces; an increase in the Rates of exchange for foreign monies.

Exchange rate determinant — Any factor other than the Rate of exchange (*see*) that determines the demand for and the supply of a currency in the Foreign exchange market (*see*).

Excise tax — A tax levied on the expenditure for a specific product or on the quantity of the product purchased.

Exclusion principle — The exclusion of those who do not pay for a product from the benefits of the product.

Exclusive dealing and tied selling — The illegal action whereby a supplier sells a product only on condition that the buyer acquire other products from the same seller and not from competitors; and forbidden under the Competition Act (*see*).

Exclusive unionism — The policies employed by a Labour union to restrict the supply of labour by excluding potential members to increase the Wages received by its members; the policies typically employed by a Craft union (*see*).

Exhaustive expenditure — An expenditure by government resulting directly in the employment of economic resources and in the absorption by government of the goods and services these resources produce; Government purchase (*see*).

Exit mechanism — Leaving a job and searching for another one to improve the conditions under which a worker is employed.

Expanding economy — An economy in which Net investment (*see*) is greater than zero (Gross investment is greater than Depreciation).

Expanding industry — An industry in which Economic profits are obtained by the firms in the industry and which will, therefore, increase its output as new firms enter the industry.

Expansionary fiscal policy — An increase in Aggregate demand brought about by an increase in Government expenditures for goods and services, a decrease in Net taxes, or some combination of the two.

Expectations — What consumers, business Firms, and others believe will happen or what conditions will be in the future.

Expected rate of net profits — Annual profits a firm anticipates it will obtain by purchasing Capital (by investing) expressed as a percentage of the price (cost) of the Capital.

Expenditure approach — The method that adds all the expenditures made for Final goods and services to measure the Gross domestic product.

Expenditures-output approach — (*See* Aggregate expenditures-domestic output approach.)

Explicit cost — The monetary payment a Firm must make to an outsider to obtain a resource.

Export controls — The limitation or prohibition of the export of certain high-technology products on the basis of foreign policy or national security objectives.

Exports — Goods and services produced in a nation and sold to customers in other nations.

Export subsidies — Government payments that reduce the price of a product to foreign buyers.

Export supply curve — An upsloping curve showing the amount of a product domestic firms will export at each World price (*see*) above the Domestic price (*see*).

Export transaction — A sale of a good or service that increases the amount of foreign money (or of their own money) held by the citizens, firms, and governments of a nation.

External benefit — (*See* Spillover benefit.)

External cost — (*See* Spillover cost.)

External debt — Debt (*see*) owed to foreign citizens, firms, and institutions.

Externality — (*See* Spillover.)

Externally held public debt — Public debt (*see*) owed to (Canadian government securities owned by) foreign citizens, firms, and institutions.

Face value — The dollar or cents value stamped on a coin.

Factors of production — Economic resources: Land, Capital, Labour, and Entrepreneurial ability.

Fair-return price — The price of a product that enables its producer to obtain a Normal profit (*see*), and that is equal to the Average total cost of producing it.

Fallacy of composition — Incorrectly reasoning that what is true for the individual (or part) is therefore necessarily true for the group (or whole).

Fallacy of limited decisions — The false notion that there are a limited number of economic decisions to be made so that, if government makes more decisions, there will be fewer private decisions to render.

Farm problem — Technological advance, coupled with a price inelastic and relatively constant demand has made agriculture a Declining industry; also the tendency for the prices farmers receive and their incomes to fluctuate sharply from year to year.

Farm products and marketing boards — The federal and provincial boards, numbering more than 100, that set marketing regulations for commodities ranging from asparagus to turkeys. The boards have the power to allocate quotas, set prices, issue licences, collect fees, and require that the commodity be marketed through them.

Featherbedding — Payment by an employer to a worker for work not actually performed.

Feedback effects — The effects a change in the money supply will have (because it affects the Interest rate, Planned investment, and the Equilibrium GDP) on the demand for money, which is itself directly related to the GDP.

Female participation rate — The percentage of the female population of working age in the Civilian labour force (*see*).

Fewness — A relatively small number of sellers (or buyers) of a good or service.

Fiat money — Anything that is Money because government has decreed it to be Money.

Final goods — Goods that have been purchased for final use and not for resale or further processing or manufacturing (during the year).

Financial capital — (*See* Money capital.)

Financial intermediary — A Chartered bank or other financial institution (trust or mortgage loan company, credit union, *caisse populaire*), which uses the funds (savings) deposited with it to make loans (for consumption or investment).

Financing exports and imports — The use of Foreign exchange markets by exporters and importers to receive and make payments for goods and services they sell and buy in foreign nations.

Firm — An organization that employs Resources to produce a good or service for profit and owns and operates one or more Plants (*see*).

Fiscal policy — Changes in government spending and tax collections designed to achieve a full-employment and noninflationary domestic output.

Five fundamental economic questions — The five questions every economy must answer: what to produce, how to produce, how to divide the total output, how to maintain Full employment, and how to assure economic flexibility.

Fixed cost — Any cost that in total does not change when the Firm changes its output; the cost of Fixed resources (*see*).

Fixed exchange rate — A Rate of exchange that is prevented from rising or falling by the intervention of government.

Fixed resource — Any resource employed by a Firm in a quantity that the firm cannot change.

Flat-rate income tax — A tax that taxes all incomes at the same rate.

Flexible exchange rate — A Rate of exchange determined by the demand for and supply of the foreign money and is free to rise or fall without government interference.

Floating exchange rate — (*See* Flexible exchange rate.)

Floor price — A price set by government that is above the Equilibrium price.

Food and Drugs Act — The federal law enacted in 1920 as outgrowth of legislation dating back to 1875; subsequently amended, the Act and its Regulations now provide for controls over all foods, drugs, cosmetics, and medical devices sold in Canada.

Foreign competition — (*See* Import competition.)

Foreign exchange — (*See* Official international reserves.)

Foreign exchange control — The control a government may exercise over the quantity of foreign money demanded by its citizens and business firms and over the

Rates of exchange in order to limit its outpayments to its inpayments (to eliminate a Payments deficit) (see).

Foreign exchange market — A market in which the money (currency) used by one nation is used to purchase (is exchanged for) the money used by another nation.

Foreign exchange rate — (See Rate of exchange.)

Foreign-trade effect — The inverse relationship between the Net exports (see) of an economy and its Price level (see) relative to foreign Price levels.

Foreign investment — (See Direct investment and Portfolio investment.)

45° line — A curve along which the value of the GDP (measured horizontally) is equal to the value of Aggregate expenditures (measured vertically).

Fractional reserve — A Reserve ratio (see) that is less than 100% of the deposit liabilities of a Chartered bank.

Freedom of choice — Freedom of owners of property resources and money to employ or dispose of these resources as they see fit, of workers to enter any line of work for which they are qualified, and of consumers to spend their incomes in a manner they deem appropriate (best for them).

Freedom of enterprise — Freedom of business Firms to employ economic resources, to use these resources to produce products of the firm's own choosing, and to sell these products in markets of their choice.

Freely floating exchange rates — Rates of exchange (see) that are not controlled and that may, therefore, rise and fall; and that are determined by the demand for and the supply of foreign monies.

Free-rider problem — The inability of potential providers of an economically desirable and indivisible good or service to obtain payment from those who benefit because the Exclusion principle (see) is not applicable.

Free trade — The absence of artificial (government-imposed) barriers to trade among individuals and firms in different nations.

Frictional unemployment — Unemployment caused by workers voluntarily changing jobs and by temporary lay-offs; unemployed workers between jobs.

Fringe benefits — The rewards other than Wages that employees receive from their employers and that include pensions, medical and dental insurance, paid vacations, and sick leaves.

Full employment — (1) Using all available economic resources to produce goods and services; (2) when the Unemployment rate is equal to the Full-employment unemployment rate and there is Frictional and Structural but no Cyclical unemployment (and the real output of the economy is equal to its Potential real output).

Full-employment unemployment rate — The Unemployment rate (see) at which there is no Cyclical unemployment (see) of the Civilian labour force (see) and, because some Frictional and Structural unemployment is unavoidable, equal to about 7.5 to 8%.

Full production — The maximum amount of goods and services that can be produced from the employed resources of an economy; occurs when both Allocative efficiency and Productive efficiency are realized.

Functional distribution of income — The manner in which national income is divided among those who perform different functions (provide the economy with different kinds of resources); the division of Net domestic income (see) into wages and salaries, corporation profits, farmers' income, unincorporated business income, interest, and rent.

Functional finance — Use of Fiscal policy to achieve a full-employment, noninflationary Gross domestic product without regard to the effect on the Public debt (see).

G-7 nations — A group of seven major industrial powers that meet regularly to discuss common economic problems and try to co-ordinate economic policies; Canada, the United States, Japan, Germany, United Kingdom, France, and Italy.

Game theory — A theory that compares the behaviour of participants in games of strategy, such as poker and chess, with that of a small group of mutually interdependent firms (an Oligopoly).

GATT — (See General Agreement on Tariffs and Trade.)

GDP — (See Gross domestic product.)

GDP deflator — The Price index (see) for all final goods and services used to adjust nominal GDP to derive real GDP.

GDP gap — Potential Real gross domestic product less actual Real gross domestic product.

General Agreement on Tariffs and Trade — The international agreement reached in 1947 in which 23 nations agreed to give equal and nondiscriminatory treatment to the other nations, to reduce tariff rates by multinational negotiations, and to eliminate import quotas. Now includes 123 nations.

Generalization — Statistical or probability statement; statement of the nature of the relation between two or more sets of facts.

Gentlemen's agreement — An informal understanding on the price to be charged among the firms in an Oligopoly (*see*).

GNP — (*See* Gross national product.)

Gold export point — The Rate of exchange for a foreign money above which — when nations participate in the International gold standard (*see*) — the foreign money will not be purchased and gold will be sent (exported) to the foreign country to make payments there.

Gold flow — The movement of gold into or out of a nation.

Gold import point — The Rate of exchange for a foreign money below which — when nations participate in the International gold standard (*see*) — a nation's own money will not be purchased and gold will be sent (imported) into that country by foreigners to make payments there.

Gorbachev's reforms — A mid-1980s series of reforms designed to revitalize the Soviet economy. The reforms stressed the modernization of productive facilities, less centralized control, improved worker discipline and productivity, more emphasis on market prices, and an expansion of private economic activity.

Government purchases — Disbursements of money by government for which government receives a currently produced good or service in return; the expenditures of all governments in the economy for Final goods (*see*) and services.

Government transfer payment — The disbursement of money (or goods and services) by government for which government receives no currently produced good or service in return.

Grievance procedure — The methods used by a Labour union and the Firm to settle disputes that arise during the life of the collective bargaining agreement between them.

Gross domestic product (GDP) — The total market value of all Final goods (*see*) and services produced annually within the boundaries of Canada, whether by Canadian or foreign-supplied resources.

Gross national product (GNP) — The total market value of all Final goods (*see*) and services produced annually by land, labour, and capital, and entrepreneurial talent supplied by Canadian residents, whether these resources are located in Canada or abroad.

Gross private domestic investment — Expenditures for newly produced Capital goods (*see*) — machinery, equipment, tools, and buildings — and for additions to inventories.

Guaranteed annual income — The minimum income a family (or individual) would receive if a Negative income tax (*see*) were to be adopted.

Guaranteed Income Supplement — A 1966 amendment to the Old Age Security Act (*see*) provides for the payment of a full supplement to pensioners with no other income and a partial supplement to those with other, but still low, income.

Guiding function of prices — The ability of price changes to bring about changes in the quantities of products and resources demanded and supplied. (*See* Incentive function of price.)

Herfindahl index — A measure of the concentration and competitiveness of an industry; calculated as the sum of the squared market shares of the individual firms.

Homogeneous oligopoly — An Oligopoly in which the firms produce a Standardized product (*see*).

Horizontal axis — The "left–right" or "west–east" axis on a graph or grid.

Horizontal combination — A group of Plants (*see*) in the same stage of production owned by a single Firm (*see*).

Horizontal merger — The merger of one or more Firms producing the same product into a single Firm.

Horizontal range — The horizontal segment of the short-run Aggregate supply curve, indicating much slack in the economy.

Household — An economic unit (of one or more persons) that provides the economy with resources and uses the money paid to it for these resources to purchase goods and services to satisfy material wants.

Human capital investment — Any action taken to increase the productivity (by improving the skills and abilities) of workers; expenditures made to improve the education, health, or mobility of workers.

Hyperinflation — A very rapid rise in the price level.

IMF — (*See* International Monetary Fund.)

Immobility — The inability or unwillingness of a worker or another resource to move from one geographic area or occupation to another or from a lower-paying to a higher-paying job.

Imperfect competition — All markets except Pure competition (*see*); Monopoly, Monopolistic competition, Oligopoly (*see all*).

Implicit cost — The monetary income a Firm sacrifices when it employs a resource it owns to produce a product rather than supplying the resource in the market; equal to what the resource could have earned in the best-paying alternative employment.

Import competition — Competition that domestic firms encounter from the products and services of foreign suppliers.

Import demand curve — A downsloping curve showing the amount of a product that an economy will import at each World price (*see*) below the Domestic price (*see*).

Import quota — A limit imposed by a nation on the quantity of a good may be imported during some period of time.

Imports — Spending by individuals, Firms, and governments for goods and services produced in foreign nations.

Import transaction — The purchase of a good or service that decreases the amount of foreign money held by citizens, firms, and governments of a nation.

Incentive function of price The inducement that an increase (a decrease) in the price of a commodity offers to sellers of the commodity to make more (less) of it available; and the inducement that an increase (decrease) in price offers to buyers to purchase smaller (larger) quantities; the Guiding function of prices (*see*).

Incentive pay plan — A compensation scheme that ties worker pay directly to performance. Such plans include piece rates, bonuses, commissions, and profit sharing.

Inclusive unionism — A union that attempts to include all workers employed in an industry as members.

Income approach — The method that adds all the incomes generated by the production of Final goods and services to measure the Gross domestic product.

Income effect — The effect of a change in price of a product on a consumer's Real income (purchasing power) and thus on the quantity of the product purchased, after the Substitution effect (*see*) has been determined and eliminated.

Income elasticity of demand — The ratio of the percentage change in the Quantity demanded of a good to the percentage change in income; it measures the responsiveness of consumer purchases to income changes.

Income inequality — The unequal distribution of an economy's total income among persons or families.

Income-maintenance system — The programs designed to eliminate poverty and to reduce inequality in the distribution of income.

Incomes policy — Government policy that affects the Nominal incomes of individuals (the wages workers receive) and the prices they pay for goods and services and alters their Real incomes; (*see* Wage-price policy).

Income velocity of money — (*See* Velocity of money.)

Increase in demand — An increase in the Quantity demanded of a good or service at every price; a shift in the Demand curve to the right.

Increase in supply — An increase in the Quantity supplied of a good or service at every price; a shift in the Supply curve to the right.

Increasing-cost industry — An Industry in which expansion through the entry of new firms increases the prices the Firms in the Industry must pay for resources and, therefore, increases their cost schedules (shifts their cost curves upward).

Increasing returns — An increase in the Marginal product (*see*) of a resource as successive units of the resource are employed.

Independent goods — Goods or services for which there is no relationship between the price of one and the demand for the other; when the price of one rises or falls the demand for the other remains constant.

Independent variable — The variable causing a change in some other (dependent) variable.

Indifference curve — A curve showing the different combinations of two products that give a consumer the same satisfaction or Utility (*see*).

Indifference map — A series of indifference curves (*see*), each representing a different level of Utility; and which together are the preferences of the consumer.

Indirect taxes — Such taxes as Sales, Excise, and business Property taxes (*see all*), licence fees, and Tariffs (*see*), which Firms treat as costs of producing a product and pass on (in whole or in part) to buyers of the product by charging them higher prices.

Individual demand — The Demand schedule (*see*) or Demand curve (*see*) of a single buyer of a good or service.

Individual supply — The Supply schedule (*see*) or Supply curve (*see*) of a single seller of a good or service.

Induction — A method of reasoning that proceeds from facts to Generalization (*see*).

Industrial Disputes Investigation Act — The 1907 law that marked the beginning of federal labour legislation; it required disputes in the federal jurisdiction to be submitted to a Board of Conciliation and Investigation; replaced by Canada Labour Code (*see*).

Industrial policy — Any policy in which government takes a direct and active role in promoting firms or industries to expand output and achieve economic growth.

Industrial regulation — The older and more traditional type of regulation in which government is concerned with the prices charged and the services provided the public in specific industries; in contrast to Social regulation (*see*).

Industrial union — A Labour union that accepts as members all workers employed in a particular industry (or by a particular firm).

Industrially advanced countries (IACs) — Countries such as Canada, the United States, Japan, and the nations of western Europe that have developed Market economies based on large stocks of technologically advanced capital goods and skilled labour forces.

Industry — A group of (one or more) Firms that produce identical or similar products.

Inelastic demand — The Elasticity coefficient (*see*) is less than one; the percentage change in Quantity demanded is less than the percentage change in Price.

Inelastic supply — The Elasticity coefficient (*see*) is less than one; the percentage change in Quantity supplied is less than the percentage change in Price.

Inferior good — A good or service of which consumers purchase less (more) at every price when their incomes increase (decrease).

Inflating — Finding the Real gross domestic product (*see*) by increasing the dollar value of the Gross domestic product produced in a year in which prices are lower than in the Base year (*see*).

Inflation — A rise in the general (average) level of prices in the economy.

Inflation premium — The component of the nominal interest rate that reflects anticipated inflation.

Inflationary expectations — The belief of workers, business Firms, and consumers that there will be substantial inflation in the future.

Inflationary gap — The amount by which equilibrium GDP exceeds full employment GDP.

Inflationary recession — (*See* Stagflation.)

Infrastructure — The capital goods usually provided by the Public sector for the use of its citizens and Firms (e.g., highways, bridges, transit systems, waste-water treatment facilities, municipal water systems, and airports).

Injection — An addition of spending to the income-expenditure stream: Investment Government purchases, and Exports.

Injunction — A court order directing a person or organization not to perform a certain act because the act would do irreparable damage to some other person or persons; a restraining order.

In-kind investment — Nonfinancial investment (*see*).

In-kind transfer — The distribution by government of goods and services to individuals and for which the government receives no currently produced good or service in return; a Government transfer payment (*see*) made in goods or services rather than in money.

Innovation — The introduction of a new product, the use of a new method of production, or the employment of a new form of business organization.

Inpayments — The receipts of (its own or foreign) money that the individuals, Firms, and governments of one nation obtain from the sale of goods and services, investment income, Remittances, and Capital inflows from abroad.

Insurable risk — An event — the average occurrence of which can be estimated with considerable accuracy — that would result in a loss that can be avoided by purchasing insurance.

Interest — The payment made for the use of money (of borrowed funds).

Interest income — Income of those who supply the economy with Capital (*see*).

Interest rate — The Rate of interest (*see*).

Interest-rate effect — The tendency for increases (decreases) in the Price level to increase (decrease) the demand for money; raise (lower) interest rates; and, as a result, to reduce (expand) total spending in the economy.

Intergovernmental grant — A transfer payment from the federal government to a provincial government or from a provincial to a local government. (*See* Conditional grant and Unconditional grant.)

Interindustry competition — Competition or rivalry between the products of one industry (*see*) and the products of another Industry (or of other Industries).

Interlocking directorate — A situation where one or more members of the board of directors of a Corporation are also on the board of directors of a competing Corporation; and which is illegal in the United States — but not in Canada — when it tends to reduce competition among the Corporations.

Intermediate goods — Goods that are purchased for resale or further processing or manufacturing during the year.

Intermediate range — The upsloping segment of the Aggregate supply curve lying between the Horizontal range and the Vertical range (*see both*).

Internal economic goal — (*See* Domestic economic goal.)

Internal economies — The reduction in the unit cost of producing or marketing a product that results from an increase in output of the Firm [*see* Economies of (large) scale].

Internally held public debt — Public debt (*see*) owed to (Government of Canada securities owned by) Canadian residents, Firms, and institutions.

International Bank for Reconstruction and Development — (*See* World Bank.)

International economic goal — Assumed to be a current-account balance of zero.

International gold standard — An international monetary system employed in the nineteenth and early twentieth centuries in which each nation defined its money in terms of a quantity of gold, maintained a fixed relationship between its gold stock and money supply, and allowed the free importation and exportation of gold.

International Monetary Fund (IMF) — The international association of nations that was formed after World War II to make loans of foreign monies to nations with temporary Payments deficits (*see*) and to administer the Adjustable pegs (*see*); and which today creates Special Drawing Rights (*see*).

International monetary reserves — The foreign monies — in Canada mostly U.S. dollars — and such other assets as gold and Special Drawing Rights (*see*) that a nation may use to settle a Payments deficit (*see*).

International value of the dollar — The price that must be paid in foreign currency (money) to obtain one Canadian dollar.

Intrinsic value — The value in the market of the metal in a coin.

Inverse relationship — The relationship between two variables that change in opposite directions, for example, product price and quantity demanded.

Investment — Spending for (the production and accumulation of) Capital goods (*see*) and additions to inventories.

Investment curve (schedule) — A curve (schedule) that shows the amounts firms plan to invest (along the vertical axis) at different income (Gross domestic product) levels (along the horizontal axis).

Investment-demand curve (schedule) — A curve (schedule) that shows real Rates of interest (along the vertical axis) and the amount of Investment (along the horizontal axis) at each Rate of interest.

Investment in human capital — (*See* Human capital investment.)

Invisible hand — The tendency of Firms and resource suppliers seeking to further their self-interests in competitive markets that furthers the best interest of society as a whole (the maximum satisfaction of wants).

Jurisdictional strike — A Labour union's withholding of its labour from an employer because of the union's dispute with another Labour union over which is to perform a specific kind of work.

Keynesian economics — The macroeconomic generalizations that lead to the conclusion that a capitalist economy does not always employ its resources fully and that Fiscal policy (*see*) and Monetary policy (*see*) can be used to promote Full employment (*see*).

Keynesianism — The philosophical, ideological, and analytical views pertaining to Keynesian economics (*see*).

Kinked demand curve — The demand curve for a noncollusive oligopolist, based on the assumption that rivals will follow a price decrease and will ignore a price increase.

Labour — The physical and mental talents (efforts) of people that can be used to produce goods and services.

Labour force — (*See* Civilian labour force.)

Labour force participation rate — The percentage of the working-age population that is actually in the labour force.

Labour-intensive commodity — A product that requires much labour to produce.

Labour productivity — Total output divided by the quantity of labour employed to produce the output; the Average product (*see*) of labour or output per worker per hour or per year.

Labour theory of value — The Marxian notion that the economic value of any commodity is determined solely by the amount of labour required to produce it.

Labour union — A group of workers organized to advance the interests of the group (to increase wages, shorten the hours worked, improve working conditions, and so on).

Laffer curve — A curve showing the relationship between tax rates and the tax revenues of government and on which there is a tax rate (between 0 and 100%) where tax revenues are at a maximum.

Laissez-faire capitalism — (*See* Pure capitalism.)

Land — Natural resources ("free gifts of nature") used to produce goods and services.

Land-intensive commodity — A product requiring a relatively large amount of Land to produce.

Law of conservation of matter and energy — The notion that matter can be changed to other matter or into energy but cannot disappear; all production inputs are ultimately transformed into an equal amount of finished product, energy, and waste (potentially pollution).

Law of demand — The inverse relationship between the price and the Quantity demanded (*see*) of a good or service during some period of time.

Law of diminishing marginal utility — As a consumer increases the consumption of a good or service, the Marginal utility (*see*) obtained from each additional unit of the good or service decreases.

Law of diminishing returns — When successive equal increments of a Variable resource (*see*) are added to the Fixed resources (*see*), beyond some level of employment, the Marginal product (*see*) of the Variable resource will decrease.

Law of increasing opportunity cost — As the amount of a product produced is increased, the Opportunity cost

(*see*) — the Marginal cost (*see*) — of producing an additional unit of the product increases.

Law of supply — The direct relationship between the price and the Quantity supplied (*see*) of a good or service during some period.

Leakage — (1) A withdrawal of potential spending from the income-expenditures stream: Saving (*see*), tax payment, and Imports (*see*); (2) a withdrawal that reduces the lending potential of the Chartered banking system.

Leakages-injections approach — Determination of the Equilibrium gross domestic product (*see*) by finding the GDP at which Leakages (*see*) are equal to Injections (*see*).

Least-cost combination rule (of resources) — The quantity of each resource a Firm must employ if it is to produce an output at the lowest total cost; the combination in which the ratio of the Marginal product (*see*) of a resource to its Marginal resource cost (*see*) (to its price if the resource is employed in a competitive market) is the same for all resources employed.

Legal cartel theory of regulation — The hypothesis that industries want to be regulated so that they may form legal Cartels (*see*) and that government officials (the government) provide the regulation in return for their political and financial support.

Legal tender — Anything that government has decreed must be accepted in payment of a debt.

Lending potential of an individual chartered bank — The amount by which a single Chartered bank can safely increase the Money supply by making new loans to (or buying securities from) the public; equal to the Chartered bank's Excess cash reserve (*see*).

Lending potential of the banking system — The amount the Chartered banking system (*see*) can increase the Money supply by making new loans to (or buying securities from) the public; equal to the Excess reserve (*see*) of the Chartered banking system multiplied by the Money multiplier (*see*).

Less-developed countries (LDCs) — Many countries of Africa, Asia, and Latin America that are characterized by a lack of capital goods, primitive production technologies, low literacy rates, high unemployment, rapid population growth, and labour forces heavily committed to agriculture.

Liability — A debt with a monetary value; an amount owed by a Firm or an individual.

Limited liability — Restriction of the maximum loss to a predetermined amount; for the owners (stockholders) of a Corporation, the maximum loss is the amount they paid for their shares of stock.

Limited-liability company — An unincorporated business whose owners are protected by Limited liability (*see*).

Liquidity — Money or things that can be quickly and easily converted into Money with little or no loss of purchasing power.

Loaded terminology — Terms that arouse emotions and elicit approval or disapproval.

Loanable funds theory of interest — The concept that the supply of and demand for loanable funds determines the equilibrium rate of interest.

Log-rolling — The trading of votes by legislators to secure favourable outcomes on decisions to provide public goods and services.

Long run — A period of time long enough to enable producers of a product to change the quantities of all the resources they employ; in which all resources and costs are variable and no resources or costs are fixed.

Long-run aggregate supply curve — The aggregate supply curve associated with a time period in which input prices (especially nominal wages) are fully responsive to changes in the price level.

Long-run competitive equilibrium — The price at which the Firms in Pure competition (*see*) neither obtain Economic profit nor suffer losses in the Long run and the total quantity demanded and supplied at that price are equal; a price equal to the minimum long-run average total cost of producing the product.

Long-run farm problem — The tendency for agriculture to be a declining industry as technological progress increases supply relative to an inelastic and relatively constant demand.

Long-run supply — A schedule or curve showing the prices at which a Purely competitive industry will make various quantities of the product available in the Long run.

Lorenz curve — A curve showing the distribution of income in an economy; and when used for this purpose, the cumulated percentage of families (income receivers) is measured along the horizontal axis and the cumulated percentage of income is measured along the vertical axis.

Loss-minimizing case — The circumstances where a firm loses less than its Total cost; when the price at which the firm can sell its product is less than Average total but greater than Average variable cost.

Lotteries — Games of chance where people buy numbered tickets and winners are drawn by lot; a source of provincial government revenue.

Lump-sum tax — A tax that is a constant amount (the tax revenue of government is the same) at all levels of GDP.

M1 — The narrowly defined Money supply; the Currency (coins and Paper money) and Demand deposits in chartered banks (*see*) not owned by the federal government or banks.

M2 — Includes, in addition to M1, Canadian dollar personal savings deposits and nonpersonal notice deposits at chartered banks.

M2+ — Includes, in addition to M2, deposits at trust and mortgage loan companies, and deposits and shares at *caisses populaires* and credit unions.

M3 — Includes, in addition to M2, Canadian dollar nonpersonal fixed term deposits plus all foreign currency deposits of Canadian residents booked at chartered banks in Canada.

Macroeconomics — The part of economics concerned with the economy as a whole; with such major aggregates as the households, business, international trade, and governmental sectors and with totals for the economy.

Managed floating exchange rate — An Exchange rate allowed to change (float) to eliminate Payments deficits and surpluses and is controlled (managed) to eliminate day-to-day fluctuations.

Marginal analysis — Decision making that involves a comparison or marginal ("extra" or "additional") benefits.

Marginal cost — The extra (additional) cost of producing one more unit of output; equal to the change in Total cost divided by the change in output (and in the short run to the change in total Variable cost divided by the change in output).

Marginal labour cost — The amount the total cost of employing Labour increases when a Firm employs one additional unit of Labour (the quantity of other resources employed remaining constant); equal to the change in the total cost of Labour divided by the change in the quantity of Labour employed.

Marginal product — The additional output produced when one additional unit of a resource is employed (the quantity of all other resources employed remaining constant); equal to the change in total product divided by the change in the quantity of a resource employed.

Marginal productivity theory of income distribution — The contention that the distribution of income is equitable when each unit of each resource receives a money payment equal to its marginal contribution to the firm's revenue (its Marginal revenue product).

Marginal propensity to consume — Fraction of any change in Disposable income spent for Consumer goods; equal to the change in consumption divided by the change in Disposable income.

Marginal propensity to import — The fraction of any change in income (Gross domestic product) spent for imported goods and services; equal to the change in Imports (*see*) divided by the change in income.

Marginal propensity to save — Fraction of any change in Disposable income that households save; equal to change in Saving (*see*) divided by the change in Disposable income.

Marginal rate of substitution — The rate (at the margin) at which a consumer is prepared to substitute one good or service for another and remain equally satisfied (have the same total Utility); and equal to the slope of an Indifference curve (*see*).

Marginal resource cost — The amount the total cost of employing a resource increases when a Firm employs one additional unit of the resource (the quantity of all other resources employed remaining constant); equal to the change in the total cost of the resource divided by the change in the quantity of the resource employed.

Marginal revenue — The change in the Total revenue of the Firm that results from the sale of one additional unit of its product; equal to the change in Total revenue divided by the change in the quantity of the product sold (demanded).

Marginal-revenue–marginal-cost approach — The method that finds the total output where Economic profit (*see*) is a maximum (or losses a minimum) by comparing the Marginal revenue (*see*) and the Marginal cost (*see*) of additional units of output.

Marginal revenue product — The change in the Total revenue of the Firm when it employs one additional unit of a resource (the quantity of all other resources employed remaining constant); equal to the change in

Total revenue divided by the change in the quantity of the resource employed.

Marginal tax rate — The fraction of additional (taxable) income that must be paid in taxes.

Marginal utility — The extra Utility (*see*) a consumer obtains from the consumption of one additional unit of a good or service; equal to the change in total Utility divided by the change in the quantity consumed.

Market — Any institution or mechanism that brings together the buyers (demanders) and sellers (suppliers) of a particular good or service.

Market demand — (*See* Total demand.)

Market economy — An economy in which only the private decisions of consumers, resource suppliers, and business Firms determine how resources are allocated; the Market system (*see*).

Market failure — The failure of a market to bring about the allocation of resources that best satisfies the wants of society (that maximizes the satisfaction of wants). In particular, the over- or underallocation of resources to the production of a particular good or service (because of Spillovers) and no allocation of resources to the production of Public (social) goods (*see*).

Market for externality rights — A market in which the Perfectly inelastic supply (*see*) of the right to pollute the environment and the demand for the right to pollute would determine the price a polluter would have to pay for the right.

Market period — A period in which producers of a product are unable to change the quantity produced in response to a change in its price; in which there is Perfect inelasticity of supply (*see*); and where all resources are Fixed resources (*see*).

Market policies — Government policies designed to reduce the market power of Labour unions and large business firms and to reduce or eliminate imbalances and bottlenecks in labour markets.

Market socialism — An economic system (method of organization) in which property resources are publicly owned and markets and prices are used to direct and co-ordinate economic activities.

Market system — All the product and resource markets of the economy and the relationships among them; a method that allows the prices determined in these markets to allocate the economy's Scarce resources and to communicate and co-ordinate the decisions made by consumers, business firms, and resource suppliers.

Median-voter model — The view that under majority rule the median (middle) voter will be in the dominant position to determine the outcome of an election.

Medium of exchange — Money (*see*); a convenient means of exchanging goods and services without engaging in Barter (*see*); what sellers generally accept and buyers generally use to pay for a good or service.

Microeconomics — The part of economics concerned with such individual units within the economy as Industries, Firms, and Households, and with individual markets, particular prices, and specific goods and services.

Minimum wage — The lowest Wage (rate) employers may legally pay for an hour of Labour.

Mixed capitalism — An economy in which both government and private decisions determine how resources are allocated.

Monetarism — An alternative to Keynesianism (*see*); the macroeconomic view that the main cause of changes in aggregate output and the price level are fluctuations in the money supply; advocates a Monetary rule (*see*).

Monetary control instruments — Techniques the Bank of Canada employs to change the size of the nation's Money supply (*see*); Open-market operations (*see*) and Switching Government of Canada deposits (*see*).

Monetary policy — Changing the Money supply (*see*) in order to assist the economy to achieve a full-employment, noninflationary level of total output.

Monetary rule — The rule suggested by the Monetarists (*see*): the Money supply should be expanded each year at the same annual rate as the potential rate of growth of the Real gross domestic product; the supply of money should be increased steadily at from 3 to 5% per year.

Money — Any item that is generally acceptable to sellers in exchange for goods and services.

Money capital — Money available to purchase Capital goods (*see*).

Money income — (See Nominal income.)

Money interest rate — The Nominal interest rate (*see*).

Money market — The Market in which the demand for and the supply of Money determine the Interest rate (or the level of interest rates) in the economy.

Money multiplier — The multiple of its Excess reserve (*see*) by which the Chartered banking system (*see*) can expand deposits and the Money supply by making new loans (or buying securities); equal to one divided by the Reserve ratio (*see*).

Money supply — Narrowly defined: M1 (*see*); more broadly defined: M2, M3, and M2+ (*see*).

Money wage — The amount of Money received by a worker per unit of time (hour, day, and so on).

Money wage rate — (See Money wage.)

Monopolistic competition — A Market in which many Firms sell a Differentiated product (*see*), into which entry is relatively easy, in which the Firm has some control over its product prices, and in which there is considerable Nonprice competition (*see*).

Monopoly — (1) A Market in which the number of sellers is so few that each seller is able to influence the total supply and the price of the good or service; (2) a major industry in which a small number of Firms control all or a large portion of its output. (*See also* Pure Monopoly.)

Monopsony — A Market in which there is only one buyer of a good or service.

Moral hazard problem — The possibility that individuals or institutions will change their behaviour as the result of a contract or agreement. Example: A bank whose deposits are insured against loss may make riskier loans and investments.

Moral suasion — The statements, pronouncements, and appeals made by the Bank of Canada that are intended to influence the lending policies of Chartered banks.

Most-favoured-nation (MFN) clause — A clause in a trade agreement between Canada and another nation that provides that the other nation's Imports into Canada will be subjected to the lowest tariff rates levied then or later on any other nation's Imports into Canada.

MR = MC rule — A Firm will maximize its Economic profit (or minimize its losses) by producing the output at which Marginal revenue (*see*) and Marginal cost (*see*) are equal — provided the price at which it can sell its product is equal to or greater than Average variable cost (*see*).

MRP = MRC rule — To maximize Economic profit (or minimize losses), a Firm should employ the quantity of a resource where its Marginal revenue product (*see*) is equal to its Marginal resource cost (*see*).

Multinational corporation — A Firm that owns production facilities in other countries and produces and sells its products abroad.

Multiplier — The ratio of the change in the Equilibrium GDP to the change in Investment (*see*), or to the change in any other component in the Aggregate-expenditures schedule or to the change in Net taxes; the number by which a change in any component in the Aggregate-expenditures schedule or in Net taxes must be multiplied to find the resulting change in the Equilibrium GDP.

Multiplier effect — The effect on the Equilibrium gross domestic product of a change in the Aggregate-expenditures schedule (caused by a change in the Consumption schedule, Investment, Net taxes, Government expenditures, or Net exports).

Mutual interdependence — Situation in which a change in price (or in some other policy) by one Firm will affect the sales and profits of another Firm (or other Firms) and any Firm that makes such a change can expect the other Firm(s) to react in an unpredictable (uncertain) way.

Mutually exclusive goals — Goals that conflict and cannot be achieved simultaneously.

National income — Total income earned by resource suppliers for their contributions to the production of the Gross national product (*see*); equal to the Gross national product minus the Nonincome charges (*see*).

National income accounting — The techniques employed to measure the overall production of the economy and other related totals for the nation as a whole.

National Policy — Sir John A. Macdonald's 1879 policy of high tariff protection for Canadian (Ontario and Quebec) secondary manufacturers.

Natural monopoly — An industry in which Economies of scale (*see*) are so great the product can be produced by one Firm at a lower average total cost than if the product were produced by more than one Firm.

Natural rate hypothesis — Contends that the economy is stable in the Long run at the natural rate of unemployment; views the long-run Phillips curve (*see*) as vertical at the natural rate of unemployment.

Natural rate of unemployment — (See Full-employment unemployment rate.)

Near-money — Financial assets, the most important of which are savings, term, and notice deposits in Chartered banks, trust companies, credit unions, and other savings institutions, that can be readily converted into Money.

Negative income tax — The proposal to subsidize families and individuals with money payments when their incomes fall below a Guaranteed (annual) income (*see*); the negative tax would decrease as earned income increases (*see* Benefit-reduction rate).

Negative relationship — (*See* Inverse relationship.)

Net capital movement — The difference between the real and financial investments and loans made by individuals and Firms of one nation in the other nations of the world and the investments and loans made by individuals and Firms from other nations in a nation.

Net domestic income — The sum of the incomes earned through the production of the Gross domestic product (*see*).

Net exports effect — The notion that the impact of a change in Monetary policy (fiscal policy) will be strengthened (weakened) by the consequent change in Net exports (*see*). For example, a contractionary (expansionary) monetary policy will increase (decrease) domestic interest rates, increasing (decreasing) the foreign demand for dollars. The dollar appreciates (depreciates) and causes Canadian Net exports to decrease (increase).

Net exports — Exports (*see*) minus Imports (*see*).

Net investment — Gross investment (*see*) less Capital consumption allowances (*see*); the addition to the nation's stock of Capital during a year.

Net investment income — The interest and dividend income received by the residents of a nation from residents of other nations less the interest and dividend payments made by the residents of that nation to the residents of other nations. In Canada, always a negative quantity.

Net national income — National income (*see*).

Net national product — Gross national product (*see*) less that part of the output needed to replace the Capital goods worn out in producing the output (Capital consumption allowances [*see*]).

Net taxes — The taxes collected by government less Government transfer payments (*see*).

Net transfers — The personal and government Transfer payments made to residents of foreign nations less the personal and government Transfer payments received from residents of foreign nations.

Net worth — The total Assets (*see*) less the total Liabilities (*see*) of a Firm or an individual; the claims of the owners of a firm against its total Assets.

New classical economics — The theory that, although unanticipated price level changes may create macroeconomic instability in the Short run, the economy is stable at the full-employment level of domestic output in the Long run because of price and wage flexibility.

New global compact — A reform agenda by which Less-developed countries (*see*) seek more foreign aid, debt relief, greater access to a world market, freer immigration, and an end to neocolonialism.

NIT — (*See* Negative income tax.)

New perspective view of advertising — Envisions advertising as a low-cost source of consumer information that increases competition by making consumers more aware of substitute products.

NNP — (*See* Net national product.)

Nominal gross domestic output (GDP) — The GDP (*see*) measured in terms of the price level at the time of measurement (unadjusted for changes in the price level).

Nominal income — The number of dollars received by an individual or group during some period of time; the money income.

Nominal interest rate — The rate of interest expressed in dollars of current value (not adjusted for inflation).

Nominal wage rate — The Money wage (*see*).

Noncollusive oligopoly — An Oligopoly (*see*) in which the Firms do not act together and in agreement to determine the price of the product and the output each Firm will produce or to determine the geographic area in which each Firm will sell.

Noncompeting groups — Groups of workers in the economy who do not compete with each other for employment because the skill and training of the workers in one group are substantially different from those in other groups.

Nondiscretionary fiscal policy — The increases (decreases) in Net taxes (*see*) that occur without Parliamentary action when the Gross domestic product rises (falls) and that tend to stabilize the economy; also called Built-in stability.

Nondurable good — A Consumer good (*see*) with an expected life (use) of less than three years.

Nonexhaustive expenditure — An expenditure by government that does not result directly in the employment of economic resources or the production of goods and services; *see* Government transfer payment.

Nonfinancial investment — An investment that does not require Households to save a part of their money incomes; but that uses Surplus (unproductive) labour to build Capital goods.

Nonincome charges — Capital consumption allowances (*see*) and Indirect-taxes (*see*).

Nonincome determinants of consumption and saving — All influences on consumption spending and saving other than the level of Disposable income.

Noninterest determinants of investment — All influences on the level of investment spending other than the Rate of interest.

Noninvestment transaction — An expenditure for stocks, bonds, or second-hand Capital goods.

Nonmarket transactions — The production of goods and services not included in the measurement of the Gross domestic product because the goods and services are not bought and sold.

Nonmerchandise balance — The addition of the balances on services, investment income, and transfers in the Current account (*see*) of the Balance of payments (*see*).

Nonprice competition — The means other than decreasing the prices of their products that Firms employ to increase the sale of their products; and that includes Product differentiation (*see*), advertising, and sales promotion activities.

Nonproduction transaction — The purchase and sale of any item that is not a currently produced good or service.

Nontariff barriers (NTBs) — All barriers other than Tariffs (*see*) that nations erect to impede international trade: Import quotas (*see*), licensing requirements, unreasonable product-quality standards, unnecessary red tape in customs procedures, and so on.

Nonunion shop — A place of employment at which none of the employees are members of a Labour union (and at which the employer attempts to hire only workers who are not apt to join a union).

Normal good — A good or service whose consumption increases (decreases) when income increases (decreases).

Normal profit — Payment that must be made by a Firm to obtain and retain Entrepreneurial ability (*see*); the minimum payment (income) Entrepreneurial ability must (expect to) receive to induce it to perform the entrepreneurial functions for a Firm; an Implicit cost (*see*).

Normative economics — That part of economics pertaining to value judgements about what the economy should be like; concerned with economic goals and policies.

North American Free Trade Agreement (NAFTA) — A 1993 agreement establishing a Trade bock (*see*) comprising Canada, Mexico, and the United States. The goal is to establish free trade between the three nations.

Notice, term, and savings deposit — A deposit in a Chartered bank against which cheques may or may not be written but for which the bank has the right to demand notice of withdrawal.

NTBs — (*See* Nontariff barriers.)

Occupational discrimination — The form of discrimination that excludes women from certain occupations and the higher wages paid workers in these occupations.

Occupational licensing — The laws of provincial governments that require a worker to obtain a licence from a provincial board (by satisfying certain specified requirements) before engaging in a particular occupation.

Offers to purchase — A method of Price support (*see*) whereby the government buys the Surplus created when it sets the minimum price above the Equilibrium price (*see*).

Official international reserves — The international monetary assets (*see*) owned by the federal government and held in its behalf by the Bank of Canada in the Exchange Fund Account.

Official reserves — Official international reserves (*see*).

Okun's Law — The generalization that any one percentage point rise in the Unemployment rate above the Full-employment unemployment rate will increase the GDP gap by 2.5% of the Potential output (GDP) of the economy.

Old Age Security Act — The 1951 federal Act, as subsequently amended, by which a pension is payable to every person aged 65 and older provided the person has resided in Canada for ten years immediately preceding the approval of an application for pension; in addition a Guaranteed Income Supplement (*see*) may be paid; the pension is payable in addition to the Canada Pension (*see*).

Oligopoly — A Market in which a few Firms sell either a Standardized or Differentiated product, into which entry is difficult, in which the Firm has limited control over product price because of Mutual interdependence (*see*) (except when there is Collusion among firms), and in which there is typically Nonprice Competition (*see*).

Oligopsony — A market in which there are a few buyers.

OPEC — An acronym for the Organization of Petroleum Exporting Countries (*see*).

Open economy — An economy that both exports and imports goods and services.

Open-economy multiplier — The Multiplier (*see*) in an economy in which some part of any increase in the income (Gross domestic product) of the economy is used to purchase additional goods and services from abroad; and which is equal to the reciprocal of the sum of the Marginal propensity to save (*see*) and the Marginal propensity to import (*see*).

Open-market operations — The buying and selling of Government of Canada securities by the Bank of Canada.

Open shop — A place of employment where the employer may hire either Labour union members or workers who are not (and need not become) members of the union.

Opportunity cost — The amount of other products that must be forgone or sacrificed to produce a unit of a product.

Optimal amount of externality reduction — That reduction of pollution or other negative externality where society's marginal benefit and marginal cost of reducing the externality are equal.

Optimal social price — The price of a product that results in the most efficient allocation of an economy's resources and that is equal to the Marginal cost (*see*) of the last unit of the product produced.

Organization of Petroleum Exporting Countries — The cartel formed in 1970 by 13 oil-producing countries to control the price and quantity of crude oil exported by its members, and which accounts for a large proportion of the world's export of oil.

"Other things being equal" assumption — Assuming that the factors other than those being considered are constant.

Outpayments — The expenditures of (its own or foreign) money that the individuals, Firms, and governments of one nation make to purchase goods, services, and investment income, for Remittances, for government loans and grants, and (liquid) capital outflows abroad.

Output effect — The change in labour input resulting from the effect of a change in the wage rate on a Firm's cost of production and the subsequent change in the desired level of output, after the Substitution effect (*see*) has been determined and eliminated.

Paper money — Pieces of paper used as a Medium of exchange (*see*); in Canada, Bank of Canada notes.

Paradox of voting — A situation wherein voting by majority rule fails to provide a consistent ranking of society's preferences for public goods or services.

Partnership — An unincorporated business Firm owned and operated by two or more persons.

Patent laws — The federal laws granting to inventors and innovators the exclusive right to produce and sell a new product or machine for a period of 17 years.

Payments deficit — (*See* Balance of payments deficit.)

Payments surplus — (*See* Balance of payments surplus.)

Perestroika — The essential feature of Mikhail Gorbachev's reform program to "restructure" the Soviet economy; includes modernization, decentralization, some privatization, and improved worker incentives.

Perfect elastic demand — A change in the Quantity demanded requires no change in the price of the product or resource; buyers will purchase as much of a product or resource as is available at a constant price.

Perfect elastic supply — A change in the Quantity supplied requires no change in the price of the product or resource; sellers will make available as much of the product or resource as buyers will purchase at a constant price.

Perfect inelastic demand — A change in price results in no change in the Quantity demanded of a product or resource; the Quantity demanded is the same at all prices.

Perfect inelastic supply — A change in price results in no change in the Quantity supplied of a product or resource; the Quantity supplied is the same at all prices.

Personal consumption expenditures — The expenditures of Households for Durable, semidurable, and nondurable consumer goods and for services.

Personal distribution of income — The manner in which the economy's Personal or Disposable income is divided among different income classes or different Households.

Personal income — The income earned and unearned, available to resource suppliers and others before the payment of Personal taxes (*see*).

Personal income tax — A tax levied on the taxable income of individuals (Households and unincorporated Firms).

Personal saving — The Personal income of Households less Personal taxes (*see*) and Personal consumption expenditures (*see*); Disposable income less Personal consumption expenditures; that part of Disposable income not spent for Consumer goods (*see*).

Phillips curve — A curve showing the relationship between the Unemployment rate (*see*) (on the horizontal axis) and the annual rate of increase in the Price level (on the vertical axis).

Planned economy — An economy in which government determines how resources are allocated.

Planned investment — The amount that business firms plan or intend to invest.

Plant — A physical establishment (Land and Capital) that performs one or more of the functions in the production (fabrication and distribution) of goods and services.

P = MC rule — A Firm in Pure competition (*see*) will maximize its Economic profit (*see*) or minimize its losses by producing the output at which the price of the product is equal to Marginal cost (*see*), provided that price is equal to or greater than Average variable cost (*see*) in the short run and equal to or greater than Average total cost (*see*) in the long run.

Policy economics — The formulation of courses of action to bring about desired results or to prevent undesired occurrences (to control economic events).

Political business cycle — The tendency of Parliament to destabilize the economy by reducing taxes and increasing government expenditures before elections and to raise taxes and lower expenditures after the elections.

Portfolio investment — The buying of bonds and shares by nonresidents, the number of shares bought being insufficient to attain control of the firm. (*See also* Direct Investment.)

Positive economics — The analysis of facts or data for the purpose of establishing scientific generalizations about economic behaviour; compare Normative economics.

Positive relationship — The relationship between two variables that change in the same direction, for example, product price and quantity supplied.

Post hoc, ergo propter hoc **fallacy** — Incorrectly reasoning that when one event precedes another, the first event necessarily is the cause of the second.

Potential competition — The possibility that new competitors will be induced to enter an industry if Firms at present in that industry are realizing large economic profits.

Potential output — The real output (GDP) an economy is able to produce when it fully employs its available resources.

Poverty — An existence in which the basic needs of an individual or family exceed the means available to satisfy them.

Poverty rate — The percentage of the population with incomes below the official poverty income levels established by Statistics Canada.

Predatory pricing — A general, illegal policy of selling at prices unreasonably low with a view to eliminating competition; forbidden under the Competition Act (*see*).

Premature inflation — Inflation (*see*) that occurs before the economy has reached Full employment (*see*).

Price — The quantity of Money (or of other goods and services) paid and received for a unit of a good or service.

Price ceiling — A government-fixed maximum price for a good or service.

Price-decreasing effect — The effect in a competitive market of a Decrease in Demand or an Increase in Supply upon the Equilibrium price (*see*).

Price discrimination — The selling of a product to different buyers at different prices when the price differences are not justified by differences in production costs; an illegal trade practice under the Competition Act (*see*) when it consists of giving a trade purchaser an unfair advantage over its competitors by selling to it at a lower price.

Price elasticity of demand — The ratio of the percentage change in Quantity demanded of a product or resource to the percentage change in its price, the responsiveness or sensitivity of the quantity of a product or resource buyers demand to a change in the price of the product or resource.

Price elasticity of supply — The ratio of the percentage change in the Quantity supplied of a product or resource to the percentage change in its price; the responsiveness or sensitivity of the quantity sellers of a product or resource supply to a change in the price of the product or resource.

Price guidepost — The price charged by an Industry for its product should increase by no more than the increase in the Unit labour cost (*see*) of producing the product.

Price-increasing effect — The effect in a competitive market of an Increase in Demand or a Decrease in Supply upon the Equilibrium price (*see*).

Price index — An index number that shows how the average price of a "market basket" of goods changes through time. A price index is used to change nominal output (income) into real output (income).

Price leadership — An informal method that Firms in an Oligopoly (*see*) may employ to set the price of their product: one firm (the leader) is the first to announce a change in price and the other firms (the followers) quickly announce identical (or similar) changes in price.

Price level — The weighted average of the Prices paid for the final goods and services produced in the economy.

Price level surprises — Unanticipated changes in the price level.

Price-maker — A seller (or buyer) of a product or resource that is able to affect the product or resource price by changing the amount it sells (buys).

Price support — The minimum price government allows sellers to receive for a good or service; a price that is the established or maintained minimum price.

Price-taker — A seller (or buyer) of a product or resource that is unable to affect the price at which a product or resource sells by changing the amount it sells (or buys).

Price-wage flexibility — Changes in the prices of products and in the Wages paid to workers; the ability of prices and Wages to rise or to fall.

Price war — Successive and continued decreases in the prices charged by the firms in an oligopolistic industry by which each firm hopes to increase its sales and revenues and from which firms seldom benefit.

Primary reserve — (*See* Cash reserve.)

Prime rate — The interest rate the Chartered banks (*see*) charge on demand note loans to their best corporate customers.

Principal-agent problem — A conflict of interest that occurs when agents (workers) pursue their own objectives to the detriment of the principal's (employer's) goals.

Private good — A good or service subject to the Exclusion principle (see) and which is provided by privately owned firms to those who are willing to pay for it.

Private property — The right of private persons and Firms to obtain, own, control, employ, dispose of, and bequeath Land, Capital, and other Assets.

Private sector — The Households and business Firms of the economy.

Product differentiation — Physical or other differences between the products of different Firms that result in individual buyers preferring (so long as the price charged by all sellers is the same) the product of one Firm to the products of the other Firms.

Production possibilities curve (table) — A curve (table) showing the different combinations of two goods or services that can be produced in a Full-employment (see), Full-production (see) economy where the available supplies of resources and technology are constant.

Productive efficiency — The production of a good in the least-costly way: employing the minimum quantity of resources needed to produce a given output and producing the output at which Average total cost is a minimum.

Productivity — A measure of average output or real output per unit of input. For example, the productivity of labour may be determined by dividing hours of work into real output.

Productivity slowdown — The recent decline in the rate at which Labour productivity (see) in Canada has increased.

Product market — A market in which Households buy and Firms sell the products they have produced.

Profit — (See) Economic profit and Normal profit; without an adjective preceding it, the income of those who supply the economy with Entrepreneurial ability (see) or Normal profit.

Profit-maximizing case — The circumstances that result in an Economic profit (see) for a (competitive) Firm when it produces the output at which Economic profit is a maximum: when the price at which the Firm can sell its product is greater than the Average total cost of producing it.

Profit-maximizing rule (combination of resources) — The quantity of each resource a Firm must employ if its Economic profit (see) is to be a maximum or its losses a minimum; the combination in which the Marginal rev-enue product (see) of each resource is equal to its Marginal resource cost (see) (to its price if the resource is employed in a competitive market).

Progressive tax — A tax such that the tax rate increases as the taxpayer's income increases and decreases as income decreases.

Property tax — A tax on the value of property (Capital, Land, stocks and bonds, and other Assets) owned by Firms and Households.

Proportional tax — A tax such that the tax rate remains constant as the taxpayer's income increases and decreases.

Proprietors' income — The net income of the owners of unincorporated Firms (proprietorships and partnerships); the sum of the accrued net income of farm operators from farm production plus the net income of nonfarm unincorporated business, including rent.

Prosperous industry — (See Expanding industry.)

Protective tariff — A Tariff (see) designed to protect domestic producers of a good from the competition of foreign producers.

Public assistance programs — Programs that pay benefits to those who are unable to earn income (because of permanent handicaps or because they are dependent children), that are financed by general tax revenues, and that are viewed as public charity (rather than earned rights).

Public choice theory — Generalizations that describe how government (the Public sector) makes decisions for the use of economic resources.

Public debt — The amount owed by the Government of Canada to the owners of its securities and equal to the sum of its past Budget deficits (less its Budget surpluses).

Public finance — The branch of economics that analyzes government revenues and expenditures.

Public good — A good or service to which the Exclusion principle (see) is not applicable; and that is provided by government if it yields substantial benefits to society.

Public interest theory of regulation — The presumption that the purpose of the regulation of an Industry is to protect the public (consumers) from the abuse of the power possessed by Natural monopolies (see).

Public sector — The part of the economy that contains all its governments; government.

Public-sector failure — The failure of the Public sector (government) to resolve socioeconomic problems because it performs its functions inefficiently.

Public utility — A Firm that produces an essential good or service, that has obtained from a government the right to be the sole supplier of the good or service in an area, and that is regulated by that government to prevent the abuse of its monopoly power.

Purchasing power parity — The idea that exchange rates between nations equate the purchasing power of various currencies; exchange rates between any two nations adjust to reflect the price level differences between the countries.

Pure capitalism — An economic system in which property resources are privately owned and Markets and Prices are used to direct and co-ordinate economic activities.

Pure competition — (1) A market in which a very large number of Firms sells a Standardized product (see), into which entry is very easy, in which the individual seller has no control over the price at which the product sells, and in which there is no Nonprice competition (see); (2) a Market in which there is a very large number of buyers.

Pure monopoly — A Market in which one Firm sells a unique product (one for which there are no close substitutes), into which entry is blocked, in which the Firm has considerable control over the price at which the product sells, and in which Nonprice competition (see) may or may not be found.

Pure profit — (See Economic profit.)

Pure rate of interest — (See The Rate of interest.)

Quantity-decreasing effect — The effect in a competitive market of a decrease in Demand or a decrease in Supply on the Equilibrium quantity (see).

Quantity demanded — The amount of a good or service buyers wish (or a buyer wishes) to purchase at a particular price during some period of time.

Quantity-increasing effect — The effect in a competitive market of an increase in Demand or an increase in Supply on the Equilibrium quantity (see).

Quantity supplied — The amount of a good or service sellers offer (or a seller offers) to sell at a particular price during some period of time.

Quasi-public good — A good or service to which the Exclusion principle (see) could be applied, but which has such a large Spillover benefit (see) that government sponsors its production to prevent an underallocation of resources.

R&D — Research and development; activities undertaken to bring about progress in Technology.

Rate of exchange — The price paid in one's own Money to acquire one unit of a foreign Money; the rate at which the money of one nation is exchanged for the Money of another nation.

Rate of interest — Price paid for the use of Money or for the use of Capital; interest rate.

Rational — An adjective that describes the behaviour of an individual who consistently does those things enabling the achievement of the declared objective of the individual; describes the behaviour of a consumer who uses money income to buy the collection of goods and services that yields the maximum amount of Utility (see).

Rational expectations theory — The hypothesis that business Firms and Households expect monetary and fiscal policies to have certain effects on the economy and, in pursuit of their own self-interests, take actions that make these policies ineffective.

Rationing function of price — The ability of Price in a competitive market to equalize Quantity demanded and Quantity supplied and to eliminate shortages and surpluses by rising or falling.

Reaganomics — The policies of the United States Reagan Administration based on Supply-side economics (see) and intended to reduce Inflation and the Unemployment rate (Stagflation).

Real-balances effect — (See Wealth effect.)

Real capital — (See Capital.)

Real gross domestic product — Gross domestic product (see) adjusted for changes in the price level; Gross domestic product in a year divided by the GDP deflator (see) for that year.

Real income — The amount of goods and services an individual or group can purchase with his, her, or its Nominal income during some period of time; Nominal income adjusted for changes in the Price level.

Real interest rate — The Rate of interest expressed in dollars of constant value (adjusted for Inflation); and equal to the Nominal interest rate (see) less the expected rate of Inflation.

Real rate of interest — The Real interest rate (*see*).

Real wage — The amount of goods and services a worker can purchase with his or her Money wage (*see*); the purchasing power of the Money wage; the Money wage adjusted for changes in the Price level.

Real wage rate — (*See* Real wage.)

Recessionary gap — The amount by which equilibrium GDP falls short of full employment GDP.

Reciprocal selling — The practice in which one Firm agrees to buy a product from a second Firm, and the second Firm agrees, in return, to buy another product from the first Firm.

Reciprocal Trade Agreements Act of 1934 (U.S.) — The federal Act that gave the U.S. president the authority to negotiate agreements with other nations and lower American tariff rates by up to 50% if the other nations would reduce tariff rates on American goods, and which incorporated Most-favoured-nation clauses (*see*) in the agreements reached with these nations.

Refinancing the public debt — Paying owners of maturing Government of Canada securities with Money obtained by selling new securities or with new securities.

Regional Development Incentives Act — The federal Act of 1970 designed to create jobs in Canada's slow-growth or "designated" areas.

Regressive tax — A tax such that the tax rate decreases (increases) as the taxpayer's income increases (decreases).

Regulatory agency — An agency (commission or board) established by the federal or a provincial government to control the prices charged and the services offered (output produced) by a Natural monopoly (*see*).

Remittance — A gift or grant; a payment for which no good or service is received in return; the funds sent by workers who have legally or illegally entered a foreign nation to their families in the nations from which they have migrated.

Rental income — Income received by those who supply the economy with Land (*see*).

Rent-seeking behaviour — The pursuit through government of a transfer of income or wealth to a resource supplier, business, or consumer at someone else's or society's expense.

Required reserve — The weighted average of demand deposit and notice deposit Chartered banks were required

to keep as Vault cash (*see*) or on deposit with the Bank of Canada up to the end of 1994, when these were eliminated.

Reserve ratio — The ratio of a Chartered bank's desired reserves to its deposit liabilities.

Reserves — Cash in a Chartered bank's vault plus its deposit with the Bank of Canada.

Resource market — A market in which Households sell and Firms buy the services of resources.

Retiring the public debt — Reducing the size of the Public debt (*see*) by paying money to owners of maturing Government of Canada securities.

Revaluation — An increase in the government-defined currency brought about by the Central bank; the opposite of Devaluation.

Revenue sharing — The distribution by the federal government of some of its tax revenues to provincial governments.

Revenue tariff — A Tariff (*see*) designed to produce income for the (federal) government.

Ricardian equivalence theorem — The idea that an increase in the public debt will have little or no effect on real output and employment because taxpayers will save more in anticipation of future higher taxes to pay the higher interest expense on the debt.

Roundabout production — The construction and use of Capital (*see*) to aid in the production of Consumer goods (*see*).

Ruble overhang — The large amount of forced saving formerly held by Russian Households due to the scarcity of Consumer goods; these savings fuelled Inflation when Russian prices were decontrolled.

Rule of 70 — A method for determining the number of years it will take for the Price level to double; divide 70 by the annual rate of inflation (the rate of increase).

Sales tax — A tax levied on expenditures for a broad group of products.

Saving — Disposable income not spent for Consumer goods (*see*); equal to Disposable income minus Personal consumption expenditures (*see*).

Savings account — A deposit in a financial institution that is interest-earning and that can normally be withdrawn by the depositor at any time (though the institution may legally require notice for withdrawal).

Saving schedule — Schedule that shows the amounts Households plan to save (plan not to spend for Consumer goods, *see*) at different levels of Disposable income.

Say's Law — The (discredited) macroeconomic generalization that the production of goods and services (supply) creates an equal demand for these goods and services.

Scarce resources — The fixed (limited) quantities of Land, Capital, Labour, and Entrepreneurial ability (*see all*) that are never sufficient to satisfy the wants of human beings because their wants are unlimited.

Schumpeter-Galbraith view (of oligopoly) — The belief shared by these two economists that large oligopolistic firms are necessary for rapid technological progress (because only this kind of firm has both the means and the incentive to introduce technological changes).

SDRs — (*See* Special Drawing Rights.)

Seasonal variation — An increase or decrease during a single year in the level of economic activity caused by a change in the season.

Secular trend — The expansion or contraction in the level of economic activity over a long period of years.

Self-interest — What each Firm, property owner, worker, and consumer believes is best for itself and seeks to obtain.

Seniority — The length of time a worker has been employed by an employer relative to the lengths of time the employer's other workers have been employed; the principle that is used to determine which workers will be laid off when there is insufficient work for them all, and which will be rehired when more work becomes available.

Separation of ownership and control — Difference between the group that owns the Corporation (the stockholders) and the group that manages it (the directors and officers) and between the interests (goals) of the two groups.

Service — That which is intangible (invisible) and for which a consumer, Firm, or government is willing to exchange something of value.

Shared-cost programs — (*See* Conditional grant.)

Shirking — Attempts by workers to increase their utility or well-being by neglecting or evading work.

Shortage — The amount by which the Quantity demanded of a product exceeds the Quantity supplied at a particular (below-equilibrium) price.

Short run — A period of time in which producers of a product are able to change the quantity of some but not all of the resources they employ; in which some resources — the Plant (*see*) — are Fixed resources (*see*) and some are Variable resources (*see*); in which some costs are Fixed costs (*see*) and some are Variable costs (*see*); a period of time too brief to allow a Firm (*see*) to vary its plant capacity but long enough to permit it to change the level at which the plant capacity is utilized; a period of time not long enough to enable Firms to enter or to leave an Industry (*see*).

Short-run aggregate supply curve — The aggregate supply curve relevant to a time period in which input prices (particularly nominal wages) remain constant when the price level changes.

Short-run competitive equilibrium — The price at which the total quantity of a product supplied in the Short run (*see*) by a purely competitive industry and the total quantity of the product demanded are equal and which is equal to or greater than the Average variable cost (*see*) of producing the product; and the quantity of the product demanded and supplied at this price.

Short-run farm problem — The sharp year-to-year changes in the prices of agricultural products and in the incomes of farmers.

Short-run supply curve — A curve that shows the quantities of a product a Firm in a purely competitive industry (*see* Pure competition) will offer to sell at various prices in the Short run (*see*); the portion of the Firm's short-run Marginal cost (*see*) curve that lies above the Average variable cost curve.

Simple multiplier — The Multiplier (*see*) in an economy in which government collects no Net taxes (*see*), there are no Imports (*see*), and Investment (*see*) is independent of the level of income (Gross domestic product); equal to one divided by the Marginal propensity to save (*see*).

Single-tax movement — The attempt of a group that followed the teachings of Henry George to eliminate all taxes except one that would tax all Rental income (*see*) at a rate of 100%.

Slope of a line — The ratio of the vertical change (the rise or fall) to the horizontal change (the run) in moving between two points on a line. The slope of an upward sloping line is positive, reflecting a direct relationship between two variables; the slope of a downward sloping line is negative, reflecting an inverse relationship between two variables.

Smoot-Hawley Tariff Act — Passed in 1930, this legislation established some of the highest Tariffs in U.S. history. Its objective was to reduce imports and stimulate the American economy.

Social accounting — (*See* National income accounting.)

Social good — (*See* Public good.)

Social insurance programs — The programs that replace the earnings lost when people retire or are temporarily unemployed, that are financed by pay deductions, and that are viewed as earned rights (rather than charity).

Social regulation — The newer and different type of regulation in which government is concerned with the conditions under which goods and services are produced, their physical characteristics, and the impact of their production on society; in contrast to Industrial regulation (*see*).

Sole proprietorship — An unincorporated business Firm owned and operated by a single person.

Special Drawing Rights — Credit created by the International Monetary Fund (*see*), which a member of the IMF may borrow to finance a Payments deficit (*see*) or to increase its Official international reserves (*see*); "paper gold."

Special-interest effect — Effect on public decision making and the allocation of resources in the economy when government promotes the interests (goals) of small groups to the detriment of society as a whole.

Specialization — The use of the resources of an individual, a Firm, a region, or a nation to produce one or a few goods and services.

Speculation — The activity of buying or selling with the motive of then reselling or rebuying to make a profit.

Spillover — A benefit or cost from production or consumption, accruing without compensation to nonbuyers and nonsellers of the product (*see* Spillover benefit and Spillover cost).

Spillover benefit — A benefit obtained without compensation by third parties from the production or consumption of other parties. Example: A beekeeper benefits when the neighbouring farmer plants clover.

Spillover cost — A cost imposed without compensation on third parties by the production or consumption of other parties. Example: A manufacturer dumps toxic chemicals into a river, killing the fish sought by sport fishers.

Stabilization funds — International monetary reserves (*see*) and domestic monies used to augment the supply of,

or demand for, any Currency required to avoid or restrict fluctuations in the Rate of exchange; in Canada held in the Exchange Fund Account by the Bank of Canada on behalf of the government.

Stabilization policy dilemma — The use of monetary and fiscal policy to decrease the Unemployment rate increases the rate of Inflation, and the use of monetary and fiscal policy to decrease the rate of Inflation increases the Unemployment rate; *see* the Phillips curve.

Stagflation — Inflation accompanied by stagnation in the rate of growth of output and a high unemployment rate in the economy; simultaneous increases in both the price level and the Unemployment rate (*see*).

Standardized product — A product such that buyers are indifferent to the seller from whom they purchase it so long as the price charged by all sellers is the same; a product such that all units of the product are perfect substitutes for each other (are identical).

Staple — An exported raw material.

State ownership — The ownership of property (Land and Capital) by government (the state); in the former Soviet Union by the central government (the nation).

Static economy — (1) An economy in which Net investment (*see*) is zero — Gross investment (*see*) is equal to the Capital consumption allowances (*see*); (2) an economy in which the supplies of resources, technology, and the tastes of consumers do not change and in which, therefore, the economic future is perfectly predictable and there is no uncertainty.

Store of value — Any Asset (*see*) or wealth set aside for future use; functions of Money.

Strategic trade policy — The use of trade barriers to reduce the risk of product development by domestic firms, particularly products involving advanced technology.

Strike — The withholding of their labour services by an organized group of workers (a Labour union).

Structural deficit — The difference between federal tax revenues and expenditures when the economy is at Full employment.

Structural unemployment — Unemployment caused by changes in the structure of demand for Consumer goods and in technology; workers who are unemployed because their skills are not demanded by employers, they lack sufficient skills to obtain employment, or they cannot easily move to locations where jobs for which they have skills are available.

Subsidy — A payment of funds (or goods and services) by a government, business Firm, or Household for which it receives no good or service in return. When made by a government, it is a Government transfer payment (*see*) or the reverse of a tax.

Substitutability — The ability of consumers to use one good or service instead of another to satisfy their wants and of Firms to use one resource instead of another to produce products.

Substitute goods — Goods or services for which there is a direct relationship between the price of one and the Demand for the other; when the price of one falls (rises) the Demand for the other decreases (increases).

Substitution effect — (1) The effect a change in the price of a Consumer good would have on the relative expensiveness of that good and the resulting effect on the quantity of the good a consumer would purchase if the consumer's Real income (*see*) remained constant; (2) the effect a change in the price of a resource would have on the quantity of the resource employed by a firm if the firm did not change its output.

Superior good — (*See* Normal good.)

Supplementary labour income — The payments by employers into unemployment insurance, worker's compensation, and a variety of private and public pension and welfare funds for workers: "fringe benefits."

Supply — A Supply schedule or a Supply curve (*see both*).

Supply curve — A curve showing the amounts of a good or service sellers (a seller) will offer to sell at various prices during some period.

Supply factor — An increase in the available quantity of a resource, an improvement in its quality, or an expansion of technological knowledge, which makes it possible for an economy to produce a greater output of goods and services.

Supply schedule — A schedule showing the amounts of a good or service sellers (a seller) will offer to sell at various prices during some period.

Supply shock — One of several events of the 1970s and early 1980s that increased production costs, decreased Aggregate supply, and helped generate Stagflation in Canada.

Supply-side economics — The part of modern Macroeconomics that emphasizes the role of costs and Aggregate supply in explaining Inflation, unemployed labour, and Economic growth.

Supply-side view — The view of fiscal policy held by the advocates of Supply-side economics that emphasizes increasing Aggregate supply (*see*) as a means of reducing the Unemployment rate and Inflation and encouraging Economic growth.

Support price — (*See* Price support.)

Surplus — The amount by which the Quantity supplied of product exceeds the Quantity demanded at a specific (above-equilibrium) price.

Surplus value — A Marxian term; the amount by which the value of a worker's daily output exceeds his or her daily wage; the output of workers appropriated by capitalists as profit.

Switching Government of Canada deposits — Action of Bank of Canada to increase (decrease) backing for Money supply (*see*) by switching government deposits from (to) itself to (from) the Chartered banks (*see*).

Tacit collusion — Any method utilized in a Collusive oligopoly (*see*) to set prices and outputs that does not involve outright (or overt) collusion (formal agreements or secret meetings); and of which Price leadership (*see*) is a frequent example.

Tangent — The point where a line touches, but does not intersect, a curve.

Target dilemma — A problem arising because the central bank cannot simultaneously stabilize both the money supply and the level of interest rates.

Tariff — A tax imposed by a nation on an imported good.

Tax — A nonvoluntary payment of money (or goods and services) to a government by a Household or Firm for which the Household or Firm receives no good or service directly in return.

Tax-based incomes policies (TIP) — An Incomes policy (*see*) that would include special tax penalties for those who do not comply and tax rebates for those who do comply with the Wage-price guideposts (*see*).

Tax incidence — The income or purchasing power different persons and groups lose as a result of the imposition of a tax after Tax shifting (*see*) has occurred.

Tax shifting — The transfer to others of all or part of a tax by charging them a higher price or by paying them a lower price for a good or service.

Tax subsidy — The subsidization of individuals or industries through favourable tax treatment.

Tax-transfer disincentives — Decreases in the incentives to work, save, invest, innovate, and take risks that allegedly result from high Marginal tax rates and Transfer payment programs.

Tax "wedge" — Such taxes as Indirect taxes (*see*) and pay deductions for Social insurance programs (*see*), which are treated as a cost by business firms and reflected in the prices of their products; equal to the price of the product less the cost of the resources required to produce it.

Technology — The body of knowledge that can be used to produce goods and services from Economic resources.

Term deposit — A deposit in a Chartered bank or other Financial intermediary against which cheques may not be written; a form of savings account; part of M2, M3, and M2+ (*see all*).

Terms of trade — The rate at which units of one product can be exchanged for units of another product; the Price (*see*) of a good or service; the amount of one good or service given up to obtain one unit of another good or service.

Theory of human capital — Generalization that Wage differentials (*see*) are the result of differences in the amount of Human capital investment (*see*); and that the incomes of lower-paid workers are increased by increasing the amount of such investment.

***The* rate of interest** — The Rate of interest (*see*) that is paid solely for the use of Money over an extended period of time and that excludes the charges made for the riskiness of the loan and its administrative costs; and that is approximately equal to the rate of interest paid on the long-term and virtually riskless bonds of the Government of Canada.

Third World — The semideveloped and less-developed nations; nations other than the industrially advanced market economies and the centrally planned economies.

Tied selling — (*See* Exclusive dealing.)

Tight money policy — Contracting the nation's Money supply (*see*). See also Contractionary monetary policy.

Till money — (*See* Vault cash.)

TIP — (*See* Tax-based incomes policies.)

Token money — Coins having a Face value (*see*) greater than their Intrinsic value (*see*).

Total cost — The sum of Fixed cost (*see*) and Variable cost (*see*).

Total demand — The Demand schedule (*see*) or the Demand curve (*see*) of all buyers of a good or service.

Total demand for money — The sum of the Transactions demand for money (*see*) and Asset demand for money (*see*); the relationship between the total amount of money demanded and nominal GDP and the Rate of interest.

Total product — The total output of a particular good or service produced by a Firm, a group of Firms or the entire economy.

Total revenue — The total number of dollars received by a Firm (or Firms) from the sale of a product; equal to the total expenditures for the product produced by the Firm (or Firms); equal to the quantity sold (demanded) multiplied by the price at which it is sold — by the Average revenue (*see*) from its sale.

Total-revenue test — A test to determine whether Demand is Elastic (*see*), Inelastic (*see*), or of Unitary elasticity (*see*) between any two prices: demand is elastic (inelastic, unit elastic) if the Total revenue (*see*) of sellers of the commodity increases (decreases, remains constant) when the price of the commodity falls; or Total revenue decreases (increases, remains constant) when its price rises.

Total-revenue–total-cost approach — The method that finds the output at which Economic profit (*see*) is a maximum or losses a minimum by comparing the total receipts (revenue) and the total costs of a Firm at different outputs.

Total spending — The total amount buyers of goods and services spend or plan to spend. Also called Aggregate expenditure.

Total supply — The Supply schedule (*see*) or the Supply curve (*see*) of all sellers of a good or service.

Total utility — The total amount of satisfaction derived from the consumption of some particular amount of a product.

Trade balance — The export of merchandise (goods) of a nation less its imports of merchandise (goods).

Trade bloc — A group of nations that lowers or abolishes trade barriers among members. Examples include the European Union (*see*) and the North American Free Trade Agreement (*see*).

Trade controls — Tariffs (*see*), export subsidies, Import quotas (*see*), and other means a nation may employ to reduce Imports (*see*) and expand Exports (*see*).

Trade deficit — The amount a nation's imports of merchandise (goods) exceed its exports of merchandise (goods).

Trade-offs — The notion that one economic goal or objective must be sacrificed to achieve some other goal.

Trade surplus — The amount a nation's exports of merchandise (goods) and services exceed its imports of merchandise (goods) and services.

Trades and Labour Congress of Canada (TLC) — The federation of Craft unions (*see*) formed in 1886 and affiliated with the American Federation of Labor (*see*); amalgamated into the Canadian Labour Congress (*see*) in 1956.

Trading possibilities line — A line that shows the different combinations of two products an economy is able to obtain (consume) when it specializes in the production of one product and trades (exports) this product to obtain the other product.

Traditional economy — An economic system in which traditions and customs determine how the economy will use its scarce resources.

Traditional view of advertising — The position that advertising is persuasive rather than informative; promotes industrial concentration; and is essentially inefficient and wasteful.

Transactions demand for money — The amount of Money people want to hold to use as a Medium of exchange (to make payments); and which varies directly with the nominal GDP.

Transfer payment — A payment of Money (or goods and services) by a government or a Firm to a Household or Firm for which the payer receives no good or service directly in return.

Tying agreement — A promise made by a buyer when allowed to purchase a patented product from a seller that it will make all its purchases of certain other (unpatented) products from the same seller.

Unanticipated inflation — Inflation (*see*) at a rate greater than the rate expected in that period of time.

Unconditional grant — A transfer to a province by the federal government that goes into the general revenues of the province to be used as it sees fit; such grants are made for two reasons: (1) as an Equalization payment (*see*) and (2) to make up for the general inadequacy of provincial revenues in relation to provincial responsibilities.

Underemployment — Failure to produce the maximum amount of goods and services that can be produced from the resources employed; failure to achieve Full production (*see*).

Undistributed corporation profits — After-tax corporate profits not distributed as dividends to stockholders; corporate or business saving.

Unemployment — Failure to use all available Economic resources to produce goods and services; failure of the economy to employ fully its Civilian labour force (*see*).

Unemployment insurance — The insurance program that in Canada is financed by compulsory contributions from employers and employees and from the general tax revenues of the federal government with benefits (income) made available to insured workers who are unable to find jobs.

Unemployment rate — The percentage of the Civilian labour force (*see*) unemployed at any time.

Uninsurable risk — An event — the occurrence of which is uncontrollable and unpredictable — that would result in a loss that cannot be avoided by purchasing insurance and must be assumed by an entrepreneur (*see* Entrepreneurial ability); sometimes called "uncertainty."

Union shop — A place of employment where the employer may hire either Labour union members or nonmembers, but where nonmembers must become members within a specified period of time or lose their jobs.

Unitary elasticity — The Elasticity coefficient (*see*) is equal to one; the percentage change in the quantity (demanded or supplied) is equal to the percentage change in price.

Unit labour cost — Labour costs per unit of output; equal to the Money wage rate (*see*) divided by the Average product (*see*) of labour.

Unlimited liability — Absence of any limit on the maximum amount that may be lost by an individual and that the individual may become legally required to pay; the maximum amount that may be lost and that a sole proprietor or partner may be required to pay.

Unlimited wants — The insatiable desire of consumers (people) for goods and services that will give them pleasure or satisfaction.

Unplanned investment — Actual investment less Planned investment; increases or decreases in the inventories of business firms resulting from production greater than or less than sales.

Unprosperous industry — (See Declining industry.)

Uruguay Round — The eighth round of trade negotiations under GATT (see).

Utility — The want-satisfying power of a good or service; the satisfaction or pleasure a consumer obtains from the consumption of a good or service (or from the consumption of a collection of goods and services).

Utility-maximizing rule — To obtain the greatest Utility (see) the consumer should allocate Money income so that the last dollar spent on each good or service yields the same Marginal utility (see); so that the Marginal utility of each good or service divided by its price is the same for all goods and services.

Value added — The value of the product sold by a Firm less the value of the goods (materials) purchased and used by the Firm to produce the product; and equal to the revenue that can be used for Wages, rent, interest, and profits.

Value-added tax — A tax imposed upon the difference between the value of the goods sold by a firm and the value of the goods purchased by the firm from other firms.

Value judgement — Opinion of what is desirable or undesirable; belief regarding what ought or ought not to be (regarding what is right or just and wrong or unjust).

Value of money — The quantity of goods and services for which a unit of money (a dollar) can be exchanged; the purchasing power of a unit of money; the reciprocal of the Price level.

Variable cost — A cost that, in total, increases (decreases) when the firm increases (decreases) its output; the cost of Variable resources (see).

Variable resource — Any resource employed by a firm the quantity of which can be increased or decreased (varied) in quantity.

VAT — Value-added tax (see).

Vault cash — The Currency (see) a bank has in its safe (vault) and cash drawers; till money.

Velocity of money — The number of times per year the average dollar in the Money supply (see) is spent for Final goods and services (see).

VERs — (See Voluntary export restrictions.)

Vertical axis — The "up-down" or "north-south" axis on a graph or grid.

Vertical combination — A group of Plants (see) engaged in different stages of the production of a final product and owned by a single Firm (see).

Vertical intercept — The point at which a line meets the vertical axis of a graph.

Vertical merger — The merger of one or more Firms engaged in different stages of the production of a final product.

Vertical range — Vertical segment of the short-run Aggregate supply curve along which the economy is operating at full capacity.

Voluntary export restrictions — The limitation by firms of their exports to particular foreign nations in order to avoid the erection of other trade barriers by the foreign nations.

Wage — The price paid for Labour [for the use or services of Labour (see)] per unit of time (per hour, per day, and so on).

Wage differential — The difference between the Wage (see) received by one worker or group of workers and that received by another worker or group of workers.

Wage discrimination — The payment to women (or minority groups) of a wage lower than that paid to men (or established groups) for doing the same work.

Wage guidepost — Wages (see) in all industries in the economy should increase at an annual rate equal to the rate of increase in the Average product (see) of Labour in the economy.

Wage-price controls — A Wage-price policy (see) that legally fixes the maximum amounts Wages (see) and prices may be increased in any period of time.

Wage-price guideposts — A Wage-price policy (see) that depends upon the voluntary co-operation of Labour unions and business firms.

Wage-price inflationary spiral — Increases in wage rates that bring about increases in prices and in turn result in further increases in wage rates and in prices.

Wage-price policy — Government policy that attempts to alter the behaviour of Labour unions and business firms to make their Wage and price decisions more nearly compatible with the goals of Full employment and stable prices.

Wage rate — (See Wages.)

Wages — The income of those who supply the economy with Labour (see).

Wastes of monopolistic competition — The waste of economic resources that is the result of producing an output at which price is greater than marginal cost and average cost is greater than the minimum average cost.

Wealth effect — The tendency for increases (decreases) in the price level to lower (raise) the real value (or purchasing power) of financial assets with fixed money values; and, as a result, to reduce (expand) total spending in the economy.

Welfare programs — (*See* Public assistance programs.)

(The) "will to develop" — Wanting economic growth strongly enough to change from old to new ways of doing things.

World Bank — A bank supported by 151 nations, which lends (and guarantees loans) to less-developed nations to assist them to grow; formally, the International Bank for Reconstruction and Development.

World Price — The international price of a good or service, determined by world demand and supply.

World Trade Organization (WTO) — An organization established in 1994 by GATT (*see*) to oversee the provisions of the Uruguay Round (*see*) and resolve any disputes stemming therefrom.

X-inefficiency — Failure to produce any given output at the lowest average (and total) cost possible.

National Income Statistics, 1926-1994

NATIONAL INCOME AND RELATED STATISTICS FOR SELECTED YEARS, 1926–1967

National income statistics are in billions of current dollars

			1926	1929	1933	1939	1940	1942	1945	1946	1949	1950	1951
THE	1	Personal consumption expenditure	$3.508	$4.583	$2.974	$3.972	$4.464	$5.466	$6.972	$8.012	$11.463	$12.576	$13.973
SUM	2	Government current purchases of goods and services	0.390	0.469	0.392	0.566	1.048	3.622	3.576	1.655	1.722	1.928	2.811
OF	3	Gross investment	0.949	1.413	0.208	0.969	1.097	1.200	0.890	1.877	3.676	4.596	5.515
	4	Net exports of goods and services	0.368	–0.016	0.234	0.391	0.460	0.273	0.855	0.702	0.506	0.091	–0.137
	5	Statistical discrepancy	0.139	–0.049	–0.085	–0.018	–0.082	–0.064	–0.230	–0.079	–0.020	–0.066	0.118
EQUALS	6	**GDP at market prices**	**5.354**	**6.400**	**3.723**	**5.880**	**6.987**	**10.497**	**12.063**	**12.167**	**$17.347**	**$19.125**	**$22.280**
	7	Net investment income from nonresidents	–0.208	–0.261	–0.231	–0.259	–0.274	–0.232	–0.200	–0.282	–0.355	–0.425	–0.391
EQUALS	8	**GNP at market prices**	**5.146**	**6.139**	**3.492**	**5.621**	**6.713**	**10.265**	**11.863**	**11.885**	**$16.992**	**$18.700**	**$21.889**
LESS	9	Indirect taxes less subsidies	0.627	0.711	0.547	0.759	0.859	1.133	1.084	1.371	1.878	2.065	2.548
	10	Capital consumption allowances	0.572	0.726	0.532	0.671	0.786	1.091	1.042	1.071	1.657	1.889	2.108
	11	Statistical discrepancy	–0.139	0.050	0.085	0.019	0.083	0.064	0.231	0.080	0.020	0.067	–0.119
EQUALS	12	**Net national income at factor cost**	**4.086**	**4.652**	**2.328**	**4.172**	**4.985**	**7.997**	**9.506**	**9.363**	**$13.437**	**$14.679**	**$17.352**
PLUS	13	Government transfer payments	0.074	0.092	0.180	0.226	0.204	0.218	0.542	1.102	0.944	1.025	1.026
	14	Transfers from nonresidents	0.017	0.015	0.013	0.014	0.013	0.014	0.036	0.026	0.017	0.015	0.018
	15	Interest on the public debt	0.231	0.235	0.283	0.275	0.273	0.310	0.512	0.554	0.572	0.544	0.609
	16	Interest on consumer debt (transfer portion)	0.005	0.006	0.004	0.007	0.008	0.007	0.005	0.007	0.021	0.029	0.038
LESS	17	Corporation income taxes	0.034	0.048	0.037	0.115	0.327	0.629	0.599	0.654	0.723	0.993	1.431
	18	Undistributed corporation profits	0.189	0.225	–0.045	0.271	0.168	0.360	0.367	0.480	0.738	0.869	1.031
	19	Government investment income	0.075	0.076	0.027	0.064	0.104	0.184	0.310	0.263	0.242	0.280	0.285
	20	Other earnings not paid out to persons	0.058	–0.014	–0.051	–0.106	–0.088	–0.169	0.033	–0.232	–0.222	–0.238	–0.648
EQUALS	21	**Personal income**	**4.057**	**4.665**	**2.840**	**4.350**	**4.972**	**7.522**	**9.292**	**9.887**	**$13.510**	**$14.388**	**$16.944**
LESS	22	Personal taxes	0.069	0.093	0.088	0.143	0.174	0.604	0.938	0.937	1.013	0.977	1.356
EQUALS	23	**Personal disposable income**	**3.988**	**4.572**	**2.752**	**4.207**	**4.798**	**6.918**	**8.354**	**8.950**	**$12.497**	**$13.411**	**$15.588**
LESS	24	Personal consumption expenditure	3.508	4.583	2.974	3.972	4.464	5.466	6.972	8.012	11.463	12.576	13.973
	25	Interest paid by consumers to corporations	0.005	0.006	0.004	0.007	0.008	0.007	0.005	0.007	0.021	0.029	0.038
	26	Current transfers to nonresidents	0.042	0.044	0.016	0.026	0.026	0.024	0.026	0.038	0.032	0.036	0.044
EQUALS	27	**Personal saving**	**0.433**	**–0.061**	**–0.242**	**0.202**	**0.300**	**1.421**	**1.351**	**0.893**	**$0.981**	**$0.770**	**$1.533**

RELATED STATISTICS			1926	1929	1933	1939	1940	1942	1945	1946	1949	1950	1951
	28	Real GDP (in 1986 dollars)	43.986	52.997	38.331	56.265	63.722	84.925	89.170	87.177	97.234	104.821	109.492
	29	Growth rate of real GDP (annual %)		0.9	–7.2	7.5	13.3	17.6	–2.4	–2.2	4.5	7.8	4.5
	30	Consumer price index (1986 = 100)	14.0	13.9	10.7	11.6	12.1	13.4	13.9	14.4	18.5	14.0	21.1
	31	CPI change (annual %)	1.6	–0.2	–7.1	0	3.9	5.5	0.5	3.3	3.4	2.7	11.1
	32	Money supply, M3 less foreign currency (in billions of dollars in December)	2.01	2.27	1.99	2.90	2.99	3.76	5.88	6.74	8.05	8.51	8.68
	33	Growth rate of money supply (M3) (annual %)	3.9	–2.1	–1.3	13.3	3.3	13.1	13.3	14.7	4.8	5.7	2.1
	34	3-month Treasury Bill yield-year's low	–	–	2.00	0.56	0.64	0.52	0.36	0.36	0.41	0.51	0.63
	35	3-month Treasury Bill yield-year's high	–	–	2.99	0.88	0.78	0.55	0.37	0.40	0.51	0.63	0.90
	36	Unemployment (in thousands)	108	116	826	529	423	135	73	163	153	186	1.26
	37	Unemployment as % of civilian labour force	3.0	2.9	19.3	11.4	9.2	3.0	1.6	3.4	3.0	3.6	2.4

NATIONAL INCOME AND RELATED STATISTICS FOR SELECTED YEARS, 1926–1967   (cont'd)

National income statistics are in billions of current dollars

1952	1953	1954	1955	1956	1957	1958	1959	1960	1961	1962	1963	1964	1965	1966	1967	
$15.282	$16.296	$17.078	$18.543	$20.273	$21.699	$23.064	$24.643	$25.780	$26.240	$27.985	$29.846	$32.042	$34.714	$37.952	$41.068	1
3.620	3.824	3.825	4.036	4.426	4.573	4.854	4.976	5.281	6.166	6.567	6.923	7.526	8.269	9.643	11.092	2
5.823	6.583	5.773	7.047	9.379	9.228	8.584	9.421	9.253	8.870	9.928	10.673	12.260	14.960	17.200	16.453	3
0.511	-0.137	-0.079	-0.268	-0.866	-0.838	-0.486	-0.765	-0.494	-0.154	-0.038	0.350	0.502	-0.113	-0.020	0.700	4
-0.066	-0.171	-0.066	-0.108	-0.310	-0.195	-0.327	-0.398	-0.372	-0.236	-0.034	-0.114	-0.139	-0.307	-0.387	-0.249	5
$25.170	$26.395	$26.531	$29.250	$32.902	$34.467	$35.689	$37.877	$39.448	40.886	44.408	47.678	52.191	57.523	64.388	69.064	6
-0.324	-0.301	-0.339	-0.385	-0.461	-0.563	-0.525	-0.609	-0.616	-0.722	-0.771	-0.848	-0.908	-0.992	-1.120	-1.240	7
$24.846	$26.094	$26.192	$28.865	$32.441	$33.904	$35.164	$37.268	$38.832	40.164	43.637	46.830	51.283	56.531	63.268	67.824	8
2.799	2.994	3.042	3.321	3.731	3.975	4.036	4.401	4.587	4.767	5.369	5.628	6.357	7.181	7.918	8.729	9
2.347	2.648	2.947	3.366	3.838	4.184	4.155	4.478	4.769	4.919	5.297	5.658	6.148	6.684	7.369	7.881	10
0.066	0.171	0.066	0.109	0.310	0.195	0.327	0.399	0.373	0.237	0.035	0.115	0.139	0.307	0.388	0.250	11
$19.634	$20.281	$20.137	$22.069	$24.562	$25.550	$26.646	$27.990	$29.103	30.241	32.936	35.429	38.639	42.359	47.593	50.964	12
1.347	1.452	1.628	1.723	1.760	2.072	2.619	2.732	3.099	2.732	2.934	3.007	3.220	3.452	3.781	4.683	13
0.032	0.034	0.034	0.036	0.039	0.039	0.045	0.050	0.052	0.076	0.075	0.082	0.089	0.098	0.098	0.109	14
0.651	0.620	0.650	0.664	0.718	0.774	0.826	1.023	1.093	1.184	1.316	1.431	1.546	1.676	1.862	2.080	15
0.045	0.058	0.065	0.075	0.087	0.088	0.100	0.110	0.123	0.136	0.146	0.147	0.166	0.198	0.224	0.256	16
1.403	1.244	1.115	1.310	1.443	1.378	1.350	1.615	1.588	1.649	1.753	1.891	2.101	2.197	2.355	2.396	17
1.009	1.136	1.089	1.531	1.680	1.346	1.511	1.445	1.373	1.440	1.658	1.894	2.419	2.711	2.802	2.769	18
0.368	0.378	0.373	0.420	0.537	0.490	0.542	0.604	0.649	0.721	0.795	0.899	0.982	1.080	1.226	1.479	19
0.159	-0.031	0.069	-0.132	-0.217	-0.068	-0.047	-0.120	-0.023	-0.004	-0.087	-0.021	-0.004	-0.323	-0.122	-0.429	20
$18.770	$19.718	$19.868	$21.438	$23.723	$25.377	$26.880	$28.361	$29.883	30.563	33.288	35.433	38.162	42.118	47.297	51.877	21
1.670	1.832	1.849	1.934	2.224	2.456	2.338	2.668	3.028	3.191	3.436	3.655	4.226	4.801	6.185	7.445	22
$17.100	$17.886	$18.019	$19.504	$21.499	$22.921	$24.542	$25.693	$26.855	27.372	29.852	31.778	33.936	37.317	41.112	44.432	23
15.282	16.296	17.078	18.543	20.273	21.699	23.064	24.643	25.780	26.240	27.985	29.846	32.042	34.714	37.952	41.068	24
0.045	0.058	0.065	0.075	0.087	0.088	0.100	0.110	0.123	0.136	0.146	0.147	0.166	0.198	0.224	0.256	25
0.050	0.056	0.065	0.071	0.079	0.087	0.090	0.096	0.098	0.105	0.101	0.110	0.109	0.124	0.128	0.157	26
$1.723	$1.476	$0.811	$0.815	$1.060	$1.047	$1.288	$0.844	$0.854	0.891	1.660	1.675	1.619	2.281	2.808	2.951	27
1952	1953	1954	1955	1956	1957	1958	1959	1960	1961	1962	1963	1964	1965	1966	1967	
118.627	124.526	123.163	134.889	146.523	150.179	153.439	159.484	164.126	169.271	181.264	190.672	203.382	216.802	231.519	238.306	28
8.3	5.0	-1.1	9.5	8.6	2.5	2.2	3.9	2.9	3.1	7.1	5.2	6.7	6.6	6.8	2.9	29
21.6	21.4	21.5	21.5	21.8	22.5	23.1	23.4	23.7	23.9	24.2	24.6	25.1	25.7	26.6	27.6	30
2.4	-.9	0.5	0.0	1.4	3.2	2.7	1.3	1.3	0.8	1.3	1.7	2.0	2.4	3.5	3.8	31
9.22	9.21	9.99	10.85	11.16	11.38	12.83	12.64	13.22	14.37	14.91	15.87	17.03	19.08	20.31	23.59	32
6.2	-0.2	8.5	8.6	2.9	1.9	12.8	-1.5	4.6	8.7	3.8	6.4	7.3	12.0	6.5	16.1	33
0.89	1.34	1.06	0.88	2.52	3.62	0.87	3.28	1.70	2.26	3.07	3.19	3.58	3.62	4.63	4.00	34
1.30	1.97	1.81	2.56	3.67	4.03	3.49	5.50	4.61	3.28	5.47	3.78	3.88	4.54	5.19	5.95	35
155	162	250	245	197	278	432	372	446	466	390	374	324	280	267	315	36
2.9	3.0	4.6	4.4	3.4	4.6	7.0	6.0	7.0	7.1	5.9	5.5	4.7	3.9	3.6	4.1	37

NATIONAL INCOME AND RELATED STATISTICS FOR SELECTED YEARS, 1968–1994

National income statistics are in billions of current dollars

			1968	1969	1970	1971	1972	1973	1974	1975	1976	1977	1978
THE	1	Personal consumption expenditure	$44.842	$49.093	$51.853	$56.271	$63.021	$72.069	$84.231	$97.566	$111.500	$123.555	$137.427
SUM	2	Government current purchases of goods and services	12.685	14.186	16.448	18.228	20.136	22.851	27.480	33.266	38.274	43.411	47.386
OF	3	Gross investment	17.229	19.621	19.250	21.941	24.660	30.722	39.371	43.213	49.037	52.090	55.632
	4	Net exports of goods and services	0.980	0.139	2.248	1.642	0.958	1.743	0.439	−2.408	−1.027	−0.069	1.100
	5	Statistical discrepancy	−0.318	−0.013	−0.683	−0.792	−0.146	−0.013	0.590	−0.097	0.140	−1.108	0.059
EQUALS	6	**GDP at market prices**	**75.418**	**83.026**	**89.116**	**97.290**	**108.629**	**127.372**	**152.111**	**171.540**	**197.924**	**217.879**	**241.604**
	7	Net investment income from nonresidents	−1.221	−1.207	−1.351	−1.506	−1.461	−1.730	−2.238	−2.538	−3.536	−4.571	−5.950
EQUALS	8	**GNP at market prices**	**74.197**	**81.819**	**87.765**	**95.784**	**107.168**	**125.642**	**149.873**	**169.002**	**194.388**	**213.308**	**235.654**
LESS	9	Indirect taxes less subsidies	9.520	10.544	11.095	12.053	13.627	15.311	17.867	17.087	20.992	23.188	24.819
	10	Capital consumption allowances	8.412	9.753	9.948	10.764	11.734	13.628	16.447	18.760	21.454	23.798	26.619
	11	Statistical discrepancy	0.318	0.013	0.684	0.792	0.147	0.014	−0.590	0.098	−0.141	1.109	−0.059
EQUALS	12	**Net national income at factor cost**	**55.947**	**62.109**	**66.038**	**72.175**	**81.660**	**96.689**	**116.149**	**133.057**	**152.083**	**165.213**	**184.275**
PLUS	13	Government transfer payments	5.465	6.123	6.991	8.294	9.981	11.272	13.929	17.259	19.656	22.356	25.185
	14	Transfers from nonresidents	0.110	0.109	0.123	0.171	0.182	0.215	0.229	0.258	0.279	0.331	0.394
	15	Interest on the public debt	2.390	2.767	3.252	3.622	4.137	4.788	5.425	6.538	8.101	9.268	11.589
	16	Interest on consumer debt (transfer portion)	0.364	0.466	0.538	0.553	0.625	0.812	1.176	1.351	1.570	1.670	1.918
LESS	17	Corporation income taxes	2.852	3.221	3.070	3.346	3.920	5.079	7.051	7.494	7.128	7.238	8.188
	18	corporation profits	3.310	3.396	2.960	3.544	4.449	6.983	8.978	8.019	9.863	10.333	12.384
	19	Government investment income	1.752	2.276	2.724	3.217	3.739	4.423	6.009	7.176	8.446	9.978	12.467
	20	Other earnings not paid out to persons	−0.626	−0.505	−0.034	−0.569	−1.026	−2.547	−3.898	−2.804	−1.875	−3.549	−4.841
EQUALS	21	**Personal income**	**56.988**	**63.186**	**68.222**	**75.277**	**85.503**	**99.838**	**118.768**	**138.578**	**158.127**	**174.838**	**195.163**
LESS	22	Personal taxes	8.844	10.881	12.606	14.130	15.647	18.091	22.364	25.257	29.888	33.464	35.697
EQUALS	23	**Personal Disposable income**	**48.144**	**52.305**	**55.616**	**61.147**	**69.856**	**81.747**	**96.404**	**113.321**	**128.239**	**141.374**	**159.466**
LESS	24	Personal consumption expenditure	44.842	49.093	51.853	56.271	63.021	72.069	84.231	97.566	111.500	123.550	137.427
	25	Interest paid by consumers to corporations	0.364	0.466	0.538	0.553	0.625	0.812	1.176	1.351	1.570	1.670	1.918
	26	Current transfers to nonresidents	0.130	0.185	0.176	0.181	0.215	0.237	0.247	0.258	0.269	0.292	0.294
EQUALS	27	**Personal saving**	**2.808**	**2.561**	**3.049**	**4.142**	**5.995**	**8.692**	**10.750**	**14.146**	**14.900**	**15.862**	**19.827**

RELATED STATISTICS			1968	1969	1970	1971	1972	1973	1974	1975	1976	1977	1978
	28	Real GDP (in 1986 dollars)	251.064	264.508	271.372	286.998	303.447	326.848	341.235	350.113	371.688	385.122	402.737
	29	Growth rate of real GDP (annual %)	5.4	5.4	2.6	5.8	5.7	7.7	4.4	2.6	6.2	3.6	4.6
	30	Consumer price index (1986 = 100)	28.7	30.0	31.0	31.9	33.4	36.0	39.9	44.2	47.5	51.3	55.9
	31	CP change (annual %)	4.0	4.5	3.3	2.9	4.7	7.8	10.8	10.8	7.5	8.0	9.0
*32		Money supply, M3 (in billions of dollars in December)	26.72	27.72	34.60	37.72	43.31	52.68	64.09	73.66	88.57	101.04	118.87
	33	Growth rate of money supply (annual %)	13.3	3.8	10.9†	9.0	14.8	21.6	21.7	14.9	20.2	16.5	14.3
	34	3-month Treasury Bill yield-year's low	5.48	6.38	4.40	3.00	3.36	3.90	6.07	6.26	8.14	7.05	7.13
	35	3-month Treasury Bill yield-year's high	6.99	7.81	7.78	4.68	3.73	6.53	9.11	8.64	9.13	8.04	10.46
	36	Unemployment (in thousands)	382	382	495	552	562	520	514	690	727	850	911
	37	Unemployment as % of civilian labour force	4.8	4.7	5.9	6.4	6.3	5.6	5.3	6.9	7.1	8.1	8.4

* Prior to 1970, this series *excluded* foreign currency booked in Canada as well as the liabilities of the chartered banks' majority–owned subsidiaries. Thus there is a discontinuity between 1969 and 1970.

† Growth rate of discontinued series.

NATIONAL INCOME AND RELATED STATISTICS FOR SELECTED YEARS, 1968–1994   (cont'd)

National income statistics are in billions of current dollars

1979	1980	1981	1982	1983	1984	1985	1986	1987	1988	1989	1990	1991	1992	1993	1994	
$153.390	$172.416	$196.191	$210.509	$231.452	$251.645	$274.503	$296.810	$322.769	$349.937	$378.077	398.208	411.960	422.515	436.542	452.859	1
52.286	59.250	68.792	78.655	84.571	89.089	95.519	100.337	105.836	114.472	123.718	133.781	161.279	166.106	167.970	167.522	2
68.428	72.624	87.305	71.574	78.329	89.460	96.479	104.122	119.788	136.585	149.898	137.207	112.372	109.098	114.175	125.250	3
1.794	5.646	3.879	14.053	13.612	15.403	11.531	4.490	4.914	2.925	-1.692	-1.361	-7.956	-6.065	-3.164	5.615	4
0.198	-0.045	-0.173	-0.349	-2.247	-0.862	-0.044	-1.128	-1.710	1.987	-0.085	0.008	-1.178	-1.882	-2.668	-1.193	5
276.096	309.891	355.994	374.442	405.717	444.735	477.988	504.631	551.597	605.906	649.916	667.843	676.477	690.122	712.855	750.053	6
-7.155	-7.827	-11.337	-12.670	-11.603	-13.486	-14.332	-16.548	-16.444	-18.712	-21.503	-24.256	-21.869	-24.242	-23.991	-26.272	7
268.941	302.064	344.657	361.772	394.114	431.249	463.656	488.083	535.153	587.194	628.413	643.587	654.608	665.880	688.864	723.781	8
26.635	27.272	36.457	38.908	40.135	42.714	47.212	53.532	59.719	67.790	75.844	75.231	79.878	84.389	88.731	93.662	9
30.743	35.527	40.677	44.356	47.060	50.884	55.926	60.214	64.116	68.128	72.411	76.184	82.331	85.305	87.904	92.973	10
-0.199	0.045	0.173	0.350	2.247	0.863	0.045	1.128	1.710	-1.987	0.085	-0.009	1.179	1.883	2.668	1.193	11
211.762	239.220	267.350	278.158	304.672	336.788	360.473	373.209	409.608	453.263	480.073	492.181	491.220	494.303	509.561	535.953	12
26.697	30.864	35.307	44.453	51.253	54.180	58.515	62.221	66.438	71.415	77.096	85.260	98.551	107.531	112.972	113.346	13
0.450	0.519	0.545	0.600	0.610	0.629	0.681	0.774	0.821	0.849	0.853	0.935	1.102	1.194	1.303	1.426	14
13.810	16.790	22.268	27.072	29.419	34.752	40.183	42.916	45.903	50.410	58.075	63.596	40.978	39.490	39.240	40.126	15
2.855	3.713	5.362	5.132	3.785	3.791	4.233	4.624	5.268	6.205	8.244	9.036	7.854	5.933	4.834	4.432	16
10.038	12.078	12.796	11.755	12.320	14.984	15.563	14.383	16.990	17.586	18.518	16.851	15.010	14.423	14.475	16.890	17
18.522	18.825	11.418	-0.498	11.657	16.971	19.827	15.481	24.172	28.970	22.426	6.660	-.068	.340	9.220	20.120	18
14.932	17.940	20.934	22.309	25.267	28.182	29.656	28.833	29.573	32.527	36.208	37.677	12.665	12.876	12.487	13.179	19
-7.385	-6.627	-7.531	-2.988	-2.557	-2.236	-1.160	-1.351	-3.888	-2.983	-2.002	0.269	6.131	-.964	-1.651	-2.098	20
219.467	248.890	293.215	324.837	343.052	372.239	400.199	426.398	461.191	506.042	549.191	589.551	605.967	621.776	633.379	647.192	21
39.615	45.237	55.533	61.976	67.039	71.893	78.862	89.244	99.756	111.807	117.951	135.921	140.024	143.618	144.917	149.835	22
179.852	203.653	237.682	262.861	276.013	300.346	321.337	337.154	361.435	394.235	431.240	453.630	465.943	478.158	488.462	497.357	23
153.390	172.416	196.191	210.509	231.452	251.645	274.503	296.810	322.769	349.937	378.077	398.208	411.960	422.515	436.540	452.859	24
2.855	3.713	5.362	5.132	3.785	3.791	4.233	4.624	5.268	6.205	8.244	9.036	7.854	5.933	4.834	4.432	25
0.347	0.364	0.385	0.443	0.473	0.500	0.554	0.574	0.629	0.709	0.780	0.820	.777	.941	.990	1.048	26
23.260	27.160	35.744	46.777	40.303	44.410	42.047	35.146	32.769	37.384	44.139	45.566	45.352	48.769	46.096	39.018	27
1979	1980	1981	1982	1983	1984	1985	1986	1987	1988	1989	1990	1991	1992	1993	1994	
418.328	424.537	440.127	425.970	439.448	467.167	489.437	504.631	526.730	552.958	565.779	563.060	555.052	559.305	571.722	597.936	28
3.9	1.5	3.7	-3.2	3.2	6.3	4.8	3.3	4.2	5.0	2.4	-0.2	-1.8	0.8	2.2	4.6	29
61.0	67.2	75.5	83.7	88.5	92.4	96.0	100.0	104.4	108.6	114.0	119.5	126.2	128.1	130.4	130.7	30
9.1	10.2	12.4	10.9	5.7	4.4	3.9	4.2	4.4	4.0	5.0	4.8	5.6	1.5	1.8	0.2	31
141.99	162.13	181.5	181.28	178.77	191.03	200.97	218.83	233.637	257.899	291.315	314.243	383.265	408.447	419.684	442.022	32
19.8	16.3	13.2	4.5	1.6	3.1	6.6	7.7	11.0	8.7	11.9	10.3	6.5	5.1	4.9	3.9	33
10.78	10.06	14.41	9.80	9.12	9.73	8.53	8.09	6.8	8.29	10.94	11.47	7.48	5.17	3.91	3.63	34
13.66	17.01	20.82	16.33	9.71	12.73	11.27	11.55	9.58	10.95	12.37	13.80	10.64	8.56	6.56	7.14	35
838	867	898	1,305	1,436	1,399	1,328	1,236	1,150	1,031	1,018	1,109	1,417	1,640	1,649	1,541	36
7.5	7.5	7.6	11.0	11.9	11.3	10.5	9.6	8.8	7.8	7.5	8.1	10.3	11.3	11.2	10.4	37

Sources: Statistics Canada: National Income and Expenditure Accounts; Bank of Canada Review, Bank of Canada printouts.

INDEX

STUDENT REPLY CARD

In order to improve future editions, we are seeking your comments on
    Macroeconomics: Canada in the Global Economy Seventh Canadian Edition
by McConnell, Brue, and Barbiero. After you have read this text, please answer the
following questions and return this form via Business Reply Mail. *Your opinions
matter! Thank you in advance for your feedback!*

Name of your college or university: ————————————————

Major program of study: ——————————————————————

Course title: ———————————————————————————

Were you required to buy this book?   ——— yes ——— no

Did you buy this book new or used?   ——— new ——— used ($ ———)

Do you plan to keep or sell this book? ——— keep ——— sell

Is the order of topic coverage consistent with what was taught in your course?

Are there chapters or sections of this text that were not assigned for your course?
Please specify:

Were there topics covered in your course that are not included in this text?
Please specify:

What did you like most about this text?

What did you like least?

If you would like to say more, we'd love to hear from you. Please write to us at the
address shown on the reverse of this card.